Corporate Compliance

Corporate Compliance

Carole Basri
CORPORATE COMPLIANCE PROGRAM ADVISOR AND
ADJUNCT PROFESSOR OF LAW
FORDHAM UNIVERSITY SCHOOL OF LAW
VISITING PROFESSOR
PEKING UNIVERSITY SCHOOL OF TRANSNATIONAL LAW
VISITING PROFESSOR
PERICLES LAW SCHOOL, MOSCOW

CAROLINA ACADEMIC PRESS
Durham, North Carolina

ISBN 978-1-5310-2869-5
eISBN 978-1-63282-106-5
LCCN 2016956309

Carolina Academic Press, LLC
700 Kent Street
Durham, North Carolina 27701
Telephone (919) 489-7486
Fax (919) 493-5668
www.cap-press.com

Printed in the United States of America
2023 printing

To my husband, Ken Steinberg, for his love and support.

To my mother, Annette Basri, for her love and caring.

To my brothers, Ray Basri and Bill Basri and their wives Ava and Nancy, for their love and caring.

To my late father, Dr. Albert Basri, for his love and devotion to learning.

To my sons, Joshua Heiliczer and Ephrim Heiliczer and their wives Allison and Shimrit, for their love.

To my son Alex Steinberg , daughter-in-law Bari Steinberg and to Julie Steinberg, for their love.

To my grandchildren, Shmuel, Esther, Avigail and Jeremiah, for their love.

To my friends Cheryl, Suzy, Donna, Laurie, Janis, Desiree, Rhonda, Naava, Hannah, Arlene, Isabel, Deborah, Marsha, Lyric, Oksana, Vicki, Pakeeza, Susan, Janet, Basma, Sylvia, Ellen, Ann, Ferial, Tamara and Nina.

Contents

Table of Cases

Acknowledgments

Carolina Academic Press
John Cashin
Brian S. Cousin
Nestor Davidson
Donald C. Dowling, Jr.
Toni Fine
Ellen Flynn
Fordham University Law School
JoAnn Glaccum
Sean Griffith
Hebrew University Law School
Nina Kulmala
Joseph Lee
LexisNexis
Chen Lu
Paul McNulty
Ran Nui
Anthony M. Palma
Peking University School of Transnational Law
Pericles Law School, Moscow, Russia
Ann Rakoff
Iulia Toplean
University of Pennsylvania Law School
Gabe Shawn Varges

Corporate Compliance

Chapter 1

What Is Corporate Compliance and Creating a Basic Compliance Program*

What Is Corporate Compliance?

Introduction

Corporate compliance is the system of self-governance established by a business organization seeking to conform its conduct to the demands of public policy. Practically speaking, it is the means by which a company transforms its ethical values into the more tangible reality of ethical conduct. As recently as November 2012, U.S. enforcement officials recognized that effective compliance programs "promote an organizational culture that encourages ethical conduct and a commitment to compliance with the law."

Compliance covers a broad spectrum of preventative and remedial efforts, and it must address a potentially wide range of legal risks depending on the nature of an organization's commercial activity. In recent years, compliance has moved to the forefront of corporate business strategy as government enforcement actions against corporations have increased. It is a central consideration for corporations expanding operations overseas or considering the acquisition of a company with an uncertain ethical culture.

The subject of compliance is by no means a new concept. For decades, government restrictions on trade, monopolies, and other issues have encouraged companies to establish internal controls to prevent employee misconduct. Many companies operate in highly regulated industries, such as transportation, insurance, and banking, which have long been the subject of extensive government oversight. For some time, the risk of financial mismanagement dominated the compliance concerns of corporate leaders, especially those in publicly-traded companies. But as enforcement risks have expanded into new areas of public concern, including foreign corruption and privacy, the challenges of corporate compliance have grown more difficult.

---

* Special thanks to Paul McNulty, Partner, Baker & McKenzie for his contributions. This chapter is adapted from Paul McNulty, *What is Corporate Compliance?* in CORPORATE COMPLIANCE PRACTICE GUIDE: THE NEXT GENERATION OF COMPLIANCE, Chapter 1 (Carole Basri, Release 8, 2016).

4

Compliance programs are formal systems of policies and procedures adopted by corporations and other organizations that are designed to detect and prevent violations of law by employees and other agents and to promote ethical business cultures. One of the primary goals of compliance programs is to control the risk of legal and regulatory violations. In other words, companies adopt compliance programs, in part, to attempt to minimize the risk to the organization of an employee or other agent violating law, regulation or company policy.

Beginning in the mid-1970s, it became increasingly common for companies to adopt programs to attempt to prevent and detect certain types of legal violations, such as violations of the antitrust or anti-bribery laws.[1] In 1991, with the promulgation of the United States Sentencing Guidelines for Organizations (the "Sentencing Guidelines"), the United States government offered companies an important incentive to implement broad-based programs to prevent and detect violations of law.[2] The Sentencing Guidelines achieved this by making the existence of an effective compliance program a potentially significant factor in determining the penalty assessed against an organization for corporate crimes.[3] In addition, the Sentencing Guidelines tended to increase the penalties to which organizations would be subject, thus making the mitigating effect of a compliance program even more valuable. Formal compliance programs became an important part of the corporate landscape in the United States in the 1990s.[4] And, partially as a result of the many corporate debacles of the past few years, compliance programs are experiencing renewed importance.[5]

The increasing popularity of compliance programs is not limited to the United States. Many United States corporations are disseminating their compliance programs on a global scale, and compliance programs are being adopted by an ever-increasing number of non-United States organizations and fostered by other countries and multi-lateral organizations. This chapter explores some of the reasons behind the growth of compliance programs and provides some practical guidance on how companies can effectively implement compliance programs, while avoiding some common pitfalls.

---

1. John D. Copeland, *The Tyson Story: Building an Effective Ethics and Compliance Program*, 5 Drake J. Agric. L. 305, 313–17 (2000) (detailing the development of compliance programs in response to the bribery scandals of the 1970s and the defense and financial industry scandals of the 1980s).

2. United States Sentencing Guidelines Manual § 8C2.5(f) (2002).

3. *Id.*

4. See Jeffrey M. Kaplan, *The Sentencing Guidelines: The First Ten Years*, Ethikos (Nov/Dec 2001) at 1.

5. This is evidence by recent legislation and regulations that include compliance requirements. For example, section 406 of the Sarbanes-Oxley Act requires companies to disclose in periodic reports whether or not they have adopted a code of ethics for senior financial officers, and if not, why not. Pub. L. No. 170-204, § 406, 116 Stat. 745, 789 (2002) (codified at 15 U.S.C. § 7264). In addition, corporate governance rules promulgated by the New York Stock Exchange and the Nasdaq in 2003 require listed companies to adopt and disclose codes of business conduct and ethics applicable to all directors, officers and employees. NYSE Rule 303A.10; Nasdaq Rule 4350(n).

William C. Dudley, President and Chief Executive Officer, Fed. Reserve Bank of N.Y., Speech, Enhancing Financial Stability by Improving Culture in the Financial Services Industry

(Oct. 20, 2014) (available at https://www.newyorkfed.org/
newsevents/speeches/2014/dud141020a.html)

Remarks at the Workshop on Reforming Culture and Behavior in the Financial Services Industry, Federal Reserve Bank of New York, New York City, As prepared for delivery

The Existing Culture Problem

In recent years, there have been ongoing occurrences of serious professional misbehavior, ethical lapses and compliance failures at financial institutions. This has resulted in a long list of large fines and penalties, and, to a lesser degree than I would have desired employee dismissals and punishment. Since 2008, fines imposed on the nation's largest banks have far exceeded $100 billion. The pattern of bad behavior did not end with the financial crisis, but continued despite the considerable public sector intervention that was necessary to stabilize the financial system. As a consequence, the financial industry has largely lost the public trust. To illustrate, a 2012 Harris poll found that 42 percent of people responded either "somewhat" or "a lot" to the statement that Wall Street "harms the country"; furthermore, 68 percent disagreed with the statement: "In general, people on Wall Street are as honest and moral as other people."

I reject the narrative that the current state of affairs is simply the result of the actions of isolated rogue traders or a few bad actors within these firms. As James O'Toole and Warren Bennis observed in their *Harvard Business Review* article about corporate culture: "Ethical problems in organizations originate not with 'a few bad apples' but with the 'barrel makers.'" That is, the problems originate from the culture of the firms, and this culture is largely shaped by the firms' leadership. This means that the solution needs to originate from within the firms, from their leaders.

What do I mean by the culture within a firm? Culture relates to the implicit norms that guide behavior in the absence of regulations or compliance rules—and sometimes despite those explicit restraints. Culture exists within every firm whether it is recognized or ignored, whether it is nurtured or neglected, and whether it is embraced or disavowed. Culture reflects the prevailing attitudes and behaviors within a firm. It is how people react not only to black and white, but to all of the shades of grey. Like a gentle breeze, culture may be hard to see, but you can feel it. Culture relates to what "should" I do, and not to what "can" I do.

A number of factors have contributed to the cultural failures that we have seen. An important question is whether the sheer size, complexity and global scope of large financial firms today have left them "too big to manage." Large problems can originate in small corners of these firms, as illustrated by the Financial Products Group experience at AIG, and the "London Whale" episode at JPMorgan. Differences in attitudes and business practices across countries can also be difficult to reconcile within a firm's overall compliance function. Recent fines against BNP Paribas for violating U.S. sanctions programs and providing dollar funding to a country engaged in genocide and against Credit Suisse for facilitating tax evasion by U.S. citizens, point to these challenges. Another important element affecting culture has been the shift in the prevailing business model away from traditional commercial and investment banking activities to trading; that is, from client-oriented to transaction-oriented activities. Clients became counterparties—the other side of a trade—rather than partners in a long-term business relationship. In general, interactions became more depersonalized, making it easier to rationalize away bad behavior, and more difficult to identify who would be harmed by any unethical actions.

High-powered pay incentives linked to short-term profits, combined with a flexible and fluid job market, have also contributed to a lessening of firm loyalty—and, sometimes, to a disregard for the law—in an effort to generate larger bonuses. Often allegiance to an external network of traders has been more important than the ties the trader has to his or her particular employer. This is particularly evident in the illegal manipulations of the London Interbank Offered Rate (LIBOR), and with respect to reference rates in the foreign exchange markets.

Although cultural and ethical problems are not unique to the finance industry, financial firms are different from other firms in important ways. First, the financial sector plays a key public role in allocating scarce capital and exerting market discipline throughout a complex, global economy. For the economy to achieve its long-term growth potential, we need a sound and vibrant financial sector. Financial firms exist, in part, to benefit the public, not simply their shareholders, employees and corporate clients. Unless the financial industry can rebuild the public trust, it cannot effectively perform its essential functions. For this reason alone, the industry must do much better.

As was discussed earlier, in the U.K., seven of its largest banking institutions have recently founded the Banking Standards Review Council under the leadership of Sir Richard Lambert, who joined us today. I would strongly encourage the largest institutions based here in the United States to work to develop collaborative solutions aimed at improving culture and rebuilding the public trust.

The Key Role for Senior Leadership

Correcting this problem must start with senior leadership of the firm. The "tone at the top" and the example that senior leaders set is critical to an institution's culture—it largely determines the "quality of the barrel." As a first step, senior leaders need to hold up a mirror to their own behavior and critically examine behavioral norms at their firm. Sustainable change at any firm will take time. Turning around a firm's culture is a marathon not a sprint. Senior leaders must take responsibility for the solution and communicate frequently, credibly and consistently about the importance of culture. Boards of directors have a critical role to play in setting the tone and holding senior leaders accountable for delivering sustainable change. A healthy culture must be carefully nurtured for it to have any chance of becoming self-sustaining.

Firms must take a comprehensive approach to improving their culture that encompasses recruitment, onboarding, career development, performance reviews, pay and promotion. All of these elements need to be aligned with the desired culture. Through our supervisory process, we have seen that a number of firms have started this process by developing or refining employee surveys and 360 feedback processes to target issues of behavior and culture. Some firms are incorporating case study discussions into training programs to highlight ethical dilemmas and decision-making. Some are revamping senior level promotion criteria to reinforce what are the desired characteristics and behaviors of leaders. These efforts are at various stages in terms of their depth, breadth and maturity. Supervisors will need to see how these frameworks evolve, and more importantly, see evidence of how these efforts yield results in the form of more open and routine escalation of issues, consistent application of "should we" versus "could we" in business decisions, rigor in identifying and controlling of conduct risk, and how compliance breaches factor into compensation.

Measurement and accountability for progress in developing a healthier culture across the industry is paramount to us as supervisors and central bankers. An important measurement of progress is employees' assessment of their firm's culture. To this end, we encourage the industry to harness the various individual efforts that have been initiated at a number of firms in order to develop a comprehensive culture survey. This anonymous survey would be fielded across firms each year by an independent third-party and the results shared with supervisors. Having a common survey instrument would promote benchmarking of, and accountability for, progress on culture and behavior.

A core element of any firm's mission and culture must be a respect for law. Federal Reserve guidance advises that banks should strive to "[m]aintain a corporate culture that emphasizes the importance of compliance with laws and regulations and consumer protection." To maintain such a culture, senior leaders must promote effective self-policing. If audit uncovers an instance of fraud in one unit, the firm's leadership should ask, "Where else could this behavior occur?" If the press reports fraud at a competitor in a particular business line, the same self-assessment should apply. "Could this happen to us, could we have a similar problem here?" When fraud is detected, boards and senior leaders must ensure that they are informed promptly, and that a thorough inquiry is undertaken at once. The senior leaders of financial firms, and those who report to them, must also be proactive in reporting illegal or unethical activity. Early self-reporting sends a powerful message to employees and to regulators about a firm's respect for law. This is one important reason why those who self-report in a timely way should be treated preferentially, compared to those that drag their feet and whose bad behaviors are only uncovered by enforcement investigations.

How will a firm know if it is making real progress? Not having to plead guilty to felony charges or being assessed large fines is a good start. Firms should also pay closer attention to how they and the industry are broadly viewed by the public. Internally, one important marker for progress is the frequency of problems, and whether small problems stay small, or instead, grow into large problems. A healthy culture is one where problems are identified early and promptly addressed.

In addition to a strong compliance function, firms need to foster an environment that rewards the free exchange of ideas and views. Individuals should feel that they can raise a concern, and have confidence that the issues will be escalated and fully considered. This is a critical element to prevention. A firm's employees are its best monitors, but this only works well if they feel a shared responsibility to speak up, expect to be heard and their efforts supported by senior management.

Let me give you an example to take this from the abstract to the more specific. As I noted in a speech a few weeks ago on the issue of reference rate reform, in the case of the LIBOR setting process, the information barriers between the traders and LIBOR submitters were paper thin and porous. At times, traders and LIBOR submitters colluded to manipulate LIBOR for the gain of the traders and the firm.

What should have happened instead goes like this: A trader asks the LIBOR submitter to adjust the submitted rate. The submitter says "no way," tells the trader that this request is inappropriate and that the trader will be reported to compliance. The submitter reports the trader's attempt at manipulation to legal and compliance. Compliance investigates to confirm the facts. The trader is fired and is fully prosecuted for any criminal actions. For this all to happen, a firm doesn't just have to have the right rules and procedures in place, but it also needs the right culture to ensure that those rules and procedures are followed, that the bad behavior sees the light of day immediately and that the transgressors are punished in a way that is known broadly throughout the firm — that is, a clear example of the consequences is demonstrated to others.

Compelling Reasons for Launching an Effective Compliance Program

There are several compelling reasons for an effective compliance program. Recurring corporate scandals and the ongoing financial crisis have made the necessity of an effective compliance program critical not only for each major corporation in the U.S. and abroad, but also vital to the integrity of the entire global financial system. This systemic importance cannot be overemphasized in creating the need for global corporate good citizenship

In essence, an effective compliance program can help insulate a company, and its officers, directors and employees from criminal and civil penalties; protect its officers and directors from personal liability; and create a culture of a "good citizen" corporation. In fact, an effective compliance program can be a mitigating factor even if it failed to prevent a criminal offense.

However, a poorly constructed compliance program can serve as a roadmap for prosecutors; damage employee morale; and encourage fraud and unethical conduct to continue. Moreover, a poorly constructed program lacking in sufficient leadership, funding and resources will create the view, among employees, that the code of conduct/ethics, and, indeed, the whole compliance program, is a sham.

Prior Reasons for an Effective Compliance Program

The justifications for implementing an effective corporate compliance program have traditionally been found in the U.S. Sentencing Guidelines released in November 1991, the landmark decision, *In re Caremark Int'l Deriv. Litig.*, 698 A.2d 959 (Del. Ch. 1996), which mandated personal liability for directors for oversight of compliance, the government-imposed corporate integrity agreements, as well as the Supreme Court employment discrimination decisions in the *Faragher v. City of Boca Raton*, 118 S. Ct. 2275 (1998), and *Ellerth v. Burlington Industries, Inc.*, 118 S. Ct. 2257 (1998).

In the beginning of the twenty-first century, the necessity of implementing corporate compliance programs was underscored by the Enron, WorldCom and Tyco debacles, and later by FIFA, Petrobras and Volkswagen, as well as the large settlements between corporations and the government where corporations lacked an effective compliance program.

U.S. Securities and Exchange Commission
Litigation Release No. 20829 (Dec. 15, 2008)
Accounting and Auditing Enforcement Release No. 2911
Securities and Exchange Commission v. Siemens Aktiengesellschaft,
Civil Action No. 08 CV 02167 (D.D.C.)
http://www.sec.gov/litigation/litreleases/2008/lr20829.htm

SEC Files Settled Foreign Corrupt Practices Act Charges Against Siemens AG for Engaging in Worldwide Bribery With Total Disgorgement and Criminal Fines of Over $1.6 Billion

The Securities and Exchange Commission filed a settled enforcement action on December 12, 2008, in the U.S. District Court for the District of Columbia charging Siemens Aktiengesellschaft ("Siemens"), a Munich, Germany-based manufacturer of industrial and consumer products, with violations of the anti-bribery, books and records, and internal controls provisions of the Foreign Corrupt Practices Act ("FCPA"). Siemens has offered to pay a total of $1.6 billion in disgorgement and fines, which is the largest amount a company has ever paid to resolve corruption-related charges. Siemens has agreed to pay $350 million in disgorgement to the SEC. In related actions, Siemens will pay a $450 million criminal fine to the U.S. Department of Justice and a fine of €395 million (approximately $569 million) to the Office of the Prosecutor General in Munich, Germany. Siemens previously paid a fine of €201 million (approximately $285 million) to the Munich Prosecutor in October 2007.

The SEC's complaint alleges that:

Between March 12, 2001 and September 30, 2007, Siemens violated the FCPA by engaging in a widespread and systematic practice of paying bribes to foreign government officials to obtain business. Siemens created elaborate payment schemes to conceal the nature of its corrupt payments, and the company's inadequate internal controls allowed the conduct to flourish. The misconduct involved employees at all levels, including former senior management, and revealed a corporate culture long at odds with the FCPA.

During this period, Siemens made thousands of payments to third parties in ways that obscured the purpose for, and the ultimate recipients of, the money. At least 4,283 of those payments, totaling approximately $1.4 billion, were used to bribe government officials in return for business to Siemens around the world. Among others, Siemens paid bribes on transactions to design and build metro transit lines in Venezuela; metro trains and signaling devices in China; power plants in Israel; high voltage transmission lines in China; mobile telephone networks in Bangladesh; telecommunications projects in Nigeria; national identity cards in Argentina; medical devices in Vietnam, China, and Russia; traffic control systems in Russia; refineries in Mexico; and mobile communications networks in Vietnam. Siemens also paid kickbacks to Iraqi ministries in connection with sales of power stations and equipment to Iraq under the United Nations Oil for Food Program. Siemens earned over $1.1 billion in profits on these transactions.

An additional approximately 1,185 separate payments to third parties totaling approximately $391 million were not properly controlled and were used, at least in part, for illicit purposes, including commercial bribery and embezzlement.

From 1999 to 2003, Siemens' Managing Board or "Vorstand" was ineffective in implementing controls to address constraints imposed by Germany's 1999 adoption of the Organization for Economic Cooperation and Development ("OECD") anti-bribery convention that outlawed foreign bribery. The Vorstand was also ineffective in meeting the U.S. regulatory and anti-bribery requirements that Siemens was subject to following its March 12, 2001, listing on the New York Stock Exchange. Despite knowledge of bribery at two of its largest groups — Communications and Power Generation — the company's tone at the top was inconsistent with an effective FCPA compliance program and created a corporate culture in which bribery was tolerated and even rewarded at the highest levels of the company. Employees obtained large amounts of cash from cash desks, which were sometimes transported in suitcases across international borders for bribery. Authorizations for payments were placed on post-it notes and later removed to eradicate any permanent record. Siemens used numerous slush funds, off-books accounts maintained at unconsolidated entities, and a system of business consultants and intermediaries to facilitate the corrupt payments.

Siemens failed to implement adequate internal controls to detect and prevent violations of the FCPA. Elaborate payment mechanisms were used to conceal the fact that bribe payments were made around the globe to obtain business. False invoices and payment documentation was created to make payments to business consultants under false business consultant agreements that identified services that were never intended to be rendered. Illicit payments were falsely recorded as expenses for management fees, consulting fees, supply contracts, room preparation fees, and commissions. Siemens inflated U.N. contracts, signed side agreements with Iraqi ministries that were not disclosed to the U.N., and recorded the ASSF payments as legitimate commissions despite U.N., U.S., and international sanctions against such payments.

In November 2006, Siemens' current management began to implement reforms to the company's internal controls. These reforms substantially reduced, but did not entirely eliminate, corrupt payments. All but $27.5 million of the corrupt payments occurred before November 15, 2006. The company conducted a massive internal investigation and implemented an amnesty program to its employees to gather information.

Siemens violated Section 30A of the Securities Exchange Act of 1934 (Exchange Act) by making illicit payments to foreign government officials in order to obtain or retain business. Siemens violated Section 13(b)(2)(B) of the Exchange Act by failing to have adequate internal controls to detect and prevent the payments. Siemens violated Section 13(b)(2)(A) of the Exchange Act by improperly recording the payments in its books.

Without admitting or denying the Commission's allegations, Siemens has consented to the entry of a court order permanently enjoining it from future violations of Sections 30A, 13(b)(2)(A), and 13(b)(2)(B) of the Exchange Act; ordering it to pay $350 million in disgorgement of wrongful profits, which does not include profits factored into Munich's fine; and ordering it to comply with certain undertakings regarding its FCPA compliance program, including an independent monitor for a period of four years. On December 15, 2008, the court entered the final judgment. Since being approached by SEC staff, Siemens has cooperated fully with the ongoing investigation, and the SEC considered the remedial acts promptly undertaken by Siemens. Siemens' massive internal investigation and lower level employee amnesty program was essential in gathering facts regarding the full extent of Siemens' FCPA violations.

Notes and Comments

Siemens is a notable example of global compliance failures which resulted in the largest penalty, until that time, imposed on a company for violation of the Foreign Corrupt Practices Act. Siemens is a German corporation with its executive offices in Munich, Federal Republic of Germany. Siemens manufactures industrial and consumer products and builds locomotives, traffic control systems and electrical power plants. The Company also manufactures building control systems, medical equipment and electrical components, and formerly manufactured communications networks. At this time, Siemens employed approximately 428,200 people and operated in approximately 190 countries worldwide.

As related in this case, and following the investigations of both the United States and German Securities and Exchange Commission and the Department and Justice, it appeared that Siemens Aktiengesellschaft violated the Foreign Corrupt Practices Act between 2001 and 2007 by engaging in a "widespread and systematic practice of paying bribes to foreign government officials to obtain business." The Company created payment schemes to conceal the nature of its corrupt payments, and the Company's inadequate internal controls allowed the illicit conduct to flourish.

During this period, Siemens made thousands of separate payments to third parties in ways that obscured the purpose for, and the ultimate recipients of, the money. Among the transactions on which Siemens paid bribes were those to design and build metro transit lines in Venezuela and to construct metro trains and signaling devices in China. Siemens also paid kickbacks to Iraqi ministries in connection with sales of power stations and equipment to Iraq under the United Nations Oil for Food Program. Siemens earned over $1.1 billion in profits on these fourteen categories of transactions that comprised 332 individual projects or individual sales.

Moreover, the misconduct involved employees at all levels of the Company, including former senior management, and revealed a corporate culture that had long been at odds with the Foreign Corrupt Practices Act. Siemens implemented certain improvements to its compliance program in response to the situation in Italy. These included an anti-bribery speech delivered by the then-CFO to high-level business managers in summer 2004 and the establishment of a Corporate Compliance Office in October 2004. In addition, the Company issued policies on bank accounts, including requirements relating to the initiation and use of Company accounts and authorizations regarding cash.

However, it was not until one year later, in June 2005, that the Company issued mandatory rules governing the use of business consultants, e.g., prohibiting success fees and requiring compliance officers to sign off on business consulting agreements. While these measures appear to have been partially effective, improper payments continued at least until the Dawn Raid in November 2006. On December 15, 2008, Siemens agreed to pay monetary sanctions of $800 million, each to the United States and Germany.

According to the Department of Justice, Siemens failed to establish a "sufficiently empowered and competent" compliance department. Indeed, the Department of Justice alleged that the Corporate Compliance Department was severely understaffed according to the number of its employees. The Department of Justice used a 2005 benchmarking analysis comparing Siemens' compliance infrastructure to that of General Electric. The comparison then identified "serious deficiencies" in compliance resources and that no action was taken to remedy the problem.

Moreover, the Department of Justice upheld that regional compliance officers received minimal training or direction regarding their compliance responsibilities. Finally, it cited an "inherent conflict in [the] mandate" of the Corporate Compliance Department as along with being charged with preventing compliance breaches it had to defend the company against government investigations. Therefore, the Department of Justice indicated that Siemens "lacked sufficient anti-bribery compliance policies and procedures to control significant FCPA risks."

Press Release, U.S. Department of Justice, *HSBC Holdings Plc. and HSBC Bank USA N.A. Admit to Anti-Money Laundering and Sanctions Violations, Forfeit $1.256 Billion in Deferred Prosecution Agreement*

(Dec. 11, 2012) (available at http://www.justice.gov/opa/pr/hsbc-holdings-plc-and-hsbc-bank-usa-na-admit-anti-money-laundering-and-sanctions-violations)

Bank Agrees to Enhanced Compliance Obligations, Oversight by Monitoring Connection with Five-year Agreement

HSBC Holdings plc (HSBC Group)—a United Kingdom corporation headquartered in London—and HSBC Bank USA N.A. (HSBC Bank USA) (together, HSBC)—a federally chartered banking corporation headquartered in McLean, Va.—have agreed to forfeit $1.256 billion and enter into a deferred prosecution agreement with the Justice Department for HSBC's violations of the Bank Secrecy Act (BSA), the International Emergency Economic Powers Act (IEEPA) and the Trading with the Enemy Act (TWEA). According to court documents, HSBC Bank USA violated the BSA by failing to maintain an effective anti-money laundering program and to conduct appropriate due diligence on its foreign correspondent account holders. The HSBC Group violated IEEPA and TWEA by illegally conducting transactions on behalf of customers in Cuba, Iran, Libya, Sudan and Burma—all countries that were subject to sanctions enforced by the Office of Foreign Assets Control (OFAC) at the time of the transactions.

The announcement was made by Lanny A. Breuer, Assistant Attorney General of the Justice Department's Criminal Division; Loretta Lynch, U.S. Attorney for the Eastern District of New York; and John Morton, Director of U.S. Immigration and Customs Enforcement (ICE); along with numerous law enforcement and regulatory partners. The New York County District Attorney's Office worked with the Justice Department on the sanctions portion of the investigation. Treasury Under Secretary David S. Cohen and Comptroller of the Currency Thomas J. Curry also joined in today's announcement.

A four-count felony criminal information was filed today in federal court in the Eastern District of New York charging HSBC with willfully failing to maintain an effective anti-money laundering (AML) program, willfully failing to conduct due diligence on its foreign correspondent affiliates, violating IEEPA and violating TWEA. HSBC has waived federal indictment, agreed to the filing of the information, and has accepted responsibility for its criminal conduct and that of its employees.

"HSBC is being held accountable for stunning failures of oversight—and worse—that led the bank to permit narcotics traffickers and others to launder hundreds of millions of dollars through HSBC subsidiaries, and to facilitate hundreds of millions more in transactions with sanctioned countries," said Assistant Attorney General Breuer. "The record of dysfunction that prevailed at HSBC for many years was astonishing. Today, HSBC is paying a heavy price for its conduct, and, under the terms of today's agreement, if the bank fails to comply with the agreement in any way, we reserve the right to fully prosecute it."

"Today we announce the filing of criminal charges against HSBC, one of the largest financial institutions in the world," said U.S. Attorney Lynch. "HSBC's blatant failure to implement proper anti-money laundering controls facilitated the laundering of at least $881 million in drug proceeds through the U.S. financial system. HSBC's willful flouting of U.S. sanctions laws and regulations resulted in the processing of hundreds of millions of dollars in OFAC-prohibited transactions. Today's historic agreement, which imposes the largest penalty in any BSA prosecution to date, makes it clear that all corporate citizens, no matter how large, must be held accountable for their actions."

"Cartels and criminal organization are fueled by money and profits," said ICE Director Morton. "Without their illicit proceeds used to fund criminal activities, the lifeblood of their operations is disrupted. Thanks to the work of Homeland Security Investigations and our El Dorado Task Force, this financial institution is being held accountable for turning a blind eye to money laundering that was occurring right before their very eyes. HSI will continue to aggressively target financial institutions whose inactions are contributing in no small way to the devastation wrought by the international drug trade. There will be also a high price to pay for enabling dangerous criminal enterprises."

In addition to forfeiting $1.256 billion as part of its deferred prosecution agreement (DPA) with the Department of Justice, HSBC has also agreed to pay $665 million in civil penalties—$500 million to the Office of the Comptroller of the Currency (OCC) and $165 million to the Federal Reserve—for its AML program violations. The OCC penalty also satisfies a $500 million civil penalty of the Financial Crimes Enforcement Network (FinCEN). The bank's $375 million settlement agreement with OFAC is satisfied by the forfeiture to the Department of Justice. The United Kingdom's Financial Services Authority (FSA) is pursuing a separate action.

As required by the DPA, HSBC also has committed to undertake enhanced AML and other compliance obligations and structural changes within its entire global operations to prevent a repeat of the conduct that led to this prosecution. HSBC has replaced almost all of its senior management, "clawed back" deferred compensation bonuses given to its most senior AML and compliance officers, and has agreed to partially defer bonus compensation for its most senior executives—its group general managers and group managing directors—during the period of the five-year DPA. In addition to these measures, HSBC has made significant changes in its management structure and AML compliance functions that increase the accountability of its most senior executives for AML compliance failures.

The AML Investigation

According to court documents, from 2006 to 2010, HSBC Bank USA severely understaffed its AML compliance function and failed to implement an anti-money laundering program capable of adequately monitoring suspicious transactions and activities from HSBC Group Affiliate's, particularly HSBC Mexico, one of HSBC Bank USA's largest Mexican customers. This included a failure to monitor billions of dollars in purchases of physical U.S. dollars, or "banknotes," from these affiliates. Despite evidence of serious money laundering risks associated with doing business in Mexico, from at least 2006 to 2009, HSBC Bank USA rated Mexico as "standard" risk, its lowest AML risk category. As a result, HSBC Bank USA failed to monitor over $670 billion in wire transfers and over $9.4 billion in purchases of physical U.S. dollars from HSBC Mexico during this period, when HSBC Mexico's own lax AML controls caused it to be the preferred financial institution for drug cartels and money launderers.

A significant portion of the laundered drug trafficking proceeds were involved in the Black Market Peso Exchange (BMPE), a complex money laundering system that is designed to move the proceeds from the sale of illegal drugs in the United States to drug cartels outside of the United States, often in Colombia. According to court documents, beginning in 2008, an investigation conducted by ICE Homeland Security Investigation's (HSI's) El Dorado Task Force, in conjunction with the U.S. Attorney's Office for the Eastern District of New York, identified multiple HSBC Mexico accounts associated with BMPE activity and revealed that drug traffickers were depositing hundreds of thousands of dollars in bulk U.S. currency each day into HSBC Mexico accounts. Since 2009, the investigation has resulted in the arrest, extradition, and conviction of numerous individuals illegally using HSBC Mexico accounts in furtherance of BMPE activity.

As a result of HSBC Bank USA's AML failures, at least $881 million in drug trafficking proceeds—including proceeds of drug trafficking by the Sinaloa Cartel in Mexico and the Norte del Valle Cartel in Colombia—were laundered through HSBC Bank USA. HSBC Group admitted it did not inform HSBC Bank USA of significant AML deficiencies at HSBC Mexico, despite knowing of these problems and their effect on the potential flow of illicit funds through HSBC Bank USA.

The Sanctions Investigation

According to court documents, from the mid-1990s through September 2006, HSBC Group allowed approximately $660 million in OFAC-prohibited transactions to be processed through U.S. financial institutions, including HSBC Bank USA. HSBC Group followed instructions from sanctioned entities such as Iran, Cuba, Sudan, Libya and Burma, to omit their names from U.S. dollar payment messages sent to HSBC Bank USA and other financial institutions located in the United States. The bank also removed information identifying the countries from U.S. dollar payment messages; deliberately used less-transparent payment messages, known as cover payments; and worked with at least one sanctioned entity to format payment messages, which prevented the bank's filters from blocking prohibited payments.

Specifically, beginning in the 1990s, HSBC Group affiliates worked with sanctioned entities to insert cautionary notes in payment messages including "care sanctioned country," "do not mention our name in NY," or "do not mention Iran." HSBC Group became aware of this improper practice in 2000. In 2003, HSBC Group's head of compliance acknowledged that amending payment messages "could provide the basis for an action against [HSBC] Group for breach of sanctions." Notwithstanding instructions from HSBC Group Compliance to terminate this practice, HSBC Group affiliates were permitted to engage in the practice for an additional three years through the granting of dispensations to HSBC Group policy.

Court documents show that as early as July 2001, HSBC Bank USA's chief compliance officer confronted HSBC Group's Head of Compliance on the issue of amending payments and was assured that "Group Compliance would not support blatant attempts to avoid sanctions, or actions which would place [HSBC Bank USA] in a potentially compromising position." As early as July 2001, HSBC Bank USA told HSBC Group's head of compliance that it was concerned that the use of cover payments prevented HSBC Bank USA from confirming whether the underlying transactions met OFAC requirements. From 2001 through 2006, HSBC Bank USA repeatedly told senior compliance officers at HSBC Group that it would not be able to properly screen sanctioned entity payments if payments were being sent using the cover method. These protests were ignored.

"Today HSBC is being held accountable for illegal transactions made through the U.S. financial system on behalf of entities subject to U.S. economic sanctions," said Debra Smith, Acting Assistant Director in Charge of the FBI's Washington Field Office. "The FBI works closely with partner law enforcement agencies and federal regulators to ensure compliance with federal banking laws to promote integrity across financial institutions worldwide."

"Banks are the first layer of defense against money launderers and other criminal enterprises who choose to utilize our nation's financial institutions to further their criminal activity," said Richard Weber, Chief, Internal Revenue Service-Criminal Investigation (IRS-CI). "When a bank disregards the Bank Secrecy Act's reporting requirements, it compromises that layer of defense, making it more difficult to identify, detect and deter criminal activity. In this case, HSBC became a conduit to money laundering. The IRS is proud to partner with the other law enforcement agencies and share its world-renowned financial investigative expertise in this and other complex financial investigations."

Manhattan District Attorney Cyrus R. Vance Jr., said, "New York is a center of international finance, and those who use our banks as a vehicle for international crime will not be tolerated. My office has entered into Deferred Prosecution Agreements with two different banks in just the past two days, and with six banks over the past four years. Sanctions enforcement is of vital importance to our national security and the integrity of our financial system. The fight against money laundering and terror financing requires global cooperation, and our joint investigations in this and other related cases highlight the importance of coordination in the enforcement of U.S. sanctions. I thank our federal counterparts for their ongoing partnership."

Queens County District Attorney Richard A. Brown said, "No corporate entity should ever think itself too large to escape the consequences of assisting international drug cartels. In particular, banks have a special responsibility to use appropriate due diligence in monitoring the cash transactions flowing through their financial system and identifying the sources of that money in order not to assist in criminal activity. By allowing such illicit transactions to occur, HSBC failed in its global responsibility to us all. Hopefully, as a result of this historical settlement, we have gained the attention of not only HSBC but that of every other major financial institution so that they cannot turn a blind eye to the crime of money laundering."

―――――――――

Notes and Comments

HSBC failed to monitor more than $670 billion in wire transfers and more than $9.4 billion in purchases of U.S. currency from HSBC Mexico, allowing for money laundering of Mexico and Colombia's drug cartels. According to the Department of Justice, $881 million through HSBC and a Mexican unit have been laundered. Therefore, on December 11, 2012, the Department of Justice filed a complaint charging HSBC with violations of the Bank Secrecy Act ("BSA"), including, *inter alia*, willfully failing to maintain an effective anti-money laundering ("AML") program.

On the same day the government filed the Complaint, the Department of Justice also filed a Deferred Prosecution Agreement, a Statement of Facts, and a Corporate Compliance Monitor agreement. In this deferred prosecution agreement, HSBC acknowledged it failed to maintain an effective program against money laundering and failed to conduct basic due diligence on some of its account holders.

―――――――――

United States Ex Rel. Bilotta v. Novartis Pharm. Corp.

50 F. Supp. 3d 497 (S.D.N.Y. 2014)

BACKGROUND

I. FACTS

A. The Alleged Kickback Scheme

Plaintiffs allege that from January 2002 through at least November 2011, Novartis systematically bribed doctors to induce them to prescribe drugs from Novartis's cardiovascular division for their patients. (See U.S. Am. Cmplt. (Dkt. No. 62) ¶¶ 1, 66; N.Y. Cmplt. (Dkt. No. 61) ¶¶ 2, 3, 57) These drugs include Lotrel, Diovan, Diovan HCT, Tekturna, Tekturna HCT, Exforge *502, Exforge HCT, Valturna, Tekamlo, and Starlix.3 (See U.S. Am. Cmplt. (Dkt. No. 62) ¶ 66; N.Y. Cmplt. (Dkt. No. 61) ¶ 57) Novartis sold these drugs through a network of sales representatives who met with health care professionals throughout the United States. (U.S. Am. Cmplt. (Dkt. No. 62) ¶ 67; N.Y. Cmplt. (Dkt. No. 61) ¶ 58)

Novartis induced doctors to prescribe these drugs primarily through the use of "sham" speaker events. (U.S. Am. Cmplt. (Dkt. No. 62) ¶¶ 1–3; N.Y. Cmplt. (Dkt. No. 61) ¶¶ 2–4) According to Novartis's internal policies, speaker events were intended to be educational programs; Novartis would pay doctors to educate other doctors and health care professionals about Novartis drugs by presenting slides prepared by Novartis. (U.S. Am. Cmplt. (Dkt. No. 62) ¶ 2; N.Y. Cmplt. (Dkt. No. 61) ¶ 4) These events were organized and conducted by Novartis sales representatives. (U.S. Am. Cmplt. (Dkt. No. 62) ¶ 72; N.Y. Cmplt. (Dkt. No. 61) ¶ 69) They chose the speaker, topic, and venue for the events, as well as the attendees. (See U.S. Am. Cmplt. (Dkt. No. 62) ¶¶ 72–73, 81; N.Y. Cmplt. (Dkt. No. 61) ¶¶ 6, 69)

Novartis held thousands of speaker events at which few or no slides were shown, however, and at which the attendees spent little or no time discussing the drugs that were allegedly the focus of the programs. (U.S. Am. Cmplt. (Dkt. No. 62) ¶¶ 2, 95; N.Y. Cmplt. (Dkt. No. 61) ¶¶ 4, 82) These events thus served as little more than up-scale social outings designed to induce doctors to write prescriptions for Novartis drugs. (U.S. Am. Cmplt. (Dkt. No. 62) ¶¶ 1, 77, 121, 135–36; N.Y. Cmplt. (Dkt. No. 61) ¶¶ 2, 4, 82, 86–87)

According to Plaintiffs, the sham nature of these events was apparent from the attendees, speakers, subject matter, and venues. (U.S. Am. Cmplt. (Dkt. No. 62) ¶ 95; N.Y. Cmplt. (Dkt. No. 61) ¶ 82) Frequently, groups of the same doctors would repeatedly attend speaker events on the same topic within a short period of time, with the doctors taking turns in the roles of attendees and "speakers." (U.S. Am. Cmplt. (Dkt. No. 62) ¶¶ 95–120, 126; N.Y. Cmplt. (Dkt. No. 61) ¶¶ 82–85) For example, one doctor attended the same presentation ten times between July 2010 and October 2011, and the same three doctors were consistently present at nine of those events. (U.S. Am. Cmplt. (Dkt. No. 62) ¶ 97; N.Y. Cmplt. (Dkt. No. 61) ¶ 84) Moreover, Novartis hosted many of its speaker events at high-end restaurants or sports bars without private rooms, making it difficult or impossible to hear the speaker or show slides; it was common for no slides to be shown at such events. (U.S. Am. Cmplt. (Dkt. No. 62) ¶¶ 121, 125–28, 130, 133–34; N.Y. Cmplt. (Dkt. No. 61) ¶¶ 86–90) Other venues were similarly inappropriate for the types of "educational" events that Novartis purported to be hosting, such as "round table" programs at Hooters restaurants and fishing trips. (U.S. Am. Cmplt. (Dkt. No. 62) ¶¶ 122–24)

Sales representatives frequently asked speakers who they should invite as attendees to these events, and doctors used this as an opportunity to invite their friends. (Id. ¶ 136; N.Y. Cmplt. (Dkt. No. 61) ¶ 91) Often the drug that was supposed to be the subject of the speaker program was *503 never discussed. (U.S. Am. Cmplt. (Dkt. No. 62) ¶ 137; N.Y. Cmplt. (Dkt. No. 61) ¶ 92)

The doctors who Novartis designated as "speakers" for these events were paid "honoraria" by Novartis, even though they spent little or no time discussing the drugs that were supposedly the subject of the programs. (U.S. Am. Cmplt. (Dkt. No. 62) ¶¶ 3, 78; N.Y. Cmplt. (Dkt. No. 61) ¶¶ 4, 92) "Speakers" were paid between $750 and $1500 for each event, with some speakers being paid as much as $3000. (U.S.

Am. Cmplt. (Dkt. No. 62) ¶ 79; N.Y. Cmplt. (Dkt. No. 61) ¶ 67) In some instances, speaker events reflected in Novartis records never took place, or doctors recorded as attending were not, in fact, present; nevertheless, the designated "speakers" were compensated for these non-existent events. (U.S. Am. Cmplt. (Dkt. No. 62) ¶ 138–44; N.Y. Cmplt. (Dkt. No. 61) ¶ 93)

Novartis's internal analysis showed that its speaker programs had a high "return on investment," as doctors who attended the events—as either speakers or attendees—wrote an increased number of prescriptions for Novartis drugs. (U.S. Am. Cmplt. (Dkt. No. 62) ¶¶ 3, 145–48; N.Y. Cmplt. (Dkt. No. 61) ¶¶ 94–96) Novartis found that the more incentives doctors received in the form of meals, entertainment, and honoraria from these events, the more Novartis prescriptions the doctors would write. (U.S. Am. Cmplt. (Dkt. No. 62) ¶ 147; N.Y. Cmplt. (Dkt. No. 61) ¶ 95) The highest return on investment came from doctors who were paid to "speak" at the events. (U.S. Am. Cmplt. (Dkt. No. 62) ¶ 3) Novartis considered its speaker programs to be a "key component of [Novartis's] promotional activities aimed at increasing its sales of drugs" from 2002 to at least 2011. (Id. ¶ 71; N.Y. Cmplt. (Dkt. No. 61) ¶ 61) Novartis spent more than $65 million for more than 38,000 speaker programs ostensibly about Lotrel, Starlix, and Valturna between January 1, 2002 and November 2011. (U.S. Am. Cmplt. (Dkt. No. 62) ¶ 71; N.Y. Cmplt. (Dkt. No. 61) ¶ 61)

Novartis intended its speaker programs to increase prescription-writing, and doctors knew this. (U.S. Am. Cmplt. (Dkt. No. 62) ¶ 147–50; N.Y. Cmplt. (Dkt. No. 61) ¶¶ 97–99) Doctors were chosen to be speakers if they wrote a high number of prescriptions for Novartis cardiovascular division drugs, and they had to maintain or increase that level of prescription-writing in order to be invited to appear as a "speaker" again. (U.S. Am. Cmplt. (Dkt. No. 62) ¶ 149; N.Y. Cmplt. (Dkt. No. 61) ¶ 98) Accordingly, once they began receiving honoraria, many doctors significantly increased the number of prescriptions that they wrote for Novartis drugs, or started prescribing Novartis drugs if they had not done so before. (U.S. Am. Cmplt. (Dkt. No. 62) ¶¶ 150–58; N.Y. Cmplt. (Dkt. No. 61) ¶¶ 99–124) Doctors often continued to increase their prescription-writing as the amount of honoraria they received increased. (U.S. Am. Cmplt. (Dkt. No. 62) ¶¶ 150–58; N.Y. Cmplt. (Dkt. No. 61) ¶¶ 99–124) Novartis placed no limit on the number of programs a doctor could attend or how often a doctor could attend the same program. (U.S. Am. Cmplt. (Dkt. No. 62) ¶ 84; N.Y. Cmplt. (Dkt. No. 61) ¶ 71)

Novartis also encouraged sham events by creating incentives for its sales representatives to host them. Sales representatives in the cardiovascular division were compensated based upon the number of prescriptions that doctors wrote for Novartis drugs. (U.S. Am. Cmplt. (Dkt. No. 62) ¶ 75; N.Y. Cmplt. (Dkt. No. 61) ¶¶ 6, 64) They were given budgets to use on speaker events, and they were pressured to exhaust their budgets for such events. *504 (U.S. Am. Cmplt. (Dkt. No. 62) ¶ 76) Although Novartis policies provided for caps on the price per meal for attendees at these events, sales representatives could avoid these caps by attributing costs that exceeded the caps to "unmet minimums," i.e., the difference between a restaurant's minimum spending requirement for an event and the amount that sales representatives were permitted to spend per attendee under the caps. (Id. ¶¶ 87–88; N.Y. Cmplt. (Dkt. No. 61) ¶¶ 74–75) By inviting few attendees and attributing the excess to a restaurant's "unmet minimum" cost, speakers could spend lavishly on food and alcohol well beyond the caps. (U.S. Am. Cmplt. (Dkt. No. 62) ¶ 88; N.Y. Cmplt. (Dkt. No. 61) ¶ 75) Accordingly, spending for dinners frequently exceeded the caps, with hundreds of dollars being spent on each individual attendee's meal. (U.S. Am. Cmplt. (Dkt. No. 62) ¶¶ 88, 130–32; see N.Y. Cmplt. (Dkt. No. 61) ¶ 75)

Novartis also turned a blind eye as to whether its speaker programs were being used for illegitimate purposes. (U.S. Am. Cmplt. (Dkt. No. 62) ¶ 5; N.Y. Cmplt. (Dkt. No. 61) ¶ 6) Novartis did not require signatures on attendance sheets at speaker events, and it was the sales representatives themselves who were responsible for reviewing the accuracy of receipts from speaker event venues. (U.S. Am. Cmplt. (Dkt. No. 62) ¶¶ 91–92; N.Y. Cmplt. (Dkt. No. 61) ¶¶ 78–79) There was no system in place to prevent sales representatives from repeatedly selecting the same doctors as attendees at speaker programs on the same topics, or to prevent them from arranging for the same doctors to take turns speaking and attending each other's programs repeatedly. (U.S. Am. Cmplt. (Dkt. No. 62) ¶ 84; N.Y. Cmplt. (Dkt. No. 61) ¶ 71) When sales representatives were reported for misconduct, Novartis's only punishment was a "slap on the wrist," such as placing a "conduct memo" in the employee's file. (U.S. Am. Cmplt. (Dkt. No. 62) ¶¶ 5, 169–71; N.Y. Cmplt. (Dkt. No. 61) ¶ 6) In some circumstances, sales representatives who were reported for non-compliance were even later promoted. (U.S. Am. Cmplt. (Dkt. No. 62) ¶ 5; N.Y. Cmplt. (Dkt. No. 61) ¶ 6)

When doctors wrote increased prescriptions for Novartis drugs as a result of kickbacks—which pharmacies then filled, submitting claims for reimbursement to federal and state healthcare programs—they violated federal and state anti-kickback laws. According to Plaintiffs, compliance with these laws is a precondition for reimbursement. (U.S. Am. Cmplt. (Dkt. No. 62) ¶¶ 17–18, 175–82; N.Y. Cmplt. (Dkt. No. 61) ¶¶ 135–44) Accordingly, as a result of the kickbacks it offered to physicians, Novartis caused thousands of false claims to be submitted for payment to federal healthcare programs—including Medicare, Medicaid, TRICARE, and the Veterans Administration healthcare program, (U.S. Am. Cmplt. (Dkt. No. 62) ¶¶ 6, 20–56, 175)—and state healthcare programs, including New York Medicaid. (N.Y. Cmplt. (Dkt. No. 61) ¶¶ 7, 135–46)

B. Alleged Off-Label Promotion

Novartis allegedly promoted one of its cardiovascular—Valturna—for off-label use. (Relator Third Am. Cmplt. ("TAC") ¶¶ 104–25)

Prior to June 2010, Novartis had been selling Diovan, a "blockbuster" hypertension drug. (See id. ¶¶ 104, 108) Diovan generated more than $4 billion for Novartis in 2009. (Id. ¶ 104) Novartis's patent for Diovan was set to expire in 2012. (Id.)

To make up for anticipated losses resulting from the expiration of the Diovan patent, Novartis sought to build the market share of Valturna. (Id. ¶ 105) Novartis's strategy was to market Valturna to diabetic patients who might experience high blood pressure, as opposed to hypertensive patients who were already adequately controlled on existing therapies. (Id. ¶ 106) Novartis did so by training sales representatives in off-label sale and marketing practices, and using promotional materials and speaker events to suggest that hypertensive diabetics would benefit from Valturna, even though the drug was not indicated for that particular patient population. (Id. ¶¶ 109–11, 113) Novartis's promotional materials also included data from trials on rodents; sales representatives were instructed to present the data in such a way that doctors would assume that the data reflected results in humans. (Id. ¶ 112)

When healthcare providers prescribed Valturna and subsequently submitted claims for payment, they were required to certify—as a pre-condition to payment—that the services for which they were billing were "medically indicated and necessary for the health of the patient." (Id. ¶ 114) Relator alleges that Novartis's off-label promotion of Valturna caused healthcare providers to submit claims for reimbursement that were false, because the drug was neither medically indicated nor necessary for the treatment of diabetic patients. (Id.)

C. Novartis's 2010 Settlement

In September 2010, Novartis entered into an agreement with the United States Department of Justice and several states, including New York, to settle a number of FCA claims that had been brought against it. (See U.S. Am. Cmplt. (Dkt. No. 62) ¶ 4; N.Y. Cmplt. (Dkt. No. 61) ¶ 5) In the settlement agreement, Novartis acknowledged that it had "provided illegal remuneration, through mechanisms such as speaker programs, advisory boards, and gifts (including entertainment, travel and meals), to health care professionals to induce them to promote and prescribe the [Novartis] drugs Diovan, Zelnorm, Sandostatin, Exforge, and Tekturna, in violation of the Federal Anti-Kickback Statute, 42 U.S.C. 1320a-7b(b)." (U.S. Am. Cmplt. (Dkt. No. 62) ¶ 63; N.Y. Cmplt. (Dkt. No. 61) ¶ 54) By offering kickbacks to health care professionals, Novartis had caused false claims—in the form of claims for reimbursement for prescriptions for those drugs—to be submitted to federal and state healthcare programs. (See U.S. Am. Cmplt. (Dkt. No. 62) ¶ 4; N.Y. Cmplt. (Dkt. No. 61) ¶ 5)

In connection with the 2010 settlement, Novartis signed a Corporate Integrity Agreement ("CIA") with the U.S. Department of Health and Human Services Inspector General's Office in which Novartis agreed to implement a rigorous compliance program to comply with the Anti-Kickback Statute and the FCA. (See U.S. Am. Cmplt. (Dkt. No. 62) ¶ 4; N.Y. Cmplt. (Dkt. No. 61) ¶ 5) The CIA required Novartis to "ensure that [its] Policies and Procedures address ... appropriate ways to conduct Promotional Functions in compliance with all applicable Federal healthcare program requirements, including, but not limited to the federal anti-kickback statute ... and the False Claims Act," and to enact policies and procedures that "address ... programs to educate sales representatives, including but not limited to presentations by [health care professionals]" in order "to ensure that the programs are used for legitimate and lawful purposes...." (U.S. Am. Cmplt. (Dkt. No. 62) ¶ 64; N.Y. Cmplt. (Dkt. No.

61) ¶55) The CIA further required Novartis to enact compliance policies that "address ... compensation (including ... salaries, bonuses, and contests) for ... sales representatives" "to ensure that financial incentives d[id] not inappropriately motivate such individuals to engage in improper promotion, *506 sales, and marketing of Novartis'[s] Government Reimbursed Products." (U.S. Am. Cmplt. (Dkt. No. 62) ¶65; N.Y. Cmplt. (Dkt. No. 61) ¶56)

Notes and Comments

In the *Novartis* case, a former Novartis sales employee filed a federal claim against the company, alleging that it violated the False Claims Act ("FCA") and related state laws, the Anti-Kickback Statute and other related state laws. Indeed it has been held that Novartis "systematically bribed doctors to induce them to prescribe drugs from Novartis's cardiovascular division for their patients." The United States and the State of New York have intervened as to the kickback claims.

Indeed, plaintiffs allege that from January 2002 through at least November 2011, Novartis systematically bribed doctors to induce them to prescribe drugs from Novartis's cardiovascular division for their patients and that as a result of the kickbacks it offered to physicians, Novartis caused thousands of false claims to be submitted for payment to federal healthcare programs—including Medicare, Medicaid, TRI-CARE, and the Veterans Administration healthcare program, and state healthcare programs, including New York Medicaid.

As a result, one of the issues was whether an intent, standing alone, could constitute proof of intent under the Anti-Kickback statute and the Court answered positively, holding that "Novartis's conduct—as alleged in the pleadings—violates each of these policies, raising a strong inference that Novartis acted knowingly and willfully in using the speaker events to induce prescription-writing in violation of the anti-kickback laws."

The court emphasized the importance of employee adherence to corporate policies and procedures where such policies exist and are enforced. Although Novartis is a pharmaceutical company, this decision and its implications extend outside the scope of the health care industry. This decision should be considered by all regulated industries.

Emerging Justifications under Sarbanes-Oxley for an Effective Compliance Program

The corporate scandals of Enron, Worldcom and Tyco culminated in the enactment of the Sarbanes-Oxley Act ("SOX"), effective July 30, 2002. Under Section 406 of SOX, the SEC must require corporations to adopt codes of ethics for senior financial officers. Such codes of ethics for senior financial officers are a basic component of any "effective" compliance program, and every public company should formulate a global code of ethics (also known as a code of conduct) in anticipation of these rules.

Section 302 of the SOX requires that public company CEOs and CFOs must certify, among other things, in the company's annual and quarterly report that: he or she has reviewed the reports and they are not misleading; he or she is responsible for establishing and maintaining internal controls; and he or she has evaluated the effectiveness of the company controls within the 90 days preceding the report. As such, an effective corporate compliance program is imperative to enable CEO and CFO to attest that internal controls are adequate.

SOX requires audit committees to establish procedures for "the confidential, anonymous submission by employees of [the corporation] regarding questionable accounting or auditing matters." *See* Section 301(4). In this regard, according to the 2008 Report on Fraud of the Association of Certified Fraud Examiners,[6] hotlines can lower the amount of fraud by 50%. The most effective way to catch corporate criminals is through employee hotlines according to the 2014 Report on Fraud by the Association of Certified Fraud Examiners.[7] More than 40 percent of the cases included in the 2014 study were detected by a tip. SOX also prohibits the destruction, alteration or concealment of any record or document with the "intent to impede, obstruct or influence the investigation or proper administration of any matter within the jurisdiction of any department or agency of the United States...," and a new felony carries a fine and maximum 20-year prison sentence. *See* Sections 802(a) and 1102(c) (Corporate Fraud Accountability Act of 2002).

Thus, document destruction, as an important component of a document management program, must be performed in accordance with an established company-wide document management program to avoid the stiff penalties under SOX. This also means there must be a process that includes litigation holds as well as proper administration of the company paper and electronic documents to prevent the spoliation, including alteration or concealment, of documents.

Compelling Reasons under Sarbanes-Oxley Final Rule Commentary

Since the implementation of SOX, over 10 years ago, the legal necessity of a Code of Conduct has been clear. While SOX only requires a code of conduct/ethics for senior corporate officers, in fact the Sarbanes-Oxley Final Rule Commentary strongly encourages an overall code of conduct for all employees tailored to the needs of the specific corporation. The Sarbanes-Oxley Final Rule Commentary, provided by the

---

6. http://www.acfe.com/uploadedfiles/acfe_website/content/documents/2008-rttn.pdf.

7. http://www.acfe.com/rttn/docs/2014-report-to-nations.pdf.

Securities and Exchange Commission ("SEC"), states that "We [the SEC] continue to believe that ethics codes do, and should, vary from company to company and that decisions as to the specific provisions of the code, compliance procedures and disciplinary measures for ethical breaches are best left to the company. Such an approach is consistent with our disclosure based regulatory scheme. Therefore, the rules do not specify every detail that the company must address in its code of ethics, or prescribe any specific language that the code of ethics must include. They further do not specify the procedures that the company should develop, or the types of sanctions that the company should impose, to ensure compliance with its code of ethics. We [the SEC] strongly encourage companies to adopt codes that are broader and more comprehensive than necessary to meet the new disclosure requirements." Thus, the "broader and more comprehensive" codes probably would encompass providing the code of conduct/ethics to all employees. As recently as November 2015, in the Resource Guide to the FCPA,[8] the SEC and the U.S. Department of Justice (DOJ) reiterated that "when assessing a compliance program, DOJ and SEC will review whether the company has taken steps to make certain that the code of conduct remains current and effective and whether a company has periodically reviewed and updated its code."

Moreover, the SEC states that there may even be a need for separate codes of conduct for different types of officers within the corporation. As it states, "We [the SEC] have added an instruction to the code of ethics disclosure item indicating that a company may have separate codes of ethics for different types of officers." This anticipates tiered policies as well as training for different groups of senior officers. For example, those senior officers who travel abroad should be charged in the code of conduct and trained on the need not to provide bribes to foreign officials since this would be a violation of the Foreign Corrupt Practices Act, UK Bribery Act and the OECD Anti-bribery Statutes.

Additionally, according to Sarbanes Oxley Final Rule Commentary[9] provided by the SEC, "A copy of the code of ethics should be an exhibit to the annual report. Alternatively, it can be posted on an internet website or set forth in the annual report that the company will send a copy of the code of ethics on request at no charge." Clearly, the need to provide and post the code of conduct/ethics where it is easily available to all employees, officers, directors and shareholders is critical to the success of the compliance program.

Further, the SEC makes it clear in the Commentary that changes to the code of conduct/ethics must be provided and posted so that they are easily available to all corporate constituencies. The SEC states, "Any amendment or waiver of an ethics provision of the code of ethics must be disclosed through Form 8-K within five business days or, in the alternative, in the Form 10-K and on its internet website."

---

8. http://www.justice.gov/sites/default/files/criminal-fraud/legacy/2015/01/16/guide.pdf.
9. https://www.sec.gov/rules/final/34-47262.htm.

Compelling Reasons under the New York Stock Exchange Rule 303A and NASD Rule 4350

Rule 303A.10 of the New York Stock Exchange (now succeeded by the Financial Industry Regulatory Authority ("FINRA")) requires NYSE-listed companies to adopt codes of business conduct and ethics for directors, officers, and employees which codes are to be posted publicly. Further, waivers of the code for directors or executives must be promptly disclosed to shareholders. Thus, it is anticipated by the New York Stock Exchange and FINRA that all employees will be made aware of the code of conduct/ethics. Similarly, Rule 4350 of the NASD (succeeded by FINRA) requires NASD-listed companies to adopt a code of conduct for directors, officers and employees which codes are to be posted publicly. Further, waivers of the code must be disclosed on a Form 8-K within five days.

The Importance of the U.S. Department of Justice Memoranda on Compliance Programs

The United States Department of Justice has provided guidance on prosecutorial decisions with respect to corporate criminal wrongdoing initially in the 1999 Holder Memorandum, followed by the 2003 Thompson Memorandum, the 2007 McNulty Memorandum and the 2008 Filip Memorandum. These memoranda provide that, in determining whether to charge a corporation for the criminal misconduct of its employees, prosecutors should consider the existence and adequacy of the corporation's compliance program.

The use by federal prosecutors of the waiver of the corporate client's attorney-client privilege, prompted by the Department of Justice's Holder and Thompson Memoranda, as a lever to pressure companies under investigation to "cooperate" and also to isolate employees, has evoked strong criticism from in-house counsel and business associations. As a result of such criticism, the Department of Justice purported to moderate its approach in the McNulty Memorandum, requiring prosecutors to seek approval from senior officials in Washington before requesting a company's results of internal investigations.

Further, the September 9, 2015, Yates Memorandum discusses the need for corporations "in order to qualify for cooperation credit" to provide the Justice Department "all relevant facts relating to the individuals responsible for the misconduct." These "individuals" may be corporate employees who perpetrated the wrongdoing." The Yates memorandum states as follows:

> Such accountability is important for several reasons: it deters future illegal activity, it incentivizes changes in corporate behavior, it ensures that the proper parties are held responsible for their actions and it promotes the public's confidence in our justice system.

The guidance in this memo reflects six key steps as set forth below:

(1) in order to qualify for any cooperation credit, corporations must provide to the Department all relevant facts relating to the individuals responsible for the misconduct; (2) criminal and civil corporate investigations should focus on individuals from the inception of the investigation; (3) criminal and civil attorneys handling corporate investigations should be in routine communication with one another; (4) absent extraordinary circumstances or approved departmental policy, the department will not release culpable individuals from civil or criminal liability when resolving a matter with a corporation; (5) Department attorneys should not resolve matters with a corporation without a clear plan to resolve related individual cases, and should memorialize any declinations as to individuals in such cases; and (6) civil attorneys should consistently focus on individuals as well as the company and evaluate whether to bring suit against an individual based on considerations beyond than individual's ability to pay.

In conclusion: "Companies cannot pick and choose what facts to disclose. That is, to be eligible for any credit for cooperation, the company must identify all individuals involved in or responsible for the misconduct at issue, regardless of their position, status or seniority, and provide to the Department all facts relating to that misconduct."

Further, in the decision of *United States v. Stein*, 495 F. Supp. 2d 390 (S.D.N.Y. 2007), the U. S. Court of Appeals for the Second Circuit dismissed the charges against thirteen KPMG former partners and employees finding that the Department of Justice had violated the Sixth Amendment rights of these individuals by pressuring KPMG to stop paying their legal fees. The court held that not advancing legal fees to these employees "followed as a direct consequence of the government's overwhelming influence ..." The KPMG case coupled with criticism of the McNulty Memorandum from in-house counsel and business associations led to a desire by the Department of Justice to seemingly soften their position on pressuring corporations as to legal defense funds and waiving the attorney-client privilege as to the results of internal investigations.

This position was further moderated on August 28, 2008, by Mark R. Filip, Deputy Attorney General, in the "Principles of Federal Prosecutions of Business Organizations," also known as the "Filip Memorandum." The Department of Justice would no longer consider whether a corporation waived the attorney client privilege or work product protection in determining whether a corporation has cooperated with the government's investigation under the corporate charging guidelines. Prosecutors are no longer permitted to request a waiver of the attorney-client privilege.

However, one of the revised nine guideline factors that the Department of Justice will still consider in determining whether to prosecute or investigate a corporation involves cooperation. One of the factors is, "the corporation's timely and voluntary disclosure of wrongdoing and its cooperation with the government's investigation." Principles of Federal Prosecution of Business Organizations, United States Attorney Manual ch.9-28.700 (Aug. 2008).

Therefore, beware of the need to create and keep logs on cooperation with the U.S. Attorneys Offices to show the corporation's willingness to assist the prosecutors where possible since, generally, U.S. Attorneys keep such logs of their interactions with corporate defendants.

Further, the Yates Memorandum of September 9, 2015, discusses the need to charge all individuals who may have participated in the commission of corporate wrongdoing while an employee. This clearly indicates that to receive cooperation credit from the Department of Justice, the corporation must disclose to the Justice Department all individuals who may have committed misconduct while employees.

The Revised November 1, 2004, and November 1, 2010, U.S. Sentencing Guidelines

Developments in recent years have provided new reasons for corporations to implement effective corporate compliance programs. One of the most important developments has been the revisions of the U.S. Sentencing Guidelines on November 1, 2004, and November 1, 2010. The November 1, 2004, revisions of the U.S. Sentencing Guidelines require a "culture" of ethics and a risk assessment (or "best practice gaps" analysis) to support the underlining structure of the corporate compliance program. They also discuss the need, along with standards and procedures, for processes including internal controls to promote compliance. Additionally, the U.S. Sentencing Guidelines promote the role of the Board of Directors in overseeing the compliance program. Further, they discuss the need to set up incentives as well as discipline to promote the compliance program.

In 2010, Sentencing Guidelines Amendment 744 heightened the requirement to respond to criminal conduct under § 8B2.1(b)(7) by specifically mentioning restitution to identifiable victims, self-reporting and cooperation with authorities. The 2010 Amendment also changed the calculation of the culpability score under § 8C2.5(f). The 2010 Amendment allows corporations to receive a deduction in the culpability score if four criteria are established: (1) compliance officers have direct reporting obligations to the governing authority, (2) the compliance program detected the offense before outside discovery, (3) the corporation promptly reported the offense to the governmental authorities, and (4) no compliance officer participated in, condoned, or was willfully ignorant of the offense.

Deferred Prosecutions Agreements Requiring Compliance Programs

Effective ethics and compliance programs are frequently required in the deferred prosecution agreements between corporations and the government. There have been over one hundred deferred prosecutions which required corporations to establish compliance programs costing millions of dollars, overseen by a court-appointed representative, and lasting for periods of up to five years. Therefore, failure to have an effective compliance program can lead to the costly and time-consuming remedy of a court-installed compliance program mandated by a deferred-prosecution agreement.

Declination of Prosecution

In 2012, the U.S. Department of Justice (DOJ) and the Securities and Exchange Commission (SEC) granted Morgan Stanley a Declination of Prosecution for the violations of the Foreign Corrupt Practices Act (FCPA) conducted by Garth Peterson, the managing director of the company's real estate business in China. During the investigation process, Morgan Stanley's Compliance Officers cooperated with the authorities and conducted a thorough internal investigation with the purpose of determining the scope of the improper conduct and illegal payments involved in the alleged charges. According to a press release published on April 25, 2012, by the Office of Public Affairs of the U.S. Department of Justice, the following facts of Morgan Stanley's effective compliance program played a key role in the DOJ's decision to sign the Declination, these are:

(1) Morgan Stanley maintained a system of internal controls meant to ensure accountability for its assets and to prevent employees from offering, promising or paying anything of value to foreign government officials.

(2) Morgan Stanley's internal policies, which were updated regularly to reflect regulatory developments and specific risks, prohibited bribery and addressed corruption risks associated with the giving of gifts, business entertainment, travel, lodging, meals, charitable contributions, and employment.

(3) Morgan Stanley frequently trained its employees on its internal policies, the FCPA and other anti-corruption laws. The company was able to provide evidence that showed the training efforts conducted between 2002 and 2008. As part of this evidence, Morgan Stanley proved that it trained various groups of Asia-based personnel on anti-corruption policies 54 times; trained Peterson on the FCPA seven times, and reminded him to comply with the FCPA at least 35 times.

(4) Morgan Stanley's compliance personnel regularly monitored transactions, randomly audited particular employees, transactions and business units, and tested to identify illicit payments.

(5) Morgan Stanley conducted extensive due diligence on all new business partners and imposed stringent controls on payments made to business partners.

(6) United States Government Contracting under the Federal Acquisition Regulations Mandating Compliance Programs.

Additionally, in the government contracting area, as of December 12, 2008, government contractors and subcontractors are subject to new regulations, as part of the Federal Acquisition Regulation ("FAR"), that require, among other things, the implementation and maintenance of compliance programs including the elements of an "effective" compliance and ethics program described in the United States Sentencing Guidelines. *See* 73 Fed. Reg. 67064, FAR Case 2007-006, Contractor Business Ethics Compliance Program and Disclosure Requirements (Nov. 12, 2008); United States Sentencing Guidelines Manual § 8B2.1 (2011).

U.S. Department of Health and Human Services Guidance on Effective Compliance Programs

The U.S. Department of Health and Human Services ("HHS" has provided extensive guidance to the health care sector on how to create an effective corporate compliance program. This guidance has come from the Office of Inspector General of HHS as well as from corporate integrity agreements between HHS and individual health care companies. This is an important source of guidance on a developed industry — health care — which can provide insights to help create effective corporate compliance programs in other less compliance "conscious" segments of the economy.

Compliance Failure and the Global Debt Crisis

The global debt crisis and its aftermath have further highlighted the failure of current compliance laws, regulations and guidance to avert the disastrous effects of a financial debacle. Could more compliance requirements, different compliance strategies, and/or better enforcement of existing laws and regulations have stemmed the global financial crisis?

It is clear that the global financial crisis and its aftermath underscored the importance of effective compliance programs. Further, creating an effective compliance program in the current economic environment is particularly important in alleviating the ongoing economic strains and in ensuring the integrity of government rescue actions globally. In the U.S., the American Recovery and Reinvestment Act of 2009 ("the Stimulus Act"), signed into law on Feb. 17, 2009, imposes sweeping changes to the executive compensation and corporate governance standards applicable to all recipients of government funds under the Troubled Asset Relief Program ("TARP"), including requiring CEO/CFOs to certify compliance with the executive compensation and corporate governance standards. See H.R. 1, Division B, Title VII, § 7001 et seq. Similarly, sponsors of asset-backed securities ("ABS") admitted to Federal Reserve's Term Asset-Backed Securities Loan Facility ("TALF") are subject to the executive compensation restrictions passed as section 111 of the Emergency Economic Stabilization Act ("EESA") of 2008 and applicable to recipients of TARP assistance. The enforcement and implementation of these requirements and certifications, under the TARP and TALF bailout actions, cannot succeed unless robust compliance programs are created. This presents the opportunity to create compliance programs to deal with these regulations.

Creating a basic compliance program can be a fairly easy process if there is a basic culture of ethics in the company as well as adequate time and resources. To create and enhance this culture of ethics within the corporation, it is important for all constituencies of the corporation to be aware of the compelling reasons for an effective compliance program. Further, it is important to have a strategy in creating a basic compliance program which includes the seven steps of the Sentencing Guidelines, including commencing with the foundational element of a risk assessment.

Strategy for Creating an Effective Compliance Program

Strategic Analysis of the Components

There are seven elements necessary for the creation of an effective corporate compliance program coupled with a risk assessment (or best practices/gaps analysis). The elements are based on the U.S. Sentencing Guidelines for Organizations ("Sentencing Guidelines"), as amended on November 1, 2004. *See* United States Sentencing Guidelines Manual § 8B2.1 (2011). Moreover, an effective compliance program must ensure that the organization "(1) exercise due diligence to prevent and deter criminal conduct; and (2) otherwise promote an organizational culture that encourages ethical conduct and a commitment to compliance with the law." *See* United States Sentencing Guidelines Manual § 8B2.1(a) (2011).

The U.S. Sentencing Guidelines provide the framework for the design and implementation of the corporate compliance program. Its cornerstone is the risk assessment or best practices/gaps analysis. This analysis includes looking at the history of the corporation for vulnerabilities as well as best practices and gaps within the corporation to assess its risks and strengths. This is the underlying basis for considering the seven steps of an effective compliance program.

The Part C Risk Assessment (Best Practice and Gaps Analysis) and the seven elements described in the U.S. Sentencing Guidelines for an effective compliance program are as follows:

Part C Risk Assessment

The Part C Risk Assessment (Best Practice and Gaps Analysis) is required by the November 1, 2004, Amendments to the US Sentencing Guidelines. It is the foundation of an "effective" compliance program. The Part C Risk Assessment requires regular legal risk assessments of the company. These should be done, according to industry best practice, at least yearly but may be performed quarterly or monthly, as necessary. It should include all legal risk including industry specific and country specific risks. The risk assessment should include an inventory of relevant documents including the code of conduct, training materials, litigation logs and insurance policies; interview reports for key officers and employees; heatmaps and dashboards prioritizing risk areas and risk process areas; and an executive summary of the risk assessment.

The First Element: Standards, Procedures, and Processes for a Corporate Compliance Program

The standards, procedures, and processes for an effective compliance program should be drafted by the compliance/ethics office. This can be done in consultation with the legal department and risk management department, and, if appropriate, the human resources, finance, and information technology departments. The compliance/ethics office may also be assisted by the ethics committee if one is created. Critical to this first element of the compliance program is alignment of the standards, procedures and processes.

Written Policies and Procedures

Examples of the types of written policies and procedures include the following documents: mission statement; a letter from the CEO/President on the importance of compliance; code of conduct/ethics; employee handbook; statement of policies addressing specific risk areas; and corporate compliance program guidelines. All of these documents provide standards and procedures to guide the officers, directors and employees in performing their respective responsibilities.

Alignment

Further, the policies and procedures, set forth above, must be aligned with each other and, in particular, with the mission statement, code of conduct/ethics, standard policies, employee handbook, and corporate compliance program guidelines. Alignment is critical to the integrity of the compliance program. If the mission statement is inconsistent with the spirit and tone of the code of conduct/ethics, the program could lack a coherent message.

Further, is the code of conduct/ethics merely the spirit of the program, or does it include the letter of the law? This is a strategic decision to be made at the outset of the program. For example, General Electric ("GE") actually provides a two-part code of conduct/ethics entitled the "Spirit" and the "Letter of the Law." The "Spirit" is a short version of the code of conduct/ethics, applicable to all employees globally, regardless of country or industry. The "Letter of the Law" is customized to the specific code of conduct/ethics needs of a particular country and industry. Again, as the GE example illustrates, alignment is critical in determining how different written policies and procedures such as the code of conduct/ethics should be constructed for a particular corporation.

Moreover, alignment is important not only in looking at the mission statement coupled with the code of conduct/ethics, but also as it relates to the other standard policies, employee handbook, and corporate compliance guidelines.

For example, if the phrase "sexual harassment and discrimination" is used in the code of conduct/ethics, is it explained using the same terminology in the human resources policies and employee handbook concerning "sexual harassment and discrimination"? Additionally, do the corporate compliance guidelines including, for example, how hotline inquiries are handled on "sexual harassment and discrimination" issues, all align in terminology and procedures? If alignment does not occur, this could create confusion for employees as to what is "sexual harassment and discrimination."

Further, the corporation will have difficulty in disciplining, firing and prosecuting employees for such misconduct. Finally, the corporation will have difficulty in defending itself if there are inconsistent statements as to what constitutes "sexual harassment and discrimination." Alignment is critical to training employees as well as auditing and monitoring the success or the lack thereof of the compliance program.

Internal Controls

Internal controls, based on risk assessment, should be conducted in areas including, but not limited to, the following: Anti Money-Laundering; Attorney-Client Privilege; Advertising/Marketing; Antitrust/Competition; Corporate Governance; Corporate Social Responsibility; Customs; Conflicts of Interest; eDiscovery; E-mails; Employment; Environmental; ERISA; Executive Compensation; Export Controls; False and Deceptive Advertising; Foreign Corrupt Practices Act/Anti-bribery; Fraudulent Financial Reporting; Gifts and Gratuities; Government contracting (FAR); Immigration/Migration; Insider Trading/Securities; Intellectual Property; Lobbying, Political Contributions and other political activities; New Business "Alliances"; Procurement of Goods/Services; Records Management; Protection Security/Wiretapping; Privacy, Data and Information Security; Sexual Harassment; Subcontractors and Contract Labor; Tax; and Workplace Safety. An example of an internal control is a mandatory two-week yearly holiday for all traders at banks and financial institutions. Further, industry-specific areas should be included based on the particular product line and/ or services offered by the company. For example, a pharmaceutical company needs to be aware of U.S. Food and Drug Administration ("FDA") requirements.

The Second Element: Responsible Individuals (Chief Compliance Officer and Compliance Officers, the General Counsel, Board of Directors and Top Management of the Corporation) to Oversee and Manage the Compliance Program

The Board of Directors should be knowledgeable about corporate compliance and oversee the compliance office. This requires regular semi-annual, quarterly and/or monthly reports on the activities of the compliance office to the Board of Directors and/or the Audit Committee of the Board of Directors. Such reports should be provided by the compliance office or through the legal department. In some cases, reporting is through the finance department. There are different advantages to each of these reporting choices, and the particular dynamics of the corporations should be considered.

The CEO/President of the corporation should provide leadership for the compliance program. This includes launching the compliance program with the message from the CEO/President. This leadership at the top sets the tone for the compliance program and is an essential element of creating a culture of compliance within the corporation.

Further, top management must ensure the effectiveness of the compliance office by providing necessary personnel and funding. Top management should take a leadership role in fostering the compliance program by supporting the program in their daily activities.

Finally, "specific high-level personnel," which usually consists of the compliance officers in the compliance office, should be designated with the responsibility for the day-to-day operation of the compliance program. The chief compliance officer is critical to the success of the compliance program. For the compliance effort to succeed, the chief compliance officer should be afforded access to the CEO/President and the Board of Directors, as well as sufficient funding and staff. A chief compliance officer should be appointed to coordinate the activities of individual compliance "officers" at subsidiaries. Finally, it is vital that the chief compliance officer and all other compliance officers be known for their integrity and high ethical standards.

The compliance officer's responsibilities include: overseeing and monitoring the implementation of the compliance program; reporting on a regular basis to the CEO/President and the Board of Directors/Audit Committee; periodically revising the program in light of new developments; developing, coordinating and participating in a multifaceted educational and training program that focuses on the elements of the compliance program; assisting the financial management in coordinating internal compliance reviews; monitoring high legal risk activities of the company; independently investigating and acting on matters related to compliance, including the flexibility to design and coordinate internal investigations; developing policies and programs that encourage managers and employees to report suspected fraud and other improprieties without fear of retaliation. These activities are only a few of the responsibilities of an effective compliance officer.

The Third Element: Exclusion of Certain Persons from the Corporate Compliance Function

Under this element of the Sentencing Guidelines, the General Counsel and the Director of Human Resources should undertake reasonable efforts not to include in the compliance function any personnel of questionable integrity. This entails background checks on all employees involved in the administration and coordination of corporate compliance. In particular, the background of the chief compliance officer should be carefully investigated before his or her appointment. Background checks are essential to maintain the integrity of compliance office and its personnel. Remember that background checks can only be performed at the time of hire or at the time of promotion or a salary increase.

The Fourth Element: Effective Communication of Compliance Standards and Procedures through Training

The compliance office should take reasonable steps to communicate periodically, and, in a practical manner, its standards and procedures to directors, officers, and employees, by conducting effective training programs. Training should include, for example, the following areas: code of conduct/ethics; employment issues; antitrust and competition issues; information management, intellectual property, privacy issues, conflict of interests, and other relevant issues for the company. Such training programs should be tailored to the needs of particular segments of the company. For example, sales and marketing personnel should receive training in antitrust and competition, and senior officers and those travelling outside the U.S. should be trained on the Foreign Corrupt Practices Act ("FCPA"), UK Bribery Act and the OECD Anti-bribery Statutes.

Further, training programs should include train-the-trainer programs where feasible, as well as internet-based training programs. While it may not be feasible for the compliance office to train everyone, a cascading training program featuring a small initial group from fifteen to twenty people taught by their immediate supervisor can be particularly effective in training on ethical issues encompassed in the code of conduct/ethics. Indeed, creating a culture of ethics is difficult without such highly effective train-the-trainer programs. Small training programs can also be particularly helpful, for example, in explaining the concept of attorney-client privilege and document management.

Also, once the train-the-trainer program is completed, internet refreshers programs are extremely effective. The compliance office along with the human resources department should coordinate training to occur at the time of hiring as well as at regularly scheduled intervals at least once or twice a year. A corporate compliance program cannot be effective without an adequate training program for all employees that is customized to the needs of the each employee.

The Fifth Element: Auditing, Monitoring and Reporting for the Compliance Program

The compliance office should develop effective methods of auditing, monitoring and reporting. These activities encompass creating an anonymous hotline, publicizing the reporting system, protecting whistle blowers, setting up a regular auditing and monitoring schedule, providing for on-site visits and spot checks, publicize the results of the compliance program, and conducting exit interviews. Auditing, including spot auditing, and monitoring on all aspects of corporate compliance, with the assistance of the internal controls department and the finance department, should be performed at least quarterly and reported to the General Counsel and the Board of Directors/audit committee of the Board of Directors, on a quarterly basis.

Further, the use of testing and surveillance for major areas of compliance risk, as a type of auditing and monitoring, should be conducted regularly. Testing of all auditing and monitoring systems as well as surveillance of all employees should be conducted on a continuing basis. This is an excellent way to promote best practices within the company. Further, supporting such comprehensive and effective compliance testing and surveillance systems lends credibility to the auditing, monitoring and reporting function of the compliance program.

Under this element of the U.S. Sentencing Guidelines, the compliance office should coordinate with the anonymous company-wide compliance hotline to flag problems concerning corporate compliance. This hotline can be done through adding prompts and changing prioritizations for follow-up on hotline communications. The hotline can be external, through one of the international hotline service providers or internal with a dedicated hotline unit established within the company in a segregated location.

The Sixth Element: Consistent Enforcement through Corrective Actions, Penalties and Incentives to Reinforce the Compliance Program

The compliance office should develop written policies on disciplinary standards and maintain an incentives system to encourage and promote the compliance program. These incentives and disciplinary standards should be disseminated to all new and existing employees. The policies should be incorporated in the employee handbook and adherence to compliance policies and procedures should be part of the annual review of an employee.

The Seventh Element: Continual Update and Renewal of the Compliance Program

The compliance office should create a system to continually review and update the compliance guidelines. This will encourage best practices to be maintained in the training programs as well as in the auditing, monitoring, and reporting procedures. Further, the mission statement, policies and procedures, and internal controls should be reviewed and updated as necessary to meet the needs of the internal and external information flow, technological advances, and evolving legal requirements.

At least every year, a complete risk assessment (best practices gaps analysis) should be performed by the compliance office to benchmark against comparable companies and ensure that the compliance program is conforming to best practices. This risk assessment is different from the compliance testing and surveillance of employees on compliance risks since it is part of the Part C Risk Assessment rather than part of the ongoing auditing, monitoring and reporting requirements of the fifth element of the U.S. Sentencing Guidelines.

Chart of Phases for Creating a Corporate Compliance Program

Phase I	Phase II	Phase III	Phase IV	Phase V
High Level Compliance Assessment	Develop an Overall Corporate Compliance Blueprint	Evaluate and Develop Policies in Substantive Areas	Communication, Training and Implementation	Continual Refining of the Program, Auditing, Testing and Surveillance, Monitoring and Reporting
High Level Review	Code of Conduct	Antitrust/ Competition	Introduce Code of Conduct and Program	Internal Controls
Inventory of Company's Documents Interview Reports Heatmaps and Dashboards	Corporate Compliance Program Guide-lines	Document Management	Ongoing Communication Plan including Hotline System	Internal Audits
Best Practices and Gaps Analysis/Risk Assessment Executive Summary		Employment	Training Plan	Incentive and Discipline System
Work Plan		Environmental Anti-Money Laundering	Training Material including train the trainer and internet training programs	Publicize reporting results to all corporate constituencies
Senior Management Meeting		Foreign Corrupt Practices/UK Bribery Act/ OECD Anti-Bribery Act/ Local and State Anti-Bribery	Training Schedule	Survey of all employees concerning corporate risks assessment
		Intellectual Property		Compliance risk assessment by the compliance office or outside service provider
		Securities/Insider Trading		Marketing the compliance program
		Other Risk Areas		

Phase I: Conducting a High-Level Compliance Risk Assessment

During Phase I, a compliance/ethics committee should be formed to be composed of at least the CEO or President, the General Counsel, CFO, and the Internal Audit Director. The Committee should report to the audit committee of the Board of Directors or directly to the Board of Directors. This committee is the key to involvement by senior corporate officers in the compliance program. In turn, the reporting of the compliance/ethics committee to the audit committee of the Board of Directors or directly to the Board of Directors should achieve buy-in from the corporate entity.

The corporate compliance/ethics committee should designate an individual who will become the chief compliance officer to operate as the "point person" for the compliance/ethics committee. The chief compliance officer will be responsible for collecting the company's documents, such as current policies and procedures, litigation logs, and insurance policies as part of an inventory of documents. The compliance officer will also be responsible for conducting all interviews. However, the chief compliance officer may wish to share this responsibility in order to gain outside expertise and/or try to invoke attorney-client privilege which is, at best, tenuous. The chief compliance officer may use outside legal providers and/or outside counsel to assist in interviewing key officers and employees of the company and all subsidiaries.

These interviews should include the following senior officers: the president; vice president for business development/sales and marketing; general counsel/outside counsel; chief financial officer; human resources director; environmental health and safety director (if any); and other key officers and employees, as necessary.

A report on risk assessment or best practices/gaps analysis should be prepared and presented to the compliance/ethics committee based on the following questions: what are your key risk areas; what are the standards and procedures that you now have in place in these risk areas; what are the areas you have successfully limited risk and how; what areas could you improve to limit risk and how; what is happening in such key areas as antitrust, environmental, employment, intellectual property and securities; describe the company culture toward corporate compliance and limiting risk.

In presenting the report on risk assessment or best practices/gaps analysis, the following should be provided: the report should indicate the risk assessments for relevant areas of law including heatmaps and dashboards; the report should be presented to senior officers and the Board of Directors; the report should be presented to the officers of all subsidiaries who were interviewed; buy-in on the report should be encouraged; and a workplan should be created which includes a timetable and an action plan.

Phase II: Develop an Overall Compliance Blueprint

In Phase II, an overall compliance blueprint should be developed, and other codes of conduct should be reviewed. The chief compliance officer should work with the compliance/ethics committee formed in Phase I and focus groups to develop a code of conduct/ethics customized to the company culture.

It is important to make sure that the code of conduct/ethics is suitable for all employees, and is user-friendly and attractively packaged. A mission statement and letter from the CEO/President should be prepared to accompany the code and conduct/ethics when it is distributed to all employees of the corporation.

Finally, the compliance program should be institutionalized through the compliance program guidelines.

These compliance program guidelines should be created simultaneously with the code of conduct/ethics. While they can be modified in the future, it is critical that the compliance program be institutionalized at the earliest opportunity.

Phase III: Evaluate and Develop Policies and Procedures in Substantive Areas

In Phase III, policies and procedures in substantive areas should be evaluated and developed by the chief compliance officer.

First, the chief compliance officer should inventory all existing policies and procedures. Next, the chief compliance officer should align the existing policies and procedures, code of conduct/ethics and employee handbook. Finally, the chief compliance officer should develop new policies and procedures, in coordination with the legal department, human resources department, finance department, information technology department, and other departments as necessary. New policies and procedures should be developed where gaps exist, as indicated from the report on risk assessment or best practices/gaps analysis. Best practices should be borrowed, where necessary, from the policies of company subsidiaries or the material of outside organizations and individuals (e.g., trade associations, industry practice groups, law firms, and consultants).

Phase IV: Communication, Training and Implementation

Phase IV is communication, training and implementation, where the chief compliance officer should launch the compliance program. This should begin by creating awareness for the need for a compliance program and the introduction of the code of conduct/ethics with the mission statement and the letter from the CEO/President.

At the same time, the ongoing communications plan including the hotline system should be inaugurated. The training plan should be commenced for all employees including new hires. The training materials on the code of conduct/ethics including train-the-trainer and internet training programs should be introduced to all employees.

Finally, the training schedule for training on specific areas such as antitrust/competition, securities, intellectual property, Foreign Corrupt Practices/anti-bribery should be customized for all employees.

Phase V: Continual Refinement, Auditing, Testing, Surveillance, Monitoring and Reporting

Phase V is continual refinement, auditing, testing, surveillance, monitoring and reporting, where the chief compliance officer continuously spearheads the refreshment and reinvigoration of the compliance program. The chief compliance officer should oversee regular risk assessments, internal controls for compliance including reporting to the Board of Directors at regular intervals, update the internal audit system, maintain an incentive and discipline system, and publicize reporting results to all corporate constituencies. An effective corporate compliance program is an early warning system for risk control through risk assessment processes, monitoring, reporting, and training sessions.

Further, to make the compliance program memorable, a variety of tools can be used. These tools include mementos (tombstones, plastic cubes, post-it notes), screen savers, calendars, intranet sites, and formal announcements and invitations to compliance events. The rollout and maintenance of the compliance program is a marketing campaign, where the product is the compliance program and the audience is the employees of the corporation.

Sample Checklist for General Corporate Risk Areas

- Antitrust/Competition
- Conflicts of Interest
- Employment
  - Age Discrimination
  - Gender Discrimination
  - National Origin Discrimination
  - Wage and Hour Issues
  - Retaliation
  - Independent Contractors
  - Drug Testing
  - Wrongful Discharge
  - Exit Interviews
  - Ethics and Compliance Training
  - Family Medical Leave Act (FMLA)
  - Americans with Disabilities Act
  - Executive Compensation

- Competitive Behavior
- Customs
- E-mails
- Environmental
- Advertising
- Fraudulent Financial Reporting
- Government Contracting
- Intellectual Property
- Lobbying, Political Contributions and Other Political Activities
- Procurement of Goods/Services
- Security
- Sexual Harassment
- Tax
- US Patriot Act
- Fair Credit Reporting Act
  - Race Discrimination
  - Religion Based Discrimination
  - Sexual Harassment
  - I-9
  - Labor Unions/Collective Bargaining Agreements
  - Background Checks and Fair Credit Reporting Act
  - Privacy Issues
  - Hiring Practices
  - Disciplinary Actions
  - Workplace Violence
  - Military Family Leave
  - Discrimination Against Veterans
- New Business "Alliances"
- Records Management
- Privacy of Communications
- Subcontractors and Contract Labor
- Workplace Safety
- Anti Money Laundering Act
- Export Controls

- Foreign Corrupt Practices Act/OECD
- Antibribery Statutes
- Gifts and Gratuities
- Insider Trading
- Cybersecurity
- Document Management

Assignments

- Create Semester Teams: Financial Institution (e.g., J.P. Morgan); Pharmaceutical Company (e.g., Pfizer); and Manufacturing Corporation (e.g., General Electric).
- Read the Code of Conduct, 10K, 8Ks, and other SEC filings (This can be found on the Edgar System available at http://www.sec.gov/edgar.shtml.).

Chapter 2

Creating Ethics Awareness, An Ethical Culture and Tone at the Top

Introduction

The downfall of Enron was a watershed moment in the history of American business not because it revealed the dangers in accounting for special purpose offshore vehicles, or even because it was, for a brief time, the largest bankruptcy to date. Enron became legend because it was the story of a few very bright, wily, morally lax individuals who created their own universe — one in which short-term results were all that mattered and others were left to pay the long-term consequences.

Few corporate scandals have so fascinated the American public and so clearly demonstrated the destructive power of poor ethical culture. In the years since Enron, the American public has taken a renewed interest in the ethics of organizations because the public now understands that it has a vested interest in companies being successful in honest, sustainable ways.[1] As a result, corporate commitment to ethics is now seen as a necessity and a business advantage to a greater extent than ever before. Above all, creating ethics awareness, an ethical culture, and tone at the top seem to be essential.

Press Release 2004-18, SEC, SEC Charges Jeffrey K. Skilling, Enron's Former President, Chief Executive Officer and Chief Operating Officer, with Fraud

(Feb. 19, 2004) (available at https://www.sec.gov/news/press/2004-18.htm)

Seeks disgorgement of all ill-gotten gains, including compensation; civil money penalties; a permanent bar from acting as a director or officer of a publicly held company; and injunction from future violations of federal securities laws

---

1. *See* Leeds, Roger, Ph.D., *Enron and On,* Center for International Business and Public Policy at the Johns Hopkins University, Paul H. Nitze School of Advanced International Studies, available at: http://www.sais-jhu.edu/centerslbizgovcenter/worldlink.htm.

The Securities and Exchange Commission announced that it has charged Jeffrey K. Skilling, Enron Corp.'s former President, Chief Executive Officer and Chief Operating Officer, with violating, and aiding and abetting violations of, the antifraud, lying to auditors, periodic reporting, books and records, and internal controls provisions of the federal securities laws. The charges, which amend the Commission's Complaint filed against Richard A. Causey, Enron's former Chief Accounting Officer, in U.S. District Court in Houston, allege that Skilling and others engaged in a wide-ranging scheme to defraud by manipulating Enron's publicly reported financial results.

The Amended Complaint alleges that Skilling and others improperly used reserves within Enron's wholesale energy trading business, Enron Wholesale, to manufacture and manipulate reported earnings; manipulated Enron's "business segment reporting" to conceal losses at Enron's retail energy business, Enron Energy Services ("EES"); manufactured earnings by fraudulently promoting Enron's broadband unit, Enron Broadband Services ("EBS"); and improperly used special purpose entities ("SPEs") and the LJM partnerships to manipulate Enron's financial results. In addition, the Amended Complaint alleges that Skilling made false and misleading statements concerning Enron's financial results and the performance of its businesses, and that these misrepresentations were also contained in Enron's public filings with the Commission. The Amended Complaint further alleges that Skilling sold Enron stock while in possession of material, non-public information that generated unlawful proceeds of approximately $63 million.

"In this scandal, as in others, we are by now all too familiar with executives who bask in the attention that follows the appearance of corporate success, but who then shout their ignorance when the appearance gives way to the reality of corruption. Let there be no mistake that today's enforcement action against Mr. Skilling places accountability exactly where it belongs," said SEC Enforcement Division Director Stephen M. Cutler.

Added Deputy Director Linda Chatman Thomsen, "Mr. Skilling embraced the sophisticated fraud underlying Enron's false reported financial results. To do otherwise would have discredited his much publicized business initiatives."

Specifically, the Commission's Amended Complaint alleges as follows:

- **Manufacturing and Manipulating Reported Earnings through Improper Use of Reserves.** From the third quarter of 2000 through the third quarter of 2001, Skilling and others fraudulently used reserve accounts within Enron Wholesale to mask the extent and volatility of its windfall trading profits, particularly its profits from the California energy markets; avoid reporting large losses in other areas of its business; and preserve the earnings for use in later quarters. By early 2001, Enron Wholesale's undisclosed reserve accounts contained over $1 billion in earnings. Skilling and others improperly used hundreds of millions of dollars of these reserves to ensure that analysts' expectations were met. In addition, Skilling and others improperly used the reserves to conceal hundreds of millions of dollars in losses within Enron's EES business unit from the investing public.

- Further, Skilling and others approved the improper release of reserves in certain quarters prior to 2001, in order for Enron to make or exceed analysts' earnings estimates. For example, in mid-July 2000, well after the end of the second quarter, Skilling and others decided to beat Wall Street analysts' quarterly earnings expectations by two cents a share and publicly report an earnings-per-share figure of 34 cents. They did this despite knowing that Enron's performance for the quarter did not support the 34-cent earnings-per-share figure. In order to achieve this goal, they caused a senior Enron executive to release improperly millions of dollars of "prudency" reserves from Enron's energy trading business into earnings.

- **Concealing EES Failures.** Skilling and others concealed massive losses in EES by fraudulently manipulating Enron's "business segment reporting." At the close of the first quarter of 2001, Skilling and others approved moving a large portion of EES's business into Enron Wholesale under the guise of reorganizing Enron's business segments. Skilling and others knew that the reorganization was designed to fraudulently conceal hundreds of millions of dollars in losses at EES, Enron's heavily touted retail energy trading business, losses which Enron otherwise would have had to report. Enron moved the losing portion of EES's business into Enron Wholesale because Enron Wholesale had ample earnings, including the massive reserve accounts described above, to absorb EES's huge losses while continuing to meet Enron's budget targets.

- **Promoting EBS to Manufacture Earnings.** Skilling and others fraudulently promoted EBS at Enron's January 20, 2000 corporate analyst conference and manufactured earnings from the resulting increase in Enron's stock price. At the analyst conference, Skilling and others knowingly made false and misleading statements about the status of EBS's broadband network, EBS's proprietary "network control software," and the "conservative" value — $30 billion — of EBS's business. In reality, EBS had neither the broadband network that Skilling claimed, nor the critical proprietary network control software to run it. In addition, Skilling inflated the value of EBS by billions of dollars over what both internal and external valuations had advised.

- Knowing about the planned EBS presentation, Skilling and others — prior to the analyst conference — constructed and approved a scheme that allowed Enron to recognize approximately $85 million in earnings from the increase in the value of its stock. The earnings were recorded through a partnership interest Enron held in a large energy investment named JEDI that held, as one of its investment holdings, Enron stock. In connection with the January 20, 2000 analyst conference, Enron and JEDI purportedly executed a series of transactions, known as "Project Grayhawk," that allowed JEDI's income to increase as the price of Enron's stock increased. Project Grayhawk allowed Enron to recognize, through its partnership interest in JEDI, approximately $85 million in earnings as a result of the manufactured increase in Enron stock from the false and misleading presentation at the analyst conference.

- **Use of SPEs and LJM Partnerships to Manipulate Financial Results.** Enron entered into fraudulent transactions with LJM Cayman, L.P and LJM2 Co-Investment, L.P. (collectively "LJM"), two unconsolidated partnerships created and managed by Andrew Fastow, Enron's then-Chief Financial Officer, when Skilling and others knew that LJM was not a legitimate third party acting independently from Enron. Enron used transactions with LJM to manipulate its financial results.

- For example, Enron and LJM engaged in a series of financial transactions with four SPEs called Raptor I, Raptor II, Raptor III and Raptor IV (collectively referred to as the "Raptors"). Skilling, Causey, Fastow and others used the Raptors to manipulate fraudulently Enron's reported financial results. They designed Raptor I, among other things, to protect Enron from having to report publicly decreases in value in large portions of its energy "merchant asset portfolio" and technology investments by allowing Enron to "hedge" the value of those investments with an allegedly independent third party, known as Talon. The Raptor I structure, however, was invalid under applicable accounting rules because, among other things, (i) Talon was not independent from Enron and LJM's investment in Talon was not at risk, and (ii) Causey and Fastow had entered into an oral side agreement that LJM would receive its initial investment in Talon ($30 million) plus a large profit ($11 million) from Enron, all prior to Talon engaging in any of the hedging transactions. As a quid pro quo for this payment, Fastow agreed with Causey that Enron employees could use Raptor I to manipulate Enron's financial statements, including by allowing Enron employees, without negotiation or due diligence by LJM, to select the values at which the Enron assets were hedged with Talon. Skilling was informed of and approved Fastow's deal with Causey in order to ensure that Enron achieved the financial reporting goals for which Raptor I was designed, even though it was clear that the Raptor I structure was not a true hedging device.

- In another transaction — the "Cuiaba project" — Skilling and others used LJM to move a poorly performing asset temporarily off Enron's balance sheet, when in fact such off-balance-sheet treatment was improper. When no true third-party buyer could be found, Skilling and others caused Enron to "sell" a portion of Enron's interest in the Cuiaba project to LJM for $11.3 million. LJM agreed to "buy" this interest only because Skilling, Causey, Fastow and others, in an undisclosed side deal, agreed that Enron would buy back the interest, if necessary, at a profit to LJM. Based on this purported "sale," which was in fact an asset parking or warehousing arrangement, Enron improperly recognized approximately $65 million in income in the third and fourth quarters of 1999. In the spring of 2001, even though the project was approximately $200 million over budget, Skilling, Causey and Fastow agreed that Enron would buy back LJM's interest in the Cuiaba project at a considerable profit to LJM. After agreeing to execute the repurchase, Skilling, Causey, Fastow and others delayed consummating the deal until Fastow sold his interest in LJM so that Fastow's role in the transaction would not have to be publicly disclosed. In the "Nigerian barge" transaction, Skilling and others agreed to a sham "sale" of an interest in certain power-producing barges off the coast of Nigeria to Merrill Lynch so that Enron could meet its fourth quarter 1999 budget targets. In order to induce Merrill Lynch to enter into the transaction, Enron promised—in an oral and undisclosed "handshake" deal—that Merrill Lynch would receive a return of its investment plus an agreed-upon profit within six months. As a result, Merrill Lynch's equity investment was not "at risk" and Enron should not have treated the transaction as a sale from which it could record earnings and cash flow. In June 2000, Enron delivered on its "handshake" promise. Causey and Fastow ensured that LJM re-purchased the Nigerian barges from Merrill Lynch at the agreed-upon profit.

- **Insider Trading.** Skilling profited from the scheme to defraud by selling large amounts of Enron stock at the inflated prices. These trades also occurred while Skilling was in possession of material non-public information, including information about Enron's actual financial performance and the failure of its business units as described above. From April 2000 to September 2001, Skilling sold over one million shares of Enron stock that generated unlawful proceeds of approximately $63 million.

The Commission brought this action in coordination with the Department of Justice Enron Task Force, which filed related criminal charges against Skilling.

———————

To better understand the lack of ethical leadership and "tone at the top" at Enron, the allegations in the complaint against Jeffrey K. Skilling, Kenneth L. Lay, and Richard A. Causey are very illuminating. These facts vividly explain how corporate culture can be subverted by unethical conduct by key officers of the corporation.

———————

SEC v. Lay

United States District Court, Southern District of Texas
Civil Action No. H-04-0284 (Harmon)

Second Amended Compliant
Jury Demand

Plaintiff Securities and Exchange Commission (the "Commission") for its Second Amended Complaint alleges as follows:

SUMMARY

1.   Kenneth L. Lay, Jeffrey K. Skilling, and Richard A. Causey, all former senior executives of Enron, engaged in a multi-faceted scheme to defraud in violation of the federal securities laws. From at least 1999 through late 2001, Lay, Skilling, Causey, and others manipulated Enron's publicly reported financial results and made false and misleading public statements about Enron's financial condition and its actual performance. As an objective and result of their scheme to defraud, Lay, Skilling, Causey, and others made millions of dollars in the form of salary, bonuses, and the sale of Enron stock at prices they had inflated by fraudulent means. Skilling and

Causey made at least $103 million and $23 million, respectively, in illicit gains. Lay also made millions of dollars in illicit gains, and was unjustly enriched when he secretly dumped massive amounts of his own Enron stock at the same time he falsely portrayed that all was well at Enron. Although defendants owed fiduciary duties to act in the best interests of their company and shareholders, their scheme to defraud revealed in the end a troika of executives who acted for their own personal gain, leaving in their wake a bankrupt company, employees on the street, and worthless stock in the hands of shareholders and investors they had fooled.

2.   The Commission requests that this Court permanently enjoin Lay, Skilling, and Causey from violating the federal securities laws cited herein, prohibit each permanently and unconditionally from acting as an officer or director of any issuer of securities that has a class of securities registered pursuant to Section 12 of the Securities Exchange Act of 1934 ("Exchange Act") or that is required to file reports pursuant to Section 15(d) of such Act, order each to disgorge all ill-gotten gains, to pay civil penalties, to have the amount of such penalties added to and become part of a disgorgement fund for the benefit of the victims of their unlawful conduct, and order such other and further relief as the Court may deem appropriate.

JURISDICTION AND VENUE

3.   The Court has jurisdiction over this action pursuant to Sections 21(d), 21(e), and 27 of the Exchange Act [15 U.S.C. §§ 78u(d) and (e) and 78aa] and Sections 20(b), 20(d)(1) and 22(a) of the Securities Act of 1933 ("Securities Act") [15 U.S.C. §§ 77t(b), 77t(d)(1) and 77v(a)].

4.   Venue lies in this District pursuant to Section 27 of the Exchange Act [15 U.S.C. § 78aa] and Section 22 of the Securities Act [15 U.S.C. § 77v(a)] because certain acts or transactions constituting the violations occurred in this District.

5.   In connection with the acts, practices, and courses of business alleged herein, Lay, Skilling, and Causey, directly or indirectly, made use of the means and instruments of transportation and communication in interstate commerce, and of the mails and of the facilities of a national securities exchange.

6.   Lay, Skilling, and Causey, unless restrained and enjoined by this Court, will continue to engage in transactions, acts, practices, and courses of business as set forth in this Second Amended Complaint or in similar illegal acts and practices.

DEFENDANTS

7.   Kenneth L. Lay resides in Houston, Texas. Lay served as the Chairman of the Board of Directors of Enron (the "Board") from its formation in 1986 until January 23, 2002. He was the Chief Executive Officer ("CEO") of Enron from 1986 until February 2001 and from August 14, 2001 until January 23, 2002. Lay resigned from the Board on February 4, 2002. Lay presided as Chairman at board meetings, where the Board reviewed Enron's performance and financial condition. Lay, however, did not fully disclose to the Board at various times certain negative information concerning Enron that he was aware of and possessed at the time he sold shares of Enron stock. Lay also attended meetings of the Board's Finance Committee, the Audit and Com-

pliance Committee, and the Executive Committee, where the company's operations and financial condition were discussed. In his capacity as CEO, Lay had oversight of Enron's business units and supervised the senior executives and managers of these units. Lay regularly attended management meetings with these individuals and others, where the business and financial condition of Enron and its business units were discussed. Lay signed Enron's annual reports filed on Form 10-K with the SEC. Lay also signed quarterly and annual management representation letters to Enron's auditors, registration statements for the offer and sale of securities by Enron, and letters to shareholders accompanying Enron's annual reports to shareholders.

8. Jeffrey A. Skilling resides in Houston, Texas. He was employed by or acted as a consultant to Enron from at least the late 1980s through early December 2001. From 1979 to 1990, Skilling was employed by the consulting firm of McKinsey & Co., where he provided consulting services to Enron. In August 1990, Enron hired Skilling. He held various positions at Enron and in January 1997, Enron promoted Skilling to President and Chief Operating Officer ("COO") of the entire company, reporting directly to Lay. In February 2001, Skilling became CEO of Enron and retained his position as COO. On August 14, 2001, with no forewarning to the public, Skilling resigned from Enron. Lay resumed the CEO position at that time. Along with Lay, Skilling attended meetings of the Board's Finance Committee, the Audit and Compliance Committee, and the Executive Committee, where the company's operations and financial condition were discussed. Skilling also had oversight of Enron's business units and supervised the senior executives and managers of these units. Skilling regularly attended management meetings with these individuals and others, where the business and financial condition of Enron and its business units were discussed. Skilling signed Enron's annual reports filed on Form 10-K with the SEC and he signed quarterly and annual representation letters to Enron's auditors. Skilling also signed registration statements for the offer and sale of securities by Enron, and letters to shareholders accompanying Enron's annual reports to shareholders.

9. Richard A. Causey resides in Houston, Texas. He was and is a certified public accountant and worked for Enron from 1991 through early 2002. From 1986 until 1991, while an employee of the accounting firm Arthur Andersen LLP ("Andersen"), Causey provided audit services to Enron on behalf of Andersen, Enron's outside auditor. In 1991, Enron hired Causey as Assistant Controller of Enron Gas Services Group. From 1992 until 1997, Causey served in various executive positions at Enron. In 1998, Causey was made Chief Accounting Officer ("CAO") of Enron and an Executive Vice-President. As Enron's CAO, Causey managed Enron's accounting practices and reported directly to Lay and Skilling. Lay, Skilling, and Causey, along with Enron's Chief Financial Officer ("CFO") Andrew S. Fastow, its Treasurer Ben F. Glisan, Jr., and others were the principal managers of Enron's finances. Causey also was a principal manager of Enron's financial disclosures to the investing public, and he regularly participated in conferences with investment analysts and in other public forums where he discussed Enron's financial condition. Causey signed Enron's annual reports on Form 10-K and its quarterly reports on Form 10-

Q filed with the SEC, and signed quarterly and annual representation letters to Enron's auditors. Causey also signed registration statements for the offer and sale of securities by Enron.

ENTITIES AND OTHER PERSONS INVOLVED

10.   Enron Corp. is an Oregon corporation with its principal place of business in Houston, Texas. During the relevant time period, the common stock of Enron was registered with the Commission pursuant to Section 12(b) of the Exchange Act and traded on the New York Stock Exchange. Because it was a public company, Enron and its directors, officers, and employees were required to comply with federal securities laws, including rules and regulations requiring the filing of true and accurate financial information. Enron's stock price was influenced by factors such as Enron's reported financial information, credit rating, and its ability to meet revenue and earnings targets and forecasts. Investors considered this information important in making investment decisions. Likewise, the information was important to credit rating agencies and influenced the investment-grade ratings for Enron's debt, which were critical to Enron's ongoing business operations and ability to secure loans and to sell securities. During the time that defendants engaged in the fraudulent conduct alleged herein, Enron raised millions in the public debt and equity markets. Enron was the nation's largest natural gas and electric marketer with reported annual revenue of more than $150 billion. Enron rose to number seven on the Fortune 500 list of companies. By December 2, 2001, when it filed for bankruptcy, Enron's stock price had dropped in less than a year from over $80 per share to less than $1 per share.

11.   Enron Energy Services (EES) was formed by Enron in late 1996 to provide energy products and services to industrial, commercial, and residential customers in both regulated and deregulated markets. In Enron's segment disclosures, EES' results were reported separately as Retail Energy Services. Accurate segment disclosure reporting is required under generally accepted accounting principles and SEC rules and regulations for those companies operating in multiple significant industries.

12.   Enron Wholesale Services (Wholesale) was Enron's largest business segment in 2000 and 2001. Wholesale consisted of several business units, including Enron North America (ENA). ENA was the largest and most profitable business unit within Wholesale and included Enron's wholesale merchant energy business across North America. In Enron's segment disclosures, ENA's results were reported within the Wholesale segment.

13.   Enron Broadband Services, Inc. (EBS) was a wholly-owned subsidiary of Enron engaged in the telecommunications business. Its two principal business lines were Bandwidth Intermediation (the buying and selling of bandwidth) and Content Services (the delivery of high bandwidth, media rich content, such as video streaming, high capacity data transport, and video conferencing). EBS also made investments in companies with related technologies and with the potential for capital appreciation. In Enron's segment disclosures, EBS' results were reported separately as Broadband Services.

14.   Numerous other Enron executives and senior managers engaged in the scheme to defraud with Lay, Skilling, and Causey. The others included, but were not limited to, former Enron employees named as defendants in other Enron-related cases brought by the SEC in the Southern District of Texas: Fastow (SEC v. Fastow, H-02-3666); Glisan (SEC v. Glisan, H-03-3628); former ENA and EES CEO David W. Delainey, who reported to Skilling (SEC v. Delainey, H-03-4883); former ENA CAO Wesley Colwell, who reported to Causey and Delainey and managed the accounting for Enron's wholesale energy business (SEC v. Colwell, H-03-4308); and former Enron Global Finance Managing Director Michael Kopper, who reported to Fastow and conducted structured finance activities for Enron (SEC v. Kopper, H-02-3127). Others assisted in various aspects of the scheme to defraud, including Merrill Lynch and certain of its employees (SEC v. Merrill Lynch, et al., HO-03-0946), J.P. Morgan Chase & Co. (SEC v. J.P. Morgan Chase & Co., H-03-2877), Canadian Imperial Bank of Commerce and certain of its employees (SEC v. CIBC, et al., H-03-5785); and Citigroup (In the Matter of Citigroup, Inc., SEC Administrative Proceeding, File No. 3-11192).

FACTUAL ALLEGATIONS The Objectives And Roots Of The Scheme To Defraud

15.   The objectives of the scheme to defraud carried out by defendants and others were, among other things, (a) to falsely present Enron as a profitable successful business; (b) to report recurring earnings that falsely appeared to grow by approximately 15 to 20 percent annually; (c) to meet or exceed the published expectations of industry analysts forecasting Enron's reported earnings-per-share and other results; (d) to maintain an investment-grade credit rating; (e) to conceal the true magnitude of Enron's losses, growing debt and other obligations; (f) to artificially inflate Enron's stock price; and (g) to personally profit from the unlawful conduct, including gains from the sale of inflated Enron stock.

16.   As a result of the scheme to defraud carried out by defendants and others, the descriptions of Enron's business and finances in public filings and public statements by defendants and others were false and misleading, and bore no resemblance to its actual performance and financial condition.

17.   Lay, Skilling, Causey, and others planned and carried out various parts of the scheme to defraud. They and others set annual and quarterly financial targets, including earnings and cash flow targets ("budget targets"), for Enron and each of its business units. The budget targets were based on the numbers necessary to meet or exceed analysts' expectations, not on what could be realistically achieved by legitimate business operations.

18.   On a quarterly and year-end basis, Skilling, Causey, and others assessed Enron's progress toward its budget targets. Often, Enron did not meet the budget targets from business operations and had earnings and cash flow shortfalls that were at times in the hundreds of millions of dollars. Within Enron, these shortfalls were referred to variously as the "gap," "stretch," and/or "overview." When this occurred, the targets were met by unlawful means, including those described below.

Use of Special Purpose Entities and LJM Partnership to Manipulate Financial Results

19.   As part of the scheme to defraud, Skilling, Causey, and others transferred assets and liabilities to Special Purpose Entities ("SPEs"). Under applicable accounting rules, Enron did not need to consolidate the SPE on its balance sheet if an independent investor had made a substantive investment in the SPE (at least 3% of the SPE's equity), had control of the SPE, and had the risks and rewards of owning the SPE assets. Through the use of SPEs, Enron would, among other things, record earnings and cash flows while hiding debt.

Creation of LJM Partnership

20.   In June 1999, Skilling, Causey, and others sought and obtained the approval of the Board for Fastow to create and serve as the managing partner of an investment partnership named LJM Cayman, L.P. (LJM1). The Board later approved Fastow's participation, as an equity and managing partner, in another even larger partnership used to fund SPEs by Enron named LJM2 Co-Investment, L.P. (LJM2) (the LJM entities are collectively referred to as "LJM" unless otherwise noted). These entities were created to invest in SPEs for Enron.

21.   As Skilling, Causey, and others knew, LJM was not a legitimate independent third party because Fastow controlled LJM. This permitted Skilling, Causey, and others to use LJM as Enron's own vehicle for fraudulent means.

22.   From approximately July 1999 through October 2001, Enron entered into fraudulent transactions with LJM. The transactions enabled defendants and others to manipulate Enron's reported financial results by, among other things: (a) improperly moving poorly performing assets off-balance sheet; (b) concealing Enron's poor operating performance; (c) manufacturing earnings through sham transactions; and (d) improperly inflating the value of Enron's investment portfolio by backdating documents.

"Raptor" Hedges

23.   Beginning in the spring of 2000, Enron and LJM engaged in a series of financial transactions with four SPEs called Raptor I, Raptor II, Raptor III and Raptor IV (collectively referred to as the "Raptors"). The Raptors were capitalized mainly with Enron stock. Skilling, Causey, and others used the Raptors to manipulate fraudulently Enron's reported financial results. They used Raptor I, among other things, to protect Enron from having to report publicly in its financial results decreases in value in large portions of its energy merchant asset portfolio and technology investments by purportedly hedging the value of those investments with an allegedly independent third party created by Enron and LJM, known as Talon.

24.   However, Skilling, Causey, and others knew the Raptor I structure was invalid under applicable accounting rules because Talon was not independent from Enron, since LJM2's investment in Talon was not sufficiently at risk to qualify as outside equity. Causey and Fastow had an oral side-deal that LJM2 would receive its initial $30 million investment in Talon plus a profit of $11 million from Enron, all prior to Talon engaging in any of the hedging transactions for which it was created. Enron

could then use Raptor I to manipulate Enron's financial statements, including by allowing Enron employees to arbitrarily select the values at which the Enron assets were hedged with Talon. Skilling was informed of and approved the deal.

25.   The side-deal between Causey and Fastow was satisfied by Causey and others by manufacturing an illicit transaction between Enron and Talon that generated a $41 million payment to LJM2. Specifically, Causey and others caused Enron to purchase a "put" on its own stock from an entity involved in the "Raptor" structure, which had no business purpose for Enron but ensured that LJM2 received the complete return of its $30 million investment in the first "Raptor" structure, together with a profit of $11 million.

26.   After satisfying the side-deal by providing LJM2 with a guaranteed return of and on its investment, Enron began to use Raptor I to hedge the value of Enron's assets. Enron employees manipulated the book values of Enron assets, many of which were expected to decline in value, before they were hedged, knowing that the Raptor I structure ensured that Enron would not suffer the financial reporting consequences of subsequent declines or large fluctuations in the value of those assets. Causey and others further used Raptor I fraudulently to promote Enron's financial position by back-dating the effective date of the Raptor hedge to Enron's advantage, capturing the all-time high stock value of one of the Enron assets, stock in a company named AVICI, at a time when they knew that value already had declined. The basic structure used in Raptor I, including the oral side-deal between Causey and Fastow, was repeated in the three successor fraudulent hedging devices known as Raptors II, III and IV.

27.   As with Raptor I, the Raptor successors were used to manipulate fraudulently Enron's reported financial results. These vehicles did not offer true economic hedges. Because the vehicles were dependent on the value of Enron stock, if the price of Enron stock declined the hedging obligations of the Raptors could not be met, thus creating losses that would have to be reflected on Enron's financial statements.

28.   Lay approved of the Raptors and understood they did not provide a true economic hedge, and were designed and used solely to manipulate Enron's financial statements. Lay was advised at various times in 2000 that the Raptors did not transfer economic risk and that a decline in Enron's stock price would impair the hedging ability of the Raptors. By no later than August 2001, Lay was aware that the Raptors were beyond salvage, and Enron's stock price had declined below the minimum required for the Raptors to meet their hedging obligations. As a result of the fraudulent use of the Raptors, Enron reported over $1 billion in fictitious earnings on its books that should never have been recognized. Further, as set forth below, Lay made false and misleading public statements about the Raptors.

Manufacturing Earnings and Concealing Debt through Purported Sales to LJM

29.   In addition to the fraudulent Raptor hedging devices, Skilling, Causey, and others used LJM for other transactions, including purported asset sales. These generated reported earnings and cash flow and moved poorly performing assets temporarily off

Enron's balance sheet. Skilling, Causey, and others made undisclosed side agreements that guaranteed LJM against risk in certain of its transactions with Enron.

Cuiaba

30.   One such transaction involved LJM's "purchase" of Enron's interest in a company that was building a power plant in Cuiaba, Brazil (the "Cuiaba project"). On September 30, 1999, when no true third-party buyer could be found, Skilling, Causey, and others caused Enron to "sell" a portion of Enron's interest in the Cuiaba project to LJM for $11.3 million. LJM agreed to "buy" this interest only because Skilling, Causey, and others, in an undisclosed side-deal, agreed that Enron would buy back the interest, if necessary, at a profit to LJM. Based on this purported "sale," which was in fact an asset parking or warehousing arrangement, Enron improperly recognized approximately $65 million in income in the third and fourth quarters of 1999, income that was needed to meet budget targets and earnings-per-share goals.

31.   By 2001, the Cuiaba project was approximately $200 million over budget. Nonetheless, in the spring of 2001, Skilling, Causey, and others caused Enron to agree to buy back LJM's interest in the Cuiaba project at a considerable profit to LJM, pursuant to the undisclosed oral side-deal. Enron did not disclose the repurchase agreement in its second quarter 2001 financial reports because Skilling, Causey, and others did not want to announce the deal until after Fastow had sold his interest in LJM.

Nigerian Barges

32.   In the fourth quarter of 1999, Enron engaged in a bogus asset sale to Merrill Lynch as part of an effort to meet budget targets. Enron "sold" Merrill Lynch an interest in electricity-generating power barges moored off the coast of Nigeria. When Enron was unable to find a true buyer for the barges by December 1999, it parked the barges with Merrill Lynch so that Enron could record $12 million in earnings and $28 million in cash flow needed to meet budget targets.

33.   Enron induced Merrill Lynch to enter into the Nigerian barge transaction by making a secret oral promise to Merrill Lynch that Merrill Lynch would receive a return of its investment plus an agreed-upon profit within six months. Skilling and Causey knew that the promise was concealed from Enron's auditors and the public. Because Merrill Lynch's equity investment was not sufficiently "at risk," Enron should not have treated the transaction as a sale nor recorded earnings and cash flow from the transaction. In June 2000, Enron delivered on its promise to Merrill Lynch by producing LJM as a buyer for the Nigerian barges, while secretly promising to take LJM out of the Nigerian barge deal at a profit plus a large fee. The Nigerian barge transaction is the subject of the SEC's action in this District against former Merrill Lynch executives involved in the transaction, SEC v. Merrill Lynch et al., No. H-03-0946.

Global Galactic

34.   Between approximately July 2000 and September 2000, Causey, Fastow, and others reached an agreement on fulfilling the unlawful side-deals between Enron and LJM. Fastow and Causey memorialized and initialed the agreement which came to be known as the "Global Galactic" agreement. Among other things, Causey and Fastow

reaffirmed the side-deals between Enron and LJM concerning the Nigerian barges and Cuiaba. In addition, Causey and Fastow agreed that the put on ENE stock in Raptor I would be backdated to August 3, 2000, which would cause $41 million to be disbursed from Enron to LJM. LJM would then "invest" approximately $6 million of the $41 million in a Raptor vehicle in order to increase the alleged outside equity.

Manufacturing Earnings by Fraudulently Manipulating Asset Values

35.   Enron executives and senior managers, including Causey, engaged in a pattern of fraudulent conduct designed to generate earnings needed to meet budget targets by artificially increasing the book value of certain assets in Enron's large merchant asset portfolio. This portfolio included many interests in energy-related businesses that were not publicly traded and, therefore, were valued by Enron according to its own internal valuation models. Causey and others manipulated these models in order to produce results desired to meet earnings targets. For example, in the fourth quarter of 2000, under the direction of Causey and others, Enron personnel fraudulently increased the value of one of Enron's largest merchant assets, Mariner Energy, by $100 million in order to help close a budget gap.

Use Of Disguised Loans As Asset "Sales" To Hide Debt And Report Fictitious Earnings

36.   As part of the scheme to manipulate Enron's financial results and inflate its stock price, Causey, aided and abetted by others, caused Enron to obtain loans from certain financial institutions and report the transactions as sales of assets to generate purported cash from operating activities. These transactions were sham asset sales. Under Financial Accounting Standards 125 and 140, Enron "sold" assets to various SPEs it had established with various financial institutions ("FAS 140 transactions"). Through FAS 140 transactions, Causey and others removed those assets from Enron's balance sheet and generated income and cash flow, while at the same time retaining control over the assets. From 1998 through 2001, Enron used FAS 140 transactions to obtain disguised loans, keeping more than $2.6 billion of debt off its balance sheet, generating more than $1 billion in earnings and $2 billion in operating cash flow.

37.   As Causey and others knew, Enron provided the Canadian Imperial Bank of Commerce ("CIBC") with oral promises that its three percent "equity" in certain entities, including a vehicle known as "Hawaii 125-0," which was used by Enron repeatedly to move assets off-balance sheet and record earnings, would be repaid. For example, in or about October 2000, Fastow provided such an oral promise to CIBC. As Causey and others knew, under FAS 140, these oral guarantees violated the off-balance sheet accounting treatment of assets "sold" to the vehicles because CIBC's "equity" was not sufficiently at risk to qualify the vehicles as separate from Enron. Thus, the transactions did not qualify as asset sales and Enron should have disclosed the loans as debt on its financial statements, not as earnings and cash flow.

Concealing EES Failures

38.   In presentations to the investing public, Lay, Skilling, Causey, and others touted EES as a major reason for past and projected increases in the value of Enron's

stock. However, defendants and others were warned of major problems at EES in early 2001. For example, on January 22, 2001, Lay met with several Enron executives to discuss the problem of uncollectible receivables of EES in the amount of $500 million. Lay and others engaged in a fraudulent scheme to hide the uncollectible receivables by transferring them to ENA. The concealment of EES losses in this manner materially affected EES' reported operating results.

39.   In the Spring of 2001, defendants and others were warned by EES management that EES was in extremely bad shape, was unlikely to meet its year-end target of $225 million in income before interest and taxes ("IBIT"), and that EES would require at least a year before becoming truly profitable. Enron hid the magnitude of EES' business failure from the investing public at the close of the first quarter 2001 by moving large portions of EES' business—which Lay, Skilling, Causey, and others knew at the time otherwise would have to report hundreds of millions of dollars in losses—into Wholesale, which was the Enron business segment housing most of the company's wholesale energy trading operations and income. As Lay, Skilling, Causey, and others knew, Wholesale would have ample earnings to absorb the losses that, in fact, were attributable to EES while at the same time continuing to meet Enron's budget targets.

40.   Lay, Skilling, Causey, and others falsely explained to the public that the change in segment reporting was solely a means to improve efficiency. As detailed below, defendants also falsely stated publicly that EES was continuing to perform profitably and as expected, despite their knowledge of the hidden losses.

41.   EES-related losses recorded by ENA materially affected Enron and Wholesale's first quarter 2001 operating results. Had EES properly taken the losses, EES' IBIT for the first quarter of 2001 would have decreased from a positive $40 million to a negative $694 million and would have likely caused Enron to miss its highly touted estimated IBIT of $225 million. Promoting EBS to Manufacture Earnings and Concealing Failure of EBS

42.   In 1999, technology stocks, traded at a premium compared to stocks of more traditional businesses. To take advantage of this market condition, Skilling and others sought to artificially pump up Enron's stock price by heavily promoting EBS, a costly telecommunications business that ultimately failed.

"Project Grayhawk"

43.   Enron scheduled a high profile presentation to analysts about its new EBS business for January 20, 2000. Knowing the presentation would cause an immediate increase in Enron's stock price, Skilling, Causey, and others constructed and approved a scheme to allow Enron to record and report approximately $85 million as a result of the spike in Enron's stock price as earnings from operations.

44.   The scheme required a maneuver relating to Enron's recorded earnings from a partnership interest it held in a large energy investment named JEDI. The investment holdings of the JEDI partnership consisted, in part, of Enron stock. When Enron's stock price rose, the value of JEDI rose. However, in September 1999, JEDI hedged its Enron stock holdings through a transaction with Enron that fixed the value of the

Enron stock held by JEDI at a set price. As a result of this hedge, an increase in the value of Enron stock held by JEDI did not increase JEDI's income, and therefore did not generate a corresponding increase in Enron's share of JEDI's income.

45.   In anticipation of an increase in Enron's stock price from the January 20, 2000 analyst conference, however, Enron executed a series of transactions, known as "Project Grayhawk," that temporarily removed the JEDI hedge to allow JEDI's income to increase if the price of Enron's stock increased. After the price of Enron stock rose following the analyst conference, Enron and JEDI—through a new hedging arrangement— once again fixed the value of Enron stock held by JEDI, this time at a higher price.

46.   Enron removed the original hedge to enable Enron to recognize earnings brought about by the dramatic increase in Enron's stock price as a result of its January 20, 2000 analyst conference. Skilling and others then improperly publicly reported this gain as recurring operating income in its energy business. Skilling and others failed to disclose that the income resulted from the increase in Enron's own stock price caused by the false and misleading statements outlined below. Skilling, Causey, and others planned and approved the scheme.

January 20, 2000 Analyst Conference

47.   At the January 20, 2000 analyst conference, Skilling and others knowingly made false and misleading statements about EBS. Skilling stated, among other things, that EBS "has already established the superior broadband delivery network"; that EBS has "built this network ... and we are turning on the switch"; that the critical "network control software" was in Enron's possession and incorporated and used in its network; and that Enron valued the business at $30 billion, which Skilling called a "conservative" valuation. In Skilling's presence, EBS' co-CEO Joseph Hirko stated that EBS possessed advance network control software and that it was no "pipe dream." In reality, EBS had neither the claimed broadband network in place, nor the critical proprietary network control software to run it. The claims about EBS remained only unproven concepts and laboratory demonstrations, and Skilling was advised before the analyst conference that the network he publicly described would take years to complete and might never be realized. In addition, the valuation of the business was inflated by billions of dollars over internal and external valuations.

First Quarter 2000 Earnings from Enron's Own Stock

48.   Skilling's and others' plan to boost Enron's stock price by aggressively touting EBS, and to record earnings from that boost, succeeded. On January 11, 2000, the date on which Enron purportedly altered the original hedge on the Enron stock in JEDI as part of Project Grayhawk, Enron stock traded at approximately $47 per share. After the analyst conference on January 20, 2000, Enron stock rose to approximately $67 per share. The fraudulent Project Grayhawk maneuver allowed Enron to recognize, through JEDI, approximately $85 million in earnings from the manufactured stock price. Enron, Skilling, and others then misleadingly described these earnings in later presentations to analysts and in SEC filings as ordinary and recurring operating earnings from its energy business. Enron, Skilling, and others did not disclose Project

Grayhawk to the investing public, nor did they disclose that approximately 20 percent of the earnings of Enron's energy business for the first quarter 2000 resulted solely from an increase in Enron's own stock price.

Concealment of EBS Failure

49.   By late 2000, Skilling, Causey, and others knew that EBS was a struggling business that was hemorrhaging money. However, they took steps to hide this fact and falsify EBS' financial results. For example, during 2000, Enron structured a series of misleading, one-time financial transactions in EBS, known as Project Braveheart and Backbone Trust, which were designed to manufacture earnings and give the false impression that EBS would generate operating profits. Even with these transactions, EBS still was facing much larger than expected losses during the first quarter of 2001. In order to ensure that EBS did not record losses in the first quarter of 2001 that exceeded Enron's annual budgeted loss target for EBS, and in order to ensure that the quarterly budgeted loss target for the first quarter 2001 was met, Causey and others fraudulently reduced EBS' expenses for the first quarter of 2001. They did so by shifting numerous EBS costs off EBS' books, changing the depreciable life of certain of EBS' assets from five to ten years, and halving the bonus accrual for EBS employees.

Manufacturing and Manipulating Reported Earnings through Improper Use of Reserves Third Quarter 2000 through Third Quarter 2001

50.   During 2000 and 2001, the profitability of Enron's energy trading business, primarily based in Wholesale, dramatically increased for various reasons, including rapidly rising energy prices in the western United States, especially in California. If disclosed to the public, this sudden and large increase in trading profits, which exceeded $1 billion, would have made it apparent that Wholesale's revenues were tied to the market price of energy, meaning Enron was exposed to the risk of a decline in such prices. This would have revealed Enron as a speculative (and therefore risky) trading company. To conceal the extent and volatility of Enron's energy trading profits, Skilling, Causey, and others fraudulently hid hundreds of millions of dollars in trading profits in reserve accounts maintained on an internal Enron ledger called "Schedule C." By early 2001, these reserves contained over $1 billion in unreported earnings.

51.   Skilling, Causey, and others then fraudulently used funds in the "Schedule C" reserve accounts to avoid reporting large losses in other areas of Enron's business. For example, in the first quarter of 2001, Skilling, Causey, and others improperly used "Schedule C" reserves to conceal from the investing public hundreds of millions of dollars in losses within Enron's EES business unit.

Second Quarter 2000

52.   In mid-July 2000, weeks after the end of the second quarter 2000, Skilling, Causey and others carried out a plan to publicly report a 34 cents earnings-per-share figure in the second quarter, as opposed to the 32 cents earnings per share figure predicted by analysts. Skilling and Causey were aware that Enron's performance for this quarter, even after Enron manipulated its budget targets, did not support a 34 cents earnings-per-share figure.

53.   To achieve the fraudulent earnings-per-share figure, Skilling, Causey, and others caused a senior Enron executive to improperly release into earnings millions of dollars from a "prudency" reserve account in Enron's energy trading business. This release of reserves, which had no legitimate business purpose, artificially increased the second quarter earnings-per-share figure and Enron's stock price.

"Prepays"—Use Of Disguised Loans To Fraudulently Inflate Cash Flows

54.   Enron, aided and abetted by certain financial institutions, manipulated its financial results through a series of structured transactions, called "prepays." Enron used prepays to report loans as cash flow from operating activities, rather than financing activities in its balance sheet. By using prepays as a means to increase its operating cash flow, Enron was able to match its so-called mark-to-market earnings (paper earnings based on changes in the market value of certain assets held by Enron) with operating cash flow. Enron used this tool to convince analysts and credit rating agencies that its reported mark-to-market earnings were real, i.e., that the value of the underlying assets would ultimately be converted to cash. In addition, Enron failed to disclose that the prepays were actually debt and failed to disclose the extent to which Enron was using prepays in its balance sheet during relevant periods. As of April 30, 2001, Enron's undisclosed prepays totaled $3.9 billion.

55.   By no later than April 2001, by virtue of informative presentations on prepays to Lay by Fastow and others, Lay was aware of the use, importance, and magnitude of prepays to create cash flow; that the prepays were undisclosed debt; and that credit agencies were not told of the magnitude of Enron's prepay obligations.

Failure To Disclose Goodwill Impairment

56.   In or about October 2001, Lay, Causey, and others failed to disclose the substantial impairment to the goodwill value attributable to one of its major assets, Wessex Water Services. Goodwill is an asset created when one entity acquires another entity. Goodwill is initially calculated as the excess of the sum of the amounts assigned to assets acquired over the amounts of liabilities assumed in an acquisition. By August 2001, Lay, Causey, and others undertook to determine the probable impact of a new goodwill rule on Enron, because goodwill losses would need to be disclosed to the market via SEC filings in the third quarter of 2001.

The new rule was Statement of Accounting Standard No. 142, "Goodwill and Other Intangible Assets" (FAS 142). FAS 142 eliminated a company's ability to amortize or reduce goodwill gradually over a period of years. Instead, the new rule required a periodic assessment of the value of goodwill and any impairment loss.

57.   By September 2001, as Lay and Causey knew, Enron's internal accountants had determined that the amount of goodwill attributable to Wessex Water Services ("Wessex") was approximately $700 million. Enron possessed a direct and indirect interest in Wessex, a water utility company purchased at a high cost of $2.4 billion. A rate cut imposed in April 2000 affected the future revenue of Wessex and made its post-acquisition value dubious at best. By the beginning of October 2001, Enron's internal accountants determined that Wessex's goodwill was impaired and that Enron

would have to disclose the impairment unless Enron was able to assert that the company would once again pursue a water growth strategy backed by Enron. Enron's internal accountants had estimated that pursuing such a strategy would require Enron to expend between $1.5 and $28 billion.

58.   Lay and Causey knew that Enron did not intend to pursue a water growth strategy and that Enron did not have the necessary capital for such a pursuit. Lay and Causey also knew that disclosure of the impairment would be unfavorable to Enron's financial statements and might have a negative impact on Enron's precarious credit rating. Nevertheless, on or about October 12, 2001, Lay, Causey, and others falsely claimed, including in representations to its auditors, that Enron was committed to developing a water growth strategy and failed to disclose an impairment of Wessex goodwill.

False and Misleading Representations to Investing Public

59.   In furtherance of the scheme to manipulate Enron's financial results and inflate its stock price, Lay, Skilling, Causey, and others participated in the presentation of knowingly false and misleading statements about Enron's financial results, the performance of its businesses, the manner in which its stock was and should be valued, and the sale of personally held Enron stock. These statements were disseminated to the investing public in conferences, employee meetings, conference calls, press releases, interviews, SEC filings, and statements to members of the media.

First Quarter 2000 Analyst Conference Call

60.   On April 12, 2000, Enron held its quarterly analyst conference call to discuss its earnings for the first quarter of 2000. Skilling and Causey were among the senior Enron managers who prepared for and participated in the call. Skilling knowingly made false and misleading statements. Skilling stated that Enron's Wholesale business recorded earnings of $220 million for the quarter; that those earnings were "attributable to increased earnings from Enron's portfolio of energy-related and other investments;" that "this was a pretty good quarter for the energy-related investment business in contrast to the drag it was over the last year;" and that the upswing in earnings in Wholesale was "basically the performance of the existing asset portfolios." Skilling omitted to disclose that approximately $85 million of the $220 million in earnings were unrelated to the operating performance of Enron's energy business. Rather, as Skilling knew, through "Project Grayhawk," these earnings were solely attributable to a scheme to generate earnings by manufacturing an increase in Enron's own stock price.

Fourth Quarter 2000 Analyst Conference Call

61.   On January 22, 2001, Enron held its quarterly analyst conference call to discuss its earnings for the fourth quarter of 2000. Skilling and Causey were among the senior Enron managers who prepared for and participated in the call. Skilling knowingly made false and misleading statements including: "for Enron, the situation in California had little impact on fourth quarter results. Let me repeat that. For Enron, the situation in California had little impact on fourth quarter results." He further stated that "nothing can happen in California that would jeopardize" Enron's earnings targets for 2001 and

that California business was "small" for Enron. In reality, as Skilling knew, Enron reaped huge profits in 2000 from energy trading in California and concealed hundreds of millions of dollars of those earnings in undisclosed reserve accounts for later use. Also, by late January 2001, as Skilling knew, California utilities owed EES hundreds of millions of dollars that EES could not collect and these uncollectible receivables had been offset by large reserves concealed within Wholesale's books.

62.   In support of Enron's claims that EBS continued to be successful and a positive factor contributing to Enron's stock price, a senior Enron manager misled analysts during the call about the source of EBS' earnings in the fourth quarter of 2000. After being directed by Skilling to answer a question about the source of EBS' earnings, the senior manager said that one-time, nonrecurring transactions such as sales of "dark fiber" and a "monetization," or sale, of part of EBS' nascent video-on-demand venture with the Blockbuster company accounted for only "a fairly small amount" of EBS' earnings. In truth, as Skilling, Causey, and others knew, the sale of projected future revenues from the Blockbuster video-on-demand venture, which Enron abandoned just two quarters later, accounted for $53 million of EBS' $63 million in fourth quarter 2000 earnings.

January 25, 2001 Analyst Conference

63.   Enron held its annual analyst conference in Houston on January 25, 2001. At that conference, Skilling and others knowingly made false and misleading statements, including: (a) Skilling called all of Enron's major businesses, including EBS and EES, "strong franchises with sustainable high earnings power," (b) Skilling said of EBS that "I think we have a solid position. Our network is in place. We have customers and specific procedures and [devices] for the marketplace," (c) Skilling asserted that Enron's stock, which was then trading at over $80 per share, should be valued at $126 per share, attributing $63 of that alleged stock value to EBS and EES, and (d) Skilling stated that Enron was "not a trading business."

64.   In reality, as Skilling knew, EBS was performing very poorly and had made little commercial progress in 2000; EBS personnel had recommended shutting down or selling EBS' network; EBS had few revenue prospects for the upcoming year; and EBS had an unsupportable cost structure that, without correction, could potentially lead to substantial losses well in excess of those Enron had publicly forecast. Skilling also knew that EES was an unsuccessful business as well. Its modest earnings during 2000 largely resulted from one-time sales of investments unrelated to its retail energy contracting business; its existing retail energy contracts were overvalued by hundreds of millions of dollars; and it had hundreds of millions of dollars of uncollectible receivables that Enron was concealing within Wholesale.

March 23, 2001 Analyst Conference Call

65.   Enron held a special analyst conference call on March 23, 2001 in an effort to dispel growing public concerns about Enron's stock, which had fallen from over $80 per share to under $60 per share in less than two months. Skilling prepared for and participated in the call. Skilling knowingly made false and misleading statements,

and omitted to disclose facts necessary to make his statements not misleading. Among other things, he stated that "Enron's business is in great shape" and "I know this is a bad stock market but Enron is in good shape." He stated that Enron was "highly confident" of its income target of $225 million for the year for EES, and that EES was seeing the "positive effect" of "the chaos that's going on out in California."

66.   Skilling further stated that EBS "is coming along just fine" and that the company was "very comfortable with the volumes and targets and the benchmarks that we set for EBS." He said that EBS' two profit-and-loss centers, intermediation and content services, were "growing fast" and that EBS was not laying off employees but rather "moving people around inside EBS" and that this was "very good news." In reality, as Skilling knew, EBS was continuing to fail. Senior personnel at EBS had reported internally that the unit had an unsupportable cost structure and unproven revenue model. One senior EBS executive estimated that Enron would need to write-off (that is, record as a loss) approximately half of EBS' $875 million book value. EBS was laying off employees and Skilling had told employees based in Portland, Oregon that EBS would be centralized in Houston and jobs would be cut because of a "total meltdown" in the broadband industry.

First Quarter 2001 Analyst Conference Call

67.   Enron held an analyst conference call to discuss its first quarter 2001 results on April 17, 2001. Skilling and Causey were among the senior Enron managers who prepared for and participated in the call. Skilling made false and misleading statements in the call and omitted to disclose facts necessary to make his statements not misleading.

68.   Skilling talked about continued "big, big numbers" in EES' energy contracting business. He falsely explained Enron's movement of EES' energy contract portfolio into Wholesale, omitting any reference to EES' large losses or their transfer to Wholesale and stated, "[W]e have such capability in our wholesale business that we were— we just weren't taking advantage of that in managing our portfolio at the retail side. And this retail portfolio has gotten so big so fast that we needed to get the best—the best hands working risk management there." While Enron reported modest first quarter earnings for EES of $40 million, in reality, as Skilling and Causey knew, EES was facing losses approaching one billion dollars and had concealed those losses in Wholesale.

69.   Skilling also made knowingly false and misleading statements, and omitted to disclose facts necessary to make his statements not misleading, about the success of EBS. He stated that "[o]ur network is now substantially complete" and that it "is just not the case" that Enron was reducing staff of EBS because it was getting out of the content services business. Skilling also stressed that the reported losses in the unit were on target and "anticipated" and that the unit's capital expenditures were being reduced because it was "able to get access to connectivity without having to build it." In reality, as Skilling knew, the cost-cutting measures at EBS were instituted because

the unit was continuing to fail, and was incurring much larger than expected losses that could not be offset with projected future revenues.

70.   A senior Enron manager made further false and misleading statements about EBS in the call, including that revenues from selling portions of EBS' content business, as opposed to recurring earnings from operations, were only "about a third" of EBS' overall earnings and that EBS had only done "a little bit" of such sales in the past two quarters. In reality, as Skilling knew, the sale of a portion of EBS' content business was the principal mechanism by which the unit had generated revenue in the last two quarters and accounted for the majority of EBS' earnings for the first quarter of 2001. Only a very small percentage of the unit's revenues in either quarter was due to operations that could be expected to recur. Moreover, EBS had only been able to meet its target of $35 million in losses for the first quarter of 2001 through the combined efforts of the sale of portions of its content services business and the manipulation of the accounting for many of its expenses and allocations under the supervision of Causey.

Second Quarter 2001 Analyst Conference Call

71.   Enron held an analyst conference call to discuss its second quarter 2001 results on July 12, 2001. Skilling and Causey were among the senior Enron managers who prepared for and participated in the call. Skilling made knowingly false and misleading statements about the condition of Enron, including that Enron had a "great quarter." He further stated that EES "had an outstanding second quarter" and was "firmly on track to achieve our 2001 target of $225 million" in earnings; that losses in EBS were due to "industry conditions" and "dried up" revenue opportunities; and that Enron's "new businesses are expanding and adding to our earnings power and valuation, and we are well positioned for future growth." A senior Enron manager in the presence of Skilling and Causey also misled analysts about the movement of EES' losses into Wholesale, stating, "We just took the risk management functions and combined them because we just—we were trying to get some more efficiency out of management of the overall risk management function."

72.   In reality, as Skilling and the manager knew, by the close of the second quarter of 2001, EBS had failed and its increased losses were because it had stopped the one-time sales of portions of its business that had previously been the only significant source of its earnings. EES was facing hundreds of millions of dollars in concealed losses. As a whole, Enron was less than five months from bankruptcy, and the accelerating pace of the company's decline was well known to Lay, Skilling, and Causey.

August 14, 2001: Skilling Leaves Enron

73.   On July 13, 2001, Skilling unexpectedly told Lay he wanted to leave Enron because he could not do anything about Enron's declining stock price. On August 13, 2001, Skilling informed the Board that he was resigning for personal reasons. On August 14, 2001, Enron issued a press release, with Lay's approval, that announced Skilling had resigned and stated that the resignation was for personal reasons. Lay took the title of CEO and continued his control and oversight of Enron.

74. On the same day, despite his knowledge of substantial problems at Enron as described above, Lay made the following false and misleading statements to securities analysts in a conference call: (a) "there are absolutely no problems that had anything to do with Jeff's departure ... there are no accounting issues, no trading issues, no reserve issues ... unknown, previously unknown problems, issues ... I can honestly say that the company is probably in the strongest and best shape ... that it's probably ever been in" and (b) regarding EES "we've been doubling revenue and doubling income quarter on quarter, year on year for now about the last three years. We expect that to continue to grow very, very strong.... [M]ost of us inside the company believe that the Enron Energy Services component could become as large as or larger than our wholesale business within a 5 or 6 year period or so."

August 16, 2001 Employee Meeting

75. In an August 16, 2001 meeting, Lay made false and misleading statements to his own employees, fully aware that they were heavily invested in Enron stock, including in Enron's 401K plan. Lay stated: "Enron Energy Services just keeps banging away and just keeps growing at a tremendous rate ... almost a doubling from second quarter last year to this year. And we've been kind of doing that systematically over the last four years ... tremendous growth. Of course, revenue is growing. But a very, very solid business."

August 20, 2001 Interview

76. Despite his knowledge of substantial problems at Enron, Lay made the following false and misleading statements in an August 20, 2001 interview with Business Week Online: (a) "There are no accounting issues, no trading issues, no reserve issues, no previously unknown problem issues," and (b) "There is no other shoe to fall ... The company is probably in the strongest and best shape that it has even been in. There are no surprises. We did file our 10-Q a few days ago. And if there were any serious problems, they would be in there." Lay also revealed his awareness of the legal implications of his conduct: "If there's anything material and we're not reporting it, we'd be breaking the law."

Lay Learns Of Additional Problems, August–September 2001

77. Lay became aware of additional negative information about Enron during the last two weeks of August 2001 and the first week of September 2001. In this time period, Lay was briefed by numerous Enron employees on Enron's mounting and undisclosed financial and operational problems, including overvaluation of Enron's assets and business units by billions of dollars.

78. As a result of Enron's deteriorating financial condition, Lay, Causey, and others privately considered a range of potential solutions, including mergers, restructurings, and even divestment of Enron's pipelines, assets that Lay considered to be the crown jewels of the company.

79. On or about August 23 and 28, 2001, Lay, Causey, and others participated in Management Committee meetings where reports were presented showing earnings shortfalls in virtually every Enron business unit, totaling approximately $1 billion. On

September 6 and 7, 2001, Enron's Management Committee, including Lay and Causey, attended a retreat at The Woodlands resort near Houston, Texas. They discussed serious problems at Enron, including underperforming business units and troubled assets. Among other things, Lay, Causey, and others were involved in discussions regarding the need to take at least a $1 billion charge in the third quarter of 2001 and that Enron had committed an accounting error in the amount of $1.2 billion.

80.   Throughout September 2001, Lay, Causey, and other Enron executives engaged in a series of high-level meetings to discuss the growing undisclosed financial crisis at Enron and the likely impact on Enron's credit rating and stock price. Lay, Causey, and others learned that the total amount of losses attributable to Enron's assets and business units was at least $7 billion. Also at this time, Lay, Causey, and others learned that Enron's outside auditors changed its previous position regarding the accounting treatment of the Raptors. Enron's auditors determined that Enron's treatment of the Raptors violated clear accounting rules. Lay, Causey, and others were then faced with the prospect of restating Enron's earnings and admitting the error.

September 26, 2001 Employee Forum

81.   Lay participated in an Enron employee on-line forum on September 26, 2001 and made the following false and misleading statements, including: (a) "[t]he third quarter is looking great. We will hit our numbers. We are continuing to have strong growth in our businesses, and at this time I think we're positioned for a very strong fourth quarter," (b) "we have record operating and financial results," and (c) "the balance sheet is strong."

82.   Lay also made false and misleading statements to his employees about his trading in Enron stock. Despite the fact that during the prior two months he had made net sales of over $20 million in Enron stock to Enron, sales that he knew his employees did not know about, Lay falsely and misleadingly stated: "I have strongly encouraged our 16B officers to buy additional Enron stock. Some, including myself, have done so over the last couple of months and others will probably do so in the future ... My personal belief is that Enron stock is an incredible bargain at current prices."

October 12, 2001 Call To Credit Rating Agency

83.   On or about October 12, 2001, Lay made false and misleading statements to a representative of a prominent credit rating agency in a telephone call. Among other things, Lay stated that Enron and its auditors had "scrubbed" the company's books and that no additional write-downs would be forthcoming. In fact, as Lay knew, Enron's international assets were being carried on Enron's books for billions of dollars in excess of their fair value. Lay also knew that he and other Enron employees had failed to disclose and would not report the $700 million Wessex goodwill impairment, and had falsely claimed to others, including Andersen, that Enron would pursue a growth strategy in the water business. In addition, as Lay knew, Enron's auditors had not completed their work regarding asset valuations or goodwill and had not yet provided a final opinion regarding the necessity of additional write-downs.

Third Quarter 2001 Earnings Release—October 16, 2001

84.   By October 2001, Lay knew, among other things, that: (a) Enron had incorrectly accounted for the Raptor transactions, and that due to the massive accounting error, shareholders' equity needed to be reduced by $1.2 billion; (b) the Raptors were being terminated and, combined with other write-downs, this would result in an earnings charge of $1.01 billion; and (c) these two items were unrelated, and the $1.2 billion reduction to shareholders' equity was required, whether or not the Raptors were terminated. Despite this knowledge, Lay made false and misleading statements about these items.

85.   On October 16, 2001, Enron issued an earnings release, reviewed and approved by Lay, that reported a "non-recurring" earnings charge of $1.01 billion, a majority of the charge relating to the unwind of certain vehicles. Lay did not disclose that the vehicles at issue were the Raptors. Lay knew that the characterization of the termination of the vehicles as "nonrecurring" losses, that is, a one-time or unusual earnings event, was erroneous and inconsistent with Enron's past treatment of Raptor earnings as recurring operating earnings. Lay and others knowingly omitted any reference to the separate $1.2 billion equity reduction in the press release.

86.   Enron had a conference call with analysts on October 16, 2001 to discuss the earnings release. Lay, Causey, and others prepared for and participated in the call. Lay made false and misleading statements in the call. Lay again falsely described the hundreds of millions of dollars in losses as "nonrecurring." Lay also falsely stated that "in connection with the early termination, shareholders' equity will be reduced by approximately $1.2 billion." Lay and Causey did not disclose that the vehicles unwound (as part of the $1 billion charge) were the Raptors nor disclose that the $1.2 billion equity reduction was principally due to a significant accounting error.

87.   In the same call, Lay made false and misleading statements regarding the valuation of Enron's international assets. In response to questions regarding the value of Elektro, a Brazilian power plant, which Enron carried on its books in excess of $2 billion, Lay stated that "[w]e may well have that asset and operate that asset for quite some time. It's not a bad asset, it's a good asset, just like a lot of the other assets in this portfolio." This statement was misleading, in that Lay knew that Elektro was overvalued by as much as $1 billion and classified internally as a "troubled" asset.

88.   Lay further stated that Enron "and its outside auditors have recently completed our preliminary evaluation of goodwill." Lay represented that, based upon that review, "up to $200 million goodwill adjustment may be necessary, and will be recorded as required by the accounting principles in the first quarter of 2002." In fact, as Lay knew, the adjustment did not include the impaired Wessex goodwill of approximately $700 million and Enron's auditors had not completed even a preliminary evaluation of goodwill.

89.   Lay and other senior Enron managers hosted a series of meetings with analysts and large institutional investors after the announcement of Enron's third quarter earnings results. In these meetings, Lay and the senior managers falsely and misleadingly

portrayed EES as rapidly increasing in profitability, quarter to quarter and year to year. Lay additionally distributed materials at the meetings that falsely and misleadingly described the value of Enron's international portfolio as $6.5 billion, when Lay knew this figure vastly overstated the true value of the international assets by billions of dollars.

October 23, 2001 Analyst Call

90.   In an effort to calm deepening public concern regarding the decline in Enron's stock price, Lay and Causey prepared for and participated in an Enron analyst conference call on October 23, 2001. In that call, Lay made the following false and misleading statements: "[we're] not trying to conceal anything. We're not hiding anything," "[w]e're really trying to make sure that the analysts and the shareholders and the debt holders really know what's going on here. So, we are not trying to hold anything back," and "I'm disclosing everything we've found." In response to questioning, Lay again falsely stated that the $1.2 billion reduction to shareholder equity was a result of "unwinding" certain vehicles, failing to disclose that the cause of the equity write-down was principally due to a massive accounting error.

October 23, 2001 Employee Meeting

91.   By October 2001, in addition to other problems known to Lay as described above, Lay knew that Enron had serious liquidity issues. Lay knew that Enron had been forced to offer its prized pipelines as collateral for a $1 billion bank loan. He also knew that the only source of liquidity was a $3 billion bank line of credit, which, if drawn, would highlight Enron's worsening financial situation. Despite this knowledge, on October 23, 2001, Lay made false and misleading statements to his employees during an all-employee meeting. Lay falsely stated, "[o]ur liquidity is fine. As a matter of fact, it's better than fine, it's strong ..." Three days later, Lay authorized the drawdown of the entire $3 billion line of credit.

92.   Lay also made misleading statements about Enron stock and its prospects. Lay misleadingly stated, "as sad as the current market price is—and I've certainly lost a substantial portion of my net worth and my family's net worth—at current prices the market value [of Enron] is about $17 or $18 billion. It was $2 billion when we started in '85. But I also know that many of you who were a lot wealthier six to nine months ago are now concerned about the college education for your kids, maybe the mortgage on your house, maybe your retirement ... But we're going to get it back." Lay also stated that he thought a fair price for Enron stock was in the $50–$60 range and "that doesn't mean we can't get back up to the $80s or $90s in the no-too-distant future." At the time, Enron stock was trading at approximately $19.79 per share. Lay did not disclose that he had substantially reduced his personal exposure to the declining stock price, having sold over $65 million of Enron stock in 2001. Lay also knew, and failed to disclose, that he had no reasonable basis to forecast an increase in Enron's stock price.

November 12, 2001 Analyst Call

93.   Lay participated in an analyst conference call with analysts on November 12, 2001. During the call, Lay made the following false and misleading statements: "We

don't have anything we're trying to hide … I'm disclosing everything we've found." Lay failed to disclose all of the negative information about Enron that he was well aware of by this point in time. Collapse of Scheme

94.   For a time, the scheme to defraud succeeded and supported Enron's stock price and its credit rating. In early 1998, Enron's stock traded at approximately $30 per share. By January 2001, even after a 1999 stock split, Enron's stock had risen to over $80 per share and Enron had become the seventh-ranked company in the United States, according to the leading index of the "Fortune 500." Until late 2001, Enron maintained an investment-grade credit rating. However, the scheme quickly collapsed after Enron's announcement on October 16, 2001 revealed enormous losses. On October 22, 2001, Enron announced that it was the subject of an SEC investigation. The next day, Lay authorized Enron to enter into merger discussions with Dynegy, Inc. On October 29 and November 1, 2001, the two leading credit rating agencies downgraded Enron's credit rating. On November 8, 2001, Enron announced its intention to restate its financial statements for 1997 through 2000 and the first and second quarters of 2001 to reduce previously reported net income by an aggregate of $586 million. On November 9, 2001, Enron filed an 8-K with a merger agreement signed by Lay announcing a merger between Enron and Dynegy, which falsely stated, among other things, that Enron's prior public filings were true and accurate. On November 21, 2001, Enron's credit rating was downgraded to "junk" status. On December 2, 2001, Enron filed for bankruptcy, making its stock, which was trading at over $80 per share less than a year earlier, virtually worthless.

False and Misleading Filings With The SEC

95.   In furtherance of the scheme to manipulate Enron's financial results and inflate its stock price, Lay, Skilling, Causey, and others filed and caused to be filed with the SEC false and misleading reports of Enron, including:

Annual and Quarterly Reports

Form 10-Q for the Third Quarter 1999 (filed on or about November 15, 1999);

Form 10-K for the Fiscal Year 1999 (filed on or about March 30, 2000);

Form 10-Q for the First Quarter 2000 (filed on or about May 15, 2000);

Form 10-Q for the Second Quarter 2000 (filed on or about August 14, 2000);

Form 10-Q for the Third Quarter 2000 (filed on or about November 14, 2000);

Form 10-K for Fiscal Year 2000 (filed on or about April 2, 2001);

Form 10-Q for the First Quarter 2001 (filed on or about May 15, 2001);

Form 10-Q for the Second Quarter 2001 (filed on or about August 14, 2001)

Registration Statements

Form S-3 filed on or about April 4, 2000;

Form S-3 filed on or about June 15, 2000;

Form S-3 filed on or about July 19, 2000;

Form S-3 filed on or about January 26, 2001; and

Form S-3 filed on or about June 1, 2001 and Amendment dated July 13, 2001

Other

Form 8-K dated November 9, 2001

96.   The reports caused to be filed by Lay, Skilling, Causey, contained, among other things, materially false and misleading financial statements that overstated Enron's actual revenues and earnings, understated Enron's actual debt and expenses, and contained materially false and misleading management descriptions and analysis of Enron's business.

Defendants' Illegal Gains

97.   As officers and/or directors of Enron, Lay, Skilling, and Causey each owed a fiduciary duty to Enron and its shareholders to act solely in the best interests of Enron and its shareholders. Lay, Skilling, and Causey also signed employment and/ or consulting agreements with Enron in which each acknowledged this fiduciary duty and agreed that each owed a duty of trust and confidence to Enron, and that personal use of confidential information of Enron was prohibited. The employment and/or consulting agreements signed by Lay, Skilling, and Causey were in effect during the time period relevant to the Second Amended Complaint.

98.   Lay, Skilling, Causey, and others made illegal gains from the scheme to defraud in the form of salary, bonuses, and other forms of compensation. During 2001, Lay received a salary of $1 million, a bonus of $7 million, and $3.6 million in long term incentive payments, all proceeds of the scheme to defraud. Between 1998 and 2001, Skilling received at least $14 million in salary and bonuses, all proceeds of the scheme to defraud. Between 1998 and 2001, Causey received more than $4 million in salary and bonuses, all proceeds of the scheme to defraud. Moreover, as detailed below, the defendants and others also made additional illegal gains by selling large amounts of Enron stock at the inflated prices they engineered.

99.   Defendants' trading in Enron stock also occurred while they were in possession of material non-public information, including information about Enron's actual financial position and the performance of its business units as described above, that the stock price was inflated, and that Enron and its executives and senior managers, including defendants, had supplied and were continuing to supply materially false and misleading information to the investing public, including, but not limited to, Enron's publicly reported financial results and public statements of Enron's executives and senior managers. Defendants knew or were reckless in not knowing that the information they possessed was confidential and that trading while in possession of that information was a breach of a fiduciary duty or similar relationship of trust and confidence that they owed to Enron and its shareholders.

100.   By selling shares of Enron stock at the market price, defendants represented that the market price was a reliable way to value their shares, vouching for the integrity of Enron's financial statements and the public statements they and others made about Enron's financial condition. This representation was false and misleading as the market price was not a reliable indicator of value because that price had been materially distorted

by defendants' release of inaccurate information. Defendants intended that Enron and the market rely on the accuracy of the stock market price as a fair way to value their shares. A true picture of Enron as of the dates of defendants' stock sales was far different than that represented in Enron's financial reports and defendants' public statements, leading defendants to receive unduly excessive value for their Enron shares.

Lay's Illegal Gains From Sales Of Enron Stock

101. Lay profited from the scheme to defraud, in part, by selling large amounts of Enron stock at prices that did not reflect the true value of Enron stock. In 2001, Lay sold over $70 million in Enron stock to repay cash advances on an unsecured Enron line of credit. In addition, Lay amended two preexisting program trading plans to enable him to sell an additional $20 million in Enron stock. Lay's gains and losses avoided from the sales constitute illegal gains resulting from the scheme to defraud.

Lay's Sales Of Enron Stock Back To Enron

102. Lay's unsecured line of credit allowed him to borrow up to $4 million (later increased to $7.5 million) directly from Enron. In May 1999, at Lay's request, Enron permitted Lay to repay amounts due on the line of credit in shares of Enron stock, to be valued at the closing price on the date he gave notice of his intent to repay. Lay preferred this method of repayment because, among other things, he could avoid disclosure of his stock sales at the time the sales occurred. All repayments by Lay were through sales of Enron stock to the company.

103. From January 25, 2001 to November 27, 2001, Lay took advances on his line of credit in the total amount of $77,525,000. Thereafter, despite having other assets at his disposal, Lay repaid balances on the line of credit by selling $70,104,762 worth of Enron stock to the company twenty times, at prices he knew did not reflect accurately Enron's true financial condition. For example, after learning of Enron's undisclosed plan to hide over $500 million in EES losses in ENA, Lay sold 1,086,571 shares of Enron common stock back to the company, in 11 transactions, for a total of $34,081,558. Following Skilling's resignation on August 14, 2001, at a point when Lay was learning more about Enron's deteriorating financial condition, Lay sold 918,104 shares of Enron common stock back to the company, in five transactions, totaling $26,066,474. As Lay learned more negative information following Enron's third quarter earnings release on October 16, 2001, Lay sold 362,051 shares of Enron stock back to the company, in four transactions, totaling $6,050,232. The transactions executed by Lay are set forth in the attached table, and incorporated as if fully set forth here.

104. Lay's sales of Enron stock were not reported by Lay to the SEC on a Form 5 or otherwise revealed publicly until February 2002, over two months after Enron filed for bankruptcy protection.

105. Had Lay disclosed the substantial sales of his Enron stock at the time the sales occurred, this fact would have had a significant detrimental impact on the share price of Enron stock. By avoiding public disclosure of his stock sales, and even giving the impression to his employees and others that he was buying Enron stock,

Lay was able to use artificially priced Enron shares to reduce his line of credit balance and avoid significant losses that he would have suffered had he retained his Enron shares.

106. In addition to the benefit Lay obtained from the Enron stock sales at inflated prices, Lay took advances on his line of credit in the amount of $7.5 million, an amount drawn in six advances between October 24 and November 27, 2001, while he knew Enron's financial condition was crumbling.

Lay's Sales Of Enron Stock Pursuant To Amended 10b5-1 Plan

107. Under Rule 10b5-1 of the Exchange Act, if a stock trading plan is entered into by a person before he becomes aware of material non-public information, such a plan can provide an affirmative defense to insider trading. However, any amendment to a plan is considered a new plan, and no affirmative defense is available if the amendment occurs after becoming aware of material non-public information.

108. On November 1, 2000, Lay established two program sales plans pursuant to Rule 10b5-1 of the Exchange Act. One plan was for Lay and his wife (the "Lay Plan") and the other plan was for a family partnership (the "Partnership Plan"). Under the Lay Plan, Lay could sell 3,534 shares of Enron stock every trading day at the market price from November 1, 2000 through January 31, 2001 and 1,500 shares every trading day from February 1, 2001 through January 31, 2002. Under the Partnership Plan, Lay could sell 500 Enron shares each trading day from November 1, 2000 through January 31, 2002.

109. On February 1, 2001, Lay amended the Lay Plan, increasing the sales to 2,500 shares each day. On May 1, 2001, Lay amended the Partnership Plan, increasing the sales to 1,000 shares each day. Lay terminated both plans effective July 31, 2001.

110. At the time Lay amended both plans he was in possession of material non-public information concerning Enron as described above. Thus, Lay cannot use the affirmative defense provided under Rule 10b5-1.

111. From February 1, 2001 through the termination date of July 31, 2001, under the Lay Plan, Lay sold 295,000 Enron shares at prices ranging from $43.66 to $80.81, for total proceeds of approximately $17,329,630. From May 1, 2001 through the termination date of July 31, 2001, under the Partnership Plan, Lay sold 64,000 shares at prices ranging from $43.65 to $63.07, for total proceeds of $3,278,510. The transactions executed by Lay are set forth in the attached table and incorporated as if fully set forth here.

Skilling's Illegal Gains From Sales Of Enron Stock

112. Skilling sold shares of Enron stock that generated total proceeds of $62,626,401.90 as follows:

Trade	Date	Shares	Sale Price(s)	Gross Proceeds
A	April 25, 2000	10,000	$73.875 $73.9375	$738,893.75
B	April 26, 2000	86,217	$74.00 $73.875 $72.50	$6,338,183.00
C	August 30, 2000	15,000	$86.125	$1,291,875.00
D	September 1, 2000	60,000	$87.00 $86.875 $87.25	$5,220,000.00
E	September 5, 2000	11,441	$85.00	$972,485.00
F	November 1, 2000	72,600	$83.2406 $83.0625	$6,041,023.50
G	November 2, 2000	20,000	$82.3381	$1,646,762.00
H	November 7, 2000	46,068	$82.5872	$3,804,627.13
I	November 15, 2000– June 19, 2001	10,000 per week, 31 weeks per sales plan	$84.00 to $49.90	$20,985,247.42
J	September 17, 2001	500,000	$31.5061 $31.0822	$15,587,305.10

Causey's Illegal Gains From Sales Of Enron Stock

113. Causey sold shares of Enron stock and generated total proceeds of $10,316,807.83 as follows:

Trade	Date	Shares	Sale Price(s)	Gross Proceeds
A	January 21, 2000	45,000	$72.00 $71.00	$3,220,000.00
B	September 28, 2000	80,753	$87.8829	$7,096,807.83

False And Misleading Statements To Enron's Accountants

114. On or about the dates set forth below, Skilling, Causey, and others, while agreeing that they were "responsible for the fair presentation of the financial statements," falsely represented to Enron's accountants that, among other things, (a) the statements and representations made in Enron's financial statements were true; (b) Enron properly recorded or disclosed in its financial statements all agreements to repurchase assets previously sold; (c) Enron properly recorded or disclosed in its financial statements guarantees, whether written or oral, under which Enron was contingently liable; (d) Enron's unaudited quarterly financial data fairly summarized, among other things, the operating revenues, net income and per share data based upon that income for each quarter; (e) there was no material fraud or any other irregularities that, although not material, involved management or other employees who had a significant role in Enron's system of internal control, or fraud involving other employees that could have a material effect on the financial statements; (f) there were no material liabilities or gain or loss contingencies (including those that might exist relating to oral guarantees) that were required to be disclosed in accordance with SFAS No. 5; (g) all related-party transactions, including sales, were properly recorded and disclosed;

(h) no events occurred subsequent to the balance sheet date that had a material effect on the financial statements and that should have been disclosed in order to keep those financial statements from being misleading; (i) Enron made available to the accountants all financial records and related data; (j) Enron's system of internal controls was adequate and had no significant deficiencies; and (k) the accounting records underlying Enron's financial statements accurately and fairly reflected, in reasonable detail, the transactions of Enron, well knowing that these statements were false. Skilling, Causey, and others made the false representations in representation letters to Enron's accountants as follows:

Count	Defendant(s)	Date	Statement to Auditors
A	JEFFREY K. SKILLING RICHARD A. CAUSEY	March 13, 2000	Annual Representation Letter in Connection with Enron Form 10-K for Year 1999
B	JEFFREY K. SKILLING RICHARD A CAUSEY	May 12, 2000	Quarterly Representation Letter in Connection with Enron Form 10-Q for First Quarter 2000
C	JEFFREY K. SKILLING RICHARD A. CAUSEY	August 11, 2000	Quarterly Representation Letter in Connection with Enron Form 10-Q for Second Quarter 2000
D	JEFFREY K. SKILLING RICHARD A. CAUSEY	November 13, 2000	Quarterly Representation Letter in Connection with Enron Form 10-Q for Third Quarter 2000
E	JEFFREY K. SKILLING RICHARD A. CAUSEY	February 23, 2001	Annual Representation Letter in Connection with Enron Form 10-K for Year 2000
F	JEFFREY K. SKILLING RICHARD A. CAUSEY	May 15, 2001	Quarterly Representation Letter in Connection with Enron Form 10-Q for First Quarter 2001
G	RICHARD A. CAUSEY	August 14, 2001	Quarterly Representation Letter in Connection with Enron Form 10-Q for Second Quarter 2001

Ethics Awareness

In today's global economic climate, directors, officers and employees in leadership roles, particularly those based in the United States, are far less likely than those in the past to challenge the creation and implementation of a compliance program. In the past, executive management often raised challenges in the form of "Why now?" or "Do we really need this program?" as a means of deprioritizing the creation of a compliance program in favor of bottom line direct profit projects. If Sarbanes-Oxley legislation did not already answer these questions for the majority of executive management leading U.S. businesses, the November 1, 2010, amendments to the U.S. Sentencing Guidelines by the U.S. Sentencing Commission has all but put the doubts to rest. The Amendments require company leadership to take reasonable steps to remediate an already committed violation and to prevent further criminal conduct and, to this end, to make revisions to the compliance program that will insure its effectiveness.

2010 Federal Sentencing Guidelines Manual
Chapter Eight — Sentencing of Organizations
Part B — Remedying Harm from Criminal Conduct, and Effective Compliance and Ethics Program
2. Effective Compliance and Ethics Program

Historical Note: Effective November 1, 2004 (*see* Appendix C, amendment 673)
http://www.ussc.gov/guidelines-manual/2010/2010-8b21

§ 8B2.1. Effective Compliance and Ethics Program

(a) To have an effective compliance and ethics program, for purposes of subsection (f) of § 8C2.5 (Culpability Score) and subsection (c)(1) of § 8D1.4 (Recommended Conditions of Probation — Organizations), an organization shall:

(1) exercise due diligence to prevent and detect criminal conduct; and

(2) otherwise promote an organizational culture that encourages ethical conduct and a commitment to compliance with the law.

Such compliance and ethics program shall be reasonably designed, implemented, and enforced so that the program is generally effective in preventing and detecting criminal conduct. The failure to prevent or detect the instant offense does not necessarily mean that the program is not generally effective in preventing and detecting criminal conduct.

(b) Due diligence and the promotion of an organizational culture that encourages ethical conduct and a commitment to compliance with the law within the meaning of subsection (a) minimally require the following:

(1) The organization shall establish standards and procedures to prevent and detect criminal conduct.

(2)(A) The organization's governing authority shall be knowledgeable about the content and operation of the compliance and ethics program and shall exercise reasonable oversight with respect to the implementation and effectiveness of the compliance and ethics program.

(B) High-level personnel of the organization shall ensure that the organization has an effective compliance and ethics program, as described in this guideline. Specific individual(s) within high-level personnel shall be assigned overall responsibility for the compliance and ethics program.

(C) Specific individual(s) within the organization shall be delegated day-to-day operational responsibility for the compliance and ethics program. Individual(s) with operational responsibility shall report periodically to high-level personnel and, as appropriate, to the governing authority, or an appropriate subgroup of the governing authority, on the effectiveness of the compliance and ethics program. To carry out such operational responsibility, such individual(s) shall be given adequate resources, appropriate authority, and direct access to the governing authority or an appropriate subgroup of the governing authority.

(3) The organization shall use reasonable efforts not to include within the substantial authority personnel of the organization any individual whom the organization knew, or should have known through the exercise of due diligence, has engaged in illegal activities or other conduct inconsistent with an effective compliance and ethics program.

(4)(A) The organization shall take reasonable steps to communicate periodically and in a practical manner its standards and procedures, and other aspects of the compliance and ethics program, to the individuals referred to in subparagraph (B) by conducting effective training programs and otherwise disseminating information appropriate to such individuals' respective roles and responsibilities.

(B) The individuals referred to in subparagraph (A) are the members of the governing authority, high-level personnel, substantial authority personnel, the organization's employees, and, as appropriate, the organization's agents.

(5) The organization shall take reasonable steps—

(A) to ensure that the organization's compliance and ethics program is followed, including monitoring and auditing to detect criminal conduct;

(B) to evaluate periodically the effectiveness of the organization's compliance and ethics program; and

(C) to have and publicize a system, which may include mechanisms that allow for anonymity or confidentiality, whereby the organization's employees and agents may report or seek guidance regarding potential or actual criminal conduct without fear of retaliation.

(6) The organization's compliance and ethics program shall be promoted and enforced consistently throughout the organization through (A) appropriate incentives to perform in accordance with the compliance and ethics program; and (B) appropriate disciplinary measures for engaging in criminal conduct and for failing to take reasonable steps to prevent or detect criminal conduct.

(7) After criminal conduct has been detected, the organization shall take reasonable steps to respond appropriately to the criminal conduct and to prevent further similar criminal conduct, including making any necessary modifications to the organization's compliance and ethics program.

(c) In implementing subsection (b), the organization shall periodically assess the risk of criminal conduct and shall take appropriate steps to design, implement, or modify each requirement set forth in subsection (b) to reduce the risk of criminal conduct identified through this process.

Commentary

Application Notes:

1. <u>Definitions</u>.—For purposes of this guideline:

"Compliance and ethics program" means a program designed to prevent and detect criminal conduct.

"Governing authority" means the (A) the Board of Directors; or (B) if the organization does not have a Board of Directors, the highest-level governing body of the organization.

"High-level personnel of the organization" and "substantial authority personnel" have the meaning given those terms in the Commentary to § 8A1.2 (Application Instructions—Organizations).

"Standards and procedures" means standards of conduct and internal controls that are reasonably capable of reducing the likelihood of criminal conduct.

2. <u>Factors to Consider in Meeting Requirements of this Guideline</u>.—

(A) <u>In General</u>.—Each of the requirements set forth in this guideline shall be met by an organization; however, in determining what specific actions are necessary to meet those requirements, factors that shall be considered include: (i) applicable industry practice or the standards called for by any applicable governmental regulation; (ii) the size of the organization; and (iii) similar misconduct.

(B) <u>Applicable Governmental Regulation and Industry Practice</u>.—An organization's failure to incorporate and follow applicable industry practice or the standards called for by any applicable governmental regulation weighs against a finding of an effective compliance and ethics program.

(C) <u>The Size of the Organization</u>.—

(i) <u>In General</u>.—The formality and scope of actions that an organization shall take to meet the requirements of this guideline, including the necessary features of the organization's standards and procedures, depend on the size of the organization.

(ii) <u>Large Organizations</u>.—A large organization generally shall devote more formal operations and greater resources in meeting the requirements of this guideline than shall a small organization. As appropriate, a large organization should encourage small organizations (especially those that have, or seek to have, a business relationship with the large organization) to implement effective compliance and ethics programs.

(iii) <u>Small Organizations</u>.—In meeting the requirements of this guideline, small organizations shall demonstrate the same degree of commitment to ethical conduct and compliance with the law as large organizations. However, a small organization may meet the requirements of this guideline with less formality and fewer resources than would be expected of large organizations. In appropriate circumstances, reliance on existing resources and simple systems can demonstrate a degree of commitment that, for a large organization, would only be demonstrated through more formally planned and implemented systems.

Examples of the informality and use of fewer resources with which a small organization may meet the requirements of this guideline include the following: (I) the governing authority's discharge of its responsibility for oversight of the compliance and ethics program by directly managing the organization's compliance and ethics efforts; (II) training employees through informal staff meetings, and monitoring through regular "walk-arounds" or continuous observation while managing the organization; (III) using available personnel, rather than employing separate staff, to carry out the compliance and ethics program; and (IV) modeling its own compliance and ethics program on existing, well-regarded compliance and ethics programs and best practices of other similar organizations.

(D) Recurrence of Similar Misconduct.—Recurrence of similar misconduct creates doubt regarding whether the organization took reasonable steps to meet the requirements of this guideline. For purposes of this subparagraph, "similar misconduct" has the meaning given that term in the Commentary to §8A1.2 (Application Instructions—Organizations).

3.Application of Subsection (b)(2).—High-level personnel and substantial authority personnel of the organization shall be knowledgeable about the content and operation of the compliance and ethics program, shall perform their assigned duties consistent with the exercise of due diligence, and shall promote an organizational culture that encourages ethical conduct and a commitment to compliance with the law.

If the specific individual(s) assigned overall responsibility for the compliance and ethics program does not have day-to-day operational responsibility for the program, then the individual(s) with day-to-day operational responsibility for the program typically should, no less than annually, give the governing authority or an appropriate subgroup thereof information on the implementation and effectiveness of the compliance and ethics program.

4. Application of Subsection (b)(3).—

(A) Consistency with Other Law.—Nothing in subsection (b)(3) is intended to require conduct inconsistent with any Federal, State, or local law, including any law governing employment or hiring practices.

(B) Implementation.—In implementing subsection (b)(3), the organization shall hire and promote individuals so as to ensure that all individuals within the high-level personnel and substantial authority personnel of the organization will perform their assigned duties in a manner consistent with the exercise of due diligence and the promotion of an organizational culture that encourages ethical conduct and a commitment to compliance with the law under subsection (a). With respect to the hiring or promotion of such individuals, an organization shall consider the relatedness of the individual's illegal activities and other misconduct (i.e., other conduct inconsistent with an effective compliance and ethics program) to the specific responsibilities the individual is anticipated to be assigned and other factors such as: (i) the recency of the individual's illegal activities and other misconduct; and (ii) whether the individual has engaged in other such illegal activities and other such misconduct.

5. <u>Application of Subsection (b)(6)</u>. — Adequate discipline of individuals responsible for an offense is a necessary component of enforcement; however, the form of discipline that will be appropriate will be case specific.

6. <u>Application of Subsection (b)(7)</u>. — Subsection (b)(7) has two aspects.

First, the organization should respond appropriately to the criminal conduct. The organization should take reasonable steps, as warranted under the circumstances, to remedy the harm resulting from the criminal conduct. These steps may include, where appropriate, providing restitution to identifiable victims, as well as other forms of remediation. Other reasonable steps to respond appropriately to the criminal conduct may include self-reporting and cooperation with authorities.

Second, the organization should act appropriately to prevent further similar criminal conduct, including assessing the compliance and ethics program and making modifications necessary to ensure the program is effective. The steps taken should be consistent with subsections (b)(5) and (c) and may include the use of an outside professional advisor to ensure adequate assessment and implementation of any modifications.

7. <u>Application of Subsection (c)</u>. — To meet the requirements of subsection (c), an organization shall:

(A) Assess periodically the risk that criminal conduct will occur, including assessing the following:

(i) The nature and seriousness of such criminal conduct.

(ii) The likelihood that certain criminal conduct may occur because of the nature of the organization's business. If, because of the nature of an organization's business, there is a substantial risk that certain types of criminal conduct may occur, the organization shall take reasonable steps to prevent and detect that type of criminal conduct. For example, an organization that, due to the nature of its business, employs sales personnel who have flexibility to set prices shall establish standards and procedures designed to prevent and detect price-fixing. An organization that, due to the nature of its business, employs sales personnel who have flexibility to represent the material characteristics of a product shall establish standards and procedures designed to prevent and detect fraud.

(iii) The prior history of the organization. The prior history of an organization may indicate types of criminal conduct that it shall take actions to prevent and detect.

(B) Prioritize periodically, as appropriate, the actions taken pursuant to any requirement set forth in subsection (b), in order to focus on preventing and detecting the criminal conduct identified under subparagraph (A) of this note as most serious, and most likely, to occur.

(C) Modify, as appropriate, the actions taken pursuant to any requirement set forth in subsection (b) to reduce the risk of criminal conduct identified under subparagraph (A) of this note as most serious, and most likely, to occur.

Background. This section sets forth the requirements for an effective compliance and ethics program. This section responds to section 805(a)(2)(5) of the Sarbanes-Oxley Act of 2002, Public Law 107-204, which directed the Commission to review and amend, as appropriate, the guidelines and related policy statements to ensure that the guidelines that apply to organizations in this chapter "are sufficient to deter and punish organizational criminal misconduct."

The requirements set forth in this guideline are intended to achieve reasonable prevention and detection of criminal conduct for which the organization would be vicariously liable. The prior diligence of an organization in seeking to prevent and detect criminal conduct has a direct bearing on the appropriate penalties and probation terms for the organization if it is convicted and sentenced for a criminal offense.

Historical Note: Effective November 1, 2004 (see Appendix C, amendment 673). Amended effective November 1, 2010 (see Appendix C, amendment 744).

Widespread wrongdoing by self-interested members of the board, management or employees; failure by regulators to perform their oversight duties; and outright fraud has led to the demise of what, the majority of Americans, consider to be the "safe" companies and has contributed to the serious financial crisis we face today. Obvious examples are Lehman Brothers and Bear Stearns, which until their demise, were viewed by many as almost indestructible entities.

There may exist an erroneous assumption by some directors or officers that the compliance issue is no longer an urgent one as most companies have, post-Enron, implemented some type of protocols to prevent corporate violative behavior. That assumption would be wrong as evidenced by the continuing large numbers of, and the staggering scope of, abuses uncovered daily, weekly, and monthly.

The following provide a glimpse of the ongoing violatory behavior regulators will aggressively seek to foreclose and indicate a change in climate on the tolerance barometer:

Insider Trading

A former U.S Food and Drug Administration ("FDA") chemist was charged with using his access to the agency's drug approval process to profit in the amount of $3.8 million. As stated by the SEC in its formal complaint, the case involved "serial insider trading" being carried out by Cheng Yi Lang, a chemist employed by the Food and Drug Administration was charged with trading on material inside information. Specifically the SEC complaint outlines how Liang traded in advance of an FDA announcement approving Clinical Data's application for the drug Viibryd. Liang accessed a confidential FDA database that contained critical documents and information about the FDA's review of Clinical Data's application, and then used that information to purchase more than 46,000 shares of Clinical Data at a cost of more than $700,000. After the markets closed on Friday, Jan. 21, 2011, the FDA issued a press release approving Viibryd. Clinical Data's stock price rose by more than 67 percent the following Monday and Liang sold his entire Clinical Data position in less than 15 minutes for a profit of approximately $380,000.[2]

As part of his plea, he agreed to forfeit the entirety of the $3.8 million in bank and brokerage accounts and his home in Gaithersburg, Maryland. Assistant Attorney General Lanny Brewer, who oversees the Justice Department's criminal division, had this to say as a warning to others who might use their position to illegally profit: from inside information "Now, like many others on Wall Street and elsewhere, he [Cheng Yi Lang] is facing the significant consequences of trading stocks on inside information."[3]

The former head of Galleon Group, Raj Rajaratnam, was sentenced to 11 years in jail for his involvement in insider trading deals worth $64 million. In an interview with Newsweek, Mr. Rajaratnam appeared to indicate that insider trading was "a business as usual" affair on Wall Street. If so, this sentence would appear designed to send a strong message that this type of business is not being viewed by the government or the courts as "usual" and, further, that those who continue in their attempts to make it so will be severely punished. Rajat Gupta, the former Director of the Goldman Sachs Group, was also convicted of insider trading for leaking inside information to Raj Rajaratnam. Gupta was formerly the leader of the global consulting firm, *McKinsey & Co.*[4]

Fraud

One illustration of fraud, such as bribery and kickback schemes, involved a former program manager for the U.S. Army Corps of Engineers. The program manager was sentenced to 19 years and seven months in prison on federal charges stemming from his leadership of a ring of corrupt public officials and government contractors that engaged in bribery and kickbacks and that stole over $30 million through inflated and fictitious invoices.[5] Individuals involved in the kickback scheme used the monies to purchase Rolex watches, BMWs, designer clothes, and first class travel. The former employees were charged with bribery, money laundering, and wire fraud. One Senator from New Hampshire summed up the perspective as follows: "We cannot allow this

2. https://www.sec.gov/news/press/2011/2011-76.htm.

3. http://www.justice.gov/usao/md/Public-Affairs/press_releases/press08/FDAChemistPleadsGuilty toUsingInsiderInformationToTradeonPharmaceuticalStock.html.

4. http://www.thedailybeast.com/newsweek/2011/10/23/exclusive-raj-rajaratnam-reveals-why-he-didn-t-take-a-plea.html.

5. https://www.fbi.gov/washingtondc/press-releases/2013/former-u.s.-army-corps-of-engineers-manager-sentenced-to-more-than-19-years-in-prison-in-30-million-bribery-and-kickback-scheme.

kind of fraud to run unchecked. This kind of waste erodes trust in our government and makes our already difficult fiscal situation that much worse."[6]

Retaliation

Employees' tolerance level for employers' wrongdoing is also quite low and many employees are not simply paying lip service to compliance, they are living it. Employers who attempt to bully or intimidate employees into wrongful actions will find the tables turned. An example in point: 18 employees of Countrywide filed formal charges against Countrywide (which became part of Bank of America), claiming the company punished them for pushing back against corrupt practices and that the corruption reached the upper levels of management. In one of the concluded proceedings in San Francisco, the U.S. Department of Labor's Occupational Safety and Health Administration (OSHA) found Bank of America in violation of the whistleblower protection provisions of the Sarbanes-Oxley Act for improperly firing an employee after that employee reported widespread and pervasive wire, mail, and bank fraud involving Countrywide high level management. The bank was ordered to reinstate and pay the employee approximately $930,000, which included back wages, interest, compensatory damages, and attorney fees. The findings followed an investigation by OSHA's San Francisco Regional Office, which was initiated after receiving a complaint from the Los Angeles-area employee.[7]

"It's clear from our investigation that Bank of America used illegal retaliatory tactics against this employee," said OSHA Assistant Secretary Dr. David Michaels. "This employee showed great courage reporting potential fraud and standing up for the rights of other employees to do the same ..." "Whistleblowers play a vital role in ensuring the integrity of our financial system, as well as the safety of our food, air, water, workplaces and transportation systems," said Michaels. "This case highlights the importance of defending employees against retaliation when they try to protect the public from the consequences of an employer's illegal activities."[8]

In some cases, whistleblowers are making public documents that "tell the story" rather than themselves blowing the whistle to the SEC. The Japanese camera maker Olympus found itself defending the leaking of a Price Waterhouse report, which report advised that Olympus may face regulatory and legal scrutiny for $687 million in payments to advisers totally; the advice related to an acquisition. Olympus has threatened a lawsuit against its former CEO whistleblower for illegally publishing the report, however, its share price declined precipitously since the report was made public and its three major shareholders are demanding additional information to demonstrate validity of the payments.

---

6. http://shaheen.senate.gov/news/press/release/?id=413e1617-67fc-4e36-bf01-ea11d175101d.

7. http://www.dol.gov/opa/media/press/osha/OSHA20111351.htm.

8. http://www.dol.gov/opa/media/press/osha/OSHA20111351.htm.

Foreign Violations

It is not just within the United States that government tolerance levels have been exhausted. Compliance actions are on the increase around the world in an effort to bring under control behavior that injures not only corporations but the overall economic health of the country. For instance, in the UK, despite a billionaire's thousands of pounds in donations for Labour causes, Victor Dahdaleh, described as a friend of Lord Mandelson, was charged with bribery and money laundering over an alleged $600 million fraud matter. He is alleged to be the middle man in a four-year scam to overcharge an aluminum firm controlled by the Bahraini royal family by bribing officials. He was charged with corruption following a two-year investigation by the Serious Fraud Office, in conjunction with the U.S. Department of Justice and the Swiss authorities.[9]

Former Taiwan President Chen Shui-bian was sentenced to 18 years for his part in bribery involving a series of bank mergers and stripped of his civil rights for 11 years. His wife was sentenced to 11 years and stripped of her civil rights for eight years. They were together fined $5.95 million.[10]

These and other cases demonstrate that companies and individuals, now more than ever, should assure that a robust and effective compliance program is in place to prevent this and other types of violative behavior.

Today, those who downplay the importance of an effective compliance program do so at the peril of bringing upon the company, quite possibly irreversible financial and reputational damage, as a result of a Department of Justice ("DOJ") prosecution. The Board that fails to remediate illegal conduct and to prevent further criminal conduct to the best of its ability will likely find itself defending a shareholder suit for failure to appropriately fulfill the duties required of their positions, or, possibly, hiring criminal counsel to avoid jail time.

In spite of this increased responsibility, however, in the current economy, a compelling business case still needs to be made to the board of directors, management and employees for the creation and implementation of an effective compliance program because such an effort requires serious time, energy, funding, and attention by all directors, officers and employees. The Board and management may still prioritize projects that will boost the profit line on the balance sheet, which may translate to a bonus payout at the end of the year, while the benefits reaped from an effective compliance program are not as immediately visible or rewarding. When presenting a new compliance program, the corporate compliance department should highlight trends in sanctions and penalties against companies as compared to the costs the new compliance program would cost to implement.

---

9. http://www.telegraph.co.uk/news/politics/8846813/Billionaire-labour-donor-charged-over-600m-fraud.html.

10. http://www.taipeitimes.com/News/front/archives/2011/10/14/2003515694.

So the "Why" and "How" for creating ethics awareness is still the first relevant hurdle to overcome in achieving a successful rollout of an effective compliance program and in creating a lasting ethical culture.

Creating Ethics Awareness

So how does one create ethics awareness and lay the groundwork with the board of directors, management and employees? While members of the board and/or executive management may be generally aware of the heightened level of responsibility their positions hold, they may not be aware of the more specific duties they hold as fiduciaries of the corporation, including the duty of care in monitoring and reporting and the duty of loyalty.

We should note the first and second amendments to the U.S. Sentencing Guidelines of November 1, 2010, where the U.S. Sentencing Commission voted to amend the U.S. Sentencing Guidelines to insure companies take adequate steps to address wrongful behavior and to prevent further inappropriate conduct upon detection of the initial criminality. The November 1, 2010, amendment commentary, provided above, states that upon learning of wrongful conduct, the company should:

  • take reasonable steps, as warranted under the circumstances, to remedy the harm resulting from the criminal conduct. These steps may include, where appropriate, "providing restitution to identifiable victims, as well as other forms of remediation. Other reasonable steps to respond appropriately to the criminal conduct may include self-reporting and cooperat[ing] with authorities."

  • act appropriately to prevent further similar conduct, including assessing the compliance and ethics program and making modifications necessary to ensure the program is effective. The steps taken should be consistent with subsections (b)(5) and (c) [which require periodic evaluations of the program, and periodic risk assessment] and may include the use of an outside professional advisor to ensure adequate assessment and implementation of any modifications.

The second amendment affects high level management and the board as it mandates direct access to the board by those with operational responsibility for the company's compliance and ethics programs and imposes a direct reporting obligation on those employees who hold responsibility for the compliance program. The language provides a definition of employees falling within this group. Thus, the Commission considers a person affected by this new direct reporting obligation to be a person who holds the express authority to communicate personally to the governing authority or an appropriate subgroup thereof (i.e., this could be the ethics or audit committees) promptly on any matter involving criminal conduct or potential criminal conduct. The reporting must occur no less than annually and must also cover the implementation and effectiveness of the compliance program.

As noted, an important benefit available to companies with effective compliance programs is the ability to avoid prosecution. The Commission, in the voted amendment language, takes aim at executive management and boards that have been paying lip service to compliance programs without adding the teeth or accountability. Thus, the Guidelines specify that the reduction in an organization's culpability score is not to be applied where there is a delay in reporting the violation to appropriate governmental authorities, or high level personnel within the organization or relevant business units participated in, condoned or willfully ignored the violation.

The Commission, however, has used a bit of the carrot approach here in that it has added language that allows a corporation to still avail itself of a lower culpability score and fine reductions despite the involvement of executive management or board, provided that: a) individuals with operational responsibility for the compliance program have direct reporting obligations to the governing authority; b) the mechanics of the compliance program are sufficiently robust such that the violation was discovered outside of the organization or before such discovery was reasonably likely; c) the organization promptly reported the violation to appropriate governmental authorities; and d) there were not any individuals holding responsibility for the compliance program that participated in, condoned or were willfully ignorant of the violation.

Even employees, not in executive positions, have fiduciary responsibilities to the corporation which are the same duties of care and loyalty with respect to the performance of their job. Further, the responsibility of the board of directors and executive management is especially important, and often unappreciated by expatriate executives, seconded to the United States who are not as familiar with the stringency of the United States legal and regulatory environment.

Fiduciary Duties of the Board of Directors for Purposes of Creating Ethics Awareness

A board of directors oversees the activities of a company or organization. The directors may be owners, managers or other individuals. They may be either inside directors, employed by or otherwise working for the company, or outside directors. Whether they are directors of a publically held corporation or directors of a privately held corporation, sometimes acting as executive management, all directors are responsible, under the duty of care, for overseeing and monitoring the corporation as the directors, officers and employees carry out their respective responsibilities. The board of directors would arguably run afoul of their oversight obligations should they fail to implement an effective compliance program as defined under the Federal Sentencing Guidelines. These broad obligations encompass monitoring of the compliance program itself as well as the responsibility to modify or revise the program to prevent criminal conduct.

Historically, directors had to exhibit the level of care and skill which was expected of a director, under the duty of care as provided by case law and industry custom and practice. However, in today's world, directors assume much greater obligations than in the past because the duty of care, as explained more clearly in dicta by the *Caremark* case. *In re Caremark Int'l*, 698 A.2d 959 (Del. Ch. 1996). Since 1996, the *Caremark* case has articulated and clarified the oversight and monitoring responsibilities under the duty of care for the board of directors.

As noted above, the Board of Directors should not become complacent in their duties and make a fatal error in assuming that personal liability is not a likely risk. Tolerance for waste in these days of marches on Wall Street is low, especially where waste is caused by an indifferent Board. Those affected by the waste are no longer sitting idly on their rights; they are eager to seek retribution and one route is a personal liability lawsuit. One example is the case wherein a committee representing unsecured creditors of a Pittsburgh century-old nursing home that had entered bankruptcy after several years of staggering losses, filed suit against the directors and officers, seeking personal liability, based upon the argument that management decision-making was so flawed, none of the Directors or Officers were entitled to the protection normally afforded them when their actions have been done in good faith (the "Business Judgment Rule").[11] The Court of Appeals considered the following factors in ruling in favor of the committee.

- The directors continued to rely on reports from the administrator of the home, even though she was working a part-time basis only and had accumulated a string of deficiency-ridden surveys during her tenure.

- The directors left the treasurer's position unfilled for a prolonged period, and failed to appoint a finance committee as called for by its bylaws. As a result, there was poor oversight of accounting staff.

- The directors and officers held similar positions in a sister nonprofit, and the bankruptcy was orchestrated in a manner that benefitted the sister nonprofit.

- The directors and officers should have been aware of the deepening insolvency of the home and delayed too long before filing bankruptcy.

The disarray of corporate record-keeping provided an additional factor in favor of the Court's determination that personal liability was warranted in this case.

Board of Directors/Officers should heed the lessons of this case and undertake due diligence in all of their duties. Based off the sanctions that have been issued by the SEC and the DOJ it should be clear that relying on subordinates without independent study of the issues prior to delivering a decision is not an acceptable excuse for lack of attention and could ultimately create personal liability for all of some members of a Board.

---

11. *Official Comm. of Unsecured Creditors ex rel. Estate of Lemington Home for the Aged v. Baldwin (In re Lemington Home for the Aged)*, 659 F.3d 282 (3d. Cir 2011).

Office of the United States Attorneys, U.S. Attorney Manual, Title 9 9-28.000 — Principles of Federal Prosecution of Business Organizations

http://www.justice.gov/usam/usam-9-28000-principles-federal-prosecution-business-organizations#9-28.300

9-28.300 — Factors to Be Considered

A. General Principle: Generally, prosecutors apply the same factors in determining whether to charge a corporation as they do with respect to individuals. *See* USAM 9-27.220 *et seq*. Thus, the prosecutor must weigh all of the factors normally considered in the sound exercise of prosecutorial judgment: the sufficiency of the evidence; the likelihood of success at trial; the probable deterrent, rehabilitative, and other consequences of conviction; and the adequacy of noncriminal approaches. *See id.* However, due to the nature of the corporate "person," some additional factors are present. In conducting an investigation, determining whether to bring charges, and negotiating plea or other agreements, prosecutors should consider the following factors in reaching a decision as to the proper treatment of a corporate target:

1. the nature and seriousness of the offense, including the risk of harm to the public, and applicable policies and priorities, if any, governing the prosecution of corporations for particular categories of crime (*see* USAM 9-28.400);

2. the pervasiveness of wrongdoing within the corporation, including the complicity in, or the condoning of, the wrongdoing by corporate management (*see* USAM 9-28.500);

3. the corporation's history of similar misconduct, including prior criminal, civil, and regulatory enforcement actions against it (*see* USAM 9-28.600);

4. the corporation's willingness to cooperate in the investigation of its agents (*see* USAM 9-28.700);

5. the existence and effectiveness of the corporation's pre-existing compliance program (*see* USAM 9-28.800);

6. the corporation's timely and voluntary disclosure of wrongdoing (*see* USAM 9-28.900);

7. the corporation's remedial actions, including any efforts to implement an effective corporate compliance program or to improve an existing one, to replace responsible management, to discipline or terminate wrongdoers, to pay restitution, and to cooperate with the relevant government agencies (*see* USAM 9-28.1000);

8. collateral consequences, including whether there is disproportionate harm to shareholders, pension holders, employees, and others not proven personally culpable, as well as impact on the public arising from the prosecution (*see* USAM 9-28.1100);

9. the adequacy of remedies such as civil or regulatory enforcement actions (*see* USAM 9-28.1200); and

10. the adequacy of the prosecution of individuals responsible for the corporation's malfeasance (*see* USAM 9-28.1300)

Further, under the duty of loyalty, directors have an obligation to act honestly and in good faith, and to exercise their powers for a proper purpose. In accordance with the amendments to the Federal Sentencing Guidelines, acting in good faith requires action in accordance with the compliance program to prevent illegal behavior by employees of the company. This then would require not only the implementation of a robust compliance program (and modifications where necessary based on knowledge of violations under the new reporting obligation), but also the creation of an ethical culture that encourages an unimpeded information flow to the board about possible violations. A board would arguably not be acting in good faith if it allowed, through benign neglect or intentional complacency, a prosecution to be brought against the company for illegal behavior of its employees, where action could have been taken to prevent, or at the least, to attempt to prevent, such conduct from occurring.

Directors, acting in the best interest of the corporation, from a financial perspective, may sometimes have a conflict with their ethical obligations with respect to laws and regulations. Thus, most directors understand that they cannot take actions which directly benefit themselves for an improper personal purpose or act in conflict with an interest of the corporation by inappropriately and/or illegally using corporate property, corporate opportunity or corporate information. Directors should intrinsically understand that they cannot compete, directly, or indirectly, with the company to benefit their financial interests. But, they may not understand that actions taken to obtain profits on behalf of the corporation may be problematic from a compliance perspective.

It is conceivable that the board of directors could be acting in the best financial interest of the corporation and still be subject to criminal and/or civil liability if the financial success was brought about as a result of violations of laws and/or regulations or that they acted unethically to achieve that result on behalf of the corporation.

In today's global environment, directors owe a duty of care and duty of loyalty which encompasses such considerations as the following:

(1) The company's reputation;

(2) The company's interests and/or impact upon the employees;

(3) The long term consequences of the decisions on the company's five (5) year and ten (10) year business plans;

(4) The company's social impact, through its business operations, on the environment and the community;

(5) The company's continued viability with customers, suppliers, banks and other third parties;

(6) The company's effect on international business; and

(7) If the company is publicly held, the impact of board decisions on stock prices.

A primary responsibility of the board of directors is to ensure that the corporation's officers and management are properly preventing and detecting any unethical or unlawful behavior because a corporation can be held criminally liable for any criminal act carried out by one of its agents and/or employees. This responsibility cannot be properly carried out if the board remains intentionally unaware of possible violations by restricting access and/or creating an atmosphere, either economically or otherwise, that dissuades employees from disclosing possible violations.

With the trend towards broadening the scope of protected whistleblower activity, heightened attention to detection and reporting is prudent.

Menendez v. Halliburton[12] is demonstrative in that the decision substantially lowers the bar for SOX whistleblowers respecting the requirement of establishing the plaintiff suffered a legally actionable adverse employment action. In this case, the Department of Labor's Administrative Review Board (ARB) held that Menendez had suffered an "adverse action" under the whistleblower protection provisions of the Sarbanes-Oxley Act (SOX) as a result of the disclosure of his identity by Halliburton to management and co-workers in violation of Halliburton's Audit Committee Complaint procedures. Menendez had raised concerns soon after his hire respecting Halliburton's revenue recognition practices, believing them to be improper under the SEC's standards and generally accepted accounting principles. He reported those concerns to the SEC subsequent to a review undertaken by KPMG, Halliburton's outside auditors, that no action was warranted. Upon receipt of Menendez' complaint, the SEC initiated an investigation. Halliburton, upon receiving notification of the investigation, disclosed Menendez' identity as associated with the investigation and, thereafter, he was shunned by his co-workers and KPMG employees, necessitating a paid administrative leave request, which was granted by Halliburton. The SEC ultimately declined to take any enforcement action against Halliburton. Halliburton, thereafter, summoned Menendez back to work but advised him that, although he would assume his same position as prior to leave, he would now report to the director of external auditing rather than to the Chief Accounting Officer, which was Menendez' reporting structure previous to the filing of the SEC complaint. The ARB interpreted the term, "adverse action" substantially broader than the meaning of the same term under Title VII to conclude that Menendez was subjected to retaliation for assertion of protected activity.

Similarly, in *Bonds v. Leavitt*,[13] the United States Court of Appeals for the Fourth Circuit held the plaintiff's disclosure to be protected activity. In reversing the lower court's grant of summary judgment in favor of the Defendant, the Fourth Circuit found that Dr. Duane Bonds's disclosure to a supervisor that the National Institute of Health (NIH) unlawfully retained cell lines created from the blood of participants in a clinical trial without their consent was a protected disclosure under the Whistle-

12. Case No. 09-002, 2011 DOL Ad. Rev. Bd. LEXIS 83 (ARB Sept. 13, 2011).
13. 629 F.3d 369 (4th Cir. 2011).

blower Protection Act (WPA).[14] The Court suggested that *Huffman v. Office of Pers. Mgmt.*,[15] a Federal Circuit decision creating a "duty speech" loophole in the WPA, may not apply to the Fourth Circuit. And assuming *Huffman* even applies, the Court held that Bonds went beyond her normal job duties when she disclosed the illegal activity to a supervisor, because there was no evidence that Bonds had a responsibility to report any concerns to that supervisor. The Court also rejected the argument that its 2001 decision in *Hooven Lewis v. Caldera* requires that, to constitute protected conduct, the report must be made to a person the would-be whistleblower believes has actual authority to correct the wrongdoing.

For example, if an employee acts within the scope of his or her employment for the benefit of the corporation, it is in the interest of the board of directors to ensure that the board is in a position to, not only obtain all relevant information prior to making any decisions, but to assure that the business deal does not contribute to a culture driven by bottom line profits. The requirement that individuals with operational responsibility for the compliance program have "direct reporting obligations" to the governing authority or an appropriate subcommittee enables the board to obtain the information it requires to act responsibly in conducting the everyday business of the company.

Fiduciary Duties of Officers, Management and Employees for Purposes of Creating Ethics Awareness

Like directors, all officers, managers and employees have a fiduciary duty to the company. They are all covered by the duty of care and duty of loyalty.

Further, corporate liability can be based on the unlawful conduct of low level employees who may be acting contrary to their managers expressed directions and written company policy. At the end of the day, directors, officers and managers can be held responsible for actions that are taken on behalf of the corporation by its employees. Also, employees can be held liable for violating their fiduciary duties. Thus, the directors, officers and managers as well as employees are exposed to liability if there is a lack of early detection mechanisms in place to warn of behavior that can lead to civil and criminal liability for the corporation. Indeed, directors, officers, managers, and employees could be jointly and severally liable.

Fiduciary Duties under the Sarbanes-Oxley Act

The Sarbanes-Oxley Act (SOX) imposed new standards of accountability on boards of directors of companies that are listed on the United States stock exchanges. The

---

14. 5 U.S.C. § 1201.
15. 263 F.3d 1341 (Fed. Cir. 2001).

amendments to the federal sentencing guidelines can be viewed as increasing this responsibility, at least with respect to responding to criminal conduct and preventing further similar conduct by increasing the effectiveness or comprehensiveness of the company's compliance program. This legislation imposes large fines and prison sentences in the event of unlawful accounting behavior; however, processes implemented to adhere to the SOX legislation do not change the need for a broad scale effective compliance program which is, in actuality much larger in scope than that provided under the SOX legislation. Indeed, while SOX deals with financial issues, it is still silent on such compliance areas as environmental, antitrust, intellectual property, and employment issues. Thus, the compliance program is the umbrella under which SOX compliance falls. An effective compliance program should address each and every area that the company conducts its business and should provide the means for management to reduce its exposure to criminal and/or civil liability.

Checklist of Benefits for Creating Ethics Awareness of the Need for a Compliance Program

There are many positive attributes associated with the implementation of a compliance program. These should be brought to manage ment's attention in gaining the "buy in" from the board of directors for the creation and implementation of such a compliance program. Some of these positive attributes, which provide a competitive advantage for a corporation, are as follows:

• Protects the corporation's business reputation and image (a company that is highlighted in the media as having corrupt management is not a company that prospers for long);

• Sustains an ability to focus on growth and profit instead of diverting attention and monies to the defense of criminal and civil proceedings;

• Fosters support from investors (companies with effective compliance programs are less likely to be investigated by the government); and

• Bolsters customer confidence (customers feel more secure that the corporation is acting properly in safeguarding the customers' interest, when there is a compliance program).

Some of the benefits for the board of directors include:

• Providing clear rules for accountability for employees and managers;

• Off-setting power inequalities by creating a level playing field for all employees and managers;

• Creating a transparent culture for all employees and managers where they can raise issues without the fear of retaliation;

• From a human resources perspective, enhancing the high performance of employees because the rules are aligned to the company's reward system;

- From a human resources perspective, ensuring that employees are treated fairly regardless of their position; and

- Streamlining the decision-making process.

Additional benefits of an effective compliance program are that it allows the corporation to detect misconduct at an early stage, thereby, allowing the organization to act quickly to minimize any adverse consequences. It also can be used as evidence of corporate good faith in avoiding government investigations; minimizing and defending government prosecutions; and reducing sentencing after conviction by the government. This is especially critical for the board since directors can suffer personal liability, under the Caremark decision, for failure to oversee the compliance program, and is especially relevant under the amendments to the federal sentencing guidelines. While reporting on program implementation and effectiveness were existing responsibilities under the previous set of Federal Sentencing Guidelines, the amendments now formally require such reporting to qualify for exception to prosecution or reduction of fines. To meet the fiduciary duty of care, the board should assure compliance with the Guidelines so as to enable the company to obtain the benefits associated with avoidance of prosecution and reduction of fines.

Finally, an effective compliance program is a cost saving device for the corporation because employee misconduct often results in hard costs and loss of profitability for the corporation. Failure to have an effective compliance program can result in costly defensive law suits and/or settlements. The soft costs that result from a failure to have an effective compliance program include reputational damage, lost employee productivity, disruption of business operations, and damage to employee morale.

Rollout and Launch

Full engagement and support of the chief executive officer, officers, executive management, management, and directors is critical to mobilize all employees to enthusiastically embrace the ideas and elements of the compliance program. The compliance program will ultimately not be effective and the objectives and/or benefits of the compliance program, as discussed above, will not inure to the benefit of the corporation without delivering a unified messaging about the compliance program at its launch.

The human resources department can be an effective means to communicate that change is coming to the corporation; that change is good for the corporation and its employees, and that employees should work with the compliance office, especially in the reporting of violations to the board or high-level personnel. The human resources department should also develop messaging that paves the way for the expectation of possible initial chaos and conflict resulting from the initial launch of the compliance program.

Managing the compliance program's challenges will be a learning process for all. This can be enhanced by the creation of an ethics committee. The ethics committee should at least include the following members:

- CEO or President

- General Counsel

- CFO

- Internal Audit Directors

- Chief Compliance Officer

- Human Resources Director

Marketing Campaign to Create Ethics Awareness

Thus, there is a need for a marketing campaign around the launch of the program to communicate, as broadly and effectively as possible, a culture of ethics awareness that will permeate the company environment as a whole and remain a constant in employees' minds as they go about their usual business responsibilities.

There should be some brainstorming done amongst the CEO, Chief Compliance Officer, the ethics committee members as well as other executive management to determine the most effective rollout methodology and to gain buy-in from these constituencies.

Ideally, the rollout should occur early in the year at a meeting where all executive management and, at least the majority of the managers of the company, will be present. A good opportunity would be at a meeting where the year's priority business plans are being rolled out.

The CEO should communicate the initial introduction of the program so that the employees receive the message that the compliance program is a business priority and enjoys the endorsement of the highest levels of the corporation. Two examples of such letters, found at the introduction of the code of conduct from two CEOs of major financial institutions, are provided below.

––––––––––

Morgan Stanley
Culture, Values and Conduct
A Message from James Gorman

http://www.morganstanley.com/about-us-governance/
pdf/ms-code-of-conduct.pdf

Morgan Stanley's culture and reputation differentiate us from our peers. Our future success relies on a client-centered culture of dedicated professionals doing the right thing to deliver the best of the Firm. At a time when global financial institutions are under intense scrutiny in all aspects of their business, we are reminded almost daily that our reputation is our most precious asset. Once damaged or lost, it is very difficult to restore. That is why our unwavering commitment to the highest standards of ethical conduct has been instrumental in enabling the Firm to prosper and thrive over our long history and continues to be paramount to our future success.

Our Code—Culture, Values and Conduct—reflects our continued commitment to conducting all our business activities in accordance with our core values and fostering a culture where Doing the Right Thing means delivering first-class business in a first-class way and in full alignment with the letter and spirit of applicable laws, regulations and our policies. Our values inform everything we do: Putting Clients First, Leading with Exceptional Ideas, Doing the Right Thing and Giving Back.

The purpose of this Code is to help guide all of us to live the core business principles that underlie our success. Please read it carefully and consider what it says. If you are aware of any actions that violate this Code and put us at risk, we depend on you to speak up. We prohibit retaliation against anyone who makes a good faith report of known or suspected misconduct.

Like you, I am proud to be part of a Firm that has such a distinguished history and promising future. In 1935, the Firm's founding partners understood that maintaining the trust of their clients was essential to their success, and they stayed true to this guiding principle. Thank you for doing your part to uphold our proud heritage.

James P. Gorman
Chairman and Chief Executive Officer

Bank of America
Code of Conduct

http://investor.bankofamerica.com/phoenix.zhtml?c=
71595&p=irol-govconduct#fbid=5yhTQRz70zP

Letter from the CEO

To my teammates:

Every day, millions of individuals, families and businesses rely on us to help make their financial lives better. As we work with our customers and clients to achieve their financial goals, it is important that we do business the right way—with honesty, integrity and fairness. Our Code of Conduct is our guide to fulfilling this responsibility.

The Code of Conduct is based on our company's values. It translates our values into the actions we should take as we compete in the marketplace and engage with customers, clients, shareholders, vendors and each other.

Each of us is required to review, acknowledge and understand our Code of Conduct. This information is posted on Bank of America's public website. If you have questions, please talk with your manager.

Thank you for upholding our ethical standards and demonstrating our values in all you do every day for our customers and clients.

Brian T. Moynihan
Chief Executive Officer
Bank of America

Training Sessions to Create Ethics Awareness

To create awareness, the rollout should be accompanied by training sessions conducted in small groups (not more that 15–20 employees per group), during which time, interesting and informative educational vignettes, on DVDs and/or interactive computer modules, are provided and discussed. The DVDs and interactive computer modules used for training should address relevant sections of the code of conduct/ethics (i.e., covering all the company's primary business areas) and the relevant federal and/or state laws (i.e., civil rights, sexual harassment).

Preferably, the training should be done in a train the trainer format where the training cascading down from the CEO through senior management to line employees. The training should be conducted by the CEO for senior managers; by senior managers for lower level managers; lower level managers for line employees; line employees for line employees. This allows immediate managers to train their direct reports or employees to train fellow employees. This type of training is the best mechanism for instilling group values.

Grey ethical areas often exist for such basic issues as what constitutes "stealing." For example, is it stealing for an employee to take a pen and a pad of paper home to use to finish a company assignment? What if an employee takes a box with 200 pens and 200 pads of paper home?

The training sessions should be scheduled so that employees have time for questions and answers during and at the end of the sessions. Also, information that is easily understood about the hotline process should be delivered. The code of conduct/ethics brochures and/or pamphlets should be distributed during the training sessions. Other marketing and communication tools should be used as part of the training sessions if they enhance the substantive points of the compliance program.

Marketing and Communication Tools to Create Ethics Awareness

Besides the brochures, pamphlets and/or DVDs on the code of conduct/ethics, and on the hotline, these marketing and communication tools could include calendars, work plans, and mementos, such as tombstones, plastic cubes and post-it notes, personalized with compliance information. Additionally, the "Why" question that can be anticipated from employees as to the reason that the company is placing its time and resources against the rollout of the compliance program can be ideally reinforced in these materials.

Equally appropriate to address in marketing and communication tools is the "How" of the administration of the compliance program. Emphasis should be placed on assuring that the employees understand the process for voicing issues or complaints through their managers, the Chief Compliance Officer and/or the hotline. Such an open door policy to receive employee complaints is essential to an effective compliance program.

Each employee should receive printed materials that they can retain and later use for reference and/or access to user friendly interactive websites to refresh their recollection of the training sessions. Managers must be held responsible for engaging their direct report employees in understanding the necessity for an effective compliance program, using the training sessions and the compliance marketing and communication tools to support their efforts.

The rollout should be accompanied by other highly visible communication devices which could include posters on the topics that are most relevant to the company's business.

Often, the partnering hotline company, if an outside provider is used, can provide a variety of interesting posters. Therefore, the company will need to assess which messages might be most appropriately highlighted through this vehicle. For example, if the company is involved in manufacturing, it can post messages about safety and environmental best practices. Another example: if the company has previously incurred issues with employee misunderstanding or abusing the travel and expense policy, it could use the posters to act as a reminder of the company's expectations of behavior.

Finally, the compliance training process should be rolled into the new employee orientation trainings to ensure each new employee joining the company is receiving the same ethics awareness exposure.

Subsequent to the rollout, ongoing communications to employees about compliance issues relevant to the company's business areas should occur.

One method would be through the use of monthly or quarterly newsletters which could highlight the company's particular compliance program elements, including a reminder as to the relevant roles of such constituent members of the compliance team as the Chief Compliance Officer and Deputy Compliance Officers. The newsletter could contain examples of current issues in the news that highlight unethical and/or illegal conduct (i.e., discrimination in hiring or firing, sexual harassment, financial fraud, false advertising, manufacturing environmental cases) to illustrate for the board and all employees "real life" situations involving wrongdoing that occur in today's global economic environment.

Additionally, newsletters could provide reports on surveys of current employee views on what constitutes a culture of ethics, and on internal audits to assess financial and other risks. Further, newsletters should try to harmonize the various elements of the compliance program as well as reminding the employees that the compliance program is a fully integrated part of the company's portfolio of risk and culture assessment tools. Review of the results generated by these and other assessment tools will allow the company to determine if the employees are "living" the values and best practices as expressed in the code of conduct/ethics as they go about their daily business activities.

Refreshing Company Values to Create Ethics Awareness

Finally, the company's value statement should be reinvigorated throughout the years as part of creating a culture of ethics based on an effective compliance program, using the newsletters, posters, training sessions, interactive compliance websites, DVDs, interactive computer modules, mementos, employee surveys, risk assessments, and open door communication policy including the hotline, the company's value statement can be aligned with the code of conduct/ethics. At such time, the company's value statement and the code of conduct/ethics will become a relevant foundation for an effective compliance program which the board of directors, officers and executive management oversee.

Sample Compliance Office Authorization Memorandum

DATE: _____
TO: Board of Directors/Executive Management
FROM: Designated Representative of the company Ethics Committee
CC: _____

RE: Proposed Launch of a Compliance Program

As previously discussed, we need to create a culture of ethics. This company needs to construct, organize and implement a corporate compliance program for rollout in Year _____. To ensure success of our compliance program, and in accordance with the amendments issued by the U.S. Sentencing Commission, it is not only necessary for upper management to understand the elements of a compliance program since the program must be "sponsored and endorsed" by the highest levels of the company to assure widespread acknowledgement, acceptance and buy-in of all employees, but to grant unimpeded personal access of information respecting possible violations. Additionally, there is a need for direct involvement and positive action steps by executive management to ensure the successful implementation of the compliance program, including actions to address violations as well as to modify or revise elements of the compliance program, including the Code of Conduct to prevent civil and criminal violations.

Therefore, please take the time to review the below information and to advise me, as the designated representative of the company ethics committee, of any questions or concerns you may have in moving forward toward implementation. In order to do this I would like to provide you with the compliance program rationale as well as an understanding of the seven elements of an effective compliance program.

A. Compliance Program Rationale:

Why do we need the compliance program? Why do we want to put this in place? These are questions I am sure you are all asking. Here is the rationale for instituting our compliance program as follows:

1. Sets an ethical tone and promotes a corporate atmosphere which discourages wrongdoing (intentional or otherwise), reducing the likelihood that employees will commit crimes;

2. Detects misconduct at an early stage, allowing for the company to act quickly to minimize adverse consequences;

3. Can be used as evidence of good faith in case of a government investigation and avoids or minimizes the possibility of government action, providing the company has abided by the requirements of the amendments; i.e., direct reporting obligations to the board by those with operational authority; compliance program robust enough to surface violations/offenses before discovery of outside organization; company promptly reported offense to appropriate governmental authorities and there was not an individual with operational responsibility that participated in, condoned or willfully ignored the violation/offense. If there is a conviction, the company can use the existence of such a program to reduce exposure under the U.S. Sentencing Guidelines (if found guilty, often times, the government will dictate to the company the terms of the compliance program it must institute and will require continual government oversight). More importantly, pursuant to the recent policy issued by Department of Justice, existence of an effective compliance program can help avoid criminal charges;

4. Avoids personal liability for the directors of the company (court cases hold that directors can be held personally liable for damages suffered by a corporation if they have not instituted and overseen the compliance program); and

5. Reduces costs since employee misconduct imposes hard costs in defense of lawsuits, settlement of action, etc. but also "soft costs" such as damage to reputation, lost employee productivity, disruptions to business operations, damage to employee morale, etc.

However, please note that a poorly implemented compliance program, can be worse than none at all because prosecutors' and plaintiffs' attorneys can show, once they have read the compliance materials in discovery, what the corporation understood to be risks. If the corporation did not act to prevent such risks, it can be deemed an admission of wrongdoing by the company.

B. Seven Essential Elements for an Effective Compliance Program:

The U.S. Sentencing Guidelines are the government's first all-embracing articulation of what is an effective compliance program. Most major corporations have compliance programs that comply with what the government has opined to be an effective compliance program. These corporations wish to operate within a type of "safe harbor." This requires that a Part C Risk Assessment of all legal risks (Best Practice and Gaps Analysis), including an inventory of documents, interview reports, heat maps and dashboards, and an executive summary and all the seven elements of the U.S. Sentencing Guidelines be followed as provided:

1. Tailoring the program: Compliance standards and procedures must be tailored to company's particular business and risk areas. This requires a "liability inventory" that can be prepared with the assistance of an "expert" in the compliance field. With the expert, I plan to interview key personnel, review all documents and logs concerning recent investigations, litigation, audits, customer and employee complaints, review industry sources for best practices and review applicable government standards as they apply to the company's business (i.e., regulations, etc.).

Further, the company must establish written standards of ethical business conduct and compliance procedures to be provided to all employees and develop more specific business standards, to be disseminated as appropriate, targeting risk areas specific to the services and products this company offers. The compliance standards and procedures we institute must be reasonably capable of reducing the prospect of criminal conduct. Establishing effective standards involves making compliance a part of each employee's job description and should be included as part of each employee's annual performance review.

There are three things to remember in setting up the compliance program. First, the "mere" circulation of corporate policy statements is not enough to convince investigators and prosecutors of effective training, monitoring and evaluation/enforcement of compliance protocols. Second, with respect to tailoring efforts, we reviewed and are continuing to review benchmarking data to understand what level of compliance program is most appropriate to our size, business, industry, etc. Third, the areas most frequently covered by the compliance program, either within the code of conduct/ethics or by policy, are the antitrust law including relations with competitors; corporate political activity; environmental law; employee relations; securities law (insider trading, etc.); intellectual property, including the confidentially of corporate information; use of corporate communication systems; misappropriation of corporate assets; customer/supplier relations; use of company funds; civil rights, including sexual harassment; bribes and kickbacks; and document management/destruction.

2. Oversight Responsibilities: High level personnel must be assigned overall responsibility and accountability for overseeing the compliance program including developing appropriate standards and procedures. Corporations are titling this function in various ways, including Chief Compliance Officer, Director of Compliance and Integrity, Ethics Director/Officer, etc. Larger companies have formed compliance committees. The appointed Chief Compliance Officer must regularly report to the CEO and the Board of Directors on compliance matters; i.e., not less than annually on implementation and effectiveness of the compliance program.

3. Delegation of Authority: The company must use due care not to delegate substantial discretionary authority to individuals that have propensity to engage in illegal activities. Basically, this translates into using due diligence including background checks of key personnel. This includes reviewing previous history of employment and education as part of the background check. Of course, such background checks must comply with current laws pertaining to employee privacy issues. Further, background checks can only occur at the time of hire, upon promotion, or when a salary increase occurs.

4. Training and Education: The company must take steps to insure that the standards and procedures are effectively communicated, in a tailored manner, to each employee constituency including professional and non-professional staff, new and long-standing employees, executives, etc. Acceptable training methods include focus groups, and discussions using case studies, simulations, role-playing exercises, DVDs and computer-based training. For your information, as the designated representative of the ethics committee, I have met with several training organizations and have reviewed their web-based training modules. For the first year rollout, I am considering train the trainer programs as well as web-based training. I will let you know as soon as a determination is made. In any case, the first area that we will provide compliance training on will be on the Code of Conduct/Ethics.

5. Auditing, Monitoring, and Reporting: Auditing, monitoring, and reporting must be part of an effective compliance program for this company. Spot auditing and routine audits of high-risk areas (i.e., audit for violation of environmental statutes, software copyright laws, antitrust laws) are critical to the success of the program. Under the U.S. Sentencing Guidelines corporations must provide adequate funding for auditing, monitoring and reporting as well as all other elements of an effective compliance program. Auditing should include tracking the distribution of the Code of Conduct/Ethics to all employees; certification that all employees have received and read the Code of Conduct/Ethics; and monitoring and reporting all complaints received from employees or others. Many companies utilize web-based training because such computerized training can automatically provide tracking, auditing and reporting on compliance training for employees. Finally, reporting systems must be established whereby employees and other agents of the company may report issues without fear of retribution. For this reason, most companies establish a hotline managed by a third party who reports hotline calls to the Chief Compliance Officer. It is critical to the effectiveness of the compliance program that all employees are adequately informed about the hotline, as well as other methods to report violations of the Code of Conduct/Ethics and other problems. This step, for all the reasons previously discussed above, takes on added importance under the amendments to the federal sentencing guidelines.

6. Incentives and Discipline: Incentives and discipline are important in maintaining an effective compliance program. There is a spectrum of compliance incentives that can be used including positive performance reviews, certificates of recognition and bonuses as well as a spectrum of disciplinary tools such as informal and formal reprimands, financial penalties, suspension and discharge.

7. Response and Prevention: A key to maintaining the effectiveness of the compliance program over many years is creating a process to continually renew, refresh, and improve the program. This requires annual surveys of employees, annual risk assessments, and reviewing best practices at similar corporations. As discussed above, the company may need to undertake modifications and/or revisions to the program in order to meet the "act appropriately to prevent further criminal conduct" requirement of the amendments to the federal sentencing guidelines.

Areas for further discussion include: whether the planned program, especially Code of Conduct/Ethics, is harmonious with our company culture, including those of parent, subsidiary and affiliated companies. I look forward to examining these issues for you.

I appreciate your interest in the compliance area and look forward to working with you to create an effective compliance program.

———————

Assignment

- **Hypothetical:** You are the Chief Compliance Officer at your Team's Corporation. Create a master strategy for raising ethics awareness, promoting an ethical culture and establishing an ethical Tone at the Top.

Chapter 3

Risk Assessment[*]

Introduction

Risk is at the heart of nearly every economic enterprise. One highly regarded report on risk assessment, prepared by the Committee of Sponsoring Organizations (COSO), defines it as "the identification and analysis of relevant risks to achievement of the [entity's] objectives, forming a basis for determining how the risks should be managed."

Business leaders grapple with many risks to achievement of goals, where failure will bring serious negative consequences. They worry about having the right strategy for succeeding in the current economic environment. Have they done enough to protect the safety of their employees? Are they adequately protected against fraud, embezzlement and other financial risks? Is their compliance program sufficiently designed and implemented to prevent and detect criminal conduct within their corporation? Managing these strategic, operational, financial and legal risks demands the attention and skill of employees in every component of an enterprise.

The Necessity of Risk Assessment in Corporate Compliance

The purpose of a corporate compliance program is to manage a company's wide range of legal risks. An assessment of that risk is, as U.S. regulators have recognized, "fundamental to developing a strong compliance program." Equally important is implementation of standards and controls to address those risks. As the U.S. Department of Justice (DOJ) and the U.S. Securities and Exchange Commission (SEC) affirmed in their November 2012 Foreign Corrupt Practices Act (FCPA) enforcement guidance, "Effective compliance programs are tailored to the company's specific business and to the risks associated with that business." Accordingly, the agencies expect compliance programs to be "dynamic and evolve as the business and the markets change."

---

[*] Special thanks to Paul McNulty, Partner, Baker & McKenzie for his contributions. This chapter is adapted from Paul McNulty, *Risk Assessment* in CORPORATE COMPLIANCE PRACTICE GUIDE: THE NEXT GENERATION OF COMPLIANCE, Chapter 3 (Carole Basri, Release 8, 2016).

The Justice Department and SEC are clear that "in a global marketplace, an effective compliance program is a critical component of a company's internal controls," yet, as the above mentioned guidance states, "effective policies and procedures require an in-depth understanding of the company's business model, including its products and services, third-party agents, customers, government interactions, and industry and geographic risks."

For example, a business involved in the exportation of technology outside of the U.S. must consider whether such technology is restricted in some manner from exportation for reasons of national security. If international trade is generally permissible, are there risks of re-exportation to sanctioned countries? In addition, what is the likelihood that a third-party distributor of the technology will bribe a foreign official in order to obtain substantial business in a foreign country? These are just a few of the many questions this company must ask in the hope of avoiding costly legal sanctions.

As corporations look to expand business into emerging markets, effective risk assessment becomes even more important. Many emerging markets are plagued by corruption, and local business or channel partners are too often willing to engage in corrupt practices. The world's most ethical companies give serious consideration to such legal risks and the controls necessary to address those risks when setting their strategic goals and developing their business plans.

Enforcement officials are raising the bar on what constitutes a strong compliance program. Expenditure of substantial resources on internal controls and training, backed by a good "tone at the top" will not be enough to impress prosecutors if there is no clear record of regular risk assessment. There may even be a suspicion that the program is intended to be one of form over substance. Enforcement agencies have spoken clearly on this point: a company's compliance program should be "tailored to an organization's specific needs, risks, and challenges" and a company should implement a corporate compliance program "most appropriate for that particular business organization." Furthermore, internal controls and training programs should be updated in a timely manner as new risks are identified.

Settlement Agreement | Re: Lender Processing Services, Inc. Foreclosure Fraud $35M Settlement

United States Department of Justice, Criminal Division (Feb. 14, 2013)
http://stopforeclosurefraud.com/2013/02/19/settlement-agreement-re-lender-processing-services-inc-foreclosure-fraud-35m-settlement/

[Lender Processing Services Inc. (LPS), a publicly traded mortgage servicing company based in Jacksonville, Fla., has agreed to pay $35 million in criminal penalties and forfeiture to address its participation in a six-year scheme to prepare and file more than 1 million fraudulently signed and notarized mortgage-related documents with property recorders' offices throughout the United States. The NPA-Non-Prosecution Agreement with the Department of Justice remarks that LPS took measures to remediate the wrongdoings including the acceptable enhanced Risk Management Program.]

Washington, D.C. 20530

February 14, 2013

Paul J. McNulty, Esq.
Joan Meyer, Esq.
Baker & McKenzie LLP
815 Connecticut Ave,
NW Washington, DC 20006-4078

Re: Lender Processing Services, Inc.

Dear Mr. McNulty and Ms. Meyer:

On the understandings specified below, the United States Department of Justice, Criminal Division, Fraud Section and the United States Attorney's Office for the Middle District of Florida (collectively, the "Government") will not criminally prosecute Lender Processing Services, Inc. and its subsidiaries and affiliates (collectively, "LPS"), for any crimes (except for criminal tax violations, as to which the Government cannot and does not make any agreement) related to the preparation and recordation of mortgage-related documents as described in the attached Appendix A, which is incorporated in this Non-Prosecution Agreement ("Agreement").

It is understood that LPS admits, accepts, and acknowledges responsibility for the conduct set forth in Appendix A, and agrees not to make any public statement contradicting Appendix A.

The Fraud Section enters into this Agreement based, in part, on its consideration of the following factors:

(a) LPS has made a timely, voluntary, and complete disclosure of the facts described in Appendix A.

(b) LPS conducted a thorough internal investigation of the misconduct described in Appendix A, reported its findings to the Government, cooperated with the Government's investigation of this matter, and sought to effectively remediate any problems it discovered.

1. Although LPS's self-disclosure and cooperation commenced after a whistleblower complaint brought the misconduct to the government's attention, since the misconduct described in Appendix A was first reported, LPS has taken substantial remedial actions, including:

a. Within approximately six months of discovering the misconduct, LPS wound down all operations of its wholly-owned subsidiary DocX, LLC ("DocX") in Alpharetta, Georgia, where the primary misconduct described in Appendix A took place.

b. LPS took action to remediate certain of the filings made by DocX from March to October 2009, including re-executing with proper signatures and notarizations, approximately 30,000 mortgage assignments.

c. Within weeks of the disclosure, LPS terminated DocX's president, Lorraine Brown. Later, after conducting its internal investigation, LPS terminated Ms. Brown's immediate supervisor at LPS for, among other reasons, failure to supervise Ms. Brown and the DocX operation.

2. The Government received substantial information from LPS, as well as from federal and state regulatory agencies, demonstrating LPS has recently made important and positive changes in its compliance, training, and overall approach to ensuring its adherence to the law.

a. On April 13, 2011, LPS entered into a consent order (the "2011" Consent Order") with the Board of Governors of the Federal Reserve System, the Office of the Comptroller of the Currency, the Federal Deposit Insurance Corporation, and the Office of Thrift Supervision (collectively, the "Banking Agencies"). The 2011 Consent Order has a number of conditions with which LPS is required to comply, including:

(i) delineating a methodology for reviewing document execution practices and remediating identified issues;

(ii) establishing an acceptable compliance program and timeline for implementation;

(iii) acceptably enhancing its risk management program;

(iv) acceptably enhancing its internal audit program;

(v) retaining an independent consultant to review and report on LPS's document execution practices, and assess related operational, compliance, legal, and reputational risks; and

(vi) to the extent that the independent consultant identifies any financial harm stemming from the document execution practices to mortgage servicers or borrowers, establish a plan for reimbursing any such financial injury.

To date, LPS has complied with the conditions of the 2011 Consent Order. That work is ongoing and is subject to review and approval by the Banking Agencies.

b. LPS has agreed in a multi-state settlement with a number of state attorneys general (the "Multi-State Resolution") to undertake additional steps, including assisting homeowners with remediating specific documents as necessary and appropriate.

c. Including this Agreement, LPS has paid to date over $160 million to state and federal authorities related to the DocX conduct.

This recent record is commendable, and partially mitigates the adverse implications of the prior history of misconduct at the DocX subsidiary.

3. The primary misconduct set forth in Appendix A took place at DocX, a subsidiary acquired by an LPS predecessor company in 2005, which constituted less than 1% of LPS's overall corporate revenue.

4. The Government's investigation has revealed, as set forth in Appendix A, that Lorraine Brown and others at DocX took various steps to actively conceal the misconduct taking place at DocX from detection, including from LPS senior management and auditors.

This Agreement does not provide any protection against prosecution for any crimes except as set forth above, and applies only to LPS and not to any other entities or to any individuals, including but not limited to employees or officers of LPS. The protections provided to LPS shall not apply to any acquirer or successor entities unless and until such acquirer or successor formally adopts and executes this Agreement.

This Agreement shall have a term of two years from the date of this Agreement, except as specifically provided below. It is understood that for the two-year term of this Agreement, LPS shall: (a) commit no crime whatsoever; (b) truthfully and completely disclose non-privileged information with respect to the activities of LPS, its officers and employees, and others concerning all matters about which the Government inquires of it, which information can be used for any purpose, except as otherwise limited in this Agreement; (c) bring to the Government's attention all potentially criminal conduct by LPS or any of its employees that relates to violations of U.S. laws (i) concerning fraud or (ii) concerning mortgage or foreclosure document execution services; and (d) bring to the Government's attention all criminal or regulatory investigations, administrative proceedings or civil actions brought by any governmental authority in the United States against LPS, its subsidiaries, or its employees that alleges fraud or violations of the laws governing mortgage or foreclosure document execution services.

Data Protection

With the increase of data storage, all institutions will need to protect their expanded amount of information, because it might constitute sensitive personal data; companies' valuable and confidential information, trade secrets or government-restricted data. All these situations are important examples of well-established protective measures that any institution—private or public, profit or non-profit—must take regarding the protection of the ever-growing agglomeration of stored data.

A cyber risk assessment program revealed to be necessary for entities subject to cyber risks. A recent example of a cyberattack on a major company resulted in Target agreeing to pay a total of up to $19 million to issuers of MasterCard payment cards over losses and expenses they incurred as a result of the retailer's massive 2013 breach.

Press Release, *Target Confirms Unauthorized Access to Payment Card Data in U.S. Stores*

(Dec. 19, 2013) https://corporate.target.com/press/releases-1/2013/12/
target-confirms-unauthorized-access-to-payment-car

Target today confirmed it is aware of unauthorized access to payment card data that may have impacted certain guests making credit and debit card purchases in its U.S. stores. Target is working closely with law enforcement and financial institutions, and has identified and resolved the issue.

"Target's first priority is preserving the trust of our guests and we have moved swiftly to address this issue, so guests can shop with confidence. We regret any inconvenience this may cause," said Gregg Steinhafel, chairman, president and chief executive officer, Target. "We take this matter very seriously and are working with law enforcement to bring those responsible to justice."

Approximately 40 million credit and debit card accounts may have been impacted between Nov. 27 and Dec. 15, 2013. Target alerted authorities and financial institutions immediately after it was made aware of the unauthorized access, and is putting all appropriate resources behind these efforts. Among other actions, Target is partnering with a leading third-party forensics firm to conduct a thorough investigation of the incident.

The Target settlement announced April 15, 2015, is contingent on issuers of at least 90 percent of the eligible MasterCard accounts accepting their offers by May 20, 2015. If sufficient issuers accept the offer, Target said they will be paid by the end of June 2015. Target said the 2013 breach compromised at least 40 million payment cards and might have caused the pilfering of personal information from as many as 110 million people. The retailer has reported that its breach costs have totaled at least $252 million so far, with $90 million covered by insurance.

Press Release, *Target Reports Third Quarter 2015 Earnings*

(Nov. 18, 2015) http://investors.target.com/phoenix.zhtml?c=
65828&p=irol-newsArticle&ID=2113534

| | Nine Months Ended | | | | | |
| | October 31, 2015 | | | November 1, 2014 | | |
(millions, except per share data)	Pretax	Net of Tax	Per Share Amounts	Pretax	Net of Tax	Per Share Amounts
GAAP diluted earnings per share from continuing operations			$2.98			$2.33	27.7%
Adjustments[1]						
Data Breach-related costs	$38	$27	$0.04	$140	$90	$0.14

One of the most recent risks for global corporations is cybersecurity and customer data security. Any risk assessment should include this important area.

Risk Assessment and the Sentencing Guidelines

In 2004 when the U.S. Sentencing Commission modified the Organizational Sentencing Guidelines of 1991, it highlighted a small number of "best practices" which had developed since the guidelines were first promulgated. Among this set of practices was risk assessment. The Commission added a provision applicable to all seven elements of an effective compliance program, which are listed in subsection (b) of Section 8B2.1. This provision reads as follows:

> (c) In implementing subsection (b), the organization shall periodically assess the risk of criminal conduct and shall take appropriate steps to design, implement, or modify each requirement set forth in subsection (b) to reduce the risk of criminal conduct identified through this process (8B2.1(c)).

In the commentary on this provision, the Commission offers a description of what is required for adequate risk assessment. In essence, companies are instructed to conduct risk assessments on a periodic basis in an effort to determine whether criminal conduct will occur. They should consider the nature and seriousness of such conduct,

---

1. [*(b)*] For the three and nine months ended October 31, 2015, we recorded $26 million and $38 million of pretax Data Breach-related expenses. Along with legal and other professional services, these expenses include adjustments to the accrual necessary to reflect our current loss expectations for the remaining potential Data Breach-related claims. For the three and nine months ended November 1, 2014, we recorded $12 million and $186 million of pretax expenses, respectively. We also recorded expected insurance proceeds of $46 million for the nine months ended November 1, 2014, for net pretax expenses of $140 million.

the likelihood that it will occur because of the nature of the organization's business, and the prior history of the organization. Business organizations should also set priorities periodically for their compliance actions to ensure that they are addressing the criminal conduct that is most serious and most likely to occur. Finally, the Commission directs companies to modify their compliance programs when appropriate to reduce the risk of misconduct.

The Commission has identified some common sense considerations for effective risk assessment: the frequency with which it should occur; what it should consider; and how risk assessment findings should impact compliance programs. With regard to the scope of the assessment, the Commission encourages business organizations to review the adequacy of its controls that were designed to manage the company's risks. In other words, robust risk assessment looks not only at external factors which can lead to misconduct, but it also examines honestly the internal efforts that should be preventing compliance failures.

Risk Assessment in Anti-Corruption Compliance

The critical importance of risk assessment in an effective compliance program is well illustrated in the context of corporate anti-corruption efforts. Global enterprises must anticipate the significant possibility that their employees will be coerced into paying bribes to foreign officials in order to obtain business. The reality is that such payments are a common occurrence in many parts of the world. It is noteworthy that the United Kingdom's guidance on "adequate procedures" for preventing bribery includes the principle of risk assessment — a commercial organization "assessing the nature and extent of its exposure to potential external and internal risks of bribery."

A properly designed and implemented anti-corruption program must anticipate where the risks of bribery are the strongest. Consideration of external and internal risk factors is a useful way to identify these risks. Such a program must carefully examine the organization's business practices. The use of agents or intermediaries, for example, increases the risk of corruption because these third parties are outside the direct control of a company and its anti-bribery restrictions. Therefore, adequate controls should be established to prevent this conduct from occurring or to detect it after it happens.

Judicial/Regulatory Perspective

Enforcement officials will not look favorably upon a "check-the-box" approach to designing and implementing a compliance program. The absence of a credible effort to assess risks unique to an individual company and build a compliance program which prioritizes the most significant of those risks would be judged by enforcement officials as a major compliance short-coming. The Department of Justice Principles of Federal Prosecution of Business Organizations direct prosecutors to carefully review the substance of compliance programs to ensure they are not "paper programs." The Department confirmed this approach in the guidance stating that the Justice Department and the SEC "will give meaningful credit to a company that implements in good faith a comprehensive, risk-based compliance program, even if that program does not prevent an infraction in a low risk area because greater attention and resources had been devoted to a higher risk area." Companies should remain aware of their evolving risks through regular risk assessments, real-time monitoring, and risk-based auditing, and update their controls and training programs in a timely manner, in order to demonstrate the effectiveness of their compliance program.

To this end, an extraordinarily helpful tool has been created by Berlin-based Transparency International (TI), a non-profit educational and advocacy organization devoted to the elimination of public corruption throughout the world. TI issues an annual "Corruption Perception Index" (CPI) which surveys public perceptions about the level of corruption within international business environments. The CPI ranks nearly 200 countries from the least corrupt to the most corrupt. This index is a vital place to begin a risk assessment when developing an anti-corruption compliance program. https://www.transparency.org/cpi2014).

Risk Assessment Process and Checklist

A well-designed compliance program begins with a thorough risk assessment and ensures that the company undertakes further risk assessments on a regular basis, updating the program as the company's business operations and legal risks evolve. In fact, many best practice compliance programs build regular risk assessments into the program's annual plan.

A risk assessment, whether it be an initial risk assessment or subsequent assessment updates, can be undertaken in four fundamental steps. The first step is to gather information about the company's business operations and practices and determine the scope of the review. This is called an inventory of documents. In particular, information on the company structure, sector, locations, client base, business partners, third party engagement, existing standards, policies, internal controls, training protocols, and procedures should be gathered, along with any plans addressing strategic business initiatives under consideration. Further, all applicable laws and regulatory regimes should be identified at this stage. As the corporate trend toward globalization continues, it is essential that a company understands the legal framework and regulatory environment within which it operates if it is to maintain risk mitigation mechanisms that effectively address these requirements.

Sample Request for Inventory of Documents for
Best Practice/Gaps Analysis Risk Assessment
Interoffice Memorandum

To: Officers, Department Heads and Managers
From: Compliance Officer
Date: _____

Subject: Request for Inventory of Documents for Best Practice/Gaps Analysis Risk Assessment

As I have mentioned to many of you, we will be undertaking the development and implementation of a corporate compliance program commencing on _____. This risk assessment will require some attention by each of you as the programs relate to the business area which you represent as officers, department heads and managers. An essential starting point for the development of the corporate compliance program is the gathering of all the existing relevant information, which we currently have at each of your areas. Accordingly, I am asking each of you to gather the following documents and information (to extent it exists) relating to the area you represent and forward it to my attention at your earliest convenience:

– Organizational charts reflecting Company partnerships or affiliations and management responsibilities

– Business plans, annual reports, and other materials describing business operations and strategic business initiatives

– Handbooks and any other policies or procedures reflecting Company standards or operational protocols

– Existing compliance structure or program and any previous internal or external reviews or assessments of the compliance program

– Business partner inventory lists, including any government officials or entities with whom the Company interacts

– Training curriculum and related materials (diversity, sexual harassment, etc.)

– Corporate audit document checklist

– Previous internal or external reviews and investigations of reports received through a whistleblower hotline or other misconduct reporting mechanisms

– Litigation lists and settled cases for past five years

– Crisis management policies and/or manuals

– Data retention policies and/or manuals

– Employee application forms

– Human resources annual reports

– Exit/termination checklists

– Interview checklist or evaluation form

– Insider trading guides

– Environmental policies and reports

– Community Right to Know reports

– Advertising materials

Many thanks in advance for your help in advancing this very important project.

The second step of a risk assessment involves the conduct of interviews. Following a review and analysis of the materials collected thus far, key stakeholders with knowledge of the company's operations and relevant personnel on the ground should be identified and interviewed. Understanding firsthand how the company operates in practice and the compliance culture within the company is key to identifying areas of risk.

The third step of a risk assessment is to evaluate all information gathered and develop a report that provides both a risk profile and recommendations on how to enhance a company's compliance program to address those risks. The information collated in the preceding steps is analyzed in detail to identify both the nature and extent of the risks, any "red flags" within the company and the areas of risk that need to be addressed as a priority. Issues requiring additional review and investigation may be identified during this stage of a risk assessment. Further review into such matters should be conducted prior to finalizing the assessment or, in the alternative, they should be highlighted for follow up review. This should include heat maps of the risk areas as well as a dashboard of the risk review process.

The last step of a risk assessment, following consideration and review of any outstanding items from the previous stages of the assessment, is to finalize the report and develop a plan for implementing program enhancements. This should include an executive summary of the final report and heat maps and dashboards to illustrate the findings. Program enhancement recommendations included as part of the report should be prioritized based on the nature of the legal risk, the complexities surrounding implementation of the enhancement, and the amount of time implementation is expected to take. Finally, a detailed action plan should be developed that assigns responsibility for implementing the recommendations to specific departments or individuals in order to ensure timely adoption of the recommendations.

A valuable tool for this initial risk assessment process is a checklist of key areas of concern frequently encountered in the pursuit of ethical business activity. Some of the most pertinent questions will vary from one business sector to another. For example, companies in the IT or telecommunications business that maintain large quantities of customer data should be especially concerned about risks associated with data security and privacy. Similarly, financial institutions must pay close attention to anti-money laundering issues. For these organizations, a checklist of the most significant risk-related questions will need to address such topics.

Many questions, however, apply to a wide range of corporate interests. They relate to issues regularly encountered by or concerns common to virtually every enterprise engaging in risk assessment. Here are ten questions that should be included in an effective risk analysis. They are just a sample of the types and categories of questions that may need to be asked.

1. Who are the partners within the stream of business, including all third parties and joint venture partners?

2. What are the compensation arrangements with third parties? Commissions? Percentage of deals? Margin?

3. Who are the customers? Are they government agencies or instrumentalities?

4. Where and how is business conducted outside of the U.S.?

5. How extensive are the internal controls? How frequently are they reviewed and modified?

6. Is the leadership sufficiently engaged in the compliance program?

7. Where does compliance fit within the organizational structure? Does it have sufficient authority and independence from the business units, access to the Board of Directors, and support and resources?

8. Have there been past violations of law or credible allegations of misconduct within the company?

9. What are the enforcement priorities and policies of the governments where substantial business is done? (For example, the European Commission is vigorously enforcing antitrust laws.)

10. What are the best practices for compliance within the industry for benchmarking a compliance program?

Answering these questions and completing a comprehensive risk assessment is just the start of risk management. The chapters that follow in this treatise will address best practices for protecting a company from the harm that results when red flags become actual violations of law.

Additionally, Department of Justice Criminal Division created a Resource Guide to understand the Foreign Corrupt Practices Act (FCPA). This Resource Guide, in Chapter 5 Guiding Principles of Enforcement, provides guidance on risk assessment in creating an FCPA compliance program. However, this guidance provides helpful best practices applicable to any compliance program.

U.S. Department of Justice Criminal Division & SEC Enforcement Division, Resource Guide to the U.S. Foreign Corrupt Practices Act

http://www.justice.gov/sites/default/files/criminal-fraud/legacy/2015/01/16/guide.pdf

Risk Assessment

Assessment of risk is fundamental to developing a strong compliance program, and is another factor DOJ and SEC evaluate when assessing a company's compliance program. One-size-fits-all compliance programs are generally ill-conceived and ineffective because resources inevitably are spread too thin, with too much focus on low risk markets and transactions to the detriment of high-risk areas. Devoting a disproportionate amount of time policing modest entertainment and gift-giving instead of focusing on large government bids, questionable payments to third-party consultants, or excessive discounts to resellers and distributors may indicate that a company's compliance program is ineffective. A $50 million contract with a government agency in a high-risk country warrants greater scrutiny than modest and routine gifts and entertainment.

Similarly, performing identical due diligence on all third party agents, irrespective of risk factors, is often counterproductive, diverting attention and resources away from those third parties that pose the most significant risks. DOJ and SEC will give meaningful credit to a company that implements in good faith a comprehensive, risk-based compliance program, even if that program does not prevent an infraction in a low risk area because greater attention and resources had been devoted to a higher risk area. Conversely, a company that fails to prevent an FCPA violation on an economically significant, high-risk transaction because it failed to perform a level of due diligence commensurate with the size and risk of the transaction is likely to receive reduced credit based on the quality and effectiveness of its compliance program.

As a company's risk for FCPA violations increases, that business should consider increasing its compliance procedures, including due diligence and periodic internal audits. The degree of appropriate due diligence is fact-specific and should vary based on industry, country, size, and nature of the transaction, and the method and amount of third-party compensation. Factors to consider, for instance, include risks presented by: the country and industry sector, the business opportunity, potential business partners, level of involvement with governments, amount of government regulation and oversight, and exposure to customs and immigration in conducting business affairs. When assessing a company's compliance program, DOJ and SEC take into account whether and to what degree a company analyzes and addresses the particular risks it faces.

———————

Risk Assessment Tools

Heat Map

Risk assessment is a critical step in risk management. It involves evaluating the likelihood and potential impact of identified risks. A heat map is a managerial tool that presents the risk assessment results in a visually and precise way. The heat map below is one of the many examples of how organizations can map probability ranges to common qualitative characterizations of risk event likelihood, and a ranking scheme for potential impacts.

An organization needs to have in mind what would be considered a material risk to that entity, how much risk is to be accepted, how to define the parameters to evaluate the likelihood of risk events and the impact that they might have on the business in order to map the potential risk events to the heat map.

Figure 3.1 Heat Map

Likelihood	Insignificant 1	Minor 2	Moderate 3	Major 4	Catastrophic 5
Rare 1	2	3	4	5 (Low)	6 (Low)
Unlikely 2	3	4	5 (Low)	6 (Low)	7 (Moderate)
Possible 3	4	5 (Low)	6 (Low)	7 (Moderate)	8 (Moderate)
Likely 4	5 (Low)	6 (Low)	7 (Moderate)	8 (Moderate)	9 (High)
Almost Certain 5	6 (Low)	7 (Moderate)	8 (Moderate)	9 (High)	10 (EXTREME!!!!!)

Assignments

- **Hypothetical:** You are the Chief Compliance Officer at your Team's Corporation. Draft a sample request of inventory of documents for Best Practice/Gap Analysis Risk Assessment and draft sample interview questions for inventory of documents for Best Practice/Gap Analysis Risk Assessment.

- Create a list of risk areas to look for in a prototype global corporation.

Chapter 4

Global Codes of Conduct[*]

Introduction

Most major multinationals—particularly those based in the United States—have issued global codes of conduct spelling out baseline rules that apply across their worldwide operations. But these conduct codes vary substantially as to their purpose, content and focus. In fact, "code of conduct" is not even a term of art; it is just a broad label applied to a range of multinational and nongovernmental organization policies. The International Labour Organisation website used to say that "global codes of conduct do not have any authorized definition ... [T]here is a great variance in the way these statements are drafted." For that matter, many policies labeled "code of conduct" have little to do with employment relationships: There are antitrust compliance codes of conduct, environmental-protection codes of conduct and advisory codes of conduct on topics like intellectual property and computer programming. These non-employment-related codes, while vital, are only loosely connected to a multinational's cross-border efforts at legal and ethical human resources compliance.

Our discussion focuses on global conduct codes in the international employment context. We begin by drawing the critical distinction between external *supplier codes of conduct* that protect the staff of a multinational's suppliers from so-called "sweatshop" conditions, versus *internal codes of conduct or ethics* that impose compliance rules on a multinational's in-house personnel worldwide. In a sense, these two types of conduct codes are actually opposites: external supplier codes seek to *protect* employees not on the code issuer's payroll, while internal ethics codes seek to *restrain* a code issuer's in-house staff. Sometimes a multinational tries to cobble these two very different documents together into a single text, but effectively merging them is hard because both the goals and intended audiences differ.

A multinational ready either to issue a new global code of conduct or to update an old one needs to take three steps: First, clarify which of the two types of conduct codes is necessary. Second, determine what the code should say. Third, implement the code across global operations. Accordingly, the first part of our discussion dis-

---

[*] Special thanks to Donald C. Dowling, Jr., International Employment Lawyer in New York City, for his contributions. This chapter is adapted from Donald C. Dowling, Jr., *Global Codes of Conduct* in CORPORATE COMPLIANCE PRACTICE GUIDE: THE NEXT GENERATION OF COMPLIANCE, Chapter 4 (Carole Basri, Release 8, 2016).

tinguishes the two types of conduct codes with a focus on supplier ("sweatshop") codes. The second part offers a checklist of topics to address when drafting an internal code of business conduct or ethics. And the third part lists the steps to take when launching or implementing an internal code of business conduct or ethics.

Because external supplier codes of conduct differ substantially from internal codes of business conduct or ethics, any multinational employer contemplating a conduct code first needs to decide which of these two very different types of codes it needs — or whether it needs both.

Two Types of Codes of Conduct: The Supplier Code of Conduct and the Internal Code of Conduct

Global supplier or "sweatshop" codes of conduct first got traction in the 1990s when American human rights activists championed them as a weapon to fight perceived overseas labor abuses and to promote workers' rights in the developing world. U.S. labor union activists interested in job security for American workers — "protecting American jobs" — jumped on this bandwagon and promoted supplier codes, too. Then California passed a law effective since 2012, the Supply Chain Transparency Act, which required companies to confirm they are not complicit in human trafficking or slavery. More recently, the 2013 Rana Plaza factory collapse in Bangladesh actually reinvigorated the supplier code of conduct movement, even though a building collapse has nothing to do with labor standards and everything to do with real estate construction code standards.

Today, human rights activists and U.S. organized labor continue to urge those multinationals that resell third-world-sourced product in rich first-world markets to impose supplier codes of conduct and to police the labor conditions of the overseas workers working for companies that sell goods to multinationals.[1] That said, trade unions in developing countries tend to *oppose* overzealous American attempts to protect third world workers — too much protection threatens the jobs of the very workers ostensibly protected.[2]

The multinationals that issue robust supplier codes of conduct tend to be businesses that source low-cost manufactured product from the developing world — technology hardware marketers like Apple and Samsung, athletic shoe companies like Nike and Adidas, mass-market retailers like Wal-Mart and Target, mid-market fashion marketers like Liz Claiborne and Donna Karan, sports equipment and toy makers like Mattel and Reebok. Some oil and mining companies and some global manufacturing conglomerates (General Electric, for example) also impose supplier codes. And supplier codes pop up in unexpected sectors, like the Starbucks "fair trade" sourcing protocols

---

1. *See* W. Martucci, et al., *International Workers, Companies and Consumers*, Law360, Aug. 19, 2013.

2. *See* Thomas Friedman, *Don't Punish Africa*, N.Y. Times, Mar. 7, 2000.

and New York University's Statement of Labor Values (which made headlines in May 2014). But supplier codes of conduct are far from ubiquitous. They remain relatively rare in industries from food and restaurants to finance, professional services, industrial supply, business-to-business sectors and most all services industries. In fact, supplier codes of conduct are not even much of an issue among high-end luxury goods brands that source product from rich countries.

External Focus: Supplier codes of conduct are external, neither addressed to nor meant to protect the multinational issuer's in-house staff on its own payroll. Rather, supplier codes protect workers on the payrolls of the multinationals' unaffiliated *suppliers*. While some codes purport to reach both supplier employees and the multinational code issuer's own staff, internal compliance rarely matters to anyone, because any multinational that goes to the trouble of issuing a supplier code thinks of itself as a conscientious employer not operating "sweatshops" of its own. Indeed, even the activists and labor unions that complain about foreign sweatshops rarely accuse multinationals themselves of shoddy labor practices in their own in-house operations (but there are a few exceptions, like discount retailers).

Developing and Underdeveloped Country Focus: External supplier codes of conduct almost always purport to reach a multinational's suppliers worldwide, across rich and poor countries alike. But as a practical matter, these codes only concern suppliers in the developing world. While labor abuses occur everywhere, no activist who decries sweatshops sees domestic labor abuses as a pressing social issue in, say, Canada, Denmark or Japan. So while multinationals nominally extend their sweatshop codes to suppliers in rich countries, rich-country suppliers often ignore them. No one seems to complain.

Supplier Code Content

Supplier codes of conduct require the multinational's sellers to meet whatever minimum labor protections the code spells out. The specific minimum labor standards covered differ widely from code to code. Some supplier codes focus on just a single issue or two—child labor, slave labor or human trafficking, for example. But most supplier codes cover a range of potential workplace abuses, like these topics plus rest periods, bathroom breaks, anti-discrimination, health/safety, unionization, work hours, pay rates and payroll. An emerging additional issue, especially in the Arab world, is recruitment fees and withholding immigrant workers' passports.

Not surprisingly, when *organized labor* champions supplier codes, the most vital provision becomes the code clause on union organization ("right to organize"). Be strategic in addressing unionization within a supplier code. Consider merely committing to follow applicable labor unionization laws. Indeed, a conservative but viable approach to drafting an entire supplier conduct code is to anchor it in a commitment to follow applicable law without second-guessing local legislatures by adding too many additional rights.

While some supplier conduct codes list core labor protections specifically, others incorporate by reference model industry code templates, local employee-protection laws or International Labour Organization (ILO) conventions. Many of the industries in which supplier conduct codes are common have issued sample codes — forms, models and examples setting out recommended content, or entire codes meant to be incorporated by reference. Be careful adopting some interest group's or industry group's model code; it may contain provisions unworkable in your operations. In particular, the too-common practice of incorporating ILO conventions into a global supplier conduct code can cause unintended consequences. ILO standards are a bad fit for a multinational's supplier code of conduct because the ILO addresses its conventions to nation-states, not corporations. Just as no U.S. domestic employee handbook would ever incorporate the U.S. Constitution's bill of rights, to incorporate ILO standards into a supplier conduct code misconstrues what ILO standards are meant to do. (In 2006, the ILO did issue a "Tripartite Declaration of Principles Concerning Multinational Enterprises and Social Policy," but this declaration merely offers broad suggestions and is directed only to multinationals, not to their overseas suppliers.) Incorporating the core ILO right to *freedom of association* opens the door to the argument that the multinational code issuer estopped itself and its suppliers from opposing union drives and resisting certain union initiatives worldwide. "Freedom of association" has widely divergent meanings around the world, and academic literature within the labor movement interprets the free association concept expansively. Never incorporate ILO standards, particularly not the "free association" right, into a supplier code of conduct without embracing the significant ramifications.

Example:

> *"We adhere to the principles of the International Labor Organization, we support and apply the core principles relating to human rights, labor and environment"*

Implementation and monitoring: Multinationals usually impose supplier conduct codes as appendices to the supply contracts and sourcing agreements they enter into with the "business partners" around the world that sell them goods. This structure is a lot more awkward and a lot less effective than proponents of supplier conduct codes ever seem to admit. The lurking legal challenge here is *privity of employment contract:* Multinationals that buy product in arm's-length sales transactions from unaffiliated foreign sellers are mere customers in cross-border sales of goods transactions. In the normal course of business, a customer — especially one overseas — has little information about and zero say over the seller's internal terms and conditions of employment. Legally as opposed to economically, customers tend to be powerless to dictate and monitor day-to-day human resources conditions and operations inside the businesses that sell them goods. Indeed, in most all other contexts, business partners are careful to *avoid* setting terms and conditions of workers they do not employ, as a precaution against findings of co-/dual-/joint-employer liability.

Supplier codes of conduct try to change all this by usurping human resources powers from sellers and bestowing them on customers. But even a customer empowered to set a seller's labor terms has a tough time establishing and then policing them. *The Wall Street Journal* has acknowledged "the difficulties Western companies sometimes face in assessing working conditions at the foreign plants that manufacture their products."[3] According to "an extensive investigation by *The New York Times*," many "Western companies'" supplier code of conduct "inspection system[s] intended to protect [suppliers'] workers and ensure manufacturing quality [are] riddled with flaws."[4]

After a multinational customer drafts a supplier code of conduct and gets its overseas sellers to agree to it, then what happens? How does the customer (or its agents) access the foreign seller's premises to monitor their work conditions? What does a customer do if it finds minor violations at a seller's overseas factories that otherwise are better than industry standards, or if it finds violations that do not justify cutting the seller off? These questions get asked a lot, but there are no easy answers.

Supplier codes rarely ever—and certainly should never—*require* the multinational customer to monitor sellers' code compliance. Some class action lawsuits filed in U.S. courts, albeit almost uniformly unsuccessful ones, have sought to enforce supplier codes against multinational customers on behalf of overseas supplier factory workers by asserting a third-party-beneficiary theory, arguing the multinational failed to monitor.[5] The best defense to these lawsuits is to be able to show the monitoring provision in the operative code was voluntary, not mandatory.

Service sector codes: Until now the supplier code of conduct movement has targeted institutional buyers of tangible goods, even though most all of the social, compliance, public relations and business-case arguments for supplier conduct codes apply equally powerfully to sellers of *services*. Will the next frontier be imposing supplier codes on outsourced call centers and other low-wage, back-office services operations from India to the Philippines and beyond?

Internal Code of Conduct Content: A Checklist of Topics
Checklist of Topics in an Internal ("Ethics") Code of Conduct or Code of Ethics

When launching or updating an internal code of business conduct or ethics designed to impose compliance standards on staff across a multinational's worldwide operations, the first question that gets asked is inevitably the question of code content:

---

3. M. Bustillo, *Sex Abuse Alleged at Apparel Maker*, Wall St. J., June 20, 2011.
4. S. Clifford, *Fast and Flawed Inspections of Factories Abroad*, N.Y. Times, Sept. 1, 2013.
5. *See Doe v. Wal-Mart*, 572 F. 3d 677 (9th Cir. 2009).

What should our code of ethics say? Which topics should we include? Which topics can we omit?

A Google search for "code of conduct" yields dozens of excellent sample internal ethics codes. The easy temptation in drafting one of these codes is just to copy somebody else's document—or at least to use someone else's code as a first draft. Resist this temptation. The problem with cloning another organization's code is that each multinational's particular business operation spawns unique business needs. A code of business conduct should confine itself only to those topics the issuing organization really needs to regulate. Yet business needs differ widely from one multinational to the next. Needs of government contractors differ from needs of professional services organizations, which differ from needs of manufacturers. The needs of a publicly-traded company differ from those of a privately held business, which in turn differ from those of a nonprofit. Needs of businesses operating in the world's business centers differ from needs of organizations serving the world's trouble spots. Needs differ by business sector—an oil company's needs differ from a bank's. Needs also vary by headquarters country—a Japanese trading company drafting an internal code of ethics has very different priorities from a U.S.-headquartered conglomerate.

A well-drafted internal code of ethics meets the issuing organization's own business needs by tailoring a provision on each topic the code issuer needs to align across borders while omitting each topic the issuing organization can afford to leave out. Copying some other company's ethics code (or adopting the code of some trade organization or advocate group) is dangerous because the model code was drafted by an outsider responding to the outsider's own agenda. A code drafted by an outsider will inevitably omit necessary provisions and will contain superfluous provisions. For example, a global, privately held shipping company's ethics code needs a human trafficking provision but does not need an insider trading clause. The opposite is true of a publicly traded professional services firm.

When drafting an internal code of ethics, steer clear of provisions addressing everyday human resources topics best relegated to local HR policies, individual or collective employment agreements, or employee handbooks. An internal ethics code differs fundamentally from an employee handbook, although there is some overlap. Employee handbooks generally address quotidian aspects of human resources that differ from country to country—topics best relegated to local employee communications, like employee benefits, dress code, smoking, office hours, performance evaluations, expense reimbursement, holidays, vacation, payroll and overtime. By contrast, a well-drafted internal code of conduct or ethics addresses minimum baseline compliance standards that reach across borders.

To take an organic approach when drafting or revising a code of business conduct or ethics, use a topic-by-topic checklist to craft a bespoke code that meets your actual business needs without including anything superfluous. Consider the business case for each of the following topics commonly found in ethics codes, then tailor provisions on these topics to meet your specific business needs:

- **Introduction stating core values**

Internal codes of business conduct or ethics usually open with a statement, typically from the president or chief executive officer, explaining the organization's core values and reasons for imposing the code, sending the message "from the top" that code compliance is a vital business priority. This is often referred to as the "mission statement."

Example of values statement across industries:

PHARMACEUTICAL/HEALTHCARE

"Values"

Integrity — Acting ethically

We commit to maintain the highest ethical and quality standards.

Respect — Embracing Difference

We recognize and respect the diversity and needs of our people, patients and partners, ensuring transparent and constructive interactions through mutual trust.

Solidarity — Socially responsible

We are united in shared responsibility for our actions, our people, the wellbeing of our patients and in achieving a sustainable impact on the environment.

OIL INDUSTRY

Safety

Safety is good business. Everything we do relies upon the safety of our workforce and the communities around us. We care about the safe management of the environment. We are committed to safely delivering energy to the world.

Respect

We respect the world in which we operate. It begins with compliance with laws and regulations. We hold ourselves to the highest ethical standards and behave in ways that earn the trust of others. We depend on the relationships we have and respect each other and those we work with. We value diversity of people and thought. We care about the consequences of our decisions, large and small, on those around us.

Excellence

We are in a hazardous business and are committed to excellence through the systematic and disciplined management of our operations. We follow and uphold the rules and standards we set for our company. We commit to quality outcomes, have a thirst to learn and to improve. If something is not right, we correct it.

Courage

What we do is rarely easy. Achieving the best outcomes often requires the courage to face difficulty, to speak up and stand by what we believe. We always strive to do the right thing. We explore new ways of thinking and are unafraid to ask for help. We are honest with ourselves and actively seek feedback from others. We aim for an enduring legacy, despite the short-term priorities of our world.

One Team

Whatever the strength of the individual, we will accomplish more together. We put the team ahead of our personal success and commit to building its capability. We trust each other to deliver on our respective obligations.

HI-TECH INDUSTRY

"Values"

Customer Orientation

- Listen and respond to our customers, suppliers and stakeholders
- Deliver innovative and competitive products and services
- Excel at customer satisfaction

Discipline

- Conduct business with uncompromising integrity and professionalism
- Ensure a safe, clean and injury-free workplace
- Properly plan, fund and staff projects

Quality

- Achieve the highest standards of excellence
- Do the right things right
- Continuously learn, develop and

Improve

- Take pride in our work
- Continuously innovate

Risk Taking

- Foster innovation and creative thinking, encourage informed risk taking
- Embrace change and challenge the status quo
- Learn from our successes and mistakes

Great Place to Work

- Promote a challenging work environment that develops our diverse workforce
- Work as a team with respect and trust for each other

Results Orientation

- Set competitive goals
- Focus on results
- Be accountable
- Constructively confront and solve problems

BANKING INDUSTRY

"Values"

Dependable and do the right thing

Stand firm for what is right, deliver on commitments, be resilient and trustworthy

Open to different ideas and cultures

Communicate openly, honestly and transparently, value challenge and learn from mistakes. Listen, treat people fairly, be inclusive, value different perspectives

Connected to customers, communities, regulators and each other

Build connections, be aware of external issues, and collaborate across boundaries

Comparison table of Values Statement:

While every corporation in the market list honesty, integrity and fairness as their core values, some values can be specific to the industry:

Pharmaceutical	Oil company	Hi-Tech	Banking/Financial Services
Values	Values	Values	Values
Integrity—Acting ethically	Safety	Customer Orientation	Integrity/Do the right thing
Respect—Embracing Difference	Environment/Respect	Discipline	Fair treatment
Solidarity—Socially responsible	Excellence	Quality	Respect for customers, communities, regulators and each other
	Courage	Innovation	
		Risk taking	

The U.S. Federal Sentencing Guidelines, November 1, 1991, as revised on November 1, 2004, provided for a "Culture of Ethics." For an effective compliance program, it is essential that the company can show "tone at the top," which is the emanating of positive ethical values from the top executives to the lowest level of the corporate ladder.

The 2015 Volkswagen case is an example of a lack of alignment between, on the one hand, the Global Code of Conduct and the 2014 Sustainability Report and, on the other hand, the actions taken by the Volkswagen.

The Volkswagen 2010 Global Code of Conduct[6] beings as follows:

By introducing the following Code of Conduct, we, the Volkswagen Group, have taken another resolute step in the exercise of our global and local responsibility.

---

6. http://en.volkswagen.com/content/medialib/vwd4/de/Volkswagen/Nachhaltigkeit/service/download/corporate_governance/Code_of_Conduct/_jcr_content/renditions/rendition.file/the-volkswagen-group-code-of-conduct.pdf.

Our products help to ensure that mobility is environmentally friendly, efficient, and safe. In this context, the future obligates us to promote mobility in the interest of the common good, while doing justice to individual needs, ecological concerns, and the economic requirements placed on a global enterprise.

Further, Volkswagen's 2014 Sustainability Report[7] illustrates the action areas it intends to operate under *"to become the world's most sustainable automaker"* broken down into the three dimensions, *"Economy, People, and Environment,"* as follows:

First of all, we need to better protect the environment and further reduce carbon dioxide emissions in the future …

Setting Global Standards

By 2018, the Volkswagen Group is aiming to be the world's most environmentally compatible automaker. In order to achieve this goal, we have set ourselves some ambitious targets, particularly with regard to environmental protection. In 2014 we continued our consistent pursuit of these goals. Our Environmental Strategy embraces all of our brands and regions, and extends through-out every stage of the value chain.

Press Release, *EPA, California Notify Volkswagen of Clean Air Act Violations/Carmaker allegedly used software that circumvents emissions testing for certain air pollutants*

(Sept. 18, 2015) https://yosemite.epa.gov/opa/admpress.nsf/0/
dfc8e33b5ab162b985257ec40057813b

Today, EPA is issuing a notice of violation (NOV) of the Clean Air Act (CAA) to Volkswagen AG, Audi AG, and Volkswagen Group of America, Inc. (collectively referred to as Volkswagen). The NOV alleges that four-cylinder Volkswagen and Audi diesel cars from model years 2009–2015 include software that circumvents EPA emissions standards for certain air pollutants. California is separately issuing an In-Use Compliance letter to Volkswagen, and EPA and the California Air Resources Board (CARB) have both initiated investigations based on Volkswagen's alleged actions.

"Using a defeat device in cars to evade clean air standards is illegal and a threat to public health," said Cynthia Giles, Assistant Administrator for the Office of Enforcement and Compliance Assurance. "Working closely with the California Air Resources Board, EPA is committed to making sure that all automakers play by the same rules. EPA will continue to investigate these very serious matters."

---

7. http://www.volkswagenag.com/content/vwcorp/info_center/en/publications/2015/04/group-sustainability-report-2014.bin.html/binarystorageitem/file/Volkswagen_Sustainability_Report_2014.pdf.

"Working with US EPA we are taking this important step to protect public health thanks to the dogged investigations by our laboratory scientists and staff," said Air Resources Board Executive Officer Richard Corey. "Our goal now is to ensure that the affected cars are brought into compliance, to dig more deeply into the extent and implications of Volkswagen's efforts to cheat on clean air rules, and to take appropriate further action."

As described in the NOV, a sophisticated software algorithm on certain Volkswagen vehicles detects when the car is undergoing official emissions testing, and turns full emissions controls on only during the test. The effectiveness of these vehicles' pollution emissions control devices is greatly reduced during all normal driving situations. This results in cars that meet emissions standards in the laboratory or testing station, but during normal operation, emit nitrogen oxides, or NOx, at up to 40 times the standard. The software produced by Volkswagen is a "defeat device," as defined by the Clean Air Act.

The Clean Air Act requires vehicle manufacturers to certify to EPA that their products will meet applicable federal emission standards to control air pollution, and every vehicle sold in the U.S. must be covered by an EPA-issued certificate of conformity. Motor vehicles equipped with defeat devices, which reduce the effectiveness of the emission control system during normal driving conditions, cannot be certified. By making and selling vehicles with defeat devices that allowed for higher levels of air emissions than were certified to EPA, Volkswagen violated two important provisions of the Clean Air Act.

EPA and CARB uncovered the defeat device software after independent analysis by researchers at West Virginia University, working with the International Council on Clean Transportation, a non-governmental organization, raised questions about emissions levels, and the agencies began further investigations into the issue. In September, after EPA and CARB demanded an explanation for the identified emission problems, Volkswagen admitted that the cars contained defeat devices.

NOx pollution contributes to nitrogen dioxide, ground-level ozone, and fine particulate matter. Exposure to these pollutants has been linked with a range of serious health effects, including increased asthma attacks and other respiratory illnesses that can be serious enough to send people to the hospital. Exposure to ozone and particulate matter have also been associated with premature death due to respiratory-related or cardiovascular-related effects. Children, the elderly, and people with pre-existing respiratory disease are particularly at risk for health effects of these pollutants.

VW may be liable for civil penalties and injunctive relief for the violations alleged in the NOV.

The allegations cover roughly 482,000 diesel passenger cars sold in the United States since 2008.

Affected diesel models include:

Jetta (MY 2009–2015)

Jetta Sportwagen (MY 2009–2014)

Beetle (MY 2012–2015)

Beetle Convertible (MY 2012–2015)

Audi A3 (MY 2010–2015)

Golf (MY 2010–2015)

Golf Sportwagen (MY 2015)

Passat (MY 2012–2015)

It is incumbent upon Volkswagen to initiate the process that will fix the cars' emissions systems. Car owners should know that although these vehicles have emissions exceeding standards, these violations do not present a safety hazard and the cars remain legal to drive and resell. Owners of cars of these models and years do not need to take any action at this time.

———————

In testimony before the House Committee on Energy and Commerce Subcommittee on Oversight and Investigations on October 8, 2015, Michael Horn, former President and CEO of Volkswagen Group of America, Inc. stated:

> My name is Michael Horn, and I am the President and CEO of Volkswagen Group of America, a subsidiary of Volkswagen AG, headquartered in Wolfsburg, Germany. I have volunteered to come before this Committee at the very outset of these inquiries in an effort to show our commitment to cooperation. We have not had the opportunity to review all aspects of this matter, indeed the investigation is just beginning. Therefore, my testimony and my answers to your questions will, by necessity, have to be considered preliminary and based on my best current recollection and information.
>
> On behalf of our company, and my colleagues in Germany, I would like to offer a sincere apology for Volkswagen's use of a software program that served to defeat the regular emissions testing regime.
>
> In the spring of 2014 when the West Virginia University study was published, I was told that there was a possible emissions non-compliance that could be remedied. I was informed that EPA regulations included various penalties for non-compliance with the emissions standards and that the agencies can conduct engineering tests; which could include "defeat device" testing or analysis. I was also informed that the company engineers would work with the agencies to resolve the issue. Later in 2014, I was informed that the technical teams had a specific plan for remedies to bring the vehicles into compliance and that they were engaged with the agencies about the process.
>
> On September 3, 2015, Volkswagen AG disclosed at a meeting with the California Air Resources Board ("CARB") and the U.S. Environmental Protection Agency ("EPA") that emissions software in four cylinder diesel vehicles from model years 2009–2015 contained a "defeat device" in the form of hid-

den software that could recognize whether a vehicle was being operated in a test laboratory or on the road. The software made those emit higher levels of nitrogen oxides when the vehicles were driven in actual road use than during laboratory testing.

In Volkswagen's recent ongoing discussions with the regulators, we described to the EPA and CARB that our emissions control strategy also included a software feature that should be disclosed to and approved by them as an auxiliary emissions control device ("AECD") in connection with the certification process. As a result, we have withdrawn the application for certification of our model year 2016 vehicles. We are working with the agencies to continue the certification process.

These events are deeply troubling. I did not think that something like this was possible at the Volkswagen Group. We have broken the trust of our customers, dealerships, and employees, as well as the public and regulators.

Let me be clear, we at Volkswagen take full responsibility for our actions and we are working with all relevant authorities in a cooperative way. I am here to offer the commitment of Volkswagen AG to work with this Committee to understand what happened, and how we will move forward. EPA, CARB, the U.S. Department of Justice, State Attorneys General, as well as other authorities, are fulfilling their duties to investigate this matter.

We are determined to make things right. This includes accepting the consequences of our acts, providing a remedy, and beginning to restore the trust of our customers, dealerships, employees, the regulators, and the American public. We will rebuild the reputation of a company that more than two million people worldwide, including dealers and suppliers, rely upon for their livelihoods.

Our immediate goal is to develop a remedy for our customers. While much work is still to be done, I'd like to talk today about how we get from where we are now to that goal.

First, we are conducting investigations on a world-wide scale into how these matters happened. Responsible parties will be identified and held accountable. Thorough investigations have already begun, but any information developed at this stage is preliminary. We ask for your understanding as we complete this work.

Second, it is important for the public to know that, as the EPA has said, these vehicles do not present a safety hazard and remain safe and legal to drive.

Third, technical teams are working tirelessly to develop remedies for each of the affected groups of vehicles. These solutions will be tested and validated, and then shared with the responsible authorities for approval. There are three groups of vehicles involved, each containing one of the three generations of the 2.0L diesel engine. Each will require a different remedy, but these remedies can only be our first step for our customers.

Fourth, we will examine our compliance, processes, and standards at Volkswagen and adopt measures to make certain that something like this cannot happen again.

Fifth, we commit to regular and open communication with our customers, dealers, employees, and the public as we move forward. As first steps, we have set up a designated service line and website to be a channel for this communication, and I have sent a letter to every affected customer.

I can offer today this outline of a path forward toward the goal of making things right. Nevertheless, Volkswagen knows that we will be judged not by words but by our actions over the coming weeks and months.

These events are fundamentally contrary to Volkswagen's core principles of providing value to our customers, innovation, and responsibility to our communities and the environment. They do not reflect the company that I know and to which I have dedicated 25 years of my life. It is inconsistent that the company involved in this emissions issue is also a company that has invested in environmental efforts to reduce the carbon footprint in our factories around the world.

Volkswagen Group has a deep commitment to preserving our environment. As one of the world's largest automobile manufacturers, our commitment to the environment extends throughout every aspect of our business in the more than 150 countries in which we operate.

For example, here in the United States, Volkswagen's manufacturing facility in Chattanooga, Tennessee serves as a model for Volkswagen plants around the world for increasing energy efficiency and reducing emissions, water, and materials usage and waste. In recognition of the plant's efficiency, Volkswagen Chattanooga received a platinum certification from the U.S. Green Building Council's Leadership in Energy and Environmental Design ("LEED") program.

The facility is the first and only automotive manufacturing plant in the world to receive the Platinum Certification. As environmental protection and sustainability are central to Volkswagen's core values, these events have been particularly troubling. Our conduct in the events that bring us here today belittle the efforts of Volkswagen to lead in environmental responsibility.

Over the 60 years Volkswagen has been in the United States, it has become part of the American culture. There are more than 6,000 Americans employed directly by Volkswagen Group of America in its 60 facilities across the United States: from a customer relations center in Auburn Hills, Michigan and a testing lab in Golden, Colorado, to a parts distribution center in Haslet, Texas, and our state-of-the-art manufacturing facility in Chattanooga, Tennessee. That factory, alone, employs more than 2,200 people and is expanding. We are part of communities all across the country. Thousands more hardworking men and women are employed at our parts suppliers and the network of about 1,000 dealerships across the United States.

In closing, I again apologize on behalf of everyone at Volkswagen. We will fully cooperate with all responsible authorities. We will find remedies for our customers, and we will work to ensure that this will never happen again.[8]

———————

Volkswagen Group installed manipulated software in the emissions-control module of eleven million Volkswagen and Audi diesel vehicles sold worldwide. The software allowed the car to spew up to 40 times the U.S. Environmental Protection Agency's maximum allowed level of nitrogen oxides and air pollutants that can cause respiratory problems and smog in the atmosphere.

This led to a large vehicle recall, an apology from the now former CEO, and several investigations as well as legal actions in the U.S. and Europe.

Volkswagen's case highlights the difficulty in determining whether the manipulation of the emission control software in millions of vehicles worldwide was the result of few rouge engineers or massive corporate wrongdoing.

Moreover, there are studies in the U.S. on the impact of Volkswagen's actions on people's health.

According to an Associated Press statistical and computer analysis, Volkswagen pollution emission has killed between five and 20 people in the United States annually in recent years:

"Statistically, we can't point out who died because of this policy, but some people have died or likely died as a result of this," said Carnegie Mellon environmental engineer professor Peter Adams. Volkswagen "computer software allowed diesel cars to spew between 10 to 40 times more nitrogen oxides (NOx) than allowed by regulation, making this a serious concern for air quality and public health."

Adams and other [experts] said the lost lives — valued at $8.6 million apiece — overwhelm other costs such as lost workdays or hospital costs. The overall annual cost of the extra pollutants from the VW diesels ranged from $40 million to $170 million, environmental engineering professors calculated.[9]

Statement of Compliance Philosophy

Any multinational that imposes a global code of ethics across its worldwide workforces does so both to impose its own policies and in an effort to comply with applicable laws. This raises the question of what laws in the global context are "applicable."

———————

8. docs.house.gov/meetings/IF/IF02/20151008/104046/HHRG-114-IF02-Wstate-HornM-2015 1008.pdf. Oct. 8, 2015, Michael Horn.

9. http://bigstory.ap.org/article/a6925f0af82e44aaa1a1ed4b55d030f6/ap-analysis-dozens-deaths-likely-vw-pollution-dodge.

Drafters of global ethics codes too often forget that the overwhelming majority of applicable laws are the *local laws of the host countries where the multinational operates*. Yes, certain "extraterritorial" (internationally applicable) laws of the multinational's headquarters country are often vital as well. Indeed, it is overseas compliance with the handful of *U.S.* extraterritorial business laws reaching the overseas workplace (FCPA, SOX, Dodd-Frank, securities laws, international trade sanctions and "trading with the enemy" laws, employment discrimination laws and a few others) that pushes many American multinationals to implement ethics codes in the first place.

The code-drafting issue here is that multinationals too often get their compliance priorities backwards. Too many American-drafted codes focus so intently on compliance with less than a dozen U.S. extraterritorial laws that they all but ignore the tens of thousands of local laws that apply across every overseas workplace. Avoid this mistake. Craft a global code that enforces not only the few vital headquarters extraterritorial laws, but also the huge number of applicable overseas local laws.

A related mistake is for a global conduct code to instruct employees worldwide that they have to follow *all* American "state and federal" laws. That instruction is wrong. Only a few American laws reach extraterritorially and into workplaces overseas. A code of conduct should never by its terms extend all American laws abroad.

One often-overlooked challenge as to applicable laws in a global code of ethics is explaining to overseas employee readers that headquarters-jurisdiction extraterritorial laws *really do* reach abroad. Without explaining extraterritoriality to overseas staff, foreign readers of a U.S. multinational's conduct code will doubt they really have to follow U.S. laws—just as, for example, auto workers at Toyota's plant in Georgetown, Kentucky and secretaries at Toyota's regional headquarters in California inevitably assume their actions stateside lie beyond the reach of Japanese law.

In wording any compliance mandate in a code that addresses extraterritorial laws, be careful not to violate doctrines in some Eastern European and other countries that prohibit imposing foreign laws locally.

Some companies' codes use "Question and Answer" to address the topic of extraterritorial laws and illustrate how different laws relate and what is their scope of application.

Illustration of a "Question & Answer" that addresses the application of the code to employees:

> *Q: Many of the topics don't seem to apply to me. Why should I be concerned with this booklet?*
>
> *A: As a company-wide document, some sections and topics may be more relevant to certain functions or departments than to others. However, it may be helpful to be aware of how business is conducted in different areas of the Company.*
>
> *Q: Why do we have one standards booklet? Why don't we have regional booklets that address issues that are more relevant to particular locations?*
>
> *A: Because our principles are universal.*

Illustration of a "Question and Answer" that compares the U.K. Bribery Act to the U.S. Foreign Corrupt Act:

Q: How does the U.K. Bribery Act compare to the U.S. Foreign Corrupt Practices Act?

A: The U.K. Bribery Act is broader. It prohibits not only bribery of a government official, but also commercial bribery and receipt of bribes. Additionally, companies with operations in the United Kingdom can be held strictly liable for failing to prevent bribery by persons associated with such companies unless the companies can demonstrate that they had adequate procedures in place to prevent and detect such conduct.

Discrimination/equal employment opportunity: Because prohibiting illegal discrimination across worldwide operations is a vital, legally mandated goal, U.S. multinationals sometimes transplant their robust American anti-discrimination ("equal employment opportunity") provisions from their U.S. handbooks straight into their global codes of ethics. But in drafting an ethics code, first deconstruct U.S.-drafted discrimination rules, then rebuild them to account for the global context.

A key issue here is listing *protected groups*. While U.S. discrimination laws focus on protected groups, some countries (Belgium and Chile, for example) actually impose a vague, all-but-chaotic obligation of total equality, prohibiting employers from singling out any group that a judge agrees to protect—even a group not mentioned in applicable discrimination statutes. Another hurdle here is the problem that certain groups protected in the United States are not protected abroad (for example, veteran status, genetic makeup, workers compensation claimant status), while many countries outside the United States protect their own categories not protected stateside (for example, family status, traveler status, political opinion, caste). And age discrimination clauses in codes of conduct raise big problems in countries where multinationals impose mandatory retirement, from the UK to India to Germany and beyond.

The knee-jerk solution is to insert a catch-all clause in the ethics code discrimination provision's listing of protected groups (*"... or any other group protected by applicable law"*). But a catch-all clause may not be fully effective under the canon of construction by which included factors control over omitted ones (*inclusio unis est exclusio alterius*). One viable if less-than-ideal strategy is to omit mention of specific protected groups entirely, and simply prohibit all discrimination illegal under "applicable law."

Another issue when drafting a discrimination provision in a global code is accounting for the extraterritorial reach of U.S. discrimination laws. U.S. discrimination laws reach abroad only in the limited respect that they protect a tiny sub-set of most U.S. multinationals' overseas workforces: overseas-working U.S. citizens. Too many global conduct code discrimination provisions extend American-style discrimination protections to everyone abroad. This lets the "tail wag the dog."

Illustration of an anti-discrimination provision listing protected categories with a catch-all provision:

*We are committed to providing a work environment that promotes the equal opportunity, dignity and respect. Our policies promote equal employment opportunity without discrimination on the basis of race, color, religion, creed, age, sex, gender, sexual orientation, national origin, citizenship, disability, marital and civil partnership or union status, pregnancy, veteran status, genetic information **or any other characteristics protected by law.***

Illustration of an Equal Employment opportunity and Discrimination provision listing protected categories without a catch-all provision:

Our company prohibits all forms of discrimination on grounds of:

- *gender;*
- *age;*
- *origin;*
- *religion;*
- *sexual orientation;*
- *physical appearance;*
- *health;*
- *disability;*
- *trade union membership.*

Harassment: Harassment provisions lifted from U.S. handbooks and dropped into international codes of conduct fall far short in jurisdictions like Brazil, Chile, Venezuela and much of Europe that impose a broad concept of "moral harassment," "bullying," "mobbing," "psycho-social harassment" or "employee dignity" and "personality rights" (concepts that used to be known stateside as non-actionable "equal-opportunity harassment" and that U.S. states have proven reluctant to regulate as "abusive work environment"). Too many U.S. multinationals' international harassment provisions persist in defining "harassment" narrowly, as unwelcome behavior *based on the victim's membership in a protected class.* This definition falls short in the growing number of overseas jurisdictions that legislatively protect employee dignity and prohibit abusive workplace behavior unlinked to protected-group status. Global conduct codes that use the restrictive American-style harassment definition simply miss lots of behaviors illegal abroad that would be perfectly legal stateside. An effective harassment prohibition needs to be broad enough to prohibit all actionable harassment. A broader definition of harassment is necessary in many jurisdictions.

Illustration of a harassment provision that is narrowly construed:

Our company values a work environment that is free of verbal or physical harassment. This includes any unwelcome comments or actions regarding race, color, ethnicity, religion, gender, sexual orientation, age, gender identity or gender expression, national origin, marital status, pregnancy, childbirth or related medical condition, genetic information, military service, medical condition the presence of a mental or physical disability, or veteran status.

Illustration of a harassment provision that is broadly construed (modified from Merck):

We strive to maintain an environment free of harassment, where all employees are respected. In many cases, workplace harassment is a form of discrimination that is generally defined as any verbal or physical conduct that occurs because of a certain individual's characteristic such as race, gender, age or religious belief. Workplace harassment is generally defined as any action that inappropriately or unreasonably creates an intimidating, hostile or offensive work environment.

Some companies introduce "Question & Answer" to explain differences among jurisdictions on several types of harassment.

Illustration of a "Question & Answer" on sexual Harassment:

Q: I know that sexual harassment is prohibited in the United States, but what about other locations?

A: Our company policies apply globally. If you have doubts about a certain conduct, you are encouraged to consult with the Human Resources department and inquiry whether such conduct is consistent with a work environment of respect and local laws.

A separate problem is that U.S. drafted code of conduct harassment provisions tend to impose overly aggressive *co-worker dating restrictions*. In many countries, these provisions (even ones that merely require reporting a relationship to management) are offensive and all but unenforceable.

Illustration of Facebook corporate policy that allows co-worker dating and subjects to mere disclosure in cases of potential conflicts of interest:

Facebook does not prohibit dating among Facebook Personnel, nor does it prohibit relatives from working together within, for or on behalf of the company. However, if a potentially conflicting relationship, romantic or otherwise, involves two employees in a direct reporting relationship, in the same chain of command, or otherwise creates an actual or apparent conflict of interest, the employees must disclose the relationship to Human Resources.

Diversity: U.S. multinationals sometimes include diversity provisions in their global codes of ethics, often lifted directly from the organization's domestic U.S. handbook or diversity program communications. But robust U.S.-style diversity programs need radical reinvention outside the United States. Never include a diversity provision in a globally applicable code of conduct unless the international diversity program, goals and metrics have been tailored for the international environment.

Illustration of a provision that might not be understood in homogenous societies:

Our company is committed to diversity.

Illustration of a provision that might be understood also in homogenous societies:

Our company is committed to diversity. We value the unique contribution that each person brings to us. We accomplish more when people from diverse back-

grounds and with different talents and ideas work together in an environment where everyone can contribute and make full use of their talents.

Conflicts of interests: Many global codes of conduct and ethics include provisions on employee conflicts of interest and prohibit, for example, contracting with relatives on behalf of the organization and hiring certain relatives and former government officials. These provisions also may address moonlighting—employee holding a side job or position on a board of directors at a competitor, supplier or customer. Craft a cross-border conflict of interest clause to be flexible enough for regions like the Middle East and Latin America where family relationships play a vital part in everyday business.

Illustration of conflict of interests that might occur across different industries internationally:

> • *Having a personal financial interest in a supplier, customer, competitor or distributor;*
>
> • *Having a close family member (e.g., spouse, domestic partner, parent, sibling or child of a domestic partner), work for a supplier, customer, competitor or distributor;*
>
> • *Having an intimate relationship with another employee who can influence decisions such as salary, performance rating or promotion.*
>
> • *Having a personal interest or potential for gain in any Company transactions;*
>
> • *Serving on an Advisory Board and/or Board of Directors of an association or company that is in a similar market/industry;*
>
> • *Having a close family member work at a governmental agency that has oversight of the company;*
>
> • *Hiring an employee/consultant due to their family/relationship with government decision makers;*
>
> • *Having outside (paid or non-paid) employment with an organization that competes with the company;*
>
> • *Having investments, including those of close relatives, which might influence or appear to influence employee's judgment.*

Bribery and improper payments: Multinationals—particularly those that sell to or need licenses from foreign governments—must communicate, train on and enforce tough bribery and improper payments prohibitions, both because local laws around the world prohibit bribing local government officials and because extraterritorial laws in the United States, the UK and Organisation for Economic Cooperation and Development (OECD) countries prohibit multinationals from making improper payments to *foreign* government officials. The U.S. extraterritorial bribery law, the Foreign Corrupt Practices Act, is an aggressively enforced statute that prohibits both bribes and deceptive accounting notations of improper payments. And the UK Bribery Act, in some respects tougher than the U.S. FCPA, might reach bribery outside the UK committed by U.S. entities with UK offices. For these reasons a conduct code bribery provision is vital, unless the organization has a separate, freestanding bribery/improper payment policy.[10]

Business gifts to *nongovernment* contacts: U.S. FCPA law prohibits improper payments only to overseas government and political officials. A growing trend is for conduct codes (and even some countries' local laws) to prohibit improper payments to *nongovernment* recipients. These prohibitions may reach payments made to nongovernmental customers and gifts received from nongovernmental suppliers.

A payment to procure business from a private company differs in important respects from a bribe or an improper payment to a government official or political party. Never improperly conflate these concepts. Think through any business gifts provision in a code of ethics.

The blunt, U.S.-centric approach here is simply to have the code prohibit all business gifts worth more than some set nominal value. But cultural issues come into play: "[I]n Asia, gift giving is customary on the occasions of marriage and death. This presents a tricky situation [where] company policy may [prohibit] gifts from customers, vendors or suppliers [while] refusal of such an offering may be interpreted as a hostile or insulting gesture."[11]

Judicial/Regulatory Perspective

Foreign Corrupt Practices Act compliance has become its own legal specialty. As a best practice, the bribery/FCPA provision of a global code of conduct should be reviewed by an expert, particularly where the company has a UK presence and may trigger the UK Bribery Act operations.

Money laundering/financing terrorism: Employers in the financial services sector need to impose "know your customer/client" mandates and rules or code provisions on money laundering. Codes of ethics also commonly address compliance with the U.S. executive orders and regulations meant to restrict terrorism financing—so-called "list-scrubbing" obligations that prohibit payments to and from named suspected terrorists (an issue particularly acute for nonprofits).

Trade sanctions and embargo/anti-boycott: Extraterritorial U.S. trade laws embargo or boycott (prohibit doing business in) black-listed countries. U.S. law also prohibits complying with the Arab boycott of Israel. U.S. multinationals often impose code of conduct provisions that address compliance with these U.S. trade laws. But some jurisdictions, particularly in Eastern Europe, prohibit multinationals from requiring

---

10. *See* M. Swanton, *Combating Corruption: GCs Aim to Establish Global Ethics Codes*, Inside-Counsel, Jan. 2011.

11. S. Hirschfeld, *Global Employee Handbooks Must Balance Compliance with Culture*, Soc'y for Human Res. Mgmt., Nov. 18, 2013, https://www.shrm.org/hrdisciplines/global/articles/pages/global-employee-handbooks-compliance.aspx.

locals to follow foreign laws; code provisions that strictly require following U.S. trade laws can cause problems in these jurisdictions. The text of any trade provision in an ethics code needs to be nuanced enough to account for this.

Illustration of provisions that impose U.S. anti-boycott laws:

- *Our company complies with U.S. anti-boycott laws prohibiting....*
- *Our company requires to report any request to participate in a boycott other than those imposed by the U.S.*

And overseas jurisdictions impose their own trade sanctions. Never draft a cross-border trade sanctions clause cognizant only of U.S. trade law.

Antitrust/competition, non-collusion and trade practices: Global codes of conduct often instruct employees not to commit basic antitrust violations like collusion and price fixing. Codes often tell employees where to find further guidance on these matters. Antitrust laws differ from country to country, and so these code provisions must take a broad view. The best approach is to introduce references to Antitrust Policies and Procedures applicable in the relevant country and suggest to contact the Legal Department for clarifications.

Illustration:

For more information, please refer to the Antitrust Policy/Procedure available at [insert link] *and contact the Legal Department for any clarification or inquiry.*

Insider trading: Publicly traded multinationals need global rules or code provisions that ban insider trading in the company's own stock. And professional services firms that offer their employees access to inside information about publicly traded clients need to impose tough *client* insider trading restrictions.

Illustration of a provision formulating a broad insider trade rule:

"Insider trading." It is illegal to buy or sell securities (for example, stocks, bonds or options) of a company when you are aware of material, non-public information (inside information) relating to the company. Securities laws and our company policy prohibit you from using or disclosing any inside information that you gained through your employment with the Company before this information is known publicly, to buy or sell the securities of our Company or any other company with which we have a relationship or we might start a relationship with. Securities laws and our Company policy equally prohibits you to give inside information to anyone else so that they can trade. These restrictions apply not only to you, but also to your spouse and minor children....

Audit/accounting fraud, SOX and Dodd-Frank: Sarbanes-Oxley-regulated multi-nationals are subject to audit/accounting rules that reach company operations worldwide. Conduct codes often impose global SOX and Dodd-Frank accounting and compliance standards that explain why compliance is vital. Indeed, as a best practice even certain *non-SOX-regulated* multinationals insert audit/accounting provisions into their codes. Again, though, some jurisdictions, such as in Eastern Europe, prohibit imposing foreign laws locally; code text needs to account for this.

U.S. federal sentencing guidelines: Violations of some U.S. laws with extraterritorial effect can lead to U.S. criminal liability and convictions. Multinationals should therefore draft global codes of conduct cognizant of the U.S. federal sentencing guidelines that offer credit for certain human resources policies meant to curtail illegal conduct. Of course, codes of conduct do not *mention* U.S. federal sentencing guidelines explicitly; the drafting issue is imposing human resources rules and punishments robust enough to earn sentencing credit.

Data privacy/processing: Data protection laws in the European Union,[12] Argentina, Canada, Hong Kong, Israel, Japan, Mexico, Peru, Philippines, Uruguay, and beyond impose tough rules on multinationals that run global human resources information systems. Multinational compliance initiatives should impose guidelines or rules on employees who "process" personal data such as employee, supplier and customer data. International conduct codes often (but not always) set out data privacy rules. Some organizations, though, handle data law compliance outside the code.

Monitoring communications and reserving right to search: A best practice for a U.S. domestic employee handbook is to defeat employees' "expectations of privacy" in employer-provided communications systems. U.S. handbooks expressly reserve the employer's right to monitor employee emails, handheld devices, telephone calls and the like. Some U.S. employers also reserve a right to search offices, desks, lockers—even lunch boxes. Additional monitoring issues come up in the BYOD (bring your own device) context, and as to drug testing.

American employers that draft global codes of conduct and ethics want to extend their American-style right-to-monitor/search provisions globally. The challenge is that in many jurisdictions these provisions are not, themselves, very effective. The American approach of using an employee communication to defeat expectations of privacy falls short in many countries.

There is no "magic bullet" here, no single clause with which a code of conduct can confer on a multinational power to search employees worldwide however it

---

12. Despite the absence of a data protection law in the U.S. the European Commission allowed the free transfer of personal data from EU member states to companies in the U.S. under the Safe Harbor Principles and accompanying frequently Asked Questions issued by the Department of Commerce of the United States (Commission Decision 2000/520/EC of 20 July 2000, hereafter: "the Safe Harbour Decision"). The Court of Justice of the European Union with a ruling of 6 October 2015 in Case C-362/14 declared the Safe Harbor invalid. The consequences of the judgment brought the Art.29 Working Party—the independent advisory board that brings together representatives all of Data Protection Authorities across Europe, to issue a preliminary statement specifying that data transfer can be done via Standard Contractual Clauses ("SCCs") or Binding Corporate Rules ("BCRs"). The use of BCRs thus allows personal data to move freely among the various entities of a corporate group worldwide—dispensing with the need to have contractual arrangements between each and every corporate entity—while ensuring that the same high level of protection of personal data is complied with throughout the group by means of a single set of binding and enforceable rules. Having a single set of rules creates a simpler and more effective system, which is easier for staff to implement and for data subjects to understand.

wants. An employee-monitoring provision in a global conduct code needs careful structuring to account for the employer's needs and for restrictions in the jurisdictions at issue. The multinational must understand that its search clause is just a starting point, not an end point, in the legal analysis of whether and when it can electronically monitor or search overseas employees. Regardless of what employer monitoring rights a global code of conduct purports to reserve, employers in many jurisdictions will need legal advice before invoking purportedly reserved monitoring rights. Before monitoring overseas, understand how employer monitoring plays out in each relevant jurisdiction.

Environmental protection: Some global ethics codes require employees to comply with local environmental laws, and some codes require compliance with the most protective of local environmental law, U.S. law or global environmental standards. Obviously environmental clauses are vital in industries like manufacturing, oil and mining, but are mostly irrelevant in service industries.

Intellectual property: Some global codes of conduct contain intellectual property provisions that instruct employees to respect others' copyrights, such as in photo-copying, copying software, or emailing copyrighted materials.

Restrictive covenants and trade secrets: Some global conduct codes purport to impose on worldwide workforces restrictive-covenant-like prohibitions—confidentiality, post-termination non-compete and non-solicitation of employees and customers. But for the most part, a code of conduct is the wrong medium to impose these restrictions. Remember that ethics codes do not bind ex-employees. Restrictive-covenant-like rules are best built into *employment contracts*. Enforceability standards for these covenants differ widely by country; many countries require extra consideration paid after separation, which makes a one-size-fits-all global approach to restrictive covenants infeasible. It often makes sense to omit entirely from a code of conduct restrictive covenant topics (at least beyond a confidentiality clause), other than perhaps a short statement in the code declaring the employer's commitment to enforce any employee-signed covenants.

Workplace safety and pandemic response: Most every country imposes detailed workplace safety laws broadly analogous to U.S. OSHA. A global code of conduct cannot replicate every jurisdiction's safety rules, but many conduct codes contain provisions requiring compliance with applicable safety rules and imposing accident reporting procedures. Some multinationals impose detailed global safety frameworks and crisis response protocols that address, for example, pandemic or disaster response and "cardinal safety rules"—but usually these appear separate from the conduct codes in a freestanding global safety policy.

Another safety issue is on-premises possession of guns and weapons. This may be less of an issue outside the United States, perhaps more appropriately relegated to domestic U.S. employee handbooks.

A related issue is duty of care—protecting business travelers and expatriates. This is a vital issue, but one that does not usually merit coverage in a global conduct code.

Drugs and alcohol: While the recent trend of U.S. states legalizing marijuana may change things, for years U.S. domestic employers have been inclined toward a "zero-tolerance" approach to drugs and alcohol in the workplace, refusing to hire applicants who test positive even where positive test results offer no evidence of work-time impairment. U.S. domestic employers even occasionally fire good performers whose drug test results demonstrate only off-hours drug use. And countless U.S. employers have fired staff caught drinking on the job, even while still sober.

Outside the United States and Canada, on-job alcohol use is less of an evil and workplace drug testing is often virtually impossible. Zero-tolerance workplace alcohol policies outside the United States are impractical and come across as puritanical; in countries like Germany and Mexico, company cafeterias and vending machines serve beer and wine, and alcohol can be ubiquitous at business lunches and company parties. Further, some drugs that remain illegal in much of the United States are legal elsewhere and so are all but impossible for employers to prohibit using off-hours. A zero-tolerance cannabis policy, for example, makes little sense in the Netherlands where menus in the ubiquitous "coffeehouses" openly offer varieties of hash and marijuana across a range of price points. Dismissal for off-hours drug use abroad would not amount to good cause, even if an ethics code tried to maintain otherwise.

Rethink any U.S. domestic zero-tolerance drug/alcohol policy for the global context. Do a reality check by running a draft of a proposed drugs and alcohol conduct code provision past overseas local human resources overseas.

Labor rights: Some internal ethics codes of business conduct contain clauses on labor rights, ILO standards and freedom of association, although (as addressed in our discussion of supplier codes) these provisions are often a bigger issue in "sweatshop" codes. In an ethics code just as in a supplier code, beware of adopting a free-association clause or any provision that incorporates ILO standards.

Child labor, human trafficking and slavery: Codes of ethics in industries where child labor, human trafficking and slavery (forced and prison labor) are a risk, like shipping, fishing and mining, might contain clauses on these topics. But otherwise, child labor, human trafficking and slavery may be too remote to merit a mention in many employers' internal ethics codes. An internal code should not address a topic just to "touch the base" if that topic looks silly in context. A child labor, human trafficking and slavery provision might look silly in the internal code of ethics of, for example, a financial services or professional services firm or a media sector business.

Media contact and social media: Multinationals are constantly subjects of stories in the business press, and employees might get contacted by professional reporters. But that scenario is remote compared to the much bigger issue of social media—employees tweeting and posting comments about the employer organization. For these reasons, global codes of conduct often contain provisions instructing employees on press relations, fielding media inquiries—and social media. Fortunately, the U.S. domestic labor law doctrine of "protected concerted activity" and social media policies tends not to be an issue abroad, not even in Canada.[13] Therefore, social media provisions in global codes need not account for this uniquely U.S.-domestic issue, except to the extent the code applies domestically in the United States.

Compliance, cooperation and investigations: Some internal codes of conduct impose provisions that require employees to follow both the code and all company rules set out elsewhere (such as in the employer's local human resources polices, handbooks, intranet, reimbursement procedures, clocking-in rules, safety protocols and the like). Separately, some codes purport to impose mandatory reporting rules that ostensibly require staff who find out about co-worker wrongdoing to denounce their fellows. Be careful with these clauses—they are not strictly enforceable in many jurisdictions. Indeed, including a mandatory reporting clause sometimes can be grounds for a foreign court to invalidate a unilaterally implemented code of conduct.[14]

Also, some ethics codes affirmatively require employees to cooperate in internal investigations. These cooperation clauses seem unobjectionable to Americans, but in many countries they may be unenforceable as improperly implemented mandatory reporting clauses. (Forcing a reluctant employee witness to cooperate in an investigation amounts to a mandatory reporting obligation.) Local laws overseas may not support discipline imposed for non-cooperation in an investigation, even where the code expressly purports to require cooperation.

Sanctions clauses: Many U.S.-drafted internal codes of conduct contain clauses exposing employees who violate the code to discipline up to discharge. Outside the United States, though, for an employer simply to declare that certain acts will be subject to punishment or discharge does not necessarily make it so. Local laws on good-cause discipline may prohibit employer sanctions even for blatant violations of rules clearly set out in an ethics code. For example, a mandatory reporting clause in a code of conduct may purport to force employee witnesses to denounce their co-workers who break rules, but local law in many jurisdictions will not support discipline for failing to blow the whistle, even if this failure violates an express reporting mandate. Also, in jurisdictions from the UK to France and beyond, locally mandated disciplinary procedures often trump a discipline clause in a global conduct code.

In drafting any global conduct code sanctions clause, factor in the rules that regulate employer discipline outside U.S. employment-at-will.

Complaint system/whistleblowing hotlines: Sarbanes-Oxley requires imposing "anonymous" whistleblower hotline "procedures," and Dodd-Frank implicitly encourages company whistleblower hotlines to the extent that the Dodd-Frank bounty program might lure whistleblowers over to the U.S. SEC. These days even many non-SOX-regulated multinationals impose global reporting procedures, outsourcing hot-

---

13. *See* "NLRB and Social Media," www.nlrb.gov.
14. *See* Wal-Mart, Wuppertal Labor Court, 5th Div., 5 BV 20/05 (June 15, 2005) (Germany).

lines to outside providers. But workplace whistleblower hotlines are heavily regulated in the European Union and increasingly elsewhere. Any global code of conduct provision that addresses reporting procedures and that describes a whistleblowing hotline needs careful strategy. Treat the launch of an international whistleblower hotline as separate from the launch of a global code of conduct.

Acknowledgment: Many global codes of business conduct end with an acknowledgement page for employees to sign, agreeing to follow the code. But signed employee acknowledgements outside the United States raise a number of logistical problems. Acknowledgments overseas can actually backfire, offering ammunition to non-signers who violate the code. Carefully consider any acknowledgement provision.

How to Implement a Global Internal Code of Conduct or Code of Ethics

A multinational headquarters launching a global code of business conduct, code of ethics, work rules or international employee handbook or any of these cross-border workplace initiatives tends to focus chiefly on content. In essence, headquarters asks: *What should the text of our new cross-border policy, code, rule or plan say?* But drafting a global code's text merely gets these projects started. As soon as headquarters crafts workable language for its latest cross-border code, policy or plan document, the project should shift to answering an entirely separate, often more complex question: *How are we going to launch this document and impose it on our staff overseas?*

That is, while "phase one" of any global code of conduct, HR policy or benefits plan project is indeed drafting the document, "phase two"—the often overlooked but tougher phase—needs to be implementing the cross-border initiative by effectively imposing it on affiliate employees worldwide. Too many cross-border workplace initiatives gloss over this vital second phase.

Step 1: Number of Versions

A multinational rolling out a new cross-border code of conduct, HR policy or benefits plan should decide whether to issue one single global document worldwide, whether to bifurcate a headquarters version from a "rest-of-the-world" version, or whether to spin off distinct local versions or riders for each relevant country.

These three approaches differ significantly. None works best every time. Selecting the most appropriate of the three approaches depends in part on the global initiative topic: Topics like ethics, insider trading and bribery lend themselves to a single global version. Topics like discrimination and harassment can be more appropriate for a bifurcated U.S. headquarters plus "rest-of-the-world" version. Inherently local topics like holidays, vacation and overtime are most appropriate for local country-by-country versions or riders.

Single Global Version

Sticking with just one single global code, HR policy or benefits plan document offers a multinational a streamlined and uniform global approach. Using one global version is always simplest and best promotes cross-border alignment. Therefore the single-version approach is usually the default; indeed, multinationals sometimes claim they *need* just one global document, to impose a uniform global rule, to streamline employee communications and to promote global unity.

But sometimes a single global document is not ideal. Rules, provisions and benefits appropriate for headquarters employees sometimes need tweaking or reworking abroad. For example:

• An anti-harassment policy that ties the harassment prohibition to U.S. protected group status is too narrow for jurisdictions that prohibit so-called "moral harassment," "bullying," "mobbing" or "psycho-social harassment."

• A detailed "use it or lose it" vacation policy or overtime pay policy cannot work internationally without local modifications, because of differences among local laws.

• A severance plan, equity plan or other employee benefits plan may be unworkable internationally unless modified locally to account for local employment, benefits, securities and tax laws. For example, clawback provisions in plan documents are particularly susceptible to local interpretations.

Bifurcated Headquarters versus Rest-of-the-World Versions

U.S. multinationals often decide to launch a U.S. domestic code of conduct, HR policy or benefits plan plus a separate "rest-of-the-world" version for their overseas employees. The bifurcated two-version approach lets the multinational account for issues from a non-U.S. perspective without watering down nuances unique to the U.S. employment-at-will environment. This approach is ideal for topics like diversity and reduction-in-force selection, where U.S. principles differ intrinsically from best practices abroad. The bifurcated two-version approach is common among multinationals that have most of their workforce stateside, with only smaller employee populations spread out abroad.

Local Versions or Riders

Every country's employment laws are different. The most compliant way to impose any global workforce initiative across more than one country is to tweak the documentation locally, tailoring for each jurisdiction a version or rider that accounts for local nuances. Coming up with local versions/riders can get unwieldy, expensive and slow, and can weaken the unifying character of a single global document. But accounting for local differences is always a best practice.

Highlighting this, a recent Australian case struck down a U.S. multinational's otherwise-robust global sex harassment policy because it glossed over a few Australia-specific nuances and "made no reference to the legislative foundation in Australia for the prohibition on sexual harassment."[15] The only way the multinational in that case could have issued an Australia-compliant sex harassment policy would have been to issue a local Australian version or rider.

Step 2: Non-Conforming Documents

Never issue a new or revised international code of conduct, HR policy or benefits plan by imposing it "on high" from headquarters, "damn the torpedoes," heedless of existing earlier versions. Always start by repealing or aligning all existing HR documents now in place. This step implicates three sub-issues: Repeal obsolete cross-border offerings; align local HR policies; and harmonize formal work rules.

Repeal Obsolete Cross-Border Offerings

A multinational that issues a revised or updated international code of conduct, HR policy or benefits plan needs to repeal all earlier versions floating around. Too often headquarters slaps its latest initiative onto its intranet without bothering to dig out and eradicate each extant now-obsolete version. Later, some hapless foreign employee stumbles across an old version and assumes it still controls. Or worse, some clever employee threatened with discipline for breaching the new policy (or held to less-generous terms under a new benefits plan) exploits the organization's sloppiness and insists the looser, earlier version still controls.

Align Local HR Policies

A more complex scenario is reconciling a new cross-border code of conduct, HR policy or benefits plan with existing, still-in-force—but inconsistent—*local* offerings. Global headquarters initiatives often contain provisions that clash with existing local HR communications on related topics. For example, a global code of conduct may address discrimination, harassment, conflicts of interest, expense reimbursement, business gifts, on-job smoking and alcohol in ways inconsistent with local affiliate protocols on similar topics. Or else a global severance pay plan may not align with severance pay clauses in overseas employment agreement forms. Even absent a head-on conflict, any global rule or offering that overlaps with local HR policies probably uses language inconsistent in some respects.

Failing to harmonize a global initiative with local offerings can cause real problems. Think of a local employee who commits some act that, while compliant with an on-point local policy, violates a stricter headquarters code or rule. The employer will argue the newer headquarters policy trumps the local subsidiary's laxer local policy, but local employees, local managers and even local judges may favor the looser local rule over the tougher, more distant headquarters edict—especially if the local rule is in the local language while the headquarters rule is in English (and even if the

---

15. *Richardson v. Oracle Corp. Aust. Pty. Ltd*, 2013 FCA 102, at ¶¶ 161–64.

global document has a boilerplate clause saying that, in case of conflict with another policy, the "standard that requires the higher degree of ethical conduct controls").

In every affected jurisdiction, repeal or reconcile dissonant local HR policies or offerings. Align them with the new cross-border code, policy or plan. This can be a big job, but failing to do it gives locals leverage to flout headquarters edicts.

Harmonize Formal Work Rules

Jurisdictions including Belgium, Chile, Colombia, France, Greece, Japan, Korea, Poland and Slovakia force local employers to issue formal work rules or so-called "internal work regulations" that list every infraction for which the boss can impose discipline. (In some jurisdictions this mandate reaches only workforces exceeding a minimum size—ten employees in Japan, for example.) The policy behind these work rules laws is workplace due process analogous to the American criminal procedure ban on *ex post facto* laws: Employers should not be allowed to discipline staff for acts the employer never previously prohibited.

These formal work rules mandates amount to a real hurdle when U.S. headquarters launches a cross-border code of conduct or HR policy. Imagine this hypothetical scenario: A multinational's Tokyo affiliate has issued its Japanese work rules, which contain, say, 23 specific grounds for discipline. But none of the 23 grounds happens to mention bribery. Then U.S. headquarters issues a tough global FCPA policy. Next, some ambitious Japanese "salaryman" entertains a Japanese government minister in a way that violates the FCPA policy but not the work rules. If the employer disciplines or fires the salaryman, he will argue discipline is illegal because none of the 23 posted grounds for discipline apply. A Japanese court will likely agree, even reinstating the salaryman with back pay.

Actively amend local work rules to accommodate (or incorporate by reference) global headquarters mandates.

Step 3: Dual Employer

Multinationals' overseas staff typically work on the payroll of locally incorporated subsidiary affiliates. From the point of view of an employee working for an overseas subsidiary, headquarters is merely the employer stockholder, not the employer of record. When a headquarters entity imposes some new code of conduct, HR policy or benefits plan directly on employees of foreign affiliates, it triggers a significant but often-overlooked "dual-employer" challenge: How can a parent corporation impose work rules that order around people (staff of local foreign affiliates) whom it does not employ? As to a global benefits plan, how can headquarters compensate people it does not employ?

If a parent corporation presumes to impose rules on (or pay benefits to) subsidiary staff it does not directly employ and with whom it has no privity of contract, then the headquarters entity risks being deemed a dual-/co-/joint-employer also liable (along with the subsidiary) for employment claims. This dual-co-joint-employer scenario raises three problems.

Permanent establishment and headquarters co-defendant: The first dual-employer problem is that when a corporate parent imposes some cross-border human resources code or policy directly on staff working for subsidiary entities (or pays benefits to foreigners abroad), headquarters arguably starts transacting business in the foreign jurisdiction. This scenario risks triggering a local "permanent establishment" subject to corporate registration and tax-filing obligations. Another risk is that employees asserting claims in local employment litigation against the local subsidiary might also sue the headquarters parent as a co-defendant. Certainly it can work this way stateside.[16]

Void rule: The second dual-employer problem is that some jurisdictions will reject or nullify a workplace code, policy or plan unless the local employer took the steps necessary under local corporate law to impose it on local staff. A headquarters work rule not ratified locally may be unenforceable. For example, Russia requires that the "management body" (board of directors) of a local Russian employer entity formally approve and implement workplace policies.

Impotent rule: The third dual employer problem is the scenario of a clever overseas employee raising the "my non-compliance is your problem" argument. An employee disciplined for violating a headquarters-issued work rule argues the rule is powerless and does not reach him because his boss, the local employer affiliate, never implemented it. In essence he argues: *That rule came from the shareholder of my employer. My employer never imposed it on me, so you can't discipline me for violating it. Following that rule is not my responsibility. My non-compliance is your problem, not mine.*

Fortunately there is a simple way to resolve these dual-employer problems: Headquarters imposes all cross-border codes of conduct, all international HR polices and certain global and regional benefits plans *on foreign affiliate* entities rather than on overseas staff directly. Each affiliate entity, in turn, duly ratifies the global initiative and imposes it directly on its own staff.

A related issue is imposing a code of conduct or rule on contractors. The texts of multinationals' global codes and rules often purport to reach contractors and business partners—but of course third parties need not follow rules unless they expressly agreed to follow them contractually. Where appropriate (and where consistent with contractor classification), include a code-compliance or rule-compliance clause in contracts with business partners.

Step 4: Collective Consultation

In many jurisdictions abroad, employee representatives are common—works councils, trade union "cells," health and safety committees, employee advocates, employee delegations, worker ombudsmen and the like. Labor laws from Europe to China and beyond impose a consultation requirement analogous to the U.S. labor

---

16. *Brown v. Daiken America, Inc.*, 756 F.3d 219 (2d Cir. 2014) (Japanese parent corporation held "single integrated enterprise with its American subsidiary to be properly named as a co-defendant" in employment litigation).

union concept of "mandatory subject of bargaining": An employer cannot add or change certain workplace rules until it sits down and discusses, negotiates or "informs and consults" (in Germany, "co-determines") the proposed changes with employee representatives.

This consultation or bargaining step can easily reach new codes of conduct, HR policies and benefits plans. Unionized American bosses understand exactly how this works, because U.S. labor law requires employers to bargain over an HR policy change as benign as a new dress code.[17]

Overseas, countries like China, France and Germany regularly nullify HR policies and codes that the employer unilaterally implemented in violation of this vital obligation.[18]

A multinational launching some new international code of conduct, HR policy or benefits plan needs to slow down and first involve its own overseas *management-side* labor liaisons (the team that bargains with worker representatives on behalf of management). Give your management-side labor liaisons a "heads-up" about the incoming cross-border initiative. Discuss with them local employee-representative consultation strategy and timing. Then take whatever steps are necessary to comply with local employee consultation obligations.

Step 5: Translation

Many American organizations consider English to be their official company language and assume their subsidiary employees worldwide are fluent. Many organizations issue global codes of conduct, HR policies and benefits plans in English only, sometimes posting an English-only version on the company intranet.

But before headquarters issues some new HR document meant to apply abroad, it should consider translation requirements and strategy. In Belgium, Chile, France, Iraq, Mongolia, Portugal, Quebec, Turkey, Venezuela, much of Central America and elsewhere, local laws require that work rules or "obligations," including mandates imbedded in a cross-border HR code, policy or plan, be communicated in the local language. In these jurisdictions English-language policies are not only unenforceable, they can be flatly *illegal*. One multinational once got fined €500,000 plus €20,000 per day because it distributed English-language HR documents to French staff in violation of the *Loi Toubon* French language law. Even in jurisdictions that do not impose local-language mandates, courts may prove reluctant to enforce English-language HR policies. Translations always buttress enforceability.

---

17. *Salem Hospital Corp.*, 360 NLRB No. 95 (2014), www.nlrb.gov/cases-decisions/weekly-summaries-decisions/summary-nlrb-decisions-week-april-28-may-2-2014.

18. *See Hou*, Beijing Intermediate People's Ct. no. 4, 11/26/09 (employer's unilateral change in handbook void because employees never consulted over the change).

Step 6: Communication, Distribution and Acknowledgement

A multinational cannot quietly slip a new code of conduct, HR policy or benefits plan onto its intranet and expect affiliate employees worldwide to find it, read it, understand it, and comply with it. Develop a proactive strategy for communicating and distributing any cross-border HR document to overseas staff in a way that requires them to comply. Remember: if some overseas employee later disciplined for a violation claims ignorance of the headquarters initiative, the employer bears the burden to prove it had implemented and communicated the global rule. To ensure a new international code, policy or plan binds foreign staff, be ready to prove each foreign employee actually received the documents, and (ideally) agreed to comply.

In addition, local law and best practices in jurisdictions from Austria to Czech Republic to Finland and beyond all but require *employee-signed acknowledgements* when an employer changes or adds new workplace rules. Also, many American multinationals believe the U.S. Foreign Corrupt Practices Act, U.S. Sarbanes-Oxley, U.S. Dodd-Frank, and U.S. federal sentencing guidelines require that American organizations be able to demonstrate they communicated compliance policies to overseas employees. Further, some countries look to whether a workplace code, policy, rule or benefit is "contractual." Those systems (which include common law countries outside the U.S. such as Australia, Canada, England and Ireland as well as certain civil law jurisdictions like Belgium, Germany, Norway) elevate at least some workplace policies to the level of employment contracts and require that any new "contractual" policy integrate into employees' written work contracts. Executing "contractual" policies in these jurisdictions usually requires employee signatures or assents. In effect, the policies become amendments to earlier-executed individual employment contracts.

For these reasons, multinational headquarters often decides to collect acknowledgements or consents from affiliate employees worldwide. Each employee signs onto the organization's new global code of conduct, HR policy or benefits plan. Staff signs (or electronically mouse-clicks) acknowledgements saying they received and read the new initiative and agree to comply.

At first this strategy sounds logical, but *collecting* signed employee acknowledgements from staff across borders raises four serious logistical challenges:

Presumptive coercion: Courts in parts of Continental Europe and beyond hold employee-signed acknowledgments void as presumptively coerced, because of the inherent inequality of bargaining power between an employer and staff—almost like a contract with a minor or someone mentally disabled. (What choice does a worker have when his boss instructs him to sign a consent?) In these jurisdictions, signed staff acknowledgements might be worthless because they are presumed void.

Presumptive employment contract: As mentioned, some jurisdictions treat an employee's signed acknowledgement as an amendment to the employment agreement. In these countries, properly executed acknowledgements may indeed make a code, HR policy or benefits plan enforceable as "contractual." But casually-signed or electronically mouse-clicked acknowledgements may prove unenforceable under local law to the extent they fall short of local employment-contract-execution strictures. Where an employee acknowledgement amounts to a "contractual" amendment, draft and execute it as a full-blown contractual amendment. An online click ("I agree") is almost always insufficient.

Non-signers: A 100% return rate on employee code/policy/plan acknowledgements is all but impossible across big global employee populations. Local foreign staff may prove skeptical, sometimes even hostile, to new cross-border headquarters initiatives. Some employees will openly refuse to sign acknowledgements while others will passive-aggressively neglect to return them even after repeated reminders from local HR staff. Indeed, hapless foreign HR staff may be all but powerless to force locals to sign or click "I accept," especially where local HR teams feel intimidated pestering superiors. Remember that local HR has little leverage: away from U.S. employment-at-will, there is no good cause to discipline staff for refusing or neglecting to acknowledge something.[19]

Non-signers of a headquarters code, policy or plan acknowledgement raise a serious "Achilles' heel" problem: A non-signer who later violates the rule can argue he was exempt precisely because he never signed. Brandishing his co-workers' signed (or computer-clicked) acknowledgements *in his own favor*, the scofflaw non-signer declares the cross-border HR initiative reaches only those of his colleagues who agreed to follow it. At that point the multinational realizes, too late, that it would have been better off not collecting any signed acknowledgements in the first place.

Before embarking on an effort to collect staff acknowledgements to some new cross-border code, policy or plan, first devise a viable strategy for handling non-signers.

Proof problems: In-house human resources teams have unimpressive records retaining and tracking employee acknowledgements over time. Years after staff across far-flung offices were thought to have signed or mouse-click-accepted some company code, policy or plan acknowledgement, it can prove maddeningly difficult for HR to dig out that one specific acknowledgement of that one particular employee who now needs to be punished for violating a provision he claims he never saw. HR is sure the scofflaw executed an acknowledgement, but where is it?

A second proof problem is that new hires who "onboard" after a cross-border code or HR policy launch may never get asked to sign acknowledgements.

A third proof problem is that *mouse-click* acknowledgements are notoriously tough to verify after the fact, when a dispute later goes to court. Meeting the employer's burden to prove a given employee actually clicked "I accept" can be all but impossible years later, under inflexible and antiquated local evidence rules in foreign courts with uncertain electronic signature proof requirements.

---

19. *See Hou, supra*, Beijing Intermediate People's Ct. no. 4, 11/26/09 (reinstating chief guard fired for refusing to sign acknowledgement consenting to a changed handbook).

Before embarking on any initiative to collect acknowledgements from employees across borders, first work up a fool-proof plan for storing the acknowledgements in a way that they are readily accessible and admissible in court, years later.

Because overseas employee acknowledgements implicate these four tough logistical challenges, always think carefully before deciding to ask local staff worldwide to execute code/policy/plan acknowledgements. Consider alternatives. One alternative is to get collective buy-in from employee representatives, not individual employee buy-in. Another alternative is for local HR representatives personally to distribute the new cross-border document, or for HR to hand it out during training sessions; then HR representatives themselves sign forms or log sheets recording the date and circumstances by which each employee received and got trained on the new initiative. Yet another alternative is to time acknowledgements to coincide with some discretionary bonus payment, stock award or pay raise. Distribute the bonus, award or raise only in exchange for a singed acknowledgement.

Step 7: Government Filings

Publicly traded American companies regularly file their codes of conduct, insider trading policies, whistleblower hotline policies and stock option plans with a U.S. federal government agency—the SEC. Obligations to file HR documents with government agencies also exist overseas, but American organizations tend to chafe at *foreign* government filing mandates for HR documents.

Filing or registering certain HR codes, policies or plans with foreign government agencies, while cumbersome, may be necessary to make the document effective locally. For example, French employers must file codes of conduct with France's Labor Inspectorate or a French labor court. Chilean employers must file any HR policy inconsistent with company work rules *(Reglamentos Internos de Orden, Higiene y Seguridad)* with the Chilean Labor Board or Ministry of Health. And data protection authorities across much of Europe require employers to disclose or file internal HR policies and systems that "process" employee data (human resources information systems, whistleblower hotlines and the like). Be sure to make necessary filings.

Step 8: Vested Rights

In discussing steps for launching a new international code of conduct, HR policy or benefits plan, we have assumed the headquarters initiative is neutral to employees, or at least does not materially cut pay or terms/conditions of employment. But sometimes a new headquarters code, policy or plan *does* materially reduce employment packages of at least some staff. And sometimes a new headquarters initiative is susceptible to an argument that it materially restricts the workplace environment.

Where a new global initiative materially cuts existing terms or conditions of employment abroad, the employer must account for vital additional steps to address the infringement on staff's "vested rights." Outside employment-at-will, all employees enjoy vested rights in their current terms/conditions of employment, and bosses cannot necessarily abrogate these rights unilaterally.

Step 9: Backstopping

The above eight steps for launching a new international code of conduct, HR policy or benefits plan address what to do before the initiative "goes live." But many cross-border initiatives that multinationals consider already in place today originally got rolled out without the employer scrupulously accounting for these eight steps. This leaves many existing multinational codes, rules, policies and plans vulnerable to challenge—findings of unenforceability or nullity.

A best practice for a multinational that failed properly to implement its current package of cross-border codes of conduct, work rules, HR policies and international benefits offerings is to "backstop"—go back and correct past oversights in implementation.

Assignments

- **Hypothetical:** You are the Chief Compliance Officer at your [Team's] Corporation. Get the Code of Conduct of your Company and compare risks with that of another company in the same industry. You should have a list of the top 5 risks indicated by the Code of Conduct and news articles on each company.

Chapter 5

Setting Up the Compliance Office and Defining the Role of the Compliance Officer

Introduction

Setting up the compliance office so that it is integrated into the corporate structure is a critical step in creating an effective compliance program.

On October 2008, the Federal Reserve System published the Supervisory Letter SR 08-8/CA 08-11 on *Compliance Risk Management Programs and Oversight at Large Banking Organizations with Complex Compliance Profiles* endorsing the principles set forth in *Compliance and the Compliance Function in Banks*, a high level paper published by the Basel Committee on Banking Supervision on April 2005. The *Compliance and the Compliance Function in Banks* provides a basic guidance for banks that embody ongoing efforts to address bank supervisory issues and enhance sound practices applicable to the compliance programs of financial institutions.

As part of the establishment of the compliance office, the role of the chief compliance officer as well as compliance officers, deputy compliance officers and other compliance personnel should be defined. Creating the corporate compliance guidelines for the corporation is the key step in creating the compliance office and defining the role of the compliance officer.

It is critical that this process of establishing the compliance office is undertaken at the commencement of compliance activities and is part of the work plan and rollout process.

Board of Governors of the Federal Reserve System
SR 08-8/CA 08-11

(Oct. 16, 2008) http://www.federalreserve.gov/
boarddocs/srletters/2008/sr0808.htm

TO THE OFFICER IN CHARGE OF SUPERVISION AND APPROPRIATE SUPER-
VISORY AND EXAMINATION STAFF AT EACH FEDERAL RESERVE BANK AND
CERTAIN ORGANIZATIONS SUPERVISED BY THE FEDERAL RESERVE

SUBJECT: Compliance Risk Management Programs and Oversight at Large Banking
Organizations with Complex Compliance Profiles

In recent years, banking organizations have greatly expanded the scope, complexity, and global nature of their business activities. At the same time, compliance requirements associated with these activities have become more complex. As a result, organizations have confronted significant risk management and corporate governance challenges, particularly with respect to compliance risks that transcend business lines, legal entities, and jurisdictions of operation. To address these challenges, many banking organizations have implemented or enhanced firmwide compliance risk management programs and program oversight.

While the guiding principles of sound risk management are the same for compliance as for other types of risk, the management and oversight of compliance risk presents certain challenges. For example, quantitative limits reflecting the board of directors' risk appetite can be established for market and credit risks, allocated to the various business lines within the organization, and monitored by units independent of the business line. Compliance risk does not lend itself to similar processes for establishing and allocating overall risk tolerance, in part because organizations must comply with applicable rules and standards. Additionally, existing compliance risk metrics are often less meaningful in terms of aggregation and trend analysis as compared with more traditional market and credit risk metrics. These distinguishing characteristics of compliance risk underscore the need for a firmwide approach to compliance risk management and oversight for large, complex organizations. A firmwide compliance function that plays a key role in managing and overseeing compliance risk while promoting a strong culture of compliance across the organization is particularly important for large, complex organizations that have a number of separate business lines and legal entities that must comply with a wide range of applicable rules and standards.

The Federal Reserve has, primarily through the examination process, emphasized the need for effective firmwide compliance risk management and oversight at large, complex banking organizations. While firmwide compliance risk management programs and oversight at the largest supervised banking organizations have generally improved, the level of progress at individual banking organizations varies and opportunity for improvement remains. The Federal Reserve strongly encourages large banking organizations with complex compliance profiles to ensure that the necessary resources are dedicated to fully implementing effective firmwide compliance risk management programs and oversight in a timely manner.

The Federal Reserve's expectations for all supervised banking organizations are consistent with the principles outlined in a paper issued in April 2005 by the Basel Committee on Banking Supervision, entitled *Compliance and the compliance function in banks* (Basel compliance paper). The principles in the Basel compliance paper have become widely recognized as global sound practices for compliance risk management and oversight, and the Federal Reserve endorses these principles. Nevertheless, some banking organizations have sought clarification as to the Federal Reserve's views regarding certain compliance risk management and oversight matters. This SR/CA letter clarifies Federal Reserve views applicable to large banking organizations with complex compliance profiles in the following areas where guidance has been requested:

I. Organizations that should implement a firmwide approach to compliance risk management and oversight;

II. Independence of compliance staff;

III. Compliance monitoring and testing; and

IV. Responsibilities of boards of directors and senior management regarding compliance risk management and oversight.

I. Firmwide Compliance Risk Management and Oversight

Overview

Organizations supervised by the Federal Reserve, regardless of size and complexity, should have effective compliance risk management programs that are appropriately tailored to the organizations' risk profiles. The manner in which the program is implemented and the type of oversight needed for that program can vary considerably depending upon the scope and complexity of the organization's activities, the geographic reach of the organization, and other inherent risk factors. Larger, more complex banking organizations tend to conduct a wide range of business activities that are subject to complex compliance requirements that frequently transcend business lines and legal entities and, accordingly, present risk management and corporate governance challenges. Consequently, these organizations typically require a firmwide approach to compliance risk management and oversight that includes a corporate compliance function. In contrast, smaller, less-complex banking organizations are not generally confronted with the types of compliance risks and challenges that require a comprehensive firmwide approach to effectively manage and oversee compliance risk. The following discussion, therefore, is *not* directed at smaller, less-complex banking organizations.

Firmwide compliance risk management refers to the processes established to manage compliance risk across an entire organization, both within and across business lines, support units, legal entities, and jurisdictions of operation. This approach ensures that compliance risk management is conducted in a context broader than would take place solely within individual business lines or legal entities. The need for a firmwide approach to compliance risk management at larger, more complex banking organizations is well demonstrated in areas such as anti-money laundering, privacy, affiliate transactions, conflicts of interest, and fair lending, where legal and regulatory requirements may apply to multiple business lines or legal entities within the banking organization. Certain other compliance risks may also warrant a firmwide risk management approach to address similar rules and standards that apply to the organization's operations across different jurisdictions. In all such instances, compliance risk management benefits from an aggregate view of the organization's compliance risk exposure and an integrated approach to managing those risks.

The processes established for managing compliance risk on a firmwide basis should be formalized in a compliance *program* that establishes the framework for identifying, assessing, controlling, measuring, monitoring, and reporting compliance risks across the organization, and for providing compliance training throughout the organization. A banking organization's compliance risk management program should be documented in the form of compliance policies and procedures and compliance risk management standards.

Firmwide compliance oversight refers to the processes established to oversee compliance risk management across the entire organization, both within and across business lines, legal entities, and jurisdictions of operation. In addition to the oversight provided by the board of directors and various executive and management committees of an organization, a key component of firmwide compliance oversight in larger, more complex banking organizations is a corporate compliance function that has day-to-day responsibility for overseeing and supporting the implementation of the organization's firmwide compliance risk management program, and that plays a key role in controlling compliance risks that transcend business lines, legal entities, and jurisdictions of operation.

Federal Reserve Supervisory Policies

Large Banking Organizations with Complex Compliance Profiles. Although balance sheet size is not the defining indication of a banking organization's compliance risk management needs, experience has demonstrated that banking organizations with $50 billion or more in consolidated total assets typically have multiple legal entities that pose the type of compliance risks and challenges that call for a comprehensive firmwide approach to appropriately control compliance risk and provide effective oversight. Accordingly, such organizations should generally implement firmwide compliance risk management programs and have a corporate compliance function.

Compliance programs at such organizations should include more robust processes for identifying, assessing, controlling, measuring, monitoring, and reporting compliance risk, and for providing compliance training throughout the organization in order to appropriately control the heightened level and complexity of compliance risk. The corporate compliance function should play a key role in overseeing and supporting the implementation of the compliance risk management program, and in controlling compliance risks that transcend business lines, legal entities, and jurisdictions of operation.

Large Banking Organizations with Less-Complex Compliance Profiles. In some instances, banking organizations that meet the $50 billion asset threshold may have few legal entities, be less complex in nature, and may engage in only a very limited range of business activities. Such organizations may be able to effectively manage and oversee compliance risk without implementing a comprehensive firmwide approach. Alternatively, these organizations may choose to implement a firmwide approach whose scope is highly risk-focused on particular compliance risks that exist throughout the organization. In lieu of relying on a corporate compliance function to play a key role in providing day-to-day oversight of the compliance program, these organizations may rely on executive and management committees that are actively involved in providing ongoing corporate oversight of the compliance risk management program. An organization that adopts this approach, however, should ensure that its compliance program incorporates controls that effectively address compliance risks that transcend business lines, legal entities, and jurisdictions of operation; that appropriate firmwide standards are established for the business lines to follow in managing compliance risk and reporting on key compliance matters; and that the organization is appropriately overseeing the implementation of its compliance risk management program.

Foreign Banking Organizations. Each foreign banking organization supervised by the Federal Reserve should implement a compliance program that is appropriately tailored to the scope, complexity, and risk profile of the organization's U.S. operations. The program should be reasonably designed to ensure that the organization's U.S. operations comply with applicable U.S. rules and standards, and should establish effective controls over compliance risks that transcend business lines or legal entities. Foreign banking organizations with large, complex U.S. operations should implement compliance programs for these operations that have more robust processes for identifying, assessing, controlling, measuring, monitoring, and reporting compliance risk, and for providing compliance training, than would be appropriate for foreign banking organizations with smaller, less-complex U.S. operations.

With respect to oversight, foreign banking organizations should provide effective oversight of compliance risks within their U.S. operations, including risks that transcend business lines or legal entities. A foreign banking organization, however, has flexibility in organizing its oversight structure. Compliance oversight of U.S. activities may be conducted in a manner that is consistent with the foreign banking organization's broader compliance risk management framework. Alternatively, a separate function may be established specifically to provide compliance oversight of the organization's U.S. operations. Regardless of the oversight structure utilized by a foreign banking organization, its established oversight mechanisms, governing policies and procedures, and supporting infrastructure for its U.S. operations should be sufficiently transparent for the Federal Reserve to assess their adequacy.

II. Independence of Compliance Staff

Federal Reserve supervisory findings at large, complex banking organizations consistently reinforce the need for compliance staff to be appropriately independent of the business lines for which they have compliance responsibilities. Compliance independence facilitates objectivity and avoids inherent conflicts of interest that may hinder the effective implementation of a compliance program. The Federal Reserve has observed compliance independence to be an area in which there is considerable variation in practices, some of which do not consistently meet supervisory standards.

A particular challenge for many organizations is attaining an appropriate level of independence with respect to compliance staff operating within the business lines.

The Federal Reserve does not prescribe a particular organizational structure for the compliance function. Large banking organizations with complex compliance profiles are encouraged, however, to avoid inherent conflicts of interest by ensuring that accountability exists between the corporate compliance function and compliance staff within the business lines. Such accountability would provide the corporate compliance function with ultimate authority regarding the handling of compliance matters and personnel decisions and actions relating to compliance staff, including retaining control over the budget for, and remuneration of, all compliance staff. Compliance independence should not, however, preclude compliance staff from working closely with the management and staff of the various business lines. To the contrary, compliance functions are generally more effective when strong working relationships between compliance and business line staff exist.

The Federal Reserve recognizes, however, that many large, complex banking organizations have chosen to implement an organizational structure in which compliance staff within a business line have a reporting line into the management of the business. In these circumstances, compliance staff should also have a reporting line through to the corporate compliance function with respect to compliance responsibilities. In addition, a banking organization that chooses to implement such a dual reporting structure should ensure that the following minimum standards are observed in order to minimize potential conflicts of interest associated with this approach:

(1) In organizations with dual reporting line structures, the corporate compliance function should play a key role in determining how compliance matters are handled and in personnel decisions and actions (including remuneration) affecting business line compliance and local compliance staff, particularly senior compliance staff. Furthermore, the organization should have in place a process designed to ensure that disputes between the corporate compliance function and business line management regarding compliance matters are resolved objectively. Under such a process, the final decision-making authority should rest either with the corporate compliance function, or with a member or committee of senior management that has no business line responsibilities.

(2) Compensation and incentive programs should be carefully structured to avoid undermining the independence of compliance staff. Compliance staff should not be compensated on the basis of the financial performance of the business line. Such an arrangement creates an improper conflict of interest.

(3) Banking organizations with dual reporting line structures should implement appropriate controls and enhanced corporate oversight to identify and address issues that may arise from conflicts of interest affecting compliance staff within the business lines. For example, in these circumstances, the process for providing corporate oversight of monitoring and testing activities performed by compliance staff within the business lines should be especially robust.

III. Compliance Monitoring and Testing

Robust compliance monitoring and testing play a key role in identifying weaknesses in existing compliance risk management controls and are, therefore, critical components of an effective firmwide compliance risk management program. Federal Reserve supervisory findings at large, complex banking organizations indicate that opportunities for improving compliance monitoring and testing programs at many of these organizations remain.

Risk Assessments and Monitoring and Testing Programs. Risk assessments are the foundation of an effective compliance monitoring and testing program. The scope and frequency of compliance monitoring and testing activities should be a function of a comprehensive assessment of the overall compliance risk associated with a particular business activity. Many larger, more complex banking organizations, however, remain in the process of implementing comprehensive risk assessment methodologies. This presents a challenge to the effectiveness of compliance monitoring and testing programs as the effectiveness of these programs relies upon comprehensive risk assessments. Larger, more complex banking organizations are strongly encouraged to complete the implementation of comprehensive risk assessment methodologies and to ensure that compliance monitoring and testing activities are based upon the resulting risk assessments.

Testing. Although the Federal Reserve has generally observed considerable progress in the level of compliance monitoring, there continues to be room for improvement regarding the testing of compliance controls. Compliance testing is necessary to validate that key assumptions, data sources, and procedures utilized in measuring and monitoring compliance risk can be relied upon on an ongoing basis and, in the case of transaction testing, that controls are working as intended. The testing of controls and remediation of deficiencies identified as a result of testing activities are essential to maintaining an effective internal control framework.

The scope and frequency of compliance testing activities should be based upon the assessment of the specific compliance risks associated with a particular business activity. Periodic testing of compliance controls by compliance staff is strongly encouraged as this practice tends to result in an enhanced level of compliance testing. If, however, compliance testing is performed exclusively by the internal audit function, particular care should be taken to ensure that high-risk compliance elements are not otherwise obscured by a lower overall risk rating of a broadly defined audit entity. Otherwise, the scope and frequency of audit coverage of higher-risk compliance elements tends to be insufficient.

IV. Responsibilities of the Board of Directors and Senior Management

The primary responsibility for complying with applicable rules and standards rests with the individuals within the organization as they conduct their day-to-day business and support activities. The board, senior management, and the corporate compliance function are responsible for working together to establish and implement a comprehensive and effective compliance risk management program and oversight framework that is reasonably designed to prevent and detect compliance breaches and issues.

Boards of Directors. Boards of directors are responsible for setting an appropriate culture of compliance within their organizations, for establishing clear policies regarding the management of key risks, and for ensuring that these policies are adhered to in practice. The following discussion is intended to clarify existing Federal Reserve supervisory views with regard to responsibilities of the board related to compliance risk management and oversight, and to differentiate these responsibilities from those of senior management.

To achieve its objectives, a sound and effective firmwide compliance risk management program should have the support of the board and senior management. As set forth in applicable law and supervisory guidance, the board and senior management of a banking organization have different, but complementary, roles in managing and overseeing compliance risk.

The board has the responsibility for promoting a culture that encourages ethical conduct and compliance with applicable rules and standards. A strong compliance culture reinforces the principle that an organization must conduct its activities in accordance with applicable rules and standards, and encourages employees to conduct all activities in accordance with both the letter and the spirit of applicable rules and standards. The board should have an appropriate understanding of the types of compliance risks to which the organization is exposed. The level of technical knowledge required of directors to fulfill these responsibilities may vary depending on the particular circumstances at the organization.

The board should ensure that senior management is fully capable, qualified, and properly motivated to manage the compliance risks arising from the organization's business activities in a manner that is consistent with the board's expectations. The board should ensure that its views about the importance of compliance are understood and communicated by senior management across, and at all levels of, the organization through ongoing training and other means. The board should ensure that senior management has established appropriate incentives to integrate compliance objectives into the management goals and compensation structure across the organization, and that appropriate disciplinary actions and other measures are taken when serious compliance failures are identified. Finally, the board should ensure that the corporate compliance function has an appropriately prominent status within the organization. Senior management within the corporate compliance function and senior compliance personnel within individual business lines should have the appropriate authority, independence, and access to personnel and information within the organization, and appropriate resources to conduct their activities effectively.

The board should be knowledgeable about the general content of the compliance program and exercise appropriate oversight of the program. Accordingly, the board should review and approve key elements of the organization's compliance risk management program and oversight framework, including firmwide compliance policies, compliance risk management standards, and roles and responsibilities of committees and functions with compliance oversight responsibilities. The board should oversee management's implementation of the compliance program and the appropriate and timely resolution of compliance issues by senior management. The board should exercise reasonable due diligence to ensure that the compliance program remains effective by at least annually reviewing a report on the effectiveness of the program. The board may delegate these tasks to an appropriate board-level committee.

Senior Management. Senior management across the organization is responsible for communicating and reinforcing the compliance culture established by the board, and for implementing measures to promote the culture. Senior management also should implement and enforce the compliance policies and compliance risk management standards that have been approved by the board. Senior management of the corporate compliance function should establish, support, and oversee the organization's compliance risk management program. The corporate compliance function should report to the board, or a committee thereof, on significant compliance matters and the effectiveness of the compliance risk management program.

Senior management of a foreign banking organization's U.S. operations should provide sufficient information to governance or control functions in its home country, and should ensure that responsible senior management, including in the home country, maintain a thorough understanding of the risk and control environment governing U.S. operations. U.S. management should assess the effectiveness of established governance and control mechanisms on an ongoing basis, including processes for reporting and escalating areas of concern and implementation of corrective action as necessary.

V. Conclusion

This SR/CA letter should be disseminated to all large, complex banking organizations, and other institutions supervised by the Federal Reserve as Reserve Bank staff believes appropriate. Questions may be directed to Karen El Kochta, Senior Supervisory Financial Analyst, Compliance Risk, Division of Banking Supervision and Regulation, at (202) 452-5206; Chris Laursen, Manager, Risk Policy & Guidance, Division of Banking Supervision and Regulation, at (202) 452-2478; or Phyllis Harwell, Manager, Division of Consumer and Community Affairs, at (202) 452-3658. In addition, questions may be sent via the Board's public website.

Strategy for Setting Up a Compliance Office and Defining the Role of the Compliance Officer

Understanding Why

Setting up the compliance office and defining the role of the compliance officer are two functions that are intertwined. Therefore, there should be an analysis of the goals of the compliance program, the mission of the compliance office in implementing these goals and the responsibilities of the compliance officer in achieving these goals. This critical analysis sets the stage for establishing the compliance office and properly defining the role of the compliance officer.

It is critical to have a focused, articulated rationale and objective.

Proactive Objective	Reactive Objective
Understanding the business need	Issues arise
Serve customers	Bad Publicity (under investigation)
Efficiency	

The strategy for setting up a compliance office and properly defining the role of the compliance officer is critical to the success of an effective compliance program. There are several different methodologies for setting up the compliance office. These methodologies depend upon whether the compliance office is separate from the office of general counsel, human resources department, the finance department, or a part of one of these departments.

Key Considerations

General:

- Leadership
- Independence
- Organizational firm-reporting lines
- "Risk-based"
- Talent
  - Generalist
  - Specialists
- Staging
- Potential overlaps with other roles and functions

Company Specific:

- Size/complexity
- Culture
- Organizational Structure

If the compliance office is separate from the office of the general counsel, human resources department, and the finance department, this avoids potential conflict of interest issues. For example, if the hotline receives a complaint about the finance department or the human resources department, it may be difficult for the compliance officer to pursue a complaint and open an investigation. Therefore, the autonomy of the compliance office is a key to creating an effective compliance program. In fact, this is the recommendation of the Health and Human Services Guidelines for health related organizations covered by the Health and Human Services Guidelines.

Principle 5 of *Compliance and the Compliance Function in Banks* states: "The bank's compliance function should be independent." In the principle's commentary, the Basel Committee adds "The concept of independence of does not mean that the compliance function cannot work closely with management and staff in the various business units … rather, it should be viewed as safeguards to help ensure the effectiveness of the compliance function."

However, while an effective compliance program can exist where the compliance program is under the control of another functional department, this is much more difficult because of the potential conflicts of interest. Mixing the compliance function with other corporate functions may increase conflicts of interest, make reporting issues more difficult, and may have a negative impact on the effective implementation of a compliance program. This may be remedied by making sure there is direct reporting to the Board of Directors by the designated compliance officer. Corporate culture, size of the company, and personnel available to perform the compliance function are critical factors in determining where the compliance function should reside.

In the Federal Reserve System's Supervisory Letter, SR 08-8/CA 08-11, it sets forth minimum standards that should be observed in order to minimize potential conflicts of interests associated with a dual reporting structure. The Letter outlined four key areas where guidance was requested:

I.   **Organizations that should implement a firm wide approach to compliance risk management and oversight:** The manner in which a program is implemented is dependent upon the scope and complexity of the organization's activities, the geographic reach of the organization, and other risk factors. This process should be formalized in a compliance program that establishes the framework for identifying, assessing, controlling, monitoring, reporting compliance risks and providing training throughout the organization.

II. **Independence of compliance staff:** Compliance independence facilitates objectivity and avoids inherent conflicts of interest that my hinder the effective implementation of a compliance program.

III. **Compliance monitoring and testing:** Risk assessments are the foundation of an effective compliance monitoring and testing program. The scope and frequency of compliance monitoring and testing activities should be a function of a comprehensive assessment of the overall compliance risk associated with the particular business activity.

IV. **Responsibilities of boards of directors and senior management regarding compliance risk management and oversight:** To achieve the objectives of a compliance program, a sound and effective firm wide compliance risk management program should have the support of the board and senior management. There should be clear support from the top.

This is a frequent practice in many corporations; however, one should still be aware of potential conflicts of interest between the compliance function and the legal function. However, corporate culture and availability of personnel can mitigate this. The most common mixing of the compliance function with other functions is where the compliance officer is also the general counsel. If there is a conflict of interest, the General Counsel should recuse himself or herself and the Board of Directors or other designee should supervise the process to resolve the conflict.

Further, in setting up a compliance office, it is not only important to create a compliance office that is autonomous, but it is also critical to have reporting lines that provide direct access to the CEO/President as well as the Board of Directors and/or the Audit Committee of the Board of Directors.

In determining reporting lines, the emphasis should be on creating the most effective compliance program that will enhance the ethical culture of the corporation. In addition to the direct reporting line from the compliance officer to the CEO/President as well as the Board of Directors and/or the Audit Committee of the Board of Directors, some alternative reporting line options include the following:

- Compliance Officer Reporting to the General Counsel;
- Compliance Officer Reporting to the Chief Financial Officer;
- Compliance Officer Reporting to the CEO/President only;
- Compliance Officer Reporting to the Board of Directors/Audit Committee of the Board only;
- Compliance Officer Reporting to Compliance Executive Team only.

When setting up a compliance office it is importance to evaluate what type of reporting system would be most efficient for the particular corporate model. There are multiple approaches to creating reporting lines.

Direct vs. Indirect Reporting Lines

Direct reporting within a corporation requires that the Chief Compliance Officer report directly to the Board of Directors and Chief Executive Officer of the Corporation. Indirect reporting would require that the Chief Compliance Officer first report to the Chief Legal Officer, the Chief Legal Officer will then report to the Board of Directors and Chief Executive Officer.

Note: Even if a corporation implements Indirect reporting, there should be a dotted line (indirect) reporting permitted from the Chief Compliance Officer to the Board of Directors.

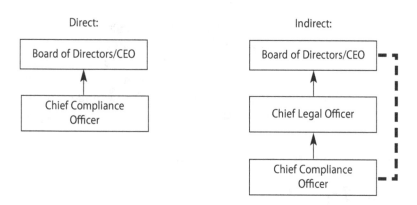

Centralized vs. Decentralized Reporting Lines

Corporations are no longer single entities but rather many operate as parents for various subsidiaries located worldwide. Centralized approach to reporting lines requires that the compliance office of the subsidiary report directly to the Board of Directors and Chief Executive Officer of the parent company. A Decentralized approach requires that the Chief Compliance Officer of the subsidiary report directly to the subsidiary's Chief Executive Officer and Board of Directors; then the subsidiary Chief Executive Officer or Board will report to the parent company. This approach has no direct reporting from the subsidiary to the parent; it can make it difficult for executive and board leadership to look across the organization and understand compliance risks. Decentralization could result in inconsistent application of compliance policies—different regions can create their own approach on compliance issues. Therefore, if a corporation does select to apply a decentralized reporting system, there should be a unifying thread-either office, person, or technology that is designed to confirm that risks are being accounted for, addressed, and resolved.

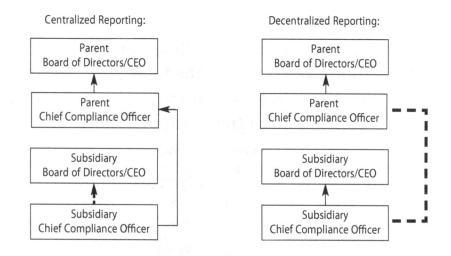

Specialists vs. Generalists

Another important factor to determine is how many specialists and generalists the compliance office will employ. Specialists are individuals that specialize in a particular field that is pertinent to the corporate function. These can include specialists in Intellectual Property, Taxation, and Employment to name just a few. Generalists are individuals that have a more comprehensive understanding of the business and its key components, as well as a general understanding of corporate law.

Below are examples of specialists various industries may seek to employ.

Petroleum Company

Extract/Oil Laws	Patent Law
Environmental Law	Securities/Insider Trading
Marketing/Advertising	Anti-Trust
Cyber Security	

Pharmaceutical Company

Anti-Bribery/FCPA/U.K. Bribery Act	FDA
Drug Trials	Intellectual Property
Anti-trust	Environmental Law
Employment Law	Cyber Security

Financial Institution

Anti-Money Laundering	Know Your Customer
Secrecy Act	Anti-Bribery/FCPA/U.K. Bribery Act
Cyber Security	Sarbanes-Oxley/Dodd-Frank
Consumer Protection	Securities/Insider Trading

Passing a Resolution by the Board of Directors and/or Audit Committee of the Board to Create a Compliance/Ethics Committee to Oversee the Creation of the Compliance Office

As the first step in creating an effective compliance program, the Board of Directors and/or Audit Committee of the Board of Directors need to pass resolutions to appoint the compliance/ethics committee to oversee the creation of the compliance office. The Board's approval demonstrates that the Board of Directors has exercised its corporate governance and oversight responsibilities with respect to the compliance area.

Principle 1 of *Compliance and the Compliance Function in Banks* states: "The bank's board of directors for overseeing the management of the bank's compliance risk. The Board should approve the bank's compliance policy, including a formal document establishing a permanent and effective compliance function. At least once a year, the Board of Directors should assess the extent to which the bank is managing its compliance risk effectively." In the principle's commentary, the Basel Committee adds "the board should oversee the implementation of the policy, including ensuring that compliance issues are resolved effectively and expeditiously by senior management with the assistance of the compliance function. The board may delegate these tasks to an appropriate board level committee (e.g., its audit committee)."

In re Caremark Int'l Derivative Suit
698 A.2d 959 (Del. Ch. 1996)

Chancellor Allen delivered the memorandum opinion.

[Parties to a derivative suit seeking to impose personal liability on members of board of directors proposed settlement for court approval. The suit involves claims that the members of Caremark International, Inc.'s ("Caremark") board of directors (the "Board") breached their fiduciary duty of care to Caremark in connection with alleged violations by Caremark employees of federal and state laws and regulations applicable to health care providers.]

I. BACKGROUND

Caremark, a Delaware corporation with its headquarters in Northbrook, Illinois, was created in November 1992 when it was spun-off from Baxter International, Inc. ("Baxter") and became a publicly held company listed on the New York Stock Exchange. The business practices that created the problem pre-dated the spin-off. During the relevant period Caremark was involved in two main health care business segments, providing patient care and managed care services. As part of its patient care business, which accounted for the majority of Caremark's revenues, Caremark provided alternative site health care services, including infusion therapy, growth hormone therapy, HIV/AIDS-related treatments and hemophilia therapy. Caremark's managed care services included prescription drug programs and the operation of multi-specialty group practices.

A substantial part of the revenues generated by Caremark's businesses is derived from third party payments, insurers, and Medicare and Medicaid reimbursement programs. The latter source of payments are subject to the terms of the Anti-Referral Payments Law ("ARPL") which prohibits health care providers from paying any form of remuneration to induce the referral of Medicare or Medicaid patients. From its inception, Caremark entered into a variety of agreements with hospitals, physicians, and health care providers for advice and services, as well as distribution agreements with drug manufacturers, as had its predecessor prior to 1992. Specifically, Caremark did have a practice of entering into contracts for services (e.g., consultation agreements and research grants) with physicians at least some of whom prescribed or recommended services or products that Caremark provided to Medicare recipients and other patients. Such contracts were not prohibited by the ARPL but they obviously raised a possibility of unlawful "kickbacks."

As early as 1989, Caremark's predecessor issued an internal "Guide to Contractual Relationships" ("Guide") to govern its employees in entering into contracts with physicians and hospitals. The Guide tended to be reviewed annually by lawyers and updated. Each version of the Guide stated as Caremark's and its predecessor's policy that no payments would be made in exchange for or to induce patient referrals. But what one might deem a prohibited *quid pro quo* was not always clear.

In August 1991, the HHS Office of the Inspector General ("OIG") initiated an investigation of Caremark's predecessor. Caremark's predecessor was served with a subpoena requiring the production of documents, including contracts between Caremark's predecessor and physicians (Quality Service Agreements ("QSAs")). Under the QSAs, Caremark's predecessor appears to have paid physicians fees for monitoring patients under Caremark's predecessor's care, including Medicare and Medicaid recipients. Sometimes apparently those monitoring patients were referring physicians, which raised ARPL concerns.

In March 1992, the Department of Justice ("DOJ") joined the OIG investigation and separate investigations were commenced by several additional federal and state agencies.[1] During the relevant period, Caremark had approximately 7,000 employees and ninety branch operations. It had a decentralized management structure. By May 1991, however, Caremark asserts that it had begun making attempts to centralize its management structure in order to increase supervision over its branch operations.

The first action taken by management, as a result of the initiation of the OIG investigation, was an announcement that as of October 1, 1991, Caremark's predecessor would no longer pay management fees to physicians for services to Medicare and Medicaid patients. Despite this decision, Caremark asserts that its management, pursuant to advice, did not believe that such payments were illegal under the existing laws and regulations. During this period, Caremark's Board took several additional steps consistent with an effort to assure compliance with company policies concerning the ARPL and the contractual forms in the Guide. In April 1992, Caremark published a fourth revised version of its Guide apparently designed to assure that its agreements either complied with the ARPL and regulations or excluded Medicare and Medicaid patients altogether. In addition, in September 1992, Caremark instituted a policy requiring its regional officers, Zone Presidents, to approve each contractual relationship entered into by Caremark with a physician.

---

1. [2] In addition to investigating whether Caremark's financial relationships with health care providers were intended to induce patient referrals, inquiries were made concerning Caremark's billing practices, activities which might lead to excessive and medically unnecessary treatments for patients, potentially improper waivers of patient co-payment obligations, and the adequacy of records kept at Caremark pharmacies.

Throughout the period of the government investigations, Caremark had an internal audit plan designed to assure compliance with business and ethics policies. In addition, Caremark employed Price Waterhouse as its outside auditor. On February 8, 1993, the Ethics Committee of Caremark's Board received and reviewed an outside auditors report by Price Waterhouse, which concluded that there were no material weaknesses in Caremark's control structure.[2] Despite the positive findings of Price Waterhouse, however, on April 20, 1993, the Audit & Ethics Committee adopted a new internal audit charter requiring a comprehensive review of compliance policies and the compilation of an employee ethics handbook concerning such policies.[3]

During 1993, Caremark took several additional steps, which appear to have been aimed at increasing management supervision. These steps included new policies requiring local branch managers to secure home office approval for all disbursements under agreements with health care providers and to certify compliance with the ethics program. In addition, the chief financial officer was appointed to serve as Caremark's compliance officer. In 1994, a fifth revised Guide was published.

On August 4, 1994, a federal grand jury in Minnesota issued a 47-page indictment charging Caremark, two of its officers (not the firm's chief officer), an individual who had been a sales employee of Genentech, Inc., and David R. Brown, a physician practicing in Minneapolis, with violating the ARPL over a lengthy period. In reaction to the Minnesota Indictment and the subsequent filing of this and other derivative actions in 1994, the Board met and was informed by management that the investigation had resulted in an indictment; Caremark denied any wrongdoing relating to the indictment and believed that the OIG investigation would have a favorable outcome. Management reiterated the grounds for its view that the contracts were in compliance with law.

The original complaint, dated August 5, 1994, alleged, in relevant part, that Caremark's directors breached their duty of care by failing adequately to supervise the conduct of Caremark employees, or institute corrective measures, thereby exposing Caremark to fines and liability. After each complaint was filed, defendants filed a motion to dismiss. According to defendants, plaintiffs had failed to state a cause of action due to the fact that Caremark's charter eliminates directors' personal liability for money damages, to the extent permitted by law.

B. Directors' Duties To Monitor Corporate Operations

The complaint charges the director defendants with breach of their duty of attention or care in connection with the on-going operation of the corporation's business. The claim is that the directors allowed a situation to develop and continue which exposed the corporation to enormous legal liability and that in so doing they violated a duty to be active monitors of corporate performance.

---

2. [3] At that time, Price Waterhouse viewed the outcome of the OIG Investigation as uncertain. After further audits, however, on February 7, 1995, Price Waterhouse informed the Audit & Ethics Committee that it had not become aware of any irregularities or illegal acts in relation to the OIG investigation.

3. [4] Price Waterhouse worked in conjunction with the Internal Audit Department.

1. Potential liability for directoral decisions: Director liability for a breach of the duty to exercise appropriate attention may, in theory, arise in two distinct contexts. First, such liability may be said to follow *from a board decision* that results in a loss because that decision was ill advised or "negligent." Second, liability to the corporation for a loss may be said to arise from an *unconsidered failure of the board to act* in circumstances in which due attention would, arguably, have prevented the loss. *See generally* Veasey & Seitz, *The Business Judgment Rule in the Revised Model Act ...* 63 Texas L. Rev. 1483 (1985). However, compliance with a director's duty of care can never appropriately be judicially determined by reference to *the content of the board decision* that leads to a corporate loss, apart from consideration of the good faith *or* rationality of the process employed. That is, whether a judge or jury considering the matter after the fact, believes a decision substantively wrong, or degrees of wrong extending through "stupid" to "egregious" or "irrational," provides no ground for director liability, so long as the court determines that the process employed was either rational or employed in *a good faith* effort to advance corporate interests.

2. Liability for failure to monitor: The second class of cases in which director liability for inattention is theoretically possible entail circumstances in which a loss eventuates not from a decision but, from unconsidered inaction. Financial and organizational disasters raise the question, what is the board's responsibility with respect to the organization and monitoring of the enterprise to assure that the corporation functions within the law to achieve its purposes?

Modernly this question has been given special importance by an increasing tendency, especially under federal law, to employ the criminal law to assure corporate compliance with external legal requirements, including environmental, financial, employee and product safety as well as assorted other health and safety regulations. In 1991, pursuant to the Sentencing Reform Act of 1984,[4] the United States Sentencing Commission adopted Organizational Sentencing Guidelines, which impact importantly on the prospective effect these criminal sanctions might have on business corporations. The Guidelines set forth a uniform sentencing structure for organizations to be sentenced for violation of federal criminal statutes and provide for penalties that equal or often massively exceed those previously imposed on corporations.[5] The Guidelines offer powerful incentives for corporations today to have in place compliance programs to detect violations of law, promptly to report violations to appropriate public officials when discovered, and to take prompt, voluntary remedial efforts.

In 1963, the Delaware Supreme Court in *Graham v. Allis-Chalmers Mfg. Co.*[6] addressed the question of potential liability of board members for losses experienced by the corporation as a result of the corporation having violated the anti-trust laws

---

4. [21] *See* Sentencing Reform Act of 1984, Pub. L. 98-473, Title II, §212(a)(2)(1984); 18 U.S.C.A. §§3551–3656.

5. [22] *See* United States Sentencing Commission, Guidelines Manuel, Chapter 8 (U.S. Government Printing Office November 1994).

6. [23] 41 Del.Ch. 78, 188 A.2d 125 (1963).

of the United States. There was no claim in that case that the directors knew about the behavior of subordinate employees of the corporation that had resulted in the liability. Rather, as in this case, the claim asserted was that the directors *ought to have known* of it and if they had known they would have been under a duty to bring the corporation into compliance with the law and thus save the corporation from the loss.

The Delaware Supreme Court concluded that, under the facts as they appeared, there was no basis to find that the directors had breached a duty to be informed of the ongoing operations of the firm. In notably colorful terms, the court stated that "absent cause for suspicion there is no duty upon the directors to install and operate a corporate system of espionage to ferret out wrongdoing which they have no reason to suspect exists." The Court found that there were no grounds for suspicion in that case and, thus, concluded that the directors were blamelessly unaware of the conduct leading to the corporate liability.

A broader interpretation of *Graham v. Allis-Chalmers*—that it means that a corporate board has no responsibility to assure that appropriate information and reporting systems are established by management—would not, in any event, be accepted by the Delaware Supreme Court in 1996, in my opinion. In stating the basis for this view, I start with the recognition that in recent years the Delaware Supreme Court has made it clear—especially in its jurisprudence concerning takeovers, from *Smith v. Van Gorkom* through *Paramount Communications v. QVC*[7]—the seriousness with which the corporation law views the role of the corporate board. Secondly, I note the elementary fact that relevant and timely *information* is an essential predicate for satisfaction of the board's supervisory and monitoring role under Section 141 of the Delaware General Corporation Law. Thirdly, I note the potential impact of the federal organizational sentencing guidelines on any business organization. Any rational person attempting in good faith to meet an organizational governance responsibility would be bound to take into account this development and the enhanced penalties and the opportunities for reduced sanctions that it offers.

In light of these developments, it would, in my opinion, be a mistake to conclude that our Supreme Court's statement in *Graham* concerning "espionage" means that corporate boards may satisfy their obligation to be reasonably informed concerning the corporation, without assuring themselves that information and reporting systems exist in the organization that are reasonably designed to provide to senior management and to the board itself timely, accurate information sufficient to allow management and the board, each within its scope, to reach informed judgments concerning both the corporation's compliance with law and its business performance.

Thus, I am of the view that a director's obligation includes a duty to attempt in good faith to assure that a corporate information and reporting system, which the

---

7. [26] *E.g., Smith v. Van Gorkom,* Del. Supr., 488 A.2d 858 (1985); *Paramount Communications v. QVC Network,* Del. Supr., 637 A.2d 34 (1994).

board concludes is adequate, exists, and that failure to do so under some circumstances may, in theory at least, render a director liable for losses caused by non-compliance with applicable legal standards.

III. ANALYSIS OF THIRD AMENDED COMPLAINT AND SETTLEMENT

On balance, after reviewing an extensive record in this case, including numerous documents and three depositions, I conclude that this settlement is fair and reasonable. In light of the fact that the Caremark Board already has a functioning committee charged with overseeing corporate compliance, the changes in corporate practice that are presented as consideration for the settlement do not impress one as very significant. Nonetheless, that consideration appears fully adequate to support dismissal of the derivative claims of director fault asserted, because those claims find no substantial evidentiary support in the record and quite likely were susceptible to a motion to dismiss in all events.

In order to show that the Caremark directors breached their duty of care by failing adequately to control Caremark's employees, plaintiffs would have to show either (1) that the directors knew or (2) should have known that violations of law were occurring and, in either event, (3) that the directors took no steps in a good faith effort to prevent or remedy that situation, and (4) that such failure proximately resulted in the losses complained of, although under *Cede & Co. v. Technicolor, Inc.,* Del. Supr., 636 A.2d 956 (1994), this last element may be thought to constitute an affirmative defense.

Since it does appears that the Board was to some extent unaware of the activities that led to liability, I turn to a consideration of the other potential avenue to director liability that the pleadings take: director inattention or "negligence." Generally where a claim of directorial liability for corporate loss is predicated upon ignorance of liability creating activities within the corporation, as in *Graham* or in this case, in my opinion only a sustained or systematic failure of the board to exercise oversight — such as an utter failure to attempt to assure a reasonable information and reporting system exists — will establish the lack of good faith that is a necessary condition to liability. Such a test of liability — lack of good faith as evidenced by sustained or systematic failure of a director to exercise reasonable oversight — is quite high. But, a demanding test of liability in the oversight context is probably beneficial to corporate shareholders as a class, as it is in the board decision context, since it makes board service by qualified persons more likely, while continuing to act as a stimulus to *good faith performance of duty* by such directors.

Here the record supplies essentially no evidence that the director defendants were guilty of a sustained failure to exercise their oversight function. To the contrary, insofar as I am able to tell on this record, the corporation's information systems appear to have represented a good faith attempt to be informed of relevant facts. If the directors did not know the specifics of the activities that lead to the indictments, they cannot be faulted.

Notes and Comments

Under the *Caremark* decision, the members of the Board of Directors have personal liability for overseeing the corporate compliance program. By creating a compliance/ethics committee to oversee the creation of the compliance office, the Board of Directors clearly indicates, at the launch of the compliance program, the necessity for board supervision of the compliance process. Further, it memorializes the Board of Directors' independent authority and jurisdiction over compliance and the Board's intent to receive auditing and monitoring reports once the compliance program is rolled out as part of its ongoing oversight responsibility. Finally, the Board resolution creating the compliance/ethics committee should delineate the steps necessary to establish the compliance office by the compliance/ethics committee.

Moneygram International, Inc.

Compliant filed in the Southern District of New York
Dec. 18, 2014

The Financial Crimes Enforcement Network (FinCEN) issued a $1 million civil money penalty (CMP) against Mr. Thomas E. Haider for failing to ensure that his company abided by the anti-money laundering (AML) provisions of the Bank Secrecy Act (BSA). Concurrently, FinCEN's representative, the U.S. Attorney's Office for the Southern District of New York (SDNY), filed a complaint in U.S. District Court that seeks to enforce the penalty and to enjoin Mr. Haider from employment in the financial industry.

The complaint alleges the following:

Since at least 2003, MoneyGram has operated a money transfer service that enables customers to transfer money from one location to another through a global network of agents and outlets. Money gram outlets are independently owned entities that are authorized to transfer money through MoneyGram's money transfer system. MoneyGram agents are the owners and/or operators of such outlets.

As a money transmitter, MoneyGram is subject to, and must comply with various requirements set forth in the BSA and its implementing regulations. MoneyGram is also required to implement and maintain an effective anti-money laundering ("AML") program. MoneyGram was also required to file with FinCEN suspicious activity reports ("SARs").

MoneyGram's Chief Compliance Officer was responsible for ensuring that the Company implemented and maintained an effective AML program and complied with its SAR filing obligations. From at least 203 through on or about May 23, 2008, Haider was MoneyGram's Chief Compliance Officer. Haider's employment at MoneyGram ended on or about May 23, 2008.

Notwithstanding Haider's obligations as MoneyGram's Chief Compliance Officer, Haider failed to ensure that MoneyGram (1) implemented and maintained an effective

AML program and (2) fulfilled its obligation to file timely SARs. Haider's failures included the following:

- *Failure to Implement a Discipline Policy.* Haider failed to ensure that MoneyGram implemented a policy for disciplining agents and outlets that MoneyGram personnel knew or suspected were involved in fraud and/or money laundering.

- *Failure to Terminate Known High-Risk Agents/outlets.* Haider failed to ensure that MoneyGram terminated agents and outlets that MoneyGram personnel understood were involved in fraud and/or money laundering, including outlets that Haider himself was on notice posed an unreasonable risk of fraud and/or money laundering.

- *Failure to File Timely SARs.* Haider failed to ensure that MoneyGram fulfilled its obligation to file timely SARs, including because Haider maintained Money-Gram's AML program so that individuals responsible for filling SARs were not provided with information possessed by MoneyGram's Fraud Department.

- *Failure to Conduct Effective Audits of Agents/outlets.* Haider failed to ensure that MoneyGram conducted effective audits of agents and outlets, including outlets that MoneyGram personnel knew or suspected were involved in fraud and/or money laundering.

- *Failure to Conduct Adequate Due Diligence on Agents/Outlets.* Haider failed to ensure that MoneyGram conducted adequate due diligence on prospective agents, or existing agents seeking to open additional outlets, which resulted in, among other things, MoneyGram (1) granting outlets to agents who had previously been terminated by other money transmission companies and (2) granting additional outlets to agents who MoneyGram personnel knew or suspected were involved in fraud and/or money laundering.

Pursuant to 31 C.F.R. § 103.125, and AML Compliance Officer must, among other things, ensure that (1) "[t] he properly filed reports ... in accordance with applicable requirements of [31 C/F/R/ Part 103]"; (2) "[t] he compliance program is updated as necessary to reflect current requirements of [31 C.F.R. Part 103], and related guidance issued by the Department of the Treasury; and (3) "provides appropriate training and education in accordance with [31 C.F.R. § 103.125(d)(3)]." In late 2004, FinCEN issues "Interpretive Release 2004-01" through which it clarified that, pursuant to 31 C.F.R. 103.125, a Money Services Businesses that do business through agents or counterparties located outside of the United must implement and maintain as part of their AML program risk-based policies, procedures, and controls designed to identify and minimize money laundering and terrorist financing risks associated with such foreign agents and counterparties.

As a result of Haider's AML failures, agents and outlets that MoneyGram personnel knew or suspected were involved in fraud and/or money laundering were allowed to continue to use MoneyGram's money transfer system to facilitate their fraudulent schemes. Haider's failures resulted in MoneyGram's customers suffering substantial losses.

As a result of Haider's failures, FinCEN has assessed a civil money penalty against him for $1 million. The Government seeks an order reducing FinCEN's assessment to judgment, and awarding the Government judgment against Haider in the amount of $1 million. The Government also seeks an order enjoining Haider from participating, directly or indirectly, in the conduct of the affairs of any financial institution that is located in the United States or conducts business within the United States, for a term of years sufficient to prevent future harm to the public.

Rich Ex. Rel. Fuqi International Inc. v. Chong
66.3d 963 (Del. Ch. 2013)

Glasscock, Vice Chancellor:

I. OVERVIEW

The Plaintiff here, a stockholder, made a demand to the Defendant Corporation, asking the corporation to prosecute claims against its officers and directors for violating their *Caremark* duties. The individual Defendants not only failed to respond to the demand over the next two years, but also allegedly took actions making a meaningful response to the demand unlikely if not impossible. Under these facts, the Plaintiff may pursue an action on behalf of the corporation derivatively, notwithstanding Court of Chancery Rule 23.1.

This Opinion concerns a motion brought by Defendant Fuqi International, Inc. and its directors to dismiss a derivative complaint alleging breaches of fiduciary duty. Fuqi, a Delaware entity whose sole asset is stock of a Chinese jewelry company, completed a public offering in the United States in 2009. In March 2010, Fuqi announced the need for restatement of its 2009 financial statements. Following this announcement, Fuqi disclosed additional problems it had, including the transfer of $120 million of cash out of the company to third parties in China. In July 2010, Plaintiff George Rich, Jr., a Fuqi stockholder, made a demand to the board of directors to remedy breaches of fiduciary duty and weaknesses in Fuqi's internal controls. Fuqi's Audit Committee commenced an investigation, which was abandoned in January 2012 upon management's failure to pay the fees of the Audit Committee's advisors. Fuqi's independent directors have since resigned.

Plaintiff Rich brought this action in June 2012, alleging breaches of fiduciary duty under *Caremark*. Now, the Defendants have moved to dismiss the Complaint under Rule 23.1, because the Fuqi board has not yet rejected the Plaintiff's demand. Having found that the Plaintiff has pled particularized facts that raise a reasonable doubt that the directors acted in good faith in response to the demand, I deny the Rule 23.1 Motion. Second, Fuqi moved to dismiss under Rule 12(b)(6) for failure to state a claim upon which relief can be granted. Notwithstanding the well-known difficulty of prevailing on a *Caremark* claim, the Plaintiff has pled facts that, assumed true, lead me to reasonably infer that the Fuqi directors knew that its internal controls were deficient, yet failed to act. Therefore, I deny the Motion to Dismiss under Rule

12(b)(6). Finally, the Defendant has moved to dismiss or stay this case under the *McWane* doctrine, in favor of several prior-filed cases in New York. I deny that Motion as well, because I doubt that courts sitting in New York have personal jurisdiction over the Defendants.

In summary, the Defendants' Motion to Dismiss or Stay this case is denied.

II. BACKGROUND FACTS

Fuqi's primary operations are conducted through a wholly-owned subsidiary, Fuqi International Holdings Co., Ltd., a British Virgin Islands corporation ("Fuqi BVI") and its wholly owned subsidiary, Shenzhen Fuqi Jewelry Co., Ltd. ("Fuqi China"), a company established under the laws of China.

On March 16, 2010, Fuqi announced that its fourth quarter 10-Q and 10-K for 2009 would be delayed because Fuqi had discovered "certain errors related to the accounting of the Company's inventory and cost of sales." The press release stated that the errors identified were expected to have a material impact on Fuqi's previously issued quarterly financial statements for 2009 and that "at least one of the identified deficiencies ... constitutes a material weakness...." This press release was followed by another dated April 7, 2010, in which Fuqi disclosed that it had received a notification letter from NASDAQ that Fuqi was no longer in compliance with NASDAQ rules requiring the timely filing of SEC reports. On September 8, 2010, Fuqi announced that the SEC had initiated a formal investigation into Fuqi, related to Fuqi's failure to file timely periodic reports, among other matters.

After Fuqi announced that its 2009 financial statements needed restatement, Fuqi stockholders filed several securities and derivative lawsuits on behalf of Fuqi against the Individual Defendants in federal and state courts. Ten securities class action lawsuits were filed in the United States District Court for the Southern District of New York within weeks of the March 16, 2010 press release. Three derivative suits were filed on behalf of Fuqi in April 2010, two in federal court and one in New York State court. The derivative suits allege that the directors and certain officers of Fuqi breached their fiduciary duties by failing to adequately supervise and control Fuqi, which resulted in the filing of false financial statements. Each of the claims brought in federal court—including the derivative actions and the securities class actions— were subsequently consolidated for discovery purposes on July 26, 2010 (the "Federal Action"), and a lead plaintiff was selected. The parties to the Federal Action agreed that the plaintiffs would file an amended complaint in that action after Fuqi files its restated financial statements. Fuqi has not yet filed audited financial statements, so the Federal Action remains stayed. At oral argument, the parties noted that very little has been done so far in the Federal Action since the case has been stayed. With regard to the derivative claims, most relevant for this Court's purposes, the defendants have not all been served in the Federal Action.

On July 19, 2010, Plaintiff Rich made a demand to the Fuqi Board to commence an action against certain directors and executive officers of Fuqi (the "Demand Letter"). The Demand Letter asked the board of directors to "take action to remedy breaches of fiduciary duties by the directors and certain executive officers of the Company" as well as to "correct the deficiencies in the Company's internal controls that allowed the misconduct to occur." The Demand Letter also informed the board that if Fuqi did not respond to the letter within a reasonable period, the Plaintiff would commence a stockholder derivative action on behalf of Fuqi. Fuqi never responded to the Demand Letter in writing.

On October 29, 2010, Fuqi announced the appointment of Kim K.T. Pan as a new independent member of the board of directors. In response to the demand, the directors formed a "Special Internal Investigation Committee" and appointed Pan and Chen to serve as its members (the "Special Committee"). The board authorized the Special Committee to retain experts and advisors to investigate whether the claims in the demand were meritorious. Disclosure of the Special Committee's formation was the only information Fuqi ever disclosed to the stockholders regarding the Special Committee. The Plaintiff contends that the Special Committee "never conducted any investigation or any other activity during its short-lived existence." Furthermore, by March 2012 the Special Committee effectively ceased to exist after losing both of its members, Pan and Chen, due to Chen's resignation and Pan's appointment as CEO.

B. *Caremark* Claim

The Plaintiff alleges that Fuqi's directors are liable for failure to oversee the operations of the corporation. Fuqi argues that the Complaint fails to plead facts that show that the directors "consciously and in bad faith failed to implement any reporting or accounting system or controls." Such claims for bad-faith failure to monitor are known colloquially as "*Caremark* actions." The Defendants have moved to dismiss the action against the board generally. Because they have not articulated that claims against the Individual Defendants should be dismissed on a defendant-by-defendant basis, I refrain from undertaking that analysis.

The essence of a *Caremark* claim is a breach of the duty of loyalty arising from a director's bad-faith failure to exercise oversight over the company. A *Caremark* claim is "possibly the most difficult theory in corporation law upon which a plaintiff might hope to win a judgment." I am conscious of the need to prevent hindsight from dictating the result of a *Caremark* action; a bad outcome, without more, does not equate to bad faith. To survive a motion to dismiss, the plaintiff must plead facts that allow a reasonable inference that the defendants breached their fiduciary duties.

In *Stone v. Ritter*,[8] the Supreme Court clarified that *Caremark* claims are breaches of the duty of loyalty, as opposed to care, preconditioned on a finding of bad faith. The Supreme Court affirmed this Court's language in *Caremark* holding that "only a sustained or systematic failure of the board to exercise oversight — such as an utter failure to attempt to assure a reasonable information and reporting system exists — will establish the lack of good faith that is a necessary condition to liability." Demonstrating lack of good faith is the reef upon which most *Caremark* claims founder.

---

8. [*Stone v. Ritter*, 911 A.2d 362 (Del. 2006). — Ed.]

There are two possible scenarios in which a plaintiff can successfully assert a *Caremark* claim. The Supreme Court described these scenarios as being either:

> (a) the directors utterly failed to implement any reporting or information system or controls, or (b) having implemented such a system or controls, consciously failed to monitor or oversee its operations thus disabling themselves from being informed of risks or problems requiring their attention.

Under either scenario, a finding of liability is conditioned on a plaintiff's showing that the directors knew they were not fulfilling their fiduciary duties. "Where directors fail to act in the face of a known duty to act, thereby demonstrating a conscious disregard for their responsibilities, they breach their duty of loyalty by failing to discharge that fiduciary obligation in good faith." Examples of directors' "disabling themselves from being informed" include a corporation's lacking an audit committee, or a corporation's not utilizing its audit committee.

The defendant directors, officers, and employees each moved to dismiss the complaint. In deciding whether the complaint should be dismissed, then-Vice Chancellor Strine illustrated the effect of the requirement, under 12(b)(6), that he draw all reasonable inferences in favor of the plaintiffs:

> Although the Stockholder Plaintiffs provide detailed allegations about the illegal transactions and schemes that proliferated at AIG, they are not able to tie all of the defendants directly with the specific facts to all of the schemes. In some instances ... the Complaint only outlines the misconduct that occurred, or pleads the involvement of other [defendants]. But, as discussed above, this is a motion to dismiss, and thus I must grant the Stockholder Plaintiffs the benefit of all reasonable inferences. Even the transactions that cannot be tied to specific defendants support the inference that, given the pervasiveness of the fraud, [the defendants] knew that AIG was engaging in illegal conduct.

The Court explained that, if the case was analyzed under Rule 23.1, certain defendants would be "well positioned" to argue that the complaint needed more specifics to adequately plead knowledge on the part of the defendants. However, because the Court decided the case under Rule 12(b)(6) and because of the pervasiveness and materiality of the alleged fraud, the Court inferred that the defendants knew that AIG's internal controls were inadequate. For the purposes of a 12(b)(6) motion to dismiss, the Court inferred that "even when [the defendants] were not directly complicitous in the wrongful schemes, they were aware of the schemes and knowingly failed to stop them." I find the Court's analysis in AIG helpful here. My analysis follows.

a. Fuqi Had No Meaningful Controls in Place.

One way a plaintiff may successfully plead a *Caremark* claim is to plead facts showing that a corporation had no internal controls in place. Fuqi had some sort of compliance system in place. For example, it had an Audit Committee and submitted financial statements to the SEC in 2009. However, accepting the Plaintiff's allegations as true, the mechanisms Fuqi had in place appear to have been woefully inadequate.

In its press releases, Fuqi has detailed its extensive problems with internal controls. For example, Fuqi disclosed its "incorrect and untimely recordkeeping of inventory movements of retail operation." Problems with inventory are particularly troubling here, because Fuqi is a jewelry company, specializing in precious metals and gemstones, which are valuable and easily stolen. Nonetheless, the Fuqi directors allowed the corporation to operate few to no controls over these vulnerable assets. Fuqi's self-disclosed accounting inadequacies include:

> (i) incorrect carve-out of the retail segment from the general ledger; (ii) unrecorded purchases and accounts payable; (iii) inadvertent inclusion of consigned inventory; (iv) incorrect and untimely recordkeeping of inventory movements of retail operation; and (v) incorrect diamond inventory costing, unrecorded purchases and unrecorded accounts payable.

These disclosures lead me to believe that Fuqi had no meaningful controls in place. The board of directors may have had regular meetings, and an Audit Committee may have existed, but there does not seem to have been any regulation of the company's operations in China. Nonetheless, even if I were to find that Fuqi had some system of internal controls in place, I may infer that the board's failure to monitor that system was a breach of fiduciary duty.

b. The Board of Directors Ignored Red Flags.

As the Supreme Court held in *Stone v. Ritter*, if the directors have implemented a system of controls, a finding of liability is predicated on the directors' having "consciously failed to monitor or oversee [the system's] operations thus disabling themselves from being informed of risks or problems requiring their attention." One way that the plaintiff may plead such a conscious failure to monitor is to identify "red flags," obvious and problematic occurrences that support an inference that the Fuqi directors knew that there were material weaknesses in Fuqi's internal controls and failed to correct such weaknesses. It is unclear how far back in time Fuqi's internal controls have been inadequate. At the very least, the Fuqi board had several "warnings" that all was not well with the internal controls as far back as March 2010.

First, Fuqi was a preexisting Chinese company that gained access to the U.S. capital markets through the Reverse Merger. Thus, Fuqi's directors were aware that there may be challenges in bringing Fuqi's internal controls into harmony with the U.S. securities reporting systems. Notwithstanding that fact, according to the Complaint, the directors did nothing to ensure that its reporting mechanisms were accurate. Second, the board knew that it had problems with its accounting and inventory processes by March 2010 at the latest, because it announced that the 2009 financial statements would need restatement at that time. In the same press release, Fuqi also acknowledged the likelihood of material weaknesses in its internal controls. Third, Fuqi received a letter from NASDAQ in April 2010 warning Fuqi that it would face delisting if Fuqi did not bring its reporting requirements up to date with the SEC.

It seems reasonable to infer that, because of these "red flags," the directors knew that there were deficiencies in Fuqi's internal controls. Furthermore, NASDAQ's letter to Fuqi put the board on notice that these deficiencies risked serious adverse consequences. The directors acknowledged as much in their March 2010 press release.

An analysis of the dates of Fuqi's disclosures demonstrates that it is reasonable, based on the facts pled, to infer that the directors knew that the internal controls were inadequate and failed to act in the face of a known duty. Fuqi announced to stockholders that it was restating its 2009 financial statements and investigating possible "material weaknesses" in its controls in March 2010. Rich sent the Demand Letter in July 2010, and the board appointed the Special Committee in October 2010. In March 2011, Fuqi announced that the cash transfer transactions had occurred between September 2009 and November 2010.

These dates indicate that (1) Fuqi's directors knew that there were material weaknesses in Fuqi's internal controls at the latest in March of 2010; (2) Rich's stockholder demand in July 2010 (as well as the myriad securities litigation suits filed) put the directors on notice that the stockholders would carefully scrutinize what was going on at Fuqi; (3) Fuqi had purportedly already begun to "act" on Rich's demand by November 2010; and (4) despite their knowledge of the weaknesses in Fuqi's internal controls, the directors allowed $130 million in cash to be transferred out of the company, some as late as November 2010. The Plaintiffs have derived these facts directly from Fuqi's public disclosures. Facially, these disclosures are enough to allow me to reasonably infer scienter on the part of the Defendants.

That these cash transfers were not discovered until March of 2011, when Fuqi's auditor discovered them, reinforces the inference that the internal controls were (and possibly still are) grossly inadequate. That Chong was able to transfer $130 million out of the company's coffers, without the directors knowing about it for over a year, strains credulity. Either the directors knew about the cash transfers and were complicit, or they had zero controls in place and did not know about them. If the directors had even the barest framework of appropriate controls in place, they would have prevented the cash transfers.

When faced with knowledge that the company controls are inadequate, the directors must act, i.e., they must prevent further wrongdoing from occurring. A conscious failure to act, in the face of a known duty, is a breach of the duty of loyalty. At the very least, it is inferable that even if the Defendants were not complicit in these money transfers, they were aware of the pervasive, fundamental weaknesses in Fuqi's controls and knowingly failed to stop further problems from occurring. This knowing failure, as alleged by the Plaintiff, states a claim for breach of the duty of good faith under *Caremark*.

Finally, as then-Vice Chancellor Lamb explained in *David B. Shaev Profit Sharing Account v. Armstrong*, failing to establish an audit committee or failing to utilize an existing audit committee are examples of directors' "disabling themselves from being informed." Fuqi management's failure to pay the fees of the Audit Committee's advisors is a deliberate failure to utilize the Audit Committee. Therefore, I may infer that the board has disabled itself from being informed.

For the reasons above, I find that the Plaintiff has stated a claim under Caremark upon which relief can be granted.

IV. CONCLUSION

Having found that the Plaintiff pled particularized facts that raise a reasonable doubt that the directors acted in good faith in failing to respond to the demand, I deny the Motion to Dismiss under Rule 23.1. Likewise, I deny the Defendants' Motion to Dismiss under Rule 12(b)(6) because the Plaintiff has pled facts that, when assumed true, lead me to reasonably infer that the Fuqi directors knew that its internal controls were deficient, and failed to correct such deficiencies. Finally, I deny the Defendants' Motion to Stay or Dismiss under McWane, as well, because I doubt that courts sitting in New York have personal jurisdiction over the Defendants. In summary, the Defendants' Motion to Dismiss or Stay this case is DENIED. An appropriate order accompanies this Opinion.

———————

Financial Crimes Enforcement Network is following through on its promises to increasingly hold individuals responsible for lapses in corporate controls.

- **FINRA Fines Brown Brothers Harriman A Record $8 Million for Substantial Anti-Money Laundering Compliance Failures.** In February 2014, Financial Industry Regulatory Authority fined Harold Crawford, Brown Brothers Harriman's Global anti-money-laundering compliance officer. BBH did not have an adequate supervisory system to prevent the distribution of unregistered securities. BBH's former Global AML Compliance Officer Harold Crawford was also fined $25,000 and suspended for one month.

  Complaint:

  1. BBH and Crawford failed to establish and implement an adequate AML program, in violation of NASD Rule 3011(a) and FINRA Rules 3310(a) and 2010.

     a. Throughout the relevant period, Crawford, as the Firm's Global AML Compliance Officer, was responsible for ensuring that the AML program was adequately tailored to the Firm's business and appropriately monitoring, detecting, and reporting suspicious activity. In addition, Crawford managed the Firm's AML staff, was personally, or through his designee, responsible for making determination as to whether to file SARs on behalf of the Firm and was ultimately responsible for establishing and implementing a program reasonably excepted to detect and cause the reporting of suspicious activity when appropriate.

Organizing the Compliance/Ethics Committee

Based on the Board of Directors resolution to create the compliance/ethics committee, the following members should constitute the compliance/ethics committee: the CEO/President, the General Counsel, the Chief Financial Officer, the Internal

Audit Director and the VP of Human Resources. Optional members of the compliance/ethics committee may include the following: the Director of Information Technology, Vice President for Business Development, Vice President for Sales and Marketing, and Director of Environmental, Health and Safety.

Creating a Mission Statement for the Compliance Program by the Compliance/Ethics Committee

First, the compliance/ethics committee should evaluate the current state of the corporation against best practices to define the mission statement and goals of the compliance program. Then, the compliance/ethics committee should create a mission statement for the compliance program. This mission statement should be brief and delineate the goals of the compliance program. The mission statement should be written in plain English, user-friendly and suitable for all employees regardless of location and industry line. There also should be a letter prepared by the CEO/President to accompany the mission statement. This letter should reinforce the importance of the mission statement and demonstrate that the CEO/President is leading the rollout of the compliance program. This also ensures "tone at the top" support. The mission statement should, ultimately, align with the code of conduct and the corporate compliance program guidelines when they are created.

Establishing the Selection Criteria for the Compliance Officer by the Compliance/Ethics Committee

Next, the compliance/ethics committee should establish the criteria for the selection of the compliance officer based on the goals of the compliance program, the mission statement of the compliance program, the letter from the CEO/President, and the anticipated responsibilities of the compliance officer in achieving these goals and mission of the compliance program. The selection criteria for the compliance officer should include the following: knowledge of the industry; knowledge of compliance and applicable international, federal, state and local laws and regulations; knowledge of best practices in compliance; high-level experience in compliance; known for integrity and high ethical standards; auditing and monitoring skills; investigation skills; leadership and teambuilding skills; communications skills; and cross-cultural awareness. These selection criteria can be used in the future as the basis for creating the job description in the corporate compliance program guidelines.

Selecting the Compliance Officer by the Compliance/Ethics Committee

Using the above-adapted criteria, the compliance officer should be selected from within or outside the corporation. The compliance officer should be selected through an interview process that includes background searches and reference checks conducted by the human resources department in conjunction with the compliance/ethics committee. A designated member of the compliance/ethics committee in coordination can lead this process with an outside service provider and/or the in-house human resources department. Use of internet postings and referrals from compliance/ethics organizations such as the Society for Corporate Compliance and Ethics and Ethics Officers Association are excellent starting points.

Creating a Budgeting and Staffing Proposal for the Compliance Office by the Compliance/ Ethics Committee

Adequate budgeting and staffing are critical to the success of an effective compliance program. Even before the compliance office can be set up, there must be a tentative budget and staffing allocation for the compliance office. This should be proposed by the compliance/ethics committee based on the goals of the compliance program and the mission statement for the compliance program. Sufficient funding and staffing can be determined by looking at best practices in other comparable corporations as well as various studies conducted by such organizations as the Ethics Officers Association. Further, the human resources and finance department should be enlisted to help determine the costs of setting up a new department within the corporation.

Passing Resolutions by the Board of Directors and/or Audit Committee of the Board to Approve the Mission Statement, Approve the Appointment of the Compliance Officer, and Authorize the Budget and Staffing of the Compliance Office

Once the mission statement has been crafted, the compliance officer has been selected, and the budget and staffing proposal for the compliance office has been recommended, the next step is for the compliance/ethics committee to request that the Board of Directors and/or the Audit Committee of the Board of Directors pass resolutions to approve the mission statement, appoint the compliance officer, and adopt the budget and staffing allocations. This is a critical step in creating Board oversight of the compliance program under the *Caremark* decision.[9] Further, the passage of Board resolutions on the mission statement, the appointment of the compliance officer the approval of the adoption of the budget and staffing creates the foundation for the compliance office.

Once the Board resolutions are passed, the compliance office will be on a firm foundation to create the compliance office. The continued utility of the compliance/ ethics committee depends upon the culture of the company and whether such a committee will enhance the effectiveness of the corporate compliance program. For the purpose of this chapter, it is anticipated that the compliance/ethics committee will expire once the corporate compliance guidelines establishing the compliance office are adopted. However, the example in Part III of the Corporate Compliance Program Guidelines anticipates continuing the compliance/ethics committee.

Installing the Compliance Officer

Once the Board resolution appointing the Compliance Officer is passed by the Board of Directors and/or Audit Committee of the Board of Directors, the next step is installing the Compliance Officer in the Compliance Office. The Compliance Officer should preferably have his or her own office since confidential information, such as hotline complaints and reports, will be sent to the Compliance Officer to review. The Compliance Officer should have access to locked drawers and shredding machines. Security of information is vital to maintaining the integrity and confidentiality necessary to implement and administer an effective compliance program.

Creating the Work plan for the Compliance Program

The compliance officer should create a work plan for the rollout of the compliance program. If the compliance/ethics committee still exists, it should be consulted in creating the work plan. The work plan should show the phases necessary for the completion of the rollout phase of the compliance program as well as the expected timeframe. The progress on the work plan should be tracked and the work plan should be updated on a monthly basis. Work plans are important to making the process of implementing the compliance program transparent. It helps employees and management feel more comfortable with what to expect as the compliance program is rolled out.

The corporate compliance program should be fully rolled out within a one-year period, or as soon as practical, of the Board resolution to implement the compliance program, depending upon the size and location of the corporation. For example, if multiple languages and industries are covered globally, the program launch would

---

9. *See In re Caremark Int'l,* 698 A.2d 959 (Del. Ch. 1996).

probably take a longer time than the launch of a program in one country, in one language and in one industry.

The work plan should include the timing for the best practice/risk assessment, the establishment of the hotline, the development of the code of conduct, the development of policies and procedures, the launching of the training schedule, and the rollout of the auditing, monitoring and reporting systems. The work plan is the essential timetable for project managing the delivery of the completed compliance program.

Creating the Corporate Compliance Program Guidelines to Establish the Compliance Office

The final and important step in setting up the compliance office and defining the role of the compliance officer is creating the corporate compliance program guidelines. This is a significant step because it formalizes the compliance office and its functions and makes these functions transparent. An effective compliance program is not the result of a particular compliance officer since compliance officers can be changed through promotion, termination, illness or death. An effective compliance program is the result of establishing the compliance office so that it is not run on the whim of any individual but the result of transparent and thoughtful process. The corporate compliance program guidelines, along with the code of conduct, should be posted on the company intranet and available to every employee. The corporate compliance program guidelines should include job descriptions explaining the duties and responsibilities of all parties involved in the administration of the compliance function, including, but not limited to, the following: Board of Directors, Board Audit Committee, Compliance Executive Team, President/Chief Executive Officer, Chief Compliance Officer, Chief Human Resource Officer, Compliance Program Team, Deputy Compliance Officer for Operations, Deputy Compliance Officer for Intellectual Property, Deputy Compliance Officer for Employment, Deputy Compliance Officer for Antitrust, Division Compliance Officers, Operating Company Compliance Officers, Operating Company Board of Directors, Operating Company Chief Executive Officers, Compliance Department Coordinator/Paralegal, Compliance Office Ethics Committee, Managers, and Employees.

Further, the following areas need to be addressed in the corporate compliance program guidelines: establishing standards, procedures and internal controls; aligning the mission statement, code of conduct, policies and procedures and employee handbook; implementing background check methodology; setting up the hotline; creating a document management system; training on the code of conduct, policies and procedures; monitoring, auditing and reporting; creating annual assessments on the compliance program; commencing and conducting of internal or external investigations; reporting to senior management, the Board of Directors, and/or the Audit Committee of the Board of Directors on the corporate compliance program; reporting violations to the government; issuing public disclosures; setting up consistent incentives and disciplinary processes; modifying and reviewing the corporate compliance program on a regular basis for continual renewal. Other areas should be considered as needed.

Alternatively, it may be appropriate to establish separate investigation guidelines at the time of the establishment of the Compliance Office.

Additionally, Department of Justice Criminal Division created a Resource Guide to understand the Foreign Corrupt Practices Act (FCPA). This Resource Guide, in Chapter 5 Guiding Principles of Enforcement, provides guidance on the Hallmarks of an Effective Compliance Program. This guidance is provided for FCPA compliance programs; however, it provides helpful best practices applicable to any compliance program.

U.S. Department of Justice Criminal Division & SEC Enforcement Division, Resource Guide to the U.S. Foreign Corrupt Practices Act

http://www.justice.gov/sites/default/files/criminal-fraud/legacy/2015/01/16/guide.pdf

Hallmarks of Effective Compliance Programs

Individual companies may have different compliance needs depending on their size and the particular risks associated with their businesses, among other factors. When it comes to compliance, there is no one-size-fits-all program.

Thus, the discussion below is meant to provide insight into the aspects of compliance programs that DOJ and SEC assess, recognizing that companies may consider a variety of factors when making their own determination of what is appropriate for their specific business needs. Indeed, small- and medium-size enterprises likely will have different compliance programs from large multi-national corporations, a fact DOJ and SEC take into account when evaluating companies' compliance programs.

Compliance programs that employ a "check-the-box" approach may be inefficient and, more importantly, ineffective. Because each compliance program should be tailored to an organization's specific needs, risks, and challenges, the information provided below should not be considered a substitute for a company's own assessment of the corporate compliance program most appropriate for that particular business organization. In the end, if designed carefully, implemented earnestly, and enforced fairly, a company's compliance program—no matter how large or small the organization—will allow the company generally to prevent violations, detect those that do occur, and remediate them promptly and appropriately.

Commitment from Senior Management and a Clearly Articulated Policy Against Corruption

Within a business organization, compliance begins with the board of directors and senior executives setting the proper tone for the rest of the company. Managers and employees take their cues from these corporate leaders. Thus, DOJ and SEC consider the commitment of corporate leaders to a "culture of compliance" and look to see if this high-level commitment is also reinforced and implemented by middle managers and employees at all levels of a business. A well-designed compliance program that is not enforced in good faith, such as when corporate management explicitly or implicitly encourages employees to engage in misconduct to achieve business objectives, will be ineffective. DOJ and SEC have often encountered companies with compliance programs that are strong on paper but that nevertheless have significant FCPA violations because management has failed to effectively implement the program even in the face of obvious signs of corruption. This may be the result of aggressive sales staff preventing compliance personnel from doing their jobs effectively and of senior management, more concerned with securing a valuable business opportunity than enforcing a culture of compliance, siding with the sales team. The higher the financial stakes of the transaction, the greater the temptation for management to choose profit over compliance.

A strong ethical culture directly supports a strong compliance program. By adhering to ethical standards, senior managers will inspire middle managers to reinforce those standards. Compliant middle managers, in turn, will encourage employees to strive to attain those standards throughout the organizational structure.

In short, compliance with the FCPA and ethical rules must start at the top. DOJ and SEC thus evaluate whether senior management has clearly articulated company standards, communicated them in unambiguous terms, adhered to them scrupulously, and disseminated them throughout the organization.

Code of Conduct and Compliance Policies and Procedures

A company's code of conduct is often the foundation upon which an effective compliance program is built. As DOJ has repeatedly noted in its charging documents, the most effective codes are clear, concise, and accessible to all employees and to those conducting business on the company's behalf. Indeed, it would be difficult to effectively implement a compliance program if it was not available in the local language so that employees in foreign subsidiaries can access and understand it. When assessing a compliance program, DOJ and SEC will review whether the company has taken steps to make certain that the code of conduct remains current and effective and whether a company has periodically reviewed and updated its code.

Whether a company has policies and procedures that outline responsibilities for compliance within the company, detail proper internal controls, auditing practices, and documentation policies, and set forth disciplinary procedures will also be considered by DOJ and SEC. These types of policies and procedures will depend on the size and nature of the business and the risks associated with the business.

Effective policies and procedures require an in-depth understanding of the company's business model, including its products and services, third-party agents, customers, government interactions, and industry and geographic risks. Among the risks that a company may need to address include the nature and extent of transactions with foreign governments, including payments to foreign officials; use of third parties; gifts, travel, and entertainment expenses; charitable and political donations; and facilitating and expediting payments. For example, some companies with global operations have created web-based approval processes to review and approve routine gifts, travel, and entertainment involving foreign officials and private customers with clear monetary limits and annual limitations. Many of these systems have built-in flexibility so that senior management, or in-house legal counsel, can be apprised of and, in appropriate circumstances, approve unique requests. These types of systems can be a good way to conserve corporate resources while, if properly implemented, preventing and detecting potential FCPA violations. Regardless of the specific policies and procedures implemented, these standards should apply to personnel at all levels of the company.

Oversight, Autonomy, and Resources

In appraising a compliance program, DOJ and SEC also consider whether a company has assigned responsibility for the oversight and implementation of a company's compliance program to one or more specific senior executives within an organization. Those individuals must have appropriate authority within the organization, adequate autonomy from management, and sufficient resources to ensure that the company's compliance program is implemented effectively. Adequate autonomy generally includes direct access to an organization's governing authority, such as the board of directors and committees of the board of directors (e.g., the audit committee).

Depending on the size and structure of an organization, it may be appropriate for day-to-day operational responsibility to be delegated to other specific individuals within a company. DOJ and SEC recognize that the reporting structure will depend on the size and complexity of an organization. Moreover, the amount of resources devoted to compliance will depend on the company's size, complexity, industry, geographical reach, and risks associated with the business. In assessing whether a company has reasonable internal controls, DOJ and SEC typically consider whether the company devoted adequate staffing and resources to the compliance program given the size, structure, and risk profile of the business.

Risk Assessment

Assessment of risk is fundamental to developing a strong compliance program, and is another factor DOJ and SEC evaluate when assessing a company's compliance program. One-size-fits-all compliance programs are generally ill-conceived and ineffective because resources inevitably are spread too thin, with too much focus on low risk markets and transactions to the detriment of high-risk areas. Devoting a disproportionate amount of time policing modest entertainment and gift-giving instead of focusing on large government bids, questionable payments to third-party consultants, or excessive discounts to resellers and distributors may indicate that a company's compliance program is ineffective. A $50 million contract with a government agency in a high-risk country warrants greater scrutiny than modest and routine gifts and entertainment.

Similarly, performing identical due diligence on all third party agents, irrespective of risk factors, is often counterproductive, diverting attention and resources away from those third parties that pose the most significant risks. DOJ and SEC will give meaningful credit to a company that implement in good faith a comprehensive, risk-based compliance program, even if that program does not prevent an infraction in a low risk area because greater attention and resources had been devoted to a higher risk area. Conversely, a company that fails to prevent an FCPA violation on an economically significant, high-risk transaction because it failed to perform a level of due diligence commensurate with the size and risk of the transaction is likely to receive reduced credit based on the quality and effectiveness of its compliance program.

As a company's risk for FCPA violations increases, that business should consider increasing its compliance procedures, including due diligence and periodic internal audits. The degree of appropriate due diligence is fact-specific and should vary based on industry, country, size, and nature of the transaction, and the method and amount of third-party compensation. Factors to consider, for instance, include risks presented by: the country and industry sector, the business opportunity, potential business partners, level of involvement with governments, amount of government regulation and oversight, and exposure to customs and immigration in conducting business affairs. When assessing a company's compliance program, DOJ and SEC take into account whether and to what degree a company analyzes and addresses the particular risks it faces.

Training and Continuing Advice

Compliance policies cannot work unless effectively communicated throughout a company. Accordingly, DOJ and SEC will evaluate whether a company has taken steps to ensure that relevant policies and procedures have been communicated throughout the organization, including through periodic training and certification for all directors, officers, relevant employees, and, where appropriate, agents and business partners. For example, many larger companies have implemented a mix of web-based and in-person training conducted at varying intervals. Such training typically covers company policies and procedures, instruction on applicable laws, practical advice to address real-life scenarios, and case studies. Regardless of how a company chooses to conduct its training, however, the information should be presented in a manner appropriate for the targeted audience, including providing training and training materials in the local language. For example, companies may want to consider providing different types of training to their sales personnel and accounting personnel with hypotheticals or sample situations that are similar to the situations they might encounter. In addition to the existence and scope of a company's training program, a company should develop appropriate measures, depending on the size and sophistication of the particular company, to provide guidance and advice on complying with the company's ethics and compliance program, including when such advice is needed urgently. Such measures will help ensure that the compliance program is understood and followed appropriately at all levels of the company.

Incentives and Disciplinary Measures

In addition to evaluating the design and implementation of a compliance program throughout an organization, enforcement of that program is fundamental to its effectiveness. A compliance program should apply from the board room to the supply room—no one should be beyond its reach. DOJ and SEC will thus consider whether, when enforcing a compliance program, a company has appropriate and clear disciplinary procedures, whether those procedures are applied reliably and promptly, and whether they are commensurate with the violation. Many companies have found that publicizing disciplinary actions internally, where appropriate under local law, can have an important deterrent effect, demonstrating that unethical and unlawful actions have swift and sure consequences.

DOJ and SEC recognize that positive incentives can also drive compliant behavior. These incentives can take many forms such as personnel evaluations and promotions, rewards for improving and developing a company's compliance program, and rewards for ethics and compliance leadership. Some organizations, for example, have made adherence to compliance a significant metric for management's bonuses so that compliance becomes an integral part of management's everyday concern. Beyond financial incentives, some companies have highlighted compliance within their organizations by recognizing compliance professionals and internal audit staff. Others have made working in the company's compliance organization a way to advance an employee's career.

SEC, for instance, has encouraged companies to embrace methods to incentivize ethical and lawful behavior:

> [M]ake integrity, ethics and compliance part of the promotion, compensation and evaluation processes as well. For at the end of the day, the most effective way to communicate that "doing the right thing" is a priority, is to reward it. Conversely, if employees are led to believe that, when it comes to compensation and career advancement, all that counts is short-term profitability, and that cutting ethical corners is an acceptable way of getting there, they'll perform to that measure. To cite an example from a different walk of life: a college football coach can be told that the graduation rates of his players are what matters, but he'll know differently if the sole focus of his contract extension talks or the decision to fire him is his win loss record.

No matter what the disciplinary scheme or potential incentives a company decides to adopt, DOJ and SEC will consider whether they are fairly and consistently applied across the organization. No executive should be above compliance, no employee below compliance, and no person within an organization deemed too valuable to be disciplined, if warranted. Rewarding good behavior and sanctioning bad behavior reinforces a culture of compliance and ethics throughout an organization.

Conclusion

Establishing an effective Compliance Office and Program has become necessary to protect any highly regulated organization. A Compliance Program protects an organization and its Officers and Directors by detecting, preventing, and promoting adherence to the organizations regulatory and ethical obligations. While one size does not fit all, the core components of an Effective Compliance Office and Program must exist. As a result, Compliance has evolved into a *culture* of conducting business and not solely adherence to policies and regulations.

Exhibit A to Chapter 5
Sample Corporate Compliance Program Guidelines
ABC, INC. CORPORATE COMPLIANCE PROGRAM GUIDELINES

Contents

I. OBJECTIVES OF ABC, INC. CORPORATE COMPLIANCE PROGRAM

II. CORPORATE COMPLIANCE GUIDELINES

III. ABC, INC. COMPLIANCE ORGANIZATION STRUCTURE

IV. PROGRAM ADMINISTRATION

- Purpose
- Board of Directors
  Audit Committee of the Board of Directors
- President/Chief Executive Officer
  Compliance Officer
  Compliance Department Coordinator/Paralegal
- Compliance Office
- Ethics Committee
- Managers
- Employees

V. STANDARDS AND PROCEDURES

VI. COMMUNICATION AND TRAINING

VII. EMPLOYMENT PRACTICES

VIII. MONITORING AND AUDITING

IX. OBLIGATION TO REPORT

X. INVESTIGATIONS

XI. CORRECTIVE ACTIONS AND RESPONSES TO VIOLATIONS

XII. COMPLIANCE REPORTS

XIII. REPORTS TO PRESIDENT/CEO, BOARD OF DIRECTORS, AUDIT COMMITTEE OF THE BOARD OF DIRECTORS, ETHICS COMMITTEE AND/OR GENERAL COUNSEL

XIV. REPORTING VIOLATIONS TO THE GOVERNMENT AND PUBLIC DISCLOSURE

XV. INCENTIVES

XVI. DISCIPLINARY ACTION

XVII. PROGRAM REVIEW AND MODIFICATION

XVIII. CODE OF ETHICS TRAINING AND DISCLOSURE

I. Objectives of ABC, Inc. Corporate Compliance Program

The objectives of the Corporate Compliance Program (the "Program") are to ensure that ABC, Inc. and its subsidiaries ("ABC") implement and maintain compliance policies and procedures so that all employees conducting business on behalf of ABC comply with applicable laws and regulations and with the ABC Code of Ethics (the "Code").

The Corporate Compliance Program Guidelines ("Guidelines") set forth the structure, roles and responsibilities and are intended to assure that effective compliance systems are in place and functioning. For example, today ABC has encouraged compliance training and performs compliance audits in many functional areas such as environmental and quality audits under ISO 14001 and 9000/2000. These and other similar processes are not expected to change in connection with implementing the Program. ABC's existing compliance procedures and managerial structure should be considered the front line defense in preventing, detecting and correcting compliance issues. ABC's Compliance Office and the ABC Hot Line should be used if issues are not being resolved through normal channels.

II. Corporate Compliance Guidelines

To achieve the objectives of the Program, these Guidelines have been developed to define the structure and process for implementing and administrating the Program. These Guidelines serve as a framework and vehicle for implementing the Program. These Guidelines are intended to provide continued guidance to ABC and its employees. The Compliance Office, under the direction of the Compliance Officer, administers the Program.

These Guidelines provide the process for the administration of the Program. The Guidelines are being distributed to the Board of Directors, Audit Committee of the Board of Directors, President/Chief Executive Officer, Compliance Officer, Director of Corporate Communications, Compliance Department Coordinator/Paralegal, Ethics Committee, General Counsel, Director Human Resources and Chief Financial Officer, who will assist the Compliance Office in implementing and administering the Program. The Guidelines will be posted on the company intranet site for purposes of transparency. If you have questions regarding these Guidelines or the Program, contact the Compliance Office. (Add contact information here.)

III. ABC's Compliance Organization Structure

[Insert organizational structure.]

IV. Program Administration

Purpose

This section of the Guidelines defines the compliance responsibilities for the Program's administration among various groups and individuals within ABC that have compliance responsibilities.

Board of Directors

The Board of Directors has the following compliance related responsibilities:

- Abide by the Code;
- Demonstrate a strong commitment to the Program;
- Provide oversight regarding the overall Program effectiveness; and
- Review reports from the Compliance Officer regarding the status of the Program, corrective actions and improvement plans.

Audit Committee of the Board of Directors

The Audit Committee of the Board of Directors will oversee the effectiveness and the operation of the Program. The Audit Committee of the Board of Directors may invite non-members of the Committee and outside consultants to meet with the Audit Committee of the Board of Directors, as appropriate. The Audit Committee of the Board of Directors has the following responsibilities:

- Abide by the Code;
- Provide oversight regarding the Program's effectiveness and operation;
- Review periodic reports prepared by the Compliance Officer regarding the Program; and
- Periodically report to the Board of Directors regarding the Program as appropriate.

President/Chief Executive Officer

The President/CEO has the following compliance related responsibilities:

- Abide by the Code;
- Demonstrate a strong commitment to the Program;
- Provide oversight regarding the overall Program effectiveness;
- Review the status of the Program, corrective actions and improvement plans with the Compliance Officer as appropriate;
- Serve on the Ethics Committee; and
- Report as appropriate to the Board of Directors.
- Compliance Officer

The Compliance Officer has the following compliance related responsibilities:

Oversight

- Abide by the Code;
- Administrate and manage the Program;
- Ensure that appropriate action is taken on reports provided to the Compliance Office;
- Keep the President/CEO informed about the Program;
- Attend and report to the Board and/or Audit Committee of the Board of Directors at all meetings

- Coordinate and communicate with the Legal Department;
- Work with the Human Resources Department to ensure appropriate training programs are being implemented;
- Coordinate with the Finance Department to ensure auditing and monitoring of compliance programs
- Work with the Corporate Communications Department on rolling out and internal marketing of the Program
- Oversee the implementation of the compliance training sessions;
- Identify current and ongoing potential compliance issues;
- Ensure that the Human Resources Department is made appropriately aware of compliance issues, initiatives and corrective actions, so that they may appropriately fulfill their compliance responsibilities;
- Monitor with the Legal Department, federal, state, and local statutory and regulatory developments to update compliance related issues; and
- Ensure that the investigations are conducted in accordance with the ABC, Inc. Investigation Guidelines.

Program Improvements

- Oversee continual improvement of the Program through benchmarking, assessments, surveys, audits, best practice reviews and training; and
- Coordinate revisions to the Program.

Operations

- Communicate compliance messages (through such media as presentations, DVDs, person-to-person meetings, internet, and written materials);
- Oversee compliance monitoring efforts;
- Consult with Human Resources on disciplinary actions related to compliance;
- Implement mechanisms to facilitate compliance reporting by employees through the ABC Hot Line;
- Follow up on identified compliance issues received from the ABC Hot Line or other sources;
- Investigate or delegate the investigation as appropriate and document compliance issues;
- Provide corrective action to remedy violations of the law and/or the Code;
- Create, oversee and analyze employee assessments on risk areas such as antitrust; employment; environmental and OSHA; conflicts of interest; gifts and entertainment; travel and expenses; intellectual property; records retention; subcontractors, suppliers and distributors; and
- Provide reports on complaints to the Board of Directors, Audit Committee of the Board of Directors, and the Ethics Committee as appropriate.

Compliance Department Coordinator/Paralegal

The Compliance Department Coordinator/Paralegal has the following compliance related responsibilities:

- Abide by the Code;
- Support the compliance initiatives of the Compliance Officer;
- Coordinate with the Compliance Officer, Ethics Committee, Legal Department, Finance Department, Human Resources Department, and the Corporate Communications Department;
- Compile, analyze and report on all employee assessments for risk areas such as antitrust; employment; environmental and OSHA; conflicts of interest; gifts and entertainment; travel and expenses; intellectual property; records retention; subcontractors, suppliers and distributors;
- Analyze the overall compliance program process to enhance coordination;
- Provide an early warning as to any gaps in the compliance program, including issues involving reporting, violations of the law and/or the Code, training deficits, risk areas needing to be audited and best practices that should be integrated into the Program;
- Monitor the reports of various complaints based on violations of the law and/or the Code, including those made to the ABC Hot Line and the Human Resources Department;
- Notify all employees as to their specific training and assessment requirements and ensure that all applicable training sessions are completed;
- Research and analyze best practices in related companies;
- Coordinate distribution of the Code to the subcontractors, suppliers and distributors; and
- Research and analyze the ABC Hot Line brochure and protocols as necessary in coordination with the Compliance Officer.

Compliance Office

The role of the Compliance Office is to support the Compliance Officer and the performance of his or her compliance responsibilities. The Compliance Office will be staffed as necessary and appropriate.

Ethics Committee

The Ethics Committee is composed of the President/Chief Executive Officer, Chief Financial Officer, Vice President of Human Resources, General Counsel, Director of Corporate Communications, and Compliance Officer. The Ethics Committee has the following compliance related responsibilities:

- Provide oversight regarding the overall Program effectiveness;
- Meet at least quarterly;

- Review the status of the Program, corrective actions and improvement plans with the Compliance Office, as appropriate;
- Agree on a consensus of action regarding complaints concerning the Code and the Program; and
- Receive quarterly reports from the Compliance Officer on the ABC Hot Line.

Managers

Managers have the following compliance related responsibilities:

- Abide by Code;
- Support compliance initiatives by the Compliance Office and Compliance Officer;
- Work with the Compliance Office, Corporate Communications Department, Legal Department, Finance Department and/or Human Resource Department to provide guidance to subordinates on compliance related matters;
- Coordinate with Human Resources Department, and the Compliance Officer, to identify appropriate incentives and/or disciplinary/corrective actions;
- Support the Program by including compliance in the performance evaluation process; and
- Serve as a good example to others.

Employees

All Employees have the following compliance related responsibilities:

- Abide by the Code;
- Comply with appropriate laws and regulations affecting their responsibilities;
- Ask questions and seek the help of others, if uncertain;
- Report potential instances of non-compliance through established mechanisms; and
- Attend compliance-training sessions.

V. Principles of the Code and Program and Standard Operating Procedures

Principle

The Code and Program have been established to ensure and promote an ethical environment for ABC and its employees. This section provides references to Standard Operating Procedures that assist employees.

Standard Operating Procedures

The values and compliance standards of ABC are embodied in the Code. The Code is the cornerstone of the Program, and sets forth standards of conduct to which employees will be held.

The Code will be updated periodically to ensure continued compliance with applicable requirements and standards, and the Compliance Officer is responsible for ensuring that this is accomplished. More specific information and guidance can be found in the various sources of policies and procedures that are retained by the Human Resources Department.

VI. Communication and Training

Principle

The Code and the Program will be communicated to all employees. Effective communication and training facilitates employees' understanding of compliance responsibilities and the importance of complying with laws, regulations and the Code.

The goal of the communication and training process is to provide a continuing communication channel for compliance matters; to deliver compliance messages to employees; to train and educate employees about their compliance responsibilities and to support the Code and the Program. Communications and training to introduce the Program to employees will include presentations, DVDs, person-to-person meetings, website materials and written materials.

Standard Operating Procedures

Employees will receive communications on developments affecting the Code and the Program from the Compliance Office. The Compliance Office will coordinate, in a working group, with Human Resources to develop a comprehensive training and communication plan regarding the Code and the Program. Human Resources will keep the Compliance Officer informed as to compliance training and communication efforts for coordination and efficiency purposes.

All existing and new employees will receive the Code and training on the Program and the Code. The Compliance Office and Human Resources will document the compliance training. Human Resources will also ensure that all employees sign annual certifications that they have complied with the Code and provide the original certification to the Compliance Office to retain.

Meetings are an effective forum for training and conveying information and are useful for reinforcing compliance messages. Management is encouraged to add compliance topics to appropriate meeting agendas. The Compliance Office and Human Resources will be available to conduct presentations and training for various meetings.

VII. Employment Practices

Principle

ABC is committed to hiring employees consistent with the elements of an effective compliance program. Appropriate levels of background checks are performed for all new employees based on the position.

Standard Operating Procedures

Background Checks

Background checks will be performed for new employees with substantial discretionary authority to make decisions. Appropriate due diligence will be performed as a prerequisite for promotion of existing employees to positions with substantial discretionary authority, which may include background checks. ABC performs background checks in accordance with applicable law. The application process requires applicants to disclose any criminal conviction. The Human Resources Department will be responsible for performing background checks. Background checks may include 1) employment verification; 2) education verification; 3) reference checks; 4) credit checks; and 5) criminal convictions.

Exit Interviews

Human Resources may arrange exit interviews with those leaving ABC. The exit interview should identify if an individual's departure relates to a potential non-compliance issue in order to investigate activities or modify the Program.

VIII. Monitoring and Auditing

Principle

The purpose of monitoring is to ensure detection and deterrence of misconduct and promote corrective actions to foster continual improvement of the Program.

Standard Operating Procedures

The Compliance Office has primary responsibility for auditing, monitoring and reporting on the Compliance Program. This includes spot checks, onsite visits, routine audits, and ABC Hot Line reporting and audits of the compliance risk areas.

The Compliance Office will ensure the appropriate monitoring processes are in place for assessments of the Program in such areas as antitrust; compliance generally; conflicts of interest; employment; environment; gifts and entertainment; intellectual property; records retention; subcontractors, suppliers and distributors; security (including use of tangible property); and travel and expenses.

Since the Finance Department is an independent function established by ABC, it can also plan and execute a broad and comprehensive program of audits at the same time on related compliance areas. The Finance Department will assist the Compliance Office, where requested by the Compliance Office, to perform appropriate audits to review business practices for compliance with policies and procedures, including the Sarbanes Oxley Act of 2002. The Compliance Office will provide input to the Finance Department on compliance areas that need to be audited, and will coordinate the use of external compliance resources as necessary.

IX. Obligation to Report

Principle

ABC employees acting in good faith are required to report actual or potential violations of the law and/or the Code. There shall be no reprisals for any good faith report. ABC promotes open communication to resolve employee concerns about compliance and provides several reporting channels to their Managers.

Standard Operating Procedures

Means of Communication

Employees should communicate compliance questions or concerns to their Managers or to the Human Resources Department, Legal Department and/or Compliance

Office. Each of the aforementioned parties has a responsibility to communicate with the Compliance Office. Employees may also report actual or potential violations of the law and/or the Code to the ABC Hot Line.

ABC Hot Line

ABC has established the ABC Hot Line for use by all employees 24 hours a day, 7 days a week, available on a confidential basis. The ABC Hot Line does not replace existing means of communication (e.g., reporting to Managers). The ABC Hot Line should be used if an employee believes that compliance issues are not being resolved through existing channels.

Trained communication specialists answer calls to the ABC Hot Line. After reviewing the information given by the caller, the specialist may assign a control number to use as identification during follow-up, if the call is anonymous. A written report will be forwarded to the Compliance Officer. The Compliance Officer will be responsible for referring the matter to the appropriate function for investigation. Confidentiality will only be preserved where it will not interfere with the best interests of the Company. All reports of actual or potential non-compliance received will be documented.

Analysis of Reports

ABC assesses the effectiveness of the Program by monitoring the nature of reports received through various reporting channels for compliance matters. The Compliance Officer will monitor the frequency and nature of inquiries and respond appropriately through revised compliance policies, increased training or increased compliance auditing activity.

What to Report

Actual or potential violations of the law, regulations or the Code that employees believe are not being handled properly should be reported immediately, including but not limited to:

- Discrimination;
- Sexual Harassment;
- Workplace Violence;
- Substance Abuse;
- Destruction of property and theft;
- Conflicts of Interest;
- Gifts and Entertainment;
- Environmental;
- Antitrust;
- Confidentiality;
- Accuracy, retention and disposal of records;

- Personal use of ABC resources; and
- Bribes and Kickbacks.

X. Investigations

Principle

ABC is committed to responding appropriately to compliance issues that may constitute violations of law, regulations or the Code. To determine whether a violation has occurred requires a process, which involves significant judgment and should be based on the facts and circumstances.

Standard Operating Procedures

Actual or potential violations of law, regulations or the Code reported to Managers in the ordinary course of business will be investigated through established procedures as set forth in the ABC, Inc. Investigation Guidelines under the direction of the appropriate function or by an external agency where appropriate. The Compliance Officer will investigate or cause to be investigated by the appropriate function reports of actual or potential violations received by the Compliance Office.

The Compliance Officer or designated representative will coordinate and supervise the investigation. The Compliance Officer will maintain a record, with all supporting documentation. The record will be maintained in a secured file with limited access. A record of all files removed will also be maintained. The Compliance Officer, in coordination with the Legal Department, will determine the manner of investigation with consideration to preservation of the attorney-client privilege.

XI. Corrective Actions and Responses to Violations

Principle

The Program is designed to ensure that appropriate corrective action is taken whenever an investigation results in a determination that a violation has occurred.

Standard Operating Procedure

Corrective action resulting from investigations in the ordinary course of business will be implemented under the direction of the appropriate function. An investigation should be conducted or caused to be conducted by the Compliance Officer, in consultation with other functions, such as the Legal Department or Human Resources Department or externally, as appropriate. Corrective action should be taken to ensure that the violation or problem does not reoccur (or at a minimum reduce the likelihood that it will reoccur) and be based on an analysis of the root cause of the problem. In addition, the corrective action will include, whenever possible, a review of the effectiveness of the corrective action following its implementation. If such a review establishes that a corrective action plan has not been effective, then additional or new corrective actions will be designed and implemented.

Corrective actions may include, but are not limited to, the following: (1) informing and discussing with the offending employee, both the violation and how it should be avoided in the future; (2) providing remedial training (formal or informal) to ensure that the employee understands the applicable rules and regulations; (3) conducting a follow up review to ensure that the problem is not recurring; (4) conducting repeated cycles of remedial education and focused audits, and/or; (5) disciplining the offending employee, if necessary and as appropriate.

In addition, if it appears that a larger, systemic problem may exist, then possible modification or improvement of ABC's compliance business practices will be considered. Such action might include, for instance, creating new procedures, or modifying existing procedures, so as to ensure that similar errors will not reoccur in the Program. Possible changes or additions to procedures will be reviewed with the Compliance Officer, the President/CEO and the Ethics Committee, as appropriate. Other corrective actions might also include working with a specific function to formulate new or revised compliance policies or procedures for an area or department, and conducting formal or informal training on specific issues.

XII. Compliance Reports

Principle

The purpose is to establish adequate corporate information and reporting systems that are reasonably designed to provide the Compliance Officer, the President/CEO, and the Ethics Committee of ABC with timely and accurate information regarding actual or potential violations of laws and regulations of the Code.

Standard Operating Procedures

The Compliance Department Coordinator/Paralegal will be responsible for preparing Compliance Reports substantially in the form attached as Appendix A and submitting them to the Compliance Officer as soon as appropriate or sooner where serious threat to persons or property is presented. The Compliance Officer may change the frequency of reporting depending on the number of issues surfaced, the severity of issues reported, and other appropriate considerations.

XIII. Reports to the President/CEO, Board of Directors, Audit Committee of the Board of Directors, Ethics Committee and/or General Counsel

Principle

Some violations may require reporting to the President/CEO, Board of Directors, Audit Committee of the Board of Directors, Ethics Committee and/or General Counsel.

Standard Operating Procedures

In determining whether matters should be communicated to the President/CEO, Board of Directors, Audit Committee of the Board of Directors, Ethics Committee and/or General Counsel, consideration should be given to:

- Results of preliminary investigation;
- Pervasiveness of the issue;
- Severity of the issue;
- Criminal intent, and/or;
- Impact on the ABC® Brand, reputation or well-being.

XIV. Reporting Violations to the Government and Public Disclosure

Principle

ABC will report violations to government authorities and make disclosures as appropriate.

Standard Operating Procedures

Reports to government authorities resulting from investigation in the ordinary course of business should be handled through established procedures under the direction of the appropriate function.

When an investigation is conducted by the Compliance Officer, the Compliance Officer, in consultation with other functions as appropriate, will determine whether it is appropriate to report a matter to the government. The Compliance Officer will then present a recommendation to the President/CEO, and/or the Ethics Committee as appropriate. The Compliance Officer will coordinate with the Corporate Communications Department for all communications with the public, including disclosure to the government.

XV. Incentives

Principle

Incentives should be used to encourage employees to obey the law and the code since this promotes an ethical culture with in ABC.

Standard Operating Procedures

Human Resources, in consultation with the Compliance Office, will encourage managers to provide incentives to all employees for attending compliance training sessions, performing their duties with integrity, observing the law and adhering to the Code. Further, performance evaluations will include compliance as an area of appraisal and provide incentives and financial rewards for high ratings.

XVI. Disciplinary Action

Principle

Disciplinary action may be taken against employees who violate the law or the Code. The credibility of the Program rests on fair and impartial discipline for all employees.

Standard Operating Procedures

Human Resources, in consultation with the Compliance Office, will oversee all disciplinary actions arising from the investigative process. Remember, disciplinary action must be consistently applied. Examples of actions that may be taken for violations of laws or the Code are as follows:

- Retraining;
- Verbal reprimand;
- Written reprimand;
- Suspension from work with or without pay, and/or;
- Termination.

XVII. Program Review and Modification

Principle

Action regarding the Program must be conducted to ensure it is effective on a long-term basis in deterring, detecting and dealing with non-compliance. ABC will proactively evaluate the effectiveness of the Program and implement changes that are required to maintain its effectiveness. This includes reviewing revisions to government regulations, industry standards and practices as well as enforcement trends by regulatory agencies.

Standard Operating Procedures

The Compliance Officer is responsible for ensuring that the Program responds to changes in ABC's practices and procedures, business, new acquisitions or joint ventures, as well as new laws, regulations or industry trends. The Compliance Office will evaluate the results of the Program by monitoring and auditing activities, by performing risk assessments, reviewing trends in ABC's Hot Line reports, as well as other reported issues, to determine a need for developing or modifying compliance policies and procedures, the Code, these Guidelines or the Program. The Compliance Officer will oversee any modifications to these Guidelines and the Program.

XVIII. Code of Ethics Training and Disclosure Statement

Principle

Existing and new employees should participate in training sessions to enhance compliance with the Code and be asked to submit a disclosure statement as necessary.

Standard Operating Procedure

All employees should be required to participate in the compliance training sessions, whether live or via other mechanisms such as the Internet. At the end of these sessions, employees will be asked to disclose any circumstances that may result in violations of the law and/or the Code. Further, employees will be advised that they must report violations promptly whenever they know of any circumstances where a violation of the law and/or the Code has occurred. Such violations should be reported on the form attached as Appendix B. The employees are responsible for completing Appendix B and submitting it to Human Resources who will then submit it to the Compliance Office or directly to the Compliance Office.

Exhibit B to Chapter 5
PRIVATE & CONFIDENTIAL
ABC Compliance Report

Description of Compliance Issue:[1]

Date Compliance Issue Reported:

---

1. For Example: discrimination, sexual harassment, workplace violence, substance abuse, conflicts of interest, gifts and entertainment, political activities and contributions, antitrust, confidentiality, theft, bribes and kickbacks.

Compliance Issue Initially Reported to:[2]

Priority:[3]

Person Handling Issue:

Corrective Action Taken:[4]

Status of Issue:

Exhibit C to Chapter 5
ABC CODE OF ETHICS
DISCLOSURE STATEMENT

In accordance with my obligations under the ABC Code of Ethics, I disclose (*check all that apply*)

_____ To the best of my knowledge and belief, a possible violation of ABC Code of Ethics has occurred which was not previously disclosed.

_____ To the best of my knowledge and belief, a conflict of interest as described in the ABC Code of Ethics exists which I have not previously disclosed.

_____ Other.

Describe in full all facts related to the above disclosure:

_____

_____

_____

_____

Signature: _____

Print Name: _____

Date: _____

Exhibit D to Chapter 5
Sample Corporate Compliance Program Guidelines
ABC, INC. INVESTIGATION GUIDELINES

PURPOSE AND SCOPE

It is the intent of ABC, Inc. ("Company") to promote consistent awareness and behavior throughout the organization by providing guidelines and assigning respon-

---

2. MS = Manager: F = Functional Department (e.g., Human Resources, Legal, Finance): CO = Compliance Officer: HL = ABC Hotline.

3. A = Actual or potential violation of the law and/or the Code requiring immediate action; presents an immediate threat to a person or property; could result in significant reputational risk: B = Actual or potential violation of the law and/or the Code not requiring immediate action; not an immediate threat to person or property but could result in significant reputational risk: C = Compliance or ethics questions not requiring immediate response; response may require research.

4. For example: verbal warning, written warning, suspension with or without pay, rewrite policies and procedures, clarify the Code, employee retained, employee terminated, or investigation commenced.

sibility for the management and ownership of internal controls as well as guidance in conducting the investigation process.

The purpose of the ABC, Inc. Investigation Guidelines ("Investigation Guidelines") is to facilitate the development of internal controls, which will aid in the prevention and detection of potential violations of ABC's Code of Ethics ("Code") and/or policies and procedures.

These Investigation Guidelines apply to any violation of, or suspected violation of the Code and/or Company policies and procedures involving employees, consultants, vendors, contractors, customers, outside agencies doing business with employees of such agencies, and/or any other parties with a business relationship to the Company. Any investigative activity required will be conducted without regard to the suspected wrongdoer's length of service, position/title, or relationship to the Company.

These Investigation Guidelines include the investigation of criminal acts, fraud and any other acts that would warrant an investigation. Fraud is generally defined as the intentional, false representation or concealment of a material fact for the purpose of inducing another to act upon it to his or her injury.

Process owners and business group leaders are responsible for the detection and prevention of fraud, misappropriations, and other inappropriate conduct that may have adverse impact to the Company. All key process owners and leaders should be familiar with the types of improprieties that might occur within their area of responsibility, and be alert for any indication of irregularity.

ACTIONS THAT MAY WARRANT INVESTIGATION

Any actions contrary to the Code and/or Company policies and procedures include, *but are not limited to*:

- Actions contrary to the Code and/or Company policies and procedures;

- Any dishonest or fraudulent act;

- Forgery or alteration of any document of record (financial or otherwise) or account belonging to the Company;

- Misappropriation of funds, data or assets;

- Impropriety in the handling or reporting of cash, cash equivalents, data, and/or financial transactions;

- Profiteering as a result of insider knowledge of Company activities;

- Disclosing confidential and proprietary information to outside parties;

- Accepting or seeking anything of value from contractors, vendors or persons providing services/materials to the Company;

- Destruction, removal or inappropriate use of records, furniture, fixtures, and equipment; and

- Any criminal act.

REPORTING POTENTIAL VIOLATIONS & RESPONSIBILITIES

The Compliance Office or its designee has the primary responsibility for determining the nature and extent of internal or external investigations and coordinating such investigations. Any employee who suspects potential violations of the Code and/or Company policies and procedures should immediately notify one of the respective contacts below:

- The Compliance Officer, the General Counsel, Vice President Finance, Chief Information Officer and Treasurer are the designated lead contacts for any violations that are not related to employee relation matters;
- The Director of Human Resources is the designated lead for routine employee relations internal investigations (e.g., workplace harassment, workplace safety, discrimination); or
- The Hotline at 1-800-XXX-XXXX which is available 24 hours a day, seven days a week.

NO EMPLOYEE SHOULD ATTEMPT TO PERSONALLY CONDUCT INVESTIGATIONS, INTERVIEWS OR INTERROGATIONS *AT ANY LEVEL* WITH REGARD TO *ANY* SUSPECTED VIOLATION OF COMPANY GUIDELINES WITHOUT FIRST CONSULTING THE ABOVE CONTACTS.

Members of the Compliance Office or its designee involved in conducting the investigation will have:

- Free and unrestricted access to all Company records including electronic data; and
- The authority to examine, copy, transmit, and/or remove all or any portion of the contents of files, whether on computers, servers, hard drives or in desks, cabinets, and other storage facilities considered company property without prior knowledge or consent of any individual who may use or have custody of any such items.

CONFIDENTIALITY & DISCLOSURE

Information related to the reporting and investigation will be treated confidentially as deemed appropriate. Investigation results *will not* be disclosed or discussed with anyone other than those who have a legitimate need to know. This is important to avoid damaging the reputations of persons suspected but subsequently found innocent of wrongful conduct.

All inquiries concerning the activity under investigation from the suspected individual, their attorney or representative, or any other inquirer *should be* directed to the Compliance Office designee. Any information concerning the status of an investigation should only be disclosed by the member of the Compliance Office or its designee investigating the issue. Under *no* circumstances should any reference be made to "the allegation," "the crime," "the fraud," "the misappropriation," or any other similar reference.

REPORTING PROCEDURES

Due professional care must be taken in the course of the investigation to avoid mistaken accusations or alerting suspected individuals that an investigation is under way. Based on results of the investigation the Compliance Office or its designee will recommend involvement and/or notification of appropriate law enforcement, regulatory agencies, as well as, notifying internally the Legal Department, Human Resources Department, Senior Management, and/or the Board.

If an investigation results in a recommendation to terminate an individual, the recommendation will be reviewed and communicated by the General Counsel and the Director of Human Resources before any such action is taken.

ADMINISTRATION

The Compliance Office will be responsible for administration of these Investigation Guidelines.

Assignment

- **Hypothetical:** You are the Chief Compliance Officer at your [Team's] Corporation. Create an organizational chart for the Compliance Department and then create an organizational chart for the reporting lines for Compliance Department within the Company including subsidiaries located in London, Paris, Hong Kong and Beijing, and the parent company located in New York City and registered as a Delaware corporation.

Chapter 6

Background Checks and Their Importance for the Compliance Program[*]

Introduction

Background checks are an important component of an effective compliance program under the United States Sentencing Guidelines Manual § 8B2.1(b)(3) (2011). If the personnel involved in promulgating the compliance program are known as people of integrity, then the compliance program will be perceived as the result of a sincere effort to create a culture of ethics within the corporation.

Since the integrity of the senior management, compliance officer, and the compliance office personnel is critical to the effectiveness of the compliance program, enhanced background checks need to be conducted on all personnel who are involved in the conduct and dissemination of the compliance program. These background checks should be conducted at the time of employment, promotion, salary increase or change of position to a compliance related function. Typically, conducting background checks on certain prospective employees can be an important part of the employee selection process for any company.

Background checks may also be advisable for employees considered for promotion or transfer into managerial or sensitive positions, or those positions, which involve unsupervised employee contact with customers. This practice should be reinforced throughout the company in hiring all employees since every employee is involved in promoting and participating in the compliance program.

---

[*] Special thanks to Brian S. Cousin and Neil Capobianco for their contributions. This chapter is adapted from Brian S. Cousin and Neil Capobianco, *Background Checks and Their Importance for the Compliance Program* in CORPORATE COMPLIANCE PRACTICE GUIDE: THE NEXT GENERATION OF COMPLIANCE, Chapter 6 (Carole Basri, Release 8, 2016).

Steps Involved in the Background Check Process

While seemingly straightforward, the steps required to conduct a legal background check are full of traps for the unwary. As a matter of federal law (and the law of many states), the process involves the following steps:

1. Obtain written consent for a background check from the applicant or employee;

2. Obtain and analyze the results of the background check;

3. Provide a copy of the background check to the applicant (if the results are relevant to the selection process) along with a written statement of rights and request a response;

4. Provide the applicant with an opportunity to respond with written comments to the background check results;

5. Consider the applicant's written comments and the background check results in making a final determination as to whether the applicant will be hired, promoted, or transferred; and

6. Provide the applicant with written notice (if the background check results are relevant to the selection process) of the fact that the background check results played a part in the selection process and that the applicant was not selected as a result.

These steps are more than just a set of best practices, they are designed to help an employer fully comply with the requirements of the Fair Credit Reporting Act ("FCRA"). Failing to follow one or more of these steps when using background checks for employment decisions can leave a company open to class action or single plaintiff lawsuits.

Originally passed by Congress in 1970, the Fair Credit Reporting Act regulates "consumer reporting agencies" and any company or individual who seeks to rely on a "consumer report" in connection with making an employment decision, extending credit or insurance, or other decisions in connection with a "consumer." While the FCRA is not limited to employment decisions, this chapter focuses on the effects of the FCRA on the employment relationship. In the employment context, the "consumer" is either an applicant for employment or a current employee (hereinafter, collectively "applicant").

What Is a "Consumer Report"?

It is broadly defined in the FCRA as any written, oral, or other communication of any information by a consumer reporting agency bearing on a consumer's "credit worthiness, credit standing, credit capacity, character, general reputation, personal characteristics, or mode of living" which is used as a factor to determine the consumer's eligibility for credit or insurance, employment purposes, or business transactions. 15 U.S.C. § 1681a(d)(1). In the employment context, it covers any report from a consumer reporting agency describing a current or potential employee's arrests, convictions, or credit history.

What Is a "Consumer Reporting Agency"?

Any person or company which — for monetary fees, dues, or on a cooperative nonprofit basis — regularly engages in the practice of assembling or evaluating consumer credit information or other information on consumers for the purpose of furnishing consumer reports to third parties. 15 U.S.C. § 1681a(f). In the employment context, any company that provides an employer with information about an applicant's arrest, conviction, or credit history for a fee is a "consumer reporting agency."

There are numerous state laws that regulate the use of background checks for use in the employment context. This is particularly the case with criminal background checks.

The Federal Trade Commission ("FTC") has recently said that companies that conduct social media background checks are "consumer reporting agencies" under the FCRA. Thus, companies that decide to use a third party to conduct social media background checks must follow the steps outlined in this section. Alternatively, if the company does the social media check in-house, it is not required to follow these steps.

Social media background checks can reveal information about a candidate or employee's membership in a protected class. Companies must be vigilant not to rely on such information. Employers who conduct social media checks themselves are not subject to FCRA regulation. Third party service providers that conduct social media background checks for employers, however, must be careful when conducting searches because they must comply with FCRA requirements. The FTC has fined companies that provide social media background checks. For example, in 2012, the FTC assessed an $800,000 penalty against Spokeo, a data collector that the commission claimed had violated FCRA by compiling and selling people's personal information for use by potential employers in screening applicants. Spokeo failed to maintain reasonable procedures to verify who its users were and that the consumer report information would be used for a permissible purpose, to ensure accuracy of consumer reports, and to provide a user notice to any person that purchased its consumer reports.[1]

Step One: Obtain Written Consent from the Applicant or Employee

Before any background check is requested on any applicant, the employer must provide "a clear and conspicuous disclosure" in writing to the applicant that a consumer report may be obtained for employment purposes. 15 U.S.C. § 1681b(b)(2)(A)(i). This written disclosure must be "in a document that consists solely of the disclosure." In other words, it must be provided in a stand-alone document that cannot be provided with other information to the employee or applicant.

---

1. *See* United States v. Spokeo, No. 2:12-cv-05001-MMM-SH (C.D. Cal., June 19, 2012); FTC, *Spokeo to Pay $800,000 to Settle FTC Charges* (June 12, 2012), https://www.ftc.gov/news-events/press-releases/2012/06/spokeo-pay-800000-settle-ftc-charges-company-allegedly-marketed.

However, the FTC has issued an opinion that the written disclosure may be on the same form as used to obtain the applicant's written consent. The applicant must authorize the procurement of the report for the employer in writing. 15 U.S.C. § 1681b(b)(2)(A)(ii). Obtaining a report on an individual without that individual's consent is a violation of the FCRA, for which the employer may be liable for actual damages between $100 and $1,000, punitive damages, and attorney's fees. 15 U.S.C. § 1681n(a). However, if the applicant fails or refuses to authorize the employer to obtain a report, the position may be denied to the individual on that basis.

Additionally, the employer must also provide certification to the credit reporting agency stating that (a) it provided the necessary disclosure to the applicant or employee, (b) it will comply with the requirements regarding adverse action, and (c) it will not use the report in violation of any applicable federal or state equal opportunity law or regulation. 15 U.S.C. § 1681b(b)(1)(A). Typically, the credit reporting agency will require that this certification be signed by a responsible official from the employer before any report is provided. However, it is important for the employer to recognize that these are not meaningless boilerplate representations. Failure to comply with the certifications can expose the employer to a damages claim by the disappointed applicant.

Step Two: Obtain and Analyze the Results of the Background Check

Once the results of the background check are in, the employer must determine whether it raises any concerns about the applicant's integrity and suitability for the employment position at issue. Indeed, if a report has been obtained for a current employee in connection with a possible promotion or transfer, the report may raise questions about the employee's integrity and suitability for his or her current position.

If the background check results do not raise any issues concerning the applicant's integrity and suitability for the position, then an offer can be made to the applicant without any further FCRA obligation. Alternatively, if the background check does not raise any concerns, but the applicant is not selected for some other reason — such as a decision to offer the position to a better qualified applicant or a decision not to fill the position at all — then there is similarly no further FCRA obligation.

However, if something in the background check raises questions in the employer's view about the applicant's integrity and suitability for the position, then the employer must next determine whether it would be legal to deny the applicant the position on the basis of the background check. If the employer concludes that it would be legal to deny the position on that basis, then the employer may move on to step three.

As of October 2015, at least 14 states have enacted laws that limit the use of criminal background checks for employment purposes. These states include Alaska, Arkansas, California, Connecticut, Illinois, Louisiana, Massachusetts, Michigan, Nebraska, New York, North Dakota, Pennsylvania, Rhode Island, and Wisconsin. Some of these states prohibit an employer from considering a criminal conviction in connection with an employee selection process unless the conviction is reasonably related to the employment in question. For example, California restricts employers from requesting or using conviction records relating to certain marijuana convictions that are over two (2) years old. As of October 2015,[2] 17 states have also passed ban-the-box legislation, a legislative effort to require employers to remove the check box on their hiring applications that asks if applicants have a criminal record. Under ban-the-box legislation, employers must typically wait until later in the hiring process to conduct a background check. States that have passed such legislation include California, Colorado, Connecticut, Delaware, Georgia, Hawaii, Illinois, Maryland, Massachusetts, Minnesota, Nebraska, New Jersey, New Mexico, Rhode Island, Ohio, Vermont, and Virginia. Over 100 cities and counties throughout the country have passed similar legislation. For example, New York City passed ban-the-box-legislation on June 11, 2015, but New York State has thus far failed to follow suit.

Whether a conviction is reasonably related to the employment is a somewhat vague standard. It does not give the employer much guidance in determining whether a particular conviction for a crime may legally be used by the employer to deny employment for a particular position. The public policy behind these statutes, prohibiting discrimination against individuals convicted of criminal offenses, is to allow such individuals to obtain employment and thus to reduce the likelihood that the individual will commit further crimes. As a policy goal, these statutes are understandable. They clarify that an employer may not automatically disqualify an employee or applicant from a position simply because of any conviction regardless of how remote in time or how unrelated to the employment position at issue.

Further, be advised that, in many states, employers may not inquire about arrest records where no conviction has occurred. For example, Michigan prohibits the use of information regarding an arrest that did not lead to a conviction in connection with an application for employment. M.C.L. §37.2205a.

The employer, however, may also be sued for negligent hiring if it obtained—or could have obtained—information about the applicant's conviction that would have alerted the employer to the risk that the applicant might commit the same or a similar crime against a co-worker, vendor, or customer.

Federal law and regulations may actually require criminal background checks for some jobs and industries. For example, an individual convicted of a crime involving dishonesty or a breach of trust cannot work as a bank employee or insurance for a designated period. 12 U.S.C. § 1829(a)(1); 18 U.S.C. § 1033(e).

In other words, the employer faces possible liability to the disappointed applicant if it declines to hire him or her based on a prior conviction and possible liability to

---

2. A list of all states and cities that implemented ban-the-box laws can be found at National Employment Law Project, http://www.nelp.org/page/-/SCLP/Ban-the-Box-Fair-Chance-State-and-Local-Guide.pdf.

a person injured or damaged by the employee hired despite the conviction at issue. For prior convictions involving violence, this concern is most acute.

In New York, for example, it is an unlawful discriminatory practice to deny employment to an individual convicted of one or more criminal offenses unless:

(1) There is a direct relationship between one or more of the previous criminal offenses and the specific employment sought or held by the individual; or

(2) The granting or continuation of the employment would involve an unreasonable risk to property or to the safety or welfare of specific individuals or the general public.

In making a determination under this standard, the employer is supposed to consider the following factors:

(a) The public policy of [New York] to encourage the employment of persons previously convicted of one or more criminal offenses.

(b) The specific duties and responsibilities necessarily related to the employment sought or held by the person.

(c) The bearing, if any, the criminal offense or offenses for which the person was previously convicted will have on his fitness or ability to perform one or more such duties or responsibilities.

(d) The time which has elapsed since the occurrence of the criminal offense or offenses.

(e) The age of the person at the time of occurrence of the criminal offense or offenses.

(f) The seriousness of the offense or offenses.

(g) Any information produced by the person, or produced on his behalf, in regard to his rehabilitation and good conduct.

(h) The legitimate interest of the employer in protecting property, and the safety and welfare of specific individuals or the general public.

New York law absolutely prohibits an employer from discriminating against an applicant because of an arrest that was ultimately terminated—on the merits or otherwise—in the applicant's favor. New York Executive Law § 296(16).

The listing of the above factors requires the employer to consider and weigh each factor in determining whether it would be lawful to refuse to hire or promote the employee based on a prior conviction. There are no bright line tests. The employer is required to consider that New York public policy encourages the employment of previously convicted persons, but should also consider the safety and welfare of coworkers, vendors, or customers. The employer is also required to consider the seriousness of the offense, the applicant's age when it was committed, and how much time has passed since the offense occurred. Presumably, offenses committed long ago or when the applicant was young and immature should not be disqualifying for current employment.

Most importantly, the employer is required to consider the specific duties and responsibilities of the employment position and whether the criminal offense at issue will have any "bearing" on the applicant's "fitness or ability to perform one or more such duties or responsibilities." Clearly, a recent drunk driving conviction could disqualify an applicant for a position that requires driving on the employer's behalf. Similarly, a recent child molestation conviction would likely disqualify an applicant for a position as a child care worker.

Beyond these clear-cut examples, however, the employer runs the risk of a claim of conviction discrimination if it attempts to disqualify an applicant for a prior conviction, especially for older convictions or those for which the applicant has presented a certificate of rehabilitation. The Equal Employment Opportunity Commission ("EEOC") has taken the position that a policy that automatically disqualifies applicants for criminal convictions is per se discriminatory. In 2013, the EEOC filed complaints against BMW and Dollar General, claiming that the companies' use of criminal background checks violated Title VII and had a disparate impact against black applicants.[3] While decisions on these cases are still pending, the Fourth Circuit most recently ruled against the EEOC in a Title VII case, holding that the EEOC failed to show proof, through reliable statistical evidence, that a specific employment practice conducted by Freeman, a company that provides services for corporate events, resulted in a disparate impact.[4] Nevertheless, employers should continue to take steps, as outlined in this chapter, to ensure that their conduct is defensible.

Step Three: Provide a Copy of the Background Check to the Applicant along with a Written Statement of Rights and Request a Response

If the employer is considering not hiring the applicant or not promoting the employee because of something the employer has learned from the background check report, the employer must provide the applicant or employee with three things:

1. A copy of the report;

2. A written explanation that the employer is considering taking adverse action based on the results of the background check and requesting any response, comments, or additional information that the applicant or employee would like the employer to consider; and

3. A written summary of rights under the Fair Credit Reporting Act (available at www.ftc.gov/bcp/edu/pubs/consumer/credit/cre35.pdf).

The employer is prohibited from making a final decision prior to giving the applicant a reasonable opportunity to respond and considering any comments or in-

---

3. *See* EEOC v. BMW Mfg. Co., LLC, No. 7:13-cv-01583 (D. S.C., filed June 11, 2013); No. EEOC v. Dollar General, 1:13-cv-04307 (D. Ill., filed June 11, 2013).

4. *See* EEOC v. Freeman, 778 F.3d 463 (4th Cir. 2015).

formation that the applicant provides. However, the employer is not required to specify or explain precisely what in the report is motivating its reasons for considering adverse action or why it considers the report to be disqualifying. For example, the following letter is sufficient to comply with these requirements:

Dear Applicant:

The purpose of this letter is to inform you that we have received a consumer report from [**name of consumer reporting agency**] upon which we intend to rely in considering your employment application. Enclosed please find a copy of this consumer report. Also enclosed is A Summary of Your Rights Under the Fair Credit Reporting Act.

If you have any additional information that you would like us to consider regarding the information provided in the enclosed report or your employment application, please provide it to us within five (5) business days of your receipt of this letter.

Step Four: Provide the Applicant with an Opportunity to Respond with Written Comments to the Background Check Results

As explained in the above sample letter, the applicant must be given a reasonable opportunity to offer additional information, which the employer is legally required to consider.

Effectively, this means that the employer cannot hire another applicant for the position until it receives and considers the additional information that the applicant has the legal right to submit.

It is important that the applicant be given a specific, reasonable deadline within which to provide the additional information because the applicant is not required to submit any additional information and the employer cannot legally make a final determination until either the information is received or the time deadline has expired.

Step Five: Consider the Applicant's Written Comments and the Background Check Results in Making a Final Determination as to Whether the Applicant Will Be Hired, Promoted, or Transferred

Once the applicant has submitted his or her written comments or other information, the employer may consider the background check results and any comments or information submitted by the applicant to make a final decision about the position at issue. The employer should be guided by the requirements for the position as well as the applicable legal obligations discussed in Step Two above.

If the employer decides to hire the applicant in view of the applicant's written comments or for any other reason, then the employer need only inform the applicant of his or her selection for the position. There are no further FCRA requirements if the employer decides to hire the applicant. However, if the employer decides not to hire the applicant, then the employer must determine whether the background check results played a role in the decision not to hire the applicant. Having already informed the applicant that it was considering taking adverse action as a result of the background check results, it would generally seem likely that such results played a role in the employer's ultimate decision not to hire the applicant. Nonetheless, it is possible that the employer will decide not to hire the applicant for some reason unrelated to anything in the background check results.

For example, the employer might accept the applicant's explanation of the prior conviction as being irrelevant to the employment position in question or that the background check results are erroneous, but determine that some other applicant is better qualified for the position. Any applicant who reaches Step Five is likely to suspect that the background check results are what caused him or her not to be selected for the position and may bring a claim against the employer if the employer does not follow-up with the requirements of Step Six.

Therefore, it may be advisable for an employer who decides not to hire the applicant for a reason unrelated to the background check to inform the applicant of the reason for not selecting the applicant. However, the employer is not legally required to inform the applicant of any reason that is not related to the background check results.

Step Six: Provide the Applicant with Written Notice of the Fact that the Background Check Results Played a Part in the Selection Process and that the Applicant Was Not Selected as a Result

If the employer determines not to hire the applicant and that the background check results played a part in that decision, then the employer must provide the applicant with written notice of that fact, the name, address, and telephone number of the consumer reporting agency, and a statement that the consumer reporting agency did not make the adverse employment decision. 15 U.S.C. § 1681m(a)(1), (2).

Along with written notice that the consumer report played a role in the decision not to hire the applicant, the employer must also provide the applicant with notice of the applicant's right to obtain a free copy of the report and to dispute the accuracy of the report. 15 U.S.C. § 1681m(a)(3). Even though the applicant should already have a copy of the results of the background check (from Step Three above), the employer is legally required to provide the applicant with notice of the right to obtain a copy of the report for free and to dispute its accuracy with the credit reporting agency.

The following sample letter complies with these requirements:

Dear Applicant:

This notice is provided to you in accordance with the Fair Credit Reporting Act ("FCRA"). In our letter to you dated _____, we provided you with a copy of a consumer report, pre-authorized by you, that the Company obtained as part of its hiring process and advised you that the Company intended to rely upon it in considering your application for employment. We offered you the opportunity to provide any additional information that you wanted us to consider.

The Company has considered the additional information you provided along with the information it already possessed, including the consumer report, and the Company has decided not to offer you employment based, at least in part, on the information contained in the consumer report.

Pursuant to your rights under the FCRA, the Company is obligated to inform you of the following:

- The consumer report was provided to the Company by a consumer reporting agency, [**name, address, and telephone number of consumer reporting agency**].

- [**Consumer reporting agency**] did not make the decision not to offer employment, and cannot explain the specific reasons for the decision.

- At your request, [**consumer reporting agency**] must provide you with a free copy of its consumer report. This request must be made, in writing, to [**consumer reporting agency**] at the above address, and must be received by [**consumer reporting agency**] within 60 days of the date of this notification. You have the right to dispute with the consumer reporting agency the accuracy or completeness of any information in a consumer report.

Once the employer completes Step Six, its obligations under the FCRA will be fully satisfied.

However, the applicant has the right to contest with the consumer reporting agency—not the employer—the accuracy of any information in the background check. Notably, it is not the employer's obligation to ensure the accuracy of the consumer report. The employer is legally entitled to assume the accuracy of and rely upon the information set forth in the consumer report, even if the applicant claims that certain information is inaccurate. As long as the employer has properly followed the above steps and informed the applicant that it has relied upon information provided by a disclosed consumer reporting agency, the employer's obligations under the FCRA have been met.

Application of Background Checks to Compliance

The six steps in the process of dealing with background checks should be applied when doing a check of personnel promoted or transferred to a compliance function. Make sure to do enhanced background checks on all personnel involved in compliance since they nurture the integrity of the compliance program and are critical to fostering an ethical culture. Background checks are a critical step under the United States Sentencing Guidelines Manual, § 8B2.1(b)(3) (2011) ("The organization shall use reasonable efforts not to include within the substantial authority personnel of the organization any individual whom the organization knew, or should have known through the exercise of due diligence, has engaged in illegal activities or other conduct inconsistent with an effective compliance and ethics program.").

Safeco Ins. Co. of Am. v. Burr

551 U.S. 47 (2007)

Justice Souter delivered the opinion of the Court.

The Fair Credit Reporting Act (FCRA or Act) requires notice to any consumer subjected to "adverse action ... based in whole or in part on any information contained in a consumer [credit] report." 15 U.S.C. § 1681m(a). Anyone who "willfully fails" to provide notice is civilly liable to the consumer. § 1681n(a). The questions in these consolidated cases are whether willful failure covers a violation committed in reckless disregard of the notice obligation, and, if so, whether petitioners Safeco and GEICO committed reckless violations. We hold that reckless action is covered, that GEICO did not violate the statute, and that while Safeco might have, it did not act recklessly.

I.

A.

Congress enacted FCRA in 1970 to ensure fair and accurate credit reporting, promote efficiency in the banking system, and protect consumer privacy. See 84 Stat. 1128 [2206], 15 U.S.C. § 1681;TRW Inc. v. Andrews, 534 U.S. 19, 23, 122 S. Ct. 441, 151 L. Ed. 2d 339 (2001). The Act requires, among other things, that "any person [who] takes any adverse action with respect to any consumer that is based in whole or in part on any information contained in a consumer report" must notify the affected consumer. 15 U.S.C. § 1681m(a). The notice must point out the adverse action, explain how to reach the agency that reported on the consumer's credit, and tell the consumer that he can get a free copy of the report and dispute its accuracy with the agency. Ibid. As it applies to an insurance company, "adverse action" is "a denial or cancellation of, an increase in any charge for, or a reduction or other adverse or unfavorable change in the terms of coverage or amount of, any insurance, existing or applied for." § 1681a(k)(1)(B)(i).

FCRA provides a private right of action against businesses that use consumer reports but fail to comply. If a violation is negligent, the affected consumer is entitled to actual damages. § 1681o(a) (2000 ed., Supp. IV). If willful, however, the consumer may have actual damages, or statutory damages ranging from $100 to $1,000, and even punitive damages. § 1681n(a) (2000 ed.).

B.

Petitioner GEICO writes auto insurance through four subsidiaries: GEICO General, which sells "preferred" policies at low rates to low-risk customers; Government Employees, which also sells "preferred" policies, but only to government employees; GEICO Indemnity, which sells standard policies to moderate-risk customers; and GEICO Casualty, which sells nonstandard policies at higher rates to high-risk customers. Potential customers call a toll-free number answered by an agent of the four affiliates, who takes information and, with permission, gets the applicant's credit score. This information goes into GEICO's computer system, which selects any appropriate company and the particular rate at which a policy may be issued.

For some time after FCRA went into effect, GEICO sent adverse action notices to all applicants who were not offered "preferred" policies from GEICO General or Government Employees. GEICO changed its practice, however, after a method to "neutralize" an applicant's credit score was devised: the applicant's company and tier placement is compared with the company and tier placement he would have been assigned with a "neutral" credit score, that is, one calculated without reliance on credit history. Under this new scheme, it is only if using a neutral credit score would have put the applicant in a lower priced tier or company that GEICO sends an adverse action notice; the applicant is not otherwise told if he would have gotten better terms with a better credit score.

Respondent Ajene Edo applied for auto insurance with GEICO. After obtaining Edo's credit score, GEICO offered him a standard policy with GEICO Indemnity (at rates higher than the most favorable), which he accepted. Because Edo's company and tier placement would have been the same with a neutral score, GEICO did not give Edo an adverse action notice. Edo later filed this proposed class action against GEICO, alleging willful failure to give notice in violation of § 1681m(a); he claimed no actual harm, but sought statutory and punitive damages under § 1681n(a). The District Court granted summary judgment for GEICO, finding there was no adverse action when "the premium charged to [Edo] ... would have been the same even if GEICO Indemnity did not consider information in [his] consumer credit history." Edo v. GEICO Casualty Co., CV 02-678-BR, 2004 U.S. Dist. LEXIS 28522, *12 (D. Ore., Feb. 23, 2004), App. to Pet. for Cert. in No. 06-100, p 46a.

Like GEICO, petitioner Safeco relies on credit reports to set initial insurance premiums, as it did for respondents Charles Burr and Shannon Massey, who were offered higher rates than the best rates possible. Safeco sent them no adverse action notices, and they later joined a proposed class action against the company, alleging willful violation of § 1681m(a) and seeking statutory and punitive damages under § 1681n(a). The District Court ordered summary judgment for Safeco, on the understanding that offering a single, initial rate for insurance cannot be "adverse action."

The Court of Appeals for the Ninth Circuit reversed both judgments. In GEICO's case, it held that whenever a consumer "would have received a lower rate for his insurance had the information in his consumer report been more favorable, an adverse action has been taken against him." Reynolds v. Hartford Financial Servs. Group, Inc., 435 F.3d 1081, 1093 (2006). Since a better credit score would have placed Edo with GEICO General, not GEICO Indemnity, the appeals court held that GEICO's failure to give notice was an adverse action.

The Ninth Circuit also held that an insurer "willfully" fails to comply with FCRA if it acts with "reckless disregard" of a consumer's rights under the Act. Id., at 1099. It explained that a company would not be acting recklessly if it "diligently and in good faith attempted to fulfill its statutory obligations" and came to a "tenable, albeit erroneous, interpretation of the statute." Ibid. The court went on to say that "a deliberate failure to determine the extent of its obligations" would not ordinarily escape liability under § 1681n, any more than "reliance on creative lawyering that provides indefensible answers." Ibid. Because the court believed that the enquiry into GEICO's reckless disregard might turn on undisclosed circumstances surrounding GEICO's revision of its notification policy, the Court of Appeals remanded the company's case for further proceedings.

In the action against Safeco, the Court of Appeals rejected the District Court's position, relying on its reasoning in GEICO's case (where it had held that the notice requirement applies to a single statement of an initial charge for a new policy). Spano v. Safeco Corp., 140 Fed. Appx. 746 (2005). The Court of Appeals also rejected Safeco's argument that its conduct was not willful, again citing the GEICO case, and remanded for further proceedings.

We consolidated the two matters and granted certiorari to resolve a conflict in the Circuits as to whether § 1681n(a) reaches reckless disregard of FCRA's obligations, and to clarify the notice requirement in § 1681m(a). 548 U.S. 942, 127 S. Ct. 36, 165 L. Ed. 2d 1014 (2006). We now reverse in both cases.

II.

GEICO and Safeco argue that liability under § 1681n(a) for "willfully fail[ing] to comply" with FCRA goes only to acts known to violate the Act, not to reckless disregard of statutory duty, but we think they are wrong. We have said before that "willfully" is a "word of many meanings whose construction is often dependent on the context in which it appears," Bryan v. United States, 524 U.S. 184, 191, 118 S. Ct. 1939, 141 L. Ed. 2d 197 (1998) (internal quotation marks omitted); and where willfulness is a statutory condition of civil liability, we have generally taken it to cover not only knowing violations of a standard, but reckless ones as well, see McLaughlin v. Richland Shoe Co., 486 U.S. 128, 132–133, 108 S. Ct. 1677, 100 L. Ed. 2d 115 (1988) ("willful," as used in a limitation provision for actions under the Fair Labor Standards Act, covers claims of reckless violation); Trans World Airlines, Inc. v. Thurston, 469 U.S. 111, 125–126, 105 S. Ct. 613, 83 L. Ed. 2d 523 (1985) (same, as to a liquidated damages provision of the Age Discrimination in Employment Act of 1967); cf. United States v. Illinois Central R. Co., 303 U.S. 239, 242–243, 58 S. Ct. 533, 82 L. Ed. 773 (1938) ("willfully," as used in a civil penalty provision, includes "'conduct marked by careless disregard whether or not one has the right so to act'" (quoting United States v. Murdock, 290 U.S. 389, 395, 54 S. Ct. 223, 78 L. Ed. 381, 1934-1 C.B. 144, 1934-1 C.B. 145 (1933))). This construction reflects common law usage, which treated actions in "reckless disregard" of the law as "willful" violations. See W. Keeton, D. Dobbs, R. Keeton, & D. Owen, Prosser and Keeton on Law of Torts § 34, p 212 (5th ed. 1984) (hereinafter Prosser and Keeton) ("Although efforts have been made to distinguish" the terms "willful," "wanton," and "reckless," "such distinctions have consistently been ignored, and the three terms have been treated as meaning the same thing, or at least as coming out at the same legal exit"). The standard civil usage thus counsels reading the phrase "willfully fails to comply" in § 1681n(a) as reaching reckless FCRA violations, and this is so both on the interpretive assumption that Congress knows how we construe statutes and expects us to run true to form, see *Commissioner v. Keystone Consol. Industries, Inc.*, 508 U.S. 152, 159, 113 S. Ct. 2006, 124 L. Ed. 2d 71 (1993), and under the general rule that a common law term in a statute comes with a common law meaning, absent anything pointing another way, *Beck v. Prupis*, 529 U.S. 494, 500–501, 120 S. Ct. 1608, 146 L. Ed. 2d 561 (2000).

GEICO and Safeco argue that Congress did point to something different in FCRA, by a drafting history of § 1681n(a) said to show that liability was supposed to attach only to knowing violations. The original version of the Senate bill that turned out as FCRA had two standards of liability to victims: grossly negligent violation (supporting actual damages) and willful violation (supporting actual, statutory, and punitive damages). S. 823, 91st Cong., 1st Sess., § 1 (1969). GEICO and Safeco argue that since a "gross negligence" standard is effectively the same as a "reckless disregard" standard, the original bill's "willfulness" standard must have meant a level of culpability higher than "reckless disregard," or there would have been no requirement to show a different state of mind as a condition of the potentially much greater liability; thus, "willfully fails to comply" must have referred to a knowing violation. Although the gross negligence standard was reduced later in the legislative process to simple negligence (as it now appears in § 1681o), the provision for willful liability remains unchanged and so must require knowing action, just as it did originally in the draft of § 1681n.

Perhaps. But Congress may have scaled the standard for actual damages down to simple negligence because it thought gross negligence, being like reckless action, was covered by willfulness. Because this alternative reading is possible, any inference from the drafting sequence is shaky, and certainly no match for the following clue in the text as finally adopted, which points to the traditional understanding of willfulness in the civil sphere.

The phrase in question appears in the preamble sentence of § 1681n(a): "Any person who willfully fails to comply with any requirement imposed under this subchapter with respect to any consumer is liable to that consumer...." Then come the details, in paragraphs (1)(A) and (1)(B), spelling out two distinct measures of damages chargeable against the willful violator. As a general matter, the consumer may get either actual damages or "damages of not less than $100 and not more than $1,000." § 1681n(a)(1)(A). But where the offender is liable "for obtaining a consumer report under false pretenses or knowingly without a permissible purpose," the statute sets liability higher: "actual damages ... or $1,000, whichever is greater." § 1681n(a)(1)(B).

If the companies were right that "willfully" limits liability under § 1681n(a) to knowing violations, the modifier "knowingly" in § 1681n(a)(1)(B) would be superfluous and incongruous; it would have made no sense for Congress to condition the higher damages under §1681n(a) on knowingly obtaining a report without a permissible purpose if the general threshold of any liability under the section were knowing misconduct. If, on the other hand, "willfully" covers both knowing and reckless disregard of the law, knowing violations are sensibly understood as a more serious subcategory of willful ones, and both the preamble and the subsection have distinct jobs to do. See United States v. Menasche, 348 U.S. 528, 538–539, 75 S. Ct. 513, 99 L. Ed. 615 (1955) "'[G]ive effect, if possible, to every clause and word of a statute'" (quoting Montclair v. Ramsdell, 107 U.S. 147, 152, 2 S. Ct. 391, 27 L. Ed. 431 (1883)).

The companies make other textual and structural arguments for their view, but none is persuasive. Safeco thinks our reading would lead to the absurd result that one could, with reckless disregard, knowingly obtain a consumer report without a permissible purpose. But this is not so; action falling within the knowing subcategory does not simultaneously fall within the reckless alternative. Then both GEICO and Safeco argue that the reference to acting "knowingly and willfully" in FCRA's criminal enforcement provisions, §§1681q and 1681r, indicates that "willfully" cannot include recklessness. But we are now on the criminal side of the law, where the paired modifiers are often found, see, e.g., 18 U.S.C. §1001 (2000 ed. and Supp. IV) (false statements to federal investigators); 20 U.S.C. §1097(a) (embezzlement of student loan funds); 18 U.S.C. §1542 (2000 ed. and Supp. IV) (false statements in a passport application). As we said before in the criminal law "willfully" typically narrows the otherwise sufficient intent, making the government prove something extra, in contrast to its civil-law usage, giving a plaintiff a choice of mental states to show in making a case for liability, see n. 9, supra. The vocabulary of the criminal side of FCRA is consequently beside the point in construing the civil side.

III.
A.

In GEICO's case, the initial rate offered to Edo was the one he would have received if his credit score had not been taken into account, and GEICO owed him no adverse action notice under §1681m(a).

B.

Safeco did not give Burr and Massey any notice because it thought §1681m(a) did not apply to initial applications, a mistake that left the company in violation of the statute if Burr and Massey received higher rates "based in whole or in part" on their credit reports; if they did, Safeco would be liable to them on a showing of reckless conduct (or worse). The first issue we can forget, however, for although the record does not reliably indicate what rates they would have obtained if their credit reports had not been considered, it is clear enough that if Safeco did violate the statute, the company was not reckless in falling down in its duty.

While "the term recklessness is not self-defining," the common law has generally understood it in the sphere of civil liability as conduct violating an objective standard: action entailing "an unjustifiably high risk of harm that is either known or so obvious that it should be known." Farmer v. Brennan, 511 U.S. 825, 836, 114 S. Ct. 1970, 128 L. Ed. 2d 811 (1994); see Prosser and Keeton § 34, at 213–214. The Restatement, for example, defines reckless disregard of a person's physical safety this way:

> "The actor's conduct is in reckless disregard of the safety of another if he does an act or intentionally fails to do an act which it is his duty to the other to do, knowing or having reason to know of facts which would lead a reasonable man to realize, not only that his conduct creates an unreasonable risk of physical harm to another, but also that such risk is substantially greater than that which is necessary to make his conduct negligent." Restatement (Second) of Torts § 500, p 587 (1963–1964).

It is this high risk of harm, objectively assessed, that is the essence of recklessness at common law. See Prosser and Keeton § 34, at 213 (recklessness requires "a known or obvious risk that was so great as to make it highly probable that harm would follow").

There being no indication that Congress had something different in mind, we have no reason to deviate from the common law understanding in applying the statute. See Prupis, 529 U.S., at 500–501, 120 S. Ct. 1608, 146 L. Ed. 2d 561. Thus, a company subject to FCRA does not act in reckless disregard of it unless the action is not only a violation under a reasonable reading of the statute's terms, but shows that the company ran a risk of violating the law substantially greater than the risk associated with a reading that was merely careless.

Here, there is no need to pinpoint the negligence/recklessness line, for Safeco's reading of the statute, albeit erroneous, was not objectively unreasonable. As we said, § 1681a(k)(1)(B)(i) is silent on the point from which to measure "increase." On the rationale that "increase" presupposes prior dealing, Safeco took the definition as excluding initial rate offers for new insurance, and so sent no adverse action notices to Burr and Massey. While we disagree with Safeco's analysis, we recognize that its reading has a foundation in the statutory text, see supra, at 61, 167 L. Ed. 2d, at 1061, and a sufficiently convincing justification to have persuaded the District Court to adopt it and rule in Safeco's favor.

This is not a case in which the business subject to the Act had the benefit of guidance from the courts of appeals or the Federal Trade Commission (FTC) that might have warned it away from the view it took. Before these cases, no court of appeals had spoken on the issue, and no authoritative guidance has yet come from the FTC (which in any case has only enforcement responsibility, not substantive rulemaking authority, for the provisions in question, see 15 U.S.C. §§ 1681s(a)(1), (e)). Cf. Saucier v. Katz, 533 U.S. 194, 202, 121 S. Ct. 2151, 150 L. Ed. 2d 272 (2001) (assessing, for qualified immunity purposes, whether an action was reasonable in light of legal rules that were "clearly established" at the time). Given this dearth of guidance and the less-than-pellucid statutory text, Safeco's reading was not objectively unreasonable, and so falls well short of raising the "unjustifiably high risk" of violating the statute necessary for reckless liability.

The Court of Appeals correctly held that reckless disregard of a requirement of FCRA would qualify as a willful violation within the meaning of § 1681n(a). But there was no need for that court to remand the cases for factual development. GEICO's decision to issue no adverse action notice to Edo was not a violation of § 1681m(a), and Safeco's misreading of the statute was not reckless. The judgments of the Court of Appeals are therefore reversed in both cases, which are remanded for further proceedings consistent with this opinion.

It is so ordered.

Singleton v. Domino's Pizza, LLC

976 F. Supp. 2d 665 (D. Md. 2013)

Presently pending and ready for resolution in this action arising under the Fair Credit Reporting Act ("FCRA") is the motion to dismiss filed by Defendant Domino's Pizza, LLC ("Domino's" or "the company"). (ECF No. 22). The issues have been briefed, and the court now rules pursuant to Local Rule 105.6, no hearing being deemed necessary. For the reasons that follow, the company's motion will be denied.

I. Background

A. Factual Background

Plaintiffs Adrian Singleton and Justin D'Heilly allege the following facts in their first amended class action complaint and documents appended thereto. Domino's conducts background checks on all of its job applicants as part of a "standard screening process." (ECF No. 19 ¶ 16). In addition, it conducts background checks on existing employees "from time-to-time" during their employment. (Id.). Domino's does not perform these background checks in-house; rather, it relies on two external consumer reporting agencies ("CRAs") to run the background checks and report the results directly to the company.

Before requesting that these firms perform background checks, Domino's requires its employees to complete a "Background Investigation Information and Consent" form ("BIIC form"). (Id. ¶ 23). The BIIC form is included as "page 5" in the company's application packet. (Id.; ECF No. 19, at 35). The first two paragraphs on the form state, in relevant part:

> I understand that you intend to make an independent investigation of my background which may include references, character, past employment, education, credit and consumer information, driving history, criminal or police records, or insurance claims records ... for the purpose of confirming the information contained on my application and/or obtaining other information that may be material to my qualifications for employment (a background investigation).
>
> CONSENT. I hereby authorize you, as part of the application process, and from time to time during my employment, to the extent permitted by applicable law, to conduct a Background Investigation.... I authorize the release of such information to you. (ECF No. 19, at 35). The BIIC form also contains the following paragraph, which precedes the employee's signature authorizing Domino's to perform the background check:

> I release, without reservation, you and any person or entity which provides information pursuant to this authorization, from any and all liabilities, claims or causes of action in regards to the information obtained from any and all of the above reference sources used. I acknowledge that this is a standalone consumer notification informing me that a report will be requested and that the information obtained shall be used solely for the purpose of evaluating me for employment, promotion, reassignment, or retention as an employee.

(Id.).

In December 2008, D'Heilly applied to work as a delivery driver in one of the company's Minnesota stores. Prior to beginning work, he completed the "standard" application packet, which included the BIIC form. (ECF No. 19). D'Heilly worked for Domino's without incident through August 2009. In September 2009, however, the store stopped scheduling him for work, and D'Heilly's employment was terminated the following month. At that time, D'Heilly's general manager advised him that he could no longer work as a delivery driver "because something had come up on a background check relating to his motor vehicle history." (Id.) D'Heilly received no additional information regarding his termination, and Domino's never provided him with a copy of the background check.

Singleton, like D'Heilly, applied to work as a delivery driver at one of the company's Maryland stores during the spring of 2009. He, too, completed the "standard" application packet, including the BIIC form. (Id.). Singleton then began work. Several weeks into his employment, and just following the July 4, 2009, holiday, Singleton learned that a "potential issue" had arisen with his employment application and that he had not been scheduled to work any additional hours. (Id. ¶ 28). In an attempt to resolve the unspecified issue, Singleton submitted a second employment application, but he did not receive any work.

Instead, several days later, Singleton received a letter dated July 9, 2009, from Domino's entitled "FCRA Letter 2." (ECF No. 19, at 50). The letter stated, in relevant part:

> As part of our employment selection process, we require that a consumer report be obtained before employment commences to any applicant being considered for the position for which you applied. You previously should have received a copy of your consumer report.... This is to advise you that our offer of employment is being withdrawn and your application for employment is being denied. In evaluating your application, the consumer reporting agency listed below provided us with ... information which, in whole or in part, influenced our employment decision. Under the Fair Credit Reporting Act, you are entitled to disclosure of the information contained in your consumer report by contacting the consumer reporting agency directly, within sixty (60) days of this letter. You also have the right to dispute the completeness or accuracy of the report.

(Id.)

Contrary to the assertion in the letter, Singleton had not previously received a copy of the referenced report, and Domino's never provided him with this information.

B. Procedural Background

On July 1, 2011, Singleton filed a class action complaint against Domino's alleging multiple violations of the FCRA. Domino's subsequently moved to dismiss for failure to state a claim. Singleton and D'Heilly responded by filing an amended class action complaint on September 2, 2011. The amended complaint alleges that Domino's systematically and willfully violated the FCRA in three ways: (1) by failing to provide employees with copies of their background investigations prior to taking adverse action against them, in violation of 15 U.S.C. § 1681b(b)(3)(A); (2) by using a BIIC form that did not comply with the disclosure requirements set forth in 15 U.S.C. § 1681b(b)(2)(A)(i); and (3) by using a BIIC form that did not comply with the authorization requirements set forth in 15 U.S.C. § 1681b(b)(2)(A)(ii). On September 26, 2011, Domino's moved to dismiss the amended complaint for failure to state a claim. Plaintiffs have opposed this motion in its entirety.

II. Analysis

Domino's initially asserts, as to all counts, that Plaintiffs have failed to allege adequately that Domino's willfully violated the FCRA, a requirement to recover statutory damages under the FCRA. 15 U.S.C. § 1681n(a)(1)(A). To the extent that this argument is unavailing, Domino's further contends that counts two and three, which address the adequacy of the BIIC form, must be dismissed because: (1) they are time-barred; (2) the BIIC form complies with the FCRA's disclosure and authorization requirements; and (3) even if the BIIC form violates those requirements, Plaintiffs cannot "establish willful misconduct" because the company's interpretation of the FCRA's requirements was "not objectively unreasonable." (ECF No. 22, at 21). Each of these arguments will be addressed in turn.

A. The Amended Complaint Sufficiently Alleges Willfulness

The FCRA permits a plaintiff to recover damages when a defendant acted either negligently or willfully in violating the statute's requirements. See 15 U.S.C. § 1681o(a)(1) (providing that a plaintiff may recover actual damages in cases of negligent noncompliance); id. § 1681n(a)(1)(A) (providing for statutory damages in cases of willful noncompliance). In the absence of negligent or willful misconduct, however, a plaintiff may not recover at all. See Safeco Ins. Co. v. Burr, 551 U.S. 47, 53, 127 S. Ct. 2201, 167 L. Ed. 2d 1045 (2007). As a result, courts have routinely granted motions to dismiss where a plaintiff alleges neither that the defendant's negligence caused the plaintiff actual damages, nor that the defendant acted willfully. Shlahtichman v. 1-800 Contacts, Inc., 615 F.3d 794, 803 (7th Cir. 2010) (affirming dismissal where a complaint "alleged no actual injury" and failed to allege adequately that a defendant willfully violated the FCRA), cert. denied, 131 S. Ct. 1007, 178 L. Ed. 2d 828 (Jan. 18, 2011) (No. 10-640); Ogbon v. Beneficial Credit Servs., Inc., No. 10 CV 03760 (GBD), 2011 U.S. Dist. LEXIS 11615, 2011 WL 347222, at *3 (S.D.N.Y. Feb. 1, 2011) (granting a motion to dismiss where the plaintiff "allege[d] no facts that, if true, would demonstrate that the FCRA was violated willfully or negligently"). In the present case, Plaintiffs do not allege actual injury; rather, they contend that Domino's willfully violated the FCRA and seek only statutory damages. Domino's contends that Plaintiffs' allegations of willfulness are insufficient to survive a motion to dismiss.

In the wake of Twombly and Iqbal, a mere assertion of willful noncompliance with the FCRA will not, on its own, satisfy Rule 8(a). See, e.g., Ogbon, 2011 U.S. Dist. LEXIS 11615, 2011 WL 347222, at *3 (dismissing a complaint asserting FCRA violations where the plaintiff alleged only that "Defendants acted willfully"); Miller-Huggins v. SpaClinic, LLC, No. 09 C 2677, 2010 U.S. Dist. LEXIS 23418, 2010 WL 963924, at *2 (N.D. Ill. Mar. 11, 2010) (finding the plaintiff's allegation that the defendant "willfully disregarded the mandates of [the Fair and Accurate Credit Transactions Act]" insufficient to survive a motion to dismiss). Thus, to avoid dismissal, plaintiffs asserting that a defendant willfully failed to comply with the FCRA must set forth specific allegations to demonstrate willfulness. Ogbon, 2011 U.S. Dist. LEXIS 11615, 2011 WL 347222, at *3.

A defendant acts willfully under the FCRA by either knowingly or recklessly disregarding its statutory duty. Safeco, 551 U.S. at 57–60. Relying upon this definition, courts have found assertions that a defendant repeatedly violated the FCRA sufficient to allege reckless—and, therefore, willful-misconduct. See Smith v. HireRight Solutions, Inc., 711 F. Supp. 2d 426, 435 (E.D. Pa. 2010) (finding that a plaintiff had sufficiently alleged willfulness where the complaint indicated that the defendant had repeatedly engaged in "objectionable conduct" by reporting a single criminal history incident multiple times on a consumer report—an assertion that could, "at minimum, rise to the level of reckless disregard"); Romano v. Active Network, Inc., No. 09 C 1905, 2009 U.S. Dist. LEXIS 78983, 2009 WL 2916838, at *3 (N.D. Ill. Sept. 3, 2009) (citing the plaintiff's assertion that the defendant had repeatedly violated FACTA when concluding that the complaint's allegations of willfulness were sufficient to survive a motion to dismiss). In addition, assertions that a defendant was aware of the FCRA, but failed to comply with its requirements, are sufficient to support an allegation of willfulness and to avoid dismissal. See Kubas v. Standard Parking Corp. IL, 594 F. Supp. 2d 1029, 1031–32 (N.D. Ill. 2009) (denying a motion to dismiss where a plaintiff alleged that a defendant acted willfully by failing to comply with FACTA after credit card issuers had informed it of the law's requirements); see also Zaun v. Tuttle, Inc., No. 10-2191 (DWF/JJK), 2011 U.S. Dist. LEXIS 47916, 2011 (D. Minn. May 4, 2011) (concluding that a plaintiff had sufficiently alleged willfulness by asserting that the defendant was aware of FACTA's requirements, via information provided by a trade association, had the ability to comply with those requirements, and simply decided not to do so).

Here, in each count of the amended complaint, Plaintiffs allege that Domino's acted "willfully" in violating the FCRA, and they support this assertion with allegations analogous to those set forth in the cases above. With regard to count one, Plaintiffs contend that Domino's engaged in a practice of violating the FCRA by systematically failing to provide employees with copies of background checks prior to taking adverse action against them. To support this assertion, Plaintiffs emphasize that neither Singleton nor D'Heilly received such copies prior to their termination. Additionally, Plaintiffs assert that Domino's was aware — through its "general counsel's office and outside employment counsel" — that the FCRA requires employers to provide employees with copies of background checks before taking adverse action against them. (ECF No. 19 ¶ 65). According to the complaint, Domino's disregarded the FCRA by "typically" failing to provide employees with copies of their background checks. (Id. ¶ 30).

Plaintiffs set forth nearly identical allegations with regard to counts two and three. Specifically, they assert that Domino's repeatedly violated the FCRA by obtaining consumer reports for its employees, such as Singleton and D'Heilly, without providing the prerequisite disclosure and authorization information in a "stand-alone document." (Id. ¶ 71). Additionally, Plaintiffs suggest that Domino's, again through its in-house and outside counsel, knew about these requirements, an assertion supported by the company's request that employees certify the BIIC form as a "stand-alone consumer notification." (ECF No. 19, at 35). Yet despite the company's knowledge of the FCRA's disclosure and authorization requirements, Plaintiffs allege that the BIIC form did not actually qualify as a "standalone document" because it was part of the company's employment application and contained a liability release. (ECF No. 19 ¶ 71). In light of the case law above, these allegations are sufficient to support Plaintiffs' contention that Domino's willfully violated the FCRA.

Domino's makes two additional arguments in an attempt to avoid this outcome, but both are unavailing. First, the company demands more specificity and support for Plaintiffs' allegations of willfulness, asserting that repeated FCRA violations and knowledge of the FCRA's requirements are insufficient to satisfy Rule 8(a) in the wake of Twombly and Iqbal. This argument, however, is based on cases that involved decisions made on motions for summary judgment. See, e.g., Lagrassa v. Jack Gaughen, LLC, No. 1:09-0770, 2011 U.S. Dist. LEXIS 38838, 2011 WL 1257384, at *5 (M.D. Pa. Mar. 11, 2011) (granting a motion for summary judgment where the only evidence offered to support a finding of willfulness was "this single violation of the FCRA, without more"), judgment adopted by No. 09-cv-0770, 2011 U.S. Dist. LEXIS 34323, 2011 WL 1257371 (M.D. Pa. Mar. 30, 2011). On a motion to dismiss, plaintiffs need only provide allegations sufficient to demonstrate entitlement to relief; they need not prove their case at such an early stage in the proceedings. See Smith, 711 F. Supp. 2d at 438 (explaining that, while a plaintiff's assertion of repeated FCRA violations "would not necessarily withstand summary judgment scrutiny, ... a plaintiff, having set forth a legally and factually viable cause of action is entitled to the benefits of discovery before being put to his or her proofs."); see also McBurney v. Cuccinelli, 616 F.3d 393, 408 (4th Cir. 2010) (reasoning that "a Rule 12(b)(6) motion does not resolve contests surrounding ... the merits of a claim") (internal quotation marks and brackets omitted).

Domino's further contends that its defenses to Plaintiffs' willfulness allegations are plainly apparent from the documents appended to the complaint. With regard to count one, Domino's asserts that "the only plausible inference" from Singleton's termination letter is that "Domino's made a mistake by not providing Plaintiffs with a copy of their background checks." (See ECF No. 22, at 11, 13) (emphasizing that "FCRA Letter 2" stated that "[y]ou previously should have received a copy of your consumer report"). In support of this argument, Domino's cites Zaun v. J.S.H. Inc., a case in which the court granted a defendant's motion to dismiss where the plaintiff made a conclusory allegation of willfulness, but acknowledged in the complaint that the FACTA violation had resulted solely due to mistake. No. 10-2190, 2010 U.S. Dist. LEXIS 102062, 2010 WL 3862860, at *2 (Sept. 28, 2010).

Zaun, however, is distinguishable from the present case precisely because Plaintiffs' allegations do not "clearly reveal[]" that the company's failure to provide the background checks was a mistake. Brooks, 85 F.3d at 181. Indeed, Plaintiffs have presented several allegations, which were previously discussed, to support the assertion that Domino's acted willfully. They also emphasize the statement in Singleton's termination letter that directed him to contact the CRA to obtain a copy of his background check, an action that would presumably be unnecessary if Singleton had already received this information. (ECF No. 19, at 50). Taken together, and viewing the facts in the light most favorable to Plaintiffs, the parties' conflicting allegations do not "clearly reveal[]" that the failure to provide the background checks was the result of mistake. Brooks, 85 F.3d at 181. Rather, resolution of this issue goes to the merits of count one itself and is not properly the subject of a motion to dismiss. McBurney, 616 F.3d at 408.

With regard to counts two and three, Domino's alleges that it engaged in a good-faith effort to comply with the FCRA, as indicated by the BIIC form's assertion that it "is a stand-alone consumer notification." (ECF No. 19, at 35). But, once again, given Plaintiffs' contrary allegations of willfulness, it is too early in the proceedings to make such a determination. See id. Plaintiffs' allegations of willfulness are, therefore, sufficient to survive a motion to dismiss.

B. The Statute of Limitations Does Not Bar Counts Two and Three

The company's remaining arguments focus on dismissal of counts two and three, which address the adequacy of the BIIC form in light of the FCRA's disclosure and authorization requirements. To begin, Domino's contends that these claims must be dismissed as time-barred because Plaintiffs did not file suit within two years of the time they completed the BIIC form.

The FCRA statute of limitations provides that a plaintiff must file suit "not later than the earlier of—(1) 2 years after the date of discovery by the plaintiff of the violation that is the basis for such liability; or (2) 5 years after the date on which the violation that is the basis for such liability occurs." 15 U.S.C. § 1681p. The parties agree that the two-year limitations period applies in this case. According to Domino's, however, the complaint reveals that Plaintiffs filed suit outside of the limitations period. Singleton acknowledges that he completed the BIIC form prior to July 1, 2009, more than two years before filing the original class action complaint. D'Heilly similarly acknowledges that he completed the BIIC form before September 2, 2009, more than two years prior to filing the amended class action complaint. Domino's contends that because counts two and three stem from deficiencies within the BIIC form itself, Plaintiffs were on notice regarding these claims when they completed that form, a time the parties agree is outside the limitations period. While persuasive at first blush, this argument ultimately fails because it misconstrues the plain language of § 1681b(b)(2).

To be timely, Plaintiffs had to file suit under the FCRA within two years of "the date of discovery ... of the violation that is the basis for such liability." Id. (emphasis added). The company's limitations argument assumes that the violations in counts two and three occurred when Plaintiffs completed the purportedly deficient BIIC form. This assumption, however, neglects to consider that the violation was not complete until Domino's—through its external CRAs—actually obtained Plaintiffs' consumer reports. See 15 U.S.C. § 1681b(b)(2) ("[A] person may not procure a consumer report, or cause a consumer report to be procured, ... unless [it complies with these disclosure and authorization requirements]"); Davis v. Reg'l Acceptance Corp., 300 F. Supp. 2d 377, 385 (E.D. Va. 2002) ("[Section] 1681b(b)(2) prohibits any person from obtaining a consumer report ... without fulfilling enumerated [disclosure and authorization] requirements."). Thus, until these background checks were performed, no violation of § 1681b(b)(2) had occurred. See 15 U.S.C. § 1681b(b)(2)(A)(i) (explaining that the employer may provide the requisite disclosures "at any time before the report is procured").

As a result, Plaintiffs could not have discovered the violations underlying counts two and three until they learned that the background checks had taken place. Here, the complaint indicates that Singleton and D'Heilly did not discover this information until after July 1, 2009, and September 2, 2009, respectively, time periods within the statute of limitations. (See ECF No. 19 ¶ 39) (indicating that Singleton learned that he was being terminated through a letter dated July 9, 2009); (id. ¶¶ 47–48) (noting that D'Heilly learned in October 2009 that his termination resulted from information uncovered during the background check). Accordingly, contrary to the company's contention, counts two and three are timely.

C. Domino's Has Not Shown that, as a Matter of Law, the BIIC Form Complies with the FCRA's Disclosure and Authorization Requirements

Domino's next contends that counts two and three fail to state a claim for relief because the BIIC form complies with the FCRA's disclosure and authorization requirements. Relying upon the statute's plain language and guidance from the Federal Trade Commission ("FTC"), Plaintiffs disagree, alleging that the form is deficient because (1) it is included within the company's application packet, and (2) it contains a liability release. Although the parties devote substantial portions of their argument to the former issue, it need not be addressed in resolving this motion because the latter is dispositive. That is, inclusion of the liability release in the BIIC form precludes Domino's from asserting that, as a matter of law, the BIIC form satisfies the FCRA's requirements.

The parties have not identified, and the court is not aware of, any case law addressing whether an employer may lawfully include a liability release "in the document consist[ing] solely of the disclosure" that informs an employee about procurement of a consumer report for employment purposes. 15 U.S.C. § 1681b(b)(2)(A)(i). Therefore, it is appropriate to start the analysis of § 1681b(b)(2) from the beginning—with "an examination of the statute's plain text." See Broughman v. Carver, 624 F.3d 670, 675 (4th Cir. 2010) (internal quotation marks omitted), cert. denied, 131 S. Ct. 2969, 180 L. Ed. 2d 246 (June 6, 2011) (No. 10-1229). "In interpreting the plain language of a statute, [courts] give the terms their ordinary, contemporary, [and] common meaning, absent an indication Congress intended [them] to bear some different import." Crespo v. Holder, 631 F.3d 130, 133 (4th Cir. 2011).

Here, dictionary definitions of the word "solely" indicate that a document disclosing that an employer planned to obtain a consumer report would not "consist[] solely of the disclosure" if the document also contained a liability release. 15 U.S.C. § 1681b(b)(2)(A)(i). These definitions define "solely" as, inter alia, "to the exclusion of all else." Merriam Webster Online Dictionary (2011), available at http://www .merriam-webster.com; see also Oxford English Dictionary Online (2012) (defining "solely" as "alone" or "without any other as an associate"), available at http://www .oed.com; Webster's Third New Int'l Dictionary of the English Language 2168 (3d ed. 1971) (defining "solely" as "to the exclusion of alternate or competing things"). The BIIC form runs contrary to these definitions because, by containing a liability release, the form includes information that extends beyond the disclosure itself.

Domino's makes only one argument in an effort to avoid the statute's plain language. According to the company, inclusion of such a release in the disclosure document must be permissible because "the statute itself provides that a consumer authorization may be made on the disclosure document." (ECF No. 22, at 11) (internal quotation marks and brackets omitted). This contention, however, ignores the significance of congressional silence on an issue where Congress has otherwise spoken. Indeed, when mandating that an employer use a document that "consists solely of the disclosure," Congress expressly permitted employers to include language authorizing the employer to procure the consumer report. 15 U.S.C. § 1681b(b)(2)(A)(ii); see also Burghy, 695 F. Supp. 2d at 699. Had Congress intended for employers to include additional information in these documents, it could easily have included language to that effect in the statute. It did not do so, however, and its "silence is controlling." Cf. Smith v. Under Armour, Inc., 593 F. Supp. 2d 1281, 1287 (S.D. Fla. 2008) (finding Congress's failure to include language regarding e-commerce in one FCRA section instructive in determining whether that section applied to e-commerce).

In addition to the statutory text, FTC interpretations of § 1681b(b)(2) suggest that inclusion of a liability release in a disclosure form violates the FCRA. In 1998, in response to company inquiries, the FTC issued two opinion letters addressing § 1681b(b)(2)'s "consists solely" language. The first letter explicitly states that "inclusion of … a waiver [of one's FCRA rights] in a disclosure form will violate" § 1681b(b)(2) because the form will not "consist 'solely' of the disclosure." Letter from William

Haynes, Attorney, Div. of Credit Practices, Fed. Trade Comm'n, to Richard W. Hauxwell, CEO, Accufax Div. (June 12, 1998). The reasoning employed in the second letter supports this conclusion, stating that the FCRA prohibits disclosure forms "encumbered by any other information … [in order] to prevent consumers from being distracted by other information side-by-side with the disclosure." Letter from Clarke W. Brinckerhoff, Fed. Trade Comm'n, to H. Roman Leathers, Manier & Herod (Sept. 9, 1998). Domino's does not contend that the BIIC form could pass muster under this guidance.

Rather, citing Safeco, 551 U.S. 47, 127 S. Ct. 2201, 167 L. Ed. 2d 1045, Domino's argues that the court should ignore these letters because they are merely advisory opinions. Its argument, however, overstates the Supreme Court's conclusion in Safeco. Indeed, while the Safeco Court concluded that FTC advisory opinions did not constitute "authoritative guidance" on the FCRA, id. at 70 & n.19 (emphasis added), numerous courts interpreting the FCRA after Safeco have found such opinion letters persuasive, see, e.g., Owner-Operator Independent Drivers Ass'n, Inc. v. USIS Commercial, 537 F.3d 1184, 1192 (10th Cir. 2008); Morris v. Equifax Info. Servs., LLC, 457 F.3d 460, 468 (5th Cir. 2006). A similar finding is warranted in the present case.

Ultimately, both the statutory text and FTC advisory opinions indicate that an employer violates the FCRA by including a liability release in a disclosure document. Because the BIIC form contains such a release, Domino's has not shown, as a matter of law, that the form complies with the FCRA. Its attempt to have counts two and three dismissed on this ground must, therefore, fail.

D. Domino's Is Not Entitled to Dismissal of Counts Two and Three on the Ground that Its Interpretation of the FCRA "Was Not Objectively Unreasonable"

In its final argument, Domino's maintains that, even if the BIIC form did violate the FCRA, its interpretation of the statute's disclosure and authorization requirements "was, at a minimum, not objectively unreasonable." (ECF No. 22, at 21). As with the company's prior argument, because Domino's fails to show that inclusion of the liability release in the BIIC form was "not objectively unreasonable," the reasonableness of including that form within the application packet need not be addressed. (Id.).

The Supreme Court has held that a defendant does not willfully violate the FCRA "unless the [challenged] action is not only a violation under a reasonable reading of the statute's terms, but shows that the company ran a risk of violating the law substantially greater than the risk associated with a reading that was merely careless." Safeco, 551 U.S. at 69. That is, unless the defendant's interpretation of the statute is objectively unreasonable, a plaintiff will be unable to show that the defendant willfully violated the FCRA. "Where the reading has 'a foundation in the statutory text … and a sufficiently convincing justification,'" the interpretation is not objectively unreasonable, even if the reviewing court disagrees with it. Smith, 711 F. Supp. 2d at 434 (quoting Safeco, 551 U.S. at 69). Domino's clings to this language, asserting that its inclusion of the liability release in the BIIC form resulted from a reasonable reading of § 1681b(b)(2). The company's reliance on Safeco, however, is misplaced for two reasons.

First, the procedural posture of the Safeco case differed in a critical manner from the present action. "[T]he Supreme Court [in Safeco] was operating under a summary judgment standard of review. It found no genuine issue of material fact as to whether the defendant's interpretation of the statute—albeit erroneous—was objectively unreasonable." Id. at 436. In this case, however, a motion to dismiss is pending, and discovery has not yet begun. Thus, at present, there is no evidence that Domino's actually adopted the interpretation of § 1681b(b)(2) that it proposes here. See Gillespie v. Equifax Info. Servs., No. 05 C 138, 2008 U.S. Dist. LEXIS 85150, 2008 WL 4316950, at *7 (N.D. Ill. Sept. 15, 2008) (denying a motion for summary judgment where, among other reasons, a defendant had not offered evidence that it "actually adopted a particular construction" of the relevant statutory section). On similar facts, numerous courts have declined to examine the reasonableness of a defendant's statutory interpretation when ruling on motions to dismiss. See, e.g., id. at 436–37; Korman v. Walking Co., 503 F. Supp. 2d 755, 761 (E.D. Pa. 2007) (noting that, "at the motion to dismiss stage, the Court's only role is to determine" whether the complaint sufficiently alleges willfulness (citing Jordan v. Fox, Rothschild, O'Brien, & Frankel, 20 F.3d 1250, 1261 (3d Cir. 1994))).

Second, even if it were appropriate to reach this issue on a 12(b)(6) motion, Domino's would not prevail. Unlike in Safeco, where the FCRA provision at issue was "less-than-pellucid," 551 U.S. at 70, the text at issue here appears to have "a plain and clearly ascertainable meaning," Smith, 711 F. Supp. 2d at 436. See Edwards v. Toys "R" Us, 527 F. Supp. 2d 1197, 1209 (C.D. Cal. 2007) ("This case presents a different situation than Safeco because [the FCRA provision at issue] is not ambiguous or susceptible of conflicting interpretations."). Domino's has pointed to no authority that would lead to a contrary conclusion.

At bottom, the basis of the company's argument is that "the paucity of [judicial] authority on the [disputed] statutory provision" precludes the conclusion that the company acted in an objectively unreasonable manner. (ECF No. 24, at 12). This argument is unpersuasive because it ignores the guidance provided within the statutory provision itself. Where "the text of [the] statute is clear and open to only one reasonable interpretation ... a dearth of guidance does not render [a] defendant's readings plausible." Follman v. Hospitality Plus of Carpentersville, Inc., 532 F. Supp. 2d 960, 964 (N.D. Ill. 2007); Ramirez v. MGM Mirage, Inc., 524 F. Supp. 2d 1226, 1235 (D. Nev. 2007) (quoting Follman, 532 F. Supp. 2d at 964). Because the plain language of § 1681b(b)(2) indicates that inclusion of a liability release in a disclosure form violates the FCRA's disclosure and authorization requirements, Domino's fails to show that its interpretation of this section was "not objectively unreasonable." (ECF No. 22, at 21). Dismissal of counts two and three on this ground is, therefore, improper.

IV. Conclusion

For the foregoing reasons, the company's motion to dismiss the amended class action complaint will be denied. A separate Order will follow.

Notes and Comments

EEOC's investigation on Pepsi Beverages[5]

Pepsi Beverages (Pepsi), formerly known as Pepsi Bottling Group, has agreed to pay $3.13 million and provide job offers and training to resolve a charge of race discrimination filed in the Minneapolis Area Office of the EEOC. The monetary settlement will primarily be divided among black applicants for positions at Pepsi, with a portion of the sum being allocated for the administration of the claims process. Based on the investigation, the EEOC found reasonable cause to believe that the criminal background check policy formerly used by Pepsi discriminated against African Americans in violation of Title VII of the Civil Rights Act of 1964.

The EEOC's investigation revealed that more than 300 African Americans were adversely affected when Pepsi applied a criminal background check policy that disproportionately excluded black applicants from permanent employment. Under Pepsi's former policy, job applicants who had been arrested pending prosecution were not hired for a permanent job even if they had never been convicted of any offense.

Pepsi's former policy also denied employment to applicants from employment who had been arrested or convicted of certain minor offenses. The use of arrest and conviction records to deny employment can be illegal under Title VII of the Civil Rights Act of 1964, when it is not relevant for the job, because it can limit the employment opportunities of applicants or workers based on their race or ethnicity.

"The EEOC has long standing guidance and policy statements on the use of arrest and conviction records in employment," said EEOC Chair Jacqueline A. Berrien. "I commend Pepsi's willingness to re-examine its policy and modify it to ensure that unwarranted roadblocks to employment are removed."

During the course of the EEOC's investigation, Pepsi adopted a new criminal background check policy. In addition to the monetary relief, Pepsi will offer employment opportunities to victims of the former criminal background check policy who still want jobs at Pepsi and are qualified for the jobs for which they apply. The company will supply the EEOC with regular reports on its hiring practices under its new criminal background check policy.

---

5. *Pepsi to Pay $3.13 Million and Made Major Policy Changes to Resolve EEOC Finding of Nationwide Hiring Discrimination Against African American,* http://www.eeoc.gov/eeoc/newsroom/release/1-11-12a.cfm.

Press Release, N.Y. State Office of the Attorney General, *A.G. Schneiderman Announces Agreement with Party City to End Discrimination in Hiring Based on Criminal Records*

(Oct. 2, 2014) http://www.ag.ny.gov/press-release/ag-schneiderman-announces-agreement-party-city-end-discrimination-hiring-based

New York Attorney General Eric T. Schneiderman announced a settlement today with Party City, a national retailer employing nearly 5,000 people in 49 stores across New York State. The settlement will ensure that the company complies with state laws prohibiting discrimination against individuals with criminal records. Under the terms of the agreement, Party City will no longer automatically disqualify individuals with felony convictions from advancing in the company ...

"An applicant's criminal history does not give employers a right to slam the door in his face," Attorney General Schneiderman said. "Reentry efforts provide critical opportunities to reduce recidivism, ensuring that everyone gets a fair shot and ultimately making our communities safer...."

Under New York State law, before an employer can reject applicants based on their criminal history, the employer must individually assess the applicant's record to determine whether it is relevant to the job. Specifically, the employer must consider several factors, including the nature and gravity of an applicant's criminal conviction and its bearing, if any, on any specific responsibilities of the job sought, the time that has elapsed since the conviction, the age of the applicant at the time when the offense was committed, and evidence of rehabilitation ...

As part of the settlement, Party City has agreed to:

- revise its hiring policies and procedures;
- conduct training for employees to ensure fair consideration of all job applicants;
- conduct outreach and recruiting efforts with non-profits that specialize in job training and rehabilitation of individuals with criminal records;
- reconsider applications from hundreds of former applicants who may have been denied employment opportunities unlawfully;
- submit periodic reports to verify its continued compliance with the law for a period of three years; and
- pay a $95,000 penalty

Finally, the company has agreed to remove any inquiry regarding criminal history from the employment application used at its stores. By taking this step, Party City joins Bed Bath & Beyond as the second company to "Ban the Box" pursuant to enforcement efforts of the Attorney General's Office.

———

Assignments

- **Hypothetical:** You are the Chief Compliance Officer at your [Team's] Corporation. Create a checklist to be considered for background checks. Describe the different policies that a company might have to adhere to in terms of social media background checks.

- Do a background check, including social media, on yourself.

Chapter 7

Training on the Compliance Program

Introduction

This chapter serves as a summary of the key considerations and tactical steps necessary to implement an enterprise-wide compliance training program, which is designed to meet or exceed the criteria set forth under the U.S. Sentencing Guidelines of an "effective compliance and ethics program."

Training programs are not—and should not be—"one size fits all." Implementing training that does not resonate with employees is a sure-fire way of losing their attention, as well as a valuable training opportunity. Considering the increased emphasis that the Guidelines place on self-disclosure, a company is well-served to be sure to avoid such a situation. At every step described below, be sure to view the development of the training program through the lens of your organization's training needs.

Depending on a variety of factors, the design and implementation of an enterprise-wide training initiative can take as little as 8–12 weeks to launch, with an additional 12–16 weeks to drive completion rates and measure the effectiveness of the training effort. However, due to the complexity of the task and the frequent lack of dedicated internal resources available to aid in implementation, this process can take as long as a year from start to finish. It should be noted that many of the eight steps discussed below overlap; therefore, adding the relative average completion times for each step will result in an erroneously high estimate of the total time required.

Step One: Identifying the Audience

The intended audience will influence every step of the training development process. Therefore, tailoring this initiative with the organization's employee base in mind is the key to the initiative's success. In order to truly figure out who the organization's employees are, ask the following questions.

Is it prudent to verify if a comprehensive list of who works where is available? Without such a list, rolling out training will be challenging. Where do the employees work? Are they sitting in cubicles at computers (which favors eLearning) or are they driving trucks in mines (which will require a more adaptable delivery mechanism)?

What languages do they speak? Translations affect budget, so be sure to know whether the employees in Shanghai will be able to comprehend training delivered in English, or if Mandarin and/or Cantonese translations will be necessary. What education level have employees attained, on average? A group of aerospace engineers who have earned Ph.D.s will be addressed in a different manner than manufacturing staff in Malaysia. Finally, assume that the organization's employee base will be made up of different learners; some will learn textually, while others may learn verbally or contextually. All of these factors need to be considered as the training plan progresses.

Determining Training Goals

In addition to helping allocate an appropriate percentage of the organization's budget to the training program, defining training goals from the outset will provide a benchmark against which to measure progress. Typically, training focuses on knowledge, skills and attitudes.

Compliance training is different from "normal" corporate training because it does not involve teaching skills (e.g., how to use software, run a machine or fill out an expense report). Instead, compliance training is focused on knowledge and attitudes; it is designed to provide employees tools with which they can recognize potential ethics or compliance issues, information regarding the resources they may consult when they have questions and/or concerns, and an understanding as to why it is so important that they ask questions and raise concerns. Compliance training serves as an introduction to issues and a guide to assistance rather than teaching set answers. Recognition of this difference is crucial in the goal-setting context; the average employee does not need to understand all the ramifications of U.S. anti-boycott law, for example, but does need to understand that a reference to Israel in a bill of lading means they should seek guidance.

- During the goal-setting process, consider the training delivery method, which should be affected by the information gathered when identifying the training audience. The most common training options include eLearning; instructor-led training, including train-the-trainer; and document-based training (also known as "workbook training"). There are positive and negative aspects to each of these training methods. For instance, eLearning is consistent, trackable and measurable, and can be taken by the employee at a convenient time during his or her work day. ELearning is especially good for conveying complicated areas in a consistent manner. However, eLearning does not allow for face-to-face interaction, which adds a human element to compliance training efforts, and does not provide a mechanism by which an employee's questions can be instantly answered. These questions are particularly useful since they can indicate unsuspected problem areas for the compliance program and the company.

Instructor-led training, on the other hand, allows for face-to-face contact, which often leads to productive discussions amongst employees regarding the issues included in the training session as well as an opportunity for questions and answers which can raise issues of urgency and can act as a warning system to the company. Facilitators of instructor-led training should be confident of their knowledge of the material, able to engage the learners and capable of reinforcing the key learning points. They should be able to deliver the material consistently based on a well thought-out script or train-the-trainer guide. Professional trainers, human resources personnel and legal department members are excellent choices for trainers in instructor-led training on topics for which they have expertise.

Further, train-the-trainer, one type of instructor-led training, is particularly effective for the general compliance/ethics training necessary to roll out the compliance program and to provide annual refresher compliance training to all employees. Training involves the immediate supervisor or a colleague acting as the trainer teaching a small group of employees, about 15 to 20 people, on the core values and requirements of the Code of Conduct/Ethics and the general compliance program. This is a very effective method of promoting a culture of ethics within the company. The employee peer group is present with its supervisor to discuss what is unethical conduct under the Code of Conduct/Ethics.

This reinforces, for individual employees, that his or her supervisor and/or peer group is aware of what is acceptable behavior under the Code of Conduct/Ethics and that his or her supervisor is an available resource to answer questions. For example, taking a pen and a pad of paper home to do work "may not" be stealing but taking a carton of pens and a gross of pads of paper "may," in all probability, be stealing. Norms of conduct are often more easily explained in the small group settings found in train-the-trainer programs than in eLearning situations. Train-the-trainer programs should be well organized and provide step-by-step guidance on how to work with small groups. However, instructor-led training can be logistically difficult to deliver, and can require a substantial investment of human capital to develop the material and to deliver the training.

Finally, workbook learning may be the best option for employees who are remote locations not accessible to instructors and/or computers. However, it can be less effective for those who learn best when information is put in context with an instructor or eLearning, or those who have reading and/or reading comprehension issues.

Compliance training goals should also be job-specific in many instances. A mailroom employee does not need to have the same level of understanding of antitrust rules as a salesperson; thus, initial training will be general in nature, with more specific training implemented to manage job specific risk over time. It is important that these goals are reasonable and achievable. Preferably, these should be three-to-five-year goals broken down into smaller interim steps.

A best practice is to learn about the compliance training activities of peer organizations, including even industry competitors, if possible. Our survey data indicates that e-Learning is the most common mechanism by which organizations deliver code training (see Figure 1) but the answer for non-code training is not as consistent (see Figure 2).

Figure 1

Percentage of Employees Who Take the Code of Conduct Training Online

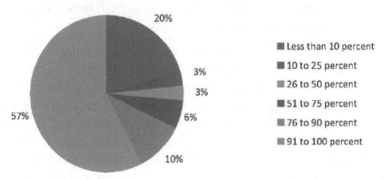

Source: 2013 ACC-Corpedia Benchmarking Survey

Figure 2

Percentage of Non-Code of Conduct Formal Training Conducted Online

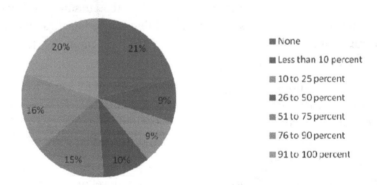

Source: 2013 ACC-Corpedia Benchmarking Survey

Determining Estimated Training Budget

When determining the organization's training budget, consider not only the actual costs that would be incurred in developing (or purchasing) training programs, but also other internal costs. For example, what would be a reasonable "budget" for the amount of time employees use attending the compliance training? Furthermore, what would be the cost of administrating the program? Would the organization outsource administration or hire/allocate internal resources to do so? Naturally, this calculation is influenced by the design of the overall compliance curriculum (see "Step Three: Create a Code of Conduct Training Plan"), but the initial financial framework and parameters should be determined upfront.

Regardless as to how it is accomplished, creating a detailed a budget estimate at the outset will be helpful when establishing the overall program's design. Often, compliance training programs are driven by budget limits, as opposed to vice-versa. The discipline of budgeting ensures that goals will be realistic and consistent with what the organization may be willing to fund.

Step Two: Assemble, Staff, and Meet with the Steering Committee

Once the preliminary goals and estimated budget have been determined, a Steering Committee, alternatively referred to as a Program Team, should be formed. While the Steering Committee should include members from headquarter divisions or operating units, it should ultimately report to whomever is directly responsible for corporate compliance (most frequently, this is the Chief Compliance Officer, the Chief Ethics Officer or the General Counsel). Typically, an effective Steering Committee includes members of all major departments affected by the initiative.

While this Steering Committee should be given the opportunity to weigh in on the training program's goals and budget, the primary mission of the Steering Committee should be to:

- Engage and obtain "buy-in" from operational units and divisions by acting as a liaison for the initiative between field and corporate;

- Ensure that the initial technological direction is compatible with the organization's infrastructure;

- Aid in creating the three-to five-year curriculum plan (see Step Four);

- Assure continued executive leadership team support;

- Collaborate on the choice of a vendor (should an outside vendor be used for consulting, programming and/or administration);

- Help in the negotiation and structure of a vendor contract (again, depending on whether a vendor is used);

- Coordinate cooperation (and police competing agendas or turf-wars) among headquarter divisions (e.g., HR, Finance, Legal, Audit, etc.); and

- Plan for the ongoing administration of the initiative once it has been launched.

Steering Committees should also carefully set and adhere to a strict project plan and timeline for launching the program.

Step Three: Create a Code of Conduct Training Plan

As the core of most compliance training programs begins with training on the Code of Conduct/Ethics ("Code"), discussions about Code training should be separated at the outset from the overall remaining compliance training curriculum (see "Step Four: Develop a Three-to Five-Year Compliance Training Program Plan").

Designing an effective Code training curriculum is rarely as simple as it might first appear. Code training needs to be examined within the context of overall training goals and objectives, as well as in relation to other compliance processes within the organization. Code training must also take into consideration the structure, culture and geographic scope of the organization.

Leading Practices of Organizations Implementing Code of Conduct eLearning

As a significant portion of Fortune 1000 companies use eLearning to train on their Codes, a number of leading practices have emerged, including those listed below.

- **Code training should be assigned to employees as soon as reasonably possible after date of hire, and should be reinforced regularly thereafter.** Many organizations that have Code training as a pillar of their compliance training programs diligently assign training to new employees as soon as possible after the date of hire (generally within 30 days). Then, employees are expected to participate in training on the Code regularly thereafter (either on an annual basis or every two years, with certification of the Code required annually).

- **Code of Conduct training programs should be interactive and include Code certification and disclosures.** An increasing number of organizations not only use Code training as an educational tool, but also to integrate other compliance-related processes. Code training programs may, for example, be used to "push down" certifications and attestations (particularly relating to financial statements). In the United States, since the enactment of the Electronic Signatures in Global and National Commerce Act in 2000, which views such electronic signatures as binding contractual acceptances, such a move has become increasingly popular.

- **Code training programs should build and reinforce compliance systems' credibility.** For example, employees may be hesitant to use reporting hotlines to report observed misconduct due to fear of retribution or a concern that the information disclosed (including their identity) may not be treated with adequate confidentiality. National survey statistics compiled by the Ethics Resource Center in 2011 indicate that 28 percent of all employees of organizations that have at least 500 employees personally observed conduct that violated the law or their employers' standards of ethical conduct. However, 45 percent of non-management employees (and 27 percent of management employees) did not report their observations of misconduct to their managers or other appropriate personnel. As such, a good Code training program does more than merely focus on "what not to do" and "what our values are"—it also emphasizes the credibility and integrity of the organization's compliance systems to ensure they are utilized. The emphasis that the 2010 revisions to the Federal Sentencing Guidelines place on self-disclosure makes this point even more critical; companies rely on employees to tell them what is happening "in the field" so that they can conduct an internal investigation and determine whether self-disclosure is appropriate.

- **Organizations with diverse operations may run different Code training programs.** As an organization's operations become increasingly diverse, either as to work performed or location, it is critical that it consider creating multiple Code training programs. For example, different programs may emphasize different risk areas depending on the functional level of the internal audience. Furthermore, for international operations, the Code training program may be localized and translated for a broad spectrum of geographic locations. Train-the-trainer programs should be localized and translated into the local language(s) and dialects. Additionally, employee location might influence the medium in which the training is delivered if train-the-trainer is not used. Since media is becoming increasingly diversified due to technological developments, new media delivery systems are helping companies reach employees through mobile learning (e-Learning delivered to iPhones, iPads, and other tablets and mobile devices), CDs, kiosk computers and other methods.

Leading Practices of Organizations Implementing Instructor-Led Training

Even as organizations rely more and more on eLearning for most training situations, instructor-led training should be considered when an enhanced understanding of a particular risk area (i.e., anti-corruption, export controls or competition law) is needed. Live instruction by lawyers or other skilled practitioners is invaluable in reaching high level management on complex issues where unanticipated questions may arise. For example, 3 or 4 high level officers of the corporation negotiating a project in a foreign country may need specific training on the Foreign Corrupt Practices Act (FCPA) or the UK Bribery Act.

There are a number of things to keep in mind when considering instructor-led training for compliance training, as follows:

- **Determine what kind of instructor-led training you intend to conduct.** There are a number of different options, including:
  - *Train-the-trainer.* Training involves the immediate supervisor or a colleague acting as the trainer teaching a small group of employees, about 15 to 20 people, on the core values and requirements of the Code of Conduct/Ethics and the general compliance program. This is a very effective method of promoting a culture of ethics within the company. The employee peer group is present with their supervisor to discuss what is unethical conduct under the Code of Conduct/Ethics. (The train-the-trainer program may be assisted by

the eLearning course network or CD if it is available. From time to time the trainer can pause the eLearning course and lead a discussion to reinforce key ideas in the main content and activities. Each pause point and the questions or statements that should be used for discussion are clearly specified in the train-the-trainer guide).

○ *Instructor-Led Courses.* If you have expert and confident trainers, comprehensive instructor-led courses based on the content, activities, and tests of your online courses are a viable option. Facilitators use a facilitator guide and PowerPoint slide deck to present information on each topic, guide discussions, and lead activities. Learners can follow the course and take notes in an optional participant guide.

○ *Enhanced Instructor-Led Courses.* If you want the most comprehensive and interactive classroom experience, you could pursue enhanced instructor-led courses. These include the facilitator guide and PowerPoint slide deck, enhanced with additional engaging activities designed specifically for live training. Facilitators can easily adapt these activities to the size of their group, from five people to 50. Again, learners can follow the course and take notes in a participant guide.

• **Determine who your trainers are going to be.** Are they subject matter experts who need support describing the best way to engage the learner's attention, how to pace and chunk the material, how to handle group interactions and how to reinforce learning? Or are they professional trainers who are going to need assistance understanding the content of the training? Do they speak the language(s) of your learners, or will you need translators in order to effectively deliver the training? This choice will have a profound influence on the kinds of materials you will need to develop for effective instructor-led training.

• **Determine what kind of activities you want to include.** Ideally, you want to choose hypothetical case studies, case study discussions, role modeling and other group activities that take advantage of the face-to-face nature of instructor-led training.

• **Determine whether your learning management system (LMS) can track instructor-led training courses.** You need the capability to track and record attendance at instructor-led training courses, so be sure that your current LMS has that capability. If it does not, seriously consider upgrading your LMS.

Step Four: Develop a Three-to-Five-Year Compliance Training Program Plan

It can be tempting to create a training program curriculum that outlines only the first year of the initiative, and then to make subsequent years' curricula decisions concurrently with the annual budgetary cycle process. However, doing so is a mistake and can result in an inherent bias of viewing compliance training programs (and implicitly the overall compliance program) as a year-by-year activity. As a result, it becomes more difficult to create a truly ongoing and sustainable process that is institutionalized into the daily operations of the organization and managed with a long-term view.

Compliance training program plans are living documents and can be updated as necessary during their three-to five-year lifespan. Certainly, training plans can (and oftentimes do) evolve as the organization grows and its risk areas change. A good three-to-five year curriculum should seek to mitigate the job-related risks discussed above through more in-depth training. Consider all of the potential delivery mechanisms for in-depth training: eLearning, instructor-led training, emailed scenarios or mini-training sessions, and presentations provided during a sales or business meeting. Broadening the delivery methods allows training to reach different groups of employees in different ways. This is increasingly important in light of the large number of employees reporting that their manager or manager's manager exerts the greatest influence on their behavior.

There are many factors that can affect a curriculum, not the least of which is the rolling out of the initiative, as this process may incur unforeseen hurdles or objections. Therefore, the best curricula, while based on a multi-year plan, are consciously and systematically revisited on an annual basis in light of the results of an organization's risk assessment.

Despite the many factors that can affect a multi-year training curriculum midstream, creating a multi-year curriculum encourages a high level of valuable discipline by forcing companies to address risk priorities, as well as surrounding budgetary and staffing issues. Paying mind to all of these factors is critical to the overall training program initiative's long-term effectiveness and success.

Step Five: Determine Technology, Deployment Strategy, and Preferences

In this day and age, chances are good that at least some elements of the compliance training plan will involve eLearning. eLearning offers significant benefits—it is trackable, measurable and repeatable, as well as simultaneously deployable to a broad cross-section of employees. In addition, for international organizations, it is often less expensive than sending the compliance officer to the four corners of the globe to deliver in-person training.

While compliance eLearning initiatives involve a substantial amount of technology issues, legal and compliance departments (or any other department charged with this task) are generally ill-equipped from both a resource and an experience perspective to properly address these issues. As such, while planning their compliance eLearning initiatives, it is critical that organizations adequately consider the important role that technology plays in compliance and ethics eLearning. For instance, it is not uncommon for an organization to do extensive due diligence on the content and curriculum for their compliance eLearning initiative, only to find that the resulting programs do not live up to expectations due to unforeseen technology-related hurdles. Commonly, these hurdles are technology issues that could have been, and *should* have been, addressed upfront in the planning process, as well as the vendor selection process (see "Step Six: Receive Proposals from Vendors; Analyze, Narrow and Negotiate Contract").

For these reasons, it is critical that the department tasked with this initiative involve the right internal parties and invest sufficient time in determining what technology requirements should be addressed and how programs will be properly deployed, administrated and tracked.

Avoiding Four Common Problems Posed by eLearning Training Initiatives

In determining a technology strategy, it is helpful to start with an understanding of what could go wrong. The four most common technological problems encountered by organizations when developing eLearning initiatives are:

- Bandwidth constraints that preclude the use of video-based programs and/or training program notifications;
- Training program notifications (when the organization uses a third-party vendor) that are blocked by spam or junk filters;
- Corruption of employee training records or separate Human Resources systems, which undermine the integrity of the records or results in employees not being enrolled in programs (or being shown as not having completed programs that they have taken); and
- Difficult integrations between vendor data and an organization's Human Resources Information System (HRIS) or LMS, requiring increased time and effort, and causing greater aggravation in administering the program.

In order to avoid these four common problems, there is a parallel set of four critical questions that need to be considered:

1. What is the required minimum network infrastructure necessary to run these training programs?
2. Will the programs be hosted internally or externally?
3. What will the organization use as an LMS?
4. How will the program be technically administered and will it be integrated to the organization's HRIS? Does the organization have a single integrated HRIS?

Leading Practices by Organizations for Technology and Recordkeeping

Leading practices employed by organizations that have had success in running a trouble-free compliance training initiative from a technology perspective include the following:

- **Companies can leverage eLearning for non-networked employees.** Despite the fact that many employees do not use computers on a regular basis, organizations have found innovative ways to harness the benefits of eLearning, such as time-efficiency, ease of administration and tracking, and content consistency. This has included using eLearning for such positions as production floor workers; high-turnover, customer-facing employees; traveling salespersons; industrial workers and so forth. Innovative approaches have included the creation of training "kiosks," *ad hoc* training centers, group eLearning sessions, home computer training credits, mobile-device eLearning delivery and so forth.

- **Companies are wise to limit the need for multiple sign-ons/passwords.** Most employees have multiple passwords with which to access secure corporate and personal computer applications. While most vendors have password protection access to training programs in order to protect the integrity of the training records, it is also important to recognize that trainees might use the same password for their training that they use to access corporate networks (despite embedded instructions to do otherwise). Leading training providers work with organizations to eliminate such "multiple sign-ons" through "handshake" authenticators, which securely log in employees who have already logged onto the corporate intranet, or other advanced means.

- **Security-conscious organizations adequately assess vendor information security.** Should an organization engage an external compliance training vendor to host training records, employee information or log-on passwords (see above), it is imperative that the organization be satisfied with the vendor's information security practices, policies and procedures. Failure to perform adequate due diligence could result in an inexperienced vendor infecting the corporate network with viruses, the corporate network being hacked or employee records being compromised, potentially in violation of data protection laws in many jurisdictions.

- **Organizations should include test integration files as part of any vendor-selection process.** The technical sophistication of compliance eLearning vendors can vary widely. As such, it is a best practice to conduct test integrations with possible vendors in advance of entering into a contractual engagement. Organizations need to know that software applications and data feeds will communicate seamlessly before undertaking large-scale implementations.

- **Companies should undergo pilot programs for filters, reverse proxies and load-testing.** It is wise, from a technology perspective, to conduct a pilot test before undertaking any large-scale launch of a training initiative. A properly executed pilot test should involve progressively larger test files being transferred between the organization and its compliance eLearning vendor. It should also examine such things as: spam blocking or junk email filters; multiple and simultaneous connection points; coded and single sign-on authentication; "key" transfer; automated plug-in downloads; and reverse proxy communications.

Step Six: Receive Proposals from Vendors; Analyze, Narrow and Negotiate Contract

Working with an external vendor that has a dedicated focus on compliance eLearning can impart numerous benefits to the average organization. Generally, engaging outside vendors is more cost and time-effective than developing programs in-house. In addition, external vendors are able to vouch for and maintain the quality of the content, and are able to play an active role in helping to design and administer the training curriculum and program. However, organizations should ensure that engaging a vendor is a thoughtful and carefully planned process; failure to do so will likely result in unmet expectations and strained relationships.

To RFP or Not RFP?—Questions to Ask Potential Providers

Some organizations conduct their vendor analysis through a formal Request for Proposal ("RFP") process. Other organizations examine vendor offerings either on a more informal basis through a series of *ad hoc* meetings with prospective vendors or through a semi-formal Request for Information ("RFI") process.

Whether an organization uses a formal RFP process or not often depends on the company's procurement policies, as well as whether or not there is sufficient time and/or personnel to run a formal, regimented and dedicated process.

Whichever process is used, the organization's Steering Committee commonly narrows down the list of prospective vendors to one or two, which then will be invited to deliver a presentation to the Committee.

Common RFP Problems to Avoid

Should an organization decide to pursue a formal RFP process, it should be prepared to dedicate adequate time and energy to crafting a well-balanced RFP. The Steering Committee Chair (or designate) will also have to diligently follow up on the responses, as an RFP process can quickly get off track and be inefficient without a strong and well-organized internal leader.

Companies often encounter common problems that result in a derailed RFP process and wasted time by all parties. In order to avoid these pitfalls, follow these simple steps:

- **Have a specific plan outlined in the RFP to which the vendors can respond.** Failing to do so can result in additional back-and-forth and confused responses to the RFP.
- **Demand the specific format in which vendors should present and break down their pricing.** Failing to do so can result in an impossible "apples to oranges" comparison among vendor responses.
- **Include sufficient technical specifications in the RFP.** Failing to do so can result in responses that are inadequate for the organization to be able to carry out information technology and security due diligence.

- **Schedule internal Steering Committee meetings in advance for analyzing RFP responses.** Failing to do so will commonly result in substantial, yet unnecessary, delay to overall project's implementation.

- **Provide an avenue by which vendors can ask questions about the RFP.** Failing to do so may result in vendors providing confused responses or terms and conditions with too many qualifying factors.

- **Inform vendors who were not chosen as to the provider of choice.** Failing to do so may undermine such vendors' willingness to participate in future RFP processes conducted by the organization, and may therefore unnecessarily limit the organization's options in the future.

In addition to the above problems, a common mistake is to fail to have pre-set criteria against which RFP responses can be measured by the Steering Committee.

Leading Practices of Organizations in Choosing an eLearning Provider

Leading practices for organizations in choosing an eLearning vendor that is best-suited for their company in the short-and long-term are set forth below:

- **Organizations need to ensure that the vendor does not have an undisclosed conflict of interest.** With heightened scrutiny of corporate governance and compliance comes higher sensitivity to potential conflicts of interests. Organizations should be vigilant about examining potential conflicts of interest and demanding that vendors disclose current conflicts of interest, both real and apparent, as well as past ethical transgressions.

- **Companies should examine vendors within the context of the broader compliance program, as opposed to simply looking at one or more training programs.** With the U.S. Sentencing Guidelines criteria for effective compliance and ethics programs extending well beyond mere training, organizations are benefiting from purchasing programs and services from fewer vendors. By consolidating purchases, a company is likely to benefit economically, and should have a better composed and focused compliance program depending on which services the organization chooses to pursue (such as training, communication plan development, risk assessment, data metrics, technology implementation and administrative services).

- **Organizations are careful to assess both vendor viability and commitment to the industry.** The advent of Sarbanes-Oxley and the ensuing optimistic projection for corporate compliance spending budgets attracted many new participants to the compliance programming industry. From loss of records and program administration and support, to having to revisit the vendor-selection process, it can be extremely disruptive to lose the services of a vendor. In order to avoid the pitfalls associated with such a loss, an organization needs to assure itself of the vendor's long-term commitment and viability.

- **A company should assess the skills of the individuals at the vendor with whom they will be working.** As enterprise-wide compliance eLearning initiatives are complex, multi-part undertakings (often including translations, customizations, integrations, etc.) that are integrated with other compliance processes, excellent project management skills on the part of the vendor are of paramount importance. An organization may oftentimes demand to meet the members of the vendor's team who will be assigned to the company's project.

- **Companies should be sure to conduct adequate technical and customer reference due diligence.** Implementing an enterprise-wide compliance training initiative is a complex and high-profile endeavor for any organization, and such programs are most effective when tightly integrated to the rest of the organization's compliance program. To conduct vendor due diligence, the reference-checking approach typically works well, as compliance officers are generally willing to share insights, opinions and best practices with peers.

- **Organizations should not forget that the vendors may have good insights.** A final leading practice is to ask the vendor to take a proactive role in providing insights as part of their response to RFIs or RFPs (or even outside of such in an *ad hoc* process). Most vendors, so far as they do not feel that they are being unjustly taken advantage of, are willing to share best practices and knowledge on program design and implementation.

Step Seven: Customize Programs, Conduct Systems Integration, and Design Communications Plan

Once the curriculum has been set, the technology and deployment strategy finalized, and the vendor chosen (or internal department designated to build and administer the programs, if the company decides to in-source), the process of customizing the programs, undertaking systems integration (as necessary) and designing the supporting communications strategy takes precedence.

Systems Integration

The issues surrounding systems integration are covered extensively in "Step Five: Determine Technology and Deployment Strategy and Preferences." Systems integration merely requires execution of the integration and deployment of the technology. So far as adequate preparation and analysis was completed in Step Five, and adequate due diligence was performed in Step Six, this process should go smoothly.

Customizing the Programs

As noted earlier, customizing the training programs to the organization's specific needs is important in ensuring that the programs are well-received and effective. The major areas that may be necessary to customize at this stage include:

- Changing the branding and look-and-feel of the trainee interface to the user organization;

- Making sure that scenarios are relevant to the company's operations;

- Customizing test questions and quizzes as necessary;

- Embedding relevant contact information (e.g., in-house ethics office, legal department and anonymous reporting hotline contact information);

- Embedding relevant company policies (the policies and procedures should preferably be segmented by content area within the program, as opposed to being presented all at once in a list form);

- Making sure that the program's visuals (e.g., diverse persons and working attire) reflect the culture and populace of the organization; and

- Customizing the emails that alert and remind employees of specific training obligations.

An organization should be sure that all parties that will be involved internally in signing off on customized visuals and content are available for and timely in providing feedback. A common mistake to avoid is neglecting to obtain sign-off from a critical stakeholder within the organization prior to the commencement of program customization. It is incredibly disruptive to any project management process to have to redevelop content or multimedia once the development process has begun.

Creating a Communications Plan

In order to have an effective training component to a corporate compliance and ethics program, an organization must have an adequate supporting internal communications program. A good communications program is well-planned, consistent and regular in frequency. In the absence of such, employees may not be sufficiently aware of training expectations, or may fail to take the training initiative seriously.

Generally, a well-designed communications program is not only focused on compliance training, but also takes into account the organization's broader compliance and ethics initiative. As the Federal Sentencing Guidelines note, it should also help *"promote an organizational culture that encourages ethical conduct and a commitment to compliance within the law."* This is commonly referred to as setting the "proper tone from the top."

The importance of an organizations' communications program is also discussed in the awareness requirements as outlined in the Department of Justice McNulty Memorandum,[1] which states,

Charging a Corporation: Corporate Compliance Programs

A. <u>General Principle</u>: Compliance programs are established by corporate management to prevent and to detect misconduct and to ensure that corporate

---

1. http://www.justice.gov/sites/default/files/dag/legacy/2007/07/05/mcnulty_memo.pdf.

activities are conducted in accordance with all applicable criminal and civil laws, regulations, and rules. The Department encourages such corporate self-policing, including voluntary disclosures to the government of any problems that a corporation discovers on its own. However, the existence of a compliance program is not sufficient, in and of itself, to justify not charging a corporation for criminal conduct undertaken by its officers, directors, employees, or agents. Indeed, the commission of such crimes in the face of a compliance program may suggest that the corporate management is not adequately enforcing its program.

B.   Comment: [I]n *United States* v. *Hilton Hotels Corp.*, 467 F.2d 1000 (9th Cir. 1972), *cert. denied*, 409 U.S. 1125 (1973), the Ninth Circuit affirmed antitrust liability based upon a purchasing agent for a single hotel threatening a single supplier with a boycott unless it paid dues to a local marketing association, even though the agent's actions were contrary to corporate policy and directly against express instructions from his superiors. The court reasoned that Congress, in enacting the Sherman Antitrust Act, "intended to impose liability upon business entities for the acts of those to whom they choose to delegate the conduct of their affairs, thus stimulating a maximum effort by owners and managers to assure adherence by such agents to the requirements of the Act. It concluded that "general policy statements" and even direct instructions from the agent's superiors were not sufficient; "Appellant could not gain exculpation by issuing general instructions without undertaking to enforce those instructions by means commensurate with the obvious risks." *See also United States v. Beusch*, 596 F.2d 871, 878 (9th Cir. 1979) ("[A] corporation may be liable for the acts of its employees done contrary to express instructions and policies, but … the existence of such instructions and policies may be considered in determining whether the employee in fact acted to benefit the corporation.") …

Prosecutors should therefore attempt to determine whether a corporation's compliance program is merely a "paper program" or whether it was designed and implemented in an effective manner. In addition, prosecutors should determine whether the corporation has provided for a staff sufficient to audit, document, analyze, and utilize the results of the corporation's compliance efforts. In addition, prosecutors should determine whether the corporation's employees are adequately informed about the compliance program and are convinced of the corporation's commitment to it.

Leading Practices of Effective Communications Programs Supporting Compliance Training

A number of leading practices with measurable impact and results have been employed successfully by organizations in recent years. Such practices include the following:

- **An organization may look to provide static and interactive online and offline supporting resources and tools.** There is no guarantee that after taking a training program, employees will retain all the legal and ethical concepts that apply to their individual job functions. Furthermore, there may be certain periods in which employees have not recently been trained in legal compliance concepts important to their job execution. As such, many companies' compliance training programs focus on building a culture of awareness and "safe communications" that can be used when guidance is needed. For example, when an employee recognizes a "red flag" event, he or she may turn to an ethics hotline or reference additionally provided materials.

- **An effective supporting communications plan is characterized by variation, frequency and consistency.** It is a mistake for an organization to only focus on compliance communications during a certain portion of the year, such as during a fiscal quarter when enterprise-wide Code training is rolled out. While it would be logical to have a greater emphasis on communications during such a focused initiative, some form of sufficiently visible communications should be present throughout the year to maintain a minimum level of awareness of ethics and compliance issues among employees.

As an example of a way to continuously promote ethics and compliance, some companies have used video podcasts of their leadership talking about real-life ethical and compliance dilemmas and how they resolved them. Other organizations have taken hotline calls or investigations, removed any identifying information, and posted those scenarios on the ethics and compliance section of their intranet.

Organizations recognize that it is important to communicate appropriate incentives and discipline relating to the compliance program.

The U.S. Sentencing Guidelines set forth principles for an effective compliance and ethics program in its Sentencing Guidelines Manual ("Guidelines"). Pursuant to Section 8 (B) (2) (1) of the Guidelines and its Commentary Section, conducting effective training programs and training employees through informal staff meetings have been demonstrated as a part of an effective compliance program. The amendments made to the Guidelines in November 2004 required trainings for a company's compliance program to target board members, all company's employees and its agents, if necessary, and that trainings should be tailored to each individual's role and responsibility within the organization.

> "The organization's compliance and ethics program shall be promoted and enforced consistently throughout the organization through (A) appropriate incentives to perform in accordance with the compliance and ethics program; and (B) appropriate disciplinary measures for engaging in criminal conduct and for failing to take reasonable steps to prevent or detect criminal conduct."

As such, it is a leading practice to inform the employee population through effective communication the pros and cons of diligently adhering to the organization's compliance program. In addition, companies have begun to commonly incentivize acting in accordance with the organization's compliance and ethics program by having a portion of an employee's performance review be based on their commitment to said program. Organizations are also increasingly tying completing all necessary training to bonus payments; some are even placing the responsibility for employees completing all training in a timely manner on their supervisor, and tying that supervisor's bonus or incentive payments to the number of reminders their direct reports required before completing training.

Companies see benefit in providing and publicizing an "ethics helpline" that can be used not only to report misconduct, but also to offer guidance.

Any company subject to Sarbanes-Oxley is required to have an anonymous reporting hotline. The U.S. Sentencing Guidelines similarly dictate that, to maintain an effective compliance and ethics program, companies must:

> *"Have and publicize a system, which may include mechanisms that allow for anonymity or confidentiality, whereby the organization's employees and agents may report or seek guidance regarding potential or actual criminal conduct without fear of retaliation."*

Many organizations have acted based on common perception that the "promise of anonymity and confidentiality" is stronger when an outside provider is used to man such anonymous hotlines. As Figure 2 illustrates, 74 percent of all companies entirely outsource their "hotline." However, it is a leading practice to also maintain an "internal hotline" through which guidance on ethical dilemmas may be received.

As further shown in Figure 3, 8% of companies use a blend of both outsourced third-party hotlines and internally-manned ethics guidance hotlines.

Figure 3

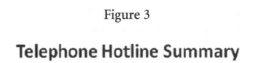

Telephone Hotline Summary

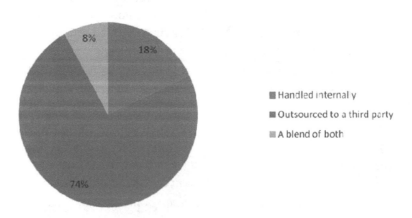

Source: 2013 ACC-Corpedia Benchmarking Survey

Some companies have benefitted from communicating summary disciplinary information to enhance the credibility of their compliance systems.

While an effective training program will proactively encourage employees to report observed misconduct by using available internal reporting channels, in practice many employees will remain reluctant to do so. Commonly, they fear retaliation and feel that the employer will not act on the report. To counter this, an increasing number of organizations are sharing details or reports on disciplinary actions with their employees.

A good compliance communications plan emphasizes employees' responsibility to report misconduct.

Hand in hand with incentives and discipline, a good communications program will specifically point out to employees, as local law allows, that, it is their responsibility to report ethical and legal misconduct through the available channels. Therefore, the best compliance communications programs make it clear to employees that failure to report observed criminal conduct, even if they are not a firsthand participant, will not insulate them in the event criminal conduct is later discovered.

The communications plan needs to set the tone from the top by including a strong message from executive leadership.

Studies have shown that employee perceptions as to the level that the organization's executive leadership is committed to compliance and ethics will have a significant impact on such employees' behavior. Some of the leading ways that organizations can heighten executive leadership team visibility in their compliance and communications program include:

- Leaders, such as the CEO and even members of the Board of Directors, record personal introductions to the training programs in a multimedia format;
- Enrollment emails assigning employees training appear to come from the CEO or another member of the executive leadership team; and
- The leadership team sends periodic email and written communications to the workforce discussing the importance of compliance and ethics, and encouraging the use of available reporting systems and other resources should employees observe misconduct or need guidance on an issue.

See the following for a sample CEO introduction derived from an actual Fortune 1000 company Code of Conduct eLearning program.

Sample CEO Introduction to Code of Conduct eLearning Program

NOTE ON PROPER USE: *The following is a model format for a CEO introduction to a compliance or ethics eLearning program, such as a Code of Conduct training program. Some corporations have successfully used different executive introductions in different programs depending on the content area (e.g., having the CFO do the introduction for a Sarbanes-Oxley program; the head of HR doing the introduction for an EEOC program; etc.). This model format should be personalized to the author of the introduction, as well as customized to the values and operations of the specific organization.*

Hello, I'm [insert name], the CEO of [your company],

This training and review program deals with a very important topic: our company's Code of Conduct. As you know, our vision is to be a global leader in our market — admired for our innovative spirit, integrity and stewardship.

This vision relates to our dedication to profitable growth through market leadership, but it is about more than business success. It also relates to how we conduct ourselves day in and day out.

Our employees are expected to act in accordance with the highest standards of ethical conduct. Our Code of Conduct summarizes the policies and principles by which we commit ourselves to the safe, honest, thoughtful and responsible operation of all our businesses and facilities.

These policies and principles support our core values:

- Integrity;
- Teamwork;
- Respect for the individual; and
- Commitment to excellence.

Our ethics and values are essential to the success of our global business. They give our customers confidence in our products, our services and our word. In addition, they give us pride in our work, and maintain our standing as a good corporate citizen.

Our dedication to integrity must take us beyond compliance with the law. We should remember that our reputation for ethical behavior is a tremendous asset of this company and its employees.

This training program is required for ALL members of our organization. This includes our own senior executive team, as well as our Board of Directors, who have already taken this same training program that we are asking you to participate in.

I am confident that you'll find this program both stimulating and thought-provoking.

[End of CEO introduction]

––––––––––

Step Eight: Launch Training Initative and Drive Completion Rates

By this stage, the organization should be well-prepared to launch the initiative, having completed customization of the programs and total systems integration. To be effective, the training initiative and supporting communications should be ongoing. Generally, curriculum allocation to trainees is interspersed throughout the calendar year, with the 6–12 week timeframe applying only to any specific and singular training program launch.

Whether it is launching an enterprise-wide Code training initiative or an antitrust training program specifically targeting sales personnel, a company should be prepared to allow for up to 12 weeks for full penetration of the target training base.

Leading Practices of Organizations Looking to Drive Training Completion Rates

There are a number of efforts that can be undertaken by an organization that will have a significant impact on the completion rate of the programs by enrolled trainees. These practices include the following:

- **An organization should conduct a test launch of a sub-group before enrolling the entire target training population for any particular training program.** At this stage, extensive technical due diligence (and perhaps a pilot test group run) should be completed. However, launching the actual training initiative in batches provides for an additional margin of safety. Typically, groups of enrollees can be separated into four to six evenly sized batches. The reason for so doing is that a corporate information technology and security environment is constantly changing and new protocols could have been put in place since the last training launch.

- **For Code training programs, best practices dictate that the Board of Directors take it first.** Having the Board of Directors complete a Code training program before other employee audiences not only helps meet U.S. Sentencing Guidelines criteria, but also educates the Board on how the compliance program works. Companies have also found that so doing helps set a stronger tone for an ethical culture throughout the organization. Additionally, when the employee population is informed that the Board of Directors has completed the same program and is subject to the same standard, completion rates for the training program are higher.

- **Programs should be short enough to allow for one-session completion.** The ideal training program for compliance and ethics is around 45 minutes. The longer a program, the less likely it is that employees will complete the session in one sitting. When training is interrupted, completion rates suffer. However, all programs should contain a bookmarking feature that tracks users' progress and allows them to pick up where they last left off, should they be interrupted.

- **Initial communications about the program should come from the executive leadership.** All initial communications informing trainees about the training program requirement and availability should be communicated by a senior executive leadership team member (preferably the CEO or President, a member of the Board of Directors, or in the case of an operating unit, the Leader/President of such unit). This is particularly true when the topic being addressed is the Code of Conduct.

- **Training deadlines should be specific, and reminder emails should be of increasing intensity.** The deadline for completing required training should not be vague, nor should the applicable incentives and discipline be unknown to the trainees. Effective training program launches aggressively communicate the availability of the program, completion timeframe expectations and surrounding factors. While training communications may be widespread, an LMS and its administrator can quickly narrow the communications, specifically and exclusively, to those employees who have failed to stay current with their required training curriculum.

- **Training programs should be launched at appropriate times of the week and year.** The period within the business and calendar cycle when the training initiative launches can have a significant impact on trainee completion rates. Research indicates that training and supporting communications should be launched early in the week and during the workday, as opposed to being sent out overnight, over the weekend or on a Thursday or Friday. Furthermore, the best times of the year to launch a training initiative (when measured on a normal calendar year basis) are the first quarter, early in the second quarter (prior to summer) and during the third quarter. It is not advisable to launch a training initiative any later than November 1 in any given year. This is due to the disruptive nature of holidays, as well as the fact that having open and ongoing training through the end of the year is not ideal for year-end reporting, which may include reports on the status of the compliance program (e.g., to the Board of Directors, in an annual corporate citizenship report, etc.).

- **Training programs should be institutionalized into the employment cycle.** By incorporating training into the employment cycle, an organization can make sure that key topics are immediately communicated to an employee upon hire. This initial communication makes an impression on the new employee regarding the importance of ethics in the organization's culture. Additionally, such a policy ensures that the training initiative is fully integrated into the employment cycle. This helps prevent the liability of having undereducated employees operating in an environment in which they could commit misconduct due to ignorance.

By implementing the above techniques, many organizations have found they routinely exceed completion rates in excess of 95 percent of the target training population by the end of the 12–16 week period. For some companies that have a highly-disciplined approach and culture, and are prepared to visibly enforce disciplinary measures for failing to complete required training, 100 percent target training population completion rates can become commonplace.

Sample Trainer's Guide

For the Introduction of the ABC Company, Inc.
Corporate Compliance Program

Trainer's Guide

This Trainer's Guide is a step-by-step guide to introduce the ABC Corporate Compliance Program to employees. It is accompanied by the following Training Kit Materials:

1. A video
2. An ABC Code of Conduct, along with the Certification Form
3. A Brochure for the ABC Integrity Hotline
4. The ABC Corporate Compliance Guidelines

You will be requested to:

1. Have attendees sign an attendance sheet, which includes the date of the meeting and who conducted the meeting.

2. Introduce yourself and the training video. The video includes messages by our President and Chairman of the Board, Zachary Bright; Compliance Officer, Alexander Smart; followed by three scenarios on various business ethics situations.

3. Respond to questions (See frequently asked questions on pages 9–11. If you are unclear on how to respond, just refer the question to the Compliance Office.)

4. Remind all employees that they need to complete the Certification Form and return it to the Compliance Office no later than December 31, 2009.

5. Send to the Compliance Office the original attendance sheet.

Scenario 1: Use of ABC Property and Destruction of Property and Theft

a. Use of ABC Property

The use of ABC property for individual profit or any unlawful, unauthorized personal or unethical purpose is prohibited by Company policy. ABC's information, technology, intellectual property, buildings, land, equipment, machines, software and cash must be used for business purposes only except as provided by Company policy or approved by your manager. Further, travel and entertainment expenses must be reasonable and substantiated by receipts as required by the Travel and Expense Reimbursement Guidelines.

b. Destruction of Property and Theft

Employees shall not intentionally damage or destroy the property of ABC and others or engage in theft.

Questions to ask:

- Are you doing the right thing or are you stealing? There are shades of gray as we saw in the above scenario.
- What kinds of things are Company property?
- Can you use Company property, such as paperclips, pens, telephones, e-mails, for personal use?
- When is personal use of Company property appropriate?
- When is personal use of Company property "stealing"?
- What should you do if you are not sure if you can make personal use of Company property?

Message:

- Always get authorization for use of Company property if in doubt;
- Never justify stealing based on the actions of others.

Scenario 2: Conflicts of Interest and Gifts and Entertainment

a. <u>Conflicts of Interest</u>

All employees occupy a position of trust with the Company and, as a result, have a duty of loyalty to the Company both during and after the employment relationship. Employees are required to avoid any relationship or activity that might create or give the appearance of a conflict between their personal interests and the interests of ABC. ABC selects its suppliers, vendors and contractors in a non-discriminatory manner and based on the quality, price, service, delivery and supply of goods and services. A decision to hire a supplier, vendor or contractor must never be based on personal interests or interests of family members but must be in the best interests of ABC and its shareholders.

Employees must disclose any relationship that appears to create a conflict of interest to their manager, or ABC's Compliance Officer. In addition, an employee or officer of the Company must seek prior approval from ABC's Compliance Officer before accepting an invitation to serve as a director or trustee of any other business or non-profit organization. If such services existed at the time of hire or upon acquisition of a new company, the employee must promptly disclose the existence of such service and seek approval to continue providing such service before doing so.

Here are examples of potential conflicts of interest that may require disclosure:

- Employee or immediate family member of employee acting as a director, partner, consultant or employee of a firm that either provides goods or services to ABC or is a competitor of ABC.
- Holding a second job that interferes with employment at ABC.
- Ownership by employees or members of their immediate family of a material financial interest, known to the employee, in a firm which is either a competitor of, or vendor to ABC.
- Using ABC's confidential information in any manner that violates the Company's confidentiality policy.

b. <u>Gifts and Entertainment</u>

Employees or the immediate family of employees shall not use their position with ABC to solicit any cash, gifts or free services from any ABC customer, vendor or contractor for personal benefit. Gifts or entertainment from others should not be accepted if they could be reasonably considered to improperly influence ABC's business relationship with or create an obligation to a customer, vendor or contractor. The following are guidelines regarding gifts and entertainment:

- Nominal gifts and entertainment, such as logo items, pens, calendars, caps, shirts and mugs are acceptable.

- Reasonable invitation to business-related meetings, conventions, conferences or product training seminars may be accepted.

- Invitations to social, cultural or sporting events may be accepted if the cost is reasonable and your attendance serves a customary business purpose such as networking (e.g., meals, holiday party and tickets).

- Invitations to sporting activities or events that are usual and customary in the conduct of business and promote good working relationships with customers and suppliers may be accepted.

Questions to Ask:

- What kinds of conflicts of interest do you encounter?

- Are there any conflicts of interest you have found in the workplace?

- How do you handle conflicts of interest?

Message:

- Suppliers must be chosen solely on the basis of what's in the best interest of the Company.

- Employees must not give or receive gifts or favors in their business dealings beyond those consistent with local custom and common courtesy.

- Employees shouldn't use Company purchasing opportunities for their own personal interests.

Scenario 3: Confidential and Proprietary Information; Financial Reporting and Records; Conflicts of Interest; and Inside Information

a. Confidential and Proprietary Information

Employees may be exposed to certain information that is considered confidential by the Company, or may be involved in the design or development of new products, procedures or inventions related to the business of the Company. All such information, products and inventions, even if the subject of a copyright or patent, is the sole property of ABC. Employees shall not disclose confidential information to persons outside the Company, including family members, and should share it only with other employees who have a "need to know."

Confidential information includes, but is not limited to

- Proposed or advance product plans;

- Projected earnings, proposed dividends, important management or organizational changes, or information about mergers or acquisitions and any other information related to the foregoing;

- Product or service design and development or training;

- Computer software and systems developed by, for or unique to the Company's business;

- Client lists (including phone numbers and addresses) or client contact information;

- Personal or financial information pertaining to any employee of the Company; and

- Advertising, marketing or pricing plans methods or strategies, and cost structures.

Employees are responsible and accountable for safeguarding Company documents and information to which they have direct or indirect access as a result of their employment with the Company, and should not leave confidential or proprietary documents or other such material in the office or elsewhere in a manner so as to invite unwanted disclosure.

b. <u>Financial Reporting and Records</u>

Each manager is responsible and accountable for maintaining an adequate system of internal controls over all areas of his or her responsibility. These controls should provide reasonable assurance that (1) (A) all transactions have been properly recorded, (B) each such transaction has been made in accordance with management authorization and applicable laws and regulations, and (C) Company assets are adequately safeguarded; and (2), as a consequence, the financial records and other reports are accurately and fairly stated. Each employee within his or her area of responsibility is expected to adhere to these established controls and the following prohibitions:

- No employee may intentionally make false or misleading entries in the Company's books and records for any reason. Any violation is ground for immediate termination, as well as civil and criminal liability.

- No employee may intentionally conceal Company information from authorized auditors or governmental regulatory agencies. Employees are required to disclose, on a timely basis, information required to evaluate the fairness of the Company's financial presentation, the soundness of its financial condition and the propriety of its operation.

- No employee may make a payment or transfer Company funds or assets that is not authorized, properly recorded and clearly accounted for on the Company's books. No employee may make or approve a payment or transfer Company funds or assets with the intention or understanding that any part of such payment or transfer is to be used except as specified in the supporting transactional documents.

- No employee shall deliberately attempt to circumvent any Company processes or controls.

c. <u>Conflicts of Interest</u>

All employees occupy a position of trust with the Company and, as a result, have a duty of loyalty to the Company both during and after the employment relationship. Employees are required to avoid any relationship or activity that might create or give the appearance of a conflict between their personal interests and the interests of ABC. ABC selects its suppliers, vendors and contractors in a non-discriminatory manner and based on the quality, price, service, delivery and supply of goods and services.

A decision to hire a supplier, vendor or contractor must never be based on personal interests or interests of family members but must be in the best interests of ABC and its shareholders.

Employees must disclose any relationship that appears to create a conflict of interest to their manager, ABC's Compliance Officer. In addition, an employee or officer of the Company must seek prior approval from ABC's Compliance Officer before accepting an invitation to serve as a director or trustee of any other business or non-profit organization. If such services existed at the time of hire or upon acquisition of a new company, the employee must promptly disclose the existence of such service and seek approval to continue providing such service before doing so.

Here are examples of potential conflicts of interest that may require disclosure:

- Employee or immediate family member of employee acting as a director, partner, consultant or employee of a firm that either provides goods or services to ABC or is a competitor of ABC.
- Holding a second job that interferes with employment at ABC.
- Ownership by employees or members of their immediate family of a material financial interest, known to the employee, in a firm which is either a competitor of, or vendor to ABC.
- Using ABC's confidential information in any manner that violates the Company's confidentiality policy.

d. Inside Information

Directors, officers and employees of ABC may, in the course of performing their duties, come into possession of "material non-public information" about ABC or other companies with whom ABC does business. "Material non-public information" is defined as any information that a reasonable investor would consider important in making a decision to buy or sell securities. In short, it includes any information that could be expected to affect the price of securities, either positively or negatively. Buying or selling securities based on such information is referred to as "insider trading" and can result in substantial fines and imprisonment.

It is illegal for ABC directors, officers, and employees to, directly or indirectly, buy or sell company stock or bonds, based on insider information or to discuss such information with others who might buy or sell securities.

For example, if in the course of your work and prior to a public announcement, you become aware of a change in dividends and earnings, an acquisition or major change in management that would materially affect ABC, you may be guilty of insider trading if you bought or sold securities of ABC or passed this information to anyone who bought or sold the securities.

Questions to Ask:

- What should be kept confidential?
- What is insider information?

- How do you keep things physically confidential?
- Do you leave important papers lying around?

Messages:
- Do not improperly share confidential information
- Do not benefit from the improper disclosure of confidential information

Frequently Asked Questions and Answers

1. *Who is covered by the ABC Code of Conduct ("Code")? I am a part-time employee. Am I covered by the Code? What about temporary employees?*

   All ABC employees are required to abide by the Code, whether full-time, part-time or temporary.

2. *Why do I need this training session? Can I just read the Code?*

   ABC employees are encouraged to attend this training session. Employees learn a lot more by attending this training session than when they read the Code on their own. Employees will also have the opportunity to ask questions and obtain explanations and clarifications.

3. *Is there any consequence if I do not attend training?*

   Employees who do not attend the training pose the risk of misunderstanding the Code and potentially violating it, which may result in disciplinary action.

4. *I read the Code of Conduct after the training and I have more questions I would like to ask. Who should I direct my questions to?*

   The first person to approach is your manager. If you need additional assistance, you may contact the Human Resources Department. If you still need additional assistance, call ABC's Compliance Office or the ABC Hotline.

5. *I'm not sure if a violation has occurred. How can I be certain before I report it?*

   It is often hard to tell whether a violation has occurred. You should seek assistance immediately if you believe in good faith that a violation may have occurred.

6. *I know about some potential violations going on in my area, but decided it was not my business to report the matter. Is there any consequence for this?*

   Unreported potential violations may cause serious damage to ABC. That is why ABC imposes a duty on employees to report in good faith actual or potential violations that they are aware of. Failure to report a violation of ABC's policy, depending on the circumstances, may result in disciplinary action.

7. *What should I do if my manager asks me to do something that I think is a potential violation of the Code?*

   You should first speak with your manager and discuss your views that the requested action could be a potential violation of the Code. If your conversation does not resolve the issue, you should discuss the situation with a level of management above your manager. If they are unable to resolve the issue or you are uncomfortable discussing the issue with them, you may report to the Human Resources Department or the ABC Compliance Office. If you feel that you cannot use any of the above mentioned channels or feel you need to report the matter anonymously, you may call the ABC Hotline.

8. *What type of training will I be required to attend?*

The additional training sessions are those you already attend as part of your job. As a result of this program, we will now have the ability to track all of the different training programs that already exist throughout the organization.

ABC Hotline

(This is an additional explanation of what is already in the brochure)

9. *What happens when I call the ABC Hotline?*

You will be connected to a trained communications specialist who will take detailed information from you and assign a control number to use as identification during follow-up. A written report will be forwarded to the ABC Compliance Office. The ABC Compliance Office will review the report and refer the matter to the appropriate department for investigation.

10. *If I report a violation to the ABC Hotline, will my call be recorded or traced? Do I need to identify myself?*

Calls will not be traced or recorded. All calls are confidential. While we encourage you to identify yourself, you do not have to.

11. *Will I be informed of the outcome of my call?*

When you make a call to the ABC Hotline, you will be given a tracking number that will allow you to call in for an update on your report.

12. *What types of issues could be channeled through the Hotline?*

While any issue can be channeled through the ABC Hotline, you should use it when reporting the following issues which involve violation of the Code: gifts and favors; antitrust and competition; inside trading; confidentiality; record keeping and document retention; personal use of ABC's resources; theft; and bribery; and complaints regarding accounting, financial reporting and financial auditing. However, ABC encourages you to first use your immediate manager for any reportable issues. If they cannot resolve the issue or you are uncomfortable using them, you may report to the Human Resources Department or ABC's Compliance Office.

13. *I placed a call to the ABC Hotline regarding how our copying machine is always out of order. Why didn't anyone come to fix it?*

The ABC Hotline is not the channel for addressing administrative issues. Administrative matters like equipment requiring maintenance or repair, and supplies needing replenishment are best communicated to your manager, department head, or other appropriate departments (e.g., building services).

14. *Should I call the ABC Hotline for questions on benefit plans and personal matters?*

No. All questions on benefit plans and personnel matters should continue to be directed to the Human Resources Department.

15. *What happens if I report in good faith an apparent violation, but it turns out that I was incorrect?*

There will be no reprisal for good faith reporting.

16. *I was out on leave when all the compliance training and distribution of compliance materials was done so I am not aware of the Compliance Program. What should I do?*

The ABC Compliance Program aims to accommodate everyone in conducting training and education. Contact your manager, department head, Human Resources or ABC Compliance Office to reschedule training.

———————

The Morgan Stanley declination from prosecution provided valuable insight into what was necessary in order to have an effective compliance program. One of the major considerations cited by the Department of Justice (DOJ) was the training that Morgan Stanley had provided to its employees. The DOJ acknowledged that Morgan Stanley provided numerous and regular trainings to its employees. Further, the DOJ highlighted the quality of training provided.

SEC v. Peterson[2]
United States District Court, Eastern District of New York
Nos. CV12-2033 and CR12-224 (2012)

THE UNITED STATES CHARGES:

At all times relevant to this Information, unless otherwise stated:

The Defendant and His Employer

1. The defendant GARTH PETERSON was a United States citizen. From 2002 to 2008, PETERSON worked for Morgan Stanley and held various positions, including Managing Director in charge of the Morgan Stanley Real Estate Group's ("MSRE") Shanghai office in the People's Republic of China ("China").

2. Morgan Stanley was a global financial-services firm with more than 61,000 employees worldwide. Its shares were listed on the New York Stock Exchange. Morgan Stanley had a class of securities registered pursuant to Section 12 of the Securities and Exchange Act of 1934 (15 U.S.C. § 78) and was required to file reports with the Securities and Exchange Commission under Section 15(d) of the Exchange Act (15 U.S.C. § 780(d)). Accordingly, Morgan Stanley was an "issuer" within the meaning of the Foreign Corrupt Practices Act.

———————

2. https://www.justice.gov/sites/default/files/criminal-fraud/legacy/2012/04/26/petersong-information.pdf. The complaint can be found at: https://www.sec.gov/litigation/complaints/2012/comp-pr2012-78.pdf.

3. Morgan Stanley, through MSRE, created and managed real-estate funds (the "MSREFs") for institutional investors and high-net-worth individuals. The MSREFs were organized as limited partnerships in Delaware.

The Foreign Corrupt Practices Act

4. Congress enacted the Foreign Corrupt Practices Act of 1977, as amended, Title 15, United States Code, Section 78dd-l et seq. ("FCPA") to prohibit covered persons and entities from acting corruptly in furtherance of an offer, promise, authorization, or payment of money or anything of value to a foreign government official for the purposes of securing any improper advantage, or assisting in obtaining or retaining business for, or directing business to, any person. Persons and entities covered by the FCPA included officers, directors, employees, or shareholders of an "issuer" acting on the issuer's behalf, and "domestic concerns," including citizens, residents, and nationals of the United States.

5. The FCPA also required issuers, including Morgan Stanley, to maintain a system of internal accounting controls sufficient to provide reasonable assurances that: (i) transactions were executed in accordance with management's general or specific authorization; (ii) transactions were recorded as necessary to (A) permit preparation of financial statements in conformity with generally accepted accounting principles or any other criteria applicable to such statements, and (B) maintain accountability for assets; (iii) access LO assets was permitted only in accordance with management's general or specific authorization; and (iv) the recorded accountability for assets was compared with the existing assets at reasonable intervals, and appropriate action was taken with respect to any differences.15 U. S.C. §78m(b) (2)(B).

6. The FCPA specifically prohibited any person from knowingly and willfully circumventing or failing to implement the required system of internal accounting controls or knowingly and willfully falsifying any book, record, or account that issuers were required to keep. 15 U.S.C. §§78m(b) (5) and 78ff (a).

Additional Relevant Persons and Entities

7. The city of Shanghai, China, is composed of several governmental districts, including the Luwan District. In December 1994, the Luwan District government incorporated a state owned, limited-liability corporation, Shanghai Yongye Enterprise (Group) Co. Ltd. ("Yongye"), to operate as the Luwan District government's real-estate-development arm. The Luwan District government owned 100 percent of Yongye' s shares. In turn, on the Luwan District government's behalf, Yongye owned much of the land in prime areas in the Luwan District.

8. Because, among other factors, the Luwan District government incorporated and owned Yongye to purchase, hold, manage, and sell the Luwan District government's real-estate investments, and to encourage, facilitate, and coordinate outside investment in the Luwan District, Yongye was an "instrumentality" of the Luwan District government within the meaning of the FCPA.

9. "Chinese Official 1," whose identity is known to the United States, was a senior executive of Yongye from 1995 to late 2006 and previously held a different position

as a public official with the Luwan District government. PETERSON and Chinese Official 1 had a close personal relationship before PETERSON joined Morgan Stanley.

10. As a senior executive of Yongye, Chinese Official 1 exercised control over Yongye and had the authority to make certain types of investment decisions for Yongye. As such, Chinese Official 1 was a "foreign official" as that term is defined in the FCPA, 15 U.S.C. §78dd-l (f) (1).

11. "Canadian Attorney 1," whose identity is known to the United States, was a Canadian citizen and partner with a Canadian law firm that maintained offices in China and elsewhere.

12. Asiasphere Holdings Limited ("Asiasphere U") was a shell company incorporated in the British Virgin Islands. Beginning on or before January I, 2006, Chinese Official 1 owned 47 percent of Asiasphere. During the same period, Canadian Attorney 1 and PETERSON indirectly owned, through another business entity that they controlled, the remaining 53 percent of Asiasphere.

Morgan Stanley's Compliance Program and Internal Controls

13. Morgan Stanley maintained an FCPA compliance program that both frequently trained Morgan Stanley employees and imposed a payment approval process that was meant to ensure, among other things, that transactions were in accordance with management's authorization and to prevent improper payments, including the transfer of things of value to officials of foreign governments and foreign government instrumentalities.

14. Between 2002 and 2008, Morgan Stanley employed over 500 dedicated compliance officers, and its compliance department had direct lines to Morgan Stanley's Board of Directors and regularly reported through the Chief Legal Officer to the Chief Executive Officer and senior management committees. Morgan Stanley employed dedicated anti-corruption specialists' who were responsible for drafting and maintaining policies and procedures; providing anti-corruption training to Morgan Stanley employees; coordinating with business units firm-wide to provide anti-corruption-related advisory services; evaluating the retention of agents; pre-clearing expenses involving non-U.S. government officials; and working with outside counsel to conduct due diligence into potential business partners. Morgan Stanley's compliance personnel regularly surveilled and monitored client and employee transactions; randomly audited selected personnel in high-risk areas; regularly audited and tested Morgan Stanley's business units; and completed additional anti-corruption initiatives by, for instance, aggregating and evaluating expense reports to attempt to detect potential illicit payments. Morgan specialized in particular regions, including China, in order to evaluate region-specific risks.

15. Morgan Stanley provided its employees with a toll free compliance hotline that was available 24 hours a day, 7 days a week. The hotline was staffed to field calls in every major language, including Chinese.

16. Morgan Stanley required each of its employees annually to certify adherence to Morgan Stanley's Code of Conduct, which included a section specifically addressing corruption risks and activities that would violate the FCPA.

17. Morgan Stanley's standing anti-corruption policy also addressed the FCPA and risks associated with the giving of gifts, business entertainment, travel, lodging, meals, charitable contributions, and employment.

18. Morgan Stanley's FCPA compliance program included live training presentations web based training, and additional FCPA reminders. Between 2000 and 2008, Morgan Stanley held at least 54 trainings for various groups of Asia-based employees on anti-corruption policies, including the FCPA.

19. Between 2002 to 2008, Morgan Stanley trained PETERSON on his duties under the FCPA at least seven times, including providing live and web-based training and a teleconference training session conducted by Morgan Stanley's Global Head of Litigation and Global Head of Morgan Stanley's Anti-Corruption Group. Among other things, Morgan Stanley specifically trained PETERSON that employees of Chinese state-owned entities could be government officials under the FCPA. Morgan Stanley also provided PETERSON at least 35 FCPA compliance reminders. These reminders included FCPA specific distributions, such as written training materials that PETERSON kept in his office; circulations and reminders of Morgan Stanley's Code of Conduct, which included policies that directly addressed the FCPA; various reminders concerning Morgan Stanley's policies on gift-giving and entertainment; the circulation of Morgan Stanley's Global Anti-Bribery Policy; guidance on the engagement of consultants; and policies addressing specific high risk events, including the Beijing Olympics.

20. Morgan Stanley required PETERSON on multiple occasions to certify his compliance with the FCPA and kept 'Chose written certifications in PETERSON's permanent employment record.

Press Release, Department of Justice, *Former Morgan Stanley Managing Director Pleads Guilty for Role in Evading Internal Controls Required by FCPA*

(Apr. 25, 2012) https://www.justice.gov/opa/pr/former-morgan-stanley-managing-director-pleads-guilty-role-evading-internal-controls-required

A former managing director for Morgan Stanley's real estate business in China pleaded guilty today for his role in a conspiracy to evade the company's internal accounting controls, announced Assistant Attorney General Lanny A. Breuer of the Justice Department's Criminal Division; U.S. Attorney Loretta E. Lynch for the Eastern District of New York; and Janice Fedarcyk, Assistant Director in Charge of the FBI's New York Field Office.

Garth Peterson, 42, an American citizen living in Singapore, pleaded guilty to one-count criminal information charging him with conspiring to evade internal accounting controls that Morgan Stanley was required to maintain under the Foreign Corrupt Practices Act (FCPA). Peterson pleaded guilty in Brooklyn, N.Y., before Senior U.S. District Judge Jack B. Weinstein.

"Mr. Peterson admitted today that he actively sought to evade Morgan Stanley's internal controls in an effort to enrich himself and a Chinese government official," said Assistant Attorney General Breuer. "As a managing director for Morgan Stanley, he had an obligation to adhere to the company's internal controls; instead, he lied and cheated his way to personal profit. Because of his corrupt conduct, he now faces the prospect of prison time."

"This defendant used a web of deceit to thwart Morgan Stanley's efforts to maintain adequate controls designed to prevent corruption. Despite years of training, he circumvented those controls for personal enrichment. We take seriously our role in detecting and prosecuting efforts to evade those controls," said U.S. Attorney Lynch.

"The defendant engaged in a pattern of self-dealing and deception that perpetuated his unjust enrichment," said FBI Assistant Director Fedarcyk. "He not only circumvented his employer's internal controls; he violated the law."

According to court documents, Morgan Stanley maintained a system of internal controls meant to ensure accountability for its assets and to prevent employees from offering, promising or paying anything of value to foreign government officials. Morgan Stanley's internal policies, which were updated regularly to reflect regulatory developments and specific risks, prohibited bribery and addressed corruption risks associated with the giving of gifts, business entertainment, travel, lodging, meals, charitable contributions and employment.

Morgan Stanley frequently trained its employees on its internal policies, the FCPA and other anti-corruption laws. Between 2002 and 2008, Morgan Stanley trained various groups of Asia-based personnel on anti-corruption policies 54 times. During the same period, Morgan Stanley trained Peterson on the FCPA seven times and reminded him to comply with the FCPA at least 35 times. Morgan Stanley's compliance personnel regularly monitored transactions, randomly audited particular employees, transactions and business units, and tested to identify illicit payments. Moreover, Morgan Stanley conducted extensive due diligence on all new business partners and imposed stringent controls on payments made to business partners.

According to court documents, Peterson conspired with others to circumvent Morgan Stanley's internal controls in order to transfer a multi-million dollar ownership interest in a Shanghai building to himself and a Chinese public official with whom he had a personal friendship. The corruption scheme began when Peterson encouraged Morgan Stanley to sell an interest in a Shanghai real-estate deal to Shanghai Yongye Enterprise (Group) Co. Ltd., a state-owned and state-controlled entity through which Shanghai's Luwan District managed its own property and facilitated outside investment in the district. Peterson falsely represented to others within Morgan Stanley that Yongye was purchasing the real-estate interest, when in fact Peterson knew the interest would be conveyed to a shell company controlled by him, a Chinese public official associated with Yongye and a Canadian attorney. After Peterson and his co-conspirators falsely represented to Morgan Stanley that Yongye owned the shell company, Morgan Stanley sold the real-estate interest in 2006 to the shell company at a discount to the interest's actual 2006 market value.

As a result, the conspirators realized an immediate paper profit of more than $2.5 million. Even after the sale, Peterson and his co-conspirators continued to claim falsely that Yongye owned the shell company, which in reality they owned. In the years since Peterson and his co-conspirators gained control of the real-estate interest, they have periodically accepted equity distributions and the real-estate interest has appreciated in value.

At sentencing, scheduled for July 17, 2012, Peterson faces a maximum penalty of five years in prison and a maximum fine of $250,000 or twice his gross gain from the offense. After considering all the available facts and circumstances, including that Morgan Stanley constructed and maintained a system of internal controls, which provided reasonable assurances that its employees were not bribing government officials, the Department of Justice declined to bring any enforcement action against Morgan Stanley related to Peterson's conduct. The company voluntarily disclosed this matter and has cooperated throughout the department's investigation.

The Securities and Exchange Commission today announced civil charges and a settlement with Peterson.

The criminal case is being prosecuted by Trial Attorney Stephen J. Spiegelhalter of the Criminal Division's Fraud Section and Assistant U.S. Attorney John Nowak of the Eastern District of New York. The Criminal Division's Office of International Affairs also provided assistance in this matter. The case was investigated by the FBI's New York Field Office.

———————

Additionally, Department of Justice Criminal Division created a Resource Guide to understand the Foreign Corrupt Practices Act (FCPA). This Resource Guide, in Chapter 5 Guiding Principles of Enforcement, provides guidance on training. This guidance is provided for FCPA compliance programs; however, it provides helpful best practices applicable to any compliance program.

———————

U.S. Department of Justice Criminal Division & SEC Enforcement Division, Resource Guide to the U.S. Foreign Corrupt Practices Act

http://www.justice.gov/sites/default/files/criminal-fraud/legacy/2015/01/16/guide.pdf

Training and Continuing Advice

Compliance policies cannot work unless effectively communicated throughout a company. Accordingly, DOJ and SEC will evaluate whether a company has taken steps to ensure that relevant policies and procedures have been communicated throughout the organization, including through periodic training and certification for all directors, officers, relevant employees, and, where appropriate, agents and business partners. For example, many larger companies have implemented a mix of web-based and in-person training conducted at varying intervals. Such training typically covers company policies and procedures, instruction on applicable laws, practical advice to address real-life scenarios, and case studies. Regardless of how a company chooses to conduct its training, however, the information should be presented in a manner appropriate for the targeted audience, including providing training and training materials in the local language. For example, companies may want to consider providing different types of training to their sales personnel and accounting personnel with hypotheticals or sample situations that are similar to the situations they might encounter. In addition to the existence and scope of a company's training program, a company should develop appropriate measures, depending on the size and sophistication of the particular company, to provide guidance and advice on complying with the company's ethics and compliance program, including when such advice is needed urgently. Such measures will help ensure that the compliance program is understood and followed appropriately at all levels of the company.

Compliance programs' effectiveness depends on compliance professionals' ability to create a culture of ethics and provide training that will effectively reduce and prevent future misconduct.

Training should be multi-tiered including in-person, train-the-trainer, and online training. Compliance professionals will need to be increasingly focused on prioritizing and addressing top risk areas, and using training to cover more risk areas even in the midst of limited training hours and pressured budgets. And, as they look to the future, leaders must be increasingly focused on laying the groundwork today to measure the effectiveness of their training investment tomorrow.

Compliance training program is a cornerstone for organizations that are committed to building an ethical culture, and protecting their employees, reputation and bottom line.[3]

Assignments

- **Hypothetical:** You are the Chief Compliance Officer at your [Team's] corporation. Create a sample anti-money laundering or anti-bribery training program.

- Create a training program including a heatmap and dashboard on the top five risks of your company.

---

3. NAVEX Global 2014 Ethics and Compliance Training Benchmark Report: http://www.navexglobal.com/file-download?file=uploads/NAVEXGlobal_2014_Training_Benchmark_Report_US_07.01.pdf&file-name=NAVEXGlobal_2014_Training_Benchmark_Report_US_07.01.pdf.

- Analyze the Morgan Stanley Declination from Prosecution to determine what kind of training and what frequency of training was considered "effective" by the Department of Justice.

Chapter 8

Auditing, Monitoring, Testing, Surveillance, and Reporting

Introduction

As the need to identify and prioritize material compliance risks becomes increasingly critical to Audit Committees, senior management and rating agency discussions, companies are moving from rules-based to risk-based compliance programs in an effort to more effectively measure and monitor the significant risks across the organization. "The migration from rules-based to risk-based compliance programs is about providing risk intelligence, not just data," says Rebecca C. Amoroso, Vice Chairman and U.S. Insurance Industry Group Leader with Deloitte LLP. "The more effective programs can proactively identify the points of greatest exposure. To align compliance reporting with areas of significant risk, companies need to employ a 'next generation' approach for data gathering, synthesis, metrics, and reporting." This is achieved through adequate testing methodologies and/or surveillance operations that, combined with other analytical tools, such as heat-maps and dashboards, allow compliance departments the ability to gather and synthesize the collected risk-exposure data in a manner that is easier to comprehend and visualize.

Furthermore, central to the uncovering of fraud and misconduct, the Sarbanes-Oxley Act of 2002 mandated the implementation of an anonymous reporting hotline to allay the fear of retaliation experienced by public company employees. Further, the Dodd-Frank Wall Street Reform and Consumer Protection Act of 2010 created a federal whistleblower protection program through which an employee may notify the government of any wrongdoing. (For a fuller discussion of these hotlines, see Chapter 9.)

For many financial services companies, achieving a risk-based compliance program remains a goal, rather than an accomplishment, particularly when the task is viewed from the highest levels of compliance management. According to the 2014 Compliance Trends Survey, a joint effort conducted by Deloitte & Touche LLP and Compliance Week Magazine, 64 percent of the staff-level compliance professional respondents (such as managers, directors and vice presidents) believe that their compliance metrics give them a true sense of the efficacy of their compliance programs, while only 52 percent of chief compliance officers are confident in the accuracy of such assessments. Additionally, 23 percent of survey respondents indicated that they do not measure the effectiveness of their compliance program at all.

Current Regulatory Environment

Companies today operate in a dynamic regulatory environment and must contend with a number of critical compliance issues. Most financial institutions are subject to exams and oversight by the Securities and Exchange Commission (SEC), Financial Industry Regulatory Authority (FINRA), and state insurance and securities departments, plus an increased level of involvement by state attorneys general. Also, financial institutions may be subject to the Commodities Future Exchange Commission (CFTC) if they engage in the sale or purchase of commodities and the National Futures Association (NFA) if they engage in the sale or purchase of futures, swaps or foreign currencies. In addition to the risks associated with regulatory sweeps and enforcement actions, companies must address the risk of private litigation, as well as the scrutiny of rating agencies, as they determine how compliance programs are designed and operated to identify and manage regulatory risks at an early stage. Finally, since most financial institutions operate in a global environment, financial institutions should be equally aware of regulations and guidance by international organizations, such as the U.N., IMF, World Bank, and OECD, as well as national and local regulators located outside the U.S.

Typically, more effective compliance programs are patterned after integrated risk management practices. Compliance has accordingly emerged as a key risk discipline within the risk management framework of companies, in addition to market, credit, actuarial, and operational risks. Compliance with laws and managing risks associated with a failure to adhere to regulatory requirements has led to the need for implementing compliance reporting systems that include key risk indicators to highlight the areas carrying the most risk. Unfortunately, there are a number of companies that have not identified appropriate metrics and lack risk reporting capabilities that could anticipate and identify risk proactively.

"Insurers are concerned with the increasing cost of noncompliance as well as the impact on their reputation," says Howard Mulls, Chief Advisor at Deloitte LLP's Insurance Industry Group and a former Superintendent of the New York State Insurance Department. "There are cost pressures out there, obviously. But if your compliance function fails, the costs to the company are often not measurable in dollars. It is not just an issue of the total amount of the fine that may result. It is also the reputational risk that can range from the mild to the extreme, which can rise to a level of exposure posing a real threat to the enterprise." In recent years, some of the world's biggest financial institutions, such as JP Morgan Chase, Bank of America, Citi, BNP Paribas and UBS, have been showcased in the headlines of international news due to the multi-billion dollar fines imposed.

- In June 2014, the French bank BNP Paribas agreed to pay $8.9 billion for disguising transfers to U.S. banks involving entities from countries that are subject to economic sanctions, including Iran, Cuba and Sudan.

- In July 2014, Citigroup paid $7 billion that, according to the Wall Street Journal's article published on July 14, 2014, included a "$4 billion civil penalty to the Justice

Department, $500 million to the Federal Deposit Insurance Corp. and several states, and $2.5 billion earmarked for 'consumer relief,' to settle the U.S. government's allegations it knowingly sold shoddy mortgages ahead of the crisis."

- In August 2014, Bank of America paid $16.7 billion to U.S. authorities for misleading investors about the quality of loans sold.

- In March 2015, Commerzbank, a German bank, reached a settlement with U.S. regulators and agreed to pay $1.45 billion for helping Olympus Corporation commit accounting fraud and for its role in concealing prohibited transactions with Sudan and Iran.

Shifting to Risk-Based Compliance Management

Leading compliance practices are moving beyond the traditional core capabilities to more advanced capabilities, such as early warning systems for high risk compliance issues and a process of continuous, formalized, and information-based risk assessments. As compliance programs mature, there has been a shift from their previous rule and value-based approaches in order to become more risk-based in their assessments, with a greater focus on the measurement and reporting of risk. In order for top management to receive a comprehensive, up-to-date analysis of the institution's risk exposure, the data collected through these assessments should be integrated into more holistic, risk-focused dashboards and heatmaps that enable senior management to have an integrated view of risks across the entire organization.

This shift to risk-based compliance is even more prudent in light of the SEC and DOJ's position on risk-based compliance. In 2012, the SEC and the DOJ published the *Foreign Corrupt Practices Act: A Resource Guide to the U.S. Foreign Corrupt Practices Act* ("*FCPA Guide*"). In the *FCPA Guide*, the DOJ and SEC stated that they would "give meaningful credit to a company that implements in good faith a comprehensive, risk-based compliance program, even if that program does not prevent an infraction in a low risk area because greater attention and resources had been devoted to a higher risk area." *FCPA Guide* at 59. In 2014, Kara Brockmeyer, chief of the SEC's FCPA Unit, emphasized the need for strong compliance programs in the context of anti-bribery and corruption and stated that the best compliance programs are geared toward the company's risks. Brockmeyer noted that by utilizing a risk-based auditing and testing, companies can identify and prioritize risks.[1]

Further, in the *FCPA Guide*, the DOJ and SEC recognize that when it comes to effective compliance programs the "one-size-fits-all" approach does not work and that "[c]ompliance programs that employ the 'check-the-box' approach may be in-

---

1. Kara Brockmeyer, Chief of the SEC FCPA Unit, 18th Annual Corporate Counsel Institute, Washington, DC (Mar. 13, 2014).

efficient and, more importantly, ineffective." *FCPA Guide* at 57. This means that companies will have to conduct their own risk assessment in order to identify, understand and prioritize their specific company risks and establish procedures, policies and protocols that address the identified issues. Additionally, because risks continue to evolve as the company, industry and regulations change, it is critical that companies monitor and reevaluate their risks and modify the associated policies, procedures and protocols, as appropriate.

In less mature compliance programs, companies have grappled with the challenges of putting compliance procedures and controls in place, frequently discovering that the procedures and controls are implemented differently within distinct business units, with varying degrees of effectiveness. This tendency to silo compliance approaches for each line of business is often seen in companies with diverse product and distribution approaches that are subject to a broad range of federal and state regulations. Lacking a strategic approach to the structure and operation of their compliance programs, companies often have inconsistent, fragmented, and uncoordinated approaches to implementation and monitoring.

As companies seek to mitigate costs, a program design that permits the compliance function to focus its resources on key risks ultimately promotes cost-effectiveness. Adopting a uniform and formal process of regular compliance risk assessment to identify the areas of significant risk allows companies to better align human resources, training, and compliance monitoring, testing, and reporting. Moreover, adopting a uniform process focuses attention on higher risk and potentially less controlled business activities and appropriately de-emphasizes those areas that have some risk but are well managed and controlled. This process also helps align the efforts of the internal control groups, such as risk management and internal audit, and provides a consistent view of the areas of significant risk, which enables a more coordinated approach toward testing and reporting.

Key Steps to Adopting a Risk-Based Compliance Program

To move toward a more effective risk-based compliance program, companies should focus on the following key steps:

- **Risk Assessments:** Develop uniform risk definitions and the overall framework for a risk assessment process to identify and evaluate significant compliance risk and controls and to help the organization assess those in the context of the overall risk profile of the organization. This should be done in concert with the other control functions so there is a coordinated and consistent set of definitions that fit into a corporate framework.

- **Risk Ranking:** Determine the inherent risk and residual risk (i.e., net risk after assessing controls to mitigate the inherent risk). Based on the likelihood and the impact of a failure that has been considered for the residual risk exposure, rank the risks in order of importance to highlight those risks requiring the most immediate attention. Heatmaps are a particularly useful tool when risk ranking. Heatmaps help visualize in a comprehensive, transparent and integrated manner an enterprise's risk exposure.

- **Compliance Metrics:** Identify and understand key risks, and develop metrics that align with those risks. These metrics will support key risk indicator reporting for the greatest potential risk areas. The 2014 Compliance Trends Survey conducted by Deloitte and Compliance Week indicated that most frequently utilized metrics for measuring the effectiveness of a compliance department are analysis of internal audit findings, hotline call analysis, completion rates for required trainings and disposition of internal investigations.

- **Executive Dashboards:** Create an executive reporting dashboard that incorporates risk-based compliance metrics, provides both exception and trend reporting, and highlights emerging problems. (Dashboards can be aligned, for example, along such themes as: People/Culture, Technology, Process, External, Legal Regulatory.)

- **Auditing:** Work closely with Internal Audit to develop a continual risk-based auditing program that focuses on areas of prior concern, emerging risk areas, cultural tone, and static ongoing operational areas.

- **Monitoring:** Establish ongoing oversight procedures to ensure the proper application of compliance program policies and to determine if there are gaps in the compliance program's coverage, including the use of testing and surveillance.

- **Testing:** Conduct "sting operations" to test the application of compliance procedures and protocols. For example, compliance personnel could call the company hotline and report a fake issue to the operator to test if proper procedures are followed in the investigation of such report.

- **Surveillance:** Implement protocols for random and targeted collection and review of paperwork, e-mail, and telephone calls. Compliance personnel should also make announced and unannounced visits to inspect and observe activities and facilities.

- **Compliance Reporting:** Implement a robust reporting process for compliance management's use to continuously assess the compliance program and to align the auditing, monitoring, testing, surveillance and reporting protocols.

Illustration 8.1

Sample Auditing, Monitoring, Testing, Surveillance and Reporting Dashboard for a global financial institution. Dashboard sets out the schedule of activities and categories the activities/results by risk level.

	1st Quarter	2nd Quarter	3rd Quarter	4th Quarter
Auditing	1. Audit of the AML Program 2. Audit of North American Branch Offices	1. Audit of the FCPA program 2. Audit of European Branch Offices 3. London Office—not following protocol with regard to travel and entertainment policy	1. Audit of the control room functions 2. Audit of Asian Offices 3. In depth, review of London Travel and entertainment policy	1. Audit of Wealth Management Compliance Group 2. Audit of South American and African Offices 3. London Travel and Entertainment Policy issue resolved
Monitoring	1. Monitor of the control room functions 2. Monitor of Asian Offices 3. Review of Control Room activities shows insufficient barriers, issues referred to CCO	1. Monitor of Wealth Management Compliance Group 2. Monitor of S. American and African Offices 3. Continued monitoring of control room shows improved barriers	1. Monitor of the AML Program 2. Monitor of North American Branch Offices 3. Control room issues resolved	1. Monitor of the FCPA program 2.Monitor of European Branch Offices
Testing	1. Hotline Testing 2. Testing of control room	1. Testing Broker-Dealer disclosures 2. Testing of Branch Offices 3. Two failures of disclosure obligations related to senior investors	1. Hotline Testing 2. Testing of control room 3. Enhanced testing of senior disclosure requirements	1. Testing Broker-Dealer disclosures 2. Testing of Branch Offices

Illustration 8.1, *continued*

	1st Quarter	2nd Quarter	3rd Quarter	4th Quarter
Surveillance	1. Surveillance of control room calls 2. Surveillance of Branch Office emails	1. Surveillance of hotline calls 2. Surveillance of communication between research and clients	1. Surveillance of control room calls 2. Surveillance of Branch Office emails 3. Enhanced Surveillance of London FCPA violators 4. Enhanced Surveillance of brokers with failed disclosures	1. Surveillance of hotline calls 2. Surveillance of communication between research and clients 3. Enhanced Surveillance of London FCPA violators 4. Enhanced Surveillance of brokers with failed disclosures
Reporting	1. Monthly reporting of results of AMTS to the CCO 2. Control Room Monitoring report to CCO 3. CCO reports on control room issues to Audit Committee	1. Monthly reporting of results of AMTS to the CCO	1. Monthly reporting of results of AMTS to the CCO	1. Monthly reporting of results of AMTS to the CCO

Risk-Based Metrics with an ICRM Approach

Integrated Compliance Risk Management (ICRM) is a unified approach to the structure, design and operation of a company's compliance program that helps management to understand and manage compliance risks across multiple business units efficiently and effectively. Three of the ICRM cornerstones are practical and well-designed risk assessments, compliance metrics, and the employment of technology in a way that allows companies to extract data from various administrative systems and provide risk-based reporting.

Increasingly, financial institutions are employing key risk-based metrics to measure significant risks. According to Deloitte and Compliance Week 2013 and 2014 Compliance Trends Survey, companies have increased the number and types of metrics that they use to assess the effectiveness of their programs.

Among the lessons learned from the recent financial and credit market crisis is the importance of sound risk management practices and reliable performance metrics. Regulatory compliance should be an important part of a company-wide risk management program, with appropriate risk measures and monitoring and reporting capabilities across all risk classes.

While the actual process of measuring the effectiveness of a compliance program is highly dependent on a company's structure, business model, regulatory environment and culture, there are a number of other areas that companies should consider when developing and quantifying metrics. These include, but are not limited to:

1. The compliance-related training curriculum and the number and types of employees trained in each of the subject areas.

2. The annual number of hotline calls in each of the pre-defined areas (e.g., procurement fraud, improper accounting, sexual harassment, etc.).

3. The number of code of conduct violations and terminations by category.

4. Results of surveys relating to the general perception of the company by shareholders, employees, customers, and other constituents.

5. The general awareness of the compliance program and code of conduct.

6. Company violations, fines, or penalties imposed by governing agencies.

7. Results of culture audits and the employees' opinions on the culture's general adherence to critical company policies.

8. The "Tone at the Top" as measured by the overall commitment to compliance with laws and regulations and represented in communications by the Board and senior management.

9. The existence of compliance-related objectives in employees' annual performance goals, their relationship with compensation, and overall evaluation.

10. Adherence to various policies and procedures that may include:
    a. Email;
    b. Record retention and destruction;
    c. Background checks;
    d. Data privacy;
    e. Gift and Entertainment;
    f. Personal Investment; and
    g. Outside Activities.

Because some compliance areas are more easily measurable than others, it is important to use all available tools which may include: internal and external surveys, human resources data, focus groups, third party data, and cultural assessments.

Intelligent Use of Technology

Compliance reporting continues to be a heavily manual process, with even automated processes requiring significant manual intervention. Regulatory reporting is generally one of the most cost-effective ways to leverage technology. IT departments should look at technology opportunities within the typical reporting life-cycle, which starts with data mining and capture, is supported by core processing systems and data repositories, and ends with reporting capabilities. Weaknesses in any phase of the life-cycle can cause significant gaps in reporting, risk assessment, and decision-making. A recent Deloitte survey indicated that 26 percent of chief compliance officers are not confident that their current IT systems have the capacity to satisfy all compliance and reporting requirements.

In the data capture process, there may be many challenges with incomplete, incorrect or missing data, as well as controlling the quality of data received from third parties, such as third-party administrators. Challenges in the core processing platforms include redundant systems, and lines of business or business units with different formats, definitions, and quality of data. Additionally, companies typically struggle with matching data across their systems as the data flows into data warehouses or repositories, and such inconsistencies result in conflicting information with no "single version of the truth." Because of these intersecting issues, the actual reporting process requires significant manual intervention to gather, assess, correct, and report the results, which introduces great risk of error and misreporting.

Many times lack of data integrity results from external inconsistencies that are outside of the company's control. Regular implementation of a front-end system of correction (at least four times a year) to review data input can help to identify external inconsistencies due to data received from outside the company. Implementing front-end systemic corrections is one of the lowest cost methods to improve data integrity, but it frequently meets resistance from operations management who view it as taxing resources and productivity. Tracking and reporting data errors can help build awareness of the problem and gain organizational consensus and discipline to implement enhanced controls.

In addition to front-end data capture, companies can invest in Master Data Management and Data Governance hubs to help improve the consistency and quality of data within their organization. Where efforts to control and manage data have not been successful, a regulatory data warehouse can be developed to support efforts to consolidate, match, and control the data required to support scheduled and ad hoc regulatory reporting needs. Frequently, these data warehouses become valuable sources of information because they hold more reliable data than is available elsewhere in the organization.

In the reporting process, technology can be leveraged in a number of ways beyond just gathering the data into a reportable format. Provision of business intelligence tools can more efficiently support ad hoc requests from regulators or internal risk management and compliance personnel. Moreover, rules can be developed that alert risk officers of compliance violations or significant deviations from policy or required conduct.

The ultimate use of technology in the reporting environment is to implement regulatory dashboards to proactively manage compliance and provide visibility of the risk profile and reporting process. Key business objectives provide transparency to operations and initiatives, reduce risk, improve enterprise-wide communications, and keep directors and management informed of performance metrics and potential issues.

Tracking the true cost of regulatory reporting can be an effective method to help justify automation throughout the reporting life-cycle. Most organizations do not recognize the total cost because it is hidden in analysts performing special data runs, in fines and unrecovered assessments, in middle-office departments that work to correct data, and in the cost of legal and regulatory actions. Identifying, measuring, and reporting these costs can build a persuasive business case to build internal controls into the organization's systems.

Compliance Auditing and Testing

Aside from the practicality associated with general compliance auditing of a company's processes and controls, the need to audit the compliance program is mandated by the Federal Sentencing Guidelines, which require "regular steps to ensure ongoing compliance through effective monitoring and auditing."

The process of auditing a compliance program is a central activity that should look across the entire enterprise in an effort to adequately and independently test policies, procedures and controls, and use the collected data to identify critical weaknesses that may lead to violations of company policy, the code of conduct, and violations of federal and state law. Adequate testing of policies and procedures should be conducted on an ongoing basis in order to determine the "effectiveness" of the compliance program. In order to improve data accuracy and facilitate an enterprise-wide analysis of the collected data, testing methodologies should be consistent throughout an institution. This would enable management to better identify any patterns or loopholes that may indicate potential weaknesses of the compliance program.

A long standing problem that continues to be discussed throughout organizations today is the ownership of compliance audit-related activities. While compliance activities typically involve monitoring, reporting, and business support, a large number of companies have engaged their compliance departments in audit-related activities. While there is no one method for approaching compliance auditing activities, it is important to recognize that whomever performs the compliance audits, needs to be competent in the area and needs to maintain independence.

When it comes to selecting the staff to perform compliance audits, there are a number of options to consider, a few of which are included below:

- Compliance Department;
- Office of the Corporate Secretary;
- Internal Audit;
- Corporate Legal;
- External Auditors; and
- Third Parties (i.e., Compliance Consultants).

When considering compliance audit options, the Chief Compliance Officer (CCO) should consider the specifics of the situation and take into account the potential need for attorney-client privilege, attorney work product privilege, self-evaluative privilege, *Kovel* privilege and other federal and state protections. (For a fuller discussion of these issues, see Corporate Compliance and Attorney-Client Privilege chapter, *supra*.) As a result of these considerations, a company may choose to take a different course of action and utilize some combination of the above mentioned resources to perform the audit. Generally, it is best to coordinate with the internal audit department regardless of who is performing the compliance audit.

Once the audit is performed, a company must then consider the distribution of the report and the various report-out options. Options include:

- Local Management;
- Senior Management;
- Audit Committee;
- Compliance/Risk Committee;
- Governance Committee; and
- General Counsel.

Typically if internal audit is associated with the compliance audit, the distribution protocol is pre-determined. Distribution options associated with the use of others in the audit process are generally dependent on company structure, compliance structure, and the specifics of the audit.

Regardless of the distribution, the Chief Compliance Officer (CCO) must ensure that the appropriate follow-up takes place to cure all identified weaknesses and findings within a reasonable amount of time. The development of an action plan that identifies responsible parties and completion dates is generally a good practice to follow. In addition, follow-up audits act as vehicles to access whether the commitments made by the business units have been achieved. The existence of an audit document with known issues without a defined plan and associated remediation activity can be damaging to a company.

Regulatory/Legal Perspective

Attorneys may be generally concerned about the existence of audit reports, measures, metrics and other types of assessments as these types of reports can be used as road maps to identify issues within in the organization when examined either by a regulator or through the discovery process related to litigation. The general perception is that this type of documentation can create risk and/or incriminating evidence that could lead to civil or criminal liability. While these are all valid concerns, the real issue arises when known issues are documented, distributed and not remediated. Accordingly, documented metrics can be considered to be a positive asset provided there is a constant commitment to remediation and the corrective actions are documented fully.

Over the years, as corporate legal and compliance divisions have grown, courts have been faced with the difficult task of defining the types of activities that should be protected by attorney-client privilege, work product privilege and/or self-evaluative privilege. In designing an auditing, monitoring, testing, surveillance and reporting program, companies must consider the defined scope of these privileges.

Upjohn Co. v. United States
449 U.S. 383 (1981)

Justice Rehnquist delivered the opinion of the Court. Chief Justice Burger filed an opinion concurring in part and concurring in the judgment.

We granted certiorari in this case to address important questions concerning the scope of the attorney-client privilege in the corporate context and the applicability of the work-product doctrine in proceedings to enforce tax summonses.

I

Petitioner Upjohn Co. manufactures and sells pharmaceuticals here and abroad. In January 1976 independent accountants conducting an audit of one of Upjohn's foreign subsidiaries discovered that the subsidiary made payments to or for the benefit of foreign government officials in order to secure government business. The accountants, so informed petitioner, Mr. Gerard Thomas, Upjohn's Vice President, Secretary, and General Counsel. Thomas is a member of the Michigan and New York Bars, and has been Upjohn's General Counsel for 20 years. He consulted with outside counsel and R. T. Parfet, Jr., Upjohn's Chairman of the Board. It was decided that the company would conduct an internal investigation of what were termed "questionable payments." As part of this investigation the attorneys prepared a letter containing a questionnaire which was sent to "All Foreign General and Area Managers" over the Chairman's signature. The letter began by noting recent disclosures that several American companies made "possibly illegal" payments to foreign government officials and emphasized that the management needed full information concerning any such payments made by Upjohn. The letter indicated that the Chairman had asked Thomas, identified as "the company's General Counsel," "to conduct an investigation for the purpose of determining the nature and magnitude of any payments made by the Upjohn Company or any of its subsidiaries to any employee or official of a foreign government." The questionnaire sought detailed information concerning such payments. Managers were instructed to treat the investigation as "highly confidential" and not to discuss it with anyone other than Upjohn employees who might be helpful in providing the requested information. Responses were to be sent directly to Thomas. Thomas and outside counsel also interviewed the recipients of the questionnaire and some 33 other Upjohn officers or employees as part of the investigation.

On March 26, 1976, the company voluntarily submitted a preliminary report to the Securities and Exchange Commission on Form 8-K disclosing certain questionable payments. A copy of the report was simultaneously submitted to the Internal Revenue Service, which immediately began an investigation to determine the tax consequences of the payments. Special agents conducting the investigation were given lists by Upjohn of all those interviewed and all who had responded to the questionnaire. On November 23, 1976, the Service issued a summons pursuant to 26 U.S.C. §7602 demanding production of:

> "All files relative to the investigation conducted under the supervision of Gerard Thomas to identify payments to employees of foreign governments and any political contributions made by the Upjohn Company or any of its affiliates since January 1, 1971 and to determine whether any funds of the Upjohn Company had been improperly accounted for on the corporate books during the same period.

> "The records should include but not be limited to written questionnaires sent to managers of the Upjohn Company's foreign affiliates, and memorandums or notes of the interviews conducted in the United States and abroad with officers and employees of the Upjohn Company and its subsidiaries."

The company declined to produce the documents specified in the second paragraph on the grounds that they were protected from disclosure by the attorney-client privilege and constituted the work product of attorneys prepared in anticipation of litigation. On August 31, 1977, the United States filed a petition seeking enforcement of the summons under 26 U.S.C. §§7402(b) and 7604(a) in the United States District Court for the Western District of Michigan. That court adopted the recommendation of a Magistrate who concluded that the summons should be enforced. Petitioners appealed to the Court of Appeals for the Sixth Circuit which rejected the Magistrate's finding of a waiver of the attorney-client privilege, 600 F.2d 1223, 1227, n. 12, but agreed that the privilege did not apply "[t]o the extent that the communications were made by officers and agents not responsible for directing Upjohn's actions in response to legal advice ... for the simple reason that the communications were not the 'client's.'" *Id.*, at 1225. The court reasoned that accepting petitioners' claim for a broader application of the privilege would encourage upper-echelon management to ignore unpleasant facts and create too broad a "zone of silence." Noting that Upjohn's counsel had interviewed officials such as the Chairman and President, the Court of Appeals remanded to the District Court so that a determination of who was within the "control group" could be made. In a concluding footnote the court stated that the work-product doctrine "is not applicable to administrative summonses issued under 26 U.S.C. §7602." *Id.*, at 1228, n. 13

II

Federal Rule of Evidence 501 provides that "the privilege of a witness ... shall be governed by the principles of the common law as they may be interpreted by the courts of the United States in light of reason and experience." The attorney-client privilege is the oldest of the privileges for confidential communications known to the common law. 8 J. Wigmore, Evidence §2290 (McNaughton rev. 1961). Its purpose is to encourage full and frank communication between attorneys and their clients and thereby promote broader public interests in the observance of law and administration of justice. The privilege recognizes that sound legal advice or advocacy serves public ends and that such advice or advocacy depends upon the lawyer's being fully informed by the client. As we stated last Term in *Trammel v. United States*, 445 U.S. 40, 51 (1980): "The lawyer-client privilege rests on the need for the advocate and counselor to know all that relates to the client's reasons for seeking representation if the professional mission is to be carried out." And in *Fisher v. United States*, 425 U.S. 391, 403 (1976), we recognized the purpose of the privilege to be "to encourage clients to make full disclosure to their attorneys." This rationale for the privilege has long been recognized by the Court, see *Hunt v. Blackburn*, 128 U.S. 464, 470 (1888) (privilege "is founded upon the necessity, in the interest and administration of justice, of the aid of persons having knowledge of the law and skilled in its practice, which assistance can only be safely and readily availed of when free from the consequences or the apprehension of disclosure"). Admittedly complications in the application of the privilege arise when the client is a corporation, which in theory is an artificial creature of the law, and not an individual; but this Court has assumed that the privilege applies when the client is a corporation, *United States v. Louisville & Nashville R. Co.*, 236 U.S. 318, 336 (1915), and the Government does not contest the general proposition.

The Court of Appeals, however, considered the application of the privilege in the corporate context to present a "different problem," since the client was an inanimate entity and "only the senior management, guiding and integrating the several operations, ... can be said to possess an identity analogous to the corporation as a whole." 600 F.2d at 1226. The first case to articulate the so-called "control group test" adopted by the court below, *Philadelphia v. Westinghouse Electric Corp.*, 210 F. Supp. 483, 485 (ED Pa.), petition for mandamus and prohibition denied *sub nom. General Electric Co. v. Kirkpatrick*, 312 F.2d 742 (CA3 1962), cert. denied, 372 U.S. 943 (1963), reflected a similar conceptual approach:

> "Keeping in mind that the question is, Is it the corporation which is seeking the lawyer's advice when the asserted privileged communication is made?, the most satisfactory solution, I think, is that if the employee making the communication, of whatever rank he may be, is in a position to control or even to take a substantial part in a decision about any action which the corporation may take upon the advice of the attorney, ... then, in effect, *he is (or personifies) the corporation* when he makes his disclosure to the lawyer and the privilege would apply." (Emphasis supplied.)

Such a view, we think, overlooks the fact that the privilege exists to protect not only the giving of professional advice to those who can act on it but also the giving of information to the lawyer to enable him to give sound and informed advice. See *Trammel, supra,* at 51; *Fisher, supra,* at 403. The first step in the resolution of any legal problem is ascertaining the factual background and sifting through the facts with an eye to the legally relevant. See ABA Code of Professional Responsibility, Ethical Consideration 4-1:

"A lawyer should be fully informed of all the facts of the matter he is handling in order for his client to obtain the full advantage of our legal system. It is for the lawyer in the exercise of his independent professional judgment to separate the relevant and important from the irrelevant and unimportant. The observance of the ethical obligation of a lawyer to hold inviolate the confidences and secrets of his client not only facilitates the full development of facts essential to proper representation of the client but also encourages laymen to seek early legal assistance."

See also *Hickman v. Taylor*, 329 U.S. 495, 511 (1947).

In the case of the individual client the provider of information and the person who acts on the lawyer's advice are one and the same. In the corporate context, however, it will frequently be employees beyond the control group as defined by the court below—"officers and agents ... responsible for directing [the company's] actions in response to legal advice"—who will possess the information needed by the corporation's lawyers. Middle-level—and indeed lower-level—employees can, by actions within the scope of their employment, embroil the corporation in serious legal difficulties, and it is only natural that these employees would have the relevant information needed by corporate counsel if he is adequately to advise the client with respect to such actual or potential difficulties. This fact was noted in *Diversified Industries, Inc. v. Meredith*, 572 F.2d 596 (CA8 1978) (en banc):

"In a corporation, it may be necessary to glean information relevant to a legal problem from middle management or non-management personnel as well as from top executives. The attorney dealing with a complex legal problem 'is thus faced with a "Hobson's choice." If he interviews employees not having "the very highest authority," their communications to him will not be privileged. If, on the other hand, he interviews only those employees with the "very highest authority," he may find it extremely difficult, if not impossible, to determine what happened.'" *Id.*, at 608–609 (quoting Weinschel Corporate Employee Interviews and the Attorney-Client Privilege, 12 B.C. Ind. & Comm. L. Rev. 873, 876 (1971)).

The control group test adopted by the court below thus frustrates the very purpose of the privilege by discouraging the communication of relevant information by employees of the client to attorneys seeking to render legal advice to the client corporation. The attorney's advice will also frequently be more significant to non-control group members than to those who officially sanction the advice, and the control group test makes it more difficult to convey full and frank legal advice to the employees who will put into effect the client corporation's policy. *See, e. g., Duplan Corp. v. Deering Milliken, Inc.*, 397 F. Supp. 1146, 1164 (DSC 1974) ("After the lawyer forms his or her opinion, it is of no immediate benefit to the Chairman of the Board or the President. It must be given to the corporate personnel who will apply it.").

The narrow scope given the attorney-client privilege by the court below not only makes it difficult for corporate attorneys to formulate sound advice when their client is faced with a specific legal problem but also threatens to limit the valuable efforts of corporate counsel to ensure their client's compliance with the law. In light of the vast and complicated array of regulatory legislation confronting the modern corporation, corporations, unlike most individuals, "constantly go to lawyers to find out how to obey the law," Burnham, The Attorney-Client Privilege in the Corporate Arena, 24 Bus. Law. 901, 913 (1969), particularly since compliance with the law in this area is hardly an instinctive matter, *see, e.g., United States v. United States Gypsum Co.*, 438 U.S. 422, 440–441 (1978) ("the behavior proscribed by the [Sherman] Act is often difficult to distinguish from the gray zone of socially acceptable and economically justifiable business conduct").[2] The test adopted by the court below is difficult to apply in practice, though no abstractly formulated and unvarying "test" will necessarily enable courts to decide questions such as this with mathematical precision. But if the purpose of the attorney-client privilege is to be served, the attorney and client must be able to predict with some degree of certainty whether particular discussions will be protected. An uncertain privilege, or one which purports to be certain but results in widely varying applications by the courts, is little better than no privilege at all. The very terms of the test adopted by the court below suggest the unpredictability of its application. The test restricts the availability of the privilege to those officers who play a "substantial role" in deciding and directing a corporation's legal response. Disparate decisions in cases applying this test illustrate its unpredictability. *Compare, e.g., Hogan v. Zletz*, 43 F.R.D. 308, 315–316 (ND Okl.1967), aff'd in part *sub nom. Natta v. Hogan*, 392 F.2d 686 (CA10 1968) (control group includes managers and assistant managers of patent division and research and development department), *with Congoleum Industries, Inc. v. GAF Corp.*, 49 F.R.D. 82, 83–85 (ED Pa.1969), aff'd, 478 F.2d 1398 (CA3 1973) (control group includes only division and corporate vice presidents, and not two directors of research and vice president for production and research).

The communications at issue were made by Upjohn employees[3] to counsel for Upjohn acting as such, at the direction of corporate superiors in order to secure legal advice from counsel. As the Magistrate found, "Mr. Thomas consulted with the Chairman of the Board and outside counsel and thereafter conducted a factual investigation to determine the nature and extent of the questionable payments *and to be in a position*

---

2. [2] The Government argues that the risk of civil or criminal liability suffices to ensure that corporations will seek legal advice in the absence of the protection of the privilege. This response ignores the fact that the depth and quality of any investigations, to ensure compliance with the law would suffer, even were they undertaken. The response also proves too much, since it applies to all communications covered by the privilege: an individual trying to comply with the law or faced with a legal problem also has strong incentive to disclose information to his lawyer, yet the common law has recognized the value of the privilege in further facilitating communications.

3. [3] Seven of the eighty-six employees interviewed by counsel had terminated their employment with Upjohn at the time of the interview. Petitioners argue that the privilege should nonetheless apply to communications by these former employees concerning activities during their period of employment. Neither the District Court nor the Court of Appeals had occasion to address this issue, and we decline to decide it without the benefit of treatment below.

to give legal advice to the company with respect to the payments." (Emphasis supplied.) Information, not available from upper-echelon management, was needed to supply a basis for legal advice concerning compliance with securities and tax laws, foreign laws, currency regulations, duties to shareholders, and potential litigation in each of these areas. The communications concerned matters within the scope of the employees' corporate duties, and the employees themselves were sufficiently aware that they were being questioned in order that the corporation could obtain legal advice. The questionnaire identified Thomas as "the company's General Counsel" and referred in its opening sentence to the possible illegality of payments such as the ones on which information was sought. A statement of policy accompanying the questionnaire clearly indicated the legal implications of the investigation. The policy statement was issued "in order that there be no uncertainty in the future as to the policy with respect to the practices which are the subject of this investigation." It began, "Upjohn will comply with all laws and regulations," and stated that commissions or payments "will not be used as a subterfuge for bribes or illegal payments" and that all payments must be "proper and legal." Any future agreements with foreign distributors or agents were to be approved "by a company attorney" and any questions concerning the policy were to be referred "to the company's General Counsel." This statement was issued to Upjohn employees worldwide, so that even those interviewees not receiving a questionnaire were aware of the legal implications of the interviews. Pursuant to explicit instructions from the Chairman of the Board, the communications were considered "highly confidential" when made, and have been kept confidential by the company. Consistent with the underlying purposes of the attorney-client privilege, these communications must be protected against compelled disclosure.

The Court of Appeals declined to extend the attorney-client privilege beyond the limits of the control group test for fear that doing so would entail severe burdens on discovery and create a broad "zone of silence" over corporate affairs. Application of the attorney-client privilege to communications such as those involved here, however, puts the adversary in no worse position than if the communications had never taken place. The privilege only protects disclosure of communications; it does not protect disclosure of the underlying facts by those who communicated with the attorney:

> "[T]he protection of the privilege extends only to *communications* and not to facts. A fact is one thing and a communication concerning that fact is an entirely different thing. The client cannot be compelled to answer the question, 'What did you say or write to the attorney?' but may not refuse to disclose any relevant fact within his knowledge merely because he incorporated a statement of such fact into his communication to his attorney." *Philadelphia v. Westinghouse Electric Corp.*, 205 F. Supp. 830, 831 (ED Pa. 1962).

See also *Diversified Industries*, 572 F.2d., at 611; *State ex rel. Dudek v. Circuit Court*, 34 Wis.2d 559, 580, 150 N.W.2d 387, 399 (1967) ("the courts have noted that a party cannot conceal a fact merely by revealing it to his lawyer"). Here the Government was free to question the employees who communicated with Thomas and outside counsel. Upjohn has provided the IRS with a list of such employees, and the IRS has already interviewed some 25 of them. While it would probably be more convenient for the Government to secure the results of petitioner's internal investigation by simply subpoenaing the questionnaires and notes taken by petitioner's attorneys, such considerations of convenience do not overcome the policies served by the attorney-client privilege. As Justice Jackson noted in his concurring opinion in *Hickman v. Taylor*, 329 U.S., at 516, 67, at 396: "Discovery was hardly intended to enable a learned profession to perform its functions ... on wits borrowed from the adversary."

Needless to say, we decide only the case before us, and do not undertake to draft a set of rules which should govern challenges to investigatory subpoenas. Any such approach would violate the spirit of Federal Rule of Evidence 501. *See* S. Rep. No. 93-1277, p. 13 (1974) ("the recognition of a privilege based on a confidential relationship ... should be determined on a case-by-case basis"); *Trammel*, 445 U.S., at 47; *United States v. Gillock*, 445 U.S. 360, 367 (1980). While such a "case-by-case" basis may to some slight extent undermine desirable certainty in the boundaries of the attorney-client privilege, it obeys the spirit of the Rules. At the same time we conclude that the narrow "control group test" sanctioned by the Court of Appeals, in this case cannot, consistent with "the principles of the common law as ... interpreted ... in the light of reason and experience," Fed. Rule Evid. 501, govern the development of the law in this area.

It is so ordered.

[Concurring opinion of Burger, C.J., is omitted.]

Notes and Comments

1. In *Upjohn*, the Court firmly rejected the control group test, and declined to adopt the subject matter test as well. Instead, the Court emphasized that it would not adopt a general rule and would decide the privilege issue on a case-by-case basis. As a result, in-house attorneys and compliance attorneys have struggled to determine whether the privilege applies to particular corporate communications.

2. The federal courts have, at times, appeared confused on how to interpret *Upjohn*, with at least one court stating that the Supreme Court implicitly adopted the modified subject matter test. *See SEC v. Gulf & W. Indus., Inc.*, 518 F. Supp. 675, 681 n.9 (D.D.C. 1981). Several federal courts have not acknowledged that *Upjohn* adopts any standard at all, only that corporate privilege cases will be decided on a case-by-case basis. Moreover, different standards may apply if the corporation becomes involved in a shareholder derivative suit, for example, rather than an action brought by a third party. *See Garner v. Wolfinbarger*, 430 F.2d 1093, 1103–04 (5th Cir. 1970), *cert. denied*, 401 U.S. 974 (1971) (holding that in a shareholder derivative suit, shareholders could defeat the attorney-client privilege asserted by the corporation through a showing of "good cause"); *see also* Weiser v. Grace, 179 Misc. 2d 116, 683 N.Y.S.2d 781 (N.Y. Sup. Ct. 1998) (holding, in a shareholder derivative action against the corporation's directors, that material prepared by counsel for a special litigation committee was

subject to disclosure); *Granite Partners, LP v. Bear, Stearns & Co.*, 184 F.R.D. 49 (S.D.N.Y. 1999) (finding that the "use of selected quotes from ... interview notes waives any privilege claimed on the unquoted portion of those notes"). But see *In re Dow Corning Corp.*, 261 F.3d 280 (2d Cir. 2001), in which the court, while refusing to block a district court order compelling the deposition of Dow Corning's general counsel in a shareholder suit against the company (because the "scanty record" did not justify the extraordinary relief of a writ of mandamus), nevertheless sent the case back for further consideration, directing the lower court to "consider, however, that relevance without more does not override the privilege and that a protective order will not adequately safeguard the privilege holder's interests such that the attorney-client privilege may be neglected." The court noted particularly: "compelled disclosure of privileged attorney-client communications, absent waiver or an applicable exception, is contrary to well established precedent."

3. There are no hard and fast rules on how to handle this situation, but the lawyer should be alert to the problem and take all steps possible to separate his or her legal and business roles. For example, the in-house lawyer might provide legal advice at one time in one written instrument and offer business advice subsequently in a separate document. The document of communication should also be written or given in such a way that makes clear that the main purpose of the document or communication is to provide legal advice, and all other matters are merely incidental to that legal advice. This does not mean that a particular memorandum submitted by counsel must be filled with the results of legal research, including a multitude of citations and case analyses, to support the advice or opinion rendered.

Recently, the District of Columbia Circuit Court added its interpretation with *In re Kellogg:*

In re Kellogg Brown & Root, Inc.
756 F.3d 754 (D.C. Cir. 2014)

Kavanaugh, Circuit Judge:

More than three decades ago, the Supreme Court held that the attorney-client privilege protects confidential employee communications made during a business's internal investigation led by company lawyers. *See Upjohn Co. v. United States,* 449 U.S. 383, 101 S. Ct. 677, 66 L. Ed. 2d 584 (1981). In this case, the District Court denied the protection of the privilege to a company that had conducted just such an internal investigation. The District Court's decision has generated substantial uncertainty about the scope of the attorney-client privilege in the business setting. We conclude that the District Court's decision is irreconcilable with *Upjohn.* We therefore grant KBR's petition for a writ of mandamus and vacate the District Court's March 6 document production order.

I

Harry Barko worked for KBR, a defense contractor. In 2005, he filed a False Claims Act complaint against KBR and KBR-related corporate entities, whom we will collectively refer to as KBR. In essence, Barko alleged that KBR and certain subcontractors defrauded the U.S. Government by inflating costs and accepting kickbacks while administering military contracts in wartime Iraq. During discovery, Barko sought documents related to KBR's prior internal investigation into the alleged fraud. KBR had conducted that internal investigation pursuant to its Code of Business Conduct, which is overseen by the company's Law Department.

KBR argued that the internal investigation had been conducted for the purpose of obtaining legal advice and that the internal investigation documents therefore were protected by the attorney-client privilege. Barko responded that the internal investigation documents were unprivileged business records that he was entitled to discover. *See generally* Fed. R. Civ. P. 26(b)(1).

After reviewing the disputed documents *in camera,* the District Court determined that the attorney-client privilege protection did not apply because, among other reasons, KBR had not shown that "the communication would not have been made 'but for' the fact that legal advice was sought." *United States ex rel. Barko v. Halliburton Co.,* No. 05-cv-1276, 37 F. Supp. 3d 1, 2014 U.S. Dist. LEXIS 36490, 2014 WL 1016784, at *2 (D.D.C. Mar. 6, 2014) (quoting *United States v. ISS Marine Services, Inc.,* 905 F. Supp. 2d 121, 128 (D.D.C. 2012)). KBR's internal investigation, the court concluded, was "undertaken pursuant to regulatory law and corporate policy rather than for the purpose of obtaining legal advice." 2014 U.S. Dist. LEXIS 36490, 2014 WL 1016784, at *3.

KBR vehemently opposed the ruling. The company asked the District Court to certify the privilege question to this Court for interlocutory appeal and to stay its order pending a petition for mandamus in this Court. The District Court denied those requests and ordered KBR to produce the disputed documents to Barko within a matter of days. *See United States ex rel. Barko v. Halliburton Co.,* No. 1:05-cv-1276, 2014 WL 929430 (D.D.C. Mar. 11, 2014). KBR promptly filed a petition for a writ of mandamus in this Court. A number of business organizations and trade associations also objected to the District Court's decision and filed an amicus brief in support of KBR. We stayed the District Court's document production order and held oral argument on the mandamus petition.

The threshold question is whether the District Court's privilege ruling constituted legal error. If not, mandamus is of course inappropriate. If the District Court's ruling was erroneous, the remaining question is whether that error is the kind that justifies mandamus. *See Cheney v. U.S. District Court for the District of Columbia,* 542 U.S. 367, 380–81, 124 S. Ct. 2576, 159 L. Ed. 2d 459 (2004). We address those questions in turn.

II

We first consider whether the District Court's privilege ruling was legally erroneous. We conclude that it was.

Federal Rule of Evidence 501 provides that claims of privilege in federal courts are governed by the "common law—as interpreted by United States courts in the light of reason and experience." Fed. R. Evid. 501. The attorney-client privilege is the "oldest of the privileges for confidential communications known to the common law." *Upjohn Co. v. United States*, 449 U.S. 383, 389, 101 S. Ct. 677, 66 L. Ed. 2d 584 (1981). As relevant here, the privilege applies to a confidential communication between attorney and client if that communication was made for the purpose of obtaining or providing legal advice to the client. *See* 1 RESTATEMENT (THIRD) IF THE LAW GOV-ERNING LAWYERS §§ 68–72 (2000); *In re Grand Jury*, 475 F.3d 1299, 1304, 374 U.S. App. D.C. 428 (D.C. Cir. 2007); *In re Lindsey*, 158 F.3d 1263, 1270, 332 U.S. App. D.C. 357 (D.C. Cir. 1998); *In re Sealed Case*, 737 F.2d 94, 98–99, 237 U.S. App. D.C. 312 (D.C. Cir. 1984); *see also Fisher v. United States*, 425 U.S. 391, 403, 96 S. Ct. 1569, 48 L. Ed. 2d 39 (1976) ("Confidential disclosures by a client to an attorney made in order to obtain legal assistance are privileged.").

In *Upjohn*, the Supreme Court held that the attorney-client privilege applies to corporations. The Court explained that the attorney-client privilege for business or-ganizations was essential in light of "the vast and complicated array of regulatory leg-islation confronting the modern corporation," which required corporations to "constantly go to lawyers to find out how to obey the law, ... particularly since com-pliance with the law in this area is hardly an instinctive matter." 449 U.S. at 392 (in-ternal quotation marks and citation omitted). The Court stated, moreover, that the attorney-client privilege "exists to protect not only the giving of professional advice to those who can act on it but also the giving of information to the lawyer to enable him to give sound and informed advice." *Id.* at 390. That is so, the Court said, because the "first step in the resolution of any legal problem is ascertaining the factual back-ground and sifting through the facts with an eye to the legally relevant." *Id.* at 390–91. In *Upjohn*, the communications were made by company employees to company attorneys during an attorney-led internal investigation that was undertaken to ensure the company's "compliance with the law." *Id.* at 392; *see id.* at 394. The Court ruled that the privilege applied to the internal investigation and covered the communications between company employees and company attorneys.

KBR's assertion of the privilege in this case is materially indistinguishable from Upjohn's assertion of the privilege in that case. As in *Upjohn*, KBR initiated an internal investigation to gather facts and ensure compliance with the law after being informed of potential misconduct. And as in *Upjohn*, KBR's investigation was conducted under the auspices of KBR's in-house legal department, acting in its legal capacity. The same considerations that led the Court in *Upjohn* to uphold the corporation's privilege claims apply here.

The District Court in this case initially distinguished *Upjohn* on a variety of grounds. But none of those purported distinctions takes this case out from under *Upjohn*'s umbrella.

First, the District Court stated that in Upjohn the internal investigation began after in-house counsel conferred with outside counsel, whereas here the investigation was conducted in-house without consultation with outside lawyers. But Upjohn does not hold or imply that the involvement of outside counsel is a necessary predicate for the privilege to apply. On the contrary, the general rule, which this Court has adopted, is that a lawyer's status as in-house counsel "does not dilute the privilege." *In re Sealed Case,* 737 F.2d at 99. As the Restatement's commentary points out, "Inside legal counsel to a corporation or similar organization ... is fully empowered to engage in privileged communications." 1 RESTATEMENT § 72, cmt. c, at 551.

Second, the District Court noted that in Upjohn the interviews were conducted by attorneys, whereas here many of the interviews in KBR's investigation were conducted by non-attorneys. But the investigation here was conducted at the direction of the attorneys in KBR's Law Department. And communications made by and to non-attorneys serving as agents of attorneys in internal investigations are routinely protected by the attorney-client privilege. *See FTC v. TRW, Inc.,* 628 F.2d 207, 212, 202 U.S. App. D.C. 207 (D.C.Cir.1980); *see also* 1 PAUL R. RICE, ATTORNEY-CLIENT PRIVILEGE IN THE UNITED STATES § 7:18, at 1230–31 (2013) ("If internal investigations are conducted by agents of the client at the behest of the attorney, they are protected by the attorney-client privilege to the same extent as they would be had they been conducted by the attorney who was consulted."). So that fact, too, is not a basis on which to distinguish *Upjohn.*

Third, the District Court pointed out that in *Upjohn* the interviewed employees were expressly informed that the purpose of the interview was to assist the company in obtaining legal advice, whereas here they were not. The District Court further stated that the confidentiality agreements signed by KBR employees did not mention that the purpose of KBR's investigation was to obtain legal advice. Yet nothing in *Upjohn* requires a company to use magic words to its employees in order to gain the benefit of the privilege for an internal investigation. And in any event, here as in *Upjohn* employees knew that the company's legal department was conducting an investigation of a sensitive nature and that the information they disclosed would be protected. *Cf. Upjohn,* 449 U.S. at 387 (Upjohn's managers were "instructed to treat the investigation as 'highly confidential'"). KBR employees were also told not to discuss their interviews "without the specific advance authorization of KBR General Counsel." *United States ex rel. Barko v. Halliburton Co.,* No. 1:05-cv-1276, 2014 U.S. Dist. LEXIS 36490, 2014 WL 1016784, at *3 n.33 (D.D.C. Mar. 6, 2014).

In short, none of those three distinctions of *Upjohn* holds water as a basis for denying KBR's privilege claim.

More broadly and more importantly, the District Court also distinguished *Upjohn* on the ground that KBR's internal investigation was undertaken to comply with Department of Defense regulations that require defense contractors such as KBR to maintain compliance programs and conduct internal investigations into allegations of potential wrongdoing. The District Court therefore concluded that the purpose of KBR's internal investigation was to comply with those regulatory requirements rather than to obtain or provide legal advice. In our view, the District Court's analysis rested on a false dichotomy. So long as obtaining or providing legal advice was one of the significant purposes of the internal investigation, the attorney-client privilege applies, even if there were also other purposes for the investigation and even if the investigation was mandated by regulation rather than simply an exercise of company discretion.

The District Court began its analysis by reciting the "primary purpose" test, which many courts (including this one) have used to resolve privilege disputes when attorney-client communications may have had both legal and business purposes. *See* 2014 U.S. District LEXIS 36490, 2014 WL 1001674, at *2; *see also In re Sealed Case,* 737 F.2d at 98–99. But in a key move, the District Court then said that the primary purpose of a communication is to obtain or provide legal advice only if the communication would not have been made "but for" the fact that legal advice was sought. 2014 U.S. District LEXIS 36490, 2014 WL 1016784, at *2. In other words, if there was any other purpose behind the communication, the attorney-client privilege apparently does not apply. The District Court went on to conclude that KBR's internal investigation was "undertaken pursuant to regulatory law and corporate policy rather than for the purpose of obtaining legal advice." 2014 U.S. Dist. LEXIS 36490, 2014 WL 1001674 at *3; *see* 2014 U.S. Dist. LEXIS 36490, 2014 WL 1001674 at *3 n.28 (citing federal contracting regulations). Therefore, in the District Court's view, "the primary purpose of" the internal investigation "was to comply with federal defense contractor regulations, not to secure legal advice." *United States ex rel. Barko v. Halliburton Co.,* No. 1:05-cv-1276, 4 F. Supp. 3d 162, 166, 2014 U.S. Dist. LEXIS 30866, 2014 WL 929430, at *2 (D.D.C. Mar. 11, 2014); *see id.* ("Nothing suggests the reports were prepared to obtain legal advice. Instead, the reports were prepared to try to comply with KBR's obligation to report improper conduct to the Department of Defense.").

The District Court erred because it employed the wrong legal test. The but-for test articulated by the District Court is not appropriate for attorney-client privilege analysis. Under the District Court's approach, the attorney-client privilege apparently would not apply unless the sole purpose of the communication was to obtain or provide legal advice. That is not the law. We are aware of no Supreme Court or court of appeals decision that has adopted a test of this kind in this context. The District Court's novel approach to the attorney-client privilege would eliminate the attorney-client privilege for numerous communications that are made for both legal and business purposes and that heretofore have been covered by the attorney-client privilege. And the District Court's novel approach would eradicate the attorney-client privilege for internal investigations conducted by businesses that are required by law to maintain compliance programs, which is now the case in a significant swath of American industry. In turn, businesses would be less likely to disclose facts to their attorneys and to seek legal advice, which would "limit the valuable efforts of corporate counsel to ensure their client's compliance with the law." *Upjohn,* 449 U.S. at 392. We reject the District Court's but-for test as inconsistent with the principle of *Upjohn* and long-standing attorney-client privilege law.

Given the evident confusion in some cases, we also think it important to underscore that the primary purpose test, sensibly and properly applied, cannot and does not draw a rigid distinction between a legal purpose on the one hand and a business purpose on the other. After all, trying to find *the* one primary purpose for a communication motivated by two sometimes overlapping purposes (one legal and one business, for example) can be an inherently impossible task. It is often not useful or even feasible to try to determine whether the purpose was A or B when the purpose was A and B. It is thus not correct for a court to presume that a communication can have only one primary purpose. It is likewise not correct for a court to try to find *the* one primary purpose in cases where a given communication plainly has multiple purposes. Rather, it is clearer, more precise, and more predictable to articulate the test as follows: Was obtaining or providing legal advice *a* primary purpose of the communication, meaning one of the significant purposes of the communication? As the Reporter's Note to the Restatement says, "In general, American decisions agree that the privilege applies if one of the significant purposes of a client in communicating with a lawyer is that of obtaining legal assistance." 1 RESTATEMENT § 72, Reporter's Note, at 554. We agree with and adopt that formulation — "one of the significant purposes" — as an accurate and appropriate description of the primary purpose test. Sensibly and properly applied, the test boils down to whether obtaining or providing legal advice was one of the significant purposes of the attorney-client communication.

In the context of an organization's internal investigation, if one of the significant purposes of the internal investigation was to obtain or provide legal advice, the privilege will apply. That is true regardless of whether an internal investigation was conducted pursuant to a company compliance program required by statute or regulation, or was otherwise conducted pursuant to company policy. *Cf.* Andy Liu et al., *How To Protect Internal Investigation Materials from Disclosure*, 56 GOVERNMENT CONTRACTOR ¶ 108 (Apr. 9, 2014) ("Helping a corporation comply with a statute or regulation — although required by law — does not transform quintessentially legal advice into business advice.").

In this case, there can be no serious dispute that one of the significant purposes of the KBR internal investigation was to obtain or provide legal advice. In denying KBR's privilege claim on the ground that the internal investigation was conducted in order to comply with regulatory requirements and corporate policy and not just to obtain or provide legal advice, the District Court applied the wrong legal test and clearly erred.

IV

We have one final matter to address. At oral argument, KBR requested that if we grant mandamus, we also reassign this case to a different district court judge. *See* Tr. of Oral Arg. at 17–19; 28 U.S.C. § 2106. KBR grounds its request on the District Court's erroneous decisions on the privilege claim, as well as on a letter sent by the District Court to the Clerk of this Court in which the District Court arranged to transfer the record in the case and identified certain documents as particularly important for this Court's review. *See* KBR Reply Br. App. 142. KBR claims that the letter violated Federal Rule of Appellate Procedure 21(b)(4), which provides that in a mandamus proceeding the "trial-court judge may request permission to address the petition but may not do so unless invited or ordered to do so by the court of appeals."

In its mandamus petition, KBR did not request reassignment. Nor did KBR do so in its reply brief, even though the company knew by that time of the District Court letter that it complains about. Ordinarily, we do not consider a request for relief that a party failed to clearly articulate in its briefs. To be sure, appellate courts on rare occasions will reassign a case sua sponte. *See Ligon v. City of New York,* 736 F.3d 118, 129 & n. 31 (2d Cir.2013) (collecting cases), *vacated in part,* 743 F.3d 362 (2d Cir.2014). But whether requested to do so or considering the matter sua sponte, we will reassign a case only in the exceedingly rare circumstance that a district judge's conduct is "so extreme as to display clear inability to render fair judgment." *Liteky v. United States,* 510 U.S. 540, 551, 114 S. Ct. 1147, 127 L. Ed. 2d 474 (1994); *see also United States v. Microsoft Corp.,* 253 F.3d 34, 107, 346 U.S. App. D.C. 330 (D.C. Cir. 2001) (en banc). Nothing in the District Court's decisions or subsequent letter reaches that very high standard. Based on the record before us, we have no reason to doubt that the District Court will render fair judgment in further proceedings. We will not reassign the case.

In reaching our decision here, we stress, as the Supreme Court did in *Upjohn,* that the attorney-client privilege "only protects disclosure of communications; it does not protect disclosure of the underlying facts by those who communicated with the attorney." *Upjohn Co. v. United States,* 449 U.S. 383, 395, 101 S. Ct. 677, 66 L. Ed. 2d 584 (1981). Barko was able to pursue the facts underlying KBR's investigation. But he was not entitled to KBR's own investigation files. As the *Upjohn* Court stated, quoting Justice Jackson, "Discovery was hardly intended to enable a learned profession to perform its functions ... on wits borrowed from the adversary." *Id.* at 396, 101 677 (quoting *Hickman v. Taylor,* 329 U.S. 495, 515, 67 S. Ct. 385, 91 L. Ed. 451 (1947) (Jackson, J., concurring)).

Although the attorney-client privilege covers only communications and not facts, we acknowledge that the privilege carries costs. The privilege means that potentially critical evidence may be withheld from the factfinder. Indeed, as the District Court here noted, that may be the end result in this case. But our legal system tolerates those costs because the privilege "is intended to encourage 'full and frank communication between attorneys and their clients and thereby promote broader public interests in the observance of law and the administration of justice.'" *Swidler & Berlin v. United States,* 524 U.S. 399, 403, 118 S. Ct. 2081, 141 L. Ed. 2d 379 (1998) (quoting *Upjohn,* 449 U.S. at 389).

We grant the petition for a writ of mandamus and vacate the District Court's March 6 document production order. To the extent that Barko has timely asserted other arguments for why these documents are not covered by either the attorney-client privilege or the work-product protection, the District Court may consider such arguments.

So ordered.

Notes and Comments

1. In August 2015, The D.C. Circuit affirmed their decision. *In re Kellogg Brown & Root, Inc.*, 796 F.3d 137 (D.C. Cir. 2015).

2. Given the importance of using tools to monitor and audit compliance programs, it is important to recognize that there are risks associated with producing these types of written reports. As a result, it is important to involve counsel when developing the reports as it may be necessary to consider whether the documents may be discoverable and/or otherwise used in litigation. There are no hard and fast rules on how to handle this situation, but the lawyer should be alert to the problem and take all steps possible to separate the two roles.

Additionally, Department of Justice Criminal Division created a Resource Guide to understand the Foreign Corrupt Practices Act (FCPA). This Resource Guide, in Chapter 3, The FCPA: Accounting Provisions, provides guidance on accounting principles related to 'books and records' provision of the FCPA as well as on "internal controls." This guidance is provided for FCPA compliance programs; however, it provides helpful best practices applicable to any compliance program.

U.S. Department of Justice Criminal Division & SEC Enforcement Division, Resource Guide to the U.S. Foreign Corrupt Practices Act

http://www.justice.gov/sites/default/files/criminal-fraud/legacy/2015/01/16/guide.pdf

THE FCPA: ACCOUNTING PROVISIONS

In addition to the anti-bribery provisions, the FCPA contains accounting provisions applicable to public companies. The FCPA's accounting provisions operate in tandem with the anti-bribery provisions and prohibit off-the-books accounting. Company management and investors rely on a company's financial statements and internal accounting controls to ensure transparency in the financial health of the business, the risks undertaken, and the transactions between the company and its customers and business partners. The accounting provisions are designed to "strengthen the accuracy of the corporate books and records and the reliability of the audit process which constitute the foundations of our system of corporate disclosure."

The accounting provisions consist of two primary components. First, under the "books and records" provision, issuers must make and keep books, records, and accounts that, in reasonable detail, accurately and fairly reflect an issuer's transactions and dispositions of an issuer's assets. Second, under the "internal controls" provision, issuers must devise and maintain a system of internal accounting controls sufficient to assure management's control, authority, and responsibility over the firm's assets. These components, and other aspects of the accounting provisions, are discussed in greater detail below.

Although the accounting provisions were originally enacted as part of the FCPA, they do not apply only to bribery-related violations. Rather, the accounting provisions ensure that all public companies account for all of their assets and liabilities accurately and in reasonable detail, and they form the backbone for most accounting fraud and issuer disclosure cases brought by DOJ and SEC.

What Is Covered by the Accounting Provisions?

Books and Records Provision

Bribes, both foreign and domestic, are often mischaracterized in companies' books and records. Section 13(b)(2)(A) of the Exchange Act (15 U.S.C. §78m(b)(2)(A)), commonly called the "books and records" provision, requires issuers to "make and keep books, records, and accounts, which, in reasonable detail, accurately and fairly reflect the transactions and dispositions of the assets of the issuer." The "in reasonable detail" qualification was adopted by Congress "in light of the concern that such a standard, if unqualified, might connote a degree of exactitude and precision which is unrealistic." The addition of this phrase was intended to make clear "that the issuer's records should reflect transactions in conformity with accepted methods of recording economic events and effectively prevent off-the-books slush funds and payments of bribes."

The term "reasonable detail" is defined in the statute as the level of detail that would "satisfy prudent officials in the conduct of their own affairs." Thus, as Congress noted when it adopted this definition, "[t]he concept of reasonableness of necessity contemplates the weighing of a number of relevant factors, including the costs of compliance."

Although the standard is one of reasonable detail, it is never appropriate to mischaracterize transactions in a company's books and records. Bribes are often concealed under the guise of legitimate payments, such as commissions or consulting fees.

In instances where all the elements of a violation of the anti-bribery provisions are not met—where, for example, there was no use of interstate commerce—companies nonetheless may be liable if the improper payments are inaccurately recorded. Consistent with the FCPA's approach to prohibiting payments of any value that are made with a corrupt purpose, there is no materiality threshold under the books and records provision. In combination with the internal controls provision, the requirement that issuers maintain books and records that accurately and fairly reflect the corporation's transactions "assure[s], among other things, that the assets of the issuer are used for proper corporate purpose[s]." As with the anti-bribery provisions, DOJ's and SEC's enforcement of the books and records provision has typically involved misreporting of either large bribe payments or widespread inaccurate recording of smaller payments made as part of a systemic pattern of bribery.

Bribes Have Been Mischaracterized As:

- Commissions or Royalties
- Consulting Fees

- Sales and Marketing Expenses
- Scientific Incentives or Studies
- Travel and Entertainment Expenses
- Rebates or Discounts
- After Sales Service Fees
- Miscellaneous Expenses
- Petty Cash Withdrawals
- Free Goods
- Intercompany Accounts
- Supplier/Vendor Payments
- Write-offs
- "Customs Intervention" Payments

Internal Controls Provision

The payment of bribes often occurs in companies that have weak internal control environments. Internal controls over financial reporting are the processes used by companies to provide reasonable assurances regarding the reliability of financial reporting and the preparation of financial statements. They include various components, such as: a control environment that covers the tone set by the organization regarding integrity and ethics; risk assessments; control activities that cover policies and procedures designed to ensure that management directives are carried out (e.g., approvals, authorizations, reconciliations, and segregation of duties); information and communication; and monitoring. Section 13(b)(2)(B) of the Exchange Act (15 U.S.C. §78m(b)(2)(B)), commonly called the "internal controls" provision, requires issuers to:

> devise and maintain a system of internal accounting controls sufficient to provide reasonable assurances that—(i) transactions are executed in accordance with management's general or specific authorization; (ii) transactions are recorded as necessary (I) to permit preparation of financial statements in conformity with generally accepted accounting principles or any other criteria applicable to such statements, and (II) to maintain accountability for assets; (iii) access to assets is permitted only in accordance with management's general or specific authorization; and (iv) the recorded accountability for assets is compared with the existing assets at reasonable intervals and appropriate action is taken with respect to any differences....

Like the "reasonable detail" requirement in the books and records provision, the Act defines "reasonable assurances" as "such level of detail and degree of assurance as would satisfy prudent officials in the conduct of their own affairs."

The Act does not specify a particular set of controls that companies are required to implement. Rather, the internal controls provision gives companies the flexibility to develop and maintain a system of controls that is appropriate to their particular needs and circumstances.

An effective compliance program is a critical component of an issuer's internal controls. Fundamentally, the design of a company's internal controls must take into account the operational realities and risks attendant to the company's business, such as: the nature of its products or services; how the products or services get to market; the nature of its work force; the degree of regulation; the extent of its government interaction; and the degree to which it has operations in countries with a high risk of corruption. A company's compliance program should be tailored to these differences. Businesses whose operations expose them to a high risk of corruption will necessarily devise and employ different internal controls than businesses that have a lesser exposure to corruption, just as a financial services company would be expected to devise and employ different internal controls than a manufacturer.

A 2008 case against a German manufacturer of industrial and consumer products illustrates a systemic internal controls problem involving bribery that was unprecedented in scale and geographic reach. From 2001 to 2007, the company created elaborate payment schemes — including slush funds, off-the-books accounts, and systematic payments to business consultants and other intermediaries — to facilitate bribery. Payments were made in ways that obscured their purpose and the ultimate recipients of the money. In some cases, employees obtained large amounts of cash from cash desks and then transported the cash in suitcases across international borders. Authorizations for some payments were placed on sticky notes and later removed to avoid any permanent record. The company made payments totaling approximately $1.36 billion through various mechanisms, including $805.5 million as bribes and $554.5 million for unknown purposes. The company was charged with internal controls and books and records violations, along with anti-bribery violations, and paid over $1.6 billion to resolve the case with authorities in the United States and Germany.

The types of internal control failures identified in the above example exist in many other cases where companies were charged with internal controls violations. A 2010 case against a multi-national automobile manufacturer involved bribery that occurred over a long period of time in multiple countries. In that case, the company used dozens of ledger accounts, known internally as "internal third party accounts," to maintain credit balances for the benefit of government officials. The accounts were funded through several bogus pricing mechanisms, such as "price surcharges," "price inclusions," or excessive commissions. The company also used artificial discounts or rebates on sales contracts to generate the money to pay the bribes. The bribes also were made through phony sales intermediaries and corrupt business partners, as well as through the use of cash desks. Sales executives would obtain cash from the company in amounts as high as hundreds of thousands of dollars, enabling the company to obscure the purpose and recipients of the money paid to government officials. In addition to bribery charges, the company was charged with internal controls and books and records violations.

Good internal controls can prevent not only FCPA violations, but also other illegal or unethical conduct by the company, its subsidiaries, and its employees. DOJ and SEC have repeatedly brought FCPA cases that also involved other types of misconduct, such as financial fraud, commercial bribery; export controls violations, and embezzlement or self-dealing by company employees.

Potential Reporting and Anti-Fraud Violations

Issuers have reporting obligations under Section 13(a) of the Exchange Act, which requires issuers to file an annual report that contains comprehensive information about the issuer. Failure to properly disclose material information about the issuer's business, including material revenue, expenses, profits, assets, or liabilities related to bribery of foreign government officials, may give rise to anti-fraud and reporting violations under Sections 10(b) and 13(a) of the Exchange Act.

For example, a California-based technology company was charged with reporting violations, in addition to violations of the FCPA's anti-bribery and accounting provisions, when its bribery scheme led to material misstatements in its SEC filings. The company was awarded contracts procured through bribery of Chinese officials that generated material revenue and profits. The revenue and profits helped the company offset losses incurred to develop new products expected to become the company's future source of revenue growth. The company improperly recorded the bribe payments as sales commission expenses in its books and records.

Companies engaged in bribery may also be engaged in activity that violates the anti-fraud and reporting provisions. For example, an oil and gas pipeline company and its employees engaged in a long-running scheme to use the company's petty cash accounts in Nigeria to make a variety of corrupt payments to Nigerian tax and court officials using false invoices. The company and its employees also engaged in a fraudulent scheme to minimize the company's tax obligations in Bolivia by using false invoices to claim false offsets to its value-added tax obligations. The scheme resulted in material overstatements of the company's net income in the company's financial statements, which violated the Exchange Act's anti-fraud and reporting provisions. Both schemes also violated the books and records and internal controls provisions.

What Are Management's Other Obligations?

Sarbanes-Oxley Act of 2002

In 2002, in response to a series of accounting scandals involving U.S. companies, Congress enacted the Sarbanes-Oxley Act (Sarbanes-Oxley or SOX), which strengthened the accounting requirements for issuers. All issuers must comply with Sarbanes-Oxley's requirements, several of which have FCPA implications.

SOX Section 302 (15 U.S.C. §7241)—Responsibility of Corporate Officers for the Accuracy and Validity of Corporate Financial Reports

Section 302 of Sarbanes-Oxley requires that a company's "principal officers" (typically the Chief Executive Officer (CEO) and Chief Financial Officer (CFO)) take responsibility for and certify the integrity of their company's financial reports on a quarterly basis. Under Exchange Act Rule 13a-14, which is commonly called the "SOX certification" rule, each periodic report filed by an issuer must include a certification signed by the issuer's principal executive officer and principal financial officer that, among other things, states that: (i) based on the officer's knowledge, the report contains no material misstatements or omissions; (ii) based on the officer's knowledge, the relevant financial statements are accurate in all material respects; (iii) internal controls are properly designed; and (iv) the certifying officers have disclosed to the issuer's audit committee and auditors all significant internal control deficiencies.

SOX Section 404 (15 U.S.C. § 7262)—Reporting on the State of a Company's Internal Controls over Financial Reporting

Sarbanes-Oxley also strengthened a company's required disclosures concerning the state of its internal control over financial reporting. Under Section 404, issuers are required to present in their annual reports management's conclusion regarding the effectiveness of the company's internal controls over financial reporting. This statement must also assess the effectiveness of such internal control and procedures. In addition, the company's independent auditor must attest to and report on its assessment of the effectiveness of the company's internal controls over financial reporting.

As directed by Section 404, SEC has adopted rules requiring issuers and their independent auditors to report to the public on the effectiveness of the company's internal controls over financial reporting. These internal controls include those related to illegal acts and fraud—including acts of bribery—that could result in a material misstatement of the company's financial statements. In 2007, SEC issued guidance on controls over financial reporting.

SOX Section 802 (18 U.S.C. §§ 1519 and 1520)—Criminal Penalties for Altering Documents

Section 802 of Sarbanes-Oxley prohibits altering, destroying, mutilating, concealing, or falsifying records, documents, or tangible objects with the intent to obstruct, impede, or influence a potential or actual federal investigation. This section also prohibits any accountant from knowingly and willfully violating the requirement that all audit or review papers be maintained for a period of five years.

Who Is Covered by the Accounting Provisions?

Civil Liability for Issuers, Subsidiaries, and Affiliates The FCPA's accounting provisions apply to every issuer that has a class of securities registered pursuant to Section 12 of the Exchange Act or that is required to file annual or other periodic reports pursuant to Section 15(d) of the Exchange Act. These provisions apply to any issuer whose securities trade on a national securities exchange in the United States, including foreign issuers with exchange traded American Depository Receipts. They also apply to companies whose stock trades in the over-the-counter market in the United States and which file periodic reports with the Commission, such as annual and quarterly reports. Unlike the FCPA's anti-bribery provisions, the accounting provisions do not apply to private companies.

Although the FCPA's accounting requirements are directed at "issuers," an issuer's books and records include those of its consolidated subsidiaries and affiliates. An issuer's responsibility thus extends to ensuring that subsidiaries or affiliates under its control, including foreign subsidiaries and joint ventures, comply with the accounting provisions. For instance, DOJ and SEC brought enforcement actions against a California company for violating the FCPA's accounting provisions when two Chinese joint ventures in which it was a partner paid more than $400,000 in bribes over a four-year period to obtain business in China. Sales personnel in China made the illicit payments by obtaining cash advances from accounting personnel, who recorded the payments on the books as "business fees" or "travel and entertainment" expenses. Although the payments were made exclusively in China by Chinese employees of the joint venture, the California company failed to have adequate internal controls and failed to act on red flags indicating that its affiliates were engaged in bribery. The California company paid $1.15 million in civil disgorgement and a criminal monetary penalty of $1.7 million.

Companies may not be able to exercise the same level of control over a minority-owned subsidiary or affiliate as they do over a majority or wholly owned entity. Therefore, if a parent company owns 50% or less of a subsidiary or affiliate, the parent is only required to use good faith efforts to cause the minority-owned subsidiary or affiliate to devise and maintain a system of internal accounting controls consistent with the issuer's own obligations under the FCPA. In evaluating an issuer's good faith efforts, all the circumstances—including "the relative degree of the issuer's ownership of the domestic or foreign firm and the laws and practices governing the business operations of the country in which such firm is located"—are taken into account.

Civil Liability for Individuals and Other Entities

Companies (including subsidiaries of issuers) and individuals may also face civil liability for aiding and abetting or causing an issuer's violation of the accounting provisions. For example, in April 2010, SEC charged four individuals—a Country Manager, a Senior Vice President of Sales, a Regional Financial Director, and an International Controller of a U.S. issuer—for their roles in schemes to bribe Kyrgyz and Thai government officials to purchase tobacco from their employer. The complaint alleged that, among other things, the individuals aided and abetted the issuer company's violations of the books and records and internal controls provisions by "knowingly provid[ing] substantial assistance to" the parent company. All four executives settled the charges against them, consenting to the entry of final judgments permanently enjoining them from violating the accounting and anti-bribery provisions, with two executives paying civil penalties. As in other areas of federal securities law, corporate officers also can be held liable as control persons.

Similarly, in October 2011, SEC brought an administrative action against a U.S. water valve manufacturer and a former employee of the company's Chinese subsidiary for violations of the FCPA's accounting provisions. The Chinese subsidiary had made improper payments to employees of certain design institutes to create design specifications that favored the company's valve products. The payments were disguised as sales commissions in the subsidiary's books and records, thereby causing the U.S. issuer's books and records to be inaccurate. The general manager of the subsidiary, who approved the payments and knew or should have known that they were improperly recorded, was ordered to cease-and-desist from committing or causing violations of the accounting provisions, among other charges.

Additionally, individuals and entities can be held directly civilly liable for falsifying an issuer's books and records or for circumventing internal controls. Exchange Act Rule 13b2-1 provides: "No person shall, directly or indirectly, falsify or cause to be falsified, any book, record or account subject to [the books and records provision] of the Securities Exchange Act."256 And Section 13(b)(5) of the Exchange Act (15 U.S.C. § 78m(b)(5)) provides that "[n]o person shall knowingly circumvent or knowingly fail to implement a system of internal accounting controls or knowingly falsify any book, record, or account...." The Exchange Act defines "person" to include a "natural person, company, government, or political subdivision, agency, or instrumentality of a government."

An issuer's officers and directors may also be held civilly liable for making false statements to a company's auditor. Exchange Act Rule 13b2-2 prohibits officers and directors from making (or causing to be made) materially false or misleading statements, including an omission of material facts, to an accountant. This liability arises in connection with any audit, review, or examination of a company's financial statements or in connection with the filing of any document with SEC.

Finally, the principal executive and principal financial officer, or persons performing similar functions, can be held liable for violating Exchange Act Rule 13a-14 by signing false personal certifications required by SOX. Thus, for example, in January 2011, SEC charged the former CEO of a U.S. issuer for his role in schemes to bribe Iraqi government officials in connection with the United Nations Oil-For-Food Programme and to bribe Iraqi and Indonesian officials to purchase the company's fuel additives. There, the company used false invoices and sham consulting contracts to support large bribes that were passed on to foreign officials through an agent, and the bribes were mischaracterized as legitimate commissions and travel fees in the company's books and records. The officer directed and authorized the bribe payments and their false recording in the books and records. He also signed annual and quarterly SOX certifications in which he falsely represented that the company's financial statements were fairly presented and the company's internal controls sufficiently designed, as well as annual representations to the company's external auditors where he falsely stated that he complied with the company's code of ethics and was unaware of any violations of the code of ethics by anyone else. The officer was charged with aiding and abetting violations of the books and records and internal controls provisions, circumventing internal controls, falsifying books and records, making false statements to accountants, and signing false certifications. He consented to the entry of an injunction and paid disgorgement and a civil penalty. He also later pleaded guilty in the United Kingdom to conspiring to corrupt Iraqi and Indonesian officials.

Criminal Liability for Accounting Violations

Criminal liability can be imposed on companies and individuals for knowingly failing to comply with the FCPA's books and records or internal controls provisions. As with the FCPA's anti-bribery provisions, individuals are only subject to the FCPA's criminal penalties for violations of the accounting provisions if they acted "willfully."

For example, a French company was criminally charged with failure to implement internal controls and failure to keep accurate books and records, among other violations. As part of its deferred prosecution agreement, the company admitted to numerous internal control failures, including failure to implement sufficient anti-bribery compliance policies, maintain a sufficient system for the selection and approval of consultants, and conduct appropriate audits of payments to purported "business consultants." Likewise, a German company pleaded guilty to internal controls and books and records violations where, from 2001 through 2007, it made payments totaling approximately $1.36 billion through various mechanisms, including $805.5 million as bribes and $554.5 million for unknown purposes.

Individuals can be held criminally liable for accounting violations. For example, a former managing director of a U.S. bank's real estate business in China pleaded guilty to conspiring to evade internal accounting controls in order to transfer a multi-million dollar ownership interest in a Shanghai building to himself and a Chinese public official with whom he had a personal friendship. The former managing director repeatedly made false representations to his employer about the transaction and the ownership interests involved.

Conspiracy and Aiding and Abetting Liability

As with the FCPA's anti-bribery provisions, companies (including subsidiaries of issuers) and individuals may face criminal liability for conspiring to commit or for aiding and abetting violations of the accounting provisions.

For example, the subsidiary of a Houston-based company pleaded guilty both to conspiring to commit and to aiding and abetting the company's books and records and anti-bribery violations. The subsidiary paid bribes of over $4 million and falsely characterized the payments as "commissions," "fees," or "legal services," consequently causing the company's books and records to be inaccurate. Although the subsidiary was not an issuer and therefore could not be charged directly with an accounting violation, it was criminally liable for its involvement in the parent company's accounting violation.

Similarly, a U.S. subsidiary of a Swiss freight forwarding company that was not an issuer was charged with conspiring to commit and with aiding and abetting the books and records violations of its customers, who were issuers and therefore subject to the FCPA's accounting provisions. The U.S. subsidiary substantially assisted the issuer-customers in violating the FCPA's books and records provision by masking the true nature of the bribe payments in the invoices it submitted to the issuer-customers. The subsidiary thus faced criminal liability for its involvement in the issuer-customers' FCPA violations even though it was not itself subject to the FCPA's accounting provisions.

Auditor Obligations

All public companies in the United States must file annual financial statements that have been prepared in conformity with U.S. Generally Accepted Accounting Principles (U.S. GAAP). These accounting principles are among the most comprehensive in the world. U.S. GAAP requires an accounting of all assets, liabilities, revenue, and expenses as well as extensive disclosures concerning the company's operations and financial condition. A company's financial statements should be complete and fairly represent the company's financial condition. Thus, under U.S. GAAP, any payments to foreign government officials must be properly accounted for in a company's books, records, and financial statements.

U.S. laws, including SEC Rules, require issuers to undergo an annual external audit of their financial statements and to make those audited financial statements available to the public by filing them with SEC. SEC Rules and the rules and standards issued by the Public Company Accounting Oversight Board (PCAOB) under SEC oversight, require external auditors to be independent of the companies that they audit. Independent auditors must comply with the rules and standards set forth by the PCAOB when they perform an audit of a public company. These audit standards govern, for example, the auditor's responsibility concerning material errors, irregularities, or illegal acts by a client and its officers, directors, and employees. Additionally, the auditor has a responsibility to obtain an understanding of an entity's internal controls over financial reporting as part of its audit and must communicate all significant deficiencies and material weaknesses identified during the audit to management and the audit committee.

Under Section 10A of the Exchange Act, independent auditors who discover an illegal act, such as the payment of bribes to domestic or foreign government officials, have certain obligations in connection with their audits of public companies. Generally, Section 10A requires auditors who become aware of illegal acts to report such acts to appropriate levels within the company and, if the company fails to take appropriate action, to notify SEC.

———

Regulatory compliance is an important risk class in a growing number of companies. These companies are recognizing that adopting risk-based compliance programs with integrated measurement, auditing and reporting capabilities provides them with the tools and information they need to manage regulatory exposure in a cost-effective manner. While no compliance program can provide absolute assurance that a company will not encounter regulatory challenges, companies that migrate from rules-based compliance programs to a risk-based approach, significantly increase their ability manage risk, minimize potential sanctions, avoid possible damage to reputation, and promote shareholder value.

Assignments

- Should a pharmaceutical company and a financial services company have auditing, monitoring, testing, surveillance and reporting programs that are substantially similar? Explain.

- Identify and describe two reasons why it is critical that a company have an auditing, monitoring, testing, surveillance and reporting program in place.

- Compare the analysis in *In re Kellogg* with the analysis in *Upjohn*. Consider the facts in the *In re Kellogg* case and the larger role that in house legal departments play in 2014 as compared to 1981.

Chapter 9

Setting Up an Ethics and Compliance Hotline/Helpline and Whistleblowing Protection

Introduction

Establishing a hotline is an important part of an ethics and compliance program. An ethics hotline provides a confidential resource for employees to turn to, should they need clarification of policies or to report any concerns. A compliance hotline directs employee questions to the appropriate source so they can receive the guidance and information they require. A hotline may also be the last internal stop for whistleblowers.

A method of confidential and anonymous reporting of misconduct, fraud, incidents, or other concerns without fear of retribution became a requirement for corporations under the Sarbanes-Oxley Act of 2002 (SOX) and the amended Organizational Sentencing Guidelines. A whistleblower hotline is endorsed by this legislation and guidelines as a vehicle and as an essential part of an "effective" ethics and compliance program. Further, with the passage of the Dodd-Frank Act Whistleblower Provisions, which became effective on July 22, 2010, and the Whistleblower Improvement Act of 2011, employees have a monetary incentive to voluntarily come forward with high quality, original information that may potentially lead an SEC enforcement action over $1,000,000. However, employees are required to report any information related to a misconduct to their employer before reporting such information to the Securities and Exchange Commission (SEC) or the Commodities Futures and Trading Commission (CFTC). Only in specific instances prescribed by law, an employee may contact the national whistleblower hotline before notifying his employer and still be able to collect the award granted by law.

Hotlines have also been proven effective in providing an early warning of issues or business misconduct. In the Association of Certified Fraud Examiners 2014 Report to the Nation on Occupational Fraud and Abuse, tips continue to be the number one channel for fraud detection and over 40 percent of all cases were detected by a tip. According to the Report, the presence of a reporting hotline had a substantial impact on the initial fraud detection method and tips were the most common detection method for organizations with and without hotlines, but the benefit was much more pronounced in organizations with them. The Report also noted that these organizations experienced frauds that were 41 percent less costly, and they detected frauds 50 percent more quickly.

Whistleblowing. "Pursuant to Section 922 of the Dodd-Frank Wall Street Reform and Consumer Protection Act ("Dodd-Frank Act"), the U.S. Securities and Exchange Commission ("Commission" or "SEC") created a whistleblower program designed to encourage the submission of high-quality information to aid Division of Enforcement ("Enforcement") staff in discovering and prosecuting violations of the federal securities laws. There are three integral components of the Commission's whistleblower program—monetary awards, retaliation protection, and confidentiality protection—each of which is equally important to the continued success of the program.

On September 22, 2014, the Commission authorized an award of more than $30 million to a whistleblower who provided key original information that led to a successful enforcement action. The whistleblower in this matter provided information of an ongoing fraud that otherwise would have been very difficult to detect. The award is the largest made by the SEC's whistleblower program to date and the fourth award to a whistleblower living in a foreign country, demonstrating the program's international reach.

During Fiscal 2014 Year, the Office worked with other SEC staff to ensure that those who work with whistleblowers or who may review whistleblower information understand their confidentiality obligations under the Dodd-Frank Act and the Commission's implementing regulations."[1]

Considerations before Setting Up a Hotline

Initial Considerations: Outsource versus In-Source

There are many considerations to review before setting up a hotline. Questions must be posed and different decisions makers must be consulted, especially the Board, executives, and management, whose support is crucial. One of the most important decisions to make before determining capabilities, scope, policies, and procedures is to determine whether to insource or outsource the hotline.

There are multiple vendors that provide hotline services, and this option does offer real benefits, as these parties have years of background, experience, and expertise in the industry. Not only does the administration become seamless by engaging a third party but there is also an assurance of unbiased results which can also increase comfort that the hotline will be an effective avenue by which to raise concerns. Vendors are experts in call intake, with special call centers available 24/7/365. They can

---

1. *See* SEC, Annual Report to Congress on the Dodd-Frank Whistleblower Program (Nov. 2014).

handle any type of volume and have invested in the most advanced technological infrastructure. They typically offer multilingual services and additional guarantees of anonymity and confidentiality for callers. Organizations have the added benefit of utilizing the integrated information intake and management functionality that third party vendors offer. Those outsourced hotline vendors that are nationally recognized as leaders in information intake and management include NAVEX Global, The Network and In Touch.

On the surface, insourcing seems to be the lower-cost option and allows information, which could be proprietary, to remain internal. However, to create an internal system requires an investment in facilities, hardware, software, and personnel. Depending on the size and locations of the organization, insourcing could lead to many administrative and logistical challenges.

Capabilities and Scope

Once an organization has determined the sourcing of its hotline, it must consider how the hotline will function. The types of allegations should be clearly defined and might include Human Resources, Financial, Health, Environment, Safety, Business Integrity, Workplace Respect, and many others that may be industry specific. Defining these issues will be critical in the future to help an organization best track the types of allegations or incidents it is receiving; thus, careful planning can improve the utility of the resulting data down the road.

There are many functionality issues to determine, and many are tied directly to the logistics, location, and type of organization. Depending on the geographic locations of an organization, consideration would need to be given to multilingual capabilities and required interpretation. In addition to accommodating language differences, an organization should also look at cultural and operational differences in the countries it conducts business. Also, an organization may have multiple subsidiaries or lines of business. How these parts work together could indicate that the organization would need a separate line for each. Also, inclusion may need to reach agents, vendors, and contractors. In addition to these groups, the hotline may need to be extended to customers, patients, or shareholders. If these groups are included, a separate line may need to be considered in order to appropriately manage issue types.

There are also more basic capabilities to take into account. Availability needs to be 24/7/365, to accommodate time zones and employee schedules. Accessibility is another issue. Phone and web reporting mechanisms are available. Regardless of the industry, there are often employees who do not have access to both vehicles. There is also the consideration that some individuals feel more confident making a report through either the phone or the web. Organizations need to decide which best meets the needs of its employees and determine if they should utilize phone, web, or both. Beyond these two vehicles, an organization should also be prepared to receive reports from its employees via written letter, e-mail, and voice mail.

Policies, Procedures and Investigation Protocols

Before establishing a hotline, an organization should have in place certain policies and procedures. Protecting the confidentiality of the reporter is a top priority. Only those with a strict need to know for investigation or resolution matters should be privy to such information. This is particularly important if a hotline might receive calls from countries outside the U.S., which place a high premium on the protection of the caller's identity, and attach legal liability to a failure in that regard. The reporter should also be informed of his or her duty to keep the matter confidential.

Reporters also need to be assured they will not suffer any retaliation, which is also a clear mandate of SOX, the Sentencing Guidelines, and the Dodd Frank Whistle-blower provisions. Monitoring and investigating policies must be in place to create a culture where employees are not afraid of retaliation should they make a claim or allegation.

The investigation process should also be mapped out beginning with what internal department(s) and designees will receive reports. Once reports are received, there should be specific individuals or groups that handle these allegations and delineation of issues must be decided; this could be based on allegation type, location, or some other basis. Investigation policies should also include:

- Timeframe for investigation and resolution;
- Establishing a repository for all reports;
- Documentation of the investigation process;
- Communication with the reporter including follow-up;
- Handling responses to anonymous reporters;
- Security and data privacy issues; and
- Summary reports presented to Board and senior management.

Regarding regular reporting to the Board and senior management, there should be a report format in place that determines the type of information and in what context it will be presented so that the reports are meaningful and representative of the concerns or allegations being made.

Some issues are outside the realm of all these policies and should be considered special cases. Certain allegations, as determined by the organization, require immediate escalation to the Board or senior management. Other special cases might include allegations made against executive management or those that receive and/or investigate reports. These special cases require specific policies and alternate distribution for investigation. Essentially, the organization should be prepared for anything.

Communication and Positioning

After addressing all relevant considerations, the hotline must be positioned in a way to potential users that encompasses your organization's message and helps facilitate an effective ethics and compliance program. The hotline should be communicated to your employees as a tool and resource for their benefit as well as the organization's. Before launch of the hotline, an integrated communications campaign is necessary and likely should include a combination of the following most-common communication mediums: e-mail, posters, brochures, wallet cards, newsletter, website, Code of Conduct, and training.

Advice and Best Practices Regarding Hotlines

Implementing a hotline should be considered as one tool for employees to utilize to report concerns or alleged misconduct, but it should not be viewed or presented as a substitute for other channels. Human Resources and direct chain of management that offer an open door policy are important and should be positioned as desired channels. The hotline is an alternate source when employees do not feel comfortable discussing issues with internal personnel. This is also consistent with the views of data protection regulators of the European Union, discussed later in the chapter.

In designing the optimal approach for a hotline, the end user or employee perspective should be considered. Don't refuse any types of calls. Users may not be able to articulate an allegation in a way that fits within specific categories, but this type of allegation could lead to secondary reports that uncover serious misconduct. For example, a high level of Human Resource-related calls could ultimately indicate financial issues. Regardless of the initial issue, do not turn down information from employees.

Not all users are comfortable using the hotline telephony option; some are more comfortable writing, so a web reporting mechanism is useful for this type of employee. For those who do prefer the phone, the reporter should be able to speak to a live person and in his or her native language. A hotline that is solely a voice mailbox does not convey that the organization views the hotline as a serious mechanism to make a claim. Also, having live operators, like that of a third party vendor, ensures immediacy of the report at the time the reporter is prompted to place the report. Having both reporting methods available 24/7/365 gives users the ability to make contact when it is most appropriate for them.

Hotlines, in order to be most effective, must offer and ensure anonymity, which means that callers should not have to leave voicemails nor should calls be recorded. Place the burden on an intake specialist, who has been specifically trained to cover every detail, seek out information, and create an actionable report. This will also give the caller the assurance of confidentiality and non-retaliation.

Users do not want to have to struggle to file a report so they will be most conducive when reporting channels are available in their native languages. This ensures accuracy as well, since there is a likelihood for incorrect word choices or miscommunication when a reporter is speaking in his/her native language.

Finally, not only treat the reporter with respect but also the accused. Not until a thorough investigation has been completed should any action against an employee be commenced. This advice is particularly important for those hotlines that must meet data protection rules in other countries, discussed below.

The other perspective to consider in best practices is that of the investigator(s). Ensure report distribution protocols are in place and that all parties are aware of their assignments and the expectations. Commit to and conduct timely investigations by individuals who have received necessary training and have specific expertise. And do not launch reporting mechanisms until you are ready to respond to issues.

Best practices also include testing and auditing the line sporadically to ensure consistency. Testing for timely answers, appropriate interview style and customization by the intake specialist as well as quality of report and timely receipt of it ensures that the hotline is a resource for information and allegations and that those responsible for the hotline, internal and external, are performing as expected.

Issues/Concerns Facing Practitioner

There are multiple concerns associated with implementing a hotline. Management is certain to have some trepidation when establishing a hotline. Anonymous calls, vindictive callers with personal agendas, using the hotline to bypass the management chain, turf battles in handling issues, and impact of collective bargaining agreements are all possible concerns.

Management may worry that anonymous calls do not have any value. This topic has long been discussed in the ethics and compliance world. Many assume that anonymous reports are likely to be unsubstantiated. Managers often fear that anonymous reports will be used as a way for employees to deliberately make false allegations against a colleague or boss. Some even argue that anonymity should not be an option when making reports. They say, *"If they aren't willing to give their name then they shouldn't raise the issue."*

Will the hotline just be a way for employees to blow off steam? This is always a possibility, but this tends to be the exception rather than the rule. Utilizing a robust case management system allows users to track calls and notate trends. When an organization is able to look at all allegations in a broad sense, it is much easier to identify these types of calls.

Will the hotline become the preferred vehicle for employees to voice allegations or report issues, rather than utilizing management? This concern can be curtailed by how an organization communicates the hotline and its benefits to its employees. Emphasize that this is an alternative but not a substitute for an open door policy. If management prefers that employees communicate issues to their supervisors then the organization should support a culture of transparency and integrity.

Management does not want to get involved in turf wars over handling issues that come via the hotline. This is a waste of time and resources. That is why it is very important to have an investigation team and policy in place that can be shared with management. Make sure they feel confident that investigations and resolution of issues will be handled in a consistent manner.

Collective bargaining agreements also need to be taken into consideration when setting up a hotline. Certain issues raised by employees who are members of unions are covered by a required grievance process under most agreements. If collective bargaining agreements are in place, it is important to be sure there is a plan in place to properly direct any hotline reports received that are covered by a grievance process. Note also the requirement in certain countries, particularly in Europe, that an organization consult with employees' works councils before implementing a hotline, as discussed below.

Legislative Compliance

For publicly traded companies, Section 301 of SOX mandates that a method of confidential and anonymous reporting of concerns regarding auditing or accounting be in place. The reporting mechanism is also referenced under the Sentencing Guidelines. It is important for organizations to comply; even organizations that are not publicly traded must follow these protocols as best practices to not only mitigate risk but to be proactive in discovering any misconduct.

The Dodd-Frank Act Whistleblower Provisions, effective July 22, 2010, made the penalties for corporate wrongdoing increase dramatically. Any whistleblower, including in house counsel, can receive up to 30 percent of any amount the "watchdog" government collector collects over $1,000,000 for tips on corporate wrongdoing that lead to financial penalty.

International Considerations/Compliance

The operation of a "whistleblowing" hotline in other countries implicates some issues that a U.S.-based company may not appreciate. Specifically, data protection rules and employment/labor issues in some countries can affect the implementation of a hotline. Those issues reflect inconsistencies between U.S. law and the law of other nations that complicate the operation of a hotline.

To appreciate the significance of each of those issues and how they might affect a hotline, background regarding data privacy must be understood. In order to be compliant in other countries, an organization must take into account and comply with foreign regulations.

Data Protection

The European Union ("EU") has adopted a "Charter of Fundamental Rights of the European Union" (the "Charter") of which Article 8 recognizes that (1) "everyone has the right to the protection of personal data concerning him or her"; (2) "such data must be processed fairly for specified purposes and on the basis of the consent of the person concerned or some other legitimate basis laid down by law. Everyone has the right of access to data which has been collected concerning to him or her, and the right to have it rectified"; and (3) "compliance with these rules shall be subject to control by an independent authority." Those rights underlie the EU's Directive 95/46/EC "on the protection of individuals with regard to the processing of personal data and on the free movement of such data" (the "Directive").

Countries within the EU have implemented the protections contained within the Directive and the Charter by enacting data protection legislation. The Directive provides the juridical basis for the legislation of member states, but it does not directly affect citizens of those member states. The member states' laws apply directly to operations within their jurisdiction and the enforcement of those laws is delegated to data protection authorities ("DPAs") within those states.

The EU established an entity to develop consistent practices under the Directive across the entire EU. That group, the Article 29 Working Party (the "Working Party"), has issued a number of documents that explore various issues that arise within the Directive's scope.

In an opinion in which it specifically discussed the application of data protection rules to hotlines, the Working Party stated the following about issues that it believed arise in the course of setting up and managing a whistleblowing hotline:

- "the implementation of whistleblowing schemes will in the vast majority of cases rely on the processing of personal data (i.e., on the collection, registration, storage, disclosure and destruction of data related to an identified or identifiable person), meaning that data protection rules are applicable"

- "Applying data protection rules to whistleblowing schemes means giving specific consideration to the issue of the protection of the person who may have been incriminated in an alert"

- "The establishment of a reporting system should have the purpose of meeting a legal obligation imposed by Community (EU) or Member State law, and more specifically a legal obligation designed to establish internal control procedures in well-defined areas"

- "whistleblowing schemes should be built in such a way that they do not encourage anonymous reporting as the usual way to make a complaint"

- "whistleblowing schemes should focus on the data subject's rights, which damage the whistleblower's ones"

The Working Party's opinion—and subsequent decisions by various countries' DPAs—reflects a strong dislike of whistleblowing hotlines. As the DPAs in the EU countries have analyzed their countries' respective data protection laws within the context of the Directive, the rules regarding the collection, processing, and transfer of personal data have become more involved, which has created more issues for companies to consider. A short review of some of the issues that have been addressed il-luminate some of the difficulties that face international business operations that want to meet the expectations of U.S. regulators and laws.

The Permissible Scope of Allegations
Accepted on a Whistleblowing Hotline

The Directive states that personal data can be processed only for legitimate pur-poses and, with respect to a corporate hotline, the relevant purposes are that the "processing is necessary for compliance with a legal obligation to which the [data] controller is subject" and that "processing is necessary for the purposes of the le-gitimate interests pursued by the [data] controller ... except where such interests are overridden by the interests for fundamental rights and freedoms of the data subject which require protection under Article 1(1)" of the Directive. Different countries have issued opinions on this issue. The Article 7 of the Directive states that EU Member States shall provide that personal data may be processed only if:

(a) the data subject has unambiguously given his consent; or

(b) processing is necessary for the performance of a contract to which the data subject is party or in order to take steps at the request of the data subject prior to entering into a contract; or

(c) processing is necessary for compliance with a legal obligation to which the controller is subject; or

(d) processing is necessary in order to protect the vital interests of the data subject; or

(e) processing is necessary for the performance of a task carried out in the public interest or in the exercise of official authority vested in the controller or in a third party to whom the data are disclosed; or

(f) processing is necessary for the purposes of the legitimate interests pursued by the controller or by the third party or parties to whom the data are dis-closed, except where such interests are overridden by the interests for fun-damental rights and freedoms of the data subject which require protection under Article 1 (1).

Caller Anonymity

One issue that troubled the Working Party is the possibility that whistleblowing systems might receive anonymous reports. According to the Working Party, "anony-mous reports raise a specific problem with regard to the essential requirement that personal data should only be collected fairly. As a rule, the Working Party considers that only identified reports should be communicated through whistleblowing schemes in order to satisfy this requirement."

According to the Working Party, "some whistleblowers may not always be in a position or have the psychological disposition to file identified reports. It is also aware of the fact that anonymous complaints are a reality within companies, even and especially in the absence of organised confidential whistleblowing systems, and that this reality cannot be ignored. The Working Party therefore considers that whistleblowing schemes may lead to anonymous reports being filed through the scheme and acted upon, but as an exception to the rule and under the following conditions.

"The Working Party considers that whistleblowing schemes should be built in such a way that they do not encourage anonymous reporting as the usual way to make a complaint. In particular, companies should not advertise the fact that anonymous reports may be made through the scheme. On the contrary, since whistleblowing schemes should ensure that the identity of the whistleblower is processed under conditions of confidentiality, an individual who intends to report to a whistleblowing system should be aware that he/she will not suffer due to his/her action. For that reason a scheme should inform the whistleblower, at the time of establishing the first contact with the scheme, that his/her identity will be kept confidential at all the stages of the process and in particular will not be disclosed to third parties, either to the incriminated person or to the employee's line management. If, despite this information, the person reporting to the scheme still wants to remain anonymous, the report will be accepted into the scheme. It is also necessary to make whistleblowers aware that their identity may need to be disclosed to the relevant people involved in any further investigation or subsequent judicial proceedings instigated as a result of the enquiry conducted by the whistleblowing scheme.

"The processing of anonymous reports must be subject to special caution. Such caution would, for instance, require examination by the first recipient of the report with regard to its admission and the appropriateness of its circulation within the framework of the scheme. It might also be worth considering whether anonymous reports should be investigated and processed with greater speed than confidential complaints because of the risk of misuse. Such special caution does not mean, however, that anonymous reports should not be investigated without due consideration for all the facts of the case, as if the report were made openly."

Transfer of Hotline Reports to a Parent Corporation in Another Country

The Working Party recognized the need for transfers between affiliated companies, such as from a company within the EU to a parent corporation outside the EU, even if the country in which the other company is does not adequately protect personal information by law. The Working Party stressed that the nature of the offense identified in a report should determine if the information is shared and that as a rule groups should deal with issues locally. The Working Party did recognize, however, that "data received through the whistleblowing system may be communicated within the group if such communication is necessary for the investigation."

However, "Where the third country to which the data will be sent does not ensure an adequate level of protection, as required pursuant to Article 25 of Directive 95/46/EC, data may be transferred on the following grounds:

[1] where the recipient of personal data is an entity established in the US that has subscribed to the Safe Harbor Scheme;

[2] where the recipient has entered into a transfer contract with the EU company transferring the data by which the latter adduces adequate safeguards, for example based on the standard contract clauses issued by the European Commission in its Decisions of 15 June 2001 or 27 December 2004;

[3] where the recipient has a set of binding corporate rules in place which have been duly approved by the competent data protection authorities."

Deletion or Retention of Data

The Directive provides that data "which permits identification of data subjects [must be kept] for no longer than is necessary for the purposes for which the data were collected or for which they are further processed." The Working Party interpreted this to mean that "personal data processed by a whistleblowing scheme should be deleted, promptly, and usually within two months of completion of the investigation of the facts alleged in the report."

Article 29 Data Protection Working Party Opinion 1/2006 provides guidance on how internal whistleblowing schemes can be implemented in compliance with the EU data protection rules enshrined in Directive 95/46/EC.2.[2]

Article 29 Data Protection Working Party
Opinion 1/2006 on the application of EU data protection rules to internal whistleblowing schemes in the fields of accounting, internal accounting controls, auditing matters, fight against bribery, banking and financial crime

(adopted Feb. 1, 2006) http://ec.europa.eu/justice/policies/
privacy/docs/wpdocs/2006/wp117_en.pdf

Management of whistleblowing schemes

Whistleblowing schemes require careful consideration of how the reports are to be collected and handled. While favouring internal handling of the system, the Work-

---

2. OJ L 281, 23.11.1995, p. 31, available at http://europa.eu.int/comm/internal_market/privacy/law_en.htm.

ing Party acknowledges that companies may decide to use external service providers to which they outsource part of the scheme, mainly for the collection of the reports. These external providers must be bound by a strict obligation of confidentiality and commit themselves to complying with data protection principles. Whatever the system established by a company, the company must comply in particular with Articles 16 and 17 of the Directive.

i) Specific internal organisation for the management of whistleblowing schemes

A specific organisational must be set up within the company or the group dedicated to handling whistleblowers' reports and leading the investigation. This organisation must be composed of specially trained and dedicated people, limited in number and contractually bound by specific confidentiality obligations. This whistleblowing system should be strictly separated from other departments of the company, such as the human resources department.

It shall ensure that, insofar as is necessary, the information collected and processed shall be exclusively transmitted to those persons who are specifically responsible, within the company or the group to which the company belongs, for the investigation or for taking the required measures to follow up the facts reported. Persons receiving this information shall ensure that the information received is handled confidentially and subject to security measures.

ii) Possibility of using external service providers

Where companies or groups of companies turn to external service providers to outsource part of the management of the whistleblowing scheme, they still remain responsible for the resulting processing operations, as those providers merely act as processors within the meaning of Directive 95/46/EC.

External providers may be companies running call centres or specialised companies or law firms specialising in collecting reports and sometimes even conducting part of the necessary investigations. These external providers will also have to comply with the principles of Directive 95/46/EC. They shall ensure, by means of a contract with the company on behalf of which the scheme is run, that they collect and process the information in accordance with the principles of Directive 95/46/EC; and that they process the information only for the specific purposes for which it was collected. In particular, they shall abide by strict confidentiality obligations and communicate the information processed only to specified persons in the company or the organisation responsible for the investigation or for taking the required measures to follow up the facts reported. They will also comply with the retention periods by which the data controller is bound. The company which uses these mechanisms, in its capacity as data controller, shall be required to periodically verify compliance by external providers with the principles of the Directive.

iii) Principle of investigation in the EU for EU companies and exceptions

The nature and structure of multinational groups means the facts and outcome of any reports may need to be shared throughout the wider group, including outside the EU.

Taking the proportionality principle into account, the nature and seriousness of the alleged offence should in principle determine at what level, and thus in what country, assessment of the report should take place. As a rule, the Working Party believes that groups should deal with reports locally, i.e. in one EU country, rather than automatically share all the information with other companies in the group.

The Working Party acknowledges some exceptions to this rule, however. The data received through the whistleblowing system may be communicated within the group if such communication is necessary for the investigation, depending on the nature or the seriousness of the reported misconduct, or results from how the group is set up. Such communication will be considered as necessary to the requirements of the investigation, for example if the report incriminates a partner of another legal entity within the group, a high level member or a management official of the company concerned. In this case, data must only be communicated under confidential and secure conditions to the competent organisation of the recipient legal entity, which provides equivalent guarantees as regards the management of whistleblowing reports as the organisation in charge of handling such reports in the EU company.

* * *

Compliance with notification requirements

In application of Articles 18 to 20 of the Data Protection Directive, companies which set up whistleblowing schemes have to comply with the requirements of notification to, or prior checking by, the national data protection authorities. In Member States providing for such a procedure, the processing operations might be subject to prior checking by the national data protection authority in as much as those operations are likely to present a specific risk to the rights and freedoms of the data subjects. This could be the case where national law allows the processing of data relating to suspected criminal offences by private legal entities under specific conditions, including prior checking by the competent national supervisory authority. This could also be the case where the national authority considers that the processing operations may exclude reported individuals from a right, benefit or contract. The evaluation of whether such processing operations fall under prior checking requirements depends on the national legislation and the practice of the national data protection authority.

* * *

Employment Law

In many member states of the EU, workers have rights based on statute that in the U.S. exist, if at all, by means of negotiated contractual terms, especially in the context of organized labor. Among those rights in EU member states is that of "information and consultation." This has an impact on whistleblower hotlines.

Those statutes mandate that certain types of changes in working conditions must be discussed with "works councils" — statutory entities that represent workers' interests. In some respects, this might be analogized to those types of issues that must be negotiated with workers in the U.S. who have organized into unions or undertaken steps to that end.

————————

The establishment and operation of a hotline has been held to be a subject that must be presented to and discussed with a company's works councils, at least in Germany. Wal-Mart's effort to inaugurate a whistleblowing hotline for its German operations was the subject of a decision by a court, which prevented Wal-Mart from proceeding with its plan. That court held that the introduction of a standard or code of conduct by the company unilaterally violated the German statutes that mandate that certain issues must be submitted for "consultation" with the works councils. Though the use of the hotline was not mandated in that situation according to the company, the court still held that encouraging employees to use the anonymous hotline constituted an effort to monitor employee conduct that could result in disciplinary action, thus requiring Works Council involvement.

Another issue that arises relates to the requirement in some jurisdictions that materials used in the employment context must be issued in the local language. This will apply to the materials used to introduce and to publicize a whistleblowing hotline. These requirements are not universal and may arise at various governmental levels, so caution is advised when operating in other countries. The applicable rules must be carefully examined and mapped out to assure complete compliance.

Case Cycle Time

One key data point that is examined in program reviews is the amount of time it takes to answer an inquiry or complete an investigation and close matters that employees have raised to the ethics and compliance department—case cycle time. This is very important because if matters take a long time to review, employees will interpret this to mean that nothing is going to be done about their call or that the company does not take calls seriously.

Best practice is to close inquiries within two days and the majority of investigations within 30 days. Obviously some cases are very complex and will take longer to investigate; however, reasonably prompt resolution not only conveys to the caller that their concern has been responded to, it is also good for the organization because a potential issue is reviewed and addressed in a timely way to minimize the additional risk of potential ongoing wrongdoing. In any event, periodic updates to the reporter if the investigation takes longer than the normal time would be advised.

Implementing a Hotline

The basics of hotline implementation are logistical and depend mostly on an organization's decision to outsource or insource. If outsourcing the hotline, the vendor takes care of the set-up requirements. If opting to initiate in-house, the first step is involving the telecommunications department.

The organization should then identify expected standards of quality in the process, regardless whether the hotline is internal or external. The quality of information in the report is also a key factor in the report being substantiated or not and further impacts the efficiency and effectiveness of the investigation process. The information in the report needs to be detailed, accurate, and actionable. If outsourcing, a vendor has highly trained representatives that will know how to perform a call intake, but an organization can determine specific questions or information that it feels relevant. If the hotline is internal, then the responsible party that takes calls should be trained to illicit the kind of information needed to proceed with an investigation. This may be additionally hard with anonymous calls, and a different type of approach or questions may be necessary.

The implementation process should be seamless if the proper due diligence has and planning have been performed at the onset, wherein the organization has fully considered and determined all those elements included in scope, capabilities, policies, and procedures, including:

- Identification of desired allegations categories;
- Identification of priority allegations requiring immediate notification;
- Identification of methods by which you will receive reports, including by telephone or web;
- Identification of process to redirect calls that are solely seeking information or guidance;
- Establish method/system for repositing all report information and ensure information security—built into service with outsourced vendors;
- Identification of individuals that will receive and process the reports;
- Identification of method to handle any emergency or critical reports received;
- Identification of individuals that will investigate the reports from open through closed status;
- Establish method for providing answers to reporters as well as possible resolution;
- Establish method/system for tracking investigations and repositing case history—built into service with outsourced vendors;
- Establish what will be acceptable timeline for completing investigations.

Once these factors are made into policies and procedures, the naming and positioning of the hotline becomes forefront. Some organizations consider branding the hotline and website; while others stick with a more generic name: ethics line, assist line, or compliance line. Promotional materials can then be developed and distributed. Consistent messaging regarding the hotline is critical. Employees need to know about the existence and appropriate use of the hotline, and buy-in from the Board, executives, and middle management ensures that employees will identify the hotline as legitimate resource.

The most important plan to have in place during implementation is appointing and establishing resources to manage the hotline program administration and guide efforts of report receipt, distribution, and incident management. The hotline should be included in the duties and responsibilities of a particular employee or department. This strengthens the hotline as a tool in an effective ethics and compliance program and ensures accountability.

Timeline for Completing Hotline Setup from Inception to Completion

When working with a vendor for implementation, the basic set-up normally takes two to three weeks for hotline and website. If a website has many customizable features, extra time is usually required. For international access, specifically an international toll-free service (ITFS) or Global Inbound Service (GIS) line, the timeline can be many months longer. Four to six weeks is usually needed for the concept, development, and production of promotional materials detailing the hotline and the organization's messaging regarding it. Depending on the organizational hierarchy, resources, technology, and other factors, the time to develop protocols for report receipt, distribution, and investigation vary.

A testing cycle is also an important part to factor into the timeline. Testing can take from two days to three weeks, contingent on the features and complexity of the program. Testing of international hotline numbers requires the organization to coordinate internal resources in multiple countries, so it can take a few weeks to complete.

Timeline Checklist

Pre-Implementation Phase
- Define Program Features
  - Allegations and definitions
  - Program contacts (roles, permissions, access)
  - Report delivery (recipients and formats)
  - Special handling protocols (when to escalate and to whom)
  - Referral instructions
  - Custom data fields and questions
  - Website text and format

Implementation Phase
- Telephony
  - Order and program Parent company toll-free number

  - ◦ Order and program of international toll-free number(s), if applicable
  - ◦ Record customized greeting(s) for callers
- Program Data Implementation
  - ◦ Set-up of designated program features
- Web
  - ◦ URL designation
  - ◦ Home page text
  - ◦ Links
  - ◦ Contacts
  - ◦ Defined parameters of information on report form
- Quality Assurance
  - ◦ Program testing and QA by both vendor and organization
  - ◦ Telephony and web

Additional Items

- Staff Training
  - ◦ Case Management system
  - ◦ Additional training needed if program is internal (report intake, report distribution, etc.)
- Communications materials to employees

Ongoing Maintenance of the Hotline Program

Trending and Tracking

Once a hotline has been launched, there will be ongoing maintenance that needs to occur, as well as looking more closely at data to better analyze the issues being raised in reports. Tracking and trending of data is key to effectively getting the most from your hotline data. The type of data that is most important to review includes:

- Total number of contacts (including inquiries, requests for guidance and information)
- Issue types
- Where the calls are coming from
- Number of anonymous calls (as a percentage of calls)
- Percent of contacts that are inquiries and percent that include allegations
- Percent of substantiated allegations

- Disciplinary actions taken by level of employee
- Timely case closure times (the average is 30 days for investigations and two days for questions)
- Trends in level, location, type of issue, etc.

However, just interpreting the data in this way might not elicit the type of information the organization, specifically the Board and upper management, wants to see. The information needs to mean something or have context in order to be best interpreted. If the data is not meaningful, then Boards and executives become complacent about the program and miss the organizational implications that can be gleaned from well-analyzed hotline data. Is there an easy way to perfectly mine data so that relevant information is readily at hand? The short answer is no. And sometimes the analytical process is an art as much as a science. But there are approaches and resources which can dramatically change the way your organization looks at (and benefits from) its hotline data. Thus, an organization can utilize benchmarking to create meaningful data.

Benchmarking

There are two ways to benchmark your reporting system data. The first is to compare data internally within the organization. The second is to compare the data to external organizations both within your industry and across all industries. Each approach will provide valuable insights and each is necessary to understand the full picture.

Internal Benchmarking

Internal benchmarking throughout an organization's various businesses and locations provides important context, particularly when observing deviations from the internal norms over time. Here, the sophistication of an organization's case management system will determine how robust the analysis can be—more tracked data, more context, and more opportunity for actionable conclusions. By looking at reports over time, an organization can compare trends, detect trouble spots, and measure the effectiveness of its program. For example, if an organization has a significant spike in the number of reports received, there could be several causes including:

- Employee perception that other channels of communication are not effective or cannot be trusted.
- Extremely high employee awareness of this reporting channel versus others, perhaps due to recent education through training or publicity.

In this situation, an organization could consider two courses of action based on their sudden increase in call volume:

- If training or a publicity campaign related to reporting awareness had recently been conducted, the level of reports should be monitored for the next three quarters.

- If neither is the case, the organization could conduct an employee survey or targeted focus groups to determine the root cause of the spike in call volume in a given area or location.

As noted earlier, a sophisticated case management system, one that allows tracking and analysis of critical data fields, will pay great dividends in evaluating program effectiveness. The system (and resulting analysis) can only be as good as the data entered. Accurate, consistent, and timely entry of data—and most specifically data points concerning case closure and outcomes information—will provide the most reliable analyses. There are two data fields in particular that will yield valuable insights: (1) whether or not the report was substantiated and (2) the case closure time.

Report substantiation rates provide important information on the "quality" of reports received. A high substantiation rate (typically over 40% of the allegations) indicates that employees know the types of issue that should be reported and are providing enough information to conduct a thorough investigation.

There are two factors that would generally lead to a lower percentage of substantiated reports. One factor is the type of methods (or lack thereof) used to educate employees on the reporting process. If employees do not understand the process or the types of issues that should be reported, then the system will be dealing with "low quality" reports.

Second, a low substantiation rate could be an indicator of a need to review and/or improve the investigation process. One organization reviewed had zero substantiated allegations during an entire year. While the organization could rationalize this data point by assuming the calls were "junk level," a "zero substantiation rate" is highly unusual. In fact, we urge deeper examination whenever substantiation rates are below 20%. One should encourage the organization with no substantiated allegations to review the investigations conducted that year to ensure that they were properly and thoroughly completed—i.e. effective.[3]

Case closure time is also an important measure of program effectiveness because long case resolution times will cause employees to believe that the company does not take them, or their issues, seriously. Employees are more likely to report genuine issues if their concerns are addressed in a timely fashion. While any organization will have investigations that are complex and take longer to review, best practice organizations close the majority of cases within 30 days. Tracking this statistic by "investigating department" will also help highlight those areas that may need additional or different resources for timelier case resolution.

There are other ways to look at internal data. An organization could also correlate two or more variables. For example, if fraud-related allegations spike after training about fraud recognition, the organization may wish to determine if the percentage of substantiated fraud-related allegations increased. This could serve as a measurement of training effectiveness.

---

3. See above for the percentage of rates.

Another essential aspect of internal benchmarking is the comparison of different business units, departments, or locations across the total organization. This comparison allows a better examination of how different parts of the operations are performing in relation to ethics and compliance. If there are more reports in certain areas, it could indicate a need for intervention. When looking at data as a whole, without trending or grouping, this would not be so obvious. Internal data mining and benchmarking do not always lead to an answer, but they can clarify which questions to ask. This may also lead to questions best answered by external benchmarking.

External Benchmarking

There is one question that Boards and executives always ask: *How does our ethics and compliance program stack up against those of others in our field?* By benchmarking within the industry, an organization can, for example, compare itself against the call statistics reported by its peers. This can inform an organization whether certain allegations are more common in the industry than others, or if the organization itself has higher numbers than its competitors.

In addition to looking within your own industry, benchmarking across all industries adds another useful perspective to your data analysis. Looking at the larger context of all industries can assist in drawing conclusions such as certain types of allegations may be unique to one industry or more prevalent in some than others.

Other Maintenance and Ongoing Considerations

Different types of documents may need to be retained for a certain amount of time, depending on the issues raised or if the event was escalated. A system should be in place to address this, though it must be consistent with and integrated into the company's records management policies and procedures, as well as satisfy the legal requirements, such as those in international jurisdictions discussed above.

In addition to providing meaningful reports to the Board, more general results can be communicated to employees to continue to enforce transparency and an ethical culture. Continuous and regular communication regarding the hotline, and it as a part of the ethics and compliance program, keep ideas of integrity and ethical behavior top of mind.

The Dodd-Frank Act amended the Securities Exchange Act of 1934 (the "Exchange Act") by, among other things, adding Section 21F, entitled "Securities Whistleblower Incentives and Protection."

Section 21F directs the Commission to make monetary awards to eligible individuals who voluntarily provide original information that leads to successful Commission enforcement actions resulting in monetary sanctions over $1,000,000, and successful related actions.

Awards are required to be made in an amount equal to 10 to 30% of the monetary sanctions collected. To ensure that whistleblower payments would not diminish the amount of recovery for victims of securities law violations, Congress established a separate fund, called the Investor Protection Fund ("Fund"), out of which eligible whistleblowers would be paid.

2014 Annual Report to Congress on the Dodd Frank Whistleblower Program

http://www.sec.gov/about/offices/owb/annual-report-2014.pdf

Message From the Chief of the Office of the Whistleblower

Pursuant to Section 922 of the Dodd-Frank Wall Street Reform and Consumer Protection Act ("Dodd-Frank Act"), the U.S. Securities and Exchange Commission ("Commission" or "SEC") created a whistleblower program designed to encourage the submission of high-quality information to aid Division of Enforcement ("Enforcement") staff in discovering and prosecuting violations of the federal securities laws. There are three integral components of the Commission's whistleblower program—monetary awards, retaliation protection, and confidentiality protection—each of which is equally important to the continued success of the program. During Fiscal Year 2014, the Office of the Whistleblower ("OWB" or "Office") administered the Commission's whistleblower program with an eye to furthering each of these objectives.

Fiscal Year 2014 was historic for the Office in terms of both the number and dollar amount of whistleblower awards. The Commission issued whistleblower awards to more individuals in Fiscal Year 2014 than in all previous years combined. Since the inception of the whistleblower program, the Commission has authorized awards to fourteen whistleblowers. The SEC authorized awards to nine of these whistleblowers in Fiscal Year 2014. Each of these whistleblowers provided original information that led or significantly contributed to a successful enforcement action.

Not only did the number of whistleblower awards rise significantly, but the magnitude of the award payments was record-breaking. On September 22, 2014, the Commission authorized an award of more than $30 million to a whistleblower who provided key original information that led to a successful enforcement action. The whistleblower in this matter provided information of an ongoing fraud that otherwise would have been very difficult to detect. The award is the largest made by the SEC's whistleblower program to date and the fourth award to a whistleblower living in a foreign country, demonstrating the program's international reach. We hope that awards like this one will incentivize company and industry insiders, or others who may have knowledge of possible federal securities law violations, both in the U.S. and abroad, to come forward and report their information promptly to the Commission.

Two other whistleblower awards made this year drive home another important message—that companies not only need to have internal reporting mechanisms in place, but they must act upon credible allegations of potential wrongdoing when voiced by their employees. For example, the Commission's Final Order of July 31,

2014 reflects that the whistleblower in that matter worked aggressively internally to bring the securities law violations to the attention of appropriate company personnel. The whistleblower brought the information to the SEC only after the company failed to take corrective action. Similarly, on August 29, 2014, the Office announced a whistleblower award to a company employee with audit and compliance responsibilities who reported the securities violation internally and then reported the violation to the SEC after the company failed to take appropriate, timely action in response to the information. Persons with internal audit or compliance-related functions may be eligible under the program in certain limited circumstances, including where the individual reports the securities law violation internally and then waits 120 days before reporting the information to the Commission.

Fiscal Year 2014 also saw significant additional payments being made to individuals who had received awards in previous years. Because of the Commission's collection efforts, additional amounts were recovered in certain actions which, in turn, increased the amounts paid to whistleblowers in those matters. For example, our very first award recipient has seen the whistleblower award increase from the initial payout of nearly $50,000 to over $385,000, more than seven times the original payment amount.

Last year, OWB reported that it was coordinating actively with Enforcement staff to identify matters where retaliatory measures were taken against whistleblowers. On June 16, 2014, the Commission brought its first enforcement action under the anti-retaliation provisions of the Dodd-Frank Act. In that case, the head trader of Paradigm Capital Management reported to the SEC that the company had engaged in prohibited principal transactions. After learning that the head trader reported the potential misconduct to the SEC, the firm engaged in a series of retaliatory actions, including changing the whistleblower's job function, stripping the whistleblower of supervisory responsibilities and otherwise marginalizing the whistleblower. The Commission ordered the firm to pay $2.2 million to settle the retaliation and other charges. The Commission's action sends a strong message to employers that retaliation against whistleblowers in any form is unacceptable.

The SEC also filed amicus curiae briefs in several private cases pending in the federal courts to address the scope of the anti-retaliation employment protections established by the Dodd-Frank Act. The Commission argued that the anti-retaliation protections should not be interpreted narrowly to reach only individuals who make disclosures directly to the Commission. Rather, the employment protections should be understood to protect individuals at publicly-traded companies from employment retaliation who internally report potential securities law violations. The SEC explained that the whistleblower program was designed to encourage employees to report internally instances of potential securities violations and was not meant to replace or undercut corporate compliance programs. But any refusal to provide anti-retaliation protection to individuals who report wrongdoing internally at publicly-traded companies could create the unintended result of causing whistleblowers to forgo internal compliance programs and instead report directly to the SEC.

Confidentiality protection for whistleblowers also is one of the Office's paramount objectives. Confidentiality may be particularly important in cases where the whistleblower currently is employed at the company that is the subject of his or her tip or continues to work in the same or similar industry. During Fiscal Year 2014, the Office worked with other SEC staff to ensure that those who work with whistleblowers or who may review whistleblower information understand their confidentiality obligations under the Dodd-Frank Act and the Commission's implementing regulations.

As a result of the Commission's issuance of significant whistleblower awards, enforcement of the anti-retaliation provisions, and protection of whistleblower confidentiality, the agency has continued to receive an increasing number of whistleblower tips. In Fiscal Year 2014, OWB received 3,620 whistleblower tips, a more than 20% increase in the number of whistleblower tips in just two years. The Office also staffs a public hotline to answer questions from whistleblowers or their counsel concerning the whistleblower program or how to go about submitting information to the agency. In the past fiscal year, we returned over 2,731 calls from members of the public.

Finally, OWB encourages anyone who believes they have information concerning a potential securities law violation, including whether they were retaliated against for reporting the information, to submit the tip via the online portal on OWB's webpage (http://www.sec.gov/whistleblower) or by submitting a Form TCR by mail or fax, also located on OWB's webpage. If a whistleblower or his or her counsel has any question about how or whether to submit a tip to the Commission, or any other questions about the program, they should call the whistleblower hotline at (202) 551-4790.

* * *

Claims For Whistleblower Awards

Whistleblower Awards

Since the inception of the Commission's whistleblower program in August 2011, the Commission has authorized awards to fourteen whistleblowers, with awards being made to nine whistleblowers during Fiscal Year 2014. In each instance, the whistleblower provided high-quality original information that allowed the Commission to more quickly uncover and investigate the securities law violation, thereby better protecting investors from further financial injury and helping to conserve limited agency resources.

Commission's Largest Award To Date

On September 22, 2014, the Commission authorized an award of more than $30 million to a whistleblower who provided original information that led to a successful SEC enforcement action. This whistleblower award is more than double the amount of the previous highest award made under the SEC's whistleblower program.

The information provided by this whistleblower allowed the Commission to discover a substantial and ongoing fraud that otherwise would have been very difficult to detect.

The whistleblower's information not only led to a successful Commission enforcement action, but also to successful related actions. This is the fourth award to a whistleblower living in a foreign country. In issuing the award, the Commission specifically noted that allowing foreign nationals to receive awards under the program best effectuates the clear Congressional purpose underlying the award program, which was to further the effective enforcement of the U.S. securities laws by encouraging individuals with knowledge of violations of these U.S. laws to voluntarily provide that information to the Commission.

In the Commission's view, there is a sufficient U.S. territorial nexus whenever a claimant's information leads to the successful enforcement of a covered action brought in the United States, concerning violations of the U.S. securities laws, by the Commission.

In reaching the award determination, the Commission considered the significance of the claimant's information, the assistance provided by the claimant, and the law enforcement interests at issue. The Commission also considered the claimant's delay in reporting the securities violations, which was found to be unreasonable.

The Commission determined that the claimant delayed coming to the Commission after first learning of the violation, during which time investors continued to suffer significant monetary injury that might otherwise have been avoided. The Commission also recognized, however, that some of the period of delay occurred before the whistleblower award program was established by the Dodd-Frank Act, and noted that, in the Commission's discretion, it determined not to apply the unreasonable delay consideration as severely as it might otherwise have done had the delay occurred entirely after the program's creation.

Individual With Compliance or Internal Audit Responsibilities Receives Award After Reporting Internally

On August 29, 2014, the Office announced that the Commission had made an award of over $300,000 to a whistleblower who provided critical information to the Commission that led to a successful enforcement action. Under the whistleblower rules, information provided by persons with compliance or internal audit responsibilities is not considered to be "original information" unless an exception applies. One of these exceptions permits such individuals to be eligible for a whistleblower award if they reported the violations internally to designated persons at least 120 days before providing the information to the Commission. In this case, the Commission applied this exception to permit an award to the whistleblower upon determining that the claimant had reported the information through the proper channels at least 120 days before reporting it to the Commission.

The Commission also denied another individual's claim for award in the same matter.

Enforcement staff responsible for the matter had not received any information from the claimant that related to the particular covered action upon which the claimant was seeking an award.

Aggressive Internal Reporting Considered in SEC Award

On July 31, 2014, the Commission awarded more than $400,000 to a whistleblower who reported a fraud to the SEC after the company failed to address the issue Internally. The whistleblower aggressively worked internally to bring the securities law violation to the attention of appropriate personnel in an effort to obtain corrective action.

The Commission recognized the whistleblower's persistent efforts in reporting the information to the Commission after learning that an inquiry by a self-regulatory organization ("SRO") into the matter had been closed and that the whistleblower's internal efforts would not protect investors from future harm.

Rule 21F-4(a)(1)(ii) under the Exchange Act provides that a whistleblower's submission to the Commission will not be treated as "voluntary" if the whistleblower received a previous request relating to the same subject matter in connection with an SRO investigation. On the unique facts of this case, however, the Commission found it in the public interest and consistent with the protection of investors to invoke its general exemptive authority under Section 36(a) of the Exchange Act and waive the "voluntary" requirement in order to make an award to the whistleblower.

$875,000 Awarded to Two Whistleblowers

On June 3, 2014, the Commission awarded a total of $875,000, to be shared by two whistleblowers. These whistleblowers acted in concert to voluntarily provide information and assistance that helped the SEC bring a successful enforcement action.

As a result, the Commission split the award evenly between the two whistleblowers.

Of particular note, a portion of the disgorgement and prejudgment interest in the Commission's action was deemed satisfied by the respondents' payment of that amount in another governmental action. The Commission included those funds for purposes of calculating the award payment to the two whistleblowers.

Additionally, Department of Justice Criminal Division created a Resource Guide to understand the Foreign Corrupt Practices Act (FCPA). This Resource Guide, in Chapter 8, Whistleblower Provisions and Protections, provides guidance on the 2010 Dodd-Frank Act addressing whistleblower incentives and protections. This guidance is provided for FCPA compliance programs; however, it provides helpful best practices applicable to any compliance program.

U.S. Department of Justice Criminal Division & SEC Enforcement Division, Resource Guide to the U.S. Foreign Corrupt Practices Act

http://www.justice.gov/sites/default/files/criminal-fraud/legacy/2015/01/16/guide.pdf

WHISTLEBLOWER PROVISIONS AND PROTECTIONS

Assistance and information from a whistleblower who knows of possible securities law violations can be among the most powerful weapons in the law enforcement arsenal. Through their knowledge of the circumstances and individuals involved, whistle-blowers can help SEC and DOJ identify potential violations much earlier than might otherwise have been possible, thus allowing SEC and DOJ to minimize the harm to investors, better preserve the integrity of the U.S. capital markets, and more swiftly hold accountable those responsible for unlawful conduct.

The Sarbanes-Oxley Act of 2002 and the Dodd-Frank Act of 2010 both contain provisions affecting whistleblowers who report FCPA violations. Sarbanes-Oxley prohibits issuers from retaliating against whistleblowers and provides that employees who are retaliated against for reporting possible securities law violations may file a complaint with the Department of Labor, for which they would be eligible to receive reinstatement, back pay, and other compensation. Sarbanes-Oxley also prohibits retaliation against employee whistleblowers under the obstruction of justice statute.

In 2010, the Dodd-Frank Act added Section 21F to the Exchange Act, addressing whistleblower incentives and protections. Section 21F authorizes SEC to provide monetary awards to eligible individuals who voluntarily come forward with high quality, original information that leads to an SEC enforcement action in which over $1,000,000 in sanctions is ordered. The awards range is between 10% and 30% of the monetary sanctions recovered by the government. The Dodd-Frank Act also prohibits employers from retaliating against whistleblowers and creates a private right of action for employees who are retaliated against. Furthermore, businesses should be aware that retaliation against a whistleblower may also violate state, local, and foreign laws that provide protection of whistleblowers.

On August 12, 2011, the final rules for SEC's Whistleblower Program became effective. These rules set forth the requirements for whistleblowers to be eligible for awards consideration, the factors that SEC will use to determine the amount of the award, the categories of individuals who are excluded from award consideration, and the categories of individuals who are subject to limitations in award considerations. The final rules strengthen incentives for employees to report the suspected violations internally through internal compliance programs when appropriate, although it does not require an employee to do so in order to qualify for an award.

Individuals with information about a possible violation of the federal securities laws, including FCPA violations, should submit that information to SEC either online through SEC's Tips, Complaints, and Referrals (TCR) Intake and Resolution System (available at https://denebleo.sec.gov/TCRExternal/disclaimer.xhtml) or by mailing or faxing a completed Form TCR to the Commission's Office of the Whistleblower.

Whistleblowers can submit information anonymously. To be considered under SEC's whistleblower program as eligible for a reward, however, the information must be submitted on an anonymous whistleblower's behalf by an attorney. Whether or not a whistleblower reports anonymously, SEC is committed to protecting the identity of a whistleblower to the fullest extent possible under the statute. SEC's Office of the Whistleblower administers SEC's Whistleblower Program and answers questions from the public regarding the program. Additional information regarding SEC's Whistleblower Program, including answers to frequently asked questions, is available online at http://www.sec.gov/whistleblower.

Assignment

Setting Up an Ethics and Compliance Hotline/Helpline

- **Hypothetical:** You are Chief Compliance Officer at your [Team's] Corporation. Set up a hotline script and priorities and create a sample employee evaluation form. Create a work plan to update the compliance program.

Chapter 10

Incentives and Disciplinary Procedures to Promote and Protect the Compliance Program[*]

Introduction

One of the most important lessons of the recent financial crises is that misaligned incentives are as dangerous as ineffective controls. Even companies with advanced internal control systems are not immune to the phenomenon of back-door vulnerability that arises from improperly calibrated compensation and rewards systems. Absence of calibration can be as detrimental as the absence of an appropriate system. It is vital to understand that financial incentives create *a force of their own* capable of clouding and distorting individual and corporate perceptions of both risk and strategic interests. On the highest level, they may lead to a decision to acquire a company with less than clear prospects in regard of long-term profitability if such acquisition happens to help the short-term goal of increased market share. They may also influence more routine but essential daily operational decisions on all levels, such as reduction of spending on local equipment maintenance that allows the department to meet the target on cost saving and be rewarded with a bonus.[1]

For legal and compliance functions, these are instructive insights. Above all, they remind of the importance of ensuring that the company's compliance approach is not focused only toward the control and disciplinary end of what may be called "*the compliance spectrum.*" This end of the spectrum is largely about detection of non-compliance and correction of transgressions that allows achievement of deterrence through fear of discovery and disciplinary action. This emphasis on control and discipline can be very helpful for addressing intentional fraud or other clear black-and-white areas, but may be less effective in the grayer areas of corporate decision-making—those involving more subtle legal, ethical or economic nuances.

---

[*] Special thanks to G.S. Varges for his contributions. This chapter is adapted from G.S. Varges, *Incentives and Disciplinary Procedures to Promote and Protect the Compliance Program*, CORPORATE COMPLIANCE PRACTICE GUIDE: THE NEXT GENERATION OF COMPLIANCE, Chapter 10 (Carole Basri, Release 8, 2016).

1. For more on the risks of remuneration systems, see G.S. Varges, *Governing Remuneration, in* S. EMMENEGGER, CORPORATE GOVERNANCE (University of Bern Press 2011).

A more holistic or *integrated* approach to compliance needs to cover the whole spectrum, including actions designed to inspire employees, motivate the right behaviors, and reward those who excel in terms of desired conduct and ethical leadership. These efforts tend to be more focused on prevention, on incentives, on guidance, and on increasing each employee's ability to make sounder decisions. Unfortunately, there are limitations associated with preventive and empowering approaches, as they lack the means of timely detection and deterrence of intentional wrongdoing, particularly lacking a credible corrective component. Hence, the importance of ensuring appropriate compliance activity throughout its full spectrum.

This chapter addresses the elements of the compliance spectrum as depicted below and suggests possible strategies for pursuing a more balanced, integrative approach. Such approach of necessity connects the compliance program to (1) performance management and (2) compensation and reward system of the company. Importantly, all employees must be included, with special provisions for the employees in areas of compliance, risk management, audit, and similar functions. The chapter ends with a brief discussion on enforcement and disciplinary measures.

Analysis of Compliance Spectrum: From Incentives and Compensation to Disciplinary Actions

Understanding and Mapping the Spectrum

A compliance function can define in various ways how it will pursue its mission.

A *risk-based* approach focuses on the risks that could impair the attainment of company's objectives.

Under common risk categorization, legal, regulatory, compliance, and reputational risk may be either considered as a part of operational risk or it may be set aside in one or more separate categories. *Operational risk* is commonly defined as the risk of something going wrong as a result of a failure by people, systems, or processes. Examples of operational risk include a situation where the company does not have an adequate compliance policy or process for a specific regulatory obligation, or a situation where a manager ignores or circumvents such policy or process, even if it is present and adequate.

A risk-based approach in general involves:

- The identification of key risks that could imperil important organizational goals;
- The assessment of identified risks to determine the likelihood of their occurrence and the likely cost or impact on agreed goal attainment of an occurrence;
- A decision of which of these risks are acceptable without any action and which require a specific mitigation, transfer, or control.

Under this approach, identified risks are assessed and agreed upon, actions are monitored, and targeted controls are applied to ensure that the agreed response actions take place and that the risks that remain (the "retained" or "net" risks) stay within agreed parameters. Retained risks may include those where the company assesses the cost of remediation as outweighing the cost of consequences if such risks are realized. An audit function may separately conduct investigations in high-risk areas and formulate the opinion whether the risk and control activities are operating as intended and attaining their objectives. The language of the risk-based approach documents is often colored with notions of threats and of defense against such threats; thus, the frequent reference to various "lines of defense," whereby particularly risk managers, compliance officers, and internal auditors are referred to as "control functions"[2] or "gatekeepers."

A *values-based* approach has a different starting point. It frames the efforts less in terms of "risks" and more in terms of values and obligations. If a company has a legal obligation to do X, the compliance function's role is to ensure the company meets such obligation:

- Even if the possibility of detection of non-observance by the authorities or the public is low, or;
- Even if the discovery of non-observance would have no major financial or reputational impact on the company.

Consequently, the values-based vocabulary is focused less on coercive and more on enabling terminology, less on erecting control barriers and more on influencing corporate culture and corporate decision-making. Under a values-based approach, the compliance officer is viewed less as a "soldier of control" but rather as a guardian of the values who has leadership, motivational, and other pro-active responsibilities to fulfill.

A combined or integrated risk and values-based approach joins the best aspects of both perspectives. It recognizes the benefit of risk assessment, risk prioritization, controls, and enforcement measures. At the same time, it works to ensure that decision-making incorporates considerations of value and that corporate investment is directed at activities such as training and culture building that may have limited immediate deterrent effect but increase longer-term preventive value. This approach uses the risk cost-benefit methodology but enriches it with the imperative that the impact on the company's ethical fabric be given as much weight as the impact on the balance sheet.

Thus, while a pure risk approach might give relatively little weight to a bribing incident at a small foreign subsidiary that is successfully contained internally (assuming the company is under no legal obligation to self-report), the combined risk/values approach would view such incident with much greater concern, as to reflect

---

2. The shorthand term "control functions" is gaining international currency and is increasingly being used in new international standards. *See, e.g.*, Basel Commission on Bank Supervision, Corporate Governance Principles for Banks (BIS Oct. 2014) (consultative version), *available at* http://www.bis .org/publ/bcbs294.pdf. The latter defines control functions as "those functions that have a responsibility independent from management to provide objective assessment, reporting and/or assurance. This includes the risk management function, the compliance function and the internal audit function."

the potentially corrosive effect on company culture and values, even if the incident has no reputational impact. A values approach would also tend to show more concern than a risk approach to violations that result in minor fines, seeing these (particularly if high in number) as being long-term detrimental to the integrity of the company.

Notes and Comments

A company needs to make a conscious choice of which approach or combination of approaches it will pursue. This should be reflected in a formal *compliance strategy paper* that at many companies is either worked out with or approved by the Board of Directors or its Audit Committee. Such strategy should be reviewed regularly.

Equally important, the company should determine the position of its compliance focus on the spectrum. Having the focal point too close to one of the ends of the spectrum may represent a potential exposure for the company. This analysis is best achieved by formally mapping each of the compliance-relevant activities on the spectrum, thus determining the appropriate choice of preventive, detective, or corrective goals. Additionally, this mapping may reveal mismatches, gaps, or inefficiencies. For example, it may uncover low (rather than robust) detective activity in areas having potential criminal penalties such as antitrust, or it may show excessively burdensome controls in areas where sensitizing communications and employee training may be adequate, such as in respect to employee use of the company e-mail system.

Connecting to Performance Management

Over the past two decades, both the compliance practice and the managerial practices on evaluating employee and corporate performance were evolving. The crucial ideological influences of that evolution were the notions of total quality management, human capital, and corporate development. As a result, HR departments and executive management at large and small companies have been particularly active in recent years in reviewing—sometimes at the behest of the Board of Directors—how to improve their approach to these areas. Some of the terminology used includes "people," "talent," or "performance" management.

Typical objectives include:

- Attracting new talent;
- Developing existing personnel;
- Implementing methodologies for more reliable, fairer and consistent performance reviews of employees;
- Aggregating enterprise-wide performance review data;
- Doing so-called talent inventories where employees are grouped into categories regarding their "promotability" and potential for technical, managerial or leadership growth;

- Striving to retain the best talent while using performance and other measures to further train or separate from personnel who do not meet the expected standards.

The most recent innovation involves so-called "calibrations" whereby annual performance data are aggregated and analyzed across different categories, such as level of seniority, departments, divisions, regions, et cetera. The results are used to make adjustments to employees' final evaluations or ratings. Typically done by a committee or in conjunction with guidance from the executive board or CEO, these calibrations seek to compensate for possible "grade inflation" or other potential distortions or inconsistencies that tend to arise in a system with numerous and diverse managers and evaluators.

For the work of compliance functions, these can be welcomed innovations *if appropriately designed and carried out.* As these innovations assemble a more formalized process and improve objectivity of employee evaluations, they can provide a useful tool on which a compliance program can "piggy back" to advance its goals. Thus, the compliance officer will wish to gain a deep understanding of the company's performance management philosophy and practice and seek to populate appropriate HR processes with the right compliance elements.

Naturally, if the existing company performance management philosophy or practice is inconsistent with the company's compliance and ethical goals, then the task is to bring change to it. See the discussion on rewards and recognition below.

In the above efforts, the compliance officer should consider focusing on (1) the standard employee performance evaluation form, (2) the annual objective setting by individuals, (3) the periodic company-wide or unit-wide setting of objectives, and (4) the periodic assessment and ranking of units, as used at some companies.

Employee Performance Evaluation Forms

Most companies have a standard form used for employee annual or more frequent performance reviews. At some companies, the form is modified frequently, at others the same form may be in place for years. Either way, the compliance officer needs to review the form carefully to determine (a) whether anything in it may be inconsistent with the company's values and compliance goals, and (b) whether there is sufficient integration in the form of compliance elements, including the appropriate recognition of managers who excel in ethics and compliance areas.

Successfully integrating compliance considerations in the evaluation form of employees serves as a clear signal to the employee and the reviewing manager that compliance performance is also considered an important component of doing well at the company.

Ideally, the evaluation form should be specific for the conduct expectations on the employee in regard of compliance. In some companies, the above is framed in terms of negative conduct: "did the employee breach any compliance rule?" or "did the employee fail to take any required compliance training?" In other companies, the approach may also include examples of positive conduct: "did the employee excel in her efforts to learn the regulations that apply to her job?" or "during the review period did employee exhibit any particularly exemplary conduct reflecting the company's ethical and other values?"

Human resource departments tend to be, not without reason, protective of their processes and forms, and the compliance officer may encounter resistance in some cases. The most frequent objection from the HR departments refers to form inflation: "I can't put in my forms the wishes from all departments. If I put in compliance criteria, then IT, or Security, or other departments would want me to do the same." Overcoming such resistance is primarily a factor of strong leadership by the compliance officer such that he or she persuasively demonstrates to HR and executive management the value of compliance integration into the company's performance review process. Most compliance officers find HR and similar departments to be willing partners in achieving the goal of making the company a more responsible organization. However, some "upward" education may be needed, including development of new skills by the CEO.[3]

Appropriate positioning is one of the decisive factors of how quickly or how deeply the compliance officer can influence HR processes. If the compliance officer does not report directly to the Board of Directors or the company President, or is not deemed at least a peer to the head of Human Resources, he or she may have more hurdles to overcome to bring about change to the established HR and other corporate practices. This underscores the importance of reviewing the governance structure of the company to ensure that compliance officers have sufficient anchoring of governance and are positioned, both hierarchically and in terms of reporting, in a way to give them appropriate leverage and maximize their ability to have impact. Such impact should not only exist at the disciplinary part of the compliance spectrum; it should also affect those portions of the spectrum that motivate employees to appreciate compliance as requiring excellence in personal performance.

Employee Annual Objective Setting Process

Ensuring that compliance is represented in the evaluation form of employees is an important step; however, it will attain less value if compliance elements are not periodically reflected in the yearly employee objective setting process used by many companies. Often referred to as *MBO* (management by objectives), this approach is commonly deployed on multiple levels of the organization. If done correctly, the specific goals set through such process would serve to support the strategic and operational direction established by the Board of Directors and senior management. Viewed collectively, these goals are in effect the truest reflection of the character of the company — not only the tone from the top but from the middle and "lower decks" as

---

3. See G.S. Varges, *Working with the Chief Compliance Officer: A New CEO Skill*, European CEO (Jan. 13, 2013), *available at* http://www.europeanceo.com/business-and-management/working-with-the-chief-compliance-officer-a-new-ceo-skill/.

well. They describe through concrete annual or other periodic targets what the company considers important for employees in helping to achieve the company's mission. If no compliance goals are found in these targets over several years, this can be indicative of compliance not being on the priorities list of the company.

The MBO approach, therefore, should be seen as another opportunity for determining the aims of the compliance program. For example:

- If the company is implementing a new code of conduct, the compliance officer might negotiate with the Board of Directors or company President that all managers above X level include in their annual goals specific actions in support of the implementation of and training on such code in the units for which they are responsible.

- If a company has had problems with its sales force adhering to client entertainment guidelines aimed at preventing conflicts of interest, a possible annual goal for each manager that supervises salespersons might be not to have a failure rate of more than 1% when audits of spending are conducted.

- If a company beset by litigation is having trouble with managers not giving enough attention to "litigation hold" or document preservation orders, it might include in such managers' annual objectives such goals as to personally reinforce to their employees each time a litigation hold order is received from the legal department, regularly monitor observance of such orders in their unit, and report adherence and performance to the legal or compliance department on a monthly basis.

In each of the above examples, an express employee performance objective is set to support a specific compliance goal. While one might argue that the employees involved already have an obligation to do the task in question independent of the annual objective set, the employment of the MBO approach for these purposes makes use of a positive incentive to help increase the compliance success rate or implementation quality. Expressed otherwise, this approach rests on *performance* principles, not just on *control* principles. Like other corporate goals (e.g., achieving high customer satisfaction rates), many compliance goals cannot be reduced to an all-or-nothing grade. Depending on many factors—such as the quality of the effort by the persons involved, their skills, the extent of support they receive, the time allotted for completion, etc.—the actual performance levels in relation to compliance goals may significantly differ among employees. For a compliance program the task is to figure out *which factors can influence employee compliance performance the most*, i.e., which levers can be pulled (and how far) to most effectively increase compliance goal achievement. With this in mind, the compliance officer must remember that controls and disciplinary action are not the only applicable and appropriate levers.

Company or Unit Objectives

As suggested above, the annual process of objective setting for employees can be a useful lever. An additional lever is found in the collective goals or plans that companies tend to set annually or over a period of years. These may be company-wide or be specific to particular divisions, regions, departments or other units. Although organizational goals may be tied to the individual objective setting process (e.g., a division manager may have the attainment of a certain division goal as part of his or her individual objectives), organizational goals have the advantage of (a) carrying institutional weight since they represent a collective aim, and (b) benefitting from the positive pressure that comes when a particular goal is openly communicated within the company. For example, if a company announces to its employees a project to redefine its brand and indicates that the new brand positioning will be launched by X date, such communication creates an additional stimulus for those involved in the rebranding effort to work hard on their objective and deliver by the announced date.

If the company's practice incorporates the use of such kind of company- or unit-wide objectives, the compliance officer would want to consider:

- Setting a *distinct* company- or unit-wide objective in a particular compliance area which is then specifically communicated to employees, or
- Including a compliance component in a company or unit objective that will be pursued by another division or department of the company.

For example, if a company is aiming to increase front-line employee IT skills and formally sets a two-year company-wide target to train 80% of such employees, the compliance officer may wish to review the objective to determine if a compliance training element can be integrated into this IT company-wide initiative. The benefit for compliance in leveraging off the IT goal is not only in achieving cost or other efficiencies, but in acquiring additional employee exposure since the IT initiative is likely to receive a high level of visibility within the company. Such exposure could add to employee familiarity with the compliance program and serve as a further signal of the importance of compliance in the corporate agenda.

Periodic Unit Assessments

Practices described above address goals that may be set periodically for the whole organization or any of its units or departments. A number of companies have gone a step further: they have introduced regular grading of units or lines of business against specific indicators as part of performance management or *execution management*. Some companies may choose only two or three key indicators (e.g., customer payment defaults, percentage of returned products, sales per customer, etc.) or a whole dashboard of indicators (sometimes referred to as a "balanced score card"). Under either approach, the company tracks the indicators by business division, line of business, or other criteria as part of measuring the ongoing health of the organization, or the progress made in executing particular strategies or attaining specific goals. In some companies, these unit evaluations may be qualitative (descriptive); in others they may be quantitative (a number, color, or letter grade). In either case, unit managers usually work hard to ensure that their units receive a favorable assessment or rating.

The potential for integrating compliance criteria in such regular unit assessments is obvious. Thus, it is not surprising that compliance measures have found their way onto performance dashboards or balanced score cards used at a number of companies. How compliance criteria is incorporated varies widely and is usually focused on areas of specific importance or concern to the company, such as:

- Timely response to customer complaints under a particular regulatory standard;
- Accuracy in filing of regulatory reports;
- Regulatory fines paid;
- Law suits filed alleging violations, such as misrepresentation of products or safety flaws;
- Completion rate of compliance training by employees in the unit;
- Successful resolution of any open audit points from the internal or external auditors;
- Unit responsiveness to and cooperation with requests made by the central legal or compliance department, etc.

Based on the performance by the unit in the measured areas, the compliance department issues its assessment or grade, which, along with the other measures for the unit in question, becomes part of the report card of that unit for the specific period of time.

Among other things, the described practice allows for measuring comparative performance across units and historically, thus facilitating trend analyses and early identification of problematic units or areas within the company. If compliance indicators were a part of such analysis, obtained data would constitute critical intelligence for guiding the compliance program and reporting to the Board of Directors.

Connecting to the Compensation and Rewards System

Whether approached from a values-based or risks-based perspective, the compensation and rewards system of a company should be of interest to the compliance officer.

- From a values perspective, a key question is whether such system is designed and operated consistent with good governance principles and promotes goals and behaviors supportive of company values, such as avoiding conflicts of interest, balancing the interests of the company's stakeholder, and sustaining long-term enterprise value.[4]

---

4. The challenge is that each of these goals may require different types or at least differently calibrated incentives. Increasingly the market and regulators are aiming to reduce these conflicts by requesting a longer horizon for measuring performance—beyond the traditional one-year performance period. The compliance officer thus will need to probe not only the types of compensation performance

- From a risk perspective, a key question is whether the compensation and rewards system has any component that creates unacceptable incentives such as motivating employees to go beyond the risk appetite or exceed the risk limits approved by the Board of Directors or to circumvent any compliance policies.

Four areas relating to the compensation and reward system are particularly fertile for the compliance officer to review and seek to impact: (1) compensation architecture and governance, (2) compensation's connection to performance management, (3) bonus pools for units, and (4) compensation for personnel in control functions.

Impacting Compensation Architecture and Governance

The challenge for the compliance officer wishing to have an impact in this area has to do both with the complexity of compensation and reward systems as well as with the fact that historically most companies considered design of such systems and setting of compensation levels to be an especially sensitive domain restricted to a fairly small circle of senior decision-makers.

With respect to program design, compensation funding, and general compensation levels, the lead at well-governed companies is usually by the Compensation Committee of the Board of Directors, though a good deal of the leg work may be done by the HR department and executive management. The compensation committee sometimes also relies on external compensation consultants.

To achieve the most objectivity, such consultants should be hired by and report to the Board of Directors, not to management. At companies where the Board of Directors has not established clearly its leadership in the remuneration area, the main architecture and the levels of proposed compensation may be largely driven by executive management and HR, sometimes with the help of management-hired compensation consultants. While the approval of the Board of Directors is naturally sought, the experience of past years has shown that at some companies the review by the Board of Directors of compensation proposals that originate with the management may not be as thorough and independent as would be desirable.

Complexity is another challenge. Compensation and reward systems, particularly for more senior managers, have tended over the years to become more intricate. They often involve multiple components — cash, shares, options, personal and family fringe benefits, life insurance, signing and departure bonuses, tax equalization payments, loans, etc., — and have various conditional requirements and vesting periods. Since

---

measures the company uses but whether the time horizon is long enough. In recent years, the so-called vesting period for certain kinds of variable pay has been increasing, sometimes going well beyond three years.

employees come to rely on the payouts from the remuneration system and since the interests of the other company's stakeholders also need to be taken into account, making major changes on remuneration is often like trying to change the direction of a large tanker—it can be slow and arduous, even for well-intentioned individuals committed to reform.

Whether the current debate on executive compensation will stimulate companies in all industries to review on their own the long-term viability of their compensation approaches is an open question, though there are some signs of this beginning to happen. An important factor is the presence of internal leaders in the company who champion remuneration reform. There is no reason why the chief ethics or compliance officer should abstain from becoming one of such leaders.

The current public debate is both national and international. Following the issuance particularly of the Financial Stability Board's remuneration principles in 2009, many jurisdictions, including the USA, have begun taking various legal and regulatory initiatives to address perceived malfunctioning of corporate compensation systems.[5] Some of these, such as the European Union caps on bonuses that took effect on January 1, 2014, have some extraterritorial reach, reminding of the need to have an overview of relevant regulation in all jurisdictions where the company does business.[6] The public perception of the compensation debate sometimes focuses on the levels of compensation, such as whether pay of certain senior executives is disproportionate given the specific conditions of their performance, overall market, or in comparison to other employees in the company. Other times the debate focuses less on the amounts and more on the "how," such as on (a) the governance of the compensation process,[7] e.g., how are levels of remuneration decided: who decides, with which controls, with what levels of transparency etc., (b) the conditions on which compensation rests, such as whether it is connected too much to short-term sales, profit, share price or other such criteria or whether it is connected to longer-term value creating criteria, and (c) whether compensation is sufficiently risk-discounted, i.e., adjusted for actual risk and cost incurred by the company associated with the actions for which the ex-

---

5. In the U.S., for example, important developments include the Dodd-Frank Act, including more recently the compensation elements of the Volcker Rule and the rules for bank holding companies and foreign banks. *See* https://www.sec.gov/about/laws/wallstreetreform-cpa.pdf; http://www.federal reserve.gov/newsevents/press/bcreg/20131210a.htm; http://www.federalreserve.gov/aboutthefed/board meetings/memo_20140218.pdf.

6. The EU remuneration rules are part of the Capital Requirements Directive (CRD IV). The rules to implement CRD IV are issued by the European Banking Authority. *See* http://ec.europa.eu/ internal_market/bank/regcapital/legislation-in-force/index_en.htm; http://eur-lex.europa.eu/LexUri Serv/LexUriServ.do?uri=OJ:L:2013:176:0338:0436:EN:PDF; https://www.eba.europa.eu/regulation- and-policy/remuneration.

7. The concern with the "how," not just the absolute amounts paid, creates the natural link to governance, risk, and compliance. Thus, while the market, shareholders, board of directors, and senior management are better positioned to determine the appropriate amounts to be paid, the risk manager and compliance officer can be of help with ensuring that compensation decisions take properly into account risk, compliance, and ethical considerations as well. *See, e.g.,* G.S. Varges, *Governing Remuneration, supra* note 1.

ecutive is being compensated. As part of the review at his or her company, the compliance officer should ensure that all necessary aspects of compensation and rewards are considered both in terms of the design and in terms of aspects of the operation of the system.

Within the above context, the compliance officer has to study and strategize how he or she can best have impact in the compensation area. While it is important to recognize the authority of those who are formally responsible for the compensation and reward system, there is a strong case to be made that compliance (and risk management) functions have a role, or even a duty, in helping promote (a) the proper governance of the compensation and reward system, (b) its proper alignment with the company's compliance and risk management goals, and (c) compliance by the company to its internal compensation rules and to relevant laws and regulations. The potential ways of contributing and influencing could include:

- Participating in a formal company task force to revise the existing compensation and rewards system;

- Preparing proactively for the Compensation Committee of the Board of Directors an independent compliance and values review of the existing compensation and rewards system, even if there are no current plans to do a formal company-wide review of such system;

- Proposing a "Compensation Integrity Committee" or similar body to monitor the operation of the compensation and rewards system to ensure it is being operated fairly and consistently with approved policy and that any exception or non-adherence to such policy is being reported to the Board of Directors. Such committee might also review the company's disclosure practices on compensation and determine where additional disclosures, beyond what is legally required, might be of benefit to the company and its stakeholders;

- Proposing a process for reviewing from the perspective of risk and/or compliance the contemplated performance objectives of, for example, a high risk unit, managers above X level, employees with major sales responsibilities, etc.; such review could focus on ensuring that such objectives, particularly those with specific profit or sales targets, are not structured in a way that may induce unwise risk-taking or compromise ethical or other key company principles;

- Proposing that in order to remain eligible for a bonus, option or share award a manager must remain in compliance with the company's code of conduct and other company policies and must not take any risks outside of the approved risk parameters; to the extent possible, this would be formally incorporated in employment contracts and in the compensation and rewards policy documents; a variant of this policy would go even further and require the returning (the so-called clawback) of an already vested or received bonus if the compliance and risk assumptions under which the bonus or award was granted turn out not to have been met (e.g., the recipient invested in non-approved securities, made a misrepresentation on his unit's financials, knowingly allowed non-compliant marketing practices that later led to fines, engaged in unlawful discriminatory conduct, etc.).[8]

• Developing a robust compliance process for encouraging and verifying that management, human resources, and others involved in the administration of the remuneration system are adhering to the established rules; this may include establishing a reporting process by the compliance officer to the Board of Directors.

Naturally, any such tie of compensation to risk or compliance conduct would need thorough legal review to ensure, among other things, no conflict with pre-existing contractual obligations, collective bargaining agreements, labor laws, and the like. For banks and other regulated industries it would also mean taking into account the rules or expectations of their regulator on compensation.[9]

———————

Sample Employee Evaluation Form

Employee Name: _____   Department: _____

Job Title: _____   Immediate Supervisor: _____

Date of Review: _____   Next-Level Supervisor: _____

Evaluation Period: _____   Too New to Evaluate: Yes ___ No ___

Summary of Performance: Performance Definitions:

O   Outstanding   Performance is superior on a consistent and sustained basis

E   Exceeds Expectations   Performance exceeds normal job requirements

M   Meets Expectations   Performance meets position requirements

NI   Needs Improvement   Performance meets some position requirements

U   Unsatisfactory   Performance does not meet position requirements; immediate attention to improvement is required

N/A   Not Applicable   Criterion does not apply to this position

———————

8. Since it involves monies the ownership of which has already transferred to the employee, a clawback is among the most legally challenging instruments in the compensation area. Yet a clawback is perceived as a powerful tool for discouraging improper conduct since it maintains the compensation at risk beyond the vesting period. In the UK proposals are currently under consultation that would create one of the most rigorous regimes on clawbacks. See http://www.bankofengland.co.uk/pra/Documents/publications/policy/2014/clawbackcp6-14.pdf.

9. For example, some jurisdictions have introduced regulations that affect not only the way a financial institution remunerates its executives but even the levels of such remuneration. Thus, as of January 2014, new European Union rules for banks and certain other financial institutions limit a bonus to one time the base salary for certain level of managers, absent shareholder approval to go up to two times base. See n. 5 *supra*. Other jurisdictions, including the United States, have put in place certain compensation restrictions on institutions receiving governmental financial support. *See, e.g.,* the Troubled Assets Relief Program under the Emergency Economic Stabilization Act, *available at* http://www.treasury.gov/initiatives/financial-stability/TARP-Programs/executive-comp/Pages/default.aspx.

It is the company's policy to evaluate employees for their complete performance. This includes their contribution to the company's financial, people, risk, and compliance goals. The evaluation will be a guide for providing feedback to the employee, identifying, improving needs, and determining the recommendation for any promotions as well any salary increase or bonus.

Please see the sample performance evaluation below. Additional space is provided for evaluator comments. The evaluator should write a few words supporting the evaluation. Please note that as part of the performance evaluation, the manager should take into account input received from the company's compliance department with regard to the employee's fulfillment of compliance obligations, including compliance training.

	Description	Rating	Further Explanation	Suggestions for Improvement
Core Competencies				
Quality of Work	Completes assigned work efficiently and in an organized manner within an established time frame, works to complete objectives and sees a task through to the end while taking into consideration current responsibilities and workload			
Individual Effectiveness	Displays a cooperative attitude in the workplace, exhibits tact and sincerity with others to achieve objectives			
Communication	Expresses ideas and information in writing and verbally, in a manner that is complete, clear, concise, organized and appropriate to the audience. Conveys information to supervisors, peers, and customers in a clear, timely and concise manner. Listens to others, and is open-minded to and evaluates suggestions from others			
Service Focus	Takes a personal interest in both internal and external customers, creates a pleasant atmosphere for interaction and takes appropriate action to meet their needs			
Judgment and Decision Making	Realistically weighs and evaluates information, separates the important from the unimportant, assesses probable consequences and takes appropriate action, and			

	Description	Rating	Further Explanation	Suggestions for Improvement
	demonstrates the ability to make sound and timely decisions. Accountable for results and selects decision alternatives that meet the objectives of the department			
Team Building	Actively seeks and achieves group participation to improve work, set priorities, is innovative and solves problems			
Job Knowledge	Demonstrates comprehension of techniques, skills, processes, procedures and materials necessary to perform job			
Ongoing Skills Improvement	Displays an interest in and uses initiative to not only maintain current skills, but also continuously upgrade skills to meet changing requirements of the job			
Dependability	Exhibits reliability in being available for work, sometimes without close supervision, and takes ownership in the work to be performed			
Enhanced Competencies				
Leadership	Exhibits leadership qualities			
Business Growth	Helps develop and expand the company's business lines and relationships			
Ethics	Displays ethical behavior and decision-making			
Business Reputation	Aids in maintaining the ethical reputation of the company			
Adaptability	Demonstrates flexibility and adaptability in difficult or changing work and work-related circumstances. Thinks quickly on his/her feet			
Compliance	The employee has not violated any compliance procedure or rule/regulation of the company			

Would you recommend this employee for an alternative position at our company? Please provide an explanation.

Do you believe this employee is well suited for his/her role; is a valuable asset and should continue being employed? Please provide an explanation.

Please provide general and any additional comments below.

It is my understanding that the employee will have access to the information in this evaluation.

Supervisor name: _____

Supervisor position: _____

Date: _____

Signature: _____

Signature of employee: _____

Date: _____

_____

Impacting Compensation by Influencing Performance Management

Whether or not the compliance officer is successful in helping the company focus on the larger questions surrounding the governance and components of its compensation and rewards system, he or she still has an opportunity to have influence in a different way: by influencing the criteria that lead to compensation allocation decisions.

To the extent that a company reliably uses the results of the performance evaluation process to make compensation decisions, it establishes thereby the desirable *connection between pay and performance*. Consequently, if the forms and processes used to evaluate and document an employee's performance contain compliance elements, then the employee's compliance performance also becomes a factor in the determination of how much compensation the employee receives (whether as a salary increase, a bonus, or in any other form). If done correctly, this has the advantage of adding another tool to the compliance arsenal, a tool for providing a financial incentive to guide employees toward the right behaviors.

Compensation, however, is not the only form of rewards within a company. Another important component are promotions and other career advancement decisions. Thus, to ensure it can more amply affect the incentives portion of the compliance spectrum, the compliance officer may wish to consider how the compliance performance of an individual employee can also be brought to bear on any decision by the company to promote, transfer, or offer other career enhancements to such employee. For example, at some companies there is a clear division between management and non-management roles. To be considered for a management role, the individual may need to meet certain criteria, such as demonstrating that he or she possesses the appropriate organizational, people-management, and leadership skills.

For the compliance officer the above represents an additional opportunity for furthering the compliance agenda. He or she might wish to ensure, for example, that before a person is considered for a promotion—particularly one where such person will play a key leadership role, such as becoming a regional or divisional manager or a member of the company's management committee—consideration must also include an assessment of the quality of such person's *compliance performance* as an individual and (if applicable) as a manager. Thus, if the head of the smaller Asian Division is now being proposed for the larger role as head of the Pacific Division, consideration should include an assessment of how well the Asian Division did on compliance criteria under his or her leadership. In addition, review should include such person's past performance on individual compliance goals. Some of the questions that may be asked: did he or she resist compliance training; were there any incidents raising doubts on his or her ethical judgment; were there any complaints from employees he or she managed regarding any potentially discriminatory or other inappropriate behavior? Alternatively, was this manager particularly known for his or her support of compliance goals and for insisting that the company's values not be compromised to achieve a particular business goal?

Influencing Bonus Pools

As previously discussed, some companies assess and grade departments or units through the use of certain indicators or performance criteria. Such grading helps the company monitor performance by unit and make necessary adjustments. At the same it allows management (as the individual evaluations and rankings are not always shared with the Board of Directors) to form views regarding the capabilities of those in leadership positions in the units in question. In some companies, these unit assessments also lead to compensation consequences. One distribution method is through the establishment of specific bonus pools by division or other unit. Either the size of such pool or the percentage payout under the pool can be dependent on the actual performance of the unit in regard of the specific targets or indicators. Naturally, if the compliance officer has succeeded in embedding compliance criteria in the unit assessments, then he or she has also succeeded in influencing the bonus pool or the payout under the bonus pool received by those in the unit.

In some companies, there are practices where compliance performance has an even more direct impact on the bonus pool. One such practice involves deducting from the bonus pool of a unit all regulatory fines incurred due to any non-compliance within such unit. A more comprehensive approach would deduct related legal and other costs and might also include the cost of civil law suits that were clearly triggered by a compliance lapse or gap at the unit.

What these practices have in common is that they provide another stimulus for the unit's management to give high focus to minimizing noncompliance incidents. This may influence not only conduct but also decisions on ensuring adequate compliance staff and funding. Thus, whereas previously management may have perceived any additional spending on compliance as a further cost that merely reduces the unit's profitability (on which compensation often rests only partially), under these approaches, the unit's management may better appreciate the benefit of appropriate local compliance investment and preventive activity. After all, if successful, these efforts could lead to a larger bonus pool or payout for the unit. While not a replacement for controls or other compliance practices, the use of these types of financial incentives can play a healthy complementary role provided they are properly designed, implemented, and communicated. For if they are not, there is the risk that such incentives could be perceived as compromising the company's values in that they may appear to replace the *ethical* incentive with a *pecuniary* one.

While not yet an established compliance practice, the notion of, in effect, making a company unit "pay" for its compliance shortcomings could theoretically be extended further and be tied to the capital provision. Some company management teams already use the "carrot" of more parent-provided funding and the "stick" of reduced parent-provided funding to incent company units to meet certain financial performance targets, particularly in terms of profitability or return on capital. Units that exceed the set targets receive a larger share of funding (and thus more opportunity to grow their business) than those that do not. Leveraging on this model, it would be conceivable for a company to also add compliance criteria to their funding or capital provision practices, amounting almost to a kind of "play or pay" compliance concept—in other words, do less well on compliance and your unit will have less money with which to work. A variant of this approach would involve giving the units that meet their compliance goals the right to retain more of their earnings, i.e., to dividend up or transfer up less capital to the parent company. A further variant would make those units that underperform on compliance pay for parent-provided or ordered compliance remediation or set up more reserves to cover the realization of potential compliance risks. The latter approach would resemble the additional capital buffers that banks and other financial institutions have to put in place for certain kinds of risks under the regulation in certain jurisdictions.

Shaping the Compensation of Personnel in Control Functions

A recommendation from a number of national and international bodies reacting to the recent financial crises is for companies and regulators to review the way those in control functions (compliance, risk management, audit, etc.) are compensated. The concern is that if not properly structured, the remuneration of control functions could create (or give the appearance of creating) potential conflicts of interest and compromise objectivity and effectiveness of these control functions.

Another element of concern is *who* evaluates and determines the compensation of a person in a control function. For example, consistent with leading practices, in an increasing number of companies, the compliance officer reports directly to the CEO or other senior member of management who evaluates the compliance officer at the end of the year and determines his or her bonus. A dilemma thereby emerges, since in order to achieve effective overall compliance, the compliance officer should report to the highest possible level of the management hierarchy, unless the less common practice of reporting directly to the Board of Directors is followed (see discussion below). At the same time, reporting to the CEO or other senior member of management and being in effect beholden to such person for career advancement might impact how vigorously the compliance officer pursues matters on which such senior manager is of a different opinion or is implicated. Some of the checks-and-balances may be lost even unconsciously, in spite of genuine efforts by the compliance officer to maintain objectivity.

The potential reporting conflict is not sufficiently diminished by having the compliance officer report to the company's general counsel or another intermediary, for as long as such person reports to the CEO or other senior member of management, and not to the Board of Directors. In this connection, several distinct approaches may be considered with regard to the extent of "reporting" to the Board of Directors by a compliance officer:

(a) Reporting in terms of the right to bring to the Board's attention, without the need of any other person's approval, a violation or other significant issue;

(b) Everything in (a), plus the ongoing (i.e., several times a year) obligation to report to the Board on the compliance program strategy, progress, resources, barriers, etc., but on the latter only with the prior approval or clearance of content by some other person (e.g., the general counsel, the CEO, or some other non-Board person);

(c) All in (a) and (b), except with the right to report to the Board on program strategy, progress, etc., without the need to seek the approval or clearance on content from any other non-Board person; and

(d) All in (c), along with having the compliance officer's performance evaluated by the Board directly (with input from those executives with whom the compliance officer deals the most); the Board in such case would also decide on the compliance officer's compensation, promotion, etc.

For maximum effectiveness, compliance officers may aim to have (c) or (d) apply to them. Being able to report to the Board only when something is wrong (the right "to ring the alarm") under (a) above would not meet today's compliance best practices. Where the Board of Directors is not prepared to entertain direct functional reporting by the compliance officer (or where the CEO opposes this), one potential solution for addressing the reporting conflict issue is for the evaluation and compensation decisions regarding the compliance officer to be done, not by one person, but by a committee which ideally should include a senior representative of a control function, such as the head auditor or the general counsel.

The dilemma outlined above goes beyond deciding on the aspects and structuring of the reporting responsibilities of the compliance officer. It extends to the *components and measures* for compensation. For example, some argue that awarding shares or options to personnel engaged in control functions is, on balance, less healthy than simply offering only cash remuneration. Others see the problem as being less related to the compensation components and more to the performance measures. For example, if the compliance officer's compensation includes a bonus that is connected to the company attaining certain financial results, it is sometimes argued that this taints his or her objectivity to the extent any action or inaction by the compliance officer could influence the outcome (e.g., delaying the launch of an internal investigation that may substantially add to the company's costs and potentially impede the company from reaching a cost-saving target on which compliance officer's bonus depends).

With respect to risk managers, some believe that lessons of the recent years, specifically, the apparent failure to oppose strongly enough the practice of investment into risky instruments is at least partly explainable by the fact that—as long as these instruments were contributing markedly to the company's annual financial performance, on which the bonus and other awards of the risk managers were in part dependent—there was a disincentive for the risk managers to challenge robustly enough management's investment policies.

While some of these concerns and lines of argumentation might seem to stretch plausibility, they are not to be taken lightly. However founded or unfounded such concerns may be, the fact that specific compensation practices may raise even a perception of a potential conflict of interest means that compliance and other control functionaries need to review how they are compensated and recommend any necessary adjustments to senior management and the Board of Directors.

The challenge is how to accomplish the above while ensuring that the divisions of the company entrusted with control functions remain able to achieve their own personnel needs. These include (a) attracting and retaining the best talent, (b) incentivizing better performance through higher pay, (c) not disadvantaging financially those in control functions vis-à-vis personnel not in control functions, and (d) staying competitive in the relevant compensation market. With the "war for talent" having reached compliance and other control areas in recent years, these considerations are not without merit.

The reality of competition for talent within the same company cannot be underestimated. Particularly in larger companies, control functions need also to be able to draw the best talent from elsewhere in the organization. To do this, a compliance department for example needs to become known within the company as a division offering competitive career and salary development, and where high potential individuals can excel and find career satisfaction.

What solution appropriately balances all the relevant interests will depend in large part on the specifics of each company, including the peculiarities of its existing compensation plans. The compliance officer seeking reform in this area will have to take into account all possibly existing practical or political obstacles to the goal of setting up a compensation structure for personnel in control functions that differs in a meaningful way from that of other personnel in the company.

The following principles may be helpful to consider in developing an approach to compensation for personnel in control functions, including compliance:

(a) A person in a control function is not exempt from the expectation of performance but the measures of performance *should not create any disincentives for such person to carry out his or her duties objectively and robustly.*

(b) Because of the risk of a conflict of interest, a member of a control functions department should not be compensated based on the completion or non-completion of a particular commercial or financial transaction, nor on the attainment of a financial short-term goal by a unit that is overseen, evaluated, or investigated by that person.

(c) Compensation for control personnel based on company-wide goals or performance measures is not by itself a cure to any potential conflicts; each such goal and measure needs to be reviewed to ensure it passes the disincentive test under (a) above.

(d) In some cases, extending the relevant time horizon may help reduce the potential conflict or appearance of a conflict. For example, if for non-control personnel a bonus depends on profit of the company over X period of time, for the control personnel's compensation could be based on results over an extended timeframe, such as X plus an additional period of time.

(e) Where a company creates bonus pools for different units or categories of employees, one possibility is creating a bonus pool unique to control functions. The size of such pool ideally is decided by or in conjunction with the Compensation (or Audit) Committee of the Board of Directors. The payout and allocation to such pool can be done based on objective criteria agreed upon among the control functions, the Compensation (or Audit) Committee, and management.

(f) Where options or shares are part of the compensation of a person in a control function, the exercise of options or the sale of shares by such person (a) may be subject to longer vesting or holding periods and (b) should require at least as much review and clearance as is required of board members, senior management, and others with access to potentially price-sensitive information. If a company keeps a list of insiders, restricted persons or similar, those in control functions should be included on such lists and be subject to the same trading restrictions as others on the list (such as being prohibited from trading during close or restricted periods). This should be considered even for junior members of a control function who may not necessarily have access to price sensitive information so as to avoid the appearance of conflicts. All these measures help eliminate any potential chance of a control person—a part of the company's vanguard—using, or being perceived as using, any non-public job related information for personal trading advantage.

Regardless of the specifics of the approach a company ultimately takes in respect of compensation of control functions, it is essential for the compliance officer to be an active part of that debate, to offer thoughtful leadership, and to continue to monitor the chosen approach to ensure it remains viable and consistent with the ethical, compliance and risk principles of the company.

William C. Dudley, President and Chief Executive Officer, Fed. Reserve Bank of N.Y., Speech, Enhancing Financial Stability by Improving Culture in the Financial Services Industry

(Oct. 20, 2014) (available at https://www.newyorkfed.org/
newsevents/speeches/2014/dud141020a.html)

Remarks at the Workshop on Reforming Culture and Behavior in the Financial Services Industry, Federal Reserve Bank of New York, New York City, As prepared for delivery

How Can Better Incentives Help?

In my example, for matters to work properly, I think it is important that all the players—traders, compliance, risk and legal, have the right incentives to behave in the way that is appropriate and that aligns their interests with the broader interests of the firm in rooting out bad behaviors. One way in which incentives can be shaped is through the structure of compensation. I believe that a proper compensation system can be an important tool for enhancing culture, promoting financial stability and rebuilding the public trust in the financial industry.

Incentives matter for individual behaviors and decisions in all industries, including the financial industry. Some might argue, however, that risk-takers are drawn to finance like they are drawn to Formula One racing, and that regardless of risk or reward, these types of individuals will always want to push the boundaries. This logic might lead one to conclude that incentives are unlikely to be an effective tool to limit excessive risk-taking and to promote more ethical behavior in the financial sector. I disagree. First, the degree to which an industry attracts risk-takers is not pre-ordained, but reflects the prevailing incentives in the industry. After all, risk-takers have options. Second, and, more importantly, incentives matter even for risk-takers.

In my speech on ending too big to fail, I stressed the importance of reducing the likelihood that large financial firms would face insolvency, as well as the need for a credible resolution plan that does not involve taxpayer money. Compensation policies can play a useful role in reducing excessive risk-taking. Similarly, compensation policies can complement an improved culture, and play a role in reducing unethical and fraudulent behavior. Individuals who decide to bend the rules or to step over the line usually do this in the context of an assessment of the expected risks and rewards of their actions.

This implies that one objective should be to rebalance the scales so that the expected risks from unwanted behaviors are more likely to outweigh the expected rewards. The expected risks are a function of the likelihood that an individual (or set of individuals) is caught and the attendant consequences. The expected rewards include any financial and psychic benefits to the individual from the behavior if undetected. Improved culture helps to tip the balance in the favor of better behaviors by increasing the likelihood that an individual will both feel an obligation to behave properly, and be prevented by others from carrying out bad behavior. In addition, a strong culture can also reduce the rewards some employees may hope to enjoy. In its simplest form, a strong culture means that individuals who get away with unethical or illegal activities will not have the satisfaction of "bragging rights" about their actions because there are no congratulations for breaking the law or outwitting compliance. A strong culture will reinforce the simple reward of having done the right thing. A clear conscience can be a powerful reward.

A well-designed compensation structure can also help favorably tip the balance by effectively extending the time horizon of senior management and material risk-takers, and by forcing them to more fully internalize the consequences of their actions. There are two important dimensions of the structure of compensation—first, how much compensation is paid out immediately versus deferred into the future, and second, the form of the compensation that is deferred—cash, equity, equity options or debt. For deferred compensation, the rules for how it vests and under what conditions it can be forfeited are important. Getting the balance right is critical. For my part, I believe that in order to improve financial stability and rebuild the public trust, more compensation in finance needs to be deferred and for longer periods. Also, I think there needs to be a shift in the mix of deferred compensation away from equity and towards debt.

The optimal structure of deferred compensation likely differs with respect to the goals of providing incentives to support prudent risk-taking versus encouraging the right culture. For example, consider trades that might appear to be highly profitable on a mark-to-market basis, but take some time to be closed out and for the profits to be realized in fact, not just on paper. In this case, as long as deferred compensation is set at a horizon longer than the life of the trade, this can ensure the firm's and the trader's incentives are aligned and the "trader's option" is effectively mitigated. This component of deferred compensation could take the form of either cash or equity.

However, in contrast to the issue of trading risk, unethical and illegal behavior may take a much longer period of time—measured in many years—to surface and to be fully resolved. For this reason, I believe that it is also important to have a component of deferred compensation that does not begin to vest for several years. For example, the deferral period might be five years, with uniform vesting over an additional five years. Given recent experience, a decade would seem to be a reasonable timeframe to provide sufficient time and space for any illegal actions or violations of the firm's culture to materialize and fines and legal penalties realized. As I will argue below, I also believe that this longer vesting portion of the deferred compensation should be debt as opposed to equity.

I noted earlier that improving a financial firm's culture will take sustained determination and commitment from its senior leaders. Deferred compensation can play a useful role in reinforcing buy-in of senior leadership to this endeavor. As I discussed last November, an important element of a Title II resolution under Dodd-Frank is that there is sufficient long-term unsecured debt at the holding company level to recapitalize a failing bank. I indicated in my remarks that it would be useful if a meaningful component of this debt was contributed by the senior management and the firm's material risk-takers. That is, if a bank ran into solvency problems, this component of deferred compensation would be used to recapitalize the restructured bank. The goal is to incent senior management and the material risk-takers to focus on maximizing the long-term "enterprise" value of the firm, not just the short-term share price. In this framework, I would expect the relative size of the debt component of deferred compensation to increase as one moved up the management ranks to the senior managers of the firm. That is, the individuals who have the greatest impact on a firm's strategic direction should have the strongest incentives to maximize the firm's long-term enterprise value.

If we have this deferred compensation structure in place for financial firms, then we can leverage it to strengthen the incentives for senior leaders to design and implement the necessary changes to improve their firm's culture. That is, this deferred debt compensation can be used as a "performance bond." Performance bonds are used in many situations such as security deposits on rental properties. Today, when a financial firm is assessed a large fine it is paid by the shareholders of the firm. Although senior management may own equity in the firm, their combined ownership share is likely small, and so management bears only a small fraction of the fine. Now, having shareholders pay may create market discipline in that they have an incentive to better monitor the firm's actions. However, financial firms are not transparent enterprises, and it would be difficult even for a diligent shareholder to be able to know when these bad behaviors are taking place, much less to be able to take actions to prevent them. This limits the potential effectiveness of market discipline exerted by shareholders.

How can we improve on this situation? Assume instead that a sizeable portion of the fine is now paid for out of the firm's deferred debt compensation, with only the remaining balance paid for by shareholders. In other words, in the case of a large fine, the senior management and the material risk-takers would forfeit their performance bond. This would increase the financial incentive of those individuals who are best placed to identify bad activities at an early stage, or prevent them from occurring in the first place. In addition, if paying the fine were to deplete the pool of deferred debt below a minimum required level, the solution could be to reduce the ratio of current to deferred pay until the minimum deferred compensation debt requirement is again satisfied—that is, until a new performance bond is posted.

Not only would this deferred debt compensation discipline individual behavior and decision-making, but it would provide strong incentives for individuals to flag issues when problems develop. Each individual's ability to realize their deferred debt compensation would depend not only on their own behavior, but also on the behavior of their colleagues. This would create a strong incentive for individuals to monitor the actions of their colleagues, and to call attention to any issues. This could be expected to help to keep small problems from growing into larger ones. Importantly, individuals would not be able to "opt out" of the firm as a way of escaping the problem. If a person knew that something is amiss and decided to leave the firm, their deferred debt compensation would still be at risk. This would reinforce the incentive for the individual to stay at the firm and to try to get the problem fixed.

This might work for senior managers, but what about those material risk-takers who are early in their careers at a firm and do not have much wealth tied up through deferred compensation to serve as an effective performance bond? How do we provide strong incentives for these traders not to put the firm at risk by their potential illegal behavior? In these cases, we can create the performance bond in a slightly different manner. Individuals who enter finance have generally invested heavily to develop the specialized skills required in the field. These skills typically have a higher return in finance than they do in any other occupation. That is, workers in finance earn a premium relative to their next best alternative job outside of the industry. Over the course of a career, this premium can be expected to add up to a significant sum of money. This cumulative premium can act like a performance bond. For this to be the case, however, an individual who is convicted of illegal activities, or who violates a firm's code of conduct would need to face the risk of being permanently denied employment in the financial industry. Rather than paying for the performance bond upfront, the bond is posted in terms of the privilege to continue to work in the industry.

There are several steps that can be taken to implement this concept. The first step is to make it more difficult for employees in finance who cross ethical boundaries to be able to move from one firm to another in order to escape the consequences. Currently, lenders who are considering making a loan to a borrower can look up the borrower's credit score which reflects the borrower's performance on past loans. In a similar manner, it would be helpful if financial firms, prior to making a hiring decision, could look up a candidate's "ethics and compliance score" that reflects the individual's past performance at other financial firms.

Along these lines, one approach would be to create a central registry that tracks the hiring and firing of traders and other financial professionals across the industry. There would be many details to sort out regarding how to do this in a manner that was both transparent and consistent with due process. The database could be maintained by the official sector — specifically, by financial institution supervisors — based on information provided by supervised financial institutions. A similar regime already exists in the broker-dealer context, in which supervised institutions are required to file U4 and U5 forms when they hire and part ways with licensed professionals. Banking supervisors could consider whether it was appropriate to import these concepts to the banking industry. To help support the completeness and accuracy of the filings, the filing firms could be subject to a safe harbor, akin to the civil immunity for filing a Suspicious Activity Report, so that employers do not fear liability for good faith reporting. Under this approach, new regulations could also require that all financial institutions search the database prior to hiring any trader or financial professional; so that any prior reported events could be taken into account in the course of a hiring decision. As I mentioned, there would, of course, need to be adequate safeguards for employees to challenge an entry, consistent with due process.

Furthermore, as a complementary step to the registry, it would be helpful if individuals in finance who are convicted of an illegal activity were prohibited from future employment in the financial services industry. Currently, Section 19 of the Federal Deposit Insurance Act prohibits anyone convicted of a crime of dishonesty, breach of trust, or money laundering from working at an insured depository institution or bank holding company. One possibility could be to amend Section 19 to cover the entire financial services industry. The precise formulation of an amendment would need to be worked out, but the application should be sufficiently broad so that it also covers asset managers, hedge funds and private equity funds. Like the registry, a broad and permanent industry prohibition changes the time horizon for the perceived costs of misconduct—from a one-time fine, or perhaps a few years in prison, to a lifetime prohibition from earning a living in finance, regardless of the type of employer involved. I would welcome the industry's participation in developing this concept.

Conclusion

To ensure the behavior that is required for a safe, sound and trusted financial system, we must also be effective in our role as regulators and supervisors. As part of this, we as supervisors must continually work to improve our own cultures to ensure that we can successively carry out our responsibilities. But it also requires good culture at the institutions that we supervise. Supervisors simply do not have sufficient "boots on the ground" to ferret out all forms of bad behavior within a giant, global, financial institution. Moreover, regardless what supervisors want to do, a good culture cannot simply be mandated by regulation or imposed by supervision.

In conclusion, if those of you here today as stewards of these large financial institutions do not do your part in pushing forcefully for change across the industry, then bad behavior will undoubtedly persist. If that were to occur, the inevitable conclusion will be reached that your firms are too big and complex to manage effectively. In that case, financial stability concerns would dictate that your firms need to be dramatically downsized and simplified so they can be managed effectively. It is up to you to address this cultural and ethical challenge. The consequences of inaction seem obvious to me—they are both fully appropriate and unattractive—compared to the alternative of improving the culture at the large financial firms and the behavior that stems from it. So let's get on with it.

Thank you for your attention.

Connecting to Enforcement and Disciplinary Measures

This chapter has emphasized the value of recognizing compliance as part of more than just the disciplinary system of a company. It is not the case, however, that such emphasis is meant to suggest non-presence in the disciplinary space. Indeed, an integrated compliance approach also requires giving the right level of focus to those activities closer to the right hand side of the spectrum as depicted in above. This includes those measures that a company must take when its efforts at providing incentives, motivation and guidance to employees fail to prevent an employee transgression.

It is beyond the scope of this chapter to cover the various labor law, contractual and other legal considerations that are involved in designing and applying disciplinary measures against non-compliant employees. From a compliance management standpoint, however, the following principles might be of value in developing a compliance strategy in regard of disciplinary measures:

Compliance Involvement. It is essential for the credibility and effectiveness of the compliance function to have a role in enforcing the company's rules. In many ways, a compliance officer is a facilitator: he or she helps and guides employees, and provides support to the business so that they can meet their compliance obligations. However, it is not without good reason that the persons entrusted with compliance responsibilities also bear the title of "officer." The "officer" part of the compliance professional requires him or her to claim a stake in enforcement and in what follows any violation of company's rules by an employee.

Partnering. While the compliance officer should be involved in the disciplinary side of the compliance spectrum, he or she should obviously not occupy that space alone. The involvement of HR and the legal department are critical not just for the evident reasons of organizational competences, legal advice, legal privilege, and the like, but also as a further reflection of the kind of partnering an effective compliance function needs to pursue.

Independence. Partnering on disciplinary matters, however, does not mean necessarily giving up the independent nature of judgment in the area of compliance. As part of appropriate governance checks-and-balances, the compliance officer should retain the ability to offer his or her recommendation on the appropriate disciplinary action to be taken given the facts at hand. In cases of significant differences of opinion or where something touches on a material interest or a fundamental value of the company, the compliance officer should have the ability to consult with the Board of Directors.

Objectivity. As with the involvement of any other company representative, the compliance officer's involvement in disciplinary proceedings or disciplinary decisions also needs to meet the tests of objectivity and absence of conflicts of interest.

For example, if Compliance Officer A conducted the investigation that leads to the decision to recommend disciplining an employee, it would be advisable (and in most cases necessary) for objectivity for Compliance Officer B rather than Compliance

Officer A to be involved in the specific disciplinary decision-making. In some cases, the need for objectivity may render the involvement of the entire compliance department inappropriate (such as, perhaps, where an employee is challenging whether the guidance he received from the compliance department was adequate). The point is that while in many instances compliance officer involvement can add to objectivity in the disciplinary process, there may be cases where such involvement could compromise it.

Fairness and Consistency. Subject to the test of objectivity discussed above, the involvement of a compliance officer in the disciplinary process is generally desirable given his or her role as a defender of the company's values and ethics. Disciplinary measures must meet the company's value of fairness. Fairness in this context means not only procedural and substantive fairness but also consistency of application. The compliance officer must ensure that disciplinary measures are consistently applied regardless of the level of seniority of the manager or other employee involved (and regardless of how "profitable" such person may be to the company). Subject to differences in legal requirements, the measures should also be applied consistently across the various divisions and locations of the company. Cumulative and individual information about disciplinary procedures and outcomes can be valuable information to help determine how well the compliance program is doing. The compliance officer may wish to report on a regular basis to the Board of Directors the most relevant of this data, including trends.

Gradation. Part of fairness is ensuring that any disciplinary action meets the test of reasonableness and proportionality. To this end, the compliance officer will wish to ensure that there is an appropriate range of disciplinary responses and sufficient predetermined guidance as to when each response is suitable. There should be healthy deliberation among the relevant divisions of the company to define such range, ideally with the involvement and ultimate approval from the Board of Directors. In many companies, the disciplinary range may include a requirement that the employee attend training to improve his knowledge in the area where his violation took place; a verbal admonition (with or without the employee's manager being informed); a written admonition which does not go into the employee's permanent HR records; a written admonition that does go into the employee's HR records; a formal warning with clear indication of what will happen if there is another compliance violation or lapse by the employee, and so on until coming to more drastic measures such as a demotion, suspension from employment, permanent dismissal, bringing legal action against the employee, etc. Part of the dialog the compliance officer needs to have with management, HR, and the law department is which department takes the lead in a specific category of cases, which department plays a review or supportive role, how a decision is taken, who can review a decision before it is communicated to the employee and implemented, etc. Toward this end, a best practice is having a formal table of competences or responsibilities in disciplinary matters where the role of each relevant department or officer of the company is spelled out.

Additionally, the Department of Justice Criminal Division created a Resource Guide to understand the Foreign Corrupt Practices Act (FCPA). This Resource Guide, in Chapter 6, FCPA Penalties, Sanctions, and Remedies, provides guidance on incentives and discipline. However, this guidance provides helpful best practices applicable to any compliance program.

U.S. Department of Justice Criminal Division & SEC Enforcement Division, Resource Guide to the U.S. Foreign Corrupt Practices Act

http://www.justice.gov/sites/default/files/criminal-
fraud/legacy/2015/01/16/guide.pdf

What Are the Potential Consequences for Violations of the FCPA?

The FCPA provides for different criminal and civil penalties for companies and individuals.

Criminal Penalties

For each violation of the anti-bribery provisions, the FCPA provides that corporations and other business entities are subject to a fine of up to $2 million. Individuals, including officers, directors, stockholders, and agents of companies, are subject to a fine of up to $250,000 and imprisonment for up to five years. For each violation of the accounting provisions, the FCPA provides that corporations and other business entities are subject to a fine of up to $25 million. Individuals are subject to a fine of up to $5 million and imprisonment for up to 20 years.

Under the Alternative Fines Act, 18 U.S.C. § 3571(d), courts may impose significantly higher fines than those provided by the FCPA—up to twice the benefit that the defendant obtained by making the corrupt payment, as long as the facts supporting the increased fines are included in the indictment and either proved to the jury beyond a reasonable doubt or admitted in a guilty plea proceeding. Fines imposed on individuals may not be paid by their employer or principal.

U.S. Sentencing Guidelines

When calculating penalties for violations of the FCPA, DOJ focuses its analysis on the U.S. Sentencing Guidelines (Guidelines) in all of its resolutions, including guilty pleas, DPAs, and NPAs. The Guidelines provide a very detailed and predictable structure for calculating penalties for all federal crimes, including violations of the FCPA. To determine the appropriate penalty, the "offense level" is first calculated by examining both the severity of the crime and facts specific to the crime, with appropriate reductions for cooperation and acceptance of responsibility, and, for business entities, additional factors such as voluntary disclosure, cooperation, preexisting compliance programs, and remediation.

The Guidelines provide for different penalties for the different provisions of the FCPA. The initial offense level for violations of the anti-bribery provisions is determined under § 2C1.1, while violations of the accounting provisions are assessed under § 2B1.1. For individuals, the initial offense level is modified by factors set forth in Chapters 3, 4, and 5 of the Guidelines to identify a final offense level. This final offense level, combined with other factors, is used to determine whether the Guidelines would recommend that incarceration is appropriate, the length of any term of incarceration, and the appropriate amount of any fine. For corporations, the offense level is modified by factors particular to organizations as described in Chapter 8 to determine the applicable organizational penalty.

For example, violations of the anti-bribery provisions are calculated pursuant to § 2C1.1. The offense level is determined by first identifying the base offense level; adding additional levels based on specific offense characteristics, including whether the offense involved more than one bribe, the value of the bribe or the benefit that was conferred, and the level of the public official; adjusting the offense level based on the defendant's role in the offense; and using the total offense level as well as the defendant's criminal history category to determine the advisory guideline range. For violations of the accounting provisions assessed under § 2B1.1, the procedure is generally the same, except that the specific offense characteristics differ. For instance, for violations of the FCPA's accounting provisions, the offense level may be increased if a substantial part of the scheme occurred outside the United States or if the defendant was an officer or director of a publicly traded company at the time of the offense.

For companies, the offense level is calculated pursuant to §§ 2C1.1 or 2B1.1 in the same way as for an individual — by starting with the base offense level and increasing it as warranted by any applicable specific offense characteristics. The organizational guidelines found in Chapter 8, however, provide the structure for determining the final advisory guideline fine range for organizations. The base fine consists of the greater of the amount corresponding to the total offense level, calculated pursuant to the Guidelines, or the pecuniary gain or loss from the offense. This base fine is then multiplied by a culpability score that can either reduce the fine to as little as five percent of the base fine or increase the recommended fine to up to four times the amount of the base fine. As described in § 8C2.5, this culpability score is calculated by taking into account numerous factors such as the size of the organization committing the criminal acts; the involvement in or tolerance of criminal activity by high-level personnel within the organization; and prior misconduct or obstructive behavior. The culpability score is reduced if the organization had an effective preexisting compliance program to prevent violations and if the organization voluntarily disclosed the offense, cooperated in the investigation, and accepted responsibility for the criminal conduct.

Civil Penalties

Although only DOJ has the authority to pursue criminal actions, both DOJ and SEC have civil enforcement authority under the FCPA. DOJ may pursue civil actions for anti-bribery violations by domestic concerns (and their officers, directors, employees, agents, or stockholders) and foreign nationals and companies for violations while in the United States, while SEC may pursue civil actions against issuers and their officers, directors, employees, agents, or stockholders for violations of the anti-bribery and the accounting provisions.

For violations of the anti-bribery provisions, corporations and other business entities are subject to a civil penalty of up to $16,000 per violation. Individuals, including officers, directors, stockholders, and agents of companies, are similarly subject to a civil penalty of up to $16,000 per violation, which may not be paid by their employer or principal.

For violations of the accounting provisions, SEC may obtain a civil penalty not to exceed the greater of (a) the gross amount of the pecuniary gain to the defendant as a result of the violations or (b) a specified dollar limitation. The specified dollar limitations are based on the egregiousness of the violation, ranging from $7,500 to $150,000 for an individual and $75,000 to $725,000 for a company. SEC may obtain civil penalties both in actions filed in federal court and in administrative proceedings.

Collateral Consequences

In addition to the criminal and civil penalties described above, individuals and companies who violate the FCPA may face significant collateral consequences, including suspension or debarment from contracting with the federal government, cross-debarment by multilateral development banks, and the suspension or revocation of certain export privileges.

Debarment

Under federal guidelines governing procurement, an individual or company that violates the FCPA or other criminal statutes may be barred from doing business with the federal government. The Federal Acquisition Regulations (FAR) provide for the potential suspension or debarment of companies that contract with the government upon conviction of or civil judgment for bribery, falsification or destruction of records, the making of false statements, or "[c]ommission of any other offense indicating a lack of business integrity or business honesty that seriously and directly affects the present responsibility of a Government contractor or subcontractor." These measures are not intended to be punitive and may be imposed only if "in the public's interest for the Government's protection."

Under the FAR, a decision to debar or suspend is discretionary. The decision is not made by DOJ prosecutors or SEC staff, but instead by independent debarment authorities within each agency, such as the Department of Defense or the General Services Administration, which analyze a number of factors to determine whether a company should be suspended, debarred, or otherwise determined to be ineligible for government contracting. Such factors include whether the contractor has effective internal control systems in place, self-reported the misconduct in a timely manner, and has taken remedial measures. If a cause for debarment exists, the contractor has the burden of demonstrating to the satisfaction of the debarring official that it is presently responsible and that debarment is not necessary. Each federal department and agency determines the eligibility of contractors with whom it deals. However, if one department or agency debars or suspends a contractor, the debarment or suspension applies to the entire executive branch of the federal government, unless a department or agency shows compelling reasons not to debar or suspend the contractor.

Although guilty pleas, DPAs, and NPAs do not result in automatic debarment from U.S. government contracting, committing a federal crime and the factual admissions underlying a resolution are factors that the independent debarment authorities may consider. Moreover, indictment alone can lead to suspension of the right to do business with the government. The U.S. Attorney's Manual also provides that when a company engages in fraud against the government, a prosecutor may not negotiate away an agency's right to debar or delist the company as part of the plea bargaining process. In making debarment determinations, contracting agencies, including at the state and local level, may consult with DOJ in advance of awarding a contract. Depending on the circumstances, DOJ may provide information to contracting authorities in the context of the corporate settlement about the facts and circumstances underlying the criminal conduct and remediation measures undertaken by the company, if any. This information sharing is not advocacy, and the ultimate debarment decisions are squarely within the purview of the independent debarment authorities. In some situations, the contracting agency may impose its own oversight requirements in order for a company that has admitted to violations of federal law to be awarded federal contracts, such as the Corporate Integrity Agreements often required by the Department of Health and Human Services.

Cross-Debarment by Multilateral Development Banks

Multilateral Development Banks (MDBs), like the World Bank, also have the ability to debar companies and individuals for corrupt practices. Each MDB has its own process for evaluating alleged corruption in connection with MDB-funded projects. When appropriate, DOJ and SEC work with MDBs to share evidence and refer cases. On April 9, 2010, the African Development Bank Group, the Asian Development Bank, the European Bank for Reconstruction and Development, the Inter-American Development Bank Group, and the World Bank Group entered into an agreement under which entities debarred by one MDB will be sanctioned for the same misconduct by other signatory MDBs. This cross-debarment agreement means that if a company is debarred by one MDB, it is debarred by all.

Loss of Export Privileges

Companies and individuals who violate the FCPA may face consequences under other regulatory regimes, such as the Arms Export Control Act (AECA), 22 U.S.C. § 2751, *et seq.*, and its implementing regulations, the International Traffic in Arms Regulations (ITAR), 22 C.F.R. § 120, *et seq.* AECA and ITAR together provide for the suspension, revocation, amendment, or denial of an arms export license if an applicant has been indicted or convicted for violating the FCPA. They also set forth certain factors for the Department of State's Directorate of Defense Trade Controls (DDTC) to consider when determining whether to grant, deny, or return without action license applications for certain types of defense materials. One of those factors is whether there is reasonable cause to believe that an applicant for a license has violated (or conspired to violate) the FCPA; if so, the Department of State "may disapprove the application." In addition, it is the policy of the Department of State not to consider applications for licenses involving any persons who have been convicted of violating the AECA or convicted of conspiracy to violate the AECA. In an action related to the criminal resolution of a U.K. military products manufacturer, the DDTC imposed a "policy of denial" for export licenses on three of the company's subsidiaries that were involved in violations of AECA and ITAR.

When Is a Compliance Monitor or Independent Consultant Appropriate?

One of the primary goals of both criminal prosecutions and civil enforcement actions against companies that violate the FCPA is ensuring that such conduct does not occur again. As a consequence, enhanced compliance and reporting requirements may be part of criminal and civil resolutions of FCPA matters. The amount of enhanced compliance and kind of reporting required varies according to the facts and circumstances of individual cases.

In criminal cases, a company's sentence, or a DPA or NPA with a company, may require the appointment of an independent corporate monitor. Whether a monitor is appropriate depends on the specific facts and circumstances of the case. In 2008, DOJ issued internal guidance regarding the selection and use of corporate monitors in DPAs and NPAs with companies. Additional guidance has since been issued. A monitor is an independent third party who assesses and monitors a company's adherence to the compliance requirements of an agreement that was designed to reduce the risk of recurrence of the company's misconduct. Appointment of a monitor is not appropriate in all circumstances, but it may be appropriate, for example, where a company does not already have an effective internal compliance program or needs to establish necessary internal controls. In addition, companies are sometimes allowed to engage in self-monitoring, typically in cases when the company has made a voluntary disclosure, has been fully cooperative, and has demonstrated a genuine commitment to reform.

Factors DOJ and SEC Consider When Determining Whether a Compliance Monitor Is Appropriate Include:

- Seriousness of the offense
- Duration of the misconduct
- Pervasiveness of the misconduct, including whether the conduct cuts across geographic and/or product lines
- Nature and size of the company
- Quality of the company's compliance program at the time of the misconduct
- Subsequent remediation efforts

In civil cases, a company may similarly be required to retain an independent compliance consultant or monitor to provide an independent, third-party review of the company's internal controls. The consultant recommends improvements, to the extent necessary, which the company must adopt. When both DOJ and SEC require a company to retain a monitor, the two agencies have been able to coordinate their requirements so that the company can retain one monitor to fulfill both sets of requirements.

The most successful monitoring relationships are those in which the company embraces the monitor or consultant. If the company takes the recommendations and suggestions seriously and uses the monitoring period as a time to find and fix any outstanding compliance issues, the company can emerge from the monitorship with a stronger, long-lasting compliance program.

———

If managed appropriately, an integrated approach to compliance can contribute significantly to the effectiveness of a compliance program and lead to much better protection of the company. Through this approach, a compliance officer has a more complete view of the various levers within the compliance spectrum that can be operated to deal with risks and provide positive impact on organizational and individual conduct. As such, the compliance officer can be in a better position to prioritize and determine where and how compliance program leadership or involvement can bring the most value.

This chapter suggests that in making such prioritization it is as important for the compliance officer to give as much attention to the middle and left hand side of the compliance spectrum—the part encompassing education, motivation, provision of incentives and rewards to employees—as to the right hand side which deals more with controls and enforcement. This includes giving due attention to the company's compensation and performance management systems, both as they regard all employees as well as the employees in control functions, including compliance.

Assignment

- **Hypothetical:** You are the Chief Compliance Officer at your [Team's] Corporation. Perform a compliance risk assessment on incentives and determine which incentives require changes or updating.
- **Hypothetical:** You are the Chief Compliance Officer at your [Team's] Corporation. Create a systematic set of discipline for violations of the Code of Conduct.

Chapter 11

Continually Reevaluating and Updating the Compliance Program

Introduction

Effectiveness is the keyword word that should be the focus for a corporation when initially setting up a compliance program and remains the keyword after implementation. Retention of the effectiveness of a company's compliance program must be assured and an evaluation process is essential to the defense of such a program in the face of allegations of illegal or unethical behavior. The effectiveness of a compliance program has taken on increased importance in light of the November 1, 2010, amended Sentencing Guidelines, which provide increased focus on a company's behavior as it relates to violations of ethical obligations or illegal actions.

Chapter 8 (Section 8B2.1) of the U.S. Sentencing Guidelines outlines seven steps for an "effective" compliance program including the seventh step, which is taking "reasonable steps to respond to and prevent further similar offenses upon detection of a violation."

The U.S. Sentencing Commission has voted to amend this section to insure companies take adequate steps to address wrongful behavior and to prevent further inappropriate conduct upon earnest detection of the initial criminality. The November 1, 2010 amendment commentary provides that upon learning of wrongful conduct, the company should:

- Take reasonable steps, as warranted under the circumstances, to remedy the harm resulting from the criminal conduct. These steps may include, where appropriate, "providing restitution to identifiable victims, as well as other forms of remediation." Other reasonable steps to respond appropriately to the criminal conduct may include self-reporting and cooperating with authorities.

- Act appropriately to prevent further similar conduct, including assessing the compliance and ethics program and making modifications necessary to ensure the program is effective. The steps taken should be consistent with subsections (b)(5) and (c) [which require periodic evaluations of the program, and periodic risk assessment] and may include the use of an outside professional advisor to ensure adequate assessment and implementation of any modifications.

A compliance program is not a one-time expenditure of time, effort, or funding. In fact, it is critically important that the board and/or executive management understands that the corporation has a continued responsibility to maintain the viability of its compliance program. The compliance program should remain very much alive for as long as the corporation is in existence. Some continued efforts are required to assure the ongoing effectiveness of the compliance program.

To remain effective, a corporation must, in a timely manner, incorporate sections into its written compliance program materials to address new laws or regulations that could adversely impact risk to the corporation. It is important to note that laws or regulations differ between countries and may have varying jurisdictional breadth. This requires that corporations adapt the compliance program including the code of conduct, policies, procedures, and internal controls. The corporation needs to then republish the updated compliance materials to all employees. As an example, many companies may be impacted by the UK Bribery Act, the reach of which affects any company having a UK presence, thus reaching instances not only where U.S. companies have established formal offices in the UK but also extending to subsidiaries and general operations as well.[1] The ability of a U.S. company to successfully defend a charge under this corporate offense will depend on whether it can demonstrate that it had, in effect at the time of the charge, policies, systems, controls, and training programs (i.e., adequate procedures) that should have prevented the bribe is critical (indeed, it is the only defense currently available).

If the company fails to stay abreast of legal developments, its compliance program fails in its effectiveness. The risk is greater today than before as there is clearly a movement towards greater scrutiny of compliance procedures in the determination of whether companies have done enough to comply with their obligations to prevent corporate misconduct.

Given the heightened review of corporate compliance procedures, an area that should be reviewed as part of a compliance program's effectiveness is third party compliance. While there is not a standard approach to this point in the compliance field at this time, due consideration is warranted nonetheless because relationships with third parties who themselves have failed to institute within their own organizations, appropriate compliance procedures, can result in the ineffectiveness of the compliance program in place at the outsourcing company, which may otherwise be effective. Thus, the fact that a company has outsourced some of its business responsibilities to a third party does not necessarily shield that company from liability in the event that the outsourcing entity commits a violation of law in the course of carrying out those outsourced responsibilities.

There are a host of examples where third-party actions have created liability for the outsourcing entity. A number of significant defense industry procurement prosecutions have arisen from the actions of third-party business representatives and independent sales agents have been the subject of sales practices abuse cases in the life insurance industry. Other examples include manufacturing companies who have suf-

---

1. United Kingdom Bribery Act, Ch. 23 § 7(5)(a) (2010), *available at* http://www.legislation.gov.uk/ukpga/2010/23/pdfs/ukpga_20100023_en.pdf.

fered severe reputational harm from the labor practices of their suppliers. And recently, corrupt practices by agents and distributors have been the basis for numerous FCPA prosecutions.

As noted above, this is as yet an evolving area in compliance and there is not one "gold" standard that can be used as a "best practice model." As in the development of an overall compliance program, the starting point should be a determination of the specific risk areas most likely to lead to company liability. Who are your suppliers and subcontractors? Are they U.S. companies or foreign-led? Do they have the "capacity" to commit certain types of wrongdoing, such as antitrust where they have access to pricing and distribution information? If foreign, have they received training on the compliance and regulatory business environment in the U.S.?

Companies are handling this challenge in differing ways. Some companies are requiring third parties to submit for review their Code of Ethics or other such evidentiary compliance document so that the outsourcing entity can determine if it meets industry standards while others are requiring an executed document by an authorized principal of the third party attesting that the third party will uphold the standards of the outsourcing company's Code of Ethics. Still others are simply requiring the third party to affirm that they have an effective Compliance Program, or at the minimum, have in place standard consistent protocols. Thus, this is an area to continue to monitor as additional guidelines are developed and more consistency is obtained. For the moment, it appears to be an area of potential risk in the heightened enforcement environment for many companies. The Society of Corporate Compliance and Ethics (SCCE) notes that,

> [d]espite the proliferation of third party relationships in business, relatively few companies set ethics and compliance expectations on the companies that they rely on to act on their behalf. The SCCE survey found that only about half of companies (47%) disseminate their internal, employee code of conduct to third parties. Just 26% require that third parties certify to their codes of conduct, and only 17% of organization have a code of conduct that is applicable to third parties.[2]

Given the objective of the government in setting forth the U.S. Sentencing Guidelines, i.e., to detect and prevent violations of law by employees and other agents and to promote ethical business cultures, a corporation must necessarily determine if the employees have actually understood the compliance programs' components and, are indeed, adhering to these practices as they conduct business on behalf of the company. It would obviously not benefit a corporation to rollout a compliance program that facially addresses the essential seven elements of an "effective" compliance program, if after the rollout, the employees lock the materials in a cabinet in their offices and have failed to incorporate the best practices, as set forth in the compliance program,

---

2. *See* Rebecca Walker, *A Benchmarking Survey on Third-Party Codes of Conduct*, Compliance and Ethics Professional (SCCE Dec., 2009).

into their daily business activities. This is exactly the purpose of the amendments; i.e., to prevent sham or paper compliance without engaged board oversight and action. The Enron compliance program is an example of a program that attempted to meet some of the facial requirements of the U.S. Sentencing Guidelines, such as a code of conduct/ethics, but failed to create an *effective* compliance program and, in fact, created a "roadmap for prosecutors."

The recent November 1, 2010, amendment language imposes a mandatory obligation on high level personnel to act effectively in preventing further criminal conduct in light of information received by those with operational responsibility for the compliance program (or other employees) and directly correlates those obligations to a company's ability to forestall prosecution. Thus, DOJ employees receive a set of guidelines for federal investigation and prosecution purposes. The existence of an effective compliance program has been one of the factors set forth in those guidelines that the DOJ employees may consider in determining whether to bring charges against a company and, in the past, companies have successfully lowered their Culpability Score and lessened the severity of the Conditions of Probation by presenting evidence of the effectiveness or comprehensiveness of the company's compliance program. The language of the amendments restricts the discretion of DOJ employees to grant such leniency where the organization has unreasonably delayed reporting the offense to appropriate governmental authorities or where high-level personnel have participated in, condoned or willfully ignored the offense.

The Securities and Exchange Commission non-prosecution agreement with Ralph Lauren provides an excellent example of the importance of continually renewing the compliance program. Ralph Lauren undertook to provide an enhanced compliance program that lead to the uncovering of FCPA violations and self-reporting to the Department of Justice.

Press Release, *SEC Announces Non-Prosecution Agreement with Ralph Lauren Corporation Involving FCPA Misconduct*

(Apr. 22, 2013) http://www.sec.gov/News/PressRelease/
Detail/PressRelease/1365171514780

The Securities and Exchange Commission announced a non-prosecution agreement (NPA) with Ralph Lauren Corporation in which the company will disgorge more than $700,000 in illicit profits and interest obtained in connection with bribes paid by a subsidiary to government officials in Argentina from 2005 to 2009. The misconduct was uncovered in an internal review undertaken by the company and promptly reported to the SEC.

The SEC has determined not to charge Ralph Lauren Corporation with violations of the Foreign Corrupt Practices Act (FCPA) due to the company's prompt reporting of the violations on its own initiative, the completeness of the information it provided, and its extensive, thorough, and real-time cooperation with the SEC's investigation.

Ralph Lauren Corporation's cooperation saved the agency substantial time and resources ordinarily consumed in investigations of comparable conduct.

The NPA is the first that the SEC has entered involving FCPA misconduct. NPAs are part of the SEC Enforcement Division's Cooperation Initiative, which rewards cooperation in SEC investigations. In parallel criminal proceedings, the Justice Department entered into an NPA with Ralph Lauren Corporation in which the company will pay an $882,000 penalty.

"When they found a problem, Ralph Lauren Corporation did the right thing by immediately reporting it to the SEC and providing exceptional assistance in our investigation," said George S. Canellos, Acting Director of the SEC's Division of Enforcement. "The NPA in this matter makes clear that we will confer substantial and tangible benefits on companies that respond appropriately to violations and cooperate fully with the SEC."

Kara Brockmeyer, the SEC's FCPA Unit Chief, added, "This NPA shows the benefit of implementing an effective compliance program. Ralph Lauren Corporation discovered this problem after it put in place an enhanced compliance program and began training its employees. That level of self-policing along with its self-reporting and cooperation led to this resolution."

According to the NPA, Ralph Lauren Corporation's cooperation included:

- Reporting preliminary findings of its internal investigation to the staff within two weeks of discovering the illegal payments and gifts.
- Voluntarily and expeditiously producing documents.
- Providing English language translations of documents to the staff.
- Summarizing witness interviews that the company's investigators conducted overseas.
- Making overseas witnesses available for staff interviews and bringing witnesses to the U.S.

According to the NPA, the bribes occurred during a period when Ralph Lauren Corporation lacked meaningful anti-corruption compliance and control mechanisms over its Argentine subsidiary. The misconduct came to light as a result of the company adopting measures to improve its worldwide internal controls and compliance efforts, including implementation of an FCPA compliance-training program in Argentina.

As outlined in the NPA, Ralph Lauren Corporation's Argentine subsidiary paid bribes to government and customs officials to improperly secure the importation of Ralph Lauren Corporation's products in Argentina. The purpose of the bribes, paid through its customs broker, was to obtain entry of Ralph Lauren Corporation's products into the country without necessary paperwork, avoid inspection of prohibited products, and avoid inspection by customs officials. The bribe payments and gifts to Argentine officials totaled $593,000 during a four-year period.

Under the NPA, Ralph Lauren Corporation agreed to pay $593,000 in disgorgement and $141,845.79 in prejudgment interest.

The SEC took into account the significant remedial measures undertaken by Ralph Lauren Corporation, including a comprehensive new compliance program throughout its operations. Among Ralph Lauren Corporation's remedial measures have been new compliance training, termination of employment and business arrangements with all individuals involved in the wrongdoing, and strengthening its internal controls and its procedures for third party due diligence. Ralph Lauren Corporation also conducted a risk assessment of its major operations worldwide to identify any other compliance problems. Ralph Lauren Corporation has ceased operations in Argentina.

It is far worse for a corporation to roll out a compliance program and then fail to take steps to ensure that it is effective in preventing unethical or improper conduct than to not have a program in place at all. Especially, in today's environment with the recent financial instabilities affecting the global economy, and at least partially attributable to the lack of ethical behavior, the government is not likely to accept lip service and window dressing in place of concrete corporate action on compliance. The amendments provide little doubt that failure to modify a compliance program to incorporate lessons learned from past violations will lead to vigorous prosecution of the lax company. Thus, the compliance office should engage in a check and balance process that adequately demonstrates effectiveness and should take documented steps to place itself in a position where it could evidence the continued effectiveness of its compliance program.

One critical measure of effectiveness is the actions taken by a company to assure compliance with program elements. Thus, a company must be in a position to demonstrate that it has adequate procedures to detect a violation and that appropriate enforcement is taken after detection. Internal investigation procedures should be consistent, in accord with sound legal principles, results oriented, and preferably the subject of a written document that can be produced to authorities as evidence to support the company's integrity in assuring effectiveness. Again, while there is not one gold standard to be followed, at a minimum, the document should address: 1) the ease and transparency of the reporting process for employees; 2) the "when" of employee reporting (i.e., that employees are encouraged to report any and all possible violations); 3) the actual reporting procedure in progressive steps (i.e., to the immediate supervisor first; to local management next; to local compliance committee; to the corporate compliance committee; to the audit committee, etc.); 4) the "owner" of the complaint; 5) protection of the reporting employee (i.e., reporting can be anonymous); 5) protection and rights of the accused (i.e., notification/appeals process); 6) guidelines for investigation process (i.e., purposes/objectives; investigation plan; written documentation; outside legal advisement; independence and impartiality; confidentiality; responsibilities of the investigator and execution of investigation, including closure protocols).

There are several approaches being assumed by companies, depending on size, type of business, type and amount of risk, etc. For example, some larger entities in the financial or securities area have a separate internal investigations unit and the investigations are, in the first instance, managed by lawyers with specific financial expertise. Some smaller companies not involved in finance, are allocating the responsibility to human resources personnel.

Below is a checklist of items that are relevant to the process of effectively reevaluating and updating the compliance program.

1. Best practice gaps analysis—review risk areas then and now risk assessment considers the likelihood that criminal conduct will occur, the nature and seriousness of the conduct, and the prior history of the organization. Business models and practices should be examined, the location of the work and the legal restrictions and policies of the governments where the work is performed; i.e., tailoring of the program to eradicate the risks;

2. Work Plan—beginning of the project, revisions as the project advances;

3. Development of separate departmental work plans for updating the compliance program;

4. Assessment questionnaires for beta testing, high level, mid level and all;

5. Identification of company representatives for broader assessment participation;

6. Choice of company to perform tabulation;

7. Updating of compliance department guidelines;

8. International considerations, i.e., harmonization with international company guidelines;

9. Review of policy/harmonization between human resources department, the code of conduct/ethics and the assessments;

10. Acquisition/Divestiture considerations;

11. Identification of selected employees to receive assessments;

12. Evaluation of electronic interactive options, if the compliance program is not already interactive;

13. Development of targeted training modules based upon results of assessments;

14. Incorporation of assessment results into employee orientation training;

15. Targeted newsletters based on beta testing and assessment results;

16. Review and reinvigoration of company values;

17. Evaluation of assessments to existing modules beginning with the code of conduct/ethics;

18. Harmonize and incorporate assessment results to company tracking tools such as manager surveys and/or risk/best practice tools;

19. Develop new marketing literature to target the identified assessment results;

20. Review/harmonization of the employee handbook;

21. Review of all investigations and actions taken by the company as a result of the investigations;

22. Review of the reporting obligations of those employees holding operational responsibility for the compliance program

23. Review of modifications to the compliance program; i.e., to prevent further criminal conduct based on historical violations.

Additionally, the Department of Justice Criminal Division created a Resource Guide to understand the Foreign Corrupt Practices Act (FCPA). This Resource Guide, in Chapter 5, Guiding Principles of Enforcement, provides a case study to illustrate the importance of continuously improving your compliance program through periodic testing and review. In this case, while the company was not charged, the Department of Justice and Securities and Exchange Commission declined enforcement against the company, the executive plead guilty to conspiracy to violate the FCPA internal control provisions. The "robust" FCPA compliance program, in the case study, illustrates how continually reevaluating and updating the compliance program can demonstrate that the company in the case study should not be prosecuted. This FCPA case study provides helpful guidance on best practices for continually reevaluating and updating any compliance program.

U.S. Department of Justice Criminal Division & SEC Enforcement Division, Resource Guide to the U.S. Foreign Corrupt Practices Act

http://www.justice.gov/sites/default/files/criminal-fraud/legacy/2015/01/16/guide.pdf

Compliance Program Case Study

Recent DOJ and SEC actions relating to a financial institution's real estate transactions with a government agency in China illustrate the benefits of implementing and enforcing a comprehensive risk-based compliance program. The case involved a joint venture real estate investment in the Luwan District of Shanghai, China, between a U.S.-based financial institution and a state-owned entity that functioned as the District's real estate arm. The government entity conducted the transactions through two special purpose vehicles ("SPVs"), with the second SPV purchasing a 12% stake in a real estate project. The financial institution, through a robust compliance program, frequently trained its employees, imposed a comprehensive payment-approval process designed to prevent bribery, and staffed a compliance department with a direct reporting line to the board of directors. As appropriate given the industry, market, and size and structure of the transactions, the financial institution (1) provided extensive FCPA training to the senior executive responsible for the transactions and (2) conducted extensive due diligence on the transactions, the local government entity, and the SPVs. Due diligence on the entity included reviewing Chinese government records; speaking with sources familiar with the Shanghai real estate market; checking the government entity's payment records and credit references; conducting an on-site visit and placing a pretextual telephone call to the entity's offices; searching media sources; and conducting background checks on the entity's principals. The financial institution vetted the SPVs by obtaining a letter with designated bank account information from a Chinese official associated with the government entity (the "Chinese Official"); using an international law firm to request and review 50 documents from the SPVs' Canadian attorney; interviewing the attorney; and interviewing the SPVs' management. Notwithstanding the financial institution's robust compliance program and good faith enforcement of it, the company failed to learn that the Chinese Official personally owned nearly 50% of the second SPV (and therefore a nearly 6% stake in the joint venture) and that the SPV was used as a vehicle for corrupt payments. This failure was due, in large part, to misrepresentations by the Chinese Official, the financial institution's executive in charge of the project, and the SPV's attorney that the SPV was 100% owned and controlled by the government entity. DOJ and SEC declined to take enforcement action against the financial institution, and its executive pleaded guilty to conspiracy to violate the FCPA's internal control provisions and also settled with SEC.

The Resource Guide also provides guidance on continuous improvement of a compliance program.

U.S. Department of Justice Criminal Division & SEC Enforcement Division, Resource Guide to the U.S. Foreign Corrupt Practices Act

http://www.justice.gov/sites/default/files/criminal-fraud/legacy/2015/01/16/guide.pdf

Continuous Improvement: Periodic Testing and Review

Finally, a good compliance program should constantly evolve. A company's business changes over time, as do the environments in which it operates, the nature of its customers, the laws that govern its actions, and the standards of its industry. In addition, compliance programs that do not just exist on paper but are followed in practice will inevitably uncover compliance weaknesses and require enhancements. Consequently, DOJ and SEC evaluate whether companies regularly review and improve their compliance programs and not allow them to become stale. According to one survey, 64% of general counsel whose companies are subject to the FCPA says there is room for improvement in their FCPA training and compliance programs. An organization should take the time to review and test its controls, and it should think critically about its potential weaknesses and risk areas. For example, some companies have undertaken employee surveys to measure their compliance culture and strength of internal controls, identify best practices, and detect new risk areas. Other companies periodically test their internal controls with targeted audits to make certain that controls on paper are working in practice. DOJ and SEC will give meaningful credit to thoughtful efforts to create a sustainable compliance program if a problem is later discovered. Similarly, undertaking proactive evaluations before a problem strikes can lower the applicable penalty range under the U.S. Sentencing Guidelines. Although the nature and the frequency of proactive evaluations may vary depending on the size and complexity of an organization, the idea behind such efforts is the same: continuous improvement and sustainability.

Review of Relevant Materials

Updating of the compliance program requires a holistic approach pursuant to which the compliance office takes into account the company's business structure and risks as they existed at the inception of the compliance program but, more importantly, for this second phase, at the time the reevaluation is undertaken. Therefore, the compliance office should review the initial work plan; best practice gaps analysis and compliance department guidelines to determine if the risks that had been identified during that process have been adequately addressed. The new amendments promulgated by the U.S. Sentencing Commission dictate the need for intense scrutiny in this area. Thus, if gaps have been identified, the amendments are intended to encourage companies to quickly close those gaps. Additionally, the review should consider if there has been a change in the company's risk position relevant to its internal or external organizational structure, inclusive of the ethics committee and if there has been additional acquisitions or divestitures of businesses, or if there are additional regulations or laws that would now be applicable to the company's present business based on the company's current business position and employee population. Moreover, a review of current company policies should be undertaken to determine whether those that exist are appropriately referenced in the code of conduct/ethics and the employee handbook and have been distributed to the entirety of the employee population. Review of hotline calls and any resulting investigations should be conducted to enable a broader assessment query into those departmental areas that were subject to higher call volume. As noted above, under the amendments, knowledge of violations without an accompanying rational response to address the violation and revise program components to reduce the possibility of future misconduct, is equivalent to asking for a DOJ prosecution. Equally relevant for review would be crisis team reports, which will highlight the areas where deeper probing in the assessment process is warranted. Reviews should also be conducted as to the scope of training that has been provided to employees to draft appropriate assessment questions based on the knowledge that the employee base should have obtained through these trainings and to determine if there is a need to expand or update these trainings.

Work Plan

Once these tasks have been accomplished, the compliance office should draft a general work plan for updating the compliance program. This work plan should envision a timeline for which the overall updating will occur and should also specify a timeline for development of departmental work plans with a specific focus on those departments that the earlier reviews of hotline and crisis records have flagged as possible "hotbeds" of aberrant compliance activities. Per the discussion immediately above, a critical focus of the plan should be company actions in response to violations of the program elements, including any planned modifications and/or revisions to the program that are intended to address the initial misconduct and prevent further misconduct. The work plan should also include any required updates to the compliance departmental organizational chart, accounting for change in personnel and/or the creation of job descriptions for Deputy Compliance Officers. In light of the amendments, reporting obligations, for those with operational authority should be specified, highlighting that these employees have the authority to report any type of criminal offense. Additionally, the work plan should address the identity and the name of the outsourcing company that will perform the assessment tabulations work as well as the identity of the assessment areas and the criteria that will be used for those assessments. For example, if the company is engaged in sales and marketing, an antitrust assessment must be included in the assessments to be conducted. Ideally, the compliance office should use the code of conduct/ethics as the guide post. Each subject area addressed in the code of conduct/ethics should also be assessed in the work plan. Finally, the work plan should reflect that there will be a meeting of the ethics committee to discuss and approve the elements and process for updating the compliance program.

Minutes of this meeting should be recorded, transcribed and retained in a compliance binder kept by the Chief Compliance Officer in the event documentation is needed to be produced as to the efforts undertaken by the company to retain or increase the effectiveness of its compliance program. Previously identified gap areas (i.e., record retention program, disaster recovery, contract management) should also be identified and included for assessment in the work plan. The company should also highlight its strategic decision to utilize outside professional advisors. The amendment language provides that a company "may" include use of these types of persons to ensure adequate assessments and implementation of any modifications. Thus, the board or high-level management should consider, in accordance with their duty of care to the corporation, whether this is required or not in the remediation action plan. If there have been serious violations committed, logic would dictate that the company's response be equally serious and, in such a case, outside advisors may bring an additional layer of validation to the company's efforts to increase effectiveness. Additionally, if the modifications themselves are fairly complicated, that may also lean in favor of outside assistance in the remediation effort. And, finally, if implementation of the revisions is likely to meet with internal resistance, outside assistance may be required, as an independent party may need to provide the mechanism of oversight to assure the changes are actually installed.

Beta Testing/Communication of New Program Phase

Prior to rolling out an updated phase of the compliance program, consideration needs to be given to the communication that should preview the assessment process. A communication issued jointly from the CEO, the compliance office, and the ethics committee and perhaps the human resources team should communicate clearly the objectives of the assessments. It would be best to first remind employees of the current state of affairs (i.e., the rollout of the program X number of years ago, the elements of the compliance program, i.e., the code of conduct/ethics booklet, the hotline material, training materials delivered, etc.). The communication should explain that the company has an obligation to update its compliance program and modify it, as may be necessary, to help the employees understand their roles in acting in accordance with the laws and regulations governing their industry. Employees should be made aware of the November 1, 2010 amendments to the sentencing guidelines and the relevancy of such to the company; i.e., increased training being provided in response to departmental "hotbeds," etc. The communication should also explain that X percentage of the corporation's employees will be asked to complete assessments which will be a series of questions in specific business subject areas or areas in the code of conduct/ethics.

Care should be taken to assure employees that individual responses will be received anonymously although on a departmental level, certain departments will receive subject area questions that are directly relevant to that department (i.e., sales department will receive assessments concerning antitrust questions, marketing will receive questions addressing advertising practices, etc.) in addition to the more general questions areas such as, conflict of interest or travel and expense policies.

The communication should explain to employees that an initial Beta testing will be conducted pursuant to which a few employees from each department will be requested to "preview" the assessments and provide feedback so that further refinements and adjustments for clarity and understanding could be done prior to the rollout of the online assessment survey to the larger employee population. To receive honest feedback and gain the employees willing cooperation, it is important to explain that the assessments will not be used to identify violators or terminate employees, but rather for issue spotting so that the company can determine if its compliance program elements require modification and are serving the employees needs for guidance and direction in the areas that affect their day to day business activities.

Assessments

As noted above, the assessment questions should target the key takeaways and best practices from each subject area of the code of conduct/ethics. The questions should be direct, simple and in a language that is easily understood and should be drafted to allow for a "yes" or "no" answer with a section for brief further comments by the employee where further information would be helpful in digging deeper into a particular subject area. Thus, for the general compliance assessment, the questions would seek to obtain whether employees are aware of the company's compliance program, its code of conduct/ethics, its hotline and each of its other elements; whether they received training and understood the materials; whether they know the process for filing complaints; and whether they feel comfortable asserting complaints. Questions should be included to elicit knowledge of violations of current criminal conduct as well as an understanding of reporting obligations.

Conclusion

Prior to rolling out an updated phase of the compliance program, consideration needs to be given to the communication that should preview the assessment process. A communication issued jointly from the CEO, the compliance office, and the ethics committee and perhaps the human resources team should communicate clearly the objectives of the assessments. It would be best to first remind employees of the current state of affairs (i.e., the rollout of the program X number of years ago, the elements of the compliance program, i.e., the code of conduct/ethics booklet, the hotline material, training materials delivered, etc.). The communication should explain that the company has an obligation to update its compliance program and modify it, as may be necessary, to help the employees understand their roles in acting in accordance with the laws and regulations governing their industry. Employees should be made aware of the November 1, 2010, amendments to the sentencing guidelines and the relevancy of such to the company; i.e., increased training being provided in response to departmental "hotbeds," etc. The communication should also explain that X percentage of the corporation's employees will be asked to complete assessments which will be a series of questions in specific business subject areas or areas in the code of conduct/ethics.

Assignments

- **Hypothetical:** You are the Chief Compliance Officer at your Team's Corporation. Perform a compliance risk assessment and determine which areas of your Company require updating.

Chapter 12

Corporate Compliance Programs in the Context of Deferred and Non-Prosecution Agreements

Introduction

A deferred prosecution agreement (DPA) or a non-prosecution agreement (NPA) is frequently used as a tool by the Department of Justice (DOJ) to implement an "effective" compliance program in a corporation. A DPA, which is very similar to an NPA, is a voluntary alternative to adjudication in which a prosecutor agrees to grant amnesty in exchange for the defendant fulfilling certain requirements. For instance, a case of corporate fraud might be settled by means of a deferred-prosecution agreement in which the defendant agrees to pay fines, implement corporate reforms, and fully cooperate with the investigation. Fulfillment of the specified requirements will then result in dismissal of the charges.

Under a DPA, DOJ files a charging document with the court, but it simultaneously requests that the prosecution be deferred, that is, postponed for the purpose of allowing the company to demonstrate its good conduct. DPAs generally require a defendant to agree to pay a monetary penalty, waive the statute of limitations, cooperate with the government, admit the relevant facts, and enter into certain compliance and remediation commitments, potentially including a corporate compliance monitor. DPAs describe the company's conduct, cooperation, and remediation, if any, and provide a calculation of the penalty pursuant to the U.S. Sentencing Guidelines. In addition to being publicly filed, DOJ places all of its DPAs on its website. If the company successfully completes the term of the agreement (typically three to five consecutive years), DOJ will then move to dismiss the filed charges. A company's successful completion of a DPA is not treated as a criminal conviction.

Under a non-prosecution agreement, DOJ maintains the right to file charges but refrains from doing so to allow the company to demonstrate its good conduct during the term of the NPA. Unlike a DPA, an NPA is not filed with a court but is instead maintained by the parties. The requirements of an NPA are similar to those of a DPA, and generally require a waiver of the statute of limitations, ongoing cooperation, admission of the material facts, and compliance and remediation commitments, in addition to payment of a monetary penalty. If the company complies with the agreement throughout its term, DOJ does not file criminal charges. If an individual complies with the terms of his or her NPA, truthful and complete cooperation and continued law-abiding conduct, DOJ will not pursue criminal charges.[1]

NPAs and DPAs look fairly similar — although the DPAs (for the most part) resemble documents that are filed with a court (paragraph numbers, case style, etc.). An NPA usually takes the form of a letter from the particular DOJ component investigating the entity. (With a DPA, a case number is assigned by the federal court once a charging document is filed and the DPA is often filed into the record. NPAs are not filed with the court, but a company may have a duty to file the agreement as a material definitive agreement under the federal securities laws. Both agreements are signed by the government and the entity.

According to the Gibson Dunn 2015 Mid-Year Update on Corporate NPAs and DPAs, "in the first six months of 2015, Department of Justice (DOJ) entered into five Deferred Prosecution Agreements (DPA) and 23 Non Prosecution Agreements (NPA). In addition to DOJ's 28 agreements, the SEC entered into one DPA in the first part of 2015, bringing its total overall NPA and DPA count to eight." The first six months of 2015 a total of 29 "overall agreements vastly exceeds agreement counts from recent years," with 2014 having 13, and 2013 having 12 by the first six months of the year.

In fact, "2015's NPA and DPA count has already exceeded the overall number of NPAs and DPAs in 2013, when there were only 28, and it is closely approaching last year's overall count of 30."

As demonstrated by Illustration 12.1, NPAs and DPAs have played an increasingly important and consistent role in resolving allegations of corporate wrongdoing since 2000. There have typically been at least 20 agreements per year since 2006, with highs reached in 2007 and 2010 at 39 and 40 agreements, respectively. In the first six months of 2015, with 29 agreements and the prospect of many more "through the DOJ Tax Swiss Bank Program, it is highly likely that 2015 will substantially exceed historical highs."

Illustration 12.2 below shows the total monetary recoveries related to NPAs and DPAs from 2000 through 2015. At over $4.2 billion, the first six months of 2015 "agreements — as in 2014 — have already exceeded the overall recovery value for 2013, which was approximately $2.9 billion." This is largely the result of one "DOJ DPA with Deutsche Bank AG, which involved a recovery of $2.369 billion, and several other settlements in the millions and hundreds of millions."

---

1. https://www.documentcloud.org/documents/515229-a-resource-guide-to-the-u-s-foreign-corrupt.html.

Illustration 12.1

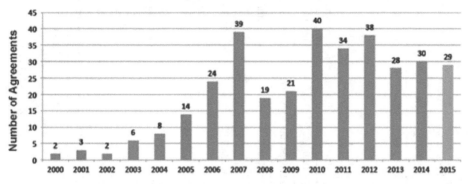

Chart 1: Corporate NPAs and DPAs, 2000 – 2015

http://www.gibsondunn.com/publications/pages/2015-Mid-Year-Update-Corporate-Non-Prosecution-Agreements-and-Deferred-Prosecution-Agreements.aspx.

NPAs and DPAs continue to be important resolution tools, which involve some of the largest and most successful global corporations, "either through parent companies or their subsidiaries. NPAs and DPAs are crucial in allowing companies that are otherwise good corporate citizens to continue to do business while implementing the significant reforms, reporting, and ongoing cooperation that these agreements typically require."

Illustration 12.2

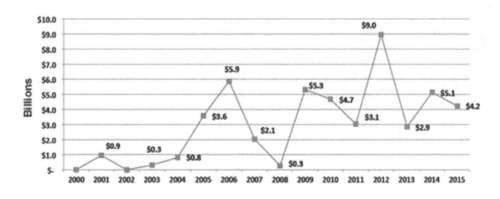

Chart 2: Total Monetary Recoveries Related to NPAs and DPAs, 2000 – 2015

http://www.gibsondunn.com/publications/pages/2015-Mid-Year-Update-Corporate-Non-Prosecution-Agreements-and-Deferred-Prosecution-Agreements.aspx.

The following chart summarizes the agreements concluded by DOJ and the SEC during the first half of 2015.

Deferred and Non-Prosecution Agreements in 2015

Company	Agency	Alleged Violation	Type	Penalties	Monitor	Term of DPA/NPA
Ansun Biopharma	S.D. Cal.	Fraud; False Claims Act	DPA	$2,149,600	No	6 months
Banca Credinvest SA	DOJ Tax	Tax-Related and Monetary Transactions Offenses	NPA	$3,022,000	No	48 months
Bank Linth LBB AG	DOJ Tax	Tax-Related and Monetary Transactions Offenses	NPA	$4,150,000	No	48 months
Bank of Mingo	S.D. W. Va.	Bank Secrecy Act	DPA	$2,200,000	No	12 months
Bank Sparhafen Zurich AG	DOJ Tax	Tax-Related and Monetary Transactions Offenses	NPA	$1,810,000	No	48 months
Berner Kantonalbank AG	DOJ Tax	Tax-Related and Monetary Transactions Offenses	NPA	$4,619,000	No	48 months
BSI SA	DOJ Tax	Tax-Related and Monetary Transactions Offenses	NPA	$211,000,000	No	48 months
Commerce West Bank	DOJ Consumer Protection	FIRREA	DPA	$4,900,000	No	24 months
Commerzbank A.G.	DOJ AFMLS; S.D.N.Y.	Trade Sanctions/IEEPA/Export; BSA	DPA	$1,452,000,000	Yes	36 months
Deutsche Bank AG	DOJ Fraud; DOJ Antitrust	Fraud	DPA	$2,369,000,000	Yes	36 months
Digital Reveal, LLC	E.D.N.C.	Anti-Gambling Compliance	NPA	$0	No	60 months and 56 days (expires July 1, 2020)
Ersparniskasse Schaffhausen AG	DOJ Tax	Tax-Related and Monetary Transactions Offenses	NPA	$2,066,000	No	48 months
Exide Technologies	C.D. Cal.	Environmental	NPA	$133,000,000	Yes	120 months
Finter Bank AG	DOJ Tax	Tax-Related and Monetary Transactions Offenses	NPA	$5,414,000	No	48 months
Hunter Roberts Construction Group, LLC	E.D.N.Y.	Fraud (Overbilling)	NPA	$7,007,046	Yes	24 months

IAP Worldwide Services, Inc.	DOJ Fraud; E.D. Va.	FCPA	NPA	$7,100,000	Yes	36 months and 7 days
LBBW (Schweiz) AG	DOJ Tax	Tax-Related and Monetary Transactions Offenses	NPA	$34,000	No	48 months
MediBank AG	DOJ Tax	Tax-Related and Monetary Transactions Offenses	NPA	$826,000	No	48 months
PBSJ Corporation	SEC	FCPA	DPA	$3,407,875	No	24 months
Privatbank Von Graffenried AG	DOJ Tax	Tax-Related and Monetary Transactions Offenses	NPA	$287,000	No	48 months
Ripple Labs, Inc.	N.D. Cal.	Anti-Money Laundering Compliance	NPA	$700,000	Yes	36 months
Rothschild Bank AG	DOJ Tax	Tax-Related and Monetary Transactions Offenses	NPA	$11,510,000	No	48 months
Scobag Privatbank AG	DOJ Tax	Tax-Related and Monetary Transactions Offenses	NPA	$9,090	No	48 months
Sierra Software LLC	E.D.N.C.	Anti-Gambling Compliance	NPA	$0	No	No set term
Société Générale Private Banking (Lugano-Svizzera) SA	DOJ Tax	Tax-Related and Monetary Transactions Offenses	NPA	$1,363,000	No	48 months
Société Générale Private Banking (Suisse) SA	DOJ Tax	Tax-Related and Monetary Transactions Offenses	NPA	$17,807,000	No	48 months
TNT Software, LLC	E.D.N.C.	Anti-Gambling Compliance	NPA	$0	No	60 months and 56 days (expires July 1, 2020)
Vadian Bank AG	DOJ Tax	Tax-Related and Monetary Transactions Offenses	NPA	$4,253,000	No	48 months
White Sands Technology, LLC	E.D.N.C.	Anti-Gambling Compliance	NPA	$0	No	60 months and 56 days (expires July 1, 2020)

http://www.gibsondunn.com/publications/pages/2015-Mid-Year-Update-Corporate-Non-Prosecution-Agreements-and-Deferred-Prosecution-Agreements.aspx.

The figures for "Penalties" may include amounts not strictly limited to an NPA or a DPA, such as fines, penalties, forfeitures, and restitution requirements imposed by other regulators and enforcement agencies, as well as amounts from related settlement agreements, all of which may be part of a global resolution in connection with the NPA or DPA, paid by the named entity and/or subsidiaries. "Monitor" includes traditional compliance monitors, self-reporting arrangements, and other monitorship arrangements found in settlement agreements.

Background on DPAs and NPAs

DPAs and NPAs consist of agreements between the DOJ and a corporation used to end criminal investigation that could have led to prosecution. (The DOJ also has ability to prosecute under the Criminal Division, Civil Division, Environmental Crimes and Natural Resources Division and the Antitrust Division.) The difference between an NPA and DPA is whether charges are filed in court. The terms of DPAs vary; often they include admissions of wrongdoing; regular reporting to Pretrial Services; obeying the law; and refraining from publicly discussing the case. If the case goes to trial, the defendant generally cannot contest any admitted facts. In a DPA, the Justice Department files the agreement along with an information, but agrees to hold the charges in abeyance pending the company's successful satisfaction of the DPA. There is minimal judicial review of the terms of a DPA and only the prosecutor determines whether the company has successfully met them. If the government is satisfied, the charges are dismissed; if not, the prosecutor commonly seeks broader charges from a grand jury and takes the case to trial. The terms of an entity DPA, which commonly are in place for a year or more, may include payment of restitution, admission of wrongful conduct, ongoing cooperation with the government's investigation, new or enhanced compliance programs, and internal reforms ranging from changes in corporate governance structure to personnel actions.

With an NPA no charging document is filed, but the investigation remains pending until the entity fulfills the terms of the NPA. If the company complies with the agreement, that is the end of the matter. If the Justice Department concludes that the company has fallen short of its obligations under an NPA, the prosecutor will present the case to a grand jury and proceed to trial, as with a DPA. An NPA would contain the same sort of cooperation and remediation provisions as a DPA, but would not include any admission of wrongdoing. The substantive result of both is the same: no criminal conviction for the company.

Most of the terms found in the agreements are fairly uniform. The company (1) admits to wrongdoing, (2) waives the statute of limitations (sometimes broadly), (3) agrees that the agreement is admissible in court, (4) agrees that the company will no longer violate the law; (5) agrees the company will help the government prosecute any wrongdoers (e.g., make employees available to testify for grand jury or trial and provide documents and other evidence to the DOJ), and (6) agrees that company employees will not contradict the terms of the agreement.

In return, the DOJ agrees to dismiss the case (in the case of a DPA) or not bring one (in the case of an NPA). The agreement also has an expiration date, an appeals process if the DOJ thinks the company violated the agreement and provisions dealing with penalties, restitution, and/or forfeiture.

Both the DPA and NPA allow the entity to avoid the stigma of criminal conviction and associated collateral consequences, which can vary depending on industry and structure of the organization. For some companies this may mean reputational harm—criminal convictions are not a popular marketing tool. For others it may mean they can no longer do business with the government (i.e., debarment) or continue to exist (e.g., Arthur Andersen).

The SEC's Encouragement to Cooperate

Cooperation has been a conundrum for the Securities and Exchange Commission (SEC). As a civil enforcement agency, the SEC inherently has less to offer potential cooperators than the Justice Department, since the SEC cannot put people in jail or destroy companies simply by indicting them. Moreover, since the SEC is held only to a preponderance-of-the-evidence burden of proof, it may have felt that cooperating witnesses were not as essential as they are viewed by criminal prosecutors, who must prove their cases beyond a reasonable doubt. Yet the SEC has also long recognized that it does not have the resources to investigate every case from scratch; to have the greatest deterrent effect, it needs cooperators to bring potential violations to its attention and voluntarily provide key pieces of evidence. The SEC has not had a process analogous to a DPA, where it would bring a case but hold it in abeyance pending cooperation. With respect to corporations and other entities, the SEC's cooperation policy has, since 2002, been governed by the so-called Seaboard Report.[2]

The SEC recently elaborated on some of the criteria it will employ in determining what actions to bring, if any, against publicly reporting companies for securities law violations. In *In the Matter of Gisela de Leon-Meredith*,[3] the SEC issued a relatively unusual Report of Investigation under Section 21(a) of the Securities Exchange Act of 1934.

The Report of Investigation, commonly known as the "Seaboard Report," highlights the value placed by the SEC on timely internal investigations that are followed by

---

2. Under that policy, a timely internal investigation, followed by prompt self-reporting, cooperation with the SEC staff's requests for documents and witnesses, discipline of the individuals responsible and establishment of controls designed to prevent future misconduct would weigh in a company's favor under a sliding scale of cooperation. A company like Seaboard, which provided "complete cooperation" to the SEC, might be granted the "extraordinary step of taking no enforcement action". Exchange Act Release No. 44969 (the "Seaboard Report"), Oct. 23, 2001, available at http://www.sec.gov/litigation/investreport/34-44969.htm; see also SEC Enforcement Division Manual, available at www.sec.gov/divisions/enforce/enforcementmanual.pdf, at 80–81.

3. Securities Exchange Act Release No. 44969, Oct. 23, 2001.

prompt disclosure of the misconduct to the public, cooperation with the SEC, discipline of those responsible, and establishment of more effective controls and procedures designed to prevent a recurrence of the misconduct.

The Seaboard Report is notable, however, for more than its non-exhaustive list of factors the SEC may consider in seeking sanctions against a company. The report also emphasizes the importance of a public company employing outside counsel with little, if any, prior engagement with the company to conduct the requisite internal investigation. While signaling its preference for independent outside counsel to handle internal investigations, the SEC stopped short of requiring disclosure to the SEC and government investigators of any report of an investigation by counsel, with the possibility of attendant waiver of the attorney-client privilege and other protections. Instead, the SEC chose to just encourage such disclosure.

SEC, The Seaboard Report
Release No. 44969 (Oct. 23, 2001)

Report of Investigation Pursuant to Section 21(a) of the Securities Exchange Act of 1934 and Commission Statement on the Relationship of Cooperation to Agency Enforcement Decisions

Today, we commence and settle a cease-and-desist proceeding against Gisela de Leon-Meredith, former controller of a public company's subsidiary. Our order finds that Meredith caused the parent company's books and records to be inaccurate and its periodic reports misstated, and then covered up those facts.

We are not taking action against the parent company, given the nature of the conduct and the company's responses. Within a week of learning about the apparent misconduct, the company's internal auditors had conducted a preliminary review and had advised company management who, in turn, advised the Board's audit committee, that Meredith had caused the company's books and records to be inaccurate and its financial reports to be misstated. The full Board was advised and authorized the company to hire an outside law firm to conduct a thorough inquiry. Four days later, Meredith was dismissed, as were two other employees who, in the company's view, had inadequately supervised Meredith; a day later, the company disclosed publicly and to us that its financial statements would be restated. The price of the company's shares did not decline after the announcement or after the restatement was published. The company pledged and gave complete cooperation to our staff. It provided the staff with all information relevant to the underlying violations. Among other things, the company produced the details of its internal investigation, including notes and transcripts of interviews of Meredith and others; and it did not invoke the attorney-client privilege, work product protection or other privileges or protections with respect to any facts uncovered in the investigation.

The company also strengthened its financial reporting processes to address Meredith's conduct—developing a detailed closing process for the subsidiary's accounting personnel, consolidating subsidiary accounting functions under a parent company

CPA, hiring three new CPAs for the accounting department responsible for preparing the subsidiary's financial statements, redesigning the subsidiary's minimum annual audit requirements, and requiring the parent company's controller to interview and approve all senior accounting personnel in its subsidiaries' reporting processes.

Our willingness to credit such behavior in deciding whether and how to take enforcement action benefits investors as well as our enforcement program. When businesses seek out, self-report and rectify illegal conduct, and otherwise cooperate with Commission staff, large expenditures of government and shareholder resources can be avoided and investors can benefit more promptly. In setting forth the criteria listed below, we think a few caveats are in order:

First, the paramount issue in every enforcement judgment is, and must be, what best protects investors. There is no single, or constant, answer to that question. Self-policing, self-reporting, remediation and cooperation with law enforcement authorities, among other things, are unquestionably important in promoting investors' best interests.

Second, we are not adopting any rule or making any commitment or promise about any specific case; nor are we in any way limiting our broad discretion to evaluate every case individually, on its own particular facts and circumstances.

Third, we do not limit ourselves to the criteria we discuss below.

In brief form, we set forth below some of the criteria we will consider in determining whether, and how much, to credit self-policing, self-reporting, remediation and cooperation—from the extraordinary step of taking no enforcement action to bringing reduced charges, seeking lighter sanctions, or including mitigating language in documents we use to announce and resolve enforcement actions.

1. What is the nature of the misconduct involved? Did it result from inadvertence, honest mistake, simple negligence, reckless or deliberate indifference to indicia of wrongful conduct, willful misconduct or unadorned venality? Were the company's auditors misled?

2. How did the misconduct arise? Is it the result of pressure placed on employees to achieve specific results, or a tone of lawlessness set by those in control of the company? What compliance procedures were in place to prevent the misconduct now uncovered? Why did those procedures fail to stop or inhibit the wrongful conduct?

3. Where in the organization did the misconduct occur? How high up in the chain of command was knowledge of, or participation in, the misconduct? Did senior personnel participate in, or turn a blind eye toward, obvious indicia of misconduct? How systemic was the behavior? Is it symptomatic of the way the entity does business, or was it isolated?

4. How long did the misconduct last? Was it a one-quarter, or one-time, event, or did it last several years? In the case of a public company, did the misconduct occur before the company went public? Did it facilitate the company's ability to go public?

5. How much harm has the misconduct inflicted upon investors and other corporate constituencies? Did the share price of the company's stock drop significantly upon its discovery and disclosure?

6. How was the misconduct detected and who uncovered it?

7. How long after discovery of the misconduct did it take to implement an effective response?

8. What steps did the company take upon learning of the misconduct? Did the company immediately stop the misconduct? Are persons responsible for any misconduct still with the company? If so, are they still in the same positions? Did the company promptly, completely and effectively disclose the existence of the misconduct to the public, to regulators and to self-regulators? Did the company cooperate completely with appropriate regulatory and law enforcement bodies? Did the company identify what additional related misconduct is likely to have occurred? Did the company take steps to identify the extent of damage to investors and other corporate constituencies? Did the company appropriately recompense those adversely affected by the conduct?

9. What processes did the company follow to resolve many of these issues and ferret out necessary information? Were the Audit Committee and the Board of Directors fully informed? If so, when?

10. Did the company commit to learn the truth, fully and expeditiously? Did it do a thorough review of the nature, extent, origins and consequences of the conduct and related behavior? Did management, the Board or committees consisting solely of outside directors oversee the review? Did company employees or outside persons perform the review? If outside persons, had they done other work for the company? Where the review was conducted by outside counsel, had management previously engaged such counsel? Were scope limitations placed on the review? If so, what were they?

11. Did the company promptly make available to our staff the results of its review and provide sufficient documentation reflecting its response to the situation? Did the company identify possible violative conduct and evidence with sufficient precision to facilitate prompt enforcement actions against those who violated the law? Did the company produce a thorough and probing written report detailing the findings of its review? Did the company voluntarily disclose information our staff did not directly request and otherwise might not have uncovered? Did the company ask its employees to cooperate with our staff and make all reasonable efforts to secure such cooperation?

12. What assurances are there that the conduct is unlikely to recur? Did the company adopt and ensure enforcement of new and more effective internal controls and procedures designed to prevent a recurrence of the misconduct? Did the company provide our staff with sufficient information for it to evaluate the company's measures to correct the situation and ensure that the conduct does not recur?

13. Is the company the same company in which the misconduct occurred, or has it changed through a merger or bankruptcy reorganization?

We hope that this Report of Investigation and Commission Statement will further encourage self-policing efforts and will promote more self-reporting, remediation and cooperation with the Commission staff. We welcome the constructive input of all interested persons. We urge those who have contributions to make to direct them to our Division of Enforcement. The public can be confident that all such communications will be fairly evaluated not only by our staff, but also by us. We continue to reassess our enforcement approaches with the aim of maximizing the benefits of our program to investors and the marketplace.[4]

The Seaboard Report offers what the SEC has referred to as an "enticing carrot" in its implicit promise that good corporate behavior after discovery of misconduct can help mitigate the SEC's response, and, in the right circumstances, even help a company avoid an SEC enforcement action altogether. For companies that fail to heed Seaboard's call to investigate, disclose, undertake remediation and cooperate, look for the SEC to pursue cases even more vigorously through an array of available sanctions, including the SEC's newly rediscovered remedy of barring individual violators from future service as officers or directors "if their conduct demonstrates substantial unfitness to serve" in such capacities.

The Seaboard Report provides a highly instructive, but non-exhaustive, list of factors the SEC may employ in determining what, if any, action to bring against a publicly reporting company in connection with misconduct resulting in securities laws violations. It provides a useful road map for any company — publicly reporting or privately held — to follow in considering what measures to take in the days and weeks after the discovery of misconduct.

In 2008 the DOJ implemented a new policy dealing with the selection of corporate monitors in DPAs and NPAs — the Morford Memo now found at Section 163 of the DOJ Criminal Resources Manual. *See* Memorandum from Craig Morford, Acting Deputy Att'y Gen., U.S. Dep't of Justice, to Heads of Dep't Components, note 2 (Mar. 7, 2008), *available at* http://www.usdoj.gov/dag/morford-useofmonitorsmemo-03072008.pdf. When substantial business reforms are incorporated into a DPA or an NPA, a monitor can provide oversight that ordinarily the probation office or the court would provide in the event the entity was prosecuted and convicted. Otherwise, busy federal prosecutors would have little or no way to confirm that an entity was keeping its end of the bargain. It is, therefore, unsurprising that as DPAs/NPAs with negotiated business reforms and compliance programs have increased, so have monitors. The Morford Memo provides guidance to prosecutors on how to address po-

---

4. [In the Seaboard Report, the SEC seized the opportunity to explain some factors it will use to determine how to credit companies for their affirmative efforts in connection with the discovery and remediation of misconduct. The SEC identified four major criteria: self-policing/nature of the conduct; self-reporting; remediation; cooperation with law enforcement. The Seaboard Report provides no "safe harbor" for reporting companies that have violated securities laws. The SEC made clear in the Seaboard Report that the SEC was not making any commitments about the outcome of any specific case, and it noted that "there may be circumstances where conduct is so egregious, and harm so great, that no amount of cooperation or other mitigating conduct can justify a decision not to bring any enforcement action at all." — Eds.]

tential issues that may arise with the selection and appointment of a monitor as well as the monitor's duties. The purpose of the memorandum is to present a series of principles for drafting provisions pertaining to the use of monitors in connection with DPA and NPA with corporations. A monitor's primary responsibility is to assess and monitor a corporation's compliance with the terms of the agreement specifically designed to address and reduce the risk of recurrence of the corporation's misconduct, and not to further punitive goals.

The Morford Memo makes clear that a monitor is "an independent third-party, not an employee or agent of the corporation or of the Government." The role of the monitor under the Morford Memo is "to evaluate whether a corporation has both adopted and effectively implemented ethics and compliance programs to address and reduce the risk of recurrence of the corporation's misconduct. A well-designed ethics and compliance program that is not effectively implemented will fail to lower the risk of recidivism."

The new policy mandates that DOJ components (including U.S. Attorney's Offices) establish a selection committee and review a panel of qualified candidates before selecting a monitor as part of a DPA or NPA. The committee must include: (1) the ethics officer for the applicable DOJ component, (2) the criminal chief or DOJ component chief, and (3) an experienced prosecutor. Ideally, the committee must consider at least three qualified candidates. The amount of DOJ input will vary depending on the agreed upon selection process. (The Morford Memo notes: "there is no one method of selection that should necessarily be used in every instance. For example, the corporation may select a monitor candidate, with the Government reserving the right to veto the proposed choice if the monitor is unacceptable. In other cases, the facts may require the Government to play a greater role in selecting the monitor.") In every case, the Deputy Attorney General will have the final say on the monitor and the monitor must be impartial and avoid working for the company for at least a year after the monitorship expires.

The Morford Memo notes that the duration of the monitorship varies depending on the agreement. The memo provides a list of non-exhaustive factors: (1) the nature and seriousness of the underlying misconduct; (2) the pervasiveness and duration of misconduct within the corporation, including the complicity or involvement of senior management; (3) the corporation's history of similar misconduct; (4) the nature of the corporate culture; (5) the scale and complexity of any remedial measures contemplated by the agreement, including the size of the entity or business unit at issue; and (6) the stage of design and implementation of remedial measures when the monitorship commences.

U.S. Dep't of Justice, Office of the Deputy Attorney General, Memorandum for Heads of Department Components United States Attorneys ("Morford Memorandum")

http://www.justice.gov/sites/default/files/dag/legacy/2008/
03/20/morford-useofmonitorsmemo-03072008.pdf

Selection and Use of Monitors in Deferred Prosecution Agreements and Non-Prosecution Agreements with Corporations

The Department of Justice's commitment to deterring and preventing corporate crime remains a high priority. The Principles of Federal Prosecution of Business Organizations set forth guidance to federal prosecutors regarding charges against corporations. A careful consideration of those principles and the facts in a given case may result in a decision to negotiate an agreement to resolve a criminal case against a corporation without a formal conviction—either a deferred prosecution agreement or a non-prosecution agreement.

The purpose of this memorandum is to present a series of principles for drafting provisions pertaining to the use of monitors in connection with deferred prosecution and non-prosecution agreements (hereafter referred to collectively as "agreements") with corporations. Given the varying facts and circumstances of each case—where different industries, corporate size and structure, and other considerations may be at issue—any guidance regarding monitors must be practical and flexible. This guidance is limited to monitors, and does not apply to third parties, whatever their titles, retained to act as receivers, trustees, or perform other functions.

In negotiating agreements with corporations, prosecutors should be mindful of both: (1) the potential benefits that employing a monitor may have for the corporation and the public, and (2) the cost of a monitor and its impact on the operations of a corporation. Prosecutors shall, at a minimum, notify the appropriate United States Attorney or Department Component Head prior to the execution of an agreement that includes a corporate monitor. The appropriate United States Attorney or Department Component Head shall, in turn, provide a copy of the agreement to the Assistant Attorney General for the Criminal Division at a reasonable time after it has been executed. The Assistant Attorney General for the Criminal Division shall maintain a record of all such agreements.

This memorandum sets forth nine basic principles in the areas of selection, scope of duties, and duration.

II. SELECTION

1. Principle: Before beginning the process of selecting a monitor in connection with deferred prosecution agreements and non-prosecution agreements, the corporation and the Government should discuss the necessary qualifications for a monitor based on the facts and circumstances of the case. The selection process must, at a minimum, be designed to: (1) select a highly qualified and respected person or entity based on suitability for the assignment and all of the circumstances; (2) avoid potential

and actual conflicts of interests, and (3) otherwise instill public confidence by implementing the steps set forth in this Principle.

To avoid a conflict, first, Government attorneys who participate in the process of selecting a monitor shall be mindful of their obligation to comply with the conflict-of interest guidelines set forth in 18 U.S.C. § 208 and 5 C.F.R. Part 2635. Second, the Government shall create a standing or ad hoc committee in the Department component or office where the case originated to consider monitor candidates. United States Attorneys and Assistant Attorneys General may not make, accept, or veto the selection of monitor candidates unilaterally. Third, the Office of the Deputy Attorney General must approve the monitor. Fourth, the Government should decline to accept a monitor if he or she has an interest in, or relationship with, the corporation or its employees, officers or directors that would cause a reasonable person to question the monitor's impartiality. Finally, the Government should obtain a commitment from the corporation that it will not employ or be affiliated with the monitor for a period of not less than one year from the date the monitorship is terminated.

Subsequent employment or retention of the monitor by the corporation after the monitorship period concludes may raise concerns about both the appearance of a conflict of interest and the effectiveness of the monitor during the monitorship, particularly with regard to the disclosure of possible new misconduct. Such employment includes both direct and indirect, or subcontracted, relationships.

Where practicable, the corporation, the Government, or both parties, depending on the selection process being used, should consider a pool of at least three qualified monitor candidates. Where the selection process calls for the corporation to choose the monitor at the outset, the corporation should submit its choice from among the pool of candidates to the Government. Where the selection process calls for the Government to play a greater role in selecting the monitor, the Government should, where practicable, identify at least three acceptable monitors from the pool of candidates, and the corporation shall choose from that list.

III. SCOPE OF DUTIES

A. INDEPENDENCE

2. Principle: A monitor is an independent third-party, not an employee or agent of the corporation or of the Government.

B. MONITORING COMPLIANCE WITH THE AGREEMENT

3. Principle: A monitor's primary responsibility should be to assess and monitor a corporation's compliance with those terms of the agreement that are specifically designed to address and reduce the risk of recurrence of the corporation's misconduct, including, in most cases, evaluating (and where appropriate proposing) internal controls and corporate ethics and compliance programs.

4. Principle: In carrying out his or her duties, a monitor will often need to understand the full scope of the corporation's misconduct covered by the agreement, but the

monitor's responsibilities should be no broader than necessary to address and reduce the risk of recurrence of the corporation's misconduct.

C. COMMUNICATIONS AND RECOMMENDATIONS BY THE MONITOR

5. Principle: Communication among the Government, the corporation and the monitor is in the interest of all the parties. Depending on the facts and circumstances, it may be appropriate for the monitor to make periodic written reports to both the Government and the corporation.

6. Principle: If the corporation chooses not to adopt recommendations made by the monitor within a reasonable time, either the monitor or the corporation, or both, should report that fact to the Government, along with the corporation's reasons. The Government may consider this conduct when evaluating whether the corporation has fulfilled its obligations under the agreement

D. REPORTING OF PREVIOUSLY UNDISCLOSED OR NEW MISCONDUCT

7. Principle: The agreement should clearly identify any types of previously undisclosed or new misconduct that the monitor will be required to report directly to the Government. The agreement should also provide that as to evidence of other such misconduct, the monitor will have the discretion to report this misconduct to the Government or the corporation or both.

IV. DURATION

8. Principle: The duration of the agreement should be tailored to the problems that have been found to exist and the types of remedial measures needed for the monitor to satisfy his or her mandate.

The following criteria should be considered when negotiating duration of the agreement (not necessarily in this order): (1) the nature and seriousness of the underlying misconduct; (2) the pervasiveness and duration of misconduct within the corporation, including the complicity or involvement of senior management; (3) the corporation's history of similar misconduct; (4) the nature of the corporate culture; (5) the scale and complexity of any remedial measures contemplated by the agreement, including the size of the entity or business unit at issue; and (6) the stage of design and implementation of remedial measures when the monitorship commences. It is reasonable to forecast that completing an assessment of more extensive and/or complex remedial measures will require a longer period of time than completing an assessment of less extensive and/or less complex ones. Similarly, it is reasonable to forecast that a monitor who is assigned responsibility to assess a compliance program that has not been designed or implemented may take longer to complete that assignment than one who is assigned responsibility to assess a compliance program that has already been designed and implemented.

9. Principle; In most cases, an agreement should provide for an extension of the monitor provision(s) at the discretion of the Government in the event that the corporation has not successfully satisfied its obligations under the agreement. Conversely, in most cases, an agreement should provide for early termination if the corporation

can demonstrate to the Government that there exists a change in circumstances sufficient to eliminate the need for a monitor.

If the corporation has not satisfied its obligations under the terms of the agreement at the time the monitorship ends, the corresponding risk of recidivism will not have been reduced and an extension of the monitor provision(s) may be appropriate. On the other hand, there are a number of changes in circumstances that could justify early termination of an agreement. For example, if a corporation ceased operations in the area that was the subject of the agreement, a monitor may no longer be necessary. Similarly, if a corporation is purchased by or merges with another entity that has an effective ethics and compliance program, it may be prudent to terminate a monitorship.

Finally, the Department of Justice Criminal Division created a Resource Guide to understand the Foreign Corrupt Practices Act (FCPA). This Resource Guide in Chapter 7 provides explanations for different types of resolutions with the DOJ. These include DPAs, NPAs, as well as plea agreements, and declinations from prosecution. This Resource Guide is helpful in understanding the concept of DPAs and NPAs as distinguishing these from other types of resolutions with the DOJ and other U.S. government departments.

U.S. Department of Justice Criminal Division & SEC Enforcement Division, Resource Guide to the U.S. Foreign Corrupt Practices Act

http://www.justice.gov/sites/default/files/criminal-fraud/legacy/2015/01/16/guide.pdf

RESOLUTIONS

What Are the Different Types of Resolutions with DOJ?

Criminal Complaints, Informations, and Indictments

Charges against individuals and companies are brought in three different ways under the Federal Rules of Criminal Procedure: criminal complaints, criminal informations, and indictments. DOJ may agree to resolve criminal FCPA matters against companies either through a declination or, in appropriate cases, a negotiated resolution resulting in a plea agreement, deferred prosecution agreement, or non-prosecution agreement. For individuals, a negotiated resolution will generally take the form of a plea agreement, which may include language regarding cooperation, or a non-prosecution cooperation agreement. When negotiated resolutions cannot be reached with companies or individuals, the matter may proceed to trial.

Plea Agreements

Plea agreements—whether with companies or individuals—are governed by Rule 11 of the Federal Rules of Criminal Procedure. The defendant generally admits to the facts supporting the charges, admits guilt, and is convicted of the charged crimes when the plea agreement is presented to and accepted by a court. The plea agreement may jointly recommend a sentence or fine, jointly recommend an analysis under the U.S. Sentencing Guidelines, or leave such items open for argument at the time of sentencing.

Deferred Prosecution Agreements

Under a deferred prosecution agreement, or a DPA as it is commonly known, DOJ files a charging document with the court, but it simultaneously requests that the prosecution be deferred, that is, postponed for the purpose of allowing the company to demonstrate its good conduct. DPAs generally require a defendant to agree to pay a monetary penalty, waive the statute of limitations, cooperate with the government, admit the relevant facts, and enter into certain compliance and remediation commitments, potentially including a corporate compliance monitor. DPAs describe the company's conduct, cooperation, and remediation, if any, and provide a calculation of the penalty pursuant to the U.S. Sentencing Guidelines. In addition to being publicly filed, DOJ places all of its DPAs on its website. If the company successfully completes the term of the agreement (typically two or three years), DOJ will then move to dismiss the filed charges. A company's successful completion of a DPA is not treated as a criminal conviction.

Non-Prosecution Agreements

Under a non-prosecution agreement, or an NPA as it is commonly known, DOJ maintains the right to file charges but refrains from doing so to allow the company to demonstrate its good conduct during the term of the NPA. Unlike a DPA, an NPA is not filed with a court but is instead maintained by the parties. In circumstances where an NPA is with a company for FCPA-related offenses, it is made available to the public through DOJ's website. The requirements of an NPA are similar to those of a DPA, and generally require a waiver of the statute of limitations, ongoing cooperation, admission of the material facts, and compliance and remediation commitments, in addition to payment of a monetary penalty. If the company complies with the agreement throughout its term, DOJ does not file criminal charges. If an individual complies with the terms of his or her NPA, namely, truthful and complete cooperation and continued law-abiding conduct, DOJ will not pursue criminal charges.

Declinations

As discussed above, DOJ's decision to bring or decline to bring an enforcement action under the FCPA is made pursuant to the Principles of Federal Prosecution, in the case of individuals, and the Principles of Federal Prosecution of Business Organizations, in the case of companies. As described, in the case of individuals, the Principles of Federal Prosecution advise prosecutors to weigh all relevant considerations, including:

- Federal law enforcement priorities;
- The nature and seriousness of the offense;
- The deterrent effect of prosecution;

- the person's culpability in connection with the offense;
- the person's history of criminal activity;
- The person's willingness to cooperate in the investigation or prosecution of others; and
- The probable sentence or other consequences if the person is convicted.

The Principles of Federal Prosecution provide additional commentary about each of these factors. For instance, they explain that prosecutors should take into account federal law enforcement priorities because federal law enforcement and judicial resources are not sufficient to permit prosecution of every alleged offense over which federal jurisdiction exists. The deterrent effect of prosecution should also be kept in mind because some offenses, "although seemingly not of great importance by themselves, if commonly committed would have a substantial cumulative impact on the community."

As discussed above, the Principles of Federal Prosecution of Business Organizations require prosecutors to consider nine factors when determining whether to prosecute a corporate entity for an FCPA violation, including the nature and seriousness of the offense; the pervasiveness of wrongdoing within the company; the company's history of similar conduct; the existence and effectiveness of the company's pre-existing compliance program; and the adequacy of remedies, such as civil or regulatory enforcement actions.

Pursuant to these guidelines, DOJ has declined to prosecute both individuals and corporate entities in numerous cases based on the particular facts and circumstances presented in those matters, taking into account the available evidence. To protect the privacy rights and other interests of the uncharged and other potentially interested parties, DOJ has a long-standing policy not to provide, without the party's consent, non-public information on matters it has declined to prosecute. To put DOJ's declinations in context, however, in the past two years alone, DOJ has declined several dozen cases against companies where potential FCPA violations were alleged.

As mentioned above, there are rare occasions in which, in conjunction with the public filing of charges against an individual, it is appropriate to disclose that a company is not also being prosecuted. That was done in a recent case where a former employee was charged but the former corporate employer was not.

What Are the Different Types of Resolutions with SEC?

Civil Injunctive Actions and Remedies

In a civil injunctive action, SEC seeks a court order compelling the defendant to obey the law in the future. Violating such an order can result in civil or criminal contempt proceedings. Civil contempt sanctions, brought by SEC, are remedial rather than punitive in nature and serve one of two purposes: to compensate the party injured as a result of the violation of the injunction or force compliance with the terms of the injunction.

Where a defendant has profited from a violation of law, SEC can obtain the equitable relief of disgorgement of ill-gotten gains and pre-judgment interest and can also obtain civil money penalties pursuant to Sections 21(d)(3) and 32(c) of the Exchange Act. SEC may also seek ancillary relief (such as an accounting from a defendant). Pursuant to Section 21(d)(5), SEC also may seek, and any federal court may grant, any other equitable relief that may be appropriate or necessary for the benefit of investors, such as enhanced remedial measures or the retention of an independent compliance consultant or monitor.

Civil Administrative Actions and Remedies

SEC has the ability to institute various types of administrative proceedings against a person or an entity that it believes has violated the law. This type of enforcement action is brought by SEC's Enforcement Division and is litigated before an SEC administrative law judge (ALJ). The ALJ's decision is subject to appeal directly to the Securities and Exchange Commission itself, and the Commission's decision is in turn subject to review by a U.S. Court of Appeals.

Administrative proceedings provide for a variety of relief. For regulated persons and entities, such as brokerdealers and investment advisers and persons associated with them, sanctions include censure, limitation on activities, suspension of up to twelve months, and bar from association or revocation of registration. For professionals such as attorneys and accountants, SEC can order in Rule 102(e) proceedings that the professional be censured, suspended, or barred from practicing before SEC. SEC staff can seek an order from an administrative law judge requiring the respondent to cease and desist from any current or future violations of the securities laws. In addition, SEC can obtain disgorgement, pre-judgment interest, and civil money penalties in administrative proceedings under Section 21B of the Exchange Act, and also can obtain other equitable relief, such as enhanced remedial measures or the retention of an independent compliance consultant or monitor.

Deferred Prosecution Agreements

A deferred prosecution agreement is a written agreement between SEC and a potential cooperating individual or company in which SEC agrees to forego an enforcement action against the individual or company if the individual or company agrees to, among other things: (1) cooperate truthfully and fully in SEC's investigation and related enforcement actions; (2) enter into a long-term tolling agreement; (3) comply with express prohibitions and/ or undertakings during a period of deferred prosecution; and (4) under certain circumstances, agree either to admit or not to contest underlying facts that SEC could assert to establish a violation of the federal securities laws. If the agreement is violated during the period of deferred prosecution, SEC staff may recommend an enforcement action to the Commission against the individual or company for the original misconduct as well as any additional misconduct. Furthermore, if the Commission authorizes the enforcement action, SEC staff may use any factual admissions made by the cooperating individual or company in support of a motion for summary judgment, while maintaining the ability to bring an enforcement action for any additional misconduct at a later date.

In May of 2011, SEC entered into its first deferred prosecution agreement against a company for violating the FCPA. In that case, a global manufacturer of steel pipe products violated the FCPA by bribing Uzbekistan government officials during a bidding process to supply pipelines for transporting oil and natural gas. The company made almost $5 million in profits when it was subsequently awarded several contracts by the Uzbekistan government. The company discovered the misconduct during a worldwide review of its operations and brought it to the government's attention. In addition to self-reporting, the company conducted a thorough internal investigation; provided complete, real-time cooperation with SEC and DOJ staff; and undertook extensive remediation, including enhanced anti-corruption procedures and training. Under the terms of the DPA, the company paid $5.4 million in disgorgement and prejudgment interest. The company also paid a $3.5 million monetary penalty to resolve a criminal investigation by DOJ through an NPA.

For further information about deferred prosecution agreements, see SEC's Enforcement Manual.

Non-Prosecution Agreements

A non-prosecution agreement is a written agreement between SEC and a potential cooperating individual or company, entered into in limited and appropriate circumstances, that provides that SEC will not pursue an enforcement action against the individual or company if the individual or company agrees to, among other things: (1) cooperate truthfully and fully in SEC's investigation and related enforcement actions; and (2) comply, under certain circumstances, with express undertakings. If the agreement is violated, SEC staff retains its ability to recommend an enforcement action to the Commission against the individual or company.

For further information about non-prosecution agreements, see SEC's Enforcement Manual.

Termination Letters and Declinations

As discussed above, SEC's decision to bring or decline to bring an enforcement action under the FCPA is made pursuant to the guiding principles set forth in SEC's Enforcement Manual. The same factors that apply to SEC staff 's determination of whether to recommend an enforcement action against an individual or entity apply to the decision to close an investigation without recommending enforcement action. Generally, SEC staff considers, among other things:

- The seriousness of the conduct and potential violations;
- The resources available to sec staff to pursue the investigation;
- The sufficiency and strength of the evidence;
- The extent of potential investor harm if an action is not commenced; and
- The age of the conduct underlying the potential violations.

SEC has declined to take enforcement action against both individuals and companies based on the facts and circumstances present in those matters, where, for example, the conduct was not egregious, the company fully cooperated, and the company identified and remediated the misconduct quickly. SEC Enforcement Division policy is to notify individuals and entities at the earliest opportunity when the staff has determined not to recommend an enforcement action against them to the Commission. This notification takes the form of a termination letter.

In order to protect the privacy rights and other interests of the uncharged and other potentially interested parties, SEC does not provide non-public information on matters it has declined to prosecute.

What Are Some Examples of Past Declinations by DOJ and SEC?

Neither DOJ nor SEC typically publicizes declinations but, to provide some insight into the process, the following are recent, anonymized examples of matters DOJ and SEC have declined to pursue:

Example 1: Public Company Declination

DOJ and SEC declined to take enforcement action against a public U.S. company. Factors taken into consideration included:

- The company discovered that its employees had received competitor bid information from a third party with connections to the foreign government.

- The company began an internal investigation, withdrew its contract bid, terminated the employees involved, severed ties to the third-party agent, and voluntarily disclosed the conduct to DOJ's Antitrust Division, which also declined prosecution.

- During the internal investigation, the company uncovered various FCPA red flags, including prior concerns about the third-party agent, all of which the company voluntarily disclosed to DOJ and SEC.

- The company immediately took substantial steps to improve its compliance program.

Example 2: Public Company Declination

DOJ and SEC declined to take enforcement action against a public U.S. company. Factors taken into consideration included:

- With knowledge of employees of the company's subsidiary, a retained construction company paid relatively small bribes, which were wrongly approved by the company's local law firm, to foreign building code inspectors.

- When the company's compliance department learned of the bribes, it immediately ended the conduct, terminated its relationship with the construction company and law firm, and terminated or disciplined the employees involved.

- The company completed a thorough internal investigation and voluntarily disclosed to DOJ and SEC.

- The company reorganized its compliance department, appointed a new compliance officer dedicated to anti-corruption, improved the training and compliance program, and undertook a review of all of the company's international third-party relationships.

Example 3: Public Company Declination

DOJ and SEC declined to take enforcement action against a U.S. publicly held industrial services company for bribes paid by a small foreign subsidiary. Factors taken into consideration included:

- The company self-reported the conduct to DOJ and SEC.
- The total amount of the improper payments was relatively small, and the activity appeared to be an isolated incident by a single employee at the subsidiary.
- The profits potentially obtained from the improper payments were very small.
- The payments were detected by the company's existing internal controls. The company's audit committee conducted a thorough independent internal investigation. The results of the investigation were provided to the government.
- The company cooperated fully with investigations by DOJ and SEC.
- The company implemented significant remedial actions and enhanced its internal control structure.

Example 4: Public Company Declination

DOJ and SEC declined to take enforcement action against a U.S. publicly held oil-and-gas services company for small bribes paid by a foreign subsidiary's customs agent. Factors taken into consideration included:

- The company's internal controls timely detected a potential bribe before a payment was made.
- When company management learned of the potential bribe, management immediately reported the issue to the company's General Counsel and Audit Committee and prevented the payment from occurring.
- Within weeks of learning of the attempted bribe, the company provided in-person FCPA training to employees of the subsidiary and undertook an extensive internal investigation to determine whether any of the company's subsidiaries in the same region had engaged in misconduct.
- The company self-reported the misconduct and the results of its internal investigation to DOJ and SEC.
- The company cooperated fully with investigations by DOJ and SEC.
- In addition to the immediate training at the relevant subsidiary, the company provided comprehensive FCPA training to all of its employees and conducted an extensive review of its anti-corruption compliance program.
- The company enhanced its internal controls and record-keeping policies and procedures, including requiring periodic internal audits of customs payments.
- As part of its remediation, the company directed that local lawyers rather than customs agents be used to handle its permits, with instructions that "no matter what, we don't pay bribes" — a policy that resulted in a longer and costlier permit procedure.

Example 5: Public Company Declination

DOJ and SEC declined to take enforcement action against a U.S. publicly held consumer products company in connection with its acquisition of a foreign company. Factors taken into consideration included:

- The company identified the potential improper payments to local government officials as part of its pre-acquisition due diligence.

- The company promptly developed a comprehensive plan to investigate, correct, and remediate any FCPA issues after acquisition.

- The company promptly self-reported the issues prior to acquisition and provided the results of its investigation to the government on a real-time basis.

- The acquiring company's existing internal controls and compliance program were robust.

- After the acquisition closed, the company implemented a comprehensive remedial plan, ensured that all improper payments stopped, provided extensive FCPA training to employees of the new subsidiary, and promptly incorporated the new subsidiary into the company's existing internal controls and compliance environment.

Example 6: Private Company Declination

In 2011, DOJ declined to take prosecutorial action against a privately held U.S. company and its foreign subsidiary. Factors taken into consideration included:

- The company voluntarily disclosed bribes paid to social security officials in a foreign country.

- The total amount of the bribes was small.

- When discovered, the corrupt practices were immediately terminated.

- The conduct was thoroughly investigated, and the results of the investigation were promptly provided to DOJ.

- All individuals involved were either terminated or disciplined. The company also terminated its relationship with its foreign law firm.

- The company instituted improved training and compliance programs commensurate with its size and risk exposure.

Assignments

- **Hypothetical:** You are the Chief Compliance Officer at your [Team's] Corporation. Draft a memorandum on DOJ release regarding declination from prosecution of Morgan Stanley.

- Your [Team's] Company is under DPA with the US Justice Department for FCPA violations, create a position paper for your [Team's] Company based on Morford agreement on how to be involved in choosing a monitor and working with a monitor.

- Review current NPA and DPA agreements with the US Justice Department and make an outline of what steps need to be added to the your [Team's] Company compliance program.

Chapter 13

Corporate Governance and the Role of the Board of Directors in Corporate Compliance

Introduction

Directors are charged with managing the affairs of a corporation. Directors typically delegate to corporate officers the day to day management of the corporation. *See In re Walt Disney Co. Derivative Litig.*, 907 A.2d 693, 761 n.490 (Del. Ch. 2005), *aff'd*, 906 A.2d 27 (Del. 2006). While often divorced from the day to day operations, directors' oversight responsibility dictates that they have in place systems and controls to monitor the corporation's compliance with applicable laws, rules, and regulations. This oversight responsibility is imposed by a variety of laws, regulations, and private guidelines. While historically the province of state law, federal law and regulations are playing an ever-increasing role in director responsibilities, as are private entities, such as the stock exchanges and rating agencies. The consequences for breaching these obligations can mean liability for the corporation and personal financial liability for the director. This chapter will explore the sources and the parameters of this oversight responsibility.

Summary of Fiduciary Duties

Directors owe a triad of fiduciary duties to the corporation and its shareholders: a duty of care, a duty of loyalty, and a duty of good faith. As a general proposition the duties of care, loyalty, and good faith that govern a director's conduct can be described as follows:

Duty of Care: The duty of care imposes the obligation of informed decision making. "The fiduciary duty of care requires that directors of a Delaware corporation 'use that amount of care which ordinarily careful and prudent [individuals] would use in similar circumstances,' and 'consider all material information reasonably available' in making business decisions, and that the deficiencies in the directors' process are actionable only if the directors' actions are grossly negligent." *In re Walt Disney Co. Derivative Litig.*, 907 A.2d 693, 749 (Del. Ch. 2005) (citation omitted), *aff'd*, 906 A.2d 27 (Del. 2006); *see also* N.Y. Bus. Corp. §717 (a)(1)–(3) ("A director shall perform his duties as a director, including his duties as a member of any committee of the board upon which he may serve, in good faith and with that degree of care which an ordinarily prudent person in a like position would use under similar circumstances. In performing his duties, a director shall be entitled to rely on information, opinions, reports or statements including financial statements and other financial data, in each case prepared or presented by: (1) one or more officers or employees of the corporation ... (2) counsel, public accountants or other persons as to matters which the director believes to be within such person's professional or expert competence, or (3) a committee of the board upon which he does not serve, duly designated in accordance with a provision of the certificate of incorporation or the bylaws, as to matters within its designated authority, which committee the director believes to merit confidence, so long as in so relying he shall be acting in good faith and with such degree of care, but he shall not be considered to be acting in good faith if he has knowledge concerning the matter in question that would cause such reliance to be unwarranted...."); Model Bus. Corp. Act § 8.30(b) ("The members of the board of directors or a committee of the board, when becoming informed in connection with their decision-making function or devoting attention to their oversight function, shall discharge their duties with the care that a person in a like position would reasonably believe appropriate under similar circumstances.").

Duty of Loyalty: "[T]he duty of loyalty mandates that the best interest of the corporation and its shareholders takes precedence over any interest possessed by a director, [or] officer ... and not shared by the stockholders generally." *Cede & Co. v. Technicolor, Inc.*, 634 A.2d 345, 361 (Del. 1993); *see also Foley v. D'Agostino*, 21 A.D.2d 60, 66–67 (1st Dep't 1964) ("'Officers and directors of a corporation owe [to it] their undivided and unqualified loyalty.... They should never be permitted to profit personally at the expense of the corporation. Nor must they allow their private interests to conflict with the corporate interests. These are elementary rules of equity and business morality....'" (citation omitted)). The classic example of a transaction where the duty of loyalty is implicated is when an officer or director engages in a transaction with the corporation. *See Aronson v. Lewis*, 473 A.2d 805, 812 (Del. 1984), *overruled on other grounds by Brehm v. Eisner*, 746 A.2d 244 (Del. 2000). The duty of loyalty is also implicated in other circumstances where the director or officer at issue does not receive a financial benefit, including instances developed more fully below where a director consciously disregards his duties of oversight. *Stone v. Ritter*, 911 A.2d 362, 369–70 (Del. 2006).

Good Faith: The duty of good faith is a "'subsidiary element[,]' i.e., a condition, 'of the fundamental duty of loyalty.'" *Id.* at 370 (quoting *Guttman v. Huang*, 823 A.2d 492, 506 n.34 (Del. Ch. 2003)) (alteration in original). Unlike a more traditional breach of duty of loyalty claim where a director puts his own interests ahead of the corporation, the duty of good faith encompasses those circumstances where the director fails to act in the corporation's best interests, but not necessarily for personal gain. The classic example is where "directors fail to act in the face of a known duty to act, thereby demonstrating a conscious disregard for their responsibilities," e.g., utterly failing to implement a compliance system or consciously failing to monitor its operations. *Id.*; *see also* Model Bus. Corp. Act § 8.31 cmt. at 8-233 (2013 Revision) ("[I]t has been stated that a lack of good faith is presented where a board 'lacked an actual intention to advance corporate welfare'... [']or is known to constitute a violation of applicable positive law.'" (quoting *Gagliardi v. TriFoods Int'l Inc.*, 683 A.2d 1049 (Del. Ch. 1996)). Conversely, the Delaware Supreme Court has identified at least two types of conduct that would constitute bad faith: (1) subjective bad faith, i.e., "fiduciary conduct motivated by an actual intent to do harm"; and (2) "intentional dereliction of duty, a conscious disregard for one's responsibilities." *In re Walt Disney Co. Derivative Litig.*, 906 A.2d 27, 64, 66 (Del. 2006).

Business Judgment Rule: No discussion of the duties of directors would be complete without reference to the business judgment rule—a "presum[ption] that 'in making a business decision the directors of a corporation acted on an informed basis, in good faith, and in the honest belief that the action taken was in the best interests of the company.'" *Walt Disney*, 906 A.2d at 52; *see also* Model Bus. Corp. Act § 8.31 cmt. at 8-232 (2013 Revision) ("[The business judgment rule] ... presumes that, absent self-dealing or other breach of the duty of loyalty, directors' decision-making satisfies the applicable legal requirements."). The business judgment rule reflects courts' deference to business decisions made by independent directors in good faith and on an informed basis. The focus in such an inquiry is the process employed, as opposed to the substance of the decision reached by the board. *In re Citigroup Inc. S'holder Derivative Litig.*, 964 A.2d 106, 124 (Del. Ch. 2009); *cf. Auerbach v. Bennett*, 393 N.E.2d 994, 1002 (N.Y. 1979). "Those presumptions can be rebutted if the plaintiff shows that the directors breached their fiduciary duty of care or of loyalty or acted in bad faith." *Walt Disney*, 906 A.2d at 52. Once the presumption is rebutted, "the burden then shifts to the director defendants to demonstrate that the challenged act or transaction was entirely fair to the corporation and its shareholders." *Id.*; *see also Wolf v. Rand*, 685 N.Y.S.2d 708, 711 (N.Y. App. Div. 1999) ("[S]ince the business judgment rule does not protect corporate officials who engage in fraud or self-dealing ... or corporate fiduciaries when they make decisions affected by inherent conflict of interest, the burden shifts to defendants to prove the fairness of the challenged acts[.]").

Notes and Comments

In certain circumstances that are not the subject of this chapter, specific applications of these duties are called for, such as under the corporate opportunity doctrine, *Broz v. Cellular Info. Sys.*, 673 A.2d 148, 155 (Del. 1996) (providing "guidelines to be considered by a reviewing court" when determining "whether or not a director has appropriated for himself something that in fairness should belong to the corporation" (internal quotation marks omitted)), the so-called *Unocal* standard, *Unocal Corp. v. Mesa Petroleum Co.*, 493 A.2d 946 (Del. 1985) (addressing the standard to be applied where a board adopts defensive measures to defeat a hostile takeover) or the *Revlon* principles, *Revlon, Inc. v. MacAndrews & Forbes Holdings, Inc.*, 506 A.2d 173 (Del. 1986) (addressing the standard to be applied where a sale or break-up of a company becomes inevitable).

The focus of this chapter will be on the duties of loyalty and good faith as they relate to the officers' and directors' obligation to ensure the corporation has in place systems and controls to monitor the corporation's compliance with applicable laws, rules, and regulations.

Relevant Authorities

The directors' and officers' oversight responsibility is imposed by a variety of laws, regulations, and guidelines. Historically directors' and officers' duties were dictated largely by state law. However, federal law and regulations are playing an ever-increasing role in director responsibilities, as are private sources, such as the stock exchanges and rating agencies.

State Law

The law of the state of incorporation typically governs the duties, responsibilities, and obligations of directors of corporations. *See McDermott, Inc. v. Lewis*, 531 A.2d 206, 215 (Del. 1987) ("The traditional conflicts rule developed by courts has been that internal corporate relationships are governed by the laws of the forum of incorporation."). Delaware law, because of its well-developed body of law regarding corporations and the duties of officers and directors, is often looked to for guidance by courts outside of Delaware.

- Del. Code Ann. tit. 8, § 141(a): "The business and affairs of every corporation organized under this chapter shall be managed by or under the direction of a board of directors...."

- N.Y. Bus. Corp. § 701: "[T]he business of a corporation shall be managed under the direction of its board of directors...."

- Model Bus. Corp. Act § 8.01(b): "All corporate powers shall be exercised by or under the authority of the board of directors of the corporation, and the business and affairs of the corporation shall be managed by or under the direction, and subject to the oversight, of its board of directors...."

Core Cases:

- *In re Caremark Int'l Inc. Derivative Litig.*, 698 A.2d 959, 970 (Del. Ch. 1996): "[A] director's obligation includes a duty to attempt in good faith to assure that a corporate information and reporting system, which the board concludes is adequate, exists, and that failure to do so under some circumstances may, in theory at least, render a director liable for losses caused by non-compliance with applicable legal standards."

- *Stone v. Ritter*, 911 A.2d 362, 370 (Del. 2006): "*Caremark* articulates the necessary conditions predicate for director oversight liability: (a) the directors utterly failed to implement any reporting or information system or controls; *or* (b) having implemented such a system or controls, consciously failed to monitor or oversee its operations thus disabling themselves from being informed of risks or problems requiring their attention."

Federal Law

While traditionally the province of state law, federal law is increasingly encroaching on corporate governance duties and obligations.

- Sarbanes-Oxley Act of 2002 § 301, 15 U.S.C. § 78j-1(m): mandating certain functions for audit committees of boards of directors, including requiring that an audit committee establish procedures for the receipt, retention and treatment of complaints regarding accounting and internal audit controls, as well as procedures for employees to submit confidential and anonymous submissions concerning questionable accounting and auditing matters.

- Sarbanes-Oxley Act of 2002 § 404, 15 U.S.C. § 7262(a): directing the SEC to prescribe rules requiring companies to "state the responsibility of management for establishing and maintaining an adequate internal control structure and procedures for financial reporting," as well as assess and annually attest to "the effectiveness of the internal control structure and procedures of the issuer for financial reporting."

- Dodd-Frank Wall Street Reform and Consumer Protection Act, 15 U.S.C. § 78j-3: outlining requirements for independent compensation committees.

- Sarbanes-Oxley Act of 2002, 15 U.S.C. § 7264: directing the SEC to prescribe rules requiring companies "to disclose whether or not" the company "has adopted a code of ethics," meaning "such standards as are reasonably necessary to promote," among other things, "compliance with applicable governmental rules and regulations."

- Investment Advisers Act of 1940, 15 U.S.C. § 80b-3(e)(6): subjecting investment advisers to liability for a failure to supervise.

- Standard Instructions for Filing Forms Under the Securities Act of 1993 and the Securities Act of 1934, 17 C.F.R. § 229.407(h): requiring the disclosure in a proxy statement of "the extent of the board's role in the risk oversight of the registrant, such as how the board administers its oversight function, and the effect that this has on the board's leadership structure."

- U.S. Sentencing Guidelines Manual §§ 8B2.1, 8C2.5(f) (2015): an effective compliance and ethics program designed to detect and prevent criminal misconduct may reduce a corporation's culpability score for the purposes of determining fines and penalties.

- U.S. Sentencing Guidelines Manual § 8C2.5(f)(3)(C) & cmt. (2015): Corporations may be given sentencing credit for an effective compliance and ethics program even though high-level personnel were involved in the offense if "(i) the individual or individuals with operational responsibility for the compliance and ethics program ... have direct reporting obligations to the governing authority or an appropriate subgroup thereof (e.g., an audit committee of the board of directors); (ii) the compliance and ethics program detected the offense before discovery outside the organization or before such discovery was reasonably likely; (iii) the organization promptly reported the offense to appropriate governmental authorities; and (iv) no individual with operational responsibility for the compliance and ethics program participated in, condoned, or was willfully ignorant of the offense."

- United States Attorneys' Manual, Principles of Federal Prosecution of Business, §§ 9-28.300, 9-28.800, http://www.justice.gov/usam/usam-9-28000-principles-federal-prosecution-business-organizations#9-28.300: "In evaluating compliance programs [in connection with an investigation or a determination of whether to pursue or accept a plea from a corporation], prosecutors may consider whether the corporation has established corporate governance mechanisms that can effectively detect and prevent misconduct. For example, do the corporation's directors exercise independent review over proposed corporate actions rather than unquestionably ratifying officers' recommendations; ... and have the directors established an information and reporting system in the organization reasonably designed to provide management and directors with timely and accurate information sufficient to allow them to reach an informed decision regarding the organization's compliance with the law." (citing *In re Caremark*, 698 A.2d at 698–70).

- Securities and Exchange Commission ("SEC") Division of Enforcement, Enforcement Manual, § 6.1.2, http://www.sec.gov/divisions/enforce/enforcement manual.pdf: The SEC "considers in determining whether, and to what extent, it grants leniency" whether the company engaged in "[s]elf-policing prior to the discovery of the misconduct, including establishing effective compliance procedures and an appropriate tone at the top."

- Dodd-Frank Wall Street Reform and Consumer Protection Act, 15 U.S.C. § 78n-1: say-on-pay provision providing shareholders a non-binding vote on executive compensation.

- Dodd-Frank Wall Street Reform and Consumer Protection Act, 15 U.S.C. § 78j-4: instituting additional three-year clawback against former and current executive officers upon the company's accounting restatement.

Other Authority

There are additional sources of obligations imposed on officers and directors of public companies.

- NYSE Listed Company Manual § 303A.10: "Listed companies must adopt and disclose a code of business conduct and ethics for directors, officers and employees, and promptly disclose any waivers of the code for directors or executive officers."

- NYSE Listed Company Manual § 303A.07(b)(i)(A): "The audit committee must have a written charter that addresses: (i) the committee's purpose—which, at minimum, must be to: (A) assist board oversight of (1) the integrity of the listed company's financial statements, (2) the listed company's compliance with legal and regulatory requirements, (3) the independent auditor's qualifications and independence, and (4) the performance of the listed company's internal audit function and independent auditors...."

- NASDAQ Listing R. 5610: "Each Company shall adopt a code of conduct applicable to all directors, officers and employees, which shall be publicly available. A code of conduct satisfying this rule must comply with the definition of a 'code of ethics,' set out in Section 406(c) of the Sarbanes-Oxley Act of 2002 ... and any regulations promulgated thereunder by the Commission.... In addition, the code must provide for an enforcement mechanism."

- FINRA Rules R. 3130(b): "Each member shall have its chief executive officer(s) (or equivalent officer(s)) certify annually ... that the member has in place processes to establish, maintain, review, test and modify written compliance policies and written supervisory procedures reasonably designed to achieve compliance with applicable FINRA rules, MSRB rules and federal securities laws and regulations, and that the chief executive officer(s) has conducted one or more meetings with the chief compliance officer(s) in the preceding 12 months to discuss such processes."

- Rating agency corporate governance assessments, which include a review of audit committee and risk oversight.

Duty to Monitor

In re Caremark Int'l Inc. Derivative Litigation

698 A.2d 959 (Del. Ch. 1996)

Allen, Chancellor

Pending is a motion pursuant to Chancery Rule 23.1 to approve as fair and reasonable a proposed settlement of a consolidated derivative action on behalf of Caremark International, Inc. ("Caremark"). The suit involves claims that the members of Caremark's board of directors (the "Board") breached their fiduciary duty of care to Caremark in connection with alleged violations by Caremark employees of federal and state laws and regulations applicable to health care providers. As a result of the alleged violations, Caremark was subject to an extensive four year investigation by the United States Department of Health and Human Services and the Department of Justice. In 1994 Caremark was charged in an indictment with multiple felonies. It thereafter entered into a number of agreements with the Department of Justice and others. Those agreements included a plea agreement in which Caremark pleaded guilty to a single felony of mail fraud and agreed to pay civil and criminal fines. Subsequently, Caremark agreed to make reimbursements to various private and public parties. In all, the payments that Caremark has been required to make total approximately $250 million.

This suit was filed in 1994, purporting to seek on behalf of the company recovery of these losses from the individual defendants who constitute the board of directors of Caremark. The parties now propose that it be settled and, after notice to Caremark shareholders, a hearing on the fairness of the proposal was held on August 16, 1996.

A motion of this type requires the court to assess the strengths and weaknesses of the claims asserted in light of the discovery record and to evaluate the fairness and adequacy of the consideration offered to the corporation in exchange for the release of all claims made or arising from the facts alleged. The ultimate issue then is whether the proposed settlement appears to be fair to the corporation and its absent shareholders. In this effort the court does not determine contested facts, but evaluates the claims and defenses on the discovery record to achieve a sense of the relative strengths of the parties' positions. Polk v. Good, Del. Supr., 507 A.2d 531, 536 (1986). In doing this, in most instances, the court is constrained by the absence of a truly adversarial process, since inevitably both sides support the settlement and legally assisted objectors are rare. Thus, the facts stated hereafter represent the court's effort to understand the context of the motion from the discovery record, but do not deserve the respect that judicial findings after trial are customarily accorded.

Legally, evaluation of the central claim made entails consideration of the legal standard governing a board of directors' obligation to supervise or monitor corporate performance. For the reasons set forth below I conclude, in light of the discovery record, that there is a very low probability that it would be determined that the directors of Caremark breached any duty to appropriately monitor and supervise the enterprise. Indeed the record tends to show an active consideration by Caremark management and its Board of the Caremark structures and programs that ultimately led to the company's indictment and to the large financial losses incurred in the settlement of those claims. It does not tend to show knowing or intentional violation of law. Neither the fact that the Board, although advised by lawyers and accountants, did not accurately predict the severe consequences to the company that would ultimately follow from the deployment by the company of the strategies and practices that ultimately led to this liability, nor the scale of the liability, gives rise to an inference of breach of any duty imposed by corporation law upon the directors of Caremark.

I. BACKGROUND

For these purposes I regard the following facts, suggested by the discovery record, as material. Caremark, a Delaware corporation with its headquarters in Northbrook, Illinois, was created in November 1992 when it was spun-off from Baxter International, Inc. ("Baxter") and became a publicly held company listed on the New York Stock Exchange. The business practices that created the problem pre-dated the spin-off. During the relevant period Caremark was involved in two main health care business segments, providing patient care and managed care services. As part of its patient care business, which accounted for the majority of Caremark's revenues, Caremark provided alternative site health care services, including infusion therapy, growth hormone therapy, HIV/AIDS-related treatments and hemophilia therapy. Caremark's managed care services included prescription drug programs and the operation of multi-specialty group practices.

A. Events Prior to the Government Investigation

A substantial part of the revenues generated by Caremark's businesses is derived from third party payments, insurers, and Medicare and Medicaid reimbursement programs. The latter source of payments are subject to the terms of the Anti-Referral Payments Law ("ARPL") which prohibits health care providers from paying any form of remuneration to induce the referral of Medicare or Medicaid patients. From its inception, Caremark entered into a variety of agreements with hospitals, physicians, and health care providers for advice and services, as well as distribution agreements with drug manufacturers, as had its predecessor prior to 1992. Specifically, Caremark did have a practice of entering into contracts for services (e.g., consultation agreements and research grants) with physicians at least some of whom prescribed or recommended services or products that Caremark provided to Medicare recipients and other patients. Such contracts were not prohibited by the ARPL but they obviously raised a possibility of unlawful "kickbacks."

As early as 1989, Caremark's predecessor issued an internal "Guide to Contractual Relationships" ("Guide") to govern its employees in entering into contracts with physicians and hospitals. The Guide tended to be reviewed annually by lawyers and updated. Each version of the Guide stated as Caremark's and its predecessor's policy that no payments would be made in exchange for or to induce patient referrals. But what one might deem a prohibited quid pro quo was not always clear. Due to a scarcity of court decisions interpreting the ARPL, however, Caremark repeatedly publicly stated that there was uncertainty concerning Caremark's interpretation of the law.

To clarify the scope of the ARPL, the United States Department of Health and Human Services ("HHS") issued "safe harbor" regulations in July 1991 stating conditions under which financial relationships between health care service providers and patient referral sources, such as physicians, would not violate the ARPL. Caremark contends that the narrowly drawn regulations gave limited guidance as to the legality of many of the agreements used by Caremark that did not fall within the safe-harbor. Caremark's predecessor, however, amended many of its standard forms of agreement with health care providers and revised the Guide in an apparent attempt to comply with the new regulations.

B. Government Investigation and Related Litigation

In August 1991, the HHS Office of the Inspector General ("OIG") initiated an investigation of Caremark's predecessor. Caremark's predecessor was served with a subpoena requiring the production of documents, including contracts between Caremark's predecessor and physicians (Quality Service Agreements ("QSAs")). Under the QSAs, Caremark's predecessor appears to have paid physicians fees for monitoring patients under Caremark's predecessor's care, including Medicare and Medicaid recipients. Sometimes apparently those monitoring patients were referring physicians, which raised ARPL concerns.

In March 1992, the Department of Justice ("DOJ") joined the OIG investigation and separate investigations were commenced by several additional federal and state agencies.

C. Caremark's Response to the Investigation

During the relevant period, Caremark had approximately 7,000 employees and ninety branch operations. It had a decentralized management structure. By May 1991, however, Caremark asserts that it had begun making attempts to centralize its management structure in order to increase supervision over its branch operations.

The first action taken by management, as a result of the initiation of the OIG investigation, was an announcement that as of October 1, 1991, Caremark's predecessor would no longer pay management fees to physicians for services to Medicare and Medicaid patients. Despite this decision, Caremark asserts that its management, pursuant to advice, did not believe that such payments were illegal under the existing laws and regulations.

During this period, Caremark's Board took several additional steps consistent with an effort to assure compliance with company policies concerning the ARPL and the contractual forms in the Guide. In April 1992, Caremark published a fourth revised version of its Guide apparently designed to assure that its agreements either complied with the ARPL and regulations or excluded Medicare and Medicaid patients altogether. In addition, in September 1992, Caremark instituted a policy requiring its regional officers, Zone Presidents, to approve each contractual relationship entered into by Caremark with a physician.

Although there is evidence that inside and outside counsel had advised Caremark's directors that their contracts were in accord with the law, Caremark recognized that some uncertainty respecting the correct interpretation of the law existed. In its 1992 annual report, Caremark disclosed the ongoing government investigations, acknowledged that if penalties were imposed on the company they could have a material adverse effect on Caremark's business, and stated that no assurance could be given that its interpretation of the ARPL would prevail if challenged.

Throughout the period of the government investigations, Caremark had an internal audit plan designed to assure compliance with business and ethics policies. In addition, Caremark employed Price Waterhouse as its outside auditor. On February 8, 1993, the Ethics Committee of Caremark's Board received and reviewed an outside auditors report by Price Waterhouse which concluded that there were no material weaknesses in Caremark's control structure. Despite the positive findings of Price Waterhouse, however, on April 20, 1993, the Audit & Ethics Committee adopted a new internal audit charter requiring a comprehensive review of compliance policies and the compilation of an employee ethics handbook concerning such policies.

The Board appears to have been informed about this project and other efforts to assure compliance with the law. For example, Caremark's management reported to the Board that Caremark's sales force was receiving an ongoing education regarding the ARPL and the proper use of Caremark's form contracts which had been approved by in-house counsel. On July 27, 1993, the new ethics manual, expressly prohibiting payments in exchange for referrals and requiring employees to report all illegal conduct to a toll free confidential ethics hotline, was approved and allegedly disseminated. The record suggests that Caremark continued these policies in subsequent years, causing employees to be given revised versions of the ethics manual and requiring them to participate in training sessions concerning compliance with the law.

During 1993, Caremark took several additional steps which appear to have been aimed at increasing management supervision. These steps included new policies requiring local branch managers to secure home office approval for all disbursements under agreements with health care providers and to certify compliance with the ethics program. In addition, the chief financial officer was appointed to serve as Caremark's compliance officer. In 1994, a fifth revised Guide was published.

D. Federal Indictments Against Caremark and Officers

On August 4, 1994, a federal grand jury in Minnesota issued a 47 page indictment charging Caremark, two of its officers (not the firm's chief officer), an individual who had been a sales employee of Genentech, Inc., and David R. Brown, a physician practicing in Minneapolis, with violating the ARPL over a lengthy period. According to the indictment, over $1.1 million had been paid to Brown to induce him to distribute Protropin, a human growth hormone drug marketed by Caremark. The substantial payments involved started, according to the allegations of the indictment, in 1986 and continued through 1993. Some payments were "in the guise of research grants," Ind. P20, and others were "consulting agreements," Ind. P19. The indictment charged, for example, that Dr. Brown performed virtually none of the consulting functions described in his 1991 agreement with Caremark, but was nevertheless neither required to return the money he had received nor precluded from receiving future funding from Caremark. In addition the indictment charged that Brown received from Caremark payments of staff and office expenses, including telephone answering services and fax rental expenses.

In reaction to the Minnesota Indictment and the subsequent filing of this and other derivative actions in 1994, the Board met and was informed by management that the investigation had resulted in an indictment; Caremark denied any wrongdoing relating to the indictment and believed that the OIG investigation would have a favorable outcome. Management reiterated the grounds for its view that the contracts were in compliance with law.

Subsequently, five stockholder derivative actions were filed in this court and consolidated into this action. The original complaint, dated August 5, 1994, alleged, in relevant part, that Caremark's directors breached their duty of care by failing adequately to supervise the conduct of Caremark employees, or institute corrective measures, thereby exposing Caremark to fines and liability.

On September 21, 1994, a federal grand jury in Columbus, Ohio issued another indictment alleging that an Ohio physician had defrauded the Medicare program by requesting and receiving $134,600 in exchange for referrals of patients whose medical

costs were in part reimbursed by Medicare in violation of the ARPL. Although uniden-
tified at that time, Caremark was the health care provider who allegedly made such
payments. The indictment also charged that the physician, Elliot Neufeld, D.O., was
provided with the services of a registered nurse to work in his office at the expense
of the infusion company, in addition to free office equipment.

An October 28, 1994 amended complaint in this action added allegations concerning the Ohio indictment as well as new allegations of over billing and inappropriate
referral payments in connection with an action brought in Atlanta, Booth v. Rankin.
Following a newspaper article report that federal investigators were expanding their
inquiry to look at Caremark's referral practices in Michigan as well as allegations of
fraudulent billing of insurers, a second amended complaint was filed in this action.
The third, and final, amended complaint was filed on April 11, 1995, adding allegations that the federal indictments had caused Caremark to incur significant legal fees
and forced it to sell its home infusion business at a loss.

After each complaint was filed, defendants filed a motion to dismiss. According
to defendants if a settlement had not been reached in this action, the case would have
been dismissed on two grounds. First, they contend that the complaints fail to allege
particularized facts sufficient to excuse the demand requirement under Delaware
Chancery Court Rule 23.1. Second, defendants assert that plaintiffs had failed to state
a cause of action due to the fact that Caremark's charter eliminates directors' personal
liability for money damages, to the extent permitted by law.

Settlement Negotiations

In September, following the announcement of the Ohio indictment, Caremark
publicly announced that as of January 1, 1995, it would terminate all remaining financial relationships with physicians in its home infusion, hemophilia, and growth
hormone lines of business. In addition, Caremark asserts that it extended its restrictive policies to all of its contractual relationships with physicians, rather than
just those involving Medicare and Medicaid patients, and terminated its research
grant program which had always involved some recipients who referred patients to
Caremark.

Caremark began settlement negotiations with federal and state government entities
in May 1995. In return for a guilty plea to a single count of mail fraud by the corporation, the payment of a criminal fine, the payment of substantial civil damages,
and cooperation with further federal investigations on matters relating to the OIG
investigation, the government entities agreed to negotiate a settlement that would
permit Caremark to continue participating in Medicare and Medicaid programs. On
June 15, 1995, the Board approved a settlement ("Government Settlement Agreement")
with the DOJ, OIG, U.S. Veterans Administration, U.S. Federal Employee Health
Benefits Program, federal Civilian Health and Medical Program of the Uniformed
Services, and related state agencies in all fifty states and the District of Columbia.

No senior officers or directors were charged with wrongdoing in the Government
Settlement Agreement or in any of the prior indictments. In fact, as part of the sen-

tencing in the Ohio action on June 19, 1995, the United States stipulated that no senior executive of Caremark participated in, condoned, or was willfully ignorant of wrongdoing in connection with the home infusion business practices.

The federal settlement included certain provisions in a "Corporate Integrity Agreement" designed to enhance future compliance with law. The parties have not discussed this agreement, except to say that the negotiated provisions of the settlement of this claim are not redundant of those in that agreement.

Settlement negotiations between the parties in this action commenced in May 1995 as well, based upon a letter proposal of the plaintiffs, dated May 16, 1995. These negotiations resulted in a memorandum of understanding ("MOU"), dated June 7, 1995, and the execution of the Stipulation and Agreement of Compromise and Settlement on June 28, 1995, which is the subject of this action. The MOU, approved by the Board on June 15, 1995, required the Board to adopt several resolutions, discussed below, and to create a new compliance committee. The Compliance and Ethics Committee has been reporting to the Board in accord with its newly specified duties.

After negotiating these settlements, Caremark learned in December 1995 that several private insurance company payors ("Private Payors") believed that Caremark was liable for damages to them for allegedly improper business practices related to those at issue in the OIG investigation. As a result of intensive negotiations with the Private Payors and the Board's extensive consideration of the alternatives for dealing with such claims, the Board approved a $98.5 million settlement agreement with the Private Payors on March 18, 1996. In its public disclosure statement, Caremark asserted that the settlement did not involve current business practices and contained an express denial of any wrongdoing by Caremark. After further discovery in this action, the plaintiffs decided to continue seeking approval of the proposed settlement agreement.

F. The Proposed Settlement of this Litigation

In relevant part the terms upon which these claims asserted are proposed to be settled are as follows:

1. That Caremark, undertakes that it and its employees, and agents not pay any form of compensation to a third party in exchange for the referral of a patient to a Caremark facility or service or the prescription of drugs marketed or distributed by Caremark for which reimbursement may be sought from Medicare, Medicaid, or a similar state reimbursement program;

2. That Caremark, undertakes for itself and its employees, and agents not to pay to or split fees with physicians, joint ventures, any business combination in which Caremark maintains a direct financial interest, or other health care providers with whom Caremark has a financial relationship or interest, in exchange for the referral of a patient to a Caremark facility or service or the prescription of drugs marketed or distributed by Caremark for which reimbursement may be sought from Medicare, Medicaid, or a similar state reimbursement program;

3. That the full Board shall discuss all relevant material changes in government health care regulations and their effect on relationships with health care providers on a semi-annual basis;

4. That Caremark's officers will remove all personnel from health care facilities or hospitals who have been placed in such facility for the purpose of providing remuneration in exchange for a patient referral for which reimbursement may be sought from Medicare, Medicaid, or a similar state reimbursement program;

5. That every patient will receive written disclosure of any financial relationship between Caremark and the health care professional or provider who made the referral;

6. That the Board will establish a Compliance and Ethics Committee of four directors, two of which will be non-management directors, to meet at least four times a year to effectuate these policies and monitor business segment compliance with the ARPL, and to report to the Board semi-annually concerning compliance by each business segment; and

7. That corporate officers responsible for business segments shall serve as compliance officers who must report semi-annually to the Compliance and Ethics Committee and, with the assistance of outside counsel, review existing contracts and get advanced approval of any new contract forms.

II. LEGAL PRINCIPLES

A. Principles Governing Settlements of Derivative Claims

As noted at the outset of this opinion, this Court is now required to exercise an informed judgment whether the proposed settlement is fair and reasonable in the light of all relevant factors. Polk v. Good, 507 A.2d 531 (1986). On an application of this kind, this Court attempts to protect the best interests of the corporation and its absent shareholders all of whom will be barred from future litigation on these claims if the settlement is approved. The parties proposing the settlement bear the burden of persuading the court that it is in fact fair and reasonable. Fins v. Pearlman, 424 A.2d 305 (1980).

B. Directors' Duties To Monitor Corporate Operations

The complaint charges the director defendants with breach of their duty of attention or care in connection with the on-going operation of the corporation's business. The claim is that the directors allowed a situation to develop and continue which exposed the corporation to enormous legal liability and that in so doing they violated a duty to be active monitors of corporate performance. The complaint thus does not charge either director self-dealing or the more difficult loyalty-type problems arising from cases of suspect director motivation, such as entrenchment or sale of control contexts. The theory here advanced is possibly the most difficult theory in corporation law upon which a plaintiff might hope to win a judgment. The good policy reasons why it is so difficult to charge directors with responsibility for corporate losses for an alleged breach of care, where there is no conflict of interest or no facts suggesting suspect motivation involved, were recently described in Gagliardi v. TriFoods Int'l Inc., Del.Ch., 683 A.2d 1049 (1996).

1. Potential liability for directoral decisions

Director liability for a breach of the duty to exercise appropriate attention may, in theory, arise in two distinct contexts. First, such liability may be said to follow from a board decision that results in a loss because that decision was ill advised or "negligent." Second, liability to the corporation for a loss may be said to arise from an unconsidered failure of the board to act in circumstances in which due attention would, arguably, have prevented the loss. See generally Veasey & Seitz, The Business Judgment Rule in the Revised Model Act, 63 TEXAS L. REV. 1483 (1985). The first class of cases will typically be subject to review under the director-protective business judgment rule, assuming the decision made was the product of a process that was either deliberately considered in good faith or was otherwise rational. See Aronson v. Lewis, 473 A.2d 805 (1984); Gagliardi v. TriFoods Int'l Inc., Del.Ch. 683 A.2d 1049 (1996). What should be understood, but may not widely be understood by courts or commentators who are not often required to face such questions, is that compliance with a director's duty of care can never appropriately be judicially determined by reference to the content of the board decision that leads to a corporate loss, apart from consideration of the good faith or rationality of the process employed. That is, whether a judge or jury considering the matter after the fact, believes a decision substantively wrong, or degrees of wrong extending through "stupid" to "egregious" or "irrational," provides no ground for director liability, so long as the court determines that the process employed was either rational or employed in a good faith effort to advance corporate interests. To employ a different rule—one that permitted an "objective" evaluation of the decision—would expose directors to substantive second guessing by ill-equipped judges or juries, which would, in the long-run, be injurious to investor interests. Thus, the business judgment rule is process oriented and informed by a deep respect for all good faith board decisions.

Indeed, one wonders on what moral basis might shareholders attack a good faith business decision of a director as "unreasonable" or "irrational." Where a director in fact exercises a good faith effort to be informed and to exercise appropriate judgment, he or she should be deemed to satisfy fully the duty of attention. If the shareholders thought themselves entitled to some other quality of judgment than such a director produces in the good faith exercise of the powers of office, then the shareholders should have elected other directors. Judge Learned Hand made the point rather better than can I. In speaking of the passive director defendant Mr. Andrews in Barnes v. Andrews, Judge Hand said:

> True, he was not very suited by experience for the job he had undertaken, but I cannot hold him on that account. After all it is the same corporation that chose him that now seeks to charge him.... Directors are not specialists like lawyers or doctors.... They are the general advisors of the business and if they faithfully give such ability as they have to their charge, it would not be lawful to hold them liable. Must a director guarantee that his judgment is good? Can a shareholder call him to account for deficiencies that their votes assured him did not disqualify him for his office? While he may not

have been the Cromwell for that Civil War, Andrews did not engage to play any such role.

In this formulation Learned Hand correctly identifies, in my opinion, the core element of any corporate law duty of care inquiry: whether there was good faith effort to be informed and exercise judgment.

2. Liability for failure to monitor

The second class of cases in which director liability for inattention is theoretically possible entail circumstances in which a loss eventuates not from a decision but, from unconsidered inaction. Most of the decisions that a corporation, acting through its human agents, makes are, of course, not the subject of director attention. Legally, the board itself will be required only to authorize the most significant corporate acts or transactions: mergers, changes in capital structure, fundamental changes in business, appointment and compensation of the CEO, etc. As the facts of this case graphically demonstrate, ordinary business decisions that are made by officers and employees deeper in the interior of the organization can, however, vitally affect the welfare of the corporation and its ability to achieve its various strategic and financial goals. If this case did not prove the point itself, recent business history would. Recall for example the displacement of senior management and much of the board of Salomon, Inc.; the replacement of senior management of Kidder, Peabody following the discovery of large trading losses resulting from phantom trades by a highly compensated trader; or the extensive financial loss and reputational injury suffered by Prudential Insurance as a result its junior officers misrepresentations in connection with the distribution of limited partnership interests. Financial and organizational disasters such as these raise the question, what is the board's responsibility with respect to the organization and monitoring of the enterprise to assure that the corporation functions within the law to achieve its purposes?

Modernly this question has been given special importance by an increasing tendency, especially under federal law, to employ the criminal law to assure corporate compliance with external legal requirements, including environmental, financial, employee and product safety as well as assorted other health and safety regulations. In 1991, pursuant to the Sentencing Reform Act of 1984, the United States Sentencing Commission adopted Organizational Sentencing Guidelines which impact importantly on the prospective effect these criminal sanctions might have on business corporations. The Guidelines set forth a uniform sentencing structure for organizations to be sentenced for violation of federal criminal statutes and provide for penalties that equal or often massively exceed those previously imposed on corporations. The Guidelines offer powerful incentives for corporations today to have in place compliance programs to detect violations of law, promptly to report violations to appropriate public officials when discovered, and to take prompt, voluntary remedial efforts.

In 1963, the Delaware Supreme Court in Graham v. Allis-Chalmers Mfg. Co., addressed the question of potential liability of board members for losses experienced by the corporation as a result of the corporation having violated the anti-trust laws of the United States. There was no claim in that case that the directors knew about the behavior of subordinate employees of the corporation that had resulted in the liability. Rather, as in this case, the claim asserted was that the directors ought to have known of it and if they had known they would have been under a duty to bring the corporation into compliance with the law and thus save the corporation from the loss. The Delaware Supreme Court concluded that, under the facts as they appeared, there was no basis to find that the directors had breached a duty to be informed of the ongoing operations of the firm. In notably colorful terms, the court stated that "absent cause for suspicion there is no duty upon the directors to install and operate a corporate system of espionage to ferret out wrongdoing which they have no reason to suspect exists." The Court found that there were no grounds for suspicion in that case and, thus, concluded that the directors were blamelessly unaware of the conduct leading to the corporate liability.

How does one generalize this holding today? Can it be said today that, absent some ground giving rise to suspicion of violation of law, that corporate directors have no duty to assure that a corporate information gathering and reporting systems exists which represents a good faith attempt to provide senior management and the Board with information respecting material acts, events or conditions within the corporation, including compliance with applicable statutes and regulations? I certainly do not believe so. I doubt that such a broad generalization of the Graham holding would have been accepted by the Supreme Court in 1963. The case can be more narrowly interpreted as standing for the proposition that, absent grounds to suspect deception, neither corporate boards nor senior officers can be charged with wrongdoing simply for assuming the integrity of employees and the honesty of their dealings on the company's behalf. See 188 A.2d at 130–31.

A broader interpretation of Graham v. Allis Chalmers—that it means that a corporate board has no responsibility to assure that appropriate information and reporting systems are established by management—would not, in any event, be accepted by the Delaware Supreme Court in 1996, in my opinion. In stating the basis for this view, I start with the recognition that in recent years the Delaware Supreme Court has made it clear—especially in its jurisprudence concerning takeovers, from Smith v. Van Gorkom through QVC v. Paramount Communications—the seriousness with which the corporation law views the role of the corporate board. Secondly, I note the elementary fact that relevant and timely information is an essential predicate for satisfaction of the board's supervisory and monitoring role under Section 141 of the Delaware General Corporation Law. Thirdly, I note the potential impact of the federal organizational sentencing guidelines on any business organization. Any rational person attempting in good faith to meet an organizational governance responsibility would be bound to take into account this development and the enhanced penalties and the opportunities for reduced sanctions that it offers.

In light of these developments, it would, in my opinion, be a mistake to conclude that our Supreme Court's statement in Graham concerning "espionage" means that corporate boards may satisfy their obligation to be reasonably informed concerning the corporation, without assuring themselves that information and reporting systems exist in the organization that are reasonably designed to provide to senior management and to the board itself timely, accurate information sufficient to allow management and the board, each within its scope, to reach informed judgments concerning both the corporation's compliance with law and its business performance.

Obviously the level of detail that is appropriate for such an information system is a question of business judgment. And obviously too, no rationally designed information and reporting system will remove the possibility that the corporation will violate laws or regulations, or that senior officers or directors may nevertheless sometimes be misled or otherwise fail reasonably to detect acts material to the corporation's compliance with the law. But it is important that the board exercise a good faith judgment that the corporation's information and reporting system is in concept and design adequate to assure the board that appropriate information will come to its attention in a timely manner as a matter of ordinary operations, so that it may satisfy its responsibility.

Thus, I am of the view that a director's obligation includes a duty to attempt in good faith to assure that a corporate information and reporting system, which the board concludes is adequate, exists, and that failure to do so under some circumstances may, in theory at least, render a director liable for losses caused by non-compliance with applicable legal standards. I now turn to an analysis of the claims asserted with this concept of the directors duty of care, as a duty satisfied in part by assurance of adequate information flows to the board, in mind.

III ANALYSIS OF THIRD AMENDED COMPLAINT AND SETTLEMENT

A. The Claims

On balance, after reviewing an extensive record in this case, including numerous documents and three depositions, I conclude that this settlement is fair and reasonable. In light of the fact that the Caremark Board already has a functioning committee charged with overseeing corporate compliance, the changes in corporate practice that are presented as consideration for the settlement do not impress one as very significant. Nonetheless, that consideration appears fully adequate to support dismissal of the derivative claims of director fault asserted, because those claims find no substantial evidentiary support in the record and quite likely were susceptible to a motion to dismiss in all events.

In order to Show that the Caremark directors breached their duty of care by failing adequately to control Caremark's employees, plaintiffs would have to show either (1) that the directors knew or (2) should have known that violations of law were occurring and, in either event, (3) that the directors took no steps in a good faith effort to prevent or remedy that situation, and (4) that such failure proximately resulted in the losses complained of, although under Cede & Co. v. Technicolor, Inc., 636 A.2d 956 (1994) this last element may be thought to constitute an affirmative defense.

1. Knowing violation for statute: Concerning the possibility that the Caremark directors knew of violations of law, none of the documents submitted for review, nor any of the deposition transcripts appear to provide evidence of it. Certainly the Board

understood that the company had entered into a variety of contracts with physicians, researchers, and health care providers and it was understood that some of these contracts were with persons who had prescribed treatments that Caremark participated in providing. The board was informed that the company's reimbursement for patient care was frequently from government funded sources and that such services were subject to the ARPL. But the Board appears to have been informed by experts that the company's practices while contestable, were lawful. There is no evidence that reliance on such reports was not reasonable. Thus, this case presents no occasion to apply a principle to the effect that knowingly causing the corporation to violate a criminal statute constitutes a breach of a director's fiduciary duty. See Roth v. Robertson, N.Y. Sup. Ct., 64 Misc. 343, 118 N.Y.S. 351 (1909); Miller v. American Tel. & Tel Co., 507 F.2d 759 (3rd Cir. 1974). It is not clear that the Board knew the detail found, for example, in the indictments arising from the Company's payments. But, of course, the duty to act in good faith to be informed cannot be thought to require directors to possess detailed information about all aspects of the operation of the enterprise. Such a requirement would simple be inconsistent with the scale and scope of efficient organization size in this technological age.

2. Failure to monitor: Since it does appears that the Board was to some extent unaware of the activities that led to liability, I turn to a consideration of the other potential avenue to director liability that the pleadings take: director inattention or "negligence." Generally where a claim of directorial liability for corporate loss is predicated upon ignorance of liability creating activities within the corporation, as in Graham or in this case, in my opinion only a sustained or systematic failure of the board to exercise oversight — such as an utter failure to attempt to assure a reasonable information and reporting system exits — will establish the lack of good faith that is a necessary condition to liability. Such a test of liability — lack of good faith as evidenced by sustained or systematic failure of a director to exercise reasonable oversight — is quite high. But, a demanding test of liability in the oversight context is probably beneficial to corporate shareholders as a class, as it is in the board decision context, since it makes board service by qualified persons more likely, while continuing to act as a stimulus to good faith performance of duty by such directors.

Here the record supplies essentially no evidence that the director defendants were guilty of a sustained failure to exercise their oversight function. To the contrary, insofar as I am able to tell on this record, the corporation's information systems appear to have represented a good faith attempt to be informed of relevant facts. If the directors did not know the specifics of the activities that lead to the indictments, they cannot be faulted.

The liability that eventuated in this instance was huge. But the fact that it resulted from a violation of criminal law alone does not create a breach of fiduciary duty by directors. The record at this stage does not support the conclusion that the defendants either lacked good faith in the exercise of their monitoring responsibilities or conscientiously permitted a known violation of law by the corporation to occur. The claims asserted against them must be viewed at this stage as extremely weak.

B. The Consideration For Release of Claim

The proposed settlement provides very modest benefits. Under the settlement agreement, plaintiffs have been given express assurances that Caremark will have a more centralized, active supervisory system in the future. Specifically, the settlement mandates duties to be performed by the newly named Compliance and Ethics Committee on an ongoing basis and increases the responsibility for monitoring compliance with the law at the lower levels of management. In adopting the resolutions required under the settlement, Caremark has further clarified its policies concerning the prohibition of providing remuneration for referrals. These appear to be positive consequences of the settlement of the claims brought by the plaintiffs, even if they are not highly significant. Nonetheless, given the weakness of the plaintiffs' claims the proposed settlement appears to be an adequate, reasonable, and beneficial outcome for all of the parties. Thus, the proposed settlement will be approved.

Notes and Comments

Directors and the boards on which they serve have an obligation to ensure that the company has information and reporting systems in place to monitor compliance with applicable laws. *In re Caremark Int'l Inc. Derivative Litig.*, 698 A.2d 959, 970 (Del. Ch. 1996). The duty to monitor is also referred to as the duty to supervise or the duty of oversight.

The Delaware Court of Chancery, in *Caremark*, was the first court to articulate and expand upon a director's and board's duty of oversight. In that case, as part of its business, Caremark International, Inc. ("Caremark"), a health service provider, entered into agreements and contracts with doctors, for example, in exchange for services or counsel. These agreements were regulated by law, principally because of the prohibition against allowing a company like Caremark from paying remuneration to induce doctors to refer Medicare and Medicaid patients to Caremark. *Id.* at 961–962. But because physicians that had contracted with Caremark had also been issuing such referrals, federal and state agencies began investigating the company. *Id.* at 962. Eventually, the company was indicted and pled guilty to mail fraud, in part, as a result of significant payments made to a doctor to induce him to distribute a drug marketed by Caremark. *Id.* at 964–65. Shortly thereafter, several shareholder derivative complaints were filed against the company alleging that the Caremark directors had breached their fiduciary duty by failing to oversee Caremark employees or institute remedial action, and that such failure had resulted in the government investigations, and the penalties and exposure faced by the company. *Id.* at 964. Subsequently, the parties reached a settlement and moved the court for approval.

In connection with its review of the settlement, the court was required to evaluate the strength of the derivative plaintiff's claims, including the allegation that the directors had failed to monitor Caremark's operations, i.e., liability premised on "unconsidered inaction," not a board decision. The court explained that the duty to monitor requires the board "[to] assur[e itself] that information and reporting systems exist in the organization that are reasonably designed to provide to senior management and to the board itself timely, accurate information sufficient to allow management and the board, each within its scope, to reach informed judgments concerning both the corporation's compliance with law and its business performance." *Id.* at 970.

The court then established the standard for determining liability for a board's failure to monitor the company or its business, officers, or employees: "[O]nly a sustained or systematic failure of the board to exercise oversight — such as an utter failure to attempt to assure a reasonable information and reporting system exists — will establish the lack of good faith that is a necessary condition to liability." *Id.* at 971. The court recognized that this test was a high standard but reasoned that such a demanding threshold was necessary to continue to encourage board service. *Id.*

Stone v. Ritter

In *Stone v. Ritter*, 911 A.2d 362 (Del. 2006), the Delaware Supreme Court approved of the oversight liability standard articulated in *Caremark* and clarified how the important concepts of good faith and the duty of loyalty relate to *Caremark* claims. *Id.* at 369–70. The court held that "*Caremark* articulates the necessary conditions predicate for director oversight liability: (a) the directors utterly failed to implement any reporting or information system or controls; *or* (b) having implemented such a system or controls, consciously failed to monitor or oversee its operations thus disabling themselves from being informed of risks or problems requiring their attention." *Id.* at 370. In both cases liability is predicated on "a showing that the directors knew that they were not discharging their fiduciary obligations." *Id.*

In *Stone*, the court clarified that *Caremark* or "oversight" liability is characterized by a lack of good faith. The court further explained that the "the obligation to act in good faith does not establish an independent fiduciary duty that stands on the same footing as the duties of care and loyalty." *Stone*, 911 A.2d at 370. Thus, a failure to act in good faith indirectly subjects a director to liability:

> The purpose of [this] formulation is to communicate that a failure to act in good faith is not conduct that results, *ipso facto*, in the direct imposition of fiduciary liability. The failure to act in good faith may result in liability because the requirement to act in good faith "is a subsidiary element[,]" i.e., a condition, "of the fundamental duty of loyalty." It follows that because a showing of bad faith conduct ... is essential to establish director oversight liability, the fiduciary duty violated by that conduct is the duty of loyalty.

Id. at 369–70 (second alteration in original) (quoting *Guttman v. Huang*, 823 A.2d 492, 506 n.34 (Del. Ch. 2003)).

The court reiterated that a *Caremark* violation requires a lack of good faith on behalf of the director or officer. Thus, it summarized the prime examples of conduct recognized by the Delaware courts that could establish such bad faith:

- "[W]here the fiduciary intentionally acts with a purpose other than that of advancing the best interests of the corporation";

- "[W]here the fiduciary acts with the intent to violate applicable positive law"; or

- "[W]here the fiduciary intentionally fails to act in the face of a known duty to act, demonstrating a conscious disregard for his duties."

Id. at 369. The last instance represents the lack of good faith necessary to subject a director to liability for a failure to supervise under *Caremark. Id.*

The Model Business Corporation Act

The duty to monitor is included within the oversight responsibilities listed by the Model Business Corporation Act ("MBCA") for boards of public companies. Model Bus. Corp. Act § 8.01(c). Those responsibilities include attention to "(1) business performance and plans; (2) major risks to which the corporation is or may be exposed; (3) the performance and compensation of senior officers; (4) policies and practices to foster the corporation's compliance with law and ethical conduct; (5) preparation of the corporation's financial statements; (6) the effectiveness of the corporation's internal controls; (7) arrangements for providing adequate and timely information to directors; (8) the composition of the board and its committees, taking into account the important role of independent directors." *Id.* The MBCA's Official Comment, citing *Caremark*, explains that "subsection (c)(7) reflects that the board of directors should devote attention to whether the corporation has information and reporting systems in place to provide directors with appropriate information in a timely manner in order to permit them to discharge their responsibilities." *Id.* § 8.01 cmt. at 8-5-6 (2013 Revision).

In addition to detailing particular areas which should be monitored by the boards of public companies, the MBCA provides that directors may be liable to the company or its shareholders if they fail to comply with their *Caremark*-type duty:

(a) A director shall not be liable to the corporation or its shareholders for any decision to take or not to take action, or any failure to take any action, as a director, unless the party asserting liability in a proceeding establishes that:

. . .

(2) the challenged conduct consisted or was the result of:

. . .

(iv) a sustained failure of the director to devote attention to ongoing oversight of the business and affairs of the corporation, or a failure to devote timely attention, by making (or causing to be made) appropriate inquiry, when particular facts and circumstances of significant concern materialize that would alert a reasonably attentive director to the need therefore[.]

Id. § 8.31.

Conduct Breaching the Duty To Monitor

As discussed further below, Delaware courts applying *Caremark* have found that plaintiffs adequately alleged breaches of the duty to monitor where egregious behavior by directors evidenced their knowledge of inadequate internal controls. In addition, they have found breaches alleged where directors failed to adequately monitor a Delaware corporation's foreign operations. Moreover, a Delaware court applying *Caremark* held directors liable after trial for breach of the duty to monitor where no internal controls or monitoring systems were in place at all.

Egregious Behavior

In *American International Group v. Greenberg*, 965 A.2d 763 (Del. Ch. 2009), the court found that stockholder plaintiffs' allegations that directors had engaged in significant wrongdoing, such that their activity resembled a "criminal organization," adequately stated a *Caremark* theory of failure to monitor because the directors' involvement in the wrongdoing demonstrated that they knew the company's internal controls were inadequate and could easily be bypassed.

In that case, the purported scheme alleged in the complaint included: misstating the company's financial performance to deceive investors, e.g., "staged" reinsurance transactions to dress up the balance sheet and the use of "secret offshore subsidiaries" to hide losses; engaging in various "schemes" to avoid taxes, such as falsely claiming that workers' compensation policies were other types of insurance; conspiring with others to rig markets and competitive auctions; and selling its experience in "balance sheet manipulation." *Id.* at 775. The defendants argued, however, that the complaint was not properly pled in that the alleged facts did not show their involvement in the alleged schemes. The court disagreed, finding that the complaint set out sufficient facts to survive a motion to dismiss and to demonstrate that the defendants would have been involved in, monitored, or supervised the transactions at issue because of their positions within the company and their financial experience. *Id.* at 797–99.

The court found that the alleged "pervasive misconduct" had "permeated AIG's way of doing business." *Id* at 777. "The Complaint fairly supports the assertion that AIG's Inner Circle led a—and I use this term with knowledge of its strength—criminal organization." *Id.* at 799. The court acknowledged that "[a] cosmic wrong may have been done to the Inner Circle Defendants, whose members were victimized by a large number of lower level employees who, despite good faith efforts at oversight and the use of internal controls by the Inner Circle Defendants, were able to avoid detection and engage in widespread financial fraud." *Id.* at 777. However, at the motion to dismiss stage of the proceedings, "the pleading of direct involvement by … the Inner Circle Defendants in many of the specific alleged wrongs gives rise to a fair inference that the defendants knew that AIG's internal controls and compliance efforts were inadequate." *Id.* at 777. Therefore the court declined defendants' motion to dismiss the complaint, finding that plaintiffs had stated a breach of loyalty claim against the defendants for "knowingly tolerating inadequate internal controls and knowingly failing to monitor their subordinates' compliance with legal duties." *Id.* at 799.

Notes and Comments

The court in the AIG case analyzed the complaint under the traditional and plaintiff-friendly pleading standard of Rule 12 (b)(6), rather than the more difficult particularized pleading standard of Rule 23.1 because of the procedural posture of the case. *Am. Int'l Group*, 965 A.2d at 778. The AIG board had created a special litigation committee to determine what action the corporation should take with respect to the derivative complaint, and vested full authority in the special committee, including whether to pursue the claims set out in the derivative complaint or whether to have them dismissed. Following its investigation, the special committee decided to "remain neutral" with respect to the relevant defendants. Therefore, any demand on the board would have been futile and was excused. As such, defendants' motion to dismiss was evaluated under Rule 12(b)(6). *Compare* Del. Ct. Ch. R. 12(b)(6), *with* Del. Ct. Ch. R. 23.1(a).

Failure to Adequately Monitor Foreign Operations

In three cases involving Delaware corporations with operations in China—*In re Puda Coal, Inc. Stockholders Litig.*, C.A. No. 64786-CS (Del. Ch. Feb. 6, 2013) (transcript), *Rich v. Chong*, 66 A.3d 963 (Del. Ch. 2013), *reargument denied* 2013 Del. Ch. LEXIS 165 (Del. Ch. July 2, 2013), and *In re China Agritech, Inc. S'holder Deriv. Litig.*, 2013 Del. Ch. LEXIS 132 (Del. Ch. May 21, 2013)—the Court of Chancery refused to dismiss *Caremark* claims against directors of Delaware corporations who, if the facts were as alleged, failed to adequately monitor operations in China. In these cases, the courts emphasized that directors of a Delaware corporation have duties of oversight with respect to the corporation's foreign operations.

In *Puda Coal*, the Court of Chancery elaborated on directors' oversight duties in companies with foreign operations. There, the court refused to dismiss a breach of fiduciary duty claim against independent directors of a Delaware corporation where "the entire asset base of the company was sold out from under the independent directors nearly two years before they discovered it." C.A. No. 64786-CS, at 19. To make matters worse, the directors were not even the ones to discover what had happened. *Id.* When they were alerted to what had happened, rather than "cause the company to sue" or otherwise remedy the situation, "they simply quit." *Id.* at 23. In these circumstances, the court declined to dismiss the breach of fiduciary duty claim. The court concluded that "the magnitude of what happened[,] … the length of time it went undiscovered, [and] the repetitive filing of statements saying that the company owned assets [it] didn't" gave "rise to a *Caremark* claim." *Id.* at 19. In so concluding, the court elaborated on the oversight duties of directors of a Delaware corporation with assets and operations in China, explaining that as a director, in order to meet the obligation of good faith, you "better have your physical body in China an awful lot ... [and] have in place a system of controls to make sure that you know that [the corporation] actually own[s] the assets." *Id.* at 17–18. Additionally, you "better have the language skills to navigate the environment in which the company is operating." *Id.* at 18.

In *Rich v. Chong*, the court found that a plaintiff had pled facts sufficient for the court "to reasonably infer that the [defendant] directors" of a Delaware corporation that held stock in a Chinese jewelry company as its sole asset "knew that [the company's] internal controls were deficient, yet failed to act." 66 A.3d at 966. Based on the alleged facts, the compliance system appeared "woefully inadequate." *Id.* at 982. For example, the inadequate inventory controls were "particularly troubling" because the company was "a jewelry company, specializing in precious metals and gemstones which are valuable and easily stolen." *Id.* at 983. Though the company had an audit committee, "there [did] not seem to have been any regulation of the company's operations *in China.*" *Id.* at 983. Additionally, the board allegedly ignored numerous "red flags" that should have led the board to improve internal controls, including an earnings restatement, acknowledgment of "the likelihood of material weaknesses in [the company's] internal controls," and a letter from NASDAQ warning of possible delisting due to deficient reporting. *Id.* at 983–84. The court found it reasonable "to infer that the directors knew that the internal controls were inadequate and failed to act in the face of a known duty." *Id.* at 984. Reinforcing "the inference that the internal control were ... grossly inadequate," was the fact that $130 million was transferred out of the company "without the directors knowing about it for over a year." *Id.* The court explained that "[e]ither the directors knew about the cash transfers and were complicit, or they had zero controls in place and did not know about them. If the directors had even the barest framework of appropriate controls in place, they would have prevented the cash transfers." *Id.*

Rich Ex Rel. Fuqi Int'l, Inc. v. Yu Kwai Chong

66 A.3d 963 (Del. Ch. 2013)

GLASSCOCK, Vice Chancellor

I. OVERVIEW

The Plaintiff here, a stockholder, made a demand to the Defendant corporation, asking the corporation to prosecute claims against its officers and directors for violating their Caremark duties. The individual Defendants not only failed to respond to the demand over the next two years, but allegedly took actions making a meaningful response to the demand unlikely if not impossible. Under these facts, the Plaintiff may pursue an action on behalf of the corporation derivatively, notwithstanding Court of Chancery Rule 23.1.

This Opinion concerns a motion brought by Defendant Fuqi International, Inc. and its directors to dismiss a derivative complaint alleging breaches of fiduciary duty. Fuqi, a Delaware entity whose sole asset is stock of a Chinese jewelry company, completed a public offering in the United States in 2009. In March 2010, Fuqi announced the need for restatement of its 2009 financial statements. Following this announcement, Fuqi disclosed additional problems it had, including the transfer of $120 million of cash out of the company to third parties in China. In July 2010, Plaintiff George Rich, Jr., a Fuqi stockholder, made a demand to the board of directors to remedy breaches of fiduciary duty and weaknesses in Fuqi's internal controls. Fuqi's Audit Committee commenced an investigation, which was abandoned in January 2012 upon management's failure to pay the fees of the Audit Committee's advisors. Fuqi's independent directors have since resigned.

Plaintiff Rich brought this action in June 2012, alleging breaches of fiduciary duty under Caremark. Now, the Defendants have moved to dismiss the Complaint under Rule 23.1, because the Fuqi board has not yet rejected the Plaintiff's demand. Having found that the Plaintiff has pled particularized facts that raise a reasonable doubt that the directors acted in good faith in response to the demand, I deny the Rule 23.1 Motion. Second, Fuqi moved to dismiss under Rule 12(b)(6) for failure to state a claim upon which relief can be granted. Notwithstanding the well-known difficulty of prevailing on a Caremark claim, the Plaintiff has pled facts that, assumed true, lead me to reasonably infer that the Fuqi directors knew that its internal controls were deficient, yet failed to act. Therefore, I deny the Motion to Dismiss under Rule 12(b)(6). Finally, the Defendant has moved to dismiss or stay this case under the McWane doctrine, in favor of several prior-filed cases in New York. I deny that Motion as well, because I doubt that courts sitting in New York have personal jurisdiction over the Defendants.

In summary, the Defendants' Motion to Dismiss or Stay this case is denied.

II. BACKGROUND FACTS

A. Parties

Plaintiff George Rich, Jr. is, and at all relevant times has been, a stockholder of Fuqi International, Inc. ("Fuqi"). Nominal Defendant Fuqi is a Delaware corporation whose principle offices are located in the People's Republic of China. Fuqi is engaged in selling high quality, precious metal jewelry. Fuqi shares were traded on the NASDAQ until they were delisted in March of 2011 and now trade on the pink sheet market for approximately $1 per share.

Defendant Yu Kwai Chong ("Chong") is the principal founder of Fuqi and has served as Chairman of the Board since Fuqi's inception. Chong also served as Fuqi's CEO from April 2011 until June 2011. Defendant Lie Xi Zhuang ("Zhuang") has served as Fuqi's COO since April 2001 and as a director since 2008. Defendant Ching Wan Wong ("Wong") served as Fuqi's CFO from January 2004 until his resignation in July 2011; Wong also served as a Fuqi director from 2008 until he resigned in June 2011. Defendant Lily Lee Chen ("Chen") served as a Fuqi director from June 2007 until her resignation in March 2012. Defendants Eileen B. Brody ("Brody") and Victor A. Hollander ("Hollander") served as Fuqi directors, and as members of the Audit Committee, from June 2007 until their resignations in January 2012. Defendant Jeff Haiyong Liu ("Liu") has served as a director of Fuqi from June 2007 to the present, and has also served as a member of the Audit Committee. Collectively, I refer to Defendants Chong, Zhuang, Wong, Chen, Brody, Hollander, and Liu as the "Individual Defendants."

B. Fuqi's Background and Organizational Structure.

Fuqi's primary operations are conducted through a wholly-owned subsidiary, Fuqi International Holdings Co., Ltd., a British Virgin Islands corporation ("Fuqi BVI") and its wholly owned subsidiary, Shenzhen Fuqi Jewelry Co., Ltd. ("Fuqi China"), a company established under the laws of China.

Fuqi was born of a reverse-merger transaction (the "Reverse Merger") involving Fuqi BVI and VT Marketing Services, Inc. ("VT"), a corporation formed as part of the Chapter 11 reorganization plan of visitalk.com, Inc. Prior to the Reverse Merger, Chong was the sole stockholder of Fuqi BVI. On November 20, 2006, Chong, Fuqi BVI, and VT entered into a share exchange agreement to effect the Reverse Merger. Under the agreement, Chong agreed to exchange all of his shares of Fuqi BVI for shares of VT, and VT agreed to acquire all of the issued and outstanding capital stock of Fuqi BVI. The Reverse Merger closed on November 22, 2006, and VT issued 11,175,543 shares of common stock in exchange for all of the issued and outstanding shares of Fuqi BVI. Upon the Reverse Merger's closing, VT became the 100% parent of Fuqi BVI and assumed the operations of Fuqi BVI and Fuqi China as its sole business. On December 8, 2006, VT reincorporated in Delaware, having previously been organized under the laws of Nevada, and changed its corporate name from "VT Marketing Services, Inc." to "Fuqi International, Inc."

C. Fuqi's Public Offering and Associated Disclosures.

Fuqi's Reverse Merger facilitated Fuqi's access to the U.S. capital markets. Following the Reverse Merger, Fuqi began issuing press releases and filings with the SEC that reported strikingly strong growth. On July 31, 2009, Fuqi completed a public offering of 5.58 million of shares of common stock at a price of $21.50 per share. Gross proceeds were approximately $120 million.

D. Fuqi Announces Material Weakness in Accounting Methods.

On March 16, 2010, Fuqi announced that its fourth quarter 10-Q and 10-K for 2009 would be delayed because Fuqi had discovered "certain errors related to the accounting of the Company's inventory and cost of sales." The press release stated that the errors identified were expected to have a material impact on Fuqi's previously issued quarterly financial statements for 2009 and that "at least one of the identified deficiencies ... constitutes a material weakness...." This press release was followed by another dated April 7, 2010, in which Fuqi disclosed that it had received a notification letter from NASDAQ that Fuqi was no longer in compliance with NASDAQ rules requiring the timely filing of SEC reports. On September 8, 2010, Fuqi announced that the SEC had initiated a formal investigation into Fuqi, related to Fuqi's failure to file timely periodic reports, among other matters.

E. Fuqi Stockholders File Securities and Derivative Actions Outside of Delaware.

After Fuqi announced that its 2009 financial statements needed restatement, Fuqi stockholders filed several securities and derivative lawsuits on behalf of Fuqi against the Individual Defendants in federal and state courts. Ten securities class action lawsuits were filed in the United States District Court for the Southern District of

New York within weeks of the March 16, 2010 press release. Three derivative suits were filed on behalf of Fuqi in April 2010, two in federal court and one in New York State court. The derivative suits allege that the directors and certain officers of Fuqi breached their fiduciary duties by failing to adequately supervise and control Fuqi, which resulted in the filing of false financial statements. Each of the claims brought in federal court—including the derivative actions and the securities class actions— were subsequently consolidated for discovery purposes on July 26, 2010 (the "Federal Action"), and a lead plaintiff was selected. The parties to the Federal Action agreed that the plaintiffs would file an amended complaint in that action after Fuqi files its restated financial statements. Fuqi has not yet filed audited financial statements, so the Federal Action remains stayed. At oral argument, the parties noted that very little has been done so far in the Federal Action since the case has been stayed. With regard to the derivative claims, most relevant for this Court's purposes, the defendants have not all been served in the Federal Action.

F. Plaintiff Rich Makes a Demand to the Fuqi Board of Directors.

On July 19, 2010, Plaintiff Rich made a demand to the Fuqi Board to commence an action against certain directors and executive officers of Fuqi (the "Demand Letter"). The Demand Letter asked the board of directors to "take action to remedy breaches of fiduciary duties by the directors and certain executive officers of the Company" as well as to "correct the deficiencies in the Company's internal controls that allowed the misconduct to occur." The Demand Letter also informed the board that if Fuqi did not respond to the letter within a reasonable period, the Plaintiff would commence a stockholder derivative action on behalf of Fuqi. Fuqi never responded to the Demand Letter in writing.

G. Fuqi Appoints the Special Internal Investigation Committee.

On October 29, 2010, Fuqi announced the appointment of Kim K.T. Pan as a new independent member of the board of directors. In response to the demand, the directors formed a "Special Internal Investigation Committee" and appointed Pan and Chen to serve as its members (the "Special Committee"). The board authorized the Special Committee to retain experts and advisors to investigate whether the claims in the demand were meritorious. Disclosure of the Special Committee's formation was the only information Fuqi ever disclosed to the stockholders regarding the Special Committee. The Plaintiff contends that the Special Committee "never conducted any investigation or any other activity during its short-lived existence." Furthermore, by March 2012 the Special Committee effectively ceased to exist after losing both of its members, Pan and Chen, due to Chen's resignation and Pan's appointment as CEO.

H. Fuqi Discloses Material Weaknesses and Cash-Transfer Transactions.

From the time the Plaintiff sent the Demand Letter to the present, Fuqi has released additional negative information about its accounting errors, lack of internal controls, and mismanagement of corporate resources. For instance, on March 16, 2011, Fuqi filed a Form NT 10-K with the SEC announcing that the financial statements for the quarterly periods ending March 31, 2009; June 30, 2009; and September 30, 2009 would be restated due to accounting errors. These accounting errors related to:

> (i) incorrect carve-out of the retail segment from the general ledger; (ii) unrecorded purchases and accounts payable, (iii) inadvertent inclusion of consigned inventory, (iv) incorrect and untimely recordkeeping of inventory movements of retail operation; and (v) incorrect diamond inventory costing, unrecorded purchases and unrecorded accounts payable.

In other words, Fuqi's financial statements were replete with basic accounting errors. The Form NT 10-K further disclosed that Fuqi had identified material weaknesses in its disclosure controls, procedures, and internal control over financial reporting. These material weaknesses include Fuqi's failure to "maintain effective controls ... over its accounting and finance personnel..., the inventory and purchasing cycles, the accounting of complex and non-routine transactions, internal audit function, and treasury function."

Two weeks later, Fuqi announced that its Audit Committee was conducting an investigation relating to certain cash-transfer transactions that had been discovered by Fuqi's independent auditor during Fuqi's preparation of its restated quarterly financial statements for 2009. Fuqi made the cash-transfer transactions, between September 2009 and November 2010, to parties that are "registered legal entities in China." Chong, Fuqi's Chairman of the board, authorized the transfers pursuant to an oral agreement with Fuqi's bank. The entities receiving these cash transfers are Chinese entities, "but the Company has not been able to confirm the accuracy of their business addresses nor determine the extent and nature of their business operations, if any." As of March 2011, the company had found no evidence that the receiving entities were related to any of Fuqi's managers or directors. Fuqi has represented that "all of the outgoing cash transfers made by the Company were repaid in full by the recipient companies on a short-term basis, with no loss resulting from the transfers." However, Fuqi has not produced audited financial statements to confirm that these amounts have been repaid. The aggregate amount of the cash transfers totaled $86.3 million for 2009 and $47.5 million for 2010.

In essence, Fuqi transferred cash out of the company to third parties, outside of the U.S., who have yet to be verified as legitimate businesses. Fuqi has asserted, but not demonstrated, that the cash has been restored. The press release disclosing these events concluded with "[t]he internal investigation is ongoing." Since this press release in 2011, Fuqi has provided no additional information about the investigation to the stockholders.

The following day, because of Fuqi's ongoing failure to file timely financial statements, NASDAQ delisted Fuqi stock from the exchange. Although it once traded at close to $30 per share, Fuqi stock now trades on the pink sheets for approximately $1 per share.

I. Fuqi's Investigation.

Although there is no evidence that the Special Committee performed any investigation, the Audit Committee did begin an investigation into Fuqi's accounting problems. Fuqi's Audit Committee, which apparently predates its disclosure problems, consisted of board members Hollander, Brody and Liu. Fuqi contends that the Audit Committee has "conducted a lengthy assessment and remediation of its internal and financial controls" resulting in "significant progress."

Fuqi's auditors requested that the Audit Committee perform an expedited investigation of the cash-transfer transactions. The Audit Committee retained a Chinese law firm to investigate the transactions and determine whether Fuqi had violated Chinese or U.S. law. In February 2011, the Audit Committee engaged special investigative counsel and a forensic accountant after Fuqi's auditors requested that the Audit Committee conclude its investigation. After the Audit Committee shared its preliminary findings with its auditors, the auditors requested that the Audit Committee expand the investigation.

Whatever progress the Audit Committee made in uncovering and correcting the causes of Fuqi's problems has allegedly stalled. According to Brody and Hollander (two of the three former members of the Audit Committee), Fuqi management failed to pay the fees of the Audit Committee's outside legal counsel, forensic specialists, and auditor. As a result, these professionals have either withdrawn from advising or suspended their services to the Audit Committee. In January 2012, Brody and Hollander resigned as Fuqi directors, and as members of the Audit Committee, in protest of the defunding.

Because the Audit Committee has failed to complete its audits of years 2009, 2010, and 2011, Fuqi has not filed any audited financial statements for over three years. As of March 28, 2012, Fuqi has represented to the SEC and to this Court that it is unable to estimate when it will file its audited financial statements.

Although Fuqi has still not completed its investigation, Fuqi has disclosed to its stockholders that the cash-transfer transactions were the result of material weaknesses in Fuqi's internal controls. For example, Fuqi has acknowledged "the Company's treasury controls did not require that internal fund transfer applications identify any specific business purpose or be accompanied by supporting documentation, such as a copy of a relevant invoice, purchase order, contract, or pre-payment statement."

J. Fuqi Experiences Mass Defections in Leadership.

From June 2010 until March 2012, Fuqi's board of directors and executive team experienced mass defections. These defections are detailed below:

- On June 11, 2010, Xi Zhou Zhuo resigned as Marketing Director of Fuqi;

- On June 16, 2011, Wong resigned as a director but remained as Fuqi's CFO;

- On June 17, 2011, Chong resigned as Fuqi's CEO and was replaced by the previously independent director, Kim Pan;

- On July 30, 2011, Wong resigned as Fuqi's CFO, and CEO Pan also became Interim CFO, which he remained until the time of the Complaint;

- On January 3, 2012, Brody and Hollander resigned as directors;

- On January 16, 2012, Frederick Wong resigned as Vice President of Special Projects; and

- On March 31, 2012, Chen resigned as a director.

Xi Zhou Zhuo, Wong, Chong, Frederick Wong, and Chen reportedly resigned for "personal reasons." However, Brody and Hollander expressly resigned because of management's failure to pay the fees of legal, auditing, and other professional-service providers engaged by the Audit Committee, and because of management's assumption of responsibility and authority for engaging a professional accounting firm without the approval of the Audit Committee. In their words, Brody and Hollander felt compelled to resign "[b]ecause the Audit Committee's efforts to serve the shareholders of Fuqi have been completely frustrated by Management."

Fuqi responded publicly to Brody and Hollander's grievances in a Form 8-K filed on January 3, 2012. Fuqi argued that the Audit Committee's expenses had not been paid due to discrepancies with its insurer. It further contended that management had the right to select its own auditor. Brody and Hollander responded to these defenses via a letter to the Board on January 9, 2012. Without going into the details of this letter, it suffices to say that Brody and Hollander dispute the board's characterization.

K. The Allegations against the Individual Defendants.

As a procedural matter, the Plaintiff argues that he should not have to prove demand futility because (1) he made a demand, and (2) "the Board has not acted, is not acting, and will not act in response to the Demand." The Plaintiff draws support for this statement from the fact that the Board's Special Committee has had no meetings, released no progress reports, and now has no members. Finally, the Plaintiff alleges that the Defendants have had sufficient time to investigate this matter since over two years has passed since the Demand Letter was written.

Substantively, the Plaintiff alleges that the Individual Defendants breached their fiduciary duty of loyalty. Specifically, the Plaintiff contends that

each of the Individual Defendants knowingly, and in a sustained and systematic manner, failed to institute and maintain adequate internal controls over Fuqi's accounting and financial reporting, failed to make a good faith effort to correct or prevent the deficiencies and accounting and financial problems caused thereby, and knowingly caused or allowed the Company to disseminate to shareholders false and misleading financial statements.

The Plaintiff alleges that the Individual Defendants were aware that Fuqi's public filings grossly misstated Fuqi's financial position. He contends that the Individual Defendants had this knowledge because they "had knowingly engaged in improper financial reporting and accounting practices, including, but not limited to, improperly reporting revenues, expenses and net income." The Plaintiff also alleges that Fuqi had "virtually no meaningful internal accounting and financial reporting controls, and ... the Individual Defendants willfully ignored the Company's obvious and pervasive lack of controls and made no good faith effort to correct or prevent the disaster that would ensue as a result." As damages, the Plaintiff seeks the costs and expenses incurred in connection with the accounting-restatement process, the SEC's investigation, and NASDAQ's delisting of Fuqi.

L. Related Actions and Procedural History.

It should be noted that these parties are involved in a contemporaneous suit before this Court and before a federal court. On July 21, 2010, before filing this action, the Plaintiff filed a complaint seeking an order compelling Fuqi to hold its annual stockholder meeting as required by 8 Del. C. § 211. I granted summary judgment for the Plaintiff and ordered Fuqi to hold its annual stockholder meeting by December 17, 2012. Fuqi asked me to certify an interlocutory appeal of that order on the grounds that holding an annual stockholder meeting was "physically impossible" for Fuqi because it had not filed audited financial statements for three years and holding such a meeting would therefore be in contravention of SEC rules. I denied certification of that question for interlocutory appeal because I found that the standards under Supreme Court Rule 42 were not met. Fuqi then sought leave to appeal my order from the Supreme Court. The Supreme Court denied Fuqi's request on November 9, 2012.

Fuqi then sought relief from my Order from the United States District Court for the District of Delaware, seeking "a declaration that Regulations 14A and 14C promulgated by the Securities and Exchange Commission under Section 14 of the Exchange Act preempt Section 211 of the Delaware General Corporation Law." Fuqi sought injunctive relief, as well as a temporary restraining order, against my order compelling Fuqi to hold its annual stockholder meeting. The District of Delaware heard Fuqi's motion for a temporary restraining order on an expedited basis, and, in a ruling from the bench on November 16, 2012, denied Fuqi's motion. Fuqi then moved for a preliminary injunction, which was likewise denied on December 17, 2012. Since that time, Plaintiff Rich has moved to hold Fuqi in contempt of my Order.

The Complaint in this action was filed on June 13, 2012. Fuqi moved to dismiss the Complaint on July 16, 2012. Following briefing on the motion, oral argument was held on January 7, 2013, after which I reserved decision. A further conference in this matter was held on February 11, 2013. This is my Opinion on Defendant Fuqi's Motion to Dismiss or Stay this action.

III. ANALYSIS

A. The Demand Requirement.

As a threshold matter, I must decide whether Fuqi's failure to respond to the Demand justifies the Plaintiff's prosecution of this suit derivatively. Court of Chancery Rule 23.1 permits a stockholder to pursue an action on behalf of a corporation derivatively, where "the corporation ... [has] failed to enforce a right which may properly be asserted by it...." The Rule requires a stockholder to make (or justify excusal of) a demand to the board of directors before the stockholder may bring a suit derivatively. A stockholder plaintiff must allege with particularity "the efforts, if any, made by the plaintiff to obtain the action he desires from the directors ... and the reasons for his failure to obtain the action or for not making the effort." Where a plaintiff seeks to proceed without a demand, he may satisfy the Rule where he alleges particular facts that raise a reasonable doubt, because of a conflict of interest or lack of independence, that the board could render a response to a demand without violating its duty of loyalty. Similarly, where the plaintiff has made a demand, the Rule is satisfied and the plaintiff may proceed derivatively where he raises a reasonable doubt that the board's failure to acquiesce to his demand is in compliance with its fiduciary duties; that is, was wrongful.

Once a stockholder has made a demand, he is precluded from arguing that a demand is excused. The board of directors is entitled to a reasonable period of time to respond to the demand. Until the board has responded to a demand, the stockholder generally may not move forward with a derivative action. The demand requirement preserves a core function of the board of directors—to determine whether litigation on behalf of the corporation should proceed—and balances this function with the right of stockholders to pursue the interests of the corporation in the face of the board's wrongful refusal or inability to act.

By making a litigation demand on a board of directors, a stockholder concedes that the board is able to evaluate the demand, free from concerns of conflicts of interest or lack of independence. Once the stockholder makes a demand, the board has an affirmative duty to evaluate the demand and to determine if the litigation demanded is in the best interest of the stockholders. Where the board fails to accede to the plaintiff's demand, Rule 23.1 requires that the plaintiff plead with particularity why that failure to accede is wrongful.

If the board rejects the demand, the plaintiff may satisfy his burden under Rule 23.1 by raising a reasonable doubt that the denial was in compliance with the board's fiduciary duties. Similarly, as described in more detail below, where the board has not responded to a demand, the plaintiff satisfies the rule, and may proceed, upon raising a reasonable doubt that the board's lack of a response is consistent with its fiduciary duties.

Relatively few Delaware cases have arisen in which a stockholder attempts to move forward with a derivative suit before a board formally responds to the stockholder's demand. Where the board has taken no action and has simply failed to address the demand, the stockholder satisfies Rule 23.1 and may proceed derivatively if he demonstrates that the failure to act is wrongful, an analysis that in past cases has turned on the time available to the board for response in light of the allegations in the demand.

Other cases, however, including this case, involve board action which has not yet resulted in a formal response to the demand, and a request by the board that the plaintiff's action be dismissed so that the board's investigation may continue. In such cases, once a demand has been made, the board has taken some action in response, and the demanding stockholder has then sued as a derivative plaintiff before the board has responded to the demand, the methods and manner in which the board has chosen to act on the demand represent judgments entitled to the benefit of the business judgment rule if taken in a manner that was informed and in good faith. That benefit is that the Court must presume that the actions of the board are in the corporation's interest, and the Court will accordingly dismiss the derivative action. The business judgment rule, however, provides no protection in cases of bad-faith conduct, such as "where the fiduciary intentionally acts with a purpose other than that of advancing the best interests of the corporation, where the fiduciary acts with the intent to violate applicable positive law, or where the fiduciary intentionally fails to act in the face of a known duty to act, demonstrating a conscious disregard for his duties." Similarly, the business judgment rule does not apply if directors fail to inform themselves of all material information reasonably available to them and fail to act with requisite care. If the plaintiff is able to raise a reasonable doubt that the directors are acting in good faith or with due care, the directors' actions taken in response to a demand are not entitled to the business judgment rule's presumption that the directors are acting in the corporate interest. Therefore, where the plaintiff by particularized pleading has raised a reasonable doubt that the board's actions are in compliance with its fiduciary duties, Rule 23.1 is satisfied and the plaintiff may proceed derivatively.

In Thorpe v. CERBCO, Inc., then-Chancellor Allen applied a business judgment rule analysis to the actions of the CERBCO board in considering a stockholder demand. There, a stockholder made a demand to the CERBCO board of directors to investigate breaches of fiduciary duty arising under a controlling stockholder's sale of its shares. Two months later, the CERBCO board appointed two directors to serve on a special litigation committee to review the demand. Within six months from its appointment, the special litigation committee conducted an investigation and prepared a report detailing its findings. The members of the special litigation committee then resigned from the CERBCO board of directors. CERBCO never showed the contents of the report to its stockholders, nor did the directors formally respond to the plaintiff's demand. By the time of the Court's decision, ten months had passed from the time the special litigation committee finished its report, and the board of directors still had not acted on the report.

Then-Chancellor Allen found that, since the plaintiff had made a pre-suit demand on the CERBCO board of directors, the plaintiff had conceded the board's independence and ability to investigate the alleged wrongdoing. Applying the business judgment rule, the Court assessed whether the CERBCO board had acted in good faith:

It may be that the special committee did function in good faith and prudently.... One cannot know that yet, but the alleged resignation of the members of the committee from the board following submission of the report is not inconsistent with that possibility. The board however has apparently not acted on that report. No action at all has been taken so far as the complaint (or the record otherwise) shows. How in these circumstances can the committee's investigation, even if it is presumed to be in good faith and reasonable, itself preclude judicial review of the claim of corporate injury by the self-interested controlling shareholder? Even if one is required to presume the independence of a majority of the board and if one assumes that the special committee operated in good faith and reasonably, nevertheless, the circumstances alleged (the failure of the board to act on the report, the failure to disclose it to the stockholders after request and the resignation of the committee members from the board), if considered to be true, do raise a reasonable doubt concerning the whole board's good faith and justify my conclusion that the requisites of Rule 23.1 have been satisfied here.

As in Thorpe, the Fuqi board has taken action in response to the Plaintiff's demand, and asks that I allow it to continue its consideration of the demand, a consideration that has occupied, theoretically, some two-and-one-half years. Also consistent with Thorpe, the Plaintiff here has pled facts providing me reason to doubt the good faith of the Fuqi board. The Plaintiff sent the Demand Letter to the Fuqi board of directors on July 19, 2010. As a result, the Plaintiff will be deemed to have conceded the independence and disinterestedness of the board. Because Fuqi has not formally rejected the Demand Letter, I must determine whether the Plaintiff has pled particular facts creating a reasonable doubt that the Fuqi board is acting in good faith and with due care in investigating the facts underlying the Demand to assess whether the Plaintiff has satisfied Rule 23.1 and may proceed derivatively.

The Plaintiff has alleged that (1) he made a demand; (2) Fuqi took steps to begin an investigation; (3) that investigation appears to have uncovered some amount of corporate mismanagement; (4) Fuqi has not acted on the information uncovered; (5) the Special Committee appointed by the Board to investigate the demand became defunct before making a recommendation; (6) by de-funding the advisors to the Audit Committee, Fuqi has deliberately abandoned that investigation, and has taken no action through the Audit Committee for at least 12 months; and (7) the independent directors have left the company, some in protest of management's actions.

Fuqi's argument that these allegations are insufficient to raise a reasonable doubt that the Board has acted in good faith is unpersuasive. First, if I consider the Fuqi board's abandonment of the investigation as an abdication of its duty to investigate the demand, then the protections of the business judgment rule do not apply. Specifically, the business judgment rule "has no role where directors have either abdicated their functions, or absent a conscious decision, failed to act." Here, the Plaintiff has pled facts with particularity that show that the Fuqi board has abdicated its responsibilities because the investigation has been left in limbo, with no progress, for several months. Under that view of the facts, Fuqi management is not entitled to the business judgment rule's protections. Beyond that, Fuqi management has refused to pay for the professional advisors—including auditors and legal counsel—of the Audit Committee performing the investigation. This lack of payment has thwarted what efforts could have been taken by the Audit Committee to investigate. To make matters worse, the independent directors, who could have conducted a meaningful investigation on behalf of the company, have resigned from their posts. Thus, the Plaintiff has alleged with particularity that the board has not only failed to move the investigation forward, but has also impeded that investigation. Nor does the record indicate that the investigation continues. It has been abandoned.

The Plaintiff has pled with particularity facts that create a reasonable doubt that the Fuqi board has acted in good faith in investigating the Plaintiff's demand. Therefore, I find that the requirements of Rule 23.1 have been satisfied. I assess the remainder of Fuqi's grounds for dismissal under the more lenient pleading standards of Rule 12(b)(6).

B. Caremark Claim and 12(b)(6) Analysis.

The Plaintiff alleges that Fuqi's directors are liable for failure to oversee the operations of the corporation. Fuqi argues that the Complaint fails to plead facts that show that the directors "consciously and in bad faith failed to implement any reporting or accounting system or controls." Such claims for bad-faith failure to monitor are known colloquially as "Caremark actions." The Defendants have moved to dismiss the action against the board generally. Because they have not articulated that claims against the Individual Defendants should be dismissed on a defendant-by-defendant basis, I refrain from undertaking that analysis.

1. Standard of Review Under 12(b)(6).

Under Court of Chancery Rule 12(b)(6), the Court will dismiss a complaint if the plaintiff has failed to state a claim upon which relief can be granted. The standard for reviewing a plaintiff's claims under Rule 12(b)(6) is "reasonable conceivability."

When considering a defendant's motion to dismiss, a trial court should accept all well-pleaded factual allegations in the Complaint as true, accept even vague allegations in the Complaint as "well-pleaded" if they provide the defendant notice of the claim, draw all reasonable inferences in favor of the plaintiff, and deny the motion unless the plaintiff could not recover under any reasonably conceivable set of circumstances susceptible of proof.

Dismissal is improper if, accepting all such inferences, "there is a reasonable possibility that a plaintiff could recover."

2. The Elements of a Caremark Claim.

The essence of a Caremark claim is a breach of the duty of loyalty arising from a director's bad-faith failure to exercise oversight over the company. A Caremark claim is "possibly the most difficult theory in corporation law upon which a plaintiff might hope to win a judgment." I am conscious of the need to prevent hindsight from dictating the result of a Caremark action; a bad outcome, without more, does not equate to bad faith. To survive a motion to dismiss, the plaintiff must plead facts that allow a reasonable inference that the defendants breached their fiduciary duties.

In Stone v. Ritter, the Supreme Court clarified that Caremark claims are breaches of the duty of loyalty, as opposed to care, preconditioned on a finding of bad faith. The Supreme Court affirmed this Court's language in Caremark holding that "only a sustained or systematic failure of the board to exercise oversight — such as an utter failure to attempt to assure a reasonable information and reporting system exists — will establish the lack of good faith that is a necessary condition to liability." Demonstrating lack of good faith is the reef upon which most Caremark claims founder. There are two possible scenarios in which a plaintiff can successfully assert a Caremark claim. The Supreme Court described these scenarios as being either:

(a) the directors utterly failed to implement any reporting or information system or controls, or (b) having implemented such a system or controls, consciously failed to monitor or oversee its operations thus disabling themselves from being informed of risks or problems requiring their attention.

Under either scenario, a finding of liability is conditioned on a plaintiff's showing that the directors knew they were not fulfilling their fiduciary duties. "Where directors fail to act in the face of a known duty to act, thereby demonstrating a conscious disregard for their responsibilities, they breach their duty of loyalty by failing to discharge that fiduciary obligation in good faith." Examples of directors' "disabling themselves from being informed" include a corporation's lacking an audit committee, or a corporation's not utilizing its audit committee.

I must analyze the facts alleged here under the lenient pleading standard of Rule 12(b)(6), drawing all reasonable inferences in favor of the Plaintiff, to see if it is reasonably conceivable that he may prevail. Because I find it so, the Motion to Dismiss for failure to state a claim must be denied.

In re American International Group, Inc. ("AIG") illustrates how Rule 12(b)(6)'s lenient pleading standard eases this Court's scrutiny of a Caremark claim at the motion-to-dismiss stage. In AIG, the underlying bases of the Caremark claims were several transactions, practices, and deceptive behaviors that caused AIG to restate its shareholder equity by $3.5 billion and to pay $1.6 billion to settle government investigations. Without going into the specific allegations of that case, which were quite complex, the plaintiffs alleged that the defendants had engaged in transactions designed to hide AIG's true financial situation, implemented illegal schemes to avoid taxes, sold illegal financial products to other companies, and rigged markets. The largest fraudulent transaction alleged was a $500 million phony reinsurance transaction designed to prop up AIG's financial statements.

The defendant directors, officers, and employees each moved to dismiss the complaint. In deciding whether the complaint should be dismissed, then-Vice Chancellor Strine illustrated the effect of the requirement, under 12(b)(6), that he draw all reasonable inferences in favor of the plaintiffs:

> Although the Stockholder Plaintiffs provide detailed allegations about the illegal transactions and schemes that proliferated at AIG, they are not able to tie all of the defendants directly with the specific facts to all of the schemes. In some instances ... the Complaint only outlines the misconduct that occurred, or pleads the involvement of other [defendants]. But, as discussed above, this is a motion to dismiss, and thus I must grant the Stockholder Plaintiffs the benefit of all reasonable inferences. Even the transactions that cannot be tied to specific defendants support the inference that, given the pervasiveness of the fraud, [the defendants] knew that AIG was engaging in illegal conduct.

The Court explained that, if the case was analyzed under Rule 23.1, certain defendants would be "well positioned" to argue that the complaint needed more specifics to adequately plead knowledge on the part of the defendants. However, because the Court decided the case under Rule 12(b)(6) and because of the pervasiveness and materiality of the alleged fraud, the Court inferred that the defendants knew that AIG's internal controls were inadequate. For the purposes of a 12(b)(6) motion to dismiss, the Court inferred that "even when [the defendants] were not directly complicitous in the wrongful schemes, they were aware of the schemes and knowingly failed to stop them." I find the Court's analysis in AIG helpful here. My analysis follows.

a. Fuqi Had No Meaningful Controls in Place.

One way a plaintiff may successfully plead a Caremark claim is to plead facts showing that a corporation had no internal controls in place. Fuqi had some sort of compliance system in place. For example, it had an Audit Committee and submitted financial statements to the SEC in 2009. However, accepting the Plaintiff's allegations as true, the mechanisms Fuqi had in place appear to have been woefully inadequate. In its press releases, Fuqi has detailed its extensive problems with internal controls. For example, Fuqi disclosed its "incorrect and untimely recordkeeping of inventory movements of retail operation." Problems with inventory are particularly troubling here, because Fuqi is a jewelry company, specializing in precious metals and gemstones which are valuable and easily stolen. Nonetheless, the Fuqi directors allowed the corporation to operate few to no controls over these vulnerable assets. Fuqi's self-disclosed accounting inadequacies include:

> (i) incorrect carve-out of the retail segment from the general ledger; (ii) unrecorded purchases and accounts payable, (iii) inadvertent inclusion of consigned inventory, (iv) incorrect and untimely recordkeeping of inventory movements of retail operation; and (v) incorrect diamond inventory costing, unrecorded purchases and unrecorded accounts payable.

These disclosures lead me to believe that Fuqi had no meaningful controls in place. The board of directors may have had regular meetings, and an Audit Committee may have existed, but there does not seem to have been any regulation of the company's operations in China. Nonetheless, even if I were to find that Fuqi had some system of internal controls in place, I may infer that the board's failure to monitor that system was a breach of fiduciary duty.

b. The Board of Directors Ignored Red Flags.

As the Supreme Court held in Stone v. Ritter, if the directors have implemented a system of controls, a finding of liability is predicated on the directors' having "consciously failed to monitor or oversee [the system's] operations thus disabling themselves from being informed of risks or problems requiring their attention." One way that the plaintiff may plead such a conscious failure to monitor is to identify "red flags," obvious and problematic occurrences, that support an inference that the Fuqi directors knew that there were material weaknesses in Fuqi's internal controls and failed to correct such weaknesses. It is unclear how far back in time Fuqi's internal controls have been inadequate. At the very least, the Fuqi board had several "warnings" that all was not well with the internal controls as far back as March 2010.

First, Fuqi was a preexisting Chinese company that gained access to the U.S. capital markets through the Reverse Merger. Thus, Fuqi's directors were aware that there may be challenges in bringing Fuqi's internal controls into harmony with the U.S. securities reporting systems. Notwithstanding that fact, according to the Complaint, the directors did nothing to ensure that its reporting mechanisms were accurate. Second, the board knew that it had problems with its accounting and inventory processes by March 2010 at the latest, because it announced that the 2009 financial statements would need restatement at that time. In the same press release, Fuqi also acknowledged the likelihood of material weaknesses in its internal controls. Third, Fuqi received a letter from NASDAQ in April 2010 warning Fuqi that it would face delisting if Fuqi did not bring its reporting requirements up to date with the SEC.

It seems reasonable to infer that, because of these "red flags," the directors knew that there were deficiencies in Fuqi's internal controls. Furthermore, NASDAQ's letter to Fuqi put the board on notice that these deficiencies risked serious adverse consequences. The directors acknowledged as much in their March 2010 press release.

An analysis of the dates of Fuqi's disclosures demonstrates that it is reasonable, based on the facts pled, to infer that the directors knew that the internal controls were inadequate and failed to act in the face of a known duty. Fuqi announced to stockholders that it was restating its 2009 financial statements and investigating possible "material weaknesses" in its controls in March 2010. Rich sent the Demand Letter in July 2010, and the board appointed the Special Committee in October 2010. In March 2011, Fuqi announced that the cash transfer transactions had occurred between September 2009 and November 2010. These dates indicate that (1) Fuqi's directors knew that there were material weaknesses in Fuqi's internal controls at the latest in March of 2010; (2) Rich's stockholder demand in July 2010 (as well as the myriad securities litigation suits filed) put the directors on notice that the stockholders would carefully scrutinize what was going on at Fuqi; (3) Fuqi had purportedly already begun to "act" on Rich's demand by November 2010; and (4) despite their knowledge of the weaknesses in Fuqi's internal controls, the directors allowed $130 million in cash to be transferred out of the company, some as late as November 2010. The Plaintiffs have derived these facts directly from Fuqi's public disclosures. Facially, these disclosures are enough to allow me to reasonably infer scienter on the part of the Defendants.

That these cash transfers were not discovered until March of 2011, when Fuqi's auditor discovered them, reinforces the inference that the internal controls were (and possibly still are) grossly inadequate. That Chong was able to transfer $130 million out of the company's coffers, without the directors knowing about it for over a year, strains credulity. Either the directors knew about the cash transfers and were complicit, or they had zero controls in place and did not know about them. If the directors had even the barest framework of appropriate controls in place, they would have prevented the cash transfers.

When faced with knowledge that the company controls are inadequate, the directors must act, i.e., they must prevent further wrongdoing from occurring. A conscious failure to act, in the face of a known duty, is a breach of the duty of loyalty. At the very least, it is inferable that even if the Defendants were not complicit in these money transfers, they were aware of the pervasive, fundamental weaknesses in Fuqi's controls and knowingly failed to stop further problems from occurring. This knowing failure, as alleged by the Plaintiff, states a claim for breach of the duty of good faith under Caremark.

Finally, as then-Vice Chancellor Lamb explained in David B. Shaev Profit Sharing Account v. Armstrong, failing to establish an audit committee or failing to utilize an existing audit committee are examples of directors' "disabling themselves from being informed." Fuqi management's failure to pay the fees of the Audit Committee's advisors is a deliberate failure to utilize the Audit Committee. Therefore, I may infer that the board has disabled itself from being informed.

For the reasons above, I find that the Plaintiff has stated a claim under Caremark upon which relief can be granted.

C. Whether this Suit Should be Stayed.

The decision of whether to stay a case in favor of a first-filed action is discretionary. As a general rule, litigation should be confined to the state in which the first suit is filed. However, Delaware actions will not be stayed as a matter of right in favor of a prior-filed, out-of-state action. Instead, the Court should "freely" exercise its discretion in favor of a stay where there is a prior action pending elsewhere, in a court capable of doing prompt and complete justice, involving the same parties and the same issues. In deciding this issue, the Court must be mindful of comity and the public policy behind one party's not being "permitted to defeat the [original] plaintiff's choice of forum in a pending suit by commencing litigation involving the same cause of action in another jurisdiction of its own choosing." These rules were articulated by the Delaware Supreme Court in McWane Cast Iron Pipe Corp. v. McDowell-Wellman Engineering Co. The Supreme Court noted that the policies driving the McWane factors were goals of avoiding inconsistent or contradictory judgments between courts, as well as avoiding an unseemly race to the courthouse.

Here, Fuqi argues that this Court should stay or dismiss this suit in favor of cases that are consolidated and pending before the United States District Court for the Southern District of New York. In particular, there are several securities actions and two derivative actions pending. In the alternative, Fuqi argues that "because Rich's Complaint essentially seeks indemnification, and is contingent on the resolution of the SEC investigation and restatement process, this Court should stay this case pending the outcome of those actions."

1. A Stay in Favor of the Restatement Process or SEC Investigation is Not Appropriate at this Time.

I must deny the Defendants' request that this suit should be stayed until audited financial statements are released or the SEC investigation is completed. Parts of the Plaintiff's claims may be contingent on the results of the SEC investigation; for example, some of the harm Fuqi has suffered may not be quantifiable at this time since the investigations are pending. However, that some of the harms are contingent in nature does not require that the adjudication of the Plaintiff's other claims be placed on hold, perhaps indefinitely, until the restatement process is finished. There are certainly circumstances where a stay would be appropriate where necessary evidence was forthcoming, and not yet available. Here, however, Fuqi has been unable to identify or even suggest when the restatement process will be complete. Four years have passed without the stockholders' receiving reliable audited financial statements. Just as it cannot indefinitely delay its obligation to hold an annual stockholders meeting, Fuqi management cannot indefinitely delay facing appropriately brought derivative claims.

2. This Court has the Discretion Not to Stay this Matter in Favor of the Federal Action.

McWane instructs me to freely exercise my discretion in favor of a stay where there is a prior action pending elsewhere, in a court capable of doing prompt and complete justice, involving the same parties and the same issues. I doubt that courts sitting in New York have personal jurisdiction over the Individual Defendants, many of whom are residents of China. Delaware has jurisdiction over each of the Individual Defendants because they are directors of a Delaware corporation. Because New York likely does not have jurisdiction over the Individual Defendants, I do not consider the courts in the Federal Action to be courts capable of doing prompt and complete justice in this matter. As a result, I decline to stay this case.

IV. CONCLUSION

Having found that the Plaintiff pled particularized facts that raise a reasonable doubt that the directors acted in good faith in failing to respond to the demand, I deny the Motion to Dismiss under Rule 23.1. Likewise, I deny the Defendants' Motion to Dismiss under Rule 12(b)(6) because the Plaintiff has pled facts that, when assumed true, lead me to reasonably infer that the Fuqi directors knew that its internal controls were deficient, and failed to correct such deficiencies. Finally, I deny the Defendants' Motion to Stay or Dismiss under McWane, as well, because I doubt that courts sitting in New York have personal jurisdiction over the Defendants. In summary, the Defendants' Motion to Dismiss or Stay this case is DENIED. An appropriate order accompanies this Opinion.

———

In *China Agritech*, the court concluded that the shareholders' factual allegations supported a "reasonable inference" that the members of the company's audit committee had acted in bad faith by consciously disregarding their duties of oversight. 2013 Del. Ch. LEXIS 132, at *56. In particular, the alleged facts showed that the audit committee failed to meet, and there was "no documentary evidence" that it had ever met. *Id.* at *52–53. The company's outside auditor resigned and sent a letter under a provision indicating that the auditor believed an illegal act had occurred and the company had not taken appropriate remedial action. *Id.* at *53. Additionally, "[d]iscrepancies in the Company's public filings with governmental agencies reinforce[d] the inference of an Audit Committee that existed in name only." *Id.* at *54. In particular, the company's public filings in China reported losses while the company's public filings in the Unites States for the same periods reported profits. *Id.* at *54–55. The court distinguished this complaint from "the parade of hastily filed *Caremark* complaints that Delaware courts have dismissed," explaining that "like those rare *Caremark* complaints that prior decisions have found adequate, the Complaint supports these allegations with references to books and records ... and with inferences that this Court can reasonably draw from the *absence* of books and records that the company could be expected to produce." *Id.* at *58.

No Internal Controls or Monitoring Systems

In *ATR-KIM ENG Financial Corp. v. Araneta*, No. 489-N, 2006 Del. Ch. LEXIS 215 (Dec. 21, 2006), two executives were held liable following a full trial for *Caremark* violations even though there was no allegation that they participated in, approved of, or profited from wrongdoing. The court found that their lack of knowledge of the wrongdoing was not an excuse but, in essence, a confession of their failure to comply with their oversight duties.

There, a minority shareholder brought an action against three directors for breaches of their fiduciary duties. The allegations against the first director were "clear-cut claims of self-dealing by a controlling shareholder and director" who had transferred the company's most valuable asset to his family without consideration. But as to the remaining directors, the complaint did not allege that they participated in, approved of, or directly profited from the illicit conduct. Therefore the issue before the court was whether the remaining directors had breached their duties of loyalty by failing to monitor the brazen wrongdoing by the first director.

It was clear to the court that the remaining directors had, in fact, breached their *Caremark* duties. For instance, no reporting system had ever been instituted and internal controls had never even been contemplated. *Id.* at *73. Further, no board meetings had been held and the remaining directors had conceded that they were entirely deferential to the dominating director, who had looted the company. *Id.* at *73–76. In fact, the court explained that their admission of inaction in response to the dominating, looting director's actions amounted to an admission of the violation of their fiduciary duty to monitor, and thus found them jointly liable for the first director's conduct. *Id.* at *75–77.

The court explained: "Under Delaware law, it is fundamental that a director cannot act loyally towards the corporation unless she tries—i.e., makes a genuine, good faith effort—to do her job as a director. One cannot accept the important role of director in a Delaware corporation and thereafter consciously avoid any attempt to carry out one's duties." *Id.* at *71.

No Violation of the Duty To Monitor

Equally as important as the cases above, which illustrate facts supporting *Caremark* claims, are cases in which courts have rejected different *Caremark* theories of director liability. The three cases below illustrate types of scenarios where the courts have not imposed liability. One court rejected an attempt to extend the Caremark theory to a failure to monitor business risk, as opposed to a failure to monitor wrongdoing or illegal conduct, and another court found that a monitoring system's failure to detect fraud generally will not be a predicate for liability. Additionally, one court refused to extend the duty of oversight to encompass a duty to monitor the private affairs of the company's CEO.

Business Risk

In *In re Citigroup Inc. Shareholder Derivative Litigation*, 964 A.2d 106 (Del. Ch. 2009), the court rejected the plaintiffs' attempt to impose liability on directors for a failure to monitor business risks, specifically the purported failure to monitor the bank's exposure to the subprime mortgage market. In *Citigroup*, the court expressed hostility to the attempt to extend *Caremark* obligations to liability predicated on the purported failure to monitor business risks: "While it may be tempting to say that directors have the same duties to monitor and oversee business risk, imposing *Caremark-type* duties on directors to monitor business risk is fundamentally different." *Id* at 131. The bank, the court noted, was in the business of balancing risk and return. *Id.* Courts are not. "To impose oversight liability on directors for failure to monitor 'excessive' risk would involve courts in conducting hindsight evaluations of decisions at the heart of the business judgment of directors." *Id.*

The court noted that taking plaintiffs' theory—that defendants should be liable for their failure to foresee the extent of the problems in the sub-prime mortgage market—to its logical conclusion would mean that defendants could be found similarly liable for their failure to predict the problem and profit from it. *Id.* at 131 n.78. "If directors are going to be held liable for losses for failing to accurately predict market events, then why not hold them liable for failing to profit by predicting market events that, in hindsight, the directors should have seen because of certain red (or green?) flags?" *Id.*

While the court did not rule out the possibility that under some set of facts directors could possibly be held liable for their failure to monitor a company's business risk, *id.* at 125–26, "[o]versight duties under Delaware law are not designed to subject directors, even expert directors, to *personal liability* for failure to predict the future and to properly evaluate business risk." *Id.* at 131.

While the plaintiffs cast their claims as a failure of the duty to monitor the risk of Citigroup's exposure to the sub-prime mortgage market, the court found that the plaintiffs' claims were more accurately characterized as an attack on "business decisions that, in hindsight, turned out poorly for the Company." *Id.* at 124. "To the extent the Court allows shareholder plaintiffs to succeed on a theory that a director is liable for a failure to monitor business risk, the Court risks undermining the well settled policy of Delaware law by inviting Courts to perform a hindsight evaluation of the reasonableness or prudence of directors' business decisions." *Id.* at 126. In fact, the court noted that the "essence of the business judgment of managers and directors is deciding how the company will evaluate the trade-off between risk and return." *Id.* Application of *Caremark* obligations to this decision process would invite the very type of "judicial second guessing" that the business judgment rule is designed to prevent. *Id.* at 126, 131.

The court ultimately dismissed the *Caremark* claims, finding that the derivative plaintiffs had "failed to state a *Caremark* claim sufficient to excuse demand based on a theory that the directors did not fulfill their oversight obligations by failing to monitor the business risk of the company." *Id.* at 128. The court cited a number of factors in support of its decision. For instance, the plaintiffs did not dispute that Citigroup had a number of procedures and controls in place to monitor and evaluate risk. *Id.* at 127. The plaintiffs nevertheless argued that "red flags" should have alerted the directors of the pending losses Citigroup would face. *Id.* at 127–28. But the court rejected this argument, finding that the "red flags" were merely signs of the deteriorating economic condition, rather than evidence that would support a finding of liability, i.e., red flags that demonstrated that the directors had been aware of wrongdoing at Citigroup or that they were consciously disregarding their duties owed to Citigroup. *Id.* at 128.

Well-Functioning Monitoring Systems with No Knowledge of Wrongdoing

In *David Shaev Profit Sharing Account v. Armstrong*, No. 1449-N, 2006 Del. Ch. LEXIS 33 (Feb. 13, 2006), *aff'd*, 911 A.2d 802 (Del. 2006), the Delaware Court of Chancery held that directors could not be held liable under *Caremark* on a "bald allegation that directors bear liability where a concededly well-constituted oversight mechanism, having received no specific indications of misconduct, failed to discover fraud." *Id.* at *15–16. In *Shaev*, the derivative plaintiff filed a complaint, attempting to hold Citigroup directors liable in connection with Citigroup's transactions related to Enron and WorldCom. The plaintiff acknowledged that the directors had no knowledge of the alleged fraud and that the company had oversight mechanisms in place. *Id.* at *17–18. The plaintiff maintained, however, that "only a board violating its fiduciary duties could possibly have remained ignorant of Citigroup's allegedly corrupt relationships with Enron and WorldCom." *Id.* at *17. The court rejected the premise, holding that "these allegations are precisely the type of conclusory statements that do not constitute a *Caremark* claim." *Id.* at *18. The court reasoned that there were no allegations regarding inadequate controls or red flags that had alerted the board to potential misconduct. *Id.*

The *Shaev* decision and the case of *Guttman v. Huang*, 823 A.2d 492, 506–07 (Del. Ch. 2003) each dismissed a *Caremark* claim, and in so doing, the decisions are instructive in that they set out examples of the type of conduct that could be found to be a predicate for a *Caremark* claim:

- Lack of "an audit committee or other important supervisory structures" (*Shaev*, 2006 Del. Ch. LEXIS 33, at *16);
- The failure of the company's audit committee to meet (*Id.* at *17);
- The existence of "an audit committee [that] met only sporadically and devoted patently inadequate time to its work" (*Guttman*, 823 A.2d at 507);
- The board or audit committee ignored or failed to investigate notice of serious improprieties or misconduct (*Id.*; *Shaev*, 2006 Del. Ch. LEXIS 33, at *17), or;
- The board or audit committee learned of irregularities and encouraged their continuation (*Guttman*, 823 A.2d at 507).

Personal Affairs

In *Beam ex rel. Martha Stewart Living Omnimedia, Inc. v. Stewart*, 833 A.2d 961, 972 (Del. Ch. 2003), the Delaware Court of Chancery found that "the defendant directors had no duty to monitor [Martha] Stewart's personal actions." In *Beam*, a derivative action was filed against various directors of Martha Stewart Living Omnimedia, Inc. based, in part, on their alleged failure to monitor Martha Stewart's personal, financial, and legal affairs. *Id.* at 970–71. These allegations stemmed from Martha Stewart's alleged trading of stock of ImClone Systems, Inc. on inside information. *Id.* at 968. The court dismissed plaintiff's claim as an unreasonable extension of the board's oversight responsibilities. *See id.* at 971–72.

Judicial Perspective: Correct Demand Futility Standard for *Caremark* Claims

On a motion to dismiss a derivative complaint on the grounds that a plaintiff has failed to adequately plead that the required pre-suit demand on the board would be futile, the court will analyze plaintiff's demand futility allegations under Rule 23.1 which requires that such allegations be specified with particularity. *See, e.g.*, Del. Ct. Ch. R. 23.1(a). Where the underlying allegations relate to a challenged transaction or a business decision — i.e., board action, the *Aronson* test is applied: "[The] plaintiffs must provide particularized factual allegations that raise a reasonable doubt that '(1) the directors are disinterested and independent [or] (2) the challenged transaction was otherwise the product of a valid exercise of business judgment.'" *In re Citigroup*, 964 A.2d at 120 (quoting *Brehm v. Eisner*, 746 A.2d 244, 253 (Del. 2000), and *Aronson v. Lewis*, 473 A.2d 805, 814 (Del. 1984) (second alteration in original)). But where the shareholder has objected to board inaction, as is the case with *Caremark* claims, the *Rales* test governs: "[The complaint] must allege particularized facts that 'create a reasonable doubt that, as of the time the complaint is filed, the board of directors could have properly exercised its independent and disinterested business judgment in responding to a demand.'" *Id.* (quoting *Rales v. Blasband*, 634 A.2d 927, 934 (Del. 1993)).

Exculpation Provision May Be Inapplicable to Breach of Loyalty Claim

Delaware

When discussing director liability, the Delaware courts often reference whether or not a corporation has adopted a "section 102(b)(7) provision." Under title 8, section 102(b)(7) of the Delaware Code, which governs the provisions of a corporation's articles of incorporation, a corporation may adopt:

> [a] provision eliminating or limiting the personal liability of a director to the corporation or its stockholders for monetary damages for breach of fiduciary duty as a director, provided that such provision shall not eliminate or limit the liability of a director: (i) For any breach of the director's duty of loyalty to the corporation or its stockholders; [or] (ii) for acts or omissions not in good faith or which involve intentional misconduct or a knowing violation of law[.]

Del. Code Ann. tit. 8, § 102(b)(7). This is an important provision as it "can exculpate directors from monetary liability for a breach of the duty of care." *Stone*, 911 A.2d at 367. Put another way, if a corporation has adopted this provision in its articles of incorporation, directors will not be subject to liability if they were involved in a board decision that was not well-informed, a result of an inadequate process, or grossly negligent.

Notes and Comments

It is important to note that directors will not be protected by a section 102(b)(7) provision for breaches of the duty to monitor, as these violations are a breach of a director's duty of loyalty and necessarily involve a failure to act in good faith. *See, e.g.*, *In re Citigroup*, 964 A.2d at 125 ("[O]ne can see a similarity between the standard for assessing oversight liability and the standard for assessing a disinterested director's decision under the duty of care when the company has adopted an exculpatory provision pursuant to § 102(b)(7). In either case, a plaintiff can show that the director defendants will be liable if their acts or omissions constitute bad faith."); *Guttman*, 823 A.2d at 506 ("Functionally, *Caremark* ... matches the liability landscape for most corporate directors, who are insulated from monetary damage awards by exculpatory charter provisions.").

The Model Business Corporation Act

The MBCA provision exculpating directors under certain circumstances, provides that a corporation's articles of incorporation may contain:

> a provision eliminating or limiting the liability of a director to the corporation or its shareholders for money damages for any action taken, or any failure to take any action, as a director, except liability for (A) the amount of a financial benefit received by a director to which the director is not entitled; (B) an intentional infliction of harm on the corporation or the shareholders; ... or (D) an intentional violation of criminal law.

Model Bus. Corp. Act § 2.02(b)(4).

The MBCA provision precludes exculpation of liability for conduct that would constitute "intentional infliction of harm" or "intentional violation of criminal law." *Id.*; *see also id.* § 2.02 cmt. at 2–35 (2013 Revision). In contrast, Delaware precludes exculpation of liability for conduct that constitutes a "breach of the director's duty of loyalty" or "acts or omissions not in good faith or which involve intentional misconduct or a knowing violation of law." Del. Code Ann. tit. 8, § 102(b)(7)(i)–(ii). The drafters of the MBCA suggest that requiring that directors be held liable for "intentional" conduct is more precise, because it is directed at a board member with actual knowledge to harm the corporation, rather than a director that acted "knowingly," which necessitates a general, not specific, intent. Model Bus. Corp. Act § 2.02 cmt. at 2–20 (2013 rev.).

Board Assessment and Checklist

Given the diverse nature of companies, the markets they operate in and the products they sell, as well as the complex nature of the oversight obligations, a one-size-fits-all checklist is impossible. The following, which is based on the U.S. Sentencing Guidelines Manual § 8B2.1 (2015), is offered as a guide, rather than a minimal standard or complete prescription for compliance.

1) Does the company have standards and procedures in place to prevent and detect illegal conduct, such as a compliance and ethics program?

2) Has the Board of Directors assigned a committee, such as the Audit Committee, to oversee the implementation and effectiveness of the compliance and ethics program?

3) Is a specific company employee "delegated day-to-day operational responsibility for the compliance and ethics program"?

4) Does that person report periodically to senior management and a committee of the Board of Directors (e.g., Audit Committee) on the effectiveness of the compliance and ethics program?

5) Does that person have adequate resources, authority and access to senior management and a committee of the Board of Directors (e.g., Audit Committee)?

6) Does the company "take reasonable steps to communicate periodically" the standards and procedures of the compliance and ethics program within the organization, such as through training or dissemination of the program's standards and procedures?

7) Does the company take reasonable steps to ensure that the "compliance and ethics program is followed," such as monitoring and auditing for illegal activity?

8) Does the company periodically evaluate the effectiveness of the compliance and ethics program?

9) Does the company have and publicize a mechanism for employees to anonymously and confidentially report illegal conduct?

10) Does the company periodically assess the risk of illegal activity, and modify the program to address any changed risk assessment?

Assignment

- **Hypothetical:** You are the Chief Compliance Officer at your [Team's] Corporation. Perform a compliance risk assessment and determine which areas of compliance within your Company require updating.

Chapter 14

Corporate Compliance and Attorney-Client Privilege

Introduction

Privileges play a critical role in fostering the open exchange of information that is vital to the mission of any compliance professional. Without the assurance of confidentiality, employees are less likely to impart complete and accurate information, the lifeblood of any valuable compliance review or internal investigation. In the context of a corporation, multiple privileges potentially affording such confidentiality are potentially applicable, including the attorney-client, work product, and self-critical analysis privileges.

Today's complex regulatory environment presents multiple challenges to compliance professionals. Among those challenges is to meet the informational demands of regulatory agencies while protecting the sanctity of privileged information. Increasingly, regulatory agencies have demanded access to privileged information that would be otherwise unavailable to an adversary in ordinary discovery in litigation, and, increasingly, many compliance and legal professionals have felt that, because of the power wielded by certain regulatory agencies, they have no choice but to comply with those demands and, thereby, waive applicable privileges. In this light, it is crucial for compliance professionals to be familiar with the scope and applicability of the available privileges and to be able to assess the consequences of waivers.

Attorney-Client Privilege — The Basics

The attorney-client privilege is a rule of evidence that protects the confidentiality of communications between an attorney and client. According to the Supreme Court, the purpose of the privilege

> is to encourage full and frank communication between attorneys and their clients and thereby promote broader public interests in the observance of law and the administration of justice. The privilege recognizes that sound legal advice or advocacy serves public ends and that such advice or advocacy depends upon the lawyer's being fully informed by the client.

Upjohn Co. v. United States, 449 U.S. 383, 389 (1981). The attorney-client privilege is relatively simple in formulation, but extremely complex in application. The complexity in application is caused by a number of factors, including that the privilege varies according to state law, is often not susceptible to bright-line rules and can be highly fact-specific. That complexity is especially pronounced in the context of communications to or from a corporate client.

The application of the privilege to the communications between a lawyer and an individual client is comparatively straightforward. However, its application to a corporate client, a juridical entity, is significantly more complicated because any number of people can act for or speak on behalf of a corporation, including its officers, directors, employees or other agents. In this light, the identity of the "client," may not be clear and courts have grappled with how to define the "client," in the corporate context for purposes of the application of the privilege. Other than the fact that virtually all courts reject the proposition that any employee or agent of the corporation is the "client," such that the privilege can be maintained even if a privileged communication has been disclosed to hundreds or thousands of corporate employees, there is a good deal of uncertainty as to what constitutes the "client" in the corporate context. Accordingly, there is uncertainty as to which employees or agents of a corporation privileged communications can be disclosed without causing a waiver.

The privilege applies only if:

> (1) the asserted holder of the privilege is or sought to become a client; (2) the person to whom the communication was made (a) is a member of the bar of a court, or his subordinate and (b) in connection with this communication is acting as a lawyer; (3) the communication relates to a fact of which the attorney was informed (a) by his client (b) without the presence of strangers (c) for the purpose of securing primarily either (i) an opinion on law or (ii) legal services or (iii) assistance in some legal proceeding, and not (d) for the purpose of committing a crime or tort; and (4) the privilege has been (a) claimed and (b) not waived by the client.

U.S. v. United Shoe Machinery Corp., 89 F. Supp. 357 (D. Mass. 1950).

The privilege applies in both directions: to communications from the client to the attorney, and to communications from the attorney to the client. *Schwimmer v. U.S.*, 232 F.2d 855 (8th Cir.), *cert. denied*, 352 U.S. 833 (1956); *Green v. IRS*, 556 F. Supp. 79, 85 (N.D. Ind. 1982), *aff'd without op.*, 734 F.2d 18 (7th Cir. 1984). It protects communications, including documents that consist of or reflect the substance of advice given by an attorney based on facts, but not necessarily the facts themselves. *Upjohn Co. v. United States*, 449 U.S. 383, 395–96 (1981). The attorney-client privilege also extends to communications between agents of a client and the client's attorney, assuming the other conditions of the privilege are satisfied. *Golden Trade v. Lee Ansarel Co.*, 143 F.R.D. 514, 518 (S.D.N.Y. 1992) ("[I]f the purpose of the communication is to facilitate the rendering of legal services by the attorney, the privilege may also cover communications between the client and his attorney's representative, between the client's representative and the attorney, and between the attorney and his representative.") Courts generally define the term "agent" broadly to encompass a range of individuals, from expert consultants to relatives to insurance agents, whose presence is necessary to the purpose of the meeting and to the rendering of advice. *See, e.g., Kevlick v. Goldstein*, 724 F.2d 844, 849 (1st Cir. 1984) (client's father); *Foseco Int'l. v. Fireline Inc.*, 546 F. Supp. 22, 25 (N.D. Ohio 1982) (patent agent); *Miller v. Haulmark*, 104 F.R.D. 442, 445 (E.D. Pa. 1984) (insurance agent); *Harkobusic v. General American*, 31 F.R.D. 264, 265 (W.D. Pa. 1962) (brother-in-law).

Whether an attorney-client relationship exists depends on the understanding of the client. "The professional relationship for purposes of the privilege hinges upon the belief that one is consulting a lawyer and his intention to seek legal advice." *Wylie v. Marley Co.*, 891 F.2d 1463, 1471 (10th Cir. 1989). Accordingly, the privilege applies to confidential communications between an individual and a person he reasonably believes to be his attorney, even if the attorney ultimately elects not to represent the client, and even if the attorney is not a member of the bar. *See U.S. v. Mullen*, 776 F. Supp. 620, 621 (D. Mass. 1991) ("the attorney-client privilege may apply to confidential communications made to an accountant when the client is under the mistaken, but reasonable, belief that the professional from whom legal advice is sought is in fact an attorney."); *U.S. v. Tyler*, 745 F. Supp. 423, 425–26 (W.D. Mich. 1990); *U.S. v. Boffa*, 513 F. Supp. 517, 523 (D. Del. 1981).

The "Control Group" Test

The "control group" test was designed to answer the question of who, short of all employees or agents of the corporation, constitutes the "client" for the purposes of application of the privilege in the corporate context. In *City of Philadelphia v. Westinghouse Elec. Corp.* 210 F. Supp. 486 (E.D. Pa. 1962), the case in which the "control group" test originated, Judge Kirkpatrick of the United States District Court for the Eastern District of Pennsylvania held that information obtained from employees of Westinghouse Corporation during interviews of employees by the corporation's attorneys was not privileged because the employees who were interviewed were not members of the "control group," i.e., they did not have the power or authority to act on the advice rendered by the corporation's attorneys.

The decision rejected the virtually unlimited scope of the corporate attorney-client privilege announced in *U.S. v. United Shoe Machinery Corp.* 89 F. Supp. 357 (D. Mass. 1950), i.e., that the privilege extended to communications between any employee of the corporation and counsel, and announced the more limited "control group" test:

> Keeping in mind that the question is, "is it the corporation which is seeking the lawyer's advice when the asserted privileged communication is made?," the most satisfactory solution, I think, is that if the employee making the communication, of whatever rank he may be, is in a position to control or even to take a substantial part in a decision about any action which the corporation may take upon the advice of the attorney, or if he is an authorized

member of a body or group which has that authority, then, in effect, he is (or personifies) the corporation when he makes his disclosure to the lawyer and the privilege would apply. In all other cases the employee would be merely giving information to the lawyer to enable the latter to advise those in the corporation having the authority to act or refrain from acting on the advice.

City of Philadelphia v. Westinghouse Elec. Corp., 210 F. Supp. 483, 485 (E.D. Pa. 1962).

Hickman v. Taylor. 329 U.S. 495 (1947), served as a basis for Judge Kirkpatrick's decision to reject *United Shoe*. In *Hickman*, the Supreme Court held that an attorney's notes of interviews with his corporate client's employees, were not protected by the attorney-client privilege. According to Judge Kirkpatrick, this holding "very clearly shows the distinction between statements by employees of the client and statements by the client itself." *City of Philadelphia*, 210 F. Supp. at 485. However, in *Hickman*, the Supreme Court stopped short of "delineat[ing] the content and scope of ... [the] [attorney-client] privilege as recognized in the federal courts," and limited its holding to the facts of the case: "th[e] privilege does not extend to information which an attorney secures from a witness while acting for his client in anticipation of litigation."

City of Philadelphia did not give concrete guidance regarding which employees were members of the "control group." The court recognized that this would likely vary from corporation to corporation and could depend upon factors such as which departments or divisions within a corporation the matter upon which the advice is sought concerns. *Id.* at 486 ("Of course, there may be cases where an employee is actually authorized to make a decision after consultation with an attorney. An example might be the head of the Claims Department, who frequently has authority to settle damage claims without any action by the Board of Directors or the chief officers, or without their even being advised of it. In such case the communication would be privileged because the claims executive was the person who could act upon the lawyer's advice and he was the person receiving it.").

The "control group" test was subsequently adopted by the Third, Sixth and Tenth Circuit Courts of Appeal and by various district courts within those Circuits as well as in the Second, Fourth, Fifth, and Ninth Circuits. The "control group" test has been criticized however. Indeed, the control group test arguably frustrated the very purpose of the privilege—to foster the full and frank communication between an attorney and client—because it did not account for the fact that attorneys are often required to obtain information from employees outside of the control group in order to give advice to the members of the control group; and that unless such information were privileged to the same extent as the advice based on that information, attorneys would be hamstrung in their efforts to give informed legal advice. Edna Selan Epstein, The Attorney-Client Privilege and the Work-Product Doctrine 102 (ABA, Section of Litigation, 4th ed.)

The Subject Matter Test

In 1970, the Seventh Circuit rejected the control-group test and opted for a "subject matter" test. In *Harper & Row Publishers v. Decker* (423 F.2d 487 (7th Cir. 1970), *aff'd* 400 U.S. 348 (1971)), the Seventh Circuit Court of Appeals held that the subject matter of a communication between a corporate employee and the corporation's counsel, rather than the employee's authority over the matter in question, was determinative of whether the communication was privileged. Specifically, the court granted a petition for a writ of mandamus compelling the district court to vacate an order, based upon application of the control group test, permitting the plaintiffs to inspect documents withheld by the defendants on the grounds of privilege:

> We conclude that an employee of a corporation, though not a member of its control group, is sufficiently identified with the corporation so that his communication to the corporation's attorney is privileged where the employee makes the communication at the direction of his superiors in the corporation and where the subject matter upon which the attorney's advice is sought by the corporation and dealt with in the communication is the performance by the employee of the duties of his employment.

Upjohn Company v. United States

In *Upjohn Company v. United States,* 449 U.S. 383 (1981), the Supreme Court rejected the "control group" test but "decline[d] to lay down a broad rule or series of rules" to govern future questions regarding the scope or application of the attorney-client privilege. *Id.* 386. (For more information on *Upjohn*, see Chapter 8, *supra*.)

In *Upjohn*, the company commenced an internal investigation to determine whether and the extent to which a foreign subsidiary had made questionable payments to foreign government officials to obtain government contracts. As part of the investigation, the company's counsel sent a questionnaire to all foreign managers seeking information concerning the payments. In addition, the company's counsel conducted interviews with the recipients of the questionnaire as well as with various company officers and employees. Subsequently, the Internal Revenue Service commenced an investigation and issued a subpoena demanding the production of the questionnaires and the memoranda and notes of the interviews with company personnel. The company refused to produce the documents on the grounds that they were protected from disclosure by the attorney-client and work product privileges.

In a proceeding brought by the government to enforce the subpoena, the district court held that the company had waived the attorney-client privilege and that the government had made a sufficient showing of necessity to overcome the work product doctrine. On appeal, the Sixth Circuit found that although there had been no waiver of privilege, under the "control group" test, the privilege did not apply because the individuals who responded to the questionnaires and who were interviewed were not members of the "control group."

The Supreme Court reversed and explicitly rejected the "control group" test, finding that it "frustrates the very purpose of the privilege by discouraging the communication of relevant information by employees of the client to attorneys seeking to render legal advice to the client corporation." *Upjohn*, 449 U.S. at 392. The Court recognized that the "control group" test did not take account of the fact that employees outside of the "control group" "can, by actions within the scope of their employment, embroil the corporation in serious legal difficulties, and it is only natural that these employees would have relevant information needed by corporate counsel if he is adequately to advise the client with respect to such actual or potential difficulties." *Id.* at 391. Accordingly, if the privilege protected only communications between an attorney and the control group, "it [is] difficult for corporate attorneys to formulate sound advice," and "threatens to limit the valuable efforts to corporate counsel to ensure their client's compliance with the law." *Id.* at 392.

Ultimately, the Court held that the communications at issue were privileged because they were made by company employees to company counsel at the direction of corporate superiors in order to secure legal advice from counsel. Specifically:

> Information, not available from upper-echelon management, was needed to supply a basis for legal advice concerning compliance with securities and tax laws, foreign laws, currency regulations, duties to shareholders, and potential litigation in each of these areas. The communications concerned matters within the scope of the employees' corporate duties, and the employees themselves were sufficiently aware that they were being questioned in order that the corporation could obtain legal advice.

Id. at 394.[1]

Exceptions to the Attorney-Client Privilege

The attorney-client privilege is not inviolable. Indeed, there are at least five well recognized exceptions to the privilege, i.e., circumstances where, notwithstanding the fact that all elements of the privilege are satisfied, an otherwise privileged communication will not be treated as such. These five exceptions can be generally described as: the Fiduciary Exception, the Crime-Fraud Exception, the Common-Interest Exception, the Attorney Self-Defense Exception and the Death of a Testator Exception. The Crime-Fraud Exception is addressed below.

The attorney-client privilege does not extend to communications made in connection with a client seeking advice on how to commit a criminal or fraudulent

---

1. In August 2015, the United States Court of Appeals for the D.C. Circuit, citing *Upjohn*, ruled that documents produced in connection with an internal investigation were protected by attorney-client privilege and the work product doctrine. *In re Kellogg Brown & Root, Inc.*, 796 F.3d 137 (D.C. Cir. 2015). The court stated that if the documents from KBR's internal investigation relating to fraud were required to be turned over to the plaintiff it would "erode the confidentiality of an internal investigation in a manner squarely contrary to the Supreme Court's guidance in *Upjohn*." *Id.* at 150.

act. *See In re Grant Jury Subpoena Duces Tecum (Marc Rich)*, 731 F.2d 1032, 1041 (2d Cir. 1984) ("Advice sought in furtherance of a future or ongoing fraud is unprivileged; communications with respect to advice as to past frauds are within the privilege."). Nor will a client's statement of intent to commit a crime be privileged, even if the client was not seeking advice about how to commit the crime. *In re Grand Jury Proceedings (Doe)*, 102 F.3d 748, 749–51 (4th Cir. 1996) (crime/fraud exception applied to communications between attorneys and client even though attorneys were unaware that their advice was being used to conceal client's fraud).

A party seeking discovery of privileged communications based upon the crime-fraud exception must make a threshold showing that the legal advice was obtained in furtherance of the fraudulent activity and was closely related to it. The party seeking disclosure does not satisfy this burden merely by alleging that a crime or fraud has occurred and then asserting that disclosure of privileged communications might help prove the crime or fraud. There must be a specific showing that a particular document or communication was made in furtherance of the client's alleged crime or fraud. *See In re Grand Jury Investigation (Schroeder)*, 842 F.2d 1223 (11th Cir. 1988).

Selective Waiver

Today, the most vexing privilege issue facing corporations is "selective waiver," i.e., whether to waive privilege at the request of a government agency that is conducting an investigation and run the risk that doing so will affect a universal waiver vis à vis the rest of the world, including plaintiffs in civil actions against the corporation.

Often, in response to allegations of wrongdoing by its employees, a corporation will conduct an internal investigation. If a government investigation is commenced to inquire into the same allegations of wrongdoing, the government will often ask the corporation to waive privilege so that the government can have access to the results of the corporation's counsel's investigation. Although there are incentives to "cooperating" with the government by waiving privilege, "selective waiver" is not universally accepted and, as a result, a waiver vis à vis the government can constitute a waiver vis à vis the rest of the world, including class action plaintiffs; and more often than not, where there is a government investigation of a public corporation, there is a civil class-action lawsuit against that corporation.

Although the Eighth Circuit created the concept of selective waiver of the attorney-client privilege in 1977 in *Diversified Industries, Inc. v. Meredith,* 572 F.2d 596 (8th Cir. 1977), the majority of courts that have considered the issue since then, have rejected selective waiver (that is, held that a waiver to one party is a waiver to all parties). For example, according to the D.C. Circuit, "[t]he client cannot be permitted to pick and choose among his opponents, waiving the privilege for some and resurrecting the claim of confidentiality to obstruct others." *Permian Corp. v. United States,* 665 F.2d 1214, 1221 (D.C. Cir. 1981).

The Ninth Circuit addressed selective waiver in *In re Pac. Pictures Corp.*, 679 F.3d 1121 (9th Cir. 2012).

Pac. Pictures Corp. v. United States Dist. Court

679 F.3d 1121 (9th Cir. 2012)

AMENDED OPINION

Opinion by Judge O'SCANNLAIN, Circuit Judge:

We must decide whether a party waives attorney-client privilege forever by voluntarily disclosing privileged documents to the federal government.

I

In the 1930s, writer Jerome Siegel and illustrator Joe Shuster joined forces to create the character that would eventually become Superman. They ceded their intellectual property rights to D.C. Comics when they joined the company as independent contractors in 1937.[2] Since the Man of Steel made his first appearance in 1938, he has been fighting for "truth, justice, and the American way." Shuster, Siegel, their heirs ("Heirs"), and D.C. Comics have been fighting for the rights to his royalties for almost as long.

Marc Toberoff, a Hollywood producer and a licensed attorney, stepped into the fray around the turn of the millennium. As one of his many businesses, Toberoff pairs intellectual property rights with talent and markets these packages to movie studios. Having set his sights on Superman, Toberoff approached the Heirs with an offer to manage preexisting litigation over the rights Siegel and Shuster had ceded to D.C. Comics. He also claimed that he would arrange for a new Superman film to be produced. To pursue these goals, Toberoff created a joint venture between the Heirs and an entity he owned. Toberoff served as both a business advisor and an attorney for that venture. The ethical and professional concerns raised by Toberoff's actions will likely occur to many readers, but they are not before this court.

While the preexisting litigation was pending, Toberoff hired a new lawyer to work for one of his companies. This attorney remained in Toberoff's employ for only about three months before allegedly absconding with copies of several documents from the Siegel and Shuster files. Unsuccessful in his alleged attempt to use the documents to solicit business from the Heirs, this attorney sent the documents to executives at D.C. Comics. While he did not include his name with the package, he did append a cover letter, written in the form of a timeline, outlining in detail Toberoff's alleged master plan to capture Superman for himself.

This happened no later than June 2006, and the parties have been battling over what should be done with these documents ever since. Rather than exploiting the documents, D.C. Comics entrusted them to an outside attorney and sought to obtain them through ordinary discovery in the two ongoing lawsuits over Superman. Con-

---

2. [1] The name and corporate structure of the real party in interest has changed a number of times since 1938. For simplicity, we refer to it as "D.C. Comics."

sidering every communication he had with the Heirs to be privileged—regardless of whether the communication was in his capacity as a business advisor or an attorney—Toberoff resisted all such efforts. Ultimately, in April 2007, a magistrate judge ordered certain documents, including the attorney's cover letter, turned over to D.C. Comics. A few months later, Toberoff at long last reported the incident to the authorities (specifically the Federal Bureau of Investigation). In December 2008, Toberoff finally produced at least some of the documents.

In 2010, D.C. Comics filed this lawsuit against Toberoff, the Heirs, and three entities in which Toberoff owned a controlling interest (collectively, the "Petitioners"), claiming that Toberoff interfered with its contractual relationships with the Heirs. The attorney's cover letter formed the basis of the lawsuit and was incorporated into the complaint. Toberoff has continued to resist the use of any of the documents taken from his offices, including those already disclosed to D.C. Comics and especially the cover letter.

About a month after the suit was filed, Toberoff asked the Office of the United States Attorney for the Central District of California to investigate the theft. In response to a request from Toberoff, the U.S. Attorney's Office issued a grand jury subpoena for the documents as well as a letter stating that if Toberoff voluntarily complied with the subpoena the Government would "not provide the ... documents ... to non-governmental third parties except as may be required by law or court order." The letter also confirmed that disclosure would indicate that "Toberoff has obtained all relevant permissions and consents needed (if any) to provide the ... documents ... to the government." Armed with this letter, Toberoff readily complied with the subpoena, making no attempt to redact anything from the documents.

D.C. Comics immediately requested all documents disclosed to the U.S. Attorney, claiming that the disclosure of these unredacted copies waived any remaining privilege. Examining the weight of authority from other circuits, the magistrate judge agreed that a party may not selectively waive attorney-client privilege. The magistrate judge reasoned that, because a voluntary disclosure of privileged materials breaches confidentiality and is inconsistent with the theory behind the privilege, such disclosure waives that privilege regardless of whether the third party is the government or a civil litigant. Having delivered the documents to the government, the magistrate judge concluded, Petitioners could not rely on the attorney-client privilege to shield them from D.C. Comics.

However, the magistrate judge noted that this circuit has twice declined to decide whether a party may selectively waive the attorney-client privilege, and stayed his order to allow Petitioners to seek review. The district court denied review. Petitioners seek to overturn the magistrate's order through a writ of mandamus.

II

A writ of mandamus is an extraordinary remedy. A party seeking the writ has the "burden of showing that [his] right to the issuance of the writ is clear and indisputable." *Bauman v. U.S. Dist. Ct.*, 557 F.2d 650, 656 (9th Cir. 1977) (internal quotation marks omitted). In evaluating whether a petitioner has met that burden, we consider: (1) whether he "has no other adequate means" of seeking relief; (2) whether he "will be damaged or prejudiced in a way not correctable on appeal" after final judgment; (3) whether the "district court's order is clearly erroneous as a matter of law"; (4) whether the order "is an oft-repeated error"; and (5) whether the order "raises new and important problems, or issues of first impression." *Id.* at 654–55. We have established no specific formula to weigh these factors, but failure to show what is generally listed as the third factor, error, is fatal to any petition for mandamus. *See Burlington N. & Santa Fe. Ry. v. U.S. Dist. Ct.*, 408 F.3d 1142, 1146 (9th Cir. 2005).[3]

III

Under certain circumstances, the attorney-client privilege will protect communications between clients and their attorneys from compelled disclosure in a court of law. *See Upjohn Co. v. United States*, 449 U.S. 383, 389, 101 S. Ct. 677, 66 L. Ed. 2d 584 (1981). Though this in some way impedes the truth-finding process, we have long recognized that "the advocate and counselor [needs] to know all that relates to the client's reasons for seeking representation" if he is to provide effective legal advice. *Trammel v. United States*, 445 U.S. 40, 51, 100 S. Ct. 906, 63 L. Ed. 2d 186 (1980); *see also* 8 John Henry Wigmore, Evidence § 2290 (John T. McNaughton, ed. 1961). As such, we recognize the privilege in order to "encourage full and frank communication between attorneys and their clients and thereby promote broader public interests in the observance of law and administration of justice." *Upjohn Co.*, 449 U.S. at 389.[4]

Nonetheless, because, like any other testimonial privilege, this rule "contravene[s] the fundamental principle that the public has a right to every man's evidence," *Trammel*, 445 U.S. at 50 (internal alterations and quotation marks omitted), we construe it narrowly to serve its purposes, *see, e.g., United States v. Martin*, 278 F.3d 988, 999 (9th Cir. 2002).[5] In particular, we recognize several ways by which parties may waive the privilege. *See, e.g., Hernandez v. Tanninen*, 604 F.3d 1095, 1100 (9th Cir. 2010). Most pertinent here is that voluntarily disclosing privileged documents to third parties will generally destroy the privilege. *Id.* The reason behind this rule is that, "'[i]f clients themselves divulge such information to third parties, chances are that they would also have divulged it to their attorneys, even without the protection of the

---

3. [2] Petitioners assert that, because this case presents an issue of first impression, they must demonstrate simple rather than clear error. We have not always been precise as to whether we look for "error" or "clear error" where our sister circuits have addressed an issue, but we have not. *Compare Anon. Online Speakers v. U.S. Dist. Ct.*, 661 F.3d 1168 (9th Cir. 2011) (applying the clear error standard in a circuit split situation), *with San Jose Mercury News, Inc. v. U.S. Dist. Ct.*, 187 F.3d 1096 (9th Cir. 1999) (applying the simple error standard when other circuits had weighed in on parts of an issue). We assume but do not decide that Petitioners need show only error.

4. [3] Because Petitioners have never challenged the district court's application of federal law, we assume but do not decide that this was correct even though this case involves diversity claims to which state privilege law would apply. *Lewis v. United States*, 517 F.2d 236, 237 n.2 (9th Cir. 1975) (per curiam).

5. [4] Because no one challenges whether these communications would have been privileged absent waiver, we do not address that issue. For example, we assume but do not decide that these communications were all made for the purpose of obtaining legal as opposed to business advice. *Cf. United States v. Ruehle*, 583 F.3d 600, 608 n.8 (9th Cir. 2009) (noting that business advice does not fall within the purview of attorney-client privilege even if the advisor is a lawyer).

privilege.'" Comment, *Stuffing the Rabbit Back into the Hat: Limited Waiver of the Attorney-Client Privilege in an Administrative Agency Investigation*, 130 U. Pa. L. Rev. 1198, 1207 (1982). Under such circumstances, there simply is no justification to shut off judicial inquiry into these communications.

Petitioners concede that this is the general rule, but they assert a number of reasons why it should not apply to them.

A

Petitioners' primary contention is that because Toberoff disclosed these documents to the government, as opposed to a civil litigant, his actions did not waive the privilege as to the world at large. That is, they urge that we adopt the theory of "selective waiver" initially accepted by the Eight Circuit, *Diversified Industries, Inc. v. Meredith*, 572 F.2d 596 (8th Cir. 1978) (en banc), but rejected by every other circuit to consider the issue since, see *In re Qwest Communs. Int'l*, 450 F.3d 1179, 1197 (10th Cir. 2006); *Burden-Meeks v. Welch*, 319 F.3d 897, 899 (7th Cir. 2003); *In re Columbia/HCA Healthcare Corp. Billing Practices Litig.*, 293 F.3d 289, 295 (6th Cir. 2002) [hereinafter "In re Columbia"]; *United States v. Mass. Inst. of Tech.*, 129 F.3d 681, 686 (1st Cir. 1997); *Genentech, Inc. v. United States Int'l Trade Comm'n*, 122 F.3d 1409, 1416–18 (Fed. Cir. 1997); *In re Steinhardt Partners, L.P.*, 9 F.3d 230, 236 (2d Cir. 1993); *Westinghouse Elec. Corp. v. Republic of Philippines*, 951 F.2d 1414, 1425 (3d Cir. 1991); *In re Martin Marietta Corp.*, 856 F.2d 619, 623–24 (4th Cir. 1988); *Permian Corp. v. United States*, 665 F.2d 1214, 1221, 214 U.S. App. D.C. 396 (D.C. Cir. 1981).

As the magistrate judge noted, we have twice deferred judgment on whether we will accept a theory of selective waiver. *United States v. Bergonzi*, 403 F.3d 1048, 1050 (9th Cir. 2005) (per curiam); *Bittaker v. Woodford*, 331 F.3d 715, 720 n.5 (9th Cir. 2003) (en banc). But we share the concerns expressed by many of our sister circuits about the cursory analysis behind the Diversified rule. The Eighth Circuit—the first court of appeals to consider the issue—adopted what has become a highly controversial rule only because it concluded that "[t]o hold otherwise may have the effect of thwarting the developing procedure of corporations to employ independent outside counsel to investigate and advise them in order to protect stockholders." Diversified, 572 F.2d at 611. This apprehension has proven unjustified. Officers of public corporations, it seems, do not require a rule of selective waiver to employ outside consultants or voluntarily to cooperate with the government. *See, e.g., Westinghouse Elec. Corp.*, 951 F.2d at 1426.

More importantly, such reasoning does little, if anything, to serve the public good underpinning the attorney-client privilege. That is, "selective waiver does not serve the purpose of encouraging full disclosure to one's attorney in order to obtain informed legal assistance; it merely encourages voluntary disclosure to government agencies, thereby extending the privilege beyond its intended purpose." *Id.* at 1425.

It may well be that encouraging cooperation with the government is an alternative route to the ultimate goal of promoting adherence to the law. *In re Columbia*, 293 F.3d at 311 (Boggs, J., dissenting). And there are those who assert that "an exception to the third-party waiver rule need [not] be moored to the justifications of the attorney-client privilege." *Id.* at 308 (emphasis omitted). We disagree. If we were to unmoor a privilege from its underlying justification, we would at least be failing to construe the privilege narrowly. *Cf. Univ. of Pa. v. EEOC*, 493 U.S. 182, 189, 110 S. Ct. 577, 107 L. Ed. 2d 571 (1990) (citing *Trammel*, 445 U.S. at 50; *United States v. Bryan*, 339 U.S. 323, 331, 70 S. Ct. 724, 94 L. Ed. 884) (1950)). And more likely, we would be creating an entirely new privilege. *In re Qwest Communs. Int'l*, 450 F.3d 1179; *Westinghouse*, 951 F.2d at 1425.

It is not beyond our power to create such a privilege. *Univ. of Pa.*, 493 U.S. at 189 (noting that Fed. R. Evid. 501 provides certain flexibility to adopt privilege rules on a case-by-case basis). But as doing so requires balancing competing societal interests in access to evidence and in promoting certain types of communication, the Supreme Court has warned us not to "exercise this authority expansively." *Id.*; *see also United States v. Nixon*, 418 U.S. 683, 710, 94 S. Ct. 3090, 41 L. Ed. 2d 1039 (1974). Put simply, "[t]he balancing of conflicting interests of this type is particularly a legislative function." *Univ. of Pa.*, 493 U.S. at 189.

Since Diversified, there have been multiple legislative attempts to adopt a theory of selective waiver. Most have failed. Report of the Advisory Committee on Evidence Rules, May 15, 2007, at 4, available at http://www.uscourts.gov/uscourts/RulesAnd Policies/rules/Reports/2007-05-Committee_Report-Evidence.pdf (reporting the selective waiver provision separately from the general proposed rule); SEC Statement in Support of Proposed Section 24(d) of the Securities Exchange Act of 1934, 16 Sec. Reg. & L. Rep. 456, 461 (Mar. 2, 1984). But see H.R. Rep. No. 870, 96th Cong., 1st Sess. (1980), codified at 15 U.S.C. § 1312. Given that Congress has declined broadly to adopt a new privilege to protect disclosures of attorney-client privileged materials to the government, we will not do so here. *Univ. of Pa.*, 493 U.S. at 189 (requiring federal courts to be particularly cautious when legislators have "considered the relevant competing concerns but [have] not provided the privilege").

B

Petitioners next assert that even if we reject selective waiver as a general matter, we should enforce a purported confidentiality agreement based upon the letter from the U.S. Attorney's Office. Though no circuit has officially adopted such a rule, at least two have "left the door open to selective waiver" where there is a confidentiality agreement. *In re Columbia*, 293 F.3d at 301 (discussing *Steinhardt and Dellwood Farms, Inc. v. Cargill*, 128 F.3d 1122 (7th Cir. 1997)); *see also In re Qwest Communs Int'l*, 450 F.3d at 1192–94 (describing such a rule as a "leap" but declining to reject it completely).

Assuming that this letter constitutes a confidentiality agreement, Petitioners have provided no convincing reason that post hoc contracts regarding how information may be revealed encourage frank conversation at the time of advice. Indeed, as the Sixth Circuit has noted, while this approach "certainly protects the expectations of the parties to the confidentiality agreement, it does little to serve the 'public ends' of adequate legal representation that the attorney-client privilege is designed to protect." *In re Columbia*, 293 F.3d at 303. Instead, recognizing the validity of such a contract "merely [adds] another brush on an attorney's palette [to be] utilized and manipulated to gain tactical or strategic advantage." *Steinhardt*, 9 F.3d at 235; *cf. Permian Corp.*, 665 F.2d at 1221. And it would undermine the public good of promoting an efficient judicial system by fostering uncertainty and encouraging litigation. *Upjohn*, 449 U.S. at 393 (noting that an "uncertain privilege ... is little better than no privilege at all").

The only justification behind enforcing such agreements would be to encourage cooperation with the government. But Congress has declined to adopt even this limited form of selective waiver. *See Statement of Congressional Intent Regarding Rule 502 of the Federal Rules of Evidence*, 154 Cong. Rec. H. 7817 (2008), *reprinted in* Fed. R. Evid. 502 addendum to comm. n subdivision (d) (noting that Rule 502 "does not provide a basis for a court to enable parties to agree to a selective waiver of the privilege, such as to a federal agency conducting an investigation"). As such, we reject such a theory here.

D

Petitioners also argue that they should be treated differently because Toberoff produced these documents subject to a subpoena. Involuntary disclosures do not automatically waive the attorney-client privilege. *United States v. De La Jara*, 973 F.2d 746, 749–50 (9th Cir. 1992). But without the threat of contempt, the mere existence of a subpoena does not render testimony or the production of documents involuntary. *Westinghouse Elec. Corp.*, 951 F.2d at 1414; *see also United States v. Plache*, 913 F.2d 1375, 1380 (9th Cir. 1990). Instead, whether the subpoenaed party "chose not to assert the privilege when it was appropriate to do so is [also] relevant to the waiver analysis." *In re Grand Jury Proceedings*, 219 F.3d 175, 187 (2d Cir. 2000); *cf. In re Subpoenas Duces Tecum*, 738 F.2d 1367, 1369–70, 238 U.S. App. D.C. 221 (D.C. Cir. 1984).

Toberoff both solicited the subpoena and "chose not to assert the privilege when it was appropriate to do so...." *In re Grand Jury Proceedings*, 219 F.3d at 187. That is, even though the subpoena specifically contemplated that Toberoff may choose to redact privileged materials, he did not. Petitioners assert that the U.S. Attorney would not have been satisfied with redacted documents, but we will never know because Toberoff never tried. As such, we conclude that the district court properly treated the disclosure of these documents as voluntary.[6]

V

Because Petitioners have not established error, we need not discuss the other *Bauman* factors. The petition for mandamus is **DENIED**.

---

6. [5] As these preexisting documents were "sought for [their] own sake rather than to learn what took place before the grand jury" and as their "disclosure will not compromise the integrity of the grand jury process," Petitioners' argument that the disclosure was protected by Federal Rule of Criminal Procedure 6(e)(2)(B) is similarly without merit. *United States v. Dynavac, Inc.*, 6 F.3d 1407, 1411–12 (9th Cir. 1993).

Notes and Issues

1. In rejecting selective waiver, the Ninth Circuit joined the First, Second, Third, Fourth, Sixth, Tenth, and D.C. Circuits. *United States v. Mass. Inst. of Tech.*, 129 F.3d 681 (1st Cir. 1997); *In re John Doe Corp.*, 675 F.2d 482 (2d Cir. 1982); *Westinghouse Elec. Corp. v. Republic of Philippines*, 951 F.2d 1414 (3d Cir. 1991); *In re Martin Marietta Corp.*, 856 F.2d 619 (4th Cir. 1988); *In re Columbia/HCA Healthcare Corp. Billing Practices Litig.*, 293 F.3d 289 (6th Cir. 2002); *In re Qwest Commns. Int'l*, 450 F.3d 1179 (10th Cir. 2006). In the Second Circuit there is not a per se rule against selective waiver. Rather, the Second Circuit has held that courts should assess selective waiver on a case-by-case basis. *Salomon Bros. Treasury Litig. v. Steinhardt Partners, L.P. (In re Steinhardt Partners, L.P.)*, 9 F.3d 230 (2d Cir. 1993) (rejected by *Tenn. Laborers Health & Welfare Fund v. Columbia/HCA Healthcare Corp. (In re Columbia/HCA Healthcare Corp. Billing Practices Litig.)*, 293 F.3d 289 (6th Cir. 2002)).

2. Would you expect the U.S. Attorney to support the concept of selective waiver? Why or why not?

3. The court, quoting *Westinghouse Elec. Corp.*, stated "selective waiver does not serve the purpose of encouraging full disclosure to one's attorney in order to obtain informed legal assistance; it merely encourages voluntary disclosure to government agencies, thereby extending the privilege beyond its intended purpose." 951 F.2d at 1426. In addition to encouraging voluntary disclosure to government agencies, would allowing selective waivers encourage any other potentially beneficial activities?

4. Courts are split on the issue of selective waiver. If you had the power to settle the issue, how would you decide? Explain your rationale.

There are some cases holding that disclosure of privileged materials to a government agency pursuant to a confidentiality agreement does not waive privilege vis-à-vis private litigants. For example, Judge Crotty of the Southern District of New York held that a defendant did not waive either the attorney-client privilege or the work-product privilege by producing privileged documents to the SEC and the U.S. Attorney's office. The court reasoned that the defendant "produced the Privileged Materials to the government, not private litigants, pursuant to confidentiality agreements that provide for non-waiver." *Police & Fire Ret. Sys. v. Safenet, Inc.*, 2010 U.S. Dist. LEXIS 23196 (S.D.N.Y. Mar. 11, 2010). Similarly, a Magistrate Judge in the Northern District of New York held that "documents shared with an adversarial government agency pursuant to a confidentiality, non-waiver agreement, did not waive a disclosing party's privileges." *Plug Power, Inc. v. UBS AG*, 2008 U.S. Dist. LEXIS 82396 (N.D.N.Y Oct. 15, 2008) (*see also E.I. du Pont de Nemours & Company v. Kolon Indus.*, 2010 U.S. Dist. LEXIS 36530 (E.D. Va. Apr. 13, 2010)) (sharing confidential information with government investigators did not waive work product privilege). Authority for this proposition is limited and significant uncertainty continues to surround the issue of selective waiver. Indeed, in contrast to the authorities discussed immediately above, a recent decision from a district court in New Jersey firmly upheld the Third Circuit's rejection of selective waiver—even where the party that had produced the documents to the government did so pursuant to an express non-waiver agreement. *See In re Merck & Co.*, 2012 U.S. Dist. LEXIS 144850, 2012 WL 4764589 (D.N.J. Oct. 5, 2012).

Certain courts have treated selective waiver of work product differently than selective waiver of attorney-client privilege. For example, although in *In re Martin Marietta*, the Fourth Circuit rejected selective waiver of the attorney-client privilege, it approved selective waiver with respect to opinion work product.

The issue of selective waiver has been a source of much controversy. The controversy results from the Justice Department's policy of effectively pressuring corporations into waiving the attorney-client and work product privileges by making it policy to consider whether a corporation has waived privileged in connection with corporate charging decisions.

Under the "Principles of Federal Prosecution of Business Organizations," issued by then Deputy Attorney General Larry D. Thompson on January 20, 2003 (the "Thompson Memorandum"), federal prosecutors were ordered to consider the "authenticity" of a corporation's cooperation with the Justice Department's investigations in assessing whether to charge the corporation with crimes. One of the express factors to be considered in making that assessment was the corporation's willingness to waive the attorney-client privilege.

In response to significant criticism of that policy, the Justice Department revised the Thompson Memorandum in the form of the "McNulty Memorandum." The McNulty Memorandum, issued by then Deputy Attorney General Paul J. McNulty on December 12, 2006, does not fundamentally change the Justice Department's policy; a prosecutor can still consider a corporation's decision to waive privilege in connection with a charging decision. The revisions to the policy were mostly procedural. For example, to seek a complete waiver, prosecutors are now required to obtain approval from the Deputy Attorney General.

On August 28, 2008, the Department of Justice jettisoned the McNulty Memo and issued new guidelines authored by Deputy Attorney General Mark Filip. The new guidelines provide that the Justice Department will no longer judge a corporate defendant's cooperation, for purposes of a charging decision, on whether it waives privilege. In addition, prosecutors are prohibited from requesting that companies disclose non-factual attorney-client privileged communications or work product, except in the limited circumstances when either (a) a company is asserting an advice-of-counsel defense against criminal charges or (b) the communications fall within the "crime fraud" exception, i.e., the privileged communications were made in furtherance of a crime. The "Filip Guidelines," unlike the previous Thompson and McNulty memoranda, was incorporated in the United States Attorneys Manual, which is binding on all federal prosecutors.

In remarks to New York University School of Law on September 10, 2015, Deputy Attorney General Sally Quillian Yates announced a change in Justice Department policy relating to cooperation credit for companies that are being investigated for corporate wrongdoing. Yates stated that "if a company wants any consideration for its cooperation, it must give up the individuals, no matter where they sit within the company." And if the corporations do not know who is responsible, the Justice Department will require corporations to conduct an investigation to "identify the responsible parties, then provide all non-privileged evidence implicating those individuals" in order to receive cooperation credit. This change in policy reflects the Justice Department's shift in focus to addressing wrongdoings of individuals through both civil and criminal enforcement.

Similar to the Justice Department's policy under the McNulty Memorandum, in its 2015 Enforcement Manual, the Securities and Exchange Commission addressed the assertion of privilege by corporations, stating that "staff must respect legitimate assertions of the attorney-client privilege and attorney work product protection." SEC Enforcement Manual §4.3 (June 4, 2015). Further, the SEC Manual requires that its staff "not ask a party to waive the attorney-client privilege or work product protection without prior approval of the Director or Deputy Director" and that any such waiver is not necessary for the corporation to receive cooperation credit. *Id.*

The Self-Critical Analysis Privilege

In response to growing corporate misconduct suits during the past few decades, as well as increased regulatory complexity, corporations have adopted in-depth self-evaluative procedures in order to root out misconduct and thereby protect themselves from potential liability. *See* Donald P. Vandegrift, Jr., *Legal Development, The Privilege of Self-Critical Analysis: A Survey of the Law*, 60 Alb. L. Rev. 171, 172 (1996). Internal checks and balances enable corporations "to detect early, and thereby correct promptly, business procedures which are unlawful, unsafe, or unfair, and which may result in heavy fines or civil damages awards." *Id.* However, such measures simultaneously subject corporations to increased risks of liability because courts may deem internal corporate controls discoverable. *Id.* at 173. Thus, modern corporations face a difficult dilemma of whether to critically analyze themselves. *Id.*

In response to that dilemma, some jurisdictions have recognized the "self-evaluative" or "self-critical analysis" privilege. This privilege may protect information developed by a corporation in connection with a compliance audit or other review designed to uncover and deter unlawful or inappropriate conduct. The purpose of the privilege is to promote the public interest in having corporate entities conduct internal audits or reviews by protecting the results of those reviews from discovery.

The self-critical analysis privilege is far from universally recognized and, even if recognized, can differ significantly in scope and context between jurisdictions. To the extent that jurisdictions have recognized the privilege, four elements are generally required for its application: (1) the information must result from a critical self-analysis by the party asserting the privilege; (2) the public must have a strong interest in preserving the free flow of the type of information sought; (3) the information must be of the type whose flow would be curtailed if discovery were allowed; and (4) no document will be accorded a privilege unless it was prepared with the expectation that it would be kept confidential, and has in fact been kept confidential. *See Dowling v. Am. Haw. Cruises, Inc.* 971 F.2d 423, 426 (9th Cir. 1992), quoting from Note, *The Privilege of Self-Critical Analysis*, 96 Harv. L. Rev. 1083, 1086 (1983). *See also* Ronald G. Blum & Andrew J. Turro, *Self-Evaluative Privilege in the Second Circuit: Dead or Alive?*, 75 N.Y.B.J. 44 (June 2003).

The privilege of self-evaluation has become an important issue in several corporate compliance contexts, including medical malpractice, equal employment, securities regulation, and tax. For example, in *Bredice v. Doctors Hospital, Inc.*, the United States District Court for the District of Columbia concluded that self-critical analysis documents should not be disclosed because they are "essential to the effective functioning of staff meetings; and these meetings are essential to the continued improvement in the care and treatment of patients." *Id.* at 178; 50 F.R.D. 249 (D.D.C. 1970), *aff'd*, 479 F.2d 920 (D.C. Cir. 1973). Similarly, in *In re Crazy Eddie Securities Litigation*, a court "applied the self-critical analysis privilege and protect[ed] from discovery the firm's internal review of a 1987 audit of Crazy Eddie's operations and 1987 peer review report on internal quality controls." 792. F. Supp. 197 (E.D.N.Y. 1992). In *Bracco Diagnostics, Inc. v. Amersham Health Inc.*, 2006 U.S. Dist. LEXIS 75359 (D.N.J. Oct. 16, 2006), a magistrate judge applied the privilege in denying an informal motion to compel the production of documents concerning a sales and marketing audit performed by PriceWaterhouseCoopers (PWC) for Amersham Health Inc. The audit was conducted for the purpose of assisting Amersham in complying with the many laws and regulations governing the marketing and sales of prescription pharmaceuticals.

Proponents of self-critical analysis argue that such information should be privileged so that socially useful activities, such as providing health care, can occur. Jason M. Healy, et al., *Confidentiality of Health Care Provider Quality of Care Information*, 40 Brandeis L.J. 595, 595 (2002). Proponents argue that self-evaluation is necessary in order to provide quality service, and to take action to ensure compliance with contemporary America's increasingly complex regulatory framework. *Id.* In contrast, advocates of a more restricted approach to privilege argue that "the economic efficiencies, the accuracy of financial reporting and the improvement of business standards achieved by internal auditing programs and management control studies are so integral to the success of a business that the free flow of information is not likely to be stemmed by the possibility of future disclosure." 60 Alb. L. Rev. 171, 185 (1996).

The development of the privilege has been hampered by the United States Supreme Court decision in *University of Pennsylvania v. Equal Employment Opportunity Commission*, 493 U.S. 182 (1990). In that case, a unanimous Supreme Court refused to recognize a privilege against the disclosure of "peer review materials" in a Title VII race and sex discrimination suit against the university. In its decision, the Supreme Court "cautioned federal courts to create or expand federal privileges only with extreme reluctance." *Brunt v. Hunterdon County*, 183 F.R.D. 181, 184 (D.N.J. 1998) (*citing University of Penn.*, 493 U.S. at 189).

The Work Product Doctrine

Hickman v. Taylor

329 U.S. 495 (1947)

Mr. Justice MURPHY delivered the opinion of the Court.

This case presents an important problem under the Federal Rules of Civil Procedure * * * as to the extent to which a party may inquire into oral and written statements of witnesses, or other information, secured by an adverse party's counsel in the course of preparation for possible litigation after a claim has arisen. Examination into a person's files and records, including those resulting from the professional activities of an attorney, must be judged with care. It is not without reason that various safeguards have been established to preclude unwarranted excursions into the privacy of a man's work. At the same time, public policy supports reasonable and necessary inquiries. Properly to balance these competing interests is a delicate and difficult task.

On February 7, 1943, the tug 'J. M. Taylor' sank while engaged in helping to tow a car float of the Baltimore & Ohio Railroad across the Delaware River at Philadelphia. The accident was apparently unusual in nature, the cause of it still being unknown. Five of the nine crew members were drowned. Three days later the tug owners and the underwriters employed a law firm, of which respondent Fortenbaugh is a member, to defend them against potential suits by representatives of the deceased crew members and to sue the railroad for damages to the tug.

A public hearing was held on March 4, 1943, before the United States Steamboat Inspectors, at which the four survivors were examined. This testimony was recorded and made available to all interested parties. Shortly thereafter, Fortenbaugh privately interviewed the survivors and took statements from them with an eye toward the anticipated litigation; the survivors signed these statements on March 29. Fortenbaugh also interviewed other persons believed to have some information relating to the accident and in some cases he made memoranda of what they told him. At the time when Fortenbaugh secured the statements of the survivors, representatives of two of the deceased crew members had been in communication with him. Ultimately claims were presented by representatives of all five of the deceased; four of the claims, however, were settled without litigation. The fifth claimant, petitioner herein, brought suit in a federal court under the Jones Act on November 26, 1943, naming as defendants the two tug owners, individually and as partners, and the railroad.

One year later, petitioner filed 39 interrogatories directed to the tug owners. The 38th interrogatory read: "State whether any statements of the members of the crews of the Tugs 'J. M. Taylor' and 'Philadelphia' or of any other vessel were taken in connection with the towing of the car float and the sinking of the Tug 'John M. Taylor.'

Attach hereto exact copies of all such statements if in writing, and if oral, set forth in detail the exact provisions of any such oral statements or reports."

Supplemental interrogatories asked whether any oral or written statements, records, reports or other memoranda had been made concerning any matter relative to the towing operation, the sinking of the tug, the salvaging and repair of the tug, and the death of the deceased. If the answer was in the affirmative, the tug owners were then requested to set forth the nature of all such records, reports, statements or other memoranda.

The tug owners, through Fortenbaugh, answered all of the interrogatories except No. 38 and the supplemental ones just described. While admitting that statements of the survivors had been taken, they declined to summarize or set forth the contents. They did so on the ground that such requests called "for privileged matter obtained in preparation for litigation" and constituted "an attempt to obtain indirectly counsel's private files." It was claimed that answering these requests "would involve practically turning over not only the complete files, but also the telephone records and, almost, the thoughts of counsel."

In connection with the hearing on these objections, Fortenbaugh made a written statement and gave an informal oral deposition explaining the circumstances under which he had taken the statements. But he was not expressly asked in the deposition to produce the statements. The District Court for the Eastern District of Pennsylvania, sitting en banc, held that the requested matters were not privileged. 4 F. R. D. 479. The court then decreed that the tug owners and Fortenbaugh, as counsel and agent for the tug owners forthwith "Answer Plaintiff's 38th interrogatory and supplemental interrogatories; produce all written statements of witnesses obtained by Mr. Fortenbaugh, as counsel and agent for Defendants; state in substance any fact concerning this case which Defendants learned through oral statements made by witnesses to Mr. Fortenbaugh whether or not included in his private memoranda and produce Mr. Fortenbaugh's memoranda containing statements of fact by witnesses or to submit these memoranda to the Court for determination of those portions which should be revealed to Plaintiff." Upon their refusal, the court adjudged them in contempt and ordered them imprisoned until they complied.

The Third Circuit Court of Appeals, also sitting en banc, reversed the judgment of the District Court. It held that the information here sought was part of the "work product of the lawyer" and hence privileged from discovery under the Federal Rules of Civil Procedure. The importance of the problem, which has engendered a great divergence of views among district courts, led us to grant certiorari. * * *

The pre-trial deposition-discovery mechanism established by Rules 26 to 37 is one of the most significant innovations of the Federal Rules of Civil Procedure. Under the prior federal practice, the pre-trial functions of notice-giving issue-formulation and fact-revelation were performed primarily and inadequately by the pleadings.[7] In-

---

7. [2] "The great weakness of pleading as a means for developing and presenting issues of fact for trial lay in its total lack of any means for testing the factual basis for the pleader's allegations and

quiry into the issues and the facts before trial was narrowly confined and was often cumbersome in method. The new rules, however, restrict the pleadings to the task of general notice-giving and invest the deposition-discovery process with a vital role in the preparation for trial. The various instruments of discovery now serve (1) as a device, along with the pre-trial hearing under Rule 16, to narrow and clarify the basic issues between the parties, and (2) as a device for ascertaining the facts, or information as to the existence or whereabouts of facts, relative to those issues. Thus civil trials in the federal courts no longer need be carried on in the dark. The way is now clear, consistent with recognized privileges, for the parties to obtain the fullest possible knowledge of the issues and facts before trial.

There is an initial question as to which of the deposition-discovery rules is involved in this case.

[U]nder the circumstances we deem it unnecessary and unwise to rest our decision upon this procedural irregularity, an irregularity which is not strongly urged upon us and which was disregarded in the two courts below. It matters little at this later stage whether Fortenbaugh fails to answer interrogatories filed under Rule 26 or under Rule 33 or whether he refuses to produce the memoranda and statements pursuant to a subpoena under Rule 45 or a court order under Rule 34. The deposition-discovery rules create integrated procedural devices. And the basic question at stake is whether any of those devices may be used to inquire into materials collected by an adverse party's counsel in the course of preparation for possible litigation. The fact that the petitioner may have used the wrong method does not destroy the main thrust of his attempt. Nor does it relieve us of the responsibility of dealing with the problem raised by that attempt. It would be inconsistent with the liberal atmosphere surrounding these rules to insist that petitioner now go through the empty formality of pursuing the right procedural device only to reestablish precisely the same basic problem now confronting us. We do not mean to say, however, that there may not be situations in which the failure to proceed in accordance with a specific rule would be important or decisive. But in the present circumstances, for the purposes of this decision, the procedural irregularity is not material. Having noted the proper procedure, we may accordingly turn our attention to the substance of the underlying problem.

In urging that he has a right to inquire into the materials secured and prepared by Fortenbaugh, petitioner emphasizes that the deposition-discovery portions of the Federal Rules of Civil Procedure are designed to enable the parties to discover the true facts and to compel their disclosure wherever they may be found. It is said that inquiry may be made under these rules, epitomized by Rule 26, as to any relevant matter which is not privileged; and since the discovery provisions are to be applied as broadly and liberally as possible, the privilege limitation must be restricted to its narrowest bounds. On the premise that the attorney-client privilege is the one involved in this case, petitioner argues that it must be strictly confined to confidential com-

denials." Sunderland, 'The Theory and Practice of Pre-Trial Procedure,' 36 Mich.L.Rev. 215, 216. See also Ragland, Discovery Before Trial (1932), ch. I.

munications made by a client to his attorney. And since the materials here in issue were secured by Fortenbaugh from third persons rather than from his clients, the tug owners, the conclusion is reached that these materials are proper subjects for discovery under Rule 26.

As additional support for this result, petitioner claims that to prohibit discovery under these circumstances would give a corporate defendant a tremendous advantage in a suit by an individual plaintiff. Thus in a suit by an injured employee against a railroad or in a suit by an insured person against an insurance company the corporate defendant could pull a dark veil of secrecy over all the pertinent facts it can collect after the claim arises merely on the assertion that such facts were gathered by its large staff of attorneys and claim agents. At the same time, the individual plaintiff, who often has direct knowledge of the matter in issue and has no counsel until some time after his claim arises could be compelled to disclose all the intimate details of his case. By endowing with immunity from disclosure all that a lawyer discovers in the course of his duties, it is said, the rights of individual litigants in such cases are drained of vitality and the lawsuit becomes more of a battle of deception than a search for truth.

But framing the problem in terms of assisting individual plaintiffs in their suits against corporate defendants is unsatisfactory. Discovery concededly may work to the disadvantage as well as to the advantage of individual plaintiffs. Discovery, in other words, is not a one-way proposition. It is available in all types of cases at the behest of any party, individual or corporate, plaintiff or defendant. The problem thus far transcends the situation confronting this petitioner. And we must view that problem in light of the limitless situations where the particular kind of discovery sought by petitioner might be used.

We agree, of course, that the deposition-discovery rules are to be accorded a broad and liberal treatment. No longer can the time-honored cry of "fishing expedition" serve to preclude a party from inquiring into the facts underlying his opponent's case. Mutual knowledge of all the relevant facts gathered by both parties is essential to proper litigation. To that end, either party may compel the other to disgorge whatever facts he has in his possession. The deposition-discovery procedure simply advances the stage at which the disclosure can be compelled from the time of trial to the period preceding it, thus reducing the possibility of surprise. But discovery, like all matters of procedure, has ultimate and necessary boundaries. As indicated by Rules 30(b) and (d) and 31(d), limitations inevitably arise when it can be shown that the examination is being conducted in bad faith or in such a manner as to annoy, embarrass or oppress the person subject to the inquiry. And as Rule 26(b) provides, further limitations come into existence when the inquiry touches upon the irrelevant or encroaches upon the recognized domains of privilege.

We also agree that the memoranda, statements and mental impressions in issue in this case fall outside the scope of the attorney-client privilege and hence are not protected from discovery on that basis. It is unnecessary here to delineate the content and scope of that privilege as recognized in the federal courts. For present purposes, it suffices to note that the protective cloak of this privilege does not extend to information which an attorney secures from a witness while acting for his client in anticipation of litigation. Nor does this privilege concern the memoranda, briefs, communications and other writings prepared by counsel for his own use in prosecuting his client's case; and it is equally unrelated to writings which reflect an attorney's mental impressions, conclusions, opinions or legal theories.

But the impropriety of invoking that privilege does not provide an answer to the problem before us. Petitioner has made more than an ordinary request for relevant, non-privileged facts in the possession of his adversaries or their counsel. He has sought discovery as of right of oral and written statements of witnesses whose identity is well known and whose availability to petitioner appears unimpaired. He has sought production of these matters after making the most searching inquiries of his opponents as to the circumstances surrounding the fatal accident, which inquiries were sworn to have been answered to the best of their information and belief. Interrogatories were directed toward all the events prior to, during and subsequent to the sinking of the tug. Full and honest answers to such broad inquiries would necessarily have included all pertinent information gleaned by Fortenbaugh through his interviews with the witnesses. Petitioner makes no suggestion, and we cannot assume, that the tug owners or Fortenbaugh were incomplete or dishonest in the framing of their answers. In addition, petitioner was free to examine the public testimony of the witnesses taken before the United States Steamboat Inspectors. We are thus dealing with an attempt to secure the production of written statements and mental impressions contained in the files and the mind of the attorney Fortenbaugh without any showing of necessity or any indication or claim that denial of such production would unduly prejudice the preparation of petitioner's case or cause him any hardship or injustice. For aught that appears, the essence of what petitioner seeks either has been revealed to him already through the interrogatories or is readily available to him direct from the witnesses for the asking.

The District Court, after hearing objections to petitioner's request, commanded Fortenbaugh to produce all written statements of witnesses and to state in substance any facts learned through oral statements of witnesses to him. Fortenbaugh was to submit any memoranda he had made of the oral statements so that the court might determine what portions should be revealed to petitioner. All of this was ordered without any showing by petitioner, or any requirement that he make a proper showing, of the necessity for the production of any of this material or any demonstration that denial of production would cause hardship or injustice. The court simply ordered production on the theory that the facts sought were material and were not privileged as constituting attorney-client communications.

In our opinion, neither Rule 26 nor any other rule dealing with discovery contemplates production under such circumstances. That is not because the subject matter is privileged or irrelevant, as those concepts are used in these rules. Here is simply an attempt, without purported necessity or justification, to secure written statements, private memoranda and personal recollections prepared or formed by an adverse party's counsel in the course of his legal duties. As such, it falls outside the arena of discovery and contravenes the public policy underlying the orderly prosecution and defense of legal claims. Not even the most liberal of discovery theories can justify unwarranted inquiries into the files and the mental impressions of an attorney.

Historically, a lawyer is an officer of the court and is bound to work for the advancement of justice while faithfully protecting the rightful interests of his clients. In performing his various duties, however, it is essential that a lawyer work with a certain degree of privacy, free from unnecessary intrusion by opposing parties and their counsel. Proper preparation of a client's case demands that he assemble information, sift what he considers to be the relevant from the irrelevant facts, prepare his legal theories and plan his strategy without undue and needless interference. That is the historical and the necessary way in which lawyers act within the framework of our system of jurisprudence to promote justice and to protect their clients' interests. This work is reflected, of course, in interviews, statements, memoranda, correspondence, briefs, mental impressions, personal beliefs, and countless other tangible and intangible ways—aptly though roughly termed by the Circuit Court of Appeals in this case as the "Work product of the lawyer." Were such materials open to opposing counsel on mere demand, much of what is now put down in writing would remain unwritten. An attorney's thoughts, heretofore inviolate, would not be his own. Inefficiency, unfairness and sharp practices would inevitably develop in the giving of legal advice and in the preparation of cases for trial. The effect on the legal profession would be demoralizing. And the interests of the clients and the cause of justice would be poorly served.

We do not mean to say that all written materials obtained or prepared by an adversary's counsel with an eye toward litigation are necessarily free from discovery in all cases. Where relevant and non-privileged facts remain hidden in an attorney's file and where production of those facts is essential to the preparation of one's case, discovery may properly be had. Such written statements and documents might, under certain circumstances, be admissible in evidence or give clues as to the existence or location of relevant facts. Or they might be useful for purposes of impeachment or corroboration. And production might be justified where the witnesses are no longer available or can be reached only with difficulty. Were production of written statements and documents to be precluded under such circumstances, the liberal ideals of the deposition-discovery portions of the Federal Rules of Civil Procedure would be stripped of much of their meaning. But the general policy against invading the privacy of an attorney's course of preparation is so well recognized and so essential to an orderly working of our system of legal procedure that a burden rests on the one who would invade that privacy to establish adequate reasons to justify production through a subpoena or court order. That burden, we believe, is necessarily implicit in the rules as now constituted.

Rule 30(b), as presently written, gives the trial judge the requisite discretion to make a judgment as to whether discovery should be allowed as to written statements secured from witnesses. But in the instant case there was no room for that discretion to operate in favor of the petitioner. No attempt was made to establish any reason why Fortenbaugh should be forced to produce the written statements. There was only a naked, general demand for these materials as of right and a finding by the District Court that no recognizable privilege was involved. That was insufficient to justify discovery under these circumstances and the court should have sustained the refusal of the tug owners and Fortenbaugh to produce.

But as to oral statements made by witnesses to Fortenbaugh, whether presently in the form of his mental impressions or memoranda, we do not believe that any showing of necessity can be made under the circumstances of this case so as to justify production. Under ordinary conditions, forcing an attorney to repeat or write out all that witnesses have told him and to deliver the account to his adversary gives rise to grave dangers of inaccuracy and untrustworthiness. No legitimate purpose is served by such production. The practice forces the attorney to testify as to what he remembers or what he saw fit to write down regarding witnesses' remarks. Such testimony could not qualify as evidence; and to use it for impeachment or corroborative purposes would make the attorney much less an officer of the court and much more an ordinary witness. The standards of the profession would thereby suffer.

Denial of production of this nature does not mean that any material, non-privileged facts can be hidden from the petitioner in this case. He need not be unduly hindered in the preparation of his case, in the discovery of facts or in his anticipation of his opponents' position. Searching interrogatories directed to Fortenbaugh and the tug owners, production of written documents and statements upon a proper showing and direct interviews with the witnesses themselves all serve to reveal the facts in Fortenbaugh's possession to the fullest possible extent consistent with public policy. Petitioner's counsel frankly admits that he wants the oral statements only to help prepare himself to examine witnesses and to make sure that he has overlooked nothing. That is insufficient under the circumstances to permit him an exception to the policy underlying the privacy of Fortenbaugh's professional activities. If there should be a rare situation justifying production of these matters, petitioner's case is not of that type.

Affirmed.

Mr. Justice JACKSON, concurring.

The primary effect of the practice advocated here would be on the legal profession itself. But it too often is overlooked that the lawyer and the law office are indispensable parts of our administration of justice. Law-abiding people can go nowhere else to learn the ever changing and constantly multiplying rules by which they must behave and to obtain redress for their wrongs. The welfare and tone of the legal profession is therefore of prime consequence to society, which would feel the consequences of such a practice as petitioner urges secondarily but certainly.

Counsel for the petitioner candidly said on argument that he wanted this information to help prepare himself to examine witnesses, to make sure he overlooked nothing. He bases his claim to it in his brief on the view that the Rules were to do away with the old situation where a law suit developed into 'a battle of wits between counsel.' But a common law trial is and always should be an adversary proceeding. Discovery was hardly intended to enable a learned profession to perform its functions either without wits or on wits borrowed from the adversary.

The real purpose and the probable effect of the practice ordered by the district court would be to put trials on a level even lower than a "battle of wits." I can conceive of no practice more demoralizing to the Bar than to require a lawyer to write out and deliver to his adversary an account of what witnesses have told him. Even if his recollection were perfect, the statement would be his language permeated with his inferences. Everyone who has tried it knows that it is almost impossible so fairly to record the expressions and emphasis of a witness that when he testifies in the environment of the court and under the influence of the leading question there will not be departures in some respects. Whenever the testimony of the witness would differ from the "exact" statement the lawyer had delivered, the lawyer's statement would be whipped out to impeach the witness. Counsel producing his adversary's "inexact" statement could lose nothing by saying, "Here is a contradiction, gentlemen of the jury. I do not know whether it is my adversary or his witness who is not telling the truth, but one is not." Of course, if this practice were adopted, that scene would be repeated over and over again. The lawyer who delivers such statements often would find himself branded a deceiver afraid to take the stand to support his own version of the witness's conversation with him, or else he will have to go on the stand to defend his own credibility-perhaps against that of his chief witness, or possibly even his client.

Every lawyer dislikes to take the witness stand and will do so only for grave reasons. This is partly because it is not his role; he is almost invariably a poor witness. But he steps out of professional character to do it. He regrets it; the profession discourages it. But the practice advocated here is one which would force him to be a witness, not as to what he has seen or done but as to other witnesses' stories, and not because he wants to do so but in self-defense.

And what is the lawyer to do who has interviewed one whom he believes to be a biased, lying or hostile witness to get his unfavorable statements and know what to meet? He must record and deliver such statements even though he would not vouch for the credibility of the witness by calling him. Perhaps the other side would not want to call him either, but the attorney is open to the charge of suppressing evidence at the trial if he fails to call such a hostile witness even though he never regarded him as reliable or truthful.

Having been supplied the names of the witnesses, petitioner's lawyer gives no reason why he cannot interview them himself. If an employee-witness refuses to tell his story, he, too, may be examined under the Rules. He may be compelled on discovery as fully as on the trial to disclose his version of the facts. But that is his own disclosure — it can be used to impeach him if he contradicts it and such a deposition is not useful to promote an unseemly disagreement between the witness and the counsel in the case.

I agree to the affirmance of the judgment of the Circuit Court of Appeals which reversed the district court.

Mr. Justice FRANKFURTER joins in this opinion.

Notes and Issues

1. Generally speaking, the "work product privilege" protects from discovery documents prepared in anticipation of litigation. Specifically, Federal Rule of Civil Procedure 26(b)(3) provides that "[o]rdinarily, a party may not discover documents and tangible things that are prepared in anticipation of litigation or for trial by or for another party or its representatives."

2. The doctrine protects from disclosure any documents prepared by the attorney "in anticipation of litigation," including written statements, private memoranda and personal recollections of the attorney. However, the protection is not inviolable and may be overcome by a showing that the party seeking production of the materials "has substantial need for the materials to prepare its case and cannot, without undue hardship, obtain their substantial equivalent by other means." Fed. R. Civ. P. 23(b)(3)(A)(i). This "exception," however, applies only with respect to factual work product materials, as opposed to opinion or strategy work product materials. Fed. R. Civ. P. 23(b)(A)(B) specifically provides that if a court orders production of work product materials, it "must protect against disclosure of the mental impressions, conclusions, opinions, or legal theories of a party's attorney ... concerning the litigation." Would privilege apply if the president of the company was the one who interviewed witnesses? Why or why not?

3. How would the analysis change if Fortenbaugh had made audio recordings of the interviews that he conducted with the survivors?

4. What if instead of conducting witness interviews in anticipation of the litigation associated with the accident, Fortenbaugh had conducted interviews with the tug boat employees one year prior to the accident to discover if the company's safety protocols were being followed, would privilege apply? Why or why not?

The application of the term "prepared in anticipation of litigation," is not crystal clear. For some time it was widely held that only those communications prepared in anticipation of actual litigation would be treated as work product. Accordingly, documents that were prepared to assess the prospect or likelihood of litigation that might result from certain actions were not necessarily protected. *Weil Ceramics & Glass, Inc. v. Work*, 110 F.R.D. 500, 505 (E.D.N.Y. 1986) (citing *Westhemeco Ltd. v. N.H. Ins. Co.*, 82 F.R.D. 702, 708 (S.D.N.Y. 1979)), *modified on other grounds sub nom. Commercial Union Ins. Co. v. Albert Pipe & Supply Co.*, 484 F. Supp. 1153 (1980) (the party seeking the privilege must demonstrate a "substantial probability" of litigation at the time the documents were created). However, generally, courts now take a less rigid approach and correspondingly have somewhat expanded the scope of the protection available under the work product doctrine. For example, documents prepared in connection with regulatory investigations have been found to have been prepared in "anticipation-of-litigation" for purposes of the application of the work product doctrine. *See Martin v. Bally's Park Place Hotel & Casino*, 983 F.2d 1252, 1261 (3d Cir. 1993) (documents prepared in connection with OSHA inquiry protected as work product); *Martin v. Monfort, Inc.*, 150 F.R.D. 172, 173 (D. Colo. 1993) (citations omitted) (internal studies created in connection with Department of Labor investigation protected as work product).

In *United States v. Adlman*, 134 F.3d 1194 (2d Cir. 1998), the Second Circuit Court of Appeals expanded the scope of work product protection and infused some clarity into the application of the doctrine when it found that documents prepared "because of litigation" and not just those prepared "primarily or exclusively for litigation" are entitled to protection from disclosure. Thus, the court held that a document that was created both to inform a business decision and in anticipation of litigation was "prepared in anticipation of litigation" for the purposes of the application of the work product doctrine.

Another question that frequently arises in the context of the work product doctrine is whether materials need to have been prepared by an attorney in order to qualify for protection. Fed. R. Civ. P. 23(b)(3)(A) specifically provides that materials prepared by an "attorney, consultant, surety, indemnitor, insurer or agent," are entitled to be protected. However, in order to be protected, the materials in question must have been created at the direction of, and managed closely by, lawyers. *See Nat'l Petrochemical Co. of Iran v. M/T Stolt Sheaf*, 930 F.2d 240, 244 (2d Cir. 1991); *United States v. Nobles*, 422 U.S. 225, 236–40 (1975); *United States v. Dist. Council of N.Y.C.*, 1992 U.S. Dist. LEXIS 12307 (S.D.N.Y. Aug. 18, 1992) (citations omitted). The fact that materials were created at the direction of or managed by lawyers is not itself dispositive of work product protection. For example, in *Assured Guaranty Municipal Corp. v. UBS Real Estate Securities, Inc.*, the district court held that certain documents created by a working group that was working under the direction of outside counsel to analyze the claims of a party threatening litigation were not privileged. There, a financial guaranty insurer demanded that UBS repurchase certain mortgages that were part of trusts that had issued mortgage-backed securities that the plaintiff had insured. In response to these demands, UBS hired outside counsel and created an internal working group to work with outside counsel to assess the transactions and the repurchase demands. The court found that communications between the non-lawyer working group members were not privileged, holding that "[t]here is no privilege for communications between non-lawyers merely because they were purportedly done for the purposes of assisting outside litigation counsel." Nos. 12-1579, 12-7322 (S.D.N.Y. Mar. 25, 2013).

The Privilege Internationally

To United States lawyers, the attorney-client privilege is a bedrock principle of the United States legal system which regularly guides the manner in which they practice.

However, the attorney-client privilege is not necessarily applicable outside of the United States and, as such, advice given by foreign lawyers to a person or entity may not be privileged. *See, e.g., Duttle v. Bandler & Kass,* 127 F.R.D. 46 (S.D.N.Y. 1989) (although German law recognizes the privilege, court held that it was inapplicable because the role of tax advisors and notaries involved were more akin to accountants than lawyers); *Detection Sys., Inc. v. Pittway Corp.,* 96 F.R.D. 152 (W.D.N.Y. 1982) (court found that privilege was unclear in Japan or Mexico); *Honeywell, Inc. v. Minolta Camera Co.,* 1990 U.S. Dist. LEXIS 5954 (D.N.J. May 15, 1990) (although a member of Minolta's patent department in Japan was acting as the functional equivalent of an attorney, court held individual was not licensed to practice law and was not registered as a patent agent and privilege did not attach to his communications); *Bristol-Myers Squibb Co. v. Rhone-Poulenc Rorer, Inc.,* 188 F.R.D. 189, 52 U.S.P.Q.2d 1897 (S.D.N.Y. 1999) (French patent agent's communications and memoranda not privileged unless agent acting under authority of an American attorney). In addition, even to the extent that a foreign jurisdiction recognizes the attorney-client privilege, the rules and or scope of the privilege may be different. For example, certain jurisdictions draw a distinction between in-house lawyers and outside counsel and do not recognize any privilege in connection with internal communications by in-house counsel.

Specifically, in its ruling in *Akzo Nobel Chemicals Limited-v-Commission* on September 17, 2007, the European Court of First Instance (CFI), refused to extend the privilege in connection with EU competition investigations, to communications between companies and their in-house lawyers. The CFI followed the European Court of Justice's ruling in *AM & S Europe-v-Commission* (1982) by holding that privilege, in connection with documents uncovered during a Commission investigation, only applied to communications with outside counsel who were independent, i.e., not subject to an employer/employee relationship. In September 2010, the CFI's decision was affirmed by the European Union's highest court. However, this is not necessarily the rule throughout Europe. In March 2013, in a case involving Belgian telecommunications company Belgacom, the Brussels Court of Appeal issued a decision that rejected the applicability of the CFI's decision in Akzo to national competition proceedings. In that decision, the Belgian court held that under Belgian law, legal advice provided by in-house attorneys and related correspondence was effectively privileged.

Finally, the application of the privilege in foreign jurisdictions is not only relevant in the context of litigation in courts outside of the United States. The determination by a court in the United States of whether documents are privileged may well depend upon the law of a foreign jurisdiction. Indeed, the general rule is that "communications that relate to activity in a foreign country are governed by that country's privilege law, while communications that 'touch base' with the United States are controlled by the United States privilege law." Tulip Computers Int'l B.V. v. Dell Computer Corp., 210 F.R.D. 100, 104 (D. Del. 2002), *aff'd and adopted,* 2003 U.S. Dist. LEXIS 26542 (D. Del. Feb. 10, 2003).

Conclusion

The scope of the attorney-client privilege and work product doctrine in the context of the complex regulatory environment that exists today remains far from settled, and a determination of whether a privilege will apply will rely on the specific facts of the case as well as the jurisdiction involved. Because of the significant liabilities that may be associated with a determination that privilege does not apply, it is critical that a company and its attorneys have thoughtfully considered all relevant factors when determining a course of action.

Assignments

- **Hypothetical:** You are the General Counsel of a major U.S. pharmaceutical company that has recently been served with a class action lawsuit alleging that the plaintiffs suffered a variety of serious health consequences as a result of taking the Company's newest allergy medication. Obviously, the Company's CEO wants to ensure that the Company is as protected by privilege as possible and has requested that you draft an email to be distributed to employees outlining the "dos" and "don'ts" for employees in connection with the pending litigation. What should you include in this email and to whom should it be distributed?

- What additional issues should you consider if the drug was also partially-developed, manufactured, and distributed in Europe?

- Just before the trial is about to begin, you receive a request from the Department of Justice asking for all documents related to the internal investigation conducted by the Company in connection with allergy medication class action. The DOJ has offered to provide a non-disclosure agreement in connection with any documents that you produce and will give credit for your cooperation in determining whether to file criminal charges. What factors should you consider when determining whether or not to provide the documents to the DOJ?

Chapter 15

Corporate Compliance and Records Management[*]

Introduction

In 2015, there were over 205 billion emails sent and received worldwide every day, 112 billion of which were business-related.[1] By 2019, those figures are projected to rise to over 246 billion emails sent and received worldwide every day, almost 129 billion of which will be business-related.[2] In 2012, there were 2,837 *exabytes*[3] of data in the world, almost one third of it in the United States.[4] The top three industries in the U.S. with the most data, investment services, banking, and manufacturing, accounted for 7,595 terabytes of data.[5] The figures are staggering, to say the least, and this explosion of data is unprecedented. Part of the reason for this incredible volume of data is the evolution and proliferation of new business technologies. Twenty years ago, a well-equipped office may have consisted of a telephone, desktop computer, fax machine and copier. Important business documents were still generated on paper and stored in file folders stuffed into metal filing cabinets. And the latest in communications technology, electronic mail or "email," was only starting to gain traction. Companies that were parties in litigation had to rely on lawyers meticulously paging through hundreds of documents by hand to identify relevant documents. Today, a

---

[*] Special thanks to Joseph Lee for his contributions. This chapter is adapted from Joseph Lee, *Corporate Compliance and Records Management*, in CORPORATE COMPLIANCE PRACTICE GUIDE: THE NEXT GENERATION OF COMPLIANCE, Chapter 20 (Carole Basri, Release 8, 2016).

1. *Email Statistics Report, 2015–2019*, The Radicati Group, Inc. (March 2015), available at http://www.radicati.com/wp/wp-content/uploads/2015/02/Email-Statistics-Report-2015-2019-Executive-Summary.pdf.

2. *Id.*

3. For context, conversions for common units of digital information are provided here:
   1024 bytes = 1 Kilobyte (KB)
   1024 KB = 1 Megabyte (MB)
   1024 MB = 1 Gigabyte (GB)
   1024 GB = 1 Terabyte (TB)
   1024 TB = 1 Petabyte (PB)
   1024 PB = 1 Exabyte (EB)

4. Susan Lund et al., *Game changers: Five opportunities for US growth and renewal*, McKinsey Global Institute (July 2013), http://www.mckinsey.com/insights/americas/us_game_changers.

5. *Id.*

smartphone, no larger than a deck of cards, can take the place of a telephone, computer, fax machine and copier, as well as a camera, voice recorder, and a dozen other gadgets, and can store millions of documents electronically. Instant messaging has replaced emails in some industries as the preferred, faster means of communication, and social media has the capacity to reach millions of consumers instantly with just a few keystrokes. Applying sophisticated learning software across hundreds of millions of documents can quickly identify documents relevant to litigation. Indeed, times have changed; and along with it, so have the risks companies now face and the role of the in-house legal and compliance departments that are tasked to manage it.

The sheer volume of data and the risks associated with new, rapidly evolving and relatively untested business technologies present issues that corporations have never had to face before. A single corporation can stockpile hundreds of terabytes of electronic information that can be very expensive to maintain; many others still hoard millions of hardcopy documents in warehouses managed by third-party archive services. A corporation can churn through a tremendous amount of information everyday making it difficult, if not impossible, to find relevant documents in litigation. Cloud computing has made it difficult to know where the data is even stored; servers that actually house the data may be located in foreign jurisdictions with stringent data privacy laws. Non-traditional forms of data like voice data or image files may be impossible to track unless it is properly cataloged. Bring Your Own Device or "BYOD" policies may comingle personal information with corporate data, raising privacy concerns. The list of challenges seems endless. In-house legal and compliance departments are tasked with identifying and mitigating these risks by actively managing the corporate information infrastructure, typically through enterprise data management plans ("EDM"), such as mobile device management plans ("MDM"), document retention policies and litigation readiness plans. Information governance and the effective management of this enormous universe of data and new technologies has become an essential component for an organization's success.

Role of In-House Legal Departments and Effective Data Management Plans

In this modern, frenzied information age, in-house legal and compliance departments must adapt quickly to keep up with day-to-day business operations, identify and mitigate risks that come with new technologies and the growing volume of data, and prepare the company for unforeseen events, such as litigation and investigations. Lawyers must expand beyond traditional legal roles and become proficient in technology and the corporation's information infrastructure. They must understand how data is generated, transmitted, stored and destroyed. To do so, they must work with various internal and external parties, including for example, information technology ("IT") and records management departments that are directly involved in handling the company's systems and data, human resource ("HR") departments that track the employees that actually use the data, and regulatory departments that make sure the company is abiding by applicable rules and regulations, including document retention laws. Outside the organization, in-house lawyers may engage third-party archive services, e-discovery vendors, and technology consultants to handle large-scale data management or discovery.

With so many parties to account for, the skyrocketing volume of data, and constantly evolving business technologies, having some roadmap or EDM is imperative to keep the business organized, compliant with relevant laws, and ready to act in the event of litigation. An effective EDM will identify points of contact and delegate responsibility, and provide instruction about how data should be managed and how certain technologies should be utilized. An EDM may include a number of discrete policies and procedures depending on an organization's size, sophistication and particular need, such as document retention policies, litigation readiness plans, BYOD policies, and social media acceptable use policies. A blueprint or "data map" of all of the organization's systems and data is also important to help navigate through the corporation's information landscape.

Consequences of Mismanaged Data

Having clear, well thought-out policies that govern the maintenance and disposition of data is good business practice. Plain and simple, it helps to be organized. Some industries are required by law to maintain certain records for a period of time. And if a company is faced with a lawsuit, having a comprehensive data management plan that includes coherent document retention policies and litigation readiness protocols will help mitigate some of the pains associated with discovery, and help prevent discovery mishaps that can lead to sanctions. And the consequences of failing to properly navigate through this landscape because of mismanaged data or ineffective policies can be severe.[6] There are now dozens of cases that serve as cautionary tales in how to properly navigate through an organization's information landscape and manage discovery. Courts have doled out sanctions, including adverse inference instructions and millions of dollars in monetary fines for discovery failures.

---

6. *See, e.g.,* Calderon v. Corporacion Puertorriqueña de Salud, 992 F. Supp. 2d 48 (D.P.R. 2014) (imposing adverse inference sanction for failing to preserve text messages and photos on a cell phone while selectively saving others); SK Hynix Inc. v. Rambus Inc., 2013 U.S. Dist. LEXIS 66554, *77 (N.D. Cal. 2013) (finding defendant willfully destroyed documents when litigation was reasonably foreseeable, and awarding a monetary sanction of $250,000,000 to be applied as a credit against defendant's judgment against plaintiff); Green v. Blitz, U.S.A., Inc., 2011 U.S. Dist. LEXIS 20353, *36–37 (E.D. Tex. 2011), sanctions order vacated, 2014 U.S. Dist. LEXIS 83907 (E.D. Tex. 2014) (sanctions including $250,000 in civil contempt sanctions, a $500,000 "purging" sanction, extinguishable if the defendant furnishes a copy of the order to every plaintiff in every lawsuit against it for the past two years, and ordered to file a copy of the order with its first pleading or filing in all new lawsuits for the next five years); Qualcomm Inc. v. Broadcom Corp., 2008 U.S. Dist. LEXIS 911, *42 (S.D. Cal. 2008), vacated in part, 2008 U.S. Dist. LEXIS 16897 (S.D. Cal. 2008) (court initially sanctioned defendant $8.5 million and referred the attorneys to the California State Bar for possible disciplinary proceeding).

Information Governance and Elements of an Effective Data Management Plan

While every organization has its own unique set of needs, there are a handful of basic building blocks upon which any EDM should be built. A successful EDM should include: (i) attorney competence; (ii) a comprehensive "data map" of the corporate information infrastructure; (iii) formal, written policies and procedures; (iv) dedicated personnel responsible for oversight; and (v) proactive monitoring and compliance.

Attorney Competence

An effective data management plan begins with competence. In-house lawyers, for example, must become experts in the corporation's information infrastructure and know what action to take when the company is faced with circumstances outside the ordinary course of business, such as litigation or investigations. In August 2012, the ABA amended Comment 6 of the Model Rules of Professional Conduct Rule 1.1, and raised the bar for attorneys to become more adept in the use of technology. To be competent, "a lawyer should keep abreast of changes in the law and its practice, including the benefits and risks associated with relevant technology."[7] The ABA Commission on Ethics noted that the amendment "would offer greater clarity in this area and emphasize the importance of technology to modern law practice."[8] But there is still a steep learning curve. According to a survey of federal district and magistrate judges published in February 2015, one of the biggest problems among attorneys is their "lack of knowledge about their clients' e-discovery environment."[9] It goes without saying, but it is important for in-house lawyers to understand that their clients are not in the business of generating and stockpiling enormous amounts of its own data for the sake of it. And they are not in the business of being sued. These are collateral effects of modern business practice. But there is tremendous risk in letting data accumulate unchecked, and it is the lawyers' job to evaluate and mitigate the risk by knowing how to handle the data.

Policies, Procedures, and Data Maps

It is critical to have formal, written policies and procedures in place to manage the corporation's data. In the context of litigation, simply knowing where the data

---

7. Model Rules of Prof'l Conduct R. 1.1, cmt. 8.

8. ABA Comm. on Ethics 20/20, *Report to the House of Delegates,* 105A (August 2012).

9. Daniel Miller & Tina Miller, *What the judges think: e-discovery practices and trends,* Lawyers Journal, The Journal of the Allegheny County Bar Association, Vol. 17 No. 7 (Apr. 3, 2015) ("Fifty percent of respondents noted that the typical amount of electronically stored information in cases has grown substantially over the past five years, yet the judges see significant gaps in attorneys' understanding of e-discovery principles."), http://www.ediscoverylaw.com/files/2015/04/What-the-judges-think.pdf.

is stored, what it looks like, and how to get it out can reduce risk, streamline productions, and help alleviate some of the pain associated with discovery. In fact, some courts expect that companies have formal data management plans in place, and if they do not and it results in discovery issues, the court may consider it a factor in determining sanctions.[10]

Magaña v. Hyundai Motor Am.

2009 Wash. LEXIS 1066 (Nov. 25, 2009) (en banc)

Opinion

[As amended by order of the Supreme Court April 20, 2010.]

Sanders, J.—

Trial courts need not tolerate deliberate and willful discovery abuse. Given the unique facts and circumstances of this case, we hold that the trial court appropriately diagnosed Hyundai's willful efforts to frustrate and undermine truthful pretrial discovery efforts by striking its pleadings and rendering an $8,000,000 default judgment plus reasonable attorney fees. This result appropriately compensates the other party and hopefully educates and deters others inclined to similar behavior.

We determine the trial court acted well within its discretion and reverse the Court of Appeals, which improvidently reversed the trial court.

FACTS AND PROCEDURAL HISTORY

On February 15, 1997 Jesse Magaña was a passenger in a 1996 Hyundai Accent, two-door hatchback driven by Ricky Smith (Smith). Angela Smith was also a passenger. As they drove over a hill they saw an oncoming truck driven by Dennis Nylander that appeared to be in their lane. Smith swerved the Accent to avoid the truck, causing his car to veer off the road. The car hit several trees and spun violently. Magaña was thrown out of the rear window and landed about 50 to 100 feet away from where the car eventually stopped. He was rendered a paraplegic due to the accident. Smith suffered a concussion, and Angela broke her collarbone, leg, and shoulder blade.

Magaña filed suit on February 8, 2000 in Clark County Superior Court against Hyundai Motor America and Hyundai Motor Company (collectively Hyundai), the Smiths, and the Nylanders. Magaña alleged his injuries were proximately caused by

---

10. *See, e.g.,* Phillip M. Adams & Assoc. v. Dell, 621 F. Supp. 2d 1173, 1193–94 (D. Utah 2009) ("'The absence of a coherent document retention policy' is a pertinent factor to consider when evaluating sanctions. Information management policies are not a dark or novel art. Numerous authoritative organizations have long promulgated policy guidelines for document retention and destruction." (citations omitted); Magaña v. Hyundai Motor Am., 167 Wash. 2d 570, 586, 220 P.3d 191, 199 (Wash. Sup. Ct. 2009) (en banc) (finding that defendant had willfully violated discovery obligations and entered default judgment against defendant in the amount of $8,000,000) ("Hyundai had the obligation not only to diligently and in good faith respond to discovery efforts, but to maintain a document retrieval system that would enable the corporation to respond to plaintiff's requests. Hyundai is a sophisticated multinational corporation, experienced in litigation.").

a design defect in the car which allowed the seat to collapse and by the negligent driving of Smith and Nylander. On January 11, 2002 the trial court granted the Nylanders summary judgment of dismissal, and they were dismissed from the lawsuit.

During discovery in 2000–2001 Magaña requested many documents from Hyundai. Hyundai refused to directly answer Magaña's requests but reworded and limited their scope. Hyundai never sought a protective order to narrow the scope of discovery, and Magaña never sought a motion to compel Hyundai to answer these discovery requests before the first trial.

In request for production Magaña requested Hyundai produce "copies of any and all documents including but not limited to complaints, answers, police reports, photographs, depositions or other documents relating to complaints, notices, claims, lawsuits or incidents of alleged seat back failure on Hyundai products for the years 1980 to present." Clerk's Papers (CP) at 3728. Hyundai responded in April 2000 that the request was "overly broad and not reasonably calculated to lead to the discovery of admissible evidence" and that there were "no personal injury or fatality lawsuits or claims in connection with or involving the seat or seat back of the Hyundai Accent model years 1995–1999." CP at 2379.

In interrogatory 12 Magaña also requested Hyundai to "[i]dentify with name and model number all Hyundai vehicles that used the same (or substantially similar) front right seat as the 1996 Hyundai Accent." CP at 3722. Hyundai responded that the 1995–1999 "Hyundai Accents used the same or substantially similar right front seat as the 1996 Hyundai Accent" and that "[n]o other Hyundai model automobile uses the same or substantially similar design for the right front seat...." CP at 2376.

A jury trial commenced on June 3, 2002. At trial one of Magaña's expert witnesses, Dr. Joseph Burton, testified that an alternative seat belt design, known as an integrated seat belt design, would have prevented Magaña's injuries. Hyundai objected because there was no discussion about an integrated seat belt design in Dr. Burton's deposition during discovery, but the trial court overruled the objection. Four days later the trial court decided it should have sustained Hyundai's objection to Burton's testimony and struck his testimony. However it did not advise the jury that the testimony had been stricken because of concerns it would highlight the evidence.

Magaña prevailed at the jury trial by a vote of 10–2 and was awarded over $8,000,000 in damages. The jury attributed 60 percent of the fault to Hyundai and 40 percent to Smith. Smith and Hyundai appealed. The Court of Appeals reversed and remanded in 2004 as to Hyundai, determining the trial court's failure to instruct the jury that the expert's testimony had been stricken misled the jury as to which evidence was properly before it, and the error was not harmless. Magaña v. Hyundai Motor Am., 123 Wn. App. 306, 316, 319, 94 P.3d 987 (2004). The retrial was to be limited to the issue of liability without disturbing the jury's damages verdict. The mandate was issued on April 4, 2005. Magaña did not seek review in this court.

On May 23, 2005 the trial court set the retrial date for January 17, 2006. On September 13, 2005 Magaña's counsel requested that Hyundai update its responses to

Magaña's previous discovery requests in 2000. Magaña believed Hyundai's initial response to interrogatory 12 (his request to discover other Hyundai vehicles with the same or similar seats to the 1996 Accent) was inaccurate because he had found a recliner mechanism in another Hyundai model that looked identical to the one in the 1996 Accent. Magaña also requested Hyundai update its response to request for production 20 regarding other incidents of seat back failure in Hyundai vehicles without limiting the response to 1995–1996 Accents because it was clear other Hyundai vehicles had the same recliner mechanism. Hyundai told Magaña it would provide him with information relating to alleged seat back failure in the 1995–1999 Accents and the 1992–1995 Hyundai Elantras. Magaña continued to request all seat back failure claims in Hyundai products from 1980 to the present.

On October 25, 2005 Hyundai updated its response to Magaña's request for production 20 by objecting but stating it would produce complaints and claims of alleged seat back failure in 1995–1999 Hyundai Accents and in 1992–1995 Hyundai Elantras. Hyundai also supplemented its response to Magaña's interrogatory 12, stating that only the 1995–1999 Hyundai Accents used the same or similar right front seat as the 1996 Accent and that although not asked by Magaña, the 1992–1995 Hyundai Elantras had a recliner on the right front seat that was substantially similar to the front recliner on the 1996 Hyundai Accent.

Hyundai also produced documents of two claims relating to seat back failure from 2000 (Matthew Dowling claim) and 2002 (Janelle Bobbitt and Joshua Chastagner claim). Hyundai represented these two claims were the only seat back failure claims involving 1995–1999 Hyundai Accents or 1992–1995 Hyundai Elantras other than Magaña's claim.

On October 27, 2005 Magaña filed a motion to compel Hyundai to produce all documents relating to other seat back failures in Hyundai vehicles as he had previously requested in the requests for production served on Hyundai in 2000. Hyundai opposed the motion, arguing it was too burdensome and would not lead to the discovery of admissible evidence. However, Hyundai never requested a protective order to narrow the scope of discovery.

On November 18, 2005 the trial court ordered Hyundai to produce "Police Reports, legal claims, Consumer Complaints and Expert Reports or Depositions and Exhibits and photographs thereto with respect to all consumer complaints and lawsuits involving allegations of seat back failure on all Hyundai vehicles with single recliner mechanisms regardless of incident date and regardless of model year." CP at 961–62. On November 21, 2005 Hyundai produced numerous documents that related to other complaints of seat back failure. On December 1, 2005 Hyundai produced additional documents including police reports, photographs, expert records, deposition transcripts, and for the first time, records from its consumer "hotline" database. Nine reports of seat back failure involving 1995–1999 Accents were included in these documents.

On December 23, 2005 Magaña moved for a default judgment against Hyundai, arguing that it would be impossible to prepare a proper case with the other, similar incidents that had just been produced by Hyundai. Magaña also argued that evidence was lost due to the delay. Magaña argued a continuance would only reward Hyundai's behavior. Magaña claimed Hyundai (1) failed to comply with production requests, (2) falsely answered interrogatories, (3) willfully spoiled evidence of other similar incidents, and (4) failed to produce documents related to rear impact crash tests. Magaña's experts argued that the information of other similar incidents would have been invaluable and useful during the first trial.

On January 4, 2006 Magaña requested an evidentiary hearing on his motion for sanctions. He also filed a motion to amend his complaint to add a failure to warn claim. Hyundai produced the last of the documents on January 6, 2006, less than two weeks before the scheduled trial and argued it had been relieved of the obligation to produce other similar incidents of seat back failure per an agreement between the parties in July 2001. Hyundai also asserted that any prejudice against Magaña was speculative and that it had truthfully answered interrogatory 12. Hyundai did admit to failing to disclose documents from an earlier lawsuit, CP at 2361–66 (Acevedo v. Hyundai, Amended Complaint and Jury Demand, No. ATL-L-2276-01 (N.J. Sup. Ct. 2002)), and a "sled test."

On January 13, 2006 the trial court granted Magaña's motion for an evidentiary hearing, stating it would primarily focus on whether Magaña was prejudiced in preparing for the retrial since the remand by the Court of Appeals. The court denied Hyundai's request for a continuance after Magaña withdrew his motion to amend his complaint.

The evidentiary hearing took place from January 17 to January 20, 2006, during which witnesses testified and the court considered many pleadings and declarations. After the hearing the trial court imposed a default judgment against Hyundai supported by numerous findings of fact. The court found the discovery violations alleged by Magaña were real and serious. The court found (1) there was no agreement between the parties to limit discovery, (2) Hyundai falsely responded to Magaña's request for production and interrogatories, (3) Magaña was substantially prejudiced in preparing for trial, and (4) evidence was spoiled and forever lost. The trial court considered lesser sanctions but found that the only suitable remedy under the circumstances was a default judgment. Hyundai then appealed.

The Court of Appeals reversed in a two-to-one decision and remanded for a new trial. Magaña v. Hyundai Motor Am., 141 Wn. App. 495, 170 P.3d 1165 (2007) (Magaña II). The Court of Appeals majority found that Hyundai had willfully violated Magaña's discovery request but there was "no prejudice to Magaña's ability to retry his case resulting from Hyundai's discovery violations" and lesser sanctions would have sufficed. Id. at 500, 511. We granted review. Magaña v. Hyundai Motor Am., 164 Wn.2d 1020, 195 P.3d 89 (2008).

STANDARD OF REVIEW

We review a trial court's discovery sanctions for abuse of discretion. Wash. State Physicians Ins. Exch. & Ass'n v. Fisons Corp., 122 Wn.2d 299, 338, 858 P.2d 1054 (1993). "A trial court exercises broad discretion in imposing discovery sanctions under

CR 26(g) or 37(b), and its determination will not be disturbed absent a clear abuse of discretion." Mayer v. Sto Indus., Inc., 156 Wn.2d 677, 684, 132 P.3d 115 (2006) (citing Fisons, 122 Wn.2d at 355–56). "A trial court abuses its discretion when its order is manifestly unreasonable or based on untenable grounds." Fisons, 122 Wn.2d at 339 (citing Holbrook v. Weyerhaeuser Co., 118 Wn.2d 306, 315, 822 P.2d 271 (1992)). "A discretionary decision rests on 'untenable grounds' or is based on 'untenable reasons' if the trial court relies on unsupported facts or applies the wrong legal standard; the court's decision is 'manifestly unreasonable' if 'the court, despite applying the correct legal standard to the supported facts, adopts a view 'that no reasonable person would take.'" Mayer, 156 Wn.2d at 684 (internal quotation marks omitted) (quoting State v. Rohrich, 149 Wn.2d 647, 654, 71 P.3d 638 (2003)).

"There is a natural tendency on the part of reviewing courts, properly employing the benefit of hindsight, to be heavily influenced by the severity of outright dismissal as a sanction for failure to comply with a discovery order." Nat'l Hockey League v. Metro. Hockey Club, Inc., 427 U.S. 639, 642, 96 S. Ct. 2778, 49 L. Ed. 2d 747 (1976). However since the trial court is in the best position to decide an issue, deference should normally be given to the trial court's decision. Fisons, 122 Wn.2d at 339. A trial court's reasons for imposing discovery sanctions should "be clearly stated on the record so that meaningful review can be had on appeal." Burnet v. Spokane Ambulance, 131 Wn.2d 484, 494, 933 P.2d 1036 (1997). If a trial court's findings of fact are clearly unsupported by the record, then an appellate court will find that the trial court abused its discretion. Mayer, 156 Wn.2d at 684. An appellate court can disturb a trial court's sanction only if it is clearly unsupported by the record. See Ermine v. City of Spokane, 143 Wn.2d 636, 650, 23 P.3d 492 (2001) (noting that a reasonable difference of opinion does not amount to abuse of discretion).

ANALYSIS

We are asked to determine whether the trial court abused its discretion to grant a default judgment against Hyundai as a discovery sanction. Under the authority of CR 37(d), the trial court entered a default judgment against Hyundai. CR 37 sets forth the rules regarding sanctions when a party fails to make discovery. CR 37(d) authorizes a court to impose the sanctions in CR 37(b)(2), which range from exclusion of evidence to granting default judgment when a party fails to respond to interrogatories and requests for production. See Smith v. Behr Process Corp., 113 Wn. App. 306, 324, 54 P.3d 665 (2002).

Broad discovery is permitted under CR 26. "It is not ground for objection that the information sought will be inadmissible at the trial if the information sought appears reasonably calculated to lead to the discovery of admissible evidence." CR 26(b)(1). A party must answer or object to an interrogatory or a request for production. If the party does not, it must seek a protective order under CR 26(c). CR 37(d). If the party does not seek a protective order, then the party must respond to the discovery request. The party cannot simply ignore or fail to respond to the request. "[A]n evasive or misleading answer is to be treated as a failure to answer." CR 37(d). Hyundai never sought a protective order under CR 26(c) but ignored or evaded Magaña's discovery requests, asserting the requests were overbroad and not reasonably calculated to lead to the discovery of admissible evidence.

If a trial court imposes one of the more "harsher remedies" under CR 37(b), then the record must clearly show (1) one party willfully or deliberately violated the discovery rules and orders, (2) the opposing party was substantially prejudiced in its ability to prepare for trial, and (3) the trial court explicitly considered whether a lesser sanction would have sufficed. Burnet, 131 Wn.2d at 494. "The purposes of sanctions orders are to deter, to punish, to compensate and to educate." Fisons, 122 Wn.2d at 356.

Willfulness

"Fair and reasoned resistance to discovery is not sanctionable." Fisons, 122 Wn.2d at 346. "A party's disregard of a court order without reasonable excuse or justification is deemed willful." Rivers v. Wash. State Conference of Mason Contractors, 145 Wn.2d 674, 686–87, 41 P.3d 1175 (2002) (citing Woodhead v. Disc. Waterbeds, Inc., 78 Wn. App. 125, 130, 896 P.2d 66 (1995)).

The trial court found Hyundai willfully violated the discovery rules. The Court of Appeals held "it was reasonable for the trial court to conclude that Hyundai's failure to timely disclose similar incidents of seat back failure was willful." Magaña II, 141 Wn. App. at 511. The trial court did not abuse its discretion in finding Hyundai willfully violated the discovery rules.

The trial court held, and the Court of Appeals agreed, Hyundai's responses to Magaña's request for production 20 and interrogatory 12 were false, misleading, and evasive. Id. The record supports this finding. Hyundai failed to inform Magaña in its response to request for production 20 that there were in fact several claims of alleged seat back failure of which Hyundai was aware, including the Martinez, McQuary, and Salizar claims. Id. at 527–28. In fact, Hyundai falsely represented to Magaña that there were no claims involving the seat back of 1995–1999 Hyundai Accents. Then Hyundai failed to supplement its incorrect responses, as required under CR 26(e)(2), when it learned about other claims involving seat back failure, including the Wagner, Bobbitt, Pockrus, and Powell claims, before the June 2002 trial. Id. Additionally, Hyundai's responses to interrogatory 12 were inaccurate because it misrepresented there were no identical recliner mechanisms in other Hyundai vehicles as in the 1996 Accent.

A corporation must search all of its departments, not just its legal department, when a party requests information about other claims during discovery. Here Hyundai searched only its legal department. Hyundai's counsel told the trial court that in response to request for production 20, Hyundai's search "was limited to the records of the Hyundai legal department" and that "no effort was made to search beyond the legal department, as this would have taken an extensive computer search." CP at 5319. As the trial court correctly found, "[t]here is no legal basis for limiting a search for documents in response to a discovery request to those documents available in the corporate legal department. This would be the equivalent of limiting the responses in [Behr, 113 Wn. App. 306,] to a search for chemical tests which were on record in the corporate legal office, without disclosing that the search was so limited." CP at

5319–20. The trial court went on to say, "the legal department at Hyundai worked closely with the Consumer Affairs Department with respect to customer complaints and claims, including product liability claims. The vehicle owners' manual directed customers to call the Consumer Affairs number." CP at 5320. Hyundai had the obligation to diligently respond to Magaña's discovery requests about other similar incidents. It failed to do so by using its legal department as a shield. The trial court also found, "Hyundai had the obligation not only to diligently and in good faith respond to discovery efforts, but to maintain a document retrieval system that would enable the corporation to respond to plaintiff's requests. Hyundai is a sophisticated multinational corporation, experienced in litigation." Id. Hyundai willfully and deliberately failed to comply with Magaña's discovery requests since Magaña's initial requests in 2000 and continued to do so.

The record fully supports the trial court's other conclusions: there was no agreement between the parties to limit discovery, Hyundai's definition of "claims" was too narrow because Magaña's discovery request was broad, and the seats in the Hyundai Elantra were similar to the seats in the Hyundai Accent. These findings of fact also support the conclusion Hyundai willfully violated the discovery rules.

The trial court's finding that Hyundai willfully violated the discovery rules was based on reasonable grounds and substantial evidence in the record. The trial court did not abuse its discretion as to the willfulness element of the three-part test.

Prejudice

The trial court found Magaña suffered substantial prejudice in preparing for his second trial. However the Court of Appeals asserted that finding was unfounded and that "the trial court abused its discretion in sanctioning Hyundai with a default judgment." Magaña II, 141 Wn. App. at 515. The Court of Appeals stated "that on the record presented, there is insufficient evidence to show that the delay occasioned by Hyundai's late production substantially prejudiced Magaña." Id. at 516.

The Court of Appeals argued Magaña could complete his inquiry into other similar accidents if he had more time to do so. Id. But as Magaña testified during the evidentiary hearing, his inquiry into other similar incidents was futile and time would not have cured that. After finally receiving the discovery responses from Hyundai and shortly before the evidentiary hearing, Magaña attempted to contact 18 complainants. Of those 18 complainants, only one produced relevant files for Magaña. Twelve of the complainants were unreachable, did not remember enough to be helpful, or had purged their records. Five of them had not responded to Magaña's calls and messages at the time of the evidentiary hearing. More time would not have benefited Magaña because most of the evidence had gone stale. After an extensive evidentiary hearing, the trial court found, "it is very difficult if not impossible to adequately investigate and develop the OSI [other similar incidents] information at this late date.... Even if this time were now available, evidence has been lost and much of the information is stale." CP at 5331.

The Court of Appeals also criticized Magaña's "choice of strategy in pursuing the case," asserting that Magaña requested additional discovery and then complained that "the time required to investigate would have substantially prejudiced his case." Magaña II, 141 Wn. App. at 518–19. This assertion completely misses the mark. Magaña was entitled to the discovery he requested. Hyundai never requested a protective order, and the discovery requests were reasonably calculated to lead to the production of admissible evidence. The discovery requested should have been given to Magaña in a timely manner. Magaña need not have continually requested more discovery and updates on existing requests. Additionally Magaña should not have needed to file a motion for an order to compel Hyundai to produce the documents Hyundai was required to produce by the discovery requests themselves, nor does this opinion rest on the existence of a discovery order. But the Court of Appeals faults Magaña for continually requesting discovery materials that should have been submitted in the first place, and as Judge Bridgewater accurately asserts in his dissent, "the fault should lie with Hyundai, not Magaña." Id. at 528 (Bridgewater, J., dissenting).

The trial court held, "Reasonable opportunity to conduct discovery is a fundamental part of due process of law. If disclosed in the 2000 to 2001 time frame the information regarding other seat back failures in Hyundai vehicles would have been investigated and further evidence would have been developed by the plaintiff.... Plaintiff would have had the opportunity to contact witnesses and to preserve evidence and would have done so." CP at 5329. Instead evidence was lost and much of what remained was too stale for effective use. The Court of Appeals argues, "many of the incidents were already several years old when Magaña first requested them." Magaña II, 141 Wn. App. at 518. But that is not the point. Hyundai knew about these claims but willfully failed to disclose them, thereby prejudicing Magaña's ability to prepare for trial.

In Behr the trial court found the plaintiffs were substantially prejudiced in preparing for trial because "'the discovery violations complained of suppressed evidence that was relevant, because it goes to the heart of the plaintiffs' claims, and it supports them.'" 113 Wn. App. at 325 (quoting court proceedings). As Judge Bridgewater articulated, "On remand, the sole issue was whether Hyundai was liable for the allegedly defective occupant restraint system." Magaña II, 141 Wn. App. at 531 (Bridgewater, J., dissenting). Hyundai suppressed relevant evidence, which included many documents about other similar claims against Hyundai that would have supported Magaña's claims.

The Court of Appeals also uses the wrong standard when it asserts Magaña was not prejudiced in obtaining a fair trial. Magaña II, 141 Wn. App. at 516–18. This prong of the test looks to whether Magaña was prejudiced in preparing for trial, not obtaining a fair trial. Burnet, 131 Wn.2d at 494; Behr, 113 Wn. App. at 325–26. The Court of Appeals asserts, "This does not demonstrate prejudice to his ability to obtain a fair trial when (1) he did not request additional discovery until shortly before trial, (2) the parties litigated the scope of permissible discovery, and (3) Hyundai timely produced documentation of other similar incidents in compliance with the court's order." Magaña II, 141 Wn. App. at 516–17 (emphasis added). Each of these assertions by the Court of Appeals was contradicted by the trial court's findings of fact and conclusions of law, which were supported by substantial evidence. On the facts of this case, Magaña could not have obtained a fair trial, let alone properly prepare for a trial.

The Court of Appeals concluded, "If [Magaña] tries to find experts and they are unable to analyze the evidence and would have been able to analyze it if it had been provided earlier, then and only then could irrevocable prejudice be shown that may warrant the trial court's usurping of the right to trial and directing a verdict in Magaña's favor." Id. at 520. But the problem is Magaña is unable to find the evidence because others who had accidents involving Hyundai vehicles are no longer living, have disappeared, or have discarded their evidence. The evidence that could be analyzed by experts has been lost because of the time that has elapsed between when Hyundai should have disclosed the information and the time it was compelled to do so — more than five years late.

Magaña's ability to prepare for trial was substantially prejudiced because of Hyundai's egregious actions during discovery. The Court of Appeals substituted its own discretion for the trial court's, which is inconsistent with the abuse of discretion standard. The record supports the findings of the trial court that Magaña was prejudiced in preparing for trial.

Lesser Sanctions

A court should issue sanctions appropriate to advancing the purposes of discovery. Burnet, 131 Wn.2d at 497. The discovery sanction should be proportional to the discovery violation and the circumstances of the case. Id. at 496–97. "[T]he least severe sanction that will be adequate to serve the purpose of the particular sanction should be imposed. The sanction must not be so minimal, however, that it undermines the purpose of discovery. The sanction should insure that the wrongdoer does not profit from the wrong." Fisons, 122 Wn.2d at 355–56 (footnote omitted). "Before resorting to the sanction of dismissal, the trial court must clearly indicate on the record that it has considered less harsh sanctions under CR 37. Its failure to do so constitutes an abuse of discretion." Rivers, 145 Wn.2d at 696.

"The right of trial by jury shall remain inviolate." Const. art. I, §21; see also CR 38. "Due process is satisfied, however, if, before entering a default judgment or dismissing a claim or defense, the trial court concludes that there was 'a willful or deliberate refusal to obey a discovery order, which refusal substantially prejudices the opponent's ability to prepare for trial.'" Behr, 113 Wn. App. at 330 (internal quotation marks omitted) (quoting White v. Kent Med. Ctr., Inc., 61 Wn. App. 163, 176, 810 P.2d 4 (1991)).

Here the trial court adequately and explicitly considered on the record whether lesser sanctions such as a monetary fine, a continuance, striking counterclaims, and admitting into evidence all or some of the other similar incidents of seat back failure would suffice. However, it determined the only suitable remedy was to enter a default judgment against Hyundai for its continued willful and deliberate failure to comply with Magaña's discovery requests.

The Court of Appeals agreed that Hyundai should have been sanctioned but stated, "Lesser sanctions here could adequately address the goal of encouraging good faith compliance with discovery requests and timely trial preparation." Magaña II, 141 Wn. App. at 520. The Court of Appeals asserted, "[D]efault judgment is tantamount to awarding Magaña a several million dollar verdict without requiring him to prove his case." Id. Hyundai argued a default judgment does not allow a jury to decide if the seat back did in fact cause the accident.

The trial court did acknowledge a default judgment would reinstate the prior verdict, which was substantial, but went on to say, "The remedy of default is not dependent upon the amount of potential verdict or in this case, actual damages verdict." CP at 5334. While the amount reinstated is large, this is not because of any wrongdoing on Magaña's part; rather it is due to Hyundai's atrocious behavior in failing to respond to discovery requests throughout the lawsuit.

In addressing whether a monetary fine would suffice, the trial court found it would be difficult to know what amount would be suitable since "Hyundai is a multi-billion dollar corporation." CP at 5332–33. It also found a monetary sanction would not address the prejudice to Magaña or to the judicial system. Since there were no counterclaims in this case, the trial court could not strike those as a remedy. The trial court also denied a continuance, which Hyundai had proposed. The trial court held that sanctions for discovery violations should not reward the party who has committed the violations and that granting a continuance would only exacerbate the situation. The Court of Appeals disagreed, claiming, "Allowing Magaña to investigate the incidents of seat failure will shed light on whether Hyundai manufactured and sold a defective product." Magaña II, 141 Wn. App. at 519. But as aforementioned, time will not allow Magaña to investigate other incidents because much of that evidence is lost or stale.

Finally the trial court found that admitting into evidence all the other similar incidents of seat back failure would not be adequate because Magaña did not have time to develop those incidents. Both parties agreed it would not be workable to admit other incidents of seat back failure without examination or challenge.

Hyundai argues a default judgment is appropriate only if the discovery violations irremediably deprived the opposing party of a fair trial on its claims or defenses. Hyundai misstates this prong of the test. As aforementioned, the record must show that the discovery violation prejudiced the opposing party's ability to prepare for trial. The test looks at preparing for trial, not having a fair trial.

Attorney Fees and Expenses

In addition to the discovery sanctions issued, the court may require the party failing to respond to discovery to pay reasonable expenses to the other party, including attorney fees. CR 37(d). In its findings of fact the trial court awarded to Magaña the fees and costs incurred because of Hyundai's discovery violations, which would be determined at another hearing.

An award of attorney fees is reviewed for abuse of discretion. Mayer v. City of Seattle, 102 Wn. App. 66, 79, 10 P.3d 408 (2000). "Attorney fee decisions under CR 37 require the exercise of judicial discretion that will not be disturbed on appeal except upon a clear showing of abuse of discretion." Eugster v. City of Spokane, 121 Wn. App. 799, 815, 91 P.3d 117 (2004) (citing Reid Sand & Gravel, Inc. v. Bellevue Props., 7 Wn. App. 701, 705, 502 P.2d 480 (1972)). A trial court must enter findings of fact and conclusions of law supporting an award of attorney fees. Mahler v. Szucs, 135 Wn.2d 398, 435, 957 P.2d 632, 966 P.2d 305 (1998). The court reviewing the award needs to know if the attorney's services were reasonable or essential to the successful outcome. Id. Here the trial court entered findings of fact and conclusions of law detailing the necessary and reasonable work of Magaña's attorneys. This finding awarding Magaña attorney fees and costs should be reinstated since default judgment against Hyundai was proper.

In accordance with RAP 18.1(b) Magaña also requested in his opening brief attorney fees and expenses for responding to the second appeal. Under RAP 18.1(a) a party can recover attorney fees and expenses, if applicable law grants the right to such recovery. Magaña should recover attorney fees and expenses for responding to the second appeal because CR 37(d) is the applicable rule that grants the right to recovery of attorney fees and expenses.

CONCLUSION

Appellate courts may not substitute their discretion for that vested in the trial court, absent abuse. Where there is no abuse of trial court discretion, we may not reverse simply because there are other possible ways the trial court could have possibly exercised it. The trial court properly imposed a default judgment against Hyundai for its willful and deliberate failure to comply with discovery. Accordingly we reverse the Court of Appeals and award Magaña reasonable attorney fees and expenses for responding to this appeal.

———

Enterprise data management may include MDM, BYOD policies, document retention policies and litigation readiness plans, each with very unique issues to consider. For example, the proliferation of mobile devices in the workplace may present greater risk of security breach, as handheld devices can be lost more easily. BYOD policies, where employees are allowed to use their personal devices for work, increase the possibility of commingling personal and business information, which may lead to privacy issues. Many industries are required by law to keep certain business records. But taking a "save everything" approach is not only expensive; it may also expose the company to greater liability. A coherent, well thought-out document retention policy that allows for the regular disposal of obsolete information is imperative in these instances. And litigation readiness plans are particularly important for companies that are prone to lawsuits, because they provide the framework to respond quickly to discovery demands.

Data management plans should also include "data maps" of the entire corporate information infrastructure, including for example, email systems, telephone networks, and departmental folders, and track all hardware, such as servers, desktop computers and mobile devices. A review of the inventory of all data stores, such as hard drives, optical discs and tapes, may be important to ensure the organization is not keeping more data than it should. Holding on to obsolete data may be very expensive and may expose the company unnecessarily to legal issues. It is also important to note that some data may be managed by third parties, like data storage and document archive services, and it may be just as important to understand how these entities handle the client's data. For example, many archives are designed solely as a place to store data and may not be equipped to run sophisticated Boolean searches across millions of documents. An organization's ability to search through vast quantities of data and retrieve information quickly may be an important factor to consider in negotiating discovery demands in litigation.

It is also important to consider the types of data that are being generated, how the data flows through the systems and hardware, and where the data is ultimately stored. Some data by nature may be difficult to sort. For example, voice data and image files may be impossible to identify unless it is properly cataloged. Depending on the settings, some email platforms may save copies of emails on local hard drives as they travel through the network. Cloud computing may mean data is stored on servers thousands of miles away, halfway around the world. The emergence of the Internet of Things ("IoT")—the notion that all kinds of gadgets, such as smartphones, wearable technology, medical devices, and appliances, can connect with the internet and to each other with no human intervention—adds an entirely new dimension to data mapping and understanding its flow.[11] As this concept is applied to business, lawyers will likely have to contend with unprecedented legal issues as complex as the IoT itself.

Corporate data management plans, policies and procedures, and data maps, help organize and make sense of the information infrastructure. They provide direction not only in the ordinary course of business, but also in the event of contingencies like litigation, investigations, and even natural disasters. And when these events occur, there is usually very little time to figure out where relevant systems are located, what data must be preserved, and how to access and collect it. Being prepared is half the battle. Sound policies also speak to the defensibility of the overall process, and shows that the process more reliable, credible and less susceptible to challenges. Document retention policies that provide for the destruction of obsolete data can trump preservation obligations, so long as the policies are reasonable and responsible.[12] This notion is also contemplated in the "safe harbor" provision of Rule 37(e) of the Federal Rules of Civil Procedure.[13]

---

11. *See, e.g.,* Ignatius A. Grande & Mark E. Michels, *The Internet of Things: "You Ain't Seen Nothin' Yet,"* (Oct. 2014), available at http://www.hugheshubbard.com/PublicationDocuments/IOT%20 Georgetown-final-10-27-14.pdf.

12. *See, e.g.,* Phillip, 621 F. Supp. 2d at 1193–94 ("An organization should have reasonable policies and procedures for managing its information and records." (quoting Guideline 1, The Sedona Guidelines: Best Practice Guidelines & Commentary for Managing Information & Records in the Electronic Age (Nov. 2007)) (The court references a number of other authorities that have promulgated guidelines for document retention and destruction, and cautioned, "'[u]tilizing a system of record-keeping which conceals rather than discloses relevant records, or makes it unduly difficult to identify or locate them, [renders] the production of the documents an excessively burdensome and costly expedition. To allow a defendant whose business generates massive records to frustrate discovery by creating an inadequate filing system, and then claiming undue burden, would defeat the purposes of the discovery rules.'" (quoting Kozlowski v. Sears, Roebuck 73 F.R.D. 73 (D. Mass. 1976)).

13. Fed. R. Civ. P. 37(e) ("[A] court may not impose sanctions under these rules on a party for failing to provide electronically stored information lost as a result of the routine, good-faith operation

Dedicated Personnel Responsible for Oversight

Managing a corporation's information infrastructure is no longer the sole responsibility of IT or records management departments. Effective data management in many large corporations may require collaboration among various internal departments, and sometimes with outside parties. It takes a village. Within the organization, for example, legal departments may have to interface with IT, records management, HR, regulatory and compliance departments. Outside the company, in-house lawyers may have to work with technology consultants, third-party data archives, paper document warehouses, e-discovery vendors, as well as outside counsel. Oversight of what can be a very complicated, massive scheme of policies, procedures and protocols should be centralized in order for it to be managed efficiently. In large organizations, this may require a consortium of designated representatives from a number of departments, but the in-house lawyer is uniquely situated to identify and address any legal ramifications of sometimes very technical decisions.

A large corporation will rely primarily on its IT department to set up the sophisticated network of systems to run its business. It is imperative that in-house lawyers work with the IT department to understand how data is generated, transmitted and stored within the organization, and proactively manage the data to keep the business compliant with applicable laws and ready for litigation. Electronic data may be easily manipulated and even destroyed, so it is especially important, for example, for in-house lawyers to know how to suspend automated deletion protocols when a litigation hold is in effect. Decisions may have to be made very quickly and very early in the process when unintended events like litigation occur, so being prepared is critical. Records management departments, traditionally tasked with maintaining hard copy documents, may now also be responsible for managing information in electronic form. Records management departments are usually responsible for retention policies and the disposition of old information. In-house lawyers should work with records management departments to make sure the policies are reasonable and applied consistently. HR will help onboard new employees and integrate them into the corporate systems, but it may be as important to know what to do with documents that belonged to employees who left the organization. If a departing employee is a relevant custodian in a lawsuit, for example, the employee's documents may be subject to a litigation hold and must be preserved. In-house lawyers may also work with the regulatory department to make sure the organization is abiding by applicable data retention laws, and compliance to ensure that the employees are following the policies and procedures governing corporate data. And there may be many policies and procedures to consider — document retention policies, personal use policies, BYOD programs, litigation holds — and in-house lawyers and compliance professionals must be vigilant in making sure every employee follows the

---

of an electronic information system."); Fidelity Nat'l Title Ins. Co. of New York v. Intercompany Nat'l Title Ins. Co., 412 F.3d 747, 750 (7th Cir. 2005) ("There is nothing wrong with a policy of destroying documents after the point is reached at which there is no good business reason to retain them.").

rules. At the very least, this may require regular reminders about the policies, periodic audits, and written confirmation from employees indicating that they are in compliance. And if they are not, organizations should consistently enforce some formal system of penalties.

Proactive Monitoring and Compliance

In addition to having a coherent data management plan and dedicated personnel to oversee its execution, companies must proactively monitor compliance, particularly in the context of a lawsuit.[14] Organizations should periodically conduct audits to make sure their employees are abiding by the rules. In the event of a lawsuit and a company is subject to a litigation hold, employees should confirm in writing that they are in compliance with the hold and preserving relevant materials. Lawyers are accountable should discovery issues arise. Under the "signature requirement" of Rule 26(g)(1) of the Federal Rules of Civil Procedure, by signing a disclosure, discovery request, response, or objection, an attorney certifies that the disclosure is complete and correct based on the attorney's knowledge, information, and belief "formed after a reasonable inquiry."[15] Under Rule 26(g)(3), "sanctions can be imposed if an attorney fails in his or her 'duty to make a reasonable investigation to assure that their clients have provided all available responsive information and documents.'"[16]

Pension Comm. of the Univ. of Montreal Pension Plan v. Banc of Am. Sec., LLC

685 F. Supp. 2d 456 (S.D.N.Y. 2010)

AMENDED OPINION AND ORDER

SHIRA A. SCHEINDLIN, U.S.D.J.:

I. INTRODUCTION

In an era where vast amounts of electronic information is available for review, discovery in certain cases has become increasingly complex and expensive. Courts cannot and do not expect that any party can meet a standard of perfection. Nonetheless, the

---

14. *See, e.g.,* Pension Comm. of the Univ. of Montreal Pension Plan v. Banc of America Sec., LLC, 685 F. Supp. 2d 456, 463 (S.D.N.Y. 2010) (court found that plaintiffs "failed to timely institute written litigation holds and engaged in careless and indifferent collection efforts after the duty to preserve arose...." leading to the loss or destruction of documents, and awarded monetary sanctions and adverse inference instructions to the jury.); Zubulake v. UBS Warburg LLC, 229 F.R.D. 422, 432 (S.D.N.Y. 2004) ("[c]ounsel must take affirmative steps to monitor compliance so that all sources of discoverable information are identified and searched.").

15. Fed. R. Civ. P. Rule 26(g).

16. Brown v. Tellermate Holdings LTD., 2014 U.S. Dist. LEXIS 90123, *47 (S.D. Ohio 2014) (*quoting* Bernal v. All American Investment Realty, Inc., 479 F. Supp. 2d 1291, 1333 (S.D. Fla. 2007)).

courts have a right to expect that litigants and counsel will take the necessary steps to ensure that relevant records are preserved when litigation is reasonably anticipated, and that such records are collected, reviewed, and produced to the opposing party. As discussed six years ago in the Zubulake opinions, when this does not happen, the integrity of the judicial process is harmed and the courts are required to fashion a remedy. Once again, I have been compelled to closely review the discovery efforts of parties in a litigation, and once again have found that those efforts were flawed. As famously noted, "[t]hose who cannot remember the past are condemned to repeat it." By now, it should be abundantly clear that the duty to preserve means what it says and that a failure to preserve records—paper or electronic—and to search in the right places for those records, will inevitably result in the spoliation of evidence.

In February, 2004, a group of investors brought this action to recover losses of 550 million dollars stemming from the liquidation of two British Virgin Islands based hedge funds in which they held shares: Lancer Offshore, Inc. and OmniFund Ltd. (the "Funds"). Plaintiffs have asserted claims under the federal securities laws and under New York law against former directors, administrators, the auditor, and the prime broker and custodian of the Funds. The Funds were managed by Lancer Management Group LLC ("Lancer") and its principal, Michael Lauer. The Funds retained Citco Fund Services (Curacao) N.V. ("Citco NV") to perform certain administrative duties, but it eventually resigned as administrator of the Funds. On April 16, 2003, Lancer filed for bankruptcy. On July 8, 2003, the Funds were placed into receivership in the Southern District of Florida.

In October, 2007, during the discovery process, Citco NV, its parent company, the Citco Group Limited, and former Lancer Offshore directors who were Citco officers (collectively with Citco NV, the "Citco Defendants") claimed that substantial gaps were found in plaintiffs' document productions. As a result, depositions were held and declarations were submitted. This occurred from October, 2007 through June, 2008. Following the close of this discovery, the Citco Defendants moved for sanctions, alleging that each plaintiff failed to preserve and produce documents— including those stored electronically—and submitted false and misleading declarations regarding their document collection and preservation efforts. The Citco Defendants seek dismissal of the Complaint—or any lesser sanction the Court deems appropriate—based on plaintiffs' alleged misconduct.

Because this is a long and complicated opinion, it may be helpful to provide a brief summary up front. I begin with a discussion of how to define negligence, gross negligence, and willfulness in the discovery context and what conduct falls in each of these categories. I then review the law governing the imposition of sanctions for a party's failure to produce relevant information during discovery. This is followed by factual summaries regarding the discovery efforts—or lack thereof—undertaken by each of the thirteen plaintiffs against whom sanctions are sought, and then by an application of the law to those facts. Based on my review of the evidence, I conclude that all of these plaintiffs were either negligent or grossly negligent in meeting their discovery obligations. As a result, sanctions are required.

II. AN ANALYTICAL FRAMEWORK AND APPLICABLE LAW

From the outset, it is important to recognize what this case involves and what it does not. This case does not present any egregious examples of litigants purposefully destroying evidence. This is a case where plaintiffs failed to timely institute written litigation holds and engaged in careless and indifferent collection efforts after the duty to preserve arose. As a result, there can be little doubt that some documents were lost or destroyed.

The question, then, is whether plaintiffs' conduct requires this Court to impose a sanction for the spoliation of evidence. To answer this question, there are several concepts that must be carefully reviewed and analyzed. The first is plaintiffs' level of culpability—that is, was their conduct of discovery acceptable or was it negligent, grossly negligent, or willful. The second is the interplay between the duty to preserve evidence and the spoliation of evidence. The third is which party should bear the burden of proving that evidence has been lost or destroyed and the consequences resulting from that loss. And the fourth is the appropriate remedy for the harm caused by the spoliation.

A. Defining Negligence, Gross Negligence, and Willfulness in the Discovery Context

While many treatises and cases routinely define negligence, gross negligence, and willfulness in the context of tortious conduct, I have found no clear definition of these terms in the context of discovery misconduct. It is apparent to me that these terms simply describe a continuum. Conduct is either acceptable or unacceptable. Once it is unacceptable the only question is how bad is the conduct. That is a judgment call that must be made by a court reviewing the conduct through the backward lens known as hindsight. It is also a call that cannot be measured with exactitude and might be called differently by a different judge. That said, it is well established that negligence involves unreasonable conduct in that it creates a risk of harm to others, but willfulness involves intentional or reckless conduct that is so unreasonable that harm is highly likely to occur.

It is useful to begin with standard definitions of each term and then to explore the conduct, in the discovery context, that causes certain conduct to fall in one category or another.

[Negligence] is conduct "which falls below the standard established by law for the protection of others against unreasonable risk of harm." [Negligence] is caused by heedlessness or inadvertence, by which the negligent party is unaware of the results which may follow from [its] act. But it may also arise where the negligent party has considered the possible consequences carefully, and has exercised [its] own best judgment.

The standard of acceptable conduct is determined through experience. In the discovery context, the standards have been set by years of judicial decisions analyzing allegations of misconduct and reaching a determination as to what a party must do to meet its obligation to participate meaningfully and fairly in the discovery phase of a judicial proceeding. A failure to conform to this standard is negligent even if it results from a pure heart and an empty head.

"Gross negligence has been described as a failure to exercise even that care which a careless person would use." According to a leading treatise — Prosser & Keeton on Torts — most courts find that gross negligence is something more than negligence "and differs from ordinary negligence only in degree, and not in kind."

The same treatise groups willful, wanton, and reckless into one category that requires "that the actor has intentionally done an act of an unreasonable character in disregard of a known or obvious risk that was so great as to make it highly probable that harm would follow, and which thus is usually accompanied by a conscious indifference to the consequences."

Applying these terms in the discovery context is the next task. Proceeding chronologically, the first step in any discovery effort is the preservation of relevant information. A failure to preserve evidence resulting in the loss or destruction of relevant information is surely negligent, and, depending on the circumstances, may be grossly negligent or willful. For example, the intentional destruction of relevant records, either paper or electronic, after the duty to preserve has attached, is willful. Possibly after October, 2003, when Zubulake IV was issued, and definitely after July, 2004, when the final relevant Zubulake opinion was issued, the failure to issue a written litigation hold constitutes gross negligence because that failure is likely to result in the destruction of relevant information.

The next step in the discovery process is collection and review. Once again, depending on the extent of the failure to collect evidence, or the sloppiness of the review, the resulting loss or destruction of evidence is surely negligent, and, depending on the circumstances may be grossly negligent or willful. For example, the failure to collect records — either paper or electronic — from key players constitutes gross negligence or willfulness as does the destruction of email or certain backup tapes after the duty to preserve has attached. By contrast, the failure to obtain records from all employees (some of whom may have had only a passing encounter with the issues in the litigation), as opposed to key players, likely constitutes negligence as opposed to a higher degree of culpability. Similarly, the failure to take all appropriate measures to preserve ESI likely falls in the negligence category. These examples are not meant as a definitive list. Each case will turn on its own facts and the varieties of efforts and failures is infinite. I have drawn the examples above from this case and others. Recent cases have also addressed the failure to collect information from the files of former employees that remain in a party's possession, custody, or control after the duty to preserve has attached (gross negligence) or the failure to assess the accuracy and validity of selected search terms (negligence).

B. The Duty to Preserve and Spoliation

Spoliation refers to the destruction or material alteration of evidence or to the failure to preserve property for another's use as evidence in pending or reasonably foreseeable litigation. The right to impose sanctions for spoliation arises from a court's inherent power to control the judicial process and litigation, but the power is limited to that necessary to redress conduct "which abuses the judicial process." The policy underlying this inherent power of the courts is the need to preserve the integrity of the judicial process in order to retain confidence that the process works to uncover the truth.... The courts must protect the integrity of the judicial process because, "[a]s soon as the process falters ... the people are then justified in abandoning support for the system."

The common law duty to preserve evidence relevant to litigation is well recognized. The case law makes crystal clear that the breach of the duty to preserve, and the resulting spoliation of evidence, may result in the imposition of sanctions by a court because the court has the obligation to ensure that the judicial process is not abused. It is well established that the duty to preserve evidence arises when a party reasonably anticipates litigation. " '[O]nce a party reasonably anticipates litigation, it must suspend its routine document retention/destruction policy and put in place a 'litigation hold' to ensure the preservation of relevant documents.' " A plaintiff's duty is more often triggered before litigation commences, in large part because plaintiffs control the timing of litigation.

C. Burdens of Proof

The third preliminary matter that must be analyzed is what can be done when documents are no longer available. This is not an easy question. It is often impossible to know what lost documents would have contained. At best, their content can be inferred from existing documents or recalled during depositions. But this is not always possible. Who then should bear the burden of establishing the relevance of evidence that can no longer be found? And, an even more difficult question is who should be required to prove that the absence of the missing material has caused prejudice to the innocent party.

The burden of proof question differs depending on the severity of the sanction. For less severe sanctions—such as fines and cost-shifting—the inquiry focuses more on the conduct of the spoliating party than on whether documents were lost, and, if so, whether those documents were relevant and resulted in prejudice to the innocent party. As explained more thoroughly below, for more severe sanctions—such as dismissal, preclusion, or the imposition of an adverse inference—the court must consider, in addition to the conduct of the spoliating party, whether any missing evidence was relevant and whether the innocent party has suffered prejudice as a result of the loss of evidence.

On the question of what is "relevant," the Second Circuit has provided the following guidance:

> [O]ur cases make clear that "relevant" in this context means something more than sufficiently probative to satisfy Rule 401 of the Federal Rules of Evidence. Rather, the party seeking an adverse inference must adduce sufficient evidence from which a reasonable trier of fact could infer that "the destroyed or unavailable evidence would have been of the nature alleged by the party affected by its destruction."

It is not enough for the innocent party to show that the destroyed evidence would have been responsive to a document request. The innocent party must also show that the evidence would have been helpful in proving its claims or defenses—i.e., that the innocent party is prejudiced without that evidence. Proof of relevance does not necessarily equal proof of prejudice.

In short, the innocent party must prove the following three elements: that the spoliating party (1) had control over the evidence and an obligation to preserve it at the time of destruction or loss; (2) acted with a culpable state of mind upon destroying or losing the evidence; and that (3) the missing evidence is relevant to the innocent party's claim or defense.

Relevance and prejudice may be presumed when the spoliating party acted in bad faith or in a grossly negligent manner. "Where a party destroys evidence in bad faith, that bad faith alone is sufficient circumstantial evidence from which a reasonable fact finder could conclude that the missing evidence was unfavorable to that party." Although many courts in this district presume relevance where there is a finding of gross negligence, application of the presumption is not required. However, when the spoliating party was merely negligent, the innocent party must prove both relevance and prejudice in order to justify the imposition of a severe sanction. The innocent party may do so by "adduc[ing] sufficient evidence from which a reasonable trier of fact could infer that 'the destroyed [or unavailable] evidence would have been of the nature alleged by the party affected by its destruction.'" "In other words, the [innocent party] must present extrinsic evidence tending to show that the destroyed e-mails would have been favorable to [its] case." "Courts must take care not to 'hold[ ] the prejudiced party to too strict a standard of proof regarding the likely contents of the destroyed [or unavailable] evidence,' because doing so 'would ... allow parties who have ... destroyed evidence to profit from that destruction.'"

No matter what level of culpability is found, any presumption is rebuttable and the spoliating party should have the opportunity to demonstrate that the innocent party has not been prejudiced by the absence of the missing information. If the spoliating party offers proof that there has been no prejudice, the innocent party, of course, may offer evidence to counter that proof. While requiring the innocent party to demonstrate the relevance of information that it can never review may seem unfair, the party seeking relief has some obligation to make a showing of relevance and eventually prejudice, lest litigation become a "gotcha" game rather than a full and fair opportunity to air the merits of a dispute. If a presumption of relevance and prejudice were awarded to every party who can show that an adversary failed to produce any document, even if such failure is completely inadvertent, the incentive to find such error and capitalize on it would be overwhelming. This would not be a good thing.

To ensure that no party's task is too onerous or too lenient, I am employing the following burden shifting test: When the spoliating party's conduct is sufficiently egregious to justify a court's imposition of a presumption of relevance and prejudice, or when the spoliating party's conduct warrants permitting the jury to make such a presumption, the burden then shifts to the spoliating party to rebut that presumption.

The spoliating party can do so, for example, by demonstrating that the innocent party had access to the evidence alleged to have been destroyed or that the evidence would not support the innocent party's claims or defenses. If the spoliating party demonstrates to a court's satisfaction that there could not have been any prejudice to the innocent party, then no jury instruction will be warranted, although a lesser sanction might still be required.

D. Remedies

The remaining question is what remedy should the court impose. "The determination of an appropriate sanction for spoliation, if any, is confined to the sound discretion of the trial judge and is assessed on a case-by-case basis." Where the breach of a discovery obligation is the non-production of evidence, a court has broad discretion to determine the appropriate sanction. Appropriate sanctions should "(1) deter the parties from engaging in spoliation; (2) place the risk of an erroneous judgment on the party who wrongfully created the risk; and (3) restore 'the prejudiced party to the same position [it] would have been in absent the wrongful destruction of evidence by the opposing party.'"

It is well accepted that a court should always impose the least harsh sanction that can provide an adequate remedy. The choices include — from least harsh to most harsh — further discovery, cost-shifting, fines, special jury instructions, preclusion, and the entry of default judgment or dismissal (terminating sanctions). The selection of the appropriate remedy is a delicate matter requiring a great deal of time and attention by a court.

The Citco Defendants request dismissal — the most extreme sanction. However, a terminating sanction is justified in only the most egregious cases, such as where a party has engaged in perjury, tampering with evidence, or intentionally destroying evidence by burning, shredding, or wiping out computer hard drives. As described below, there is no evidence of such misconduct in this case.

Instead, the appropriate sanction here is some form of an adverse inference instruction that is intended to alleviate the harm suffered by the Citco Defendants. Like many other sanctions, an adverse inference instruction can take many forms, again ranging in degrees of harshness. The harshness of the instruction should be determined based on the nature of the spoliating party's conduct — the more egregious the conduct, the more harsh the instruction.

In its most harsh form, when a spoliating party has acted willfully or in bad faith, a jury can be instructed that certain facts are deemed admitted and must be accepted as true. At the next level, when a spoliating party has acted willfully or recklessly, a court may impose a mandatory presumption. Even a mandatory presumption, however, is considered to be rebuttable.

The least harsh instruction permits (but does not require) a jury to presume that the lost evidence is both relevant and favorable to the innocent party. If it makes this presumption, the spoliating party's rebuttal evidence must then be considered by the jury, which must then decide whether to draw an adverse inference against the spoliating party. This sanction still benefits the innocent party in that it allows the jury to consider both the misconduct of the spoliating party as well as proof of prejudice to the innocent party. Such a charge should be termed a "spoliation charge" to distinguish it from a charge where the a jury is directed to presume, albeit still subject to rebuttal, that the missing evidence would have been favorable to the innocent party, and from a charge where the jury is directed to deem certain facts admitted.

Monetary sanctions are also appropriate in this case. "Monetary sanctions are appropriate 'to punish the offending party for its actions [and] to deter the litigant's conduct, sending the message that egregious conduct will not be tolerated.'" Awarding monetary sanctions "serves the remedial purpose of compensating [the movant] for the reasonable costs it incurred in bringing [a motion for sanctions]." This sanction is imposed in order to compensate the Citco Defendants for reviewing the declarations, conducting the additional depositions, and bringing this motion.

Three final notes. First, I stress that at the end of the day the judgment call of whether to award sanctions is inherently subjective. A court has a "gut reaction" based on years of experience as to whether a litigant has complied with its discovery obligations and how hard it worked to comply. Second, while it would be helpful to develop a list of relevant criteria a court should review in evaluating discovery conduct, these inquiries are inherently fact intensive and must be reviewed case by case. Nonetheless, I offer the following guidance.

After a discovery duty is well established, the failure to adhere to contemporary standards can be considered gross negligence. Thus, after the final relevant Zubulake opinion in July, 2004, the following failures support a finding of gross negligence, when the duty to preserve has attached: to issue a written litigation hold; to identify all of the key players and to ensure that their electronic and paper records are preserved; to cease the deletion of email or to preserve the records of former employees that are in a party's possession, custody, or control; and to preserve backup tapes when they are the sole source of relevant information or when they relate to key players, if the relevant information maintained by those players is not obtainable from readily accessible sources.

Finally, I note the risk that sanctions motions, which are very, very time consuming, distracting, and expensive for the parties and the court, will be increasingly sought by litigants. This, too, is not a good thing. For this reason alone, the most careful consideration should be given before a court finds that a party has violated its duty to comply with discovery obligations and deserves to be sanctioned. Likewise, parties need to anticipate and undertake document preservation with the most serious and thorough care, if for no other reason than to avoid the detour of sanctions.

III. PROCEDURAL HISTORY

In the summer of 2003, a group of investors formed an ad hoc "policy consultative committee" to represent the interests of the Funds' investors, including "monitor[ing] the court proceedings" against Lancer and the Funds and "retain[ing] legal counsel as necessary...," On September 17 and 18, 2003, this group of investors met prospective legal counsel. Although some plaintiffs had previously retained counsel, in October or November, 2003, plaintiffs retained BRBI and Berman as lead counsel for this suit. This lawsuit was then instituted on February 12, 2004 in the Southern District of Florida. On October 25, 2005, the case was transferred to this Court as a result of defendants' motion to transfer venue.

IV. PLAINTIFFS' EFFORTS AT PRESERVATION AND PRODUCTION

Shortly after its retention in October or November, 2003, Counsel contacted plaintiffs to begin document collection and preservation. Counsel telephoned and emailed plaintiffs and distributed memoranda instructing plaintiffs to be over, rather than under, inclusive, and noting that emails and electronic documents should be included in the production. Counsel indicated that the documents were necessary to draft the complaint, although they did not expressly direct that the search be limited to those documents.

This instruction does not meet the standard for a litigation hold. It does not direct employees to preserve all relevant records—both paper and electronic—nor does it create a mechanism for collecting the preserved records so that they can be searched by someone other than the employee. Rather, the directive places total reliance on the employee to search and select what that employee believed to be responsive records without any supervision from Counsel. Throughout the litigation, Counsel sent plaintiffs monthly case status memoranda, which included additional requests for Lancer-related documents, including electronic documents. But these memoranda never specifically instructed plaintiffs not to destroy records so that Counsel could monitor the collection and production of documents.

In 2004, a stay pursuant to the Private Securities Litigation Reform Act ("PSLRA") was instituted and remained in place until early 2007. Counsel "did not focus [their] efforts ... on discovery" while the PSLRA discovery stay was in place and plaintiffs did not issue a written litigation hold until 2007. In May, 2007, the Citco Defendants made their first document requests.

Depositions of plaintiffs commenced on August 30, 2007. Those depositions revealed that there were gaps in plaintiffs' document production. By October, 2007, the Citco Defendants were dissatisfied with plaintiffs' efforts to produce missing documents. In response to a request from the Citco Defendants, the Court ordered plaintiffs to provide declarations regarding their efforts to preserve and produce documents.

Counsel spent a huge amount of time preparing the declarations, including drafting, questioning plaintiffs' employees, and attempting to locate documents that had not yet been produced. Counsel emphasized to each declarant the importance of the declarations' accuracy and that each should be carefully reviewed prior to its execution. In a systematic manner, each declaration identifies the declarant's relationship to the plaintiff and that, upon retaining Counsel in late 2003 or early 2004—if not earlier—the steps plaintiff took to locate and preserve documents relating to its Lancer investment (the "2003/2004 Search"). Most declarations also discuss receiving, and complying with, a second search request in late 2007 or early 2008 (the "2007/2008 Search"). Each declarant states that he or she believes the company located, preserved, and produced "all" Lancer-related documents in its possession at the time of either the 2003/2004 search, the 2007/2008 search, or both. Each declarant also states that no responsive documents in plaintiff's possession, custody, or control were discarded or destroyed following a specific point in time—either after the "request to preserve them," a specified date, or after the declarant arrived at the company.

Plaintiffs' declarations were submitted in the first half of 2008. At least four declarants submitted amended declarations, and at least one deponent submitted a declaration containing information not revealed prior to his deposition. The Citco Defendants then sought to depose certain declarants and other relevant individuals. The Court granted that request. The Citco Defendants found additional gaps in plaintiffs' productions. By cross referencing the productions of other plaintiffs, former co-defendants, and the Receiver in the SEC Action, the Citco Defendants were able to identify at least 311 documents from twelve of the thirteen plaintiffs (all but the Bombardier Foundation) that should have been in plaintiffs' productions, but were not included ("311 Documents"). In addition, the Citco Defendants discovered that almost all of the declarations were false and misleading and/or executed by a declarant without personal knowledge of its contents.

V. DISCUSSION

A. Duty to Preserve and Document Destruction

By April, 2003, Lancer had filed for bankruptcy, UM had filed a complaint with the Financial Services Commission of the British Virgin Islands, Hunnicutt and the Chagnon Plaintiffs had retained counsel, and the Chagnon Plaintiffs had initiated communication with a number of other plaintiffs. It is unreasonable to assume that the remaining plaintiffs—all sophisticated investors—were unaware of the impending Lancer collapse while other investors were filing suit and retaining counsel. Accordingly, each plaintiff was under a duty to preserve at that time. While, as discussed below, the duty to issue a written litigation hold might not have been well established at that time, it was beyond cavil that the duty to preserve evidence included a duty to preserve electronic records.

The burden then falls to the Citco Defendants to demonstrate that documents were destroyed after the duty to preserve arose. The Citco Defendants first point to the 311 Documents, most of which post-date the onset of plaintiffs' duty to preserve. Thus, those plaintiffs that failed to produce these documents clearly failed to preserve and produce relevant documents that existed at the time (or shortly after) the duty to preserve arose. This is not true, however, with respect to the Bombardier Foundation, Commonfund, KMEFIC, and UM. While three of these plaintiffs (all but the Bombardier Foundation) failed to produce documents that the Citco Defendants now have, those documents are older records that may not have been in plaintiffs' possession and/or control at the time the duty to preserve arose.

In addition to citing specific documents not produced by each plaintiff, the Citco Defendants next ask this Court to assume that each plaintiff also received or generated documents that have not been produced by anyone and are now presumed to be missing. Plaintiffs call such a request "absurd" and argue that any such inference would be based on no more than "rank speculation." The Citco Defendants' argument is by far the more compelling.

All plaintiffs had a fiduciary duty to conduct due diligence before making significant investments in the Funds. Surely records must have existed documenting the due diligence, investments, and subsequent monitoring of these investments. The paucity of records produced by some plaintiffs and the admitted failure to preserve some records or search at all for others by all plaintiffs leads inexorably to the conclusion that relevant records have been lost or destroyed.

B. Culpability

The age of this case requires a dual analysis of culpability—plaintiffs' conduct before and after 2005. The Citco Defendants contend that plaintiffs acted willfully or with reckless disregard, such that the sanction of dismissal is warranted. Plaintiffs admit that they failed to institute written litigation holds until 2007 when they returned their attention to discovery after a four year hiatus. Plaintiffs should have done so no later than 2005, when the action was transferred to this District. This requirement was clearly established in this District by mid-2004, after the last relevant Zubulake opinion was issued. Thus, the failure to do so as of that date was, at a minimum, grossly negligent. The severity of this misconduct would have justified severe sanctions had the Citco Defendants demonstrated that any documents were destroyed after 2005. They have not done so. It is likely that most of the evidence was lost before that date due to the failure to institute written litigation holds.

Almost all plaintiffs' pre-2005 conduct, apart from the failure to issue written litigation holds, is best characterized as either grossly negligent or negligent because they failed to execute a comprehensive search for documents and/or failed to sufficiently supervise or monitor their employees' document collection. For some plaintiffs, no further evidence of culpable conduct is offered. For others, the Citco Defendants have provided additional evidence. For example, one plaintiff—the Bombardier Foundation—admitted that it destroyed backup data in 2004, after the duty to preserve at least some backup tapes was well-established. Similarly, several plaintiffs failed to collect and preserve documents of key players—including members of investment committees and/or boards of directors. One further problem bears mention. Each plaintiff was directed by this Court to submit a declaration documenting its search efforts for two periods—2003/2004 and 2007/2008, as well as any steps taken in between. In the end, almost every plaintiff submitted a declaration that—at best—lacked attention to detail, or—at worst—was intentionally vague in an attempt to mislead the Citco Defendants and the Court. In addition, plaintiffs had a duty to adequately prepare knowledgeable witnesses with respect to these topics. Which files were searched, how the search was conducted, who was asked to search, what they were told, and the extent of any supervision are all topics reasonably within the scope of the inquiry. Several plaintiffs violated this duty.

From my review of the evidence submitted by the parties and discussed at the hearings held on October 30, 2007 and April 22, 2008, I conclude that no plaintiff engaged in willful misconduct. However, as outlined below, I find that 2M, Hunnicutt, Coronation, the Chagnon Plaintiffs, Bombardier Trusts, and the Bombardier Foundation acted with gross negligence, and the Altar Fund, L'Ecole Polytechnique, Okabena, the Corbett Foundation, Commonfund, KMEFIC, and UM acted in a negligent manner.

C. Relevance and Prejudice

For those plaintiffs that were grossly negligent, I find that the Citco Defendants have "adduced enough evidence" that plaintiffs have failed to produce relevant documents and that the Citco Defendants have been prejudiced as a result. Thus, a jury will be permitted to presume, if it so chooses, both the relevance of the missing documents and resulting prejudice to the Citco Defendants, subject to the plaintiffs' ability to rebut the presumption to the satisfaction of the trier of fact.

For those plaintiffs that were negligent, the Citco Defendants must demonstrate that any destroyed documents were relevant and the loss was prejudicial. To meet this burden, the Citco Defendants begin by pointing to the 311 Documents. While many of these documents may be relevant, the Citco Defendants suffered no prejudice because all were eventually obtained from other sources. As noted by plaintiffs, "Citco possesses every one of the 311 [D]ocuments; indeed, every one of these documents was marked as an exhibit and used by Citco at depositions." The Citco Defendants had the opportunity to question witnesses about these documents and will be able to introduce them at trial. Severe sanctions based on the failure to produce the 311 Documents is not justified.

By contrast, it is impossible to know the extent of the prejudice suffered by the Citco Defendants as a result of those emails and documents that have been permanently lost due to plaintiffs' conduct. The volume of missing emails and documents can never be learned, nor can their substance be known. "Because we do not know what has been destroyed, it is impossible to accurately assess what harm has been done to the [innocent party] and what prejudice it has suffered." Such documents may have been helpful to the Citco Defendants, helpful to plaintiffs, or of no value to any party. But it is plaintiffs' misconduct that destroyed the emails and documents. Given the facts and circumstances presented here, I can only conclude that the Citco Defendants have carried their limited burden of demonstrating that the lost documents would have been relevant. The documents that no longer exist were created during the critical time period. Key players must have engaged in correspondence regarding the relevant transactions. There can be no serious question that the missing material would have been relevant.

Prejudice is another matter. The Citco Defendants have gathered an enormous amount of discovery—both from documents and witnesses. Unless they can show through extrinsic evidence that the loss of the documents has prejudiced their ability to defend the case, then a lesser sanction than a spoliation charge is sufficient to address any lapse in the discovery efforts of the negligent plaintiffs.

D. Individual Plaintiffs

Because this motion involves the conduct of thirteen plaintiffs, and because the Citco Defendants have charged each plaintiff with distinct discovery misconduct, a factual summary as to each plaintiff is required. In addition, because the stakes are high for both sides, and because sanctions should not be awarded lightly nor should discovery misconduct be tolerated, it is important to carefully review that conduct to determine whether any plaintiff engaged in culpable conduct and, if so, what level of culpability should be assigned. Each plaintiff's discovery efforts is described below together with my determination of the adequacy of those efforts.

1. Plaintiffs that Acted in a Grossly Negligent Manner

As detailed below, 2M, Hunnicutt, Coronation, the Chagnon Plaintiffs, Bombardier Trusts, and the Bombardier Foundation were grossly negligent in their discovery efforts. In each instance, these plaintiffs' 2003/2004 Searches were severely deficient. In addition to failing to institute a timely written litigation hold, one or more of these plaintiffs failed to collect or preserve any electronic documents prior to 2007, continued to delete electronic documents after the duty to preserve arose, did not request documents from key players, delegated search efforts without any supervision from management, destroyed backup data potentially containing responsive documents of key players that were not otherwise available, and/or submitted misleading or inaccurate declarations. From this conduct, it is fair to presume that responsive documents were lost or destroyed. The relevance of any destroyed documents and the prejudice caused by their loss may also be presumed.

Because this permissive presumption is rebuttable, I find that no reasonable juror could conclude that the Citco Defendants were prejudiced by plaintiffs' failure to produce the 311 Documents. With regard to those documents that are missing or destroyed, however, the Citco Defendants are entitled to a spoliation instruction permitting the jury to presume, if it so chooses, that these documents would have been both relevant and prejudicial. The jury must then consider whether the plaintiffs have successfully rebutted this presumption. If plaintiffs succeed, no adverse inference will be drawn. If plaintiffs cannot rebut the presumption, the jury will be entitled to draw an adverse inference in favor of the Citco Defendants.

a. 2M

In his October, 2007 deposition, Letier, 2M's former Chief Financial Officer ("CFO"), testified that although he served as the lead contact with Counsel prior to leaving 2M in 2004, he was not in charge of gathering and producing documents. He further testified that he neither took any steps to ensure that emails relating to the Funds were not deleted nor was he aware of anyone else at 2M doing so. He testified that he did not recall "ever giv[ing] instructions to anyone to preserve" Lancer-related documents and never received any such instructions. On March 31, 2008, Letier submitted a declaration stating that he directed other employees to locate and preserve Lancer-related documents and that "all documents" related to Lancer had been produced to Counsel during the 2003/2004 Search. Letier also declared that to the best of his knowledge no Lancer-related documents were discarded or destroyed after Counsel instructed 2M to locate all documents in its possession in late 2003 or early 2004. Subsequently, Letier amended his declaration to clarify that only "paper documents" had been produced.

Trumpower, 2M's current CFO and General Counsel, also submitted a declaration requiring amendment. Trumpower's initial declaration indicated that 2M had searched for electronic documents prior to his arrival at 2M in 2007. In his amended declaration, Trumpower clarified that his declaration addressed only the 2007/2008 Search. Trumpower also declared that to the best of his knowledge, all relevant documents in 2M's possession at the time of the 2007/2008 Search were submitted to Counsel and no documents had been discarded or destroyed at 2M since his arrival in February 2007. Trumpower testified that no emails had been deleted from 2M's server since 2004 and personal folders were not automatically deleted from 2M's network. The Citco Defendants also complain that 2M failed to produce "reams of research" on Lancer referenced in Trumpower's deposition and another email. This research was, in fact, destroyed after April, 2003. Finally, the Citco Defendants have identified forty-six emails that were sent or received by 2M between June 9, 2003 and October 28, 2003, that were not produced by 2M. 2M "did not produce a single email or electronic document" until 2008. Then, on August 7 and 21, 2009, just days after plaintiffs submitted their opposition to this motion, 2M produced 8,084 pages of documents— more than three times the number of documents previously produced. This production included nearly seven hundred emails.

The Citco Defendants have shown that 2M took no action to collect or preserve electronic documents prior to 2007, did not produce a single email or electronic document until 2008, and then dumped thousands of pages on the Citco Defendants only when it faced the prospect of sanctions. Although 2M can verify that it has not deleted any emails from its server since 2004, there is no similar representation for the most relevant period—i.e., prior to 2004. 2M also concedes that its employees' collection lacked oversight and that no direction was given either orally or in writing to preserve documents or cease deleting emails, until a written litigation hold was issued in 2007. Finally, 2M's initial declarations were misleading as to whether 2M had conducted any electronic searches prior to 2007. These declarations, alone, would have supported a finding of bad faith. However, given that each declarant submitted an amended declaration within a reasonable time of being notified of the deficiencies in the original declaration, 2M's conduct, on the whole, amounts to gross negligence.

b. Hunnicutt

At his deposition, William Hunnicutt, President of Hunnicutt, testified that to the best of his recollection, he maintained all of the emails he sent regarding Lancer from the inception of his relationship with Lancer in April 1998 through the first quarter of 2003. However, Mr. Hunnicutt also testified that he had a practice of deleting emails unless he "felt there was an important reason to keep them" and did not recall anyone ever instructing him to discontinue that practice. In addition, Mr. Hunnicutt took no steps during the 2003/2004 Search to request documents from, or search the files of, one current and one former employee to whom Hunnicutt assigned Lancer-related work. Some of this work was done by the employees on their personal computers outside of Hunnicutt's offices. When shown emails he had sent but not produced, Mr. Hunnicutt could not explain why he had not produced them. However, when Mr. Hunnicutt submitted his declaration approximately two months later, he stated that he now recalled having accidently deleted his email "sent" file prior to March 13, 2003. The Citco Defendants have identified fifty-seven emails that Mr. Hunnicutt sent between February 3, 1999 and May 14, 2003, but did not produce.

Mr. Hunnicutt's continued deletion of emails long after 2003 is inexcusable, as is Hunnicutt's failure to seek any Lancer-related documents or emails from one current employee and one former employee who worked on the Lancer investment. These actions and inactions — including the loss of the fifty-seven emails — lead inexorably to the conclusion that relevant documents were not produced and are now lost. This conduct amounts to gross negligence.

c. Coronation

Coronation, operating out of offices in London and Cape Town, South Africa, delegated the 2003/2004 Search to Mei Hardman, an employee in the "due diligence area." Despite declaring that to the best of her knowledge Coronation located and preserved "all documents relating to Lancer," Hardman testified at her deposition that she had no experience conducting searches, received no instruction on how to do so, had no supervision during the collection, and no contact with Counsel during the search. Hardman stated that she searched only the investment team's drive on the London computer network, even though she was aware that not all emails or electronic documents on the office computers of investment team members would be on that drive. Hardman communicated the request for documents to the Cape Town office during a brief telephone conversation without imparting instructions. Hardman was also aware that Coronation kept backup tapes, but never searched them for Lancer-related documents and was unaware of anyone else doing so.

Hardman also asked only three employees — Stuart Davies, Anthony Gibson, and Maria Meadows — out of a number of other employees in the London office to search their computers for emails and electronic documents. According to an internal Coronation memorandum, Davies, Gibson, and Meadows were part of a larger "investment team" comprised of up to twenty "investment specialists" in London, including fund managers, research analysts, due diligence analysts, and risk managers. Although Hardman resisted the characterization that the other investment specialists would have been involved in Lancer-related decisions, she acknowledged that investment specialist Fred Ingham was involved in Lancer-related decisions in July, 2003. Hardman also acknowledged that the files of Amrusta Blignaut, Coronation's compliance officer and Arne Hassel, Chief Investment Officer of Coronation's investment team, were never searched, but she did not know whether either Blignaut or Hassel held those positions prior to late 2003. The Citco Defendants have identified thirty-nine emails from May 16, 2003 through September 19, 2003 that Coronation did not produce.

Coronation produced no emails or correspondence from 1998 through 1999 and only limited emails and correspondence from 2000 through 2002.

Hardman was ill-equipped to handle Coronation's discovery obligations without supervision. Given her inexperience, Hardman should have been taught proper search methods, remained in constant contact with Counsel, and should have been monitored by management. She searched only one network drive, permitted other employees to conduct their own searches, and delegated the Cape Town office search without follow-up. Hardman knew that backup tapes existed, but did not search them and, to the best of her knowledge, they have not been searched to this day.

In addition to the paucity of Coronation's document production for the years 1998 through 2002 and the recent production of emails by 2M including many that were copied to Coronation, the Citco Defendants have identified a number of employees Coronation should have searched but did not—including approximately seventeen members of the investment team, Coronation's compliance officer, and Coronation's chief investment officer. While it is not entirely clear that all of these people were involved with Lancer, it is clear that Ingham's files were not searched and there is no question that Ingham was involved with Lancer-related investments in July, 2003. Based on the all of these facts it is apparent that Coronation acted in a grossly negligent manner.

d. The Chagnon Plaintiffs

The Chagnon Plaintiffs proffered Normand Gregoire, their Vice President of Investments, as their declarant with regard to their discovery efforts. Having joined the Chagnon Plaintiffs in 2004, the majority of Gregoire's declaration pertaining to the 2003/2004 Search was based on information given to him by others. Gregoire's declaration stated that the Chagnon Plaintiffs produced "all documents"—including emails and electronic documents—in their possession to Counsel in February or March 2004. Gregoire then admitted that some emails that had been located in 2004 were not provided to Counsel until 2008.

In response to a questionnaire served on all plaintiffs, the Chagnon Plaintiffs identified at least twelve employees as having either been involved in decisions to invest in Lancer or having had some contact with Lancer on behalf of Chagnon. Of the twelve, Gregoire could only state conclusively that four were asked to search for relevant documents in the 2003/2004 Search. When some of the eight were later questioned in connection with the 2007/2008 Search, the conversations were brief—the Chagnon Plaintiffs received cursory confirmation that the employees either had no documents or had only a few that had already been produced, and the Chagnon Plaintiffs did not follow up or conduct their own search. The Citco Defendants have identified three emails from May and June 2003 that the Chagnon Plaintiffs did not produce. The Citco Defendants also note that the Chagnon Plaintiffs produced only two emails and two pieces of correspondence from 1998 through 2002. The Chagnon Plaintiffs produced an unspecified number of emails from 2003.

Gregoire's declaration was misleading and inaccurate in that it indicated "all" documents had been produced, when, as Gregoire admitted, some emails located in 2004 were not provided to Counsel until 2008. The Chagnon Plaintiffs produced an unusually small number of emails and correspondence from 1998 through 2002—a total of four. In addition, the recent production of emails by 2M included a number of emails on which the Chagnon Plaintiffs were copied. These emails were not produced by the Chagnon Plaintiffs. Two-thirds of the key players were never asked for documents during the 2003/2004 Search. When they were contacted in 2007/2008, those employees had few, if any, documents. This combination of facts supports the conclusion that the Chagnon Plaintiffs were grossly negligent.

e. Bombardier Trusts

Patricia Romanovici, who joined Bombardier Trusts as Advisor, Compliance and Committee Secretary in May, 2007, submitted a declaration and testified regarding Bombardier Trusts' search efforts. Because her arrival at Bombardier Trusts postdated the 2003/2004 Search, she relied in large part on information provided to her by another employee, Guy Dionne. Romanovici declared that Bombardier Trusts had preserved and located "all documents" in their possession in 2003, but also admitted that Bombardier Trusts failed to search for or preserve emails or electronic documents prior to 2007, despite the inherent conflict in these two statements.

In 2007, Bombardier Trusts hired a vendor to retrieve from backup tapes electronic data and email relating to Bombardier Trusts' investments in Lancer. Romanovici stated that to the best of her understanding, "it is the practice of Bombardier's Information Technology [("IT")] Department to back up electronic data and email correspondence monthly, but not necessarily to preserve it indefinitely." This practice was not suspended for any employee at any time. "For a number of months during the years 2001 and 2002," Bombardier Trusts was not able to recover emails because backup tapes either never existed or were blank. Romanovici speculated that the loss of these tapes was "possibl[y] due to systemic technological problems."

Romanovici also acknowledged that only five current and former employees were asked to produce documents in the 2003/2004 Search. At least eleven individuals on the Investment Committee of the Bombardier Trusts were not asked for any documents—paper or electronic—during the 2003/2004 Search, even though they may have been involved in the decisions to invest or redeem shares in the Funds. Romanovici did not know whether the company's central files had been searched during the 2003/2004 Search or the extent of communication between Dionne and Counsel. Romanovici also admitted that personal computers were not searched in the 2003/2004 Search and that if any documents were deleted from the server prior to the 2007/2008 Search, they would not be retrievable unless stored on a backup tape. The Citco Defendants have identified thirteen emails from June 10, 2003 through August 17, 2003 that Bombardier Trusts did not produce.

In addition to submitting a misleading and inaccurate declaration, Bombardier Trusts failed to search for, or take steps to preserve, any electronic documents prior to 2007. Instead, it admittedly collected only paper documents from its employees who worked on Lancer. That the vendor hired in 2007 was not able to retrieve emails from some backup tapes is not surprising given that the recycling of backup tapes was never suspended. In addition, at least eleven members of its Investment Committee were not asked for any documents—paper or electronic—or instructed to preserve documents, until 2007. Finally, a number of emails were never produced, including emails only recently produced by 2M on which Bombardier Trusts was copied. The combination of these actions and inactions—coupled with Bombardier Trusts' failure to produce a number of emails—amounts to gross negligence.

f. The Bombardier Foundation

Lyne Lavoie, the Bombardier Foundation's director of administration and grants, supervised the Bombardier Foundation's search efforts. Lavoie declared in 2004 that she instructed the Bombardier Foundation employees to locate and preserve "all files relating to Lancer." There is no indication that the Bombardier Foundation searched for electronic documents or emails at that time. Lavoie admitted that the Bombardier Foundation gave Counsel only those documents the Foundation "understood to be responsive," even though additional Lancer-related documents were preserved. The documents that were preserved after the 2003/2004 Search were not produced to Counsel until 2007.

The Bombardier Foundation "backs up electronic documents and e-mails for a period of one year, then overwrites the prior year's backed-up data with information from the next year." This practice was never suspended. In 2007, the Bombardier Foundation directed a vendor to search the company's servers for electronic documents and email relating to Lancer between January 1, 1999 and December 31, 2003. This search "did not capture any documents or e-mails relating to Lancer that may have been deleted prior to 2007." Noting that pursuant to the Foundation's document retention policy only backup data for the year 2003 would have been in existence in 2004, Lavoie admits that "certain electronic data and-or emails for the year 2003 [] may have been deleted from the [Foundation's] servers prior to the time of its electronic search" in 2007.

At her deposition, Lavoie testified that it was also possible that emails and electronic documents from 1999 through 2003 may have been in employees' possession but deleted after 2004. Lavoie also testified that she instructed only two employees to search and preserve files related to Lancer, but did not recall telling them to preserve electronic documents or email and did not confirm that they had done so. The documents of the members of the Foundation's Investment Committee or Board of Governors were never searched because any documents in their possession would be "duplicative." The Bombardier Foundation contends that its investment decisions were handled by Bombardier Trusts and it is unlikely that the Foundation would have any documents that the Trusts did not have. Plaintiffs provide no support for this contention. If this were correct, every document produced by the Bombardier Foundation would also have been produced by Bombardier Trusts. This is not the case. The Citco Defendants have not identified any emails or documents not produced by the Bombardier Foundation.

The Bombardier Foundation's failure to search for any electronic documents or emails related to Lancer until 2007 cannot be rectified given Lavoie's admission that relevant information has been deleted from the Foundation's servers. The Bombardier Foundation's discovery efforts failed in other significant respects: It failed to request any documents — paper or electronic — from the Foundation's Investment Committee or its Board of Governors; it never altered its practice of overwriting backup data to preserve the records of key players; and it also withheld until 2008 documents it had collected in 2004, but had independently and arbitrarily decided were not "responsive." Such conduct, coupled with the Bombardier Foundation's misleading and inaccurate declaration, amounts to gross negligence.

2. Plaintiffs that Acted in a Negligent Manner

The Altar Fund, L'Ecole Polytechnique, Okabena, the Corbett Foundation, Commonfund, KMEFIC, and UM were negligent in their discovery efforts. None of them instituted a written litigation hold in a timely manner, although all of them did so by 2007. Employees with possible Lancer involvement were not clearly instructed to preserve and collect all Lancer-related records. I have already held that after mid-2004, in the Southern District of New York, the failure to issue a written litigation hold in a timely manner amounts to gross negligence. I must therefore explain why, after careful consideration, I have found that these plaintiffs were negligent rather than grossly negligent.

The failure to institute a written litigation hold in early 2004 in a case brought in federal court in Florida was on the borderline between a well-established duty and one that was not yet generally required. Thus, the rule of lenity compels the conclusion that this conduct alone, under these circumstances, is not sufficient to find that a plaintiff acted in a grossly negligent manner. I therefore have looked to any additional errors made during the discovery phase to determine whether the conduct was negligent or grossly negligent. Here, as described below, each of the plaintiffs in this category engaged in additional negligent conduct in carrying out its discovery obligations.

a. The Altar Fund

Richard Lombardi, president of Altar Asset Management Inc., which served as investment advisor to the Altar Fund, was the sole decision-maker regarding the Altar Fund's Lancer investments. Lombardi declared that he conducted the 2003/2004 Search and everything in the Altar Fund's possession was produced. According to Lombardi, in the normal course of business, employees are instructed to print all communications, including emails, related to clients. Those hard copies are then filed and those files on Lancer and the Funds were produced. When examined at his deposition, Lombardi did not know what email systems his company used, how electronic documents were stored, and admitted that he did not personally perform any electronic searches for responsive documents. Instead, Lombardi had instructed two assistants to conduct the searches without any supervision and was unfamiliar with the extent of their search. The Citco Defendants have identified fifty-three emails from March 20, 1997 through September 19, 2003 that the Altar Fund did not produce. These documents included emails to Lauer, Lancer, other plaintiffs and investors. The Citco Defendants have also identified five paper documents, as well as Lancer Offshore financial statements for 1998 through 2000, that were not produced.

Lombardi delegated the search for records to his assistants, but failed to provide any meaningful supervision. He was unfamiliar with the Altar Fund's email systems or how the Altar Fund maintained its electronic files. Moreover, the Citco Defendants have identified nearly fifty emails sent or received by Lombardi between May 2003 and September 2003 that were not produced by the Altar Fund as well as several paper documents. Moreover, the Altar Fund failed to produce emails it received that were discovered as a result of 2M's recent production of emails. This, alone, demonstrates that the Altar Fund's effort to find and produce all relevant documents was insufficient. The totality of the circumstances supports a finding of negligence.

b. L'Ecole Polytechnique

Declarant Isabelle Poissant, Director of L'Ecole Polytechnique, supervised the 2003/ 2004 Search. In late 2003, Poissant undertook to produce and preserve "all" employees' documents, including emails. L'Ecole Polytechnique delegated the management of its assets, including recommending, monitoring, and discontinuing its investments, to its Investment Committee. Despite the Investment Committee's role in L'Ecole Polytechnique's Lancer investments, Poissant recalled asking at most five Investment Committee members to search for Lancer-related documents and asked only one to preserve Lancer-related documents prior to 2007. Francois Morin, chair of the Investment Committee during the relevant period, was the one member both asked to search and preserve his paper and electronic documents during the 2003/2004 Search, which he confirmed doing. The Citco Defendants identify an additional three individuals who they claim should have been contacted for documents: (1) Pierre Bataille, whose role is not clear from the evidence; (2) Mario Lefebvre, who was a member of the Investment Committee until March 15, 2000; and (3) Louis Lefebvre, who joined the Investment Committee in September 2003. When L'Ecole Polytechnique performed a system-wide search of its electronic documents and emails in 2007 and 2008, the only responsive emails that were located were found on Poissant's computer, because she had a practice of preserving every email that she sent or received. Poissant, however, played no role in the Investment Committee's decision to invest in Lancer and no emails were recovered for any other member of the Investment Committee. The Citco Defendants have identified nine emails from March 26, 2003 through August 17, 2003 that were sent to or from Morin that were not produced by L'Ecole Polytechnique.

L'Ecole Polytechnique failed to conduct a thorough search of its computer system for Lancer-related documents and failed to specifically direct all the members of the Investment Committee of the need to preserve Lancer-related documents. Nonetheless, the chair of the Committee and five of its members of the Committee did search their records. Bataille's records should have been searched during the 2003/2004 Search, although it is unclear whether he was even a member of the Investment Committee or played any role in L'Ecole Polytechnique's Lancer investment. Finally, the Citco Defendants have identified nine emails that were not produced by L'Ecole Polytechnique, plus an unspecified number recently produced by 2M on which L'Ecole Polytechnique was copied. Taken together, L'Ecole Polytechnique's conduct was negligent.

c. Okabena

Sherry Van Zee, Vice President of Investment Administration and Chief Compliance Officer, served as Okabena's declarant. Van Zee declared that Okabena located and preserved "all documents," including electronic data and emails, in connection with the 2003/2004 Search. She also declared that all files of employees who were involved in Okabena's Lancer investment were searched, including electronic files and all "servers" had been searched for email and electronic documents at that time. At her deposition, Van Zee testified that Okabena actually searched only certain email inboxes and the "F" drive. Van Zee also testified that although she was aware that Okabena backed up its electronic data four times a year and maintains the tapes in a safety-deposit box, these tapes were never searched. While routine searches of backup tapes are not required, they should be searched when it has been shown that relevant material existed but was not produced, or relevant material should have existed but was not produced. Because both conditions are met, Okabena is required to conduct this search or explain why it is unable to do so.

The Citco Defendants have identified thirty-nine emails from August 26, 1999 through September 19, 2003 that were not produced by Okabena and note that Okabena produced approximately ten emails for the entire relevant period. On August 7, 2009, after plaintiffs filed their opposition to this motion, Okabena produced three of the thirty-nine emails previously produced by others. Finally, when 2M produced the seven hundred new emails in August, 2009, Okabena was among those plaintiffs to whom some of them were copied. The very small number of emails produced by Okabena, the failure to produce thirty-nine emails, and the recent production of emails by 2M including many that were copied to Okabena, together with the failure to conduct a thorough search for ESI, demonstrates that Okabena was negligent in carrying out its discovery obligations.

d. The Corbett Foundation

Richard Corbett initially testified on behalf of the Corbett Foundation with regard to its discovery efforts. Corbett testified that at no point during the 2003/2004 Search had he personally instructed anyone to preserve emails and documents. He also did not know what steps were taken to search for documents, or which files, offices, and computers were searched. Corbett then clarified that his assistant, Melanie Craig, had actually directed the search. She subsequently submitted a declaration.

Craig stated that during the 2003/2004 Search, she located and preserved all responsive documents, including electronic documents and emails. She searched her own computer and Corbett's other assistant was tasked with searching the Foundation's only other computer. Craig did not oversee that search and did not search Corbett's palm pilot. The Citco Defendants have identified twenty-two emails that the Corbett Foundation received between June 23, 2003 and August 17, 2003, but that were not produced by the Corbett Foundation.

Craig admitted that she failed to search Corbett's palm pilot, which may have contained emails. Neither Corbett nor Craig instructed employees to preserve their emails or paper documents. This conduct, together with the Corbett Foundation's failure to produce the twenty-two emails identified by the Citco Defendants, demonstrates that the Corbett Foundation was negligent in meeting its discovery obligations.

e. Commonfund

John Auchincloss, Commonfund's general counsel, declared that he supervised Commonfund's 2003/2004 Search and that all Commonfund documents were located and produced in the first half of 2004. At his deposition, Auchincloss testified that he delegated the search to paralegal Carolyn Blanch. When pressed, Auchincloss did not know the details of Blanch's communication with employees regarding preservation or whether employees complied. On October 7, 2004, Blanch distributed a company-wide email directing employees to search their records for Lancer-related documents. For the same reasons discussed earlier with respect to Counsel's email directions to all plaintiffs, this email is insufficient to constitute a written litigation hold.

As far as Auchincloss was aware, no request for preservation or collection was made to Commonfund's Audit and Risk Management Committee. Although Auchincloss testified that concerns related to Lancer "may" have been communicated to the Committee, the minutes of Committee meetings "specifically mention the Lancer investment." The Citco Defendants have identified twenty-five emails between July 12, 1999 and April 10, 2002 sent between Commonfund employees and Hunnicutt, but not produced to the Citco Defendants. Twenty-four of these emails were produced by Commonfund in the SEC Action, but not identified to the Citco Defendants as Commonfund documents until September 10, 2007—after the deposition of a key Commonfund employee. The single email Commonfund never produced attached a March 1, 2000 Monthly Performance Review for Lancer. Commonfund produced the Performance Review, but not the cover email. On August 7, 2009, after plaintiffs filed their opposition to this motion, Commonfund produced minutes of meetings of its Audit and Risk Management Committee for September 20, 2002, February 15, 2003, and June 21, 2003.

Auchincloss signed his declaration without fully investigating Commonfund's 2003/2004 Search and lacked personal knowledge of the steps taken by Commonfund to preserve and produce documents. Although Commonfund contacted a number of key players to collect documents, Commonfund failed to collect documents from its Audit and Risk Management Committee. Because the Citco Defendants have demonstrated that the Committee had some involvement in Lancer—although not at the level of key decision makers—their documents should have been collected. This conduct—together with the failure to produce a variety of documents to the Citco Defendants and the late production of the Committee minutes—supports the conclusion that Commonfund was negligent in complying with its discovery obligations.

f. KMEFIC

Abdullateef Al-Tammar, who joined KMEFIC in September, 2007 as the General Manager, International Investments Division, submitted a declaration on behalf of

KMEFIC. Al-Tammar acknowledged that his understanding of KMEFIC's 2003/2004 Search stemmed from discussions with Mohamed Almarzook, KMEFIC's former General Manager. Al-Tammar stated that "all documents" were located and preserved. But his declaration reveals that the employees were directed to search their own computers and files. KMEFIC did not conduct its own search of its servers and employee hard drives until 2007. Al-Tammar also stated that Almarzook, who bore primary responsibility for monitoring KMEFIC's investments in Lancer, had informed him that Almarzook would have been copied on all Lancer-related emails. His emails were searched and produced. Prior to the 2007/2008 Search, members of KMEFIC's Investment Committee—which voted on investment decisions—were not asked to search for or retain documents.

At his deposition, Al-Tammar was unable to testify to the facts underlying the statements related to the 2003/2004 Search in his declaration. When faced with two Lancer-related emails produced by KMEFIC on which Almarzook was not copied, Al-Tammar stated that Almarzook, in fact, never told him that Almarzook was copied on all emails. Yet, Al-Tammar had previously sent an email to Counsel, copying Almarzook, stating that Almarzook had "confirmed that he would have been copied on all correspondence concerning Lancer." While the Citco Defendants have not identified any emails that KMEFIC has failed to produce, they state that KMEFIC failed to produce a 1997 executive summary. Regarding the executive summary, Al-Tammar declared that "an additional search" for the missing executive summary was conducted during the 2007/2008 Search, but he testified that he did not know whether a search for this document was ever done previously.

KMEFIC did not request documents from its Investment Committee before 2007. Key players searched their own files without supervision from management or counsel. Finally, Al-Tammar failed to carefully inquire into the details of KMEFIC's search prior to signing his declaration and relied on the possibly false assertion that one employee—Almarzook—would have been copied on any Lancer-related email. This conduct was negligent.

g. UM

Andree Mayrand, Director, Investment Management of UM, declared that at the time White & Case was retained in June, 2003, UM searched and preserved "all" Lancer-related documents, including electronic documents and email, in the possession of current and former UM employees. UM searched again when Counsel was retained in January 2004. But, in fact, UM's efforts did not include searching the electronic files of all employees. Rather, the search consisted of reviewing only UM's server's subfiles titled "Lancer." Mayrand conducted this initial search herself, but consulted UM's IT personnel, possibly as early as 2004 or as late as 2006. In early 2004, she contacted current and former members of UM's Investment Committee and asked for any Lancer-related documents. However, she did not recall asking for emails or instructing them to preserve all Lancer-related materials.

The Citco Defendants identify five documents that were never produced by UM. The first is a September 30, 1998, "lock up" letter imposing restrictions on UM's ability to redeem its shares. The second is a June 30, 2000 letter from Citco NV, containing a list of securities held by Lancer as of June 30, 1999. The third and fourth are two sets of written questions by Mathieu Poulin, an analyst at UM, regarding concerns about Lancer in April and July, 2002. Poulin testified that he drafted these questions on his computer and did not recall deleting them, but they were never produced by UM. Instead, they were produced from Poulin's current employer, the Chagnon Plaintiffs. The fifth is the 1999 Lancer Year End Review Newsletter (the "1999 Newsletter"). The 1999 Newsletter first produced by UM was missing the page that disclosed a surge in redemptions in the summer of 1998, which necessitated a liquidation of part of the portfolio resulting in losses to the Fund. Plaintiffs contend that the document was accidentally copied double sided to single sided. The document was recopied and reproduced. However, the reproduced copy did not include the same handwritten notation "copie," as did the originally produced copy.

UM did not do a complete search of its ESI. UM searched only its electronic server's subfiles titled "Lancer." This folder may, or may not, have encompassed all Lancer-related documents. UM did not check the electronic files of each employee to confirm that his or her search was complete. Although UM sought documents from the Investment Committee in 2004, that request may not have included ESI. Finally, UM's initial production of the 1999 Newsletter was—at best—sloppy and—at worst—was an attempt to suppress information. I decline to credit the latter explanation offered by the Citco Defendants. In sum, UM was negligent in meeting its discovery obligations.

E. Sanctions

The Citco Defendants have demonstrated that most plaintiffs conducted discovery in an ignorant and indifferent fashion. With respect to the grossly negligent plaintiffs—2M, Hunnicutt, Coronation, the Chagnon Plaintiffs, Bombardier Trusts, and the Bombardier Foundation—I will give the following jury charge:

> The Citco Defendants have argued that 2M, Hunnicutt, Coronation, the Chagnon Plaintiffs, Bombardier Trusts, and the Bombardier Foundation destroyed relevant evidence, or failed to prevent the destruction of relevant evidence. This is known as the "spoliation of evidence."
>
> Spoliation is the destruction of evidence or the failure to preserve property for another's use as evidence in pending or reasonably foreseeable litigation. To demonstrate that spoliation occurred, the Citco Defendants bear the burden of proving the following two elements by a preponderance of the evidence:
>
> First, that relevant evidence was destroyed after the duty to preserve arose. Evidence is relevant if it would have clarified a fact at issue in the trial and otherwise would naturally have been introduced into evidence; and

Second, that if relevant evidence was destroyed after the duty to preserve arose, the evidence loss would have been favorable to the Citco Defendants.

I instruct you, as a matter of law, that each of these plaintiffs failed to preserve evidence after its duty to preserve arose. This failure resulted from their gross negligence in performing their discovery obligations. As a result, you may presume, if you so choose, that such lost evidence was relevant, and that it would have been favorable to the Citco Defendants. In deciding whether to adopt this presumption, you may take into account the egregiousness of the plaintiffs' conduct in failing to preserve the evidence.

However, each of these plaintiffs has offered evidence that (1) no evidence was lost; (2) if evidence was lost, it was not relevant; and (3) if evidence was lost and it was relevant, it would not have been favorable to the Citco Defendants.

If you decline to presume that the lost evidence was relevant or would have been favorable to the Citco Defendants, then your consideration of the lost evidence is at an end, and you will not draw any inference arising from the lost evidence.

However, if you decide to presume that the lost evidence was relevant and would have been favorable to the Citco Defendants, you must next decide whether any of the following plaintiffs have rebutted that presumption: 2M, Hunnicutt, Coronation, the Chagnon Plaintiffs, Bombardier Trusts, or the Bombardier Foundation. If you determine that a plaintiff has rebutted the presumption that the lost evidence was either relevant or favorable to the Citco Defendants, you will not draw any inference arising from the lost evidence against that plaintiff. If, on the other hand, you determine that a plaintiff has not rebutted the presumption that the lost evidence was both relevant and favorable to the Citco Defendants, you may draw an inference against that plaintiff and in favor of the Citco Defendants — namely that the lost evidence would have been favorable to the Citco Defendants.

Each plaintiff is entitled to your separate consideration. The question as to whether the Citco Defendants have proven spoliation is personal to each plaintiff and must be decided by you as to each plaintiff individually.

In addition, all plaintiffs are subject to monetary sanctions. The Citco Defendants are entitled to an award of reasonable costs, including attorneys' fees, associated with reviewing the declarations submitted, deposing these declarants and their substitutes where applicable, and bringing this motion. The Citco Defendants shall submit a reasonable fee application to this Court for approval. Once approved, the costs are to be allocated among these plaintiffs.

I have also considered whether the Citco Defendants should be entitled to additional discovery. If a lesser sanction is appropriate that is always a better course. With regard to Coronation and Okabena, plaintiffs admit that backup tapes exist and have not been searched. They do not explain why such a search cannot still be conducted. The goal of discovery is to obtain evidence, not to issue sanctions. Thus, Coronation and

Okabena are ordered to search their backup tapes for the relevant period at their expense, or demonstrate why such backup tapes cannot be searched, within thirty days.

Further discovery is not necessary for the remaining plaintiffs. Given the number of submitted declarations and numerous depositions that have already occurred in this action, more discovery of the remaining plaintiffs would not be fruitful. At this stage, the costs of conducting further discovery would far outweigh the benefit of any results. Therefore, no further discovery is warranted.

VI. CONCLUSION

For the reasons discussed above, the Citco Defendant's motion for sanctions is granted in part. While litigants are not required to execute document productions with absolute precision, at a minimum they must act diligently and search thoroughly at the time they reasonably anticipate litigation. All of the plaintiffs in this motion failed to do so and have been sanctioned accordingly.

Zubulake v. UBS Warburg LLC

229 F.R.D. 422 (S.D.N.Y. 2004)

OPINION AND ORDER

SHIRA A. SCHEINDLIN, U.S.D.J.:

Commenting on the importance of speaking clearly and listening closely, Phillip Roth memorably quipped, "The English language is a form of communication! ... Words aren't only bombs and bullets—no, they're little gifts, containing meanings!" What is true in love is equally true at law: Lawyers and their clients need to communicate clearly and effectively with one another to ensure that litigation proceeds efficiently. When communication between counsel and client breaks down, conversation becomes "just crossfire," and there are usually casualties.

I. INTRODUCTION

This is the fifth written opinion in this case, a relatively routine employment discrimination dispute in which discovery has now lasted over two years. Laura Zubulake is once again moving to sanction UBS for its failure to produce relevant information and for its tardy production of such material. In order to decide whether sanctions are warranted, the following question must be answered: Did UBS fail to preserve and timely produce relevant information and, if so, did it act negligently, recklessly, or willfully?

This decision addresses counsel's obligation to ensure that relevant information is preserved by giving clear instructions to the client to preserve such information and, perhaps more importantly, a client's obligation to heed those instructions. Early on in this litigation, UBS's counsel—both in-house and outside—instructed UBS personnel to retain relevant electronic information. Notwithstanding these instructions, certain UBS employees deleted relevant emails. Other employees never produced relevant information to counsel. As a result, many discoverable e-mails were not produced to Zubulake until recently, even though they were responsive to a document request propounded on June 3, 2002. In addition, a number of e-mails responsive to that document request were deleted and have been lost altogether.

Counsel, in turn, failed to request retained information from one key employee and to give the litigation hold instructions to another. They also failed to adequately communicate with another employee about how she maintained her computer files. Counsel also failed to safeguard backup tapes that might have contained some of the deleted e-mails, and which would have mitigated the damage done by UBS's destruction of those e-mails.

The conduct of both counsel and client thus calls to mind the now-famous words of the prison captain in Cool Hand Luke: "What we've got here is a failure to communicate." Because of this failure by both UBS and its counsel, Zubulake has been prejudiced. As a result, sanctions are warranted.

II. FACTS

The allegations at the heart of this lawsuit and the history of the parties' discovery disputes have been well-documented in the Court's prior decisions, familiarity with which is presumed. In short, Zubulake is an equities trader specializing in Asian securities who is suing her former employer for gender discrimination, failure to promote, and retaliation under federal, state, and city law.

A. Background

Zubulake filed an initial charge of gender discrimination with the EEOC on August 16, 2001. Well before that, however—as early as April 2001—UBS employees were on notice of Zubulake's impending court action. After she received a right-to-sue letter from the EEOC, Zubulake filed this lawsuit on February 15, 2002.

Fully aware of their common law duty to preserve relevant evidence, UBS's in-house attorneys gave oral instructions in August 2001—immediately after Zubulake filed her EEOC charge—instructing employees not to destroy or delete material potentially relevant to Zubulake's claims, and in fact to segregate such material into separate files for the lawyers' eventual review. This warning pertained to both electronic and hard-copy files, but did not specifically pertain to so-called "backup tapes," maintained by UBS's information technology personnel. In particular, UBS's in-house counsel, Robert L. Salzberg, "advised relevant UBS employees to preserve and turn over to counsel all files, records or other written memoranda or documents concerning the allegations raised in the [EEOC] charge or any aspect of [Zubulake's] employment." Subsequently—but still in August 2001—UBS's outside counsel met with a number of the key players in the litigation and reiterated Mr. Salzberg's instructions, reminding them to preserve relevant documents, "including e-mails." Salzberg reduced these instructions to writing in e-mails dated February 22, 2002—immediately after Zubulake filed her complaint—and September 25, 2002. Finally, in August 2002, after Zubulake propounded a document request that specifically called for e-mails stored on backup tapes, UBS's outside counsel instructed UBS information technology personnel to stop recycling backup tapes. Every UBS employee mentioned in this Opinion (with the exception of Mike Davies) either personally spoke to UBS's outside counsel about the duty to preserve e-mails, or was a recipient of one of Salzberg's e-mails.

B. Procedural History

In Zubulake I, I addressed Zubulake's claim that relevant e-mails had been deleted from UBS's active servers and existed only on "inaccessible" archival media (i.e., backup tapes). Arguing that e-mail correspondence that she needed to prove her case existed only on those backup tapes, Zubulake called for their production. UBS moved for a protective order shielding it from discovery altogether or, in the alternative, shifting the cost of backup tape restoration onto Zubulake. Because the evidentiary record was sparse, I ordered UBS to bear the costs of restoring a sample of the backup tapes.

After the sample tapes were restored, UBS continued to press for cost shifting with respect to any further restoration of backup tapes. In Zubulake III, I ordered UBS to bear the lion's share of restoring certain backup tapes because Zubulake was able to demonstrate that those tapes were likely to contain relevant information. Specifically, Zubulake had demonstrated that UBS had failed to maintain all relevant information (principally e-mails) in its active files. After Zubulake III, Zubulake chose to restore sixteen backup tapes. "In the restoration effort, the parties discovered that certain backup tapes [were] missing." They also discovered a number of e-mails on the backup tapes that were missing from UBS's active files, confirming Zubulake's suspicion that relevant e-mails were being deleted or otherwise lost.

Zubulake III begat Zubulake IV, where Zubulake moved for sanctions as a result of UBS's failure to preserve all relevant backup tapes, and UBS's deletion of relevant e-mails. Finding fault in UBS's document preservation strategy but lacking evidence that the lost tapes and deleted e-mails were particularly favorable to Zubulake, I ordered UBS to pay for the re-deposition of several key UBS employees—Varsano, Chapin, Hardisty, Kim, and Tong—so that Zubulake could inquire about the newly-restored e-mails.

C. The Instant Dispute

The essence of the current dispute is that during the re-depositions required by Zubulake IV, Zubulake learned about more deleted e-mails and about the existence of e-mails preserved on UBS's active servers that were, to that point, never produced. In sum, Zubulake has now presented evidence that UBS personnel deleted relevant e-mails, some of which were subsequently recovered from backup tapes (or elsewhere) and thus produced to Zubulake long after her initial document requests, and some of which were lost altogether. Zubulake has also presented evidence that some UBS personnel did not produce responsive documents to counsel until recently, depriving Zubulake of the documents for almost two years.

1. Deleted E-Mails

Notwithstanding the clear and repeated warnings of counsel, Zubulake has proffered evidence that a number of key UBS employees—Orgill, Hardisty, Holland, Chapin, Varsano, and Amone—failed to retain e-mails germane to Zubulake's claims. Some of the deleted e-mails were restored from backup tapes (or other sources) and have been produced to Zubulake, others have been altogether lost, though there is strong evidence that they once existed. Although I have long been aware that certain e-mails were deleted, the redepositions demonstrate the scope and importance of those documents.

a. At Least One E-Mail Has Never Been Produced

At least one e-mail has been irretrievably lost; the existence of that e-mail is known only because of oblique references to it in other correspondence. It has already been shown that Chapin—the alleged primary discriminator—deleted relevant e-mails. In addition to those e-mails, Zubulake has evidence suggesting that Chapin deleted at least one other e-mail that has been lost entirely. An e-mail from Chapin sent at 10:47 AM on September 21, 2001, asks Kim to send him a "document" recounting a conversation between Zubulake and a co-worker. Approximately 45 minutes later, Chapin sent an e-mail complaining about Zubulake to his boss and to the human resources employees handling Zubulake's case purporting to contain a verbatim recitation of a conversation between Zubulake and her co-worker, as overheard by Kim. This conversation allegedly took place on September 18, 2001, at 10:58 AM. There is reason to believe that immediately after that conversation, Kim sent Chapin an e-mail that contained the verbatim quotation that appears in Chapin's September 21 e-mail—the "document" that Chapin sought from Kim just prior to sending that e-mail—and that Chapin deleted it. That e-mail, however, has never been recovered and is apparently lost.

Although Zubulake has only been able to present concrete evidence that this one e-mail was irretrievably lost, there may well be others. Zubulake has presented extensive proof, detailed below, that UBS personnel were deleting relevant e-mails. Many of those e-mails were recovered from backup tapes. The UBS record retention policies called for monthly backup tapes to be retained for three years. The tapes covering the relevant time period (circa August 2001) should have been available to UBS in August 2002, when counsel instructed UBS's information technology personnel that backup tapes were also subject to the litigation hold.

Nonetheless, many backup tapes for the most relevant time periods are missing, including: Tong's tapes for June, July, August, and September of 2001; Hardisty's tapes for May, June, and August of 2001; Clarke and Vinay Datta's tapes for April and September 2001; and Chapin's tape for April 2001. Zubulake did not even learn that four of these tapes were missing until after Zubulake IV. Thus, it is impossible to know just how many relevant e-mails have been lost in their entirety.

b. Many E-Mails Were Deleted and Only Later Recovered from Alternate Sources

Other e-mails were deleted in contravention of counsel's "litigation hold" instructions, but were subsequently recovered from alternative sources—such as backup tapes—and thus produced to Zubulake, albeit almost two years after she propounded her initial document requests. For example, an e-mail from Hardisty to Holland (and on which Chapin was copied) reported that Zubulake said "that all she wanted is to be treated like the other 'guys' on the desk." That e-mail was recovered from Hardisty's August 2001 backup tape—and thus it was on his active server as late as August 31, 2001, when the backup was generated—but was not in his active files. That e-mail therefore must have been deleted subsequent to counsel's warnings.

Another e-mail, from Varsano to Hardisty dated August 31, 2001—the very day that Hardisty met with outside counsel—forwarded an earlier message from Hardisty dated June 29, 2001, that recounted a conversation in which Hardisty "warned" Chapin about his management of Zubulake, and in which Hardisty reminded Chapin that Zubulake could "be a good broker." This e-mail was absent from UBS's initial production and had to be restored from backup; apparently neither Varsano nor Hardisty had retained it. This deletion is especially surprising because Varsano retained the June 29, 2001 e-mail for over two months before he forwarded it to Hardisty. Indeed, Varsano testified in his deposition that he "definitely" "saved all of the e-mails that [he] received concerning Ms. Zubulake" in 2001, that they were saved in a separate "very specific folder," and that "all of those e-mails" were produced to counsel.

As a final example, an e-mail from Hardisty to Varsano and Orgill, dated September 1, 2001, specifically discussed Zubulake's termination. It read: "LZ—ok once lawyers have been signed off, probably one month, but most easily done in combination with the full Asiapc [downsizing] announcement. We will need to document her perform-ance post her warning HK. Matt [Chapin] is doing that." Thus, Orgill and Hardisty had decided to terminate Zubulake as early as September 1, 2001. Indeed, two days later Orgill replied, "It's a pity we can't act on LZ earlier." Neither the authors nor any of the recipients of these e-mails retained any of them, even though these e-mails were sent within days of Hardisty's meeting with outside counsel. They were not even preserved on backup tapes, but were only recovered because Kim happened to have retained copies. Rather, all three people (Hardisty, Orgill and Varsano) deleted these e-mails from their computers by the end of September 2001. Apart from their direct relevance to Zubulake's claims, these e-mails may also serve to rebut Orgill and Hardisty's deposition testimony. Orgill testified that he played no role in the decision to terminate Zubulake. And Hardisty testified that he did not recall discussing Zubu-lake's termination with Orgill.

These are merely examples. The proof is clear: UBS personnel unquestionably deleted relevant e-mails from their computers after August 2001, even though they had received at least two directions from counsel not to. Some of those e-mails were recovered (Zubulake has pointed to at least 45), but some—and no one can say how many—were not. And even those e-mails that were recovered were produced to Zubulake well after she originally asked for them.

2. Retained, But Unproduced, E-Mails

Separate and apart from the deleted material are a number of e-mails that were absent from UBS's initial production even though they were not deleted. These e-mails existed in the active, on-line files of two UBS employees—Kim and Tong—but were not produced to counsel and thus not turned over to Zubulake until she learned of their existence as a result of her counsel's questions at deposition. Indeed, these e-mails were not produced until after Zubulake had conducted thirteen depositions and four re-depositions.

During her February 19, 2004, deposition, Kim testified that she was never asked to produce her files regarding Zubulake to counsel, nor did she ever actually produce them, although she was asked to retain them. One week after Kim's deposition, UBS produced seven new e-mails. The obvious inference to be drawn is that, subsequent to the deposition, counsel for the first time asked Kim to produce her files. Included among the new e-mails produced from Kim's computer was one (dated September 18, 2001) that recounts a conversation between Zubulake and Kim in which Zubulake complains about the way women are treated at UBS. Another e-mail recovered from Kim's computer contained the correspondence, described above, in which Hardisty and Orgill discuss Zubulake's termination, and in which Orgill laments that she could not be fired sooner than she was.

On March 29, 2004, UBS produced several new e-mails, and three new e-mail retention policies, from Tong's active files. At her deposition two weeks earlier, Tong explained (as she had at her first deposition, a year previous) that she kept a separate "archive" file on her computer with documents pertaining to Zubulake. UBS admits that until the March 2004 deposition, it misunderstood Tong's use of the word "archive" to mean backup tapes; after her March 2004 testimony, it was clear that she meant active data. Again, the inference is that UBS's counsel then, for the first time, asked her to produce her active computer files.

Among the new e-mails recovered from Tong's computer was one, dated August 21, 2001, at 11:06 AM, from Mike Davies to Tong that read, "received[.] thanks[,] mike," and which was in response to an e-mail from Tong, sent eleven minutes earlier, that read, "Mike, I have just faxed over to you the 7 pages of Laura's [EEOC] charge against the bank." While Davies' three-word e-mail seems insignificant in isolation, it is actually quite important.

Three hours after sending that three word response, Davies sent an e-mail to Tong with the subject line "Laura Zubulake" that reads:

> I spoke to Brad [Orgill] — he's looking to exit her asap [by the end of month], and looking for guidance from us following letter? we sent her re her performance [or does he mean PMM]

> I said you were on call with US yesterday and that we need US legal advise etc., but be aware he's looking to finalise quickly! — said if off by end August then no bonus consideration, but if still employed after aug consideration should be given?

Davies testified that he was unaware of Zubulake's EEOC charge when he spoke with Orgill. The timing of his e-mails, however — the newly produced e-mail that acknowledges receiving Zubulake's EEOC charge coming three hours before the e-mail beginning "I spoke to Brad" — strongly undercuts this claim. The new e-mail, therefore, is circumstantial evidence that could support the inference that Davies knew about the EEOC charge when he spoke with Orgill, and suggests that Orgill knew about the EEOC charge when the decision was made to terminate Zubulake. Its relevance to Zubulake's retaliation claim is unquestionable, and yet it was not produced until April 20, 2004.

Zubulake now moves for sanctions as a result of UBS's purported discovery failings. In particular, she asks—as she did in Zubulake IV—that an adverse inference instruction be given to the jury that eventually hears this case.

III. LEGAL STANDARD

Spoliation is "the destruction or significant alteration of evidence, or the failure to preserve property for another's use as evidence in pending or reasonably foreseeable litigation." "The determination of an appropriate sanction for spoliation, if any, is confined to the sound discretion of the trial judge, and is assessed on a case-by-case basis." The authority to sanction litigants for spoliation arises jointly under the Federal Rules of Civil Procedure and the court's inherent powers. The spoliation of evidence germane "to proof of an issue at trial can support an inference that the evidence would have been unfavorable to the party responsible for its destruction." A party seeking an adverse inference instruction (or other sanctions) based on the spoliation of evidence must establish the following three elements: (1) that the party having control over the evidence had an obligation to preserve it at the time it was destroyed; (2) that the records were destroyed with a "culpable state of mind" and (3) that the destroyed evidence was "relevant" to the party's claim or defense such that a reasonable trier of fact could find that it would support that claim or defense.

In this circuit, a "culpable state of mind" for purposes of a spoliation inference includes ordinary negligence. When evidence is destroyed in bad faith (i.e., intentionally or willfully), that fact alone is sufficient to demonstrate relevance. By contrast, when the destruction is negligent, relevance must be proven by the party seeking the sanctions.

In the context of a request for an adverse inference instruction, the concept of "relevance" encompasses not only the ordinary meaning of the term, but also that the destroyed evidence would have been favorable to the movant. "This corroboration requirement is even more necessary where the destruction was merely negligent, since in those cases it cannot be inferred from the conduct of the spoliator that the evidence would even have been harmful to him." This is equally true in cases of gross negligence or recklessness; only in the case of willful spoliation does the degree of culpability give rise to a presumption of the relevance of the documents destroyed.

IV. DISCUSSION

In Zubulake IV, I held that UBS had a duty to preserve its employees' active files as early as April 2001, and certainly by August 2001, when Zubulake filed her EEOC charge. Zubulake has thus satisfied the first element of the adverse inference test. As noted, the central question implicated by this motion is whether UBS and its counsel took all necessary steps to guarantee that relevant data was both preserved and produced. If the answer is "no," then the next question is whether UBS acted wilfully when it deleted or failed to timely produce relevant information—resulting in either a complete loss or the production of responsive information close to two years after it was initially sought. If UBS acted wilfully, this satisfies the mental culpability prong of the adverse inference test and also demonstrates that the deleted material was relevant. If UBS acted negligently or even recklessly, then Zubulake must show that the missing or late-produced information was relevant.

A. Counsel's Duty to Monitor Compliance

In Zubulake IV, I summarized a litigant's preservation obligations:

> Once a party reasonably anticipates litigation, it must suspend its routine document retention/destruction policy and put in place a "litigation hold" to ensure the preservation of relevant documents. As a general rule, that litigation hold does not apply to inaccessible backup tapes (e.g., those typically maintained solely for the purpose of disaster recovery), which may continue to be recycled on the schedule set forth in the company's policy. On the other hand, if backup tapes are accessible (i.e., actively used for information retrieval), then such tapes would likely be subject to the litigation hold.

A party's discovery obligations do not end with the implementation of a "litigation hold"—to the contrary, that's only the beginning. Counsel must oversee compliance with the litigation hold, monitoring the party's efforts to retain and produce the relevant documents. Proper communication between a party and her lawyer will ensure (1) that all relevant information (or at least all sources of relevant information) is discovered, (2) that relevant information is retained on a continuing basis; and (3) that relevant non-privileged material is produced to the opposing party.

1. Counsel's Duty to Locate Relevant Information

Once a "litigation hold" is in place, a party and her counsel must make certain that all sources of potentially relevant information are identified and placed "on hold," to the extent required in Zubulake IV. To do this, counsel must become fully familiar with her client's document retention policies, as well as the client's data retention architecture. This will invariably involve speaking with information technology personnel, who can explain system-wide backup procedures and the actual (as opposed to theoretical) implementation of the firm's recycling policy. It will also involve communicating with the "key players" in the litigation, in order to understand how they stored information. In this case, for example, some UBS employees created separate computer files pertaining to Zubulake, while others printed out relevant e-mails and retained them in hard copy only. Unless counsel interviews each employee, it is impossible to determine whether all potential sources of information have been inspected. A brief conversation with counsel, for example, might have revealed that Tong maintained "archive" copies of e-mails concerning Zubulake, and that "archive" meant a separate on-line computer file, not a backup tape. Had that conversation taken place, Zubulake might have had relevant e-mails from that file two years ago.

To the extent that it may not be feasible for counsel to speak with every key player, given the size of a company or the scope of the lawsuit, counsel must be more creative. It may be possible to run a system-wide keyword search; counsel could then preserve a copy of each "hit." Although this sounds burdensome, it need not be. Counsel does not have to review these documents, only see that they are retained. For example, counsel could create a broad list of search terms, run a search for a limited time frame, and then segregate responsive documents. When the opposing party propounds its document requests, the parties could negotiate a list of search terms to be used in identifying responsive documents, and counsel would only be obliged to review documents that came up as "hits" on the second, more restrictive search. The initial broad cut merely guarantees that relevant documents are not lost.

In short, it is not sufficient to notify all employees of a litigation hold and expect that the party will then retain and produce all relevant information. Counsel must take affirmative steps to monitor compliance so that all sources of discoverable information are identified and searched. This is not to say that counsel will necessarily succeed in locating all such sources, or that the later discovery of new sources is evidence of a lack of effort. But counsel and client must take some reasonable steps to see that sources of relevant information are located.

2. Counsel's Continuing Duty to Ensure Preservation

Once a party and her counsel have identified all of the sources of potentially relevant information, they are under a duty to retain that information (as per Zubulake IV) and to produce information responsive to the opposing party's requests. Rule 26 creates a "duty to supplement" those responses. Although the Rule 26 duty to supplement is nominally the party's, it really falls on counsel. As the Advisory Committee explains,

Although the party signs the answers, it is his lawyer who understands their significance and bears the responsibility to bring answers up to date. In a complex case all sorts of information reaches the party, who little understands its bearing on answers previously given to interrogatories. In practice, therefore, the lawyer under a continuing burden must periodically recheck all interrogatories and canvass all new information.

To ameliorate this burden, the Rules impose a continuing duty to supplement responses to discovery requests only when "a party[,] or more frequently his lawyer, obtains actual knowledge that a prior response is incorrect. This exception does not impose a duty to check the accuracy of prior responses, but it prevents knowing concealment by a party or attorney."

The continuing duty to supplement disclosures strongly suggests that parties also have a duty to make sure that discoverable information is not lost. Indeed, the notion of a "duty to preserve" connotes an ongoing obligation. Obviously, if information is lost or destroyed, it has not been preserved.

The tricky question is what that continuing duty entails. What must a lawyer do to make certain that relevant information—especially electronic information—is being retained? Is it sufficient if she periodically re-sends her initial "litigation hold" instructions? What if she communicates with the party's information technology personnel? Must she make occasional on-site inspections?

Above all, the requirement must be reasonable. A lawyer cannot be obliged to monitor her client like a parent watching a child. At some point, the client must bear responsibility for a failure to preserve. At the same time, counsel is more conscious of the contours of the preservation obligation; a party cannot reasonably be trusted to receive the "litigation hold" instruction once and to fully comply with it without the active supervision of counsel.

There are thus a number of steps that counsel should take to ensure compliance with the preservation obligation. While these precautions may not be enough (or may be too much) in some cases, they are designed to promote the continued preservation of potentially relevant information in the typical case.

First, counsel must issue a "litigation hold" at the outset of litigation or whenever litigation is reasonably anticipated. The litigation hold should be periodically reissued so that new employees are aware of it, and so that it is fresh in the minds of all employees.

Second, counsel should communicate directly with the "key players" in the litigation, i.e., the people identified in a party's initial disclosure and any subsequent supplementation thereto. Because these "key players" are the "employees likely to have relevant information," it is particularly important that the preservation duty be communicated clearly to them. As with the litigation hold, the key players should be periodically reminded that the preservation duty is still in place.

Counsel should instruct all employees to produce electronic copies of their relevant active files. Counsel must also make sure that all backup media which the party is required to retain is identified and stored in a safe place. In cases involving a small number of relevant backup tapes, counsel might be advised to take physical possession of backup tapes. In other cases, it might make sense for relevant backup tapes to be segregated and placed in storage. Regardless of what particular arrangement counsel chooses to employ, the point is to separate relevant backup tapes from others. One of the primary reasons that electronic data is lost is ineffective communication with information technology personnel. By taking possession of, or otherwise safeguarding, all potentially relevant backup tapes, counsel eliminates the possibility that such tapes will be inadvertently recycled.

Kier v. UnumProvident Corp. provides a disturbing example of what can happen when counsel and client do not effectively communicate. In that ERISA class action, the court entered an order on December 27, 2002, requiring UnumProvident to preserve electronic data, specifically including e-mails sent or received on six particular days. What ensued was a comedy of errors. First, before the court order was entered (but when it was subject to the common law duty to preserve) UnumProvident's technical staff unilaterally decided to take a "snapshot" of its servers instead of restoring backup tapes, which would have recovered the e-mails in question. (In fact, the snapshot was useless for the purpose of preserving these e-mails because most of them had already been deleted by the time the snapshot was generated.) Once the court issued the preservation order, UnumProvident failed to take any further steps to locate the e-mails, believing that the same person who ordered the snapshot would oversee compliance with the court order. But no one told him that.

Indeed, it was not until January 13, when senior UnumProvident legal personnel inquired whether there was any way to locate the e-mails referenced in the December 27 Order, that anyone sent a copy of the Order to IBM, who provided "email, file server, and electronic data related disaster recovery services to UnumProvident." By that time, UnumProvident had written over 881 of the 1,498 tapes that contained backup data for the relevant time period. All of this led to a stern rebuke from the court. Had counsel in Kier promptly taken the precautions set out above, the e-mails would not have been lost.

3. What Happened at UBS After August 2001?

As more fully described above, UBS's in-house counsel issued a litigation hold in August 2001 and repeated that instruction several times from September 2001 through September 2002. Outside counsel also spoke with some (but not all) of the key players in August 2001. Nonetheless, certain employees unquestionably deleted e-mails. Although many of the deleted e-mails were recovered from backup tapes, a number of backup tapes—and the e-mails on them—are lost forever. Other employees, notwithstanding counsel's request that they produce their files on Zubulake, did not do so.

a. UBS's Discovery Failings

UBS's counsel—both in-house and outside—repeatedly advised UBS of its discovery obligations. In fact, counsel came very close to taking the precautions laid out above. First, outside counsel issued a litigation hold in August 2001. The hold order was circulated to many of the key players in this litigation, and reiterated in e-mails in February 2002, when suit was filed, and again in September 2002. Outside counsel made clear that the hold order applied to backup tapes in August 2002, as soon as backup tapes became an issue in this case. Second, outside counsel communicated directly with many of the key players in August 2001 and attempted to impress upon them their preservation obligations. Third, and finally, counsel instructed UBS employees to produce copies of their active computer files.

To be sure, counsel did not fully comply with the standards set forth above. Nonetheless, under the standards existing at the time, counsel acted reasonably to the extent that they directed UBS to implement a litigation hold. Yet notwithstanding the clear instructions of counsel, UBS personnel failed to preserve plainly relevant e-mails.

b. Counsel's Failings

On the other hand, UBS's counsel are not entirely blameless. "While, of course, it is true that counsel need not supervise every step of the document production process and may rely on their clients in some respects," counsel is responsible for coordinating her client's discovery efforts. In this case, counsel failed to properly oversee UBS in a number of important ways, both in terms of its duty to locate relevant information and its duty to preserve and timely produce that information.

With respect to locating relevant information, counsel failed to adequately communicate with Tong about how she stored data. Although counsel determined that Tong kept her files on Zubulake in an "archive," they apparently made no effort to learn what that meant. A few simple questions—like the ones that Zubulake's counsel asked at Tong's re-deposition—would have revealed that she kept those files in a separate active file on her computer.

With respect to making sure that relevant data was retained, counsel failed in a number of important respects. First, neither in-house nor outside counsel communicated the litigation hold instructions to Mike Davies, a senior human resources employee who was intimately involved in Zubulake's termination. Second, even though the litigation hold instructions were communicated to Kim, no one ever asked her to produce her files. And third, counsel failed to protect relevant backup tapes; had they done so, Zubulake might have been able to recover some of the e-mails that UBS employees deleted.

In addition, if Varsano's deposition testimony is to be credited, he turned over "all of the e-mails that [he] received concerning Ms. Zubulake." If Varsano turned over these e-mails, then counsel must have failed to produce some of them.

In sum, while UBS personnel deleted e-mails, copies of many of these e-mails were lost or belatedly produced as a result of counsel's failures.

c. Summary

Counsel failed to communicate the litigation hold order to all key players. They also failed to ascertain each of the key players' document management habits. By the same token, UBS employees—for unknown reasons—ignored many of the instructions that counsel gave. This case represents a failure of communication, and that failure falls on counsel and client alike.

At the end of the day, however, the duty to preserve and produce documents rests on the party. Once that duty is made clear to a party, either by court order or by instructions from counsel, that party is on notice of its obligations and acts at its own peril. Though more diligent action on the part of counsel would have mitigated some of the damage caused by UBS's deletion of emails, UBS deleted the e-mails in defiance of explicit instructions not to.

Because UBS personnel continued to delete relevant e-mails, Zubulake was denied access to e-mails to which she was entitled. Even those e-mails that were deleted but ultimately salvaged from other sources (e.g., backup tapes or Tong and Kim's active files) were produced 22 months after they were initially requested. The effect of losing potentially relevant e-mails is obvious, but the effect of late production cannot be underestimated either. "As a discovery deadline ... draws near, discovery conduct that might have been considered 'merely' discourteous at an earlier point in the litigation may well breach a party's duties to its opponent and to the court." Here, as UBS points out, Zubulake's instant motion "comes more than a year after the Court's previously imposed March 3, 2003 discovery cutoff." Although UBS attempts to portray this fact as evidence that Zubulake is being overly litigious, it is in fact a testament to the time wasted by UBS's failure to timely produce all relevant and responsive information. With the discovery deadline long past, UBS "was under an obligation to be as cooperative as possible." Instead, the extent of UBS's spoliation was uncovered by Zubulake during court-ordered re-depositions.

I therefore conclude that UBS acted wilfully in destroying potentially relevant information, which resulted either in the absence of such information or its tardy production (because duplicates were recovered from Kim or Tong's active files, or restored from backup tapes). Because UBS's spoliation was willful, the lost information is presumed to be relevant.

B. Remedy

Having concluded that UBS was under a duty to preserve the e-mails and that it deleted presumably relevant e-mails wilfully, I now consider the full panoply of available sanctions. In doing so, I recognize that a major consideration in choosing an appropriate sanction—along with punishing UBS and deterring future misconduct—is to restore Zubulake to the position that she would have been in had UBS faithfully discharged its discovery obligations. That being so, I find that the following sanctions are warranted.

First, the jury empanelled to hear this case will be given an adverse inference instruction with respect to e-mails deleted after August 2001, and in particular, with respect to e-mails that were irretrievably lost when UBS's backup tapes were recycled. No one can ever know precisely what was on those tapes, but the content of e-mails recovered from other sources—along with the fact that UBS employees wilfully deleted e-mails—is sufficiently favorable to Zubulake that I am convinced that the contents of the lost tapes would have been similarly, if not more, favorable.

Second, Zubulake argues that the e-mails that were produced, albeit late, "are brand new and very significant to Ms. Zubulake's retaliation claim and would have affected [her] examination of every witness ... in this case." Likewise, Zubulake claims, with respect to the newly produced e-mails from Kim and Tong's active files, that UBS's "failure to produce these e-mails in a timely fashion precluded [her] from questioning any witness about them." These arguments stand unrebutted and are therefore adopted in full by the Court. Accordingly, UBS is ordered to pay the costs of any depositions or re-depositions required by the late production.

Third, UBS is ordered to pay the costs of this motion.

Finally, I note that UBS's belated production has resulted in a self-executing sanction. Not only was Zubulake unable to question UBS's witnesses using the newly produced e-mails, but UBS was unable to prepare those witnesses with the aid of those e-mails. Some of UBS's witnesses, not having seen these e-mails, have already given deposition testimony that seems to contradict the newly discovered evidence. For example, if Zubulake's version of the evidence is credited, the e-mail from Davies acknowledging receipt of Zubulake's EEOC charge at 11:06 AM on August 21, 2001, puts the lie to Davies' testimony that he had not seen the charge when he spoke to Orgill—a conversation that was reflected in an e-mail sent at 2:02 PM. Zubulake is, of course, free to use this testimony at trial.

These sanctions are designed to compensate Zubulake for the harm done to her by the loss of or extremely delayed access to potentially relevant evidence. They should also stem the need for any further litigation over the backup tapes.

C. Other Alleged Discovery Abuses

In addition to the deleted (and thus never- or belatedly produced) e-mails, Zubulake complains of two other perceived discovery abuses: the destruction of a September 2001 backup tape from Tong's server, and the belated production of a UBS document retention policy.

1. Tong's September 2001 Backup Tape

Zubulake moves for sanctions because of the destruction of Tong's September 2001 backup tape. In Zubulake III, I ordered UBS to pay 75% of the cost of restoring certain backup tapes. Understandably, one of the tapes that Zubulake chose to restore was Tong's tape for August 2001, the month that Zubulake filed her EEOC charge. That tape, however, had been recycled by UBS. Zubulake then chose to restore Tong's September 2001 tape, on the theory that "the majority of the e-mails on [the August 2001] tape are preserved on the September 2001 tape." When that tape was actually restored, however, it turned out not to be the September 2001 tape at all, but rather Tong's October 2001 tape. This tape, according to UBS, was simply mislabeled.

Zubulake has already (unintentionally) restored Tong's October 2001 tape, which should contain the majority of the data on the September 2001 tape. In addition, UBS has offered to pay to restore Varsano's backup tape for August 2001, which it has and which has not yet been restored. Varsano was Tong's HR counterpart in the United States, and was copied on many (but not all) of the e-mails that went to or from Tong. These backup tapes, taken together, should recreate the lion's share of data from Tong's August 2001 tape. UBS must therefore pay for the restoration and production of relevant e-mails from Varsano's August 2001 backup tape, and pay for any re-deposition of Tong or Varsano that is necessitated by new e-mails found on that tape.

2. The July 1999 Record Management Policy

Zubulake also moves for sanctions in connection with what she refers to as "bad faith discovery tactics" on the part of UBS's counsel. In particular, Zubulake complains of a late-produced record management policy. The existence of this policy was revealed to Zubulake at Varsano's second deposition on January 26, 2004, at which time Zubulake called for its production. Zubulake twice reiterated this request in writing, in the hopes that she would have the policy in time for Hardisty's deposition on February 5, 2004. UBS did not produce the policy, however, until February 26, 2004.

The late production of the July 1999 policy does not warrant sanctions at all. First, UBS's production of the policy was not late. Zubulake requested it at Varsano's deposition on January 26, 2004, and UBS produced it one month later, on February 26. The Federal Rules afford litigants thirty days to respond to document requests, and UBS produced the policy within that time. The fact that Zubulake wanted the document earlier is immaterial—if it was truly necessary to confront Hardisty with the policy, then his deposition should have been rescheduled or Zubulake should have requested relief from the Court. Not having done so, Zubulake cannot now complain that UBS improperly delayed its production of that document.

Second, even if UBS was tardy in producing the policy, Zubulake has not demonstrated that she was prejudiced. She suggests that she would have used the policy in the depositions of Hardisty and perhaps Chapin, but does not explain how. Nor is it at all clear how Zubulake might have used the policy. With respect to e-mail, the policy states: "Email is another priority. We will have a separate policy regarding email with appropriate reference or citation in this policy and/or retention schedules." Prior to these depositions, Zubulake had a number of UBS document retention policies that post-dated the June 1999 Policy.

V. CONCLUSION

In sum, counsel has a duty to effectively communicate to her client its discovery obligations so that all relevant information is discovered, retained, and produced. In particular, once the duty to preserve attaches, counsel must identify sources of discoverable information. This will usually entail speaking directly with the key players in the litigation, as well as the client's information technology personnel. In addition, when the duty to preserve attaches, counsel must put in place a litigation hold and make that known to all relevant employees by communicating with them directly. The litigation hold instructions must be reiterated regularly and compliance must be monitored. Counsel must also call for employees to produce copies of relevant electronic evidence, and must arrange for the segregation and safeguarding of any archival media (e.g., backup tapes) that the party has a duty to preserve.

Once counsel takes these steps (or once a court order is in place), a party is fully on notice of its discovery obligations. If a party acts contrary to counsel's instructions or to a court's order, it acts at its own peril.

UBS failed to preserve relevant e-mails, even after receiving adequate warnings from counsel, resulting in the production of some relevant e-mails almost two years after they were initially requested, and resulting in the complete destruction of others. For that reason, Zubulake's motion is granted and sanctions are warranted. UBS is ordered to:

1. Pay for the re-deposition of relevant UBS personnel, limited to the subject of the newly-discovered e-mails;

2. Restore and produce relevant documents from Varsano's August 2001 backup tape;

3. Pay for the re-deposition of Varsano and Tong, limited to the new material produced from Varsano's August 2001 backup tape; and

4. Pay all "reasonable expenses, including attorney's fees," incurred by Zubulake in connection with the making of this motion.

In addition, I will give the following instruction to the jury that hears this case:

You have heard that UBS failed to produce some of the e-mails sent or received by UBS personnel in August and September 2001. Plaintiff has argued that this evidence was in defendants' control and would have proven facts material to the matter in controversy.

If you find that UBS could have produced this evidence, and that the evidence was within its control, and that the evidence would have been material in deciding facts in dispute in this case, you are permitted, but not required, to infer that the evidence would have been unfavorable to UBS.

In deciding whether to draw this inference, you should consider whether the evidence not produced would merely have duplicated other evidence already before you. You may also consider whether you are satisfied that UBS's failure to produce this information was reasonable. Again, any inference you decide to draw should be based on all of the facts and circumstances in this case.

. . . .

VI. POSTSCRIPT

The subject of the discovery of electronically stored information is rapidly evolving. When this case began more than two years ago, there was little guidance from the judiciary, bar associations or the academy as to the governing standards. Much has changed in that time. There have been a flood of recent opinions—including a number from appellate courts—and there are now several treatises on the subject. In addition, professional groups such as the American Bar Association and the Sedona Conference have provided very useful guidance on thorny issues relating to the discovery of electronically stored information. Many courts have adopted, or are considering adopting, local rules addressing the subject. Most recently, the Standing Committee on Rules and Procedures has approved for publication and public comment a proposal for revisions to the Federal Rules of Civil Procedure designed to address many of the issues raised by the discovery of electronically stored information.

Now that the key issues have been addressed and national standards are developing, parties and their counsel are fully on notice of their responsibility to preserve and produce electronically stored information. The tedious and difficult fact finding encompassed in this opinion and others like it is a great burden on a court's limited resources. The time and effort spent by counsel to litigate these issues has also been time-consuming and distracting. This Court, for one, is optimistic that with the guidance now provided it will not be necessary to spend this amount of time again. It is hoped that counsel will heed the guidance provided by these resources and will work to ensure that preservation, production and spoliation issues are limited, if not eliminated.

———

Discovery failures can be very costly and embarrassing.[17] In one of the more creative sanctions cases, in *Green v. Blitz, U.S.A., Inc.*, the court found that the defense lawyers

17. *See, e.g.,* Brown, 2014 U.S. Dist. LEXIS 90123 (defendant and counsel sanctioned with attorneys' fees and costs to plaintiff, and preclusion of evidence in support of the defense, where defendant failed to comply with discovery obligations, largely due to counsel's failure to make reasonable inquiry into the validity of the client's false and "illogical" representations regarding discovery); Small v. University Med. Ctr. of Southern Nevada, 2014 U.S. Dist. LEXIS 114406, fn. 19 (D. Nev. 2014) (special

relied too heavily on a client who admitted to being "about as computer literate—illiterate as they get" to manage all aspects of discovery for the litigation.[18] In addition to monetary sanctions for all sorts of e-discovery failures, the court issued a "scarlet letter" sanction, where the defendant was ordered to attach a copy of the sanctions order with its first pleading in all subsequent cases for five years.[19] In another case involving e-discovery issues, in *Qualcomm Inc. v. Broadcom Corp.*, despite counsels' "impressive education and extensive experience," the court found it "inconceivable that these talented, well-educated, and experienced lawyers failed to discover" the insufficiency of their client's production of documents.[20] The court initially sanctioned the defendant corporation $8.5 million and referred the attorneys to the state bar for disciplinary proceedings,[21] but the order was subsequently vacated and remanded for further consideration.[22] On remand, although the court did not find evidence of "bad faith" and declined to impose sanctions, it did highlight again that "no attorney took supervisory responsibility for verifying that the necessary discovery had been conducted."[23] It is now more important than ever for lawyers to keep up with the rapidly evolving landscape of business technology, and become experts in their clients' information infrastructure, as well as e-discovery techniques. Lastly, as quickly as technology evolves, the policies themselves should be updated regularly to keep up with new technologies and applications, as well as new laws.

Green v. Blitz U.S.A., Inc.

2011 U.S. Dist. LEXIS 20353 (E.D. Tex. Mar. 1, 2011)

MEMORANDUM OPINION AND ORDER

Before the Court are various motions by Plaintiff Rene Green, Individually and as heir of Jonathan Edward Brody Breen, and Defendant Blitz U.S.A., Inc. ("Blitz").

---

discovery master recommendation of default judgment, automatic class certification and rebuttable presumption on various issues for failure to appropriately alert IT manager responsible for mobile devices, failure to identify relevant repositories, and failure to make proper preservation efforts for almost two years) ("these problems were exacerbated by UMC retaining less than effective counsel and electronic discovery consultants"); In re Pradaxa (Dabigatran Etexilate) Prods. Liab. Litig., 2013 U.S. Dist. LEXIS 173674, *58 (S.D. Ill. 2013) ("the duty to preserve is not a passive obligation; it must be discharged actively. The defendants had a duty to ensure that their employees understood that text messages were included in the litigation hold.").

18. Green v. Blitz, U.S.A., Inc., 2011 U.S. Dist. LEXIS 20353, at *20–21 (E.D. Tex. 2011), sanctions order vacated, 2014 U.S. Dist. LEXIS 83907 (E.D. Tex. 2014) (sanctions including $250,000 in civil contempt sanctions, a $500,000 "purging" sanction, extinguishable if the defendant furnishes a copy of the order to every plaintiff in every lawsuit against it for the past two years, and ordered to file a copy of the order with its first pleading or filing in all new lawsuits for the next five years).

19. Green, 2011 U.S. Dist. LEXIS 20353, at *36–37.

20. Qualcomm Inc. v. Broadcom Corp., 2008 U.S. Dist. LEXIS 911, *42 (S.D. Cal. 2008), vacated in part, 2008 U.S. Dist. LEXIS 16897 (S.D. Cal. 2008).

21. Qualcomm, 2008 U.S. Dist. LEXIS 911, at *63–65.

22. Qualcomm Inc. v. Broadcom Corp., 2008 U.S. Dist. LEXIS 16897 (S.D. Cal. 2008).

23. Qualcomm Inc. v. Broadcom Corp., 2010 U.S. Dist. LEXIS 33889, *11 (S.D. Cal. 2010).

(Dkt. Nos. 244, 199 & 195.) The Court DENIES Plaintiff's Motion to Re-Open the Case (Dkt. No. 199) for the reasons set forth in Magistrate Judge Everingham's January 12, 2011 Report and Recommendation (Dkt. No. 243). The Court DENIES Blitz's Motion for Reconsideration. (Dkt. No. 244.) The Court GRANTS-IN-PART and DENIES-IN-PART Plaintiff's Motion for Sanctions. (Dkt. No. 195.) The Court holds that Blitz is subject to sanctions for various discovery violations as described below in this Memorandum Opinion & Order. The Court orders Blitz to pay $250,000.00 in civil contempt sanctions to the plaintiff in this case. The Court additionally orders that Blitz has thirty (30) days from the date of this Memorandum Opinion & Order to furnish a copy of this Memorandum Opinion & Order to every Plaintiff in every lawsuit it has had proceeding against it, or is currently proceeding against it, for the past two years. The Court issues an additional $500,000.00 sanction that will be tolled for thirty (30) days from the date of this Memorandum Opinion & Order. At the end of that time period, if Blitz has certified with this Court that it has complied with the Court's order, the $500,000.00 sanction will be extinguished. Finally, for the next five years, Blitz is ordered that in every new lawsuit it participates in as a party, whether plaintiff, defendant, or in another official capacity, it must file a copy of this Memorandum Opinion and Order with its first pleading or filing in that particular court. This Court expresses no opinion as to the manner in which a particular court may use or not use such copy.

I. BACKGROUND

The instant case is one of several similar cases against Blitz, including *Delz v. Blitz*, 1:09-cv-251-LY ("the *Delz* case"), *Gaddy v. Blitz*, 2:09-cv-52-DF ("the *Gaddy* case"), and *Zecaida v. Blitz*, 6:09-cv-283 ("the *Zecaida* case"). In the motion under consideration, Ms. Green asks the Court to sanction Blitz for what she believes to be a systematic destruction of evidence and repeated discovery violations. Ms. Green levies broad allegations against Blitz—allegations that have expanded since her motions were originally filed. The Court has carefully reviewed the allegations made by Ms. Green in light of the procedural posture of this case and has attempted to evaluate the allegations based on the sworn testimony in the record related to each specific allegation. Further, the Court held a show cause hearing on February 1, 2011 as directed by Magistrate Judge Everingham's January 12, 2011 Report and Recommendation. (Dkt. No. 243 at 12.) The Court's efforts are compounded by the numerous supplements that have been filed since Ms. Green's original motion.

To understand the alleged discovery violations, it is important to understand the procedural posture of this case, the parties' positions at trial, and this case's relationship with numerous similar cases against Blitz. In 2007, Rene Green brought this products liability lawsuit, asserting that a gas can manufactured by Blitz caused the death of Brody Green. One of Green's major theories for liability was that the gas can did not include a flame arrester. (*See* Amended Complaint, Dkt. No. 33, at 5.) One of Blitz's major defense theories was that a flame arrester was not included on the gas can because flame arresters are ineffective. At the conclusion of the evidence and before the jury returned a verdict, the parties entered into a high-low settlement agreement.

(Dkt. No. 195, at 2.) The jury returned a unanimous verdict against the plaintiffs, resulting in a settlement figure at the low end of the high-low range. (*Id.*) The case was closed on November 10, 2008. Counsel for the plaintiff in this case ("the *Green* case"), however, is also counsel in the related *Delz* case in the Western District of Texas. (Dkt. No. 195, at 3.) Through discovery in that case, nearly a year after the trial in the present case, counsel learned of documents that were not produced in this case and promptly filed the present motion in February of 2010.

Ms. Green argues that Blitz failed to produce certain documents and also failed to preserve documents. The majority of these documents that were not produced relate to the flame arrester, or Blitz's interest in potentially using a flame arrester, in its gas cans. These documents are discussed in detail in the Analysis section of this Memorandum Opinion and Order. Ms. Green argues that the Court's Discovery Order required the production of all relevant documents, including electronically stored information, within 45 days of the scheduling conference, and Blitz's failure to do so violated the order. Ms. Green contends that Blitz's refusal to timely produce relevant materials was done in bad faith and has resulted in manifest injustice. She asserts that—had the withheld documents been available to her at trial—the outcome of the trial would have been different and that she would have been entitled to the high-end of the high-low settlement.

Nearly simultaneously with its motion for sanctions, Plaintiff in this case filed a motion to re-open the case. (Dkt. No. 199.) Magistrate Judge Everingham issued a Report and Recommendation to deny the motion to re-open the case (Dkt. No. 243), and that Report and Recommendation is adopted in this Memorandum Opinion and Order. Judge Everingham's primary reason for recommending denying the motion to re-open the case is because of the one-year statute of limitations under Federal Rule of Civil Procedure 60(b)(1)–(3). Therefore, the only issue left is whether sanctions are appropriate against Blitz for its alleged discovery abuse.

This case is not the only case where Blitz has been accused of discovery abuse. In the *Gaddy* case and *Zecaida* cases, for example, the plaintiffs also filed a motion for sanctions. *See* Order Granting-in-part and Denying-in-part, *Gaddy v. Blitz U.S.A., Inc.*, Dkt. No. 199 (Sept. 13, 2010). Both of these cases included product liability claims for Blitz failing to include a flame arrester in its gas cans. *Id.* at 2. The Court in *Gaddy* and *Zecaida* sanctioned Blitz by allowing evidence in those cases regarding Blitz's discovery abuses and allowing a jury instruction that Blitz failed its duties of discovery. *Id.* at 24. There are many other similar cases against Blitz as noted at the beginning of this Memorandum Opinion and Order.

II. LEGAL STANDARD

Federal Rule of Civil Procedure 37 authorizes sanctions for failure to comply with discovery orders. The Fifth Circuit has stated "we recognize that a district court always has jurisdiction to impose sanctions designed to enforce its own rules, even after that court no longer has jurisdiction over the substance of the case." *Fleming & Assocs. v. Newby & Tittle*, 529 F.3d 631, 638 (5th Cir. 2008). *See also Cooter & Gell v. Hartmarx*

Corp., 496 U.S. 384, 395–396, 110 S. Ct. 2447, 110 L. Ed. 2d 359 (1990). This Court may bar the disobedient party from introducing evidence, or it may direct that certain facts shall be "taken to be established for purposes of the action." Fed. R. Civ. P. 37(b)(2)(A)(i). Rule 37 also permits this court to strike claims from the pleadings and even to "dismiss the action … or render a judgment by default against the disobedient party." *Roadway Express, Inc. v. Piper*, 447 U.S. 752, 763, 100 S. Ct. 2455, 65 L. Ed. 2d 488 (1980); *accord* Fed. R. Civ. P. 37(b)(2)(A)(v)–(vi). "Rule 37 sanctions must be applied diligently both to penalize those whose conduct may be deemed to warrant such a sanction, [and] to deter those who might be tempted to such conduct in the absence of such a deterrent." *Roadway Express*, 447 U.S. at 763–64.

Rule 37(b)(2) requires that any sanction be just and that the sanction must be related to the particular claim that was the subject of the discovery violations. *Compaq Computer Corp. v. Ergonome Inc.*, 387 F.3d 403, 413 (5th Cir. 2004) (citations omitted). Further, the penalized party's discovery violation must be willful. *United States v. $49,000 Currency*, 330 F.3d 371, 376 (5th Cir. 2003). Finally, a severe sanction under Rule 37 is to be employed only where a lesser sanction would not substantially achieve the desired deterrent effect. *Id.*

In addition to Rule 37, this court also has inherent powers to enter sanctions. The inherent powers of this Court are those which "are necessary to the exercise of all others." *Roadway Express*, 447 U.S. at 764 (citation omitted). The contempt sanction is the most prominent inherent power, "which a judge must have and exercise in protecting the due and orderly administration of justice and in maintaining the authority and dignity of the court." *Id.* (citation omitted). The Fifth Circuit has recognized that the inherent power "is necessarily incident to the judicial power granted under Article III of the Constitution." *Gonzalez v. Trinity Marine Group, Inc.*, 117 F.3d 894, 898 (5th Cir. 1997). When inherent powers are invoked, however, they must be exercised with "restraint and discretion." *Id.* Therefore, severe sanctions should be confined to instances of "bad faith or willful abuse of the judicial process." *Id.* In any event, when parties exploit the judicial process, a court may sanction conduct beyond the reach of other rules. *Natural Gas Pipeline v. Energy Gathering, Inc.*, 2 F.3d 1397, 1407 (5th Cir. 1993).

III. ANALYSIS

A. Blitz's Discovery Abuse for Failure to Disclose Documents

Before proceeding into the specific documents at issue in the plaintiff's motion, it is important to understand how Blitz originally conducted its discovery in this case. Blitz had a single employee, Mr. Larry Chrisco, who from 2004 until his retirement in late 2007 was solely responsible for searching for and collecting documents relevant to ongoing litigation against Blitz. (Show Cause Hearing, Feb. 1, 2011, at 19.) Prior to 2004, beginning in at least the late 1990s, Mr. Chrisco shared this responsibility with another employee at Blitz—Mr. Jackson. (*Id.*) Mr. Chrisco worked in the product development department at Blitz. (*Id.* at 18.) In addition, Mr. Chrisco was Blitz's corporate representative at the trial of this case and Blitz's only witness called at the February 1, 2011 Show Cause Hearing. Mr. Chrisco described his discovery efforts as follows:

When Mr. Jackson and I were working jointly, we would meet with — we met with counsel. We were contacted regarding when a claim was filed, and that request for discoveries were made. We would sit with counsel, and at that point in time, we had no national coordinating counsel. It was strictly a local defense attorney in that particular state.

We would look at those requests, talk with him to understand what was relevant for production, and from there, we would go out — I would go and talk with areas that — that most likely documents would be in and ask — talk with them and explain to them what we were looking for. Mr. Jackson would do the same thing.

. . . .

When Mr. Jackson was no longer involved, I went through this same procedure in terms of looking at the complaint, and at that point in time, we had brought on a national coordinating counsel, Mr. Murphy, at that point, he would — we would go through the claims, the suits, the discovery requests, and so I would get an understanding of what materials that we needed to be searching for, what materials were relevant to this, and at that point in time, once I understood that, I would visit with those areas or those departments that had the potential to have those documents in their possession.

(Show Cause Hearing Transcript, at 20–21.) When visiting those departments, Mr. Chrisco noted that he was a "face-to-face" guy and he would "go talk with them about what [he was] looking for, what it was about, and explain what those documents could be, and ask them to look for those" and bring them back to him. (*Id.* at 24.) In addition, Mr. Chrisco had some documents himself that he disclosed — especially documents relating to flame arresters, given that Mr. Chrisco headed up the research and investigation around flame arresters. (*Id.* at 21.) As discussed above, documents related to flame arresters were particularly relevant in this case because one of Plaintiff's major arguments at trial was that the gas can at issue should have had a flame arrester.

In carrying out his duties to conduct discovery, Mr. Chrisco (i.e., Blitz) educated himself regarding the types of documents that were relevant and then talked to the departments and/or individuals he felt were likely to have those documents. Mr. Chrisco, however, acting as Blitz's agent for gathering discovery, did not institute a litigation-hold of documents, do any electronic word searches for emails, or talk with the IT department regarding how to search for electronic documents. These failures are in part the subject of this Memorandum Opinion & Order.

1. Blitz's Failure to Disclose Documents in the Present Case

With that background in mind, the Court discusses the particular documents that were not produced in this case. Ms. Green identifies numerous documents not produced in this case that are extremely relevant and material. Specifically, at the Show Cause Hearing held on February 1, 2011, Ms. Green focused on ten documents that were not disclosed. (*See, e.g.,* Show Cause Hearing, Feb. 1, 2011, Dkt. No. 250, Pl.'s Exs. 1, 3, 4, 5, 6, 8, 9, 10, 11, 12.) Many of these documents are similar, so the

Court's analysis focuses only on three documents, which, in this Court's view, these three items fairly represent the types of documents not disclosed by Blitz in this case.

First, the Court considers Plaintiff's Exhibit 1 presented at the Show Cause Hearing on February 1, 2011, which has come to be known as the "Wish List." (Hearing Transcript, Larry Chrisco Cross Examination, Dkt. No. 250, at 33.) This was a handwritten letter or memorandum dated August 16, 2005, from Rocky Flick, the former CEO of Blitz, to Larry Chrisco. (*Id.*) The letter had the subject label of "My Wish List" and the top line of the letter reads "Expectations for Gas Cans (To be completed in next 2 yrs)." The second point on the "Wish List" stated: "Develop & introduce device to eliminate flashback from a flame source. Water heater incidents should be the test case for this. Once this is developed we should advocate the device be standardized under ASTM req's [sic] or laws." (Show Cause Hearing, Feb. 1, 2011, Pl. Ex. 1.) This letter was written to Larry Chrisco approximately two years before this lawsuit was filed and Mr. Chrisco admits it is relevant to this case. (Show Cause Hearing Transcript, at 58.) It is undisputed, however, that the letter was not produced in the present case.

The next document is Plaintiff's Exhibit 4 presented at the Show Cause Hearing. This document is an email from Chuck Craig to Charlie Forbis, David Price, and Larry Chrisco that was sent on August 8, 2005. The email is a forwarded email from Douglas Hughes, and the email sent from Chuck Craig has the subject "FW: Flame Arrester." In the original email that was forwarded by Chuck Craig, Douglas Hughes states:

> I've been in meetings and travelling all day, so I apologize, I haven't had a chance to call you back earlier today. As far as your question for the flame arrester, the marine industry uses them in all the boat tanks, so the technology and testing has to be in place today. I am going to look through some of the Coast Guard test procedures and see if I can't come up with something.

(Show Cause Hearing, Feb. 1, 2011, Pl. Ex. 4.) Larry Chrisco, when collecting documents for discovery, stated that he talked to Charlie Forbis about documents he had relevant to this case. (Show Cause Hearing Transcript, at 26–27.) Larry Chrisco could not remember if he talked face-to-face with David Price about gathering discoverable documents, but Mr. Chrisco was sure that Mr. Price had received the message to gather relevant documents—potentially through Charlie Forbis. (*Id.* at 28–29; 48–49.) Indeed, Larry Chrisco, Charlie Forbis, and David Price were the three people at Blitz that put together the flame arrester project in 2005. Nevertheless, despite Chuck Craig, Charlie Forbis, David Price, and Larry Chrisco all having been a party to the email and the subject being "FW: Flame Arrester," it is undisputed that this email was not produced in this case.

The third and final document the Court considers is Plaintiff's Exhibit 10 at the Show Cause Hearing. Exhibit 10 is titled "Development Team Meeting: 02-08-07." (Show Cause Hearing, Feb. 1, 2011, Pl. Ex. 10.) The record is ambiguous regarding what exactly the document is, however, it appears on its face to be either a bullet list of things to be discussed at the February 8, 2007 Development Team Meeting or a bullet list—perhaps minutes—of things that were discussed at the meeting. The document states that Marion George, Grant Kernan, Todd McClain, Jim Calcagno, Kristi McClain, and Larry were in attendance. One of the bullet points in the document, under the header "Scenarios," states to "Exit gas can for 3–5 years, develop other business, and re-enter w/lower liability (?) [sic] and safer CARB product." (Show Cause Hearing, Feb. 1, 2011, Pl. Ex. 10, at 2.) It is undisputed that this document was not produced in this case, and Mr. Chrisco admitted that it would have been relevant. (Show Cause Hearing Transcript, at 59.)

2. Analysis of Blitz's Failure to Disclose

The three documents described above demonstrate the types of documents that were not disclosed by Blitz to the plaintiff in the present case. They are indisputably relevant. Other documents which were not disclosed were presented to the Court at the Show Cause Hearing, and these documents are similar to the three described above, as they are emails, reports, or other documents outlining meetings held by Blitz employees related to flame arresters. (*See, e.g.*, Show Cause Hearing, Feb. 1, 2011, Pl.'s Exs. 1, 3, 4, 5, 6, 8, 9, 10, 11, 12.)

Based on Blitz's failure to disclose these documents, the Court finds that Blitz's conduct constitutes a willful violation of the Court's Discovery Order. The Discovery Order stated that "[e]ach party ... shall provide to every other party the following: (a) a copy of all documents, data compilations, and tangible things in the possession, custody, or control of the party that are relevant to the pleaded claims or defenses involved in this action." (Dkt. No. 20, at 3.) The parties, when given the opportunity, did not object to the additional disclosures required by this Court's Discovery Order. In addition, in the Discovery Order, there is an order to supplement the disclosures. (*Id.* at 5.) Further, in the proposed pretrial order that was submitted jointly by the parties, the parties made the certification that "[t]he undersigned counsel for each of the parties in this action do hereby certify and acknowledge the following: (1) Full and complete disclosure has been made in accordance with the Federal Rules of Civil Procedure and the Court's orders." (Dkt. No. 126, at 12.) Blitz violated these provisions of the Discovery Order and made a false certification in its pretrial order by not disclosing the documents discussed above.

Additionally, the Court finds that the violation of the Discovery Order was willful given the context and the type of documents not disclosed. Exhibit 4, the August 8, 2005 email, shows the gravity of Blitz's discovery violations for failing to produce relevant documents. The email had the words "Flame Arrester" in the subject line of the email. There were four parties to the email—one person sent the email to three people. Larry Chrisco, the person at Blitz in charge of collecting documents for discovery, was a party to the email. Further, Larry Chrisco testified that he talked to some of the other parties on the email in order to collect documents to produce in this litigation. Despite all of this, the email was still not produced. Perhaps more shocking, however, is the ease in which this document could have been discovered and produced in this case. Any competent electronic discovery effort would have located this email. If Blitz performed a word search of the emails of, for example, Larry

Chrisco, then this email surely would have been discovered. The search term of "flame arrester" may have been the most obvious term to search for in electronic documents in this case, and "flame arrester" was used in the title of this email. Blitz, however, did not attempt to search electronically for emails. To make things worse, Larry Chrisco, the person in charge of discovery for Blitz, readily admits that "I am about as computer literate—illiterate as they get." (Show Cause Hearing Transcript, at 37.) But Chrisco, obviously aware of his lack of computer prowess, did not even attempt to consult with the IT Department about how electronic information could be discovered. (*Id.* at 85.) Accordingly, despite Blitz's IT Department's ability to do electronic word searches for emails, no word search was ever done.

Although the non-produced emails show Blitz's *lack of effort* in its discovery requirements, the "Wish List" (Exhibit 1) and the "Development Team Meeting" (Exhibit 10) show the *prejudice* to the plaintiff for the failure to produce the documents. The "Wish List" is written by Blitz's then CEO and states in one part that he wished to "Develop & introduce device to eliminate flashback from a flame source." (Show Cause Hearing, Feb. 1, 2011, Pl. Ex. 1.) This document would have been extremely valuable to the plaintiff to rebut Blitz's claims that flame arresters would not have helped to prevent the incident at issue because they were ineffective. The "Development Team Meeting" document would have similarly helpful to the plaintiff. Being able to show the jury a document where Blitz itself stated: "Exit gas can for 3–5 years, develop other business, and re-enter w/lower liability (?) [sic] and safer CARB product," would have undoubtedly helped the plaintiff's liability argument. (Show Cause Hearing, Feb. 1, 2011, Pl. Ex. 10, at 2.)

In addition to its failure to produce relevant documents, Blitz also objected to multiple exhibits presented by the Plaintiff at the Show Cause Hearing as being privileged. In a later filing with this Court, Blitz admitted that those exhibits were not included on any privilege log. (Dkt. No. 251, at 2.) In addition, Blitz admitted that there was a Dunbar Engineering document related to flame arresters that it did not produce because Blitz thought it was work product. Then the document, however, was left off the privilege log. (Dkt. No. 246, at 11 ("The [Dunbar Engineering] documents themselves were not originally a part of the production set because they had initially been designated as work product but were mistakenly left off the log.").) This conduct shows a further violation of the Court's Discovery Order in Blitz failing to properly disclose on its privilege logs documents that it is withholding based on a claim of privilege. (*See* Dkt. No. 20, at 4.)

Blitz argues that Federal Rule of Civil Procedure 26(g) requires only a reasonable effort to search for and produce documents responsive to a discovery request. The record before this Court does not show a reasonable effort; instead, as noted above, the Court finds that Blitz willfully violated its Discovery Order. One need not look any further than the failure to search for and produce emails that bear the title "flame arrester" in a case where the lack of a flame arrester was a key issue. Blitz's additional discovery abuses are additional proof of Blitz's blatant disregard for the Court's Discovery Order. The Court holds that sanctions are appropriate under the Court's inherent powers and pursuant to Federal Rule of Civil Procedure 37. The proper sanctions are discussed below in this Memorandum Opinion and Order.

B. Blitz's Discovery Abuse for Failure to Preserve Documents

The Court also holds that Blitz failed to properly preserve documents for litigation. When litigation commences, a party must suspend its routine document retention and destruction policy and establish a "litigation hold" to ensure the preservation of relevant documents. *Tantivy Commc'ns, Inc. v. Lucent Techs. Inc.*, Civ. No. 2:04-cv-79-TJW, 2005 U.S. Dist. LEXIS 29981, 2005 WL 2860976, at *2 (E.D. Tex. Nov. 1, 2005) (J. Ward) ("Lucent and its counsel are well aware that a party in litigation must suspend its routine document retention/destruction policy and establish a 'litigation hold' to ensure the preservation of relevant documents."); *see also Rimkus Consulting Group, Inc. v. Cammarata*, 688 F. Supp. 2d 598, 612–13 (S.D. Tex. 2010) (discussing the duty to preserve).

As discussed above, Blitz made little, if any, effort to discharge its electronic discovery obligations. But Blitz also failed to preserve its electronic documents. Far from instituting a litigation hold on relevant electronic documents, Blitz actually asked its employees to routinely delete electronic documents. From 2004 through 2007, Blitz's IT department head, Paul Hale, routinely sent emails to all Blitz employees instructing them and encouraging them to delete email. (*See generally* Dkt. No. 226, Ex. 7(a)–(t).) One email said "Will everyone delete all old emails that you can, please? (And then remember to go into the deleted folder, select all items, and delete that as well.)" (*Id.* at Ex. 7(h).) Other emails titled "Clean and Delete All E-Mail Folders, Please!" and "Don't forget the 'Sent' folder" were also sent. (*Id.* at Ex. 7(c) & 7(d).) Most of these emails were in the 2004 to 2006 time frame, and over that short time frame there are at least ten emails in the record where Paul Hale requested that all employees at Blitz to delete their emails. During this precise time period, Blitz was actively defending multiple products liability lawsuits relating to its gas cans and had a duty to preserve evidence. Paul Hale admits that when he sent these multiple emails telling employees to delete their email, the employees were not told to retain email relevant to ongoing litigation. (*Id.* at Ex. 9, page 69, lines 16–20.) Additionally, during the Feb. 1, 2011 Show Cause Hearing, Larry Chrisco admitted that he never communicated any type of "litigation hold" request to the employees at Blitz:

> THE COURT: Okay. All right. And you don't recall any conversation at any time with Mr. Paul Hale about what he might or might not do as the director of IT, information technology?
>
> THE WITNESS [Larry Chrisco]: Your Honor, I had conversations with Paul Hale, but not specific to that. Paul was a good friend. Most of mine was with Tom Jackson. He worked for us at some period of time.
>
> THE COURT: And you don't recall any conversations other—with—about searching e-mail with Mr. David Lamb.
>
> THE WITNESS: I don't recall any conversations I had with Mr. Lamb regarding e-mails, no.

THE COURT: And you don't recall ever giving any type of written direction or electronic communication all—to everyone about holding or not—holding onto all documents because litigation or anything like that?

THE WITNESS: No, sir, I—in talking with them, I just—they were aware that we were going through litigation and why we were pulling documents and asking for documents and that it was relevant we had those things, so ...

THE COURT: Well, I know. So there's no written communication, I mean—

THE WITNESS: No, sir.

THE COURT:—a memo or anything like that?

THE WITNESS: I don't recall that there was.

THE COURT: Well, are you telling me that you—when you talked to him about "We need to get these documents together; we've got these lawsuits," are you telling me that you recall or you don't recall discussing with them, "Now, make sure that you maintain all these documents?" Do you have any recollection of that type of conversation?

THE WITNESS: Sir, I don't recall that I specifically used those words, "retain all these documents."

THE COURT: Well, what do you recall that you told them about keeping the documents? I understand you've told me that you talked with these different people about they need to find the documents.

THE WITNESS: Correct.

THE COURT: Do you have those specific recollections?

THE WITNESS: I have those very specific recollections, that's correct.

THE COURT: I understand that, now, but my question is did you—what do you recall that you told them about keeping the document—preserve—whatever word you want to use when we say keeping or preserving the document, I'm not trying to put words in your mouth, however you want—what do you recall about that, or do you have any recollection?

THE WITNESS: I don't have any recollection as we sit here, Your Honor.

THE COURT: Okay. That's all. You may step down. Thank you.

(Show Cause Hearing Transcript, Dkt. No. 250, at 85:7–87:13.)

Finally, to make matters worse, Blitz rotated its backup tapes every two weeks during this time period—at such time the old backup tapes are permanently deleted—so the deleted emails by the employees are permanently lost. (*See* Dkt. No. 226, Ex. 23, 186:15–189:7.) Because of this systematic destruction of potentially relevant documents, it will never be known how much prejudice against the plaintiff was actually caused by Blitz's failure to preserve documents. The Court holds that Blitz's failure to preserve is sanctionable under the Court's inherent powers.

C. Sanctions for Blitz's Discovery Abuses

Though the analysis above outlines specific instances of discovery abuse and violations of court orders in this case, perhaps more alarming, however, is Blitz's lack of appreciation of the discovery process in general. Despite Blitz being sued in multiple districts for its allegedly defective gas cans beginning primarily in 2002 (Dkt. No. 250, at 13), Blitz failed to begin scrubbing its servers until early 2009, nearly a year after the trial in this specific case. Although such an expensive endeavor may not be required to satisfy its discovery obligations, Blitz at least had the capability to perform simple word searches of its email server files. Such a search would have surely uncovered the email titled: "Flame Arrester," as the term "flame arrester" may have been the most obvious term to search in this products liability case regarding a gas container not including a flame arrester. That Larry Crisco, Blitz's employee in charge of gathering discovery, did not know how to search for electronic documents is immaterial. Blitz had an obligation to conduct such a search. Perhaps Blitz should not appoint someone to coordinate discovery who is admittedly as "computer literate—illiterate as they get." Or, alternatively, Mr. Crisco could have at least inquired with the Blitz IT Department regarding a search for electronic documents, which he admittedly did not do.

Now that the Court has outlined the specific instances of conduct by Blitz that warrant sanctions in this case, it will turn its attention to the sanctions that will be imposed on Blitz for its blatant discovery abuses.

1. Legal Standard for Civil Contempt Sanctions

Under Federal Rule of Civil Procedure 37(b)(2)(A)(vii), the Court may "treat[] as contempt of court the failure to obey any order." Additionally, under the Court's inherent powers to impose sanctions, as noted above, the contempt sanction is the most prominent inherent power. *See Roadway Express*, 447 U.S. at 764. Judicial sanctions for civil contempt may be "employed for either or both of two purposes: to coerce the defendant into compliance with the court's order, and to compensate the complainant for losses sustained." *Am. Airlines, Inc. v. Allied Pilots Ass'n*, 228 F.3d 574, 585 (5th Cir. 2000). "The district court 'has broad discretion in the assessment of damages in a civil contempt proceeding.'" *Id.* (citations omitted). "'The purpose is to compensate for the damages sustained. The public rights that the said court orders sought to protect are important measures of the remedy.'" *Id.* (citations omitted). The Fifth Circuit has instructed that for sanctions under Rule 37(b)(2), "[f]irst, any sanction must be 'just'; second, the sanction must be specifically related to the particular 'claim' which was at issue in the order to provide discovery." *Compaq Computer Corp. v. Ergonome Incorp.*, 387 F.3d 403, 413 (5th Cir. 2004). For sanctions under the Court's inherent power, the Supreme Court has instructed that "[b]ecause inherent powers are shielded from direct democratic controls, they must be exercised with restraint and discretion." *Roadway Express*, 447 U.S. at 765.

2. Civil Compensatory Sanction of $250,000.00

The Court orders Blitz to pay $250,000.00 in civil contempt sanctions to the plaintiff in this case. This civil sanction is to compensate the plaintiff for losses sustained due to Blitz's multiple discovery violations. *See Am. Airlines*, 228 F.3d 574 (stating that civil sanctions may be issued to compensate the complainant for losses sustained). Given this Court's knowledge regarding the amount of the confidential settlement between the parties and the circumstances of that settlement, the Court finds that the settlement would have been not less than $250,000.00 higher if the plaintiff would have had the documents discussed in this Memorandum Opinion and Order. Particularly, the Court finds that the "Wish List" (Exhibit 1) and the "Development Team Meeting" (Exhibit 10), which were not disclosed to the plaintiff, would have drastically increased the settlement value. The "Wish List," for example, would have hurt, if not potentially eliminated, Blitz's defense that they did not add a flame arrester because it would not have been useful.

Given the procedural posture of this case and the fact that the case has been closed for more than a year, as discussed in Magistrate Judge Everingham's January 21, 2011 Report and Recommendation (Dkt. No. 243), the Court is limited in its ability to sanction Blitz. Besides civil contempt, none of the other potential sanctions under Rule 37(b)(2) are available at this point in this case. Under the guidelines the Fifth Circuit has given for Rule 37(b)(2) sanctions, the Court finds that the civil contempt sanction of $250,000.00 is "just" given the extreme prejudice the plaintiff suffered by not having access to important documents. Additionally, the sanction is "just" given Blitz's multiple discovery violations and the gravity of those violations. The sanction is also related to the particular claim which was at issue — the sanction compensates the plaintiff for additional recovery she could and would have received if Blitz had met its discovery obligations. Therefore, this particular civil contempt sanction of $250,000.00 is appropriate under Rule 37(b)(2). In addition, the $250,000.00 civil contempt sanction is appropriate under the Court's inherent power, although the Court need not use its inherent power to sanction for contempt in order to justify the $250,000.00. Given Blitz's policy to delete emails regularly without regard to currently pending litigation, it is hard to tell how much value that information would have had to the plaintiff's case.

3. Civil Purging Sanction of $500,000.00

The Court additionally orders that Blitz has thirty (30) days from the date of this Memorandum Opinion & Order to furnish a copy of this Memorandum Opinion & Order to every Plaintiff in every lawsuit it has had proceeding against it, or is currently proceeding against it, for the past two years. The Court issues an additional $500,000.00 sanction that will be tolled for thirty (30) days from the date of this Memorandum Opinion & Order. At the end of the thirty (30) days, if Blitz has certified with this Court that it has complied with the Court's order to provide a copy of this Memorandum Opinion & Order to such parties, the $500,000.00 civil sanction will be extinguished. The Court may impose a civil contempt sanction to coerce — known as a "purging" sanction — under Fifth Circuit law. *See Am. Airlines*, 228 F.3d 574 (stating that civil sanctions may be issued to coerce the defendant into compliance with the court's order).

4. Sanction to Encourage Future Compliance

Finally, for the next five years from the date of this Memorandum Opinion and Order, Blitz is ordered that in every new lawsuit it participates in as a party, whether plaintiff, defendant, or in another official capacity, it must file a copy of this Memorandum Opinion and Order with its first pleading or filing in that particular court. Given Blitz's consistent failure to comply discovery obligations in this and related cases, the Court finds that this sanction is necessary to ensure that Blitz complies with future discovery obligations. As noted above, the Court may impose sanctions in order to coerce the defendant into compliance. *See Am. Airlines*, 228 F.3d 574.

IV. CONCLUSION

In conclusion, the Court holds that Blitz is subject to sanctions for various discovery violations as described in this Memorandum Opinion & Order. The Court orders Blitz to pay $250,000.00 in civil contempt sanctions to the plaintiff in this case. The Court additionally orders that Blitz has thirty (30) days from the date of this Memorandum Opinion & Order to furnish a copy of this Memorandum Opinion & Order to every Plaintiff in every lawsuit it has had proceeding against it, or is currently proceeding against it, for the past two years. The Court issues an additional $500,000.00 sanction that will be tolled for thirty (30) days from the date of this Memorandum Opinion & Order. At the end of said thirty (30) days, if Blitz has certified to this Court that it has complied with the Court's order, the $500,000.00 sanction will be extinguished. Finally, for the next five years subsequent to the date of this Memorandum Opinion and Order, Blitz is ordered that in every new lawsuit it participates in as a party, whether plaintiff, defendant, or in another official capacity, it must file a copy of this Memorandum Opinion and Order with its first pleading or filing in that particular court. This Court expresses no opinion as to the manner in which a particular court may use or not use such copy.

In re Pradaxa (Dabigatran Etexilate) Prods. Liab. Litig.

2013 U.S. Dist. LEXIS 173674 (S.D. Ill. Dec. 9, 2013)

<u>CASE MANAGEMENT ORDER NUMBER 50</u>

Regarding the PSC's Second Motion for Sanctions (Doc. 302)

HERNDON, Chief Judge:

I. INTRODUCTION

Presently before the Court is the PSC's motion seeking sanctions against Boehringer Ingelheim International GMBH ("BII") and Boehringer Ingelheim Pharmaceuticals, Inc. ("BIPI") (collectively, "the defendants") for various alleged discovery abuses (Doc. 302). The defendants filed a responsive brief on November 26, 2013 (Doc. 311). The Court heard oral argument on the motion on December 2, 2013. During oral argument, the defendants requested leave to file a supplemental response to address any new information alleged by the PSC during the hearing. The request for leave was granted and the defendants filed their supplemental brief on December 4, 2013 (Doc. 317).

The PSC's motion for sanctions addresses alleged discovery violations that fall into one of four categories: (1) the defendants' failure to preserve the custodial file of Professor Thorstein Lehr (a high-level scientist formerly employed by BII intricately involved in Pradaxa), as well as the failure to identify Prof. Lehr as a custodian with potentially relevant evidence; (2) the defendants' failure to preserve evidence relating to and/or untimely disclosure and production of material in the possession of the defendants' Sales Representatives, Clinical Science Consultants and Medical Science Liaisons; (3) the production issues related to the G Drive (one of the defendants' shared networks); and (4) the failure to preserve and/or untimely production of business related text messages on certain employees' cell phones.

A number of the alleged discovery violations are tied to the defendants' duty to preserve evidence relevant to this litigation and the gross inadequacy of the litigation hold that has been adopted by the defendants' to date. In the instant case, the defendants' preservation obligation was triggered in February of 2012 (as to BIPI) and, at the latest, April 2012 (as to BII). Further, there is no question that, as of June 2012, both defendants knew that nationwide Pradaxa product liability litigation, involving hundreds of cases, was imminent. Thus, while the defendants may have been able to justify adopting a narrow litigation hold as to *some* employees prior to June 2012, they cannot justify failing to adopt a company-wide litigation hold as of June 2012— when they knew nationwide Pradaxa product liability litigation was imminent.

II. BACKGROUND DISCOVERY ABUSES

A. Cumulative Effect of Ongoing Discovery Abuses

Unfortunately, this is not the defendants' first instance of discovery issues or having to answer serious allegations of discovery abuse and defend requests for court sanctions. Almost since its inception, this litigation has been plagued with discovery problems primarily associated with misconduct on the part of the defendants. The Court is continuously being called upon to address issues relating to untimely, lost, accidentally destroyed, missing, and/or "just recently discovered" evidence. The defendants' justifications for these discovery violations include but are not limited to the following: (1) placing the blame on others such as third-party vendors (production is delayed due to "vendor issues"), their own IT departments (we told IT to give the vendors full access to the database but for some reason IT provided the vendors with limited access), their own employees (the defendants' deponent did not understand that work related day planners should have been produced or the employees did not understand that work related text messages should have been retained and produced); (2) the defendants' and/or counsel's lack of experience in addressing litigation of this size; (3) the defendants' did not know, until recently, that this would turn into a large nationwide MDL; (4) unusual technical issues (despite our best efforts, that employee's hard drive was accidentally erased during a routine windows 7 update); (5) minimizing the alleged abuses (yes, we failed to produce this database but it was only 500,000 pages of documents compared to the 3 million we already produced or yes that material was accidentally destroyed but the PSC doesn't really need it); (6) blaming the PSC for submitting too many discovery requests that are broad in scope (only as an excuse after discovery violations are alleged but never as a proactive motion to limit discovery); and (7) the defendants' did not know about the "gaps" in their production until they began a comprehensive re-check or audit of the discovery process in September 2013.

The Court has been exceedingly patient and, initially, was willing to give the defendants the benefit of the doubt as to these issues. However, as the Court has warned the defendants in the past, when such conduct continues, there is a cumulative effect that the Court not only can but should take into account. Accordingly, the Court initially reviews the issues that have arisen to date.

B. Discovery Issues Preceding the PSC's First Motion for Sanctions

1. History of Discovery Abuses Outlined in the PSC's First Motion for Sanctions

The PSC's first motion for sanctions provides an overview of the discovery issues that had arisen as of the date of its filing (September 11, 2013) (Doc. 266). The Court will not recount all of the discovery issues detailed in that motion and instead incorporates them by reference. The Court also incorporates by reference the defendants' response to that motion (Doc. 271). The Court notes, however, that, for the most part, it agrees with and adopts the list of discovery abuses as detailed by the PSC. Further, with regard to the discovery issues that had arisen as of September 2013, the Court specifically notes the matters outlined below.

2. Cancellation of Depositions to Allow Defendants to Get Their House in Order

At the status conference on June 10, 2013 the Court cancelled approximately two months of depositions. In a subsequent Case Management Order, the Court reflected on the cancellations as follows:

> At the status conference on June 10, 2013, the Court approved the parties' request to cancel approximately two months of depositions. The cancellation was necessitated by a number of document production deficiencies in relation to the custodial files of former and present BIPI and BII employees identified by the PSC as deponents. The parties indicated that, in light of the document production deficiencies, the custodial depositions should be delayed to allow the defendants to get their house in order and to ensure that the PSC had complete custodial files prior to taking the subject depositions. The parties further represented that the depositions could be cancelled and rescheduled without delaying the bellwether trial dates already in place. The Court concluded the requested cancellation was in the best interest of the litigation and directed the parties to confer and negotiate a revised document production and pretrial schedule that maintained the bellwether trial dates already in place.

(CMO 38, Doc. 231 p. 1)

3. CMO 38 and the Court's Findings Regarding Certain Discovery Abuses

The PSC alerted the Court to problematic supplemental custodial file productions that included thousands of pages of "old" documents (documents that should have already been produced) and the production of otherwise incomplete custodial files. The Court found, in relevant part, as follows:

> Although some of the supplemental productions may have been made for legitimate reasons (vendor issues, technical problems, supplemental privilege review), the Court takes issue with the lack of transparency in alerting the Court or the PSC to matters that delayed the production of complete custodial files on the dates ordered by this Court. In general, the Court finds that BIPI failed to timely produce or timely respond to discovery as outlined by the plaintiffs letter-brief.
>
> In addition, the Court is particularly concerned with what appears to be a unilateral decision by BIPI to withhold "highly confidential" documents from the custodial files of non-German custodians—without informing the Court or the PSC that such documents were being withheld.... BIPI's unilateral decision to do so violated this Court's orders. Considering the above, the Court finds that BIPI inappropriately withheld "highly confidential" documents contrary to its agreement with the PSC and with this Court's orders.

(CMO 38, Doc. 231 pp. 5–8). As a result of the Court's findings, the Court adopted a revised production schedule (CMO 37, Doc. 230). Further, the Court imposed a certification requirement on BIPI and BII (CMO 38, Doc. 231 p. 8). The certification required both defendants "to provide a certification attesting to the completeness of productions."

C. The Court's Ruling Regarding the PSC's First Motion for Sanctions

On September 18, 2013, after hearing oral argument on the PSC's first motion for sanctions, the Court ruled from the bench. The following are relevant excerpts from that ruling:

> The Court finds here today that the defendant has violated or failed to meet either the letter or spirit of the Court's orders relative to discovery in a number of respects. It's hard for the Court, in this context and on this record to determine exactly where the fault lies in relation to the questions that I gave to Mr. Schmidt. I am not provided with the information. As I asked Mr. Schmidt, there could be outright deliberate violation of the order for the purpose of delaying production. It could be that there is gross negligence on the part of employees. There could be a failure of leadership at BIPI or BII in failing to make the employees understand their responsibilities.
>
> The upshot is, however, that the defendants have simply failed to follow the Court's orders. I agree with the list that was—I asked the plaintiffs to provide a list of what they thought were failures on the part of the defendants. I agree with that list, adopt it for the purpose of this order. I find for the remedy that I will fashion that I need not rule upon the motive that

the plaintiffs suggest, but I also agree and find that there have been the additional violations since September 11, the five that Mr. Katz set out. I have in my notes the entire list, but for purposes of this order I'll simply adopt the list by reference. They're so numerous, which is one of the things that's so distressing to me.

(Doc. 277 p. 92 l. 23–p. 93 l. 22)

I've never seen a litigation where the problems are just ongoing and continual, and every month or every week there's an issue of this failure and that failure and the other failure. It just is astounding. The reason, that it's because of the volume or because of the scope or because of the breadth or because of the this or that, the vendor or this other or that other, that's fine in the early going perhaps but as the litigation matures the reasons just don't make sense and just simply can't be tolerated by the Court.

So it finally got to the point where we last met on September the 4th where I simply drew a line and said, The next time I hear of a failure we're going to talk about this in court with employees from the defendants, and it just took a matter of a few hours before I heard about the next failure. So there simply has to be a way to make this stop and to resolve once and for all this issue of failure after failure, and, in my eyes, violation after violation after violation of this Court's orders. It gets to the point where, from the Court's viewpoint, it's not simply working through rough patches and how to handle litigation, but a simple disregard of the Court's orders regardless of the motivation.

So throughout these countless discussions over these issues and defendants' counsel doing everything they could to try to minimize the overall impact of these violations, the Court has just become frustrated beyond comprehension with these violations, some causing delays, some causing extraordinary delays, others just simply being glitches in the process of trying to get these cases in a posture to either be tried or resolved. And the ultimate goal, of course, giving the medical community an answer to this issue, giving the defendant an answer to this issue, giving the plaintiffs an answer to the issues, and performing the duties that we're all here to perform.

My conclusion, therefore—and I agree with the plaintiffs. I'm not sure if Mr. Katz kept count of the number of times they used "totality" or not, as he did with the defendant's use of words, but I agree that the totality of the circumstance here is and the totality of the violations is what counts. If you violate a Court order and remedy it, you don't get to start from scratch as far as I'm concerned. Your conduct is what it is, and if the conduct continues it's—there is a cumulative effect that the Court not only can but should take into account as time goes on.

And so my finding and conclusion is that there has been a clear pattern of numerous and substantial violations of the Court's many orders that have occurred in the past. I believe these have prejudiced the Court prejudiced the plaintiffs, I'm sorry, and have held this Court and demonstrated a holding of this Court in low regard, and they have amounted to a contumacious disregard for its authority. Under Rule 37 and the Court's inherent authority, I have available to me a number of options, one of which, of course, is the option which the plaintiffs seek, which is to strike the defendant's pleadings in whole or in part. It's my finding that that is an option which is too draconian. I will not exercise my discretion in that regard. If this were a single plaintiff and a single defendant, perhaps that would be an appropriate response, but I choose not to exercise my option in that regard. However, I find that an appropriate response would be a couple of things: One, to impose a fine on the defendant, and two, to impose certain mandatory injunctions on the defendant. And my order is as follows:

In accordance with my inherent authority, in accordance with Rule 37, I hereby sanction the defendants by ordering them to pay a fine in the registry of this court in the amount of $29,540. For anybody that's done the math quickly, that amounts to $20 per case, not a very drastic amount, I don't believe. However, the defendant should understand I also believe in progressive discipline should this Court have to visit this issue again.

I further order the defense counsel, together with the five officers who appeared here today, to oversee a communication to all known witnesses — and this is the mandatory injunction part — and custodians of every known or potential source of discoverable material to do an immediate search for any yet undisclosed materials that are relevant in the broadest possible definition of that word to this litigation and to advise counsel of its existence by Monday of next week.

I understand you said you've been conducting an audit, but I absolutely do not know what that consists of, but I want some sort of communication from you folks that are involved in overseeing of this litigation something in writing that makes it quite clear to everybody that has some sort of control over discoverable material, so they have no way to mistake their duties and obligations, to make sure they search their records high and low for anything that's discoverable, and to report their results by Monday. If any — a witness or custodian is not present at the place where they maintain such records or discoverable material, they're to do so within two days of returning to said location, if they're on vacation, they're out of the office, whatever that circumstance may be.

The communication which conveys this instruction shall describe in detail what is required of the witness or custodian and shall provide the name and contact information of a person with specific legal knowledge whom the witness or custodian may communicate with for information in the event he or she has any questions about what must be disclosed. The communication must also suggest that any individual questions of inclusion — in other words, if they wonder whether a matter of material is discoverable or not, should be resolved on the side of assuming that disclosure to counsel is the best course, and counsel can thereafter examine the material for exclusion, if appropriate. This may have already been done. Mr. Schmidt referred to it in his argument, but for depositions in the past that were cancelled as a result—this continues with a mandatory injunction part. For depositions in the past that were cancelled as a result of the defendants' failure to timely produce documents and for which defendants have not already agreed to reimburse, the plaintiffs may petition the Court to have their expenses reimbursed by defendants for appearing if no part of the deposition took place. In such event, expenses of Judge Stack will be borne solely by the defendant. For future depositions, should a deposition be cancelled due to the failure of defendants to timely produce material which it was required to produce, and no part of the deposition was taken, plaintiffs may petition the Court to have their expenses reimbursed by defendants. In such event expenses of Judge Stack shall be borne solely by the defendants. Once again, if defendants agree to the reimbursement, plaintiffs need not petition the Court.

In the event of a petition by plaintiffs for reimbursement, plaintiffs shall provide the Court with detail regarding the reason for the reimbursement, an itemization for the expenses they seek reimbursement, and shall include— for the expenses they seek for reimbursement. Plaintiffs shall forward a copy to defendants, who shall have 14 days to respond. If they intend to contest the request, that is, if the Court grants the request, the action by the Court automatically means Judge Stack's expenses for the cancelled deposition shall be borne solely by the defendant.

As a further mandatory injunction, should a scheduled deposition be cancelled due to an alleged failure of defendants to abide by discovery order of this Court and is the only deposition scheduled for that location, whether that venue is outside or within the United States, the parties are hereby directed to submit the facts of the occurrence to the Court within seven days of its occurrence. In addition to the facts, the parties will submit to the Court the available dates they suggest the deposition should be reset, given the need to examine the late-filed material and the upcoming deposition schedules, together with the names of the likely lead interrogators for the deposition. Court will then select a date for the scheduled—for rescheduling the deposition and will select a venue for the deposition, most likely the city of the main office of the lead interrogator, or St. Louis, as the Court determines is the reasonable location.

Should the defendants continue to violate discovery orders this Court has entered, the Court will consider, on motion by the plaintiffs or its own motion, further sanctions, including all sanctions authorized by Federal Rule of Civil Procedure 37, or its inherent authority. Furthermore, if the Court is forced to hold such a hearing the defendant can expect to produce at that hearing certain employees as designated by the Court, pursuant to its inherent authority, for testimony so that the Court can determine the nature of defendants' good faith in complying with the Court's order announced today, as well as their good faith in complying with the discovery orders generally in this litigation.

(Doc. 277 p. 95 l. 10–p. 102 l.1)

D. The Court's Expectations with Respect to the Audit

As part of the Court's oral ruling addressing the PSC's first motion for sanctions, the Court ordered the defendants to take the necessary steps to locate any yet undiscovered material and to report back to the Court ("the audit"). The Court did not expect the "audit" it was ordering to uncover voluminous or broad based materials. Given an expected limited scoped and the already very untimely nature of the disclosures, the Court required completion within mere days. The audit has revealed some gaps in discovery that the Court expected to find. For example, emails such as those of Dr. Clemons' which were not stored in his custodial file and a few BIPI and BII custodians who reported finding some additional documents not previously disclosed. The Court does not now take umbrage with these matters because given the issues that had long plagued this litigation which were discussed at the first sanction hearing, it was anticipated that such matters, hopefully minimal in number, would be uncovered by the court-ordered audit.

There are, however, a growing number of "gaps" in production to which the Court takes considerable exception. The Court has asked repeatedly throughout the many discussions about discovery problems, and at the first sanction hearing, how these problems could be occurring and for such a duration of time. The answer is now clear to the Court. The defendants have taken a too narrow and an incremental approach to its "company-wide" litigation hold.

The Court has been relying on the common meaning of the words that that the defendants have a company-wide litigation hold on all persons who have custody of any documentation relevant to Pradaxa. The production requests of the plaintiffs are so broad as to cover any possible derivation of means to document someone's thoughts, words and deeds short of attaching electrodes to their scalps and electronically downloading what is contained in their minds. This extreme statement is meant to convey that all of the materials that are discussed in this order were clearly covered by production requests and further anticipated by the Court as subject to the "company-wide" litigation hold.

The Court has examined the defendants' "holds," submitted *in camera*, and does not take umbrage with the language or scope thereof. As it turns out, the problem was in the implementation. For example, the Court learned at the second sanction hearing that the defendants chose to incrementally place holds on certain classes of employees, and have unilaterally chosen not to hold regarding an employee because the company decided he didn't fit the description of "important enough" and wasn't specified by the PSC. Further, while their vendor was given access to one part of a computer drive, it did not have password access to a subpart with relevant material.

All of the materials discussed heretofore, should have been produced long, long before now. Some may never be able to be produced.

The defendants have had many conversations with the Court regarding discovery problems. During these conversations, the defendants did not hesitate to voice concerns regarding issues associated with the timing of producing certain documents, data or files. The defendants, however, never sought leave of Court to delay the implementation of the litigation hold on the premise that it was too burdensome—financially or logistically. Therefore, the Court relied on the presumption that the defendants were preserving all relevant documents of every description. It only came to light recently that such was not the case. The Court did not expect that nor was that the subject of specific discussion in the last sanction debate.

III. CASE-SPECIFIC BACKGROUND AND LEGAL AUTHORITY WITH RESPECT TO THE DEFENDANTS' DUTY TO PRESERVE

A. When the Duty to Preserve Arose

1. Relevant Legal Authority

The duty to preserve documents and material that may be relevant to litigation generally arises with the filing of the complaint. *See Norman-Nunnery*, 625 F.3d at 428–429. However, The Seventh Circuit has held that the obligation to preserve evidence arises when a party "knew, or should have known, that litigation was imminent." *Trask-Morton v. Motel 6 Operating L.P.*, 534 F.3d 672, 681 (7th Cir. 2008).

2. When the Duty to Preserve was Triggered in This Case

In the instant case, as the Court has previously concluded, BIPI's duty to preserve material relevant to this litigation arose in February 2012 when it received a lean letter regarding the first post-launch Pradaxa product liability suit. BII has indicated that it issued a litigation hold shortly thereafter—in April 2012. For purposes of this order, the Court concludes that BII's duty to preserve evidence relevant to this litigation arose—at the latest—in April 2012.

The Court further notes that at least as of June 2012, the defendants were acutely aware that nationwide litigation involving hundreds of cases (if not more) was imminent. On May 31, 2012, Plaintiff Vera Sellers filed a Motion for Transfer of Actions Pursuant to 28 U.S.C. § 1407. *See* MDL No. 2385 (Doc. 1), *In re Pradaxa Prod. Liab. Litig.* ("MDL Motion"). At that time, approximately 30 product liability actions involving the prescription drug Pradaxa were pending in 14 different federal district courts. The MDL Motion stated that at least "500 additional complaints" were expected to be filed in the near future (MDL Motion p. 2). In June 2012, the defendants filed their responsive brief and included the following argument regarding where the growing number of Pradaxa cases should be consolidated:

Beyond the pending actions, Plaintiff states that "more than 500 additional Complaints will be filed in the near future." Given the nationwide soliciting, the distribution of forthcoming cases would be expected to be spread across the United States. This is, in fact, what has happened. Even after the "wave" of cases were filed in the Southern

District of Illinois, followed by the instant MDL request, various plaintiffs filed cases in the Eastern District of Louisiana (including a purported class action), Middle District of Tennessee, Eastern District of Kentucky, Southern District of Florida, Northern District of Ohio, Eastern District of New York, and the District of South Carolina (removed). This distribution reinforces the national scope of the Pradaxa litigation — both in terms of where the cases stand today and where they are likely to be filed.

MDL No. 2385, *In re Pradaxa Prod. Liab. Litig* (Doc. 54 p. 9). Considering the above, there is absolutely no question that the defendants knew nationwide Pradaxa product liability litigation involving hundreds (if not more) cases was imminent. Therefore, the defendants cannot contend, in good faith, as they attempted to do at the sanctions hearing, that they did not understand the size and scope of this litigation until recently. Nor can they contend that their decision to adopt an extremely limited litigation hold was based on an appropriate good faith belief that this litigation would be limited in size.

B. Scope of Duty to Preserve

The general scope of discovery is defined by Fed. Rule Civ. Proc. 26(b)(1) as follows:

> Parties may obtain discovery regarding any nonprivileged matter that is relevant to any party's claim or defense — including the existence, description, nature, custody, condition, and location of any documents or other tangible things and the identity and location of persons who know of any discoverable matter. For good cause, the court may order discovery of any matter relevant to the subject matter involved in the action. Relevant information need not be admissible at the trial if the discovery appears reasonably calculated to lead to the discovery of admissible evidence. "The key phrase in this definition — 'relevant to the subject matter involved in the pending action' — has been construed broadly to encompass any matter that bears on, or that reasonably could lead to other matter that could bear on, any issue that is or may be in the case." *Oppenheimer Fund, Inc. v. Sanders* 437 U.S. 340, 351, 98 S. Ct. 2380, 2389, 57 L. Ed. 2d 253 (1978).

The broad scope of discovery outlined in Rule 26 is vital to our system of justice. *See Hickman v. Taylor*, 329 U.S. 495, 507, 67 S. Ct. 385, 392, 91 L. Ed. 451 (U.S. 1947) ("Mutual knowledge of all the relevant facts gathered by both parties is essential to proper litigation. To that end, either party may compel the other to disgorge whatever facts he has in his possession."). It was adopted, in part, to restore a sense of fair play and to combat a growing sense of frustration with the often contentious nature of litigation. *See e.g.*, Roscoe Pound, *The Causes of Popular Dissatisfaction with the Administration of Justice, Address Delivered Before the Convention of the American Bar Association* (Aug. 26, 1906), in 35 F.R.D. 241, 273 (1964).

As other district courts in this Circuit have recognized, this vital element of our discovery process "would be a dead letter if a party could avoid [its duty to disclose] by the simple expedient of failing to preserve documents that it does not wish to produce." *Danis v. USN Communications, Inc.*, 2000 U.S. Dist. LEXIS 16900, 2000 WL 1694325, *1 (N.D. Ill. Oct. 20 2000) (Schenkier, M.J.). "Therefore, fundamental to the duty of production of information is the threshold duty to preserve documents and other information that may be relevant in a case." *Id.*

Commiserate with Rule 26(b)(1), the scope of the duty to preserve evidence is broad, encompassing any relevant evidence that the non-preserving party knew or reasonably could foresee would be relevant to imminent or pending litigation. *See, e. g., Langley*, 107 F.3d at 514; *Melendez v. Illinois Bell Tel. Co.*, 79 F.3d 661, 671 (7th Cir. 1996); *Marrocco v. General Motors Corp.*, 966 F.2d 220, 223–225 (7th Cir. 1992). Thus, once the duty to preserve is triggered, the party owes a duty to preserve evidence that may be sought during discovery and should implement a plan to find and preserve relevant evidence. Finally, a party's duty to preserve information is not a passive obligation; it must be discharged actively. See *Marrocco*, 966 F.2d at 224–25.

C. Timeline of Issues Relevant to Duty to Preserve

The Court notes the following with respect to the defendants' preservation obligation in the instant case:

• February 2012 — BIPI's duty to preserve is triggered

• April 2012 (at the latest) — BII's duty to preserve is triggered

• June 2012 — the defendants know that nationwide litigation involving hundreds (if not more) Pradaxa product liability cases is imminent

• July 13, 2012 — The Court and Counsel for BIPI Discuss the Duty to Preserve. Counsel indicates that BIPI has established a litigation hold and represents that, with respect to custodians, the company issues a physical document preservation notice to custodians of relevant evidence

Transcript of July 13, 2012 Status Conference

Page 22 of 33

17 *THE COURT:* So one of the things that I was

18 concerned about — and it turns out it wasn't included in

19 your production order — and that is preservation. Do you

20 have a preservation direction issue corporate-wi[d]e?

21 *MR. HUDSON:* Yes, Your Honor.

22 *THE COURT:* People understand, obviously, this is

23 not your first — presume this is not your first piece of

24 litigation in this corporation.

25 *MR. HUDSON:* It's not, and the cases filed here

Page 23 of 33

1 were not the first filed cased, so there were preservation

2 orders in effect before these cases were even filed.

3 *THE COURT:* So explain to me essentially how

4 that—without revealing any attorney-client privilege, how

5 does that work and how is it maintained and how is it

6 policed in effect? Briefly. I don't need—

7 *MR. HUDSON:* Let me think about how to best explain

8 this. I know the process but I want to be careful about

9 discussing in open court the process the corporation uses

10 for this, because there are attorneys involved, but there is

11 a physical document preservation notice that is issued to

12 potential custodians of relevant evidence. There's a

13 process by which the custodians confirm acknowledgment of

14 the obligation to comply with the litigation hold, and that

15 is monitored and followed up on.

16 And I think—Your Honor, does that adequately

17 answer your question or would you like me to go into more

18 detail there?

19 *THE COURT:* No, that's fine. And in general, there

20 are officers, coordinators, employees who are charged with

21 overseeing the preservation?

22 *MR. HUDSON:* Individuals within the legal

23 department, and there are contact points identified on the

24 preservation notice as well, as far as who the people are

25 involved in that process. So the people charged with the

Page 24 of 33

1 preservation obligation receive the document preservation

2 notice, actually know who—in addition to the person who's

3 issued the letter from the legal department, but the person

4 they can go to with questions, yes.

(Doc. 57 p. 22 l.17–p. 24 l.3)

- November 5, 2012—Counsel for BII confirms that BII is aware of the Court's preservation order (Doc. 69 p. 11 l.14–17) ("As I told the Court in chambers, BII is aware of the preservation obligations, and document preservation notices went out prior to the cases being transferred to this MDL.").

IV. POTENTIALLY SANCTIONABLE CONDUCT PRESENTLY IN ISSUE

A. Thorsten Lehr

1. Background

Professor Thorsten Lehr is a pharmacometrician formerly employed by BII (Doc. 311 p. 9). While working for BII, Prof. Lehr was a high-level scientist that worked on Pradaxa and published articles on Pradaxa as a lead author (Doc. 302 p. 5). Prof. Lehr was responsible for quantitative analysis relating to the interaction between Dabigatran and specific patient populations (Doc. 302-5 p. 5). Prof. Lehr left employ at BI at the end of September 2012 — well after the defendants were under a duty to preserve evidence relevant to this litigation (Doc. 302-4 p. 6; Doc 302-5 p. 5). Dr. Lehr is currently employed by Saarland University (Doc. 302-5 p. 5). There is a cooperation agreement between BII and Saarland University under which Prof. Lehr continues to have access to certain Pradaxa clinical trial data (Doc. 302-5 p. 5).

According to the PSC, BII never disclosed Prof. Lehr in any answers to the PSC's interrogatories. Further, Prof. Lehr was not on the list of custodians with relevant knowledge provided by BII. *Id.*

The PSC did not learn of Prof. Lehr's relevance to this litigation until September 25, 2013 when Lehr was identified during the deposition of one of the defendants' employees, Martina Brueckman (Doc. 317-1 p.6). That same day, the PSC requested Prof. Lehr's custodial file be produced by October 7, 2013 (Doc. 317-1). BII did not respond to the request for production of Prof. Lehr's custodial file for two weeks and at that time indicated that it would need 45 days to produce his custodial file (invoking a case management order previously adopted by the Court) (Doc. 317-1).

On October 25, 2013, in a letter to the Court, BII stated that Prof. Lehr "was not subject to a litigation hold when he left BII because he had not been identified as a custodian" (Doc. 302-5 p. 5). On November 4, 2013, BII again informed the Court that Prof. Lehr was not subject to a litigation hold when he left the company because he had not been identified as a custodian (Doc. 302-4 p. 6), On November 7, 2013, counsel for BII (Beth S. Rose) provided an affidavit with additional information pertaining to Prof. Lehr (Doc. 302-6). The affidavit provides, in relevant part, as follows:

> Contemporaneous with this Affidavit BII is making the production of responsive e-mails from Thorsten Lehr. Thorsten Lehr is a former BII employee who formally left the company at the end of September 2012. At the time he left, Prof. Lehr was not identified as a custodian and, therefore, was not subject to the document preservation notice. We have confirmed with Prof. Lehr that when he left the company, he did not take his workstation or any other documents with him. Prof. Lehr's workstation, user share, and paper documents are not available to be collected. The only part of Prof. Lehr's custodial file available for collection is his e-mails.

(Doc. 302-6 ¶ 2). In other words, with the exception of Prof. Lehr's emails, BII failed to preserve Prof. Lehr's custodial file at a time when it was under a duty to do so.

BII has stated that they chose not to preserve Dr. Lehr's custodial file because, at the time of his departure in September 2012, he had not been identified as a custodian. This statement lends itself to one of two interpretations. Either BII is asserting that it did not realize that Prof. Lehr was a custodian with potentially relevant information and therefore failed to preserve his custodial file when he left the company; or BII is asserting that because the PSC had not yet requested Dr. Lehr's custodial file, it had no duty to preserve Dr. Lehr's custodial file (even if it contained information relevant to this litigation). Both interpretations are problematic for BII.

2. BII Cannot Believably Contend it Did Not Recognize Prof. Lehr as a Custodian with Potentially Relevant Information

BII cannot believably contend it did not know Prof. Lehr's custodial file contained information relevant to this litigation. Prof. Lehr was unquestionably a high-level scientist actively involved in working on Pradaxa. For instance, in an email dated May 31, 2012, Dr. Yasser Khder (employed by BII) introduces "Dr. Thorsten Lehr" to his "colleagues" as "our company expert for dabigatran" (Doc. 317-1 p. 16). He goes on to state that Prof. Lehr "did all the M&S for the [REDACTED BY THE COURT] program (Doc. 317-1 p. 16). Dr. Lehr will get in contact with you to further discuss the different aspects to this request" (Doc. 317-1 p. 16).

The PSC has also learned that Prof. Lehr co-authored at least 10 Dabigatran (Pradaxa) articles published between September 2011 and September 2013 (Doc. 317-1 pp. 9–14). Further, although Prof. Lehr is no longer employed by BII, he continues to work with BII scientists on future Pradaxa publications (Doc. 317-1 p. 14).

Even more telling, is a group of company emails exchanged in 2011 and 2012 reflecting an internal debate over whether a scientific paper being drafted by Prof. Lehr (the "exposure paper") should include Prof. Lehr's conclusions regarding Pradaxa's therapeutic range. In the exposure paper, Prof. Lehr (and his co-authors) concluded, in the early versions of the paper, that both safety and efficacy of dabigatran are related to plasma concentrations and conclude that there is a therapeutic range for Pradaxa and further specify what that range is. (Doc. 317-1 p. 20).

These emails reveal Dr. Lehr's desire to publish a paper that included a therapeutic range for Pradaxa was highly controversial. An email from Dr. Andreas Clemens, dated December 19, 2011, demonstrates the discussion and disagreement flowing through the company regarding Dr. Lehr's conclusions (Doc. 317-1 p. 23). As does a July 30, 2012 email from Stuart Connolly (Doc. 317-1 p. 29). Ultimately, an email from Dr. Jeffrey Friedman, dated October 23, 2012, seems to require a revised version of the exposure paper without inclusion of the therapeutic levels suggested by Prof. Lehr (Doc. 317-1 p. 31). An email from Dr. Clemens to Prof. Lehr, dated October 24, 2012, confirms that (Doc. 317-1 p. 33).

The following email describes Prof. Lehr's position on the matter at the end of October, 2012.

<u>October 31, 2012 email from Dr. Andreas Clemens</u>

Thorsten wants to tailor the message according our ideas. I see value in this manuscript especially with regard to a manuscript which will in the next step focus on lab levels (aPTT) to give the physicians an understanding what they have to expect in specific situations regarding aPTT. The world is crying for this information—but the tricky part is that we have to tailor the messages smart. Thorsten wants to do that.

(Doc. 317-1 p. 17).

Eventually, another scientist, Paul Reilly, was tasked with revising the exposure paper. The following email from Paul Reilly further demonstrates the internal debate over inclusion of an optimal therapeutic range in the exposure paper:

I have been facing heavy resistance internally on this paper about the concept of a therapeutic range, at least stating it outright. Perhaps you can help me with solving this dilemma. I am working on a revision to deal with this and I will come back to you with it. I think they just don't want the message that one range fits all, it's patient specific.

(Doc. 317-1 p. 28).

The emails also reveal the importance of keeping the debated issue confidential. Dr. Clemens October 24, 2012 email to Prof. Lehr (above) closes with a statement written in German, roughly translated as follows:

I think—"the banana is still shuttered." Please treat this confidential because Jeff currently interacts with Paul Reilly directly—and I do not know if they know this is actually on file.

(Doc. 317-1 p. 33). Prof. Lehr subsequently responded to Dr. Clemens' request for confidentiality as follows:

I will keep it absolutely confidential! I'm personally very disappointed about the exposure-response manuscript. I have put a LOT of effort and time into the analysis. But I don't like the way how the manuscript is written and the message conveyed. I'm working again on a revision of the document and I hope that Paul will consider them. It is the last time, that I agree to put people as first author who were not involved in data analysis. Let's try to get this manuscript in a shape that everybody is happy. Maybe we need a TC (Jeff, Paul, Andreas, Thorsten) to discuss open issues.

(Doc. 317-1 p. 34).

In addition, the emails exchanged during this time period demonstrate that the exposure paper and Dr. Lehr's controversial conclusions regarding an optimal dosing range for Pradaxa were being considered and discussed in the highest levels of the company and with the defendants' legal team. For example, consider the following emails:

<u>December 19, 2011 email from Dr. Janet Schnee to Dr. Andreas Clemens</u>

I noticed this email only this evening, but have now forwarded [Dr. Lehr's draft exposure paper] to the US product lawyer for an opinion.

(Doc. 317-1 p. 24)

June 4, 2012 email from Dr. Paul Reilly

Exposure response is definitely on the OC radar and I have been heavily pressed to revise and submit the manuscript. It has been "on hold" for almost 6 months. I had to wait several weeks for some analyses from Thorsten, at his request.

(Doc. 317-1 p. 25)

July 16, 2012 email from Dr. Lehr to Paul Reilly

I met Jeff last Thursday. We discussed the ER [exposure paper] analysis together with management. As management liked it (and also Jeff seemed to like it), I believe we have some tailwind. Maybe you can meet with Jeff and see how to move forward.

(Doc. 317-1 p. 26)

Considering the material pertaining to Prof. Lehr, including the email excerpts noted above and those not excerpted for confidentiality purposes but which the Court was able to read in the motions filed under seal, it is evident that Dr. Lehr was a prominent scientist at BII that played a vital role in researching Pradaxa. The defendants' management, legal team, and other top-scientists were familiar with Prof. Lehr's work and communicated with him regarding the same. The Court is stunned that Prof. Lehr was not identified by the defendants as a custodian with potentially relevant knowledge about Pradaxa. Further, given the above, it is evident that the defendants knew that Prof. Lehr's custodial file contained information relevant to this litigation in September 2012 when Prof. Lehr left his employ with BII. The emails also may lead a reasonable person to infer a motive for the defendant to abstain from placing a litigation hold on his materials, including the early versions of the exposure paper. The entire debate is relevant, or at least conceivably relevant, to this litigation and without question any documents, no matter who generated them, should have been the object of the litigation hold.

3. The Duty to Preserve is not Defined by What has or has not Been Requested by Opposing Counsel

The second possible interpretation of BII's statement regarding why it chose not to preserve Dr. Lehr's custodial file is that BII is blaming the PSC for failing to identify Dr. Lehr as a custodian. In other words, a party only has a duty to preserve relevant evidence that has actually been requested by the opposing party. This position is nonsense. The very purpose of the duty to preserve, is to protect potentially relevant material so it is available for production when and if the opposing party requests that material. Furthermore, the defendant, not the plaintiff, is in the best position to identify persons such as Dr. Lehr.

4. Final Points Regarding the Defendants' Supplemental Response

During oral argument, the PSC showed the Court draft version number 5 of the exposure paper. The PSC raised questions regarding whether draft versions 1–4 had been destroyed. In their supplemental response, the defendants contend that their productions have included seven earlier distinct drafts of the exposure paper (presumably from sources other than Prof. Lehr's custodial file), dating back to January 2011 (Doc. 317 p. 2). This argument misses the point. The defendants do not get to pick and choose which evidence they want to produce from which sources. At issue here are the missing documents and material contained in Dr. Lehr's custodial file. The question is, of the draft versions stored on Dr. Lehr's work stations, what was lost when the defendants failed to preserve Dr. Lehr's custodial file.

The defendants also argue that because their preservation obligation only attached in February of 2012, they were under no duty to produce documents created prior to February of 2012 (Doc. 317 p. 2). This contention distorts the nature of the duty to preserve. The fact that the defendants preservation obligation did not attach until February of 2012 (or, at the latest, April of 2012 for BII), does not mean that the defendants are entitled to destroy documents created prior to that date. It means that as of February 2012, the defendants have a duty to preserve any documents in the defendants' control—even those created before February 2012—that are potentially relevant to this litigation and destruction occurring after February 2012 is a violation of that duty.

Finally, the defendants contend that because they have produced discovery from other sources that reveals the internal dispute over the exposure paper and over issues relating to therapeutic range, the failure to preserve Prof. Lehr's custodial file must be innocent (Doc. 317 pp. 3–4). In light of all the other discovery abuses that have been discussed herein, this argument does not win the day. One does not know what annotations are or were contained on the personal versions of Dr. Lehr or what statements he made in his "share room" space about the controversy that was brewing. Plaintiffs are entitled to discovery on such matters for interrogation or cross examination purposes.

B. Inadequate Litigation Hold for Pradaxa Sales Representatives, MSLs and CSCs

1. Background

The Court will now address issues related to the litigation hold as it was applied (or not applied) to the defendants' Sales Representatives, Clinical Science Consultants (CSCs) and Medical Science Liaisons (MSLs). First, however, the Court will provide some background with regard to CSCs and MSLs.

CSCs are specialized sales representatives. In November 2011, CSCs began delivering unbranded disease state messages to health care providers concerning atrial fibrillation ("A-fib") (Pradaxa is used to reduce the risk of stroke and blood clots in people with A-fib not caused by a heart valve problem) (Doc. 271 p. 8). Purportedly, CSCs met with physicians to discuss A-fib without reference to Pradaxa (Doc. 271 p. 8). According to the defendants, the CSCs received Pradaxa-specific training in September 2012 to address physician questions they were receiving from physicians related to Pradaxa. Notably, the existence of the CSC sales force was never disclosed by the defendants even though this information was specifically requested by the PSC in prior discovery and in the Defendant Fact Sheet ("DFS") (Doc. 266 p. 18–19; Doc. 302-8 § II.C). Instead, the PSC discovered the existence of CSCs only when they noticed the word "CSC" in other documents the defendants had produced (Doc. 266 p. 19). The PSC began asking about the CSCs by title in July 2013 (Doc. 266 p. 19). The defendants repeatedly told the PSC that all of the CSC physician call information was contained in the VISTA database and had already been produced (Doc. 266 p. 19). The PSC was suspicious of this answer and continued to press the issue. Only after another five conversations with the defendants was it learned that there was in fact a separate field within VISTA that contained the CSC data and that this field had not been disclosed to the PSC and had not been produced (Doc. 266 p. 20). Defendants insisted that this was an unintentional oversight and on September 10, 2013 provided the PSC with the missing information (Doc. 271 p. 8).

MSLs are another separate specialized group within BIPI. The defendants describe MSLs as "individuals with medical and scientific backgrounds whose role is to interact with health care providers who are deemed to be scientific experts and key opinion leaders" (Doc. 271 p. 9). According to the PSC, MSLs were "responsible for making direct contact with a physician under the auspices of having a scientific conversation about a-fib, Warfarin and other subjects that could not be discussed as part of the direct promotion of Pradaxa" (Doc. 266 p. 20). Information about MSL visits with physicians is contained in what is known as the BOLD database. The existence of BOLD was not disclosed to the PSC in discovery or as part of the 30(b)(6) deposition process. Instead, the existence of MSLs and BOLD was disclosed to the PSC only in relation to the PSC uncovering the CSC issue and only when the PSC asked the defendants if there were any other forces that called on physicians (Doc. 266 p. 21). The defendants "[did] not dispute that the BOLD database and relevant MSLs should have been identified and produced to Plaintiffs earlier in this litigation (Doc. 271 p. 10). They insisted, however, that this failing was another innocent inadvertent mistake.

2. Inadequate Litigation Hold

In recent weeks, it has come to light that the defendants' litigation hold, as it relates to Pradaxa sales representatives, MSLs, and CSCs, has been grossly inadequate for a litigation of this scope and size. On November 4, 2013, the defendants informed the Court and the PSC that they had been "addressing questions recently raised at sales representative depositions that the volume of email produced for certain witnesses was smaller than expected," (Doc. 302-4 p. 2). The PSC had also raised concerns that individual sales representatives custodial files did not seem to go back sufficiently far in time (Doc. 311 p. 12). In reviewing these questions, the defendants decided to "examine the dates that the sales reps/CSCs/MSLs requested for the deposition became subject to the litigation hold" (Doc. 302-4 p. 2). This examination revealed following:

- When the defendants first instigated a litigation hold in February 2012, they only intended to apply the hold to the specific sales representatives who detailed specific plaintiffs physicians. It takes time, however, to identify each plaintiffs prescribing physician and the corresponding sales representative(s). Rather than taking steps (such as placing all Pradaxa sales representatives on a litigation hold) to preserve the relevant material while these specific sales representatives were identified, the defendants did nothing.

- It was not until September 26, 2012, at which point 127 cases were on file, that the defendants decided to "expand" the then non-existent litigation hold for Pradaxa sales representatives (Doc. 311-15 p. 2; Doc. 311 p. 13). Even then, however, the litigation hold was only applied to those Pradaxa sales representatives *currently* detailing Pradaxa (Doc. 311 p. 13).

- In March 2013, with 262 cases filed, the defendants finally decided to extend the litigation hold to all sales representatives who had ever detailed Pradaxa (Doc. 311 p. 13).

- The Clinical Science Consultants (CSCs) and Medical Science Liaisons (MSLs) who detailed Pradaxa were not included in the litigation hold until August 2013 (Doc. 311 p. 13). However, the only CSCs and MSLs included in *this* hold were the CSCs and MSLs who detailed the treating physicians in the bellwether cases.

- All CSCs and MSLs who detailed Pradaxa were not placed on litigation hold until sometime after August 2013 (the defendants responsive brief simply states that they "subsequently" added "the remaining CSCs and MSLs"—the Court suspects that "subsequently" means just before the defendants filed their responsive brief) (Doc. 311 p. 13).

The litigation hold described by the defendants is wholly inadequate in light of the size and scope of this litigation. The defendants were under a duty to preserve information that they knew or reasonably could foresee would be relevant to imminent or pending litigation. In the instant case, the duty to preserve arose in February 2012 for BIPI and in April 2012 (at the latest) for BII. Once the duty to preserve was triggered, the defendants owed a duty to preserve evidence that may be sought during discovery and should have implemented an adequate plan to find and preserve relevant evidence.

The defendants argue that the proportionality requirement of Rule 26 allowed them to implement an extremely narrow litigation hold. They contend it would have been unreasonable to require them to place, for example, all Pradaxa sales representatives on a litigation hold. That might be true if this was a regional case involving only a few plaintiffs with no indication of the litigation expanding into nationwide litigation. That, however, is not the scenario we are faced with. As discussed above, as of June 2012, the defendants were aware that nationwide Pradaxa product liability litigation involving hundreds of cases (if not more) was imminent. They argued this very fact before the MDL panel in June 2012. The Court is frankly amazed that the defendants could raise such an argument and now argue, before this Court, that they did not fully understand the broad scope of this litigation or the need to expand their litigation hold to *all* Pradaxa sales representatives, CSCs, and MSLs until March 2013 (sales representatives) and sometime after August 2013 (CSCs and MSLs) (*See* Doc. 311 pp. 12–13; Doc. 311 p. 13 ("Defendants expanded the scope of their sales representative preservation efforts as the litigation expanded in size"). Furthermore, there is nothing in any case management order nor can defendants point to any statement of the Court that can be interpreted as suggesting such a tailored litigation hold was acceptable. Defendants did not receive from the Court a protection order tailoring the litigation hold or managing in increments classes of employees on some timeline or on some case specific landmark when the litigation hold would kick in. There have been no regionally based markers designed to apply the litigation hold to certain sales or consulting staff based on case filings. The defendants' efforts to suggest they and they alone decided to implement such a proportionality test to the litigation hold smacks of a post-debacle argument in desperation to salvage a failed strategy regarding production evasion.

The defendants also argue that because they have produced certain databases and/or document repositories that warehouse relevant sales representative, CSC and MSL material any failings with regard to these employees' custodial files is of little or no consequence (Doc. 311 p. 10). For instance, the defendants note that they have produced approximately 45,000 pages of documents from the TEMPO database, which contains the documents used to train sales representatives about Pradaxa and the promotional pieces that the sales force is approved to use in detailing health care providers on Pradaxa, along with earlier drafts of these materials (Doc. 311 p. 10). The defendants note sales representatives have consistently testified they are not permitted to use and do not use material outside of the TEMPO database when detailing physicians (i.e. they only used the approved TEMPO material) (Doc. 311 p. 10). Obviously, the defendants contend, the PSC doesn't really need material from the sales representatives' custodial files, because the only material sales representatives used can be found in the TEMPO database.

This argument is ridiculous. The PSC is entitled to the requested material so they can determine for themselves whether the sales representatives only used approved material from the TEMPO database. In addition, they are entitled to review the files for other relevant information to utilize as a basis for cross examination. An example leaps to the fore, what if a sales representative has in his notes that he made some fraudulent representation about Pradaxa to a physician. Further, what if the rep said "as directed by so and so, I told Dr. X this and that" which is known by all to be patently false? Obviously, the training materials alone are not relevant and clearly the Court does not suggest that its hypothetical is accurate. However, if it were to prove true, the defendants' cannot deny such material is both relevant and discoverable.

C. The G Drive

The G Drive and T Drive are shared network drives made available to certain of defendants' employees. Defendants Letter to Court, October 7, 2013. According to the defendants, employees generally use these drives to store departmental data. *Id.* Within BIPI, this drive is known as the G Drive; within BII, it is known as the T Drive. Although potentially serious production issues have been identified with both the G Drive and the T Drive, only the production issues associated with the G Drive are presently before the Court.

The G Drive is not a single unified electronic storage area. It consists of over 1.8 million folders (Doc. 311 p. 17). Employees are granted access to the folders depending on the needs of their job (Doc. 311 p. 17). If an employee does not have access to a folder on the G Drive, it will not appear at all when he or she logs into the G Drive (Doc. 311 p. 17).

Pursuant to Case Management Order Number 17, the G Drive was scheduled to be produced on or before January 30, 2013 (Doc. 78 ¶ 14). In accord with the certification requirement imposed on the defendants as a result of earlier discovery violations (CMO 38 Doc. 231), the defendants provided an affidavit of completion of document production in relation to the G Drive on August 7, 2013 (Doc. 317-14 p. 43). The original G Drive production included approximately 3.5 million pages (Doc. 311 p. 18).

Shortly before the Court held a hearing on September 18, 2013 (to address the PSC's first motion for sanctions), the defendants alerted the PSC to potential problems with the G Drive production (October 7, 2013 Letter to the Court). The defendants indicated that approximately 500,000 documents/files (excluding attachments) from four out of the five G Drive directories were missed and, as a result, were not produced to the PSC (October 7, 2013 Letter to the Court). The defendants further indicated that the number of missed documents/files was expected to increase slightly when the fifth directory was searched (October 7, 2013 Letter to the Court).

Ultimately, the defendants determined that the documents/files were missed because the defendants' IT department failed to provide the third party vendor conducting the G Drive collection proper access to the G Drive (Doc. 311 pp. 17–18). More specifically, the IT department was tasked with providing the third party vendor with logins that would give the third party vendor full access to all folders in the G Drive (Doc. 311 p. 17). The IT department, however, failed to do this (Doc. 311 p. 17). Instead, the IT department gave the vendor "default" logins of the sort typically granted to new employees (Doc. 311 p. 17). These default logins did not have access to all G Drive folders, meaning the vendor was not aware of the existence of some of the folders and did not collect files from them (Doc. 311 p. 18). The defendants eventually produced the missing documents. That supplemental production contained approximately 400,000 pages. This sort of "mistake" early in this litigation would have been looked upon by the Court as just that, but as the rationale of this order makes clear, the reasonable inferences to be drawn from the actions of the defendant at this point in time are that such maneuverers are by design.

The PSC contends that the production indicates that there are numerous new G Drive storage areas that should have been revealed during 30(b)(6) depositions. It further contends that the late production has resulted in prejudice in that they do not yet know what is in it, it was produced in a disorganized manner, and they do not know who uses the new storage areas or what they are used for. The defendants contend that the production was not disorganized and complied with CMO 3 in all respects (with the exception of an error with a meta data field that has since been corrected) (Doc. 311 p. 18). The defendants further contend that no relevant documents from the G Drive have been lost because the G Drive does not have an auto delete function (Doc. 311 p. 18).

D. Text Messages

On June 28, 2012, before creation of the MDL, the PSC specifically requested that BIPI produce text messages (Doc. 302-9). The PSC made a similar request to BII on October 22, 2012 (Doc. 302-10). The defendants have admitted that the PSC did in fact request texts (Doc. 302-4 ("[t]exts were requested in discovery by both parties, and produced by neither, so far as we can tell."; Doc. 311 p. 14 (admitting that the PSC's document requests "included text messages in their boilerplate definition of 'document'"). Amazingly, the defendants' hold applicable to sales representatives, CSCs and MSLs did not expressly extend to text messages until October 18, 2013 or later (Doc. 302 p. 7). The defendants first alerted the Court and the PSC to the issue in a footnote in a letter dated October 25, 2013 (Doc. 302-5 p. 2 n.3). In the footnote, the defendants contend that they did not realize until mid-October that some employees had business related text messages on their cell/smart phones (Doc. 302-5 p. 2 n.3). The PSC (and the Court) question the plausibility of this claim considering the defendants have produced a document showing that the defendants directed their sales force to use texts to communicate with their supervisors, district managers, and others (Doc. 302-2). Further, the deposition testimony of employee Emily Baier raises further questions on this issue.

The defendants contend that they have "consistently included a broad definition of 'document' in the document preservation notices sent to potential custodians and — while the notices do not explicitly state 'text messages' — they do tell custodians to preserve all relevant documents in any form, particularly specifying that this includes electronic communications stored on hand held devices" (Doc. 311 p. 14). The defendants further contend that the late discovery of the existence of business related text messages on certain employees' phones is the fault of their employees (Doc. 311 p. 15 "Until October of 2013, however, BI custodians did not identify text messages among their responsive documents ..."). The Court does not accept this explanation. As noted above, the duty to preserve is not a passive obligation; it must be discharged actively. The defendants had a duty to ensure that their employees understood that text messages were included in the litigation hold. The defendants' own documentation directs employees to utilize text messaging as a form of business related communication. Questions should have been raised by the defendants prior to October 2013 when none of their employees were producing text messages.

Yet another, perhaps more egregious, example of the defendants failure to properly exercise a litigation hold with respect to employee text messages, is the revelation that the defendants failed to intervene in the automated deletion of employee text messages on company issued phones. The PSC has discovered that many employees utilized company issued cell phones. Apparently, the company issued cell phones were auto-programmed (by the defendants) to delete employee text messages. The defendants' failure to intervene in this automatic process places them outside of the "safe-harbor" provision provided for in Federal Rule 37(e) and subjects them to sanctions for the loss of any electronically stored information resulting from that failure. *See* Committee Comments to Fed. R. Civ. Proc. 37(f) (now 37(e)):

> Rule 37(f) applies to information lost due to the routine operation of an information system only if the operation was in good faith. Good faith in the routine operation of an information system may involve a party's intervention to modify or suspend certain features of that routine operation to prevent the loss of information, if that information is subject to a preservation obligation. A preservation obligation may arise from many sources, including common law, statutes, regulations, or a court order in the case. The good faith requirement of Rule 37(f) means that a party is not permitted to exploit the routine operation of an information system to thwart discovery obligations by allowing that operation to continue in order to destroy specific stored information that it is required to preserve. When a party is under a duty to preserve information because of pending or reasonably anticipated litigation, intervention in the routine operation of an information system is one aspect of what is often called a "litigation hold." Among the factors that bear on a party's good faith in the routine operation of an information system are the steps the party took to comply with a court order in the case or party agreement requiring preservation of specific electronically stored information.

In their supplemental response, the defendants argue that while sanctions might be appropriate for failure to turn off an auto-delete function in relation to email communications the same conduct with respect to text messages is not sanctionable (Doc. 317 p. 5). The basis for their argument seems to be that text messages are a less prominent form of communication and that the production of text messages is too burdensome (Doc. 317 p. 5). As to the former, text messages are electronically stored information, it does not matter that text messaging is a less prominent form of communication. Further, in the instant case, employees used text messaging—to some extent—for business related communication and text messages were expressly requested by the PSC. There is no question the defendants owed a duty to preserve this material. As to the latter, the Court has already addressed the issue of burden. If the defendants felt the PSC's request for text messages was overly burdensome they should have filed the appropriate motions with the Court. The defendants cannot simply make a unilateral decision regarding the burden of a particular discovery request and then allow the information that is the subject of the discovery request to be destroyed.

In their supplemental brief, the defendants also note the following: (1) although Ms. Baier utilized text messaging for work related communications, she also testified that these text messages were non-substantive and (2) the company has a policy prohibiting substantive text messaging with physicians (Doc. 317 p. 6). As a result, the defendants argue, their failure to preserve text messages is harmless (Doc. 317 p. 6). Once again, the defendants do not get to choose which evidence they want to produce and from which sources. The PSC is not required to simply accept as true the assumption that all employees followed the "no substantive communications with physicians" policy. Nor is it required to accept as true a deponent's claim about the content of her electronic communications. It is certainly common knowledge that texting has become the preferred means of communication. The PSC is entitled to the discovery requested for, among other things, the purpose of impeaching the above claims.

Finally, the defendants argue that they do not believe they are required to produce text messages anyway (Doc. 311 p. 15). This is a classic example of conduct on behalf of the defendants that has become all too familiar in this litigation. The PSC refers to the practice as "better to beg forgiveness than ask permission." If the defendants felt they did not have an obligation to produce the text messages requested by the PSC, they should have responded with a specific objection to the request or otherwise sought relief from the Court. *See* Fed. R. Civ. Proc. 34(b) and 26(c).

The defendants raised the issue that some employees use their personal cell phones while on business and utilize the texting feature of those phones for business purposes yet balk at the request of litigation lawyers to examine these personal phones. The litigation hold and the requirement to produce relevant text messages, without question, applies to that space on employees cell phones dedicated to the business which is relevant to this litigation. Any employee who refuses to allow the auto delete feature for text messages turned off or to turn over his or her phone for the examination of the relevant space on that phone will be subject to a show cause order of this Court to appear personally in order to demonstrate why he or she should not be held in contempt of Court, subject to any remedy available to the Court for such contempt.

VI. FINDINGS AND CONCLUSIONS

A. Findings as to Bad Faith and Otherwise Culpable Conduct

The Court finds the actions and omissions of the defendants, BIPI and BII, to be in bad faith. The defendants argue that their failure to produce the many thousands of documents they are now producing, and their inability to produce other documents at all, are the result of a good faith measured approach to the production of millions of documents over a fairly short period of time. They contend their failure to designate certain employees as subject to a hold is part of a reasonable hold strategy based on a measured and proportioned approach to cost benefit analysis dependent on scope of litigation. They base their failure to include one scientist in the litigation hold on a failure of their opponents to designate him and their own determination that he singularly was not important enough in light of including his coworkers whose custodial materials were being provided.

As the Court mentioned hereinbefore, the question the Court has been asking over and over again has been answered. How can these problems keep happening? One of the problems to which the Court has been referring was that the defendants kept coming up with materials in an untimely manner. Materials were being turned over months and months late—often on the eve of a deposition. It is clear to the Court that the defendants have been pursuing a policy of turning over relevant material, or withholding relevant material, on their schedule and not the Court's. In doing so, they have violated the Court's case management orders. They have made misrepresentations to the Court in open court and in chambers. The defendants have caused the Court to believe that each defendant had a litigation hold, company-wide, on all relevant personnel and all relevant documentation and data (in their broadest definitions) at all relevant times.

The Court finds that BII has specifically not applied the hold to Dr. Lehr and now failed to produce certain of his "files." To fail to do so was in violation of the Court's case management orders and in bad faith.

The Court finds both defendants failed to ensure that the auto delete feature of their employee cell phones, company owned and personal, was disengaged for the purpose of preserving text messages and, as such, this allowed countless records to be destroyed. One can only speculate about the relevance or lack thereof and what aspect of plaintiffs' case was harmed thereby. The Court finds this action to be in violation of its case management orders to produce relevant material by a date certain and in bad faith.

The Court finds the defendants failure to place a litigation hold on Sales Representatives, Clinical Science Consultants and Medical Science Liaisons at the earliest date and across the board of all such persons having any involvement with Pradaxa, and thereafter producing the relevant materials in a timely manner, in violation of the Court's case management orders, and in bad faith.

The Court finds that the failure to provide the vendor hired to provide the plaintiffs with discoverable material from the G drive with all relevant materials to be in violation of the Court's case management orders and in bad faith.

B. Sanctions Imposed

1. Professor Thorstein Lehr

The Court directs BII to produce all complete "files" of Professor Lehr within 7 days. If that proves impossible because they have been destroyed due to the fact that he was not subject to the litigation hold, defendant shall so certify to the Court. Once the Court, knows for certain what defendant's response to this order is in this regard, a further order will issue, allowing more time with possible conditions, or an order assessing sanctions pursuant to Rule 37 or the Court's inherent authority, if appropriate.

2. Inadequate Litigation Hold as to Sales Representatives, CSCs and MSLs

The defendants, BIPI and BII, are ordered to produce the complete files for those sales representatives, CSCs and MSLs that have been requested by the PSC within 14 days. If the defendants are unable to comply with this order, they shall so advise the Court and advise if more time is needed and the reason or if certain files are not available and the reason. The Court will then issue an order allowing more time with possible conditions, or an order assessing sanctions pursuant Rule 37 or the Court's inherent authority, if appropriate.

3. Failure to Preserve Text Messages

The defendants, BIPI and BII, are ordered to produce any text messages not otherwise covered by the order directed in number 2 immediately above that have been requested by the PSC within 14 days. If the defendants are unable to comply with this order, they shall so advise the Court and advise if more time is needed and the reason or if certain files are not available and the reason. The Court will then issue an order allowing more time with possible conditions, or an order assessing sanctions pursuant Rule 37 or the Court's inherent authority, if appropriate.

4. G Drive

The defendant, BIPI, is ordered to produce any relevant portions of the G drive that have been requested by the PSC within 30 days. If the defendant is unable to comply with this order, it shall so advise the Court and advise if more time is needed and the reason or if certain files are not available and the reason. The Court will then issue an order allowing more time with possible conditions, or an order assessing sanctions pursuant Rule 37 or the Court's inherent authority, if appropriate.

5. Financial Sanctions

The PSC requested a number of financial sanctions as a result of the defendants' transgressions. It asked for reimbursement for its fees and costs in pursuing the issue of the defendants' violations. The defendants agree they should be held accountable for that and the Court so orders and directs the PSC to submit an itemization with an affidavit.

The PSC requested that the Court revisit the issue raised by it through motion that the employee depositions scheduled or to be scheduled in Europe be scheduled in a place convenient to the PSC and defendants' United States counsel. This is a financial issue but also a timing issue because of the many delays caused by the defendants actions and the extraordinary time it takes to fly to Amsterdam and the logistics of setting up the necessary working space there. The Court has resisted multiple requests from the PSC on this issue, primarily on the basis that the Court had an inadequate basis for requiring it. Based on the Court's findings above, the bad faith of the defendants in withholding discovery until well after it was required to be produced, by many months, the prejudice those delays have caused the litigation herein in postponing depositions and precipitating countless hours of chambers time and courtroom time discussing and advocating issues that did not need to occur, the Court finds an appropriate sanction pursuant to its inherent powers to be to require the defendants to produce all employees for deposition in the United States. Effective immediately or as close as logistically possible thereto, understanding that depositions and teams may already be in place, depositions shall take place in New York City or such other place as the PSC, and the defendants shall unanimously agree upon. If no alternative is unanimously agreed upon, they the Court's selection shall stand.

The PSC also requested a corporate fine as well as individual fines to be paid by each defense counsel. The corporate fine sought by plaintiffs is in the nature of $20 million. In the course of their advocacy, plaintiffs argued, in essence, that the Court's last sanction, was laughable and urged the Court to put some teeth in its sanction this time. The Court did note a sigh of relief on the faces of the corporate general counsel, though no laughs from the defense side of the courtroom. The Court is not moved by such advocacy. Moreover, the Court is not generally inclined to impose sanctions. In this judge's recollection, perhaps three times in seven years on the state bench and perhaps twice in fifteen years as a federal judge, this order being the third. No judge should relish the serious obligation associated with a sanction, however, when a Court is confronted with a situation such as the instant one, it must act. But when it acts, it must do so in measured terms and in proportion to the wrongs and the prejudice before it.

The wrongs here are egregious in the eyes of the Court. As hereinbefore provided, there may be more orders yet to come; orders which take actions designed to determine what aspects of the plaintiffs' case have been prejudiced or even so damaged as to interfere with their ability to prove what they legally have to prove and for the facts of this case to come out. Going forward, based on the findings heretofore, pursuant to the Court's inherent powers, and to encourage defendants to respect this Court and comply with its orders, the Court fines both defendants, jointly and severally, $931,500.00 ($500.00 per case). The last time the Court imposed a sanction it was based on a figure around $25,000.00. The Court assessed a figure at $20.00 per case for the number of cases then pending (the total ended up being $29,500.00). Then as now, the Court's imposition of a fine is a measured action, designed to let the defendants know that the Court's order and the Court deserve respect. If a somewhat forceful reminder of those tenants in the law must be sent to defendants for their misdeeds which demonstrate something to the contrary, so be it. Never should such reminders shock any one's conscience. Here, the first one was quite modest indeed. It did not send a sufficient message, but then most if not all the deeds the Court discussed herein were well underway, just not discovered. The fine imposed today, will not impact the defendants profit margins, but hopefully together with the potential future actions the Court may be forced to take, once it learns whether the plaintiffs have been so prejudiced by this misconduct as to be unable to fully prosecute their cases, the defendants will understand once and for all time compliance with the Court's orders is not an optional part of litigation strategy. Just as the Court did not exhaust what it has available to it in this instance, as the plaintiffs urged in the first sanction hearing, its measured approach to behavior modification leaves remedies yet to be addressed should defendants continue on the path of wrong-headed litigation strategy as the Court has sanctioned herein.

Litigation Hold Memorandum

A litigation hold memorandum puts the company on notice that it is subject to a lawsuit. The memorandum should be issued when a lawsuit is reasonably anticipated, and should be a formal written document that provides a summary of the lawsuit, including for example, the relevant time period, potentially relevant custodians and documents, and instructs the company employees to preserve relevant information.[24] This means not only instructing the relevant custodians, but also instructing the IT and records management departments, for example, to suspend any auto-delete functions on electronic systems that may contain potentially relevant data and stop recycling data drives and tapes that may be overwritten.[25] The litigation hold should be communicated directly to key custodians, and should be carefully monitored for compliance, including periodic reminders to employees that the hold is in effect, and obtaining written confirmation from custodians that they are in compliance.[26] It is important to work with the HR department to account for new and former employees. As with any corporate data management plan, there should be processes in place for integrating new employees into any ongoing preservation protocol and managing the files for employees who leave the company.

There is an obvious tension between data retention policies that call for the destruction of old data and litigation hold directives that compel a company to preserve information for the duration of a lawsuit. The volume of data in large corporations can be enormous and complex litigation can go on for years, sometimes decades. Large corporations can easily spend millions of dollars just to hold on to information during a lawsuit, most of which will never see light of day during the entire litigation, let alone at trial.[27] Yet the consequences of failing to properly execute a litigation hold can be catastrophic.[28] It is imperative that litigation holds are managed properly, and in-house lawyers are vigilant in overseeing them.

Despite this tension, there is also a rational congruence between litigation hold protocols and document retention policies. Effective litigation hold protocols begin with effective document retention policies. If the process of managing data from its creation to its disposal is based on comprehensive, coherent, and reasonable business principles, and it is executed in a consistent, organized fashion, with vigilant oversight, then the universe of data that is left that is relevant to a litigation should be difficult

---

24. *See, e.g.,* Zubulake, 229 F.R.D. 422, 433–34 (S.D.N.Y. 2004) (a litigation hold should be issued at the "outset of litigation or whenever litigation is reasonably anticipated," and it should be reissued periodically to remind employees and inform new ones. Counsel should communicate directly with any custodians who are relevant to the litigation and confirm their compliance with the hold. Counsel should also instruct all employees to produce relevant information from their active files, and make sure that all other stores of information that may contain relevant information are preserved.).

25. *Id.*

26. *Id.*

27. *See, e.g.,* William H.J. Hubbard, *Preservation Costs Summary, Final Report,* Civil Justice Reform Group (February 18, 2014), available at http://www.ediscoverylaw.com/files/2014/02/Hubbard-Preservation_Costs_Survey_Final_Report.pdf.

28. *See, e.g.,* In re Actos (Pioglitazone) Prods. Liab. Litig., 2014 U.S. Dist. LEXIS 86101, *225 (W.D. La. 2014) (finding that defendant intentionally destroyed documents that should have been preserved under the litigation hold, and issuing a "permissive instruction allowing the jury to make its own determination as to *the nature of* [defendant's] conduct."); Pension Comm., 685 F. Supp. 2d 456 (S.D.N.Y. 2010); Zubulake, 229 F.R.D. 422 (S.D.N.Y. 2004).

to challenge, and will provide a solid foundation upon which the company can meet its discovery obligations.

Meet and Confer

The "meet and confer" requirement under Rule 26(f) of the Federal Rules of Civil Procedure provides that parties to the litigation meet as soon as practicable to discuss and develop a discovery plan.[29] The plan should address issues such as timing and form for disclosures, subjects of discovery, limitations regarding electronically stored information ("ESI"), and privilege concerns.[30] Corporations with complex networks and large stockpiles of data must act quickly to identify potentially relevant systems, documents, and custodians. They must also have ready support from various internal groups, including, for example, IT and records management departments, to suspend auto-delete functions and preserve old records. If outside help is necessary, in-house lawyers should be ready to engage e-discovery vendors and technology consultants. By partnering with these groups, and with the preparation and learning derived from well thought-out data management plans, data maps, and litigation hold protocols, company lawyers will be in far better position to negotiate discovery issues on behalf of the organization.

Assignments

- **Hypothetical:** You are the Chief Compliance Officer at your Corporation. Design a document management system for your company, including a document retention schedule.

---

29. Fed. R. Civ. P. Rule 26(f).
30. Fed. R. Civ. P. Rule 26(f)(3).

Chapter 16

Corporate Compliance and Internal Investigations

Introduction

The Sarbanes-Oxley Act of 2002, Pub. l. No. 107-204, 116 Stat. 745 (SOX), imposed increased responsibilities on corporate officers and directors to ensure that their company complies with all applicable laws and regulations. These responsibilities include overseeing and, at times, actively participating in internal investigations into alleged criminal or regulatory violations. Internal investigations present a variety of difficult, and at times not so obvious, challenges. Decisions a company makes at the very outset of an investigation, regarding whether and what to investigate, who will conduct the investigation and what powers they will have, can have far-reaching and unanticipated consequences. As several cases discussed below illustrate, even sophisticated corporate officials and their experienced legal advisors can make serious mistakes with far-reaching consequences when overseeing internal investigations.

A Company's Duty to Investigate Allegations of Wrongdoing

SOX places an affirmative obligation on publicly traded companies to investigate certain allegations of wrongdoing. In addition, although not imposing affirmative legal duties on a company to investigate wrongdoing, the Department of Justice's Principles of Federal Prosecution of Business Organizations (United States Attorneys' Manual 9-28.000 *et seq.*), the U.S. Sentencing Guidelines Manual, Section 8C2.5 and the Securities and Exchange Commission's "Seaboard Report," "Report of Investigation Pursuant to Section 21(a) of the Securities Exchange Act of 1934 and Commission Statement on the Relationship of Corporate Agency Enforcement Decisions, "Exch. Act Rel. no. 44969 (Oct. 23, 2001), http://www.sec.gov/litigation/investreport/34-44969.htm#P54_10935, all provide for more lenient treatment of companies that voluntarily investigate and report evidence of wrongdoing and that have implemented vigorous and effective compliance programs.

The Sarbanes-Oxley Act of 2002

Several provisions of the Sarbanes-Oxley Act place substantial responsibilities on officers and directors to ensure that their company complies with its legal obligations and investigates allegations of wrongdoing. Section 302 requires a publicly traded corporation's CEO and CFO to each certify in every quarterly and annual report, among other matters, that, based on the officer's knowledge:

1) report does not contain any untrue statement of material fact and does not omit any material fact necessary to make the statements made not misleading (15 U.S.C. §7241(a)(2));

2) financial statements fairly present in all material respects the financial condition of the company (15 U.S.C. §7241(a)(3));

3) certifying officers are responsible for "disclosure controls and procedures" and that they have designed "internal control over financial reporting" to ensure that material information is disclosed and accurate (15 U.S.C. §7241(a)(4)); and

4) there were significant changes in internal controls or otherwise that could significantly affect internal controls subsequent to the date of their evaluation, including any corrective actions regarding significant deficiencies and material weaknesses. 15 U.S.C. §7241(a)(6).

The CEO and CFO must also certify that they have disclosed to the issuer's auditors and the Audit Committee of the Board of Directors any fraud, whether or not material, that involved management or other employees who have a significant role in the issuer's internal controls. 15 U.S.C. §7241(a)(5)(B).

The SOX whistleblower provisions also encourage the reporting of wrongdoing up the corporate ladder and require the Audit Committee to ensure that there is a mechanism for responding to these complaints. Specifically, SOX Section 301 requires the Audit Committee to establish procedures for receiving and handling complaints "regarding accounting, internal controls or auditing matters" and "regarding questionable accounting or auditing matters" submitted confidentially by company employees.

In response to the financial crisis of 2008, Congress passed the Dodd-Frank Wall Street Reform and Consumer Protection Act, Pub. L. No. 111-203, 124 Stat 1841 (2010) adding Section 21F to the Securities Exchange Act of 1934 (Section 21F). Section 21F established a whistleblower program requiring the Securities and Exchange Commission (SEC) to pay an award to whistleblowers who voluntarily provide information about violations of federal securities laws that leads to a successful enforcement of an action resulting in sanctions that exceed $1,000,000 and prohibited retaliation by employers against whistleblowers. The Act took effect in August 2011 and the SEC made its first reward payment in August of 2012.

The SEC subsequently adopted rules and forms to implement Section 21F. The Implementation of the Whistleblower Provisions of Section 21F of the Securities Exchange Act of 1934 Release No. 34-64545 (Aug. 12, 2011) (Implementation of the

Whistleblower Provisions). Despite comments to its proposed rules encouraging the adoption of a rule requiring that such whistleblowers first report violations internally, the SEC declined to include such a requirement but encouraged internal reporting by creating a look-back period of 120 days after a whistleblower's internal report wherein subsequent reports to the SEC are treated as if reported to the SEC on the earlier date of internal reporting. (The Implementation of the Whistleblower Provisions). The SEC further provided that a whistleblower's voluntary participation with internal reporting and compliance programs could be considered as a factor in increasing the amount of the reward provided. (Implementation of the Whistleblower Provisions).

Despite several district court rulings to the contrary, the Fifth Circuit recently ruled that an employee dismissed after internally reporting possible violations of securities laws was not entitled to "whistleblower" protections afforded by the Dodd-Frank Act. *See* Asadi v. G.E. Energy United States, L.L.C., 720 F.3d 620 (5th Cir. 2013).

U.S. Department of Justice Guidelines

The Department of Justice's Principles of Federal Prosecution of Business Organizations (the "Principles") are guidelines that federal prosecutors are required to follow in determining whether to prosecute companies. United States Attorneys' Manual, 9-28.000 *et seq.* While these guidelines do not impose any affirmative legal duties on companies to investigate and voluntarily report evidence of wrongdoing, they do create strong incentives to do so, including potentially avoiding prosecution entirely or significantly reducing the severity of any criminal penalties. United States Attorneys' Manual, 9-28.000 *et seq.*

Office of the United States Attorneys, U.S. Attorney Manual, Title 9
9-28.000 — Principles of Federal Prosecution of Business Organizations

http://www.justice.gov/usam/usam-9-28000-principles-federal-prosecution-business-organizations#9-28.300

9-28.300 — Factors to Be Considered

A. **General Principle:** Generally, prosecutors apply the same factors in determining whether to charge a corporation as they do with respect to individuals. *See* USAM 9-27.220 *et seq.* Thus, the prosecutor must weigh all of the factors normally considered in the sound exercise of prosecutorial judgment: the sufficiency of the evidence; the likelihood of success at trial; the probable deterrent, rehabilitative, and other consequences of conviction; and the adequacy of noncriminal approaches. *See id.* However, due to the nature of the corporate "person," some additional factors are present. In conducting an investigation, determining whether to bring charges, and negotiating plea or other agreements, prosecutors should consider the following factors in reaching a decision as to the proper treatment of a corporate target:

1. the nature and seriousness of the offense, including the risk of harm to the public, and applicable policies and priorities, if any, governing the prosecution of corporations for particular categories of crime (*see* USAM 9-28.400);

2. the pervasiveness of wrongdoing within the corporation, including the complicity in, or the condoning of, the wrongdoing by corporate management (*see* USAM 9-28.500);

3. the corporation's history of similar misconduct, including prior criminal, civil, and regulatory enforcement actions against it (*see* USAM 9-28.600);

4. the corporation's willingness to cooperate in the investigation of its agents (*see* USAM 9-28.700);

5. the existence and effectiveness of the corporation's pre-existing compliance program (*see* USAM 9-28.800);

6. the corporation's timely and voluntary disclosure of wrongdoing (*see* USAM 9-28.900);

7. the corporation's remedial actions, including any efforts to implement an effective corporate compliance program or to improve an existing one, to replace responsible management, to discipline or terminate wrongdoers, to pay restitution, and to cooperate with the relevant government agencies (*see* USAM 9-28.1000);

8. collateral consequences, including whether there is disproportionate harm to shareholders, pension holders, employees, and others not proven personally culpable, as well as impact on the public arising from the prosecution (*see* USAM 9-28.1100);

9. the adequacy of remedies such as civil or regulatory enforcement actions (*see* USAM 9-28.1200); and

10. the adequacy of the prosecution of individuals responsible for the corporation's malfeasance (*see* USAM 9-28.1300)

The principles also state that prosecutors must also weigh all of the factors normally considered in the sound exercise of prosecutorial judgment used in determining whether to charge individuals. Including, for example, the sufficiency of the evidence, the likelihood of success at trial; deterrent, rehabilitative and other consequences of convictions, and the adequacy of non-criminal approaches. USAM 9-28.300 B. *Comment.*

Credit for Cooperation, Including Timely, Voluntary Reporting of Wrongdoing

Company officials considering whether to voluntarily report any evidence of criminal wrongdoing should be familiar with the Principles discussion entitled "Value of

Cooperation." USAM 9-28.700. While the Principles identify cooperation as a potential mitigating factor, the "failure to cooperate, in and of itself, does not support or require the filing of charges with respect to a corporation any more than with respect to an individual." USAM 9-28.700. However, federal prosecutors typically expect a company's full cooperation in connection with an investigation and a failure to do so will be weighed heavily against the company.

Office of the United States Attorneys, U.S. Attorney Manual, Title 9
9-28.000 — Principles of Federal Prosecution of Business Organizations

http://www.justice.gov/usam/usam-9-28000-principles-federal-
prosecution-business-organizations#9-28.300 (rev. Nov. 2015)

9-28.700 — The Value of Cooperation

Cooperation is a mitigating factor, by which a corporation — just like any other subject of a criminal investigation — can gain credit in a case that otherwise is appropriate for indictment and prosecution. Of course, the decision not to cooperate by a corporation (or individual) is not itself evidence of misconduct, at least where the lack of cooperation does not involve criminal misconduct or demonstrate consciousness of guilt (e.g., suborning perjury or false statements, or refusing to comply with lawful discovery requests). Thus, failure to cooperate, in and of itself, does not support or require the filing of charges with respect to a corporation any more than with respect to an individual.

A. **General Principle:** In order for a company to receive any consideration for cooperation under this section, the company must identify all individuals involved in or responsible for the misconduct at issue, regardless of their position, status or seniority, and provide to the Department all facts relating to that misconduct. If a company seeking cooperation credit declines to learn of such facts or to provide the Department with complete factual information about the individuals involved, its cooperation will not be considered a mitigating factor under this section. Nor, if a company is prosecuted, will the Department support a cooperation-related reduction at sentencing. *See* U.S.S.G. § 8C2.5(g), cmt. (n. 13) ("A prime test of whether the organization has disclosed all pertinent information" necessary to receive a cooperation-related reduction in its offense level calculation "is whether the information is sufficient ... to identify ... the individual(s) responsible for the criminal conduct."). If a company meets the threshold requirement of providing all relevant facts with respect to individuals, it will be eligible for consideration for cooperation credit. To be clear, a company is not required to waive its attorney-client privilege and attorney work product protection in order satisfy this threshold. *See* USAM 9-28.720. The extent of the cooperation credit earned will depend on all the various factors that have traditionally applied in making this assessment (e.g., the timeliness of the cooperation, the diligence, thoroughness and speed of the internal investigation, and the proactive nature of the cooperation).

B. Comment: In investigating wrongdoing by or within a corporation, a prosecutor may encounter several obstacles resulting from the nature of the corporation itself. It may be difficult to determine which individual took which action on behalf of the corporation. Lines of authority and responsibility may be shared among operating divisions or departments, and records and personnel may be spread throughout the United States or even among several countries. Where the criminal conduct continued over an extended period of time, the culpable or knowledgeable personnel may have been promoted, transferred, or fired, or they may have quit or retired. Accordingly, a corporation's cooperation may be critical in identifying potentially relevant actors and locating relevant evidence, among other things, and in doing so expeditiously.

This dynamic — i.e., the difficulty of determining what happened, where the evidence is, and which individuals took or promoted putatively illegal corporate actions — can have negative consequences for both the government and the corporation that is the subject or target of a government investigation. More specifically, because of corporate attribution principles concerning actions of corporate officers and employees, *see* USAM 9.28-210, uncertainty about who authorized or directed apparent corporate misconduct can inure to the detriment of a corporation. For example, it may not matter under the law which of several possible executives or leaders in a chain of command approved of or authorized criminal conduct; however, that information if known might bear on the propriety of a particular disposition short of indictment of the corporation. It may not be in the interest of a corporation or the government for a charging decision to be made in the absence of such information, which might occur if, for example, a statute of limitations were relevant and authorization by any one of the officials were enough to justify a charge under the law. Moreover, a protracted government investigation of such an issue could disrupt the corporation's business operations or even depress its stock price.

For these reasons and more, cooperation can be a favorable course for both the government and the corporation. Cooperation benefits the government by allowing prosecutors and federal agents, for example, to avoid protracted delays, which compromise their ability to quickly uncover and address the full extent of widespread corporate crimes. With cooperation by the corporation, the government may be able to reduce tangible losses, limit damage to reputation, and preserve assets for restitution. At the same time, cooperation may benefit the corporation — and ultimately shareholders, employees, and other often blameless victims — by enabling the government to focus its investigative resources in a manner that will not unduly disrupt the corporation's legitimate business operations. In addition, cooperation may benefit the corporation by presenting it with the opportunity to earn credit for its efforts.

The requirement that companies cooperate completely as to individuals does not mean that Department attorneys should wait for the company to deliver the information about individual wrongdoers and then merely accept what companies provide. To the contrary, Department attorneys should be proactively investigating individuals at every step of the process — before, during, and after any corporate cooperation. Department attorneys should vigorously review any information provided by companies and compare it to the results of their own investigation, in order to best ensure that the information provided is indeed complete and does not seek to minimize the behavior or role of any individual or group of individuals.

Department attorneys should strive to obtain from the company as much information as possible about responsible individuals before resolving the corporate case. In addition, the company's continued cooperation with respect to individuals may be necessary post-resolution. If so, the corporate resolution agreement should include a provision that requires the company to provide information about all individuals involved and that is explicit enough so that a failure to provide the information results in specific consequences, such as stipulated penalties and/or a material breach.

Credit for an "Effective" Compliance Program

Another factor that encourages corporations to voluntarily report evidence of wrongdoing is the credit given for the "existence and effectiveness of the corporation's pre-existing compliance program," USAM 9-28.300, which will be judged, in part, by whether prior incidents of wrongdoing were reported and the violators sanctioned.

Office of the United States Attorneys, U.S. Attorney Manual, Title 9
9-28.000 — Principles of Federal Prosecution of Business Organizations

http://www.justice.gov/usam/usam-9-28000-principles-federal-prosecution-business-organizations#9-28.300 (revised Nov. 2015)

9-28.800 — Corporate Compliance Programs

A. General Principle: Compliance programs are established by corporate management to prevent and detect misconduct and to ensure that corporate activities are conducted in accordance with applicable criminal and civil laws, regulations, and rules. The Department encourages such corporate self-policing, including voluntary disclosures to the government of any problems that a corporation discovers on its own. *See* USAM 9-28.900. However, the existence of a compliance program is not sufficient, in and of itself, to justify not charging a corporation for criminal misconduct undertaken by its officers, directors, employees, or agents. In addition, the nature of some crimes, e.g., antitrust violations, may be such that national law enforcement policies mandate prosecutions of corporations notwithstanding the existence of a compliance program.

B. Comment: The existence of a corporate compliance program, even one that specifically prohibited the very conduct in question, does not absolve the corporation from criminal liability under the doctrine of *respondeat superior. See United States v. Basic Constr. Co.*, 711 F.2d 570, 573 (4th Cir. 1983) ("[A] corporation may be held criminally responsible for antitrust violations committed by its employees if they were acting within the scope of their authority, or apparent authority, and for the benefit of the corporation, even if … such acts were against corporate policy or express instructions."). As explained in *United States v. Potter*, 463 F.3d 9 (1st Cir. 2006), a corporation cannot "avoid liability by adopting abstract rules" that forbid its agents from engaging in illegal acts, because "[e]ven a specific directive to an agent or employee or honest efforts to police such rules do not automatically free the company for the wrongful acts of agents." *Id.* at 25–26. *See also United States v. Hilton Hotels Corp.*, 467 F.2d 1000, 1007 (9th Cir. 1972) (noting that a corporation "could not gain exculpation by issuing general instructions without undertaking to enforce those instructions by means commensurate with the obvious risks"); *United States v. Beusch*, 596 F.2d 871, 878 (9th Cir. 1979) ("[A] corporation may be liable for acts of its employees done contrary to express instructions and policies, but … the existence of such instructions and policies may be considered in determining whether the employee in fact acted to benefit the corporation.").

While the Department recognizes that no compliance program can ever prevent all criminal activity by a corporation's employees, the critical factors in evaluating any program are whether the program is adequately designed for maximum effectiveness in preventing and detecting wrongdoing by employees and whether corporate management is enforcing the program or is tacitly encouraging or pressuring employees to engage in misconduct to achieve business objectives. The Department has no formulaic requirements regarding corporate compliance programs. The fundamental questions any prosecutor should ask are: Is the corporation's compliance program well designed? Is the program being applied earnestly and in good faith? Does the corporation's compliance program work? In answering these questions, the prosecutor should consider the comprehensiveness of the compliance program; the extent and pervasiveness of the criminal misconduct; the number and level of the corporate employees involved; the seriousness, duration, and frequency of the misconduct; and any remedial actions taken by the corporation, including, for example, disciplinary action against past violators uncovered by the prior compliance program, and revisions to corporate compliance programs in light of lessons learned. Prosecutors should also consider the promptness of any disclosure of wrongdoing to the government. In evaluating compliance programs, prosecutors may consider whether the corporation has established corporate governance mechanisms that can effectively detect and prevent misconduct. For example, do the corporation's directors exercise independent review over proposed corporate actions rather than unquestioningly ratifying officers' recommendations; are internal audit functions conducted at a level sufficient to ensure their independence and accuracy; and have the directors established an information and reporting system in the organization reasonably designed to provide management and directors with timely and accurate information sufficient to allow them to reach an informed decision regarding the organization's compliance with the law. *See, e.g., In re Caremark Int'l Inc. Derivative Litig.*, 698 A.2d 959, 968–70 (Del. Ch. 1996).

Prosecutors should therefore attempt to determine whether a corporation's compliance program is merely a "paper program" or whether it was designed, implemented, reviewed, and revised, as appropriate, in an effective manner. In addition, prosecutors should determine whether the corporation has provided for a staff sufficient to audit, document, analyze, and utilize the results of the corporation's compliance efforts. Prosecutors also should determine whether the corporation's employees are adequately informed about the compliance program and are convinced of the corporation's commitment to it. This will enable the prosecutor to make an informed decision as to whether the corporation has adopted and implemented a truly effective compliance program that, when consistent with other federal law enforcement policies, may result in a decision to charge only the corporation's employees and agents or to mitigate charges or sanctions against the corporation.

Compliance programs should be designed to detect the particular types of misconduct most likely to occur in a particular corporation's line of business. Many corporations operate in complex regulatory environments outside the normal experience of criminal prosecutors. Accordingly, prosecutors should consult with relevant federal and state agencies with the expertise to evaluate the adequacy of a program's design and implementation. For instance, state and federal banking, insurance, and medical boards, the Department of Defense, the Department of Health and Human Services, the Environmental Protection Agency, and the Securities and Exchange Commission have considerable experience with compliance programs and can be helpful to a prosecutor in evaluating such programs. In addition, the Fraud Section of the Criminal Division, the Commercial Litigation Branch of the Civil Division, and the Environmental Crimes Section of the Environment and Natural Resources Division can assist United States Attorneys' Offices in finding the appropriate agency office(s) for such consultation.

———————

A failure to report prior criminal violations may adversely affect any credit the company would otherwise receive for voluntarily reporting the instant offense. A more forceful response to the prior violation could have precluded the instant violation.

For example, when presented with evidence of an illegal kickback scheme, prosecutors can be expected to ask the company and its employees whether the company had any prior notice of similar misconduct either directly related to the scheme in question or any other such scheme. If there were such prior violations, prosecutors will ask, among other questions, whether the violators were punished, whether their conduct was reported to the authorities and whether steps were taken to strengthen the compliance program to prevent such future violations.

The Principles note that the Department has no formulaic requirements regarding corporate compliance programs but identifies as fundamental questions: Is the compliance program well designed?

Is it being applied earnestly and in good faith? Does it work? USAM 9-28.800, B. *Comment*. In answering these questions, prosecutors should consider:

1. the comprehensiveness of the compliance program;
2. the extent and pervasiveness of the criminal misconduct;

3. the number and level of the corporate employees involved;

4. the seriousness, duration, and frequency of the misconduct; and

5. any remedial actions taken by the corporation, including, for example, disciplinary action against past violators uncovered by the prior compliance program, and revisions to corporate compliance programs in light the of lessons learned. USAM 9-28.800, B. *Comment.*

Accordingly, to obtain credit for an effective compliance program, companies should ensure that their compliance program educates and encourages employees to comply with their legal responsibilities, contains an effective mechanism for detecting violations, punishes employees internally for wrongdoing and, in appropriate circumstances, reports evidence of wrongdoing to the authorities. Internal investigation of potential criminal and regulatory violations is an important aspect of any effective compliance program.

A noteworthy recent example of credit granted by the Department of Justice for the existence of an effective compliance program occurred in April 2012 when the Justice Department declined to prosecute Morgan Stanley after one of its Managing Directors pled guilty to charges stemming from violations of the Foreign Corrupt Practices Act. In its press release (which can be found at http://www.justice.gov/opa/pr/2012/April/12-crm-534.html) the Justice Department noted, "After considering all the available facts and circumstances, including that Morgan Stanley constructed and maintained a system of internal controls, which provided reasonable assurances that its employees were not bribing government officials, the Department of Justice declined to bring any enforcement action against Morgan Stanley...." The case involved a former Managing Director of Morgan Stanley conspiring "to circumvent Morgan Stanley's internal controls in order to transfer a multi-million dollar ownership interest in a Shanghai building to himself and a Chinese public official with whom he had a personal friendship." The Department of Justice highlighted Morgan Stanley's robust system of internal controls and training programs. Further, it noted that the Managing Partner in question had been trained on compliance with the Foreign Corrupt Practices Act seven times and reminded of its requirements 35 times.

United States Sentencing Guidelines Credit for an "Effective" Compliance Program

Companies should also be familiar with the factors set forth in United States Sentencing Guidelines Section 8B2.1. Chapter 8, entitled Sentencing of Organizations, sets forth certain general principles and specific calculations that must be taken into account by the court in sentencing a corporation.

While the guidelines are now only advisory, *see U.S. v. Booker*, 543 U.S. 220, (2005), they still form the starting point for all sentencing analysis. These guidelines are "designed so that the sanctions imposed upon organizations and their agents, taken together, will provide just punishment, adequate deterrence, and incentives for organizations to maintain internal mechanisms for preventing, detecting and reporting criminal conduct." U.S.S.G. Chapter 8 Introductory Commentary (2008).

Chapter 8 provides that the fine range for any organization, other than one operated primarily for criminal purposes, should be based on the seriousness of the offence and the culpability of the organization. U.S.S.G. Chapter 8 Introductory Commentary (2008). "Culpability generally will be determined by six factors that the sentencing court must consider." U.S.S.G. Chapter 8 Introductory Commentary (2008). Four of these factors increase the ultimate punishment of an organization: "(i) the involvement in or tolerance of criminal activity; (ii) the prior history of the organization; (iii) the violation of an order; and (iv) the obstruction of justice. Two factors that mitigate the ultimate punishment are (i) the existence of an effective compliance and ethics program; and (ii) self-reporting, cooperation, or acceptance of responsibility." U.S.S.G. Chapter 8 Introductory Commentary (2008).

In particular, U.S.S.G. § 8B2.1(a) provides that, to have an effective compliance and ethics program, an organization should "exercise due diligence to prevent and detect criminal conduct" and "otherwise promote an organizational culture that encourages ethical conduct and a commitment to compliance with the law." § 8B2.1(b) sets forth the elements of an effective compliance program, including that the organization's "governing authority" shall be knowledgeable about and shall "exercise reasonable oversight with respect to the implementation of and effectiveness of the compliance and ethics program." It further requires the organization to conduct "monitoring and auditing to detect criminal conduct" § 8B2.1(b)(5)(A); include "appropriate disciplinary measures for engaging in criminal conduct and for failing to take reasonable steps to prevent or detect criminal conduct." § 8B2.1(b)(6)(B); "after criminal conduct has been detected, the organization shall take reasonable steps to respond appropriately to the criminal conduct and to prevent further similar criminal conduct," § 8B2.1(b)(7); and "periodically assess the risk of criminal conduct and … take appropriate steps … to reduce the risk of criminal conduct identified through this process." § 8B2.1(c).

A corporation's prior history of either condoning or voluntarily reporting evidence of wrongdoing, whether it voluntarily reported such evidence and whether it cooperated in the investigation, will weigh heavily in the penalties a judge imposes. Thus, the Sentencing Guidelines create strong incentives for a company to investigate and voluntarily report evidence of wrongdoing.

On November 1, 2010 certain amendments to the Federal Sentencing Guidelines became effective. These amendments provide some more opportunity for companies with effective compliance programs to receive mitigated penalties. Specifically, subsection (f) of § 8C2.5 (Culpability Score) was amended to

> create a limited exception to the general prohibition against applying the 3-level decrease for having an effective compliance and ethics program when an organization's high-level or substantial authority personnel are involved

in the offense. Specifically, the amendment adds subsection (f)(3)(C), which allows an organization to receive the decrease if the organization meets four criteria: (1) the individual or individuals with operational responsibility for the compliance and ethics program have direct reporting obligations to the organization's governing authority or appropriate subgroup thereof; (2) the compliance and ethics program detected the offense before discovery outside the organization or before such discovery was reasonably likely; (3) the organization promptly reported the offense to the appropriate governmental authorities; and (4) no individual with operational responsibility for the compliance and ethics program participated in, condoned, or was willfully ignorant of the offense.

The new subsection (f)(3)(C) responds to concerns expressed in public comment and testimony that the general prohibition in § 8C2.5(f)(3) operates too broadly and that internal and external reporting of criminal conduct could be better encouraged by providing an exception to that general prohibition in appropriate cases.

The amendment also adds an application note that describes the "direct reporting obligations" necessary to meet the first criterion under § 8C2.5(f)(3)(C). The application note provides that an individual has "direct reporting obligations" if the individual has express authority to communicate personally to the governing authority "promptly on any matter involving criminal conduct or potential criminal conduct" and "no less than annually on the implementation and effectiveness of the compliance and ethics program." The application note responds to public comment and testimony regarding the challenges operational compliance personnel may face when seeking to report criminal conduct to the governing authority of an organization and encourages compliance and ethics policies that provide operational compliance personnel with access to the governing authority when necessary.

The SEC's Guidelines also Encourage Disclosure of Wrongdoing

The Principles are only applicable to federal prosecutors. Similarly, the U.S. Sentencing Guidelines only apply to federal criminal prosecutions. The factors that the SEC considers in determining whether to bring an enforcement action were set forth in its Report of Investigation in the *In re Seaboard* case (Report of Investigation Pursuant to Section 21(a) of the Securities Exchange Act of 1934 and Commission Statement on the Relationship of Corporate Agency Enforcement Decisions, Exchange Act Release No. 44969 (October 23, 2001), http:/www.sec.gov/litigation/investreport/ 34-44969.htm#P54_10935). These factors also place great emphasis on the extent of a company's cooperation and the efficacy of its compliance program. Because the

Seaboard case is a textbook example of how the SEC expects a company to handle allegations of wrongdoing, it is worth summarizing.

The Report of Investigation was issued in connection with a settlement of a cease and desist proceeding against Gisella D. Leone-Meredith, a former controller of a Seaboard company subsidiary. The SEC found that Meredith caused the parent company's books and records to be inaccurate, its periodic reports misstated, and then covered up those facts. The SEC decided not to take action against the parent company given the company's responses. As summarized in the Report of Investigation: "[w]ithin a week of learning about the apparent misconduct, the company's internal auditors had conducted a preliminary review and had advised company management, who in turn, advised the Board's audit committee, that Meredith had caused the company's books and records to be inaccurate and its financial reports to be misstated. The full Board was advised and authorized the company to hire an outside law firm to conduct a thorough inquiry."

Four days later, Meredith and two other employees who (in the company's view) had inadequately supervised her were dismissed. A day later, the company disclosed to the SEC and publicly that its financial statements would be restated. The Report of Investigation noted that the price of the company's shares did not decline after the announcement or after the restatement was published.

The company gave complete cooperation to the SEC and provided all information relative to the underlying revelations, including the details of its internal investigation and notes and transcripts of interviews with Meredith and others. It did not invoke the attorney-client privilege or work product protections with respect to any of the facts uncovered in the investigation. The company also strengthened its financial reporting processes to address the misconduct.

While noting that there is no single or constant answer in determining whether an enforcement action should be brought, that it was not creating any rights and not limiting itself to the criteria discussed below, the SEC set forth "some of the criteria we will consider in determining whether, and how much, to credit self-policing, self-reporting, remediation and cooperation" in determining whether to bring an enforcement action and then resolving any such actions. The SEC set forth thirteen factors:

1. What is the nature of the misconduct involved? Did it result from inadvertence, honest mistake, simple negligence, reckless, or deliberate indifference to indicia of wrongful conduct, willful misconduct or unadorned venality? Were the company's auditors misled?

2. How did the misconduct arise? Is it the result of pressure placed on employees to achieve specific results, or a tone of lawlessness set by those in control of the company? What compliance procedures were in place to prevent the misconduct now uncovered? Why did those procedures fail to stop or inhibit the wrongful conduct?

3. Where in the organization did the misconduct occur? How high up in the chain of command was knowledge of, or participation in, the misconduct?

Did senior personnel participate in, or turn a blind eye toward, obvious indicia of misconduct? How systemic was the behavior? Is it symptomatic of the way the entity does business, or was it isolated?

4. How long did the misconduct last? Was it a one-quarter, or one-time, event, or did it last several years? In the case of a public company, did the misconduct occur before the company went public? Did it facilitate the company's ability to go public?

5. How much harm has the misconduct inflicted upon investors and other corporate constituencies? Did the share price of the company's stock drop significantly upon its discovery and disclosure?

6. How was the misconduct detected, and who uncovered the misconduct?

7. How long after discovery of the misconduct did it take to implement an effective response?

8. What steps did the company take upon learning of the misconduct? Did the company immediately stop the misconduct? Are persons responsible for any misconduct still with the company? If so, are they still in the same positions? Did the company promptly, completely, and effectively disclose the existence of the misconduct to the public, to regulators and to self-regulators? Did the company cooperate completely with appropriate regulatory and law enforcement bodies? Did the company identify what additional related misconduct is likely to have occurred? Did the company take steps to identify the extent of damage to investors and other corporate constituencies? Did the company appropriately recompense those adversely affected by the conduct?

9. What processes did the company follow to resolve many of the issues and ferret out necessary information? Were the Audit Committee and the Board of Directors fully informed? If so, when?

10. Did the company commit to learn the truth, fully and expeditiously? Did it do a thorough review of the nature, extent, origins and consequences of the conduct and related behavior? Did management, the Board or committees, consisting solely of outside directors, oversee the review? Did company employees or outside persons perform the review? If outside persons, had they done other work for the company? Where the review was conducted by outside counsel, had management previously engaged such counsel? Were scope limitations placed on the review? If so, what were they?

11. Did the company promptly make available to our staff the results of its review and provide sufficient documentation reflecting its responses to the situation? Did the company identify possible violation in the conduct and evidence with sufficient precision to facilitate prompt enforcement actions against those who violated the law? Did the company produce a thorough and probing written report detailing the findings of its review? Did the company voluntarily disclose information our staff did not directly request and otherwise might

not have uncovered? Did the company ask its employees to cooperate with our staff and make all reasonable efforts to secure such cooperation?

12. What assurances are there that the conduct is unlikely to occur? Did the company adopt and ensure enforcement of new and more effective internal controls and procedures designed to prevent a recurrence of the misconduct? Did the company provide our staff with sufficient information for it to evaluate the company's measures to correct the situation and ensure that the conduct does not recur?

13. Is the company the same company in which the misconduct occurred, or has it changed through a merger or bankruptcy reorganization?

Report of Investigation Pursuant to Section 21(a) of the Securities Exchange Act of 1934 and Commission Statement on the Relationship of Corporate Agency Enforcement Decisions, Exchange Act Release No. 44969 (Oct. 23, 2001), http:/www.sec.gov/litigation/investreport/34-44969.htm#P54_10935.

The Seaboard factors indicate that the SEC will look more favorably on internal investigations conducted or overseen by only outside directors. The SEC will also look more favorably upon outside law firms and experts assisting in the investigation who have not previously been engaged by management.

The SEC also places particular emphasis on when the Audit Committee and Board of Directors were "fully informed." Accordingly, a careful record should be made regarding the chronology of disclosures that occur once the first report of wrongdoing is received within an organization in order to document the timeliness of disclosures up the ladder and to the SEC.

Decision to Conduct an Internal Investigation

When deciding whether to commence an investigation, a number of considerations generally apply. These considerations include: the source and specificity of the information; the potential scope of the wrongdoing; whether the allegations involve violations of criminal or regulatory laws or the company's code of conduct; whether the allegations concern fraud, particularly fraud by management or other employees who have a significant role in the company's internal controls; and whether the allegations concern the accuracy of material information the company has disclosed to the investing public or call into question the effectiveness of the company's disclosure controls or procedures or its internal controls over financial reporting.

Obviously, where allegations of wrongdoing are referred to the board by attorneys or auditors pursuant to SOX, or where they are contained in a shareholder demand or shareholder derivative lawsuit, the decision to investigate is virtually compelled by law. Similarly, where the company is put on notice of potential violations by prosecutors or regulators, often in the first instance through the service of subpoenas or investigative demand or inquiry letters, the company is generally well advised to immediately commence its own investigation to get ahead of the government in developing the relevant facts, minimize government intrusion into company business, obtain the benefits of cooperation, and prepare to defend against any unfounded allegations of wrongdoing. Even in the absence of any specific evidence of wrongdoing, companies should consider commencing internal investigations when they learn of government investigations into other companies concerning conduct for which their company is also at risk.

After deciding to commence an internal investigation, a company faces several important decisions regarding implementation. First, it must determine if the investigation will be carried out by in-house counsel, outside counsel or, in cases requiring specific expertise, a third party investigative firm. Second, it must determine to whom the investigators report. Lastly, it must determine whom to notify about the investigation. Throughout the process, it is critical for companies to protect the confidential nature of the information provided and discovered. While the attorney-client privilege and work product doctrine are typically sufficient for such purposes (*See Upjohn Co. v. United States*, 449 U.S. 383 (1981) and, most recently, *In re Kellogg Brown & Root, Inc.*, 756 F.3d 754 (D.C. Cir. 2014), *reh'g denied (en banc)*, 2014 U.S. App. LEXIS 17077 (D.C. Cir. Sept. 2, 2014)), internal investigations often require the assistance of consultants whose work may be covered by such doctrines. *See United States v. Kovel*, 296 F.2d 918 (2d Cir. 1961).

Company Official Overseeing the Investigation Should Be Conflict Free

Once the decision is made to conduct an investigation, the next question is who shall oversee the investigation. Careful consideration must be given to this question to avoid conflicts of interest, ensure the integrity of the investigation and preserve, to the extent possible, all legal privileges and protections. Several recent cases illustrate the dangers that arise when careful thought is not given to these questions.

Originally passed by Congress in 1970, the Fair Credit Reporting Act ("FCRA") regulates "consumer reporting agencies" and any company or individual who seeks to rely on a "consumer report" in connection with making an employment decision, extending credit or insurance, or other decisions in connection with a "consumer." While the FCRA is not limited to employment decisions, this chapter focuses on the effects of the FCRA on the employment relationship. In the employment context, the "consumer" is either an applicant for employment or a current employee (hereinafter, collectively "applicant").

One well-known case illustrating the pitfalls of not choosing conflict-free directors to oversee an internal investigation is *In re: Oracle Corp. Derivative Litigation*. 824 A.2d 917 (Del. Ch. 2003). *Oracle* arose from a shareholder derivative action brought against certain Oracle directors and officers based on allegations of insider trading. *In re Oracle Corp. Derivative Litig.*, 824 A.2d 917 (Del. Ch. 2003). The board of directors formed a Special Litigation Committee consisting of two newly appointed outside directors added specifically to oversee the investigation and believed to be independent. *In re Oracle Corp. Derivative Litig.*, 824 A.2d 917, 924 (Del. Ch. 2003). The SLC conducted an extensive internal investigation, (*In re Oracle Corp. Derivative Litig.*, 824 A.2d 917, 926 (Del. Ch. 2003)), determined not to join the shareholder derivative suit and moved to dismiss it. *In re Oracle Corp. Derivative Litig.*, 824 A.2d 917, 928 (Del. Ch. 2003).

The court denied the motion to dismiss on the grounds that the two members of the Special Litigation Committee were not independent, a requirement for Delaware corporations set forth in *Zapata Corp. v. Maldonado*, 430 A.2d 779, 788–789 (Del. 1981) and its progeny. *In re Oracle Corp. Derivative Litig.*, 824 A.2d 917, 948 (Del. Ch. 2003). The court was highly critical of the fact that the two SLC members, both Stanford University professors, were asked to investigate Oracle directors who had important ties to Stanford. *In re Oracle Corp. Derivative Litig.*, 824 A.2d 917, 942 (Del. Ch. 2003). The directors accused of insider trading included: (1) another Stanford professor, who previously taught one of the Special Litigation Committee members and who served as a senior fellow and a steering committee member alongside that SLC member at Stanford; (2) a Stanford alumnus who had directed millions of dollars of contributions to Stanford during recent years, served as chair of the same Advisory Board and had a Stanford conference center named for him; and (3) Oracle's CEO, who had made millions of dollars in donations to Stanford through a personal foundation and large donations indirectly through Oracle, and who was considering making additional donations during the approximate same time period the Special Litigation Committee members were added to the Oracle board." *In re Oracle Corp. Derivative Litig.*, 824 A.2d 917, 930–935 (Del. Ch. 2003). The Court held that, taken together, these and other facts caused it to "harbor a reasonable doubt at the impartiality of the Special Litigation Committee." *In re Oracle Corp. Derivative Litig.*, 824 A.2d 917, 921 (Del. Ch. 2003).

The court acknowledged that, given the tenured position of the two Special Litigation Committee members and the lack of any direct responsibilities for fundraising, it was confident that their current jobs would not be threatened by whatever good-faith decision they made as Special Litigation Committee members. *In re Oracle Corp. Derivative Litig.*, 824 A.2d 917, 930 (Del. Ch. 2003). It went on to state, however, that:

> In evaluating the independence of a special litigation committee, this court must take into account the extraordinary importance and difficulty of such a committee's responsibility. It is, I dare say, easier to say no to a friend, relative, colleague or boss who seeks assent for an act (e.g., a transaction) that has not yet occurred than it would be to cause a corporation to sue that person.... Denying a fellow director the ability to proceed on a matter important to him may not be easy, but it must, as a general matter, be less difficult than finding that there is reason to believe that the fellow director has committed serious wrongdoing and that a derivative suit should proceed against him.

The difficulty of making this decision is compounded in the special litigation committee context because the weight of making the moral judgment necessarily falls on less than the full board. A small number of directors feels the moral gravity — and social pressures — of this duty alone.

For all these reasons, the independence inquiry is critically important if the special litigation committee process is to retain its integrity....

Id. at 940.

Interestingly, the Court gave little weight to the Special Litigation Committee's argument that it was unaware of just how substantial one director's beneficence to Stanford had been. *Id.* It said this ignorance "undermines, rather than inspires, confidence that the SLC did not examine the trading defendants' ties to Stanford more closely in preparing its Report. The Report's failure to identify these ties is important because it is the SLC's [Special Litigation Committee's] burden to show independence." *Id.* The Court instructed that: "[i]n forming the SLC [Special Litigation Committee], the Oracle board should have undertaken a thorough consideration of the facts bearing on the independence of the proposed SLC [Special Litigation Committee] members from the key objectives of the investigation."

Assessment of Investigator's Independence Should Be Far-Ranging

Oracle teaches that one of the very first steps in conducting an investigation — deciding who shall conduct the investigation — is one of the most important decisions the board will make. The independence of the directors overseeing the investigation is one of the first factors a court or prosecutors will focus on in deciding how much weight and credibility to give any conclusions and recommendations reached by such directors. *Oracle* also teaches that in analyzing the question of independence, the board must not limit its inquiry to whether the committee members may be directly beholden to, or unduly influenced by, the individuals they are investigating, but must extend its analysis to any other indirect ties that may compromise the committee's ability to conduct a truly fair, unbiased, and independent investigation. It is essential that the board perform this due diligence at the outset of the investigation, before undue time and expense is wasted.

Although *Zapata* and *Oracle* only directly apply to shareholder derivative actions, prosecutors will look even more closely at whether there are any ties, direct or indirect, that may undermine the committee's independence and credibility. To maintain its credibility with the court, prosecutors and regulators, the Special Litigation Committee or Audit Committee should be forthright in disclosing all such potential ties. The Special Litigation Committee should also continuously reevaluate its composition as the investigation progresses. Newly discovered evidence may expand the scope of the investigation to include new areas of potential misconduct or new targets. This in turn may give rise to conflicts that the board could not have reasonably foreseen at the outset.

Investigators' Pre-Investigation Contacts May Be Relevant

Oracle also illustrates the dangers that may arise when an individual makes preliminary inquiries before deciding whether to participate in an investigation. In *Oracle*, the plaintiffs argued that one of the directors, Grundfest, had prejudged the matter because, prior to deciding to join the SLC, he met with two board defendants and asked them questions regarding the related federal class action. *In re Oracle Corp. Derivative Litigation*, 824 A.2d at 924. Grundfest testified that the two defendants' explanations of their conduct were plausible enough to form sufficient confidence to at least join the Oracle board but that he had not concluded that the claims in the class action had no merit. *Id.* The court rejected the plaintiffs' claim that Grundfest has prejudged the trading defendants' culpability. The court noted, however, that "it would have been a better practice for the [internal investigation] Report to have identified that Grundfest had inquired about the Federal Class Action in determining whether to join Oracle's board." *Id.*, n.11.

Thus, Special Litigation Committee members must exercise caution, even before they are formally appointed, regarding with whom they speak, what they review, and what they say, to avoid any suggestion that they have prejudged the issues. All such preliminary steps and contacts should also be accurately and fully disclosed in any report to avoid even the appearance of a partial cover-up.

The Scope of the Special Litigation Committee's Powers and Inadvertent Privilege Waivers

After the board has decided who will conduct the investigation, one of the next questions it will face is what powers to grant the Special Litigation Committee or Audit Committee. When faced with a shareholder derivative suit, *Zapata* provides clear guidance that the committee should be fully empowered to decide whether to bring, join, settle or terminate the suit without approval by the full board. However, when allegations of corporate misconduct arise from other sources, there is less clear guidance as to the powers that should be bestowed upon the committee. Boards may be reluctant to relinquish all control over whether fellow officers, directors, and possibly the company itself are reported to prosecutors and regulators for criminal prosecution or regulatory enforcement actions and whether and how to internally discipline wrongdoers.

Ryan v. Gifford

2008 Del. Ch. LEXIS 2 (Jan. 2, 2008)

MEMORANDUM OPINION

CHANDLER, Chancellor

This case involves what is now admitted stock option backdating that occurred at Maxim Integrated Products, Inc. ("Maxim" or the "Company"). On November 30, 2007, this Court issued a letter decision resolving several discovery disputes and other pre-trial issues in this case. One of the issues resolved in that November 30 decision concerned plaintiffs' motion to compel Orrick Herrington & Sutcliffe LLP ("Orrick," counsel to Maxim's "Special Committee"), and LECG Corporation (retained by Orrick for forensic accounting assistance), and Maxim (including its Special Committee) to produce all communications between Orrick and the Special Committee that occurred during their investigation into the option backdating, including Orrick's presentation of the investigation's final report to the Special Committee and to Maxim's board of directors. Maxim has now moved, pursuant to Supreme Court Rule 42, for certification of an interlocutory appeal of this limited aspect of the November 30 decision. Plaintiffs Ryan and Conrad oppose certification. For the following reasons, I deny Maxim's application for an order certifying an interlocutory appeal. Finding that there is no basis to stay the November 30 decision under Kirpat, Inc. v. Delaware Alcohol Beverages Control Commission, I further deny Maxim's motion to stay proceedings pending appeal.

I. FACTUAL BACKGROUND

To place the November 30 decision's discovery rulings in context, it is necessary to describe at some length the factual background of this dispute. This derivative action was filed on June 12, 2006, following the publication of Merrill Lynch's report asserting that stock option grants almost certainly backdated at a number of companies, including Maxim. Two days later, on June 14, 2006, Maxim established a Special Committee, comprised of a single director, Peter De Roeth, which was charged with investigating the Company's stock option grants and practices. As I noted previously, the Special Committee in this case was not an independent Special Litigation Committee under Zapata Corp. v. Maldonado. In addition, although Maxim's board could have given the Special Committee power to act without consulting the remaining members of the board (all of whom had roles in Maxim's option granting practices and some of whom were recipients of backdated options), it chose not to do so. De Roeth retained Orrick as the Special Committee's counsel, and it was Orrick that conducted the investigation with forensic accounting assistance from LECG Corporation. Together, Orrick and LECG conducted extensive interviews and collected and analyzed huge volumes of electronic and paper material.

As Maxim noted in an 8-K filing with the SEC, in the course of the investigation, the Special Committee's legal and accounting advisors identified, preserved and collected approximately thirteen terabytes of electronic data. After running the agreed-upon search terms and eliminating software applications and duplicates, 120 gigabytes of electronic information were reviewed. The Special Committee's legal and accounting advisors reviewed a total of 270,000 electronic documents (not including metadata documents) and a total of 50,000 hard copy documents. They also conducted thirty-two interviews of current and former employees, members of Maxim's board of directors and auditing partners of both firms that audited Maxim's financial statements during the relevant time period. Some individuals were interviewed on more than one occasion.

Plaintiffs' burden in this litigation also has been made even more difficult by the frequent invocation of the Fifth Amendment privilege not to testify. Defendant Carl Jasper (Maxim's former CFO), as well as other individuals who played central roles in the administration of Maxim's stock option plan (including Maxim's former treasurer, Timothy Ruehle, and stock administrator, Sheila Raymond) have asserted their Fifth Amendment privilege not to testify.

On January 18 and 19, 2007, Orrick and the Special Committee presented its final report, purportedly only orally, to Maxim's board of directors. In attendance at the board meeting were De Roeth, other members of Maxim's board of directors (including director defendants Frank Wazzan, Kipling Hagopian, and James Bergman), attorneys from Orrick, as well as attorneys from Quinn Emanuel, who represent the director defendants in this derivative action. Following this presentation, the board met on several occasions to deliberate and discuss actions in response to the Special Committee's findings and conclusions.

Notwithstanding the significant cost of the investigation, the importance of its results, and the need for transparency, no written report of the Special Committee's findings and recommendations was ever prepared, submitted or published. No board members were permitted to leave the room with any documents or notes from the meetings discussing the investigation. The presentation evidently was completed in a manner that left little, or no, paper trail. Maxim has instructed the directors in this litigation not to answer questions regarding the board meetings or their decision making.

On February 1, 2007, Maxim publicly announced the results of the Special Committee's review. Maxim noted that there were "deficiencies related to the process for granting stock options to employees and directors," and that, in certain instances, the recorded exercise price of option grants to employees and directors "differed" from the fair market value on the "actual measurement date," but otherwise publicly exonerated the directors from any wrongdoing or malfeasance. The public report did not assign responsibility to any individuals for the option anomalies, but noted that defendants Gifford and Jasper had resigned in connection with the investigation.

In Maxim's non-public report to NASDAQ, the Company was far more forthcoming regarding the Special Committee's findings than it was in its public disclosures. The Company explained:

> The Special Committee's review of Maxim's stock option grants to directors
> and rank-and-file employees between 1996 and the third quarter of fiscal

year 2006 revealed a number of misdated option grants. Among the director grants reviewed, such misdated options included (1) grant dates that appeared to have been selected after the grant date; (2) occasions on which a grant date was selected and later changed to a date with a lower price; (3) grants at relatively low market prices which lacked contemporaneous evidence of grant selection and (4) utilization of the "one day lookback" provision in the 1996 Plan, which allowed the Interim Options Committee to select as the grant date either the day on which the grant was made or the prior day.

The Special Committee's review of the thirty-eight quarterly grants to existing rank-and-file employees made between the first fiscal quarter of 1996 through the third fiscal quarter of 2006 revealed that grant dates fell at market prices that were uniquely low. The evidence also revealed the existence of general process issues, including (1) grant lists that were not entirely finalized until after the selection of the grant date; and (2) post-grant-date changes by Mr. Gifford to the number of shares recommended to particular employees.

The Special Committee was unable to locate contemporaneous documentation of a number of the grant-date selections. Some grant dates appeared to have been selected after the grant date and on some occasions a grant date appeared to have been selected and later changed to a date with a lower price.

The Special Committee found that the employees most involved in the selection of grant dates for directors were John F. Gifford, Maxim's former Chief Executive Officer, and Carl Jasper, who served as Maxim's Chief Financial Officer from April 1999 until January 2007. The Special Committee concluded that based on the evidence developed in the investigation, that Mr. Gifford and Mr. Jasper had knowledge of and participated in the selection of grant dates for director, rank and file and new hire employee option grants from 1999 through 2005 either with hindsight or prior to completion of the formal grant-approval process.

As a result of the Special Committee's investigation, Gifford's employment as a part-time strategic advisor to the Company was terminated and Jasper's employment with the Company was terminated. In addition, based upon the findings of the Special Committee, the Company decided to change the responsibilities of Ruehle and Raymond. Other than minor corporate governance changes, no other remedial actions have been taken. Despite these findings of the Special Committee, Maxim's board of directors, which itself was conflicted (since the Special Committee found that some board members received backdated options), did not take any action to recover the damages Maxim sustained from the backdating of its options and the unjust enrichment of its officers and directors from their receipt of the backdated options.

Although Maxim now asserts far-reaching privileges for the Special Committee's work, it has, as discussed above, provided details of this work to third-parties, including NASDAQ and publicly to investors (through the SEC Form 8-K). Moreover, the Special Committee itself provided a number of documents to the SEC, the United States Attorney's Office, and Maxim's current and former auditors.

Additionally, as I have previously concluded, the director defendants in this case have specifically made use of the Special Committee's findings and conclusions for their personal benefit and have argued to this Court that the Special Committee's exoneration of them should be accorded deference. The director defendants have made these arguments in a brief, opposing plaintiffs' motion to amend the complaint, in which coincidentally Maxim has expressly joined. Further, the director defendants have extensively relied upon the Special Committee's findings both in opposing plaintiffs' motion for summary judgment and in support of their own motion for summary judgment. At the time of the November 30 decision, in their unamended summary judgment brief, the director defendants explicitly rely upon the unwritten "findings" of the Special Committee that purport to absolve the director defendants of liability. In further support of their motion, the director defendants laud "the Special Committee's comprehensive investigation," which included "32 individual interviews." Interestingly, however, these same director defendants, who clearly control Maxim's litigation position, have refused to produce to plaintiffs (who prosecute this action on behalf of Maxim) materials related to the Special Committee's investigation. Even more interestingly, since the November 30 decision, the director defendants have submitted an amended brief in support of their motion for summary judgment that purports to disavow reliance on the Special Committee's findings, despite their explicit reliance thereon in the first brief in support of their motion.

In light of the above facts and the convenient and selective invocation of the attorney-client privilege, this Court on November 30, 2007, granted plaintiffs' motion to compel. Specifically, the Court ruled that Maxim, its Special Committee, and Orrick must produce all material related to the Special Committee's investigation that were withheld on grounds of attorney-client privilege. Maxim now seeks certification for an interlocutory appeal of one portion of this ruling.

II. ANALYSIS

Supreme Court Rule 42 sets forth the standards for certification of interlocutory appeals by a trial court. Under this Rule, no interlocutory appeal may be certified unless the order from which appeal is to be taken (1) determines a substantial issue, (2) establishes a legal right, and (3) meets at least one of the criteria enumerated in Supreme Court Rule 42(b)(i)–(v). Those criteria include the reasons listed in Rule 41 for certification of questions of law, questions of the trial court's jurisdiction, instances where the trial court has set aside precedent, or instances where the trial court has ruled on a dispositive issue. Usually, the Supreme Court accepts interlocutory appeals only where the circumstances are "extraordinary" or "exceptional." Maxim's application seeks immediate appellate review of what it purports is a significant question of law that is of first impression in this state. Because this Court's November 30 letter decision applied only established precedent, Maxim is incorrect, and because I conclude Maxim has failed to establish any other permissible justification for its application, I decline to certify its interlocutory appeal.

A. Maxim's interlocutory appeal would be futile: the November 30 Order provided two alternative bases for granting plaintiffs' motion to compel and Maxim has challenged only one

Maxim seeks an interlocutory appeal solely of this Court's conclusion that the Company's Special Committee's communications with the director defendants and their individual counsel constituted a waiver of attorney-client privilege. In the November 30 decision, however, I expressly determined that any claim to privilege was vitiated by plaintiffs' showing of good cause under the longstanding principle of Garner v. Wolfinbarger as adopted and applied by this Court numerous times over the past three decades. As then-Vice Chancellor Jacobs noted in 1987, Garner is technically not an exception to attorney-client privilege. Instead, where a plaintiff shareholder demonstrates good cause under the Garner framework, Delaware courts refuse to apply the privilege and permit discovery of otherwise protected materials. Such is the case here, where plaintiffs have established good cause under Garner and thereby rendered inapplicable any privilege that would protect the materials they seek.

Maxim's application for certification of interlocutory appeal does not discuss or challenge this Court's conclusion that plaintiffs demonstrated good cause under Garner; it only seeks review of the waiver analysis in the November 30 decision. Because the Garner determination provides an independent basis for the November 30 decision, however, even a successful appeal on the waiver issue would prove futile. The Committee's comment to Supreme Court Rule 42 clarifies that the rule's purpose is to "sav[e] time" and "advance the litigation." Certifying a purely academic appeal such as this one would undermine the rule's purpose.

B. The Court's November 30 Order neither determined a "substantial issue" nor established a "legal right"

Supreme Court Rule 42(b) prohibits certification of an interlocutory appeal unless the application, as a threshold matter, both determines a substantial issue and establishes a legal right. Maxim has failed to demonstrate that the Court's November 30 decision did either. Contrary to Maxim's assertion, this Court's decision did not establish a "new legal right of access to internal corporate information." Instead, the Court reiterates that, as in Fleischman, where this Court was also asked to certify under Rule 42 an order requiring production of material relating to an independent investigation of backdating, the decision "simply grants a limited procedural right to plaintiff—access to documents that defendants have expressly relied upon in support of their motion to dismiss." Here, the November 30 decision merely gave a similar limited procedural right to plaintiffs. As noted above, since the issuance of this Court's November 30 decision, the director defendants have—in a seeming coincidence of timing—filed an amended brief in support of their motion for summary judgment in which they superficially state that they do not rely on the findings of the Special Committee for the purposes of their motion. At the time of the November 30 decision, however, the director defendants explicitly asserted that the findings of the Special Committee were entitled to deference from this Court. Moreover, even if this Court ignores the suspicious timing of the director defendants' purported disavowal of reliance on the investigation, Maxim seeks to further avail itself of the Special Committee's report, which will redound to the benefit of the director defendants.

Maxim also appears to argue that the November 30 decision decided a "substantial issue" because it will affect Delaware corporate customs and long-standing principles of good corporate governance. Not only are such dire consequences exaggerated, but fears thereof are also misplaced. The decision was the result only of the application of well-settled precedent to a set of particular and specific facts. Though detailed more fully above, it is worthwhile to repeat that the relevant factual circumstances here include the receipt of purportedly privileged information by the director defendants in their individual capacities from the Special Committee. The decision would not apply to a situation (unlike that presented in this case) in which board members are found to be acting in their fiduciary capacity, where their personal lawyers are not present, and where the board members do not use the privileged information to exculpate themselves. Similarly, the decision would not affect the privileges of a Special Litigation Committee formed under Zapata, or any other kind of committee that (unlike the Special Committee here) has the power to take actions without approval of other board members.

Maxim also erroneously argues that the decision results in a waiver of privilege as a consequence of the director defendants' exercise of their duty of due care and that the decision therefore imposes conflicting duties on directors. The decision neither imposes duties on directors nor prevents directors from complying with their duty to act with due care, loyalty and in good faith. Maxim appears to fail to appreciate the difference between compliance with fiduciary duties and doing so while maintaining a privilege. In any event, the only thing that directors cannot do under the decision is receive purportedly privileged material while acting in their personal (as compared to fiduciary) capacity and still maintain the privilege.

C. Maxim has failed to establish any of the specific criteria in Supreme Court Rule 42(b)

Even if this appeal were not futile, and even if the November 30 decision did determine a substantial issue or establish a legal right, certification remains improper because Maxim has failed to prove applicable any of the criteria listed in Supreme Court Rule 42(b).

1. The November 30 decision did not decide an issue of first impression under Delaware law

Maxim's application appears to rest on the contention that the decision presents a question of first impression in Delaware because "Counsel could find no Delaware case that held that a committee of the board waived privilege over its entire investigation by reporting its findings to the full board." The Court notes that one need not consult even a single case to find the well established principle on which the November 30 decision is based. Rule 510 of the Delaware Rules of Evidence explains that privilege is destroyed whenever the holder of the privilege "voluntarily discloses or consents to disclosure of any significant part of the privileged matter." This clear codification of the principle notwithstanding, plenty of cases also rely on this bedrock principle of waiver.

Maxim appears to argue that its application presents a novel question of law simply because no case has previously applied Rule 510 in the unique factual context of this case. Such an argument must fail. The mere application of long-held precedent to new facts does not make an order worthy of appeal. Moreover, Maxim's logic is self defeating. Just as Maxim's counsel "could find no Delaware case that held that a committee of the board waived privilege over its entire investigation by reporting its findings to the full board," this Court could find no case, in which certification of an interlocutory appeal was granted, where the movant sought review of only one of two independent bases for a decision or where the movant seeks review of a decision that applies well established law to new facts. More importantly, the Court could find no case where a board's Special Committee disclosed its findings on the misconduct of director defendants to those defendants themselves and to their individual, outside counsel and later successfully claimed that such disclosure did not constitute a waiver. Indeed, had the Court found such a case, the November 30 decision may have read differently.

It is not clear that the privilege between Orrick and the Special Committee extends to the Company itself but, even if it does, that privilege was waived by disclosure to the director defendants, who attended the January meeting in their individual—not fiduciary—capacities along with their individual, outside counsel. Disclosure to outsiders has never failed to waive privilege under Delaware law. Maxim's "Chicken Little" argument that the Court's November 30 decision changes the law of privilege, therefore, is vastly overstated. The sky is not falling. Maxim has merely been struck by an acorn that it brought upon itself through its careless and suspicious practices.

2. Maxim has not established (or even attempted to establish) any of the other criteria of Rule 42(b)

Maxim does not make any other serious arguments that another of the criteria under Supreme Court Rule 42(b) applies in this case. The other reasons an interlocutory appeal may be permitted include resolution of conflicting trial court decisions, construction or application of a previously unconsidered statute, consideration of controverted jurisdiction, or consideration of an order that reverses or sets aside a prior decision of the court, a jury, or an administrative agency. None of those situations is present here. Consequently, the application for certification of interlocutory appeal is improper.

III. CONCLUSION

Maxim has failed to satisfy the requirements of Supreme Court Rule 42. First, an appeal of the waiver analysis in this Court's November 30 decision would be futile because the Court decided the privilege issue on two independent grounds and Maxim has not appealed the other basis for the decision. Second, Maxim has not proved that the decision determined a "substantial issue" or established a "legal right." Third, the November 30 decision did not address a question of first impression and none of the other specific criteria of Rule 42(b) are present in this case. Maxim's rhetorically charged application stated more cogently its position than did its brief opposing plaintiffs' motion to compel, but rhetoric alone cannot justify Maxim's attempt to keep from plaintiffs the materials I ordered the company to produce on November 30. Because Maxim has not satisfied Supreme Court Rule 42, I deny its application for certification of interlocutory appeal. I further deny Maxim's motion to stay the November 30 decision, finding the application meritless and finding no basis under Kirpat, Inc. to justify granting the motion.

IT IS SO ORDERED.

Investigators Should Be Granted Sufficient Powers

While the *Ryan* Court's holding may be limited to the unique facts of that case, it does present a number of cautionary warnings. First, boards should give careful consideration to the scope of the Audit Committee or Special Litigation Committee's authority to make decisions and take legal action based on its findings. Limitations on the committee's decision-making authority may compromise its independence in the eyes of a court or government authorities. Requiring the Special Litigation Committee to share its findings with other board members before any decisions can be made on behalf of the company may also lead to waiving the attorney-client privilege or work product protections and result in the investigative report being disclosed to third parties.

Steps to Avoid Waiver of Privilege

Even if there is no intentional disclosure of an investigative report to a third party, or other explicit waiver, Special Litigation Committee's and their legal advisors should not assume that the material compiled during their investigation will be protected from disclosure. As *Ryan* illustrates, a court may order the disclosure of attorney-client communications and work product where plaintiffs make a showing that the information contained therein is not available from any other source, particularly in jurisdictions which apply the *Garner* "good cause" factors in shareholder derivative actions. Committees can, however, take certain steps to minimize the risk of such compelled disclosure and limit the scope of the material ordered to be disclosed.

For example, investigators often decide not to memorialize the investigative findings and conclusions in written form. While this does not prevent a court from ordering the disclosure of notes or outlines of any oral presentation, if it finds that a waiver has occurred, such notes and outlines typically contain far less legal analysis than would a more formal written report. Similarly, verbatim interview memoranda are more likely to be ordered disclosed than summary interview memoranda. In addition, because interview memoranda are more likely to be ordered disclosed, legal analysis is better left to separate memoranda.

Directors serving on an Audit Committee or Special Litigation Committee should also exercise extreme caution when communicating with fellow board members so as not to improperly disclose factual findings or legal analysis that may constitute a waiver of the attorney-client or work product protections. They should recognize that the Audit Committee or the Special Litigation Committee is distinct from both the company, the board and the individual board members, and that it has its own independent attorney-client privilege and work product protections that can be inadvertently waived if the information is shared with other board members or management.

If the Special Litigation Committee decides to disclose some portion of its investigative facts and conclusions either within the company, to the government or to third parties, (such as outside auditors who may be legally entitled to demand such information) such disclosures should be structured to minimize the danger that they will be deemed a waiver of the attorney-client or work product privileges. For example, citing to public documents, disclosing underlying business records not created as part of the investigation, providing only summary conclusions of the investigation, or making witnesses available for independent interviews, are all means that should be explored to avoid opening the door to a privilege waiver claim. The issues arising from the waiver or selective waiver of the attorney-client or work product privileges are discussed at more length in a later chapter.

Press releases and other communications with the press should also be carefully scrutinized to ensure that they do not waive the attorney-client or work product privileges. Care should also be taken in what is shared with public relations firms and what they are authorized to disseminate on the company's behalf to avoid waiver of the attorney-client and work product protection and to avoid potential fraud and obstruction of justice charges based on the dissemination of false, misleading or incomplete information or details. *Compare In re Grand Jury Subpoenas,* 265 F. Sup. 2d. 321, 330–332 (S.D.N.Y. 2003), *and In re Cooper Mkt. Antitrust Litig.,* 200 F.R.D. 213, 220 (S.D.N.Y. 2001) (recognizing role of public relations firm in advising clients and extending attorney-client privilege to them), *with Haugh v. Schroder Investment Management North America, Inc.,* 2003 U.S. Dist. LEXIS 14586 (S.D.N.Y. Aug. 25, 2003) (denying extension of attorney-client privilege to consultant even though retained through attorney engagement letter because the assigned task did not constitute "legal advice" and Plaintiff did not identify "any nexus between the consultant's work and the attorney's role").

Selecting an Investigator — Factors to Consider

In most cases the person appointed to conduct an internal investigation should be an attorney. The primary benefits of selecting an attorney to conduct an investigation include availability of the attorney-client privilege and work product protection.

The attorney-client privilege and the work product doctrine are important because they provide a legal basis for keeping the results of any investigation from becoming a matter of public record or easily attainable by plaintiff's counsel.

Another question is whether in-house or outside counsel should be put in charge of an investigation. One of the most crucial factors in determining who should conduct an internal investigation is whether the impending investigation is likely to uncover conduct of a criminal nature, resulting in an investigation by the government and possible criminal charges against employees of the corporation, the corporation, or both. If it is, the best person to oversee such an investigation is one who has no vested interest in the outcome of the investigation, whose objectivity will not be questioned by the government, and who likely has had no previous relationship with the corporate entity subject to the investigation—in other words, neither inside nor the corporation's regular outside counsel. That said, the following is a list of factors that should be considered when deciding whether in-house or outside counsel should be appointed to conduct an internal investigation.

Selection Factors

- What is the nature of the conduct being investigated (criminal vs. civil) (as noted, an investigation involving criminal conduct may be better overseen by outside counsel with no prior relationship to the corporation);

- How widespread or serious is the alleged misconduct to be investigated (the more serious/widespread the alleged misconduct, the more important it is to consider hiring outside counsel);

- How high up the corporate chain of command is the alleged misconduct believed to have taken place (the higher up the targeted individuals are, the more important it is to utilize outside counsel);

- Whether the cost of conducting an investigation will be a factor (if so, use of in-house counsel would be most cost effective; but if cost drives the investigation, government may not view with favor the employer's efforts to uncover employee misconduct);

- Whether the investigation must be conducted quickly (if so, outside counsel might be more able to handle an investigation under time constraints);

- Whether in-house counsel has the necessary investigative skills (e.g., skills to conduct an investigation of criminal conduct) to conduct the investigation;

- Whether in-house counsel has the necessary subject matter expertise to conduct the investigation;

- Whether in-house counsel has sufficient independence to the conduct investigation (e.g., is a target of investigation someone to whom in-house counsel is subordinate or with whom in-house counsel has a personal relationship);

- Whether in-house counsel has a potential conflict of interest (e.g., is a potential witness to or a target of investigation);
- Whether in-house counsel has a vested interest in the outcome of the investigation;
- Whether in-house counsel's institutional knowledge of the corporation would aid investigation;
- Whether in-house counsel's employment status will encourage or discourage employees to be cooperative and forthcoming during the investigation;
- Whether in-house counsel's employment status would be viewed unfavorably by the government and diminish the value of the corporation's internal investigation and its perceived level of cooperation in addressing the unlawful conduct (particularly where in-house counsel's internal investigation failed to uncover misconduct that is the subject of a governmental inquiry); and
- Whether in-house counsel's employment status could jeopardize the corporation's ability to assert attorney-client privilege or work product protection vis-à-vis its investigatory findings in subsequent criminal, administrative, or civil proceedings.

Even when a determination has been made to use outside counsel to oversee an internal investigation, in-house counsel still may play a vital role by assisting outside counsel in identifying potential witnesses, identifying and securing relevant documentation, putting procedures in place to ensure that relevant documentation is not destroyed, and laying the necessary groundwork to ensure that employees will cooperate fully with outside counsel's investigation.

The Nuts and Bolts of an Internal Investigation

Entire treatises have been written on the myriad issues that must be taken into account in conducting an internal investigation. Such a broad treatment is beyond the scope of this chapter. That being said, the following is a summary of some of the most important rules of the road:

- Investigate promptly once provided with information warranting investigation; failure to timely investigate may hamper subsequent negotiations with government in seeking leniency based on the internal investigation;
- Prior to the investigation, clearly articulate the purpose, scope, budget, and timeline (when investigation needs to be completed) of the investigation in a written document signed by the responsible senior executive and given to the investigator;
- Determine who will oversee the entire investigation in order to ensure ongoing compliance with the purpose and scope of the investigation, that proper investigatory tactics are utilized, and that the investigator is familiar with any laws that may be implicated by the investigation (e.g., if potential witnesses are located in different states where laws may differ from one another);

- Identify the client so that employees/witnesses are not misled into believing that in-house or outside counsel represents them or that their communications are protected by attorney-client privilege that only they can waive;

- Employees questioned as part of the investigation should be advised at the outset of every interview, that: 1) counsel represents the company, or the Special Committee, as the case may be; 2) counsel is not the employee's lawyer and does not represent the employee's interests; 3) the employee is expected to be truthful and cooperate fully; 4) the interview is protected by the attorney-client privilege, but the privilege belongs to the company, not the employee; 5) in order to preserve the privilege, the employee is directed not to discuss the interview with any third party; 6) the company can choose to waive the privilege and disclose all or part of what the employee discloses during the interview, to outside parties, including outside auditors, regulators, or prosecutors. If the company has already agreed to cooperate with the government and/or waive its attorney-client privilege, it should strongly consider advising the employee of that fact and warning the employee that lying to the interviewer in such circumstances may be deemed obstruction of justice by the government;

- Determine at the outset whether the corporation's normal document destruction procedures need to be suspended in order to ensure that relevant documentation/electronic data is not inadvertently or intentionally destroyed prior to (or during) the investigation;

- Any documents generated during the investigation should be marked "Privileged and Confidential";

- Keep work product documents separate from attorney-client privilege documents; in other words, factual summaries should not contain attorney impressions;

- Information pertaining to the investigation should be conveyed to a limited number of persons in order to avoid inadvertent waiver of attorney-client privilege; and

- Weigh the pros and cons of drafting a written report versus giving an oral presentation of one's findings at the conclusion of the internal investigation.

Beware of Obstructing Justice

Company officials conducting internal investigations should be careful that they do not turn themselves into targets by running afoul of criminal laws, ethical or fiduciary duties or employees' rights. There are many traps for the unwary.

For example, SOX expanded the range of conduct that constitutes obstruction of justice and increased the penalties for such conduct. These statutes criminalize certain behavior that might not on its face appear to be obstruction of justice, such as destroying documents or other evidence of a crime before a governmental investigation has even commenced or lying to company lawyers or non-governmental investigators.

Company employees should be educated at the outset of any investigation as to the range of prohibited behavior and the severe penalties for obstructing justice.

Prior to Sarbanes-Oxley, the primary relevant federal obstruction statutes, Title 18, U.S.C., Section 1503 and 1505, required obstructive conduct to be connected to a pending judicial proceeding or a pending investigation by a federal agency. Thus, the destruction of documents, for example, prior to the convening of a grand jury or the commencement of a formal investigation did not constitute obstruction of justice under these statutes. Note, however, that under 18 U.S.C., Section 1001, a false statement to a federal agent is prosecutable absent any investigation.

Sarbanes-Oxley amended 18 U.S.C., Section 1512 to remedy this gap. Section 1512(c) now provides, in relevant part, that whoever corruptly—

(1) alters, destroys, mutilates, or conceals a record, document, or other object, or attempts to do so, with the intent to impair the objects integrity or availability for use in an official proceeding; or

(2) otherwise obstructs, influences or impedes any official proceeding, or attempts to do so shall be fined under this title or imprisoned not more than 20 years or both.

Section 1512(f) was also amended to provide that: "an official proceeding need not be pending or about to be instituted at the time of the offense." Also, it is no defense that the testimony, document or other object subject to obstruction is not admissible in evidence or is covered by a claim of privilege. 18 U.S.C. 1512(f). Section 1512 was also amended to reach individuals who actually destroy or shred documents, not just those in supervisory position to order their destruction.

Sarbanes-Oxley also added broader prohibitions against document destruction and other obstructive conduct. It created a new criminal statute, 18 U.S.C., §1519, commonly referred to as the general anti-shredding provision. Section 1519 provides:

Whoever knowingly alters, destroys, mutilates, conceals, covers up, falsifies, or makes a false entry in any record, document, or tangible object with the intent to impede, obstruct, or influence the investigation or proper administration of any matter within the jurisdiction of any department or agency of the United States or any case filed under Title 11, or in relation to or contemplation of any such matter or case, shall be fined under this title, imprisoned not more than 20 years, or both.

Troublingly, Section 1519 prohibits the destruction of documents not only once an investigation or litigation has been commenced but also in situations where an investigation is only "contemplated." The broad reach, potential for confusion, and dangers inherent in these statutes were illustrated in a recent case where an attorney was charged with obstruction of justice and destruction of evidence, for destroying a laptop computer containing child pornography that belonged to an individual, Tate, who was employed by a church the attorney represented. *United States v. Russell*, 639 F. Supp. 2d 226 (D. Conn. 2007). *Russell* arose when a church employee using Tate's laptop discovered numerous images of naked boys. The following day, church officials retained Russell, a lawyer specializing in civil and criminal litigation, to represent and advise the church in the matter. According to the indictment, Russell and two other church officials met with Tate, who acknowledged his responsibility for the images and resigned. Russell gave Tate the name of a local criminal defense attorney and took possession of the computer. The following day, Russell destroyed the computer. Unbeknownst to Russell, however, three days earlier and one day before the church employee had discovered the laptop pornography, the FBI had independently initiated an investigation into Tate's possession of child pornography.

Russell moved to dismiss the indictment arguing that it failed to allege a sufficient nexus between his actions and an official proceeding or investigation at issue, arguing that he was not aware of the FBI investigation at the time he destroyed the computer. This fact was not disputed by the government. Russell also moved to dismiss Count II, arguing that Section 1519 only prohibited the shredding of business records and documents, not the destruction of contraband such as child pornography.

The court held that, under the facts alleged in the indictment, there was more than sufficient basis for a jury to conclude that an official proceeding was reasonably foreseeable to Russell at the time he destroyed the laptop. *Id.* at 233. The court relied upon the fact that the church had treated the computer as evidence, that Russell was a criminal defense attorney, that Russell was retained by the church and not Tate, that Tate was in fact being investigated by the FBI, and that Russell gave Tate the name of a criminal defense attorney. The court also rejected Tate's argument that Section 1519 was limited to the destruction of business records and documents. *Id.* at 236–37.

The court's ruling in *Russell* is extremely disturbing. The factors relied upon by the court to find that it was reasonably foreseeable to Russell that an official proceeding might commence could equally apply to any case involving a potential criminal violation. Under the court's analysis, a company that becomes aware of evidence of a crime cannot destroy such evidence, arguably even in the ordinary course of business, without risking exposure to an obstruction of justice charge.

While this may not seem troublesome, think of the dilemma Russell faced. If he held onto the laptop containing the child pornography, he ran afoul of 18 U.S.C. § 2252 which makes it illegal to possess child pornography. However, for destroying the pornography he was charged with obstruction of justice. His only safe choice, adopting the court's reasoning, would be to disclose the evidence to the federal authorities. While such a remedy may be advisable in many instances, it is not always in a company's best interest to do so.

While it is arguable whether another court, or a jury, would reach the same result, the *Russell* court's holding should serve as a strong warning to all company officers, directors, and attorneys to proceed cautiously when deciding how to handle and dispose of potential evidence of wrongdoing, whether or not it rises to the level of contraband.

Ultimately, the U.S. Attorney's Office offered Russell a plea to misprision of a felony, in violation of 18 U.S.C. § 4, for failing to report the commission of a felony. Transcript of Change of Plea Hearing dated Sept. 27, 2007. (Document No. 62), at p. 37.

Interestingly, this statute creates additional potential issues for officials overseeing investigations. The misprision of felony statute, 18 U.S.C. § 4, provides:

> Whoever, having knowledge of the actual commission of a felony cognizable by a court of the United States, conceals and does not as soon as possible make known the same to some judge or other person in civil or military authority under the United States, shall be fined under this title or imprisoned not more than three years, or both.

On its face, this statute can be broadly applied to many instances where an individual or corporation, including its board, audit committee or directors, is aware of a felony violation and fails to report it. In practice, however, the statute is typically not applied by U.S. Attorney's Offices in such a broad reaching manner. For one thing, the statute contains an element of concealment and it has been construed by courts to require an act of active concealment as opposed to a mere passive failure to report the violation. *See, e.g., United States v. Johnson*, 546 F.2d 1225, 1227 (5th Cir. 1977); *U.S. v. Warters*, 885 F. 2d 1266, 1275 (5th Cir. 1989). Thus, mere knowledge of the commission of a felony by another individual should not be sufficient to constitute a violation of the statute.

In the *Russell* case, the destruction of the laptop was arguably a sufficient act of concealment to meet that element of the statute. Whether an audit committee's decision not to authorize a written report memorializing findings of commission of felony offenses by corporate employees rises to the level of concealment is less obvious. Destroying notes taken during interviews with employees who disclose incriminating information or evidence of wrongdoing may also constitute concealment.

The *Russell* court's holding is also troubling in another context. For example, at the end of an internal investigation, the audit committee may be informed of the commission of certain felony offenses by certain employees. For various reasons, the audit committee may well decide that the commission of these offenses is not something it is going to report to the authorities. The question then arises as to what to do with the underlying evidence, often in the form of emails or documents that would constitute evidence of the commission of these offenses. Does permitting the destruction of these materials in the ordinary course of business, pursuant to the company's otherwise appropriate document destruction policies, constitute a violation of Section 1519? Investigators need to be aware of these concerns and think through them carefully to avoid finding themselves the target of a government investigation for obstruction of justice.

Lying to an Investigator May Be Obstruction of Justice

The federal obstruction of justice statutes have recently been applied in other unexpected ways. *United States v. Kumar* (Indictment, *United States v. Kumar and Richards*, CR. No. 04-840 (S.D.N.Y. Sept. 20, 2004; superseding indictment filed May 15, 2005; second superseding indictment filed June 28, 2005), was the first known case where individuals were charged with obstructing justice based, in part, on false statements they made to non-governmental individuals, in this case private attorneys working on behalf of Computer Associates and its Audit Committee. *Kumar,* commonly known as the *Computer Associates* case, involved an investigation by the U.S. Attorney's Office for the Eastern District of New York and the SEC into accounting fraud by Computer Associates, a computer software provider. The investigation focused on a suspected company-wide practice of falsely reporting quarterly revenues associated with licensing agreements that had not been signed until at least several days or longer after that quarter ended (the "35 day month practice").

Kumar and Richards, two senior executives of Computer Associates, were indicted for conspiracy to obstruct justice, in violation of 18 U.S.C. Section 1512(c), as well as various counts of perjury, false statements, securities fraud and false filings with the SEC. The conspiracy to obstruct justice count alleged that Kumar and Richards conspired with other employees to intentionally mislead the law firm retained to represent the company in connection with the government investigations, by causing the employees, including Kumar and Richards themselves, to lie to the law firm about the existence of the 35 day month practice. *Id.* ¶¶ 78–79. The government alleged that the defendants lied to the law firm with the intent that those lies would be conveyed to and hopefully mislead the government in its investigation. *Id.* ¶¶ 80–83. The indictment also alleged that Kumar and Richards lied to a second law firm subsequently retained to conduct an internal investigation into the same allegations on behalf of the Audit Committee of Computer Associates' Board of Directors. *Id.* at *24. Both Kumar and Richards ultimately pled guilty to the obstruction and various other charges.

The *Computer Associates* case has been widely cited for the proposition that employees who lie in connection with an internal investigation can be charged with obstruction of justice, even when the lies are only made to company representatives and not directly to government agents. It is certainly debatable whether lying in connection with an internal investigation should constitute obstruction of justice where there is no active government investigation, or no reasonably foreseeable expectation by the interviewee that the contents of the interview will be shared with government authorities. However, many internal investigative interviews are conducted in circumstances similar to those in the *Computer Associates* case, where the government investigation is publicly known and the company has announced its intent to cooperate fully and share its investigative findings with the government.

Computer Associates is not the only case where federal authorities have charged individuals with violations of Section 1512(c) for lying in connection with an internal investigation. *See, e.g., United States v. Singleton.* 06 CR 080, Indictment ¶ 14 of Count 10 (S.D. Tex. Mar. 8, 2006). (charging employee with lying to outside counsel conducting internal investigation into illegal trading practices and price reporting also being investigated by the U.S. Attorney's Office and two other federal agencies; defendant's motion to dismiss on grounds that lying to private attorney did not establish sufficient nexus to an official proceeding denied; [Memorandum in support of Singleton's Motion to Dismiss Count Ten of the Superseding Indictment, *United States v. Singleton*, 06 CR-0080, n. 37, at 25.] Singleton's post trial motion for acquittal was granted); Hearing Minutes and Order, *United States v. Singleton*, 06 CR-0080 (S.D. Tex. July 31, 2006); *see also United States v. Ring*, 08-CR-274 (ESH) (D.C. Sept. 5, 2008) Indictment, Counts IX and X.

As a result of *Computer Associates* and similar cases, many white collar practitioners conducting internal investigations now make it a practice to routinely advise employees that the contents of their interview may be shared with government officials and that lying or concealing evidence may be deemed a violation of the federal obstruction of justice statutes.

The Changing Rules Regarding Cooperation with the Government

Federal prosecutors have often placed immense pressure on corporations to waive their attorney-client and work product privileges so that the government will credit them for cooperation. The United States Attorneys' Manual calls for consideration of a Company's "willingness to cooperate in the investigation of its agents" as factor in deciding the proper treatment of a corporate target. Such a factor can be interpreted as requiring such waivers. However, prosecutors' ability to induce such waivers has been significantly, albeit not entirely, curtailed based on recent changes in DOJ policy.

Waiver of Attorney-Client Privilege and Work Product Privileges

The Holder Memorandum

The origin of the Justice Department's policy concerning privilege waivers as an expected component of cooperation dates back to June 1999, when then Deputy Attorney General Eric Holder issued a non-binding memorandum to staff, entitled *Bringing Criminal Charges Against Corporations* ("Holder Memo"), the predecessor to the current Principles. The memorandum listed eight factors that prosecutors should consider in determining whether to criminally charge a corporation including: "company's timely and voluntary disclosure of wrongdoing and willingness to cooperate in investigating its employees." The Holder memorandum stated that prosecutors could view waivers of attorney-client and work product privileges as satisfying the "willingness to cooperate" factor. After the release of the Holder Memo, prosecutor requests for such waivers became far more frequent.

The Thompson Memorandum

Approximately six months after the Corporate Fraud Taskforce was established, in January 2003, the Justice Department replaced the Holder Memo with a memorandum drafted by then Deputy Attorney General Larry D. Thompson, entitled *Principles of Federal Prosecution of Business Organizations* ("Thompson Memo"). The Thompson Memo was virtually identical to the Holder Memo in that it contained the same eight factors referred to above but added a ninth factor permitting prosecutors to take into account the adequacy of alternative remedies such as civil or regulatory enforcement actions.

There were several notable differences, however. The Thompson Memorandum's guidance was binding on all federal prosecutors and there was new commentary addressing what corporate conduct should be viewed as impeding a governmental investigation (e.g., overly broad assertions of corporate representation of employees, directing employees not to cooperate with investigation, delaying production of records, and failing to promptly disclose knowledge of illegal conduct). Critics of the Thompson Memorandum viewed this commentary, along with the carry over language from the Holder Memo regarding waiver of privileges, as having reduced the role of corporate counsel to that of a deputy prosecutor.

The McNulty Memorandum

In December 2006, the Thompson Memorandum was superseded and replaced by a memorandum issued by then Deputy Attorney General Paul McNulty ("McNulty Memo"). [The McNulty Memo also replaced a Justice Department 2005 memorandum, entitled *Waiver of Corporate Attorney-Client and Work Product Protections* ("McCallum Memo")]. This revision was at least partially in response to a decision issued earlier that year by a New York federal court judge, who held that the government's actions in pressuring a corporation to stop paying the legal fees of current and former employees had the effect of unconstitutionally interfering with those individuals' rights to due process and assistance of counsel. *United States v. Stein*, 435 F. Supp. 2d 330 (S.D.N.Y. 2006). The judge's ruling challenged the legality of the Thompson Memorandum's guidance on what conduct could be viewed as impeding a governmental investigation.

The McNulty Memorandum also came on the heels of Senator Arlen Specter's (R-PA) introduction of legislation that would amend the federal Criminal Code to prohibit the Justice Department from conditioning the treatment of companies (whether or not to indict) on their waiving attorney-client and work product privileges, declining to pay their employees' legal fees, terminating employees who fail to cooperate in a governmental investigation, among other protections.

The McNulty Memorandum deviated from its predecessor memos on two important points: 1) it set forth procedures that prosecutors were required to comply with before they could request waivers of attorney-client privilege and work product protections, and 2) it barred prosecutors, except in exceptional circumstances, from considering a corporation's decision to provide legal representation to an employee when evaluating a corporation's degree of cooperation.

Under the new procedures, a prosecutor was required to obtain written authorization from senior Justice Department officials and seek the "least intrusive waiver necessary" in conducting its investigation of the corporation. The prosecutor was required to demonstrate a "legitimate need" for requesting privileged information—a hurdle not difficult to overcome. Whether a legitimate need existed depended on the following factors:

- Likelihood and degree to which privileged information will benefit government's investigation;

- Whether information can be obtained in a timely manner by using alternative means (without requesting a waiver);

- Completeness of the voluntary disclosure already provided; and

- Collateral consequences to the corporation in the event it waives.

If a legitimate need existed, prosecutors were instructed to first request factual information (which could include privileged information), referred to as "Category I" information. Examples of Category I information included: key documents, witness statements, factual summaries, or chronologies. If a corporation refused to waive its attorney-client or work product privileges in order to provide Category I information, its refusal could be used in determining the corporation's level of cooperation.

In the event that Category I information failed to permit the prosecutor to conduct a thorough investigation, a prosecutor, after obtaining written authorization, could request Category II information, which included attorney-client communications and non-factual attorney-client work product. The memorandum cautioned prosecutors that a request for Category II information should only be sought in "rare circumstances." Unlike Category I information, a prosecutor could not consider a corporation's refusal to waive its privilege to provide Category II information in determining the corporation's level of cooperation. Despite its admonition that Category II information should rarely be requested, many commentators opined that the McNulty Memorandum would not eliminate the unspoken pressure placed on corporations to disclose such information to avoid being indicted.

The McNulty Memorandum also provided that corporations cannot be penalized for advancing legal fees to its employees or agent, except in those "extremely rare cases" where it can be shown that, based on the totality of the circumstances, the advancement of such monies "was intended to impede a criminal investigation." It reiterated, however, that a company's promise of support to a culpable employee or agent (i.e., retaining the employee without disciplining him or her) or its decision to provide information to said individual about the government's investigation pursuant to a joint defense agreement still could be considered in weighing the extent and value of a corporation's cooperation.

While the McNulty Memorandum was intended to respond to criticisms that had been lodged against the Thompson Memorandum, many practitioners and commentators openly questioned whether the McNulty Memo changed much.

The Filip Memorandum

In August 2008, Mark Filip, then Deputy Attorney General, announced that DOJ had modified yet again the framework for assessing a company's cooperation in an investigation. Most significantly, credit for cooperation will no longer be dependent on a company's waiver of the attorney-client or work product privilege. In addition, prosecutors will no longer be permitted to consider the company's advancement of legal fees to employees under investigation, or the company's entry into a joint defense agreement, in assessing the extent of a company's cooperation.

The prosecution of corporate crime is a high priority for the Department of Justice. By investigating the allegations of wrongdoing and by bringing charges where appropriate The new guidelines forbid prosecutors from asking for attorney-client communications or attorney work product, except where either (i) the company is asserting an advice-of-counsel defense to criminal charges, or (ii) the communications between the company and its counsel were in furtherance of a crime.

Pursuant to the Filip Memorandum:

> Eligibility for cooperation credit is not predicated upon the waiver of attorney-client privilege or work product protection. Instead, the sort of cooperation that is most valuable to resolving allegations of misconduct by a corporation and its officers, directors, employees, or agents is disclosure of the relevant *facts* concerning such misconduct. USAM 9-28.720.

The general principle is that corporations should not be treated leniently because of their artificial nature. It further provides that "while corporations remain free to convey non-factual or 'core' attorney-client communications or work product—if and only if the corporation voluntarily chooses to do so—prosecutors should not ask for waivers and are directed not to do so." USAM 9-28710. Where a decision is made to charge a corporation, it does not necessarily follow that individual directors, officers, employees or shareholders should not also be charged. Prosecution of a corporation is not a substitute for the prosecution of criminally culpable individuals within or without the corporation. Because a corporation can act only through individuals, imposition of individual criminal liability may provide the strongest deterrent against future corporate wrongdoing.

However, the Filip Memorandum makes clear that to obtain cooperation credit: "the corporation does need to produce, and prosecutors may request, relevant factual information—including relevant factual information acquired through those interviews, unless the identical information has otherwise been provided—as well as relevant non-privileged evidence such as accounting business records and emails between non-attorneys or agents." USAM 9-28.720(a), n. 3. Thus, while prosecutors may not explicitly request that the company waive its attorney-client privilege, they can request the underlying information itself and if the company chooses to collect relevant information through attorney interviews, a common practice, it will be forced to disclose such evidence in order to obtain cooperation credit. *Id.*

The Filip Memorandum states that "exactly how and by whom the facts are gathered is for a corporation to decide." USAM 9.28.720. It notes that:

> Many corporations choose to collect information about potential misconduct through lawyers, a process that may confer attorney-client privilege or attorney work product protection on at least some of the information collected. Other corporations may choose a method of fact-gathering that does not have that effect—for example, having employee or other witness statements collected after interviews by non-attorney personnel.

> Whichever process the corporation selects, the government's key measure of cooperation must remain the same as it does for an individual: has the party timely disclosed the relevant facts about the putative misconduct? USAM 9-28.720(a).

Thus, while prosecutors are no longer permitted to explicitly request waivers of attorney-client or work product privileges, they are still empowered to request "factual information" that may only be contained in such protected work product. Accordingly, it is still extremely important at the outset of an investigation to think carefully about the manner in which evidence will be collected and memorialized to provide the company maximum flexibility to disclose factual information to the government, if it so chooses, without unnecessarily waiving its attorney-client and work product privileges.

Unfortunately, the Filip Memorandum provides little guidance as to how a corporation can disclose the relevant factual information collected pursuant to an attorney interview without waiving its attorney-client and work product protections. Its only suggestion is that a corporation may choose a method of fact gathering that does not bestow attorney-client or work product protection on the interviews, for example by having employee or other witness statements collected after interviews by non-attorney personnel. USAM 9-28.720(a). However, in most investigations involving potential violations of the securities laws or federal criminal statutes, it is unwise for a company to conduct such sensitive interviews without the assistance of experienced counsel. Accordingly, companies are left in a quandary as to how they can satisfy the still permitted request for factual information, even if only contained in otherwise protected attorney-client or work product materials, without waiving such privileges.

The Filip Memorandum also notes that a corporation may still freely waive its own privileges if it chooses to do so and that such waivers occur routinely when corporations are victimized by their employees or others, and disclose the details of its investigation to law enforcement officials to seek prosecution of the offenders. Accordingly, companies will still be obligated to make assessments as to whether they wish to voluntarily waive attorney-client and work product protections.

Prosecutors May No Longer Discourage Companies from Advancing Legal Fees to Targeted Employees

A number of other important changes have been made to the Principles. The Thompson Memorandum originally permitted prosecutors to weigh whether the corporation appeared to be protecting its culpable individuals and agents, including whether the company advanced legal fees. Thompson Memorandum at 11. It explained that: "a corporation's promise of support to culpable employees and agents, either through the advancing of attorney's fees, through retaining the employees without sanction for their misconduct, or through providing information to the employees about the government's investigation pursuant to a joint defense agreement, may be considered by the prosecutor in weighing the extent and value of a corporation's cooperation."

The McNulty Memorandum revised how prosecutors could evaluate the advancement of legal fees to employees, stating that prosecutors "generally should not take into account whether a corporation is advancing attorneys' fees to employees or agents under investigation and indictment." It noted that many state indemnification statutes grant corporations the power to advance the legal fees of officers under investigation and that many corporations enter into contractual obligations to advance attorney's fees through provisions contained in their corporate charters, bylaws, or employment agreements. McNulty Memorandum at 11. Accordingly, it provided that "a corporation's compliance with governing state law and its contractual obligations cannot be considered a failure to cooperate." McNulty Memorandum at 11. It made one exception, noting that "in extremely rare cases, the advancement of attorneys' fees may be taken into account when the totality of the circumstances show that it was intended to impede a criminal investigation." McNulty Memorandum at 11. However, it noted that the prohibition was not meant to prevent a prosecutor from asking questions about an attorney's representation of a corporation or its employees. It also still allowed prosecutors to weigh whether a company provided information to its employees about the government's investigation pursuant to a joint defense agreement. Thompson Memorandum at 7.

The Filip Memorandum reaffirmed that prosecutors should not take into account whether a corporation's advancing or reimbursing attorneys' fees or providing counsel to employees, officers, or directors under investigation or indictment. Prosecutors also "may not request that a corporation refrain from taking such action." USAM 9-28.730. It cautions, however, that if payment of attorneys' fees is used to obstruct justice: "for example, if fees were advanced on the condition that an employee adhere to a version of the facts that the corporation and the employee knew to be false," criminal sanctions will still apply. USAM 9-28.730.

Special Policy Concerns: The nature and seriousness of the crime, including the risk of harm to the public from the criminal misconduct, are obviously primary factors in determining whether to charge the corporation. In addition corporate conduct, particularly that of national and multi-national corporations, necessarily intersects with federal economic, tax and criminal law enforcement policies. In applying these principles, prosecutors must consider the practices and policies of the appropriate division of the department, and must comply with those policies to the extent required by the facts presented.

Comment : Apart from taking cognizance of federal laws, additionally prosecutors must be aware of the specific policy goals and incentive programs established by the respective divisions and the regulatory agencies. The approach of giving credit to corporations for coming forward on their own, and co-operating with governments investigations may not always be appropriate in all circumstances.

Prosecutors May No Longer Discourage Joint Defense Agreements

Finally, the Filip Memorandum also modified the McNulty Memorandum's prohibition against a company entering into a joint defense agreement with their employees. USAM 9-28.730. It stated: "the mere participation by a corporation in a joint defense agreement does not render the corporation ineligible to receive cooperation credit, and prosecutors may not request that a corporation refrain from entering into such agreements." USAM 9-28.730. However, it cautioned corporations to avoid putting themselves in the position of being disabled, by the provisions of a joint defense agreement, from providing relevant facts to the government and thereby limiting their ability to seek cooperation credit. USAM 9-28.730. Accordingly, it is important in reviewing joint defense agreements to ensure that they do not unduly limit the corporation's ability to disclose relevant facts to the government. USAM 9-28.730.

DOJ's change of policy was in response to judicial criticism and public pressure directed at federal prosecutors for pressuring KPMG to deny the advancement of legal fees to former employees in *United States v. Stein*, 435 F. Supp. 2d 330 (S.D.N.Y. 2006) (suppressing statements made by employees to investigators in face of threats of termination and refusal to pay legal fees by company).

Many legal commentators and white collar practitioners have criticized the revisions as still not going far enough to protect attorney-client and work product privileges. For example, the guidelines are limited in application to the DOJ and will not stem the pressure to waive attorney-client and work product privileges by the U.S. Securities and Exchange Commission and other regulatory bodies who often conduct parallel investigations. In addition, the guidelines do not "create any rights, substantive or procedural, enforceable at law by any party in any matter civil or criminal." Thus, corporations or individuals cannot seek enforcement in court if DOJ attorneys fail to follow their own guidelines. Moreover, the guidelines are subject to revision at any time and can be withdrawn or modified in the future.

Additionally, the Department of Justice Criminal Division created a Resource Guide to understand the Foreign Corrupt Practices Act (FCPA). This Resource Guide, in Chapter 5, Guiding Principles of Enforcement, provides guidance on what the Department of Justice considers when deciding to open an investigation or bring charges and what constitutes cooperation with the investigation by companies and individuals. This guidance is provided for FCPA compliance programs; however, it provides helpful best practices applicable to any compliance program.

———————

U.S. Department of Justice Criminal Division & SEC Enforcement Division, Resource Guide to the U.S. Foreign Corrupt Practices Act

http://www.justice.gov/sites/default/files/criminal-fraud/legacy/2015/01/16/guide.pdf

GUIDING PRINCIPLES OF ENFORCEMENT

What Does DOJ Consider When Deciding Whether to Open an Investigation or Bring Charges?

Whether and how DOJ will commence, decline, or otherwise resolve an FCPA matter is guided by the *Principles of Federal Prosecution* in the case of individuals, and the *Principles of Federal Prosecution of Business Organizations* in the case of companies.

DOJ *Principles of Federal Prosecution*

The *Principles of Federal Prosecution*, set forth in Chapter 9-27.000 of the U.S. Attorney's Manual, provide guidance for DOJ prosecutors regarding initiating or declining prosecution, selecting charges, and plea-bargaining. The *Principles of Federal Prosecution* provide that prosecutors should recommend or commence federal prosecution if the putative defendant's conduct constitutes a federal offense and the admissible evidence will probably be sufficient to obtain and sustain a conviction unless (1) no substantial federal interest would be served by prosecution; (2) the person is subject to effective prosecution in another jurisdiction; or (3) an adequate non-criminal alternative to prosecution exists. In assessing the existence of a substantial federal interest, the prosecutor is advised to "weigh all relevant considerations," including the nature and seriousness of the offense; the deterrent effect of prosecution; the person's culpability in connection with the offense; the person's history with respect to criminal activity; the person's willingness to cooperate in the investigation or prosecution of others; and the probable sentence or other consequences if the person is convicted. The *Principles of Federal Prosecution* also set out the considerations to be weighed when deciding whether to enter into a plea agreement with an individual defendant, including the nature and seriousness of the offense and the person's willingness to cooperate, as well as the desirability of prompt and certain disposition of the case and the expense of trial and appeal.

DOJ *Principles of Federal Prosecution of Business Organizations*

The *Principles of Federal Prosecution of Business Organizations*, set forth in Chapter 9-28.000 of the U.S. Attorney's Manual, provide guidance regarding the resolution of cases involving corporate wrongdoing. The *Principles Federal Prosecution of Business Organizations* recognize that resolution of corporate criminal cases by means other than indictment, including non-prosecution and deferred prosecution agreements, may be appropriate in certain circumstances. Nine factors are considered in conducting an investigation, determining whether to charge a corporation, and negotiating plea or other agreements:

- the nature and seriousness of the offense, including the risk of harm to the public;

- the pervasiveness of wrongdoing within the corporation, including the complicity in, or the condoning of, the wrongdoing by corporate management;

- the corporation's history of similar misconduct, including prior criminal, civil, and regulatory enforcement actions against it;

- the corporation's timely and voluntary disclosure of wrongdoing and its willingness to cooperate in the investigation of its agents;

- the existence and effectiveness of the corporation's pre-existing compliance program;

- the corporation's remedial actions, including any efforts to implement an effective corporate compliance program or improve an existing one, replace responsible management, discipline or terminate wrongdoers, pay restitution, and cooperate with the relevant government agencies;

- collateral consequences, including whether there is disproportionate harm to shareholders, pension holders, employees, and others not proven personally culpable, as well as impact on the public arising from the prosecution;

- the adequacy of the prosecution of individuals responsible for the corporation's malfeasance; and

- the adequacy of remedies such as civil or regulatory enforcement actions.

As these factors illustrate, in many investigations it will be appropriate for a prosecutor to consider a corporation's pre-indictment conduct, including voluntary disclosure, cooperation, and remediation, in determining whether to seek an indictment. In assessing a corporation's cooperation, prosecutors are prohibited from requesting attorney client privileged materials with two exceptions—when a corporation or its employee asserts an advice-of-counsel defense and when the attorney-client communications were in furtherance of a crime or fraud. Otherwise, an organization's cooperation may only be assessed on the basis of whether it disclosed the *relevant facts* underlying an investigation—and not on the basis of whether it has waived its attorney-client privilege or work product protection.

What Does SEC Consider When Deciding Whether to Open an Investigation or Bring Charges?

SEC's *Enforcement Manual*, published by SEC's Enforcement Division and available on SEC's website, sets forth information about how SEC conducts investigations, as well as the guiding principles that SEC staff considers when determining whether to open or close an investigation and whether civil charges are merited. There are various ways that potential FCPA violations come to the attention of SEC staff, including: tips from informants or whistleblowers; information developed in other investigations; self-reports or public disclosures by companies; referrals from other offices or agencies; public sources, such as media reports and trade publications; and proactive investigative techniques, including risk-based initiatives. Investigations can be formal, such as where SEC has issued a formal order of investigation that authorizes its staff to issue investigative subpoenas for testimony and documents, or informal, such as where the staff proceeds with the investigation without the use of investigative subpoenas.

In determining whether to open an investigation and, if so, whether an enforcement action is warranted, SEC staff considers a number of factors, including: the statutes or rules potentially violated; the egregiousness of the potential violation; the potential magnitude of the violation; whether the potentially harmed group is particularly vulnerable or at risk; whether the conduct is ongoing; whether the conduct can be investigated efficiently and within the statute of limitations period; and whether other authorities, including federal or state agencies or regulators, might be better suited to investigate the conduct. SEC staff also may consider whether the case involves a possibly widespread industry practice that should be addressed, whether the case involves a recidivist, and whether the matter gives SEC an opportunity to be visible in a community that might not otherwise be familiar with SEC or the protections afforded by the securities laws.

For more information about the Enforcement Division's procedures concerning investigations, enforcement actions, and cooperation with other regulators, see the *Enforcement Manual* at http://www.sec.gov/divisions/enforce.shtml.

Self-Reporting, Cooperation, and Remedial Efforts

While the conduct underlying any FCPA investigation is obviously a fundamental and threshold consideration in deciding what, if any, action to take, both DOJ and SEC place a high premium on self-reporting, along with cooperation and remedial efforts, in determining the appropriate resolution of FCPA matters.

Criminal Cases

Under DOJ's *Principles of Federal Prosecution of Business Organizations*, federal prosecutors company's cooperation in determining how corporate criminal case. Specifically, prosecutors consider whether the company made a voluntary and timely disclosure as well as the company's willingness to provide relevant information and evidence and identify relevant actors inside and outside the company, including senior executives. In addition, prosecutors may consider a company's remedial actions, including efforts to improve an existing compliance program or appropriate disciplining of wrongdoers. A company's remedial measures should be meaningful and illustrate its recognition of the seriousness of the misconduct, for example, by taking steps to implement the personnel, operational, and organizational changes necessary to establish an awareness among employees that criminal conduct will not be tolerated.

The *Principles of Federal Prosecution* similarly provide that prosecutors may consider an individual's willingness to cooperate in deciding whether a prosecution should be undertaken and how it should be resolved. Although a willingness to cooperate will not, by itself, generally relieve a person of criminal liability, it may be given "serious consideration" in evaluating whether to enter into a plea agreement with a defendant, depending on the nature and value of the cooperation offered.

The U.S. Sentencing Guidelines similarly take into account an individual defendant's cooperation and voluntary disclosure. Under § 5K1.1, a defendant's cooperation, if sufficiently substantial, may justify the government filing a motion for a reduced sentence. And under § 5K2.16, a defendant's voluntary disclosure of an offense prior to its discovery—if the offense was unlikely to have been discovered otherwise—may warrant a downward departure in certain circumstances.

Chapter 8 of the Sentencing Guidelines, which governs the sentencing of organizations, takes into account an organization's remediation as part of an "effective compliance and ethics program." One of the seven elements of such a program provides that after the detection of criminal conduct, "the organization shall take reasonable steps to respond appropriately to the criminal conduct and to prevent further similar criminal conduct, including making any necessary modifications to the organization's compliance and ethics program." Having an effective compliance and ethics program may lead to a three-point reduction in an organization's culpability score under § 8C2.5, which affects the fine calculation under the Guidelines. Similarly, an organization's self-reporting, cooperation, and acceptance of responsibility may lead to fine reductions under § 8C2.5(g) by decreasing the culpability score. Conversely, an organization will not qualify for the compliance program reduction when it unreasonably delayed reporting the offense. Similar to § 5K1.1 for individuals, organizations can qualify for departures pursuant to § 8C4.1 of the Guidelines for cooperating in the prosecution of others.

Civil Cases

SEC's Framework for Evaluating Cooperation by Companies

SEC's framework for evaluating cooperation by companies is set forth in its 2001 *Report of Investigation Pursuant to Section 21(a) of the Securities Exchange Act of 1934 and Commission Statement on the Relationship of Cooperation to Agency Enforcement Decisions,* which is commonly known as the *Seaboard Report*. The report, which explained the Commission's decision not to take enforcement action against a public company for certain accounting violations caused by its subsidiary, details the many factors SEC considers in determining whether, and to what extent, it grants leniency to companies for cooperating in its investigations and for related good corporate citizenship. Specifically, the report identifies four broad measures of a company's cooperation:

- self-policing prior to the discovery of the misconduct, including establishing effective compliance procedures and an appropriate tone at the top;
- self-reporting of misconduct when it is discovered, including conducting a thorough review of the nature, extent, origins, and consequences of the misconduct,

and promptly, completely, and effectively disclosing the misconduct to the public, to regulatory agencies, and to self-regulatory organizations;

- remediation, including dismissing or appropriately disciplining wrongdoers, modifying and improving internal controls and procedures to prevent recurrence of the misconduct, and appropriately compensating those adversely affected; and

- cooperation with law enforcement authorities, including providing SEC staff with all information relevant to the underlying violations and the company's remedial efforts.

Since every enforcement matter is different, this analytical framework sets forth general principles but does not limit SEC's broad discretion to evaluate every case individually on its own unique facts and circumstances. Similar to SEC's treatment of cooperating individuals, credit for cooperation by companies may range from taking no enforcement action to pursuing reduced sanctions in connection with enforcement actions.

SEC's Framework for Evaluating Cooperation by Individuals

In 2010, SEC announced a new cooperation program for individuals. SEC staff has a wide range of tools to facilitate and reward cooperation by individuals, from taking no enforcement action to pursuing reduced sanctions in connection with enforcement actions. Although the evaluation of cooperation depends on the specific circumstances, SEC generally evaluates four factors to determine whether, to what extent, and in what manner to credit cooperation by individuals:

- the assistance provided by the cooperating individual in SEC's investigation or related enforcement actions, including, among other things: the value and timeliness of the cooperation, including whether the individual was the first to report the misconduct to SEC or to offer his or her cooperation; whether the investigation was initiated based upon the information or other cooperation by the individual; the quality of the cooperation, including whether the individual was truthful and the cooperation was complete; the time and resources conserved as a result of the individual's cooperation; and the nature of the cooperation, such as the type of assistance provided;

- the importance of the matter in which the individual provided cooperation;

- the societal interest in ensuring that the cooperating individual is held accountable for his or her misconduct, including the severity of the individual's misconduct, the culpability of the individual, and the efforts undertaken by the individual to remediate the harm; and

- the appropriateness of a cooperation credit in light of the profile of the cooperating individual.

———————

Assignment

- **Hypothetical:** You are the Chief Compliance Officer at your [Team's] Corporation. Set up the protocols that you require for internal investigation within the company.

Chapter 17

Corporate Compliance and Crisis Management

Introduction

It is no secret that businesses today, regardless of the industry, face increasingly targeted scrutiny from various parties—including the government, the media, employees, stockholders, and customers. As a result, the importance of having a functioning corporate compliance program has become immeasurably magnified. However, implementing a general corporate compliance program only addresses a portion of the concerns inherent in the current business environment. That is, your compliance program has helped you identify problems within your organization; so, what do you do when you learn of a problem that reaches a "crisis" level?

Identifying the problem is of little use if you are not ready to resolve the crisis in an effective manner. Now more than ever, integrating a sound and effective crisis management plan within the structure of a comprehensive compliance program is necessary to ensure a company's continued operations, security, reputation, and profitability.

A good crisis management program has two principal components. The first component involves a dedicated crisis management team to develop and execute the plan. The second component involves the formulation of a crisis management plan. We will discuss each component in more detail below. However, this chapter provides a summary introduction into crisis management and it is not intended to be an exhaustive analysis of this highly complex and increasingly critical function.

Generally, a crisis management plan is a framework by which counsel, senior management, and key employees react to and address crisis events—threatened or realized—and, if necessary, navigate the resultant aftermath. The goal of any effective crisis management plan is to assist the compliance function in monitoring and assessing potential risks or crisis events to the company and, ultimately, ensuring timely disposition of the critical event, thereby minimizing disruption to the operation of the business, reputational harm to company, and negative impact to employee morale. The plan must be flexible in order to adapt to and confront the different types of crises or emergencies that may arise. The plan must also provide a clear, organized plan of action and a responsible team for dependable and timely responses to these events as they occur.

Formulating a successful crisis management plan requires a firm understanding of the types of risks faced by a particular business or industry. In this chapter, we will outline the process companies should consider following when determining the right crisis management plan. The process includes taking the following measures: conducting a risk assessment across the company's business divisions and enterprise in order to identify the key risks the company faces; creating prevention programs that address the issues of testing and assessment of the protocols related to monitoring and remediation of risk; designing the crisis management response program; defining the crisis management team; creating policies and procedures; and evaluating and testing the crisis management plan through innovative and dynamic role play exercises.

A crisis management team should consist of key participants who will provide the managerial authority, resources, and expertise to effectively execute the plan. More detail will be provided below.

Understanding Your Risks

Crisis Management Risk Assessment

A crisis management plan is built around identifiable risks found within your Company. To the extent the risks are unknown; the crisis management plan will be ineffective and crippled. Therefore, before a crisis management plan can be developed, Your Company needs to assess the risk it faces in the market. This includes legal and regulatory risks as well as other risks. As discussed in more detail in other parts of this casebook, companies face civil and criminal legal risks and liability they may face physical security and cyber security risks. They may face environmental and other hazardous risks to life and limb. They may face non-legal risks, such as extreme weather (hurricanes, typhoons, and tornados), earthquakes, terrorist attacks, war, and other non-legal risks. Companies must come to understand all the risks they may face through a formal crisis management risk assessment. What is a crisis management risk assessment? It is broader than legal risks assessment for compliance because it includes risks of nature, terrorism and war. A compliance risk assessment only deals with legal risks. This is a critical difference. Compliance risk assessment, as set forth in chapter 3, only deals with legal risks. Crisis risk assessment deals with all risks including but not limited to legal risks and acts of G-d.

Quite simply a crisis management risk assessment is the process of evaluating the key business operations that are vital to the company's existence and the potential threats that could disrupt these key areas. For example, Hurricane Sandy which caused flooding in many areas, including lower Manhattan, destroyed computer systems and the electric grid for many financial institutions, including the New York Stock Exchange. Another example, for many companies, a key business operation involves the successful health of its computer network systems. For some companies, a risk area may be operations in foreign jurisdictions that can trigger Foreign Corrupt Practices Act (FCPA) issues. The risk area may be the manufacturing process of chemicals or other dangerous substances. In addition, the assessment would also include the key drivers to company reputation and the potential threats that could impact these areas as well. Some companies may perceive significant risks associated with possessing and handling confidential private client information. Thus, a loss of confidential private data may not impact operations, but may significantly impact a company's reputation such that the event may rise to the level of a crisis.

For companies with international operations, understanding the risk associated with globalization is vital. For large companies with a presence outside the U.S., the risk assessment process should be conducted with business units and subsidiaries or affiliates and across borders. The key focus of the risk assessment is to provide a comprehensive understanding of the critical operations to the life of the business and all the potential threats that a company may face that rise to the level of a crisis. The nature of a risk may change depending on jurisdiction. Therefore, it is important and highly recommended that companies consider the implications of foreign laws and the nature of their foreign operations.

A great example of a company with a strong presence outside of the United States is Wal-Mart—the American multinational retail giant who employs 2.2 million people around the globe and 1.4 million within the United States. With subsidiaries in almost every continent, in 2014 Walmart was the world's largest company by revenue operating in the United Kingdom, South America, China, Japan, India, Brazil, and Mexico. A company such as this, who recently came under strong government inspection for potential violations of the FCPA in Latin America, had to strongly consider the implications of doing business abroad and plan for the associated risk.

In 2005, a whistleblower alerted Wal-Mart to irregularities within the company which prompted Wal-Mart to open an investigation. Wal-Mart confidentially shared its findings of its 2005 investigation with the Department of Justice and Securities Exchange Commission. The existence of the investigation in the following form 10-Q filed with the SEC:

SEC Form 10-Q

https://www.sec.gov/Archives/edgar/data/104169/
000119312511335177/d233066d10q.htm
(quarterly period ending Oct. 31, 2011)

"During fiscal 2012, the Company began conducting a voluntary internal review of its policies, procedures and internal controls pertaining to its global anti-corruption compliance program. As a result of information obtained during that review and from other sources, the Company has begun an internal investigation into whether certain matters, including permitting, licensing and inspections, were in compliance with the U.S. Foreign Corrupt Practices Act. The Company has engaged outside counsel and other advisors to assist in the review of these matters and has implemented, and is continuing to implement, appropriate remedial measures. The Company has voluntarily disclosed its internal investigation to the U.S. Department of Justice and the Securities and Exchange Commission. We cannot reasonably estimate the potential liability, if any, related to these matters. However, based on the facts currently known, we do not believe that these matters will have a material adverse effect on our business, financial condition, results of operations or cash flows."

A compliance program is essentially a risk assessment for a specific business unit, function or area. It should be noted that a general risk assessment may identify the need for the creation and implementation of a compliance program in areas where none existed before. Within this casebook, there are numerous examples of specific compliance programs designed to address specific practice areas or risk profiles faced by specific industries. For example, an FCPA compliance program may raise certain SEC or criminal issues that may rise to the level of a crisis.

The best example of this is the case of Petrobras. This Brazilian state owned company is now facing FCPA violations when a complex scheme or bribery and corruption that involved high ranking officers of the company as well as state government and political officials. Petrobras is now in securities litigation stemming from SEC issues that include violations of Rule 10B of the SEC Act. The suit is brought on behalf of a number of British and American investors who were ultimately affected by one company's lack of compliance program and tone at the top.

In re Petrobras Securities Litigation

United States District Court, Southern District Of New York
Case No. 1:14-cv-09662-JSR
The Universities Superannuation Scheme Limited's Further
Submission in Support of Its Motion for Appointment as
Lead Plaintiff and Approval of Counsel

Universities Superannuation Scheme, Ltd. ("USS") respectfully submits this brief in response to the Court's February 20, 2015 Order and in further support of its motion for appointment as Lead Plaintiff and approval of Counsel.

1. USS Is The Most Adequate Plaintiff

In striking contrast to the two purported "groups" alleging larger losses, USS has the largest financial interest among the qualified lead plaintiff movants and otherwise satisfies the requirement under Rule 23. To date, no other movant has even challenged USS's prima facie showing of typicality and adequacy under Rule 23. Accordingly, USS should be appointed Lead Plaintiff. See Faris v. Longtop Fin. Techs., Ltd., No. 11 Civ. 3658 (SAS), 2011 U.S. Dist. LEXIS 112970, at *11 (S.D.N.Y. Oct. 4, 2011) ("Under the PSLRA, the movant ... with the largest financial interest in the relief sought by the class, who also makes a prima facie showing of typicality and adequacy, is the presumptively 'most adequate plaintiff.' ").

Contrary to the State Retirement Systems' representations, USS has losses on two of three Petrobras note issues purchased during the Class Period:

Note Description Cusip Number
PETBRA 4.375% DUE 5/20/2023 (Cusip: US71647NAF69) PETBRA 6.125% DUE 10/06/2016 (Cusip: US71645WAL54) PETBRA 7.25% DUE 3/17/2044 (Cusip: US71647NAK54)
Gain/(Loss)
($5,446) ($13,720)
$35,541

The State Retirement Systems' representation results from netting the gains and losses on the notes, but there is no precedential support for such netting—and the State Retirement Systems have not proffered any. Indeed, the notes are separate securities for which investors with losses will be able to recover for each particular issuance. Therefore, USS has losses which ground its Article III standing to file an action on behalf of purchasers of Petrobras debt securities.

At bottom, USS is the ideal plaintiff envisioned by Congress when it enacted the PSLRA. USS has the largest individual loss among any qualified movant in this litigation and is the only movant that meets the typicality and adequacy requirements of both Rule 23 and the PSLRA. Indeed, no other movant has demonstrated the willingness and ability to adequately oversee counsel and vigorously prosecute the claims against Petrobras on behalf of the Class. Critically, USS is the only movant not overwhelmed by various inadequacies and unique defenses. Nor does USS have any ties to potentially relevant political contributions or curious arrangements with counsel, which have heretofore afflicted the alternative lead plaintiff groupings. Accordingly, USS respectfully submits that it should be appointed as Lead Plaintiff, and its Motion should otherwise be granted.

2. The SKAGEN-Danske Group Has Not Satisfied The Typicality And Adequacy Requirements Of Rule 23

The record here demonstrates that the SKAGEN-Danske Group is not the "most adequate plaintiff" because it (a) has unique defenses and/or interests antagonistic to the Class, and (b) lacks the necessary Article III standing to pursue claims on behalf of the funds comprising the group. Thus, the motion of the SKAGEN-Danske Group cannot withstand Rule 23 scrutiny, even at a prima facie level.

Although SKAGEN and the Danske entities have had the opportunity to submit the requisite evidence of assignments or legal title on behalf of the numerous separate funds they seek to represent as part of three memoranda of law and oral argument, they have failed to proffer anything in the manner of an evidentiary showing to demonstrate that they possess any right to litigate this securities action in this Court. Not only have they failed to file written proofs of assignment, they also have not proffered any evidence under governing Norwegian or Danish law that gives them a "right" to litigate this action. SKAGEN and the Danske entities should have filed such support as part of their prima facie showing in their initial motion. See generally 15 U.S.C. § 78u-4(a)(3)(A) (60-day deadline); In re Telxon Corp. Sec. Litig., 67 F. Supp. 2d 803, 818 (N.D. Ohio 1999) (the "PSLRA is unequivocal and allows for no exceptions" and "precludes consideration of ... any other pleading ... filed after the sixty (60) day window has closed") (emphasis in original).

It is long past the time of cure for such an evidentiary malady. Reply papers are not the time to proffer new evidence that could, and should, have been filed with the initial motion. Indeed, "there is no reason the [groups] could not have submitted such evidence in connection with their initial motions." Schriver v. Impac Mortgage Holdings, Inc., No. SACV 06-31 CJC RNBX, 2006 WL 6886020, at *8, n.10 (C.D. Cal. May 2, 2006). Moreover, as SKAGEN and Danske have had multiple opportunities to submit such evidence, any such proffer now should be stricken. As former Judge Baer has explained:

> [I]t is established beyond peradventure that it is improper to sandbag one's opponent by raising new matter in reply." Murphy v. Village of Hoffman Estates, 1999 U.S. Dist. LEXIS 3320, at *5–6 (N.D.Ill.1999) ("[p]roviding specifics in a reply in support of a general argument in an objection counts as new matter in reply"); see also, e.g., Wike v. Vertrue, Inc., 2007 U.S. Dist. LEXIS 19843, at *21–22 (M.D.Tenn.2007) ("the Court will not allow [movant] to sandbag the Plaintiff by first presenting the evidence in reply"); Brennan v. AT & T Corp., 2006 U.S. Dist. LEXIS 8237, at *26–27 (S.D.Ill.2006). Typically, in such situations, the Court strikes the evidence presented for the first time in reply, and does not consider it for purposes of ruling on the motion. See, e.g., Wike v. Vertrue, Inc., 2007 U.S. Dist. LEXIS 19843, at *21–22; Brennan v. AT & T Corp., 2006 U.S. Dist. LEXIS 8237, at *26–27. This Court will adopt such a remedy here, and strike Plaintiff's evidence presented with its reply brief, and not consider it for the purposes of ruling on this motion. Wolters Kluwer Fin. Serv. Inc. v. Scivantage, No. 07 CV 2352(HB), 2007 WL 1098714, at *1 (S.D.N.Y. Apr. 12, 2007).

Furthermore, SKAGEN has not adequately addressed the conflict it created when one of its funds purchased shares of Petrobras common ADS months after the last corrective disclosure was alleged in the complaints, and shortly after filing for appointment as lead plaintiff. Heretofore, SKAGEN had sold all its Class Period Petrobras common ADS for a profit. This conflict raises serious questions pertaining to the SKAGEN-Danske Group's ability to represent common ADS holders. SKAGEN has admitted to a gain on sales of its Petrobras common ADS purchases, while the Danske entities show relatively minor losses on their common ADS (only 53,500 retained shares all purchased within days of the end of the Class Period). See ECF No. 69 at 10–15, and ECF No. 87 at 2 n.2.

SKAGEN'S latest purchase of Petrobras common shares raises unique defenses, especially as to reliance, which may defeat class certification. Ordinarily such purchases are entered in order to average down the purchase price of the shares acquired during the class period. When questioned by the Court at oral argument, the "averaging down" rationale was never mentioned, which likely was because SKAGEN had liquidated its common ADS for a profit during the Class Period. This raises multiple questions as to whether SKAGEN will favor preferred ADS over common ADS Class members—as SKAGEN's losses are principally in preferred ADS—and, critically, whether SKAGEN relied on any statements by Petrobras in making its investment decisions. As other courts in the Second Circuit have noted: "[a] named plaintiff who has engaged in a post-disclosure purchase is subject to the defense that the alleged misstatements or omissions were really not a factor in the purchasing decision but rather that other investment considerations drove the decision." George v. China Auto. Sys., Inc., No. 11 CIV. 7533 KBF, 2013 WL 3357170, at *6 (S.D.N.Y. July 3, 2013) ("Such post-disclosure purchases can both defeat typicality and adequacy as well as rebut the presumption that plaintiff relied on the alleged misrepresentations or the integrity of the market in making his or her purchases."); see also Bensley v. FalconStor Software, Inc., 277 F.R.D. 231, 237–41 (E.D.N.Y.2011) (refusing to appoint fund as lead plaintiff because it was subject to unique defenses of buying subject security after corrective disclosures).

Further, SKAGEN's reliance on its representative's statement that its "interests in this case is to maximize recovery both on behalf of our unitholders and on behalf of the class," ECF No. 80 at 9, is little more than a non sequitur. SKAGEN's unitholders in the Kon-Tiki fund have a new $3.35 billion interest in Petrobras common shares that would like to see the same profitability as SKAGEN and it funds showed in selling off its earlier common ADS portfolio. While SKAGEN's representative may aspire to maximize the interests of its unitholders to whom it has fiduciary obligations to maximize the return on its latest investment in common shares, as well as maximize the Class's recovery against Petrobras, it is precisely the unique conflict between the two groups' competing interests to Petrobras' cash and liquid assets going forward that must be considered in determining whether SKAGEN can adequately represent all Petrobras shareholders. Where such a unique situation is present, defendants will surely be compelled to focus on SKAGEN's investment decisions and tailor any settlement discussions to satisfy SKAGEN's conflicting interests.

Thus, SKAGEN's unique defenses may be grounds to defeat class certification, and preclude SKAGEN from being considered either typical or adequate to represent the Class. See, e.g., Gary Plastic Packaging Corp. v. Merrill Lynch, Pierce, Fenner & Smith. Inc., 903 F.2d 176, 180 (2d Cir.1990) (explaining that "class certification is inappropriate where a putative class representative is subject to unique defenses which threaten to become the focus of the litigation ... [r]egardless of whether the issue is framed in terms of the typicality of the representatives claims ... or the adequacy of the representation....."); see also Baffa v. Donaldson, Lufkin & Jenrette Secs. Corp., 222 F.3d 52, 59–60 (2d Cir. 2000) (finding that the district court did not abuse its discretion in denying a request to intervene as class representative because of her unique possible defenses) (citing Gary Plastics Packaging Corp., 903 F.2d at 180).

CONCLUSION

For the foregoing reasons and the reasons set forth in USS's prior memoranda, USS respectfully requests that its Motion be granted.

The Nexus between Compliance and Crisis Management

The compliance function is not synonymous with crisis management. The purpose of compliance is to identify and monitor specific legal risks within a business enterprise. Crisis management involves the preparation for, response to, and remediation of a business disruption event that poses jeopardy to corporate operations, reputation, or employee and community safety or morale.

Within the context of corporate legal risks, the compliance function serves as a rapid response team looking for potential legal danger, and the crisis management plan serves as the battle plan to be executed for when any danger, legal or act of G-d, is imminent. Thus, there is and should be overlap between the compliance function and the crisis management plan for legal risks. Both functions need to understand the dangers faced by the company and need to work together to provide efficient and useful crisis management functionality on legal risks.

To the extent that the compliance function and the crisis management plan do not overlap on risks of nature, terrorism and war. They should complement each other by understanding what each is responsible for doing.

Components of a Crisis Management Plan

A well-designed crisis management plan should include, at a minimum, the following components:

1. Crisis management team, including the designation of a team leader and a public relations representative;

2. Crisis management risk assessment;

3. Crisis response plan;

4. Written policies and procedures;

5. Testing the crisis management plan, including role playing and drills;

6. Public relations team or agency; and

7. Remediation, including crisis insurance and a crisis fund.

Because much of this casebook covers the need for, and creation of, a compliance program for a variety of specific target areas, we will not directly address the compliance or risk prevention program component herein. However, it is worth highlighting that compliance and crisis management are interdependent.

It is important to review the company's insurance policies in order to ensure that the crisis team knows how to report the crisis event for insurance coverage purposes. Also, the company should have considered whether to purchase crisis insurance that will provide immediate funding for the initial crisis expenses as well as funding for business interruption. In addition, the crisis management team should report and document all expenses from the crisis fund in a timely function, whether or not the crisis fund is internally funded or funded by the insurance policy.

Assembling a Crisis Management Team

The Core Team Functions

In order to develop and execute a crisis management plan, a company must have a prepared crisis management team. The team members must have clear, identifiable roles that are related to the unique crisis management goals. Specifically, a well-defined team should be broken down into at least four distinct functions: 1) Crisis Management Plan Development; 2) Recovery Protocols; 3) Investigation; and 4) Assessment and Remediation.

Recently, in what has proven to be a major unraveling, FIFA has been charged with claims of widespread corruption amongst its top executives. In May of 2015, after an FBI investigation, the Justice Department indicted nine FIFA officials and five corporate executives for corruption charges that Attorney General Loretta E. Lynch described as "rampant, systemic, and deep-rooted." Nike was swept into the scandal for a questionable deal made with the organization in order to obtain official sponsorship of the Brazilian national team. True to form, the sportswear giant's crisis management team swiftly responded by pointing out that the indictment did not charge the company with any criminal wrongdoing.

———————

United States of America v. Hawilla

United States District Court, Eastern District of New York
https://www.justice.gov/sites/default/files/usao-edny/legacy/2015/05/27/
UNITED%20STATES%20V.%20JOSE%20HAWILLA%20ET%20AL.pdf

THE UNITED STATES ATTORNEY CHARGES:

<u>INTRODUCTION TO ALL COUNTS</u>

At all times relevant to this Information, unless otherwise indicated:

I. The Enterprise

1. The Federation Internationale de Football Association ("FIFA") and its six constituent continental confederations—the Confederation of North, Central American

and Caribbean Association Football ("CONCACAF"), the Confederacion Sudamer-icana de Futbol ("CONMEBOL"), the Union des Associations Europeennes de Football ("UEFA"), the Confederation Africaine de Football ("CAF"), the Asian Football Con-federation ("AFC"), and the Oceania Football Confederation ("OFC") together with affiliated regional federations, national member associations, and sports marketing companies, collectively constituted an "enterprise," as defined in Title 18, United States Code, Section 1961(4), that is, a group of legal entities associated in fact (here-inafter the "enterprise"). The enterprise constituted an ongoing organization whose members functioned as a continuing unit for a common purpose of achieving the objectives of the enterprise. The enterprise was engaged in, and its activities affected, interstate and foreign commerce.

2. The principal purpose of the enterprise was to regulate and promote the sport of soccer worldwide. The members of the enterprise carried out this purpose by using a variety of methods and means, including creating and enforcing uniform standards and rules, organizing international competitions, and commercializing the media and marketing rights associated with the sport. The members of the en-terprise, as well as individuals and entities employed by and associated with the en-terprise, frequently engaged in banking and investment activities with United States financial institutions.

3. The enterprise operated in the Eastern District of New York and elsewhere, in-cluding overseas.

A. FIFA

4. FIFA was the international body governing organized soccer, commonly known outside the United States as football. FIFA was an entity registered under Swiss law and headquartered in Zurich, Switzerland. FIFA was composed of as many as 208 member associations, each representing organized soccer in a particular nation or territory, including the United States and four of its overseas territories. The United States first became affiliated with FIFA in 1914; Puerto Rico first became affiliated with FIFA in 1960, with Guam, American Samoa, and the United States Virgin Islands following suit in the 1990s. At various times, FIFA maintained offices both in Zurich and elsewhere in the world, including in the United States, where FIFA maintained a development office since at least 2011.

5. Each of FIFA's member associations also was a member of one of the six con-tinental confederations recognized by FIFA: CONCACAF, CONMEBOL, UEFA, CAF, AFC, and OFC. Since at least 1996, under FIFA's statutes, no national soccer associ-ation could become a member of FIFA without first joining one of the six continental confederations. Since at least 2004, member associations were required to pay to FIFA annual dues, known as subscriptions.

6. FIFA was governed by: a congress composed of its member associations, which acted as the association's highest legislative body; an executive committee, which acted as the executive body; and a general secretariat, which acted as the administrative

body. FIFA also had a president, who represented the association worldwide and was responsible for the implementation of decisions. FIFA also operated several standing committees, including a committee that organized Olympic soccer qualifying tournaments, whose members included soccer officials from various national member associations. FIFA also operated through a number of subsidiaries, including subsidiaries that assisted with FIFA's media and marketing activities.

7. The FIFA congress was composed of delegates from each of its member associations, as well as observers appointed by each of the confederations. Among other things, the congress was responsible for amending FIFA's statutes and electing the FIFA president. The congress convened in ordinary sessions biennially or annually, and at other times in extraordinary sessions, in various countries around the world, including the United States.

8. The FIFA executive committee, often referred to as the "ExCo," was composed of the FIFA president and a number of ordinary members, some of whom also held the title vice president. The president was elected by the FIFA congress. The vice presidents and ordinary members were appointed by the confederations. Each confederation was entitled to appoint a specific number of vice presidents and ordinary members, as set forth in the FIFA statutes. Since at least 1996, the executive committee was required by FIFA statutes to meet at least twice per year. The executive committee held meetings at FIFA's headquarters in Zurich, as well as in various countries around the world, including the United States.

9. Among other duties, the executive committee was responsible for selecting the host nations of FIFA tournaments, including, among others, the World Cup, the Women's World Cup, the Confederations Cup, the Under-20 World Cup, the Under-20 Women's World Cup, the Under-17 World Cup, the Under-17 Women's World Cup and the Club World Cup.

10. The World Cup, the sport's premier event, was a quadrennial international tournament involving the senior national men's teams of 24 and, beginning in 1998, 32 nations. In selecting the host nation for the World Cup, the executive committee typically followed a process in which bid committees for the competing nations campaigned for votes among the members of the executive committee. Following this process, and at least six years prior to each World Cup, the executive committee typically held a vote in which its members cast their votes via secret ballot. The winners, or host nations, for the World Cups from 1990 to 2022, as well as the other bidding nations that maintained their bids to the end of the process, are reflected in the table below:

World Cup	Date Selected by the ExCo	Winning Nation	Other Bidding Nation/ Nations
1990	May 19, 1984	Italy	Soviet Union
1994	July 4, 1988	United States	Morocco Brazil
1998	July 2, 1992	France	Morocco
2006	July 6, 2000	Germany	South Africa England Morocco
2010	May 15, 2004	South Africa	Morocco Egypt
2018	December 2, 2010	Russia	Spain/Portugal Netherlands/Belgium England
2022	December 2, 2010	Qatar	United States South Korea Japan Australia

11. Since at least 1996, under FIFA's statutes, the six continental confederations had certain rights and obligations, including, among other things, that they comply with and enforce FIFA's statutes, regulations, and decisions and work closely with FIFA to further FIFA's objectives and organize international soccer competitions.

12. FIFA's purpose was, among other things·, to develop and promote the game of soccer globally by organizing international competitions and creating and enforcing rules that govern the confederations and member associations. FIFA financed its efforts in significant part by commercializing the media and marketing rights associated with the World Cup. According to its published income statement for the 2007–2010 financial period, FIFA had total revenues of $4.189 billion, 83% of which ($3.480 billion) was attributable to the sale of television and marketing rights to the 2010 World Cup. FIFA's profits during this same period were $631 million. FIFA, in turn, helped finance the confederations and their member associations, including by providing funds through the Financial Assistance Program and the Goal Program.

13. FIFA first instituted a written code of ethics in October 2004, which code was revised in 2006 and again in 2009 (generally, the "code of ethics"). The code of ethics governed the conduct of soccer "officials," which expressly included, among others, various individuals with responsibilities within FIFA, the confederations, member associations, leagues, and clubs. Among other things, the code of ethics provided that soccer officials were prohibited from accepting bribes or cash gifts and from otherwise abusing their positions for personal gain. The code of ethics further provided, from its inception, that soccer officials owed certain duties to FIFA and its confederations and member associations, including a duty of absolute loyalty. By 2009, the code of ethics explicitly recognized that FIFA officials stand in a fiduciary relationship to FIFA and its constituent confederations, member associations, leagues, and clubs.

1. The Crisis Management Development Plan function is responsible for:
   a. Defining the term "crisis" within the organization;
   b. Identifying all potential crisis level risks;
   c. Conducting inventory of existing formal or informal crisis management plans;
   d. Identifying routine problems or risks and developing escalation protocols;
   e. Assisting in drafting the crisis management plan;
   f. Utilizing internal company resources and external experts to development plans; and
   g. Reporting findings and analyses to specified senior and/or executive leadership.
2. The Response Protocols function is responsible for:
   a. Drafting response plans and protocols related to specific crisis events; and
   b. Providing or organizing the education and training of the response protocols to employees, management, and executive management as needed.
3. The Investigation function is responsible for:
   a. Drafting plans and protocols for internal investigations and coordinating with outside experts, as needed; and
   b. Providing or organizing the education and training of the investigation protocols to employees, management, and executive management, as needed.
4. The Remediation and Assessment function is responsible for:
   a. Drafting plans to conduct analyses of crisis events, developing lessons learned and creating best practices; and
   b. Providing or organizing the education and training of the remediation and assessment protocols to employees, management, and executive management, as needed.

Executive Oversight

The crisis management team needs strong leadership and sufficient authority. The leadership can take the form of a single individual or group that should be responsible for oversight of all four functions described above. This person or group will be responsible for securing resources and should be vested with the authority to ensure that the crisis management team has the resources and expertise to complete its task. For various reasons, companies have selected a variety of personnel to be responsible for the overall crisis management responsibility. For example, some crisis management teams are composed of the company's Chief Executive Officer (CEO), General Counsel, Chief Compliance Officer (CCO), Chief Risk Officer (CRO), Chief Operations Officer (COO), Chief Information Officer (CIO), Chief Financial Officer (CFO), a Public Relations Head, and any other related function. Some companies choose to create a working group that includes representatives from the legal department, executive management, and other key participants and decision-makers.

Internal Corporate Support

To be effective, a crisis management team needs support from senior, executive management. In addition, the team should include key internal participants from other corporate departments. For example, you should consider integrating some or all of the following into the various groups, as needed: (i) public relations; (ii) corporate governance; (iii) in-house counsel; (iv) human resources; (v) information technology ("IT") and engineering; (vi) corporate security (physical and computer); (vi) business unit; and (vii) customer services. In a well-designed plan, other key internal corporate participants will act to support the activities of management and the crisis team.

External Expertise

An effective crisis management team should have access to, and knowledge of, outside expert vendors. In order to work efficiently, the crisis management team should identify, and periodically update, its list of external experts who may be necessary to assist with each of the core team functions, including an outside legal counsel and an outside public relations specialist. Having known and qualified experts available will assist the crisis management team to resolve a crisis quickly and efficiently. In the context of a computer security crisis, looking for the right outside expert in the middle of a crisis is not the ideal time to go window shopping. Crisis events can be quite traumatic for companies and employees. Knowing who is on your team in advance of a crisis will help you in many ways.

Developing a Crisis Response Plan

After the crisis management team is established and after the risk areas have been identified, begin the process of creating a crisis response plan by taking the following steps:

(1) Define the term "crisis" as it applies to your Company and industry;

(2) Take inventory of existing crisis management plans;

(3) Include all potential crisis events in your plan; and

(4) Identify routine problems or risks that could escalate into crisis events.

Defining a "Crisis"

A crisis management plan is difficult to create and execute if you do not know what constitutes a "crisis" within your organization and industry. The very purpose of the crisis management plan is to create a known, efficient, response to a crisis. Therefore, before you can proceed with a crisis management plan, the first question to consider is, what is a crisis? The answer appears to be self-explanatory, but, in practice, it is not.

The definition of a crisis and the facts underlying a crisis will be different for every company and every industry. Generally, we define a crisis as a sudden event that significantly disrupts a company's on-going operations, personal safety, or reputation. The sources of the crisis may be internal or external to the company; they may be natural or man-made. A crisis may be either an (i) informational, (ii) behavioral, (iii) operational, or (iv) corporate crisis.

While certainly there are significantly more complex definitions, the bottom line is that each company must determine for itself what constitutes a crisis because, as we will discuss further below, the crisis management team and the crisis management plan is built around that definition. Moreover, there are many routine problems in the course of a company's daily existence that will not constitute a crisis until the problem reaches a boiling point. The issues then become how to monitor these small problems, at what point to decide as a company that the minor problem has reached a crisis, and how to respond? We will address these issues in more detail below.

Taking Inventory of Existing Crisis Management Plans

Learn from past experience and incorporate lessons learned into existing plans. Collect all existing, relevant plans across your enterprise. For many large companies, crisis management plans are not new, and many companies have existing crisis management plans. Make an effort to collect and review all the existing plans to determine whether they are useful, and to make sure they are not outdated or incomplete. The old plans may need slight revisions or may need to be replaced entirely. The focus is to use old information to assist you in understanding the risks, and crisis plans designed to respond to these risks. You may also find that some risk areas or businesses have no plans at all. Or, you may find that a plan suited for one particular line of business is a good template for another similar line of business. You may find that there are unique risks associated with one area of the business that are inapplicable everywhere else in the company.

Include All Potential Crisis Events in Your Plan

The crisis management plan should have responses for all crisis level risks associated with your Company. Crisis management is not a one size fits all program. Each crisis level risk may require a unique group of corporate participants with specific ways to address the event(s). In many cases, a model structure can be built across all business lines, but that is rare in complex organizations. An organization will probably need individual plans for specific risks.

Identify Routine Problems or Risks That Could Escalate into Crisis Events

Keep in mind that you have to create a structure that monitors routine problems and a mechanism to identify the routine problems that become big problems. An example of this is the computer security area. Most companies have routine outages of important network applications or servers. The issue is identifying who has the responsibility of monitoring these events, and deciding when the outages reach a critical point that triggers the execution of a crisis management plan.

The issue of when to escalate a routine problem into a "crisis" is the precise type of problem that will involve compliance and crisis management. You need a mechanism that ensures that small problems are tracked and reported to the crisis management team when appropriate. The risk of crisis for most large companies can be diverse, arising from such areas as product liability, antitrust issues, industrial accidents, environmental disasters, sabotage, or bribery.

Written Policies and Procedures

The crisis management team should put all policies and protocols in writing. The procedures should be written in simple, easy to understand instructions. Often, companies create written procedures that are adopted from a so-called industry standard authority. The result of using this approach is the creation of an overly complex written compliance and crisis management policy that is so large and complicated that no one reads it — company's must avoid this result.

A better solution is to draft a series of policies directed to a specific target group. It is acceptable to have a lengthy master policy, but the master policy should be supplemented with a specific policy that is written for the general employees, managers, or executives. You may want to have specifically-tailored written policies for IT professionals, engineers, or doctors. The bottom line is that employees need to read and understand the policies and protocols. In addition, the company should provide adequate education and training in the policies and protocols to ensure that employees and management have a complete understanding. Such training should be given to new employees and should be conducted on an annual basis to reinforce important lessons.

On a regular basis, companies should have compliance programs to ensure that all employees are receiving the proper training with respect to the written procedures. Make sure that a document is signed confirming that every employee has participated in the education and training.

Testing the Crisis Response Plan

It is important to evaluate and continue to refine your crisis management plan. Some innovative companies are using mock scenario or desktop exercises to test their crisis management plans. These highly recommended interactive tools are useful ways to test your plans. Since it is difficult to predict the specific crisis, the goal of a "crisis audit" should be to get an idea of the types of risks the corporation might face, and their relative possibilities. The crisis planning may be taken a further step by having drills, games, or dry runs that will help to work through logistical and other potential problems.

A good way to assess the various types of crisis that your Company is at risk for is to look at crisis events that similar companies in your industry have faced. In addition, looking to your own company's history of crisis events can also be a useful tool to predict potential future crisis events.

How does a desktop exercise work? Generally, a group of employees are brought together by a moderator to handle a crisis offered to the group as a hypothetical. The moderator leads the group through the facts of the very interactive exercise in order to understand how the crisis would be handled by the attendees. The various participants share their thoughts and expertise to resolve the problem. The exercise is an extraordinary opportunity to test whether the education and training offered to employees has been adopted.

Desktop exercises can be designed for an audience that includes executive leadership, members of the crisis management team, or other groups. The exercises can serve to detect weaknesses in the crisis management plan, knowledge, or expertise gaps. For example, a crisis management plan may include conducting an internal forensic analysis by company employees. During the course of a desktop exercise, the question is posed as to who specifically will conduct the work, and whether that individual has the requisite training and experience to perform the work. You may discover that there are no identifiable individuals to perform the task or that the individuals are not qualified without further training. One of the benefits of the desktop exercise is to test and evaluate the plans in advance of the crisis.

Remediation of the Crisis Management Plan

Periodically, a review of your crisis management plan(s) is warranted in order to bolster perceived weaknesses or refine/streamline approaches. Post incident response protocols should be created that measure the quality of the crisis, efficiency, and timeliness. The post-incident response protocols should memorialize any improvements needed and lessons learned from the event.

It is critically important that all recommendations be resolved. That is, you should assume that all records will be discovered by some litigant. The records should be prepared with that in mind. In many cases, companies spend considerable resources creating improvements and lessons learned while the remediation falls by the way side. That is, the execution of the remediation is either not done or not properly documented. Such failures can create inadvertent smoking gun memos that are not accurate. The creation of inaccurate or incomplete records is not a best practice and is fraught with litigation risks.

Great care should be made to properly and accurately record weaknesses and improvements to the plan. In that regard, you should follow or create company document destruction policies so that you do not have 10 years of risk assessments and crisis managements plans that have not been updated or that are no longer accurate or viable.

The involvement of in-house legal team and compliance staff can be helpful in assessing the records and recommendations.

A Sample Crisis Management Checklist

- Identify Risks
- Assemble a Crisis Management Team
- Review Insurance Policies
- Create a Crisis Fund
- Select a Public Relations Agency
- Coordinate with Appropriate Outside Counsel
- Develop a Crisis Response Plan
- Implement Written Policies and Protocols
- Test the Crisis Response Plan Through Drills, Games, and Dry Runs
- Revise and Retest

Sample Crisis Management Program for a Credit Card Company

The best-case scenario for any crisis management program is overall crisis avoidance. With good policies in place and adherence to these policies as well as solid reporting lines and an enabling culture of communication, it is possible to avoid a crisis. For example, in April of 2012, Forbes magazine wrote an article on the most marketable compliance officer in the world—Raja Chaterjee. Mr. Chaterjee was dubbed the "the king" of compliance officers not for the quality of his risk assessments but for the situations he was able to avoid. Forbes describes how his compliance program, which contained "the holy trinity" of reduced penalties: pre-existing compliance, self-disclosure, and cooperation ultimately resulted in avoidance of his company's prosecution. Akin to our modern-day Icarus, we aim to reach the highest of heights. A solid crisis management program reaches for the sun even if it's a miss; it contains the vision, planning, and foresight to put out some major fires.

In our crisis compliance program, we must start at the very beginning. Every crisis operates on a timeline. There are three phases to a crisis: *prevention, preparation, and recovery*. We are currently in the pre-crisis planning or prevention stage. In this stage, we must identify the type of situations that we have seen in order to determine what we might see in the future. Our pre-crisis planning begins with a realistic risk assessment. Like any major global corporation, in the universe of possible disasters [Your Company] has very likely had quite a few. It is necessary for us to ask, "What kind of disaster is our company most likely to face?" "How should we spend our time preparing?" "What should we prepare for?"

Because history often repeats itself, we turn to past events in order to determine what we should plan for in the future. *Exhibit 1* is a timeline of past disasters this company has faced. It is clear that environmental, behavioral, technological, and legal are all frequent threats for our company. While it is impossible to predict with accuracy what the next situation will be, there does seem to be a trend toward technological crises specifically with respect to data breaches. This is another major consideration when conducting our risk assessment. Risks affecting other companies and competitors are very likely to be risks affecting us.

In the case of data breaches, these events continue to occur throughout the country affecting not only credit card companies but also a myriad of industries beyond financial companies. For example, recently companies such as Neiman Marcus and Target have been victims of this kind of data breach. With each passing day, hackers become more sophisticated more and more companies such as companies, banks, and financial institutions fall prey. Therefore, we can almost bet that we will be seeing this kind of crisis in the near future and potentially on a recurring basis. To state that we need to prepare for this is an understatement.

The next step in our crisis management program after determining the potential crisis that may or may not affect [Your Company] is to do a *crisis audit* of the company. In order to plan ahead for the future it is imperative that we do a realistic assessment of not only the *types* of crisis that may occur but also the *probabilities* and *likelihood* of their occurrence. In our crisis audit, we will look at the various type of crises that are most likely to come up. Exhibit 2 is a pie chart based on a decade of past newsworthy crisis events. Based on the relative frequency of occurrence, the chart shows the relative probability that these types of crisis situations could occur again. As exemplified in the assessment, technological data breaches, antitrust issues, and money laundering are most foreseeable. Therefore, this is where the crux of our efforts should be spent in preparing.

As stated earlier, there are three phases to a crisis: *prevention, preparation, and recovery*. We are currently in the pre-crisis planning or prevention stage. As we know, it is in this stage that we must identify the type of risk situations that we have witnessed in order to determine what risks we might see in the future. Based an analysis of past crises, it has been determined that that the four type of risks that [Your Company] is susceptible to are: operational, behavioral, informational and reputational. In this comprehensive crisis program, a prototype plan will be provided for each form of crisis.

To begin with, an example of an operational crisis category that has often been seen is that of prepaid credit cards being used to launder money across the border. The most flexible of these types of credit cards tend to be those used on ATM networks and online as well as inside stores. The user friendliness of these credit cards makes them a prime target for illegal activity that reaches across borderlines.

Under the behavioral category of crisis, we have an international company under European Union scrutiny over the level of fees that tourists are charged when using its credit cards to make purchases. As it turns out the fees are much higher for the non-Europeans than that of actual Europeans. This poses a major problem for cross border trade. The main issue is the high bank fees, which tend to be even higher for premium cards, is that they end up pushing prices up thereby thwarting international trade and ultimately rewarding credit card companies and issuing banks unjustly.

Next, we have the ever-occurring informational crisis. As stated earlier, this crisis is very popular at this time. In light of technological advances, data breaches are occurring in every industry. Without exception is the credit card industry. Recently, 40 million files were put at risk in a company informational crisis when a pattern of fraudulent charges was traced back to a company in Tucson, Arizona, that processes over 15 billion dollars in transactions for a variety of merchants each year.

Finally, we have the reputational crisis. Two opposing lawyers involved in the antitrust settlement between two major competitors were involved in the improper communication and exchange of confidential information and emails regarding the case. In conclusion, these are the four types of crisis scenarios that Your Company could face. It is imperative that we prepare and do role-playing and crisis response simulations at the pre-crisis planning level in order for our responses to be second nature when the actual time comes.

To avoid these events from happening again [Your Company] must have the appropriate policies and procedures. What we had in place at time of these events clearly was insufficient in preparation for these potential scenarios. Therefore, a revamping of money laundering policy, anti-corruption policy, and anti-trust policy must occur. In addition, employees need to be trained on a more consistent basis regarding these rules. A zero-tolerance policy must be put in place. This means that our company culture must need to support this agenda. A hotline must be put in place and our employees need to know that this is what our company stands for. More responsibility lies at the top. [Your Company] must have tone at the top in order to avoid these disasters. In addition, our policy will be to hold a weekend retreat, at the beginning of the company's fiscal year, in which officers and employees will be trained and expected to run through live simulations of an entire crisis. With each passing year, our protocol and responses will be updated and altered as necessary. This is the first step that will be taken to teach all employees how to deal with every kind of crisis.

It is important to keep in mind that there is a risk associated with conducting a crisis audit. It is very likely that this document will be used during future litigation. Therefore, we must act under the assumption that it will be used in litigation in order to maintain attorney-client privilege. In order to do this, the company must delegate outside counsel to create this document. If outside consultants such as KPMG and Deloitte are hired to assist in this kind of assessment, it must be made clear upfront that we intend to maintain attorney-client privilege. This will extend to both types of privilege: attorney-client and work product. The work product states that documents are privileged when done in anticipation of litigation. This is the reason it is advantageous to operate from this standpoint from the inception.

Next, we will set up a multidisciplinary crisis team adaptable to the four types of crisis that will come into play. The core team will be kept for every crisis; however, outside consultants and varying legal specialists will be brought into play depending upon the circumstances we are confronted with. To begin with, every crisis needs a leader. Not just any employee can be a leader. This individual must possess command and grace under pressure. It is also useful for this person to be familiar with the various employees involved in crisis management. Because general counsel has access and command of a large legal team, it is easy to understand why this person may be best to lead in a certain crisis situation in our company. Thus, the first rule in the creation of [Your Company's] crisis team is that general counsel will be the core of the crisis team with various generalists and specialists reporting to her. Rule number two is that the CEO of the company will be on the team and general counsel will have a direct reporting route to the CEO. But, the remaining legal team will report to the general counsel.

The legal team will consist of 20 generalists and 35 specialists (5 lawyers assigned respectively to each of the 7 specialties) in the area of *Intellectual Property, Anti-corruptive Money Laundering/ Fraud, Corporate Finance, Real Estate, Employment, Anti-trust, and International Commercial Transactions.* The specialists will report to the generalist who in turn reports to the General Counsel. We will also have the Vice-president of Public relations on the team. This person will work in conjunction with general counsel in the crafting of statements. A spokesperson should be designated who is not the CEO. This person must be appropriate to the crisis and trained to put out holding statements. This person should be a polished, poised individual who is an expert at media Q&A. Outside law firms will be needed especially in area involving international crisis. For example, in our money-laundering crisis that occurred across the border, it would be necessary use our Latin American legal team as well as Latin American-based outside counsel to preserve privilege.

It is common to do this in situations in which litigation is foreseeable. Thus, we will need to call in a trusted and experienced third party outside law firm in order to maintain privilege and help with language issues as well as other procedural issues that come up in litigation. This firm will also be beneficial in addressing issues of document retention. It is common in some countries to conduct a dawn raid. This is especially true for Latin American countries. For example, in the recent Petrobras crisis, which occurred in Brazil, procedural rules for document retention were virtually non-existent. Therefore, the manner of obtaining documents was a dawn raid. This situation is less than ideal for any American corporation and thus must be anticipated from a legal standpoint. Moreover, pre-screened outside consultants will be needed depending upon the type of crisis as well as a pre-screened outside public relations firm. It is important to keep in mind when bringing in outside consultants that measures must be taken to maintain privilege. Our relationship with these consultants must operate in such a way that does not waive the attorney-client privilege. In planning ahead for this situation, it will be easier to protect ourselves now than in the future. Planning ahead is critical.

The next logical concern in our pre-crisis planning is financial. In the end, it's all about the money. Most of the crisis situations that we may find ourselves in involve the illegal obtaining of money; most of the regulations that we might potentially violated are costly. As a result, cleaning up the mess is expensive too. Given, the vast nature of disasters that affect our company on an ongoing basis, a crisis fund in the amount of $100,000.00 must be allocated and easily accessible to the chief compliance officer and team. Naturally, the CFO of [Your Company] will be involved in the planning and accounting of this part the plan. In addition, a big part of our crisis audit is determining whether we have the requisite crisis insurance and determining the required notification period to record the violation. It is recommended that outside consultants assist with recommending insurance policies and appropriate reporting procedures for insurance notification.

Adequate coverage must be made available for every kind of crisis that was explained above. In hiring of KPMG, it is crucial that we know when crisis insurance is triggered for the purpose of making an application. Depending upon the circumstance, we may or may not be eligible for insurance therefore it is crucial that we notify them in a prompt and timely manner. At first blush, one million dollars might seem like a steep proposition for a crisis fund. But, the reality of today's world and in light of the 2008 financial crisis, Fortune 500 companies are being heavily regulated. Profitable corporations such as MasterCard, Apple, Morgan Stanley, and Wal-Mart spend exorbitant fees cleaning up crises situations and regulatory infractions; therefore, it would be unrealistic to be too conservative in this phase of planning. In the end, the need for a crisis fund boils down to the reality and the truth sung by the Notorious B.I.G., "Mo' money, Mo' problems."

In our prototype application of crisis management scenarios, it is crucial that we prepare for extreme scenarios. This involves crisis management protocols short and long terms strategies, business interruption strategies, evacuation procedures, and data document retention. We will first analyze the reputational crisis. The first step in dealing with a crisis is to evaluate the scope of the crisis. The management of a crisis is done on a timeline and the first twenty-four hours of a crisis are crucial this is because the statements that are made during this time must be crafted very carefully. The media audience will keep track of the initial response and any contradictions coming later down the road. A spokesperson and outside public relations consultants need to be working in tandem with legal to get the message out to the public that we are working on the scene. The best practice is to avoid a crisis by implementing appropriate procedure and policy requirements so that the company does not get itself into crisis situations. But, even the best run company has to prepare for the worst. There is always the extreme scenario of the rogue employee who gets the company in trouble. For example, Wal-Mart recently found itself in a billion dollar crisis situation when a disgruntled employee who was passed over for promotion leaked evidence of corruptive practices of its Latin American subsidiary Walmex to the New York Times.

Company response in this type of situation is crucial. The best procedure to follow is if you find yourself in this type of problem is to 1) admit wrongdoing, 2) fix the problem, and 3) restore confidence. When a company finds itself in the midst of a crisis, it has an obligation to remedy the situation for the employees, families, and civilians affected. The crisis fund is useful in this situation.

In the case of the B.P. Oil Spill with the Deep Water Horizon, the crisis fund was crucial to plug up the well, rescue employees, and reunite families at the scene. It is important to note that communication is key in these situations. An emergency team needs to be in constant contact with one another. In today's age of instant messaging, this should not be a problem. Also, the company has an obligation to let the financial regulatory authorities know about the state of the company's business affairs. A filing of the company's financial situation must be made in order to alert potential market investors of the risks associated with the company. When a company finds itself in the midst of a crisis, it is important to weigh the costs of doing business against that of limiting legal liability. It is at this point in time that our regulatory and financial specialists must weigh in on regulatory considerations. For example Rule 10b-5 of the SEC prohibits the making of misstatements of material fact or the avoidance and omission of such facts from its financial reports. It is our responsibility to report the state of affairs as accurately as possible.

In the case of Petrobras, the company currently finds itself in a massive lawsuit with respect to a major violation of this rule. They hired auditors and outside consultants to assess the financial records of their company. They in conjunction with their auditors reported that the financial state of the company was far better than it truly was. They conveniently ignored funds from money laundering and bribery scheme that implicated the country's president and other high reaching political leaders. It was the company's duty to report this information in order to public investors. Because Petrobras failed to do so, it will have to pay regulatory fines. It is best to be upfront. Therefore, [Your Company's] policy will be to report financial problems promptly.

Exhibit 1

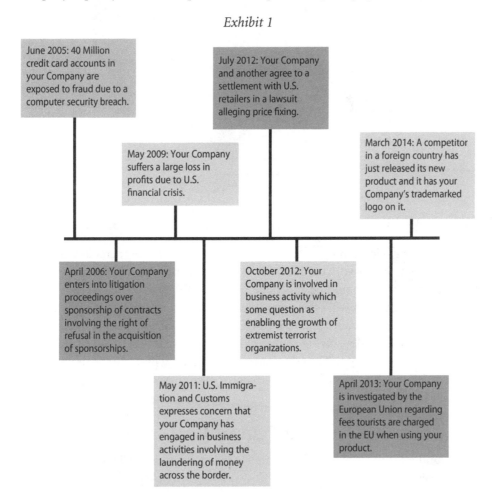

June 2005: 40 Million credit card accounts in your Company are exposed to fraud due to a computer security breach.

July 2012: Your Company and another agree to a settlement with U.S. retailers in a lawsuit alleging price fixing.

May 2009: Your Company suffers a large loss in profits due to U.S. financial crisis.

March 2014: A competitor in a foreign country has just released its new product and it has your Company's trademarked logo on it.

April 2006: Your Company enters into litigation proceedings over sponsorship of contracts involving the right of refusal in the acquisition of sponsorships.

October 2012: Your Company is involved in business activity which some question as enabling the growth of extremist terrorist organizations.

May 2011: U.S. Immigration and Customs expresses concern that your Company has engaged in business activities involving the laundering of money across the border.

April 2013: Your Company is investigated by the European Union regarding fees tourists are charged in the EU when using your product.

Below is a pie chart, based on the past events, exhibiting the relative probabilities that Your Company will face specific types of crisis situations in the future.

Exhibit 2

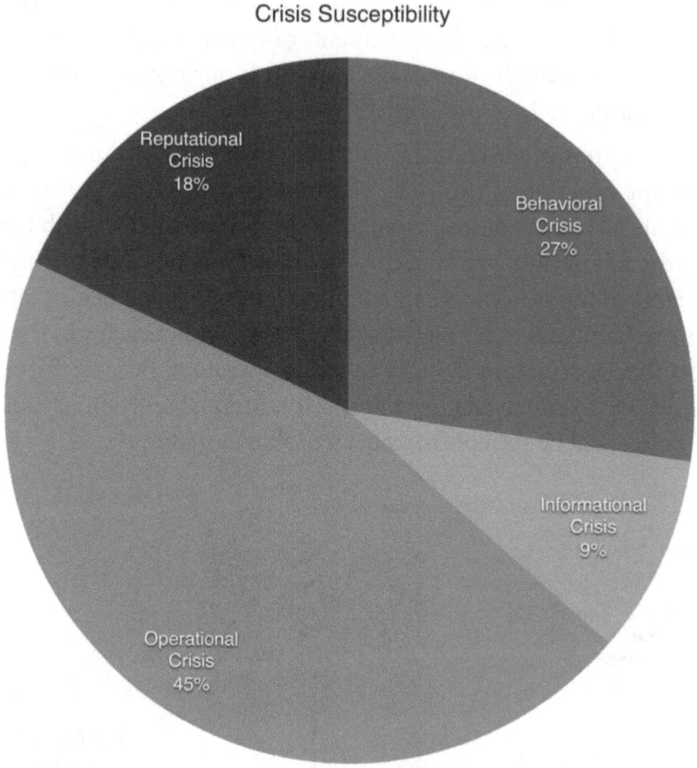

Crisis Susceptibility

Conclusion

The process of developing a crisis management plan can be incredibly difficult, costly, and labor intensive. This chapter was written to provide a high level overview of the key issues that should be addressed when creating a plan. In the end, a good crisis management plan will offer great value to Your Company by highlighting risk areas, improving compliance and response efficiencies that will assist Your Company in avoiding a crisis and resolving a crisis with little interruption to Your Company's operations and reputation. The crisis management plan will make the organization a better corporate citizen and save resources, or even lives.

Assignment

- **Hypothetical:** You are a Chief Compliance Officer at your Corporation. Create a Crisis Management Plan.

Chapter 18

Corporate Social Responsibility and Sustainability[*]

Introduction

Corporate Social Responsibility ("CSR") may be defined as a corporation's obligation to society and its "stakeholders." Stakeholders are individuals or entities affected by, or interested in, a corporation's operations. While CSR is rooted in legal compliance, it also encompasses human rights principles, ethics, governance, and philanthropic efforts. Among other things, CSR initiatives seek to manage business risks, protect brand equity and good will, and improve the lives of the corporation and its supply chain's workers and the communities in which it does business. The purpose for which corporations exist, and the means of measuring their success, has been the subject of some debate. To some, the notion of CSR is viewed as being inconsistent with the perceived single responsibility of corporations: profit maximization.

To others, CSR is "the responsibility of enterprises for their impacts on society." This is expressed in the adoption of a new policy on corporate social responsibility by the European Commission in October 2011. In order to fully meet their social responsibility, enterprises "should have in place a process to integrate social, environmental, ethical human rights and consumer concerns into their business operations and core strategy in close collaboration with their stakeholders." (Communication From The Commission To The European Parliament, The Council, The European Economic And Social Committee And The Committee Of The Regions, A renewed EU strategy 2011–14 for Corporate Social Responsibility, Brussels, Oct. 25, 2011.)

As an illustration of the CSR concept, one of the largest pharmacists in the country, CVS Caremark, has released its 2013 CSR Report. It describes that the "goal is to reinvent pharmacy and focus on solutions that benefit millions of people." The proposals of it latest CSR report are for "building healthier communities; protecting the planet; and creating economic opportunities." In the opening letter of the 2013 CSR report, Larry Merlo, President and Chief Executive Officer of CVS Caremark announced that one of the company's major changes is commitment a to better health

---

[*] Special thanks to John Cashin for his contributions. This chapter is adapted from John Cashin, *Corporate Social Responsibility and Sustainability* in CORPORATE COMPLIANCE PRACTICE GUIDE: THE NEXT GENERATION OF COMPLIANCE, Chapter 23 (Carole Basri, Release 7, 2015).

in the community by not selling cigarettes and tobacco products at its more than 7,600 stores across the country starting on October 1, 2014. According to the CSR report, this decision is consistent with the company's purpose, message, customer and activity.

Although corporations may sometimes engage in CSR by joining multi-stakeholder or multiple corporation sector-based initiatives, to some stakeholders, the "responsibility" lies with, and much of the work is done by, individual corporations. These efforts may be seen in the policies that corporations develop and the extent to which they integrate CSR practices into their daily business operations. At the individual company level, CSR initiatives are found in corporate standards, values, or operating principles, such as "Codes of Conduct." To support CSR standards corporate structures must exist to ensure that issues are identified, prioritized, and addressed efficiently. Specific criteria or benchmarks may also be used to assess the extent to which they have been implemented successfully. Each corporation also must determine how many links in the supply chain will fall under their CSR code and monitoring program. Failure to determine the proper (as determined by stakeholders) scope of review could increase the risks of reputation damage and brand deterioration in the eyes of those stakeholders. CSR initiatives emphasize social, environmental, and economic sustainability.

Although sustainability was first viewed as preserving the earth's natural resources, the 1987 World Commission on Environment and Development (the "Brundtland Commission") defined sustainability as "meeting the needs of the present without compromising the ability of future generations to meet their needs." Report on the World Commission on Environment and Development, Our Common Future, ¶ 1, U.N. Doc A/RES/42/187 (Aug. 2, 1987), *available at* http://www.un-documents.net/wced-ocf.htm. Companies embracing sustainability strive to develop operational plans aimed at sustaining economic prosperity while also taking due regard for human rights, the environment and the impact the firm's operations have on host communities.

"The term 'corporate social responsibility' is often used interchangeably with corporate responsibility, corporate citizenship, social enterprise, sustainability, sustainable development, triple-bottom line, corporate ethics, and in some cases corporate governance. Though these terms are different, they all point in the same direction. Throughout the industrialized world and in many developing countries, there has been a sharp escalation in the social roles corporations are expected to play. Companies are facing new demands to engage in public-private partnerships and are under growing pressure to be accountable not only to shareholders, but also to stakeholders such as employees, consumers, suppliers, local communities, policymakers, and society-at-large."[1]

Companies are facing new demands to engage in private-public partnerships and are being held accountable by shareholders and stakeholders. For example, the Cor-

---

1. See The Initiative Defining Corporate Social Responsibility, http://www.hks.harvard.edu/m-rcbg/CSRI/init_define.html.

porate Social Responsibility Initiative (CSRI) at the Harvard Kennedy School's Mossavar-Rahmani Center for Business and Government (M-RCBG)[2] is a multi-disciplinary and multi-stakeholder program that seeks to study and enhance the public contributions of private enterprise. Through its two primary workstreams of Governance & Accountability and Business & International Development, it explores the intersection of corporate responsibility, corporate governance, public policy, and international development. It bridges theory and practice, builds leadership skills, and supports constructive dialogue and collaboration among business, government, civil society, and academics.

The Business Cases

First, an effective CSR policy serves to protect businesses' tangible and intangible value and brand equity. Second, it may help to attract and retain talented personnel who often weigh a company's CSR policy among other factors before deciding whether to accept a position at a given company. Third, CSR policies can help drive market share. Customers may make purchasing decisions based upon the extent to which companies address CSR issues, and investors may favor companies that derive revenue from "ethically sourced" and "fair trade" products. Technology has enabled consumers to assess the social, environmental, and sustainability ratings of the products they purchase at the point of sale. Examples include the GoodGuide (http://www.good guide.com/about) and Buycott (http://www.buycott.com/about) platforms that provide participating consumers with a smartphone application which scans the product code of consumer goods and delivers ratings on how safe, green, and socially responsible those products are.

CSR programs help to address stakeholder concerns. Failure to address stakeholder concerns can lead to inquiries from and/or engagement by stakeholders, such as employees, customers, investors, and nongovernmental organizations ("NGOs"). Concerned stakeholders may mount massive, coordinated campaigns against corporations for CSR failures. A recent case in point involves Nestlé and Greenpeace.

Case of Nestle and Greenpeace

On March 17, 2010, the environmental group Greenpeace launched a social media attack on Nestlé's Kit Kat brand. In a YouTube video parodying the "Have a break; Have a Kit Kat" slogan, it highlighted the use of unsustainable forest clearing in production of palm oil used in several Nestlé products including Kit Kat. The video was

---

2. Corporate Social Responsibility Initiative, http://www.hks.harvard.edu/m-rcbg/CSRI/about/about.html.

widely viewed and ultimately Nestlé engaged with its critics and agreed to cease sourcing palm oil from unsustainable suppliers, including Sinar Mas.[3]

Press Release, Greenpeace International, *Nestlé Drives Rainforest Destruction Pushing Orangutans to Brink of Extinction, Greenpeace Launches Online Viral Exposing True Cost of "Having a Break" the KitKat Way*

(Mar. 17, 2010) http://www.greenpeace.org/international/
en/press/releases/nestle-drives-rainforest-destr/

Nestlé is using palm oil from destroyed Indonesian rainforests and peatlands, in products like KitKat, pushing already endangered orangutans to the brink of extinction and accelerating climate change, a new Greenpeace report reveals.

The damning new Greenpeace report, "*Caught Red-Handed*," exposes how Nestlé is sourcing palm oil from suppliers, including Sinar Mas, Indonesia's largest producer of palm oil, which continue to expand into the rainforest and carbon-rich peatlands, as well as into critical orangutan habitat. Sinar Mas also owns Asia Pulp and Paper, Indonesia's largest pulp and paper company, notorious for its role in rainforest destruction.

This morning, protests are taking place across Europe as around 100 Greenpeace activists, some dressed as orangutans, went to Nestlé's headquarters and factories in the UK, Germany and the Netherlands. They are calling on Nestlé staff to urge the company to stop using palm oil that's the result of forest destruction.

At 12.00pm CET/11.00am UK Greenpeace launches its "Have a Break?" video, showing what a KitKat break really means.

Nestlé, the world's leading food and drinks company, is a major consumer of palm oil. In the last three years, its annual use has almost doubled, with 320,000 tonnes of palm oil going into a range of products, including KitKat.

"Every time you take a bite out of a KitKat, you may be taking a bite out of Indonesia's rainforests, which are critical for the orangutan's survival. Nestlé needs to give the orangutan a break and stop using palm oil from suppliers that are destroying the rainforests," said Daniela Montalto, Greenpeace International campaigner.

The report's launch follows numerous attempts to persuade Nestlé to cancel its contracts with Sinar Mas. Most recently, in December, Greenpeace wrote to Nestlé with evidence that Sinar Mas is breaking Indonesian law and ignoring its commitments as a member of the Round Table on Sustainable Palm Oil (RSPO), the industry body that claims to be making the palm oil industry more sustainable. But evidence shows Sinar Mas's forest destruction continues.

---

3. *See* Aileen Ionescu-Somers & Albrecht Enders, *How Nestlé dealt with a social media campaign against it*, The Financial Times, Dec. 3, 2012, http://www.ft.com/intl/cms/s/0/90dbff8a-3aea-11e2-b3f0-00144feabdc0.html?siteedition=intl#axzz2f5RhA9J7.

In the face of its unacceptable environmental practices, several major companies, including Unilever and Kraft, have cancelled their palm oil contracts with the company.

"Other big companies are taking action, but Nestlé continues to turn a blind eye to the worst offenders which supply them, it's time for Nestlé to cancel its Sinar Mas contracts and support a halt to rainforest and peatland destruction," stressed Montalto.

Indonesia has one of the fastest rates of forest destruction on the planet, with palm oil plantations being a major cause. As a result, it is now the world's third largest greenhouse gas emitter, after China and the US.

Greenpeace & Amnesty Int'l, *The Toxic Truth About a Company Called Trafigura, a Ship Called the Probo Koala, and the Dumping of Toxic Waste in Côte d'Ivoire*

http://www.greenpeace.org/international/Global/international/
publications/toxics/ProboKoala/The-Toxic-Truth.pdf

Summary of the Key Facts of the Case

In late 2005, a multinational trading company called Trafigura decided to buy large amounts of an unrefined gasoline called coker naphtha. Trafigura intended to use the coker naphtha as a cheap blendstock for fuels, but first needed to find a way of refining it. This was done through an industrial process called caustic washing, initially carried out on land, but later at sea, on board a ship named Probo Koala.

Internal Trafigura email communications which came to light during court proceedings in the UK in 2009 confirm that the company was aware before starting the caustic washing process that the resulting waste would be hazardous and difficult to dispose of. In June 2006, after several unsuccessful attempts to dispose of the waste, Trafigura contacted a Dutch company, Amsterdam Port Services (APS), and arranged to deliver the waste in Amsterdam. The Probo Koala arrived in Amsterdam on 2 July 2006, and APS began to unload the waste on to one of its barges. However, a terrible stench emanating from the waste led APS to test it. They found it was far more contaminated than they had thought, and raised the price for treatment, from €27 per m3 to €1,000 per m.

Trafigura rejected this new quote and asked for the waste to be reloaded on to the Probo Koala. After much discussion between the Dutch authorities, this was agreed to, despite the fact that the destination of the waste was unknown.

On 19 August 2006, with the waste still onboard, the Probo Koala arrived in Abidjan in Côte d'Ivoire. Trafigura proceeded to contract a newly licensed company, called Compagnie Tommy, to dispose of the waste at a local dumpsite. There was no mention, in the handwritten contract with Tommy, of treating the waste to make it safe. The waste was unloaded into trucks and taken to the dumpsite; however, concerns about the smell led the site to close. Truck drivers then dumped the rest of the waste at approximately 18 different locations around the city of Abidjan.

On 20 August 2006, the population of Abidjan woke up to the appalling effects of the dumping. Tens of thousands of people experienced a range of similar health problems, including headaches, skin irritations and breathing problems. A major medical emergency ensued.

In September 2006 two Trafigura executives, who had arrived in Abidjan following the dumping, were charged with offences relating to breaches of Ivorian public health and environmental laws, as well as poisoning or being accessories to poisoning. Other individuals, including a number of Ivorian port and customs officials, and the head of Compagnie Tommy, were also charged with offences relating to the dumping.

On 13 February 2007 Trafigura and the government of Côte d'Ivoire reached a settlement, under which Trafigura agreed to pay the state of Côte d'Ivoire the sum of CFA95 billion (approximately US$195 million), and the government waived its right to prosecute or mount an action against the company. Neither Trafigura nor any of its executives were brought to trial in Côte d'Ivoire. Ultimately, only two individuals were convicted by a court in Abidjan: Salomon Ugborogbo, the head of Compagnie Tommy, and Essoin Kouao, a shipping agent from West African International Business Services (WAIBS).

In June 2008, the Dutch Public Prosecutor brought charges against Trafigura Beheer BV and a number of other parties for the illegal export of the waste from the Netherlands to Africa. On 23 July 2010, the Dutch court handed down a guilty verdict on a number of counts against Trafigura Beheer BV, a London-based executive of Trafigura Ltd. and the captain of the Probo Koala. The guilty verdict against Trafigura Beheer BV was upheld by the Dutch Court of Appeal in December 2011. The role played by Trafigura in relation to the dumping of toxic waste in Abidjan has never been subject to a full court proceeding.

A large portion of the settlement amount paid to the state of Côte d'Ivoire was supposed to be allocated as compensation to the victims and for clean-up. As of July 2012, clean-up was reported to be complete, but questions remain about the adequacy of the process in some of the affected areas. The status of the compensation fund is unclear, but thousands of people whose health was affected could not access the government compensation scheme.

In 2006, some 30,000 of the victims of the dumping filed a civil case against Trafigura in the United Kingdom (UK). On 23 September 2009, the High Court of England and Wales approved a UK£30 million (US$45 million) settlement between the parties. However, during the process of distributing this money to the victims in Abidjan, an organization known as the National Coordination of Toxic Waste Victims of Côte d'Ivoire (CNVDT-CI), falsely claiming to represent the claimants in the UK case, gained control of part of the money and approximately 6,000 victims did not receive their compensation. Côte d'Ivoire was plunged into political turmoil following the November 2010 elections, which led to a political stalemate and to serious human rights violations committed both by security forces loyal to the outgoing President Laurent Gbagbo and those loyal to Alassane Ouattara. All the country's state institutions virtually stopped functioning during that time. The new president, Alassane Ouattara, was sworn in on 21 May 2011. Since then, state institutions have started functioning again.

An investigation into the misappropriation of the UK compensation money was opened in 2011, and in May 2012, Côte d'Ivoire's Minister of African Integration, Adama Bictogo, was removed from his post by the President because of his alleged role in the fraud. The investigation was ongoing at the time of writing.

Despite some action by the states involved to investigate and sanction those who were involved in the dumping of the toxic waste, the victims have not seen justice done. The central actor—Trafigura—has evaded all but a limited Dutch prosecution and the UK civil action. The truth about what happened has never fully come to light. Adequate compensation has not reached all of the victims. The circumstances that allowed more than 100,000 people to experience the horror of getting sick from an unknown toxic waste dumped where they live and work continue to exist.

An effective CSR initiative may serve to safeguard companies from, or to mitigate, certain risks. Corporations without a functioning CSR program have faced economic and reputational injury. Violating labor, safety, and employment laws comes with a price, and often a price that's both tangible and intangible. Aside from possible liability for monetary payments, court costs and attorneys' fees, companies embroiled in legal defense of their actions can suffer intangible damages to reputation and corporate citizenship.

A sound Foreign Corrupt Practices Act ("FCPA") compliance program, which may work synergistically with, or as part of, a company's CSR program, addresses legal compliance issues, and will guard against litigation and potential prosecution. The risks posed by FCPA compliance challenges include investigation, multimillion-dollar fines, and being the center of antiterrorism litigation. (*See* "The Big Three FCPA Lessons from the Morgan Stanley Case," Amy Conway-Hatcher, Corporate Counsel, June 14, 2012.).

Reasons for a CSR's strategy:

1. Brand Protection

Effective CSR standards and an efficient monitoring program serve to protect corporate reputation, brands, and related good will. A good reputation can have a halo effect; it enhances or even creates competitive advantage. It has the capacity to positively impact the attitude of regulators and lawmakers, enables a business to better withstand a crisis, and helps attract and retain the best talent. Conversely, a damaged reputation potentially reduces earnings, market share, and dents stakeholder trust. According to Aon's 2013 Global Risk Management Survey, damage to reputation or brand is seen as the fourth most frequently noted risk concern by global businesses. (available at: http://www.aon.com/2013GlobalRisk/)

2. Risk Management

CSR programs help companies manage risk, including the risk of litigation. For consumer goods companies, another important risk is the potential interruption of merchandise supply because of supply chain CSR issues. Accordingly, CSR compliance effective reviews (inspections and audits, in particular) can be structured so as to evaluate concurrently product and manufacturing facility safety and illegal transshipment compliance issues.

CSR programs allow corporations to gather vast amounts of information about ever changing risks posed by their business operations and the jurisdictions in which they do business, or from which they obtain manufactured goods or natural resources.

3. Investor Relations

Mandatory environmental, social, and governance ("ESG") data and statements of investment principles ("SIP") are being sought by stakeholders. For example, in the Financial sector, the European Sustainable Investment Forum ("Eurosif") is seeking to have the European Commission ("EC") adopt "mandatory requirements for large companies to publish uniform environmental, social, and governance data and for institutional investors to disclose how they use this information to invest."[4] Eurosif seeks: 1) to update the EU Modernization Directive to oblige large companies (those with over 250 employees) to report ESG data using sector specific performance indicators, and 2) to bind institutional investors to a Statement of Investment Principle, which lays out how ESG data is used when buying and holding onto companies. In theory, combining these objectives creates a "virtuous circle" where investors reward ESG-attentive companies by buying their shares. This occurs when investors see long-term sustainability issues factored into strategy and companies that pursue sustainability strategies in order to attract investors, boost their share price and lower their cost of capital."[5]

According to data available from Institutional Shareholder Services[6] during the 2014 proxy season, investors filed over 900 shareholder resolutions which is up from 840 such proposals in 2013. In 2014, proposals on social and environmental issues, while always prevalent, comprised a majority of proposals for the first time.[7] In prior proxy seasons shareholder proposals also targeted specific companies to address human rights. Resolutions were filed with Motorola and Hewlett-Packard urging these companies to develop policies sufficient to provide assurance that their 'products and services are not used in human rights violations." A resolution filed with KBR asked the company to report on the extent to which its 'contractors and suppliers are

---

4. (Hugh Wheelan, *Eurosif steps up EU campaign on ESG reporting and lobby on stock lending*, Responsible Investor, Apr. 16, 2009. *available at* http://www.responsible-investor.com/home/article/eurosif2/)

5. http://www.responsible-investor.com/reports/.

6. https://www.issgovernance.com.

7. "Highlights of the 2014 U.S. Meeting Season," http://www.issgovernance.com/highlights-of-the-2014-u-s-meeting-season/.

implementing human rights policies in their operations, including monitoring, training, [and] addressing issues of non-compliance."[8]

4. Attracting and Retaining Employees

Socially responsible corporations may have an edge over their competition in the war for talent. They may have greater success in recruiting and retaining better employees. If CSR efforts enable companies to hire more talented employees, then the companies may have enhanced performance and better bottom-line results. Along with the intellectual challenge and financial package offered, a reputation for ethics and an atmosphere of care ranked high when prospective employees made employment decisions. "While the notion of corporate social responsibility, may have once been regarded as a corporate philanthropy, it has quickly become a crucial part of any large company's long-term strategy—not just in marketing, but in recruiting, too: As consumers are ever more concerned with where products come from, employees now want more from their employer than a paycheck. They want a sense of pride and fulfillment from their work, a purpose and importantly a company's whose values match their own."[9]

Two significant benefits of an established CSR program are attracting better employees and engaging those already there.

5. Consumer Relations

Adherence to CSR standards may provide a competitive edge for corporations, as consumers may decide to purchase products because they understand from the Company that they have been made or purchased in compliance with those standards. Some consumers may be willing to pay a higher price for products that were obtained through *fair trade* or that were *ethically sourced*.

The Fairtrade Labeling Organizations International ("FLO") (www.fairtrade.net) conducts annual inspections to ensure that the strict socioeconomic development criteria are being met using the increased fair trade revenues. Moreover, Co-op America, an active NGO, leads a grassroots effort called Adopt-a-Supermarket, where neighborhoods are encouraged to adopt a local supermarket and campaign for more Fair Trade products. Supporters are also encouraged to regularly request Fair Trade products. In the fashion industry, organic cotton produced using environmentally sustainable practices is a highly prized and marketable commodity. Popular brands such as People Tree and Edun, the brainchild of Bono and Ali Hewson, have been successful in selling ethically sourced or Fair Trade certified merchandise. (http://www.transfairusa.org/content/certification/overview.php)

Other industries have also organized certification programs aimed at establishing sustainability, labor, and environmental standards for suppliers. These include the following:

---

8. Sarah A. Altschuller & Gare A. Smith, *Making Corporate Social Responsibility Systemic*, Executive Counsel, February/March 2011, http://www.csrandthelaw.com/uploads/file/Altschuller_Smith_Executive%20Counsel(1).pdf.

9. Jeanne Meister, *Corporate Social Responsibility: A Lever For Employee Attraction & Engagement*, http://www.forbes.com/sites/jeannemeister/2012/06/07.

- Forest Stewardship Council (FSC) 11% of global forestry market
- Marine Stewardship Council (MSC) 6% of global fish market
- Roundtable on Sustainable Palm Oil 8% of global palm oil market
- UTZ Certified 5% of global coffee market
- 4C Association 30% of global coffee market
- Fair Labor Association (FLA) 75% of global athletic footwear market

6. Legal Issues

International or domestic production, importation, distribution, or sale of products may open a Pandora's Box of legal issues for corporations that have not addressed related risks through CSR efforts.

As corporations outsource production to control prices and maximize profits, there is a risk that lower costs may come at a high price, as brands, licensors, and private labelers may be held responsible by their stakeholders for illegal or sub-standard conditions that may be encountered in the locations to which production has shifted. In terms of content, some CSR code of conduct provisions are of broad applicability regardless of the specific industrial sector to which the corporation belongs. On the other hand, there are some code provisions that are designed to address specific challenges faced by companies in particular sectors. To address these issues, more and more corporations are implementing well-devised CSR programs as proactive measures to ensure that the standards are just the corporation's first words on this subject. Specifically, in the wake of reported product safety issues for toy products, and related product recalls, large toymakers are increasing their product testing regimens.

Corporations and their executives may be sued in the United States for conditions and acts that occur outside the United States. Under the Alien Tort Statute ("ATS"), district courts have original jurisdiction over any civil action brought by an alien for a tort only, committed in violation of the law of nations or a treaty of the United States (28 U.S.C. § 1350). In substance, to be liable under the ATS a corporation must violate *jus cogens* norms, which have evolved from violations of safe conduct, infringements on the rights of ambassadors, and piracy, to include conspiracy and aiding and abetting. The theory of secondary liability is nothing new to international law, as courts have concluded under appropriate circumstances that international law provides for the imposition of liability on a party that does not directly perform the acts that are the subject of a complaint.

In April 9, 2009, Southern District Judge Shira Scheindlin rejected a motion to dismiss claims asserted under the ATS that corporations allegedly aided and abetted in alleged torture and other acts that were committed during the Apartheid regime in South Africa. In re South African Apartheid Litigation, 346 F. Supp. 2d 538, 542 (S.D.N.Y. 2004), *aff'd in part, vacated in part, remanded sub nom.* Khulumani v. Barclay Nat'l Bank Ltd., 504 F.3d 254 (2d Cir. 2007), *aff'd sub nom.* Am. Isuzu Motors, Inc. v. Ntsebeza, 553 U.S. 1028 (2008). Later in 2009, the Second Circuit Court addressed another ATS lawsuit, [1]*In re South African Apartheid Litigation*, when South African plaintiffs[10] commenced multiple actions in eight district courts, alleging that the defendant-corporations "support[ed] and facilitate[d] Apartheid's destructive and civil goals ... [a]nd, these companies derived exorbitant profits and benefits from and during Apartheid." In re S. African Apartheid Litig., 346 F. Supp. 2d 538 (complaint); *see also* Ntsebeza v. Daimler AG, 617 F. Supp. 2d 228 (S.D.N.Y. 2009), reconsideration denied, 617 F. Supp. 2d 228 (S.D.N.Y.), certificate of appealability denied, 624 F. Supp. 2d 336 (S.D.N.Y. 2009), and motion to certify appeal denied, 2009 U.S. Dist. LEXIS 121559 (S.D.N.Y. Dec. 31, 2009). Back in August 2002, the Judicial Panel on Multidistrict Litigation had transferred all related actions to the Southern District. In 2009, the court denied in part the defendants' motion to dismiss the consolidated complaints, and denied the plaintiffs' motion to "re-solicit views of governments of United States and South Africa." S. African Apartheid Litig. v. Daimler AG, 617 F. Supp. 2d 228, 296 (S.D.N.Y. 2009). The district court also denied the defendants' motion for certification of an interlocutory appeal. Ntsebeza v. Daimler A.G., 624 F. Supp. 2d 336, 343 (S.D.N.Y. 2009). In October 2009, the district court granted the Union Bank of Switzerland A.G.'s motion for entry of final judgment due to the dismissal of the plaintiff's claim against this particular defendant. Khulumani v. Barclays Nat'l Bank Ltd., 2009 U.S. Dist. LEXIS 96478 (S.D.N.Y. Oct. 19, 2009). At this time, the court had not yet made any decision regarding corporate liability and thus, denied the defendants' motion for certification of interlocutory appeal on the issue of corporate liability. Ntsebeza v. Daimler AG, 2009 U.S. Dist. LEXIS 121559 (S.D.N.Y. Dec. 31, 2009).

The Second Circuit Court addressed *Khulumani v. Barclay National Bank, Ltd.*, one of the consolidated cases in *In re South African Litigation*, and discussed "whether an artificial entity that is allegedly used as a vehicle for the commission of a crime against humanity may be held vicariously liable." Khulumani v. Barclay Nat'l Bank Ltd., 504 F.3d 254, 321 (2d Cir. 2007). *Khulumani* was the first case where the Second Circuit granted jurisdiction over a multinational corporation, holding that a plaintiff may plead a theory of aiding and abetting liability under the ATS. *Id.* at 260. The Circuit Court remains split over "the standard for pleading such liability." *Id.* at 257.

Weighing in on *Twombly*'s new pleading standard, Judge Katzmann, in *Khulumani*, observed that aiding and abetting liability, much like corporate liability, "does not constitute a discrete criminal offense but only serves as a more particularized way of identifying the persons involved" in the underlying offense. Kiobel v. Royal Dutch Petroleum Co., 621 F.3d 111, 129 (2d Cir. 2010) (citing Khulumani v. Barclay Nat'l Bank Ltd., 504 F.3d 254, 254 (2d Cir. 2007)). Comparing the liability of non-state actors in *Sosa*, Sosa v. Alvarez-Machain, 542 U.S. 692 (2004), Judge Katzmann discussed that the *Sosa* principle is equally applicable to the question as to the New York. *Khulumani, supra*, 504 F.3d at 258. In 2004, the district court dismissed each of the

---

10. The plaintiffs consist of three groups: Lungisile Ntsebeza, Hermina Digwamaje, and the Khulumani Support Group.

plaintiffs' claims due to lack of subject matter jurisdiction under the ATS and failure to state a claim. *In re S. African Apartheid Litig.*, *supra*, 346 F. Supp. 2d at 554, 557. Ultimately, the Second Circuit affirmed the district court's decision in part, dismissing the consolidated class action. *In re S. African Apartheid Litig.*, *supra*; *Khulumani*, *supra*. The Court dismissed the "Digwamaje Plaintiffs' TVPA claims," *Khulumani*, *supra*, at 259, vacated and remanded "the district court's dismissal of the plaintiffs' [ATS] claims," *id.* at 260,[11] and "the district court's order denying plaintiffs' motion for leave to amend." *Id.* at 258. On remand, two amended consolidated complaints were filed, which went before the district court. S. African Apartheid Litig. v. Daimler AG, 617 F. Supp. 2d 228, 245 (S.D.N.Y. 2009) (citing Complaint, Ntsebeza v. Daimler AG (In re S. African Apartheid Litig.), 617 F. Supp. 2d 228 (S.D.N.Y. 2009); *see* Complaint, In re S. African Apartheid Litig., 346 F. Supp. 2d 538 (S.D.N.Y. 2004). The district court denied the defendants' motion for certification of an interlocutory appeal and the defendant's request for a stay. *In re S. African Apartheid Litig.*, *supra*, 624 F. Supp. 2d at 343. The district court later granted in part the defendants' motion to dismiss the source when determining "whether the scope of liability for a violation of international law should extend to aiders and abettors." Kiobel v. Royal Dutch Petroleum Co., 621 F.3d 111, 129 (2d Cir. 2010) (citing Khulumani v. Barclay Nat'l Bank Ltd., 504 F.3d 254, 283 (2d Cir. 2007). *Cf. Sosa*, *supra*, n.20 (classifying both corporations and individuals as private actor[s]). However, in previous cases, the Circuit Court made no distinction as to the issue of liability between corporations and private individuals[12] and the *Sosa* court "classif[ied] both corporations and individuals as private actors."[13] Here, the Second Circuit made this distinction between private individuals and corporations, by expanding liability and holding "that the ATS conferred jurisdiction over multinational corporations" for "aid[ing] and abet[ing] violations of customary international law."[14] Furthermore, the Second Circuit agrees that the scope of ATS liability is governed by international law.[15] Here, Judge Katzmann

---

11. The Court of Appeals justified its decision to vacate the district court's dismissal based on its belief that the district court erred in holding that aiding and abetting violations of customary international law cannot provide a basis for ATCA jurisdiction.

12. *Khulumani*, *supra*, at 282–83; *see also* Bigio v. Coca-Cola Co., 239 F.3d 440, 447 (2d Cir. 2001) (discussing whether Coca-Cola can violated 'the law of nations' as a non-governmental entity); Flores v. S. Peru Copper Corp., 414 F.3d 233, 244 (2d Cir. 2003) (stating that certain activities are of universal concern and therefore constitute violations of customary international law not only when they are committed by state actors, but also when they are committed by private individuals) (citing Kadic v. Karadzic, 70 F.3d 232, 239–240 (2d Cir. 1995)).

13. *Khulumani*, *supra*, at 283 (2d Cir. 2007) (citing *Sosa*, *supra*).

14. *Khulumani*, *supra*; Presbyterian Church of Sudan v. Talisman Energy, Inc., 582 F.3d 244, 259 (2d Cir. 2009) (citing *Khulumani*). Citing *Sosa*, Judge Katzmann adopted "that a defendant may be held liable under international law for aiding and abetting the violation of that law by another when the defendant (1) provides practical assistance to the principal which has a substantial effect on the perpetration of the crime, and (2) does so with the purpose of facilitating the commission of that crime. *Presbyterian Church of Sudan*, 582 F.3d at 259.

15. *See, e.g., Khulumani*, *supra*; *Bigio*, *supra*; Flores v. S. Peru Copper Corp., 414 F.3d 233 (2d Cir. 2003).

opined that "while domestic law might provide guidance on whether to recognize a violation of international norms, it cannot render conduct actionable under the ATS."[16]

In 2010, in *In re Chiquita Brands Int'l, Inc. Alien Tort Statute & S'holder Derivative Litig.*, 690 F. Supp. 2d 1296 (S.D. Fla. 2010), American plaintiffs commenced suit against Chiquita Brands International, Inc. in the Southern District of Florida, alleging "wrongful death, aiding and abetting wrongful death, false imprisonment, aiding and abetting false imprisonment, intentional infliction of emotional distress, aiding and abetting intentional infliction of emotional distress, negligent infliction of emotional distress, assault, and aiding and abetting assault under various state tort laws" in connection with the Colombian terrorist organization known as Fuerzas Armadas Revolucionarias de Colombia ("FARC"). *Id.* at 1299. The district court ruled that the "[p]laintiffs have sufficiently alleged aiding and abetting liability," *id.* at 1311, and granted the defendant's motion to dismiss in part and dismissed the defendant's remaining claims. *Id.* at 1317. In July 2011, the district court granted Chiquita's motions to dismiss for the plaintiffs' following ATS claims for terrorism and material support to terrorist organizations, cruel, inhuman, or degrading treatment; violation of the rights to life, liberty, and security of person and peaceful assembly and association; and consistent pattern of gross violations of human rights, Plaintiffs' state-law claims, Plaintiffs' Colombia-law claims, and Perez Plaintiffs' FARC-based claims. *Id.* at 1359. The district court also denied the plaintiffs' ATS claims for torture, extrajudicial killing, war crimes, and crimes against humanity, and TVPA claims for torture and extrajudicial killing. The trial court reasoned that the "[p]laintiffs' terrorism-based claims are not actionable under the ATS," *id.* at 1321, the plaintiffs "detailed facts supporting the requisite elements of their crimes-against-humanity claims," *id.* at 1338, and plaintiffs "sufficiently alleged that the AUC committed primary international-law violations for torture, extrajudicial killing, war crimes, and crimes against humanity." *Id.* at 1344.

In 2010, in *Abecassis v. Wyatt*, 704 F. Supp. 2d 623 (S.D. Tex. 2010), victims or families of victims of "terrorist attacks in Israel between 2000 and 2003" brought suit against defendant companies and individuals involved in the oil business for violating the United Nations Oil-for-Food Program, by "purchas[ing] oil from Iraq-either directly from Saddam Hussein's government or from third parties who had purchased the oil from Hussein-and made payments that violated the United Nations Oil-for-Food Program." *Id.* at 627.[17] The district court in Texas granted the defendants' motions to dismiss for lack of standing and motions to dismiss for failure to state a claim. After being granted leave to amend, the plaintiffs re-pled their claim under the Anti-

---

16. *Presbyterian Church of Sudan, supra*, at 258 (citing *Khulumani*).

17. The Oil-for-Food Program required anyone buying oil from Iraq to pay the purchase money into an escrow account monitored by the United Nations. Funds from this account could only be used for humanitarian purposes.

terrorism Act.[18] The district court denied the defendant's motion to dismiss, but granted the motion to dismiss the conspiracy allegations, the allegations based on violations of 18 U.S.C. §2332(d) limitations.[19]

In 2011, *Dacer v. Estrada*, 2011 U.S. Dist. LEXIS 91689 (N.D. Cal. Aug. 17, 2011), was commenced in the Northern District Court of California by family members of Salvador Dacer, "a prominent and influential publicist in the Philippines" who was tortured and killed in November 2000." The plaintiffs alleged that seven individuals were "responsible for their father's torture and death," and orchestrated his death because he was a "threat to [the individuals'] political power." The district court denied one of the defendants', Michael Ray Aquino's, motion to dismiss, stating that "Aquino has not pled exhaustion as an affirmative defense in an answer to the complaint"[20] and should file a summary judgment on the issue of exhaustion after both parties had the "opportunity to develop the evidence needed to prove and rebut the exhaustion defense." In December 2011, the district court readdressed the issue regarding exhaustion and subsequently denied the defendant's motion for summary judgment on plaintiff's claims under the ATS and TVPA. 2011 U.S. Dist. LEXIS 140664 (N.D. Cal. Dec. 7, 2011). The district court reasoned that the defendant, Aquino, "only [made] conclusory allegations that exhaustion should apply and submits no evidence on this issue,"[21] and did not meet his burden to show that exhaustion is required for plaintiffs' claims under the [ATS],"[22] and failed to "show that legal remedies in the Philippines against defendant are effective." *Id.*

On April 17, 2013 the Supreme Court issued a significant ATS decision in *Kiobel v. Royal Dutch Petroleum*, 133 S. Ct. 1659 (2013), holding that the Alien Tort Statute is subject to the "presumption against extraterritoriality" and thus will usually not apply to claims involving alleged human rights abuses or other violations of international law alleged to have occurred in foreign countries. Although the result was unanimous, the justices differed in their reasons for affirming the dismissal of the *Kiobel* plaintiff's claims.

---

18. Antiterrorism Act of 2001, 18 U.S.C. §2333.

19. No prosecution for any offense described in this section shall be undertaken by the United States except on written certification of the Attorney General or the highest ranking subordinate of the Attorney General with responsibility for criminal prosecutions that, in the judgment of the certifying official, such offense was intended to coerce, intimidate, or retaliate against a government or a civilian population. 18 U.S.C. §2332.

20. Defendant Michael Ray Aquino moved to dismiss the complaint because plaintiffs supposedly had not exhausted their legal remedies in the Philippines.

21. "To prevail on a defense of exhaustion for claims under the [ATS], defendant must first show that exhaustion is required." *Dacer, supra*, 2011 U.S. Dist. LEXIS 140664 at *5 (citing Sarei v. Rio Tinto, PLC, 550 F.3d 822, 830–31 (9th Cir. 2008)). "Exhaustion may be required if the action lacks a significant nexus to the United States or does not pertain to an offense of universal concern." *Id.* (citing *Sarei*, at 825).

22. "Although the plaintiff may rebut this showing with a demonstration of the futility of exhaustion, the ultimate burden remains with the defendant." *Id.* "While exhaustion is a statutory requirement for claims under the TVPA, it is only a prudential requirement for claims under the [ATS]." *Id.*

In *Kiobel*, a group of Nigerian citizens, on behalf of the Ogoni people of Nigeria, asserted claims for damages against Shell Petroleum Development Company of Nigeria, Ltd. (SPDC) and its parent entities claiming that these corporations had aided and abetted human rights abuses by the Nigerian Government in connection with the government's suppression of protests against SPDC's activities in Nigeria. In delivering the Court's opinion Chief Justice Roberts concluded that dismissal of the *Kiobel* plaintiff's claim was appropriate because "all the relevant conduct took place outside the United States." *Id.* at 1669. The Court further stated that, " ... even where the claims touch and concern territory of the United States, they must do so with sufficient force to displace the presumption against extraterritorial application.... Corporations are often present in many countries, and it would reach too far to say that mere corporate presence suffices. If Congress were to determine otherwise, a statute more specific than the ATS would be required." *Id.*

The *Kiobel* decision will likely not deter current initiatives by international bodies and NGO's aimed at modifying corporate conduct in countries with troubled human rights records, particularly where sufficient nexus with the United States can be alleged.

Companies are not necessarily insulated against acts that occur outside the jurisdiction in which they are headquartered or physically present through facilities, personnel or operations. They may be subject to jurisdiction in countries where there products are made. For example, in China, courts may exercise jurisdiction over a non-resident defendant in multiple ways. Regardless of whether the parent company used a local contractor, the foreign company may be tried in Chinese courts for (1) the acts of a foreign-owned entity doing business in China through the services of an independent contractor, and (2) contract disputes or disputes over property rights against a defendant who does not reside within the territory where (a) the contract is carried out in China; (b) the object of the litigation is located in China; (c) the defendant has property that can be detained in China; (d) the defendant has a representative organization in China, or; (e) the infringements of rights have taken place in China.

In the United States, there are many federal and state laws that address CSR issues. Two of the most important and far reaching federal laws are the Fair Labor Standards Act of 1938 (FLSA) and the Occupational Safety and Health Act of 1970 (OSHA) and their respective rules and regulations. Congress passed the OSHA (29 U.S.C. §651 et seq. (1970)) to ensure worker and workplace safety. Their goal was to make sure employers provide their workers a place of employment free from recognized hazards to safety and health, such as exposure to toxic chemicals, excessive noise levels, mechanical dangers, heat or cold stress, or unsanitary conditions.

The FLSA (29 U.S.C. §201 et seq. (1938)) establishes minimum wage, overtime pay, recordkeeping, and child labor standards affecting full-time and part-time workers in the private sector and in Federal, State, and local governments. Products made in violation of the FLSA may be considered "hot goods" that can be seized pursuant to court order. Companies that have manufactured or sold "hot goods" may be required to recall goods from customers; remove goods from sale; hold goods in storage at their own expense; pay monetary penalties; and disgorge profits realized from their sale.

More importantly, the United States Department of Labor may require an offending corporation to enter into a compliance agreement and implement a compliance program designed not by the corporation, but by the Department of Labor.

7. Shareholder Resolutions

Shareholder resolutions concerning CSR issues, consumer/stakeholder inquiries, and socially responsible investment (SRI) mutual fund coverage confront corporations now more than ever, particularly when environmental, social and governance issues are involved (Michael Levine, *Governance with a Conscience*, New York Law Journal, November 2008). In response to nearly 150 climate-related resolutions filed by institutional investors during the 2014 proxy season, twenty major multinational corporations have committed to set goals to reduce greenhouse gas emissions or sustainably source palm oil. An additional forty-five corporate commitments were secured related to sustainability reporting, energy efficiency and carbon asset risk. *See* http://www.ceres.org/investor-network/resolutions.

Shareholder resolutions may be used to compel management to change the way it addresses, or to cause it to focus differently upon, business issues. In March of 2014 for example, the SEC required Delta Airlines to include in its proxy materials a proposed shareholder resolution urging the board compensation committee to adopt a policy requiring that senior executives retain a significant percentage of shares acquired through equity compensation programs until reaching normal retirement age or terminating employment with the company. The proposal was requested by the International Brotherhood of Teamsters General Fund. *See* http://www.sec.gov/divisions/corpfin/cf-noaction/14a-8/2014/teamstersgeneraldeltal032614-14a8.pdf.

More recently the subject of disclosure of political contributions by public companies has come under scrutiny by pension funds and other stakeholders. A recent example is the case of the Proctor and Gamble Company (P&G) and NorthStar Asset Management Funded Pension Plan (NorthStar). NorthStar submitted a shareholder proposal to P&G asking the Company to issue and annual report analyzing any incongruities between political contributions by P&G and its PAC, the Good Government Fund (GGF), and P&G's values. This proposal arose after NorthStar observed apparent incongruities in P&G's political spending against core P&G values. The proposed shareholder resolution read as follows:

> *Resolved: Shareholders request that the Board of Directors report to shareholders annually at reasonable expense, excluding confidential information, a congruency analysis between corporate values as defined by P&G's stated policies (including our Purpose, Values and Principles, nondiscrimination policy, and Long-Term Environmental Sustainability Vision) and Company and P&G Good Government Fund political and electioneering contributions, including a list of any such contributions during the prior year which raise an issue of misalignment with corporate values, and stating the justifications for such exceptions*

P&G submitted a "No-Action" request to the SEC under Rule 14a-8 (17 C.F.R. §240.14a-8), seeking the Commission's concurrence in its decision not to include the resolution in the annual proxy materials available to shareholders. Specifically, P&G contended that the proposal may be omitted under Rule 14a-8(i)(7) if it "deals with a matter relating to the company's ordinary business operations." P&G alleged that certain tasks are "so fundamental to management's ability to run a company on a day-to-day basis that they could not, as a practical matter, be subject to direct shareholder oversight." (Citing SEC Exchange Act Release No. 40018 (May 21, 1998).)

On August 6, 2014 the SEC staff issued its opinion stating "... the proposal focuses primarily on Procter & Gamble's general political activities and does not seek to micromanage the company to such a degree that exclusion of the proposal would be appropriate. Accordingly, we do not believe that Procter & Gamble may omit the proposal from its proxy materials in reliance on rule 14a-8(i)(7)." www.sec.gov/divisions/corpfin/cf-noaction/14a-8.shtml.

Today, nearly one out of eight dollars under professional management in the United States is invested according to strategies of SRI. Meg Voorhes & Joshua Humphreys, *Recent Trends in Sustainable and Responsible Investing in the United States*, J. of Investing, Fall 2011, Vol. 20, No. 3, pp. 90–94. As SRI investments continue to gain momentum and have reached an estimated $3.74 trillion, corporate boards are taking note. As noted in the P&P example above, SRI efforts may involve shareholder challenges to management practices. SRI mutual funds use analytical research criteria ("screens") to identify and to avoid investing in alleged "sin stocks" namely companies that produce tobacco, alcohol, and munitions or to identify stocks that meet certain environmental, social and governance (ESG) criteria. SRI proponents believe there is a statistically supported business case for this investment approach. In May 1990 the Domini 400 Social Index (now the FTSE KLD 400 Index) was created, the first index to measure performance of a broad universe of socially responsible stocks in the United States. One method to determine if SRI results in lower investment returns is to compare the performance of an SRI index against a comparable traditional index like the S&P 500 or the Russell 3000. Such a study was conducted in 2011 comparing the performance of the KLD 400 against the S&P 500. Lloyd Kurtz & Dan diBartomoleo, *The Long Term Performance of a Social Investment Universe*, J. of Investing, Fall 2011, Vol. 20, No. 3, pp. 95–102. The study concluded that the SRI index slightly outperformed the traditional index over the comparable period of 1990 to 2010. Although performance differences were small, there can be meaningful differences, both positive and negative, over shorter periods.

There appears to be additional empirical support for SRI's value proposition. In a paper published in June 2012 entitled, "Sustainable Investing: Establishing Long-Term Value and Performance," the authors conclude: "100% of the academic studies agree that companies with high ratings for CSR and ESG factors have a lower cost of capital in terms of debt (loans and bonds) and equity. In effect, the market recognizes that these companies are lower risk than other companies and rewards them accordingly. This finding alone should put the issue of Sustainability squarely into the office of the Chief Financial Officer, if not the board, of every company. 89% of the studies we examined show that companies with high ratings for ESG factors exhibit market-based outperformance, while 85% of the studies show these types of company's exhibit accounting-based outperformance. Here again, the market is showing correlation between financial performance of companies and what it perceives as advantageous ESG strategies, at least over the medium (3–5 years) to long term (5–10 years)." *See* Mark Fulton, Bruce M. Kahn & Camila Sharples, *Sustainable Investing: Establishing Long-Term Value and Performance*, http://papers.ssrn.com/sol3/papers.cfm?abstract_id+2222740.

8. Action Campaigns

To be successful, a corporation must try to be better than its competitors. Equally so, a corporation must be mindful of the concerns and tactics of its stakeholders, such as nongovernmental organizations ("NGOs"), and other advocacy groups. NGOs can pressure organizations to improve conditions in their operations and those of their suppliers, particularly with respect to human and worker rights. College and University students have become increasingly engaged in supply chain CSR issues. United Students Against Sweatshops has demanded that CSR standards for licensed college and university apparel address concerns that are important to certain stakeholders, such as students who attend these institutions. When their concerns are not adequately addressed, stakeholders may mount massive, well-coordinated, and sustained campaign efforts against corporations for their CSR failures. These campaigns may include demonstrations, global media coverage, and "urgent appeals" on the Internet through such outlets as Facebook, YouTube Twitter and many others.

Regardless of size, no company is immune from the initiation or effects of a well-organized action campaign against it. For example, Oxfam, the Clean Clothes Campaign and others jointly orchestrated a global action campaign against companies that produced apparel worn in the Olympics. The campaign was launched right before the 2004 summer Olympics and as a result, numerous demonstrations broke out, including one in Athens, Greece moments before the opening ceremony. Play Fair, *Events*, www.fairolympics.org/countries/greece.html.

More recently, Starbucks was called to task by demonstrations outside its outlets in the United Kingdom over its failure to pay any UK income tax for the period 2009 to 2012 despite revenues of £400million in 2011. Although its tax filings demonstrated that the company was operating at a loss for the period, a controversial offshore structure was used to wipe out profits in the U.K. Through a series of deductions in the form of royalty payments to the Netherlands for the use of the Starbucks brand, transfer pricing of coffee from an affiliate in Switzerland and interest expenses on intercompany loans, its U.K. business became unprofitable. *Starbucks UK sales fall in wake of tax-avoidance row*, The Evening Standard, Apr. 25, 2014. Despite operating completely within the law, a company may be forced to conform to public expectations by negative consumer campaigns.

Corporations also have to contend with the impact of social media upon CSR issues. The fast growing Internet social networking phenomenon, fueled by websites such as Facebook, YouTube and Twitter, is becoming an increasingly relevant factor in CSR action campaigns. For example, when the Canadian news outlet, CBC, created a "wish list" for Canada Day on its Facebook page, the Maquila Solidarity Network ("MSN"), an NGO, reportedly used the CBC "wish list" to publicize its sourcing and anti-sweatshop campaign. With just an email or two, more than 600 Facebook users indicated that their Canada Day wish was for a sweat-free Vancouver Olympics in 2010. *See* Derek Blackadder, *Not Just Another Pretty Face(book)*, Straightgoods, Aug. 6, 2007.

The so-called "hijacking" of company social media campaigns by consumer advocates and other special interest groups has become an increasingly common tactic. It is, therefore, important to remember that when it comes to social media, no one is in charge. Positive campaigns can spiral negatively from a series of comments. Consider the case of the McDonald's 2012 Twitter campaign entitled "#McDStories." The company wanted to focus on promoting that the chain bought fresh produce from local farmers, so it introduced some Twitter hashtags, which is a tag embedded in a message posted on the Twitter microblogging service, consisting of a word within the message prefixed with a hash sign. The company posted positive commentary under the #McDStories. But positive quickly went negative as users piled on with stories about food poisoning, drug use and comparing the smell of one of the eateries to dog food. McDonald's said that the negative remarks were few in total and blamed the media for keeping the issue going a full week after the event. But experts in social media say that there are lessons to learn about what companies shouldn't do on social media. *How McDonald's Twitter campaign fell into the fire*, http://www.cbsnews.com/news/how-mcdonalds-twitter-campaign-fell-into-the-fire/.

Aspects of a Successful CSR Program

A successful CSR program is dependent on the support and commitment of top management. Those involved must be able to hold personnel in the compliance process accountable for their actions, from top executives, to line-level management, to "rank and file" employees. Compliance with CSR standards and risks of non-compliance may be part of the decision making process of key business units. CSR standards may play a role in determining where companies may do business, the locations from which they source materials or products, and the criteria according to which a third-party may become and remain a supplier to the company.

CSR and Sustainability Standards

CSR standards affect employees, the workplace, and the environment. CSR and sustainability standards often include provisions addressing topics such as forced labor, health and safety, child labor, harassment and abuse, discrimination, work hours, overtime wages, freedom of association, and collective bargaining. For example, the Fair Labor Association's ("FLA") Workplace Code of Conduct, www.fairlabor.org, prohibits the use of forced labor, from either prison, indentured, or bonded labor. In 2005, the International Labour Organization reported that at least 12.3 million people were the victims of forced labor. International Labour Organization, *International Labour Standards*, www.ilo.org/ilolex/english/convdisp1.htm. The FLA Workplace Code of Conduct also prohibits any work done by someone younger than 15 or the age for completing compulsory education, if such age is higher than 15. Fair Labor Association, www.fairlabor.org. A corporation's code of conduct will typically also have provisions concerning workers' rights to associate freely and to bargain collectively. For example, Social Accountability International's code ("SA8000") is an international CSR standard and assessment system that requires its adherents to respect workers' rights to form and join a trade union and to bargain collectively. Social Accountability International, www.sa-intl.org. SA8000 also requires that workers be paid a wage that not only meets the legal or industry minimum wage standard, but also meets the workers' basic needs, and allows for some discretionary income. www.sa-intl.org/index.cfm?fuseaction=document.showDocumentByID&nodeID=1& DocumentID=264.

Examples of Specific Codes of Conduct Initiatives

Different industries may face different challenges when it comes to CSR initiatives and means of assessing code compliance. The coffee and diamond industries have also adopted industry-specific codes. The "Common Code for the Coffee Community" ("4C") encourages the global community to improve the social, environmental, and economic conditions for people making a living off of coffee. http://www.4c-coffeeassociation.org/. The diamond industry has sought to combat the prevalence of conflict gems and diamonds. The Kimberley Process was adopted in May 2000, and was followed by the KP Certification Scheme to eliminate the use of rough diamonds by rebel movements to finance wars against legitimate governments. http://www.kimberleyprocess.com/. The Kimberley Process Certification Scheme ("KPCS") imposes extensive requirements on its members before certifying rough diamonds as "conflict-free." As of September 2014, the Kimberley Process had 54 participating members, representing 81 countries with the European Union and its Member States counting as one country. KP members account for approximately 99.8% of the global production of rough diamonds.

The apparel, retail, and footwear industries also have joint/multi-stakeholder CSR initiatives. During the Clinton Administration, the Fair Labor Association ("FLA") was formed in the wake of allegations that licensed clothing products had been made under unacceptable conditions. www.fairlabor.org. The FLA seeks to promote international labor standards and improves working conditions worldwide by employing independent monitors and reports. As a direct outcome of the Rana Plaza building collapse in Bangladesh in 2013, over 150 apparel corporations from 20 countries in Europe, North America, Asia and Australia have now signed the Accord on Fire & Building Safety in Bangladesh. The Accord is an independent, legally binding agreement that includes independent safety inspections at factories and public reporting of the results.

Even in the current economic climate, CSR continues to influence corporate behavior. Recently, Mars, the world's largest confectionary company, has publicly committed to producing its entire cocoa supply in a sustainable manner by 2020. In conjunction with the Rainforest Alliance, Mars will take steps to encourage farmers to produce cocoa while preserving the environment. http://www.rainforest-alliance.org/. Before Mars' announcement, Cadbury announced that all of the cocoa used in dairy milk products would be Fair Trade Certified™. Fair Trade products reportedly ensure that farmers are paid a minimum price for their efforts. http://www.transfairusa.org/.

Aside from pure social demands, these corporations understand that CSR efforts are good for their bottom line. Mars and Cadbury's insistence that cocoa be grown sustainably does not just make them look good in the eyes of consumers and investors, but it also reflects planning designed to ensure that cocoa will be available decades from now. http://www.worldcocoafoundation.org/info-center/fact-sheet.asp. In 2008, worldwide cocoa production fell for the fourth consecutive year in a row. Fair Trade certified cocoa persuades farmers to continue in the cocoa business. www.teacof feecocoa.org/tcc/content/download/309/2079/file/Cocoa%20Barometer%202009. Such initiatives pave the way to produce products that will serve as sustainable goods.

Aside from ensuring that a business is sustainable and continues over time, there are other commercial reasons to adopt CSR policies: they reduce costs and create efficiencies. For retailers, efforts to encourage suppliers to minimize packaging enables them to increase the amount of goods that can fit in a delivery truck. This, in turn, reduces emissions, money spent on fuel for transportation, and decreases the amount of packaging that must be discarded or recycled. Smaller package size, in turn, increases the amount of product that may be displayed and stored on retail shelves. CSR initiatives help cut costs and sustain supplies for the long haul, all while improving the corporation's public image during the economic downturn. http://www.ft.com/ cms/s/0/bc9a37ce-2def-11de-9eba-00144feabdc0.html?nclick_check=1.

Assignment

- **Hypothetical:** You are the Chief of Compliance Officer at your [Team's] corporation. Look up your company's corporate social responsibility/sustainability program and match it to the company's corporate risks.

Chapter 19

Corporate Compliance Program Coverage of Subcontractors, Subsidiaries and Consultants

Introduction

One question that may arise in implementing a corporate compliance program is whether that program needs to cover subsidiaries, consultants, subcontractors and other third parties with which a company may interact. The answer to this question will likely vary a great deal from company to company, depending, among other things, on the type of business done by the company, the company's organizational and management structure and the legal and compliance risks faced by the company.

This chapter will analyze how and to what extent a company may want to extend its corporate compliance program to external third parties on which a company may rely for its business operations. These third parties include subsidiaries, distributors, agents, subcontractors, contractors, external consultants, vendors, and end customers. The discussion will distinguish between three types of third parties: 1) subsidiaries (wholly or partially-owned) as well as contractual joint ventures; 2) "out-bound" agents, resellers, distributors, vendors and other companies with which the company engages in order to successfully sell its own products and services; and 3) third parties with which a company engages in throughout the entire supply chain.

There can be quite a bit of confusion based on terminology when talking about external third parties and this chapter does not attempt to cover all nuances or variations with respect to such parties. For purposes of this chapter, the following definitions will be used:

a. Subsidiary: shall mean any relationship where two or more parties take part in business activities that involve joint control and joint responsibility. Thus, the reference to a "subsidiary" in this chapter could mean a wholly-owned or partially-owned subsidiary or a contractual joint venture where the two parties have come together to engage in a business activity in which they will share liabilities and revenues, but where they have not registered a limited liability entity to cover that activity.

b. All other third parties involve entities with which a company interacts and does business, but with which it does not generally share a significant amount of the control and/or revenues/liabilities, even if each company may benefit (or suffer liabilities) as a result of the activities of the other company. Some examples of these types of third parties include:

1. Suppliers: entities that supply production inputs to the company.

2. Distributors: entities that purchase products and/or services from the company and resell them to other entities for their own account.

3. Agents: entities or individuals that provide marketing or other services on behalf of the company.

4. Contractors, external consultants and subcontractors: entities or individuals that are engaged to perform a specific task or project or who perform temporary labor for the company.

5. Vendors: entities that provide services for the company related to specific business process, including outsourcing Human Resources support and customs brokerage services.

6. End Customers: the entities or individuals (depending on the product or service) that buy products and services from the company and use such products or services for their own internal purposes.

This chapter will explore the need to extend corporate compliance programs to the above third parties. It will also discuss how to assess which components of the program to extend and to which types of third parties based on a risk assessment.

The chapter will then take a look at possible risk mitigation techniques based on the three types of third parties mentioned above. Finally, the chapter will look at the intersection of corporate social responsibility ("CSR") with corporate compliance programs (as many aspects of CSR focus on third-party matters), as well as industry codes of conduct.

Timeline

A company should first consider the types of third party relationships it has. Then the company should conduct one or risk assessments to identify which third parties pose the highest legal and compliance risk. Finally, the company should implement one or more risk mitigation techniques for each third party relationship identified through the risk assessment.

Checklist

1) Types of Third Party Relationships

   a) Controlled Subsidiary

   b) Minority-owned Subsidiary

   c) Suppliers

    d) Distributors

    e) Agents

    f) Contractors

    g) Vendors

    h) End Customers

2) Risk Assessment Tips and Factors to Consider in Assessing Risk:

    a) Assess the level of potential "knowledge" or control that a company has over the third party.

    b) Assess the level of involvement by the company in the decisions and actions of the third party.

    c) Identify the principal laws applicable to the business of the company and the likelihood of extra-territorial application of those laws and the likelihood of liability for violation of them based on the actions of third parties with which the company does business.

    d) Identify laws for which company officials can be held criminally liable based on actions of third parties; these likely become the "high risk" laws.

    e) For laws identified in points "c" and "d" above, identify which third parties are involved in activities subject to those laws, then evaluate the specific risk with each of those third parties.

    f) Consider the value of the transactions between the company and the third party, directly or indirectly and focus on third parties where the transaction values are higher.

    g) Consider the visibility of the company's relationship with high risk third parties to other stakeholders and likelihood of reputational damage if the third parties were to violate legal or ethical rules of the company.

    h) Consider the size of "high risk" third parties and the sophistication of their own (if any) compliance program; a company should focus more attention on less sophisticated high risk third parties.

    i) Understand the nature of the legal rules under which the third party operates in its home jurisdiction and consider where there may be confusion or lack of understanding because the home jurisdiction does not have rules similar to the rules identified in paragraph "c" or "d" above.

    j) Take into account the level of risk tolerance of the company; determine if the company willing to pay for legal fees or even penalties and damages if problems arise later in the relationship with the third party.

3) Risk Mitigation Techniques

    a) Due Diligence

    b) Contract Language

    c) Audits

d) Third Party Codes of Conduct

e) Training

f) Self-Assessments

g) Reporting

Need for Extension of Corporate Compliance Program to Third Parties Including Controlled Subsidiaries

Entrepreneurs form legal entities, or companies, primarily to be able to protect themselves from personal liability. Thus, at the highest conceptual level, no company should be liable for the activities of other companies. However, just as a company may be liable for the actions of its employees when such employees cause harm and the employees' actions at least in part were intended to benefit the company (*respondeat superior*), so too, because of certain case law, legislation and regulatory guidance developed over the years, a company may be legally liable for the actions of other companies.

The circumstances under which a company may be liable for the actions of other companies (or individuals who are clearly not employees) are more limited than the liability of companies for the actions of its employees. Unfortunately, the circumstances may not always be entirely clear and the rules in this regard are regularly changing. It seems, at least, that the direction in recent years has generally been to hold companies more often liable for the activities of other companies, provided that they have some knowledge of or connection to the activities of the third party. A company is often legally liable for the actions of its legal agents, but it may be liable for other types of third parties as well.

Companies want "effective" compliance programs in part to minimize corporate liability for violation of the law by its employees. Similarly, it would seem to make sense for companies to extend their corporate compliance programs to third parties in cases where there is an expectation that a compliance program is not effective without such extension and where a company feels by doing so that it can reduce the potential for liability for the action of the third parties. Moreover, certain legislation and regulatory trends make the case for extending compliance programs fairly compelling as it relates to the compliance areas covered by that legislation.

If your company is a U.S. registered company, a strong case can be made for extending your corporate compliance program to subsidiaries, at least subsidiaries that your company controls. Under the Securities and Exchange Act, particularly the Sarbanes-Oxley Act of 2002, company officers must certify (among other things) that their company's internal controls are sufficient to ensure that material information of the entire company, including any consolidated subsidiaries, is properly included in their SEC reports. *See* 15 U.S.C. §§ 7241; 17 C.F.R. § 240.13a-14.

Since companies are required to report on material compliance and litigation matters, a company that consolidates its financials into the United States must have a system in place that will identify to the corporate office any potential compliance problems in its subsidiaries. An effective corporate compliance program will give a parent company the visibility regarding activities of its subsidiaries that it needs to be able to accurately file its SEC reports.

More support for applying compliance programs to controlled subsidiaries is found elsewhere in the Securities and Exchange Act. The general securities investor protection provisions of Chapter 2B states, in § 78t, that a company is jointly and severally liable for the violation of Chapter 2B by controlled persons unless the controlling person "acted in good faith and did not directly or indirectly induce the act or acts constituting the violation or cause of action." *See* 15 USC § 78t. One way to show good faith is to demonstrate the presence of an effective compliance program.

Even if the parent company is a private company, registered in the United States, but not subject to the rules applicable to companies listed on U.S. Stock exchanges, there are compelling reasons for extending your corporate compliance program to your subsidiaries. The Foreign Corrupt Practices Act ("FCPA") clearly applies both to "issuers" (U.S. public companies) and "domestic concerns" (any individual or any entity with a principal place of business in the United States or organized under the laws of the United States), as well as to foreigners who do something in furtherance of the crime while in the United States. *See* 15 U.S.C. §§ 78dd-1(a), 78dd-2(a), 78c(a)(8), 78dd-2(h)(1)(B). It is imperative for US parent companies to ensure that they have effective compliance programs applicable to all of its controlled subsidiaries, at least with respect to compliance with the FCPA.

Foreign companies headquartered in countries which have signed onto the OECD Convention on Combating Bribery of Foreign Public Officials in International Business Transactions ("OECD Convention"), particularly if they have U.S.-based subsidiaries should also make sure their compliance program (at least with respect to anti-bribery compliance) extends to all controlled subsidiaries since rules of that Convention likely apply extraterritorially as well.

There are a multitude of other US laws that have clear extraterritorial application, including the U.S. Export Control and Antitrust laws, the Patriot Act of 2001, RICO, the Lanham (Trademark) Act and the laws prohibiting discrimination and retaliation. See *Extraterritorial Application of U.S. Law*, draft chapter from International Labor and Employment Laws (Supp. 2000),[1] for a good summary of the extraterritorial application of U.S. laws. It is primarily because of these concerns over extraterritorial laws that most major companies explicitly extend their corporate compliance program to controlled subsidiaries.

Finally, a number of countries outside the U.S. de facto require companies to put in place corporate compliance programs. Under Italy's law, a company can only avoid

---

1. Copyright © 2000 American Bar Association, published by BNA Books, Washington, D.C., http://apps.americanbar.org/labor/lel-aba-annual/papers/2000/outtenextra.pdf.

severe liability for criminal violations of their employees if it has in place an appropriate organizational, management and control structure in order to prevent such violation of law. Italy's requirements for "an appropriate organizational, management and control structure is modeled in part off of the U.S. Federal Sentencing guidelines. *See* Legislative Decree No. 231, Article 6 and 7 (June, 8, 2001) (Italy). A good description of this law can be found in Francesca Chiara Bevilacqua, *Corporate Compliance Programs Under Italian Law*, http://www.singerpubs.com/ethikos/html/italy.html. Other countries with compliance requirements include Korea and Australia. Thus, U.S. companies that operate in multiple countries should take into account the need to comply with local corporate compliance programs when developing and implementing their program.

Need May Vary Based on Type of Third Party and Circumstances

Whether a company will be liable for the actions of non-controlled subsidiaries and other types of third parties is much more uncertain and will vary significantly depending on the facts of the matter. Many U.S. laws have specific provisions that require companies to pay attention to the actions of third parties. A number of laws extend liability for retaliation against whistleblowers to a variety of third parties. For example, in the Sarbanes-Oxley legislation, liability for retaliation extends to contractors, subcontractors, and agents of the company. *See* 18 U.S.C. §1514A. Many health and safety laws prohibit discrimination by any person against employees who raise concerns. Thus, a company could be liable for such discrimination if, for example, it instructed a contractor to terminate one of the contractor's employees for raising a concern. See http://www.whistleblowers.gov. The Federal Acquisition Regulation (FAR) dealing with Contractor Compliance Programs requires all federal contractors to, among other things, provide training to the contractor's "principals and employees" as well as certain "agents and subcontractors." In addition, federal contractors must notify the government if it has "reasonable grounds" to believe that a "principal, employee, agent or subcontractor" has committed a violation of federal criminal law in winning or performing a federal contract. *See* 73 Fed. Reg. 67064, FAR Case 2007-006, Contractor Business Ethics Compliance Program and Disclosure Requirements (Nov. 12, 2008).

Examples of major global companies who have had brand reputational and financial harm, including loss of stock price, by third party suppliers, are as follows: Apple, whose supplier was Foxconn, and Nike, who used supplier located at Rana Plaza.

Notes and Comments

Foxconn, the company that assembles the bulk of the world's iPhones, was in the center of the corporate social responsibility scandal in 2012 along with Apple. Several Foxconn's employees committed suicide because of the brutal hours and poor living conditions. Foxconn's employees were on riot. This was brought to the attention of the Western media. Because of the strikes, Apple's products deliveries were affected.

However, as opposed to Nike and its sweatshops problem, Apple was more proactive in dealing with this situation.

As part of the FLA, Apple called on the FLA to assess working conditions and labor practices. Since the assessment, it is reported that Apple's suppliers' conditions in China has improved. For more about Apple's Foxconn and Nike, see Scott Sterling, *How Apple's Foxconn Problem Is Like Nike's Sweatshop Problem, And Why The Outcome Is The Same, Digital Trends*, Oct, 12, 2012, http://www.digitaltrends.com/apple/how-apples-foxconn-problem-is-like-nikes-sweatshop-problem-and-why-the-outcome-is-the-same/.

Press Release, Fair Labor Association, *Fair Labor Association Completes Verification at Apple Supplier Foxconn*

(Dec. 12, 2013) http://www.fairlabor.org/pressrelease/
final_foxconn_verification_report

356 of 360 action items completed on or ahead of schedule; working hours remains a challenge

The Fair Labor Association (FLA) published its final status report verifying the implementation of action items following assessments conducted by the FLA at three facilities of Apple's largest supplier, Foxconn. The final verification reviewed action items slated for completion from January through June of 2013, finding that while Foxconn did significantly reduce working hours, four of the six pending items related to hours of work had not been completed. The assessment found that while Foxconn is largely complying with the FLA 60-hour/week Code standard, it did not meet its target of full compliance with the Chinese legal limit of 36 hours of overtime per month by July 1, 2013.

Independent labor monitoring organizations engaged by the FLA returned to the three Foxconn facilities for the verification between October 28 and November 8, 2013, to conduct visual observations, review records and documentation, and inter-view workers and management. This was the third and final verification of the robust 15-month action plan Apple and Foxconn created in response to the findings from FLA's full body scan of working conditions and compliance with Chinese labor laws at three Foxconn facilities in Longhua, Guanlan and Chengdu in the first quarter of 2012. Foxconn management provided full cooperation and unrestricted access to the facilities and workers throughout the verification process.

"Foxconn's compliance with the FLA working hours standard is a significant step in the right direction," said Auret van Heerden, President & CEO of the Fair Labor Association. "FLA's expectation is that Apple, working with Foxconn, will continue to rigorously monitor working hours to ensure that they comply with the FLA standard of 60 hours per week but also make progress toward the Chinese legal limit of 49 hours per week. We welcome Foxconn's commitment to continue working toward achieving its target."

FLA assessors verified that workers at the Longhua and Chengdu facilities worked no more than 60 hours every week between March and October; the same was true in the Guanlan facility with the exception of seven weeks during this period when working hours exceeded 60 hours. The assessment found that between March and October 2013, on average more than half of the workforce had worked beyond the Chinese legal limit of 36 overtime hours per month in all three facilities.

FLA assessors found that no interns had been engaged at any of the three facilities since the January 2013 verification visits and that the internship programs had been concluded at all three facilities. Assessors also verified that construction of additional exits and toilets was underway at the three facilities, with completion slated for the end of the year.

As part of its obligations as an affiliated Participating Company, Apple is required to continue monitoring labor compliance at Foxconn and its other suppliers and to report on its monitoring efforts to the FLA on an annual basis.

Detailed status updates on each item from the action plans for the three factories can be found at http://www.fairlabor.org/report/final-foxconn-verification-status-report. The FLA Workplace Code of Conduct is available at http://www.fairlabor.org/our-work/labor-standards.

Press Release, International Labor Rights Forum, *Bangladeshi Workers Report Abusive Conditions and Violence Against Those Seeking Change*

(Dec. 14, 2015) http://www.laborrights.org/releases/bangladeshi-workers-report-abusive-conditions-and-violence-against-those-seeking-change

New interviews with Bangladeshi garment workers make clear that a climate of fear and intimidation prevails in the country's industry, two and a half years after the Rana Plaza building collapse and the launch of the first industrial reform programs to address the pervasive fire and structural hazards in Bangladeshi garment factories.

A 100-page report, *Our Voices, Our Safety: Bangladeshi Garment Workers Speak Out*, published today by the International Labor Rights Forum and based on in-depth interviews with more than 70 workers, shows that workers will not be safe without a voice at work.

"Fire, electrical, and structural safety in garment factories is essential and will save lives," said Bjorn Claeson, the author of the report. "But these renovations and repairs must be the foundation for additional reforms that address the intimidation and violence that keep workers silent, afraid to voice concerns and put forward solutions to ensure their own safety. A next phase of reforms must instill the lessons that respect for workers is as important to safety as are fire exits, that workers' perspectives on safety are as important as the findings of building engineers. Without it workers' lives and health will continue to be in jeopardy."

"We set out to talk with workers about fire, electrical, and structural safety issues," said Kalpona Akter, Executive Director of the Bangladesh Center for Worker Solidarity, whose staff conducted most of the worker interviews for the report. "But almost all workers wanted to talk to us about more than the necessary technical repairs and renovations in their factories. This report is an attempt to do justice to their words and to tell the story of safety from the point of view of the workers we interviewed."

The worker interviews presented in the report describe a chilling web of social relations of intimidation and violence that spans factories and apparel companies, workers' communities, government agencies, law enforcement, and even their families. Workers report production targets and workloads so high managers prevent them from taking necessary restroom breaks, drinking water, leaving the factory at a reasonable hour, or getting leaves from work to attend to their own or their family members' medical emergencies. They speak about wages so low they are effectively trapped in abusive conditions, and about sexual harassment and abuse for which the victims are blamed.

"Revealed in the report is a mind-blowing confluence of violence inflicted on the bodies and beings of women workers: intimidation, rape, silencing, harassment, beatings, torture, unsafe buildings, denial of breaks, dismissal of opinions, unequal pay, slave wages," said Eve Ensler, playwright and activist. "Factory owners, huge corporate chains, retailers and consumers ourselves are all complicit in a system that denies workers their voice and full participation in their own futures and well-being."

The report finds that the two main industrial reform programs, the Accord on Fire and Building Safety in Bangladesh and the Alliance for Bangladesh Worker Safety, differ markedly in their attention to the social relations that ground the violence and intimidation threatening workers' safety. Whereas the Accord enables worker organizations to engage as equals in solving safety problems, the Alliance does not provide a meaningful voice to workers or trade unions.

"A core tenant of the occupational health and safety profession is that no factory-level safety program can be effective without the genuine participation of informed, knowledgeable and active workers in identifying and correcting workplace hazards," said Garrett D. Brown, a Certified Industrial Hygienist and Coordinator of the Maquiladora Health and Safety Support Network. "Bangladesh's garment factories will not improve unless the women workers in them have a meaningful voice and are protected from retaliation and discrimination."

"The next phase of safety reforms should build on the progress achieved under the Accord," said Judy Gearhart, Executive Director of the International Labor Rights Forum. "The goal should be an end to the reprisals against workers who make their voices heard, and a safe working environment where factory owners and managers engage with workers with mutual respect. The Bangladeshi government must register unions according to the law, and investigate and publicly denounce factory owners for using thugs to silence workers through violence and intimidation. Factory owners must adopt a zero-tolerance policy for managers who threaten or inflict violence against workers, and urge the industry associations to do the same toward their members. Apparel brands and retailers must reform their purchasing practices to cease commercial demands that contribute to the silencing of workers, committing instead to prices and delivery times in line with the cost and time of producing goods in compliance with all safety and labor regulations."

It is clear, however, that whether a company can be held liable for the actions of non-controlled third parties depends a great deal on the circumstances. For example, companies are required under the FCPA to use "good faith" to the extent "reasonable" under the circumstances to cause minority-owned companies to devise and maintain a system of internal accounting controls. *See* 15 USC Section 78m (b)(6). The statute even lists the circumstances that should be considered, including the relative degree of ownership and the laws and practices governing the business operations in which the minority-owned company is based.

The settlements and deferred prosecution agreements in the last few years under the FCPA indicate that the Department of Justice ("DOJ") and SEC have very high expectations with regard to the actions a company should take to prevent bribery by all types of third parties with whom it does business. The FCPA has always prohibited companies from bribing government officials directly or indirectly. Prior to 2003, however, the DOJ's and SEC's focus with regard to third parties was primarily on legal agents of the company, rather than, for example, resellers who take ownership of a product from a company before it is resold to another company. More recent decisions make it clear that companies must scrutinize its activities with all third parties with which it does business to ensure that payments to third parties cannot be interpreted as payments enabling such third parties to pay bribes (for example when there is a sham or inflated invoice for subcontract work). *See, e.g.*, United States v. Steph, No. 4:07-cr-00307 (S.D. Tex. July 19, 2007); SEC v. The Dow Chemical Co., No. 07-cv-336 (D.D.C. Feb. 13, 2007); SEC v. Martin, No. 1:07-cv-0434 (D.D.C. March 6, 2007).

Under the FAR related to compliance, the requirements with respect to the required compliance program clearly will vary based on the type of company, how they do business, where they do business. The training and communication requirements must be extended as "appropriate" to individuals, including agents, and subcontractors.

Other Issues to Consider

In addition to legal reasons for extending a compliance program to subsidiaries, and other third parties, a company may have other reasons for doing so. For example, companies that want to list their stock on the New York Stock Exchange must adopt a code of conduct that includes a policy requiring "fair dealing" with respect to customers, suppliers, competitors and employees. *See* NYSE Rule 303A(10) (Nov. 2003). Given this rule, it might be logical for a company to adopt a code of conduct applicable to all customers, suppliers and competitors that describes how the company will ensure fair dealing among these parties.

Based on the criteria to be included in the FTSE4Good Index, including the ten principles of the UN Global Compact, there are incentives for companies to develop global codes of conduct on a variety of issues, push those codes down to suppliers, and monitor compliance. *See* FTSE4Good Index Series, http://www.ftse.com/ products/indices/FTSE4Good. Multiple organizations have principles and other non-binding rules to which companies can decide to claim adherence, such as the Tripartite Declaration of Principles Concerning Multinational Enterprises and Social Policy adopted by the International Labor Organization in 1997 and amended in 2000 and the UN Global Compact launched in July 2000. Companies join these types of indices or sign onto these types of principles in order to gain reputational value that may come from being perceived as a highly ethical and socially responsible company.

There may be certain risks, nonetheless, with extending your company's compliance program to third parties. Most importantly, if a company puts into place, for example, a supplier code of conduct, but never enforces it even if blatant violations are brought to its attention, there is a risk of reputational harm to the company. Moreover, a company that is very vocal about applying its compliance program to particular third parties may increase the risk that society will associate that company with any legal violations by such third party even if the company was not involved in any way. *See* Rebecca Walker, *Am I My Brother's Keeper? The Advantages and Potential Pitfalls of Extending Compliance Requirements to Suppliers and Other Third Parties*, ethikos (May/June 2006). Finally, there is at least an attempt (so far unsuccessful) on behalf of a purported class of non-U.S. workers at certain Wal-Mart suppliers to hold Wal-Mart liable under the Alien Torts Claims Act for Wal-Mart's alleged failure to audit and adequately monitor compliance by Wal-Mart suppliers of its supplier code of conduct. *See* Doe v. Wal-Mart, Cal. Sup. Ct. Los Angeles (Sep. 13, 2005).

Conflicts with Other Jurisdictions Outside of the United States

Another issue that can arise if a company decides to extend its compliance program to foreign subsidiaries and other third parties is conflicts of law. Three examples of this problem are laws related to bribery, whistle-blower protection and export control laws. Under the U.S. Sarbanes-Oxley legislation, companies are obligated to establish procedures to enable employees to submit anonymous complaints regarding accounting, internal accounting controls, or auditing matters. As we learned above, Sarbanes-Oxley applies also to all consolidated subsidiaries of affected parent companies. Best practices in the U.S. with regards to "hotlines" (as they are known) have developed to allow anonymous reporting for any form of compliance concern. However, in Spain, it is clearly illegal to allow employees to report anonymously on any topic and throughout Europe special procedures and care must be taken to ensure no violation of data privacy laws when investigating employee concerns. *See* Miriam Wugmeister et al., Between a Rock and a Hard Place: Whistleblowing Procedures under Sarbanes-Oxley and European Union Data Protection Laws (Apr. 2006).

The UK Bribery Act of 2010, was enacted with the purpose of responding to the various forms of bribery, since bribery consists of the giving of anything of value. The offenses listed in the Bribery Act include bribery of public officials and employees of state owned industries, as well as commercial bribery.

The UK Bribery Act is extraterritorial and provides that UK courts will have jurisdiction over any offense committed in and/or outside the UK, when the person or entity executing the bribery has a close connection with the UK by virtue of nationality (is a British national or resident in the UK) or its incorporation in the UK. Therefore, when the offense refers to the failure of a UK commercial organization to prevent bribery, there is no territorial restriction. Under such a scenario, the courts of the UK will maintain jurisdiction over the offenses committed by a corporation organized under British Law, irrespectively of where the offense had been attempted or occurred. Likewise, the UK will have jurisdiction over any offense committed by a corporation that has presence in the UK, irrespectively of the country where it was incorporated. Nonetheless, UK Bribery Act recognizes an effective compliance program through which the entity trains, monitors, and audits its employees and global business as an affirmative defense of the organization.

In the case of export control laws, under the Cuban Liberty and Democratic Solidarity (Libertad) Act of 1996 ("Helms-Burton Act"), companies owned or controlled by US persons are not allowed to do business with Cuba. *See* 22 U.S.C. §§ 6021–91 (2000). However, under the Canadian Foreign Extraterritorial Measures Act, Canadian companies are prohibited from complying with U.S. extraterritorial measures to the extent that they impede, prevent or reduce Canadian trade to Cuba. *See* RSC 1985, c. F-29. These and other conflicts of laws must be taken into account when extending a corporate compliance program to subsidiaries and other third parties.

How to Determine What Components of Compliance Program should be Extended to Third Parties (Risk Assessment)

As is seen from the above discussion, it is unlikely that a company will want to extend 100% of its corporate compliance program to all third parties with whom it does business. On the other hand, if a company does some business outside of its home country, it will likely need to extend some elements of its corporate compliance program to its subsidiaries and possibly to other third parties. For a company that has multiple foreign subsidiaries and a multitude of third party relationships, it can be overwhelming to consider how to extend your compliance program. The best way to deal with this highly complex scenario is for companies to consider third party risk issues in doing their compliance risk assessment.

In evaluating the compliance risk associated with any type of third party, it is important to understand how the company interacts with any third party, the types of legal and compliance risks faced by the company as well as the likelihood that the company could be held liable for the acts of such third party with regard to such legal and compliance risks. Below are the organization profiles for two hypothetical companies and the hypothetical risk analysis for both:

Company One: a U.S. privately-held company with 10 foreign subsidiaries, but each foreign subsidiary is completely independent (i.e., sells completely different products and makes all business decisions without input from the corporate parent other than adherence to budget and financial goals set by the parent), and the products that each company sells are highly specific to that location and well regulated in each local jurisdiction. The company does not engage any third parties to assist in selling its products; it only contracts with end users (local subsidiary to local subsidiary); and

Company Two: a U.S. company, listed on NASDAQ, with eight subsidiaries, four in Western European countries and four in the Middle East and Africa. All subsidiaries sell the same products and services to Fortune 500 customers and government agencies around the world that expect globally consistent products and services. All subsidiaries regularly engage commission agents to help sell the products and services; such commission agents receive a fixed fee for their services. All requests to pay service fees above $1 million annually to any third party must be approved by the President of the U.S. parent company.

Risk Assessment, Company One: With this hypothetical company, the parent company exercises very little control over its subsidiaries. Moreover, since the company is not listed on a US stock exchange, it is not subject to Sarbanes-Oxley rules. Thus the general risk that the company would be held liable for the acts of its subsidiaries is low. This risk is made even lower by the fact that the products sold in each jurisdiction are subject to different regulations. Finally, Company One's risk of being held liable for actions of non-subsidiary third parties is very low, since it does not use third parties for selling activities. In this scenario, the negative aspects of extending the corporate compliance programs to the foreign subsidiaries and third parties may outweigh the benefits.

Risk Assessment, Company Two: In this case, the company is subject to Sarbanes-Oxley legislation and thus there is a strong rationale for extending some form of the corporate compliance program to the company's eight subsidiaries. Moreover, the company is likely to have a high risk of legal and compliance issues with respect to the FCPA and other anti-corruption laws, at least in the four Middle Eastern Countries in which it operates. Finally, because the U.S. parent company regularly gets involved in decisions with respect to choosing agents for its sales activities in its foreign offices, the company has a higher risk of being held liable under U.S. law for the actions of those foreign offices and possibly the actions of those agents.

Thus, there are many factors to consider in assessing the level of risk that a company has with respect to any particular legal/compliance area and any particular third party:

a. Assess the level of potential "knowledge" or control that a company has over the third party.

b. Assess the level of involvement by the company in the decisions and actions of the third party.

c. Identify laws for which company officials can be held criminally liable based on actions of third parties; these likely become the "high risk" laws.

d. Identify the principal laws applicable to the business of the company and the likelihood of extra-territorial application of those laws and the likelihood of liability for violation of them based on the actions of third parties with which the company does business.

e. For laws identified in points "c" and "d" above, identify which third parties are involved in activities subject to those laws, then evaluate the specific risk with each of those third parties.

f. Consider the value of the transactions between the company and the third party, directly or indirectly and focus on third parties where the transaction values are higher.

g. Consider the visibility of the company's relationship with "high risk" third parties to other stakeholders and likelihood of reputational damage if the third parties were to violate legal or ethical rules of the company.

h. Consider the size of "high risk" third parties and the sophistication of their own (if any) compliance program; a company should focus more attention on less sophisticated high risk third parties.

i. Understand the nature of the legal rules under which the third party operates in its home jurisdiction and consider where there may be confusion or lack of understanding because the home jurisdiction does not have rules similar to the rules identified in paragraph "c" or "d" above.

j. Take into account the level of risk tolerance of the company; is the company willing to pay for legal fees or even penalties and damages if problems arise later in the relationship with the third party.

Unfortunately, for large, global companies, it can be quite difficult to accurately assess the risks associated with particular third parties and to properly prioritize the company's risk mitigation activities to the areas of highest risk. This problem is exacerbated when a company has a highly complex or distributed supply chain and when multiple groups within the company have different connections to the third parties involved.

One technique that can be helpful in sorting through these complexities is to plot the factors on a four-quadrant chart in which the horizontal axis represents the importance to the company of the activity (more important is further right on the axis) and the vertical axis shows the relative legal or reputational risk to the company (higher risk activities and/or countries are higher on the vertical axis). The company can then plot categories of relationships with third parties to help prioritize where to focus risk mitigation activities.

In addition, the level of risk associated with any particular third party may depend on the specific third party involved and the nature of the relationship with that third party. In those cases, a company may be able to assess the risk for a certain category of third parties and put in place a risk mitigation plan designed specifically for such category. Alternatively, it may be possible to design a decision guide or risk-assessment questionnaire that can be completed when a new third party is engaged. Based on the answers to the questions in such guide, the company can then decide what level of risk mitigation is required.

Risk Mitigation Techniques: How to Extend the Elements of a Corporate Compliance Program to Subsidiaries and Other Third Parties?

Subsidiaries and Controlled Joint Ventures

This section will consider each element of a compliance program. This section will also deal with the issues with which a company may be faced if it determines that it needs to extend its compliance program to its foreign subsidiaries and controlled joint ventures.

Global vs. Local Compliance Program

There are many different ways to approach the question of whether or not your compliance program is a global one or a collection of local programs. It will take many fewer resources to enforce and monitor a program that is fully consistent worldwide; however, this type of program will not take advantage of local differences that might enable a company to be more successful in such locales. It is possible to have a global code of conduct that is implemented by a dispersed staff of compliance individuals who report directly to local management and only indirectly to corporate management. Alternatively, each subsidiary could have its own code of conduct, but the compliance staff act as independent monitors of such codes, reporting directly into the corporate leadership.

In making the decision of what type of program to set up, it is important to take into account the culture of the company. Is the culture one where centralized decision-making is expected and where rules made by someone else will be adhered to? Or is the culture one where local offices expect to be able to implement different rules to take into account local business practice? Do the company's customers expect to be treated consistently around the world or are the customers different in each country and thus, consistency is not so important? A centrally run, global program will likely be quite successful if the company culture relies on centralized decision-making; however, if the local offices normally run almost autonomously, it may be difficult to make a fully global program work well. On the other hand, if customers are expecting global consistency, it might be necessary to put in place a global program, even if local subsidiaries are used to operating independently. In that situation, the company will need to consider carefully how to have both global consistency and local input and buy-in.

Codes of Conduct, Supplier Codes of Conduct and Other Policies

The same factors considered with regard to overall program structure must be taken into account when setting up the code of conduct; ideally the program structure and code of conduct would be created together. Often, though, the code and program structure (from a personnel and reporting standpoint) are done at different times. If the company chooses to have a global code of conduct, the code should be drafted using ethics or principles-based terminology, rather than rules-based terms because it is virtually impossible to avoid conflicts of law and ethics can be made more universal. Thus, the principle would be that the company and its employees, agents and other third parties operating on its behalf do not pay bribes in any form; on the other hand, in a rules-based code, the company would specify that employees must comply with the FCPA. It is possible to combine these and state the principle as well as the rule, which may be a good strategy for certain issues.

It is likely that a U.S.-listed, global company will want to establish a high-level set of principles or rules that must be followed world-wide by all controlled subsidiaries. Because ethical standards and legal rules vary from country to country, a global company that does not set out any global principles will likely see significant differences in behavior from country to country. The example of what is deemed acceptable from a speeding standpoint illustrates this problem. Everywhere in the world, it is illegal to drive over the designated speed limit. However, in most of the United States, it is deemed morally acceptable regularly to drive 5–10 miles over the speed limit. In Australia, it is now ethically unacceptable on the highway to drive above the speed limit at all, but in Italy, it is perfectly acceptable to drive 25 miles per hour or more over the speed limit. If the code of conduct for a company with offices in these countries states that it employees must drive "reasonably," then the company would see large variations in practices in each of these countries. A company should consider what rules or principles must be standard in each country in order to minimize the overall compliance risk for the whole company.

With ancillary policies, it can be easier to have localized policies. However, a company that has multiple localized policies will need to carefully consider how enforcement of those policies will be done to ensure consistent enforcement around the world. One option is to have a base policy that is globally applied and then an addendum with certain local rules that modify the base policy in limited ways. The company policy regarding the giving of gifts lends itself to this type of structure. The base policy would set out the general rules (such as no giving of gifts if something is expected in return), and the appendix sets out the country-by-country financial limits for gifts that can be given without pre-approvals. *See,* Sample Gift, Meals and Entertainment Policy in the Resources Section.

Another issue for global companies is translations. Ideally, a company's code of conduct and all significant policies would be translated into the official language of each country in which it operates. Nonetheless, for a company that operates in 50+ countries it may be prohibitively expensive and difficult to maintain codes and other policies in so many languages. Unfortunately, under the laws of most jurisdictions, it will be very difficult or impossible to strictly enforce a policy against a local employee if the policy is not in the country's official language or, at a minimum, clearly is incorporated into the employment contract as a policy to which the employee must adhere. Global companies must balance the challenges of maintaining multiple language versions of any policy against the challenges and costs of terminating employees based on English-only policies.

In some countries, such as Germany, it is extremely challenging to terminate an employee for cause, or even with notice, based on violation of a policy if that policy is not in German. Even in the case of breach of a criminal law, it is hard to terminate for cause. Moreover, employment litigation is very expensive and settlements can easily cost the company two or more years of an employee's salary. Consequently, companies that have more than a handful of employees in Germany are likely to want to translate at least the most significant policies into German. On the other hand, although it is not possible to terminate an employee in Slovakia for violation of a policy that is not in the Slovak language, it is not uncommon to be able to terminate an employee not for cause or enter into a mutual termination agreement in Slovakia for 2–3 months' salary. In such situation, it may be easier to keep the code and policies in English and accept the fact that the company may need to bear some additional costs to remove rogue employees.

Supplier codes of conduct are often found in such industries as electronics, food and clothing. If your company sources many of its products or raw materials from countries where enforcement of environmental and labor law are not stringent, supplier codes of conduct should be created. This will ensure that a company's suppliers are on notice that they must enforce safe working conditions, treat their workers with respect and dignity, and their manufacturing processes comply with international environmental standards such as ISO 14000.

Further, companies should have policies and procedures in place if violations of the supplier code of conduct are found. Indeed, they should be a corporate compliance program to deal with the suppliers. This should include a risk assessment on supplier risks including an inventory of documents, interview questions and reports, heatmaps and dash boards and an executive summary as well as policies including a supplier code of conduct, procedure and internal controls to deal with suppliers; a compliance officer charged with overseeing suppliers; background checks on all suppliers, supplier training if appropriate; auditing, monitoring and reporting on supplier facilities and activities; incentives and discipline for suppliers including supplier evaluations for contract renewals; and continually updating the supplier compliance program and protocols to investigate supplier violations of the supplier code of conduct.

Sample ABC Corporation Supplier Code of Conduct

Statement of Integrity

For more than 125 years, ABC Corporation ("ABC") has demonstrated an unwavering commitment to performance with integrity. Even as we have expanded into new businesses and new regions and built a great record of sustained growth, we have continuously built a worldwide reputation for lawful and ethical conduct. This reputation has never been stronger. In several surveys of CEOs, ABC has been named the world's most respected and admired company. We have been ranked first for integrity and governance. But none of this matters if each of us does not make the right decisions and take the right actions. At a time when many people are more cynical than ever about business, ABC must seek to earn this high level of trust every day. This includes our suppliers.

This is why we ask every supplier that conducts business with ABC to make a commitment to follow our Code of Conduct. This set of ABC policies on key integrity issues guides us in upholding our ethical commitment. All ABC suppliers must comply not only with the letter of these policies, but also with their spirit. If you have a question or concern about what is proper conduct for you or anyone else, promptly raise the issue with your manager, an ABC ombudsperson or through one of the many other channels the Company makes available to you. Do not allow anything—not "making the numbers," competitive instincts or even a direct order from a superior—to compromise your commitment to integrity. Suppliers must address employees' concerns about appropriate conduct promptly and with care and respect.

There is no conflict between excellent financial performance and high standards of governance and compliance—in fact, the two are mutually reinforcing. As we all focus on growing our businesses, we must recognize that only one kind of performance will maintain our reputation, increase our customers' confidence in us and our products and services, and enable us to continue to grow, and that is performance with integrity.

General Standards

ABC is committed to ethical business practices and we hold our suppliers to the same high standards. It is ABC policy to comply with all applicable laws and regulations of the countries and regions in which we operate and to conduct our business activities in an honest and ethical manner. The ABC Supplier Code of Conduct declares that ABC expects its suppliers to uphold the policies of ABC concerning compliance with all applicable law, respect for human rights, environmental conservation and the safety of products and services.

ABC believes that the Code of Conduct serves as an important framework for ABC businesses' suppliers to conduct their business in a socially responsible manner and to meet the expectations of ABC. This Code is maintained and updated to reflect ABC standards and supplier operations. ABC hereby requires its suppliers to comply with this "ABC Supplier Code of Conduct."

Supplier Code of Conduct

The ABC Supplier Code of Conduct establishes standards to ensure that working conditions in the business group supply chain are safe, that workers are treated with respect and dignity, and that business operations are environmentally responsible and conducted ethically. For the Code to be successful, suppliers must regard the Code as a comprehensive supply chain initiative. At a minimum, suppliers shall also require their next tier suppliers to acknowledge and implement the Code. Fundamental to adopting the Code is that a business, in all of its activities, must operate in full compliance with the laws, rules and regulations of the countries in which it operates. The Code encourages suppliers to go beyond legal compliance, drawing upon internationally recognized standards, in order to advance social and environmental responsibility and business ethics.

The Code is made up of five sections. Sections A, B, and C outline standards for Health and Safety, Environment, and Labor respectively. Section D adds standards relating to business ethics and Section E outlines the elements of a system that conforms acceptably to this Code. Finally, we attached references that helped guide the formation of this Code.

A. HEALTH AND SAFETY

Section I. Health and Safety

Worker health, safety and well-being is of the utmost importance to ABC. Suppliers shall provide and maintain a safe work environment and integrate sound health and safety management practices into its business. Workers shall have the right to refuse unsafe work and to report unhealthy working conditions.

Suppliers shall identify, evaluate, and manage potential occupational health and safety hazards through a prioritized process of hazard elimination, and engineering and administrative controls. Suppliers shall provide workers with appropriately maintained protective equipment, as well as instruction on its proper use.

Section II. Physical Injury Prevention

Integrating sound health and safety management practices is necessary to create and maintain safe working conditions and a healthy work environment for all workers. Suppliers will eliminate or minimize physical hazards where possible and will provide workers with appropriate personal protective equipment.

Section III. Prevention of Chemical Exposure

Workers will not be disciplined for raising safety concerns and will have the right to refuse unsafe working conditions without fear of reprisal. Suppliers will identify, evaluate, and control worker exposure to chemical, biological, and physical agents. Suppliers will eliminate such hazards where possible. Where such hazards cannot be eliminated, suppliers will provide appropriate measures to mitigate the risks.

Section IV. Occupational Safety Procedures and Systems

Suppliers will establish procedures and systems to manage, track, and report occupational injury and illness. Such procedures and systems will encourage workers to report any occupational injury or illness. Suppliers will classify and record work-related injury and illness cases, investigate cases, and implement corrective actions to eliminate their causes. Suppliers will also provide necessary medical treatment and facilitate employees' return to work.

Suppliers shall have a system for workers to report health and safety incidents and near-misses that includes tracking, investigation, and management of reported incidents. Suppliers shall implement corrective action to mitigate future risk, provide necessary medical treatment and facilitate workers' return to work.

Section V. Health and Safety Communication

In order to foster a safe work environment, suppliers will provide workers with appropriate workplace health and safety information and training, including written health and safety information and warnings in the language required by applicable laws and regulations. Additionally, suppliers are to provide this information in the primary language of the workers. Suppliers will post Safety Data Sheets for hazardous or toxic substances and properly train workers who may come into contact with such substances in the workplace.

Section VI. Emergency Preparedness

Emergency situations and events are to be identified and assessed by suppliers, and their impact minimized by implementing emergency plans and response procedures, including: emergency reporting, employee notification and evacuation procedures, worker training and drills, appropriate fire detection and suppression equipment, adequate exit facilities and recovery plans.

To the extent that Suppliers transport goods for ABC into the United States, Suppliers shall comply with the C-TPAT security procedures on the U.S. Customs website at www.cbp.gov (or other website established for such purpose by the U.S. government).

Section VII. Physically Demanding Work

Suppliers must identify, evaluate and control worker exposure to the hazards of physically demanding tasks, including manual material handling and heavy or repetitive lifting, prolonged standing and highly repetitive or forceful assembly tasks.

Section VIII. Sanitation, Food, and Housing

Suppliers must provide workers with ready access to clean toilet facilities, potable water, and sanitary food preparation and eating facilities where applicable. Worker dormitories provided by the supplier or a labor agent are to be clean and safe, and provided with appropriate emergency egress, hot water for bathing and showering, adequate heat and ventilation, reasonable personal space and reasonable entry and exit privileges.

Section IX. Machine Safeguarding

Production and other machinery shall be evaluated for safety hazards. Physical guards, interlocks and barriers are to be provided and properly maintained where machinery presents an injury hazard to workers.

Section X. Ergonomics

Suppliers shall identify, evaluate and control worker exposure to tasks that pose ergonomic risks, such as the use of excessive force, improper lifting positions or repetitiveness. Suppliers shall integrate this process into the development of all new or modified production lines, equipment, tools and workstations.

B. ENVIRONMENT

Section I. Environment

ABC is committed to protecting the environment, and environmental responsibility affects the core of our operations. Suppliers shall develop, implement, and maintain environmentally responsible business practices at all times, in accordance with applicable laws and regulations.

Section II. Hazardous Substance Management and Restrictions

To ensure safe handling, movement, storage, recycling, reuse, and disposal of hazardous substances, suppliers will identify and manage substances that pose a hazard if released to the environment and at a minimum, comply with applicable laws and regulations for recycling and disposal.

Section III. Solid and Hazardous Waste Management

Wastewater, solid waste, liquid waste and hazardous waste generated from operations, industrial processes and sanitation facilities are to be characterized, monitored, controlled and treated at least in accordance with applicable laws and regulations.

Section IV. Airborne Emissions Management

Suppliers will characterize, monitor, control and treat airborne emissions, at least as required by applicable laws and regulations, before and/or upon discharge.

Section V. Wastewater management

Suppliers shall implement a systematic approach to identify, control, and reduce wastewater produced by its operations. Suppliers shall conduct routine monitoring of the performance of its wastewater treatment systems.

Section VI. Storm water Management

Suppliers shall implement a systematic approach to identify and prevent contamination of storm water runoff. Suppliers shall prevent illegal discharges and spills from entering storm drains.

Section VII. Environmental Permits and Reporting

Suppliers must obtain, maintain, and keep current all required environmental permits (e.g., discharge monitoring) and registrations, and follow the operational and reporting requirements of such permits.

Section VIII. Pollution Prevention and Resource Reduction

Suppliers will use reasonable means to reduce waste of all types, including water and energy by practices such as modifying production, maintenance and facility processes, materials substitution, and conservation, recycling and reusing of materials.

Suppliers are to adhere to all applicable laws, regulations and customer requirements regarding prohibition or restriction of specific substances, including labeling for recycling and disposal.

C. LABOR

Section I. General Employee & Human Rights

ABC believes that all workers in our supply chain are entitled to a fair and ethical workplace. Workers must be treated with the utmost dignity and respect and all suppliers shall uphold the highest of standards of human rights in their treatment of employees.

Suppliers are thus committed to uphold the human rights of workers, and to treat them with dignity and respect. This applies to all workers including temporary, migrant, student, contract, direct employees, and any other type of worker. The recognized standards are set out in the annex, were used as references in preparing the Code and may be a useful source of additional information. The labor standards are:

Section II. Discrimination, Harassment & Abuse

Suppliers shall commit to a workplace environment free of harassment and abuse. There shall be no harsh and inhumane treatment or threat thereof. Harsh and inhumane treatment includes but is not limited to: sexual harassment and abuse; verbal and psychological abuse and harassment; mental or physical coercion; discrimination based on gender, ethnicity, age or any other relevant distinguishing characteristic. Disciplinary policies and procedures in support of these requirements shall be clearly presented to all workers, including management.

Section III. Involuntary Labor

Suppliers shall ensure that all work is voluntary. No forced, bonded (including debt bondage), indentured, or involuntary prison labor shall be used. Suppliers shall not engage in any form of human trafficking. Involuntary labor includes transporting, harboring, recruiting, transferring or receiving vulnerable persons by means of threat, force, coercion, abduction or fraud for the purposes of exploitation. All work must be voluntary, and workers shall be free to leave work at any time or terminate their employment.

Workers must not be required to surrender any government-issued identification, passports or work permits as a condition of employment. Supplier shall ensure that workers' contracts clearly convey the conditions of employment in a language understood by the workers. Suppliers shall not impose unreasonable restrictions on movement within the workplace or upon entering or exiting company facilities. Excessive fees are unacceptable and all fees charged to workers must be disclosed.

Suppliers shall ensure that third party recruitment agencies they patronize are compliant with the provisions of this code and the law. Suppliers shall be responsible for payment of all fees and expenses in excess of one month of the worker's anticipated net wages.

Section IV. Child Labor

Suppliers shall not engage child labor in any stage of its processes or activities. The term "child" refers to any person employed under the age of 15, or under the age for completing compulsory education, or under the minimum age for employment in the country, whichever is greatest. The use of legitimate workplace apprenticeship programs for educational benefit that are consistent with Article 6 of ILO Minimum Age Convention No. 138, or light work consistent with Article 7 of ILO Minimum Age Convention No. 138 which comply with all laws and regulations, are supported.

Section V. Juvenile Worker Protections

Where suppliers employ juveniles who are older than the applicable legal minimum age but are younger than 18 years of age, said juveniles may not perform work that might jeopardize their health, safety or morals as set forth in the ILO Minimum Age Convention No. 138. Supplier shall not require juvenile workers to work overtime or perform night work.

Section VI. Student Worker Protections

Suppliers shall ensure proper management of student workers through proper maintenance of student records, compliance with due diligence of educational partners, and protection of students' rights in accordance with applicable law and regulations. Suppliers shall provide appropriate support and training to all student workers.

Section VII. Workers' Hours

Supplier shall commit to a standard 40 hour work week, pursuant to ILO Forty-Hour Week Convention, 1935 and set a maximum limit to normal hours of work, pursuant to the ILO Hours of Work (Industry) Convention, 1919. Above standards shall include all overtime, which must be voluntary. Workers must take at least one off day every seven days except in emergencies or extraordinary circumstances.

Section VIII. Workers' Wages & Benefits

Compensation paid to workers shall comply with all applicable wage laws, including those relating to minimum wages, overtime hours and legally mandated benefits. Workers shall be compensated for overtime at the legal premium rate. Supplier shall offer vacation time, leave periods, and time off for legally recognized holidays.

Suppliers shall communicate pay structure and pay periods to all workers in a timely manner, via pay stub or similar documentation. Accurate wages shall be paid in a timely manner. Deduction from wages as a disciplinary measure shall not be permitted.

Section IX. Freedom of Association & Collective Bargaining

Supplier shall respect the rights of workers to associate freely, join or not join labor unions, seek representation and join workers' councils as well as the right of collective bargaining in accordance with applicable laws, and without interference, discrimination, retaliation or harassment. Workers shall be able to openly communicate and share grievances with management regarding working conditions and management practices without fear of reprisal, intimidation or harassment. Supplier shall ensure that workers have a mechanism to report grievances that facilitates open communication between management and workers

D. ETHICS

Section I. Ethics

To meet social responsibilities and to achieve success in the marketplace, Suppliers and their agents are to uphold the highest standards of ethics which include the following sections provided below: business integrity, anti-bribery, proper disclosure of information, intellectual property protection, fair business dealings, protecting confidentiality, and whistleblower protection.

Section II. Business Integrity

The highest standards of integrity are to be upheld in all business interactions. Suppliers shall prohibit any and all forms of bribery, corruption, extortion and embezzlement (covering promising, offering, giving or accepting any bribes). All business dealings should be transparently performed and accurately reflected on Participant's business book and records. Monitoring and enforcement procedures shall be implemented to ensure compliance with anti-corruption laws.

Section III. No Improper Advantage

Bribes or other means of obtaining undue or improper advantage are not to be offered or accepted.

Section IV. Disclosure of Information

Information regarding business activities, structure, financial situation and performance is to be disclosed in accordance with applicable regulations and prevailing industry practices. Falsification of records or misrepresentations of conditions or practices in the supply chain are prohibited.

Section V. Intellectual Property

Intellectual property rights are to be respected; transfer of technology and know-how is to be done in a manner that protects intellectual property rights.

Section VI. Fair Business, Advertising and Competition

Standards of fair business, advertising and competition are to be upheld. Means to safeguard customer information should be available.

Section VII. Protection of Identity

Programs that ensure the confidentiality and protection of supplier and employee whistleblowers are to be maintained.

Section VIII. Responsible Sourcing of Minerals

Suppliers shall have a policy to reasonably assure that the tantalum, tin, tungsten and gold in the products they manufacture does not directly or indirectly finance or benefit armed groups that are perpetrators of serious human rights abuses in the Democratic Republic of the Congo or an adjoining country. Suppliers shall exercise due diligence on the source and chain of custody of these minerals and make their due diligence measures available to customers upon customer request.

Section IX. Privacy

Suppliers are committed to protecting the reasonable privacy expectations of personal information of everyone suppliers do business with, including suppliers, customers, consumers and employees. Suppliers must comply with privacy and information security laws and regulatory requirements when personal information is collected, stored, processed, transmitted, and shared.

E. MANAGEMENT SYSTEM

Section I. Management

Suppliers shall adopt or establish a management system whose scope is related to the content of this Code. The management system shall be designed to ensure (a) compliance with applicable laws, regulations and customer requirements related to the participant's operations and products; (b) conformance with this Code; and (c) identification and mitigation of operational risks related to this Code. It should also facilitate continual improvement. The elements that should be contained by the management system are listed below.

Section II. Company Commitment

Suppliers must provide policy statements affirming Suppliers' commitment to compliance and continual improvement, endorsed by executive management.

Section III. Management Accountability and Responsibility

Suppliers clearly identify company representative[s] responsible for ensuring implementation of the management systems and associated programs. Senior management reviews the status of the management system on a regular basis.

Section IV. Legal and Customer Requirements

A process to identify, monitor and understand applicable laws, regulations and customer requirements, including the requirements of the Code.

Section V. Risk Assessment and Risk Management

Process to identify the environmental, health and safety and labor practice and ethics risks associated with Suppliers' operations. Determination of the relative significance for each risk and implementation of appropriate procedural and physical controls to control the identified risks and ensure regulatory compliance. Areas to be included in a risk assessment for environmental health and safety are production areas, warehouse and storage facilities, plant/facilities support equipment, laboratories and test areas, sanitation facilities, kitchen/cafeteria and worker housing/dormitories.

Section VI. Improvement Objectives

Written performance objectives, targets and implementation plans to improve Suppliers' social and environmental performance, including a periodic assessment of Suppliers' performance in achieving those objectives.

Section VII. Training

Programs for training managers and workers to implement Suppliers' policies, procedures and improvement objectives and to meet applicable legal and regulatory requirements.

Section VIII. Communication

Process for communicating clear and accurate information about Suppliers' policies, practices, expectations and performance to workers, suppliers and customers.

Section IX. Worker Feedback and Participation

Ongoing processes to assess employees' understanding of and obtain feedback on practices and conditions covered by this Code and to foster continuous improvement.

Section X. Audits and Assessments

Periodic self-evaluations to ensure conformity to legal and regulatory requirements, the content of the Code and customer contractual requirements related to social and environmental responsibility. Additionally, external audits should be conducted at appropriate intervals.

Section XI. Corrective Action

Process for timely correction of deficiencies identified by internal or external assessments, inspections, investigations and reviews.

Section XII. Documentation and Records

Creation and maintenance of documents and records to ensure regulatory compliance and conformity to company requirements along with appropriate confidentiality to protect privacy.

Section XIII. Supplier Responsibility

Process to communicate Code requirements to suppliers and to monitor supplier compliance to the Code.

REFERENCES

The following standards were used in preparing this Code and may be a useful source of additional information. The following standards may or may not be endorsed by each Participant.

ILO Code of Practice in Safety and Health, ww.ilo.org/public/english/protection/ safework/cops/english/download/e000013.pdf

National Fire Protection Association, http://www.nfpa.org/aboutthecodes/list_of_ codes_and_standards.asp

ILO International Labor Standards, www.ilo.org/public/english/standards/norm/ whatare/fundam/index.htm

OECD Guidelines for Multinational Enterprises, www.oecd.org

United Nations Convention Against Corruption, http://www.unodc.org/unodc/

United Nations Global Compact, www.unglobalcompact.org

Universal Declaration of Human Rights, www.un.org/Overview/rights.html ISO 14001 www.iso.org SA 8000 http://www.sa-intl.org

Ethical Trading Initiative, www.ethicaltrade.org/ OHSAS 18001 www.bsi-global.com/ index.xalter

Eco Management & Audit System, www.quality.co.uk/emas.htm

OECD Due Diligence Guidance, http://www.oecd.org/document/36/0,3746,en_2649_ 34889_44307940_1_1_1_1,00.html

Dodd-Frank Wall Street Reform and Consumer Protection Act, http://www.sec.gov/ about/laws/wallstreetreform-cpa.pdf

---

Compliance Officers

As with the discussion on the overall program, codes and policies, a company should consider carefully whether to have one global compliance officer or a network of compliance officers in each country in which the company does business. Almost certainly, the most effective structure will be a combination of the two: local compliance officers who report directly or indirectly into a global compliance officer. Having local officers will help greatly in ensuring that the code of conduct and compliance policies are understood and followed on a local basis.

One way to gain local attention without needing an army of compliance officers is to use the existing management structure in each country to host compliance councils, which meet monthly to review general compliance matters in the country and solve for local concerns that may arise. Investigations and the overall compliance training plan can be managed centrally, but the local compliance counsel can be used to facilitate the distribution and implementation of global programs. See Sample Governance Council Charter in the Resources section.

Background Checks

It can be very challenging to have a consistent set of background checks on all employees worldwide. In many jurisdictions, court and criminal records are not easily available. Thus, review of them can be slow and expensive. Moreover, in many countries it is culturally inappropriate to ask about criminal or financial records. It may be necessary to examine the risk to the company if no or minimal background checks are conducted against the cost and difficulties in obtaining them. From a U.S. perspective, however, conducting background checks on high-level employees, particularly those who have significant fiscal authority, is necessary in order to have an effective compliance program.

Training, Communications, Monitoring and Auditing, Enforcement and Corrective Actions, Detecting Criminal Violations

The remaining items in an effective compliance program all raise similar issues when a company attempts to apply them globally. It can be very challenging and costly to develop training that is understandable by employees in 50 countries. Using local examples, and relying on principles set out in the company's code of conduct can help make this process easier. Test out training modules in focus groups, consisting of employees from multiple countries before you roll out a program globally. Do not rely solely on external translation services; make sure that someone in your company (ideally a native speaker) reviews the translation before it is publicly launched. Working closing with the company employee communications team, as well as marketing, will enable the compliance team to deliver more effective global training and communications.

Global companies often have global monitoring and auditing functions, largely due to resource constraints. Even in this area, however, a company that can create an audit team with resources from multiple countries or with a variety of cultural and language backgrounds will have greater success in doing effective audits.

It is extremely important for global companies to consciously consider how to ensure that violations of the company code and policies are consistently enforced around the world. A compliance program will quickly turn into an ineffective program if employees do not believe that violators will be treated consistently. Nonetheless, due to variations in employment laws, it may be harder to discipline employees in some countries than in others; the compliance team should work closely with HR to ensure that discipline is consistently applied to the greatest extent possible.

Minority-Owned Joint Ventures

Minority-owned joint ventures pose a special challenge for companies. If it is a U.S. company that is the minority-owner, the parent company will want to be very careful not to be deemed to "control" the joint venture; non-controlled subsidiaries are treated very differently than controlled subsidiaries under U.S. accounting rules. For this reason, most companies treat minority-owned joint ventures more like agents or resellers than like subsidiaries. (See below for more suggestions on how to treat agents and resellers.) Nonetheless, because the ties to non-controlled joint ventures are closer than the ties to resellers or distributors, companies should be careful to conduct detailed due diligence before entering into any joint venture and put in as many of the suggestions listed in the next section as possible. In addition, the minority owner should use its seat or seats on the Board of Directors to ensure that the Board reviews and monitors the joint venture's compliance program.

Agents, Resellers, Distributors and Other Sales Partners

As discussed earlier, there are a number of reasons why some of a company's compliance program should be extended to agents, resellers, distributors and other sales partners. Entities that are selling on behalf of a company often pose the greatest risk for a company in terms of the likelihood that a company will be held responsible for the actions of that third party. Unfortunately, it is much harder to manage the risks from these third parties than the risk from employees or controlled subsidiaries, because the company has much less control and influence over the third party, the company has a wide variety of relationships with these third parties, within the company there are likely to be a wide variety of business "owners" of these third party relationships, and a company must always be careful to avoid unintended consequences of managing the third party relationship too closely (e.g., co-employment risks or the risk that the third party will claim it is not responsible for a breach of contract because the company did not provide sufficient resources for the third party to perform under the contract).

Prior to engaging a third party, the company should consider what type of due diligence is necessary before entering into a contract. If the third party will sell the company's products to government agencies, the U.S. government expects that the company will engage in a certain amount of research into the background of the third party to ensure that the third party does not have a history of being involved in corrupt activities. The level and nature of due diligence that is reasonable will depend on the volume of sales expected, the country in which the third party operates, the size and sophistication of the third party.

Due diligence can include some or all of the following:

a) A representation letter from the third party confirming that it has and will comply with the applicable laws.

b) The completion of a questionnaire by the third party to understand the background of the principals, the experience of the company and the company's qualifications for the work that it will perform.

c) The completion of an Internet search to see if any negative claims have been made against the third party.

d) A review of public criminal and civil records and newspaper and other print media to determine the reputation of the third party.

e) Checking references of a third party.

f) Having a third party fill out an application that sets out its qualifications and verifying some or all of the statements on the application.

g) Seeking information from the local U.S. consulate and other companies (such as law firms) about the reputation and experience of the third party.

h) Engaging a private investigator to physically inspect the premises of the third party such as criminal records.

Internet searches will be ineffective unless done in the language spoken in the third party's country. Even if done in local language, internet searches will be ineffective in countries where freedom of the press is not well-known. In addition, many countries do not have on-line searchable criminal or civil records; thus, searches in these countries may require a physical review and can be time-consuming and expensive. Finally, private investigators may be tempted to break the law to get better information for their investigation. A company should consider the legality and effectiveness of any element of due diligence before implementing it.

At a minimum, companies must make sure that they have strong contracts in place with all third parties that sell on their behalf or distribute their products and services. The contract should make it clear that the third party must comply with all applicable laws and the company should specify compliance with any laws that the third party might not otherwise need to follow, such as the FCPA and U.S. export control laws. Rather than simply refer to the law or repeat a legal citation, the contracts should describe the activity that is prohibited, such as payment of something of value to a government official or distribution of a product to an embargoed country. This sort of explanation is necessary to prevent the third party from later being able to argue that they cannot be held responsible for compliance with a law that they do not understand since it is not part of the laws of their country.

It is important to enable the company to audit the third parties that the pose the greatest risk for a company. There is some debate in the industry as to whether it is worthwhile putting in audit clauses if you never intend to exercise them. However, if the company has the right to audit, then the company will be able to and should use that clause if the third party is implicated in a high risk internal investigation, such as corruption, collusion, or significant fraud. An internal investigation may be seriously hindered if the company cannot audit third parties with whom it does business. See the Resources Section for an annotated sample audit clause.

Another solution that can be handled by contract is to require the third party to put into place its own code of conduct that meets certain minimum criteria. In this case, however, it is important to make some effort to ensure that third parties have complied with this contract requirement. Enforcement can occur up front, when the relationship is begun or it can be deferred to a time when there is a contractual dispute. If enforcement is deferred, however, the company should take care not to waive this requirement in any situation where it is possible that the company could be held responsible for a violation of law by the third party that would have been prohibited if the third party had created its own code of conduct.

Training is often the way that a company can reduce its risk of dealing with third parties in the sales context. Training can and should be targeted to third parties; in other words, usually simply requiring third parties to take the same training as employees will not work because the employee training will likely have references to company policies or other items that are not important for the third party. In addition to training or setting expectations for the third party, it is important to specifically train the company's employees on how to monitor the activities of the third party. Thus, the company's employees should be trained that if they are working with a third party who asks to have a duplicate invoice sent to them, they need to evaluate the request to ensure that there is a legitimate business reason for the duplicate invoice and that the request is not designed to enable the third party to violate any laws.

Requiring third parties to complete a compliance self-assessment in one or more areas of the law is another way to educate and evaluate third parties. However, if you decide to use self-assessments, it is important to act upon any negative information that is reported in those self-assessments. This risk mitigation technique can, therefore, be resource-intensive and should be used only when sufficient resources are available to monitor the results and ensure that any problems that are identified are resolved in a timely manner.

Other ways a company can reduce the risk of dealing with third parties is to provide them access to best practice information that the company may have on dealing with any particular compliance issues. In addition, the company can advertise the consequences of non-compliance by third parties and by company employees and can encourage all parties, including third parties doing business with the company, to report violations or misconduct to the company's compliance office.

Suppliers and Other In-Bound Vendors

Any of the above techniques can work well for suppliers and other in-bound vendors, but companies should consider carefully the trade-offs between extending elements of the company's compliance program to the supplier or vendor and the risk of making the supplier or vendor the company's agent in the process. Some suppliers or vendors will simply be an agent of the company in any case, such as a customs' broker, and thus it will be very difficult for the company to avoid liability for a violation of the law by the third party. In such situation, putting in place more contractual requirements and conducting audits and training is probably prudent.

Other suppliers, such as large manufacturers that manufacture goods for many companies (e.g., Chinese toy manufacturers), are not automatically agents of the company and in those situations, the company should be careful not to make them agents by extending too much of the company's corporate compliance program to them. In these cases, requiring the third party to create its own code of conduct and its own compliance training, may be a good alternative. Providing the company guidance on how to do this is another way to set the right expectations without trying to take too much control. There are a number of neutral resources that you can point third parties to in order to help them understand how to create their own compliance program. See Resources Section, below.

Issues that can be particularly problematic with suppliers include the acceptance of gifts, conflicts of interest and appearance of bias. In order to reduce issues in these areas, companies can advertise to their suppliers the rules under which company employees must operate, so that, for example, if a company employee asks for an inappropriate gift, the supplier can feel comfortable telling the employee, "no" because the supplier knows that the gift would cause the employee to violate his/her company's policies.

It is important for all partners (in-bound or out-bound) to know how to reach the company's corporate compliance office and to understand that the company wants suppliers to abide by their contractual commitments from a compliance standpoint, even if local management is telling them something else. Unless a company occasionally terminates a supplier or vendor for failure to comply with the terms of a contract (in the context of a compliance problem) and/or makes an employee termination for compliance issues related to third parties visible to the third parties (within the constraints imposed by employment and data privacy laws), suppliers and vendors are unlikely to listen to any plea from corporate to "do the right thing." Suppliers and vendors naturally will look first to the company managers that make the supplier/vendor buying decisions to understand how important compliance is to them. Thus, a company can improve compliance by suppliers and vendors by training company procurement managers on how to set the right tone from a compliance standpoint.

Intersection of Corporate Social Responsibility Programs and Corporate Compliance Programs for Third Parties

Particularly with regard to suppliers, it can be difficult to distinguish between activity conducted by the corporate social responsibility (CSR) program and activity conducted for the corporate compliance program. In practice, if a company has both a CSR program and a corporate compliance program, managed by different groups, significant synergies can probably be gained if the two parties work together on their compliance activities with respect to suppliers and vendors. CSR activities are typically more community-focused and less regulatory-focused than corporate compliance programs. Often the first push in CSR activities is on fundamental human rights, particularly the freedom of speech and child labor. From a compliance standpoint, most companies do not want to be responsible for monitoring compliance by their foreign suppliers with local child labor laws and it may be impossible for a company to change the way a foreign supplier deals with speech matters. Nonetheless, if a company decides to require its suppliers to sign codes of conduct for CSR reasons, it would seem logical that such code of conduct should address the areas of potentially high compliance risk as well. In addition, if a company is conducting an audit of a supplier to ensure that the supplier is not violating fundamental human rights, the company probably needs to make sure that any other compliance violations it may see during that audit (such as bribery to obtain permits) is also corrected. Thus, the CSR team needs to be fully trained on important compliance risks with suppliers and vendors and should alert the corporate compliance program when compliance red flags are spotted at a supplier or vendor.

Industry Codes of Conduct, Standardized Assessments and Other Monitoring Tools

One way to extend codes of conduct to partners, suppliers and vendors without asserting too much control over them is to require them to sign up to applicable industry codes of conduct. Companies in a number of industries have worked together to agree codes of conduct that reflect the industries views as a whole. Industry codes of conduct make sense in industries where many companies use a core set of the same suppliers. Companies can require or recommend that suppliers, partners or other third parties which it does business with adhere to these codes of conduct. A company can embed compliance with such codes into their contracts with the third parties. In some industries and some countries, industry codes of conduct are mandatory as a way of regulating the behavior of companies. See Information on Mandatory Codes of Conduct in Australia, in Resources section.

Some industries have gone further than simply creating codes of conduct; they have created standardized assessment and other monitoring tools. Industry codes of conduct and other standardized compliance tools are beneficial for both the company and the supplier, because they reduce the chance that suppliers will be subject to widely varying rules with each company with whom it works and they increase the chance that a supplier will actually put in place the necessary resources to comply with the terms of the code. Companies should be careful to consider antitrust issues in implementing these codes of conduct and assessment tools with their suppliers.

It is possible that sharing the results of any self-assessments or working with other companies in the industry to penalize any supplier that fails to comply with the code could violate antitrust laws in several countries because such results might include information on pricing, discounts and product development plans that are highly sensitive from an antitrust standpoint.

Both the importance as well as the risk issues that implementing and adhering to industry standards and codes of conducts might have over companies can be seen through the effects that the collapse of the Rana Plaza building in Bangladesh had over US and UK entities. After the collapse of Rana Plaza in 2013, global standards for the garment industry have been under scrutiny. The collapse made clear that new standards for working conditions for subcontractors with employees in under developed and developing countries are necessary, and retailers all over the world are now demanding stricter safety standards. However, U.S. companies must be careful about agreeing to standards that are overly broad or that create unexpected liability.

Assignment

- **Hypothetical:** You are the Chief Compliance Officer at your [Team's] corporation. Draft a sample contract outlining the relationship between your company and a subcontractor. Be sure to include information regarding FCPA and other legal compliance criteria.

Chapter 20

Global Corporate Compliance

Introduction

There has been a rapid convergence of global compliance standards in the first decade of the 21st century. This phenomenon has occurred largely due to a series of crises that have touched every country, on every continent, in every sector of the world economy. These crises have propelled and set in motion a global sea change in regulation and enforcement.

The series of crises began in New York City on September 11, 2001, and were followed by bombings in Madrid and London. The world became one, as the threat of international terrorism brought commerce to a full stop. World travel was halted at approximately 10:00 am on September 11, 2001. People, goods, industry and nations were yanked into the realization that terrorists could de-rail our civilization, our daily lives, and normal assumptions. A world that had shrunk due to unprecedented airline transportation and the emergence of computer technology in the 20th century linking people around the world became paralyzed by terrorism in the 21st century.

Bio-terrorism became a reality as anthrax-filled envelopes in the United States caused death and wars in Iraq, Afghanistan and Pakistan caused strains on the political and financial health of many Western nations. Oil prices soared and stock markets and banks entered into a prolonged euphoria built on financial products such as "derivatives."

The spring of 2008 brought on a global financial meltdown that ushered in the end of Wall Street as we had known it. Bear Stearns, Lehman Brothers, Merrill Lynch and AIG crumpled from their towering heights. A global real estate market that had bloomed on weak or non-existent credit standards, and that relied on ever increasing real estate values changed the landscape from Beijing to Dubai and from Dublin to Dallas. Real estate values collapsed, as values plunged below loan to value ratios. Sub-prime mortgage portfolios and complex derivatives such as credit default swaps triggered the further collapse of real estate values, causing a domino effect. The domino spiral rapidly wound downward into a deadly flattened state. The cranes stopped moving and concrete foundations were left exposed and dormant.

While the developing BRICS countries, Brazil, Russia, India, China, and South Africa continue growing at varying rates, Europe and the U.S. have suffered through

717

a prolonged economic malaise. Greece, Spain, and Portugal have suffered severe economic crises and Greece has been threatened with Eurozone expulsion. Further, the recent trend is toward large global corruption settlements and fines. Siemens is a notable example of global compliance failures which resulted in the largest penalty ever imposed on a corporation for violation of the Foreign Corrupt Practices Act. Siemens agreed to pay monetary sanctions of $800 million each to the United States and Germany. Swiss logistics company Panalpina Group paid $237 million in civil and criminal penalties to settle several foreign bribery cases with the Department of Justice and the Securities and Exchange Commission. German carmaker Daimler also paid $185 million after admitting bribery of foreign officials in 22 countries. In addition, GlaxoSmithKline (GSK), one of the world's largest healthcare and pharmaceuticals companies, agreed to pay $3 billion to the United States authorities in 2012 as a settlement for several compliance failures. Most recently, compliance failures have occurred in 2015 with Volkswagen, FIFA, and Petrobras. The extent of these failures is still unknown and, in the case of Petrobras, led to impeachment of the President of Brazil, Dilma Rousseff.

This chapter will explore the ways that law and regulation around the world have brought the dawn of a new age of corporate responsibility in reaction to a world unraveled by a series of unprecedented crises. These new laws and regulations have touched on individual liberty, data privacy, banking supervision and regulation, the import/export of goods and services, communications, education, the Internet, media and the safety and production of food and pharmaceutical products. The world we live in continues to shrink and the output of toxic emissions in Asia, Europe and the Americas continues to have a negative impact on our planet. Regulation and global enforcement of standards are growing at a startling rate as world reaction coalesces into action. Corporate citizens of the world are operating in a new and more constrained world. This trend will continue.

Major legal, regulatory and enforcement reactions to our collective 21st century crises have transformed law and regulation. In response, multinational corporations have been forced to create global strategies to survive and thrive in the face of unprecedented challenge. Multinational corporations have quickly adapted and become pragmatic world leaders. They have transformed the behavior of hundreds of thousands, and indeed millions of their workers ahead of and in anticipation of the actions of political and diplomatic bodies around the globe.

Convergence in Legal and Regulatory Responses to 21st Century Crises

Heightened security standards resulting from terrorist attacks have had far reaching effects on multiple industries. Transportation, (especially airlines and cruise ships), shipping (cargo containers, port facilities), banking, trade and the energy sector have been forced to make major changes in their operational controls.

Laws related to "know your customer" standards have changed the face of global banking, as well as the details researched and required for merger and acquisition candidates, passenger manifests or for the use of public carriers. Corporations, banks, and others are tasked with determining who they are transacting business with, the source of their funds, the origins of their products and the labor standards that were utilized in the manufacture of their products. The "Uniting and Strengthening America by Providing Appropriate Tools Required to Intercept and Obstruct Terrorism Act of 2001" ("U.S.A. Patriot Act").

The USA Patriot Act embeds this requirement into the required policies and procedures of the entire financial services sector. *See* 31 U.S.C. §§ 5311–5330; 31 C.F.R. § 103. The standards that exist for corporations today are driven by both internal and external pressures. Internally, corporations are preoccupied by the fear of reputational harm that comes from a global media presence that has a need to feed its "24/7" appetite for sensational headline grabbing news, personal liability for directors, *see In Re Caremark Int'l Inc. Derivative Litig.*, 698 A.2d 959 (Del. Ch. 1996)), as well as civil and criminal penalties.

After the Rana Plaza building collapse in Bangladesh in 2013, it is clear that new standards are necessary for working conditions for subcontractors with employees in under developed and developing countries. But U.S. companies also must be careful about agreeing to standards that are overly broad or that create unexpected liability. For instance, UK parent companies that sold the products produced in Rana Plaza, and that agreed to compensate the families of the victims, may be substantially liable for additional compensation under English Tort Law.

Siemens, Enron, Arthur Andersen, Worldcom, Exxon Valdez, Satyam, Societe General, UBS, Halliburton, Parmalat, Riggs Bank, Goldman Sachs, and BAE Systems (the Al Yamamah-U.K. crises) are just a few of the headline grabbing, reputation threatening stories that have engaged readers and television viewers from around the world. Reputational damage has killed companies. Enron, Arthur Andersen and Parmalat are probably the leading examples of death "by media." Phillip Morris successfully avoided the reputational damage of its long term tobacco litigation by using the post crises corporate name "Altria" for a number of years.

Examples of international crisis where "effective" corporate compliance programs could have limited and/or prevented the massive economic consequences and penalties for global companies include Parmalat, BAE Systems and Barclays Bank.

SEC Litigation Release No. 18527
Accounting and Auditing Enforcement Release No. 1936

(Dec. 30, 2003) https://www.sec.gov/litigation/litreleases/lr18527.htm

Securities and Exchange Commission v. Parmalat Finanziaria S.p.A., Case No. 03 CV 10266 (PKC) (S.D.N.Y.)

SEC Charges Parmalat with Financial Fraud

The Securities and Exchange Commission charged Parmalat Finanziaria S.p.A. ("Parmalat") with securities fraud. The Commission's complaint, filed in U.S. District Court in the Southern District of New York, alleges that Parmalat engaged in one of the largest and most brazen corporate financial frauds in history.

The Commission's complaint alleges as follows: From August through November 2003, Parmalat fraudulently offered $100 million of unsecured Senior Guaranteed Notes to U.S. investors by materially overstating the company's assets and materially understating its liabilities. As Parmalat acknowledged in a press release dated December 19, 2003, the assets in its 2002 audited financial statements were overstated by at least €3.95 billion (approximately $4.9 billion). In addition, Parmalat falsely stated to U.S. investors that it used its "excess cash balances"—which actually did not exist—to repurchase corporate debt securities worth €2.9 billion (approximately $3.6 billion), when in fact it had not repurchased those debt obligations and they remained outstanding. The $100 million note offering failed after Parmalat's auditors raised questions about certain Parmalat accounts.

The complaint further alleges that as of the end of 2002, Parmalat purportedly held the €3.95 billion worth of cash and marketable securities in an account at Bank of America in New York City in the name of Bonlat Financing Corporation ("Bonlat"), a wholly owned subsidiary incorporated in the Cayman Islands. Bonlat's auditors certified its 2002 financial statements based upon a false confirmation that Bonlat held these assets at Bank of America. The bank account and the assets did not exist and the purported confirmation had been forged. These non-existent assets are reflected on Bonlat's 2002 books and records and, in turn, in Parmalat's 2002 consolidated financial statements, as well as in its consolidated financial statements as at June 30, 2003, which were provided to U.S. investors to whom Parmalat offered notes from August through November 2003. The complaint further alleges that a private placement memorandum that Parmalat provided to U.S. investors in August 2003 contained numerous material misstatements about the company's financial condition. For example, the memorandum falsely states: "Liquidity is high with significant cash and marketable securities balances...."

The complaint further alleges that on December 9, 2003, Parmalat's Chairman and Chief Executive Officer, and his son, a senior Parmalat executive, met with representatives from a New York City-based private equity and financial advisory firm regarding a possible leveraged buyout of Parmalat. During that meeting, one of the New York firm's representatives noted that Parmalat's financial statements showed that the company had a large amount of cash. In response, the son stated that the cash was not there, and that Parmalat really had only €500 million in cash. Later, Parmalat's Chief Financial Officer joined the meeting. During a discussion of Parmalat's outstanding debt, the CFO stated that Parmalat's debt was actually €10 billion, much higher than the balance sheet showed. The CFO indicated that the balance sheet was incorrect because the company had not repurchased €2.9 billion of Parmalat bonds. The balance sheet falsely reflected that the bonds had been repurchased.

The complaint further alleges that based on these revelations, the New York firm's representatives offered to send members of the firm's restructuring group to meet with Parmalat representatives. The following day, representatives of the firm's restructuring group met with the Parmalat representatives, and informed them that Parmalat needed to publicly disclose the facts disclosed to the New York firm if that firm were to continue to have any involvement. When it became clear that the Parmalat representatives were unwilling to do so, the New York firm's representatives terminated their discussions with Parmalat.

The complaint further alleges that from 1998 through 2002, Parmalat and certain of its top managers and directors, including its then Chairman and CEO and its CFO, actively marketed and sold nearly $1.5 billion in notes and bonds to U.S. investors. Parmalat also sponsored an American Depositary Receipts ("ADR") program. Parmalat's ADRs were originally privately placed in the U.S. on August 9, 1996. Before December 19, 2003, the price of Parmalat ADRs had been artificially inflated by the materially false and misleading statements described above.

Parmalat is charged with violating Section 17(a) of the Securities Act of 1933. The Commission seeks against Parmalat a permanent injunction from future securities fraud violations and a substantial civil penalty.

The Commission's investigation into these events is continuing.

Press Release, U.S. Dep't of Justice, *BAE Systems PLC Pleads Guilty and Ordered to Pay $400 Million Criminal Fine*

(Mar. 1, 2010) http://www.justice.gov/opa/pr/bae-systems-plc-
pleads-guilty-and-ordered-pay-400-million-criminal-fine

BAE Systems plc (BAES) pleaded guilty today in U.S. District Court in the District of Columbia to conspiring to defraud the United States by impairing and impeding its lawful functions, to make false statements about its Foreign Corrupt Practices Act (FCPA) compliance program, and to violate the Arms Export Control Act (AECA) and International Traffic in Arms Regulations (ITAR), announced Acting Deputy Attorney General Gary G. Grindler. BAES was sentenced today by U.S. District Court Judge John D. Bates to pay a $400 million criminal fine, one of the largest criminal fines in the history of DOJ's ongoing effort to combat overseas corruption in international business and enforce U.S. export control laws.

"Today, BAE Systems pleaded guilty to knowingly and willfully making false statements to U.S. government agencies. The actions of BAE Systems impeded U.S. efforts to ensure international trade is free of corruption and to maintain control over sensitive U.S. technology," said Acting Deputy Attorney General Gary G. Grindler. "BAE Systems will pay a $400 million fine for its criminal conduct—one of the largest criminal fines ever levied in the United States against a company for business related violations. The remediation measures BAE Systems has undertaken, in conjunction with its agreement to retain an independent compliance monitor, are evidence supporting BAE Systems' stated commitment to ensure that it operates in a transparent, honest and responsible manner going forward. The Department of Justice will continue to hold accountable companies that impair the operations of the U.S. government by lying about their conduct and operations."

"Competition is one of the foundations of our economic system," said Shawn Henry, Assistant Director in Charge of the FBI's Washington Field Office. "Corporations and individuals who conspire to defeat this basic economic principle not only cause harm but ultimately shake the public's confidence in the entire system."

"Providing false statements to circumvent U.S. export laws and to defraud the U.S. Government must be vigorously prosecuted," said John Morton, assistant secretary of Homeland Security for U.S. Immigration and Customs Enforcement (ICE). "ICE is committed to working with our federal and international partners to investigate violations of U.S. export controls to assure sensitive technologies are not fraudulently and unlawfully acquired."

BAES is a multinational defense contractor with headquarters in the United Kingdom and with a U.S. subsidiary—BAE Systems Inc.—headquartered in Rockville, Md. None of the criminal conduct described in the plea involved the actions of BAE Systems Inc.

According to court documents, from approximately 2000 to 2002, BAES represented to various U.S. government agencies, including the Departments of Defense and Justice, that it would create and implement policies and procedures to ensure its compliance with the anti-bribery provisions of the FCPA, as well as similar, foreign laws implementing the Organization for Economic Cooperation and Development (OECD) Anti-bribery Convention. According to court documents, BAES knowingly and willfully failed to create mechanisms to ensure compliance with these legal prohibitions on foreign bribery. According to court documents, the gain to BAES from the various false statements and failures to make required disclosures to the U.S. government was more than $200 million.

The FCPA makes it illegal for certain businesses and individuals, or anyone taking action within U.S. territorial jurisdiction, corruptly to make payments to foreign government officials for the purpose of obtaining or retaining business. In addition, the FCPA prohibits corruptly making payments to a third party, while knowing that all or a portion of the payments will go directly or indirectly to a foreign government official for the purpose of obtaining or retaining business. Despite BAES's representations to the U.S. government to the contrary, BAES knowingly and willfully failed to create sufficient compliance mechanisms to prevent and detect violations of the anti-bribery provisions of the FCPA.

According to court documents, BAES made a series of substantial payments to shell companies and third party intermediaries that were not subjected to the degree of scrutiny and review to which BAES told the U.S. government the payments would be subjected. BAES admitted it regularly retained what it referred to as "marketing advisors" to assist in securing sales of defense items without scrutinizing those relationships. In fact, BAES took steps to conceal from the U.S. government and others its relationships with some of these advisors and its undisclosed payments to them. For example, after May 2001, BAES contracted with and paid certain advisors through various offshore shell companies beneficially owned by BAES. BAES also encouraged certain advisors to establish their own offshore shell companies to receive payments from BAES while disguising the origins and recipients of these payments. BAES admitted that it established one company in the British Virgin Islands (BVI) to conceal its marketing advisor relationships, including who the advisor was and how much it was paid; to create obstacles for investigating authorities to penetrate the arrangements; to circumvent laws in countries that did not allow such relationships; and to assist advisors in avoiding tax liability for payments from BAES.

Through this BVI entity, from May 2001 onward, BAES made payments totaling more than £135 million plus more than $14 million, even though in certain situations BAES was aware there was a high probability that part of the payments would be used to ensure that BAES was favored in foreign government decisions regarding the purchase of defense articles. According to court documents, in many instances, BAES possessed no adequate evidence that its advisors performed any legitimate activities in justification of the substantial payments.

In addition, according to court documents, BAES began serving as the prime contractor to the U.K. government in the mid-1980s, after the U.K. and the Kingdom of Saudi Arabia (KSA) entered into a formal understanding. According to court documents, the "support services" that BAES provided according to the formal understanding resulted, in part, in BAES providing substantial benefits to a foreign public official of KSA, who was in a position of influence regarding sales of fighter jets, other defense materials and related support services. BAES admitted it undertook no adequate review or verification of benefits provided to the KSA official, including no adequate review or verification of more than $5 million in invoices submitted by a BAES employee from May 2001 to early 2002 to determine whether the listed expenses were in compliance with previous statements made by BAES to the U.S. government regarding its anti-corruption compliance procedures. In addition, in connection with these same defense deals, BAES agreed to transfer more than £10 million plus more than $9 million to a bank account in Switzerland controlled by an intermediary, being aware that there was a high probability that the intermediary would transfer part of these payments to the same KSA official.

Also as part of its guilty plea, BAES admitted to making and causing to be made certain false, inaccurate and incomplete statements, and failing to make required disclosures to the U.S. government in connection with the administration of certain regulatory functions, including statements and disclosures related to applications for arms export licenses, as required by the AECA and ITAR. The AECA and ITAR prohibit the export of defense-related materials to a foreign national or a foreign nation without the required U.S. government license, and the Department of State has the power to approve or deny such applications. As part of the licensing scheme, applicants are required to identify associated commissions to the State Department — whether they are legitimate commissions or bribes — paid to anyone who helps secure the sales of defense materials.

BAES admitted that, as part of the conspiracy, it knowingly and willfully failed to identify commissions paid to third parties for assistance in soliciting, promoting or otherwise securing sales of defense items in violation of the AECA and ITAR. BAES failed to identify the commission payments paid through the BVI entity described above, in order to keep the fact and scope of its external advisors from public scrutiny. In one specific instance, BAES caused the filing of false applications for export licenses for Gripen fighter jets to the Czech Republic and Hungary by failing to tell the export license applicant or the State Department of £19 million BAES paid to an intermediary with the high probability that it would be used to influence that tender process to favor BAES.

As part of its guilty plea, BAES has agreed to maintain a compliance program that is designed to detect and deter violations of the FCPA, other foreign bribery laws implementing the OECD Anti-bribery Convention, and any other applicable anti-corruption laws, and that is designed to detect and deter violations of the AECA and ITAR, as well as similar export control laws. Under the terms of the plea agreement, BAES has agreed to retain an independent compliance monitor for three years to assess BAES's compliance program and to make a series of reports to the company and the Justice Department.

The criminal case is being prosecuted by Senior Litigation Counsel Nathaniel B. Edmonds and Deputy Chief Mark F. Mendelsohn of the Criminal Division's Fraud Section and Trial Attorney Patrick T. Murphy of the National Security Division's Counterespionage Section. The Fraud Section is responsible for all investigations and prosecutions of the Foreign Corrupt Practices Act, and conducts other investigations into sophisticated economic crimes. The Counterespionage Section supervises the investigation and prosecution of cases involving the export of military and strategic commodities and technology, including cases under the AECA and ITAR.

———————

Press Release, U.S. Dep't of Justice, *Barclays Bank PLC Admits Misconduct Related to Submissions for the London Interbank Offered Rate and the Euro Interbank Offered Rate and Agrees to Pay $160 Million Penalty*

(June 27, 2012) http://www.justice.gov/opa/pr/barclays-bank-plc-admits-misconduct-related-submissions-london-interbank-offered-rate-and

Barclays Bank PLC, a financial institution headquartered in London, has entered into an agreement with the Department of Justice to pay a $160 million penalty to resolve violations arising from Barclays's submissions for the London InterBank Offered Rate (LIBOR) and the Euro Interbank Offered Rate (EURIBOR), which are benchmark interest rates used in financial markets around the world, announced Assistant Attorney General Lanny A. Breuer of the Justice Department's Criminal Division and Assistant Director in Charge James W. McJunkin of the FBI's Washington Field Office.

As part of the agreement with the Department of Justice, Barclays has admitted and accepted responsibility for its misconduct set forth in a statement of facts that is incorporated into the agreement. According to the agreement, Barclays provided LIBOR and EURIBOR submissions that, at various times, were false because they improperly took into account the trading positions of its derivative traders, or reputational concerns about negative media attention relating to its LIBOR submissions. The Justice Department's criminal investigation into the manipulation of LIBOR and EURIBOR by other financial institutions and individuals is ongoing. The agreement requires Barclays to continue cooperating with the department in its ongoing investigation.

"LIBOR and EURIBOR are critically important benchmark interest rates," said Assistant Attorney General Breuer. "Because mortgages, student loans, financial derivatives, and other financial products rely on LIBOR and EURIBOR as reference rates, the manipulation of submissions used to calculate those rates can have significant negative effects on consumers and financial markets worldwide. For years, traders at Barclays encouraged the manipulation of LIBOR and EURIBOR submissions in order to benefit their financial positions; and, in the midst of the financial crisis, Barclays management directed that U.S. Dollar LIBOR submissions be artificially lowered. For this illegal conduct, Barclays is paying a significant price. To the bank's credit, Barclays also took a significant step toward accepting responsibility for its conduct by being the first institution to provide extensive and meaningful cooperation to the government. Its efforts have substantially assisted the Criminal Division in our ongoing investigation of individuals and other financial institutions in this matter."

"Barclays Bank's illegal activity involved manipulating its submissions for benchmark interest rates in order to benefit its trading positions and the media's perception of the bank's financial health," said Assistant Director in Charge McJunkin. "Today's announcement is the result of the hard work of the FBI Special Agents, financial analysts and forensic accountants as well as the prosecutors who dedicated significant time and resources to investigating this case."

Barclays was one of the financial institutions that contributed rates used in the calculation of LIBOR and EURIBOR. The contributed rates are generally meant to reflect each bank's assessment of the rates at which it could borrow unsecured inter-bank funds. For LIBOR, the highest and lowest 25% of contributed rates are excluded from the calculation and the remaining rates are averaged to calculate the fixed rates. For EURIBOR, the highest and lowest 15% are excluded and the remaining 70% are averaged to calculate the fixed rates.

Futures, options, swaps, and other derivative financial instruments traded in the over-the-counter market and on exchanges worldwide are settled based on LIBOR. Further, mortgages, credit cards, student loans and other consumer lending products often use LIBOR as a reference rate. According to the agreement, an individual bank's LIBOR or EURIBOR submission cannot appropriately be influenced by the financial positions of its derivatives traders or the bank's concerns about public perception of its financial health due to its LIBOR submissions.

According to the agreement, between 2005 and 2007, and then occasionally there-after through 2009, certain Barclays traders requested that the Barclays LIBOR and EURIBOR submitters contribute rates that would benefit the financial positions held by those traders. The requests were made by traders in New York and London, via electronic messages, telephone conversations and in-person conversations. The employees responsible for the LIBOR and EURIBOR submissions accommodated those requests on numerous occasions in submitting the bank's contributions. On some occasions, Barclays's submissions affected the fixed rates.

In addition, between August 2005 and May 2008, certain Barclays traders com-municated with traders at other financial institutions, including other banks on the LIBOR and EURIBOR panels, to request LIBOR and EURIBOR submissions that would be favorable to their or their counterparts' trading positions, according to the agreement.

When the requests of traders for favorable LIBOR and EURIBOR submissions were taken into account by the rate submitters, Barclays's rate submissions were false and misleading.

Further, according to the agreement, between approximately August 2007 and Jan-uary 2009, in response to initial and ongoing press speculation that Barclays's high U.S. Dollar LIBOR submissions at the time might reflect liquidity problems at Barclays, members of Barclays management directed that Barclays's Dollar LIBOR submissions be lowered. This management instruction often resulted in Barclays's submission of false rates that did not reflect its perceived cost of obtaining interbank funds. While the purpose of this particular conduct was to influence Barclays's rate submissions, as opposed to the resulting fixes, there were some occasions when Barclays's submis-sions affected the fixed rates.

The agreement and monetary penalty recognize Barclays's extraordinary cooper-ation. Barclays made timely, voluntary and complete disclosure of its misconduct. After government authorities began investigating allegations that banks had engaged in manipulation of benchmark interest rates, Barclays was the first bank to cooperate in a meaningful way in disclosing its conduct relating to LIBOR and EURIBOR. Barclays's disclosure included relevant facts that at the time were not known to the government. Barclays's cooperation has been extensive, in terms of the quality and type of information and assistance provided, and has been of substantial value in furthering the department's ongoing criminal investigation. Barclays has made a commitment to future cooperation with the department and other government authorities in the United States and the United Kingdom.

Assistant Attorney General Breuer further stated, "As today's agreement reflects, we are committed to holding companies accountable for their misconduct while, at the same time, giving meaningful credit to companies that provide full and valuable cooperation in our investigations."

In addition, Barclays has implemented a series of compliance measures and will implement additional internal controls regarding its submission of LIBOR and EU-RIBOR contributions, as required by the Commodity Futures Trading Commission (CFTC). Barclays will also continue to be supervised and monitored by the FSA.

The agreement and monetary penalty further recognize certain mitigating factors to Barclays's misconduct. At times, Barclays employees raised concerns with the British Bankers' Association, the United Kingdom Financial Services Authority (FSA), the Bank of England, and the Federal Reserve Bank of New York in late 2007 and in 2008 that the Dollar LIBOR rates submitted by contributing banks, including Barclays, were too low and did not accurately reflect the market. Further, during this time, notwithstanding Barclays's improperly low Dollar LIBOR submissions, those submissions were often higher than the contributions used in the calculation of the fixed rates.

As a result of Barclays's admission of its misconduct, its extraordinary cooperation, its remediation efforts and certain mitigating and other factors, the department agreed not to prosecute Barclays for providing false LIBOR and EURIBOR contributions, provided that Barclays satisfies its ongoing obligations under the agreement for a period of two years. The non-prosecution agreement applies only to Barclays and not to any employees or officers of Barclays or any other individuals.

In a related matter, the CFTC brought attempted manipulation and false reporting charges against Barclays, which the bank agreed to settle. The CFTC imposed a $200 million penalty and required Barclays to implement detailed measures designed to ensure the integrity and reliability of its benchmark interest rate submissions.

The FSA issued a Final Notice regarding its enforcement action against Barclays, and has imposed a penalty of £59.5 million against it.

––––––––––

Compliance professionals have been astute enough to drive cultural shifts in corporate behavior by translating and illustrating reputational harm to business leaders as equating bottom-line loss to net income. Business leaders understand the economic harm that comes from accusations of bribery, tainted food, dangerous toys or dealing with terrorists or criminals. While law and regulation respond to crises with the enactment of stricter standards, ethical business people are driven by the reputation of their company and their products in the global marketplace. A good reputation translates into positive earnings. A bad reputation leads to a decline in earnings and a sufficiently widespread scandal can lead to a total collapse (e.g., Bank of Credit and Commerce International, "BCCI," Enron, Worldcom, Anderson).

American antitrust and European competition laws have dealt severe financial repercussions to abusive players, (e.g., Kodak, Texaco, Microsoft, Intel, Monsanto, Samsung, Airline partner program cooperation agreements.). The underlying principals in this area of law and regulation are simply put: "Thou shalt not monopolize, Thou shalt not fix prices, Thou shalt not engage in unfair competition."

The details of each set of national or European Union laws and the refined set of regulations of each national regulator are similar enough to set out global standards for proper competitive conduct. European "dawn raids" of business establishments, and enormous fines have increased global attention to these laws. In 2009, "[t]he European Commission fined Intel a record 1.06 billion euros, [the equivalent of $1.45 billion] ... for abusing its dominance in the computer chip market, the strongest sign yet that regulators worldwide are serious about opening the technology sector to competition." James Kanter, *Europe Fines Intel $1.45 Billion in Antitrust Case*, N.Y. Times, May 13, 2009. In 2004, Microsoft was fined 497 million euros for blocking competition in markets for servers and media software. Intel's fine dwarfs the Microsoft penalty. South Korea fined Intel $25 million in 2008 for similar conduct. Other multinationals under scrutiny in 2009 were: Qualcomm, Rambus, Cisco Systems, I.B.M., Google and IPCom (a German technology company). European regulators have been the most proactive enforcers of anti-competitive corporate behavior.

Similarly, the basic tenet of global anti-money laundering law in over 120 nations boils down to: "Thou shalt not engage in, or aid and abet, in the transfer of proceeds from criminal conduct (illegal drugs, weapons, fraud, Ponzi schemes, terrorism, corrupt payments and sale of stolen goods)." The principals of know your customer ("KYC") policies are required and practiced in banks, insurance companies, broker dealers, hedge funds, jewelers, and auto dealers to name a few. The U.S.A. Patriot Act along with 18 U.S.C. § 1956 (Laundering of Monetary instruments) and 18 U.S.C. § 1957 (Engaging in monetary transactions in property derived from Specified Unlawful Activity) has become a ubiquitous global symbol of the need for business to do appropriate due diligence on the individuals and companies with whom they engage in business.

Riggs Bank, founded in 1836, was essentially destroyed after it ignored these rules in servicing the banking needs and accounts of individuals within foreign embassies and consulates worldwide. In July 2004, Riggs National Bank was purchased by PNC Financial Services Group who ended these international services amid accusations of terrorist financing, money laundering and the "seamier geopolitics of Big Oil." Timothy O'Brien, *A Washington Bank In a Global Mess*, N.Y. TIMES, Apr. 14, 2004. More recently, HSBC has been accused of failing to monitor because its subsidiary in Mexico allowed money-laundering. *See* Christie Smythe, *HSBC Judge Approves $1.9B Drug-Money Laundering Accord*, Jul. 3, 2014, www.bloomberg.com.

Anti-Corruption law and regulation has also become global in nature. The United States Foreign Corrupt Practices Act ("FCPA") along with the OECD Anti-Bribery Convention and UN Convention Against Corruption ("UNCAC") provided leadership in diminishing and punishing corporations who "pay to play." In addition, the United Kingdom Bribery Act came into force on July 1, 2011. The Bribery Act created the following offenses: (1) active bribery—promising or giving a financial or other advantage, (2) passive bribery—agreeing to receive or accepting a financial or other advantage, (3) bribery of foreign public officials, and (4) the failure of commercial organizations to prevent bribery by an associated person. The fourth offense essentially requires corporations to have strong global compliance programs. Further, the UK Bribery Act found business to business bribery to be illegal.

Scandals in the oil and gas industry (Petrobras, Baker Hughes, Statoil, KBR, Halliburton); automobile industry (Volkswagen, Volvo, Daimler Chrysler); telecommunications, defense industry and manufacturing sectors (Siemens), sports and entertainment (FIFA), and pharmaceutical and medical-related industries (Diagnostics Products Corporation, Micrus, Syncor, Schering-Plough) continue to grab headlines and suffer unprecedented fines. Among these core cases, the case of Siemens and its violation of the Foreign Corrupt Practices Act stand out because of the magnitude of the settlement—Siemens paid $800 million to the United States and another $800 million to Germany to settle the corruption cases.

According to court filings, the Department of Justice brought two counts against Siemens. The first count alleged that Siemens failed to maintain adequate internal controls in violation of 15 U.S.C. §§ 78m(b)(2)(B) and 78m(b)(5). Section 78m(b)(2)(B) provides that issuers of securities must, *inter alia*, "maintain a system of internal accounting controls sufficient to provide reasonable assurance that transactions are recorded as necessary to permit preparation of financial statements in conformity with generally accepted accounting principles." Section 78m(b)(5) states that "no person shall knowingly circumvent or knowingly fail to implement a system of internal accounting controls or knowingly falsify any book, record, or account...." The Justice Department made factual allegations that Siemens knowingly failed (1) to implement sufficient controls over third party bank accounts, (2) to establish a competent Corporate Compliance Office, and (3) to investigate allegations of corruption.

The second count alleged that Siemens failed to maintain adequate books and records in violation of 15 U.S.C. § 78m(b)(2)(A). Section 78m(b)(2)(A) requires issuers to "make and keep books, records, and accounts, which, in reasonable detail, accurately and fairly reflect the transactions and dispositions of assets of the issuer." To support this count, the Justice Department specifically alleged that Siemens (1) used off-books accounts as a way to conceal corrupt payments, (2) justified payments to purported business consultants based on false invoices, (3) mischaracterized bribes in the corporate books and records as consulting fees and other seemingly legitimate expenses.

The U.S. Securities and Exchange Commission also filed a complaint in the United States District Court for the District of Columbia. The complaint alleged three claims against Siemens, two of which are the same as the Justice Department's claims. The third claim, however, alleges a violation of 15 U.S.C. § 78dd-1, which prohibits, *inter alia*, any issuer from giving anything of value to "any foreign official for purposes of influencing any act or decision of such foreign official in his official capacity ..." The Commission listed numerous examples where Siemens allegedly bribed government officials: (1) Siemens paid $16.7 million in bribes to Venezuelan officials in connection with construction of a metro transit line, (2) Siemens paid $25 million in bribes to government customers in connection with an installation project of transmission lines in China, and (3) Siemens paid over $40 million in bribes to Argentinian officials to secure a $1 billion project to produce national identity cards.

Finally, in a Sentencing Memorandum to the District Court for the District of Columbia, the Department of Justice urged the court to accept the proposed plea agreement with Siemens. In the plea agreement, Siemens agreed not to contest the factual allegations involving Venezuela, Bangladesh, and Argentina. Siemens also agreed to implement rigorous compliance enhancements, including periodic testing, and to retain an independent monitor who will conduct a review of the compliance code and internal controls. In making the overall disposition of punishment, the Justice Department noted "Siemens' Exceptional Cooperation" which resulted in a two-point decrease in the culpability score from 10 to 8.

In the context of an announcement of a merger between Sun Microsystems and Oracle, a May 8, 2009 10K filing with the SEC announced a "voluntary" disclosure by Sun Microsystems to both the SEC and Department of Justice of an FCPA violation and internal investigation. Mergers and acquisitions have entered a period in which the acquiring entity does extensive due diligence to determine if it is taking on liability for prior FCPA lapses by the target of the proposed acquisition. This trend began with Lockheed Martin in its aborted acquisition of Titan Corporation (2003) and continued in a costly delay in the GE acquisition of Invision (2004–2005) under similar circumstances.

A simple global standard of behavior has become increasingly the norm. "Thou shalt not bribe foreign officials to win contracts," or more simply put, "Thou shalt not bribe in any context." In China, this point has been realized by public execution of corrupt public officials. The U.A.E. and local authorities in Dubai have taken similar positions. Transparency International led the way by publishing its indices of corrupt environments as well as by indicating countries that make corrupt payments. Doing business in Nigeria has sent shivers down the spines of almost every gas and oil company that does business there. Some corporations have begun to withhold development projects and business deals in countries that will not abide by international anti-corruption norms. A senior partner at a well-respected Tier I law firm in the U.S. commented that "doing business in Russia had become impossible because of the rampant corruption."

In addition to Transparency International, a variety of other non-governmental organizations have increased the demand for global compliance programs. The UN

Global Compact is a United Nations initiative to encourage business worldwide to adopt sustainable and socially responsible policies. The Ethics and Compliance Officer Association represents the largest group of ethics and compliance practitioners in the world. The Ethics Resource Center is a non-profit research organization that is committed to advancing high ethical standards in public and private institutions.

Global standards, led by strong European Union law in the area of data privacy and data protection, have quickly gained acceptance and active enforcement. Personal identifying data has become the subject of strict control and non-disclosure from Germany, Spain, France and Hungary to the shores of California. Recently, in *Schrems v. Data Protection Commissioner*, Judgment in Case C-362/14 of October 6, 2015, the Court of Justice of the European Union held that the U.S. Federal Trade Commission (FTC)'s safe harbor provisions are invalid. However, an accommodation has been reached for the near future using individual contracts with users.

Countries that perform outsourced customer services in places like India and Morocco (French speaking) are utilizing and abiding by the data privacy standards of the home countries who are sending work offshore (e.g., French data protection law is practiced in Morocco). A case by case analysis should be provided for each data transfer across national boundaries in outsourced data analysis.

Another example of developing global standards exist in data protection and laws related to the protection of intellectual property. These standards have been driven by the fast paced dissemination of information via cyberspace. Corporate espionage, identify theft and computer fraud have created a growing industry that seeks to protect data. Illegal duplication of films, CDs and designer goods has focused nations on the protection of trademarks, patents and other forms of intellectual property. European countries have set up data protection authorities who act as arbiters of the permissibility of certain types of access and movement of national and transnational data. These authorities were initially set up to protect individuals from human rights violations that played such a dominant role during the German Holocaust. Loss of personal data by corporations, banks, credit card companies, retailers, universities and others have brought a plethora of law suits and government intervention. Most recently, cyberwarfare has in fact occurred in the case of Sony and Twitter. Sony's data was presumably compromised by North Korea, which, under the name of "Guardians of Peace," leaked personal information, and drew apologies from Hollywood executives caught in embarrassing e-mail conversations. Ultimately, U.S. government officials stated that North Korea was behind the threats and leaks. Because the U.S. government speculated that North Korea was behind the attack on Sony's data, Sony's comedy *The Interview*, starring Seth Rogen and James Franco, about an assassination attempt on Kim Jong Un, had the movie opening canceled in most theaters. As for Twitter, it was attacked by ISIS, which threatened the founder of Twitter, Jack Dorsey, and its CEO, Dick Costolo for closing down ISIS-related Twitter accounts.

The significance of data protection as a corporate priority has increased. Chief Information Officers, security professionals and lawyers have joined forces to confront a growing risk in a computer driven society. As in other areas of law and regulation, the essential principals are quite similar from country to country. Basic principles of cyber law look to the law of the sea for guidance, with respect to the boundaries of a nation's sovereign authority, the necessity for international treaties for definitions of acceptable conduct and for the consequences of piracy.

Practical Strategies for Creating and Maintaining Global Compliance Programs

Corporate compliance has evolved dramatically over the past 25 years. In the United States where we legally hold corporations responsible for the criminal conduct of their employees, a codified set of standards has been imposed to lay down the basic elements of an acceptable corporate compliance program.

The U.S. Federal Sentencing Guidelines for Organizations (the "Sentencing Guidelines") were promulgated in 1991. In 2004, the Sentencing Commission amended Chapter 8 of the Federal Sentencing Guidelines to include (1) proper resources and structure for the office of compliance and ethics, (2) senior management oversight and accountability, and (3) periodic system of risk management as a part of effective compliance programs. In 2010, Chapter 8 was amended to allow corporations to receive a decrease in the culpability score if it meets four criteria: (1) compliance officers have direct obligations to the Board, (2) the compliance program detected the offense before outside discovery, (3) the organization promptly reported the offense to the appropriate governmental authorities, and (4) no compliance officer participated in, condoned, or was willfully ignorant of the offense.

United States Federal Sentencing Guidelines Manual § 8B2.1(a)–(e) is available at http://www.ussc.gov/guidelines-manual/guidelines-manual. The impact of these guidelines was to create an environment in which corporations were incentivized to implement formal programs to prevent and detect violations of law. Misconduct by a corporation, was to be punished by setting fines at various levels of severity that could be reduced by an ability of a corporation to demonstrate that it had an effective program to detect and prevent violations at the time of the misconduct. In 2004, these guidelines were revised to include the most important elements of an "effective" compliance program, which are the ability to demonstrate a culture of compliance and a Part C Risk Assessment of all legal risks.

The guidelines provide that to have an effective compliance and ethics program, an organization must (1) exercise due diligence to prevent and detect criminal conduct (such as money laundering, corruption, insider trading); and (2) promote an organizational culture that encourages ethical conduct and a commitment to compliance with the law. Along with Part C on Risk Assessment, which includes an inventory of documents, interview reports, heat maps and dashboards, and an executive summary, there are seven specific components:

1. The organization must establish standards and procedures to prevent and detect criminal conduct.

2. (A) The governing authority (e.g., Board of Directors) must be knowledgeable about the content and operation of the compliance and ethics program and exercise reasonable oversight with respect to its implementation and effectiveness.

   (B) High-level personnel must ensure that the organization has an effective compliance and ethics program, and specific individuals within high-level personnel must be assigned overall responsibility for the program.

   (C) Specific individuals must be delegated day-to-day operational responsibility for the program. These individuals must report periodically to high-level personnel and, as appropriate, to the board or a board committee on the program's effectiveness. They must have adequate resources, appropriate authority, and direct access to the board or a board committee.

3. The organization must use reasonable efforts not to include within substantial authority personnel anyone whom it knew, or should have known through the exercise of due diligence, has engaged in illegal activities or other conduct inconsistent with an effective compliance and ethics program.

4. The organization must take reasonable steps to communicate periodically and in a practical manner its standards and procedures, and other aspects of the compliance and ethics program, to directors, officers, employees and, as appropriate, agents, by conducting effective training programs and otherwise disseminating information appropriate to each person's roles and responsibilities.

5. The organization must take reasonable steps:

   (A) to ensure that the compliance and ethics program is followed including monitoring and auditing to detect criminal conduct;

   (B) to periodically to evaluate the effectiveness of the compliance and ethics program and;

   (C) to have and publicize a system, which may include mechanisms that allow for anonymity or confidentiality, whereby employees and agents may report or seek guidance regarding potential or actual criminal conduct *without* fear of retaliation.

6. The compliance and ethics program must be promoted and enforced consistently throughout the organization through:

   (A) appropriate incentives to perform in accordance with the program; and

   (B) appropriate disciplinary measures for engaging in criminal conduct and for failing to take reasonable steps to prevent or detect criminal conduct.

7. After criminal conduct has been detected, the organization must take reasonable steps to respond appropriately to the conduct and to prevent further similar conduct, including making necessary modifications to the compliance and ethics program.

The Guidelines set forth some factors that organizations should consider in conducting risk assessments which are now an integral and a required component of an effective compliance and ethics program:

- The nature and seriousness of potential criminal conduct;
- The likelihood that certain criminal conduct may occur because of the nature of the organization's business; and the prior history of the organization.

In Morgan Stanley, the managing director of its real estate business in China, Peterson, violated the FCPA by transferring a multimillion-dollar ownership interest in a Shanghai building to himself and a Chinese public official. This case is particularly interesting since the Department of Justice did not sue the company because the compliance program was found to be "effective." Indeed, Assistant Attorney General Lanny Breuer, notably stated that: "Because Morgan Stanley voluntarily disclosed Peterson's misconduct, fully cooperated with our investigation, and showed us that it maintained a rigorous compliance program, including extensive training of bank employees on the FCPA and other anti-corruption measures, we declined to bring any enforcement action against the institution in connection with Peterson's conduct." Moreover, Morgan Stanley had well implemented an effective compliance program with frequent training of its employees, frequent compliance reminders including written compliance materials, annual employees' certifications of anti-corruption policies, robust staffing and region-specific compliance personnel, a Compliance Hotline, continued evaluation, and improvement of compliance program and internal controls.

Strategic and Pragmatic Components for Managing a Global Compliance Program

A Global Code of Conduct

A global code of conduct must be written and become the foundation of a collective institutional understanding and commitment to global legal and ethical standards. According to the Making Sense of CSR 2010 report published by the Sethi International Center for Corporate Accountability, 514 of 1300 companies surveyed issued Corporate Social Responsibility reports. Of the 514 companies issuing Corporate Social Responsibility reports, 88 percent had company-based codes of conduct. Among the 88 percent of companies with company-based codes of conduct, which total 452 companies, 39 percent participated in an industry wide code of conduct and 32 percent also participated in a universal code of conduct.

The code of conduct must adhere to the longstanding successful principal of "KISS" (Keep it Simple Stupid). A successful code must be written in the style of "The Ten Commandments." Universal concepts of fairness must be expressed in simple, clearly understood language that resonates around the world. A good example of such a code is GE's Code of Conduct that is called "The Spirit and the Letter." Simply stated broad principles that apply universally help to create a unified conceptual framework that guides behavior globally. A good example of this in "The Spirit and the Letter" is the section on "Improper Payments," it reads in part (and can be downloaded from GE's website):

An improper payment to gain advantage in any situation is never acceptable and exposes you and GE to possible criminal prosecution. GE expressly prohibits improper payments in all business dealing, in every country around the world, with both governments and the private sector.

The "GE Code of Conduct" as differentiated from its longer "Spirit and Letter" is a very simple set of six overarching principals:

(1) Obey the applicable laws and regulations governing our business conduct worldwide.

(2) Be honest, fair and trustworthy in all your GE activities and relationships.

(3) Avoid all conflicts of interest between work and personal affairs.

(4) Foster an atmosphere in which fair employment practices extend to every member of the diverse GE community.

(5) Strive to create a safe workplace and to protect the environment.

(6) Through leadership at all levels, sustain a culture where ethical conduct is recognized, valued and exemplified by all employees.

The motto for the entire "Spirit and Letter" (which runs approximately 58 pages) is that GE's Code of Conduct sets out principals of conduct "Everywhere. Everyday and by Every GE employee." An all-inclusive ethics and compliance regime that requires ethical conduct is the bedrock of any successful corporate compliance program and key to the creation of a robust global culture. It must apply everywhere, every day and to employees and management at every level of the organization.

Leadership and Transparency

Much has been written about "Tone at the Top," "Messages in the Middle," and "Walking the Talk." Indeed, along with a Code of Conduct, a letter from the CEO with the CEO's photograph and a Mission Statement are good methods to reinforce leadership oversight and a strong "tone at the top" to encourage "effective" compliance with the program.

As simple as these slogans may be, they still constitute a basic necessary foundation for creating and sustaining corporate ethical cultures. Workers around the world respond to their immediate and direct chain of command. One's boss becomes one's role model. The boss who yells creates an environment where yelling is accepted and tolerated. A boss who is approachable, thoughtful and respectful of others is admired and becomes the model for the behavior patterns for those with whom they come in contact. The boss who orders expensive wines on corporate expense accounts teaches subordinates that this behavior is tolerated and acceptable. Senior management becomes the model for those who report directly or indirectly to them and their personal and business behavior becomes the model that is followed.

When there is a dissonance and divide between what is said, corporate expectations, observed behavior and unequal enforcement of company policy and codes of conduct between seniors and more junior staff, what ensues is a poisoned culture. Such inequality in the application of and enforcement of corporate codes of conduct between seniors, "big producers" and others in lower levels of the organization is similar to acid eating away at the core of a culture. Enron, Worldcom, Parmalat, Madoff Securities, Inc., Siemens, FIFA, Volkswagen, and Petrobras are but a few examples of dysfunctional culture.

In all societies, children model their behavior on that of their parents and older siblings. When words of instruction from their elders differ from daily observation of the behaviors of their elders, there is a clear dissonance. Children will follow what they observe, rather than what they are told. Equally, a CEO who speaks about the importance of ethical conduct, and violates his or her words is courting disaster. The collective behavior of a company, division, branch or office is determined by the leaders and management of every department within the larger organizational structure. Cues for behavior start at the top and with leadership levels throughout the organization. Employees are quick to spot disparate standards and consequences for violations of corporate codes of conduct. Lectures, pamphlets, and training that speak to issues of social or sexual harassment become the object of derision when leadership behavior is at variance with the corporate code and training.

"Bad behavior begets bad behavior." This is a truism, easily recognized by all, and agreed to without debate. The flaw, however, that lies within this truism is in its symmetrical balance created by the use of the word "bad." The issue for corporations begins before the truism is born. "Bad" behavior is defined as such because it is recognized and agreed upon at that point in time by all, or by a large majority. Action and activities frequently begin as such in a human dynamic aimed at achieving a goal. What is overlooked is that without high ethical, and even moral standards for conduct, repeated, successful, and rewarded behavior becomes socially accepted behavior. Copied behavior becomes the standard. Just as societies write law to reflect their agreed upon and acceptable social contract, companies do the same. In some societies, it is accepted, sanctioned, even legally reinforced to sell one's children or arrange binding marriages for 8–10 year old girls. In our society, Wall Street greed was rewarded by large bonus plans. Sub-prime lending in the mortgage industry was initially encouraged by compensation plans that drove ever more dramatically doomed lending to inappropriate borrowers. Sub-prime lending practices were an example of group mentality. Each corporate "society" must define for itself and those within it the "good"—not merely seek ways to create Potemkin like villages of "compliance."

A powerful tool in corporate training is to have respected and senior leaders tell "war" stories of real incidents that they observed or lived through which could have destroyed their careers or the reputation of the company. "War" stories that illustrate good ethical business decision making becomes part of a company's collective history and folklore. A CEO who utilizes this technique becomes the admired role model for subordinates, so long as he CEO, in fact, acts with integrity.

Another useful tool is to use headlines from around the world (e.g., from the Wall Street Journal and Financial Times, Straits Times) as "alerts" sent via email. The

trends or illustrations of the misbehavior of other corporations who lose their reputations at the hands of the global media become reinforcing messages when sent to
the right targeted audience within your own corporation.

Communication

Twitter, instant messaging, cell phone and email overload have become the ubiquitous communication style and symbols of the beginning of the 21st Century. This
phenomenon is as noticeable in Helsinki as it is in Bangkok, New York, Paris, Tokyo,
and Sydney. The success of creating a sustainable corporate compliance and ethics
culture is dependent on constant communication. This does not mean constant emails
or e-training to deadlines. What it means is that you use every opportunity and device
to get the "message out."

Some of the most potent messages and reminders are public relations type ad campaigns that include give away toys, and characters such as the gecko used by GEICO
Insurance Company or the duck used by Aflac.

Compliance and ethics programs need to be viewed as a product which needs to
be sold. The universal rules of effective advertising apply. Multiple channels need to
be utilized to get out the message. The advertising campaign needs to be made up
of positive images and positive words. Creating fear or messaging dire warnings of
negative consequences is not a winning strategy. The audience of negative campaign
messages quickly becomes deaf. It seldom creates a culture that supports ethical behavior. Effective advertising campaigns are clever and memorable.

Training

Training in all of its forms is an attempt to educate and effectively communicate
ideas, concepts, history, standards, law and regulation. What constitutes effective
training has been long debated. People learn in a variety of ways. Some people learn
from written words. Others learn from observation. Typically, some people can learn
a new game by reading the directions. Others will observe the game being played and
learn the game being played without reading the directions. Others need the spoken
word or some combination of reading, observing and hearing directions or rules.
Further, from the Declination of Prosecution in the Morgan Stanley Case, one can
see that an "effective" training program can help avoid corporate prosecution. In
Morgan Stanley, the Corporate Compliance Officials were able to provide evidence
that showed that between 2002–2008 the company had trained 54 times various
groups of Asia-based personnel on anti-corruption policies, and that Garth Peterson,
the convicted managing director of the company's branch in China, had been trained
seven times in six years on the FCPA, including on-line and in-person training.
Through this evidence Morgan Stanley was able to show that Garth Peterson was a
"rogue employee," who acted illegally despite an "effective" compliance program.

Compliance and ethics departments are challenged in attempting to train as if they had a monolithic work force. Employees, whether junior or senior, present themselves at various levels of readiness and with a wide variety of personal learning styles.

In the mid-1990s, corporations began exploring and utilizing "E-learning." Courses were prepared and delivered via computer terminals for workers who had access. "E-training" had the advantage of creating an inexpensive, consistent set of materials that could be viewed by thousands of workers in almost any physical environment that could support computer access. Over the past twenty years E-learning has been the most over-used channel of delivering vast quantities of training. Some of the E-training programs are creative, memorable and test comprehension of the participants for the materials delivered. Much of what passes for "E" training is too long, boring and dense to be of lasting value. It has been used to demonstrate and truthfully declare to law enforcement that a training and awareness program exists. However, twenty years of experience with this training vehicle has brought about a new era. We are now in the midst of a transformation or return to "classroom" style face-to-face training modules, often in conjunction with other types of training and communication. The need of U.S. corporations to demonstrate a "culture of compliance" has eroded the "check the box" mentality of using E-training as the sole vehicle for messaging and training.

Effective training encompasses multiple channels of communication and caters to diverse learning styles. In our age of computer overload, text messaging, "Twittering," and e-mail, alternative forms of training are necessary. Films, videos, hypothetical problem solving, activities, competitive games, contests, face-to-face teaching in large and small meeting environments, elevator installed video messaging machines and posters, plastic wallet cards, and plastic one page instruction cards all have a role to play in training. In particular, new apps on mobile devices allow for a quick advice and approval for gifts, entertainment expenses, and other advice that is country sensitive.

An important part of training in multinational companies is providing all materials and training in the language of the work force. Multinational corporations may need to translate materials into 30 or more languages. English, French, German, Spanish and Chinese are basic to any global program. Add in Japanese, Italian, Portuguese, Korean and you cover many, but not all environments.

Translations of materials should be drafted in the country and environment where the materials translated will be used. Local idiomatic expressions and formal vs. informal use of a language may make for peculiar and comedic materials when they are not vetted by locals. Training should be prepared and deliverable to relevant personnel in the time frames that are consistent with achieving specific goals.

Relying on the Navex Global's 2014 Ethics and Compliance Training Benchmark Report (2014), 76% of companies annually provide 1 to 5 training hours to employees (Senior Leaders, Middle Managers or Non-Managers).

Different kinds of formats can be used, such as online trainings or in person trainings. However, in-person training is preferably used for several reasons. First of all, it allows interaction and promotes relationships between employees and the presenter where questions and/or comments can lead to uncovering risks. Second, competitors often use this type of trainings as confirmed by the above-mentioned study, 68% of companies use this format. Finally, one of the reasons why Morgan Stanley benefited from a non-prosecution agreement in 2012 was that its rogue employee had in person training.

Training that is disruptive, time consuming and irrelevant to audiences is destined to failure. Work forces need to be divided by business, function and role. Typically, the sales and marketing function of a business has a need to become intimately familiar with key concepts of competition law and anticorruption law. Back office employees or call center personnel usually have a more compelling need to learn law and regulations related to data privacy and data protection. Selecting relevant training topics and delivering those sessions means that there must be a matrix and an analysis of your work force. The population which has the greatest exposure to certain legal and regulatory risks must learn the subject matter that places them individually, and the corporation as a whole at risk. In the anti-money laundering arena, private bankers, wealth management personnel and branch bankers face challenges on a daily basis. While the entire banking, insurance and investment community may have a need to understand "know your customer" regulations, certain functions need to understand this concept in detail. Training, tracking and testing specific targeted segments of your workforce on high risk issues in high risk environments takes a great deal of analysis and planning. A thorough annual risk assessment should highlight specific training needs to mitigate those risks.

Controls — Audits and Metrics

In the post-Enron age of Sarbanes-Oxley, auditors and audit functions have become an increasingly important element of required controllership.

All links to the Securities Commission rulemaking and reports issued under the Sarbanes-Oxley Act are available at http://www.sec.gov/spotlight/sarbanes-oxley.htm. Publicly traded corporations must adhere to specific and costly audit routines. Regardless of whether "inside" or "outside" audit teams are retained, their role is invaluable. Auditors check and verify compliance with accounting principles, law and regulation. Their job is to "kick the tires" and test for a variety of weaknesses in the day to day and year to year operation of a company. The criminal conduct engaged in by Bernard Madoff, whether acting alone or in a wider conspiracy could have and should have been captured by thorough professional external auditors. Countless frauds, mismanagement and waste of corporate assets have been uncovered by audit teams. Therefore, Chief Compliance Officers are wise to team up with and utilize internal audit functions to test vulnerabilities and behaviors within a company.

The specific focused audit of travel and living expense reports are a particularly revealing method of taking a snapshot of, and testing behaviors. The absence of such reports, or the abuse of corporate travel or entertainment standards becomes the occasion to review in greater detail the activities of certain individuals or business components. The absence of required back-up documentation is also quite telling. Expenses for dinners, alcohol consumption or golf-outings may also be revealing. Audits can be used to test and measure training, adherence to policies and procedures and to uncover fraudulent or improper books and records. A simple review of "petty cash" controls and local bank accounts can be enormously important.

In today's environment of downsizing and a contraction of the global work force, teaming has become crucial. A coordinated and concentrated effort of all controllership functions (risk, legal, finance, compliance, human resources and security/investigations) to break out of their own silos of specialization is necessary. Too much parallel and siloed information that could be useful in the review of systemic or specific problems is trapped within smaller departments and functions. Weekly or bi-monthly meetings of all controllership functions via conference call or in-person (where possible) to share incidents, trends or critical observations could sharpen and shorten internal audits, reviews, concerns or investigations. Cross functional controllership team efforts are needed in complex global organizations to pierce national, local, or office specific barriers. Field personnel typically try to deal with their own "issues" and persistently hide reportable incidents from headquarter staff. Many complex international organizations develop the local "we" culture as distinct from "them" at headquarters. Information critical to the reputational health of an organization must flow both ways between the field and headquarters and vice versa.

Metrics have gained popularity in the last five years as a method of making comparisons and making local businesses accountable for a wide variety of performance measures. In addition to sales statistics, metrics are now used to analyze information such as: training completed, turnover, due diligence completed on third-party intermediaries, number of signed annual re-acknowledgements to corporate codes of conduct, number of suspicious transactions reported, number of compliance officers per 1000 full-time employees, number of questions, complaints, and number of helpline (ombuds or anonymous reporting) contacts per month or per year by location. While metrics can assist in the review of trends and analysis of comparative data, they can also be used as a tool of deception.

The requirement that all environments demonstrate positive metrics (often shown as green on charts) and the insistence of leaders to demonstrate these results often causes a manipulation of the facts to achieve a specific result or score. Compliance and ethics officers should resist the manipulation of such information for several reasons. Data manipulation derails the need to be a role model of ethical conduct and the second most important reason is to help focus on weak points within the organization. If one zealously pursues and projects "green" light results in training statistics, then one obscures the differentiation between strong and weak or less well-trained environments. Similarly, the absence of "hot line" or anonymous reports of misconduct may be analyzed as either a completely lawful environment free from misconduct, or one in which employees either are fearful of reporting or feel that such reports might be "futile." Metrics can be useful, but they also can be traps for less wary or self-critical and less analytic management teams. The pressure, either real or perceived, to have "green" (good) results can lead to a diminished respect for an entire ethics and compliance program.

Additionally, hammering on messages to complete training in unrealistic time frames leads to negative mindsets by those who are being repeatedly reminded to complete such compliance requirements. This negativity, if allowed to reign, will diminish the capacity of the overall objective of creating a positive ethical and compliant corporate culture. This often occurs on the heels of some major revelation of misconduct by the corporation. The use of deferred prosecution agreements and monitors has increased the intensity of training demands in effected corporations. The rebound of resentment by employees can interfere with creating the ethical and desired law abiding culture. A balanced and thoughtful program is needed.

Annual assessments of the compliance programs in a multinational company goes a long way in driving consistent improvement and sustained effort in high risk environments. Human behavior can be altered by supervision and review. The old saying of "what gets measured gets done" can propel specific behaviors. Rewarding the right behaviors is a key to sustaining them. If a company measures leadership on net income, or volume and on no other factors, all effort within the leaders control will be focused on bottom line results. If, however, the company measures customer or employee satisfaction, number of complaints, on time delivery, employee turn-over or training and testing completed, the focus of management is altered.

Global compliance programs need to be managed by way of annual assessments. Leadership teams and the CEO/President of any unit, group or division of a global entity should be able to articulate what "issues keep him or her up at night" and what controllership steps have been employed to mitigate those risks. The ability to identify and rank risks, and deal with them to protect the global organization from reputational risk must be a priority. An orchestrated, standardized annual review process should be employed so that the leadership can identify, own and control their risks. Large organizations can engage in a "bottoms up"-"top down" review of issues that could potentially derail the global business. An environment and culture of open discourse aids this process. The home office, or corporate headquarter staff should provide a template of topics to be covered, and a format to be used for such an annual effort. The objective of such a "bottoms up"-"top down" review is to allow all employees an opportunity to speak up in small group settings about the ethical issues that concern them in their day-to-day roles. The mere exercise on an annual basis raises the profile and focus on ethics related business issues. Local, country, regional or global trends can be identified in this process. Annual anonymous surveys can also assist in identifying and analyzing ethical and compliance issues that make employees feel proud or concerned.

The "Helpline" or "Hotline"

In order to have an effective Compliance and Ethics Program for purposes of sentencing, the Sentencing Guidelines require that an organization "have and publicize a system, which may include mechanisms that allow for anonymity or confidentiality, whereby the organization's employees and agents may report or seek guidance regarding potential or actual criminal conduct without fear of retaliation." Federal Sentencing Guidelines Manual § 8B2.1(b)(5)(C). Indeed, the Sarbanes-Oxley Act, enacted in 2002, requires that any report made via the helpline can be anonymous. Many organizations have successfully created such systems. Those that are most successful and effective allow for multiple methodologies for reporting (both anonymous and not) via a variety of channels. These may include: in person reports to designated ombuds persons, human resources, supervisors, lawyers or compliance professionals, or via telephone to third-party "hotline" (helpline) providers, or via non-traceable protected corporate email addresses, or to supervisors outside one's chain of command. The key to a successful program is, simply put, trust. Fear of retaliation, whether instantly, or several years down the road often silences employees at every level of the organization. A lack of trust that an organization will honor its commitment to non-retaliation is a key factor. The reporting party must not feel that he/she has placed themselves and their jobs or chances for advancement at risk. Equally important is that the population in an effective system does not feel that it is futile to report because "nothing will be done" to correct the problem.

With the establishment of the Dodd Frank Act Whistleblower Provisions on July 22, 2010, in the United States, it has become important to create an environment where reporting of violations of the code of conduct and illegal activity is first reported through the company reporting system, such as the hotline. This enables the company, rather than the government, to have the first opportunity to investigate, report, and remedy the violation or illegal activity.

Perceived or real retaliation in organizations as a result of reporting acts to silence the work force. Programs can survive and thrive and give organizations real insight into misconduct if handled with great care. Celebrating, commending, encouraging and financially rewarding those individuals who are courageous enough to report difficult situations should be the model. Those who are responsible for investigating reports must identify malcontents and thoroughly review records and if necessary, interview appropriate personnel. This role must be carried out by professionals who are trained in this delicate function. They must be perceived as fair and open minded.

Best Practices

Do Not Reinvent the Wheel

Encouraging individual compliance leaders and teams to share their successful techniques can he powerful. Few problems or issues are unique. Large organizations that are global in nature are usually rich with talent, ideas, programs, training materials, and best practices. Encouraging monthly (or more frequent) discussion groups on specific topics (e.g., how to train for "dawn raids," or due diligence techniques, or anti-money laundering trends) can assist less experienced compliance individuals or groups in coming up the learning curve. Chief compliance officers should circulate and publicly applaud innovative or successful programs and techniques.

Use of Short-Term International Rotations

Newly hired, or high-potential employees capable of leading larger compliance programs can be encouraged and exposed to superior compliance programs by moving individuals into best practice model host environments for periods as short as two weeks or for as long as six months. Language proficiency and exposure to more well established and successful programs become models to take back to one's home country. Centers of excellence often exist either because of the leadership, maturity of the organization, or long standing experience with specific issues. Although budgets for expatriate packages may have declined during the current volatile economy, the need to train and clone successful processes and winning strategies has not. Short term international rotations can be used as a "hook" to attract talent as well as a retention tool to keep high potential players. They are an efficiency and productivity tool that is often overlooked.

An example of a short term international rotation would be to take a Chinese national and embed them with an Australian compliance team for a period of three months or more (depending on language proficiency). Assuming that the Australian team is a competent, mature, well-established team, there are a host of skills and processes that can be transplanted back to China by the person selected for the short-term rotation. Another twist on this idea is to embed an Australian compliance leader into the Chinese business for a period of time (3–6 months). A corporate benefit is achieved by both the importing and the exporting business as corporate leadership talent is moved into a variety of environments. The ability to promote and advance a specific corporate culture is placed on a "fast track" by utilizing internal talent in this manner. The individual employee experiences a variety of challenges and it usually turns into a "win-win" for both the host country and the business sending the talented individual.

Sharing the Wealth

Typically, business people are highly competitive. They hold onto their "secret sauce" as if it were the formula for the original Coca Cola. Compliance communities seldom exhibit this behavior, and if given the vehicle and opportunity will share their successful programs and strategies. Creating forums for such sharing is a wise use of time and talent. Monthly "best practice" sharing webinars and calls among compliance professionals spreads effective methodologies more quickly. Regional meetings and annual "in-person" compliance officer meetings can speed the institutionalization of compliance practices rapidly and effectively. These in-person meetings within a compliance organization also reinforce the sharing, friendships, and networking that lead to additional and on-going sharing. International teams get built and become interdependent when they have met, "broken bread" (have shared food and drink together) and have an opportunity to socialize. Calling up a colleague to discuss ideas and compliance techniques in several states, or countries or time zones away is facilitated by the creation of such networks. Compliance officers often feel isolated, and these opportunities to meet and share best practices either virtually or in-person promote "sharing the wealth" of ideas, strategies, and techniques for driving compliance programs to the next level of excellence.

Chief Compliance Officers Do Not Own Compliance

Chief Compliance Officers have the obligation to be specialist coaches to a business team on the field. It is every constituent member of the team who plays to win. Neither the "quarterback" CCO alone, nor the CEO alone can carry the team to success. It takes "Everyone, Everyday, Everywhere" (GE motto as described in "The Spirit and The Letter: Guiding the Way We Do Business").

It does, however, take a real leader who is a good communicator, pragmatic and a good mentor to drive a successful global compliance team. The right leader for a global compliance team will demonstrate the required gravitas, business acumen, and people skills to assist in driving the success of the program. Acting as mentor and translator are key roles for the CCO. The CCO should also be willing and able to effectively provide "air cover" for local compliance officers who are challenged by their local environments or local business leadership.

Structure

Global programs for multinational organizations require resources and talent. Large organizations will have a difficult time "touching" employees all over the world if the compliance department is solely a headquarter staff. Talent is needed in the field that is aligned with the culture and needs of each business environment. The CCO must expend a large portion of his/her executive time on selecting, promoting and training local talent. CCOs need to structure their organizations to assist their business lines and business leaders. This can be done by installing direct reports for various business lines or by having regional leaders who become responsible for leading compliance efforts in each business and country within their region (e.g., Europe, South and Central America, Asia).

A strong compliance program will have a specific number of compliance officers per 1000 employees. Mature compliance programs break up compliance related tasks into smaller bite sized program elements (e.g., policies and procedures, training, metrics, investigations) and/or into specialty subject matter expertise (e.g., anti-money laundering, anti-corruption, data protection and privacy.) Each multinational corporation can make such organizational choices based on their annual risk assessment process. Corporations that move into new emerging markets are often challenged by their lack of resource in tackling local "issues." Additionally, organizations that grow through mergers and acquisitions need to assign additional resources to give the acquired entity a chance to adjust to new demands and expectations on the legal, regulatory and cultural front. The creation of an effective global compliance program seldom happens overnight. Indeed, compliance professionals will tell you that the goal of a compliance program is not a specific destination nor does it have a finite timeline. The creation of a genuinely effective program is a journey with no end. Law, regulation and business morph constantly, so too must an effective global compliance program.

Assignment

- As General Counsel of your designated Company, come up with a risk assessment of the top five legal risks for U.S. headquarter or subsidiary and a risk assessment of the top five legal risks for your global Corporation. Compare the risks.

Index